THE PRINCIPLES OF MODERN COMPANY LAW

AUSTRALIA
The Law Book Company Ltd.
Sydney : Melbourne : Brisbane

CANADA AND U.S.A.
The Carswell Company Ltd.
Toronto

INDIA
N. M. Tripathi Private Ltd.
Bombay

ISRAEL
Steimatzky's Agency Ltd.
Jerusalem : Tel Aviv : Haifa

NEW ZEALAND
Sweet & Maxwell (N.Z.) Ltd.
Wellington

PAKISTAN
Pakistan Law House
Karachi

THE PRINCIPLES

OF

MODERN COMPANY LAW

BY

L. C. B. GOWER, LL.M.(Lond.), F.B.A.

Solicitor of the Supreme Court
Law Commissioner
Formerly Cassel Professor of Commercial Law
in the University of London

THIRD EDITION

Co-Editors

K. W. WEDDERBURN, M.A., LL.B.(Cantab.)

of the Middle Temple, Barrister-at-Law
Cassel Professor of Commercial Law
in the University of London

O. WEAVER, M.A., LL.B.(Cantab.)

of the Middle Temple, Barrister-at-Law

Taxation

A. E. W. PARK, M.A.(Oxon.)

of Lincoln's Inn, Barrister-at-Law

LONDON
STEVENS & SONS
1969

First Edition	-	-	-	1954
Second Edition		-	-	1957
Second Impression		-	-	1959
Third Impression		-	-	1961
Fourth Impression		-	-	1963
Fifth Impression		-	-	1965
Sixth Impression		-	-	1967
Seventh Impression		-	-	1968
Third Edition	-		-	1969
Second Impression		-	-	1970
Third Impression		-	-	1972
Fourth Impression		-	-	1974
Fifth Impression		-	-	1975

*Published by
Stevens & Sons of 11 New
Fetter Lane London and
printed in Great Britain
by Fletcher & Son Ltd,
Norwich*

SBN   Hardback   420   42410   5
Paperback   420   42650   7

(Sd) RES/KN 261

PREFACE

A NEW EDITION of this book is long overdue. The main excuses for the delay are: pressure of other work, the belief that the time was never ripe because comprehensive new legislation was repeatedly promised for an early date, and the fact that despite the book's increasing obsolescence it continued to sell astonishingly well both in England and abroad. However, the passage of the Companies Act 1967 made it clear that the task should not be further postponed. I was fortunately able to persuade Professor K. W. Wedderburn, Mr. Andrew Park and Mr. Oliver Weaver to assist in the work of revision and we decided to press on with it, notwithstanding the possibility of further legislation in the lifetime of the present Parliament, because we doubted whether the envisaged " wider reforms in the structure and philosophy of our company law " would in fact prove feasible so soon. We assumed that there would, instead, be legislation of a less ambitious character to implement those recommendations of the Jenkins Committee which were not dealt with in the 1967 Act; but this, we thought, could be anticipated to a considerable extent by adding, as we have, copious references to those recommendations. The wisdom of our decision not to delay further has now been proved because it appears that further legislation, either on a wider or narrower front, cannot be expected for some years.

The revision of a work on Company Law which was twelve years out of date has demanded substantial rewriting of many chapters and amendments to virtually every page. Much has occurred in those years. In the field of legislation there have been, in particular, the Prevention of Fraud (Investments) Act 1958 and the Licensed Dealers (Conduct of Business) Rules 1960, the Companies (Floating Charges) (Scotland) Act 1961, the Protection of Depositors Act 1963, the Stock Transfer Act 1963, the Finance Act 1965 (with its new scheme of corporate taxation) and the Companies Act 1967. Control of capital issues has virtually been scrapped and exchange control greatly relaxed. The major stock exchanges have federated and published new quotation requirements. The City Code on Take-overs and Mergers has been published and the Watch-dog Panel has been established and, very recently, re-furbished. Case-law developments have been many and important.

Taking account of all these changes, and of likely future developments, has inevitably meant that the book has grown in size notwithstanding the pruning of dead wood. To counteract this growth I was tempted to delete the historical matter in Chapters 2 and 3, on the basis that this would not be read more than once and could be found in the earlier editions. But my co-editors had no difficulty in persuading me that this material was rather good, and we thought that if it were deleted the likely result would be that it was not read at all, and that this would be a pity.

In the preparation of this edition I have received the most invaluable and stimulating help from my co-editors and I am deeply indebted both to them and to the many others whose brains we picked. But for the views expressed and for the errors and omissions I alone remain responsible. These would have been more numerous but for the careful scouting of the galley proofs by Mr. K. Schwarz and Mr. H. Shulman and of the page proofs by Mr. P. G. Willoughby. I am most grateful to them for their many valuable suggestions and regret that some of those made by Mr. Willoughby were received too late to be adopted in this edition.

I must also express my thanks to the publishers who have seen the work through the press with exceptional rapidity and arranged for a soft-backed students' edition at what, by modern standards, is a bargain price. They also saw to the preparation of the Tables and Index and I am particularly grateful to Mrs. A. Cozens who undertook the latter task. Last, but not least, I must thank my secretary, Miss Pat Thorne, who wrestled with illegible manuscripts and read proofs well beyond the call of duty.

The text is revised to May 1, 1969. References in it to "the Act" are to the Companies Act 1948 unless the context otherwise requires.

L. C. B. GOWER.

London,
    June 1969.

PREFACE TO THE FIRST EDITION

COMPANY LAW, to those who specialise in it, is among the most fascinating of legal subjects. But its fascination is not always readily apparent to general practitioners or to the students of law, economics, and accounting who try to master its intricacies. Indeed, they often regard it as technical and dull. This, perhaps, is because they find difficulty in viewing it in its historical and economic context and in grasping its underlying principles. This book has been written in an attempt to meet their needs. Its aim is to supply essential background material, and to emphasise the principles of common law and equity on which this branch of the law is still based, rather than the statutory provisions which supplement and amend them in detail.

The book is not intended to be an exhaustive treatise on every branch of company law. In particular, no attempt is made to deal fully with the procedure on a winding up—a subject which requires a volume to itself or a large share of a volume on bankruptcy. It is concerned with the living law of living companies, in sickness and in health. But within these limits I think it is true to say that it discusses most of the important aspects of the subject. While it emphasises principles, it is not intended to be mainly theoretical; on the contrary, an attempt has been made to concentrate on those principles which are still important in practice and to explain their purpose and how they operate. For this reason, and because of the discussion of certain problems which are ignored elsewhere, it is hoped that the book may be found useful by practitioners (lay and legal) as well as by students.

No attempt has been made to deal with systems of company law other than the English. On the other hand, attention is drawn to developments elsewhere (particularly in the U.S.A.) when these have seemed illuminating either by way of contrast or as pointers towards the possible solution of questions as yet unsolved in England. In general the footnotes have not been burdened with detailed references to American authorities as these can be readily found in any of the standard texts or casebooks.

I hope that students will not be repelled by its length, unorthodox arrangement, or price. The length is partly deceptive, for much of Part I and II is background material, not readily available elsewhere, which is essential for a proper understanding of the subject but which, once understood, will not need to be memorised in detail. Moreover, I have tried throughout to bear in mind that readability is even more important than brevity, which can sometimes be attained at too great a price.

Arrangement has been my greatest problem, and I must crave the reader's indulgence for having failed to solve it. The fact is that no one has yet discovered a method of arranging this subject which is wholly satisfactory. In essentials my attempted solution is to answer the following questions in the order stated: What is a company and how did it attain its present shape? (Part I). What are the consequences of trading as an incorporated company? (Part II). How is a company formed and floated? (Part III). What is the nature of investors' interests in a company? (Part IV). How are investors and creditors protected? (Part V). But sometimes logic has been sacrificed to convenience; thus prospectuses are dealt with wholly in Part III, rather than in Part V. Many will think that it would have been preferable to consider the formation and flotation of companies before discussing the consequences of so doing, thus reversing the order of Parts II and III. But adopting, as I have tried to do, a functional rather than a structural approach, it seemed to me better to indicate why one should want to form a company before discussing how to do so. Those who think otherwise will, I hope, find Part III intelligible if read first; indeed, within the limits indicated by cross-references, every part is intended to be self-contained and self-explanatory.

L. C. B. GOWER.

CONTENTS

PART ONE

INTRODUCTORY

PART TWO

THE CONSEQUENCES OF INCORPORATION

PART THREE

FORMATION AND FLOTATION OF COMPANIES

PART FOUR

A COMPANY'S SECURITIES

PART FIVE

INVESTOR AND CREDITOR PROTECTION

TABLE OF CASES

TABLE OF STATUTES

TABLE OF STATUTORY INSTRUMENTS

TABLE OF RULES OF THE SUPREME COURT

TABLE OF COUNTY COURT RULES

PART ONE

INTRODUCTORY

CHAPTER 1

NATURE AND FUNCTIONS OF COMPANIES

SCOPE OF THE SUBJECT

ALTHOUGH company law is a well-recognised subject in the legal curriculum and the title of a voluminous literature, its exact scope is vague, since "the word *company* has no strictly legal meaning." [1] It is clear, however, that in legal theory (though not, as we shall see, always in economic reality) the term implies an association [2] of a number [3] of people for some common object or objects. The purposes for which men and women may wish to associate are multifarious, ranging from those as basic as marriage and mutual protection against the elements to those as sophisticated as the objects of the Confederation of British Industries or the Atomic Scientists' Association. But in common parlance the word " company " is normally reserved [4] for those associated for economic purposes, *i.e.*, to carry on a business for gain.

English law now provides two main types of organisation for such associations; partnerships and companies. Although the word " company " is colloquially applied to both [5] the modern English lawyer regards companies and company law as distinct from partnerships and partnership law. Partnership law, which is now largely codified in the Partnership Act 1890, is based on the law of agency, each partner becoming an agent of the others,[6] and it therefore affords a suitable framework for an association of a small body of persons having trust and confidence in each other. A more complicated form of association, with a large and fluctuating membership, requires a more elaborate organisation which ideally should confer corporate personality on the association, that is, should recognise that it constitutes a distinct legal

---

1 *Per* Buckley J. in *Re Stanley* [1906] 1 Ch. 131 at p. 134. For attempts at a definition, see Evans, " What is a Company?" (1910) 26 L.Q.R. 259.
2 *Pace* James L.J. (that great master of the English language) in *Smith* v. *Anderson* (1880) 15 Ch.D. 247 at p. 273 : " The word ' association,' in the sense in which it is now commonly used, is etymologically inaccurate, for ' association ' does not properly describe the thing formed, but properly and etymologically describes the act of associating together, from which act of associating there is formed a company or partnership."
3 The number need not be more than two, and of these the interest of one need not be more than nominal, as in the so-called " one-man company." Nor indeed does the " company " automatically cease merely because, in the course of time, the number of members is reduced to one or none (*cf.* Companies Act 1948, ss. 31 and 222 (*d*)).
4 But not universally; we still talk about an infantry company, and a livery company. And see p. 9 *et seq., infra.*
5 So that it is common for partners to carry on business in the name of " —— & Company."
6 Partnership Act 1890, s. 5.

3

person, subject to legal duties and entitled to legal rights separate from those of its members.[7] This the modern company can obtain easily and cheaply by being formed under a succession of statutes culminating in the Companies Acts 1948 and 1967.

Briefly what occurs is that the promoters of a company prepare certain documents expressing their desire to be formed into a company with a specified name and objects and these documents are lodged with the Registrar of Companies—an official of the Board of Trade. If the documents are in order they are registered, the Registrar grants a certificate of incorporation, and the company is formed. The essential feature is public registration and this type of company is therefore described as a registered company.

Four points must, however, be stressed immediately:

Unincorporated companies

Although today there is a clear-cut legal distinction between partnerships and incorporated companies and although the latter can now be formed almost as easily and cheaply as the former, this is a relatively modern development. Little more than a century ago corporate personality could only be acquired by the dilatory and expensive process of promoting a special Act or acquiring a Royal Charter. Hence, the business world tried to adapt the partnership form to an organisation with a large and fluctuating membership and, as we shall see,[8] thanks to the equitable doctrine of the trust, their efforts met with considerable success. It was from these quasi-partnerships (rather than from chartered corporations) that the modern company was developed and until recently the borderline between them was vague. Nearly all these quasi-partnerships or unincorporated companies [9] have now either been wound up, or registered under the Companies Acts, or become incorporated by statute or charter, but until recently several important insurance companies remained as examples of the once normal earlier form.[10] These, however, are so exceptional that they need not concern us further.

---

[7] It is outside the scope of this book to discuss whether this recognition is of a pre-existing fact (as contended by the Realist school, associated with the name of Gierke) or a legal fiction. Legal personality, in the sense of the capacity to be the subject of legal rights and duties, is necessarily the creation of law whether conferred upon a single human being or a group and the Realist and other theories are of no direct concern to the lawyer (as opposed to the political scientist) except in so far as they have influenced the judges in the development of the law.

[8] Chaps. 2 and 3.

[9] An unincorporated company must not be confused with an unlimited incorporated company. The members may, if they wish, form an incorporated company but agree to accept personal responsibility for its debts. In such a case they will reap all the other advantages of corporate personality which an unincorporated association necessarily lacks. See Chap. 4, *infra.*

[10] The Sun Insurance Society and the General Life Assurance Company did not adopt the modern form until as late as 1926 and 1927 respectively. Insurance companies formed before 1844 or in 1855–56 can lawfully remain organised in the old way, and it seems that a few mutual assurance societies still are.

Choice of partnership or company

The distinction between partnerships and companies is often merely one of machinery and not of function. If a small number of persons wish to carry on business in common with a view to profit they may either form themselves into a partnership or a company. The only restraint on their freedom of choice [11] is that if their numbers are too great for that mutual trust appropriate to a partnership they must form a company. An arbitrary maximum of twenty is now imposed by the legislature, for section 434 (1) of the Companies Act 1948 (re-enacting similar provisions in the earlier Acts), provides as follows:

> "No company, association or partnership consisting of more than twenty [12] persons shall be formed for the purpose of carrying on any business . . . that has for its object the acquisition of gain by the company, association, or partnership or by the individual members thereof, unless it is registered as a company under this Act or is formed in pursuance of some other Act of Parliament, or of letters patent, or is a company engaged in working mines within the stannaries and subject to the jurisdiction of the court exercising the stannaries jurisdiction." [13]

However, by section 120 of the Companies Act 1967 this maximum does not apply to solicitors, members of a recognised body of accountants, or members of a recognised stock exchange, and the Board of Trade may, by regulations, exempt other professions or trades. [14]

Types of company

As section 434 implies, incorporation under the Companies Act is not the only way in which a company may be formed. Four types of company are referred to in that section:

(i) *Registered companies*

There is first the company formed under the Act in the manner briefly described above. This is the typical and infinitely the most important kind of company at the present day.

---

[11] But certain professions (*e.g.*, that of a solicitor) cannot be carried on by incorporated bodies, and barristers cannot even practise in partnership.

[12] Under s. 429 the figure was 10 in the case of banking partnerships but by the Companies Act 1967, s. 119, it was raised to 20 if all the members are authorised by the Board of Trade.

[13] Under subs. (2) there is an express exemption in the case of approved bodies of underwriters for reinsuring war risks under the now repealed War Risks Insurance Act 1939. In other cases Lloyd's underwriting syndicates are so organised as to avoid the implication that their members are " associated " in a business, for each member accepts several liability for his share of the risk. Lloyd's itself is now a statutory corporation but does not itself undertake insurance business.

[14] By the Partnerships (Unrestricted Size) No. 1 Regs. 1968 (S.I. 1222), certain partnerships of patent agents, surveyors, auctioneers, valuers and estate agents are exempted.

(ii) *Statutory companies*

Bodies with special types of object to which the financial profits of their members are only incidental may be formed under general public Acts, such as the Friendly Societies Acts, the Industrial and Provident Societies Acts, the Building Societies Acts, the Trade Union Acts, and the Trustee Savings Banks Acts. Although some of these bodies, particularly co-operative societies formed under the Industrial and Provident Societies Acts, closely resemble companies they fall outside the scope of this book except for purposes of distinction and comparison.[15] A company properly so called may, however, be formed by a special Act. In the past, when public utilities such as railway, gas, water and electricity undertakings were left to private enterprise, statutory incorporations by private Acts were comparatively common since the undertakings would require powers and monopolistic rights which needed a special legislative grant. During the last century therefore Public General Acts [16] were passed providing for standard clauses which are deemed to be incorporated into the private Acts, unless expressly excluded. As a result of post-war nationalisation measures, most of these statutory companies have been taken over by public boards and corporations set up by public Acts. These boards and corporations also fall outside the scope of this book except for purposes of comparison.[17] But some statutory companies remain [18] and others may be formed. Strictly speaking the statute under which they are formed need not incorporate them, but today this is invariably done.

(iii) *Chartered companies*

Section 434 thirdly refers to companies formed in pursuance of "letters patent." [19] This relates to companies granted a charter by the Crown under the Royal Prerogative or special statutory powers.[20]

---

[15] See Chap. 11 below.
[16] The Companies Clauses Acts 1845–1889. These Acts, containing the general corporate powers and duties, were supplemented in the case of particular utilities by various other "Clauses Acts," *e.g.,* the Lands Clauses Consolidation and Railways Clauses Consolidation Acts 1845, the Electric Lighting (Clauses) Act 1899, as amended by the Electricity Act 1947, and numerous Waterworks Clauses Acts, now repealed and superseded by the Water Acts 1945 and 1948, and Gasworks Clauses Acts, now repealed by the Gas Act 1948. [17] See Chap. 11 below.
[18] The *Stock Exchange Year Book,* 1968, lists 79 U.K. statutory companies—mainly water undertakings.
[19] This is, of course, the same expression as is used in connection with inventions and historically these two are closely connected. Just as the Crown might grant a monopoly of an invention by grant under its letters patent, so might it grant a charter of incorporation and the charter might confer a monopoly of trading in a particular territory. In the early days a patent for an invention was very commonly coupled with incorporation for the purposes of working it. See Chap. 2, p. 27, below.
[20] Under many *ad hoc* statutes the Crown has been granted power to grant charters in cases falling outside its prerogative powers. Moreover, by the Chartered Companies Acts 1837 and 1884, the prerogative was extended by empowering the Crown to grant charters for a limited period and to extend them. Thus the B.B.C. charter was for 10 years and has been prolonged from time to time. In many of the Canadian Provinces companies are still incorporated by letters patent but under statutory regulation.

Such a charter normally confers corporate personality, but as it was regarded as dubious policy for the Crown to confer a full charter of incorporation on an ordinary trading concern, it was empowered by the Trading Companies Act 1834 and the Chartered Companies Act 1837 to confer by letters patent all or any of the privileges of incorporation without actually granting a charter. Today an ordinary trading concern would not contemplate trying to obtain a Royal Charter, for incorporation under the Companies Acts would be far quicker and cheaper. In practice, therefore, this method of incorporation is used only by organisations formed for charitable, or quasi-charitable objects, such as learned and artistic societies, schools and colleges, which want the greater prestige that a charter is thought to confer.

Many such organisations remain unincorporated for, as Maitland pointed out in his famous essay "Trust and Corporation," [21] until recent years England, in contrast with the Continental countries, made little use of corporations in connection with associations for purposes other than those of trade, preferring to rely instead on the unique English invention of the trust. By the trust, learned societies, clubs, and professional bodies [22] (like the Inns of Court, Lloyd's and the Stock Exchanges) could function satisfactorily without incorporation by vesting their property in a small body of trustees. The more important and wealthy, such as the leading public schools and the colleges of Oxford and Cambridge, obtained Royal Charters, while others, as we have seen, became subject to special legislation. But many societies, clubs and professional bodies (including the Inns of Court, and the London Stock Exchange [23]) remain unincorporated to this day. These are not further considered here.[24] But chartered companies cannot be entirely ignored, if only because there are still a few trading companies [25] operating under charters.

(iv) *Cost-book companies*

Section 434 (1) refers finally to "a company engaged in working mines within the stannaries and subject to the jurisdiction of the court exercising the stannaries jurisdiction." Peculiar local customs have always governed the stannaries,[26] the tin mines of Devon and Cornwall,

---

21 *Collected Papers*, Vol. III, p. 321, Selected Essays (ed. Hazeltine), p. 141.
22 Including, until the legislation of the last century, building societies, friendly societies, industrial and provident societies, trade unions and trustee savings banks. Even now many of these remain unincorporated and still rely primarily on the trust (see Chap. 11 below). Even societies whose constitutions are entirely untouched by statute law may have certain statutory privileges; see the Scientific Societies Act 1843 and the Literary and Scientific Institutions Act 1854.
23 Lloyd's became incorporated by statute in 1871.
24 For an admirable account, see H. A. J. Ford, *Unincorporated Non-Profit Associations* (Oxf. 1959).
25 Only 14 chartered companies (mainly banks and insurance companies) are listed in the 1968 *Stock Exchange Year Book.*
26 For history, see Holdsworth, H.E.L., Vol. 1, pp. 151–165.

and the unincorporated partnerships (known as cost-book companies [27])
formed to work them, and these customs are now supplemented by
special statutes.[28] Until the end of the last century the law relating to
these companies was administered by special stannaries courts but the
jurisdiction is now exercised by the county courts of Cornwall.[29]
Reference has already been made to the earlier form of company which
was a hybrid partnership, and cost-book companies are a special type of
such companies and the only examples of associations for gain which
are neither incorporated nor subject to the normal partnership law [30] and
which can still lawfully be formed otherwise than under special statutory
or Crown authority. Today, however, they are so rare and unimportant
that they can be ignored.[31]

Hence this book will deal only with such companies as are incorporated, with particular emphasis on registered companies. But it will
not deal with all types of corporations. Municipal corporations and
the like will be wholly excluded—the only rules which they have in
common with companies are those which flow inevitably from the fact
that both are incorporated. Also excluded, except for the purposes
of comparison, are bodies incorporated under special public Act of
Parliament whether *ad hoc* (as in the case of the new public corporations formed to run nationalised industries) or of more general
application (such as the Building Societies and Industrial and Provident
Societies Acts).

Company law is uncodified

No attempt has ever been made to codify English company law.[32]
The Companies Act 1948 was merely a consolidation of the existing
statutory rules, and as a result of subsequent legislation, notably the
1967 Act, there is at present not even a complete consolidation. Behind
the Acts is a general body of law and equity applying to all companies
irrespective of their nature, and it is there that most of the fundamental
principles will be found.[33]

---

[27] The cost-book type of company was formerly used in connection with mines and
quarries in other districts also, *e.g.*, in Derbyshire : see High Peak Mining Customs
and Mineral Courts Act 1851 and the Derbyshire Mining Customs and Mineral
Courts Act 1852. See generally Halsbury, 3rd ed., Vol. 6, p. 806 *et seq.*, and
C. A. Cooke, *Corporation, Trust and Company* (1950), pp. 112–114.
[28] Stannaries Acts 1836, 1855, 1869 and 1887.
[29] Stannaries Court (Abolition) Act 1896.
[30] Partnership Act 1890, s. 1 (2).
[31] Indeed, nobody seems to know whether there are any left!
[32] For an attempt at a complete codification in a Commonwealth country with a
company law based on the English model, see Ghana's Companies Code 1963 (Act
179). This was based on a report by the author : see Final Report of the Commission
of Enquiry into the Working and Administration of the Company Law of Ghana
(Accra 1961).
[33] In fact, since the Acts apply to Scotland as well as to England and Wales, the
statutory rules are superimposed on two distinct common law systems. In some
respects these differ widely. This book is primarily concerned with English (not
Scottish) company law.

THE FUNCTIONS OF COMPANIES

Inadequacy of legal definitions

At the beginning of this chapter it was said that " company " implied an association of a number of persons for a common object, that object normally being the economic gain of its members. But it is no longer practicable to restrict consideration to trading concerns. In the last hundred years incorporation has become so easy and so cheap that many non-profit-making bodies, which would hitherto have remained unincorporated, have become registered under the Companies Acts and therefore become subject to the same rules as trading companies. Far from being designed to secure the economic profit of their members, these companies expressly prohibit it, and between them and normal trading companies there is nothing in common beyond the fact that they both adopt the same legal framework within which to function.[34]

Even as regard trading companies our description was legalistic rather than realistic. No doubt many of the smaller companies may properly be described as associations of a number of persons for the common object of mutual profit; if two partners convert their business into a limited company they may well continue to carry on business in common, just as they did before the incorporation. But this is not necessarily an accurate description even of small companies. A sole trader may convert his business into a company and, although he must initially bring in at least one other person, that person need have no beneficial interest in the business and need take no part in running it. In such a case, the association of a number of persons is a legal fiction.

More remarkable is the unreality of this description when applied to large public companies at the other end of the scale. A holder of 100 shares in, say, Imperial Chemical Industries is a member of the company but it is fantasy to describe him as associating with the other members in running it. The running of the business is left to the directors, or probably to the managing directors, and the shareholder, although a member, is in economic reality, but not in the eyes of the law, a mere lender of capital, on which he hopes for a return but without any effective control over the borrower. In this country the legal implications [35] of this development have been little explored, but in the United States A. A. Berle and G. C. Means, in their stimulating book *The Modern Corporation and Private Property*,[36] have drawn attention to the

---

[34] As we shall see, the legal framework is modified slightly to meet their particular needs: *infra*, p. 11.

[35] There is, of course, a considerable body of English economic literature which recognises these implications.

[36] New York, 1933 (reprinted 1968 with a new preface). This book was one of the sources relied on by James Burnham in his influential *The Managerial Revolution* (Lond. 1942). See also Arnold, *The Folklore of Capitalism* (New Haven 1937). See further, pp. 60–64, *infra*.

revolutionary change thus brought about in our traditional conceptions of the nature of property. Today the great bulk of industrial enterprise is in the hands not of individual entrepreneurs but of large public companies in which many individuals have property rights as shareholders and to the wealth of which they have directly or indirectly contributed. Investments in companies probably constitute the most important single item of property, but whether this property brings profit to its owners no longer depends on their energy and initiative but on that of the management from which they are divorced. The modern shareholder has ceased to be a quasi-partner and has become instead simply a supplier of capital. If he invests in the older forms of private property, such as a farm or his own shop, he becomes tied to that property; " he lives with it, works at it, builds his life at least partly around it with an agent or some other human mechanism devised to run it in his absence." [37] The modern public company meets the need for a new type of property in which the relationship between the owner and the property plays little part, so that the owner can recover his wealth when he needs it without removing it from the enterprise which requires it indefinitely. " The separation of ownership from management and control in the corporate system has performed this essential step in securing liquidity." [38] The modern public company is therefore one further piece of machinery (like the trust) whereby the property of individuals is managed by other individuals.

In so far as there is any true association in the modern public company it is between management and workers rather than between the shareholders *inter se* or between them and the management. But the fact that the workers form an integral part of the company is ignored by the law. In legal theory the relationship between a company and its employees is merely the contractual relationship of master and servant and the servants no more form part of the company than do its creditors. This legal theory is often doubly unreal. In the first place the true relationship today is frequently one of status rather than contract, being governed in part by general legislation, such as the Factories Acts, and in part by collective bargaining agreements, negotiated between organised bodies of employers and labour, which generally do not constitute " law " at all since they are not enforceable by the courts except in so far as they are impliedly incorporated into service agreements.[39] But more than this, the orthodox legal view is unreal in that it ignores the undoubted fact that the employees are members of the company for which they work to a far greater extent than are the shareholders whom the law persists in regarding as its

---

[37] *Op. cit.,* p. 284.
[38] *Ibid.* 285.
[39] *Ford Motor Co.* v. *A.E.F.* [1969] 1 W.L.R. 339. On collective bargaining, see the report of the (Donovan) Royal Commission on Trade Unions and Employers' Associations 1965–1968 (Cmnd. 3623).

proprietors. If the relationship between management and shareholders gives rise to problems which company law has still not satisfactorily solved, the relationship between management and labour presents problems which company law has not even recognised as being its concern.[40]

The three functions of the modern company

From a functional viewpoint therefore there are today three distinct types of companies:

1. *Companies formed for purposes other than the profit of their members, i.e.,* those formed for social, charitable or quasi-charitable purposes. In this case incorporation is merely a more modern and convenient substitute for the trust.

2. *Companies formed to enable a single trader or a small body of partners to carry on a business.* In these companies, incorporation is a device for personifying the business and divorcing its liability from that of its members despite the fact that the members retain control and share the profits.

3. *Companies formed in order to enable the investing public to share in the profits of an enterprise without taking any part in its management.* In this last type, which is economically (but not numerically) by far the most important, the company is again a device analogous to the trust, but this time it is designed to facilitate the raising and putting to use of capital by enabling a large number of owners to entrust it to a small number of expert managers. In the field of public utilities it is at present being superseded by a new type of public corporation in which the enterprise is financed by, and run for, the public as a whole (acting through State agencies), instead of by and for the investing section of the public, but in other fields it still reigns supreme.

For the first of these classes the Companies Acts provide the company limited by guarantee. For the second and third they provide the company limited by shares but, as we shall see, no longer with any meaningful distinctions recognising the different needs of the second and third.

Guarantee companies

The Companies Act 1948 does not permit a company to be created in which the members are free from any liability whatsoever, but, as an alternative to limiting their contribution to the amount payable for their shares, it enables them to agree that in the event of liquidation they will, if required, subscribe an agreed amount (generally £1 or £5). The

40 See further, Chap. 3, pp. 62–64.

Act recognises two forms of company limited by guarantee, namely, the guarantee company without a share capital [41] and the guarantee company with a share capital.[42] The former is the guarantee company in its pure form, whereas the latter is something of a hybrid.

Until very recently little or no use was made of the hybrid with a share capital but the pure form was, and is, widely used by charitable and quasi-charitable organisations, such as schools, colleges, and the " Friends " of museums and picture galleries, which thought that incorporation with limited liability would be a more convenient device than the trust. In such cases a division of the undertaking into shares would be inappropriate since no division of profits is contemplated and the members may not wish initially to put any money into the concern as they would have to do if they subscribed for shares. In recent years, however, the use of guarantee companies has spread to associations which, although not trading in the ordinary sense, wish to raise some initial capital from the members [43] and, perhaps, to distribute among the members any incidental profits that they may make.[44] This has led to a slight revival of the use of guarantee companies with a share capital.[45]

In the case of a pure guarantee company, a member is under no obligation to subscribe up to the amount of his guarantee while the company is a going concern; it is only on the company's being wound up if a contribution is needed to enable the debts to be met that any liability on the guarantee arises. But in the case of a guarantee company having a share capital a member is under a twofold liability; while the company is a going concern he is liable to pay up to the nominal amount of his shares, and once the company goes into liquidation he is liable on the guarantee as in the case of a pure guarantee company.

Companies limited by shares

A guarantee company is, however, unsuitable where the primary object is to carry on a business for profit and to divide that profit among the members. Just as a partnership agreement will need to prescribe the shares of the partners, so will a company's constitution need to define the shares of its members, and if these shares are to be transferable it will be convenient for them to be expressed in comparatively small denominations. Thus if the initial capital is to be £1,000 this will normally be divided into 1,000 shares of £1 each, even though there may initially be only two or three members. The members who

---

[41] For a model constitution, see Companies Act 1948, Sched. I, Table C.
[42] *Ibid.*, Table D.
[43] For example, management companies for large blocks of flats of which all the tenants are members: see E. F. George, *The Sale of Flats* (2nd ed.) at p. 61 *et seq.*
[44] For example, theatre clubs.
[45] Two were registered in 1965, three in 1966 and four in 1967; this was less than 1 per cent. of the number of guarantee companies without share capital registered in those years.

subscribe for the shares will be under a duty to pay the company for them in money or money's worth, and the company is accordingly said to be " limited by shares " [46]; that is to say, the members' liability [47] to contribute towards the company's debts is limited to the nominal value of the shares for which they have subscribed, and once the shares have been " paid up " they are under no further liability. A fundamental distinction between this type of company and the pure guarantee company is that the law assumes that its working capital will be, to some extent at any rate, contributed by the members. These contributions float the company on its launching and are not a mere *tabula in naufragio* to which creditors may cling when the company sinks.

Public and private companies

The company limited by shares is suitable whether the company is to be a small family concern or a large organisation to which the public is to be invited to contribute capital, but obviously some of the safeguards required in the latter case in the interest of the public investor, can be dispensed with in the former. In recognition of this the Companies (Consolidation) Act 1908 [48] exempted from some of the normal requirements a " private company " which it defined as one which (a) limited the membership to fifty, (b) restricted the right to transfer shares, and (c) prohibited any invitation to the public. Companies not coming within this definition are normally described as " public companies."

Unfortunately the legislative attempt to define " family concerns " broke down because public companies adopted the practice of operating through subsidiary companies which could come within the statutory definition of private companies and be formed as such although the public would in fact be interested in them at second hand.

Accordingly the Companies Act 1948 further subdivided private companies into exempt and non-exempt private companies [49] and laid down an elaborate definition of the former [50] which alone continued to enjoy the two most important advantages accorded to private companies, namely, freedom from the obligation to file accounts [51] and permission to make loans to the directors.[52] The complexity of the definition produced unfair and capricious results [53] and accordingly section 2 of

---

[46] For a model constitution, see Companies Act 1948, Sched. I, Tables A and B.

[47] This liability may in practice be illusory as there is no minimum nominal value of shares or of total share capital. A company (estate agents) has been registered with a share capital of ½d. divided into two ¼d. shares!

[48] This followed a tentative approach in the Act of 1900.

[49] This division was not adopted in most other Commonwealth countries.

[50] Companies Act 1948, s. 129 and Sched. 7.

[51] s. 129.

[52] s. 190.

[53] See the Report of the Jenkins Committee, Cmnd. 1749, para. 57. The provisions of ss. 2, 43 and 47 of the 1967 Act are based on the recommendations of the Committee: *ibid.* para. 63.

the Companies Act 1967 abolishes the status of exempt private companies. All companies however small are now bound to file accounts with their annual return and no company may make a loan to a director. Although the distinction between public and private companies still remains,[54] the consequences, as we shall see,[55] are minimal.

There is, therefore, no form of organisation under the Companies Acts specially devised for the small business. It is true that section 43 of the Companies Act 1967 now provides a procedure whereby limited companies may re-register as unlimited companies, and section 47 exempts most unlimited companies from the requirement to file accounts.[56] This has led some formerly exempt private companies to re-register as unlimited.[57] But unlimited companies are equally subject to most other provisions of the Companies Acts which are unnecessarily detailed and restrictive for small concerns. Hence others have been wound up and their members reverted to partnerships; a development encouraged by the rearrangement of company taxation introduced by the Finance Act 1965.[58]

The large concern designed to raise its capital from the public will, of course, become a public company,[59] although it may operate through subsidiary private companies. It is to this type of company that the Companies Acts apply in their full rigour. But the differences in the legal rules applicable to them and to private companies are few, as indeed are the differences between the rules applicable to every type of company registered under the Acts. All are formed in the same way and are subjected to the same régime, the only differences being that some sections will be inapplicable to certain types. For example, some sections of the Acts apply only to companies having a share capital and will therefore have no application to those companies limited by guarantee which have none. A few others do not apply to unlimited companies. But fundamentally, the legal organisation is the same in the case of all companies formed under the Act, irrespective of their type and function.

---

54 The Jenkins Committee recommended the abolition of the distinction: *ibid.* para. 67.
55 *Infra*, Chap. 12, pp. 250, 251.
56 The exemption does not extend to a subsidiary of a limited company or to a company controlled by two or more limited companies, to a holding company of a limited company, or to a company carrying on business as promoter of a trading stamp scheme within the meaning of the Trading Stamps Act 1964, and " limited company " includes a foreign company the liability of whose members is limited.
57 By the end of 1967, 156 companies had re-registered as unlimited (making a total of 1,341 unlimited companies). But there had been 387,697 companies (74 per cent. of the total number of private companies) which had filed the certificates required under s. 129 (1) (*b*) of the 1948 Act as exempt private companies: Board of Trade, *General Annual Report on Companies 1967*.
58 See Chap. 9, pp. 173–182.
59 At the end of 1967, excluding companies in course of liquidation or removal from the register, there were 15,344 public companies in Great Britain as compared with no less than 509,899 private companies. But the total issued capital of the public companies was £12,684 million, far greater than that of the private companies; Board of Trade, *General Annual Report on Companies 1967*.

Chartered and statutory companies on the other hand are not generally subject to the provisions of the Companies Act [60] unless they register under it. To them the rules of common law and equity apply, as modified by the express provisions of their charters and statutes. But these common law and equitable rules still prevail over a wide field and hence the differences between them and registered companies are not so great as might be imagined. Bulky though the Companies Acts undoubtedly are, they deal mainly with details, and many of the fundamental principles of company law are nowhere enshrined in them.[61]

OUTLINE OF A COMPANY'S CONSTITUTION AND ORGANS

Before proceeding further it may be useful to indicate in general terms the type of constitution adopted by companies to enable them to fulfil their economic and social functions as described above.

Today a company's original constitution is very much a matter for its promoters. This was not always so. When incorporation could only be obtained through a special statute or charter the promoters could petition for what they wanted but it rested with the legislature or the Crown to decide what they should actually have. In theory, this is still the case so far as statutory and chartered companies are concerned, but in practice the initiative has shifted to the promoters, who will draft and promote their private Bill or append a draft charter to their petition, and although this may be rejected or amended they will probably either fail completely or obtain very much what they themselves have put forward. As regards a company registered under the Companies Acts—overwhelmingly the most common type—the promoters have almost complete freedom, provided that the constitution is set out in the statutory form. This is because the modern company—as we shall see in the next chapters—developed mainly through the unincorporated partnership, the constitution of which naturally depended on the agreement of the partners.

Basic constitution and internal administration

Whether the company be statutory, chartered or registered, its regulations will almost certainly be contained in two separate documents. Its basic constitution will be set out in its statute, charter or memorandum of association, respectively, and it is to this document that it owes its existence as a corporate entity, and upon this document, construed in

---

[60] Certain sections of the Companies Acts (including the prospectus provisions) now apply with modifications to most chartered and statutory companies carrying on business for gain: see Companies Act 1948, s. 435 and Sched. 14, Companies Act 1967, s. 54, and Companies (Unregistered Companies) Regs. 1967 (S.I. 1876).

[61] Though it sometimes creates exceptions to rules which it does not state; for example, Companies Act 1948, ss. 53, 57, 58, 65–71, creating exceptions to the principle that share capital must be maintained (see Chap. 6, *infra*).

the light of the common law and general statute law, will depend its powers and duties as a legal person. To what extent the constitution is flexible will depend on the type of company and the terms of its constitution. Statutory or chartered companies will have no power to vary their constitutions unless some power to do so is conferred by their special statutes or charters. Normally, if any amendment is desired, they will have to apply to the legislature or the Crown by which they were constituted; to adopt the analogy of constitutional law, they have an inflexible constitution similar to most Federal States, and, like some Federal States, they themselves cannot amend the constitution. A statutory company which wishes to amend its constitution will have to apply to the legislature for an amending statute, and a chartered company will have to petition the Crown to amend its constitution by a supplementary charter.

In theory the position is much the same with registered companies. The memorandum of association laying down the company's constitution is only alterable to the extent permitted by the Companies Acts to which it owes its validity.[62]   In the earlier Acts the company itself had virtually no power to effect alterations, but today the constitution has become much more flexible and in one way or another every provision of the memorandum (except that fixing the country in which its registered office is to be situated) can be altered by the company itself, unless the memorandum expressly provides to the contrary, although in one case [63] the consent of the Board of Trade is required, and in others special formalities are needed.[64]   Moreover, the memorandum need only state the company's name, objects, domicile, share capital (if any) and that the liability of the members is limited (if such be the case). Everything else is regarded as a matter of administration to be dealt with in the second document, the articles of association. By contrast the constitution of a chartered or statutory company is likely to be far more detailed,[65] so that in this respect, also, registered companies enjoy far greater flexibility.

But although the dividing line between basic constitution and internal administration may be drawn at different places, it is accepted that the details of the internal administration will not be laid down in the constitution. In addition to the statute, charter or memorandum, there will be a separate set of regulations governing these matters, normally, in the case of statutory or chartered companies, called the by-laws, and in the case of registered companies, the articles of associa-

---

[62] Companies Act 1948, s. 4.

[63] For the alteration of the name : Companies Act 1948, s. 18.

[64] Companies Act 1948, ss. 5 and 23. See Chap. 5, *infra.*

[65] The Companies Clauses Consolidation Acts 1845–1889 (impliedly incorporated into the special statutes of incorporation) consist largely of matters dealt with in the articles of a registered company—indeed much of Table A of the Companies Act 1948, containing a model set of articles, is based on the Act of 1845.

tion. These, subject to certain rather ill-defined restraints on abuse,[66] are freely alterable by the company itself. Only the method of alteration and addition will be laid down in the constitution or, more probably, will depend on the general statute law. Thus, in the case of registered companies, the Companies Act 1948 [67] provides that the articles may be added to or amended by a special resolution of the company, *i.e.*, a resolution passed by a three-fourths majority of the members voting, after twenty-one days' written notice has been given of the intention to propose it as a special resolution.[68]

The company's organs

The form of these articles has become largely standardised under the influence of the model tables appended to the Companies Acts [69] and of specialist company lawyers and books of precedents.[70] They may, and do, contain regulations on many matters—on the share capital, meetings, dividends, accounts, and the like—but the most important are those relating to the company's organs.

The general meeting

A company has two primary organs, the members in general meeting and the directorate. Here, again, an analogy may be found in constitutional law. In a parliamentary democracy such as ours, legislative sovereignty rests with Parliament, while administration is left to the executive government, subject to a measure of control by Parliament through its power to force a change of government. It is much the same with a company, except, of course, that a company is not sovereign but has a limited competence only. Within these limits, supreme rule-making authority rests with a general meeting of the members. Generally a simple majority vote suffices, but in some cases a larger majority or other special formalities may be required. Thus the Companies Acts provide that certain things can only be done by an extraordinary resolution, which requires a three-fourths majority, and others by a special resolution which requires longer than the normal notice, and, again, a three-fourths majority, and the constitution

---

[66] The courts evolved the principle that by-laws must be reasonable, a rule which still applies to municipal corporations and which is expressly stated in many charters. The Companies Clauses Consolidation Act 1845 merely provides (s. 124) that by-laws shall not be " repugnant to the laws of that part of the U.K. where the same are to have effect." In the case of registered companies all that remains of the rule is the vague principle that an alteration of the articles must not be a fraud on the minority shareholders (see Chap. 24, *infra*) and s. 22 of the Act of 1948 providing that the financial obligations of members cannot be increased without their individual consent.

[67] s. 10.

[68] s. 141.

[69] Now Companies Act 1948, Sched. I.

[70] Especially Palmer's *Company Precedents* originally published in 1877 and now in its 17th ed. The unifying influence formerly exercised by this famous book is probably unparalleled elsewhere in English law.

may entrench certain rights still further by embodying them in the memorandum and providing that they shall be unalterable.[71]

The board of directors

But although it would be constitutionally possible for the company in general meeting to exercise all the powers of the company, it clearly would not be practicable (except in the case of a one- or two-man company) for day-to-day administration to be undertaken by such a cumbersome piece of machinery. Hence the statute, charter, or articles will provide for a board of directors,[72] corresponding to the executive government of the State, and will say what powers are to be performed by the board and how it is to be appointed and changed. Like the Government, the directors will be answerable to the " Parliament " constituted by the general meeting, but in practice (again like the Government) they will exercise as much control over the Parliament as that exercises over them. And the modern practice is to confer on the directors the right to exercise all the company's powers, except such as the general law expressly provides must be exercised in general meeting.[73]

Powers which are strictly legislative are not in general affected by this delegation, for, as we have seen, the Companies Act 1948 in section 10 provides that an alteration of the articles requires a special resolution of the company in general meeting. Nevertheless, the dividing line between legislation and administration is difficult to draw, and just as the modern legislature finds it necessary to delegate to the executive many powers which are of a legislative nature, so will the directors of a modern company undertake considerably more than detailed administration; it is certainly they who will make and implement most policy decisions. Indeed, their position *vis-à-vis* the company is, in many ways, more powerful than that of the Government *vis-à-vis* the Parliament at Westminster. The theory of parliamentary sovereignty means that Parliament could (in theory) override anything done by the Government notwithstanding that this was clearly within its competence as a matter of pure administration. So originally could the members in general meeting; in fact the directors seem to have been treated as their agents. The modern theory, however, is somewhat different, for, provided that the act is within the powers delegated to the directors, the members in general meeting cannot interfere with it.[74] The most they can do is to dismiss the directorate and appoint others in their place, or alter the articles so as to restrict the powers of the directors for the future. In

---

[71] Companies Act 1948, s. 23.
[72] Companies Clauses Act 1845, s. 81 *et seq.* Companies Act 1948, s. 176 *et seq.* and *cf.* Table A, Art. 75 *et seq.* The name " directors " will not necessarily be used; in many chartered and guarantee companies the equivalent officers will be called " governors "; see the definition of " directors " in Companies Act 1948, s. 455.
[73] Table A, Art. 80. The delegation under the Companies Clauses Act 1845 is only slightly less wide: see ss. 90 and 91.
[74] See further Chap. 7, pp. 130–138, *infra.*

theory, therefore, the general meeting has less power over the directorate than the British Parliament has over the Executive, although it still has more than in some other democracies where there is a complete separation of powers so that the legislature cannot dismiss the Government or curtail its powers.

Managing directors

This wide delegation of the company's powers is, however, to the directors acting as a board, not to the individual directors. But, here again, it will obviously be impractical in the case of large companies for day-to-day administration to take place at formal board meetings which will probably be held not more than once a fortnight. In the meantime other officers of the company will have to ensure that the decisions of the board are implemented and its policy carried out; under the board and directly or indirectly responsible to and appointed by the board will be found the management and secretariat. In all probability some at least of the managers and perhaps the secretary will also be directors, for the normal practice today is to provide that directors may be appointed to other paid offices in the company.[75] And, in practice, these officers will do much more than merely carry out the decisions and policy of the board; they will themselves make decisions and decide on policy. In fact, many, and perhaps most, of the company's powers which have been primarily delegated to the board will be subdelegated by them to the managing director or directors; a provision enabling this to be done has become common form in articles.[76] It is in these managers that in reality we find the closest parallel to the executive government of constitutional law; and this, indeed, is recognised by the common use of the expression " business executives " to describe, not directors as such, but the higher ranks of managers. The business of the directorate is coming more and more to be recognised as one of laying down policy in the most general terms and exercising an equally general supervision over the way in which it is carried out; everything else is left to the managers assisted by the secretariat.

Here again we may see an obvious analogy in constitutional law, the history of which, in this country, has been one of a gradual shift of control from larger executive organs to smaller. Just as power within the State has moved from the Queen in Council to the Privy Council, and from the Privy Council to the Cabinet and, at times, to an inner council within the Cabinet, so has the power within the company moved from the general meeting to the board and from the board to

---

[75] *Cf.* Companies Act 1948, Table A, Art. 84 (3). There is no such provision in the Companies Clauses Acts.

[76] *Cf.* Table A, Arts 107–109. The Companies Clauses Acts merely provide for delegation to committees of the directors: 1845 Act, s. 95.

the management. But, as in constitutional law, the law lags behind the practice. The shift of power from the general meeting to the board has received a considerable measure of legal recognition, but this is hardly true of the further shift from the board to the management. The latter is regarded in law as fully answerable to and controllable by the board [77]; there is, for example, no rule (as yet) that once the board has delegated powers to managing directors it cannot interfere with the exercise by the managers of these powers.

On the other hand there is increasing recognition of the status of management and secretariat. In many modern statutes, particularly in revenue matters, a clear distinction is drawn between " full-time service directors " and others. Similarly, the Companies Act 1948 recognises that the secretary is an important official rather than a mere servant of the company. It provides that every company must have a secretary and that a sole director [78] shall not also be the secretary [79]; it also requires that particulars of his identity shall be disclosed in the company's register and on the company's file at the Companies' Registry together with particulars of the directors.[80]

These distinctions between the functions of members in general meeting, boards of directors, and management and secretariat must not be exaggerated. They are of importance only in the case of the public company or the larger private company. In the one- or two-man private company the factual position will be the same as in a partnership, with the same few people exercising all these functions.[81] In practice they will probably not clearly distinguish between their actions in their various capacities and normally this will not matter much.

One of the main problems facing company law is to provide an adequate system of checks and balances between the various organs— and here again there is an obvious analogy in the field of government. For the present, however, it is only necessary to point out that this division of functions between separate organs is one of the features which distinguishes a company from a partnership and which enables the public company to fulfil its economic role.

Interpretation of the Constitution

The analogies which have been drawn with constitutional law must not be taken to imply that the courts, in interpreting the constitution of a company, adopt the same " large and liberal interpretation " that may be regarded as appropriate when construing the written constitution

---

[77] *Cf.* Table A, Art. 109, and Chap. 7, *infra*.

[78] Private companies need have only one director although all other companies registered after 1929 must have at least two: Companies Act 1948, s. 176.

[79] *Ibid.*, s. 177. *Cf.* also ss. 178 and 179.

[80] *Ibid.*, s. 200.

[81] Hence it was not until 1948 that a private company was required to have any directors.

of a state.[82] Though they will strive to adopt a construction which gives " business efficacy "[83] to the company's regulations, they are bound by the strict letter of the words used and, if these words are unambiguous, an argument that they produce inconvenience,[84] or even absurdity, will only be applied with great caution.[85] The result is to produce even greater strictness than in normal cases of contract, for the written regulations cannot be rectified even if they are not in accordance with the parties' intention.[86]

As already mentioned, the wording of clauses in memoranda and articles has become largely standardised and for this reason the courts will be reluctant to disturb a decision on construction which has stood for some time and upon which the title to property may depend.[87] This, however, has not always deterred them from overruling such a decision if satisfied that it is erroneous.[88]

[82] *Edwards* v. *Att.-Gen. for Canada* [1930] A.C. 124, P.C., at pp. 136–137.
[83] *Holmes* v. *Keyes* [1959] Ch. 199, C.A., see, *per* Jenkins L.J. at p. 215.
[84] *Worcester Corsetry Ltd.* v. *Witting* [1936] Ch. 640, C.A., at p. 646.
[85] *Grundt* v. *Great Boulder Proprietary Mines Ltd.* [1948] Ch. 145, C.A. " ' Absurdity ' . . . like public policy, is a very unruly horse ": *per* Greene M.R. at p. 158. See also Vaisey J. in *Rayfield* v. *Hands* [1960] Ch. 1 at p. 4.
[86] *Scott* v. *Frank Scott (London) Ltd.* [1940] Ch. 794, C.A. Within limits they can, of course, be altered for the future if the necessary majority can be obtained for passing a special resolution.
[87] *Re Warden & Hotchkiss Ltd.* [1945] Ch. 270, C.A.
[88] For a strong example, see the overruling of *Re William Metcalfe Ltd.* [1933] Ch. 142, C.A. by *Scottish Insurance Corpn.* v. *Wilsons & Clyde Coal Co.* [1949] A.C. 462, H.L., and *Re Isle of Thanet Electricity Supply Co.* [1950] Ch. 161, C.A. See *infra*, pp. 361–364.

CHAPTER 2

HISTORY OF ENGLISH COMPANY LAW TO 1825

THIS book is concerned with modern company law, but there are some branches of modern English law which cannot be properly understood without reference to their historical background, and company law is certainly one of them; indeed, of all branches of the law it is perhaps the one least readily understood except in relation to its historical development, a somewhat extended account of which is therefore essential.[1] Such an account falls conveniently into three periods: (1) until 1720 when the Bubble Act was passed; (2) from 1720 until the Bubble Act was repealed in 1825; and (3) from 1825 until the present day. The present chapter deals with the first two of these periods.

1. HISTORY OF ENGLISH COMPANIES UNTIL 1720

Early forms of commercial associations

Various forms of associations were known to medieval law and as regards some of them the concept of incorporation was early recognised. At first, however, incorporation seems to have been used only in connection with ecclesiastical and public bodies, such as chapters, monasteries and boroughs, which had corporate personality conferred upon them by a charter from the Crown or were deemed by prescription to have received such a grant.[2]

---

[1] For further details, see especially Formoy, *The Historical Foundations of Modern Company Law* (Lond. 1923); C. A. Cooke, *Corporation, Trust and Company* (Manchester, 1950); Holdsworth, H.E.L., Vol. 8, pp. 192–222; *Anglo-American Essays in Legal History*, Vol. 3, pp. 161–255 (Boston, Mass. 1909); A. B. Levy, *Private Corporations and their Control*, Vol. 1, Part 1 (Lond. 1950); Lloyd, *Unincorporated Associations*, Part 1; Horrwitz (1946) 62 L.Q.R. 375–386; W. R. Scott, *Joint Stock Companies to 1720* (Camb. 1909–1912)—especially Vol. I; C. T. Carr, *Law of Corporations* (Camb. 1905) and *Select Charters of Trading Corporations* (Selden Society, 1913); C. M. Schmitthoff, " The Origin of the Joint Stock Company " (1939) 3 Toronto L.J. 74 to 96; A. B. DuBois, *The English Business Company after the Bubble Act, 1720–1800* (N.Y. 1938); H. A. Shannon, " The Coming of General Limited Liability," and " The First 5,000 Limited Companies and their Duration " (1931–1932) Econ.Hist., Vol. 11, 267 and 396; B. C. Hunt, *The Development of the Business Corporation in England, 1800–1867* (Harvard Economic Studies, 1936); and R. B. Instone " Archaeology of the Companies Acts " (1962) 25 M.L.R. 406. The works of DuBois and Hunt are particularly fascinating accounts of the formative years which largely render obsolete earlier accounts of the periods to which they relate. Much old learning is to be found in J. Grant, *Law of Corporations* (Lond. 1850).

[2] While it is doubtful whether English law has ever unequivocally committed itself to the " fiction " theory of corporation, it seems to have fairly consistently adopted the concession theory—namely, that incorporation depends upon a State grant. But it has recognised the power of foreign States (see Chap. 28), and it may be that until the Reformation a grant of incorporation could be conferred on an English

In the commercial sphere the principal medieval associations were the Gilds of Merchants, organisations which had few resemblances to modern companies but correspond roughly to our trade protection associations, with the ceremonial and mutual fellowship of which we can see relics in the modern Freemasons. Many of these gilds in due course obtained charters from the Crown, mainly because this was the only effective method of obtaining for their members a monopoly of any particular commodity or branch of trade. Incorporation as a convenient method of distinguishing the rights and liabilities of the association from those of its members was hardly needed, since each member traded on his own account subject only to obedience to the regulations of the gild.

Trading on joint account, as opposed to individual trading subject to the rules of the gild, was carried on through partnerships, of which two types were known to the medieval law merchant. The first of these, the *commenda*, was in fact a cross between a partnership and a loan whereby a financier advanced a sum of money to the active trader upon terms that he should share in the profits of the enterprise, his position being similar to that of a sleeping partner but with no liability beyond that of the capital originally advanced. In Continental law the *commenda* developed into the *société en commandite*, a form of association which has played, and still plays, an important part in the commercial life of those countries which adopted it. But in England it never took root, possibly because we lagged behind the Continent in book-keeping technique.[3] Had it become an accepted institution of English law the history of our company law might well have been very different, but in fact it only became legalised here in 1907[4] by which time complete limitation of liability could be obtained easily and cheaply by incorporation under the Companies Act.

The other type of partnership was the *societas*, a more permanent form of association which developed into the present-day partnership, each partner being an agent of the others and liable to the full extent

religious body by the Pope. That incorporation might be granted by statute appears never to have been doubted (Holdsworth, H.E.L., Vol. 3, p. 476) but in fact it was not until the latter part of the eighteenth century that it became the practice for Acts of Parliament actually to effect the incorporation. Until then statutes were used only to amplify the royal prerogative by authorising the Crown to confer a charter of incorporation with privileges beyond those which the Crown alone could confer (this was done, for example, in the case of the Bank of England and the South Sea Co.). In a modern case (*Elve* v. *Boyton* [1891] 1 Ch. 501) it has been held that such a company is " incorporated by Act of Parliament " within the meaning of an investment clause. DuBois (*op. cit.*, pp. 87 and 88) quotes examples of incorporation granted by Scottish burghs during the eighteenth century when the question also arose of the extent to which the royal prerogative could be delegated to colonial governors. As Sir Cecil Carr pointed out long ago (*Law of Corporations*, p. 173 *et seq.*) the concession theory has worn somewhat thin now that incorporation can be obtained by mere registration.

3 See Cooke, *op. cit.*, p. 46.
4 Limited Partnerships Act 1907. It was adopted in Ireland by statute in 1781 and it seemed for a time that it might take root in Scotland : DuBois, *op. cit.*, pp. 224–225.

of his private fortune for partnership debts. The full implications of the partnership relationship were only worked out by courts of equity during the eighteenth and nineteenth centuries, but these two main elements of agency and unlimited liability were already appreciated during this period.

Merchant adventurers

The first type of English organisation to which the name " company " was generally applied was that adopted by merchant adventurers for trading overseas. Royal charters conferring privileges on such companies are found as early as the fourteenth century,[5] but it was not until the expansion of foreign trade and settlement in the sixteenth century that they became common. The earliest types were the so-called " regulated companies " which were virtually extensions of the gild principle into the foreign sphere and which retained much of the ceremonial and freemasonry of the domestic gilds. Each member traded with his own stock and on his own account, subject to obeying the rules of the company, and incorporation was not essential since the trading liability of each member would be entirely separate from that of the company and the other members. Charters were nevertheless obtained largely because of the need to acquire a monopoly of trade for members of the company and governmental power over the territory for the company itself. " Thus, in the first instance, corporate form was valued both by the king and by the merchants, not so much because it created an artificial person distinct from its members, as because it created a body endowed with these governmental powers and trading privileges. It was from the point of view of trade organisation and the foreign policy of the State, rather than from the point of the interests of the persons comprising the company—from the point of view of public rather than commercial law—that the corporate form was valued." [6] And, it may be added, it was only from these points of view that organisation as a regulated company was at all suitable.

At a later stage, however, the partnership principle of trading on joint account invaded the regulated companies which became joint commercial enterprises instead of trade protection associations.[7] At first, in addition to the separate trading by each member with his own stock and later instead of it, they started to operate on a joint account and with a joint stock. This process can be traced in the development of the famous East India Company,[8] which received its first charter in

---

[5] See C. T. Carr, *Select Charters of Trading Corporations* (Selden Society), pp. xi–xiii.
[6] Holdsworth, H.E.L., Vol. 8, 201–202.
[7] For a good account of this development and a comparison with similar developments on the Continent, see Schmitthoff (1939) 3 Toronto L.J., p. 74 *et seq.*
[8] See Scott, *op. cit.*, Vol. II, pp. 89–206.

1600, granting it a monopoly of trade with the Indies. Originally any member could carry on that trade privately, although there also existed a joint stock to which members could, if they wished, subscribe varying amounts. At first this joint stock and the profits made from it were redivided among the subscribers after each voyage. From 1614 onwards, however, the joint stock was subscribed for a period of years, and this practice subsisted until 1653 when a permanent joint stock was introduced. It was not until 1692 that private trading was finally forbidden to members. Until this date, therefore, the constitution of the East India Co. represents a compromise between a regulated company, formed primarily for the government of a particular trade, and the more modern type of company, designed to trade for the profit of its members. This new type was called a joint stock company, a name which persists until the present day,[9] although few of those who use it realise that it was adopted to distinguish the companies to which it relates from a once normal, but now obsolete, form.

Companies and incorporation

It was not until the second half of the seventeenth century that the differentiation between the two types of company was firmly established, nor was there, until very much later, any clear distinction between unincorporated partnerships and incorporated companies. Many joint stock companies were originally formed as partnerships by agreement under seal, providing for the division of the undertaking into shares which were transferable by the original partners with greater or less freedom according to the terms of the partnership agreement. At this time there was, of course, no limit to the number of partners, but in fact these were not generally very numerous, and additional capital was raised by further " leviations " or calls on the existing members rather than by invitations to the public.

On the other hand incorporation had certain clear advantages. A corporation was capable of existing in perpetuity, it could sue outsiders and its own members, and possession of a common seal facilitated the distinction between the acts of the company and those of its members. Although the transferability of shares and majority rule, which were not enjoyed by the ordinary partnership, were in practice procurable under a skilfully drafted deed of co-partnership, the legality of transferable shares, except under a power expressly conferred in a charter, was not free from doubt, for choses in action were of course not assignable at common law. However, the fact that shares were essentially a form of chose in action was not clearly recognised until

---

[9] Thus a leading textbook (" Gore-Browne ") is still entitled *A Handbook of Joint Stock Companies*. " Stock " is, of course, here used in the same sense as in " stock-in-trade " and not as in " stocks and shares."

later. The shares of the New River Company [10] were, for example, held to be realty,[11] and so they remained until the twentieth century.

Rather surprisingly the most important advantage of all those conferred by incorporation—limited liability—seems only to have been realised as an afterthought. The fact that an individual member of a corporation was not liable for its debts had been accepted in the case of non-trading corporations as early as the fifteenth century,[12] and, not without some doubts, it was eventually recognised at the end of this period in the case of trading companies.[13] But although it was recognised, it appears at first to have been valued mainly because it avoided the risk of the company's property being seized in payment of the members' separate debts,[14] rather than as a method of enabling the members to escape liability for the company's debts. This doubtless was because many charters expressly conferred a power on the company to make leviations (or calls) on the members and it was by no means clear that a company did not have this power in the absence of an express provision.[15] This being so, limited liability was illusory; the company as a person was, of course, liable to pay its debts and in order to raise money to do so it would make calls on its members. Moreover, the creditors, by a process resembling subrogation, could proceed directly against the members, if the company refrained from taking the necessary action.[16] But legal ingenuity was not long in appreciating the possibilities of expressly excluding or limiting the company's power to make levies by a bargain to that effect between the company and its members. Such agreements seem to have been in use by both incorporated and unincorporated companies, and the fact that they were only effective in the case of the former was probably not clearly grasped by lawyers and certainly not by investors.

Growth of domestic companies

By the middle of the seventeenth century powerful monopolistic companies were already coming to be regarded as anachronisms; it was

[10] Which originated in a statute of 1606 (3 Jac. 1, c. 18), was granted a charter in 1619, and became subject to no fewer than 13 later statutes culminating in the Metropolis Water Act 1902, which expressly preserved its shares as realty (s. 9 (1)) and which vested the water-supply part of the undertaking in the Metropolitan Water Board. In pursuance of a further statute the company registered under the Companies Acts in 1905 and still exists as an investment trust company.

[11] *Townsend* v. *Ash* (1745) 3 Atk. 336. The theory seems to have been that a corporation held its assets on trust for its members; *cf. Child* v. *Hudson's Bay Co.* (1723) 2 P.Wms. 207. Later equity went a stage further by recognising, both in partnerships and companies, an implied trust for conversion under which the shares became personalty irrespective of the nature of the firm's assets. In many charters and statutes of incorporation this conversion was expressly provided for; *cf.* Companies Clauses Consolidation Act 1845, s. 7, and Companies Act 1948, s. 73.

[12] Holdsworth, H.E.L., Vol. 3, 484.

[13] *Edmunds* v. *Brown & Tillard* (1668) 1 Lev. 237; *Salmon* v. *The Hamborough Co.* (1671) 1 Ch.Cas. 204, H.L.

[14] See the common form provision in petitions for charters quoted by Carr, *Select Charters*, xvii, xviii.

[15] See DuBois, *op. cit.* 98 *et seq.*   [16] *Salmon* v. *The Hamborough Co.*, *supra*.

realised that their governmental powers were properly the functions of the State itself and that their monopolies were an undue restraint on freedom of trade. Most of them atrophied; some survived for a time by converting, as did the Levant and Russia companies, from the joint stock to the regulated form (a strange reversal of the normal trend designed to allow greater freedom to their members); others, like the Royal Africa Company, by completely relinquishing their monopolies.[17] And after the Revolution of 1688 [18] it seems to have been tacitly assumed that the Crown's prerogative was limited to the right to grant a charter of incorporation, and that any monopolistic or other special powers should be conferred by statute.[19]

The decline in the foreign-trading companies was however accompanied by an immense growth in those for domestic trade. Some of these were powerful corporations chartered under statutory powers (such as the Bank of England [20]) the objects of which resembled those of the public corporations of the present day, but most were public companies only in the sense that they invited the participation of the investing public. As regards these, the close relation between incorporation and monopoly was still maintained, for most companies were incorporated in order to work a patent of monopoly granted to an inventor.[21] By the end of the seventeenth century some idea had been gleaned of one of the primary functions of the company concept—the possibility of enabling the capitalist to combine with the entrepreneur. Share dealings were common and stock-broking was a recognised profession, the abuses of which the legislature sought to regulate as early as 1696.[22] But it would be entirely misleading to suggest that there was in any sense a company law; at the most there was an embryonic law of partnership which applied to those companies which had not become incorporated and, with modifications required by the terms of the charter and the nature of incorporation, to those which had. Both deeds of partnership (or settlement, to use the later term) and charters owed much to the practice of the medieval gilds, particularly as regards the constitution of the governing body which generally consisted of a

---

[17] The Hudson's Bay Company did not do so until 1869 and still survives as a chartered company. The East India Co. also survived until the middle of the nineteenth century but as a State organ rather than as a trading concern.

[18] Previously it seems to have been assumed that the *Case of Monopolies* (1602) 11 Co.Rep. 84b, and the Statute of Monopolies 1623, had left unimpaired the Crown's power to grant a monopoly for the regulation of foreign trade and this power had been upheld by the H.L. in 1684 in *East India Co.* v. *Sandys*, 10 St.Tr. 371. But *cf. Horne* v. *Ivy* (1668) 1 Ventr. 47, showing that the courts were already placing limitations on the extent of its exercise.

[19] Even earlier this had become the practice in the case of domestic companies requiring special powers; for example, the New River Co. (see note 10, above).

[20] Incorporated, by charter preceded by statute, in 1694.

[21] See Cooke, *op. cit.*, Chap. 4.

[22] 8 & 9 Wm. 3, c. 32. It is interesting to note that this legislation followed a report of the Commissioners for Trade (the forerunners of the Board of Trade) which seems to be the first instance of this department interesting itself in a branch of company law (see pp. 38, 39, *infra*).

governor and assistant governors. From the end of the seventeenth century the term " directors " began to supersede " assistant governors." But the terminology varied and still varies.[23] It is interesting to note that although the invention of preference shares is generally attributed to the railway boom a century later, certain companies had already experimented with different classes of shares or of loan stock [24] (for the distinction between shares and debentures was not appreciated until much later).

The South Sea Bubble

The first and second decades of the eighteenth century were marked by an almost frenetic boom in company flotations which led to the famous South Sea Bubble.[25] Most company promoters were not particularly fussy about whether they obtained charters (an expensive and dilatory process), and those who felt it desirable to give their projects this hallmark of respectability found it simpler and cheaper to acquire charters from moribund companies which were able to do a brisk trade therein.[26] An insurance company acquired the charters of the Mines Royal and Mineral and Battery Works, and a company which proposed to lend money on land in Ireland and a banking partnership [27] in turn acquired the charter of the Sword Blade Company which had been formed to manufacture hollow sword blades.

Impetus was given to this boom by the grandiose scheme of the South Sea Company to acquire virtually the whole of the National Debt [28] (some £31,000,000) by buying out the holders or exchanging their holdings for the company's stock, the theory being that the possession of an interest-bearing loan owed by the state was a basis upon which the company might raise vast sums to extend its trade. This theory was not necessarily unsound—it was indeed a logical extension of the principle upon which the Bank of England, and the South Sea Company itself, had been originally formed—but unfortunately the

[23] Thus the B.B.C. and most incorporated schools and colleges still employ the term " Governors " while other corporations use the expression " Managers."
[24] Scott, *op. cit.*, Vol. I, pp. 364–365.
[25] The literature on the Bubble crisis is, of course, immense; the most scholarly treatment is still that of Scott, *op. cit.*, Vol. I, Chaps. XXI and XXII. For popular accounts, see Carswell, *The South Sea Bubble* (Lond. 1960), and Cowell, *The Great Swindle* (Lond. 1960).
[26] We cannot afford to scoff at our predecessors, for a trade is still done in registrations of defunct companies. Two centuries hence, a generation which, owing to the incidence of taxation, was prepared to pay for registrations in direct proportion to the amount of the old company's accumulated losses will probably appear just as ridiculous.
[27] Which thereupon issued " sword blade " notes and bonds, and acted as bankers for the South Sea Company.
[28] The company was originally formed, by charter preceded by statute in 1711, to incorporate the holders of the floating debt in exchange for a monopoly of trade with South America, a right which the power of Spain rendered something of a *damnosa hereditas*. The extended scheme seems to have been inspired by the financial experiments known as the Mississippi System introduced in France, with equally disastrous results, by John Law.

company had precious little trade to expand. Moreover, it had to pay dearly for its privileges by outbidding and outbribing the Bank of England.[29] And, of course, it paid too dearly—but that story belongs to our next period.

When the flood of speculative enterprises was at its height, Parliament decided to intervene to check the gambling mania which the Government had itself encouraged by sanctioning the South Sea Company's scheme. Its attempt was, however, somewhat inept. A House of Commons Resolution [30] of April 27, 1720, ignored the causes and merely emphasised the effects of the rash speculation by drawing attention to the numerous undertakings which were purporting to act as corporate bodies without legal authority, practices which "manifestly tend to the prejudices of the public trade and commerce of the kingdom." This was followed by the so-called Bubble Act [31] of the same year, which also made no attempt to put joint stock companies on a proper basis so as to further industry and trade and protect investors. Exactly what it did is, however, somewhat obscure.

The main section, 18, repeated the Resolution of the House of Commons and provided that all such undertakings as were therein described, "tending to the common Grievance, Prejudice and Inconvenience of His Majesty's subjects," should be illegal and void. The section then proceeded to give particular examples, *viz.*, the acting as a corporate body and the raising of transferable stock or the transfer of any shares therein without legal authority either by Act of Parliament or Crown charter, or acting or pretending to act under any obsolete charter. By section 21 brokers dealing in securities of illegal companies were to be liable to penalties. The remaining sections, however, exempted companies established before June 24, 1718 (which were therefore left to the common law, whatever that may have been), and also the East India and South Sea Companies and the two assurance companies authorised by the first part of the Act. Finally, in section 25, there was a vague proviso that nothing "shall extend . . . to prohibit or restrain the carrying on of any home or foreign trade in partnership in such manner as hath been hitherto usually and may be lawfully done according to the Laws of this Realm now in force."

---

[29] It is interesting to speculate on what might have happened had the Bank of England outbidden the company. Perhaps it would have been the former whose bubble reputation was so soon pricked, and the latter which acquired the mantle of respectability (with the final canon of nationalisation) in fact worn by "the old lady of Threadneedle Street."

[30] H.C.Jour. XIX, 351. This resolution was based upon the Report of a Committee appointed on Feb. 22 to inquire into certain of the projects; for its Report, see *ibid.*, p. 341 *et seq.*

[31] 6 Geo. 1, c. 18. This prolix and confusing statute, which, as Maitland said, "seems to scream at us from the Statute Book" (*Collected Papers*, Vol. 3, p. 390), is divided into two parts. The first (ss. 1–17) authorised the incorporation of the London and Royal Exchange Assurance Companies with a monopoly of the corporate insurance of marine risks. It is with the later sections only that we are at present concerned.

This statute was our first attempt at a Companies Act[32] and it clearly reflected little credit on anyone concerned with it. As Holdsworth says,[33] " What was needed was an Act which made it easy for joint stock societies to adopt a corporate form and, at the same time, safeguarded both the shareholders in such societies and the public against frauds and negligence in their promotion and management. What was passed was an Act which deliberately made it difficult for joint stock societies to assume a corporate form and contained no rules at all for the conduct of such societies, if, and when, they assumed it." But in fact the authorities were faced with a new phenomenon and had no clear idea of the issues involved. Nor is it altogether fair to blame them; a further 120 years' experience was to be needed before anything on the right lines was to be enacted, and even today we find it necessary to amend our company law every twenty years and to precede the amendment by a long and careful inquiry by an expert committee. It was obviously too much to expect the Parliament of 1720 to rush through a Companies Act comparable to that of 1948 or even 1844. Where they seem most blameworthy is not for what they omitted to do, but for the vagueness of what they in fact did, and when the courts were called upon to interpret it they found it vague indeed. But this they were not called upon to do for many years.

2. HISTORY OF ENGLISH COMPANIES FROM 1720 UNTIL THE REPEAL OF THE BUBBLE ACT IN 1825 [34]

The Bubble bursts

The passage of the Bubble Act, to which publicity was given by Royal Proclamation, and the events leading up to it must obviously have done much to sap public confidence. But what precipitated the disastrous collapse of 1720 was the institution of proceedings against some of the companies operating under obsolete charters with a view to these being forfeited.[35] This, as might perhaps have been foreseen,[36] led to a widespread panic from which the South Sea Company

---

[32] Or, perhaps, more properly, a Prevention of Fraud (Investments) Act, such as that of 1958.

[33] H.E.L., Vol. 8, 219–220.

[34] Fascinating and learned accounts of this period are now available in the pages of DuBois and Hunt. As their researches are not as well known in this country as they deserve, I have dealt with this period rather more fully.

[35] For an account of these proceedings and an attempted refutation of the generally accepted theory that they were instituted by the South Sea Company or its directors, see my article in (1952) 68 L.Q.R. 214.

[36] Although the legitimacy of the birth of the South Sea Company was beyond reproach, it was employing as its bankers a company incorporated under the Sword Blade Charter. The failure of these bankers was one of the factors which frustrated the efforts to arrest the panic by an agreement between the South Sea Company and the Bank of England.

itself never fully recovered.[37]   In June 1720, its stock had stood
at over 1,000 per cent. and immediately before the issue of the writs
it was still at 850 per cent.   A month later it had fallen to 390 and
by the end of the year it was quoted at 125.   The Government was
too much involved to allow the company to crash completely,[38] but the
subsequent investigations disclosed fraud and corruption (in which
members of the Government and the royal household were implicated)
and it never fully recovered.   With it fell many of its contemporaries,
which, not being regularly chartered nor so fortunate as to have friends
in high places, burst like the bubbles they were.   But, although they
disappeared, they were not forgotten, for public confidence in joint
stock companies and their securities was destroyed so effectively that
it was three-quarters of a century before there was a comparable boom.
If the legislature had intended the Bubble Act to suppress companies
they had succeeded beyond their reasonable expectations; if, as seems
more probable, they had intended to protect investors from ruin and to
safeguard the South Sea Company, they had failed miserably.

This result was attained almost without prosecutions under the Act,
for only one,[39] in 1723, is reported [40] until the beginning of the nineteenth century.   Nevertheless it is clear that the Bubble Act was for
long a sword of Damocles which exercised a restraining influence as
potent as the memory of the great slump.   DuBois's researches [41] have
shown how existing companies and the promoters of new enterprises
took counsel's opinion on the application to them of the Act, and it
is to this Act that he attributes the first traces of the dominant part
subsequently played by lawyers in the development of company law and
practice.

Effect of the Bubble on incorporations

Joint stock companies did not disappear completely.   On the contrary, many regularly chartered companies and a few unincorporated
ones [42] had survived the panic and were living examples of the
advantages of this type of organisation.   Others, too, still succeeded in

---

[37] The third volume of Scott, *op. cit.*, contains a graph showing the fluctuations in the
shares of the South Sea Company, the East India Company and the Bank of England
between May and September 1720.

[38] In the words of Holdsworth (H.E.L., Vol. 2, p. 210) it " dragged out a struggling
existence till 1807; and the faded splendours of its South Sea House survived long
enough to secure immortality in the Essays of Elia."   Later it became for a time
the home of the Baltic Exchange, and a building in the City of London still bears
the name having survived the blitz of the Second World War more successfully than
the company survived the financial " blitz " of an earlier century.

[39] *R.* v. *Cawood* (1724) 2 Ld.Raym. 1361.   It decided nothing of importance on the
interpretation of the Act.

[40] But contemporary news-sheets make it clear that others were instituted.

[41] *Op. cit.*, p. 3 *et seq.*   He refers particularly to the opinions of Sjt. Pengelly who
is known to have delivered opinions (which still survive) on no fewer than 27
organisations and whose views foreshadow the judicial interpretation adopted in the
succeeding century.

[42] Including the Sun Fire Office, established in 1709.

obtaining charters; but not many, for a lasting effect of the Bubble Act and the crisis of 1720 was to make the Law Officers of the Crown far more chary of advising the grant of charters,[43] and to insist on restrictive conditions in those that were granted.[44]

Nor at first was Parliament any more complaisant. It was not until towards the end of the century, with the growth of canal building, which necessarily involved an application to Parliament for special powers, that Parliament became less strict in its requirements and that direct statutory incorporation became common.[45] It is to this statutory incorporation that we owe many of the features of modern companies: in particular the method of limiting liability of the members to the nominal value of their shares.

Hence throughout the century (and beyond) the shadow of 1720 retarded the development of incorporated companies. The official view is well represented by the oft-quoted words of Adam Smith,[46] writing as late as 1776, in which he stated that a joint stock company was an appropriate type of organisation only for those trades which could be reduced to a routine, namely, those of banking, fire and marine insurance, making and maintaining canals, and bringing water to cities; others, in his view, were bound to be inefficient as businesses as well as being contrary to the public interest. Smith, therefore, put the seal of his approval on the current legislative and administrative practice, for the authorities, in their wisdom, had incorporated precisely these four types and had (with rare exceptions) refused to incorporate others.

Growth of unincorporated companies

Had the authorities granted incorporation more readily, already in the eighteenth century, incorporated companies might have become the dominant type of commercial enterprise. And had that policy been adopted, the Government, by its control over charters and statutes, would have shaped the development of business practice 200 years earlier than it attempted to do so on any large scale. Instead, as we have seen, the authorities placed almost insuperable difficulties in the way of incorporation and thus abdicated their control to businessmen and their legal advisers who sought an alternative device. This they found in the

---

[43] For an account of the difficulties which company promoters had to surmount, see DuBois, *op. cit.*, p. 12 *et seq.* " The law officers of the Crown, mindful of [the Act's] provisions, hesitated to approve of applications for charters which contemplated the creation of large stocks of transferable shares. Consequently, not only were the operations of unincorporated joint stock companies restricted by the Act, but the Act was used as an expression of policy to restrain the formation of business corporations " : *ibid.*, p. 12.

[44] *Ibid.* To this period can be traced conditions restricting the amount of capital which the company might raise. A further restraint on joint enterprise arose from the habit, introduced after 1720, of inserting in patents of invention prohibitions of assignment to more than five persons: *ibid.*, pp. 21–24.

[45] Over 100 statutory incorporations occurred during the last 40 years of the eighteenth century.

[46] *Wealth of Nations*, V, Chap. 1, Part III, Art. 1.

unincorporated association; paradoxically, the Bubble Act in the end caused a rebirth of the very type of association which it had sought to destroy. The history of the previous period had shown that it was perfectly feasible to trade with a joint stock without incorporation, and although the Bubble Act had struck at unincorporated companies it had expressly exempted partnerships carried on " in such manner as hath been hitherto usually and may be lawfully done." [47] This exemption clearly could not have covered every type of existing unincorporated company, for otherwise the Act became completely meaningless, but exactly how far partnerships could lawfully go was far from clear. The size of the membership could not be the decisive factor for at this time there was not and never had been any upper limit on numbers.[48] Professional opinion at the time [49] took the view, in fact adopted by the courts in the nineteenth century, that the basic test of illegality was the existence of freely transferable shares and for a time such unincorporated associations as were formed (and the shock of the crash of 1720 caused there to be few for many years) were careful to place severe restrictions on transfers.[50] But from the middle of the century onwards it is clear that unincorporated joint stock companies, often with a large number of proprietors,[51] were operating to a gradually increasing extent and that (as the Bubble Act came to be regarded as a dead letter) complete freedom of transfer was often permitted.

The deed of settlement company

Great legal ingenuity [52] was brought to bear to confer on these unincorporated associations nearly all the advantages of incorporation, and for this purpose use was made of the trust. The company would be formed under a deed of settlement (approximating to a cross between the modern articles of association and a debenture trust deed) under which the subscribers would agree to be associated in an enterprise with a prescribed joint stock divided into a specified number of shares; the

---

[47] s. 25.

[48] Except in the case of banking, as regards which the Bank of England's monopoly was protected by a prohibition, under a statute of 1708 (7 Anne, c. 30), of banking in England by more than five persons in association. And under the first part of the Bubble Act itself the London and Royal Exchange Assurances had a monopoly of insuring marine risks by companies or societies.

[49] See DuBois, *op. cit.*, p. 3 *et seq.*

[50] In the light of this it is interesting to note that unincorporated companies were often described as " private " companies, in contradistinction to the incorporated " public " company; restriction on transfer is, of course, the major feature of the twentieth-century private company. The use of the term " public company " to describe those formally incorporated will be found in a statute of 1767 (7 Geo. 3, c. 48), which struck at the practice of splitting shareholdings to increase voting power, by disqualifying members from voting until they had held their shares for six months.

[51] The true extent of the numbers was sometimes disguised by the device of subpartnership, *i.e.*, the original few shares would be subsequently subdivided; see DuBois, *op. cit.*, pp. 78–79.

[52] For details, see DuBois, *op. cit.*, Chap. III.

provisions of the deed would be variable with the consent of a specified majority of the proprietors; management would be delegated to a committee of directors; and the property would be vested in a separate body of trustees,[53] some of whom would often be directors also. Often it would be provided that these trustees should sue or be sued on behalf of the company, and although the legal efficacy of such a provision was by no means clear, suit by the trustees in a court of equity seems to have been generally permitted.[54] As for the right to be sued, it will be appreciated that obscurity on this point was by no means an unmixed disadvantage from the point of view of the company.

Long before the end of the century a considerable proportion of certain types of commercial enterprise was organised on this basis, which strangely enough, seems to have been encouraged rather than frowned upon by the Government, for frequent examples are found of refusal by the Law Officers to recommend charters of incorporation on the ground that " coparcenary " was a more appropriate form of organisation.[55] Unincorporated associations had a virtual monopoly of the growing activity of non-marine [56] insurance, both by companies trading for the profit of their members (where the old Sun had formed the model for the Phoenix, Norwich General, Norwich Union and a host of others) and by mutual and friendly societies.[57] They were also used extensively in the metal industries, they invaded the theatre, and were even used at times in canal building where statutory incorporation was

[53] This was by no means unusual even in the case of incorporated companies: *ibid.*, pp. 115–116.
[54] In practice considerable use was made of arbitration: *ibid.* 221.
[55] Thus on the Equitable Assurance petition in 1761 the Att.-Gen. (Yorke) said: " If the Petitioners are so sure of success there is an easy method of making the experiment by entering into a voluntary partnership of which there are several instances now subsisting in the business of insuring ": quoted in DuBois, *op. cit.* 30. Having regard to the size of these enterprises the Law Officers can hardly have been so naïve as to suppose that the " partnership " would be other than on a joint stock basis. Indeed petitions were often made by existing unincorporated companies and it was not unknown for such companies to take the opinion of the Law Officers on questions relating to their constitutions: *ibid.*, p. 313, n. 35.
[56] The first part of the Bubble Act had given the London and Royal Exchange Assurance Companies a monopoly of marine assurance by associations. During this period the value of this monopoly was diminished by individual insurances by underwriters who assembled at Lloyd's Coffee House and grew into the famous " Lloyd's " which was eventually incorporated in 1871, although policies continue to be underwritten not by the corporation but by individual underwriters: see further, Gibb, *Lloyd's of London* (Lond. 1957). For a popular account of the historical development with particular reference to life assurance, see Hartley Withers, *Pioneers of British Life Assurance* (1951).
[57] Friendly Societies became so common that they were authorised by statute in 1793 (33 Geo. 3, c. 54), the first general authorising Act from which sprang not only the modern Friendly Society but also Industrial and Provident Societies, Building Societies, and Trustee Savings Banks. Under the Act the rules had to be approved by the local justices, who probably enjoyed ratifying the rule of the Beneficent Society of Tinwold (1793) that " None shall be admitted into this Society who are suspected of being friendly to the new fangled doctrines of LIBERTY AND EQUALITY AND THE RIGHTS OF MAN as set forth by Thomas Paine and his adherents."

more common.   Indeed, the researches of DuBois into the eighteenth-century company records and counsel's opinions have made it clear that the use of joint stock companies was far more widespread than had hitherto been supposed on the basis of the paucity of incorporations and of decided cases on unincorporated companies.

On the other hand we have to wait until the nineteenth century for any outbreak of speculation in shares comparable to that of 1720. During the remainder of the eighteenth century, although the mechanism of the stock market was well understood and several rather half-hearted attempts were made by the legislature to check its abuses,[58] company shares do not seem to have been generally regarded as suitable invest-ments or gambling counters [59] for the lay public, but rather as means of enabling members of the mercantile community to acquire a permanent stake in enterprises with which they were familiar.   But the picture changed at the turn of the century, when first the exigencies of war and then the growth of the railways led to an outbreak of company promotion and of general speculation comparable to that of the Bubble period.   It was only then that the inherent disadvantages of the unincorporated type became fully apparent.

Disadvantages of unincorporated companies

As we have seen, one difficulty lay in the power to sue or be sued. In law these unincorporated companies were merely partnerships,[60] and this was before the time when the courts permitted suit in the firm's name.   On the contrary, actions at law [61] had to be brought by or against all the partners liable, and the difficulties [62] which this caused, particularly when there had been changes in the shareholdings, can be imagined.   The only satisfactory, but expensive, solution was the pro-motion of a private Act of Parliament permitting the company to sue ' or be sued in the name of one or more of its officials.   Such Acts became common towards the end of this period,[63] and the right was conferred on friendly societies by the Act of 1793.   As will be appreciated, the

---

[58] 7 Geo. 1, stat. 2, No. 8 (1721); 7 Geo. 2, c. 8 (1733); and 10 Geo. 2, c. 8 (1736).

[59] During the eighteenth century the lotteries met this need.   Their abolition in 1826 under the Lotteries Act 1823 may well have encouraged share speculation.   For Lotteries, see J. Ashton, *A History of English Lotteries* (Lond. 1893)—a most entertaining book.

[60] But even the law could not shut its eyes to all the differences between a large company and a simple partnership.   A shareholder in the former could obviously not bind the company, as a partner could the firm; anyone dealing with the com-pany must be deemed to know that powers of management were restricted to the directors.   Here we can detect the germ of the later rule in *Royal British Bank* v. *Turquand*, see Chap. 8, *infra*.

[61] As we have seen, equity was somewhat more lenient and, even at common law if the contract was with the trustees, they could sue on it for the benefit of the company: *Metcalfe* v. *Bruin* (1810) 12 East 400.

[62] They are well described in *George on Companies* (1825), p. 19 *et seq.*, quoted by Formoy, *op. cit.*, p. 33 *et seq.*

[63] DuBois, *op. cit.*, p. 142, quotes an example as early as 1730 but this was exceptional.

proprietors of the company would probably only be concerned with the possibility of suing and would be only too happy to find obstacles in the way of being sued, particularly as they would be personally liable without limitation.

This brings us to the second and most important disadvantage of the absence of incorporation—the members could not limit their personal liability. Until late in the century limited liability still seems to have been regarded as only a secondary consideration. DuBois [64] finds the earliest clear recognition of it as the motive for incorporation in the petition for incorporation by the Warmley Company in 1768, but increasingly from then on it became openly recognised as a factor of prime importance and one which incorporation alone could fully obtain. Unincorporated companies could only strive to approximate to it by expressly contracting in every case that liability should be limited to the funds of the company—a solution only practicable where the contracts were of a formal type such as insurance,[65] for it was generally believed that a statement to this effect in the deed of settlement would be ineffective even if the creditor had notice of it.[66]　Or, of course, they could make a virtue of necessity, as did the Phoenix Assurance which, when its rivals, the incorporated Royal Exchange Assurance, boasted of the advantages to their policy-holders of a ready remedy against the corporate stock, retorted by emphasising the advantages to the public of the full responsibility of its members.[67]

In truth, however, unlimited liability, though a danger to the risk-taker, was often a snare and a delusion rather than a protection to the public and no handicap at all to the dishonest promoter. The difficulties of suing a fluctuating body and the even greater difficulties of levying execution [68] made the personal liability of the members largely illusory. Moreover, the investor was supposed to become a member by signing the deed of settlement and until he did so his identity would not be known by the creditors. But in fact " stags " would deal in allotment letters or scrip certificates to bearer without signing the deed and often before any formal deed was in existence, and dishonest promoters, who alone might be under any legal liability, might disappear with the subscription

---

[64] *Op. cit.*, p. 95.

[65] In the nineteenth century these stipulations became common form in the policies of unincorporated offices. Such an express contract was ultimately held to be effective: *Hallett* v. *Dowdall* (1852) 21 L.J.Q.B. 98.

[66] But statements alleging limited liability were common form in both deeds of settlement and prospectuses. See Hunt, *op. cit.*, pp. 33–34, 72 and 99–101. They were eventually held to be ineffective in *Re Sea, Fire & Life Insurance Co.* (1854) 3 De G.M. & G. 459.

[67] Quoted by DuBois, *op. cit.*, p. 96.

[68] These difficulties are well explained in Formoy, *op. cit.*, p. 35 *et seq.* They did not disappear even if there was a private Act permitting the company to be sued in the name of its officers.

moneys.[69] Many promotions were still-born and others perished with
the slumps [70] which followed each successive boom. Some intervention
by the State was inevitable but the question was what form it should
take.

State intervention

The first form was the characteristic English expedient of reviving
an old remedy—in this case prosecution under the almost forgotten
Bubble Act. In November 1807, the Attorney-General (at the instance
of a private relator) sought a criminal information against two recently
formed unincorporated companies,[71] both of which had freely transferable shares and advertised that the liability of the members would be
limited. Lord Ellenborough [72] dismissed the applications because of the
lapse of eighty-seven years since the Act was previously invoked, but he
issued a stern warning that no one in the future could pretend that the
statute was obsolete and indicated that a " speculative project founded
on joint stock or transferable shares " was prohibited.[73] Shortly
afterwards two further associations were held illegal, apparently because
their shares were transferable.[74]

These decisions caused alarm among investors and promoters and
were probably contributory causes of the slump of 1808. However,
despite further prosecutions, confidence was gradually restored and the
years 1824–25 witnessed a boom which was compared with that of
1719–20 and which was followed by a similar slump. The various
court cases [75] did little to clarify the law; the better view seemed to
be that a company with freely transferable shares was illegal, but that
one where the right to transfer was restricted was unlawful only if it
had a mischievous tendency. On the other hand there were many who
were opposed to the whole conception of joint stock enterprise both
incorporated and unincorporated, and until the middle of the nineteenth
century bitter debates continued in which the virtues of healthy private
enterprise were contrasted with the dead hand of monopolistic

---

69 The *modus operandi* is explained in *ibid.*, p. 43. The opportunities for fraud thus
provided are immortalised by Charles Dickens's account of the " Anglo-Bengalee
Disinterested Loan and Life Assurance Company " in the pages of *Martin
Chuzzlewit*.
70 These occurred particularly in 1808, 1825–1826, and 1844–1845. See Hunt, *op. cit.*,
passim.
71 The London Paper Manufacturing Co. and the London Distillery Co.
72 *R.* v. *Dodd* (1808) 9 East 516.
73 *Ibid.*, pp. 526–528.
74 *Buck* v. *Buck* (1808) 1 Camp. 547 and *R.* v. *Stratton* (1809) 1 Camp. 549n. As we
have seen (*supra*, p. 33) this was Sjt. Pengelly's view in 1721.
75 They are summarised by Hunt, *op. cit.*, Chaps. II and III, and in Cooke, *op. cit.*,
Chap. VII. The most instructive of those reported are : *R.* v. *Webb* (1811) 14
East 406 ; *Pratt* v. *Hutchinson* (1812) 15 East 511 ; *Josephs* v. *Pebrer* (1825) 3 B. & C.
639 ; *Kinder* v. *Taylor* (1825) 3 L.J.Ch. 68. See further *Lindley on Companies*,
6th ed. (1902), pp. 180–184.

companies.[76] Lord Eldon, in particular, attacked the latter in both his legislative and judicial capacity. In the former he announced his intention of introducing further restrictive legislation but finally dropped this idea on the ground that the law as it stood was sufficiently strict [77]; had his view of it prevailed, it certainly would have been strict, for he was apparently prepared to hold that assuming to act as a corporation [78] was an offence at common law as well as under the Act.[79]

Finally, the Government felt compelled to do something to bring the law more into accord with the facts; but just as their predecessors in 1720 could think of nothing more constructive than the Bubble Act, so now they could think of nothing better than its repeal. In 1825, its Indian summer was finally ended. The repealing statute [80] was sponsored by Huskisson, the President of the Board of Trade, and it is then that this government department first started to take an active part in the development of company law.

Influence of the Board of Trade

The Board [81] was the successor of the Commissioners for Trade and Plantations, the history of which, as an *ad hoc* or standing Committee of the Privy Council, can be traced back to the beginning of the seventeenth century and whose report on stock-jobbing in 1696 led to the first legislative attempt [82] to regulate brokers. Throughout the eighteenth century examples can be found of references to the Commissioners of petitions for charters of incorporation,[83] especially in cases where the object was colonial trade (for at this time the greater part

---

[76] Admirable accounts of these will be found in Hunt, *op. cit.*, *passim*. The arguments used by the supporters of "private enterprise" are astonishingly reminiscent of those now used by the opponents of nationalisation. The company chairmen who inveigh against the menace of State enterprise would doubtless be shocked to realise that 150 years earlier very similar arguments were being used to attack their cherished companies. "The idea that a company was synonymous or at least co-extensive with monopoly persisted well into the nineteenth century ": Hunt, *op. cit.*, p. 17.

[77] *Ibid.*, pp. 38 and 39.

[78] But Eldon himself was unable to give any clear account of what this meant. The Inns of Court come close to acting as corporations, even to the extent, or so it is generally said, of using common seals and this seems to have impressed Eldon and acted as a restraining influence: see *Lloyd* v. *Loaring* (1802) 6 Ves. 773 at p. 779. But query if the Inns do, in fact, use common seals: see Lloyd, *Law of Unincorporated Associations*, p. 51, n. (*c*).

[79] He did not get a very good press; the *Morning Chronicle* said it confirmed their view that his opinions "as a Politician were seldom worth much ": March 30, 1825, quoted by Hunt, *op. cit.*, p. 39.

[80] 6 Geo. 4, c. 91. The marine-insurance monopoly had been repealed a year earlier: 5 Geo. 4, c. 114.

[81] The influence of the Board has been largely ignored by writers on the history of company law. For accounts of the Board's development, which, however, say little about its functions in connection with companies, see Llewellyn Smith, *The Board of Trade* (The Whitehall Series, 1928) and Prouty, *The Transformation of the Board of Trade 1830–1855* (Lond. 1957).

[82] 8 & 9 Wm. 3, c. 32.

[83] See DuBois, *op. cit.*, pp. 13, 57, 58, 60, 62, 66, 69, 70, 76, 89 and 172. There are also occasional examples of applications to the Commissioners for investigation of the affairs of existing companies: *ibid.* 126.

of the Commissioners' work was concerned with the colonies rather than with domestic trade). But, in general, decisions were taken by the Law Officers [84] (which in practice must often have meant the Attorney-General's devil [85]) and it was not until the Board was re-created by Pitt in 1784 that the emphasis changed and that it gradually came to be recognised that the Board was the appropriate government department to advise on incorporations and to guide the development of company law. Since Huskisson repealed the Bubble Act a century and a half ago the Board has been responsible for all company legislation and has been entrusted with gradually increasing supervisory powers over joint stock enterprises. It is appropriate that its first major intervention should have been an act of liberation rather than of control, for its policy throughout has been to allow the greatest possible freedom to private enterprise. As its official historian [86] truly says: "Broadly speaking the part played by the Board of Trade in relation to the movement which has revolutionised the structure of industry has been that of a vigilant onlooker rather than of a continuous supervisor." [87]

[84] DuBois, *op. cit.*, pp. 169–170 (n. 135) says. " The usual procedure in the case of an application for incorporation was the presentation of a petition to the Privy Council. The Privy Council would refer the matter to a subcommittee, which, if it were favourably inclined to the plan after consideration, would submit the petition to the Attorney-General or Solicitor-General. On occasion the Commissioners of Trade and Plantations would be consulted."

[85] Napier, *A Century of Law Reform* (Lond. 1901), p. 389.

[86] Llewellyn Smith, *op. cit.*, p. 168.

[87] The Board now has a General Consultative Committee and an Accountancy Advisory Committee of outside experts to assist and advise it, but the former appears to be moribund.

CHAPTER 3

HISTORY OF COMPANIES FROM 1825 TO THE PRESENT DAY

Legislative control

The repeal, like the enactment, of the Bubble Act was followed by a disastrous slump further emphasising the need for some constructive measures of control. These, however, were still lacking; the only concrete advance made by the new Act was a provision [1] enabling the Crown to declare the extent of the members' liability on the grant of incorporation, so that a charter was no longer necessarily accompanied by a complete absence of liability on the part of the members for the company's debts. This provision might have been expected to encourage greater freedom in the grant of charters, but in fact the authorities remained as strict as ever. Applications for statutory incorporation, stimulated by the boom in railway promotion, fared better but their expense was prohibitive except in the case of the largest concerns.[2]

Hence when the speculative fever broke out again in 1834 most promoters were thrown back on the unincorporated form, the legality of which was still in doubt, especially as Eldon had secured the inclusion in the repealing Act of an express recital that undertakings should be adjudged and dealt with according to common law. It was not until 1843 that doubts upon their common law legality were finally eradicated,[3] and even then little had been done to remove the disadvantages under which unincorporated associations laboured. But despite these handicaps joint stock banks,[4] insurance companies and a

---

[1] s. 2.

[2] Hunt, *op. cit.*, p. 82, quotes two railway incorporations which cost £72,868 and £40,588. Even the fees for a charter amounted to at least £402 which was a substantial sum in those days: *ibid.* The Report on Investments for the Savings of the Middle and Working Classes (1850 B.P.P., Vol. XIX, 169) quoted a chartered incorporation costing £1,134 which was alleged (surely erroneously?) to be "greater even than that of obtaining an Act of Parliament."

[3] *Garrard* v. *Hardey* (1843) 5 M. & G. 471; *Harrison* v. *Heathorn* (1843) 6 M. & G. 81; not following *Duvergier* v. *Fellows* (1828) 5 Bing. 248 and *Blundell* v. *Winsor* (1835) 8 Sim. 601. Brougham L.C. on the Bench took a more liberal view than his predecessor (*Walburn* v. *Ingilby* (1832) 1 Myl. & K. 61) although in the House he was almost equally reactionary on this matter and received an equally unfavourable press. ("The commercial part of the community have little reason to thank God, with Cobbett, that there is a House of Lords, and above all a Lord Brougham": *Morning Chronicle*, August 15, 1838 (cited in Hunt, *op. cit.* 84)—a reference to the prosecution of Cobbett in 1831 for criminal libel when he subpoenaed six members of the House of Lords and secured an acquittal largely because of the evidence of Brougham L.C.)

[4] Guided by the experience of Scotland (where joint stock banks had flourished in contrast with the failures of the English private concerns), the monopoly of the Bank of England was whittled away by Acts of 1826 (7 Geo. 4, c. 46) and 1833

host of other projects flourished as never before and joint stock companies came to play an important role in every part of the country's economy. Clearly some steps had to be taken to remove the legal confusion.

The first step was taken by the Trading Companies Act of 1834, which was intended to extend slightly the availability of corporate advantages. It empowered the Crown to confer by letters patent all or any of the privileges of incorporation (except limited liability) without actually granting a charter, thus in particular obviating the need for special Acts enabling companies to sue and be sued in the names of their officers.[5] The major importance of this highly illogical compromise was that it was the first general Act requiring public registration of members, but it expressly preserved their liability except after three years from parting with their shares. Moreover, its practical value was much diminished by the restrictive rules which the Board of Trade laid down for the granting of petitions under it.[6]

In 1837 the Board of Trade instructed a Chancery barrister, H. Bellenden Ker, to prepare a report on the law of partnership with particular reference to the expediency of introducing limited partnerships on the Continental model.[7] His report [8] was pigeon-holed and the only result was the re-enactment of the 1834 Act in the Chartered Companies Act of 1837 but with the valuable extension that personal liability of members might be expressly limited by the letters patent to a specified amount per share. In the ensuing seventeen years some fifty companies did in fact form under this Act, but most still preferred to rely on the *de facto* protection from personal liability conferred by the difficulties of suing and levying execution on the members of a fluctuating body. Many of these were from their inception fraudulent shams, particularly the bogus assurance companies such as those pilloried by Dickens in *Martin Chuzzlewit*,[9] and it was primarily the existence of these which led the Board of Trade to secure the appointment in 1841 of a Parliamentary Committee on Joint Stock Companies. In 1843 Gladstone, who had become President of the Board of Trade, assumed the chairmanship of the Committee and widened the scope of

---

(3 & 4 Wm. 4, c. 98). These Acts provided that banking companies could sue or be sued in the names of their officers and, in anticipation of the Act of 1844, provided for registration of certain essential particulars.

5 The difficulties with which a suitor might otherwise be faced have already been stressed; they are well exemplified in *Van Sandau* v. *Moore* (1825) 1 Russell 441, in which Lord Eldon, at p. 472, gave this as his principal justification for holding unincorporated companies to be illegal.

6 They are quoted by Hunt, *op. cit.* at pp. 57–58. The progressive Huskisson had retired from the Board in 1827, and in 1830 had lost his life in an accident at the opening of the Liverpool and Manchester railway—a victim of the railway boom which he had himself done so much to promote.

7 John Austin was a staunch advocate of this proposal: see 1825 *Parliamentary History and Review*, p. 711.

8 1837 B.P.P., Vol. XLIV, 399.

9 First published in 1843.

its inquiries. Its epoch-making Report [10] and the Joint Stock Companies Act 1844,[11] which followed it, were mainly due to his genius and energy.

Gladstone's legislation of 1844 and 1845

The 1844 Act introduced three main principles which have constituted the basis of our company law from that time. In the first place it drew a clear distinction between private partnerships and joint stock companies by providing for the registration of all new companies with more than twenty-five members,[12] or with shares transferable without the consent of all the members. Secondly, it provided for incorporation by mere registration as opposed to a special Act or charter; but this it did by a system, curious to modern eyes, of provisional registration, which only authorised the company to function for certain strictly limited preliminary purposes, followed by complete registration on filing a deed of settlement containing the prescribed particulars and other documents when for the first time the company became incorporated.[13] Thirdly, it provided for full publicity which ever since has been regarded as the most potent safeguard against fraud. It is to this Act, too, that we owe the Registrar of Companies [14] with whom particulars of the companies' constitution, changes therein, and annual returns are filed.

Limited liability, however, was still excluded. Although the company became incorporated, the personal liability of the members was preserved,[15] but their liability was to cease three years after they had transferred their shares by registered transfer [16] and creditors had to proceed first against the assets of the company.[17] Existing companies were compelled to register certain particulars, but did not have the privileges conferred by the Act unless they amended their deeds of settlement so as to comply with its provisions.[18] Winding up was dealt with by a separate Act [19] of the same date which made companies subject

[10] 1844 B.P.P., Vol. VII.
[11] It contained 80 sections and nine Schedules and was by far the most elaborate piece of company legislation attempted in England up to that time. It did not apply to Scotland which was left to its common law (Scottish judges were distinctly more liberal than their English colleagues) until the Act of 1856.
[12] Reduced to the present 20 by the Act of 1856. This provision was based on Ker's report of 1837 which suggested a maximum of 15. New assurance companies were also required to register irrespective of the number of members or transferability of shares: s. 2.
[13] We may detect resemblances to this " two-tier " arrangement in the modern provisions for a certificate of incorporation followed later, in the case of a public company, by a " trading certificate " (Companies Act 1948, s. 109) but there is no historical connection between the two sets of provisions.
[14] s. 19.
[15] s. 25.
[16] This provision was, of course, based on the Trading Companies Act 1834.
[17] s. 66.
[18] ss. 58–59.
[19] 7 & 8 Vict. c. 111.

to the bankruptcy law. Banking companies were also dealt with by a separate Act,[20] the provisions of which were generally similar, except that the maximum number of members of an unregistered partnership was six [21] (instead of twenty-five) and that there were stringent requirements for a minimum nominal and paid-up capital. It is perhaps surprising that these latter conditions never became established requirements of English company law for they constitute an essential feature of Continental practice [22] and appear to be a fair price to pay for the boon of simple and cheap incorporation by registration.[23]

Finally, Gladstone prepared and introduced the Bill which was passed under his successor as the Companies Clauses Consolidation Act 1845.[24] This set out the standard provisions normally included in private statutes of incorporation. These provisions were thereafter to be incorporated by reference, thus materially shortening and cheapening the process of statutory incorporation still necessary in the case of public utilities requiring powers of compulsory acquisition.

Gladstone, therefore, during his short tenure of office as President of the Board of Trade, succeeded for the first time in placing joint stock companies on a sound legal footing; he may fairly be regarded as the father of modern company law. His legislation, however, only solved the legal and not the commercial problems. It gave a company the legal status of a corporation but denied its members the most important advantage of it—freedom from personal liability. In the latter respect the only advance was the recognition that the company itself was primarily liable and that its bankruptcy did not necessarily involve bankruptcy of its members.

The Winding-up Acts

The legislation of 1844 was passed at the height of the " railway mania " and the wave of speculation led to promotions in other fields, thus bringing the man in the street into contact with companies as never before, and to an expansion of the stock markets both in London

---

20 7 & 8 Vict. c. 113.
21 Later it became 10.
22 Levy, *op. cit.*, *passim*.
23 *Cf.* O. Kahn-Freund: " Some Reflections on Company Law Reform " (1945) 7 M.L.R. 54 at pp. 57–59. Such provisions were, in fact, included in the Limited Liability Bill of 1855, but were struck out in Committee. They were reintroduced by the H.L. in an emasculated form but deleted in the Act of 1856. There are, however, requirements for a minimum capital in the case of certain types of company, *e.g.*, insurance companies.
24 A separate Act of the same date dealt with Scottish statutory companies (8 & 9 Vict. c. 17). These Acts contained the general corporate powers and duties and Table A of later Acts owed much to them. They were supplemented in the cases of particular types of utilities by other Acts of the same and later years, see Chap. 1, p. 6, note 16. As Cooke points out (*op. cit.*, p. 119), these were illustrations of a wider tendency to bring under general legislation matters which had previously been left to private Bills; other examples will be found in the fields of divorce, naturalisation and municipal corporations.

and the provinces.[25]   Inevitably, however, the boom was followed by a collapse a year later which changed the emphasis from promotions to liquidations.   In 1846 was passed a winding-up Act applying to railway companies [26] and this was followed in 1848 [27] and 1849 [28] by Acts of general application conferring winding-up jurisdiction on the Court of Chancery.   Unhappily the resulting conflicts of jurisdiction between the Courts of Bankruptcy and Chancery led to great confusion,[29] a confusion which, less unhappily, proved highly beneficial to the legal and the new-born accountancy professions.

At a later date [30] the confusion was resolved by the total removal of incorporated companies from the bankruptcy jurisdiction.   It is to these historical accidents that we owe the distinction drawn in English law (but unknown to most other systems) between bankruptcy and liquidation; with us an insolvent company is not made bankrupt but is, instead, subject to an analogous process administered under different rules by a different branch of the courts.   This development was not completed until after the general recognition of limited liability, but these earlier Acts played a part in the movement which led to this recognition since their emphasis on the administration of the company's assets as a separate estate made still more illogical the distinction drawn between incorporation and limited liability.

The struggle for limited liability

Several features of the Act of 1844 were open to criticism.   In particular the cumbersome procedure of provisional and final registration was attacked, but was left unaltered until 1856, though frequently disregarded by unscrupulous promoters [31] who dealt in scrip prior to complete registration.[32]

But, of course, the main cause of complaint was the absence of limited liability, and the next ten years saw the battle fairly joined on this issue.   It is clear that public opinion began to harden in favour of the extension of limited liability, particularly when the slump of

25 Hunt, *op. cit.*, p. 104 *et seq.*
26 9 & 10 Vict. c. 28.
27 11 & 12 Vict. c. 45.
28 12 & 13 Vict. c. 108.
29 Admirable accounts appear in Formoy, *op. cit.*, p. 93 *et seq.*, and Cooke, *op. cit.*, Chap. X.   They illustrate their accounts principally by the *Royal British Bank* liquidation (1856) 28 L.T.(o.s.) 224.   It is, of course, to this company that we are indebted for the famous rule in *Royal British Bank* v. *Turquand* (*infra*, Chap. 8).
30 The Joint Stock Companies Act 1856 and the Companies Winding Up (Amendment) Act 1857.
31 It is estimated that less than half the provisional registrations were ever followed by complete registration: Shannon (1931–32) *Econ.Hist.*, Vol. II, p. 397.   See also *ibid.*, pp. 281–282.   The defects were emphasised in the Report of the Select Committee on Assurance Associations, 1852–53, B.P.P., Vol. XXI.
32 A few amendments were made in 1847 (10 & 11 Vict. c. 78), notably the deletion of the need to file prospectuses, a retrograde step which was apparently taken without any reference to the Registrar: see his evidence before the Select Committee on Assurance Associations, *supra*, at p. 13, Q. 160.   It was not corrected until 1900.

1845–48 drew poignant attention to the consequences of its absence. But it was less clear how and to what companies it should be extended. As a result of the 1844 Act there were three principal types[33] of commercial associations:

1. Private partnerships of not more than twenty-five persons, and quasi-partnerships of unlimited dimensions formed before 1844 which had not re-formed under the Act of that year. These were unincorporated and the liability of the members was necessarily unlimited.

2. Chartered and statutory companies, which were incorporated and the members of which were normally free from liability or had their liability limited to a prescribed sum per share.

3. Companies formed or registered under the Act of 1844 which were incorporated but with unlimited liability.

The first question therefore was whether limited liability should be extended to private partnerships on the lines of the Continental *sociétés en commandite*, to registered companies, or to both.

Bellenden Ker's report of 1837 had been directed primarily to private partnerships and the desirability of the *sociétés en commandite*. The 1844 Report had given birth to the third type of association but had not extended limited liability to it; the object of the Commission was to control companies and discourage frauds, not to stimulate promotions. The *société en commandite* was outside the terms of reference of the 1844 Commission but was the main subject of consideration by the Select Committee of 1850 on Investments for the Savings of the Middle and Working Classes, which reported[34] that " the difficulties which affected the law of partnership operate with increasing severity in proportion to the smallness of the sums subscribed and the number of persons included in the association. . . . Any measures for the removal of these difficulties would be particularly acceptable to the Middle and Working Classes and would tend to satisfy them that they are not excluded from fair competition by laws throwing obstacles in the way of men with small capitals." The result, as Hunt[35] says, was that the argument for limited liability acquired a " tinge of social amelioration." Hunt's remark has a somewhat sardonic note, and it must be admitted than one can detect more than a slight whiff of Victorian humbug when

---

[33] There were also companies granted letters patent under the Trading Companies Act 1834 and Chartered Companies Act 1837, which were unincorporated (unless they registered under the 1844 Act) but with most of the advantages of chartered incorporation except limited liability.

[34] 1850 B.P.P., Vol. XIX, 169.

[35] *Op. cit.* 120. As Mr. G. Goyder emphasises (*The Future of Private Enterprise*, Lond. 1951 and *The Responsible Company*, Oxf. 1961), the hopes that limited liability would improve the relations between capital and labour have been falsified by events; workers, whose whole livelihood is dependent on the success of the undertaking for which they work, cannot be expected to take kindly to a system which enables the proprietors to limit their risks. Joint stock enterprise has also, of course, contributed to the dehumanising of the master-and-servant relationship.

one reads the evidence of Chancery barristers accepting the eager invitation of M.P.s to persuade them that limited liability was desirable in the interests of the poor. In truth, as the evidence of working class witnesses makes plain, what the working man required was an improvement in the law of friendly societies particularly as regards housing trusts, co-operative societies and building societies—and this in fact soon came about.[36]   John Stuart Mill, more realistically, pointed out [37] that " the great value of a limit of responsibility as it relates to the working classes would be not so much to facilitate the investment of their savings, not so much to enable the poor to lend to those who are rich, as to enable the rich to lend to those who are poor."

A year later a similarly constituted Select Committee considered the law of partnership. On the major issue of limited liability their report [38] was non-committal; it recommended that this vexed question should be referred to a Royal Commission " of adequate legal and commercial knowledge." It did, however, make one firm recommendation, namely, that it should be permissible to lend money at a rate of interest varying with the profits of a business without becoming a partner in the business. At this time it was supposed that such a loan automatically made the lender a partner,[39] and the Committee proposed that instead he should be a deferred creditor in the event of bankruptcy and thus placed in a position not dissimilar to that of a limited partner under a *société en commandite*.

In accordance with the recommendations of the Committee the question was referred to a strong Royal Commission [40] containing representatives from England, Scotland and Ireland.[41] They were, however, quite unable to reach unanimity. They had, they said " been much embarrassed by the great contrariety of opinion. . . . Gentlemen of great experience and talent have arrived at conclusions diametrically opposite; and in supporting these conclusions have displayed reasoning power of the highest order. It is difficult to say on which side the weight of authority in this country predominates." In the result a bare majority of five [42] signed a Report, opposing the general extension of limited liability to joint stock companies or the introduction of the *société en commandite*, and stating that they were unable to agree on the 1851 Committee's proposal regarding loans. Bramwell and Hodgson (a merchant banker), on the other hand, were wholeheartedly in favour of all three proposals. They came out uncompromisingly in favour of

---

[36] Industrial and Provident Societies Acts 1852, 1854 and 1856; Building Societies Act 1874.
[37] In his evidence at p. 78.   [38] 1851 B.P.P., Vol. XVIII, 1.
[39] *Grace* v. *Smith* (1775) 2 Wm.Bl. 997, and see Lindley, *Law of Partnership*, 12th ed., p. 74 *et seq.*
[40] 1854 B.P.P., Vol. XXVII, 445. The same commission was to consider the assimilation of the mercantile laws of the various parts of the U.K.
[41] The English legal representatives were G. W. Bramwell Q.C. (afterwards Baron Bramwell), Cresswell J. and J. Anderson, Q.C. (afterwards an Official Referee).
[42] Including Cresswell J.

laissez-faire. " If ever," said Bramwell,[43] " there was a rule established by reason, authority, and experience, it is that the interest of a community is best consulted by leaving to its members, as far as possible, the unrestricted and unfettered exercise of their own talents and industry." In his opinion the restraint on limited liability offended against this golden rule. He therefore recommended [44] that persons should be allowed as of right to form partnerships limiting the liability of all or some by private agreement followed by registration; and that where the liability of all was to be limited the partnership should be incorporated and the word " limited " added after the name. The remaining member, Anderson, was against the introduction of limited liability and *sociétés en commandite*, but in favour of the 1851 Committee's proposal regarding loans.

In effect, therefore, the majority against limited liability was six out of eight, but despite this the House of Commons immediately passed, without a division, a motion in favour of limited partnerships.[45] On this occasion the Government remained non-committal,[46] but in the following session they introduced two Bills, the Partnership Amendment Bill allowing profit-sharing loans without partnership, and the Limited Liability Bill which provided for limited liability in the case of companies securing complete registration under the 1844 Act subject to certain safeguards. Their bold action in introducing the latter is the more surprising since almost all the prior discussion had related to limited partnerships and not to incorporated companies.

Both Bills secured a second reading in the Commons [47] without a division, but thereafter the former fell a victim to time pressure and proceeded no farther. Nevertheless, the Government determined to press on with the Limited Liability Bill, which was rushed through all its stages in the Commons and given a third reading, again without a division.[48] It was then sent to the Lords who were asked to pass it that same session as a matter of urgency. Certain Lords protested vigorously,[49] and certainly it is difficult to see why the Government, which had sat on the fence for so long, should suddenly regard this as a matter of the utmost urgency at the most critical time of the Crimean War. Doubtless it was true that public opinion, at any rate as represented by the Press,[50] had at last come to favour the measure, but this

---

[43] At p. 23.
[44] At p. 29.
[45] (1854) *Hansard*, 3rd Ser., Vol. 134, at col. 752 *et seq.*
[46] Commenting on the speech of Cardwell, the President of the Board of Trade, Cobden said (*ibid.*, col. 779) that " all he could learn of the views of the right hon. gentleman was that he told them when he began that he would not offer an opinion, and he contrived very ingeniously to keep his word."
[47] *Ibid.*, Vol. 139, col. 310 *et seq.*
[48] *Ibid.*, col. 1709 *et seq.* (for Committee stage, see cols. 1348, 1378, 1445 and 1517).
[49] Fourteen voted against and nine of them minuted a formal protest (*ibid.*, col. 1918).
[50] By this time even *The Times*, formerly an uncompromising opponent, had come round. Lord Stanley of Alderley (P.B.T.) in introducing the measure in the Lords said that a hostile deputation had " candidly admitted that, with the exception

hardly explains the almost indecent haste with which it was pushed through,[51] particularly as the official view still seemed to be that it was a question of abstract principle rather than of practical importance.[52] The Committee stage before the Commons deleted a number of the safeguards which had originally been included, but others were inserted by the Lords which finally passed the Bill without a division.[53] The Commons [54] reluctantly accepted the Lords' amendments and the Bill was given the Royal Assent in August 1855.

The attainment of limited liability

The Act [55] provided for the limited liability of the members of a company on complete registration if (a) the company had at least twenty-five members holding £10 shares paid up to the extent of 20 per cent., (b) not less than three-fourths of the nominal capital was subscribed, (c) " Limited " was added to the company's name, and (d) the Board of Trade approved the auditors. The directors were to be personally liable if they paid a dividend knowing the company to be insolvent or made loans to the members, and the company had to wind up if three-fourths of the capital was lost.[56] Banks and insurance companies were excluded. The method of limitation was that already used for chartered

of the *Leeds Mercury*, there was no journal in the kingdom which would admit an article against the principle of limited liability " (*Hansard* 139, col. 1896). This seems to be an exaggeration so far as the legal Press was concerned, for the *Law Times* was still most hostile—even to the extent of describing the Bill as the " Rogues Charter "; see (1854) 24 L.T. 142; (1855) 25 L.T. 116 and 210; (1856) 26 L.T. 230; and (1858) 31 L.T. 14. Nor was it universally popular in business circles. The Manchester Chamber of Commerce declared it " so subversive of that high moral responsibility which has hitherto distinguished our Partnership Laws (!) as to call for their strongest disapproval ": Proceedings, June 13, 1855, cited by Redford, *Manchester Merchants and Foreign Trade*, p. 215, and Cooke, *op. cit.*, p. 157.

51 It may be that the altruism of 1851 had been supplanted by more selfish fears for self-preservation; by this time the fortunes of the governing classes were in commerce rather than land, there had been a number of disturbing liquidations in 1854–55 and more were to follow; at the height of the War the future could not have looked rosy. On the other hand, John Bright told the Manchester Chamber of Commerce in 1856 (cited Redford, *op. cit.*, and Cooke, *op. cit.*, *ibid.*) that the Bill was rushed through because the Palmerston administration wanted to be able to say that something had been done besides voting money for the War; but Bright was opposed to the War and hostile to the arch-apostle of limited liability, Robert Lowe (afterwards Viscount Sherbrooke) who had become Vice-President of the Board of Trade in July 1855.

52 Both Pleydell-Bouverie (the Vice-President of the Board of Trade) in the Commons (*ibid.*, col. 329), and Lord Stanley of Alderley (the President) in the Lords (*ibid.*, col. 1919) said that they thought it would prove the wisdom of Adam Smith's view (*supra*) " that in ordinary trading undertakings Joint Stock Companies could not compete with private traders " (*ibid.* 329), but that there ought to be no legal impediments in the way of competition.

53 *Ibid.*, cols. 1895 *et seq.*, 2025 *et seq.* and 2123 *et seq.*

54 *Ibid.*, col. 2127 *et seq.*

55 18 & 19 Vict. c. 133. It contained only 19 sections.

56 An existing company could take advantage of the new Act on complete registration under the 1844 Act if it made the necessary alterations to its deed of settlement by a resolution passed by a three-fourths majority of shareholders voting at a special meeting, and obtained a certificate of solvency from the Board of Trade.

companies under the Act of 1837 and for statutory companies under the Companies Clauses Act of 1845, namely, the restriction of members' liability to the nominal (unpaid) value of their shares.

The Limited Liability Act only remained in force for a few months, as it was repealed and incorporated in the Joint Stock Companies Act 1856.[57] This Act, of 116 sections and a Schedule of tables and forms, was the first of the modern Companies Acts. It did away with provisional registration, superseded deeds of settlement by the modern memorandum and articles of association,[58] and incorporated provisions for winding up. Banks and insurance companies were still excluded but, unlike the earlier Acts, it applied to Scotland. Passed as it was in the heyday of *laissez-faire* it allowed incorporation with limited liability to be obtained with a freedom amounting almost to licence; all that was necessary was for seven or more persons to sign and register a memorandum of association. Virtually, all the safeguards prescribed by the 1855 Act were deleted; there was no minimum nominal or paid-up capital or share value, only the provision for winding up on the loss of three-fourths of the capital was retained, and this, too, disappeared in 1862. Board of Trade approval of auditors was not required and even their appointment was no longer compulsory.[59] Directors were still to be liable if they paid dividends knowing the company to be insolvent, but the only other requirements were the use of the word "limited" and provisions for registration and publicity. In effect the legislature had adopted Lord Bramwell's [60] recommendations and accepted his view that those who dealt with companies knowing them to be limited had only themselves to blame if they burnt their fingers. The mystic word "Limited" was intended to act as a red flag warning the public of the dangers which they ran if they had dealings with the dangerous new invention. It is because of the arbitrary separation of personal liability from incorporation which had prevailed for eleven years that English companies still bear the label "Ltd." instead of the more logical "Inc." of the U.S.A.

[57] The Government had reintroduced the Partnership Amendment Bill at the same time (*Hansard* 140, col. 110 *et seq.*) but this ill-fated measure was ultimately withdrawn (*ibid.*, col. 2201).

[58] Model articles were appended in Table B which became the famous Table A of the 1862 and later Acts.

[59] Provisions regarding auditors were moved from the operative parts, where they had been in the Acts of 1844 and 1855, to the optional Table B. In fact these provisions continued to be adopted expressly or impliedly by most companies, so that the salutary practice of a professional audit remained customary although not again compulsory until 1900 (Companies Act 1900, *infra*). It had been reintroduced as regards banks by the Companies Act 1879. For an account of the historical development of the accounting and auditing provisions of the Acts, see Littleton & Yamey (ed.), *Studies in the History of Accounting*, 356–379.

[60] He was justly proud of the honour of having invented "Limited"; see his speech to the Institute of Bankers in 1888, *Journal of Inst.*, Vol. 9, p. 373 *et seq.* and especially p. 397. Llewellyn Smith (*op. cit.*, p. 165) says that he even suggested playfully that the word should be inscribed on his tombstone; I have been unable to find the source of this suggestion and therefore cannot say whether he envisaged it as a laudatory epitaph or a warning to posterity.

The battle for incorporation with limited liability by simple registration was now won and the issue has never been seriously reopened, although the victory has at times been unpopular.[61] Its importance has sometimes been discounted. Certainly it is true that the various devices, already described, for acquiring *de facto* freedom from liability had become perfected, and this led the *Economist* [62] to regard the issue as of no great importance. Maitland [63] seems to have taken much the same view. " If," he said, " the State had not given way we should have had in England joint stock companies, unincorporated, but contracting with limited liability. We know nowadays that men are not deterred from making contracts by the word ' limited.' We have no reason to suppose that they would have been deterred if that word were expanded into four or five lines printed at the head of the company's letter paper." Nevertheless it is clear that without legislative intervention, limited liability could never have been attained in a satisfactory and clear-cut fashion, and that it was this intervention which finally established companies as the major instrument in economic development. Of this the immediate and startling increase in promotions is sufficient proof.[64]

Subsequent developments

The subsequent history of companies belongs to the modern law and can be sketched more briefly.[65] Its main feature has been a movement away from the complete freedom allowed by the 1856 Act and the imposition of greater controls and increased provisions for publicity— the basic policy of Gladstone's Act of 1844 which had suffered partial eclipse in later Acts.

In 1857 the Act of the previous year was slightly amended,[66] banks were brought within its scope by the Joint Stock Banking Companies Act 1857, but without limited liability which was not conceded until the following year,[67] and legislation was passed dealing with frauds by directors.[68] In 1862 the various enactments were consolidated and

---

[61] The repeated bank failures during the second half of the nineteenth century caused renewed outbursts against limited liability, and in the case of the failure of Overend Gurney Ltd. in 1866 (see Hunt, *op. cit.*, p. 153 *et seq.*) these amounted almost to a panic. But had liability been unlimited the failures would have occurred just the same and the victims, although different, would probably have been just as numerous.

[62] (1854) Vol. XII, 698.

[63] *Trust and Corporation*, Collected Papers, Vol. III, p. 321 at p. 392.

[64] Between 1844 and 1856, 956 companies were completely registered under the 1844 Act; in the six years following the 1856 Act no fewer than 2,479 were registered and their paid-up capital in 1864 was over £31 millions; Shannon, *op. cit.*, p. 290. For further details, see the table at *ibid.*, p. 421.

[65] Students of the history of this later period are referred to Dr. J. B. Jefferys' London Ph.D. Thesis: " Trends in Business Organisation in Great Britain Since 1856 " which is unfortunately unpublished but is available in the London University Library. It contains an excellent account of the major trends and an invaluable bibliography.

[66] 20 & 21 Vict. c. 14.

[67] 21 & 22 Vict. c. 91.

[68] 20 & 21 Vict. c. 54. See also Larceny Act 1861, ss. 81–84.

amended in an Act which is the first to bear the brief modern title of Companies Act,[69] and which, with numerous amendments,[70] remained the principal Act until 1908. It was considerably larger than the 1856 Act, consisting of no fewer than 212 sections and three Schedules. The additions were mainly amendments to the winding-up provisions and improved and more detailed drafting, but it included insurance companies[71] and also introduced the company limited by guarantee which, as already pointed out,[72] affords a particularly suitable type of organisation for clubs and charitable or quasi-charitable associations.

Limited partnerships and private companies

Hence by 1862 two of the three[73] functions of the modern company had been provided for. Capitalists were encouraged to lend their money to industry without having themselves to operate the enterprise, and fluctuating bodies formed for social or philanthropic purposes could conveniently adopt the company rather than the trust as their *modus operandi*. But, or so it was thought, the need for limited liability within the field of the ordinary partnership or one-man business had still not been met. By the Mercantile Law (Amendment) Act 1856[74] (commonly known as Bovill's Act) it was ultimately provided that sharing of profits should not be conclusive evidence of partnership but that lenders, or sellers of goodwill, in consideration of a share of profits should be deferred creditors. At the time it was thought that this had effected a substantial advance by legalising something in the nature of limited partnerships. In fact, as the courts soon held,[75] it did no such thing; it only protected the creditor where he was not in truth associated in the running of the business, if he was he became fully liable as a partner notwithstanding that he was described as a contributor " under Bovill's Act." It therefore made no advance on the decision of the House of Lords in *Cox* v. *Hickman*[76] which had already overruled the rule in *Grace* v. *Smith*.[77] Far from protecting creditors the Act merely worsened their position by making them, in the two most common circumstances, deferred creditors in bankruptcy.

When this was realised there was a renewed outbreak of attempts to introduce full-fledged limited partnerships on the Continental model,

---

[69] The keen eye of Mr. W. H. Auden is able to detect in this Act the symptoms of a modification of the pure liberal doctrine of *laissez-faire*: *Poets of the English Language*, Vol. 5, p. xxiii.

[70] The most important were the Companies Acts of 1867, 1879 and 1880, the Companies Winding Up Act 1890, the Directors' Liability Act 1890, and the Companies Act 1900.

[71] Hitherto governed by the 1844 Act which had been revived for their benefit: 20 & 21 Vict. c. 80.

[72] *Supra*, Chap. 1, p. 12.

[73] *Supra*, Chap. 1, p. 11.

[74] This was an amended version of the ill-fated Partnership Bill of 1855.

[75] *Syers* v. *Syers* (1876) 1 App.Cas. 174, H.L.; *Pooley* v. *Driver* (1876) 5 Ch.D. 458.

[76] (1860) 8 H.L.C. 268.   [77] (1775) 2 Wm.Bl. 997, *supra*.

and it was from one such abortive attempt [78] that the Partnership Act 1890 resulted, although this in its final form merely codified the existing law. In fact, however, the Companies Acts enabled all of the advantages of limited partnerships, and more besides, to be obtained, for the requirement of seven members did not mean that so many as seven had to be beneficially interested—some could be bare nominees for the others and all could thus acquire the benefits of limited liability.[79] When this was established, as a result of the House of Lords decision in the famous case of *Salomon* v. *Salomon*,[80] the need for limited partnerships had ceased, particularly as the legislature, far from discouraging " one-man " and other small " private companies," discriminated in their favour by the Companies Acts of 1900 and 1907 by exempting them from certain of the requirements of publicity. Nevertheless, public opinion, in this instance lagging behind the law, caused limited partnerships to be legalised by the Limited Partnerships Act 1907. In practice this Act has not been much used because the private limited company involves little more trouble and expense to the members, enables the liability of *all* to be limited, and permits them to take part in the management without forfeiting their freedom from liability.

Case law developments

As already pointed out, the Companies Acts are far from being a complete code and it would be entirely misleading to give an impression that the major developments during the nineteenth century were entirely statutory. On the contrary, the courts, building on the foundations of partnership law, the law of corporations and the statutes, had for the first time evolved a coherent and comprehensive body of company law. Many of the most fundamental and salutary principles were worked out by the courts with little or no help from the statutes and their decisions constitute landmarks which later Acts have done little to obliterate. Thus the House of Lords in *Ashbury Carriage Co.* v. *Riche* [81] applied the *ultra vires* doctrine to companies and laid down that companies could only do acts expressly or impliedly authorised by their memoranda of

---

[78] See the account by the original draftsman, Sir F. Pollock, in the preface to the 12th edition of his *Law of Partnership* (reprinted in the current edition).

[79] The result, as has been well said (by O. Kahn-Freund in his notes to Renner, *The Institutions of Private Law* (Lond. 1948) at pp. 221 and 222) is that whereas in the eighteenth and early nineteenth centuries the law of partnership had been pressed into the service of joint stock enterprise, now the legal form of joint stock undertakings has come to annex the functions of the law of partnership. A similar reversal has taken place in the law of trusts into whose service the joint stock company is now pressed as a trust corporation: for a brief history of this development, see D. R. Marsh, " The Friendly Corporation," in (1951) IV *Cambridge J.* 451, and for a fuller account, the same author's *Corporate Trustees* (Lond. 1952).

[80] [1897] A.C. 22, H.L. *Infra*, p. 68.

[81] (1875) L.R. 7 H.L. 653.

association. Although, as we shall see,[82] their Lordships' intentions have been largely frustrated by the ingenuity of company draftsmen, and the practical effect of their ruling reduced by later action of the legislature, they at least prevented the misuse of corporate powers and the trafficking in incorporations which had been a scandal at the time of the South Sea Bubble. They also afforded some protection to the public against the abuses of limited liability by enunciating, in cases such as *Trevor* v. *Whitworth*[83] and *Ooregum Gold Mining Co.* v. *Roper*,[84] the principle of the raising and maintenance of capital.[85] When principles inherited from partnership law proved unduly restrictive the courts had no hesitation in rejecting them; for example, in *Andrews* v. *Gas Meter Co.*[86] they finally removed the idea that there was any implied condition that all shareholders are to be on an equality, and thus freed companies in their efforts to raise further capital by creating new preference shares.[87] And they protected the investor by laying down, in *Erlanger's* case[88] and *Gluckstein* v. *Barnes*,[89] that company promoters stood in a fiduciary position towards their fledglings[90] with all the duties of disclosure and good faith which that implies.

On the other hand, they were less successful in evolving principles which would afford adequate protection of the minority against oppression by the majority,[91] and common law rules relating to misrepresentation proved totally inadequate to protect investors against misleading statements by directors in prospectuses; the disastrous decision in *Derry* v. *Peek*[92] had to be promptly modified by the legislature[93] so far as its application to companies was concerned. Further, by construing the statutory rules for public registration as implying constructive notice to all the world of the registered data, they introduced an entirely artificial doctrine which has been fraught with complication and which has caused the basically healthy publicity principle to do almost as much harm as good.[94]

---

[82] *Infra*, Chap. 5.
[83] (1887) 12 App.Cas. 409, H.L.
[84] [1892] A.C. 125, H.L.
[85] *Infra*, Chap. 6.
[86] [1897] 1 Ch. 361, C.A., overruling *Hutton* v. *Scarborough Cliff Hotel Co.* (1865) 2 Dr. & Sm. 521.
[87] Until the 1948 Act, the model articles in Table A provided that, in accordance with partnership principles, new shares should be offered to the existing shareholders in proportion to their existing holdings. In U.S.A. this remained the common law rule; for the difficulties which it caused, see Berle & Means, *op. cit.*, p. 146 *et seq.*
[88] *Erlanger* v. *New Sombrero Phosphate Co.* (1878) 3 App.Cas. 1218, H.L.
[89] [1900] A.C. 240, H.L.
[90] See *per* Lord Macnaghten in [1900] A.C. at p. 248.
[91] See Chap. 24, *infra*.
[92] (1889) 14 App.Cas. 337, H.L.
[93] By the Directors' Liability Act 1890.
[94] We shall see examples of this harm in connection with the *ultra vires* rule (Chap. 5) and the rule in *Royal British Bank* v. *Turquand* (Chap. 8).

Twentieth-century reforms

By the end of the nineteenth century the Board of Trade had established the practice of securing the appointment of an expert committee to review company law at intervals of about twenty years and of implementing its recommendations by a statute which was immediately repealed and incorporated in a consolidating Act.[95] This convenient practice was followed more or less consistently until the present principal Act, the Companies Act 1948, though the picture was complicated by certain major pieces of legislation on closely related topics. The chief of these was the Prevention of Fraud (Investments) Act 1939,[96] which, (as amended by the 1947 Companies Act) is now replaced by an Act of the same name of 1958. This Act and the regulations made under it regulate share-pushing and impose some control over brokers and dealers, over take-over bids and over the Unit Trust industry. Again, during the war years the Government imposed restrictions on the raising of capital, and the power to exercise this control (now largely in abeyance) has been placed on a semi-permanent basis by the Borrowing (Control and Guarantees) Act 1946. This Act, like the Prevention of Fraud Act, is not restricted in its application to registered companies but it is principally in relation to them that it is important. Here again history has to some extent repeated itself, for just as the State, at the birth of companies, granted or withheld charters in what it believed to be the public interest, so now it has power to grant or withhold the right to raise capital in the same interest.

Since the 1948 Act the legislative position has become still more confused and confusing. In 1961, following a report of the Scottish Law Reform Committee,[97] the Companies (Floating Charges) (Scotland) Act [98] was passed and copious consequential amendments made to the 1948 Act in relation to Scotland. In 1963 the abuses flowing from the growing habit of companies inviting the public to deposit money with them were dealt with by the Protection of Depositors Act. In the same year, following a report of an unofficial City committee, the Stock Transfer Act simplified the machinery of transferring securities. The Finance Act 1965 was perhaps the most far-reaching post-war legislation affecting companies since, for the first time, a system of taxation was applied to incorporated business entirely different from that relating to individuals. This may well result not only in a major alteration of

---

95 The Companies (Consolidation) Act 1908 followed the reforms based on the report of the Loreburn Committee (Cd. 3052 of 1906), the Companies Act 1929 followed those recommended by the Greene Committee (Cmd. 2657 of 1926) and an earlier review by the Wrenbury Committee (Cd. 9138 of 1918), and the Companies Act 1948 followed those recommended by the Cohen Committee (Cmd. 6659 of 1945).

96 Based largely on the recommendations of the Bodkin Committee on Share-Pushing (Cmd. 5539 of 1937) and the Anderson Committee on Unit Trusts (Cmd. 5259 of 1936).

97 Cmnd. 1017.

98 The working of this Act is now being reviewed by the Scottish Law Commission (Memorandum No. 10).

companies' financial policies but also in a complete reappraisal of the advantages of incorporation.[99]   Finally, the Companies Act 1967 implemented some only of the recommendations of the Jenkins Committee,[1] the latest of the Company Law Amendment Committees, and dealt at the same time with a number of other urgent problems, especially in relation to insurance companies.   Further legislation to supplement this stop-gap measure is long overdue.   It is greatly to be hoped that when it is passed company legislation will be rearranged and reconsolidated.   At present it is in greater disarray than at any time in the last sixty years.

The issues with which the committees and the legislation of the present century have been concerned are no longer those of simple and cheap incorporation, but the improvement of the machinery of company law in a number of ways.   The first of these is, as the Cohen Committee put it in 1945, " to ensure that as much information as is reasonably required shall be made available both to the shareholders and creditors of the companies concerned and to the general public." [2]   The major developments in the Companies Acts of 1948 and 1967 in connection with disclosure of information in, for example, prospectuses, accounts and the directors' report owe much to the stringent requirements which have long been imposed by the stock exchanges as conditions for permitting and maintaining a quotation of securities.   In 1965, the London Stock Exchange and the main provincial exchanges formed a Federation of Stock Exchanges, and in 1966 the Committee of the Federation issued a number of memoranda setting out new requirements.[3]   The provisions of the Companies Acts have frequently been copied from the more developed rules of the stock exchanges (which in themselves have no legal force and until 1948 received no legal recognition [4]).   The Jenkins Report made a number of proposals to extend further the obligations placed on management to disclose information useful to actual or potential investors; but, while accepting the views of the Cohen Committee, the Report cautiously added that one must consider whether " additional information would be of any real value to persons receiving it . . . whether its ascertainment would involve an amount of work disproportionate to its value . . . [and] be detrimental to the company's business." [5]

---

[99] See Chap. 9.
[1] Cmnd. 1749 of 1962.   The appointment of this Committee was inspired by abuses in relation to take-over bids which had come to light as a result of Board of Trade investigations : see especially *Investigation into the Affairs of H. Jasper & Co. Ltd.* (H.M.S.O. 1961).
[2] Cmd. 6659, para. 5.
[3] These are published in " the Yellow Book," hereafter referred to as *Requirements*.
[4] But see the Companies Act 1948, ss. 39 and 51.   Compare the Companies Act 1967, ss. 25 (2) and 33 (10), attaching legal obligations only in respect of " quoted " shares. The Stock Exchange requirements are still markedly in advance of the legal provisions.
[5] Cmnd. 1749, para. 13.   Even on disclosure, the leading American authority called the Jenkins Report " a conservative document by American standards ": see L. Loss (1963) 80 S.A.L.J. 53 at p. 67.

The same conservative note was struck in respect of the second critical problem, described by the Cohen Report as finding " a means of making it easier for shareholders to exercise a more effective general control over the management of their companies," [6] an aim which the Jenkins Report thought " theoretically desirable " but which should be balanced by the need to give directors " a reasonably free hand to do what they think best in the interests of the company." [7]   Indeed the problems, already touched upon, of maintaining control of management by shareholders is a point where the crisis of modern company law becomes apparent.   Attempts in 1948 to reinforce such control [8] have meant little; and although the Jenkins Committee remarked that " to say that it is useless to provide investors with further safeguards which apparently they do not want and which, if provided, they will not use is a counsel of despair," [9] they too were unable to do very much to solve the intractable problem.   It seems likely that future developments here will recognise that it is unreal to expect the members of large public companies to control the management and that a State agency must do so instead.   Already steps in this direction have been taken in the Companies Act 1967 which greatly widens the investigatory powers of the Board of Trade.[10]   The alternative, control by City institutions, which is now on trial in relation to mergers and take-overs,[11] has not proved very successful and administrative machinery on the lines of that operated by the American Securities and Exchange Commission is being openly talked-of as a possibility.[12]

However, the Act of 1967 [13] has already added considerably to the legal demands for disclosure of information by management and in some respects has gone beyond the traditional philosophy of disclosure in the interests solely of investors.[14]   From a historical point of view, however, the most interesting feature of the statute is the total abolition of the exempt private company,[15] so that the small business with limited liability can no longer enjoy the secrecy which had surrounded its financial affairs.   Only if it turns itself into an unlimited company [16] can it escape the demand for disclosure of its financial condition in the annual return.   Thus, the wheel has gone full circle. As was intended

6 Cmd. 6659, para. 5.
7 Cmnd. 1749, para. 14.
8 See, for example, Companies Act 1948, s. 184.
9 Cmnd. 1749, para. 107.
10 Companies Act 1967, ss. 35–42 and 109–118.
11 *i.e.*, through the City Code and the Take-over Panel, on which see Chaps. 14 and 26.
12 Both the Governor of the Bank of England and the President of the Board of Trade have given warnings that statutory control will be inevitable if the voluntary mechanism fails: see *The Times*, Aug. 16, 1968, and *The Financial Times*, Oct. 29, 1968.
13 See on the Act, L. Leigh (1968) 31 M.L.R. 183; M. Pickering [1967] B.T.R. 384.
14 For example, in s. 25 (making certain share dealings by directors illegal), s. 18 (disclosure of number and remuneration of employees) and s. 20 (disclosure of export business).
15 s. 2.
16 See ss. 43–45 and s. 47.

in 1855, the condition on which the privilege of limited liability is granted by the State has once again become full financial disclosure. This change led, however, to criticism, largely on the ground that the Government ought to have introduced at the same time a legal mechanism for the small business more suitable than the unlimited company, the partnership, or the unincorporated enterprise, perhaps by way of a new form of incorporated partnership.[17]   Whether or not this was a mistake, the abolition of the " exempt " private company has focused new interest upon the old question: What should be the conditions on which the State permits incorporation with limited liability to be acquired by mere registration?   The question is timely since in introducing the Companies Bill to the House of Commons the then President of the Board of Trade, Mr. Jay, said that the Government would later legislate " for wider reforms in the structure and philosophy of our company law " and that it is now time " to re-examine the whole theory and purpose of the limited joint stock company, the comparative rights and obligations of shareholders, directors, creditors, employees and the community as a whole." [18]

THE FUTURE OF COMPANY LAW IN A MIXED ECONOMY

Such statements immediately reveal the wider horizon inevitably introduced by the debate about the future of company law. On this we can do no more than touch upon a few major themes to indicate both the width and the importance for society of that continuing debate. Reference has already been made to the growing divorce between ownership and control and to the likelihood of increased State control to replace the waning control of shareholders over management. In addition, the increasing concentration of capital, resulting both from the growth of individual companies and from mergers of several companies, has revived the fear of " monopoly " which, as we have seen, had been a major factor in the early development of companies. No sooner had that fear been eradicated than the new form of corporate trading began to create vast industrial empires which were seen to contain real dangers. In the United States this realisation led to anti-trust [19] legislation as early as 1899 which tried to control such combines. In a classic study of concentration and the effect which it had of divorcing most of

---

[17] See the speeches on Second Reading by Lord Goodman, H.L.Deb., Vol. 278, col. 173 *et seq.* and Lord Chorley, H.L.Deb., Vol. 278, col. 1527 *et seq.* A precedent for such a mechanism is to be found in Ghana's Incorporated Private Partnerships Act 1962 (Act 152).

[18] H.C.Deb., Vol 741, col. 359. But his successor has stated that the Government would not in this Parliament find time for that or even for the remaining proposals of the Jenkins Report.

[19] In company matters Equity has suffered badly from debasement of its terms. Not only has " equities " come to mean non-preference shares but its precious " trust " has here been applied to a monopolistic combination.

the old " owners," the shareholders, from the newly emergent managers in whom real power often lies, Berle and Means wrote in 1932:

> " The rise of the modern corporation has brought a concentration of economic power which can compete on equal terms with the modern state. . . . Where its own interests are concerned, it even attempts to dominate the state. . . . The law of corporations, accordingly, might well be considered as a potential constitutional law for the new economic state, while business practice is increasingly assuming the aspect of economic statesmanship." [20]

Modern writers have suggested that the large company today does not aim primarily at maximisation of profit and is not so much a creature of the laws of supply and demand as the creator of market conditions and consumer demands,[21] a theory which, if it is correct, would necessarily demand a reconsideration of much of our company law.

In Britain concentration of capital in corporate aggregation has increased during the last twenty years [22]; and a flood of mergers and take-overs has overtaken the economy since 1960.[23] Nevertheless, in Britain, modern legislation connected with monopolies and mergers has disclosed no consistent theme of policy.[24] Administrative investigation of monopolies by a Monopolies Commission was the policy introduced

---

[20] A. Berle and G. Means, *The Modern Corporation and Private Property* (1932), p. 357. A new analysis of recent developments, and especially by Dr. Means of corporate concentration between 1932 and 1968, is included in the revised edition of the same work (1968). The thesis of Berle and Means may be thought to derive on the one hand from the managerialist theories of Burnham: *The Managerial Revolution* (1940) and on the other from those of Marx, see, for example, *Capital*, Vol. III, Chap. XV. In his later views, A. A. Berle has developed the view that management-controlled giant companies have evolved a social conscience: see *The Twentieth Century Capitalist Revolution* (1951) and *Power without Property* (1959). For sharp exchanges between Berle and an exponent of a " free-enterprise competition " view, see his debate with H. G. Manne (1962) 62 Col.L.R. 399 and 433: and for an attack on his economic thesis and the idea of a " corporate conscience," S. Peterson (1965) 79 Quarterly J.Econ. 1. A related debate has continued in the U.S.A. around the question " For whom are corporate managers trustees?", originating in articles by Berle (1931) 43 Harv.L.R. 1049 and M. Dodd (1932) 45 Harv.L.R. 1145: see now Marsh (1966) *Business Lawyer* 35; Weiner (1964) 64 Col.L.R. 1458; chapters by E. Rostow and A. Chayes in Mason (ed.), *The Corporation in Modern Society* (1959); and Eells, *The Government of Corporations* (1962).

[21] See, for example, J. K. Galbraith, *The New Industrial State* (1967); and for a theoretical economist's similar thesis, R. Marris, *The Economic Theory of " Managerial " Capitalism* (1964). For a brief rejoinder to Galbraith, see G. C. Allen, *Economic Fact and Fantasy* (Institute of Economic Affairs, 1967).

[22] See P. Sargant Florence, *Ownership, Control and Success of Large Companies* (1961); R. Evely and I. M. D. Little, *Concentration in British Industry* (1958); but see A. Armstrong and A. Silberston (1965) J. Royal Stat.Soc. (A) Vol. 128, Pt. 3; J. M. Samuels (1965) 32 Rev.Econ. Studies (2) 106.

[23] For example, in 1967 and 1968, among other mergers were those of the giant companies G.E.C. and A.E.I. and English Electric Ltd. and Elliott Automation Ltd.; only to be followed by a merger between the new G.E.C. combine and English Electric.

[24] The inconsistencies have not been as between Labour and Conservative administrations, but in the uncertainty on the part of all Governments since the war on the extent to which very large-scale units in industry are desirable in place of the " competition " of smaller enterprises.

by the Monopolies and Restrictive Practices (Inquiry and Control) Act 1948; but the investigation of restrictive trading *agreements* was transferred to the judicial Restrictive Practices Court by the Restrictive Trade Practices Act 1956.[25] New administrative intervention by the Board of Trade was made possible by the Monopolies and Mergers Act 1965,[26] under which the Board has power, if it chooses, to refer large mergers to the Monopolies Commission, and to make an order prohibiting a merger found by the Commission to be against the public interest. In practice, the Board of Trade has referred very few mergers to the Commission,[27] but has adopted the practice of giving informal prior " approval " to mergers. By October 1968, out of more than 250 mergers considered, only eleven were referred, one more having been prevented by a threat to do so. No doubt one reason for this is the existence of the Industrial Reorganisation Corporation, established by a statute of 1966,[28] of which the main task is the employment of its £150 million loan from the Government in order to *promote* mergers likely to increase efficiency in industry, especially those which will help in increasing exports, reducing imports or assisting policies of regional development.[29] In the event, the activities of the I.R.C., sponsored by the Department of Economic Affairs, seem more likely to be effective in promoting further concentration and larger scale units than do the opposed policies or tendencies represented by the Board of Trade, the court and the Commission under the statutes of 1948, 1956 and 1965.[30]

Since 1945 another central political issue has been how far industry and trade, or at least its larger units,[31] should remain in the hands of registered companies or should be taken over by organs of the State. Although in Britain this has been regarded as an argument between capitalism and socialism, other Western European countries have

---

[25] Amended as to resale price maintenance by the Resale Prices Act 1964 and generally by the Restrictive Trade Practices Act 1968. On the working of the court, see R. B. Stevens and B. S. Yamey, *The Restrictive Practices Court* (1965); and on this area generally, V. Korah, *Monopolies and Restrictive Practices* (1968); A. Hunter, *Competition and the Law* (1966).

[26] See Chap. 26, *infra*.

[27] The factors determining the decision whether or not to refer are a mixture of considerations about the commercial and technological prospects of the merged enterprise and the over-all national interest: see V. Korah, *op. cit.*, pp. 83–86 (information from the Board of Trade). Similar considerations govern the Government's willingness to give consent under the Exchange Control Act 1947 to allow for take-overs by foreign companies: see the Minister of Technology's conditions for Chrysler Corpn. taking over Rootes Ltd.: *The Times*, Jan. 18, 1967. Not until 1968 did any Government Department seem willing to ask for assurances in respect of future *employment* prospects before permitting a take-over or merger. On the merger of English Electric and G.E.C., the companies assured the Board of Trade that they would " consult " with trade unions if redundancies seemed a likely consequence of the merger: *The Times*, Sept. 13, 1968.

[28] Industrial Reorganisation Corporation Act 1966.

[29] *First Report* of the Industrial Reorganisation Corporation (H.C. Paper 252; H.M.S.O. 1968), p. 506.

[30] It is notable that the Restrictive Trade Practices Act 1968, s. 1, now permits the Board of Trade to *exempt* an agreement from registration under the 1965 Act if, in the opinion of the Board, it is in the national interest.

[31] In Aneurin Bevan's phrase, " the commanding heights " of the economy.

experimented with State concerns within a "capitalist" economy without the experiment being thought to involve any significant process of " socialisation." [32]   In Britain, the first post-war Labour Government nationalised a number of industries, mainly of a service rather than a manufacturing character, and the *modus operandi* was to vest the undertaking in a corporation specially created by statute, subject to some measure of State control by the relevant Minister, but not itself being a branch or department of Government [33] such as the Post Office has been in the past.[34]   These " public corporations " will be considered in a later chapter,[35] but with their political or economic merits the lawyer is not as such directly concerned.   It is, however, pertinent to observe that, in the days of the giant corporation, it may be posing a false problem to speak of choosing between " monopoly " public and " competitive " private enterprise.   The modern large company is controlled by a small body of managers who are very different from the entrepreneurial owners of the nineteenth-century business who, on incorporation, were " owners " in the legal sense by virtue of being controlling shareholders.[36]   The public corporation solves the problems of the relation between shareholders and managers by abolishing the former, but this does not solve the problem of controlling the managers.   The statutes creating public corporations provided for control by the relevant Minister and by Advisory Councils to represent the consumer; but from the beginning the latter were ineffective, and the powers of the former have raised grave constitutional difficulties concerning the relationship between the Government and the corporation.   Indeed, one unexpected development has been the rise in importance of the House of Commons Select Committee on Nationalised Industries, which by its sternly independent approach in a series of detailed reports on the public corporations has provided perhaps the most effective check upon both the managers of the corporations and ministerial powers.[37]

The public corporation is, in fact, only one legal method of extending the area of public control or State intervention in industry.   The same

---

[32] See the descriptions of the French and Italian systems in A. Shonfield, *Modern Capitalism* (1965), especially Chaps. VIII and IX, and his proposals for more public supervision in Pt. 4.   Italy, with its two great State enterprises, E.N.I. and I.R.I., has gone furthest in this direction : see M. V. Posner and S. J. Woolf, *Italian Public Enterprise* (1967).

[33] For example, the National Coal Board, established by the Coal Industry Nationalisation Act 1946.

[34] In future, the Post Office will be a commercial public corporation : Post Office Bill 1969.

[35] See Chap. 11, *infra.*

[36] See on the modern analysis of " managerial capitalism " Galbraith, *op. cit.*, and other works cited in notes 20–22, *supra.*   Not everyone, however, either on the " Right " or the " Left " accepts this analysis.   Critics of the former variety are cited in the same notes; as for the latter, see *The Insiders* (Universities & Left Review Pamphlet 1958).

[37] See the various Reports of the Select Committee, and B. Crick, *Reform of Parliament* (1964) Appendix D; David Coombes, *The Member of Parliament and the Administration* (1966).

end can be achieved by acquisition of a company's shares and the appointment of Government nominees to its board.[38] When the iron and steel industry was nationalised in 1949 a public corporation acquired all the shares of nominated companies which continued in existence; and the subsequent history of denationalisation in 1953 and renationalisation in 1967 took the form first of a sale of such shares, and then of a re-acquisition of the shares of the major companies by the British Steel Corporation.[39] A new dimension to Government shareholding has now been created. As we have seen, the I.R.C. has since 1966 been able to purchase shares as part of its function of promoting more efficient industrial structures. More recently, the Industrial Expansion Act 1968 provides a new basis for Government acquisition of shares in companies by way of " industrial investment schemes " to promote industrial " efficiency," " profitability," " productive capacity " or " technological improvements." Although such schemes will be embarked upon only with the agreement of the companies concerned, the Act is likely to mark a step on the road to an increase in the number and variety of " mixed enterprises " in Britain, companies in which the State or a State agency such as the I.R.C. has a stake in the equity shareholding.

The problems of mergers and concentration and the prospect of more public money being invested in companies have re-awakened interest in a " new-look " at company law. But it is not surprising if the Government has had difficulty in working out the structure of a new philosophy, for in addition to the traditional problems of disclosure, control of management, protection of minority shareholders, and the like, discussion now embraces the law relating to " monopolies " and to labour relations and employment. All this has led to demands for more disclosure not only in the hope of enabling shareholders to play their role as controllers of management and, thereby, as the effective determinants of economic resources in a market economy,[40] but also in the wider interests of employees, consumers and the public.[41] In its extensions of compulsory disclosure, the Companies Act 1967 has already begun to tread this path.[42]

---

[38] As in the case of the British Petroleum Co. (where Government shareholding is now less than 50 per cent. but power to nominate directors still exists) or Cable and Wireless Ltd. (Cable and Wireless Act 1946).

[39] Iron and Steel Act 1949; Iron and Steel Act 1953; Iron and Steel Act 1967. The " unscrambling " of companies nationalised by acquisition of assets, rather than of shares, was much more complicated.

[40] See, for example, H. Rose, *Disclosure in Company Accounts* (Eaton Paper 1, 1963); and A. Rubner, *The Ensnared Shareholder* (1965) which also advocates compulsory distribution of profits to shareholders. See, too, F. Jarvis, *The Company Shareholder and Growth* (Hobart Papers 37, 1966).

[41] See H. Rose, *op. cit.*, p. 34, who proposed obligatory enforcement of " export sales." K. W. Wedderburn, *Company Law Reform* (Fabian Tract 363, 1965) at pp. 5–16; and N. Ross, *Workshop Bargaining* (Fabian Tract 366, 1966).

[42] See, for example, s. 18 (disclosure of remuneration of employees) and s. 20 (disclosure of export sales), which are more easily justified as disclosures in the interests of collective bargaining or in the " national interest " than for the traditional purpose of protecting investors. The proposal that limited companies should be obliged to

The vexed question of the relationship between the employees and the company which employs them is, in fact, a dominant theme in the current debate which flows over from company to labour law.[43] It is generally accepted that it is unreal for company law to ignore, as at present our law largely does, that the workers are as much, if not more, a part of the company as the members of it. One detects four main types of proposal. First, a system of co-partnership whereby employees acquire shares in their companies and thereby profit as members as well as workers. Secondly, variants on the co-partnership theme whereby employees not merely become participants in the profits but, by stages, share also in the power of control over the company. The Liberal Party has long been in favour of developments on these lines.[44] But perhaps the most far-reaching proposals have come from a business man, Mr. G. Goyder, who wants the place of workers to be recognised by company law and provision made whereby they would eventually become joint owners with the management, the shareholders being gradually bought out.[45]

A third and different theme has been pursued by those who feel that " industrial democracy " must be sought by moving towards sharing of power by means of an improved machinery of collective bargaining. In this move the contribution of company law would be largely accessory, by requiring disclosure of the necessary information, leading perhaps to " the eventual introduction of works councils into the very machinery of British company law in a way that integrates them not with management but with the structure of our trade unions,"[46] so that the informa-

bargain collectively with the employees' trade union was not accepted by the (Donovan) Royal Commission on Trade Unions and Employers' Associations (Cmnd. 3623, para. 253). Whereas the nationalised public corporations are placed under statutory obligations to consult and bargain with trade unions, companies are not; the Government's White Paper, *In Place of Strife* (Cmnd. 3888) proposes to make such bargaining a legal obligation for all employers.

43 Nationalisation does not solve this problem; see the Labour Party's *Industrial Democracy* (1967), where it is stated that after 20 years of nationalisation there is " considerable room for experiment in new forms of workers' participation " leading to " joint administration," p. 58. The Iron and Steel Act 1967 made provision for new forms of consultation and for working trade unionists to join the administering boards in the renationalised steel industry.

44 For a recent statement, see J. Livermore, *Controlling Interest—Participation and Power in Industry* (New Orbits Pamphlet 8, 1965). Schemes whereby a company provides finance to encourage its executives to acquire shares are becoming increasingly common.

45 See *The Future of Private Enterprise* (1951) and *The Responsible Company* (1961). These proposals by a practical representative of management link up with proposals by ideologically more socialist commentators that the equity shareholder should in effect become a fixed-interest creditor in the large company: see, *e.g.*, P. Derrick, *Company and the Community* (Fabian Research Series, 238, 1964). Cf. N. Ross, *The Democratic Firm* (Fabian Research Series 264, 1964) and the Evidence of H. A. Turner to the Donovan Commission, *Selected Written Evidence* (H.M.S.O. 1968) 659 at 668–670.

46 K. W. Wedderburn, *op. cit.*, p. 17 (described by H. Wincott as introducing " a real Trojan Horse for the Communists and fellow travellers ": *Investors' Chronicle*, September 10, 1965). The same approach to industrial democracy via collective bargaining appears in *Industrial Democracy* (Labour Party) and the Donovan Report (Cmnd. 3623).

tion could more readily be used for bargaining at plant level. Works councils, built by law into the structure of the enterprise, have been the subject of experiment in other systems of law, ranging from works councils that are organs of final control in Yugoslavia to bodies such as West German works councils which have limited rights of consultation.[47]

West Germany has also been the country in which a fourth type of experiment has been most highly developed. This involves introduction of "workers' directors" on the controlling boards [48] of companies.[49] This German system of *Mitbestimmung* or "Co-Determination" has had considerable influence both in Europe [50] and on certain thinkers in Britain [51] including leading members of the Labour Party.[52] Recent studies, on the other hand, suggest it is not desirable, at any rate yet, to introduce "workers' directors" on a compulsory basis [53]; the present law does not prohibit experiments along these lines on an optional basis.

Reforms in European company law will inevitably influence future British experiments,[54] and the relationship between the two will become even more important if this country either enters or forms any formal association with the European Economic Community in which, not only

---

47 For a description, see A. Sturmthal, *Workers Councils* (1964); H. Clegg, *A New Approach to Industrial Democracy* (1960); and for a critique of the latter, P. Blumberg, *Industrial Democracy* (1968), Chaps. 7 and 8.

48 It must be remembered that the German company has two " boards," the " supervisory " board on which workers' representatives sit, and the " managing " board, which includes no such representatives but does have a director who is independently concerned with " labour " matters.

49 See G. Vagts, *Reforming the Modern Corporation; Perspectives from the German* (1966) 80 Harv.L.R. 23; H. J. Spiro, *The Politics of German Co-Determination* (1957).

50 See the recent French company law reforms stemming from the Decree of August 17, 1967, No. 67/693.

51 For example, M. Fogarty, *Companies Beyond Jenkins* (P.E.P. 1965) and *Company and Corporation—One Law?* (1965), whose work has been influential in Liberal Party circles. Although trade unions have been customarily opposed to the idea (except for a minority, such as the Post Office Workers' Union, where " co-determination " has long been a formal objective), the T.U.C. was prepared to flirt with it in its evidence to the Donovan Commission: *Trade Unionism* (1967), pp. 106–107.

52 Thus, the Lord Chancellor, Lord Gardiner, introducing the Companies Bill 1966, spoke of hopes to deal in another Bill with the " very relevant question today . . . whether they [employees] ought not to have a more settled place or places on the board of directors of the company ": H.L.Deb., Vol. 278, col. 136. See also D. Jay, *Socialism in the New Society* (1962), pp. 331–333; and G. Gardiner and A. Martin (ed.), *Law Reform Now* (1964), p. 195, where it is also proposed that directors be appointed by the Government to " Enterprises of National Interest." But objections to both ideas have been pungently expressed by C. A. R. Crosland, currently President of the Board of Trade, in *The Future of Socialism* (1956), Chap. XVII, where he remarks that " Government nominees on a private board must either ' go native ' or remain suspect " (p. 358) and that workers will be suspicious of employees who " represent " them on the board, " Quisling accusations always create the deepest bitterness of all " (p. 361). Proposals for Government directors are linked with suggestions for some form of regular " efficiency audit," on which see C. D. Foster, *Labour's New Frontiers* (ed. P. Hall 1963), Chap. 2.

53 The majority of the Donovan Commission thought that a few such directors would give workers " no real share in or control over " company policy and rejected the idea (Cmnd. 3623, para. 1002).

54 For a review of all these matters in the light of West European company law systems, see *A Companies Act 1970?* (P.E.P. 1967, Vol. 33, No. 500), the first major product of a continuing study by Political and Economic Planning.

are efforts being made to "harmonise" national company laws, but a project for a supra-national "European Company," which transcends national frontiers, is already well advanced.[55]

In a world where the giant company has already assumed international proportions, either by way of trading agreements or mergers with companies in other countries, or by its own operation through subsidiaries or branches in other countries, Berle and Means' analysis of company law as part of the constitution of the new economic State [56] takes on a new significance. When a Minister can say in the House of Commons: "As the international companies develop, national governments, including the British Government, will be reduced to the status of a parish council in dealing with the large international corporations which will span the world," [57] company law reform cannot be approached in a merely insular or parochial fashion.

It is no part of the purpose of this book to advocate reforms of the law; but it seems likely that the development of Britain's mixed economy will set in train during the next decade some far-reaching changes. The lawyer of the future will have to play a major part in shaping any reforms that are resolved upon and in advising about their practicability.[58] Before he can do so he must understand the present law, not merely as an arid set of abstract rules, but as an essential part of the machinery of the modern State. The excuse for this rather lengthy historical introduction and brief outline of current problems is that this machinery is best understood in the context of an appreciation of how and why it evolved and of how it may develop in the future.

---

[55] See Chap. 28, *infra.*
[56] See p. 58, note 20, *supra.*
[57] A. Wedgwood Benn, Minister of Technology: *The Times*, Nov. 28, 1968.
[58] For example, devising separate codes to deal with the three types of company into which commentators usually divide companies—the "giants," the medium-size company, and the small owner-operated company: see *A Companies Act 1970?* (P.E.P. 1967); T. Hadden, *Control of Company Fraud* (P.E.P. 1968). The Companies Act 1967 makes a tentative step in this direction in so far as it relieves smaller companies from particular obligations, the "cut-off" point being varied in each case: see, *e.g.*, ss. 6 (6), 17 (1) and Sched. 2, para. 13A (5); ss. 18 (5), 19 (1), 20, 25 (2), 33 (10).

PART TWO

THE CONSEQUENCES OF INCORPORATION

THE CONSEQUENCES OF INCORPORATION

As we have seen, today one of the outstanding features of a company is that it is an incorporated body and, before proceeding further, it is necessary to examine the concept of corporate personality a little more closely in order to assess its legal and practical advantages and disadvantages. Its advantages, which are generally the more obvious of the two, are particularly apparent in the case of bodies carrying on business for gain, and, in the discussion which follows, the position of the incorporated company will be primarily contrasted with that of the sole trader, and with the private partnership—the main alternative to the company when a small body of persons wish to " carry on business in common with a view of profit." [1]

It must be stressed, however, that it does not follow that every unincorporated body lacks all the privileges which incorporation automatically provides. As we have seen,[2] statutes of the early nineteenth century enabled the Crown by letters patent to confer all or any of the advantages of incorporation without actually granting corporate personality, and similarly a statute may confer many of these privileges without actual incorporation. In fact, as will appear later,[3] this has been done in several cases, with the result that between the two extremes of an unincorporated club or society and the corporation there are many hybrids, which, though formally unincorporated, possess a greater or lesser number of the attributes of a corporation. Among these hybrids even partnerships ought perhaps to be included for the partners can now sue or be sued in the firm's name.[4]

---

[1] Partnership is thus defined in s. 1 (1) of the Partnership Act 1890.
[2] *Supra*, Chap. 3, p. 41. The statutes were the Trading Companies Act 1834 and the Chartered Companies Act 1837; now both obsolete although the latter is unrepealed.
[3] Chap. 11, *infra*.
[4] Under R.S.C., Ord. 81.

CHAPTER 4

THE CONSEQUENCES OF INCORPORATION

Legal entity distinct from its members

As already emphasised, the fundamental attribute of corporate personality—from which indeed all the other consequences flow—is that the corporation is a legal entity distinct from its members. Hence it is capable of enjoying rights and of being subject to duties which are not the same as those enjoyed or borne by its members. In other words, it has " legal personality " and is often described as an *artificial person* in contrast with a human being, a *natural person.*[1]

As we have seen in the previous chapter, corporate personality became an attribute of the normal joint stock company only at a comparatively late stage in its development, and it was not until *Salomon* v. *Salomon & Co.*[2] at the end of the nineteenth century that its implications were fully grasped even by the courts. The facts of this justly celebrated case were as follows:

Salomon had for many years carried on a prosperous business as a leather merchant. In 1892 he decided to convert it into a limited company and for this purpose Salomon & Co. Ltd. was formed with Salomon, his wife and five of his children as members, and Salomon as managing director. The company purchased the business as a going concern for £39,000—" a sum which represented the sanguine expectations of a fond owner rather than anything that can be called a businesslike or reasonable estimate of value." [3] The price was satisfied by £10,000 in debentures, conferring a charge over all the company's assets, £20,000 in fully paid £1 shares and the balance in cash. Seven shares were subscribed in cash by the members and the result was that Salomon held 20,001 of the 20,007 shares issued, and each of the remaining six shares was held by a member of his family apparently as a nominee for him. The company almost immediately ran into difficulties and only a year later the then holder of the debentures appointed a receiver and the company went into liquidation. Its assets were sufficient to discharge the debentures but nothing was left for the unsecured creditors. In these circumstances Vaughan Williams J. and a strong Court of Appeal held that the whole transaction

---

[1] A company, even if it has only one member is a " corporation aggregate " as opposed to the somewhat anomalous " corporation sole " in which an office, *e.g.*, that of a bishop, is personified.
[2] [1897] A.C. 22, H.L.
[3] *Per* Lord Macnaghten at p. 49.

was contrary to the true intent of the Companies Act and that the company was a mere sham, and an " alias," agent, trustee or nominee for Salomon who remained the real proprietor of the business. As such he was liable to indemnify the company against its trading debts. But the House of Lords unanimously reversed this decision. They held that the company had been validly formed, since the Act merely required seven members holding at least one share each. It said nothing about their being independent, or that they should take a substantial interest in the undertaking, or that they should have a mind and will of their own, or that there should be anything like a balance of power in the constitution of the company. Hence the business belonged to the company and not to Salomon, and Salomon was its agent not it the agent of Salomon. In the blunt words of Lord Halsbury L.C.,[4]

" Either the limited company was a legal entity or it was not. If it was, the business belonged to it and not to Mr. Salomon. If it was not, there was no person and no thing to be an agent at all; and it is impossible to say at the same time that there is a company and there is not."

Or, as Lord Macnaghten put it [5]:

" The company is at law a different person altogether from the subscribers . . . ; and, though it may be that after incorporation the business is precisely the same as it was before, and the same persons are managers, and the same hands receive the profits, the company is not in law the agent of the subscribers or trustee for them. Nor are the subscribers, as members liable, in any shape or form, except to the extent and in the manner provided by the Act." [6]

Of course this decision does not mean that a promoter can with impunity defraud the company which he forms or swindle his existing creditors. In the *Salomon* case it was argued that the company was entitled to rescind in view of the wilful overvaluation of the business sold to it. But the House held that in fact there was no fraud at all since the shareholders were fully conversant with what was being done. Had Salomon made a profit which he concealed from his fellow shareholders the position would have been different.[7] Nor was there any fraud on Salomon's existing creditors all of whom were paid off in full out of the purchase price. Otherwise they [8] or Salomon's trustee in bankruptcy [9] might have been entitled to upset the sale. And today the

---

[4] At p. 31.   [5] At p. 51.
[6] For an early statutory recognition of the same principle, see 22 Geo. 3, c. 45, which disqualified those holding Government contracts from election to Parliament but expressly provided (s. 3) that the prohibition did not extend to members of incorporated companies holding such contracts.
[7] See *infra*, Chap. 13.   [8] Under what is now s. 172 of the L.P.A. 1925.
[9] Under what is now s. 42 (1) of the Bankruptcy Act 1914. Or the transfer may constitute an act of bankruptcy and be avoided if a bankruptcy petition is presented within three months: see *Re Simms* [1930] 2 Ch. 22.

charge securing the debentures would be ineffective if liquidation followed within a year and the company could not be proved to have been solvent when the charge was granted.[10]   But, in this particular case, Salomon seems to have been one of the victims rather than the villain of the piece for he had charged his debentures and used the money to try to support the tottering company.   However, the result would have been the same if he had not, and if he had been the only creditor to receive anything from the business which was " his " in fact though not in law.

This decision opened up new vistas to company lawyers and the world of commerce. Not only did it finally establish the legality of the one-man company and showed that incorporation was as readily available to the small private partnership and sole trader as to the large public company, but it also revealed that it was possible for a trader not merely to limit his liability to the money which he put into the enterprise but even to avoid any serious risk to the major part of that by subscribing for debentures rather than shares. This result seems shocking, and the decision has been much criticised.[11]   The only justification for it is that the public deal with a limited company at their peril and know, or should know, what to expect. In particular, a search of the company's file at the Companies' Registry will show whether there are any charges on the company's assets,[12] and its last balance sheet and profit and loss account. But the latter will probably be months out of date and not everyone will be capable of understanding them. Nor does everyone having dealings with a company have the time or knowledge needed to search the file. The experienced business man with his trade protection associations can take care of himself, but the little man, whom the law should particularly protect, rarely has any idea of the risks he runs when he grants credit to a company with a high-sounding name,[13] impressive nominal capital (not paid up in cash), and with assets mortgaged up to the hilt.[14]   Nor is it practical for the unemployed workman, who is offered a job with a limited company, to decline it until he has first searched the company's file at Companies House.[15]

---

[10] Companies Act 1948, s. 322.

[11] See, for example, O. Kahn-Freund, " Some Reflections on Company Law Reform " (1944) 7 M.L.R. 54 (a most thought-provoking article still well worth study), in which it is described as a " calamitous decision."

[12] But not necessarily the amount secured; most companies grant floating charges to their bankers to secure " all sums due or to become due " on their current overdrafts and the register of charges will not give any indication of the size of the overdraft.

[13] There are undoubtedly many who think that " Ltd." is an indication of size and stability rather than a warning of irresponsibility. The fact that they do so is a testimonial to commercial morality as showing the small extent to which advantage has actually been taken of the undoubted opportunities for abuse.

[14] But no sympathy was wasted on him by the H.L. " A creditor who will not take the trouble to use the means which the statute provides for enabling him to protect himself must bear the consequences of his own negligence ": *per* Lord Watson at p. 40.

[15] The likely result would be to lose him his unemployment benefit: see National Insurance Act 1965, s. 22 (2).

Since the *Salomon* case, the complete separation of the company and its members has never been doubted. As we shall see later,[16] there are cases in which the legislature, and to a very small extent the courts, have allowed the veil of incorporation to be lifted, but in general it is opaque and impassable. The consequences, however, are not necessarily wholly beneficial to the members.[17] A landlord who carries on business through a one-man company will be unable to resist the tenant's application for a renewed tenancy on the ground that the landlord requires possession for the purpose of a business to be carried on by him.[18] If a trader sells his business to a company he will cease to have an insurable interest in its assets even although he is the beneficial owner of all the shares. If therefore he forgets to assign the insurance policies, and to obtain any necessary consents of the insurers, nothing will be payable if the assets perish.[19] Similarly, a parent company will not have an insurable interest in the assets of its subsidiary companies even though wholly owned, for the rule that a company is distinct from its members applies equally to the separate companies of a group.[20] In Professor Kahn-Freund's striking phrase [21] " sometimes *corporate entity* works like a boomerang and hits the man who was trying to use it."

It is from this fundamental attribute of separate personality that most of the particular advantages of incorporation spring.

1. Limited liability

It follows from the fact that a corporation is a separate person that its members are not as such liable for its debts. Hence in the absence of express provision to the contrary the members will be completely free from any personal liability. This is, in fact, the position as regards municipal and ecclesiastical corporations and the modern public corporations, and may be so as regards statutory and chartered companies, the members of which will only be under any personal liability if, and to the extent that, the statute or charter so provides.

But as regards a company registered under the Companies Acts a complete absence of any liability is not permitted. Such a company can either be registered as unlimited, in which case the members are in effect guarantors of its obligations without any restric-

---

16 *Infra*, Chap. 10.
17 See especially Kiralfy, " Some Unforeseen Consequences of Private Incorporation " in (1949) 65 L.Q.R. 231, and Kahn-Freund, *loc. cit.*, and *infra*, Chap. 10.
18 *Tunstall* v. *Steigmann* [1962] 2 Q.B. 593. But see Law of Property Bill 1969.
19 *Macaura* v. *Northern Assurance Co.* [1925] A.C. 619, H.L.; *Levinger* v. *Licences, etc., Insurance Co.* (1936) 54 Ll.L.R. 68.
20 As will be pointed out later (Chap. 10) inroads have been made into this principle, but it still remains the general rule.
21 *Loc. cit.* at p. 56.

tion on amount,[22] or it can be limited by shares or guarantee.[23] In the case of a company limited by shares each member is liable to contribute when called upon to do so the full nominal value (in money or money's worth) of the shares held by him in so far as this has not already been paid by him or any prior holder of those shares. In the case of a guarantee company each member is liable to contribute a specified amount to the assets of the company in the event of its being wound up while he is a member or within one year after he ceases to be a member. In effect, therefore, the member, without being directly liable to the company's creditors, is in both cases a limited guarantor of the company's debts.

When, therefore, obligations are incurred on behalf of a company, the company is liable and not the members, though the company may ultimately be able to recover a contribution from them to enable it to discharge its obligations. If the company is an unlimited one their liability to contribute will be unlimited; if it is limited by shares their liability will be limited to the unpaid nominal value of their shares and in practice their shares are today likely to be fully paid up so that they will be under no further liability. If the company is limited by guarantee they will be under no liability until it is wound up, and then, in practice, only for a derisory sum.[24] In contrast an unincorporated association, not being a legal person, cannot be liable, and obligations entered into on its behalf can only bind the actual officials who purport to act on its behalf, or the individual members if the officials have actual or apparent authority to bind them. In either event the persons bound will be liable to the full extent of their property unless they expressly or impliedly restrict their responsibility to the extent of the assets of the association, as the officials may well do.[25] Hence the extent to which the members will be liable depends on the terms of the contract of association. In the case of a club, and presumably the same applies to learned and scientific societies, there will generally be implied a term that the members are not personally liable for obligations incurred on behalf of the club.[26] But very different is the position of members of a partnership, an association carrying on business for gain. Each partner is an agent of all the others and his acts done in " carrying on in the normal way business of the kind carried on by the firm " bind the partners.[27]

---

[22] " In effect," because, of course, the *modus operandi* is different; the creditor has no direct right against the member, as he would have against a surety on default by the principal debtor.

[23] The Companies Acts (now 1948 Act, ss. 202–203) have always provided that a limited company may have directors with unlimited liability. Is is not surprising that these provisions have long been a dead letter.

[24] See Chap. 1, pp. 11, 12, *supra*.

[25] For further discussion, see Chap. 11, *infra*.

[26] *Wise* v. *Perpetual Trustee Co.* [1903] A.C. 139, P.C.

[27] Partnership Act 1890, s. 5. This, it will be seen, applies equally to Scotland, thus largely negativing the consequence of recognising the Scottish firm as a separate person.

Only if the creditor knows of the limitation placed on the partners' authority will the other members escape liability.[28] Moreover, an attempt to restrict the partners' liability to partnership funds by a provision to that effect in the partnership agreement will be ineffective even if known to the creditors [29]; they will only be able to restrict their financial liability, in respect of acts otherwise authorised, by an express agreement to that effect with the creditor concerned.[30]

There is, it is true, now a method whereby liability can be limited without forming an incorporated company; namely, by a limited partnership under the Limited Partnerships Act 1907. But this has many disadvantages in comparison with a company. In particular, it is not possible to limit the personal liability of all the partners but only some of them.[31] Moreover, even the limited partners lose their privilege of limited liability if they take any part in the management of the business.[32] This latter rule is especially inconvenient, for although a person who puts money into a business may be happy to leave the running of it to his colleagues while all goes well, he will probably want to be able to intervene if things go wrong. If a limited partner does so, his attempt to save his share from the wreck may well result in the whole of his fortune perishing.

Hence a limited company is generally found preferable. It enables the liability of all the members to be limited without restriction on the part which they play in the management, and although it involves somewhat greater formality, publicity and expense, these are not very onerous. In practice, therefore, limited partnerships are only used where for some reason an incorporated company is inappropriate (*e.g.*, in the case of certain professions which companies are not allowed to practise), but one member of the firm is not prepared to accept full liability for its debts or the other partners do not want him to play any part in the management. This may occur on the retirement from active participation of a senior partner whom it is wished to retain as a consultant or for the prestige value of his name and reputation. Save in these rare cases where limited partnerships are appropriate, the only practical alternatives are either complete personal liability on the one hand or limited liability through the medium of a company on the other.

2. Property

As the previous discussion will have suggested, one of the most obvious advantages of corporate personality is that it enables the

---

[28] *Ibid.* ss. 5 and 8.
[29] *Re Sea, Fire and Life Insurance Co.* (1854) 3 De G.M. & G. 459.
[30] *Hallett* v. *Dowdall* (1852) 21 L.J.Q.B. 98. It is a criminal offence to carry on business under a name ending with " Limited " unless duly incorporated with limited liability: Companies Act 1948, s. 439.
[31] Limited Partnerships Act 1907, s. 4 (2).
[32] *Ibid.* s. 6 (1). They may only " advise with the partners."

property of the association to be clearly distinguished from that of its members. In an unincorporated society, the property of the association *is* the joint property of the members, although the rights of the members therein differ from their rights to their separate property since the joint property must be dealt with according to the rules of the society and no individual member can claim any particular asset.[33] By virtue of the trust the obvious complications can be minimised but not completely eradicated. And the complications cause particular difficulty in the case of a trading partnership both as regards the true nature of the interests of the partners [34] and, more especially, as regards claims of creditors.[35]

These difficulties are completely avoided by incorporation. The corporate property is clearly distinguished from the members' property and members have no direct proprietary rights to the company's property but merely to their " shares."[36] A change in the membership, which causes inevitable dislocation to a partnership firm, leaves the company unconcerned; the shares will be transferred but the company's property will be untouched. No realisation or splitting up of its property will be necessary, as it will on a change in the constitution of the partnership firm. Similarly, the claims of the company's creditors will merely be against the company's property and the difficulties which arise on a firm's bankruptcy will not occur.

3. Suing and being sued

Closely allied to questions of property are those relating to legal actions. The difficulties in the way of suing or being sued by an unincorporated association have been sufficiently stressed in the previous chapters, where it was pointed out that they were partially surmounted by the trust device and, more satisfactorily, by statutory intervention. The problem is obviously of the greatest practical importance in connection with trading bodies and in fact it has now been solved in the case of partnerships by allowing a partnership to sue or be sued in the firm's name.[37] Hence there is now no difficulty so far as the pure mechanics of suit are concerned—although there may still be complications in enforcing judgment especially if bankruptcy is resorted to.

In the case of other unincorporated bodies (such as clubs and learned societies) not subject to special statutory provisions, the problems of

33 See further, Ford, *Unincorporated Non-Profit Associations*, Part I.
34 See Partnership Act 1890, ss. 20–22; *Re Fuller's Contract* [1933] Ch. 652.
35 P.A. 1890, s. 23, and Bankruptcy Act 1914, s. 33 (6). See further, Glanville Williams, *Joint Obligations*, Chap. 5.
36 " Shareholders are not, in the eye of the law, part owners of the undertaking. The undertaking is something different from the totality of the shareholdings ": *per* Evershed L.J. in *Short* v. *Treasury Commissioners* [1948] 1 K.B. 116, C.A., at p. 122 (affd. [1948] A.C. 534, H.L.).
37 R.S.C., Ord. 81. For the equivalent county court procedure, see C.C.R., Ord. 5, rr. 21–24, and Ord. 8, rr. 14 and 15.

suit are still serious. Sometimes its committee or other agents may be personally liable or entitled. Otherwise, the only course is a " representative action " whereby, under certain conditions, one or more persons may sue or be sued on behalf of all the interested parties. But resort to this procedure [38] is only available subject to compliance with a number of somewhat ill-defined conditions, and the law, which has been little explored,[39] is obscure and difficult. The result is apt to be embarrassing to the society when it wishes to enforce its rights (or, more properly, those of its members) though it has compensating advantages when it wishes to evade its duties.[40] Needless to say, none of these difficulties arises when an incorporated company is suing or being sued; the company as a legal person can take action to enforce its legal rights or be sued for breach of its legal duties. The only disadvantage is that if a limited company is plaintiff it may be ordered to give security for costs.[41]

4. Perpetual succession

One of the obvious advantages of an artificial person is that it is not susceptible to " the thousand natural shocks that flesh is heir to." It cannot become incapacitated by illness, mental or physical, and it has not (or need not have) an allotted span of life.[42] This is not to say that the death or incapacity of its human members may not cause the company considerable embarrassment; obviously this will occur if all the directors die or are imprisoned or if there are too few surviving members to hold a valid meeting, or if the bulk of the members or directors become enemy aliens.[43] But the vicissitudes of the flesh have no direct effect on the disembodied company.[44] The death of a member leaves the company unmoved; members may come and go but the company

[38] Which is of considerable importance in company law, *e.g.*, where a member, on behalf of himself and the other members is suing the company to restrain an alleged " fraud on the minority " (see Chap. 25, *infra*) or where a debentureholder starts an action, on behalf of himself and the other debentureholders, to enforce the security (see Chap. 19, *infra*).

[39] But see an invaluable discussion by Lloyd, " Actions Instituted By or Against Unincorporated Bodies " in (1949) 12 M.L.R. 409. And see *infra*, Chap. 11, p. 219.

[40] " An unincorporated association has certain advantages when litigation is desired against them " : *per* Scrutton L.J. in *Bloom* v. *National Federation of Discharged Soldiers, etc.* (1918) 35 T.L.R. 50, C.A., at p. 51.

[41] Companies Act 1948, s. 447.

[42] s. 278 of the Companies Act 1948 envisages that the period of the company's duration may be fixed in the articles, but this is never done in practice and even if it were the company would not automatically expire on the expiration of the term; an ordinary resolution would be necessary. It is otherwise with chartered companies: see Chap. 1, p. 6, n. 20, *supra*.

[43] *Cf. Daimler Co.* v. *Continental Tyre and Rubber Co.* [1916] 2 A.C. 307, H.L.

[44] As Greer L.J. said in *Stepney Corporation* v. *Osofsky* [1937] 3 All E.R. 289, C.A., at p. 291: a corporate body has " no soul to be saved or body to be kicked." This epigram is believed to be of considerable antiquity. Glanville Williams, *Criminal Law: The General Part* (2nd ed.), p. 856, has traced it back to Lord Thurlow and an earlier variation to Coke. *Cf.* the decree of Pope Innocent IV forbidding the excommunication of corporations because, having neither minds nor souls, they could not sin: see Carr, *Law of Corporations*, 73.

can go on for ever.[45]　The insanity of the managing director will not be calamitous to the company provided that he is removed promptly; he may be the company's brains but lobectomy is a simpler operation than on a natural person.

Once again, the disadvantages in the case of an unincorporated society can be minimised by the use of a trust. If the property of the association is vested in a small body of trustees the death, disability or retirement of an individual member, other than one of the trustees, need not cause much trouble. But, of course, the trustees, if natural persons, will themselves need replacing at fairly frequent intervals and the need for constant appointment of new trustees is a nuisance if nothing worse. Indeed, it may be said that the trust never functioned at its simplest until it was able to enlist the aid of its own child, the incorporated company, to act as a trust corporation with perpetual succession.

Moreover, the trust only obviates difficulties when a member or his estate has under the constitution of the association no right to be paid a share of the assets on death or retirement, which, of course, is the position with the normal club or learned society. But on the retirement or death of a partner, the partnership is automatically dissolved, so far at any rate as he is concerned,[46] and he or his estate will be entitled to be paid out his interest. The resulting dislocation of the firm's business can be reduced by special clauses in the articles of partnership providing for an arbitrary basis of valuation of his share and deferred payment, but cannot be eradicated altogether. With an incorporated company these problems do not arise. The member or his estate is not entitled to be paid out by the company. If he, or his personal representative, trustee in bankruptcy, or committee or receiver in lunacy, wishes to realise the value of his shares, these must be sold, whereupon the purchaser will, on entry in the share register, become a member in place of the former holder.[47]

The continuing existence of a company, irrespective of changes in its membership, is helpful in other directions also. When an individual sells his business to another, difficult questions may arise regarding the performance of existing contracts by the new proprietor,[48] the assignment of rights of a personal nature,[49] and the validity of agreements made

---

[45] During the war *all* the members of one private company, while in general meeting, were killed by a bomb. But the company survived; not even a hydrogen bomb could have destroyed it.

[46] And, in the absence of contrary agreement, as regards all the partners: Partnership Act 1890, s. 33.

[47] In practice it may not be so easy for the shareholder or his representatives, as the company's articles may place restraints on freedom of transfer: see Chap. 18, *infra*.

[48] *Robson* v. *Drummond* (1831) 2 B. & Ad. 303; *cf. British Waggon Co.* v. *Lea* (1880) 5 Q.B.D. 149.

[49] *Griffith* v. *Tower Publishing Co.* [1897] 1 Ch. 21 (publishing agreement held not assignable); *Kemp* v. *Baerselman* [1906] 2 K.B. 604, C.A. (agreement not assignable if question of one party's obligation depends on the other's personal " requirements "). *Cf. Tolhurst* v. *Associated Portland Cement* [1902] 2 K.B. 660, C.A.

with customers ignorant of the change of proprietorship.[50] Similar problems may arise on a change in the constitution of a partnership.[51] Where the business is incorporated and the sale is merely of the shares, none of these difficulties arises. The company remains the proprietor of the business, the company performs the existing contracts and retains the benefits of them, and the company continues to enter into future agreements. The difficulties attending vicarious performance, assignments and mistaken identity simply do not arise.

5. Transferable shares

As was pointed out in Part I, incorporation, with the resulting separation of the business from its members, greatly facilitates the transfer of the members' interests, although even without formal incorporation much the same end was achieved through the device of the trust coupled with an agreement for transferability in the deed of settlement. But this end could only be approximately attained since the member, even after transfer, would remain liable for the firm's debts incurred during the time when he was a member. Moreover, in the absence of limited liability his opportunities of transfer would in practice be much restricted.

With an incorporated company freedom to transfer, both legally and practically, can be readily attained. The company can be incorporated with its liability limited by shares, and these shares constitute items of property which are freely transferable in the absence of express provision to the contrary, and in such a way that the transferor drops out [52] and the transferee steps into his shoes. A partner has a proprietary interest which he can assign, but the assignment does not operate to divest him of his status or liability as a partner; it merely affords the assignee the right to receive whatever the firm distributes in respect of the assigning partner's share.[53] The assignee can only be admitted into partnership in the place of the assignor if the other partners agree [54] and the assignor will not be relieved of his existing liabilities as a partner unless the creditors agree, expressly or impliedly, to release him.[55]

Even in the case of an incorporated company the power to transfer may, of course, be subject to restrictions. In a private company some form of restriction is essential in order to comply with its statutory definition [56] and is, in any event, desirable if such a company is to retain

---

50 *Boulton* v. *Jones* (1857) 2 H. & N. 564.
51 See *Brace* v. *Calder* [1895] 2 Q.B. 253, C.A., where the retirement of two partners was held to operate as the wrongful dismissal of a manager. And see also P.A. 1890, s. 18. In practice such difficulties are often avoided by an implied novation.
52 Subject only, in the case of partly paid shares, to his liability to be placed on the " B " list of contributories in the event of liquidation within a year: Companies Act 1948, s. 212.
53 Partnership Act 1890, s. 31.
54 *Ibid.* s. 24 (7).
55 *Ibid.* s. 17 (2) and (3).
56 Companies Act 1948, s. 28.

its character of an incorporated private partnership. In practice these restrictions are usually so stringent as to make transferability largely illusory. Nor is there any legal objection to restrictions in the case of a public company, although such restrictions, except as regards partly paid shares, are unusual, and impracticable if the shares are to be marketed on a stock exchange.[57] But there is this fundamental difference; that in a partnership transferability depends on express agreement and is subject to legal and practical limitations, whereas in a company it exists to the fullest extent in the absence of express restriction. The partnership relationship is essentially personal; and in practice this is maintained in the case of the private company which is in economic reality a partnership though in law an incorporated company. On the other hand the relationship between members of a public company is, as we have seen,[58] essentially impersonal and financial and hence there is no reason to restrict changes in membership.

6. Borrowing

Hitherto we have considered only the advantages which flow inevitably, or at any rate naturally, from the fact of incorporation. There is, however, another matter in which, under English law, incorporation happens to confer advantages although there is no logical reason why it should necessarily do so.

This is in respect of borrowing. At first sight one would suppose that a sole trader or partners, being personally liable, would find it easier than a company to raise money by borrowing. In practice, however, this is not so since a company is often able to grant a more effective charge to secure the indebtedness. The ingenuity of equity practitioners led to the evolution of an unusual but highly beneficial type of security known as the floating charge; *i.e.,* a charge which floats like a cloud over the whole assets from time to time falling within a generic description, but without preventing the mortgagor from disposing of these assets in the usual course of business until something occurs to cause the charge to become crystallised or fixed. This type of charge is particularly suitable when a business has no fixed assets, such as land, which can be included in a normal mortgage, but carries a large and valuable stock-in-trade. Since this stock needs to be turned over in the course of business a fixed charge is impracticable because the consent of the mortgagee would be needed every time anything was sold and a new charge would have to be entered into whenever anything was bought. A floating charge obviates these difficulties; it enables the stock to be turned over but attaches to whatever it is converted into and to whatever new stock is acquired.

---

[57] See *Requirements,* App. Sched. VII, Pt. A, para. A 2.
[58] See Chap. 1, p. 9 *et seq.*

In theory there is no reason why such charges should not be granted by a sole trader or partnership as well as by a company. But there are two very good practical reasons why they are limited to the latter. In the first place, in so far as the charge attaches to chattels it would be a bill of sale within the meaning of the Bills of Sale Acts 1878–82 as an attempt to pass a proprietary interest in chattels while retaining possession of them. Hence it would need to be registered in the Bill of Sale Registry,[59] and, what is more important, as a mortgage bill it would need to be in the statutory form [60] which involves specifying the chattels in detail in a schedule. Compliance with the latter requirement is obviously impossible, since in a floating charge the chattels are, *ex hypothesi*, indeterminate and fluctuating. But the Bills of Sale Acts do not apply to charges [61] by companies; they are expressly excluded by section 17 of the Act of 1882.[62]

Secondly, the " reputed ownership " provision of the Bankruptcy Act [63] would in any case seriously restrict the efficacy of floating charges by natural persons. Under this provision goods which are " in the possession, order or disposition of the bankrupt, in his trade or business, by the consent and permission of the true owner, under such circumstances that he is reputed owner thereof " vest in his trustee in bankruptcy free from any third-party rights. This would obviously in most cases cover stock-in-trade subject to a floating charge. But although most bankruptcy rules apply in the liquidation of a company [64] the " reputed ownership " clause does not.[65]

---

[59] For some reason registration of a bill of sale against a tradesman destroys his credit, whereas registration of a debenture against a company does not. This can only be explained on the basis that the former is exceptional, whereas the latter is usual and familiarity has bred contempt.

[60] 1882 Act, s. 9; nor could it cover future goods: see s. 5. S. 6 (2) allows a limited power of replacement but not anything as fluid as a floating charge. The exemption in s. 17 is limited to " incorporated companies " and not extended to all bodies corporate, but was granted to industrial and provident societies by the Industrial and Provident Societies Act 1967.

[61] Absolute bills of sale granted by companies are within the Bills of Sale Acts: *Re Cunningham & Co., Attenborough's Case* (1885) 28 Ch.D. 682.

[62] In *Re Standard Manufacturing Co.* [1891] 1 Ch. 627, C.A., this was explained on the ground that debentures were not within the mischief of the Acts, which were designed to prevent secret charges, since debentures required registration. This explanation is now more convincing than at the time when it was given since debentures now require public registration: Companies Act 1948, Part III. In 1891 the only requirement was registration by the company and the right of inspection was restricted.

[63] Bankruptcy Act 1914, s. 38 (1) (*c*). In 1957 the Blagden Committee on Bankruptcy Law Amendment (Cmnd. 221) recommended the repeal of this provision, but no action has yet been taken on their Report.

[64] *Infra*, Chap. 27.

[65] *Gorringe* v. *Irwell Rubber Co.* (1886) 34 Ch.D. 128, C.A. In the case of debentures which require public registration this is fair enough. But it is difficult to see the policy behind the complete exemption. If I lend my car to an individual bookmaker for use in his business I run the risk of losing it if he goes bankrupt. If I lend it to his company which goes into liquidation I can recover it. Why?

Hence, use of this highly beneficial form of security is in practice restricted to companies.[66]   By virtue of it the lender can obtain an effective security on " all the undertakings and assets of the company both present and future " either alone or in conjunction with a fixed charge on its land.[67]   If, in addition, the lender requires some personal security he can insist on the members, or some of them (*e.g.,* the directors) joining as guarantors.   By so doing he can place himself in a far stronger position than if he merely had the personal security of the individual traders.   It therefore happens not infrequently that a business is converted into a company solely in order to enable further capital to be raised by borrowing.   And sometimes, as the *Salomon* case [68] shows, a trader by " selling " his business to a company which he has formed can give himself priority over his future creditors by taking a debenture, secured by a floating charge, for the purchase price.

7. Formalities, publicity and expense

Hitherto the discussion of the practical consequences of incorporation has emphasised its advantages.   But these advantages have to be paid for and we now turn to a consideration of the price demanded.

The most obvious disadvantage is that incorporation is necessarily attended with certain formalities, with a loss of privacy, and with some expense.   A partnership can be established by an agreement on a half-sheet of notepaper signed over a 6d. stamp or even by an entirely informal oral arrangement; it can conduct its affairs without any publicity,[69] and can eventually be dissolved equally cheaply and informally.   An incorporated company, on the other hand, necessarily involves certain formalities and expense at its birth, throughout its active life and on its final dissolution.   In England these are not excessive.   On original formation the promoters merely have to prepare a memorandum and articles of association and to complete and file a few simple printed forms.   Easily adaptable forms of memoranda can be obtained at any law stationers, and Table A [70] of the Companies Act can be adopted as the articles.   Alternatively, a ready-made company can be bought off the shelf from a number of agencies which make a business of forming companies and selling them to all comers.   In addition to modest registration fees payable on formation, on filing the

---

66 Effective floating charges can be created by individuals over farming stock and agricultural assets in favour of banks: Agricultural Credits Act 1928.   These also are excluded from the application of the Bills of Sale Acts and the reputed ownership clause: *ibid*. ss. 5 and 8 (1) (2) (4).

67 The implications of floating charges are discussed more fully in Chap. 19, *infra.*

68 [1897] A.C. 22, H.L., *supra.*

69 Certain simple particulars will have to be registered under the Registration of Business Names Act 1916 (as amended by the Companies Act 1947) if it trades under a name other than that of all its members, or under the Limited Partnerships Act 1907 if it is a limited partnership.

70 Or Table C, D or E if limited by guarantee or unlimited.

annual return and in certain other circumstances, capital duty is payable at 10s. per £100 of nominal capital. The Jenkins Committee felt that the advantages of incorporation could be obtained too cheaply and recommended that initial and annual registration fees should be substantially increased.[71] This has been done by the Companies Act 1967,[72] though more modestly than the Committee suggested. It is still possible to form a private company with a nominal capital of £1,000 for a total cost of under £50.

Until the middle of the last century incorporation was difficult and prohibitively expensive, but we now seem to have gone to the opposite extreme. Nor will the formalities or cost of operating such a company be disproportionately heavy; certain registers will have to be maintained, and the books will have to be audited annually,[73] but in practice this would probably be done even with a partnership. Publicity will have to be given to the company's constitution, to its directorate, to its financial position (if its liability is limited), and to charges on its assets, by filing the prescribed documents in the public registry, and proper meetings will have to be held from time to time. Care will also have to be taken to ensure that all corporate activities are undertaken in the proper name of the company which, if its liability is limited, must end with the word " limited." This, as we have seen, is intended to act as a red flag, warning those dealing with the company of the dangers which they run. Finally there will have to be a winding up [74] on dissolution, but if the company is solvent this can remain a domestic matter subject only to certain public advertisements and, of course, the filing of various documents. On the other hand winding up is considerably more expensive than formation need be; a company, like a marriage, cannot be dissolved as cheaply as it can be created.

In the case of a private company none of these requirements is unduly onerous either as regards work, expense or publicity. The burden is likely to be considerably greater in the case of a public company, for not only will it normally have a far greater share capital but it will also have to make far more information available to the public through the publication and filing of a prospectus or statement in lieu of a prospectus.[75] If, as would be the usual course, the company makes a public issue of its securities the expense will be very heavy indeed, and if, as will in practice be essential, these securities are to be quoted on a recognised stock exchange additional publicity will be necessary in order to comply with the requirements of the stock exchanges. Although

---

[71] Cmnd. 1749, para. 28.

[72] Companies Act 1967, Sched. 3.

[73] And the accounts presented in a prescribed form which, however, merely represents the minimum requirements of approved accountancy practice.

[74] Unless the Registrar can be induced to exercise his power under s. 353 of the Companies Act 1948 to strike the company off the register.

[75] As to which see Chap. 14.

English law places few restraints on company *formation* it is considerably stricter in its regulation of public *flotation*.

As we saw earlier [76] the policy of English law has been to facilitate incorporation provided that it is coupled with full disclosure. The various requirements briefly summarised are principally designed to secure this disclosure and are certainly not an extravagant price to pay for the benefits conferred.

Other differences

In addition to the advantages and disadvantages discussed in this chapter certain major consequences follow from incorporation, each of which requires a chapter to itself. Incorporated companies are subject to technical rules, from which partnerships are free, restricting the range of their activities (the *ultra vires* rule [77]) and securing the raising and maintenance of their share capital.[78] On balance these rules are probably disadvantageous from the viewpoint of the members. Agency principles [79] operate differently in their case, mainly to the members' advantage. Taxation [80] also operates differently—sometimes to the members' advantage and sometimes to their disadvantage. In some cases, too, the law regards it as unjust that the members should reap all the rewards or bear all the burdens naturally resulting from incorporation and accordingly disregards the corporate entity.[81] These are the questions discussed in the succeeding chapters.

[76] Chap. 3.
[77] Chap. 5.
[78] Chap. 6.
[79] Chaps. 7 and 8.
[80] Chap. 9.
[81] Chap. 10.

CHAPTER 5

ULTRA VIRES AND CHANGES OF OBJECTS

A COMPANY which owes its incorporation to statutory authority cannot
effectively do anything beyond the powers expressly or impliedly conferred upon it by its statute or memorandum of association—any
purported activity in excess will be ineffective even if agreed to by all the
members. Similarly, it cannot (or could not until recently) readily alter
its specified objects in order to change from one business to another.
The purpose of these restrictions is twofold. First, to protect investors
in the company so that they may know the objects in which their money
is to be employed; and, secondly, to protect creditors by ensuring that
the company's funds, to which they must look for payment, are not
dissipated in unauthorised activities.[1]

This, briefly, is the *ultra vires* doctrine as applied to companies, and
it is this which forms the subject of the present chapter. It must be
pointed out, however, that the expression *ultra vires* is also used in
practice to describe the situation when the directors of the company have
exceeded the powers delegated to them. This use is to be avoided for
it is apt to cause confusion between two entirely distinct legal principles.
When the company has exceeded its powers it is not bound by its act
because it lacks legal *capacity* to incur responsibility for it. When the
directors exceed their powers the company is not bound because its
agents have exceeded their *authority*. But unless the company's own
powers are exceeded, no question of capacity arises, and the company
may ratify what the directors have done, and may, as we shall see in a
later chapter,[2] be unable to set up the directors' lack of actual authority
when they have acted within their usual or ostensible powers.

History of the rule

The *ultra vires* rule has a long and somewhat tangled history.[3] The
early case of *Sutton's Hospital*[4] has generally been taken to establish
that a chartered corporation has all the powers of a natural person in
so far as an artificial entity is physically capable of exercising them; if it
misuses its powers by exceeding the objects in the charter, it may be that
proceedings in the nature of *quo warranto* could be taken to restrain it or

---

[1] *Per* Cairns L.C. in *Ashbury Carriage Co.* v. *Riche* (1875) L.R. 7 H.L. 653 at p. 667.
[2] Chap. 8.
[3] See especially Horrwitz in (1946) 62 L.Q.R. 66, Hornsey in (1949) 61 Jur.Rev. 263,
Holt in (1950) 66 L.Q.R. 493, and H. A. Street, *Ultra Vires* (London, 1930).
[4] (1612) 10 Co.Rep. 1a, 23a.

83

in the nature of *scire facias* to forfeit the charter, but in the meantime its actions will be fully effective.[5]

Similarly there was no question of a partnership acting *ultra vires* in the strict sense. The acts of one partner might not bind his fellow partners if the acts were outside his actual or apparent authority but they could always be ratified by all the partners.[6] Similarly no change could be made in the partnership business without the consent of all the partners,[7] but with their unanimous consent there was not, and is not, anything to stop a firm of grocers from changing to bookmakers or vice versa. The common type of joint stock company prior to 1844 was merely an enlarged partnership, and to it the *ultra vires* doctrine could have no application; the question was not whether the company had acted outside its powers (for these were unlimited) but simply whether the directors of the company had exceeded their authority.[8]

Even when joint stock companies were allowed, by the Act of 1844, to become incorporated on registration there was still really no scope for *ultra vires*. The existing form of constitution—the deed of settlement —remained unchanged and the liability of the members remained unlimited. As already stated, the object of the rule as subsequently enunciated was to protect (a) investors and (b) creditors. The former were obviously fully protected by the partnership rule requiring fundamental changes to be agreed to by all, and the latter hardly required protection so long as the liability of the members was maintained. Hence the sole question still remained whether the directors had exceeded their authority and, if so, whether their actions had been ratified by all the members, and it was on this basis that the matter continued to be treated in the cases.[9]

It is in connection with the statutory companies arising out of the railway boom that we should expect to find the germ of the modern *ultra vires* doctrine. These companies were limited, so that the need

---

5 See especially *per* Blackburn J. in *Riche* v. *Ashbury Carriage Co.* (1874) L.R. 9 Ex. 224 at pp. 263–264; Bowen L.J. in *Baroness Wenlock* v. *River Dee Co.* (1883) 36 Ch.D. 675n., C.A., at p. 685n.; *British South Africa Co.* v. *De Beers* [1910] 1 Ch. 354, C.A.; *Bonanza Creek Gold Mining Co.* v. *R.* [1916] 1 A.C. 566, P.C.; and *Jenkin* v. *Pharmaceutical Society* [1921] 1 Ch. 392.

6 See now Partnership Act 1890, s. 5 *et seq.*

7 See now Partnership Act 1890, s. 24 (8).

8 It is, nevertheless, not uncommon to apply the term *ultra vires* to the situation in which agents of an unincorporated body have acted outside their authority so that neither the members nor the funds of the association are bound: see, *e.g.*, *Abbott* v. *Sullivan* [1952] 1 K.B. 189, C.A.

9 See especially the judgments of the H.L. in the three cases arising out of the liquidation of the Agriculturist Cattle Assurance Co.: *Spackman* v. *Evans* (1868) L.R. 3 H.L. 171; *Evans* v. *Smallcombe*, *ibid.* 249; *Houldsworth* v. *Evans*, *ibid.* 263. Hornsey (*loc. cit.*) points to s. 7 of the 1844 Act providing for the registration of supplementary deeds of settlement and argues that it was the intention of the legislature that changes of objects should be made in this way and that unless so made the change would be *ultra vires* the company even although ratified by all the members. But the above cases, and others like them, were argued on the basis that the directors, and not the company as a whole, had exceeded their powers and, for reasons stated in the text, the question could only arise in this way so long as companies remained unlimited.

for the rule was apparent. Moreover, the argument that the Crown could not effectively limit the powers of chartered corporations had no application to those directly incorporated by statute, for the sovereign Parliament quite clearly could limit the potential activities of its creatures in any way it liked. If, therefore, the directors sought to enter into transactions beyond the powers of the company, not only could they be restrained on application by a shareholder, but a contract for an unauthorised purpose could be regarded as *ultra vires* and unenforceable against the company.[10] As early as 1855 Lord Cranworth could declare that: " It must therefore be now considered as a well-settled doctrine that a company incorporated by Act of Parliament for a special purpose cannot devote any part of its funds to objects unauthorised by the terms of its incorporation, however desirable such an application may appear to be." [11] It appears inevitably to follow that not even the unanimous consent of the members could render *intra vires* what a statute had forbidden, but it was not until later that the courts were called upon to draw this logical conclusion, and, indeed, the general opinion seems to have been to the contrary.[12] Moreover, the correct approach to the construction of the statutes was far from clear [13]; in opposition to the later rule—that what was not authorised expressly or by necessary implication must be taken to have been forbidden—there was powerful support for the view that the legislature must be deemed to have conferred all the powers of a natural person unless it had taken them away expressly or by necessary implication.[14]

In the meantime, the position of the normal joint stock company had changed radically when limited liability was introduced generally in 1855; then, for the first time, was there a widespread need for the application of a strict rule in the interests of creditors. Moreover, the elaboration of such a rule was facilitated by the Act of 1856 which superseded the deed of settlement and replaced it by two documents, the memorandum and articles. In the former the objects had to be stated and the Act made no provision for its alteration; the latter was expressly alterable by special resolution. If, at this time, the courts had been called upon to decide the question whether the unanimous consent of all the shareholders could have altered the memorandum, one can only surmise what the answer would have been.[15] In fact,

---

10 See the cases cited in the judgment of Cranworth L.C. in *Eastern Counties Ry.* v. *Hawkes* (1855) 5 H.L.C. 331 at p. 346 *et seq.*
11 *Ibid.* at p. 348.
12 See, for example, the dicta of Wigram V.-C. in *Foss* v. *Harbottle* (1843) 2 Hare at pp. 493 and 504, which assume that effective ratification was possible if all members agreed, and note *Phosphate of Lime Co.* v. *Green* (1871) L.R. 7 C.P. 43.
13 See, for example, the difference of judicial view in *Taylor* v. *Chichester & Midhurst Ry.* (1867) L.R. 2 Ex. 356, Ex.Ch.; (1870) L.R. 4 H.L. 628.
14 This view was maintained by many until 1874: see *per* Blackburn J. in the *Ashbury Carriage Co.* case in the Ex.Ch. (1874) L.R. 9 Ex. at p. 264.
15 Dr. Horrwitz (*loc. cit.*) surmises that the alteration would have been effective; Mr. Hornsey (*loc. cit.*) that it would not.

however, it did not arise clearly until after the passing of the Companies Act 1862, which expressly provided that, with but two exceptions,[16] " no alteration shall be made by any company in the conditions contained in its memorandum of association." [17]

In *Ashbury Carriage Co.* v. *Riche* [18] a company had been formed under the 1862 Act with the object of carrying on business as " mechanical engineers and general contractors." [19]   The directors entered into an agreement for financing the construction of a railway in Belgium.   There was some evidence that this agreement had been ratified by all the members, but later it was repudiated by the company.

It is significant of the general state of legal opinion at this time, that in the Court of Exchequer it was not even argued that ratification, if proved, would not be effective.   The argument proceeded solely on the question whether the members with full knowledge had or had not agreed.   Only on appeal to the Exchequer Chamber was the point taken that even the unanimous agreement of all the shareholders could not effectively ratify what was beyond the company's powers as expressed in the memorandum, and on this point a strong court was equally divided.[20]   Finally, the House of Lords unanimously held that ratification was legally impossible if the contract was beyond the scope of the memorandum.   For the first time the courts clearly distinguished between acts merely *ultra vires* the directors, because beyond the powers delegated to them by the articles, and acts *ultra vires* the company itself because beyond its powers in the memorandum.   And they emphasised the dual purpose of the rule, *i.e.*, protection of both investors and creditors.[21]   Anomalously, however, creditors appear normally to have no *locus standi* to sue to restrain a company from entering into an *ultra vires* transaction unless, perhaps, they have a charge on the company's undertaking.[22]

In the *Ashbury* case the courts had been called upon to decide whether they should equate registered companies with partnerships and chartered corporations, or whether they should apply to them the rule which they were slowly evolving in connection with statutory corporations.   They chose the latter solution and applied a rule stricter than any yet adopted even in the case of statutory bodies.   But shortly after-

---

[16] Reorganisation of share capital and, with consent of the Board of Trade, alteration of name.

[17] s. 12.

[18] (1875) L.R. 7 H.L. 653.

[19] There were other specified objects but it was conceded that this was the only relevant one.

[20] The decisions of the lower courts are reported in (1874) L.R. 9 Ex. 224.

[21] See especially *per* Cairns L.C. (1875) L.R. 7 H.L. at pp. 667–668.

[22] *Mills* v. *N. Ry. of Buenos Ayres* (1870) 5 Ch.App. 621 ; *Lawrence* v. *West Somerset Mineral Ry.* [1918] 2 Ch. 250.   But *cf. Hutton* v. *W. Cork Ry.* (1883) 23 Ch.D. 654, where debentureholders with a charge and some voting rights sued.

wards the strict rule was extended to such bodies,[23] leaving chartered corporations as an anomalous exception.[24] It was emphasised, however, that the rule is to be applied reasonably, so that whatever is fairly incidental to the objects expressly authorised by the memorandum or statute will, unless expressly prohibited, be *intra vires*.[25] But, subject to that limitation, whatever is not expressly or impliedly authorised must be taken to be forbidden and cannot be undertaken even by the unanimous consent of all the members. This applies not only to limitations comprised in the objects clause but to all provisions in the memorandum or statute.

Sometimes, indeed, the courts have given a still wider meaning to *ultra vires* by applying it to any activity which the company is prevented by law from carrying out. For example, as we shall see in the next chapter, the *ultra vires* doctrine has been invoked to explain the prohibition of a reduction of capital, so that in *Trevor* v. *Whitworth*[26] it was said to be *ultra vires* for a company to purchase its own shares whether or not it was empowered to do so by its memorandum. This use of the expression is confusing. It is better to restrict the expression *ultra vires* to those things which a company is incapable of doing because they are not authorised by its memorandum; there is no need to invoke it in connection with activities which are prohibited even though authorised in the memorandum.

Evasion of the ultra vires rule

It can hardly be doubted that the *ultra vires* rule was salutary in its intentions and, perhaps, to some extent in its operation. At the time it prevented trafficking in company registrations, it ensured that an investor in a gold mining company did not find himself holding shares in a fried-fish shop, and it gave those who allowed credit to a limited company some assurance that its assets would not be dissipated in unauthorised enterprises. Unhappily it was capable of causing hardships as great as those which it prevented; the individual creditor who had lent money to a company on an *ultra vires* borrowing[27] was not likely to be consoled by the thought that he had suffered for the benefit of his fellow creditors. Moreover, although it may have been valuable

---

[23] *Att.-Gen.* v. *Great Eastern Ry.* (1880) 5 App.Cas. 473, H.L.; *Baroness Wenlock* v. *River Dee Co.* (1885) 10 App.Cas. 354, H.L. This apparently extends even to unlimited companies despite the fact that it is then less needed to protect creditors: *Re Dorking Villa Building Co.* (1939) 83 S.J. 134.

[24] See *supra*, pp. 83, 84. But a chartered corporation may be restrained by injunction at the suit of a member from exceeding its expressed objects: *Jenkin* v. *Pharmaceutical Society* [1921] 1 Ch. 392; *Pharmaceutical Society* v. *Dickson* [1968] 3 W.L.R. 286, H.L.

[25] *Att.-Gen.* v. *Great Eastern Ry.*, *supra*. For recent illustrations, see *Charles Roberts & Co. Ltd.* v. *British Rlys. Board* [1965] 1 W.L.R. 396; and *Bell Houses Ltd.* v. *City Wall Properties Ltd.* [1966] 2 Q.B. 656, C.A.

[26] (1887) 12 App.Cas. 409, H.L.; *infra*, p. 111.

[27] A strong example is *Baroness Wenlock* v. *River Dee Co.*, *supra*.

to the members in restraining the activities of their directors, it was merely a nuisance in so far as it prevented the company from changing its activities in a direction upon which all were agreed. Hence business men and their legal advisers speedily found means of minimising its effects.

The intention of the legislature was that the company's objects should be set out succinctly in only one or two paragraphs; this is made clear by the objects clause in the model form of memorandum in Table B which, even in the 1948 Act, consists merely of one brief paragraph. The idea was that the promoters should simply specify in general terms the business which it was proposed to carry on; the powers (to borrow and the like) which it required as incidental to that business were not intended to be specified as these would be implied by law. And in fact, since *Att.-Gen.* v. *Great Eastern Railway*,[28] the courts have interpreted the rule in a liberal spirit and agreed that everything reasonably incidental to the specified objects will be *intra vires*. As a result there is now a considerable body of case law deciding what powers will be implied in the case of particular types of enterprise and what activities can be regarded as reasonably incidental to others.[29] But business men were reluctant to leave matters to implication; they preferred to set out in the memorandum the ancillary powers which they thought they would need. Moreover, they were not content to specify only the business which the company was initially intended to follow, but preferred also to name all the other businesses which they might conceivably want it to turn to in the future. Hence, memoranda, far from sharing the simplicity of Table B, have come to contain statements of some twenty or thirty objects and ancillary powers, covering every conceivable business and all the incidental powers which might be needed to accomplish them. This, at least, makes it less hazardous to enter into transactions with a company, for the likelihood of their being *ultra vires* is remote. On the other hand it affords little assurance of the preservation of the company's assets and less control over the activities of directors; surprising as it may seem, the modern gold mining company may quite probably have power under its memorandum to operate fried-fish shops.[30]

The high point in this development has recently been blessed by the Court of Appeal in *Bell Houses Ltd.* v. *City Wall Properties Ltd.*[31]

---

[28] *Supra.*

[29] For summaries of these decisions, see Palmer's *Company Precedents*, 17th ed., Pt. 1, p. 270 *et seq.*

[30] And an astonishing number of old-established companies are still expressly authorised to carry on the business of tallow chandlers.

[31] [1966] 2 Q.B. 656, C.A. For differing comments on the case, see Polack in [1966] Camb.L.J. 174; Wedderburn in (1966) 29 M.L.R. 673, and Baker in (1966) 82 L.Q.R. 463. For an earlier decision of the H.C. of Australia to much the same effect, see *Stephenson & Son Ltd.* v. *Gillanders, Arbuthnot & Co.* (1931) 45 C.L.R. 476.

There the objects clause included power " to carry on any other trade or business whatsoever which can, *in the opinion of the board of directors*,[32] be advantageously carried on by the company in connection with or as ancillary to any of the above businesses or the general business of the company. . . ." Although this comes close to saying that the company could carry on any business it chose, a formula which had been thought impermissible on the authority of *Re Crown Bank*,[33] the court held that it was effective to empower the company to undertake any business which the directors bona fide thought could be advantageously carried on as an adjunct to its other businesses. If objects clauses expressed in this subjective form became standard practice companies will be able to carry on any businesses that the directors choose.

Attempted curbs on evasion

The courts have striven in two ways to curb evasion. First, they have applied the *ejusdem generis* rule to the construction of objects clauses, saying that when the main objects, specified in the first few paragraphs, were followed by wide powers expressed in general words, the latter should be construed as covering their exercise only for the purposes of the main objects.[34] This, however, has been circumvented by the practice of inserting an express declaration in the objects clause to the effect that each of the specified objects or powers should be deemed to be independent and in no way ancillary or subordinate one to another. In *Cotman* v. *Brougham*,[35] although this declaration and the habit of setting out a profusion of objects were severely criticised, the device was held to be effective, so that it was not *ultra vires* for a rubber company to underwrite shares in an oil company in exercise of a general power to underwrite. Happily some limitation has recently been put on this device since the court has refused to accept that the borrowing or raising of money could possibly be an independent object but had to be construed as a power to borrow only for the purposes of an *intra vires* business.[36]

---

[32] Italics supplied.
[33] (1890) 44 Ch.D. 634. This was distinguished on the ground that it concerned a winding-up petition based on the destruction of the substratum: see *infra*. But according to Harman L.J. you " still cannot have an object to do every mortal thing you want ": [1969] 2 W.L.R. at 794H.
[34] *Re Haven Gold Mining Co.* (1882) 20 Ch.D. 151, C.A.; *Re German Date Coffee Co.*, *ibid.* 169, C.A.; *Re Crown Bank* (1890) 44 Ch.D. 634; *Re Amalgamated Syndicate* [1897] 2 Ch. 600; *Stephens* v. *Mysore Reefs* [1902] 1 Ch. 745 (the actual decision in the last case seems inconsistent with *Cotman* v. *Brougham, infra*; see *Anglo-Overseas Agencies Ltd.* v. *Green* [1961] 1 Q.B. 1.
[35] [1918] A.C. 514, H.L. If the court is asked to confirm a change of objects (see below), it may make it a condition that the declaration is deleted: *Re Cole Ltd.* [1945] 1 All E.R. 521n.
[36] *Introductions Ltd.* v. *National Provincial Bank* [1969] 2 W.L.R. 791, C.A. But *cf. Christchurch City Corpn.* v. *Flamingo Coffee Lounge* [1959] N.Z.L.R. 986 (N.Z. Sup.Ct.) where it was held *intra vires* for a company formed as drapers to operate an airport restaurant under its power to " obtain privileges, concessions or contracts "!

Secondly, it was held in the leading case of *Re German Date Coffee Co.*[37] that shareholders might petition for the winding up of a company when its whole substratum had disappeared, and that the court might order a liquidation under its power to do so whenever it is just and equitable.[38] This accordingly affords some measure of protection to investors. But it too is subject to limitations. The fact that the whole substratum has gone will not make the future activities of the company *ultra vires* providing that the activities are within the specified objects; if the members choose not to petition, that is their own affair.[39] There seems to be no remedy for a third party who has given credit to a gold mining company and sees it wasting its assets on fried-fish shops, provided that these are covered by a paragraph in its memorandum. Further, the remedy is only available, even to the members, if *all* the main objects have failed so that the *whole* substratum has been destroyed. If the company has been formed with the object of acquiring and working a certain patent and it fails to acquire it, it may be wound up.[40] If, however, it has been formed with the dual object of acquiring a particular business as a going concern *and* of carrying on business as engineers, the fact that it disposes of the particular business will not enable it to be wound up if it proposes to continue as engineers generally.[41]

The result of the foregoing practices has been largely to frustrate the whole object of the doctrine. It has ceased to be a protection to anyone and has become merely a trap for the unwary third party and a nuisance to the company itself. It is less of a nuisance than it was since the company can now change its objects quite easily.[42] But this does not make it less of a trap for the third party if the company enters into a transaction beyond its objects without first altering them.[43] The hardship that may be caused to completely innocent people is well illustrated by *Re Jon Beauforte (London) Ltd.*[44] There a company formed to make ladies' dresses decided to change to the manufacture of veneered panels—an activity which could not be brought within its objects clause however liberally construed. Unhappily no one seems to have realised this and the necessary steps to alter its objects were never taken. The company entered into contracts for the construction

---

[37] (1882) 20 Ch.D. 169, C.A.
[38] Now Companies Act 1948, s. 222 (*f*). This power applies to any statutory, chartered, or other unregistered company by virtue of s. 398 *et seq.* (see especially s. 399 (5) (*c*)). The exception in the case of railway companies (s. 398 (*a*)) is no longer of practical importance in view of the nationalisation of the railways.
[39] *Cotman* v. *Brougham* [1918] A.C. 514, H.L.
[40] *Re German Date Coffee Co., supra.*
[41] *Re Kitson & Co.* [1946] 1 All E.R. 435, C.A.; *Re Taldua Rubber Co.* [1946] 2 All E.R. 763; *Re Eastern Telegraph Co.* [1947] 2 All E.R. 104.
[42] See pp. 99–101, *infra.*
[43] It seems clear that a subsequent alteration does not validate what was previously *ultra vires.* The transaction will have to be entered into afresh and the third party cannot compel the company to do this.
[44] [1953] Ch. 131. For a more recent example, see *Introductions Ltd.* v. *National Provincial Bank, supra.*

of a factory, for the purchase of veneers, and for the purchase of coke, but failed to make a success of its new enterprise and went into liquidation. It was held that none of the three contractors [45] could prove in the liquidation. Even the supplier of coke, who argued cogently that this might equally well have been needed for an *intra vires* activity, failed because the fuel had been ordered on note-paper describing the company as " veneered panel manufacturers."

Another unhappy result has been virtually to destroy the intended distinction between objects, in the sense of authorised businesses, and incidental powers—to borrow, acquire property, and the like—needed to carry on these businesses. This, coupled with the proliferation of true objects, enables the directors to diversify or change the company's activities to fields never contemplated by the members and without any prior consultation with them.[46]

A final cause of uncertainty is that it is sometimes suggested that there is an over-riding principle that, whatever the objects clause may provide, an activity not bona fide designed to enhance the financial prosperity of the company will necessarily be *ultra vires* since " charity cannot sit at the boardroom table " and " there are to be no cakes and ale except for the benefit of the company." [47] This suggestion, however, is believed to be incorrect.[48] If, for example, it is expressly provided that one of the objects of the company is to give away its property,[49] gifts will not be *ultra vires*. They may, it is true, be liable to attack on other grounds. If the gifts were to the members themselves they might be an unlawful return of capital.[50] Whomsoever the gifts were to, the action of the directors who authorised them might be attacked on the ground that they had not exercised their powers bona fide for the benefit of the company as a whole.[51] Even if the gifts were authorised by the members in general meeting they might be liable to attack as a fraud on the minority.[52] Doubtless too, the courts will strive to construe an objects clause so as to exclude obviously improvident activities and will not regard these as within the implied powers of a commercial company

---

45 These three were selected, for the purpose of a test action, as typical of a great many others. In fact the company was left with only one *intra vires* creditor.

46 Since the Companies Act 1967 they should receive subsequent notice, since the annual directors' report is required to state " the principal activities of the company and of its subsidiaries in the course of that year and any significant change in those activities in that year ": s. 16.

47 *Per* Bowen L.J. in *Hutton* v. *W. Cork Ry.* (1883) 23 Ch.D. 654, C.A., at p. 673.

48 The suggestion, in *Re Lee Behrens & Co.* [1932] 2 Ch. 46 at 51, that, in considering whether the exercise of an express power is *ultra vires*, it is relevant to ask whether it is " for the benefit and to promote the prosperity of the company " has been expressly dissented from by Pennycuick J. in *Charterbridge Corpn. Ltd.* v. *Lloyds Bank*, November 5, 1968 (as yet unreported).

49 As might well be the case with a guarantee company formed to administer a charity.

50 See Chap. 6. But as pointed out, *supra*, p. 87, such returns of capital are frequently described as " *ultra vires*," see, for example, *Ridge Securities Ltd.* v. *I.R.C.* [1964] 1 W.L.R. 479 at p. 495.

51 See Chap. 23, and especially the discussion *post*, p. 521 of *Re Roith* [1967] 1 W.L.R. 432.

52 See Chap. 24.

or as "conducive to the attainment" of its commercial objects. But if clearly authorised by the objects clause they will not be *ultra vires*.

Indeed, while the company remains a going concern, charitable, and indeed political, donations may be within the implied powers even of commercial companies since they may well be good for business.[53] This seems to be accepted by the Companies Act 1967, which requires disclosure of such donations in the directors' report.[54] Similarly, while the company remains a going concern, voluntary pensions or redundancy payments in excess of those legally due are normally *intra vires*.[53] So may be advances by a holding company to its subsidiaries, as the tax code impliedly recognises,[55] or payments or guarantees by the holding company of the subsidiaries' debts, since default may harm the commercial reputation of the parent company. But, as the case of *Parke* v. *Daily News*[56] dramatically revealed, if the company is about to go out of business all such gratuities will be *ultra vires*, unless expressly authorised by the objects clause, and, even if expressly authorised,[57] are liable to be attacked as not a bona fide exercise of the powers of the directors or the majority, since they cannot benefit the company.

Rights of the other party under ultra vires transactions

The next question for consideration is what rights and remedies the other party has on an *ultra vires* transaction. The first point to notice is that, by a somewhat benevolent construction, the question whether a transaction is *ultra vires* at all may depend on the knowledge, actual or imputed, of the other party. If, for example, the company has powers of borrowing, although this will be construed as

---

[53] *Hutton* v. *W. Cork Ry., supra*; *Evans* v. *Brunner Mond & Co.* [1921] 1 Ch. 359; *Re Lee Behrens & Co.* [1932] 2 Ch. 46; *Parke* v. *Daily News* [1962] Ch. 927. In theory this still seems to be the somewhat cynical guise in which charity is allowed to sit at the board-room table and to a surprising extent it is still observed in practice. A study in 1957 by the Economist Intelligence Unit (*Business and the Community*) found that only 6 per cent. of charitable gifts by companies were " purely philanthropic." See, now, Shenfield, *Company Giving* (P.E.P. 1969). In the U.S.A., even in the absence of legislative authority, it has been said that " modern conditions require that corporations acknowledge and discharge social as well as private responsibilities as members of the communities within which they operate. Within this broad concept there is no difficulty in sustaining, as incidental to their proper object and in aid of the public welfare, the power of corporations to contribute corporate funds within reasonable limits in support of academic institutions ": *Smith* v. *Barlow* (1953) 98 A. 2d 581 at 586 (N.J.Sup.Ct.).

[54] s. 19. Disclosure is required if the total amount given exceeds £50 and in the case of political contributions the identity of the recipient has to be stated. Despite the attempt to define " political purposes " in subs. (3), there is some disagreement in commercial circles on whether certain bodies are political or not; the promotion of nationalisation is clearly recognised as political, the preservation of private enterprise, less clearly.

[55] See Finance Act 1967, s. 20.

[56] *Supra.* For the facts, see p. 522, *infra.*

[57] In *Parke* v. *Daily News* it was not so authorised, *quaere* if the result would have been different if it had been: see Wedderburn in [1962] Camb.L.J. 141. The final conclusion was that the ex-employees received the amount distributable to those members who assented to the gifts: *Re Daily News Ltd., The Times*, Dec. 18, 1962.

limited to borrowing for the purpose of an authorised business,[58] a loan will not be regarded as *ultra vires* unless the lender has notice that it is for the purposes of a business which in fact is unauthorised.[59] Similarly, it seems clear that the coal merchant in *Re Jon Beauforte Ltd.*[60] would have been able to recover had he not known that the coke was required in connection with veneer manufacturing, which he was deemed to know was *ultra vires*.

This loophole will, however, rarely be available, for everyone is deemed to have notice of the contents of the company's public documents,[61] which will necessarily include its objects clause. If, therefore, the transaction is unequivocally associated with a business outside these objects,[62] or if the company has no power to borrow or has only power to borrow up to a certain sum,[63] the activity will be *ultra vires* whether the other party realises it or not. And when the transaction is *ultra vires*, the other party, speaking generally, has no rights at all; the transaction, being completely void, cannot confer rights on the third party nor duties on the company. Even recovery of judgment on the *ultra vires* contract will not create an enforceable obligation,[64] unless the court specifically adjudicated on the *ultra vires* issue or unless there was a bona fide compromise of it.[65]

Despite the fact that in law an *ultra vires* transaction is void, purported transfers of property will frequently be made in the belief that it is effective. Nevertheless the *ultra vires* transaction cannot vest rights in the transferee or divest the transferor.[66] Hence the latter will be able to recover his property so long as he can identify it. This rule may even apply to money lent to the company on an *ultra vires* borrowing so long as the money can be traced, either in law or in equity, in accordance with the somewhat complicated rules laid down in *Sinclair* v. *Brougham*[67]

---

58 See *Introductions Ltd.* v. *National Provincial Bank, supra*.

59 *Ibid.*; and see *Re David Payne & Co.* [1904] 2 Ch. 608, C.A.

60 *Supra*. This slightly anomalous rule can perhaps be justified on the analogy of the rule that the contractual liability of a lunatic depends on the other party's knowledge of his insanity.

61 See Chap. 8, *infra*.

62 As in *Ashbury Carriage Co.* v. *Riche, supra*.

63 As in *Baroness Wenlock* v. *River Dee Co., supra*.

64 *Re Jon Beauforte (London) Ltd., supra*, in which two of the three applicants had in fact signed judgment, one by consent and the other in default of appearance, prior to the liquidation.

65 *Great N.W. Central Ry.* v. *Charlebois* [1899] A.C. 114, P.C.

66 This still seems to be the English theory. But it is questionable whether it would be applied where the contract had been fully executed and the property transferred absolutely. The American doctrine is that the transaction cannot then be reopened or the property recovered by either party. Some support for this can be gleaned from *Ayers* v. *S. Australian Banking Co.* (1871) L.R. 3 P.C. 548 (which, however, concerned a *chartered* company) and *National Telephone Co.* v. *St. Peter Port* [1900] A.C. 317, P.C. The cases considered below concern the continuing relationship of lender and borrower and ought perhaps to be explained as examples of intervention based on unjust enrichment.

67 [1914] A.C. 398, H.L.

and *Re Diplock*.[68]   It appears from these cases that if the money
borrowed is paid by the company into a separate account (or otherwise
earmarked), or is used to purchase a particular asset, it can be followed
and claimed by the lender.   Even if this is impossible, because the money
has been mixed with other money and therefore ceased to be physically
traceable, the lender, or indeed a whole class of lenders,[69] is entitled
in equity to a charge on the mixed fund *pari passu* with the other
claimants thereto according to their respective amounts.   This is because
the directors or other agents, who have received the money on the *ultra
vires* borrowing, stand in a fiduciary position towards the lenders,[69a] with
the result that the money is treated as if it were trust money.   Unless,
therefore, it has come into the hands of a bona fide purchaser for value
the " trust " can be enforced by recovery of the money if identifiable,
and, if not, by a charging order on the mixed fund ranking *pari passu*
with the claims of the other contributors to the fund.

   This right to trace in equity can be enforced against any volunteer,
but not against one who has given value unless he has notice that he is
receiving trust property.   Hence, in general, money obtained on an
ultra vires borrowing cannot be followed once it has been spent.   Even
in this case, however, the lenders may not be entirely devoid of remedy,
for if their money has been used to discharge *intra vires* debts, they are
entitled to rank as creditors to the extent to which the money has been
so applied.[70]   For this purpose it matters not whether the creditors know
that the borrowings from them were *ultra vires*; since the legitimate
liabilities of the company are not in fact increased, equity treats the
borrowings as valid to the extent of their legal application.[71]   Moreover,
they are entitled to hold any securities given to themselves,[72] but they
have no right to the securities held by the creditors paid with their
money.[73]

   In addition to his right to trace his property the third party may have
a personal claim against the directors or other agents with whom he has
dealt.   *Sinclair* v. *Brougham* and *Re Diplock* are based on the principle
that these agents become quasi-trustees for him, from which it seems
to follow that he has an equitable claim against them for restitution.
Whether he can claim damages must depend on normal rules of agency.

---

[68] [1948] Ch. 465, C.A.; affd. H.L., *sub nom. Min. of Health* v. *Simpson* [1951] A.C.
251.   The H.L. judgments deal only with the right of recovery *in personam*.   See
Goff & Jones, *Law of Restitution*, p. 321 *et seq.*
[69] As in *Sinclair* v. *Brougham* (the depositors in the ill-fated Birkbeck Bank).
[69a] But why?   Normally directors owe duties only to the company, not even to the
members let alone the creditors.
[70] *Ibid.* and see *Re Airedale Co-operative Worsted Society* [1933] 1 Ch. 639 and cases
there quoted.
[71] *Reversion Fund Ltd.* v. *Maison Cosway Ltd.* [1913] 1 K.B. 364, C.A.
[72] *Cunliffe Brooks & Co.* v. *Blackburn Building Society* (1883) 22 Ch.D. 61, C.A.
[73] *Re Wrexham, Mold and Connah's Quay Ry.* [1899] 1 Ch. 440, C.A.   If these
decisions are correct, the rule does not seem to be properly based on subrogation,
as is generally stated, but on a validation of the original debts: see *per* Lord Parker
in [1914] A.C. at p. 441, where the question is left open.

If the *ultra vires* transaction is a tort [74] he obviously can sue, for the agents will be the actual tortfeasors. But if it is a contract his position is less clear unless the agents have expressly contracted personally.[75] Agents who purport to contract on behalf of a company not yet formed may be personally liable,[76] but it is doubtful if the same applies when the principal is in existence but lacks capacity.[77] Another possibility is to claim in deceit, if the authority is wilfully misstated, or on a breach of implied warranty of authority,[78] but the difficulty here is that the third party may be met with a plea that he has notice of the memorandum and is therefore deemed to know of the lack of authority. The authorities appear to be based on a distinction, which is often difficult to draw, between express or implied misrepresentations of *fact*, when the directors will be liable,[79] and misrepresentations of *law*, when they will not.[80] Street probably puts the matter best when he says [81] :

> " The true position perhaps is that an outsider, being taken to know the contents of statutes and other public documents, cannot complain of any statement as to powers, the correctness of which he can estimate by reference thereto. But if he is misled by statements affecting the operation of such documents,[82] so that knowledge of the law will not help him, then the maker of such statements will be liable on a warranty of authority."

And it is submitted that if the directors wilfully misrepresent the powers of themselves or the company they will be liable in deceit if the outsider is in fact misled, and that they will not be allowed to take refuge in the argument that he ought to have read the documents and not believed the misrepresentations.[83]

Rights of the company under ultra vires transactions

On the same principles of legal and equitable tracing as those outlined above, the company may be able to recover from the other party

---

[74] It is doubtful whether the *ultra vires* doctrine has any application to torts : see *infra*.
[75] The fact that the contract is unenforceable against the company because *ultra vires* will not then prevent action against the directors.
[76] *Kelner* v. *Baxter* (1866) L.R. 2 C.P. 174, but· *cf. Newborne* v. *Sensolid (G.B.) Ltd.* [1954] 1 Q.B. 45, C.A. : see *infra*, p. 281.
[77] The point never seems to have been clearly taken ; the arguments in all the cases turned on whether the directors were liable for breach of express or implied warranty.
[78] *Chapleo* v. *Brunswick Building Society* (1881) 6 Q.B.D. 696, C.A. In respect of directors' liability it appears to make no difference whether the contract is *ultra vires* the company (as beyond its powers in the memorandum) or merely *ultra vires* the directors (as beyond their powers in the articles).
[79] *Cherry* v. *Colonial Bank of Australasia* (1869) L.R. 3 P.C. 24 ; *Weeks* v. *Propert* (1873) L.R. 8 C.P. 427 ; *West London Commercial Bank* v. *Kitson* (1883) 12 Q.B.D. 157 ; *Firbanks Exors.* v. *Humphreys* (1886) 18 Q.B.D. 54, C.A.
[80] *Rashdall* v. *Ford* (1866) L.R. 2 Eq. 750 ; *Eaglesfield* v. *Londonderry* (1876) 4 Ch.D. 693, C.A. ; affd. 38 L.T. 303, H.L.
[81] *Op. cit.* 315.
[82] *e.g.*, an express or implied statement that the limits of borrowing have not been exceeded, as in *Chapleo* v. *Brunswick Building Society*, *supra*.
[83] *Cf. Aaron's Reefs* v. *Twiss* [1896] A.C. 273, H.L.(Ir.).

any of its property which is still in his hands.[84] In addition to this right
to follow the property, there is some authority [85] for the view that the
disposition will be a breach of trust on the part of the officers of the
company who acted in the transaction so that the recipient may be
personally liable as a constructive trustee to make restoration to the
company. Moreover, those officers are liable to the company for their
breach of duty in entering into the *ultra vires* transaction on its behalf.
They must therefore make restitution to it [86] and have the usual rights
of contribution *inter se*.[87] However, officers of registered companies
may be relieved by the court under section 448 of the Companies Act
1948 if they have acted reasonably and ought fairly to be excused.[88]

It was formerly not clear whether, if the company sued on a contract,
the other party could plead as a defence that the contract was *ultra
vires* the company.[89] However, in *Bell Houses Ltd.* v. *City Wall
Properties Ltd.*, Mocatta J., at first instance, held that he could.[90]
While the Court of Appeal [91] did not find it necessary to express an
opinion on this " interesting, important and difficult question," [92] the
weight of modern authority supports the view of Mocatta J.[93] at any rate
while the contract remains executory.[94]

Tort and crime

The extent (if any) to which the *ultra vires* rule applies to torts and
crimes is one of the most popular topics of academic discussion,[95] but,

---

[84] *Cunliffe Brooks & Co.* v. *Blackburn Bldg. Society* (1883) 22 Ch.D. 61, C.A.;
(1884) 9 App.Cas. 857, H.L.

[85] See, for example, *Russell* v. *Wakefield Waterworks Co.* (1875) L.R. 20 Eq. 474 at
479; *G.E.R.* v. *Turner* (1872) L.R. 8 Ch. 149; *Hardy* v. *Metropolitan Land Co.*
(1872) 7 Ch.App. 427.

[86] *Cullerne* v. *London & Suburban Bldg. Society* (1890) 25 Q.B.D. 485.

[87] *Ashurst* v. *Mason* (1875) L.R. 20 Eq. 225; *cf. Walsh* v. *Bardsley* (1931) 47 T.L.R. 564.

[88] *Re Claridge's Patent Asphalte Co.* [1921] 1 Ch. 543. But they will not, of course,
be entitled to claim indemnification by the company against any personal liability
that they may have incurred to the third party on the *ultra vires* transaction.

[89] See Street, *Ultra Vires*, p. 30, and Furmston (1961) 24 M.L.R. 715.

[90] [1966] 1 Q.B. 207.   [91] [1966] 2 Q.B. 656, C.A.; see *supra*.

[92] *Per* Salmon L.J. at pp. 693–694—who obviously had doubts. As we have seen, *supra*,
p. 89, the C.A. held that the transaction was not *ultra vires*.

[93] See Furmston, *loc. cit.* In *Anglo Overseas Agencies Ltd.* v. *Green* [1961] 1 Q.B. 1,
it was assumed that the defendant could rely on *ultra vires*. And *cf. Smith* v.
London Transport Executive [1951] A.C. 555, where the H.L. assumed that a third
party whose interests were affected by the activities of a corporation could apply for
an injunction to restrain it from acting *ultra vires*.

[94] Salmon L.J. [1966] 2 Q.B. at p. 694, had thought it strange that the other party
could rely on the doctrine where the company had " fully performed its part under
the contract," and in *Re Staines U.D.C. Agreement* [1968] 2 All E.R. 1 at p. 7,
Cross J. took the view that his reservations were not directed to a case where the
contract was unperformed by the company. This distinction is consistent with the
view of the majority of the Alberta Supreme Court that where there is an *ultra vires*
lending the borrower cannot rely on *ultra vires* so as to deprive the lender of its
right to recover the agreed rate of interest and to rely on the security as well as its
right to recover the principal: *Beckenridge Speedway Ltd.* v. *R.* (1967) 64 D.L.R.
(2d) 488.

[95] See especially Street, *op. cit.*, p. 256 *et seq.*; Warren (1925) 2 Camb.L.J. 180;
Goodhart (1926) *ibid.* 350, and *Essays in Jurisprudence and the Common Law*, p. 91;
Welsh (1946) 62 L.Q.R. 345; Ashton-Cross (1950) 10 Camb.L.J. 419; *Winfield on*

surprisingly enough, it is one which rarely causes difficulty in practice and in consequence it can be disposed of comparatively briefly. There are three main theories in this regard:

1. That because of the *ultra vires* rule no corporation can be liable for a tort or crime. Logically, a strong case can be made out in support of this theory. If a statutory or registered company can only do what is authorised by its statute or memorandum, then it is difficult to see how it can ever be liable in tort or crime, for its objects can never include the commission of wrongs. Wrongs committed by its agents or servants ostensibly on its behalf cannot bind the company since they are acting beyond the company's powers. But despite logic and despite dicta in some of the earlier cases,[96] it is abundantly clear that this is not the law, for companies are daily made liable in tort and convicted of crimes. Indeed, if it were otherwise it is difficult to see how any unlawful act (even a breach of contract) could ever be imputed to a company.

2. That the *ultra vires* doctrine has no application except to contract and property and never applies to tortious or criminal liability. This is the view taken by the overwhelming majority of academic writers. Moreover, the *ultra vires* point never seems to have been taken in any of the modern cases on criminal liability, and there is one case which appears to be an authority in favour of the view that it has no application to tort.[97]

Nevertheless, if this is correct it reduces the whole doctrine of *ultra vires* to an absurdity.[98] Can it be seriously suggested that, in the many cases in which contracts or borrowings have been declared *ultra vires*, so that the outsider had no remedy against the company, he could have recovered by suing the company in tort if, for example, the directors had made fraudulent misrepresentations to induce him to enter into the contract? If so, the whole purpose of the *ultra vires* rule would be defeated. It would not afford any protection to the shareholders or to the creditors, for the capital of the company would be diminished just as effectively by payment of damages for tort as for breach of contract. However, the *ultra vires* doctrine has become so unreasonable anyway that perhaps we should not boggle at one crowning absurdity if that reduces its inconvenience.

3. That companies can be liable in tort and crime, but only if these are committed in the course of *intra vires* activities. This, in effect, is the view adopted by Street[99] and Goodhart[1] and is, it is submitted,

---

Tort (8th ed.), pp. 728–731: *Salmond on Torts* (15th ed.), pp. 571–574; Street, *Law of Torts* (4th ed.), pp. 470–471; Glanville Williams, *Criminal Law: The General Part* (2nd ed.), Chap. 22.

[96] *Poulton* v. *L. & S.W. Ry.* (1867) L.R. 2 Q.B. 534, *per* Blackburn J. at p. 540; *Mill* v. *Hawker* (1874) L.R. 9 Ex. 309 at pp. 318–319.

[97] *Campbell* v. *Paddington Corpn.* [1911] 1 K.B. 869.

[98] *Cf.* Wegenast, *Canadian Companies* (Toronto, 1931) at p. 133: "The crowning absurdity of the doctrine of *ultra vires* was the decision that a corporation might be liable in tort for *ultra vires* acts."

[99] *Op. cit.*

[1] *Loc. cit.*

one which can be reconciled with all the cases, except one.[2] Indeed, in more than one case the law has been expressly stated in this way.[3] In principle this seems to be the soundest view. A company may be liable for torts or crimes committed in pursuance of its stated objects but should not be liable for acts entirely outside its objects. In other words, if the objects of the company are restricted to running a tramway it will be liable for anything which its officers do within the actual or usual scope of their authority in connection with or ancillary to running trams, but will not be liable either civilly or criminally for anything which its officers do in connection with some entirely different business.

In fact, however, it can rarely make any practical difference whether we adopt the second or third rule. If the tort or crime is committed during the course of *ultra vires* activities the company will normally escape liability on the ground that its agents or servants have acted outside the scope of their authority or the course of their employment. By first asking themselves whether this scope has been exceeded the courts can normally avoid considering the further question of *ultra vires*.

Proposed reforms

That the *ultra vires* rule has outlived its usefulness has long been apparent. The Cohen Committee proposed that it should be reformed so that as regards third parties a company would have all the powers of a natural person and the objects clause in its memorandum would operate solely as a contract between the company and its members regarding the extent of the authority conferred on its directors and officers; in other words, companies would, in this respect, be equated with partnerships.[4] However, this ignored the fact that, in contrast with partnerships, those dealing with companies would still be deemed to have notice of the provisions of the memorandum of association so that, notwithstanding the rule in *Royal British Bank* v. *Turquand*,[5] third parties might be no better off, since they would be deemed to have had notice that the directors or other officers were exceeding their authority. The Jenkins Committee accordingly went further and recommended that the constructive notice rule should also be abolished,[6] and that even actual knowledge of the contents of the memorandum and articles should not deprive a third party of his right to enforce the contract if he honestly and reasonably failed to appreciate that they precluded the company or its officers from entering into the contract. If these recommendations are carried out, the sting will have been removed from the doctrine and there will be a considerable improvement both

---

[2] *Campbell* v. *Paddington Corpn.*, *supra*.
[3] *e.g.*, *Green* v. *L.G.O.C.* (1859) 7 C.B.(N.S.) 290 at p. 302; *Brownlow* v. *Met. Bd. of Works* (1864) 16 *ibid.* 546 at p. 566.
[4] Cmd. 6659, para. 12.
[5] (1856) 6 E. & B. 327. See *infra*, Chap. 8, p. 150 *et seq.*
[6] Cmnd. 1749, paras. 35–42.

in this respect and in respect of the allied *Royal British Bank* rule. In effect we shall have belatedly adopted the rule which prevails almost universally in the U.S.A. and in many Commonwealth countries. Also following the American example,[7] the Jenkins Committee further recommended that the Companies Act should contain a list of common form powers which, in the absence of express provision to the contrary, would be impliedly incorporated.[8]

Reforms already implemented

However, as yet, none of these recommendations has been carried out. All that has happened is that registered companies have been given wider powers to alter their objects. These powers are now embodied in section 5 of the Companies Act 1948, the effect of which is as follows:

1. A company may, by special resolution, alter its objects for any one of seven specified purposes.[9]
2. But, within twenty-one days [10] of the passing of the resolution, application to the court may be made by or on behalf of the holders, who have not voted in favour of the resolution,[11] of not less than 15 per cent.[12] of the nominal value of the issued share capital of any class.[13]
3. If such an application is made the alteration will not be effective except to the extent that it is confirmed by the court.[14] The court normally has an absolute discretion whether to confirm, reject or modify the alteration, and may adjourn the proceedings so that approved arrangements can be made to buy out the dissentients.[15] But if it can be shown that the alteration is not for one of the specified purposes it will, presumably, be bound

---

[7] Which has already been followed in many Commonwealth countries.

[8] Cmnd. 1749, para. 43. This, of course, would not eradicate the practice of proliferating objects.

[9] s. 5 (1). These are wide enough to cover most likely reasons for an alteration, but occasionally an attempted alteration fails on this ground: see *Re Hampstead Garden Suburb Trust Ltd.* [1962] Ch. 806.

[10] s. 5 (3). The Jenkins Committee recommended that this should be increased to 28 days: Cmnd. 1749, para. 49 (iv).

[11] This means that a nominee shareholder who has voted in favour on behalf of some beneficial owners and against on behalf of others cannot apply on behalf of the latter. The Jenkins Committee recommended the repeal of this condition: Cmnd. 1749, para. 49 (iii).

[12] The Jenkins Committee recommended that this should be reduced to 5 per cent.: Cmnd. 1749, para. 49 (ii).

[13] s. 5 (2). Or by a similar proportion of the holders of debentures secured by a floating charge and created before Dec. 1, 1947: s. 5 (2) (*b*) and (5). Notice has to be given to such debentureholders (s. 5 (5)), and notice to the trustees for debentureholders does not suffice: *Re Hampstead Garden Suburb Trust Ltd., supra.* But there is no similar requirement for notice to members without voting rights; the Jenkins Committee recommended that there should be: Cmnd. 1749, para. 49 (i).

[14] s. 5 (1).

[15] s. 5 (3). But the company's capital may not be used. The Jenkins Committee recommended that this should be permissible with the usual safeguards attending a reduction of capital: Cmnd. 1749, para. 49 (v)

to reject. And if that is the ground of objection it seems that proceedings can be taken within the twenty-one days by any member and not only by the 15 per cent.[16]

4. If, however, no application is made to the court within twenty-one days the alteration cannot subsequently be impugned [17]—even though it is not made for one of the seven specified purposes. In view of this and of the ambit of the specified purposes it is difficult to see what is served by specifying them, and the Jenkins Committee recommended that a general power should be substituted.[18]

The net effect is that so long as more than 85 per cent. of the shareholders have voted for the amendment or so long as no one takes proceedings within twenty-one days of the resolution, companies now have complete freedom to change their objects.[19] Unfortunately, as the decided cases show, companies not infrequently do not realise that an alteration is needed until it is too late.

The relaxation regarding the alteration of the objects clause has been coupled with a similar relaxation regarding other provisions of the memorandum so that there is today no very meaningful distinction between the memorandum and articles.[20] The name of the company can be altered by special resolution with the consent of the Board of Trade.[21] The nominal share capital can be altered by increasing, consolidating or dividing the shares, converting them into stock, or cancelling unissued shares [22] or by a formal reduction of capital confirmed by the court.[23] Moreover, there is now a procedure whereby a limited company can re-register as unlimited [24] or an unlimited one re-register as limited.[25] The one compulsory provision in the memorandum which remains unalterable is that stating whether the registered office is to be in England or Scotland.[26]

---

[16] But a lesser proportion will have to sue for a declaration or injunction and cannot proceed under s. 5: *Re Hampstead Garden Suburb Trust Ltd.*, *supra.* Moreover, it is doubtful who, apart from members, have a *locus standi*; *cf.* p. 86, *supra*, regarding *locus standi* to restrain an *ultra vires* activity.

[17] s. 5 (9), which expressly provides that the validity of the alteration shall not be questioned in proceedings " whether under this section or otherwise."

[18] Cmnd. 1749, para. 48.

[19] But if the company is a charity the alteration will not enable its endowments to be used otherwise than for the original charitable objects: Charities Act 1960, s. 30 (2). And if the alteration is ordered by the court on an application under s. 210 (see *infra*, Chap. 25) the company cannot without the leave of the court make any further alterations inconsistent therewith: s. 210 (3).

[20] Accordingly the Ghana Companies Code 1963 (Act 179) merges both in one document, the Regulations: s. 16.

[21] Companies Act 1948, ss. 18 and 19.

[22] *Ibid.*, s. 61. The articles must contain power to do this, but if they do not they can be altered under s. 10. The share capital of an unlimited company need not appear in the memorandum and if in the articles it can be altered under s. 10.

[23] ss. 66 and 67, see Chaps. 6 and 26, *infra.* These sections have no application to unlimited companies which can freely reduce capital.

[24] Companies Act 1967, s. 43.

[25] *Ibid.*, s. 44, replacing s. 16 of the 1948 Act.

[26] A Scottish nationalist who takes over an English company will therefore have to

Section 2 of the 1948 Act merely prescribes what must appear in the memorandum; there is nothing to stop the incorporators from inserting other provisions and this, until the 1948 Act, had the effect of making them unalterable,[27] except under a scheme of arrangement approved by the court.[28] However it is now provided [29] that anything which could lawfully have been included in the articles instead of the memorandum may be altered by special resolution subject to the right of 15 per cent. dissentients to apply to the court in the same way as under section 5 in the case of alterations of the objects clause.[30] This, however, does not permit the liability of any member to be increased without his consent [31] or the special rights of any class to be abrogated.[32] Further, it has no application where the memorandum itself provides for or prohibits the alteration of any of its conditions.[33] Hence it is still possible to entrench certain provisions by embodying them in the memorandum and providing that they are to be unalterable or alterable only by a special procedure or majority.

Accordingly there is now a great contrast between the inflexible constitutions of statutory and chartered companies and the flexible constitutions of registered companies. Indeed, a registered company now has greater freedom to change its constitution and the nature of its business than has an unincorporated partnership, where unanimity of all members will be needed. But, of course, the strict *ultra vires* doctrine has no application to partnerships or other unincorporated associations which, like any groups of individuals, have the normal capacity of individuals. Hence outsiders dealing with them are concerned only to see that the agent with whom they deal has authority actual or apparent. And even if the authority is initially lacking it can be conferred by subsequent ratification. When dealing with a company the outsider has to clear two hurdles; first the *ultra vires* doctrine dealt with in this chapter, and secondly, the possible lack of authority of the company's officials discussed in Chapter 8. It seems clear that the first hurdle is not needed and, if the recommendations of the Jenkins Committee are implemented, it will at last be removed.

---

undertake a reorganisation involving a transfer to a new company if he wishes to gratify his nationalist principles.

[27] *Ashbury* v. *Watson* (1885) 30 Ch.D. 376, C.A.

[28] Under ss. 206–208: see Chap. 26.

[29] Companies Act 1948, s. 23.

[30] s. 23 (3). But if the provision which it is desired to alter is in the objects clause, s. 5 must be complied with (*i.e.*, it can be altered only for one of the seven purposes specified in that section) and one cannot proceed under s. 23 even though the provisions need not have been in the objects clause: *Re Hampstead Garden Suburb Trust Ltd., supra.* And note that s. 5 (9) is not applied by s. 23 (3) so that if the terms of the section are not strictly complied with it will be possible to attack the validity of the alteration even after the expiration of the 21 days.

[31] The section is expressly subject to s. 22.

[32] s. 23 (2). On the meaning of this, see Chap. 22.

[33] s. 23 (3).

CHAPTER 6

THE RAISING AND MAINTENANCE OF CAPITAL

Meaning of capital

The concept of capital is of fundamental importance to a proper understanding of company law in general, and in particular to an appreciation of the distinction between individual traders and partnerships on the one hand, and incorporated limited liability companies on the other. Unhappily " capital " is a word of many different applications,[1] and even in the legal, economic [2] and accounting senses with which we are concerned, it is used loosely and to describe different conceptions at different times, although its users do not always recognise the fact.

Expressed at its simplest, we may say that whenever anyone starts a business he will put certain property into it. This property may be tangible—money, land, furniture or stock-in-trade—or intangible—patents, copyrights, trade secrets, or the goodwill and connection of a going concern. Whatever the form of this property it will probably be convenient to place a monetary value upon it, if for no other reason than because this will facilitate the preparation of accounts and enable the proprietor to see what return he is getting for the property sunk in the business. Especially is this so if two or more persons are trading in partnership; the monetary valuation of their respective contributions will then become desirable in order to quantify the shares in which they are respectively entitled. The proprietors, therefore, put into the business assets which are given a money value and they are credited with the value of their respective contributions in the books of the business.

Hence the owners of the business start with a fund of capital and their aim is to use this fund so that it increases and provides profits. These profits may either be taken out by the proprietors, or left in the business which, in the latter case, will start the next trading period with a larger capital. Of course, the object of the proprietors may be defeated; the assets may not be increased by profits but may be diminished by losses. In this event the business will start the next year with a reduced capital, unless the proprietors decide to bring in further assets.

---

[1] *Cf.* capital punishment, capital letter, capital ship, capital city, capital of a pillar, capital and labour, capital and income, and " capital! "

[2] No attempt is here made to deal with the economist's analysis of capital; such an attempt would take us into the higher flights of economic theory for which the writer has no qualifications. But the subjects discussed in this chapter presuppose some knowledge of companies' accounts and Chap. 20 should be read in conjunction with the present discussion.

In other words, with the normal business, " capital " is simply a name given to the net worth of the business—the amount by which the value of the assets exceeds the liabilities. And, since double-entry book-keeping has made it traditional to prepare financial statements so that debits and credits are balanced, in the old-style balance sheet the assets will be shown on the right-hand side and the liabilities on the left, with " capital " as the balancing item.

This explanation suggests that all the assets of the business will be revalued at the end of each accounting period—normally annually. In practice this is not so. A distinction is drawn between fixed assets and circulating or floating assets. Fixed assets are those which are to be permanently retained for the purpose of the business—its land and premises, machinery, and office furniture and equipment. Circulating, current or floating assets, on the other hand, are those turned over in the course of business—its money, trade creditors and stock-in-trade.[3] An actual revaluation of any fixed asset will not take place each year; for the purpose of calculating profits or losses it will be assumed to remain constant (until sold) subject, if the accounts are properly kept, to an annual book-keeping adjustment for depreciation.[4] But all circulating assets must be revalued annually to obtain any realistic assessment of the annual profit or loss. This is dependent not merely on whether trading receipts have exceeded payments or vice versa, but on the difference in value at the beginning and end of the trading year of all the circulating assets (stock, cash, trade debts to the firm, and the like) less current liabilities, such as trade debts due from the firm.[5]

So far as concerns the business of an individual trader or partnership this conception of capital and method of dealing with it are merely matters of convenience and accounting practice. Except to the extent that the bankruptcy and tax laws require accounts to be

---

[3] It will be appreciated that whether a particular item is fixed or floating depends on the nature of the business and not on the inherent nature of the asset. A ship in course of construction in a dry dock constitutes part of the floating assets of the shipbuilder, but once it is launched and handed over to the ship operator it becomes part of his fixed assets; for accounting purposes it ceases to float once it actually floats. The distinction, moreover, is merely one of degree and often arbitrary and difficult to draw. Sched. 8, para. 4 (2), of the Companies Act 1948, as amended by the 1967 Act, recognises that there may be assets which are neither fixed nor current.

[4] But s. 16 of the Companies Act 1967 requires the directors' report which accompanies the annual accounts to state any significant changes in fixed assets and, if the market value of land differs substantially from the figure in the balance sheet, to indicate the difference with such degree of precision as is practicable.

[5] Speaking generally the profits or losses on circulating assets will constitute the revenue or income profits or losses on which corporation tax is dependent. The description in the text of the method of calculating profits is admittedly an over-simplification; for example, in accounting practice upward adjustments of circulating capital are not made until increases are realised, nor are downward adjustments unless values fall below cost. Note that a method ot calculation acceptable for company law purposes will not always be acceptable for tax purposes: *Patrick* v. *Broadstone Mills* [1954] 1 W.L.R. 158, C.A.; *Min. of National Revenue* v. *Anaconda*

kept and profits or losses to be calculated, there is no legal requirement that the assets brought into the business should be given a
money value and credited to the proprietors as their capital, and there
is nothing to prevent capital being increased or withdrawn by the
proprietors at any time. If, in particular, they decide that the business
is over-capitalised they are perfectly free to withdraw part of the assets
and reduce the capital accordingly. Since the proprietors are fully liable
without limitation of liability it makes little difference to creditors
whether their personal wealth is treated as business capital or not; it
remains liable for payment of debts in any event.[6] The trust to be
reposed in the proprietors has therefore no relation to the capital in
the business as such. It does not even depend solely on the present
wealth of the proprietors; third parties may be prepared to place trust
in them because of their reputations and personal characters irrespective
of their existing fortunes, for, like Sir Walter Scott, they may be willing
to slave for the rest of their lives to discharge the liabilities of the
business.

Capital and credit

With a limited liability company all this is altered. It has no
personal character to be trusted; but, unless trust is reposed in it, it
will be unable to survive in competition with its rivals. It may want
to raise capital, beyond that subscribed by its members, by borrowings;
or it may need to buy commodities on credit; in any event it will
be vital, if it is to dispose of its goods or services, that third parties
shall be able to trust it properly to fulfil its contracts. The company
has only its capital to back its credit, and this being so it is essential
that capital should be more clearly defined and inviolable than is the
case with an individual or partnership. Hence the law has worked
out certain principles relating to the raising and maintaining of capital.
In effect, capital has ceased to be a name given to the fluctuating net
worth of the business and has become a rigid yardstick fixing the
minimum value of the net assets which must be raised initially and then,
so far as possible, retained in the business. These principles have no
application to unlimited companies and have been worked out in relation
only to companies limited *by shares*. They are primarily intended for
the protection of creditors (and it is upon this aspect that the following
discussion concentrates), but, like the *ultra vires* rule, they are also
designed to protect shareholders, present and future, against action by

---

American Brass Ltd. [1956] A.C. 85, P.C. Excellent discussions of these problems
will be found in the Final Report of the Royal Commission on the Taxation of
Profits and Income (Cmd. 9474 of 1955), Chap. 18, and in Chap. X of the Report
of the Jenkins Committee (Cmnd. 1749) which led to the latest revision of the
accounting provisions of the Act.

6 But in the case of a partnership it may in fact make a difference as regards the
respective priorities of business and personal creditors in the event of bankruptcy:
Bankruptcy Act 1914, s. 33 (6).

the directors which might covertly diminish the value of their shares as long-term investments.

Share capital

As we have seen, overwhelmingly the most common type of company is that limited by shares. As regards this the 1948 Act [7] expressly provides that the memorandum of association shall " state the amount of share capital with which the company proposes to be registered and the division thereof into shares of a fixed amount." The capital thus stated, the *nominal* capital, is of importance only as fixing the fees and duties payable on the formation of the company, and because the directors will normally have power to issue shares up to the limit of the authorised capital without reference to the members in general meeting. Some or all of the nominal capital will, however, have to be subscribed; thus constituting the *issued* share capital. As regards the issued shares, the Act provides [8] that the liability of the holders shall be limited " to the amount, if any, unpaid on the shares." In other words, the issued share capital may consist partly of paid up capital (representing the total of the payments made in respect of the issued shares) and partly of *uncalled* capital (representing the balance, if any, between the amount already paid and the total nominal value of the issued shares).

As previously pointed out the uncalled capital clearly constitutes something in the nature of a guarantee fund to which creditors of the company can look. It is, in effect, an asset equivalent to " sundry debtors," [9] the debtors being the members, whose personal credit is therefore retained as an element in the concept of capital. In order that this element may be made more permanent the Act provides [10] that a company may resolve that it shall only be called up in the event of winding up, in which case it is described as *reserve* capital.[11] But it is not only the uncalled capital which constitutes a fund of credit. The paid up capital is also of importance; indeed, at the present day it is most uncommon for shares to be issued otherwise than as fully payable on allotment. But obviously paid up capital could only be regarded as a fund of credit if third parties could rely on the fact that the company had received from its members assets equivalent to the amount of the

---

[7] s. 2 (4) (*a*).

[8] ss. 1 (2) (*a*) and 212 (1) (*d*). Under s. 212, on winding up existing members are liable for the uncalled amount on their shares and members who have held shares within one year previously are liable (as B List contributories) if the existing holders of their shares do not pay: see Chap. 27, p. 663.

[9] It is not in fact English accountancy practice to treat it as a balance-sheet asset until a call has actually been made, and until then only the paid up capital is shown as a notional liability. It must be stressed that, though capital is shown in the balance sheet on the same side as the liabilities, it is not a true liability; its position is merely an accounting device.

[10] s. 60.

[11] Not to be confused with capital reserve or capital redemption reserve fund: see *infra.*

shares and had not subsequently returned these assets or any part of them to the members. In other words, they must be able to rely on the fact that the capital has actually been raised by the transfer to the company of balancing assets and that these assets have been maintained.

The law therefore lays down rules which attempt to ensure that this reliance is not misplaced. For these rules we have to thank the judges of the late nineteenth century, for their decisions (although often described by them as based on the obvious intention of the legislature) in fact depend hardly at all on the express provisions of the early Companies Acts, which contained little more on the subject than those already quoted.[12] All these do is to provide that the capital shall be treated as divided into shares, that these shares shall be given a fixed value, and that the members' liability shall not exceed this value.

Raising of share capital

In the first place the courts insisted that shares could only be treated as paid up to the extent of the value actually received by the company in cash or in kind. The statutory provision, limiting the liability of the members to the amount unpaid on their shares, was construed as establishing a minimum, as well as a maximum liability; in other words, shares cannot (except now with the permission of the court in certain circumstances [13]) be issued at a discount. This was finally established by the House of Lords in *Ooregum Gold Mining Co. of India* v. *Roper* [14]—a particularly strong case since the existing shares of the same class stood at a discount and the issue was entirely bona fide and clearly for the benefit of the company.[15] The efficacy of this ruling has, however, been reduced by the fact that the law recognises that payment may be made in kind (*e.g.*, in property or services) instead of in cash [16] and that the company's valuation of the consideration will be accepted as conclusive [17] unless

---

12 American courts, interpreting very similar provisions, arrived at a totally different conclusion and allowed, subject to various safeguards against fraud, gifts of shares by the company (bonus shares—not to be confused with bonus shares in the English sense described below), issues at a discount, and the purchase by the company of its own shares.

13 s. 57. This permission is so rarely resorted to that further consideration of it is unnecessary.

14 [1892] A.C. 125, H.L.

15 This judicial legislation was the more courageous in that it has been held that a statutory company subject to the Companies Clauses Acts *may* issue shares at a discount: *Statham* v. *Brighton Marine Palace & Pier Co.* [1899] 1 Ch. 199.

16 s. 52.

17 *Re Wragg* [1897] 1 Ch. 796, C.A. Under s. 52 the documents on the company's file will show that shares have been issued for a consideration other than cash and must contain a contract evidencing the consideration. These requirements are often evaded by an arrangement whereby the vendor purports to sell for cash and to subscribe the corresponding shares for cash, he and the company exchanging cheques, or relying on a set-off without the formality of an exchange of cheques. That this amounted to an issue for cash was established by *Spargo's Case* (1873) L.R. 8 Ch.App. 407.

inadequacy appears on the face of the transaction [18] or there is evidence of fraud or of an absence of any bona fide consideration of whether the consideration was adequate.[19]   Hence, by an issue subscribed otherwise than in cash it is possible to " water " the shares by transferring to the company in payment for them something actually worth less than their nominal value.   In Continental countries this abuse is prevented by insisting on an official valuation, often coupled with the need to obtain the consent of the court,[20] but there is no such safeguard in England.

The general principle has been further weakened by the statutory permission,[21] subject to authorisation in the articles and to disclosure, allowing payment of commission not exceeding ten per cent. in consideration of an agreement to take up shares.   This was intended to permit the payment of underwriting commission, *i.e.,* a commission to ensure that, if the public did not take up the shares offered, the underwriters would do so.   Nevertheless, the section is worded widely, and more than once advantage has recently been taken of it to make a general offer of shares at par subject to an allowance of, say, 1s. commission, so that in effect £1 shares are issued at 19s.

Subject, however, to these limitations, the law does ensure that the company initially receives assets at least equivalent to the nominal amount of the paid up capital.   To this extent the insistence on shares with a fixed nominal value serves a useful purpose.   But what prevents this from being any real safeguard is the refusal of the law to prescribe any minimum to what the nominal value may be.   If a company can be formed, and one has been, with a capital of $\frac{1}{4}$d., divided into two $\frac{1}{4}$d. shares, it is clear that it is no protection to creditors to know that the company once received a halfpenny or the equivalent.   And even where the issued capital is substantial, the insistence on its *nominal* amount being raised really means no more than that the law, having insisted on a prescribed par value, will prevent the public from being misled by allowing companies to issue fully paid up shares for less than that value.   The rules now being considered do nothing to ensure that the company's capital is adequate for its requirements [22]; in so far as that is provided for, it is by the rule that shares offered to the public shall not be allotted unless there has been an adequate response to the offer.[23]

---

[18] *Re White Star Line* [1938] Ch. 458, C.A.
[19] *Tintin Exploration Syndicate* v. *Sandys* (1947) 177 L.T. 412.
[20] See Levy, *Private Corporations and their Control*, Vol. 1, p. 416 *et seq.*
[21] 1948 Act, s. 53.   It has also been held that reasonable brokerage may be paid; *Metropolitan Coal Consumers Association* v. *Scrimgeour* [1895] 2 Q.B. 604, C.A. This is impliedly recognised by s. 53 (3).
[22] A great many foreign countries, including some common law ones, provide for a minimum paid up capital.   Although the Jenkins Committee favoured this in principle they rejected it as too easily evaded: Cmnd. 1749, para. 27.
[23] *i.e.,* unless the " minimum subscription " has been received.   This question is discussed under " Flotation," in Chap. 14, *infra.*

Share premiums

There is, however, nothing to stop a company from issuing its shares at a price exceeding their nominal par value, that is, at a premium. This, indeed, is very common, especially when additional capital is raised at a later stage. Even on the inception of the company it may pay the promoters of the company to make an initial issue at a premium. If, for example, a trader is converting his business (worth £10,000) into a limited company by selling it to the company in consideration of an issue of shares to him, he will find it cheaper to form a company with £1,000 share capital than one with £10,000. Provided he obtains control of the whole of the shares it makes no other difference to him whether he obtains 1,000 £1 shares (worth £10 each) or 10,000 £1 shares (worth £1 each). Hence he will probably have 1,000 shares issued to him, in effect at a premium of £9 per share.

This example shows how arbitrary par values may be even at the beginning of the company's life. Moreover, they produce an even greater absurdity. Taking the same example once more, it is obvious that the company's assets would appear in the commencing balance sheet at a figure of £10,000. This constitutes the proprietor's capital and ought to appear as such, as it would in the accounts of an individual or partnership. But this is not possible in the case of a limited company. Capital—share capital—has necessarily been fixed at the nominal par value of £1,000; the remaining balance of £9,000 has to appear in the balance sheet, on the same side as capital, under some other title such as " Share Premiums."

Prior to 1948, share premiums could be treated totally differently from share capital. Since capital had been fixed at the nominal par value of the issued shares, that alone had to be taken into consideration in fixing the capital yardstick. Anything over and above this constituted part of the distributable surplus which the company, if it wished, could return to the shareholders by way of dividend.[24] But now section 56 of the 1948 Act provides that where a company issues shares at a premium a sum equal to the total amount of the premium shall be transferred to the " Share Premium A/c " which for most [25] purposes must be treated as though it were share capital.[26] This reform is eminently sensible but it makes par value still more of a meaningless symbol for it frankly recognises that what is important is not the arbitrary par value but the value received for the shares when issued. The section expressly applies whether the shares are issued " for cash *or otherwise*," and hence it has been held [27] that a share premium account must be established if the shares are allotted in consideration

24 *Drown* v. *Gaumont British Picture Corpn.* [1937] Ch. 402.
25 But not quite all, see s. 56 (2) (summarised *infra*, 116, n. 72) and *Re Paringa Mining and Exploration Co. Ltd.* [1957] 1 W.L.R. 1143.
26 *Cf. Re Duff's Settlement* [1951] Ch. 923, C.A.
27 *Henry Head & Co. Ltd.* v. *Ropner Holdings Ltd.* [1952] Ch. 124.

of a transfer of assets, the value of which exceeds the nominal value of the shares.[28]

Increase of capital

Hence the company's initial balance sheet will resemble that of an individual or partnership in that the right-hand side will show the assets at a valuation, balanced on the left by an equivalent amount of "capital." But, in contrast, the item "capital" may now have to be divided into two, issued share capital and share premium account, the former showing the nominal amount of the paid up capital and the latter the aggregate amounts of any premiums. Capital in this sense will only equal capital in the earlier sense of net worth if the company makes profits and annually distributes the whole of them to the shareholders by way of dividend. If it makes profits but fails to distribute them, the net worth will increase and the guarantee fund of the creditors and the value of the proprietors' shares will increase correspondingly. But because of the statutory rules it is not possible to reflect this by adding to the figures of share capital or share premium; instead, another balancing item will have to be added, to which the misleading name of "reserve" is normally given. In other words, company law makes it impossible to describe the difference between the book values of the assets and the liabilities by the one word "capital." The initial capital will have to be divided into share capital and share premiums (assuming that shares are issued for more than par) and these two items remain fixed irrespective of any fluctuations in the value of the assets and liabilities. If the net book value exceeds the capital yardstick, a further balancing item, "reserve," will have to be added.[29]

The only way in which share capital can increase is by the issue of further shares. This a company can do freely provided that it complies with the rules summarised above.[30] But just as these rules are ineffective to prevent "share-watering" by an issue for a consideration other than cash, so at this later stage they are equally ineffective to prevent "watering" by an issue even for cash. As we have seen, if the company has traded profitably and built up reserves the true value of the existing shares will exceed par. Hence in fairness to the existing shareholders, any new shares of the same class which

---

28 Professional disputation has arisen on whether this applies only when the book entries relating to the transaction indicate that there is a premium or whether the section operates whenever the company has in fact received value in excess of the shares issued. The Jenkins Committee supported the latter view and recommended that it should be clearly stated: Cmnd. 1749, paras. 161–166.

29 The same result could, of course be achieved by deliberately undervaluing the assets, but the Act now seeks to prohibit "secret reserves" of this sort: see Chap. 20, *infra*.

30 As will be pointed out later (Chap. 14, *infra*) certain regulations may have to be complied with, particularly if the shares are offered to the public generally. If the nominal capital has been exhausted it will be necessary to increase it, but this too can be effected without difficulty: s. 61.

are issued ought also to be issued at more than par and at the best price obtainable. But the rules regarding the raising of capital merely ensure that fully paid shares shall not be issued below par and that, if they are in fact issued at a premium, that premium is treated as capital. There is, it seems, no legal obligation to issue shares at the best price, thereby avoiding the dilution of the value of the existing shares,[31] so long as there is no breach of the directors' fiduciary duties [32] or fraud on the minority.[33]

It may be, however, that the company does not require any new money, but very reasonably wishes to bring the nominal amount of its issued share capital more into line with the true excess of assets over liabilities. Unless it takes this step its annual profits will appear to be disproportionately high in relation to its nominal capital and it is likely to be subjected to ignorant criticism on that account. This operation can be undertaken by means of a " bonus " or " scrip " issue, that is, by issuing more shares to the existing holders and using the funds available for dividend but retained by the company to pay for them. By this means the reserves or share premium account,[34] or some part of them, are capitalised or converted into share capital. The only result, from the shareholder's point of view is that his proportion of the capital of the business is now represented by a greater number of shares, each of which is therefore worth less [35] and this may make them more readily marketable. From the point of view of the company, the capitalisation of free, *i.e.*, voluntary, reserves [36] merely means that undistributed profits have been permanently " ploughed back " and converted into share capital which, as we shall see, cannot be returned to the members by way of dividend. Essentially a bonus issue is nothing more sinister or subtle than a formal means of restoring share capital and net book value [37] of the undertaking to something approaching equilibrium.[38]

---

[31] *Hilder* v. *Dexter* [1902] A.C. 474, H.L.; *Lowry* v. *Consolidated African Selection Trust* [1940] A.C. 648, H.L. All that can be said in favour of par values is that they place some limit on the extent of the watering.

[32] See Chap. 23, *infra*.

[33] See Chap. 24, *infra*.

[34] s. 56 (2). Or capital redemption reserve fund, see *infra*.

[35] Shareholders frequently do not realise this but think that they are being given a true tax-free bonus which they encash by selling the bonus shares. The word " bonus " is itself misleading and totally different from the sense in which it is used in America (see note 12, *supra*) where this type of issue is described as a stock dividend.

[36] If the share premium account is capitalised, there is really no difference at all from the viewpoint of the company.

[37] This expression is here used to describe the difference between the book values of the assets and liabilities. Because of the accountant's method of valuing (outlined above) it may be different from the true net worth.

[38] It may, admittedly, be used for more dubious purposes; *e.g.*, to conceal the fact that dividends are being increased—for if the number of shares is increased the amount distributed by way of dividend will also be increased although the rate per share remains the same. Formerly, too, it could be used as a means of extracting income disguised as capital thereby saving the shareholders tax.

Reduction of capital

If, however, the company trades at a loss the actual value of the capital will be reduced below the nominal value of the issued shares. Consequently the book value of the shares will be less than par, and the creditors' guarantee fund will be diminished. There is nothing the law can do about this.[39] As Lord Herschell said in *Trevor* v. *Whitworth* [40]:

> " The capital may no doubt be diminished by expenditure upon and reasonably incidental to all the objects specified. A part of it may be lost in carrying on the business operations authorised. Of this all persons trusting the company are aware and take the risk."

But, as Lord Herschell continues, creditors " have a right to rely and were intended by the legislature to have a right to rely, on the capital remaining undiminished by any expenditure ouside these limits, or by the return of any part of it to the shareholders." In other words the law can try to preserve the creditors' guarantee fund by insisting that the company shall not apply its assets for objects other than those authorised by the memorandum (the *ultra vires* doctrine [41]). And it can supplement this by seeking to ensure that no return is made to the members if this would have the effect of reducing the net worth of the company below the original yardstick fixed by the share capital and (now) share premiums. Obviously the protection of creditors would be illusory if the company's assets could be freely distributed to the members. Hence the judges, led by Jessel M.R. and Lord Macnaghten, refused to allow any repayment in reduction of the capital yardstick. This principle was ultimately established in *Trevor* v. *Whitworth* [42] which held that a company could not purchase its own shares, even though there was an express power to do so in its memorandum since this would amount to a reduction of capital.

However, it was early recognised that the rigid application of this principle might be unduly strict. In particular, if a company had consistently made losses so that its net worth was hopelessly below the figure fixed by its capital, little purpose was served by maintaining the capital yardstick at its original figure—a figure no longer represented by assets to which creditors could look for payment. This was very different from a repayment of the company's assets to the members. But even the latter might sometimes be legitimate. If the company curtailed its activities so that its net assets were greater than it needed or

---

[39] The original Limited Liability Act of 1855 did in fact provide that a company should be wound up if three-fourths of the capital was lost, but the provision was dropped from the Act of 1862: see Chap. 2, above.

[40] (1887) 12 App.Cas. 409 at p. 415.

[41] Discussed in Chap. 5, *supra*.

[42] (1887) 12 App.Cas. 409, H.L.

could profitably employ, then, provided that creditors were provided for, it was pointless to refuse to allow it to make a repayment to its members in reduction of the issued capital. Hence the legislature, by the Acts of 1867 and 1877 (now Companies Act 1948, s. 66), provided that capital might be reduced subject to certain safeguards and to the consent of the court. Reductions of capital under this section are discussed more fully in Chapter 26.

Acquisitions of the company's shares by it or by use of its assets

As we have seen, *Trevor* v. *Whitworth* [43] finally established that a company could not purchase its own shares.[44] Such purchases are dangerous, not only because they might result in the reduction of the capital yardstick to the detriment of creditors, but also because, if the company paid more than the true worth of the shares, it would dilute the value of the remainder, while if it paid too little it would increase the value of the remainder and might be used by the directors to enhance the value of their own holdings. Moreover such purchases might be used by the directors to maintain themselves in control.[45] The latter abuse can equally well occur if nothing is paid for the shares by the company but someone acquires them as a trustee for the company—yet this has been held to be legal.[46] However an attempt has been made to ban certain other devices that have much the same effect.

Thus under section 27 of the Companies Act 1948 a subsidiary company cannot become a member of its holding company [47] and if it was a shareholder of it at the commencement of the Act it may not exercise any voting rights.[48] The Jenkins Committee considered whether a similar prohibition should not extend to cross and circular holdings which are equally objectionable as a method of preserving control [49] but rejected this " somewhat reluctantly," largely because it was thought to involve too many complications.[50]

---

[43] *Supra.*
[44] In the U.S.A. the common law developed differently and such purchases are permitted, subject, now, to legislative safeguards in most states.
[45] When faced with a take-over bid (on which see Chap. 23, pp. 540–546 and Chap. 26, pp. 625–631), directors frequently seek to frustrate the bidder by buying shares on the market. They would obviously do so still more readily if they could use the company's money.
[46] *Re Castiglione's Will Trust* [1958] Ch. 549. The Jenkins Committee recommended that in such circumstances the shares should carry no right to vote so long as they were held on trust for the company: Cmnd. 1749, para. 154.
[47] Unless the subsidiary is concerned as personal representative or trustee only: subs. (2).
[48] For suggested amendments to this section, see Cmnd. 1749, para. 155.
[49] If, for example, company A holds 45 per cent. of the voting shares of company B and company B holds 45 per cent. of the shares of company A, the boards of directors of both companies are virtually irremovable, yet neither company is a holding or subsidiary company of the other and s. 27 does not bite. But the holdings will now have to be openly avowed under the Companies Act 1967, ss. 33 and 34.
[50] Cmnd. 1749, para. 153.

The provision by the company of financial assistance for the purchase or subscription of its shares is even more obviously objectionable. Yet indirectly this is a common malpractice where a take-over bidder buys the shares in a company with large liquid assets, using them to recoup the bridging loan that he has raised to pay for the shares.[51] A somewhat unsuccessful attempt to ban this has been made by the notorious section 54 of the 1948 Act—notorious because it has hit the innocent and failed to deter the guilty. Moreover, the interpretation originally given to it suggested that the only sanction for a breach was the derisory fine of £100.[52] It now seems to be fairly clear that, in addition, the section makes void for illegality any form of financial assistance to purchase the company's shares or those of its holding company and any security given by or to the company in respect of that assistance,[52] and that, further, the officers of the company responsible for the illegal transaction are liable to recoup to the company any loss it sustains.[53] The only exceptions are where the ordinary business of the company is the lending of money, and where a loan is made in the ordinary course of business [54] or to enable employees to acquire shares.[55]

The Jenkins Committee were satisfied that the section was frequently disregarded and was drafted so widely as to hit at certain transactions which were unobjectionable.[56] They accordingly suggested that the provision of financial assistance should be permissible if the transaction was approved by a special resolution of the company and a declaration of the company's solvency [57] made and filed by the directors.[58] They pointed out that these conditions should more effectively prevent the mischief against which section 54 was aimed, namely, prejudice of minority shareholders and creditors. As yet this recommendation has not been implemented.

---

[51] For a recent example of the *modus operandi*, see *Selangor United Rubber Estates Ltd.* v. *Cradock (No. 3)* [1968] 1 W.L.R. 1555.

[52] It was held in the much criticised *Victor Battery Co.* v. *Curry's Ltd.* [1946] Ch. 242 that a security given by the company to secure a loan made to finance the purchase of its shares was not avoided. Australian decisions suggested the contrary: see *Dressy Frocks Pty. Ltd.* v. *Bock* (1951) S.R.(N.S.W.) 390; *Shearer Transport Co. Pty. Ltd.* v. *McGrath* [1956] V.L.R. 361; and *E. H. Dey Pty. Ltd.* v. *Dey* [1966] V.R. 464; on which see (1968) 32 Conv.(N.S.) 6. The *Victor Battery* case was nevertheless accepted as correct by Cross J. in *Curtis's Furnishing Stores Ltd.* v. *Freedman* [1966] 1 W.L.R. 1219, though it is difficult to reconcile this with his later decision in *S. Western Mineral Water Co. Ltd.* v. *Ashmore* [1967] 1 W.L.R. 1110. Finally, Ungoed-Thomas J., in *Selangor United Rubber Estates Ltd.* v. *Cradock (No. 3), supra,* held that the loan was avoided and expressed a clear view that any security would likewise be avoided.

[53] *Steen* v. *Law* [1964] A.C. 287, P.C.

[54] s. 54 (1), proviso (*a*), on which see *Steen* v. *Law, supra,* which makes it clear that a loan deliberately made by the company for the direct purpose of financing a purchase of its shares could never be regarded as made in the ordinary course of business.

[55] s. 54 (1), provisos (*b*) and (*c*).

[56] Cmnd. 1749, paras. 170–176.

[57] *i.e.,* that the company, *after the transaction,* will be able to pay its debts as they fall due.

[58] Cmnd. 1749, paras. 177–186.

In one respect, however, the rule in *Trevor* v. *Whitworth* has been relaxed. By the Act of 1929 (now Companies Act 1948, s. 58) it was made possible to issue preference shares expressly created as redeemable.[59] The dangers are obviously less in the case of preference shares since their value is unlikely to fluctuate much and they normally do not carry voting rights.[60] Moreover steps were taken to ensure that their redemption did not lead to any reduction of the capital yardstick. They can be redeemed only when fully paid and only out of the proceeds of a fresh issue, in which case the capital of the new shares will replace the capital of those redeemed, or out of profits. In the latter event an amount equivalent to the nominal amount of the shares redeemed[61] must be transferred to what is described, not very helpfully, as the " capital redemption reserve fund "[62] and this has to be treated as if it were paid-up capital. Hence, although the shares redeemed disappear, the capital which they represented is retained for accounting purposes and there is no reduction of the capital yardstick. The section is a recognition that it is possible to allow companies to buy their own shares without opening the door to abuse. The Jenkins Committee[63] considered whether, as in the U.S.A., there should be a general power for companies to buy their own shares. Although they recognised that the needful safeguards could be provided and would not be unduly complicated, they rejected this idea largely because there was no demand for it. This illustration of the conservatism of the English legal and commercial world is regrettable, since such a power would undoubtedly be useful to private companies and to all companies wishing to introduce employee share-ownership schemes and would enable unit trusts to operate as companies instead of through the more complicated medium of a trust.[64]

Accordingly, apart from a formal reduction of capital with the court's consent, the principle[65] remains more or less intact that capital cannot be reduced.[66]

---

[59] Certain statutory companies had already been empowered to issue redeemable stock by the Statutory Companies (Redeemable Stock) Act 1915.

[60] See Chap. 16, pp. 357–364, *infra.*

[61] But not any premium payable on redemption which, however, must be provided out of profits or share premium account.

[62] The name suggests, erroneously, that it represents a sinking fund intended to provide for the redemption. In fact it is a notional liability replacing the notional liability of the redeemed share capital.

[63] Cmnd. 1749, paras. 167–169.

[64] See Chap. 11, pp. 222–227, *infra.*

[65] Though it is still nowhere stated in the Acts; the Jenkins Committee suggested that it should be: Cmnd. 1749, para. 157.

[66] There is one further exception; namely, that shares may be forfeited for non-payment of calls. This is not expressly provided for in the Act but is impliedly authorised because of the provisions of Table A, Art. 33 *et seq.* It seems that a company may accept a surrender to avoid the formalities of forfeiture: *Trevor* v. *Whitworth* (1887) 12 App.Cas. at pp. 429 and 438. Two other cases in which there is no true reduction are permitted: (i) cancellation of unissued shares: s. 61 (1) (*c*); (ii) an exchange of fully paid shares for others of a like par value: *Rowell* v. *John Rowell & Sons Ltd.* [1912] 2 Ch. 609.

Terminology has, however, now become still more complicated, for capital may now have to be divided into share capital, share premium account, and capital redemption reserve fund. Nor does it follow by any means that the total of these will represent the true net worth of the company, even on the basis of book values: it may be less than the net worth, in which case a further balancing item, " reserves," will appear on the liabilities side of the balance sheet; or it may be more, in which case there will be an item shown among the assets representing the accumulated losses.

Dividends out of capital

It is clearly not sufficient merely to ensure that the nominal amount of the capital shown as a liability is not reduced; this may prevent the creditors' guarantee fund from being whittled away by a payment to shareholders expressly made as a return of capital, but by itself it will not prevent that fund from being reduced by payments masquerading as payments of dividend.

The courts have sought to prevent this evasion by declaring that " dividends must not be paid out of capital " or, that " dividends must only be paid out of profits." [67] There was no general and direct legislative authority for either of these propositions, although the former appears in the Companies Clauses Act 1845,[68] relating to statutory companies, and the latter is expressed in most articles of association, including Table A.[69] Nevertheless, the judges were prepared to enunciate them as flowing inevitably from the golden rule that capital might not be reduced, which, as we have seen, they had deduced from the provisions of the Companies Acts. Thus, in *Flitcroft's Case* [70] in 1882, the Court of Appeal held that directors who had allowed debts, which they knew to be bad, to be credited in the accounts, thus creating fictitious profits, were liable to refund the dividends paid on their recommendation since these amounted to an unauthorised reduction of capital. It was in this case that Jessel M.R.[71] explained the basis of the whole capital concept in the clearest terms.

---

[67] The two propositions are generally assumed to be identical; *sed quaere*: see the observations of Farwell J. in *Bond* v. *Barrow Haematite Steel Co.* [1902] 1 Ch. at 365. Upon the whole of this baffling branch of the law there is an immense literature, especially on the accountancy aspects. Perhaps the best short account for legal readers is that of B. S. Yamey, " The Law Relating to Company Dividends " (1941) 4 M.L.R. 273 (reprinted in Baxter & Davidson, *Studies in Accounting Theory* (2nd ed.)).

[68] s. 121: " The company shall not make any dividend whereby their capital stock will be in any way reduced. . . ." But the section further provides that a part return of capital is permissible with the consent of all secured creditors.

[69] Art. 116.

[70] (1882) 21 Ch.D. 519, C.A.

[71] At pp. 533–534. *Cf.* the " trust fund " doctrine enunciated by Story J. in *Wood* v. *Dummer* (1824) 3 Mason 308. This may be another example of American influence playing a part in the development of English company law.

"The creditor has no debtor but that impalpable thing the corporation, which has no property except the assets of the business. The creditor, therefore, I may say, gives credit to that capital, gives credit to the company on the faith of the implied representation that the capital shall be applied only for the purposes of the business, and he has therefore a right to say that the corporation shall keep its capital and not return it to the shareholders. . . ."

Since 1908 the existence of some such principle may be regarded as tacitly recognised by the legislature because of the express provision [72] that, with the consent of the Board of Trade, a company may in certain circumstances pay *interest* out of capital where shares have been issued to defray preliminary capital expenditure which cannot bring in a return for some years.

But while it is easy to state glibly that dividends must not be paid out of capital but only out of profits, it is extraordinarily difficult to apply this rule effectively. It will be appreciated that "capital" as a clearly defined item, exists only as a statement of liability, and neither dividends, nor anything else, can be paid out of a liability. What interests creditors is not whether this item remains intact, but whether the net worth of the business is maintained and whether it has assets from which they can be paid. If therefore the principle of maintenance of capital is to be applied effectively, the law should insist that dividends are not paid if the effect would be to reduce the value of the total assets below that of the liabilities and capital.[73] Only thus can capital effectively fulfil its function as a yardstick measuring whether the company has a surplus distributable to its members.

This is the rule in some Continental countries and American states [74] and for a time it seemed that the courts, under the influence of Jessel M.R., were prepared to go thus far. But even then the principle was not as watertight as it appeared, for "value" is an uncertain concept and the courts themselves were ill-equipped to assess it. They could only proceed on the basis of the values as shown in the company's books. After a few years, therefore, the courts abdicated almost completely in favour of accountants and their businessmen clients.

[72] Now Companies Act 1948, s. 65. And by the statutory permission to reduce the share premium account by writing off preliminary expenses, the expenses of share issues and premiums paid on a redemption of redeemable preference shares or debentures: s. 56 (2).

[73] *i.e.*, paid-up share capital *plus* share premium account (if any) *plus* capital redemption reserve fund (if any). It must be emphasised that what we are here discussing is whether the company has sufficient assets to *entitle* it to pay a dividend. It does not follow that because it is entitled to pay a dividend it will, in fact, have sufficient cash (or the ability to borrow it) to enable it to pay one in money.

[74] Where the problem is now generally regulated by more explicit statutory provisions which, however, do not seem to have wholly eradicated uncertainties.

This development started with *Lee* v. *Neuchatel Asphalte Co.*[75] in 1889, in which Lindley L.J. said [76]:

> "There is nothing at all in the Act about how dividends are to be paid, nor how profits are to be reckoned; all that is left, and very judiciously and properly left, to the commercial world. It is not a subject for an Act of Parliament to say how accounts are to be kept; what is to be put into a capital account, what into an income account is left to men of business."

In so far as this suggests that the question is purely one of fact and that there are no legal rules, it seems to do less than justice to the elaborate discussions in this and later cases. In these the courts adopted with enthusiasm the accountant's distinction between fixed and circulating assets (a distinction which is now given statutory validity [77]), and, indeed, applied it with a rigidity which did not meet with the approval of all accountants.[78]

Summary of legal rules regarding dividends

The result of the cases may, it is thought, be summarised in the following rules. But, as we shall see, the Jenkins Committee made a number of recommendations regarding them which, if implemented, will change the legal position substantially.

(1) Dividends cannot be paid if this would result in the company's being unable to pay its debts as they fall due.[79] To this overriding condition of solvency all the following rules are subject.

(2) Losses of fixed assets need not be made good before treating a revenue profit as available for dividend,[80] and it is not legally essential

---

[75] (1889) 41 Ch.D. 1, C.A.
[76] At p. 21. The extent to which Lindley's view recoiled from that previously held will be apparent from the following quotation from his judgment (at pp. 22–24). "The Companies Acts do not require the capital to be made up if lost. . . . I cannot find anything in them which precludes payment of dividends so long as the assets are of less value than the original capital. . . . It appears to me that the proposition that it is *ultra vires* to pay dividends out of capital is very apt to mislead, and must not be understood in such a way as to prohibit honest trading." This may be contrasted with the dictum of Jessel M.R. cited above. Lindley, of course, always regarded company law as a branch of the law of partnership, and was therefore the more likely to leave matters in the hands of the proprietors and their advisers.
[77] Companies Act 1948, Sched. 8, which lays down that the accounts must distinguish between "fixed," "current" and other assets. But *quaere* whether the Act's (and the accountant's) "current assets" are quite the same as the judge's "circulating capital."
[78] As Yamey (*loc. cit.*) points out, nearly all the decisions were strongly criticised in the pages of the contemporary *Accountant*, and *Ammonia Soda Co.* v. *Chamberlain* (below) was decided in defiance of the evidence of an eminent accountant that the argument which prevailed was " contrary to all principles of commercial accounting."
[79] For an entertaining illustration, see the N. Irish case of *Peter Buchanan Ltd.* v. *McVey* (1950) reported at [1955] A.C. 516n., 521–522.
[80] *Lee* v. *Neuchatel Asphalte Co., supra*; *Bolton* v. *Natal Land and Colonisation Co.* [1892] 2 Ch. 124; *Verner* v. *General & Commercial Investment Trust* [1894] 2 Ch. 239, C.A.; *Re Kingston Cotton Mill Co. (No. 2)* [1896] 1 Ch. 331; [1896] 2 Ch. 279, C.A.; but see *Bond* v. *Barrow Haematite Steel Co.* [1902] 1 Ch. 353.

to make any provision for depreciation.[81]   The Jenkins Committee recommended that this should be necessary in the case of wasting assets, with a limited exception for existing companies,[82] but that there should be no general statutory obligation to make good capital losses before distributing revenue profits.[83]

(3) Losses of circulating assets in the current accounting period must be made good, however, for otherwise there is no profit. This is conceded in all the cases,[84] but seems to be true only if " circulating assets " is defined very narrowly so as to embrace only the stock-in-trade in the strictest sense.[85]   So far as other current assets are concerned it is neither accounting practice, nor, it is thought, legally necessary, to debit a fall in value to the profit and loss account.[86]

(4) A realised profit on the sale of fixed assets, may be treated as a profit available for dividend, at any rate if there is an overall surplus of fixed and circulating assets over liabilities.[87]   Whether it is then necessary to revalue *all* fixed assets is not clear, but accountants take the view that it is.[88]   The Jenkins Committee recommended that the profit should be distributable only if the directors are satisfied that the net value of the assets remaining will not be less than the book value.[89]

(5) Regarding the position of unrealised capital profits on a revaluation of assets, there is a conflict of views between the Scottish and the English courts. The former decided that such a profit was not distributable although it could be used to pay up a bonus issue.[90]   But, in England, Buckley J. expressly dissented from this view and held that unrealised profits can be distributed by way of a dividend or used

---

81 And if an allowance is made for depreciation and the directors are satisfied that the actual value of the assets in question is in excess of the depreciated value shown in the books, they may write back the appropriate part of the depreciation and thus increase the profits available for dividend : *Ammonia Soda Co.* v. *Chamberlain* [1918] 1 Ch. 266, C.A. ; *Stapley* v. *Read Bros. Ltd.* [1924] 2 Ch. 1.

82 Cmnd. 1749, paras. 349 and 350 (i).

83 *Ibid.* para. 340.

84 See especially *Re National Bank of Wales* [1899] 2 Ch. 629, C.A. ; *sub nom. Dovey* v. *Cory* [1901] A.C. 477, H.L.   This is the only case that went to the House of Lords, but the opinions delivered there did little more than to deprecate the attempt to lay down fixed rules and to reveal some misgiving as to the prevailing trend of the decisions. The effect of rules (2) and (3) was said by Lindley L.J. ([1894] 2 Ch. at p. 266) to be that " fixed capital may be sunk and lost and yet the excess of current receipts over current payments may be divided, but that floating or circulating capital must be kept up, as otherwise it will enter into and form part of such excess, in which case to divide such excess without deducting the capital which forms part of it will be contrary to law." *Bond* v. *Barrow Haematite Steel Co., supra,* may be regarded as having been decided on rule (3) but *quaere* whether the losses were in fact of circulating capital as Farwell J. thought.

85 See Swinfen Eady L.J. in *Ammonia Soda Co.* v. *Chamberlain* [1918] 1 Ch. at p. 286.

86 See Companies Act 1948, Sched. 8, para. 11 (7), which merely provides that if the directors consider that any current assets would not realise their book value a statement to that effect must be annexed to the published balance sheet.

87 *Lubbock* v. *British Bank of S. America* [1892] 2 Ch. 198 ; *Foster* v. *New Trinidad Co.* [1901] 1 Ch. 208.

88 A similar view was taken by the Royal Commission on the Taxation of Profits and Income : Cmd. 9474 of 1955, para. 805.

89 Cmnd. 1749, para. 350 (a).

90 *Westburn Sugar Refineries* v. *I.R.C.,* 1960 S.L.T. 297 ; [1960] T.R. 105.

to pay up a bonus issue.[91] The Jenkins Committee recommended that this dispute should be resolved by banning the distribution of such profits,[92] but permitting them to be used to support a bonus issue of fully paid shares.[93] They pointed out that the latter was unobjectionable since it merely increased the capital yardstick without the company parting with any assets.[94] This solution is certainly in accordance with common sense and business practice.

(6) Losses, even revenue losses on circulating assets, made in previous accounting periods need not be made good; a dividend can be paid provided there is a profit on the year's trading.[95] In other words, each accounting period is treated in isolation and, once losses have been made and the capital fund thus reduced, creditors have no right to insist that future receipts shall be appropriated to its replacement.[96] The Jenkins Committee unequivocally recommended the abrogation of this rule in relation to losses on revenue account.[97] Certainly its result is largely to destroy the whole purpose of the concept of capital as a measure of net assets which must be maintained; it has ceased to be a permanent yardstick and become one which fluctuates year by year. The company can, it seems, resume payment of dividends without a formal reduction of capital. But there are advantages in reducing since it enables the balance sheet to present a less unfavourable picture, and the same amount to be distributed but expressed as a higher percentage rate. It may also enable the company to issue further shares of a class previously quoted at a discount; indeed, without a reduction it may be difficult even to raise capital by an issue of preference shares having priority to those already existing, for investors have an irrational dislike of investing in a company with shares quoted below par even though the preference issue might be well covered by assets and earnings.

(7) If past losses do not have to be taken into account one might have supposed that past profits could not be brought forward. This, however, is not so. Undistributed profits of past years remain profits which can be distributed in future years [98] unless and until they are capitalised by using them to pay up a bonus issue. This, however,

---

[91] *Dimbula Valley (Ceylon) Tea Co.* v. *Laurie* [1961] Ch. 353.
[92] Cmnd. 1749, paras. 336 and 337. But they would have permitted a distribution of assets in specie such as shares in another company since this was equivalent to a realisation: *ibid.* para. 338.
[93] *Ibid.* para. 338.
[94] *Ibid.* para. 338.
[95] *Re National Bank of Wales, supra.* In the House of Lords, *sub nom. Dovey* v. *Cory*, Lord Davey expressed doubts on this proposition: [1901] A.C. 477 at p. 493, and these doubts were supported by Farwell J. in *Bond* v. *Barrow Haematite Steel Co., supra.* However, the validity of the rule was fully supported by the C.A. in *Ammonia Soda Co.* v. *Chamberlain, supra.*
[96] Payments in such circumstances are described in American parlance as " nimble dividends."
[97] Cmnd. 1749, paras. 341 and 350 (c).
[98] *Re Hoare & Co. Ltd.* [1904] 2 Ch. 208, C.A.

does not apply to undistributed profits of the business made before it was acquired by the company. On normal accounting principles these are capital so far as the company is concerned. The legal profession is divided on how rigidly this rule need be observed, but the Jenkins Committee strongly reaffirmed it, subject only to a modest concession to aid reconstructions and amalgamations.[99]

The foregoing rules attempt to state the strict legal position. In practice the position is already much as the Jenkins Committee wish it to be. For this there are a number of reasons. The accounts of the company must not be presented in such a way as to give a false picture of the company's position. This matter is dealt with in more detail in a later chapter.[1] Here it is sufficient to point out that section 149 of the Act specifically declares that " every balance sheet of a company shall give a true and fair view of the state of affairs of the company as at the end of its financial year,[2] and every profit and loss account shall give a true and fair view of the profit and loss of the company for the financial year." Hence, Lord Lindley's dictum [3] that, " If your earnings are less than your current expenses, you must not cook your accounts so as to make it appear that you are earning a profit," [4] is an understatement. You must not cook your accounts at all; for example, to make it appear that you are earning less profits (this is a more likely eventuality under present conditions which may lead the management to wish to present the company to the Revenue, to its workers, and to its members as less affluent than it really is). Moreover, the Act now lays down in some detail how the accounts are to be prepared and what facts are to be stated therein. This in itself acts as a deterrent against over-liberal distributions; directors who might have been prepared to recommend a dividend, although no provision had been made for past losses and depreciation, when the laconic published accounts did not make this plain, will hesitate to do so when the full position is apparent and open for criticism in the financial press and elsewhere. Further, a professional audit of the accounts is now compulsory,[5] and the auditors must certify that in their opinion the provisions of the Act have been complied with.[6] This, too, has a powerfully restraining influence, particularly as accounting practice is considerably stricter than the law

---

[99] Cmnd. 1749, paras. 342–348 and 350 (d)–(h).

[1] Chap. 20, *infra.*

[2] These words ought to make it impossible to support the view, formerly held, that a balance sheet is an historical account only and that it need only give an accurate picture of the past. Nevertheless, they do not appear to have had much effect on accounting practice regarding valuations, which, so far at any rate as fixed assets are concerned, remain on the purely historical basis of cost minus depreciation, which may bear little relation to value as at the end of the current financial year.

[3] (1889) 41 Ch.D. at p. 25.

[4] It will be appreciated that if the accounts as presented to the members are misleading, their ratification of the directors' recommendation to pay a dividend cannot be treated as evidence of men of business that there are distributable profits.

[5] See Chap. 20.

[6] See Chap. 20.

seems to be. Dividend restraint is also encouraged by the provisions for corporation tax (except in the case of close companies)[7] and by the Prices and Incomes Act 1966.[8]

Finally, it must always be borne in mind that although nothing in the memorandum or articles can widen the rules summarised above so as to authorise payment of dividends out of capital, provisions in these documents may narrow these rules by restricting the type of profits which may be distributed. Thus it is not uncommon for articles to provide that dividends shall only be paid " out of the *profits of the business.*" Such a provision will apparently preclude payments except out of profits on revenue account as opposed to a profit on fixed assets.[9]

Companies limited by guarantee

Since 1900 precisely similar rules apply to the raising and maintenance of the share capital of such guarantee companies as have a share capital.[10] But most guarantee companies have none, and in their case the only " guarantee fund " consists of the amounts which the members have undertaken to contribute in the event of a liquidation, these amounts corresponding to the uncalled liability of a company limited by shares.[11]

One would, therefore, expect to find that it is impossible for members to reduce this guarantee fund by retiring from the company, for this, of course, is subject to precisely the same objections as a reduction of uncalled capital. Strangely enough, however, it is far from clear that this is the law. It is true that the model articles for a guarantee company in Table C contain no provisions for retirement, and, in the absence of such provisions, withdrawal, except presumably by death, seems to be impossible. On the other hand, the wording of the Act[12] and of the model memorandum in Table C[13] implies that a member may " cease to be a member," and companies are certainly formed with articles which provide for retirement,[14] and the decided cases assume that these provisions are valid.[15]

It is a strange anomaly that the courts have never extended to companies limited by guarantee the rules for protecting creditors by

[7] See Chap. 9.
[8] See especially s. 12.
[9] *Wall* v. *London & Provincial Trust Ltd.* [1920] 1 Ch. 45; [1920] 2 Ch. 582, C.A. *Cf.* " realised profits " considered in *Re Oxford Benefit Building & Investment Society* (1886) 35 Ch.D. 502.
[10] See now Companies Act 1948, ss. 2 (4) (*a*), 21 (2), 212 (3).
[11] *Ibid.* ss. 1 (2) (*b*) and 212 (1) (*e*).
[12] See s. 212 regulating the liability of a " past member."
[13] Under cl. 5 of which the member undertakes to contribute if the company is wound up " while he is a member or within one year afterwards."
[14] For a precedent of such articles, see Palmer, *Company Precedents*, 17th ed., Pt. I, Form 186.
[15] *Baird's Case* [1899] 2 Ch. 593; *Re Premier Underwriting Asscn. Ltd. (No.* 1) [1913] 2 Ch. 29. This is certainly the view taken by the Board of Trade.

which they have set such store in the case of companies limited by shares. It would still be open to them to do so—for the point never seems to have been considered by an appellate court—but if they do some provision ought to be made for authorising the retirement of a member if someone else takes his place with the directors' approval. In the absence of such a provision the lot of a guarantor member would be far worse than that of a shareholder, for he would have no means of escaping liability by transferring. But it must be admitted that the question is of theoretical interest rather than of practical importance, for the guarantee, which is always purely nominal, has no real business significance.

Conclusions

To sum up, therefore, we may say that the law tries to ensure that a company with a share capital raises it and subsequently makes no return to its shareholders unless net assets are retained which equal or exceed the value of that capital. The fund of credit thus created acts as a substitute for the personal credit of a private trader or partnership and enables the company to have a chance of survival in the harshly competitive world of commerce. In particular it enables it to expand its capital by borrowings on the strength of its fund of credit; that is, to raise *loan capital* to supplement its share capital. As we have seen, thanks to the debenture conferring a floating charge a company is in fact in a stronger position than an individual or partnership in raising additional resources in this way. In law, however, loan capital is fundamentally different from share capital; it is a legally enforceable debt and not a mere book-keeping entry. It, too, will appear on the liabilities side of the balance sheet (it is a true liability not a mere balancing item) and it may be made perpetual [16] so that it, too, will not be repayable while the company remains a going concern. But this is about all that it will, in law, have in common with share capital, and none of the rules relating to the raising and maintenance of capital will apply to it. Debentures may be issued at a discount,[17] interest on them must be paid irrespective of whether there are profits, and, unless specifically made perpetual, they are repayable like any other loan. Indeed, the rules applying to share capital are largely designed precisely for the purpose of protecting the debenture holders.

The weakness of the legal rules relating to the raising and maintenance of share capital is caused mainly by four factors:

(1) There is no requirement that shares must be of a reasonable nominal value and that part of this value must be left uncalled. Hence

---

[16] Companies Act 1948, s. 89.
[17] But a provision that they are *immediately* convertible into shares at par will be invalid as an attempt to issue the shares at a discount: *Moseley* v. *Koffyfontein Mines* [1904] 2 Ch. 108, C.A. See, further, Chap. 16, p. 357, note 63.

the practice is to have shares of low denomination issued fully paid on allotment. Uncalled capital, which was envisaged as the main protection of the creditor, has virtually disappeared, thus removing any element of personal credit from the concept of capital.

(2) There is equally no requirement of a minimum paid up capital. Hence the rules which seek to secure the maintenance of paid up capital are valueless except in the case of large public companies. With private companies having small issued capital no reliance whatever can be placed on the capital as a guarantee fund. Indeed, this is recognised in practice, and such companies are treated much as partnerships, the members being required personally to guarantee any formal credit facilities. Even in the case of a public company a yardstick based on the nominal value of money is unrealistic in times of inflation.

(3) Since shares may be issued for a consideration other than cash, and since the courts will not normally investigate the adequacy of the consideration, there is not even any assurance that the company ever received assets equivalent to the nominal value of its issued capital.

(4) Even if the capital has been raised, the law cannot ensure that it is not lost in subsequent trading; at the most it can prevent its being repaid to the members. This the rules seek to accomplish, but they prevent only an open return of capital and have not been effective in preventing payment of dividends until past losses have been recouped.[18]

It is clearly desirable that the legal position should be reformed on the lines suggested by the Jenkins Committee.

No-par-value shares

It will have been apparent from the foregoing discussion that the main reason why share capital has come to have an artificial meaning is because of the insistence that shares shall be given a fixed nominal value. This nominal value need not represent their true worth even at the time of issue, and it is highly unlikely to do so after the company has been trading for some time. The fact that a share merely represents,

---

[18] There is also procedural weakness for it seems that creditors, at any rate unless they have a security which is jeopardised, cannot apply to restrain the company from paying a dividend out of capital: *Mills* v. *Northern Ry. of Buenos Ayres*, L.R. 5 Ch.App. 621; *Lawrence* v. *W. Somerset Mineral Ry.* [1918] 2 Ch. 250. The law is not entirely clear (see *Flitcroft's Case* (1882) 21 Ch.D. at p. 530, C.A. and *Coxon* v. *Gorst* [1891] 2 Ch. 73), but in practice unsecured creditors can only put the company into liquidation leaving the liquidator to bring misfeasance proceedings against the directors (as in *Re Sharpe, Re Bennett* [1892] 1 Ch. 154, C.A.) which smacks of locking the door after the horse has escaped. When an order has been made against the directors (and it will only be made against such of them as have personally broken their duties of good faith and due care—on which see Chap. 23: *Dovey* v. *Cory* [1901] A.C. 477, H.L.)—it is usual to reserve any rights they may have against the shareholders who have received any part of the capital wrongfully paid. But it seems that this right is enforceable only against such shareholders as have participated with knowledge of the wrong: *Moxham* v. *Grant* [1900] 1 Q.B. 88, C.A.

as its name implies, an aliquot part or share of the company's under-taking is obscured by the arbitrary and misleading monetary symbol attached to it. Nor is nominal value any longer the decisive factor in fixing the capital yardstick; of greater importance is the issue price, as the rules relating to share premiums now recognise.

Hence, some states, notably in the U.S.A., have for many years permitted the issue of shares of no-par-value; that is to say, the under-taking is divided into a certain number of shares, each representing a fraction of the whole share capital, the value of which will fluctuate with the value of the whole undertaking without this being obscured (as with par shares) by the attachment of a nominal par value. Until after the last war there was little public demand for the introduction of no-par shares in England [19]; the untutored people who have been misled into supposing that a £1 share is cheap if it can be bought on the market for 1s. and expensive if it costs 30s. were not sufficiently organised or influential to produce any audible outcry. In recent years, however, companies have found that a fixed nominal capital leads to ignorant criticism of the extent of their profits, which appear excessive in comparison with that capital, although fair enough in comparison with the true capital employed. And they have also found themselves subject both to criticism and, at times, to restraint and penal taxes when they sought to adjust the nominal capital to a more realistic figure by making bonus issues.

In 1954 the Gedge Committee [20] reported in favour of the legalisation of no-par equity shares,[21] but no action was taken, perhaps because the trade union movement was hostile.[22] By the time of the Jenkins Report that hostility had ceased and the Committee recommended legalisation of no-par for all types of shares.[23] An attempt to introduce legislative provisions to this effect into what became the Companies Act 1967 was unavailing, but they will presumably appear in the next, long-postponed, Bill. The case for no-par shares is a strong one. Their introduction need not lead to a weakening of any of the safeguards afforded by the present rules about the raising and maintaining capital. One expression (" stated capital " is the usual term) would be substituted for paid-up capital and share premium account, and this would set the capital yardstick and would not be reduced when redeemable preference shares were redeemed, thus also eradicating the unhappily named " capital redemption reserve fund." However, it is very doubtful whether much would be achieved if they were merely introduced on an optional basis. The real case for no-par is that it renders the true nature of a

---

[19] See, for example, the Cohen Report (Cmd. 6659), para. 18. It was at one time possible to have a guarantee company with a share capital of no-par value but this is now prevented by ss. 2 (4) (*a*) and 21 (2).

[20] Appointed to consider this one topic.

[21] Cmd. 9112.

[22] The T.U.C. representative on the Gedge Committee had dissented.

[23] Cmnd. 1749, paras. 32–34.

share more intelligible and prevents people from being misled.[24] If merely optional, the public will have to learn to understand both par and no-par, which will continue indefinitely to exist side by side causing greater confusion. And unscrupulous company promoters will continue to mislead by the use of par shares.[25] It hardly seems worthwhile at this late hour to introduce no-par shares (which will involve consequential amendments to the Companies Act and other legislation, notably the Finance Acts) unless no-par shares are made compulsory.[26]

---

[24] As even judges have been: see *Re Mackenzie & Co. Ltd.* [1916] 2 Ch. 450.
[25] For example, as in one actual case, by describing shares as 9½ per cent. £1 Preference Shares and issuing them at 25s. (and with only "the capital paid up thereon," *i.e.*, £1, repayable on a winding up).
[26] As in Ghana: Companies Code 1963 (Act 179), s. 40.

CHAPTER 7

THE COMPANY'S ORGANS AND OFFICERS

IT will have been apparent from the preceding chapters that the legal position of unincorporated associations depends largely on the law of agency.[1] Especially is this so in connection with partnerships in which each partner automatically becomes the agent of the others and, as a necessary result, stands in a fiduciary position towards his co-partners.

The law of agency is equally at the root of company law. Since the company is an artificial person it can act only through the agency of natural persons.[2] But agency principles have undergone a number of modifications in their application to companies. The present chapter discusses the nature and means of appointment of these agencies and the relationship between them. Detailed consideration of their means of functioning and of the duties which they owe to the company and its members is left for later consideration.[3]

How a company's agents are appointed

The application of agency principles to companies meets an initial difficulty: since the company is an artificial person how is it to appoint its agents? This problem does not arise in connection with unincorporated societies for the question there is simply whether the members (natural persons) have appointed other natural persons as their agents. But, with a corporation, it is the incorporated company, not its members, which is the principal and somehow certain acts have to be regarded as those of the company itself if only in order to enable it to appoint agents. The early law of corporations seems to have tried to avoid this logical dilemma by a resort to formalism—the acts of the corporation were those which were authenticated by its common seal. This, however, merely begged the question without solving it, for someone had to affix the seal and if it was affixed without lawful authority the corporation would not be bound. Moreover the insistence on the use of a seal which was only appropriate to contractual liability was, even there, totally unworkable under modern conditions and has

---

[1] See also Chap. 11, *infra*, where the legal position of such associations is considered in more detail.

[2] " The company itself cannot act in its own person, for it has no person; it can only act through directors and the case is, as regards those directors, merely the ordinary case of principal and agent ": *per* Cairns L.J. in *Ferguson* v. *Wilson* (1866) L.R. 2 Ch. at p. 89. The word " person " is, of course, here used in its popular and not in its technical legal sense.

[3] See Part V, especially Chaps. 21–24.

now been abrogated generally [4] after its earlier repeal in relation to statutory [5] and registered [6] companies.

Hence a more satisfactory solution was found by regarding the decisions of the majority of the members of the company in general meeting [7] as the acts of the company itself.[8] But this rule too has had to be supplemented since it is quite impossible for day-to-day decisions to be taken in general meeting. In practice the initial constitution of the company will provide for the appointment of a board of directors and expressly delegate all powers of management to them,[9] and they in turn are generally empowered to sub-delegate to a committee or managing director.[10] In such circumstances the theory seems to be that the company, as such, has, in its constitution, appointed its agents and clothed them with authority; the act which gives birth *to* the company operates as an appointment and delegation *by* the company.

It will be observed that authority to exercise the company's powers is delegated, not to the members, nor even to the individual directors, but only to the directors as a board, although it may, as we shall see, be sub-delegated by the board to individual managing directors and to other officers. Between the company and the board and the officers there is an agency relationship, but there is none between the company and the members or between the members *inter se*. This is in marked contrast with the partnership in which each member becomes an agent of the others. The absence of any such relationship in the case of a company is one of its distinctive features and one which is essential if the public company is to perform its economic role.

The board of directors

All registered companies must now have directors and normally there must be at least two, though one suffices for a private company or one

---

[4] Corporate Bodies Contracts Act 1960.
[5] Companies Clauses Consolidation Act 1845, s. 97.
[6] Now Companies Act 1948, s. 32.
[7] The functioning of general meetings is described in Chap. 21.
[8] *Per* Hardwicke L.C. in *Att.-Gen.* v. *Davy* (1741) 2 Atk. 212: "It cannot be disputed that wherever a certain number are incorporated a major part of them may do any corporate act; so if all are summoned, and part appear, a major part of those that appear may do a corporate act . . . it is not necessary that every corporate act should be under the seal of the corporation. . . ." This principle is at the root of the rule in *Foss* v. *Harbottle* (1843) 2 Hare 461 (see Chap. 25, p. 581 *et seq.*) in which Wigram V.-C. (at p. 493) referred to the members in general meetings as "the supreme governing body." But when a contract requires the common seal even a resolution in general meeting will not do instead: *Dunston* v. *Imperial Gas Co.* (1831) 3 B. & Ald. 125. It seems that in the absence of express provision majority rule does not prevail in unincorporated associations: *Torquay Hotel Co. Ltd.* v. *Cousins* [1969] 2 W.L.R. 289, C.A.
[9] Companies Clauses Consolidation Act 1845, s. 90; Companies Act 1948, Table A, arts. 75, 79 and 80.
[10] Companies Act 1948, Table A, arts. 102, 107 and 109. The Companies Clauses Act 1845 merely authorises delegation to committees (s. 95) and provides that the office of a director shall be vacated if he holds any office of profit under the company: ss. 85 and 86.

registered before 1929.[11]   The company must publicise the names of its directors at the Companies Registry and at its registered office,[12] and on its letter-heading.[13]

The Act says little about the means of appointing these directors, leaving this to the articles of association.   In practice, these provide for initial appointment by the subscribers to the memorandum [14] (unless actually named in the articles) and thereafter for an annual retirement of a certain proportion and for the filling of the vacancies at the annual general meeting.[15]   The Act [16] does provide that each appointment shall be voted on individually except in the case of a private company or unless the meeting shall agree *nem. con.* that two or more shall be included in a single resolution.   There is nothing in the Act to provide that an ordinary resolution suffices to elect a director, but this is the normal practice.[17]   However appointed, a director can always be removed by ordinary resolution [18] in addition to any other means of removal that may be provided in the articles.[19]   However, it is not uncommon for certain directors not to retire by rotation but to be appointed for life, or for as long as they hold some other office,[20] but these, too, can now be removed by ordinary resolution.[21]

It will therefore be appreciated that a member holding 51 per cent. of the voting shares can be sure of electing the whole of the board or, at any rate, of having a veto over the constitution of the whole of the board.   There is, in England, nothing comparable to the system of cumulative voting [22] which is optional or compulsory in most American states and which secures something like proportional representation. But this system has now been extended, on an optional basis, to some Commonwealth countries [23] with Companies Acts based on the English model, and it seems probable that its introduction here may be advocated in due course.

---

[11] Companies Act 1948, s. 176.   The Jenkins Committee recommended that a minimum of two should be required in all cases: Cmnd. 1749, para. 25.

[12] s. 200.

[13] s. 201.   But see subs. 2 (*a*) as regards pre-1917 companies.

[14] *Cf.* Table A, art. 75.

[15] *Ibid.* arts. 89–94.   It is customary to empower the directors themselves to fill a casual vacancy and to appoint additional directors within the maximum prescribed by the articles (*ibid.* art. 95), which maximum can usually be modified by ordinary resolution (*ibid.* art. 94).   Normally directors appointed by the board come up for re-election at the next A.G.M. (*ibid.* art. 95).

[16] s. 183.   This is designed to prevent the members being faced with the alternative of either accepting or rejecting the whole of a slate of nominees.

[17] Table A, art. 92.   [18] s. 184.   See *infra*, p. 133 *et seq.*

[19] These may, for example, empower certain of the directors to remove others: see *Bersel Manufacturing Co. Ltd.* v. *Berry* [1968] 2 All E.R. 552, H.L.

[20] *e.g.*, that of managing director: see Table A, art. 107.

[21] Except a life director of a private company holding office on July 18, 1945 (the date of publication of the Cohen Report): s. 184 (1).

[22] There is considerable American literature on this: see especially C. M. Williams, *Cumulative Voting for Directors* (1951, Harvard), and (1955) 33 Harv.Bus.Rev. 108, (1955) 11 *The Business Lawyer* 9; 1968 Duke L.J. 28.   Under the system a holder of, say, one-third of the voting shares can elect at least one-third of the board.

[23] *e.g.*, India, Ontario and Ghana.

Unless the articles so provide directors need not be members of the company. Formerly it was customary so to provide,[24] but now the possibility of a complete separation of " proprietors " and " managers " is recognised and Table A no longer requires a share qualification.[25] If, however, one is needed under the articles, the shares must be taken up within two months and the office will be vacated if they are not, or if they are later relinquished.[26]

Undischarged bankrupts commit a criminal offence if they act as directors without leave of the court,[27] and the court may restrain those convicted of certain offences involving fraud from acting as directors or taking part in the management of companies for a period not exceeding five years.[28] Further, articles commonly provide for the vacation of office by directors in certain events, including their resignation, prolonged absence from board meetings, or insanity.[29] The Cohen Committee also tried to ensure that directors should normally retire when they attained the age of seventy,[30] but as finally enacted this provision is so riddled with exceptions that it has proved of little value.[31]

It should perhaps be pointed out that a director need not be a natural person: another company may be appointed [32] and this device is sometimes found useful to enable a holding company to maintain complete control of a subsidiary.

Sometimes the articles entitle a director to appoint an alternate director to act for him at any board meeting that he is unable to attend. The extent of the alternate's powers and the answer to such questions as whether he is entitled to remuneration from the company or from the director appointing him will then depend on the terms of the relevant article. Some doubts have been expressed regarding the exact status of alternate directors and it was suggested to the Jenkins Committee that their position should be regulated in the Act. However the Committee thought this unnecessary as they were satisfied that he was " in the eyes

---

[24] Companies Clauses Act 1845, s. 85; Companies Act 1929, Table A, art. 66.
[25] Table A, art. 77.
[26] s. 12. The two month period runs from the declaration of the result of the vote electing the director: *Holmes* v. *Keyes* [1959] Ch. 199, C.A.
[27] s. 187.
[28] s. 188. For the flaws in this section, see Cmnd. 1749, paras. 80 and 81. Note that the period of disqualification must date from the conviction, not from the end of the prison sentence: *R.* v. *Bradley* [1961] 1 W.L.R. 398, C.C.A.
[29] Table A, art. 88. But except as authorised by the articles the directors cannot exclude one of their number from the board and can be restrained by injunction from so doing (at any rate if the directorship carries fees): *Hayes* v. *Bristol Plant Hire Ltd.* [1957] 1 W.L.R. 499.
[30] Cmd. 6659, para. 131.
[31] s. 185. Note that the age limit does not apply to private companies unless subsidiaries of public ones (subs. (8)), that it can be excluded by the articles (subs. (7)), and that an over-age director can always be appointed if " special notice " (see *infra*, p. 133) is given (subs. (5)). The Jenkins Committee recommended a simplification of these complicated provisions: Cmnd. 1749, paras. 79 and 85 (a).
[32] This is now forbidden in certain other countries of the Commonwealth and the Jenkins Committee recommended that it should be banned here: Cmnd. 1749, para. 84.

of the law in the same position as any other director." [33]　　The Committee also thought it unnecessary to do anything about the growing and potentially misleading practice of giving employees status without responsibility by appointing them " special " or " associate " directors. [34]

Division of powers between the general meeting and the board

The development referred to above raises the question of the true nature of the relationship between the company in general meeting and the board of directors.　Until at least the end of the nineteenth century it seems to have been generally assumed that the principle remained intact that the general meeting *was* the company whereas the directors were merely the *agents* of the company subject to the control of the company in general meeting.　Thus in *Isle of Wight Ry.* v. *Tahourdin* [35] the court refused an application by the directors of a statutory company for an injunction to restrain the holding of a general meeting, one purpose of which was to appoint a committee to reorganise the management of the company.　Cotton L.J. said [36]:

> " It is a very strong thing indeed to prevent shareholders from holding a meeting of the company, when such a meeting is the only way in which they can interfere, if the majority of them think that the course taken by the directors, in a matter *intra vires* of the directors, is not for the benefit of the company."

In 1906, however, the Court of Appeal, in *Automatic Self-Cleansing Filter Syndicate Co.* v. *Cuninghame*, [37] made it clear that the division of powers between the board and the company in general meeting depended in the case of registered companies entirely on the construction of the articles of association and that where powers had been vested in the board the general meeting could not interfere with their exercise. The relevant article in that case provided that the management of the company should be vested in the directors who might exercise all powers of the company which were not by the statutes or the articles expressly required to be exercised by the company in general meeting; " But subject nevertheless to the provisions of the statutes and of these presents, and to such regulations, not being inconsistent with these presents, as may from time to time be made by extraordinary resolution. . . ." The articles were held to constitute a contract by which the members had agreed that " the directors and the directors alone shall manage." [38]　Unless and until their powers were curtailed by extra-

---

[33] Cmnd. 1749, para. 83.
[34] *Ibid.* para. 82.　One difficulty, as they pointed out, was that it would be necessary to make exceptions for descriptions such as " director of research."
[35] (1883) 25 Ch.D. 320, C.A.
[36] At p. 329.
[37] [1906] 2 Ch. 34, C.A.
[38] *Per* Cozens-Hardy L.J. at p. 44.　The doctrine that the memorandum and articles constitute a contract between the members is dealt with in Chap. 12, *infra*, p. 261 *et seq.*　Lindley L.J., as he so often did, relied on partnership principles

ordinary resolution or an alteration of the articles they could ignore resolutions of the general meeting on matters of management. Hence the directors were entitled to refuse to carry out a sale agreement adopted by ordinary resolution in general meeting. *Tahourdin's* case was distinguished on the ground that the wording of section 90 of the Companies Clauses Act 1845 was different—though that section does not in fact seem to have been relied on in the earlier case.

The new approach, though cited with apparent approval by a differently constituted Court of Appeal in 1908,[39] did not secure immediate acceptance and in a case a year later [40] it was suggested that the decision in *Cuninghame's* case depended on the reference in the relevant article to an extraordinary resolution. In later cases, however, the relevant article has been equivalent to article 80 of the present Table A which provides as follows:

> "The business of the company shall be managed by the directors who . . . may exercise all such powers of the company as are not, by the Act or by these regulations, required to be exercised by the company in general meeting, subject, nevertheless, to any of these regulations, to the provisions of the Act and to such regulations, being not inconsistent with the aforesaid regulations or provisions, as may be prescribed by the company in general meeting. . . ."

Since *Quin & Axtens* v. *Salmon* [41] it has been clearly established that where this formula is employed, as it invariably is in practice, the general meeting cannot interfere with a decision of the directors unless they are acting contrary to the provisions of the Act or the articles. The final words of article 80 seem to have been deprived of any meaning.[42]

In *Shaw & Sons (Salford) Ltd.* v. *Shaw*,[43] in which a resolution of the general meeting disapproving the commencement of an action by the directors was held to be a nullity, the modern doctrine was expressed by Greer L.J. as follows [44]:

and argued that the position of the directors was analogous to that of a partner to whom all powers of management were delegated by the partnership deed and with whom the court would therefore not interfere. Weight was also placed on the fact that it would have required a special resolution to remove the directors; having regard to s. 184 of the 1948 Act this argument no longer has any validity.

[39] *Gramophone & Typewriter Ltd.* v. *Stanley* [1908] 2 K.B. 89, C.A.; see especially *per* Fletcher Moulton L.J. at p. 98 and *per* Buckley L.J. at pp. 105–106 (despite the fact that the then current edition of his book took the opposite view).

[40] *Marshall's Valve Gear Co* v. *Manning Wardle & Co.* [1909] 1 Ch. 267.

[41] [1909] 1 Ch. 311, C.A.; [1909] A.C. 442, H.L.

[42] Loreburn L.C. discussed this difficulty and inclined to the view that "regulations" throughout the article meant "articles": [1909] A.C. at p. 444. If that is correct the final words are tautologous. In *Scott* v. *Scott, infra,* Lord Clauson said that if an ordinary resolution of the general meeting could be regarded as a "regulation" within the meaning of those words it would be ineffective as "inconsistent with the aforesaid regulations"—which equally deprives the words of meaning. Possibly "regulations," when it first appears, means the existing articles and, when used in the final phrase, means any new articles adopted by special resolution.

[43] [1935] 2 K.B. 113, C.A.   [44] At p. 134.

" A company is an entity distinct alike from its shareholders and its directors. Some of its powers may, according to its articles, be exercised by directors, certain other powers may be reserved for the shareholders in general meeting. If powers of management are vested in the directors, they and they alone can exercise these powers. The only way in which the general body of the shareholders can control the exercise of the powers vested by the articles in the directors is by altering their articles, or, if opportunity arises under the articles, by refusing to re-elect the directors of whose actions they disapprove.[45] They cannot themselves usurp the powers which by the articles are vested in the directors any more than the directors can usurp the powers vested by the articles in the general body of shareholders."

Finally, in *Scott* v. *Scott* [46] it was held, on the same grounds, that resolutions of a general meeting, which might be interpreted either as directions to pay an interim dividend or as instructions to make loans, were nullities. In either event the relative powers had been delegated by Table A to the directors,[47] and until they were taken away by an amendment of the articles the members in general meeting could not interfere with their exercise. As Lord Clauson [48] rightly said, " the professional view as to the control of the company in general meeting over the actions of directors has, over a period of years, undoubtedly varied." [49]

The modern rule, therefore, is that under an article in the terms of Table A the members in general meeting cannot give directions on how the company's affairs are to be managed, nor can they overrule any decision come to by the directors in the conduct of its business. And this applies even as regards matters not specifically delegated to the directors provided they are not expressly reserved to a general meeting by the Act or the articles.[50] As the appropriate article is invariably in the terms of Table A this means that the old idea that the general meeting *is* the company whereas the board of directors are merely *agents* requires modification. It seems that both the general meeting and the board may be the company; the former when acting under the reserved powers, the latter when acting under an express or general delegation. Or, to put it in another way, both the general meeting and the board are organs, rather than agents, of the company; this, as we shall see in

---

45 They can now remove the directors by ordinary resolution: Companies Act 1948, s. 184, *infra*.
46 [1943] 1 All E.R. 582. See also the review of the cases by Plowman J. in *Bamford* v. *Bamford* [1968] 3 W.L.R. 317; affd. [1969] 2 W.L.R. 1107, C.A.
47 Expressly in the case of interim dividends (Table A, art. 115) and under the general delegation (art. 80) in the case of loans.
48 At p. 585D. Lord Clauson was sitting as a judge of the Ch.D.
49 This is very clearly seen if the judgments in the above cases are compared with that in *Foss* v. *Harbottle* (1843) 2 Hare 461; see especially at pp. 492–495.
50 *Cf.* Buckley, *Companies Act* (13th ed.), p. 60, a passage specifically approved by Greer L.J. in [1935] 2 K.B. at p. 134.

the next chapter, is how the courts have sometimes described them when considering the company's liability for their acts.

In Chapter 1 the relationship between the general meeting and the directors was compared with that between the legislature and the executive. It is now apparent that this was an over-simplification. To some extent a more exact analogy would be with the division of powers between the federal and state legislatures under a federal constitution. And, as we have seen, the residual powers are in this case with the directors. This, of course, only applies to companies registered under the Companies Act. In the case of statutory companies, the older rule still prevails because of the express terms of the Companies Clauses Act.[51] The position of chartered companies will depend on the terms of their constitutions. As most of them are old creations their constitutions may well accord more with the model of the Companies Clauses Act.

Removal of directors by the general meeting

Even in the case of registered companies the general meeting has, in law, ultimately the whip-hand. Until the 1948 Act this could only be exercised by a change in the articles, or by a refusal to re-elect directors as they came up for re-election. This was a very substantial, and probably undesirable, restriction on the members' powers; a special resolution to change the articles requires a three-fourths majority of those voting,[52] and many directors held office for life so that no question of re-election arose. Hence the control by the directors might be almost complete both for the present and the future. Only if a breach could be shown of the directors' duties would the court interfere.[53]

But by section 184 of the 1948 Act a director can be removed by *ordinary* resolution at any time. This applies notwithstanding anything in its articles or in any agreement between the company and the director,[54] but does not authorise the removal of a director in a private company holding office for life on July 18, 1945.[55] Moreover, *special notice* has to be given of any such resolution,[56] that is to say, the proposer must give twenty-eight days' notice *to* the company of his intention to propose the resolution [57] and the company must supply a

[51] s. 90. But this expressly provides that the general meeting cannot " render invalid any act done by the directors prior to any resolution passed by such general meeting."   [52] 1948 Act, s. 141 (2).
[53] *Marshall's Valve Gear* v. *Manning, Wardle & Co.* [1909] 1 Ch. 267 may be explicable on this ground. The nature of these duties is considered further, *infra*, Chap. 23.
[54] But in private companies the object of the section can apparently be frustrated by an article attaching increased votes to the director's shares on a resolution to remove him (*Bushell* v. *Faith* [1969] 2 W.L.R. 1067, C.A.) or by a voting agreement: *Stewart* v. *Schwab*, 1956 (4) S.A. 791 (Trans. P.D.).
[55] The date of publication of the Cohen Report.   [56] s. 184 (2).
[57] s. 142. The company must then give notice of the resolution in the normal notice convening the meeting (normally fourteen days, but twenty-one if an annual general meeting, s. 133), or, if that is not practicable, 21 days' notice by newspaper advertisement. " Special notice " was a new development in the 1948 Act: see

copy to the director, who is entitled to be heard at the meeting.[56] Further, he may require the company to circulate any representations which he makes.[58] The object of these restrictions is to prevent a director from being deprived of an office of profit on a snap vote and without having had a full opportunity of stating his case.[59] This is fair enough.

A more serious restraint on the members' powers of dismissal is the provision that the section shall not deprive a director of any claim for compensation or damages payable in respect of the termination.[60] If there is a contract of service between him and the company, as will be the case with most managing and working directors, the probability is that the members will be able to sack him only at the risk of imposing on the company liability to pay damages. This, it may be said, is also fair, because the company has freely bound itself by contract. But so far as the entry into service agreements is concerned the company is normally the directors, for it is they who will have the power to appoint and fix the terms of service of the managing directors.[61] The members may therefore find that the directors have entrenched themselves by contracts of service, which will be broken if the general meeting exercises its powers of dismissal. Formerly the members might know nothing about these contracts but now they have to be made available for inspection by any member.[62] Moreover the board cannot generally decide without reference to the general meeting the amount to be paid to a dismissed director by way of compensation.[63]

It must be emphasised, however, that the dismissed director will have a legal claim for compensation only if he has a binding contract entitling him either to hold his position for a fixed term or to be dismissed only after a prescribed or reasonable notice. Moreover, as will be pointed out later,[64] the articles alone do not constitute a contract between the company and a director. He will have to show that there is a separate contract of service, whether formal or informal.[65] If there is such a contract, the company cannot evade its terms by altering the articles and if the alteration gives the company a power of dismissal

---

Chap. 21, pp. 480–482, *infra*. The principal cases in which it is required are on a change of directors, or of auditors: s. 160.

[58] s. 184 (3).

[59] But apparently he can be deprived of this protection if the articles contain an express power to remove a director by ordinary resolution and the company acts under that power; s. 184 (2) and (3) are expressly limited to removals " under this section."

[60] s. 184 (6).

[61] *Cf.* Table A, art. 107.

[62] Companies Act 1967, s. 26.

[63] ss. 191 and 192. See further, Chap. 23, p. 540 *et seq.*

[64] Chap. 12, p. 261 *et seq.*

[65] For the complications which are liable to occur in the latter event, see *James* v. *Kent* [1951] 1 K.B. 551, C.A., and *Pocock* v. *A.D.A.C. Ltd.* [1952] 1 All E.R. 294n.

contrary to the terms of an existing agreement, the exercise of this power will constitute a breach of contract.[66]

Hence, the assumption of control by the members in general meeting may be an expensive luxury. Article 68 of Table A of the Companies Act 1929, relating to the appointment of a managing director, concluded by saying " his appointment shall be automatically determined if he cease from any cause to be a director or if the company in general meeting resolve that his tenure of the office of managing director or manager be determined." Diplock J. in *Shindler* v. *Northern Raincoat Co. Ltd.*[67] considered the case of a managing director with a ten-year service agreement who had been removed from his office as a director by a resolution of the company in general meeting and whose tenure as managing director had accordingly ended. It was argued, principally on the authority of a decision of Harman J. at first instance in *Read* v. *Astoria Garage (Streatham) Ltd.*,[68] that the managing director had no claim for breach of contract since the agreement must be deemed to be subject to the overriding provision for lawful determination contained in the articles. Diplock J. rejected this argument stating that in his view it was inconsistent with the decision of the House of Lords in *Southern Foundries (1926) Ltd.* v. *Shirlaw*[69] where it was held that there is an implied undertaking in the contract of service of a managing director for a given period that the company will not during that period revoke his appointment as director and will not resolve that his tenure of office be determined.

However, where a managing director has an informal service agreement or one for an unspecified duration, it appears from the decision of the Court of Appeal in *Read's* case[68] that the agreement must be deemed to be on the terms of the articles with only such security of tenure as is provided for therein. This means that many informal service agreements can be ended by either party at a moment's notice without giving rise to any claim for damages. The relevant article (107) in Table A of the 1948 Act still provides that the appointment of a managing director " shall be automatically determined if he ceases from any cause to be a director."[70] Accordingly it seems that a managing director appointed under this article with no express provision regarding tenure can walk out after resigning his directorship, or be effectively dismissed without notice by being removed from his directorship.

---

[66] *Southern Foundries* v. *Shirlaw* [1940] A.C. 701, H.L. In the light of the observations in this case it seems that the court will not grant an injunction to restrain the alteration of the articles: *contra British Murac Syndicate* v. *Alperton Rubber Co.* [1915] 2 Ch. 186. See, further, Chap. 22, *infra.*
[67] [1960] 1 W.L.R. 1038.
[68] [1952] 1 All E.R. 922, affirmed on other grounds; [1952] Ch. 637, C.A.
[69] [1940] A.C. 701.
[70] The final words of article 68 of the 1929 Table A (quoted above) have been omitted, but presumably only because they are unnecessary now that a director can always be removed by ordinary resolution.

The position seems to be different if the director is not appointed managing director under article 107, but to another office of profit (secretary, consultant or the like) under article 84 (3). If his express contract provides that he shall be entitled to remain a director so long as he retains the other office, he will, apparently, be entitled to damages under section 184 (6) if the company removes him from the directorship. Certainly, the removal from his directorship will not automatically bring his contract to an end. Why a managing director should be treated differently from any other service director is not easy to see.

The directors as primary organs of the company

The result of this discussion appears to be that the directors have ceased to be mere agents of the company. Both they and the members in general meeting are primary organs of the company between whom the company's powers are divided. The general meeting retains ultimate control, but only through its powers to amend the articles (so as to take away, for the future, certain powers from the directors) and to remove the directors and to substitute others more to its taste. Until it takes one or other of these steps the directors can, if they are so advised, disregard the wishes and instructions of the members in all matters not specifically reserved (either by the Act or the articles) to a general meeting. And, as we shall see in a later chapter,[71] the practical difficulties in the way of effectively exercising even this measure of supervision are very great owing to the directors' control over the proxy-voting machinery. The old idea that the general meeting alone is the company's primary organ and the directors merely the company's agents or servants, at all times subservient to the general meeting, seems no longer to be the law as it is certainly not the fact.

Default powers of the general meeting

It seems that if for some reason the board cannot or will not exercise the powers vested in them, the general meeting may do so. On this ground, action by the general meeting has been held effective where there was a deadlock on the board,[72] where an effective quorum could not be obtained,[73] where the directors are disqualified from voting,[74] or, more obviously, where the directors have purported to borrow in excess of the amount authorised by the articles.[75] Moreover, although the general meeting cannot restrain the directors from conducting actions in the name of the company, it still seems to be the law (as

---

[71] *Infra*, Chap. 21.
[72] *Barron* v. *Potter* [1914] 1 Ch. 895. Contrast situations in which a board is able to act but is held up by the opposition of one faction acting within its powers under the articles: see, *e.g.*, *Quin & Axtens* v. *Salmon* [1909] A.C. 442, H.L.
[73] *Foster* v. *Foster* [1916] 1 Ch. 532.
[74] *Grant* v. *U.K. Switchback Rys.* (1888) 40 Ch.D. 135, C.A.
[75] *Irvine* v. *Union Bank of Australia* (1877) 2 App.Cas. 366, P.C.

laid down in *Marshall's Valve Gear Co.* v. *Manning, Wardle & Co.*[76]) that the general meeting can commence proceedings on behalf of the company if the directors fail to do so.[77] These exceptions are convenient, but difficult to reconcile in principle with the strict theory of a division of powers. Their exact limits are not entirely clear. They can hardly mean that, although the members cannot restrain positive action by the directors, they can always take action if the directors have resolved against it. There must, it is submitted, normally be a failure by the directors validly to exercise their discretion; only then will their discretionary powers revert to the members.[78]

Moreover it is generally assumed that it is perfectly in order for the board of directors, if they so wish, to refer any matter to the general meeting either to ratify what they have done or to decide themselves on action to be taken. It is quite clear, as has recently been affirmed by the Court of Appeal in *Bamford* v. *Bamford*,[79] that any act of the directors which is voidable because, for example, it is in breach of their fiduciary duties, can be ratified by the company in general meeting if the act is within the powers of the company and the meeting acts with full knowledge and bona fide in the interests of the company.[80] It is, perhaps, less clear whether the board, without taking a decision on a matter within their powers, can initially refer it to the general meeting for a decision there. In an elaborate discussion at first instance in the *Bamford* case,[81] Plowman J. had held that the general meeting had power to act under the residual powers, but he suggested that this might depend on the terms of the memorandum and articles of the company concerned.[82] The Court of Appeal considered that this question was irrelevant to the issue before them and expressed no view on it. It seems absurd if the directors are forced improperly to take a decision and then to ask the general meeting to whitewash them, but perhaps the safest course is for them to resolve on action " subject to ratification by the company in general meeting."

If the directors have purported to exercise powers reserved to the company in general meeting their action can be effectively ratified by the company in general meeting. And for the purpose of ratifying past actions of the board, as opposed to conferring powers on the board for

---

[76] [1909] 1 Ch. 267, *supra.*
[77] *Infra,* Chap. 25, p. 583.
[78] But anomalously this does not seem to apply when it is a question of commencing legal proceedings on behalf of the company. Though the general meeting cannot interfere with the directors' decision to take proceedings (*Shaw & Sons (Salford) Ltd.* v. *Shaw, supra*) it can, apparently, reverse a decision by the directors not to take proceedings: see further, Chap. 25, *infra.* But *quaere* whether this latter rule is not limited to intra-corporate disputes.
[79] [1969] 2 W.L.R. 1107, C.A.
[80] On the meaning of this, see Chap. 24, *infra.*
[81] [1968] 3 W.L.R. 317.
[82] *Ibid.* at pp. 328–332.

the future, it is not necessary to pass a special resolution altering the articles; an ordinary resolution will suffice.[83]

Exercise of directors' powers

Where powers are conferred on the directors under clauses such as those considered above, they are conferred upon the directors collectively as a board. Prima facie, therefore, they can only be exercised at a board meeting of which due notice has been given and at which a quorum is present. In contrast with general meetings, where the procedure is laid down in some detail in the articles,[84] statute [85] or charter, directors are normally left very much to settle their own procedure.[86] But, unless the regulations provide to the contrary, due notice must be given to all of them and a quorum must be present at a meeting [87] which must be convened as such. Notice here merely means reasonable notice having regard to the practice of the company,[88] and if all in fact meet without notice they may waive this requirement if they wish, but are not bound to do so.[89] And although majority decision prevails, a meeting of the majority without notice to the minority is ineffective, for *non constat* that the persuasive oratory of the minority would not have induced the majority to change their minds.[90] But if all are agreed, a meeting may be a waste of time and hence it is usual to provide that a resolution in writing signed by all the directors shall be as valid and effectual as if it had been duly passed at a meeting.[91]

It follows that prima facie neither an individual director nor any group of directors has any powers conferred on him or them, and it seems that in the absence of an express authorisation in the articles or other appropriate constitutional document the board will have no power to delegate such powers.[92] The board will, of course, be able to appoint executive agents or servants [93] of the company but must not delegate the exercise of its discretion. Although it is very doubtful whether the board of a registered company ought any longer to be regarded as a

---

[83] *Grant* v. *U.K. Switchback Rys., supra.*
[84] *Cf.* Table A, arts. 47–74. And see ss. 130–146 of the Act. *Infra,* Chap. 21.
[85] Companies Clauses Act 1845, ss. 66–80.
[86] *Cf.* Table A, arts. 98–106. The only statutory requirement in the case of registered companies is that minutes shall be kept: s. 145.
[87] *Quaere* if this necessarily involves assembling under one roof: *cf. Collie's Claim* (1871) L.R. 12 Eq. 246 at 258, and *Ex p. Kennedy* (1890) 44 Ch.D. 472 at 481. In these days of telephonic, radio and television communication it is submitted that directors could " meet " without being physically in the same room.
[88] *Browne* v. *La Trinidad* (1887) 37 Ch.D. 1, C.A. If the practice is for the directors to meet at fixed times further notice may be unnecessary. The articles commonly provide that notice need not be given to a director who is abroad.
[89] *Barron* v. *Potter* [1914] 1 Ch. 895.
[90] *Per* Jessel M.R. in *Barber's Case* (1877) 5 Ch.D. 963, C.A., at p. 968; and see *Re Portuguese Consolidated Copper Mines* (1889) 42 Ch.D. 160, C.A.
[91] Table A, art. 106.
[92] *Cartmell's Case* (1874) L.R. 9 Ch.App. 691.
[93] But, in the absence of an express power one of the directors must not be appointed: *Kerr* v. *Marine Products* (1928) 44 T.L.R. 292.

delegate, nevertheless, the maxim *delegatus non potest delegare* is regarded as applying.

This rule, however, can be modified in two ways. Sometimes the articles may provide for " permanent " or " governing " directors and confer certain powers on them to the exclusion of the rest of the board.[94] When this occurs there is, in effect, a threefold division of powers; some are reserved to the general meeting, others to the permanent directors and only the residue are left to the general board. The company in such circumstances has three primary organs instead of two. In addition the constitution may, and invariably will, authorise delegation by the board. The Companies Clauses Act provides only for delegation to committees[95]; the implication is that statutory companies are intended to function very much on the lines of local authorities with all policy decisions taken by the board either directly or through one of its committees and with the permanent officials acting merely in an executive capacity.[96] In the case of registered companies, however, there is always an additional[97] power to appoint and delegate to managing and other service directors. Today, it is normally the managing directors who run a company, rather than the board as a whole, and their legal position requires further examination.

Division of powers between the board and a managing director

Under the normal articles, the directors are empowered to appoint one or more of their number to the office of managing director for such period and on such terms as they shall think fit.[98] In addition, a director is allowed to hold any other office or place of profit under the company in conjunction with his office of director, again on such terms as the directors think fit.[99] The result is that in most companies there will be one or more managing, service, or working directors holding office under formal or informal service agreements whereby they are bound to devote the whole or some part of their time to the service of the company. The ordinary directors will merely be expected to put in an appearance at occasional board meetings, and will receive a relatively small fee in accordance with provisions in the articles, which generally provide that fees shall be voted annually in general meeting.[1]

---

[94] As in *Shaw & Sons (Salford) Ltd.* v. *Shaw, supra.* Or one or more directors may be given a power of veto, as in *Quin & Axtens* v. *Salmon, supra.*

[95] s. 95.

[96] It may be assumed that the idea that permanent officials merely do what they are told is as unrealistic in the one case as in the other.

[97] Table A (and most articles) also provide for committees: art. 102.

[98] Table A, art. 107. Since the power to appoint is conferred on the board, a general meeting cannot interfere: *Thos. Logan* v. *Davis* (1911) 105 L.T. 419, C.A.

[99] Table A, art. 84 (3). But he cannot be appointed auditor: s. 161 (2).

[1] *Cf.* Table A, art. 76. The old practice was to pay in guineas. Hence the name " guinea-pig " applied to directors whose function was merely to add an appearance of respectability to the board by lending it their names or titles.

Service directors, on the other hand, will have to work for their living, but will probably be paid quite handsomely, normally by way of salary and commission,[2] in accordance with terms settled by their fellow directors.[3] Reference has already been made to the embarrassment that this may cause the members when they try to get rid of them.[4] It is obvious, too, that the system lends itself to abuse, since directors will be encouraged to bleed the company by voting themselves excessive salaries and expense allowances.[5] The 1948 Act attempted to minimise these dangers by providing for disclosure of the total emoluments received by directors,[6] by prohibiting tax-free salaries[7] and by invalidating payments of compensation for loss of office unless confirmed in general meeting.[8] The 1967 Act goes further by making service agreements open to inspection[9] and by providing for disclosure in greater detail of directors' emoluments.[10]

Some service directors may merely be the holders of subordinate executive posts, such as those of secretary, sales manager, branch manager or accountant,[11] which they occupy in conjunction with, but separately from, their directorships. But a managing director[12] is essentially different in that his function is to exercise some or all of the directors' powers of managing. As article 109 of Table A expresses it: " The directors may entrust to and confer upon a managing director any of the powers exercisable by them upon such terms and conditions and with such restrictions as they may think fit, and either collaterally with or to the exclusion of their own powers and may from time to time revoke, withdraw, alter or vary all or any of such powers."

---

2 Table A, arts. 84 (3) and 108. They may also be entitled to retirement benefits. The practice of paying them large sums of money on their retirement in consideration of an agreement not to compete has gone out of favour since F.A. 1950, s. 26 (now I.T.A. 1952, s. 242) made the payments liable to surtax in the hands of the recipients, but the judgment of Greene M.R. in *Associated Portland Cement* v. *I.R.C.* [1946] 1 All E.R. 68, C.A., is still worth reading as a superb example of his masterly gift of sustained irony.

3 The normal article (see Table A, art. 108) provides that a managing director shall receive such remuneration as the directors may determine. In *Re Richmond Gate Property Co. Ltd.* [1965] 1 W.L.R. 335, Plowman J. held that this precluded any question of payment being due on a *quantum meruit* where no amount had been determined. *Sed quaere*, see (1965) 28 M.L.R. 347, (1966) 29 M.L.R. 608.

4 *Supra*, p. 134 *et seq.*

5 Even if they are shareholders, it will pay them far better to receive payment by way of remuneration rather than by way of dividend. Not only will it be " earned income " for tax purposes but, their remuneration will be a deductible expense in determining the company's taxable profit: see further Chap. 9, *infra*. Moreover, they can be paid whether or not profits are earned.

6 s. 196.

7 s. 189.

8 ss. 191 and 192.

9 s. 26.

10 s. 6. Individual emoluments have to be shown only in the case of the chairman. The modesty of other directors is protected by a somewhat inadequate fig-leaf; what must be revealed is the number of directors receiving emoluments within specified points on a scale.

11 But not *auditor*: s. 161.

12 Or joint managing directors—there is often more than one.

Clearly the managing director may be appointed on the terms that he shall only perform such duties as are from time to time assigned to him by the board and that he shall conform to their orders and instructions.[13] This indeed is the usual practice and where it is adopted the board have the widest powers of curtailing the range of his activities. In *Holdsworth & Co.* v. *Caddies*[14] the appointment of a managing director of a holding company provided that he should perform the duties and exercise the powers in relation to the businesses of the holding company and its subsidiaries as should be assigned to him by the board of the holding company. After policy disagreements the board directed him that he should confine his attentions to the business of one of the subsidiaries. The House of Lords held that this was not a breach of the service agreement, notwithstanding that he was thereby deprived of any managerial functions in relation to the company employing him.[15]

However, the wording of article 109 of Table A, with its express reference to a delegation "to the exclusion of their own powers," appears to imply that the directors may effectively divest themselves of their own powers in favour of the managing director. If the service agreement with the managing director purported to confer exclusive powers upon him without expressly reserving a right of supervision it is submitted that the board could not exercise those powers during the subsistence of the agreement.

If this is correct the directors are in effect authorised to substitute [16] a managing director for themselves as one of the primary organs of the company. In such circumstances the powers of the company will be divided among three exclusive organs. The managing director will have sole power to exercise those functions entrusted to him by the board, which may, if the board thinks fit, include all its powers except such as the articles or the Companies Act require to be performed by the board itself. Any residue of powers conferred by the articles on the directors will be exercised by the board. And, finally, certain powers will be reserved to the company in general meeting. Within their respective spheres each of these three organs will have exclusive control, and be free from any interference from the others, unless and until their appointments are terminated. The general meeting has inherent power to sack both directors and managing directors [17] (but if it exercises this power in breach of contract the company will be liable to pay damages [18]). To this extent the general meeting retains (in theory) ultimate control and is

13 See Palmer's *Company Precedents*, 17th ed., Pt. I, Form 457.
14 [1955] 1 W.L.R. 352, H.L.(Sc.) and 1955 S.C.(H.L.) 27.
15 This decision (reversing a unanimous Court of Session), goes surprisingly far in ignoring the separate personalities of the various companies within a group: see *infra*, Chap. 10, p. 213.
16 It is clear that to some extent the appointment always operates by way of substitution rather than delegation. The managing director, and indeed any agent or servant, becomes an " agent," of the company, not of the board.
17 s. 184.
18 *Supra*, p. 134. And note *Bushell* v. *Faith*, *supra*, p. 133, n. 54.

more truly the company than the other organs, which it can remove while it itself is irremovable. Similarly, the board can effectively remove the managing director from the appointment which it has conferred upon him [19] although if it does so in breach of contract the company will again be liable in damages.[20]

It is submitted, therefore, that a managing director ought to be regarded as something more than a manager who happens also to be a director.[21] Even a manager who is not a director may for some external purposes be regarded as more than a mere agent or servant,[22] but he or any other employee is in a fundamentally different position so far as internal relations are concerned. The board and the managing director, as primary organs of the company, will not only be entitled to supervise his activities but will be under a duty to do so.[23] Doubtless the articles could expressly confer primary managerial powers on some official other than the board, but it is submitted that if they did so the official would in law be a director, for the Act defines director as including " any person occupying the position of director by whatever name called." [24] Any attempt, therefore, to confer exclusive power to exercise the functions normally performed by the board would seem to place the recipient of the power " in the position of director." [25]

The secretary [26]

Finally a word must be said about another important officer of the company—the secretary. Speaking generally the secretary's functions are purely ministerial and administrative and he is not, as secretary, charged with the exercise of any managerial powers. Hence, as we shall see in the next chapter, he cannot normally bind the company by entering into contracts or other commitments on its behalf except, probably, as regards such matters as the engagement of clerical staff.

---

19 This is clearly so if the articles are worded like Table A, arts. 107 and 109. But presumably the articles could provide that the board had no power to revoke an appointment which it had made.

20 *Nelson* v. *James Nelson & Sons* [1914] 2 K.B. 770, C.A.; *Shindler* v. *Northern Raincoat Co. Ltd*. [1960] 1 W.L.R. 1038.

21 Although the H.L. in *Holdsworth & Co.* v. *Caddies* (*supra*) did not seem clear on this, the decisions on the rule in *Turquand's* case, discussed in the next chapter, certainly support this view to some extent.

22 See Chap. 8, *infra*.

23 *Re City Equitable Fire Insurance Co.* [1925] Ch. 407, C.A.

24 s. 455.

25 See also ss. 124 (4), 125 (4), 195 (10) (*a*), 200 (9) (*a*) and 201 (4) (*a*) of the 1948 Act and ss. 25 (3), 27 (11) and 29 (14) of the 1967 Act, which provide that for the purposes of the sections concerned " the expression ' director ' includes any person in accordance with whose directions or instructions the directors of the company are accustomed to act." The sections in question include those relating to the register of directors' shareholdings and publication of the names of directors. Apparently therefore the company may have to publicise such people as directors although they may not in law be directors: see Chap. 24, pp. 561, 562, *infra*.

26 The position of another important official—the auditor—will be discussed when we deal with accounts: Chap. 20, *infra*.

On the other hand it is he that will be charged with the primary responsibility of ensuring that the documentation of the company is in order, that the requisite returns are made to the Companies' Registry, and that the company's registers are properly maintained.[27] Moreover it is he that will in practice be referred to in order to obtain authenticated copies of contracts and resolutions decided upon by the board,[28] and the articles will generally provide that he is one of those in whose presence the company's seal is to be affixed to documents.[29]

The 1948 Act provides that every registered company must have a secretary who must not be the sole director.[30] It also provides that anything required to be done by a director and the secretary shall not be done by the same person acting as both.[31] But the secretary can be appointed with less formality than a director; the appointment will be made by the board—not by the general meeting—and any officer of the company may be authorised by the board to act in the absence of a formally appointed secretary.[32] Further it has been recognised that those dealing with the company will be concerned to know who the secretary is, and hence the register of directors has been expanded by the 1948 Act into a register of directors and secretaries.[33] Copies of the particulars in this register must be filed at the Companies' Registry[34] and are available for inspection by the public both there and at the company's office. But the further step, of insisting that the name of the secretary shall be shown with those of the directors on the company's notepaper,[35] has not yet been taken.

Despite this statutory recognition of the increasingly important status of the secretary the courts still treat him as a subordinate servant without ostensible authority to commit the company by his actions.[36] This attitude seems both unrealistic and out of harmony with the legislative trends. To publicise the secretary may only mislead if in fact the public are not entitled to assume that he has authority to perform the normal duties now undertaken by secretaries, which duties are extensive and important.

27 Sometimes a separate professional firm is appointed to act as registrar to maintain the registers of members and debentureholders.
28 See *Mahony* v. *East Holyford Mining Co.* (1875) L.R. 7 H.L. 869, but contrast the cases cited in note 36, *infra.* All these cases are discussed more fully in the next chapter.
29 *Cf.* Table A, art. 113. Generally, too, he will be authorised to countersign cheques.
30 s. 177 (1). See also s. 178.
31 s. 179.
32 s. 177.
33 s. 200. This applies to unregistered companies also: s. 435, Sched. 14 and Companies (Unregistered Companies) Regs. 1967 (S.I. No. 1876).
34 s. 200 (4) and (5).
35 s. 201.
36 *Cf. George Whitechurch Ltd.* v. *Cavanagh* [1902] A.C. 117, H.L.: *Ruben* v. *Great Fingall Consolidated* [1906] A.C. 439, H.L.; *Houghton & Co.* v. *Nothard, Lowe & Wills* [1928] A.C. 1, H.L.; and *Kleinwort, Sons & Co.* v. *Associated Automatic Machine Corpn.* (1934) 50 T.L.R. 244, H.L.

CHAPTER 8

LIABILITIES OF THE COMPANY FOR THE ACTS OF ITS ORGANS AND OFFICERS

THE discussion in the previous chapter was concerned with the internal organisation of the company and the inter-relationship of its various agencies. In that connection certain officials or bodies have, for some purposes, ceased to be regarded as mere agents of the company and have become instead its primary organs. An exactly similar development has occurred in relation to the position of the company and its officials on the one hand, and third parties on the other.

English law has evolved an exceptionally wide doctrine of agency and vicarious liability. For most purposes, therefore, the recognition of the artificial personality of a corporation caused no great difficulty. When a natural person could be bound by the acts of his agents so could a corporation and generally this provided an adequate answer.[1]

But even English law stops short of recognising vicarious liability in all cases; sometimes it insists on personal fault as a prerequisite of liability. In such cases a corporation could never have been under any liability if the courts had continued rigidly to apply the rule that " the company . . . has no person; it can only act through directors and the case is, as regards those directors, merely the ordinary case of principal and agent." [2] Hence the courts have, once again, elected to treat the acts of certain officials as those of the company itself.

The organic theory

Strangely enough this seems to have taken place entirely independently of the comparable development in the line of cases outlined in the previous chapter and culminating in *Shaw & Sons (Salford) Ltd.* v. *Shaw* [3] and *Scott* v. *Scott*.[4] Instead, it sprang from an epoch-making judgment of Lord Haldane in *Lennard's Carrying Co.* v. *Asiatic Petroleum Co. Ltd.*[5] in 1915. In that case a company which owned a ship was seeking to take advantage of the limitation of liability under section 502 of the Merchant Shipping Act 1894. This limitation is

---

[1] *Cf.* Welsh, " The Criminal Liability of Corporations " (1946) 62 L.Q.R. 345 at p. 350 *et seq.*

[2] *Per* Cairns L.J. in *Ferguson* v. *Wilson* (1866) L.R. 2 Ch. at p. 89, *supra*, p 126.

[3] [1935] 2 K.B. 113, C.A., *supra*, p. 131.

[4] [1943] 1 All E.R. 582, *supra*, p. 132.

[5] [1915] A.C. 705, H.L. It is foreshadowed in the dictum of Neville J. in *Bath* v. *Standard Land Co.* [1910] 2 Ch. 408 at p. 416; " The Board of Directors are the brains and the only brains of the company which is the body. and the company can and does act only through them."

available only where the injury is caused without the owner's "actual fault or privity." The loss resulted from the default of Lennard, its managing director, and in holding the company liable, Viscount Haldane L.C.., in delivering the judgment of the House, said [6]:

"My Lords, a corporation is an abstraction. It has no mind of its own any more than it has a body of its own; its active and directing will must consequently be sought in the person of somebody *who for some purposes may be called an agent, but who is really the directing mind and will of the corporation, the very ego and centre of the personality of the corporation* . . . If Mr. Lennard was the directing mind of the company, then his action must, unless a corporation is not to be liable at all, have been an action *which was the action of the company itself* within the meaning of section 502. . . . It must be upon the true construction of that section in such a case as the present one that the fault or privity is the fault or privity of somebody *who is not merely a servant or agent for whom the company is liable upon the footing* respondeat superior, *but somebody for whom the company is liable because his action is the very action of the company itself.*" [7]

Lennard's case was followed in *H.M.S. Truculent,*[8] where the Third Sea Lord was held to be the "directing mind" of the Admiralty, and in *The Lady Gwendolen*[9] where it was indicated by Willmer and Winn L.JJ. that the person whose fault is to be taken as that of the corporation need not be a director. Winn L.J. said [10]:

"Wherever the fault either occurs in a function or sphere of action which the owner has retained for himself or is that of a manager independent of the owner to whom the owner has surrendered all relevant powers of control, it is 'actual fault of' the owner within the meaning of the section."

This concept is clearly capable of being used, and has been used,[11] to extend the liability of a company beyond that flowing from normal agency principles.

---

[6] At pp. 713–714.
[7] Italics supplied.
[8] [1952] P. 1.
[9] [1965] P. 294, C.A.; see Leigh (1965) 28 M.L.R. 584.
[10] At p. 355D.
[11] Examples occurred in the field of tort while common employment (abolished by Law Reform (Personal Injuries) Act 1948) remained a defence to employers. Clearly, if directors and managers of a company were regarded as in common employment with the other employees, a company would never be liable for common law negligence to its work-people. This difficulty was avoided in *Rudd* v. *Elder Dempster & Co.* [1933] 1 K.B. 566, C.A., and *Wheeler* v. *New Merton Board Mills* [1933] 2 K.B. 669, C.A., by recourse to the organic theory: *cf.* Greer L.J. in *Fanton* v. *Denville* [1932] 2 K.B. 309, C.A., at p. 329.

Crime

It is in the realm of criminal law that Lord Haldane's principle has exercised an especially powerful influence. The question whether a company ought, on grounds of public policy, to be made criminally liable, has been much debated,[12] but has been answered in the affirmative by the courts. As we have seen,[13] the *ultra vires* doctrine has been successfully by-passed. Another difficulty that has had to be overcome is that, generally speaking, there is no rule of vicarious liability in criminal law, *mens rea* on the part of the accused being an essential element.

At common law the only exceptions to the need for *mens rea* were in cases of public nuisance [14] and criminal libel.[15] Both of these offences were closely allied to their tortious counterparts; indeed the former was regarded as essentially civil in its nature although criminal in form. In both cases, therefore, the civil law principles of vicarious liability were applied and a company might be liable accordingly.[16] When, in modern times, the legislature began to create a vast number of statutory offences it was recognised by the courts that the legislature could, if it wished, dispense with the requirement of *mens rea* and make a master vicariously liable for the crimes of his servants. If it had done so,[17] then there was no reason [18] why the master should not be made liable even though it was a corporation.[19]

For many years this was as far as the courts were prepared to go, though signs of a wider doctrine were discernible.[20] In 1944, however, three cases introduced a general principle of criminal liability of companies based on the theory that certain of its officials were " agents " for which it was liable personally and not on the footing of *respondeat superior*.[21] In the first of these, *Director of Public Prosecutions* v. *Kent & Sussex Contractors Ltd.*,[22] a company was

---

12 See especially Winn in (1929) 3 Camb.L.J. 398; Welsh in (1946) 62 L.Q.R. 345; and Glanville Williams, *Criminal Law: The General Part* (2nd ed., 1961) pp. 862–865.
13 Chap. 5, pp. 96–98, *supra*.
14 *R.* v. *Stephens* (1866) L.R. 1 Q.B. 702.
15 *R.* v. *Holbrook* (1878) 4 Q.B.D. 42.
16 See the well-known dictum of Lord Blackburn in *Pharmaceutical Society* v. *London & Provincial Supply Assn.* (1880) 5 App.Cas. 857, 870.
17 There was no presumption that it had done so. The " principle of the common law applies also to statutory offences, with this difference, that it is in the power of the legislature, if it so pleases, to enact . . . that a man may be convicted and punished for an offence although there was no blameworthy condition of mind about him ": *per* Cave J. in *Chisholm* v. *Doulton* (1889) 22 Q.B.D. at p. 741.
18 Apart from procedural difficulties most of which have now been surmounted (see Welsh, *loc. cit.* at p. 362 *et seq.*) and the *ultra vires* doctrine (see Chap. 5, *supra*).
19 See Atkin J. in *Mousell Ltd.* v. *L.N.W. Ry.* [1917] 2 K.B. 836, 846.
20 They enabled Winn, writing in 1929, to enunciate the theory that later prevailed: see (1929) 3 Camb.L.J. 398.
21 They were heralded by a civil case, *Triplex Safety Glass Co. Ltd.* v. *Lancegaye Safety Glass (1934) Ltd.* [1939] 2 K.B. 395, C.A., in which it was held that a company could be guilty of criminal libel and have the malice of its directors attributed to it.
22 [1944] K.B. 146.

prosecuted under the Defence Regulations for making use of a document with intent to deceive and for making a statement which it knew to be false.[23] The offences were admittedly statutory ones, but it was clear that *mens rea* was essential and that normally a master would not have been liable for an offence committed by his servant. The local justices therefore dismissed the information. But their decision was reversed by the Divisional Court.

This decision was approved by the Court of Criminal Appeal in *R.* v. *I. C. R. Haulage Ltd.*[24] There the company was prosecuted for a *common law* conspiracy to defraud, and it was held that it could be convicted notwithstanding the fact that *mens rea* was certainly an essential element of the offence. " Whether," [25] said the court,[26] " there is evidence to go to a jury that the criminal act of an agent, including his state of mind, intention, knowledge, or belief is the act of the company and . . . whether the jury are satisfied that it has been proved, must depend on the nature of the charge, the relative position of the officer or agent and the other relevant facts and circumstances of the case." Finally, in *Moore* v. *Bresler Ltd.*,[27] a company was convicted of making use of a document with intent to deceive [28] despite the fact that the acts were not those of its directors but merely of its secretary and a branch manager.[29] Where, however, a statute draws a distinction between the criminal liability of " an employer or principal " and that of the " actual offender," it seems that a company can never be regarded as the " actual offender." [30]

In none of these criminal cases was Lord Haldane's " organic " theory referred to in the judgments. But it seems clear that they were impliedly based on his view that certain officials *are* the company and not merely agents of it. Indeed, in later decisions this has become explicit, and a limitation has been put on the ambit of the doctrine by making it clear that it is not the act or knowledge of every agent or servant of the company which will be attributed to the company,[31] but only those whom the company has made its " responsible officers " for the action in question.[32] Moreover it appears that the courts will

---

23 In order to obtain petrol coupons.
24 [1944] K.B. 551, C.C.A.
25 The word " where " appears in the report but this seems to be a misprint.
26 At p. 559.
27 [1944] 2 All E.R. 515.
28 Contrary to Finance (No. 2) Act 1940, s. 35 (2).
29 Having regard to these three decisions it is generally accepted that *R.* v. *Cory Bros.* [1927] 1 K.B. 810 (holding that a company cannot be convicted of a felony) is wrongly decided. In *R.* v. *I. C. R. Haulage*, the C.C.A. stated that it might now have been decided differently: [1944] K.B. at p. 556.
30 *Melias Ltd.* v. *Preston* [1957] 2 Q.B. 380.
31 As *Moore* v. *Bresler Ltd., supra,* had almost suggested.
32 *John Henshall (Quarries) Ltd.* v. *Harvey* [1965] 2 Q.B. 233. In this case express reliance was placed on the dictum of Denning M.R. in *Bolton (Engineering) Co. Ltd.* v. *Graham & Sons,* quoted at p. 149, *infra,* which in turn relied on Lord Haldane's statement in *Lennard's* case. These dicta were also relied on in *R.* v. *McDonnell, infra,* p. 148.

conduct a factual analysis of the workings of the company's management to discover who those officials are.[33] This identification of the company with its directing mind was carried to its logical conclusion in *R.* v. *McDonnell* [34] where it was held that the company could not conspire with the sole officer responsible for its acts and intentions.

Recent years have seen a further development whereby the rule that the acts of directors are treated as those of the company is, in effect, applied in reverse, so that the acts of the company are treated as those of its directors. Many modern statutes [35] and regulations provide that if an offence is committed by a company, every director or officer who was implicated shall be guilty of that offence and often the onus is placed on him to prove that it was committed without his consent and that he exercised due diligence to prevent its commission.

Other examples of the organic theory

Another example of the influence of the organic theory may be found in the cases relating to the determination of a company residence. This subject is dealt with more fully later.[36] Here it must suffice to say that those controlling the management of the company [37] (normally the directors or managing director) are treated as the company's " brains," [38] and wherever the brain functions, there resides the company.

The same approach is seen in cases concerned with the exercise of pressure on agents or servants of a party to a contract to induce him to break it. A person who knowingly persuades another to break his contract is liable in tort.[39] He will also be liable if he persuades a servant to render impossible the performance of his master's contract, but, in this case, only if the act of the servant is in itself wrongful.[40] If the principle that a company can only act through agents or servants were carried to its logical conclusion it would mean that the third party could always shelter behind the second and laxer rule; in other words, he could say: " I haven't induced the contracting party (the company) but only its agents (its directors)." Hence, it has been judicially declared [41]:

---

33 See, for example, *N.C.B.* v. *Gamble* [1959] 1 Q.B. 11.
34 [1966] 1 Q.B. 233.
35 For a lengthy list of illustrations, see Glanville Williams, *Criminal Law: The General Part* (2nd ed.), pp. 866–869.
36 Chap. 10, at pp. 207, 208.
37 Expressly described as " organs " by Lord Parker in a leading case on this aspect of the subject, *Daimler Co.* v. *Continental Tyre & Rubber Co. Ltd.* [1916] 2 A.C. 307, 340: " The acts of a company's organs, its directors, managers, secretary, and so forth, functioning within the scope of their authority, are the company's acts. . . ."
38 An expression used by Lord Parker in *Mitchell* v. *Egyptian Hotels* [1915] A.C. 1022 at p. 1037. *Cf.* " governing and directing minds " used by Lord Atkinson in [1916] 2 A.C. at p. 319.
39 *Lumley* v. *Gye* (1853) 2 E. & B. 216.
40 *Thomson & Co.* v. *Deakin* [1952] Ch. 646, C.A. *Cf. Mutual Finance Ltd.* v. *John Wetton & Sons* [1937] 2 K.B. 389.
41 *Per* Evershed M.R. in [1952] Ch. at p. 682.

" In the case of a company the approach to or the persuasion of a managing director, or of some person having like authority, may be regarded as being in all respects equivalent to the direct approach [to] [42] the individual contractor . . . ; but if the approach is made to other servants of the company the case . . . becomes parallel to an approach made, not to the contracting party himself, but to some servant of the contracting party, so that the intervener will only be liable if the act which he procures the servant to do is either a breach of contract towards the servant's master or is otherwise tortious in itself."

Here again we find a distinction drawn between managing directors, managers and the like who are treated as the company itself, and subordinate employees who are mere agents or servants.

Another example of the same principle is afforded by *Bolton (Engineering) Co. Ltd.* v. *Graham & Sons*,[43] where the question was whether a company could be said to intend to occupy certain premises for its own business.[44] No formal general or board meetings had been held to consider the question but the business was managed by various directors, and these managing directors had clearly manifested the requisite intention. This was held to be a sufficient indication of the company's mind. Quoting Lord Haldane's judgment in *Lennard's Carrying Co.* v. *Asiatic Petroleum*,[45] Denning L.J. said [46]:

" A company may in many ways be likened to a human body. It has a brain and nerve centre which controls what it does. It also has hands which hold the tools and act in accordance with directions from the centre. Some of the people in the company are mere servants and agents who are nothing more than hands to do the work and cannot be said to represent the mind or will. Others are directors and managers who represent the directing mind and will of the company, and control what it does. The state of mind of these managers is the state of mind of the company and is treated by the law as such. . . . So here the intention of the company can be derived from the intention of its officers and agents. Whether their intention is the company's intention depends on the nature of the matter under consideration, the relative position of the officer or agent and the other relevant facts and circumstances of the case."

These seem to be the only types of case in which the organic theory has yet been relied on. But the theory is obviously capable of application to any circumstances in which the ordinary principles of vicarious

[42] The report reads " of " but the sense seems to require " to."
[43] [1957] 1 Q.B. 159, C.A. The H.L. refused leave to appeal: [1957] 1 W.L.R. 454.
[44] The question arose under s. 30 (1) (*g*) of the Landlord and Tenant Act 1954.
[45] [1915] A.C. 705 at 713–714, *supra*, p. 145.
[46] At pp. 172–173.

liability produce injustice.[47]   It may underlie the refusal of the courts to treat the affixing of the company's signature by a director as a mere " signature by procuration " within the meaning of the Bills of Exchange Act 1882, s. 25.[48]   It might be applied in those rare cases where the law requires a document to be signed personally and not by an agent.[49] In the case of corporate bodies this normally causes no difficulty because of express statutory provisions equating signature by officials of the corporation with the signature of the corporation itself.[50]   But these provisions deal only with signatures of contracts and hence may not cover every situation.[51]

Strange as it may seem, the one case in which the courts have positively refused to apply the organic theory is in connection with their own procedure, for they have insisted that a company can never appear in person[52] or be subpoenaed to give evidence.[53]   Hence not even the managing director formally authorised by a resolution of the board will be allowed to represent the company in a High Court action.   This apparent anachronism preserves the monopoly of barristers and solicitors.

The rule in Turquand's case

Even if the officials are treated as organs, this does not obviate the need to comply with the basic principle of agency law that their acts bind the company only if they are within the actual, usual, or apparent scope of the officials' authority.   The " organic " theory is used to avoid the difficulty that in some cases an agent, even when acting within the scope of his authority, cannot bind the principal; it in no way affects the other rule that a principal is never liable if the agent is acting outside

---

[47] s. 47 (1) of the Companies Act 1967 refers to a situation where a company " to its knowledge " had been the subsidiary of another.   Would normal agency principles be applied in determining whether the company had knowledge or would the analogy of *Bolton (Engineering) Co. Ltd.* v. *Graham & Sons, supra,* be followed?

[48] See *infra,* p. 159, n. 95.

[49] The Statute of Frauds Amendment Act 1828 (Lord Tenterden's Act), s. 6; Moneylenders Act 1927, s. 6 (1); Hire Purchase Act 1965, s. 5 (1).

[50] Companies Act 1948, s. 32 (1) (*b*); Companies Clauses Act 1845, s. 97 (which requires the signature of two directors or committee men); Corporate Bodies' Contracts Act 1960.   That a signature in accordance with these provisions was a personal signature of the company was held in *Re British Games Ltd.* [1938] Ch. 240.

[51] The provision in Lord Tenterden's Act relates to actions in tort for fraudulent representations as to credit: *Banbury* v. *Bank of Montreal* [1918] A.C. 626, H.L.   If the action is in tort, s. 32 (1) (*b*) of the 1948 Act and s. 97 of the 1845 Act (*supra,* note 50), will not apply.   Hence it seems that the representation must be sealed by the company (*Hirst* v. *W. Riding Union Banking Co.* [1901] 2 K.B. 560, C.A.) unless the courts were prepared to hold that signature by a managing director or general manager was the signature of the company itself.   This possibility was argued more fully in the first edition of this book (at pp. 152–153) where it was also suggested that s. 36 of the 1948 Act might apply.

[52] *Frinton U. D. C.* v. *Walton Sand Co.* [1938] 1 All E.R. 649; *Tritonia Ltd.* v. *Equity and Law Life Assce. Society* [1943] A.C. 584, H.L.   In the county court greater freedom is allowed, as it is to a natural person: *Kinnell* v. *Harding* [1918] 1 K.B. 405, C.A.

[53] *Penn-Texas Corpn.* v. *Murat Anstalt* [1964] 1 Q.B. 40, C.A.   But under the Foreign Tribunals Evidence Act 1856 a company can be ordered to appear by its proper officer and produce specified documents: *ibid.* (No. 2) [1964] 2 Q.B. 647, C.A.

that authority. Just as a natural person may not be responsible for the acts of his organs if he has no control over them, so a company cannot be liable for its organs unless they are acting as such.

It is beyond the scope of this book to deal in detail with the general law of agency or principles of vicarious liability. Here it must suffice to say that the principal is liable if the agent is doing (i) what he is actually authorised to do, (ii) what an agent of that type would normally have authority to do, or (iii) what he has been " held out " by the principal as having authority to do, provided that, in cases (ii) and (iii) the other party to the transactions did not know that the agent was exceeding his actual authority. These rules apply equally to companies and their agents or organs. But they have received specific elaboration under what is known as the rule in *Royal British Bank* v. *Turquand*,[54] a rule which has received copious consideration elsewhere.[55]

It will be appreciated from the foregoing that a third party may allege that he has acquired rights against the company as a result of the action of the company in general meeting, or of the acts of its board of directors, its managing directors, an individual director or some subordinate official. These acts can bind the company only if, first, they are within the powers of the company under its statute, charter or memorandum, and if, secondly, the responsible agencies of the company are acting within the scope of their authority. The first of these prerequisites has already been discussed in connection with the *ultra vires* doctrine [56]; it is with the second that we are now concerned.

Where the act is that of the general meeting or the board, everything at first sight appears simple. The articles or other constitutional documents of the company will make it clear what authority is vested in the general meeting or the board and no further delegation has to be investigated. But this appearance of simplicity is deceptive. It is not so much that the original delegation of authority may, especially in the case of registered companies, have been altered, for particulars of this alteration should appear in the public documents.[57] The real difficulty is that there may be some irregularity in the operations of the organ concerned. The general or board meeting may not have been convened on proper notice, a quorum may not have been present, or a resolution may not have been properly put or carried.[58] The board may have delegated exclusive authority to a managing director,[59] or the directors, acting as the board, may not have been properly appointed. Similar

---

[54] (1856) 6 E. & B. 327.

[55] See especially Stiebel, (1933) 49 L.Q.R. 350; Montrose (1934) 50 L.Q.R. 224; Thompson (1956) 11 Univ. of Toronto L.J. 248; Campbell (1959) 75 L.Q.R. 469, (1960) 76 L.Q.R. 115; Nock (1966) 30 Conv.(N.S.) 123.

[56] *Supra*, Chap. 5.

[57] Companies Act 1948, s. 143.

[58] See Chap. 21, *infra*.

[59] The question whether the board can divest itself of control is discussed, *supra*, Chap. 7, p. 141 *et seq*.

problems may arise when a document purports to be sealed by the company; the seal may not have been affixed in accordance with a resolution of the board or not in the presence of the appropriate officials.

These difficulties are vastly increased where the agencies purport to be acting, not under a primary conferment of authority under the articles, statute or charter, but under a delegation by the board either directly or indirectly. As we have seen, an individual director prima facie has no authority to bind the company; nor *a fortiori* has a subordinate official such as a manager or secretary. But it is almost universal to confer wide authority on a managing director and a narrower one on other types of service director and on subordinate officials.

Is a third party dealing with the company bound to ensure that all the internal regulations of the company have in fact been complied with as regards the exercise and delegation of authority?

In the famous case of *Royal British Bank* v. *Turquand* [60] this question was answered in the negative. Under the registered deed of settlement [61] the board of directors were authorised to borrow on bond such sums as should from time to time be authorised by a resolution of the company in general meeting. The board borrowed money from the bank on a bond bearing the company's seal. It was held that even if no resolution had in fact been passed by the company in general meeting, the company was nevertheless bound. Jervis C.J. said [62]:

> " We may now take for granted that the dealings with these companies are not like dealings with other partnerships and that the parties dealing with them are bound to read the statute and the deed of settlement. But they are not bound to do more. And the party here, on reading the deed of settlement, would find, not a prohibition from borrowing, but a permission to do so on certain conditions. Finding that the authority might be made complete by a resolution, he would have a right to infer the fact of a resolution authorising that which on the face of the document appeared to be legitimately done."

This case was a strong one. Under the deed of settlement the directors' authority to borrow was expressly made subject to the consent of the company in general meeting. In these circumstances one might reasonably have supposed that a third party, who was bound to read the deed, would be put on inquiry to see that the requirements of the deed had been fulfilled. On the contrary, it was held that since, under the deed, the directors *might* have had authority, the third party was entitled to assume that in fact they had it.

---

[60] (1856) 6 E. & B. 327, Exch.Ch.
[61] The forerunner of the modern memorandum and articles.
[62] At p. 332.

This rule was manifestly based on business convenience, for business could not be carried on if everybody who had dealings with a company had meticulously to examine its internal machinery in order to ensure that the officials with whom he dealt had actual authority. Not only is it convenient, it is also just. The lot of creditors of a limited liability company is not a particularly happy one; it would be unhappier still if the company could escape liability by denying the authority of the officials to act on its behalf.

Nevertheless certain limitations must obviously be placed on the ambit of the rule; the mere fact that someone purports to act on behalf of the company cannot alone impose liability on the company—the *soi-disant* agent may be a complete impostor. The subsequent history of the rule has therefore seen a gradual increase in the limitations to which the rule is subject. And the limitations have become so extensive that the basic object of the rule sometimes seems to have been lost sight of. Why this should have been so, is difficult to explain; with the vast increase in the number of limited companies it might have been expected that the courts would seek to protect creditors by maintaining the rule intact. The fact remains, however, that until very recently the tendency has been to whittle it away, notwithstanding vigorous opposition by judges most familiar with commercial practice.[63] The result was that the law had become something of a jungle of irreconcilable decisions. Happily in 1964 the Court of Appeal [64] cut a path which it is hoped will not again become so overgrown.

The present law, therefore, is thought to be as set out in the following propositions :

Rule 1. Anyone dealing with a company is deemed to have notice of its public documents.[65] Hence any act which is clearly contrary to these documents will not bind the company unless subsequently ratified [66] by the company acting through its appropriate organ.

This principle is undoubted and constitutes another of the fundamental distinctions between a company and a partnership. Those dealing with a partnership are not concerned with the terms of the partnership agreement, and in the absence of actual knowledge of any limitations in it are entitled to assume that each partner has authority to carry on business in the usual way. But those dealing with companies are deemed

---

[63] Notably Wright J. (later Lord Wright) in *Kreditbank Cassel* v. *Schenkers* [1926] 2 K.B. 450; and *Houghton & Co.* v. *Nothard, Lowe & Wills* [1927] 1 K.B. 246; and Scrutton L.J. in *B.T.H.* v. *Federated European Bank* [1932] 2 K.B. 176, C.A.

[64] In *Freeman & Lockyer* v. *Buckhurst Park Properties (Mangal) Ltd.* [1964] 2 Q.B. 480, C.A.

[65] There is nothing in the Companies Act, comparable with s. 198 of the Law of Property Act 1925, providing that registration shall constitute notice, but it was so held by the H.L. in *Ernest* v. *Nicholls* (1857) 6 H.L.C. 401.

[66] It can, of course, only be ratified if within the powers of the company under its memorandum or statutes; see Chap. 5, *supra*.

to have notice of any restrictive provisions in the public documents whether in fact they have read them or not. If, for example, the articles provide that the company shall not be a party to a bill of exchange other than a cheque, the purported acceptance of a bill of exchange by the directors on behalf of the company will be ineffective. It is to this unfortunate rule that most of the difficulties are due. As we have seen, the Jenkins Committee recommended that it should be abolished,[67] and, if it is, those dealing with a company will be in much the same position as those dealing with a partnership. For the present, however, the fact that they are saddled with notice of the public documents places them in a worse position.

What then, are " public documents " for this purpose? So far as registered companies are concerned the expression is not now limited to the memorandum and articles of association, but includes some, at least, of the other documents filed at the Companies' Registry (for example, special resolutions, particulars of directors, and charges [68]). In the case of statutory and chartered companies it will similarly include their statutes and charters [69] and certain documents (for example, particulars of directors) filed at the Companies' Registry pursuant to section 435 and the Fourteenth Schedule to the Companies Act 1948. But the exact extent of the expression is doubtful. The cases on estoppel by share certificates [70] imply that it does not include the company's share register notwithstanding that this is available for public inspection, and it is not even clear that every document filed at the Registry is included. For example, it never seems to have been held that parties are affected with notice of everything in the annual return, return of allotments, or filed prospectuses.

Rule 2. But provided that everything appears to be regular so far as this can be checked from the public documents, an outsider dealing with the company is entitled to assume that all internal regulations of the company have been complied with, unless he has knowledge to the contrary or there are suspicious circumstances putting him on inquiry. Omnia praesumuntur rite ac solemniter esse acta.

As Lord Hatherley said in *Mahony* v. *East Holyford Mining Co.*[71]:

[The memorandum and articles] " are open to all who are

---

[67] Cmnd. 1749, paras. 35–42; see *supra*, pp. 98, 99.
[68] *Wilson* v. *Kelland* [1910] 2 Ch. 306, *per* Eve J. at p. 313. But notice is limited to the particulars registered and does not extend to any special provisions contained in the charge.
[69] Although these may not be in any public registry, they are public documents to which access can (albeit with difficulty) be obtained. But the by-laws of a chartered corporation are not public documents: *Montreal & St. Lawrence Light & Power Co.* v. *Robert* [1906] A.C. 196, P.C., at p. 203.
[70] See Chap. 17, pp. 381–386, *infra*.
[71] (1875) L.R. 7 H.L. 869 at pp. 893–894. Lord Hatherley in his speech seems sometimes to use the word " articles " when he means " memorandum " and " deed of partnership " when he means " articles "; the above extract has been edited accordingly.

minded to have any dealings whatsoever with the company and those who so deal with them must be affected with notice of all that is contained in those two documents. After that . . . all that the directors do with reference to what I may call the indoor management of their own concern, is a thing known to them and known to them only; subject to this observation, that no person dealing with them has a right to suppose that anything has been or can be done that is not permitted by [the memorandum or articles]. . . . When there are persons conducting the affairs of the company in a manner which appears to be perfectly consonant with the articles of association, then those so dealing with them externally are not to be affected by any irregularities which may take place in the internal management of the company."

The *Mahony* case was even stronger than the *Turquand* case. The company's bank had received what purported to be a formal copy of a resolution of the board authorising the payment of cheques signed by any two of three named " directors " and countersigned by the named " secretary." This copy was itself signed by the secretary. The bank paid cheques accordingly, but the whole company was a bubble and on its liquidation the liquidator sought to recover the amounts paid out by the bank. On investigation it proved that neither the directors nor the secretary had ever been formally appointed and no formal company or directors' meeting had ever been held. The House of Lords took the opinion of the judges and upheld their unanimous conclusion that the liquidator could not recover. According to the articles, which the bank was taken to know,[72] the directors were to be nominated by the subscribers to the memorandum and cheques were to be signed in such manner as the board might determine. The bank received formal notice in the ordinary way of the board's determination. Further than this the bank was neither bound nor entitled to look; that would have taken it into the indoor management.

It will be observed that in this and the following rules, the expression " outsider " is used to describe the person having dealings with the company. The dichotomy " insider—outsider " is borrowed from the vivid American terminology, but it must be confessed that it is not entirely clear what persons come within each class for the purposes of the *Turquand* rule. This was one of the questions discussed by Roskill J. in *Hely-Hutchinson* v. *Brayhead Ltd.*[73] where the plaintiff, a director, was seeking to enforce a contract he had made in his private capacity with the company acting through another director who was

[72] It is not clear from the report whether the bank had actually read the articles (being a bank it probably had) or whether the court regarded it as having constructive notice. In so far as the knowledge was beneficial to the bank, later cases, as we shall see, establish that mere constructive notice will not do.
[73] [1968] 1 Q.B. 549; affd. by C.A. on other grounds, *ibid.*

alleged not to have had actual authority. The defendant company argued that the plaintiff, because he was a director, could not claim he was an outsider and avail himself of the *Turquand* rule.[74] But Roskill J. upheld the plaintiff's claim, stating that even a director will not necessarily and for all purposes be an insider: the test appears to be whether the acts done by him were so closely interwoven with his position as director as to make it impossible for him not to be treated as knowing of the limitations on the powers of the officers of the company with whom he dealt.[75] He will, however, necessarily be treated as an insider unless he can satisfy the court that he was not the " responsible officer " in connection with the transactions.[76]

Rule 3.[77]   *Hence an outsider dealing with a company through an officer who is or is held out by the company as a particular type of officer (e.g., managing director) and who purports to exercise a power which that sort of officer would usually have, is entitled to hold the company liable for the officer's acts, even though the officer has not been so appointed or is in fact exceeding his actual authority. But this is not so if the officer is in fact exceeding his actual authority and*

(a) the outsider knows that the officer has not been so appointed or has no actual authority [78];

(b) the circumstances are such as to put him on inquiry [79]; *or*

(c) the public documents make it clear that the officer has no actual authority, or could not have authority unless a resolution had been passed which requires filing as a public document and no such document has been filed.[80]

If this rule applies it matters not whether the outsider has actually inspected the public documents or not.[81]

This rule, in contrast with rule 4 (below), only affords protection when the agent is purporting to exercise an authority which that sort

---

[74] Relying on *Morris* v. *Kanssen* [1946] A.C. 459, H.L., and *Howard* v. *Patent Ivory Manufacturing Co.* (1888) 38 Ch.D. 156.

[75] The judge distinguished *Morris* v. *Kanssen* and *Howard* v. *Patent Ivory Manufacturing Co.*, *supra*, on these grounds.

[76] Even then he will be bound by actual or constructive knowledge of the public documents under rule 1, *supra*.

[77] Both this rule and rule 4 are normal agency principles modified only by the doctrine of constructive notice of public documents. *Cf.* the similar rules applicable to partnerships (without such modification) as expressed in the Partnership Act 1890, ss. 5 and 10.

[78] *Howard* v. *Patent Ivory Co.* (1888) 38 Ch.D. 156.

[79] *Underwood Ltd.* v. *Bank of Liverpool* [1924] 1 K.B. 775, C.A.; *Liggett (Liverpool) Ltd.* v. *Barclays Bank* [1928] 1 K.B. 48; *Houghton & Co.* v. *Nothard, Lowe & Wills* [1927] 1 K.B. 246, C.A., affd. on other grounds [1928] A.C. 1, H.L.

[80] *i.e.*, unless rule 1 applies. See *Irvine* v. *Union Bank of Australia* (1877) 2 App.Cas. 366, P.C., where it was assumed that the resolution extending the director's borrowing powers would have required registration under what is now s. 143 of the Companies Act 1948. Contrast *Turquand's* case, *supra*, where the prescribed resolution was an ordinary one not requiring registration.

[81] This vexed point is discussed fully in connection with rule 4.

of officer would normally have, that is to say, when he is acting within the scope of his usual authority

If in fact the officer in question has been properly appointed the probability is that he will have actual authority, for he will be impliedly authorised to do what that sort of officer would usually be empowered to do unless he is expressly forbidden. If he has actual authority the third party, whether or not an outsider, is fully protected and no further question arises.[82]

If, however, the officer has not been properly appointed or if his normal authority has been curtailed, the third party will still be protected unless one of the conditions (a) (b) or (c) is established. Accordingly if he is dealing with the *de jure* or *de facto* board of directors he will be protected unless the public documents show unequivocally that the board have no power to act in the matter.[83] Similarly, since it is usual to delegate wide powers to a managing director, he will normally be protected if he is dealing with one who is a managing director or has been held out as such by the company. A good illustration is contained in the decision in *Freeman & Lockyer* v. *Buckhurst Park Properties (Mangal) Ltd.*,[84] where the Court of Appeal held that a director, who had assumed the powers of managing director with the company's approval (although he had never been so appointed) bound the company by entering into a contract with the plaintiff architects. The act of engaging architects was within the ordinary ambit of the authority of a managing director of a property company and the plaintiffs did not have to inquire whether the person with whom they were dealing was properly appointed; it was sufficient for them that under the articles there was in fact power to appoint him and that the board of directors had allowed him to act as such. Diplock L.J.[85] summarised the law by stating four conditions which must be fulfilled to entitle a contractor to enforce against a company a contract entered into on behalf of the company by an agent who has no actual authority:

"It must be shown: (1) that a representation that the agent had authority to enter on behalf of the company into a contract of the kind sought to be enforced was made to the contractor; (2) that such representation was made by a person or persons who had ' actual ' authority to manage the business of the company either generally or in respect of those matters to which the contract relates; (3) that he (the contractor) was induced by such representation to enter into the contract, that is, that he in fact relied upon it; and (4)

---

[82] It was on this ground that the Court of Appeal held that the plaintiff in *Hely-Hutchinson* v. *Brayhead Ltd.*, *supra*, was entitled to enforce the contract against the company.
[83] *Royal British Bank* v. *Turquand*, *supra*; *Mahony* v. *East Holyford Mining Co.*, *supra*.
[84] [1964] 2 Q.B. 480, C.A.
[85] At p. 506.

that under its memorandum or articles of association the company was not deprived of the capacity either to enter into a contract of the kind sought to be enforced or to delegate authority to enter into a contract of that kind to the agent."

Where, however, the outsider is dealing with some other officer his position will be much less secure. This applies even if the officer is a director who is not or has not been held out as a managing director, for a single director, as such, usually has no authority to bind the company.[86] Similarly if he is dealing with a manager, secretary or a lesser officer, he will be protected only if he can establish, which is likely to be difficult,[87] that the transaction in question is a usual one for that sort of officer, or that the officer had actual authority or that the company was estopped from denying it.[88]

To mitigate the hardship of this, the courts seem to have been prepared to hold that a chairman of directors has greater usual authority than an ordinary director [89] and that his position equates to that of a managing director [90]; why the right to take the chair should carry with it the right to manage out of the chair is difficult to see. But apart from this, unquestionably it is usual to leave certain things to individual directors. For example, it is customary to provide that documents shall be sealed in the presence, not of the whole board, but of one or more directors and the secretary. If, therefore, the third party receives a document sealed in the presence of the appropriate individuals as stated in the articles of association,[91] he is entitled to rely on its formal validity. Even if the board have never resolved that the document be sealed, he will be protected for he is not entitled to see the minutes of the board meeting which relate to a matter of "indoor management," and has no means of checking whether the internal regulations have been complied with.[92] Furthermore, he may be able to rely on section 74 of the Law of Property Act 1925, which

---

[86] *Rama Corporation* v. *Proved Tin & General Investments Ltd.* [1952] 2 Q.B. 147.
[87] *Houghton & Co.* v. *Nothard, Lowe & Wills* [1927] 1 K.B. 246, C.A.; affd. on other grounds [1928] A.C. 1; *Kreditbank Cassel* v. *Schenkers* [1927] 1 K.B. 826, C.A.; *S. London Greyhound Racecourses* v. *Wake* [1931] 1 Ch. 496; see also the observations of Willmer L.J. in *Freeman and Lockyer* v. *Buckhurst Park Properties (Mangal) Ltd.* [1964] 2 Q.B. at 494.   [88] *i.e.*, under rule 4, *infra*.
[89] It is a popular misconception, shared by lawyers and laymen (and apparently the legislature—see Companies Act 1967, s. 6), that the chairman is necessarily some sort of directorial overlord; he often is, but he may be merely an ornamental figurehead.
[90] *B.T.H.* v. *Federated European Bank* [1932] 2 K.B. 176, C.A.; *Clay Hill Brick Co.* v. *Rawlings* [1938] 4 All E.R. 100; but in *Hely-Hutchinson* v. *Brayhead, supra*, this was doubted by Roskill J. and by Lord Wilberforce: see at pp. 560D and 586G.
[91] If the articles require, say, two directors and the secretary, the outsider will not be protected if the document is sealed by *one* director only and the secretary—unless L.P.A. 1925, s. 74 (*infra*), applies.
[92] *Prince of Wales Assurance Society* v. *Athenaeum Insurance Society* (1858) 3 C.B.(N.S.) 756n.; *Re Country Life Assurance Co.* (1870) L.R. 5 Ch.App. 288; *County of Gloucester Bank* v. *Rudry Merthyr Colliery Co.* [1895] 1 Ch. 629, C.A.; *Duck* v. *Tower Galvanizing Co.* [1901] 2 K.B. 314. But see the unsatisfactory case of *S. London Greyhound Racecourses* v. *Wake* [1931] 1 Ch. 496, which appears to suggest

provides that, in favour of a purchaser, *a deed* shall be deemed to have been duly executed if it purports to be sealed in the presence of and attested by a director and the secretary. This, however, only applies if the outsider is a " purchaser," that is, one who acquires an interest in property in good faith and for valuable consideration,[93] and if the document is a deed—for a document under seal is not necessarily a deed.[94]

Similarly, it is usual to leave the signing of cheques to individual directors. Hence, again provided exception (*a*), (*b*) or (*c*) is not applicable, an outsider will be protected if cheques are signed by a director on behalf of the company.[95] It should be emphasised that whether the original recipient of the cheque will be able to sue on it depends on the validity of the main transaction in connection with which it is given, and this in turn depends on whether the officer with whom he is dealing in connection with that transaction has authority, actual, usual or apparent. But the cheque will be validly *signed* and will thus bind the company as regards the bank on whom it is drawn or subsequent holders for value. Similarly, what has been said about sealing documents relates only to execution, not to essential validity; here again subsequent transferees may be in a stronger position than the original recipient even though the document is not a negotiable instrument.[92]

But once one gets below the director level, the position becomes more problematical. Thus it is apparently not regarded as within the usual authority of a branch manager to draw bills of exchange.[96] On the other hand, it would presumably be regarded as within his usual authority to engage staff for the branch office, for it would be fantastic to suggest that a potential office-boy must inquire into the internal management before he can safely accept employment. Similarly, it is assumed that it would be within the usual authority of the secretary to engage clerical staff for the head office,[97] and *Mahoney's* case [98]

---

that, while a third party is not called upon to ensure that a resolution has been passed in general meeting, since this is a matter of internal management, he is nevertheless bound to see whether a resolution has been passed by the board of directors, which one would have thought was even more " internal." It is submitted that the decision is irreconcilable with earlier authorities, and wrong unless it can be justified on the ground that the outsider was put on inquiry.

[93] See the definition in L.P.A., s. 205 (xxi).

[94] A share certificate is not: *S. London Greyhound Racecourses* v. *Wake, supra,* which may be accepted on this point; see *R.* v. *Williams* [1942] A.C. 541, P.C.

[95] *Re Land Credit Co. of Ireland* (1869) L.R. 4 Ch.App. 460; *Mahony* v. *East Holyford Mining Co., supra.* The usual form of director's signature on behalf of a company does not seem to be treated as a " signature by procuration " within the meaning of s. 25 of the Bills of Exchange Act 1882: see the discussion in Paget, *Law of Banking* (7th ed.), pp. 327–329, and *cf.* Companies Act 1948, s. 33.

[96] *Kreditbank Cassel* v. *Schenkers, supra.*

[97] These questions are somewhat unlikely to arise because it would be rare indeed to find a case in which the manager or secretary had not *actual* authority, and even if he had no authority at all the employee would be able to recover on a *quantum meruit* for services actually rendered.

[98] *Supra.* But contrast *Houghton & Co.* v. *Nothard, Lowe & Wills, supra,* where the confirmation of a sale agreement by the secretary was held to be ineffective, for the secretary had no shadow of authority to make or confirm contracts.

appears to imply that it is within the usual scope of the secretary's authority to supply copies of board resolutions. On the other hand, the courts have displayed a strange reluctance to recognise any authority vested in the secretary even as regards those matters which, in fact, the secretary normally undertakes, such as certificating transfers.[99] This seems inconvenient and unjust, as the legislature has recognised up to a point.[1]

Rule 4. If, however, the officer is purporting to exercise an authority which that sort of officer would not usually have, the outsider will not be protected if the officer exceeds his actual authority unless the company has held him out as having authority to act in the matter and the outsider has relied thereon, that is, unless the company is estopped. But a provision in the memorandum or articles or other public documents cannot create an estoppel unless the outsider knows of the provision and has actually relied on it, and for this purpose registration at the Companies' Registry does not constitute notice.

The fundamental difference between this rule and rule 3 is that rule 3 applies where the agent is acting within the usual authority of that sort of officer, whereas rule 4 governs in other cases and imposes liability only if the company has held out the officer as having an authority greater than the normal. Both are said to be based on estoppel and the one expression, apparent or ostensible authority, is habitually used to describe them.[2] But under rule 3 the agent is held out as having power to enter into the transaction because he has been allowed to occupy a position in which it would be usual to have that power; under rule 4 he is held out as having authority to enter into the transaction although an agent in his position would not usually have authority to do so. The distinction could be important where the third party is ignorant that the officer is acting for a company but believes him to be the proprietor of the business. In that event if the officer is or has been allowed to act as managing director and is doing what a managing director would usually be empowered to do, it is submitted that under rule 3 the third party could hold the company liable as undisclosed

---

[99] *George Whitechurch Ltd.* v. *Cavanagh* [1902] A.C. 117, H.L.; *Kleinwort, Sons & Co.* v. *Associated Automatic Machine Corporation* (1934) 50 T.L.R. 244, H.L. These cases appear to depend on the now outmoded view that an act of an agent or servant will bind the principal if done for his benefit, but not if done fraudulently for the servant's own benefit. Since *Lloyd* v. *Grace, Smith & Co.* [1912] A.C. 716, H.L. they can only be regarded as anomalous exceptions to the general rule.

[1] Companies Act 1948, s. 79, partially overruling the cases cited in note 99. See Chap. 18, p. 400, *infra.*

[2] See, for example, *Freeman & Lockyer* v. *Buckhurst Park Properties (Mangal) Ltd.* [1964] 2 Q.B. 480, C.A.

principal.[3] But the chief importance of the distinction is that it affords an answer to the vexed question of how far it matters whether or not the outsider has read the company's articles.[4] When rule 3 applies it matters not at all. If the officer is doing what that sort of officer would usually be empowered to do, the company is bound unless the outsider knows or ought to have known that the officer is exceeding his authority. And if the articles (or other public documents) make it clear that the officer is exceeding his authority the company is not liable whether or not the outsider has read the articles. For example, if the articles did not empower the board to appoint and delegate powers to a managing director, the company would not be bound. That, however, would be very unusual and so long as there is such a power the company is bound whether or not the outsider knows of it. Reliance on rule 3 is in no way dependent on his having read the articles.[5] If, however, he is thrown back on rule 4 he cannot rely on a provision in the articles to establish that the officer has been held out as having authority unless he has in fact read and relied on that provision. The constructive notice doctrine does not work positively as well as negatively so as to entitle the outsider to say that he must be deemed to have relied on the provision because he has constructive notice of it.[6]

In some of the cases [7] there are dicta suggesting that if an officer is doing something unusual so that rule 3 does not apply, but there is a provision, of which the outsider was aware, in the articles whereby the board of directors might have delegated to that officer power to act, the company is thereby estopped and the outsider can rely on rule 4. This,

---

[3] *Cf. Watteau* v. *Fenwick* [1893] 1 Q.B. 346, a partnership case. It is also submitted that, not only could the third party enforce the contract against the company, but the company could enforce it against him (which suggests, *pace* the C.A. in the *Freeman & Lockyer* case, that in fact rule 3 is not based on estoppel). Under rule 4, the contract presumably cannot be enforced by the company unless it has ratified the officer's acts; until then there is no contract although the company is estopped from denying it.

[4] This question was discussed at length in the periodical literature cited in n. 55, *supra*, and in *Houghton & Co.* v. *Nothard, Lowe & Wills* [1927] 1 K.B. 246, C.A.; *Kreditbank Cassel* v. *Schenkers* [1927] 1 K.B. 826, C.A.; *British Thomson-Houston Co.* v. *Federated European Bank Ltd.* [1932] 2 K.B. 176 (where the reporter was moved to renounce his usual reticence and to append a note giving his understanding of the law); *Clay Hill Brick Co.* v. *Rawlings* [1938] 4 All E.R. 100 (where Tucker J. approved the reporter's note); *Rama Corporation* v. *Proved Tin & General Investments Ltd.* [1952] 2 Q.B. 147 (where Slade J. in an elaborate judgment dissented from the reporter's note); and *Freeman & Lockyer* v. *Buckhurst Park Properties (Mangal) Ltd.* [1964] 2 Q.B. 480 (where Willmer L.J. at p. 496 approved the reporter's note).

[5] Any doubt on this point was finally dispelled by the Court of Appeal in *Freeman & Lockyer* v. *Buckhurst Park Properties (Mangal) Ltd., supra*.

[6] Hence Diplock L.J. in the *Freeman & Lockyer* case suggested that it was preferable not to talk about constructive notice, as we have done in rule 1, since " the expression ' constructive notice ' tends to disguise that constructive notice is not a positive, but a negative doctrine, like that of estoppel of which it forms part ": at p. 504.

[7] *Houghton & Co.* v. *Nothard, Lowe & Wills, supra, Kreditbank Cassel* v. *Schenkers, supra, Rama Corporation* v. *Proved Tin & General Investments Ltd., supra*.

however, is difficult to understand. As Diplock L.J. pointed out in the *Freeman & Lockyer* case[8]: " [I]t would be necessary for him to establish first that he knew the contents of the articles[9] . . . and secondly that the conduct of the board in the light of that knowledge would be understood by a reasonable man as a representation that the agent had authority to enter into the contract sought to be enforced. . . ."[10] Clearly, the fact that there was a provision in the articles whereby the board might have delegated any of their powers to a committee of one director[11] or might have authorised someone to sign bills of exchange[12] does not amount to a representation that they have in fact done so. Knowledge of the relevant article is merely the first step towards establishing an estoppel; the second essential step will normally be lacking.[13]

Hence it is not surprising that it is difficult to find cases where the outsider has succeeded under rule 4 and there seems to be none in which a provision in the articles alone has sufficed. However *Mercantile Bank of India* v. *Chartered Bank of India*[14] affords one example where rule 4 operated. There a company, having power under its memorandum and articles to borrow and appoint agents, appointed agents by powers of attorney and authorised them to borrow and charge the company's property. The directors limited the amounts which the agents could borrow, but this limitation did not appear in the powers of attorney. Porter J. held that a charge granted to secure a borrowing in excess of the limit nevertheless bound the company. The powers of attorney, in the absence of any prohibition in the articles, estopped the company.[15]

Rule 5. An outsider who can bring himself within the protection of rule 3 or 4 will not necessarily lose his protection because the ostensible officer with whom he deals has never been validly appointed. On the other hand, that officer must at least have been held out in some way as an authorised officer of the company by one of the regularly appointed organs of the company.

That the official need not necessarily have been regularly appointed is clear. In *Mahony's* case,[16] neither the directors nor the secretary had, in fact, been properly elected to their offices, yet the company was held to be bound by their acts. Similarly, in *Biggerstaff* v. *Rowatt's*

---

[8] [1964] 2 Q.B. at p. 508.
[9] *i.e.*, that his condition 1 (see *supra*, p. 157) was fulfilled.
[10] *i.e.*, that his conditions 2 and 3 (*ibid.*) were fulfilled.
[11] As in *Houghton's* case and the *Rama* case.
[12] As in the *Kreditbank Cassel* case.
[13] " In such a case a person reading the article would be in no better a position unless he went further and inquired whether or not the directors had in fact " delegated: *per* Atkin L.J. in the *Kreditbank Cassel Case* [1927] 1 K.B. at p. 844.
[14] [1937] 1 All E.R. 231.
[15] The headnote is misleading in that it suggests that it was the articles which brought about the estoppel, whereas it is clear that it was the powers of attorney and that the articles were only of negative importance.
[16] *Mahony* v. *East Holyford Mining Co.* (1875) L.R. 7 H.L. 869, *supra*.

Wharf Ltd.,[17] *Clay Hill Brick Co.* v. *Rawlings* [18] and *Freeman & Lockyer*
v. *Buckhurst Park Properties (Mangal) Ltd.*,[19] the companies were made
liable for the acts of directors acting as managing directors although they
had never been formally appointed to these offices—a not uncommon
occurrence.

On the other hand, it would be contrary to all principle that an agent
should be allowed to clothe himself with an appearance of authority
which would bind the company without any complicity on its part. The
company itself, acting through a duly appointed organ or officer, must
either have represented the ostensible officer to have been duly
appointed, in which event it will be bound if he has done what that sort
of officer would usually have power to do,[20] or if he has done what the
company has represented him as authorised to do.[21] And if a duly
appointed organ has authorised the so-called officer to represent himself
as such or to make representations regarding the extent of his authority,
the company will be bound by the representations which he makes.[22]

For this purpose, however, there must be some regularly appointed
organ which has knowingly acquiesced. This organ may be the members
themselves acting either formally in general meeting or by (unanimous?)
informal consent even without a meeting.[23] Thus, in *Mahony's* case,
it seems that all the subscribers to the memorandum (*i.e.*, the original
members) had knowingly allowed those who acted as directors to hold
themselves out as such. Or the organ may be the directors, acting
within their actual, usual or apparent authority. Thus, in the *Biggerstaff*, *Clay Hill Brick Co.* and *Freeman & Lockyer* cases, it appears that
the directors knew that one of their number was holding himself out as
managing director, and as it was within their powers to appoint a
managing director, the company was bound by the director's acts. And,
as *Mahony's* case shows, acting directors held out as such by the
members may in turn hold out someone as secretary, with the result that
the latter's acts bind the company. However, it is difficult to see why
some of these cases were not decided on the basis that the person held
out had actual, but implied as distinct from express, authority to carry

17 [1896] 2 Ch. 93, C.A., *supra*.
18 [1938] 4 All E.R. 100, *supra*. In this case the director was also the chairman.
19 [1964] 2 Q.B. 480, *supra*.
20 Unless the outsider knows or ought to have known that he was not authorised, *i.e.*,
   unless rule 3 (*a*) (*b*) or (*c*) applies.
21 See Diplock L.J.'s condition 2 (*supra*, p. 157) and his discussion of this question at
   [1964] 2 Q.B. at pp. 504–507.
22 See *per* Greer L.J. in *British Thomson Houston Co. Ltd.* v. *Federated European
   Bank* [1932] 2 K.B. at 182; Pearson L.J. in the *Freeman & Lockyer Case* [1964]
   2 Q.B. at 499; Denning M.R. and Lord Pearson in *Hely-Hutchinson* v. *Brayhead
   Ltd.* [1968] 1 Q.B. at 583 and 593.
23 This appears to be an example of circumstances in which the veil of incorporation
   is lifted so as to allow a company to be bound by the informal consent of its
   individual members: *cf.* Chap. 10, *infra*, at pp. 208–210. It may be very important
   in the case of small private companies whose meetings tend to be mythical.

out the transactions in question.[24] If the board of directors knowingly allow one of their number to act as managing director, they will thereby impliedly authorise him to do whatever is usual for a managing director of such a company to do unless they forbid him.[25]

One may get even more complicated cases. Thus all companies today have to maintain a register of directors and secretary and to file a copy at the Companies' Registry.[26] It is submitted that if those who act as directors or secretary are shown as such in the company's register *and* the outsider has searched it (but not otherwise [27]), he is normally entitled to hold the company liable for all acts within the actual, usual or apparent scope of the official's authority in accordance with rules 2, 3 and 4. The register, however, will normally have been completed by the secretary and the filed copy signed by him. Assuming that the directors and the secretary have never been validly appointed and that the members have never acquiesced in their acting, the result, if the register estops the company, is that an acting subordinate official (the secretary) can estop the company from denying the authority of the *de facto* superior officials (the directors) and himself. It may be, therefore, that notwithstanding the particulars given on the register, the company will be bound only if the members have acquiesced in the *soi-disant* directors or secretary acting as such. This probably is the position. However, in practice it is thought that, if directors and secretary are named in the register, the onus of disproving acquiescence will be on the members. Both the register and the filed copy are open to public inspection, but although the practice is to rely on the copy in the company's file at the Registry, this seems to be dangerous, since it does not have to be filed until fourteen days after a change and may therefore not be up to date.[28]

It will also be appreciated that the names of the directors normally have to be shown on the company's notepaper and the like.[29] Presumably the company might equally be estopped from denying that those named on the notepaper were its directors. This should be so if the members knew of the statement [30] and if it was not contradicted by the register of directors, of which outsiders must be deemed to have notice.[31] Similarly, it is thought that if duly appointed directors, or those

---

[24] As in *Hely-Hutchinson* v. *Brayhead Ltd.* [1968] 1 Q.B. 549, C.A., where the chairman had never been formally appointed as managing director or expressly authorised to do what he did.

[25] *Ibid.*

[26] Companies Act 1948, s. 200, which extends to most unregistered companies: see s. 435 and Sched. 14.

[27] Rule 4. And *cf. Tower Cabinet Co.* v. *Ingram* [1949] 2 K.B. 397, which apparently establishes that this is the position as regards registration of particulars under the Registration of Business Names Act 1916.

[28] s. 200 (5).

[29] s. 201. This only applies to registered companies formed after 1916.

[30] *Tower Cabinet Co.* v. *Ingram, supra*; a partnership case in which the outsider lost because the alleged partner did *not* know that he was being held out in this way.

[31] Rule 1.

held out as such by the members, knowingly allow one of their number to describe himself on the notepaper as " managing director," the company will be estopped from denying that he occupies this position.

Another possible source of protection to the outsider is section 180 [32] of the Companies Act 1948, which provides that " The acts of a director or manager shall be valid notwithstanding any defect that may afterwards be discovered in his appointment or qualification," and which is generally supplemented by a provision in the articles on the lines of Article 105 of Table A.[33] But the decisions, and in particular that of the House of Lords in *Morris* v. *Kanssen*,[34] show that these provisions add little to the protection which an outsider would have under the *Turquand* rule. They apply only where the director concerned has been appointed but where there is some defect in the appointment. " There is, as it appears to me, a vital distinction between (a) an appointment in which there is a defect or, in other words, a defective appointment, and (b) no appointment at all." [35] And they will not protect someone who knows of the invalidity [36] nor, probably, one who is put on inquiry.[37] But it seems that the outsider may be able to invoke the section unless he himself knows (or ought to know) of the defect; " defect that may afterwards be discovered " apparently means discovered by him, not by other parties.[37]

The distinction, drawn in these cases, between a defective appointment and no appointment at all, is a fine one, and it is far from clear what is regarded as a mere defect for this purpose. As *Morris* v. *Kanssen* itself decides, an originally valid appointment which has expired is not necessarily included. The wording of the section appears to cover an appointment invalidated by the failure to take up a share qualification.[38] On the other hand, under section 182 (3) the office of director is vacated if he fails to take up his qualification within two months and according to *Morris* v. *Kanssen* a vacated appointment is no appointment at all.[39]

---

[32] Only applicable to registered companies.

[33] " All acts done by any meeting of the directors or of a committee of directors or by any person acting as a director shall, notwithstanding that it be afterwards discovered that there was some defect in the appointment of any such director or person acting as aforesaid, or that they or any of them were disqualified, be as valid as if every such person had been duly appointed and was qualified to be a director." In *Mahony* v. *East Holyford Mining Co.*, *supra*, there was an article on these lines and some reliance was placed on it, but it appears that the decision would have been the same without it.

[34] [1946] A.C. 459, H.L.

[35] *Per* Lord Simonds at p. 471.

[36] *Re Staffordshire Gas Co.* (1892) 66 L.T. 413 ; *Tyne Mutual Steamship Association* v. *Brown* (1896) 74 L.T. 283.

[37] So held by C.A. in the *Kanssen* case, *sub nom. Kanssen* v. *Rialto* (*West End*) *Ltd.* [1944] Ch. 346, but left open by H.L.

[38] So held in *Dawson* v. *African Consolidated Land & Trading Co.* [1898] 1 Ch. 6, C.A.; and *Channel Collieries Trust* v. *Dover* (*etc.*) *Light Railway Co.* [1914] 2 Ch. 506, C.A.

[39] And it might be argued that the outsider is deemed to know of the absence of share qualification because the share register is open for inspection at the company's office :

In the comparatively rare cases where the provisions apply they validate acts not only in favour of outsiders but also as between the company and its members.[38] Indeed, it seems that they are only of practical importance in the latter case, since the outsider will normally secure wider protection under the common law rule in *Turquand's* case. But although the section may validate the officer's acts, it does not entitle him to the remuneration of the office.[40]

Section 145 (3) should also be noted in this connection. This removes the onus of proof of regularity from the outsider, where decisions of general, directors' or managers' meetings are minuted, by providing that *until the contrary is proved* such proceedings shall be deemed to have been duly convened and held and all appointments of directors, managers or liquidators shall be deemed valid. It is clear that for this purpose it makes no difference that the third party has never seen the minutes; indeed, he has no right to call for them.[41]

Rule 6. If a document purporting to be sealed by or signed on behalf of the company is proved to be a forgery, it does not bind the company.[42] But the company may be estopped from disclaiming the document as a forgery if it has been put forward as genuine by an officer acting within his actual, usual, or apparent authority, and if a transaction is binding on the company under the foregoing rules the company will be liable notwithstanding that the officer has acted fraudulently or commited forgery.[43]

It is often stated that the *Turquand* rule has no application where forgery is involved. This idea appears to stem from the decision of the House of Lords in *Ruben* v. *Great Fingall Consolidated*,[44] where a company secretary had issued a share certificate to which he had affixed the company's seal and forged the signatures of the directors in whose presence it purported to be affixed. A transferee claimed damages from the company on the basis that the company was estopped from denying the truth of the certificate. It was held that the document was a forgery and that therefore it could not bind the company unless some official acting within his authority had warranted

---

see s. 110. But as already pointed out (*supra*, p. 154), the register does not seem to be treated as a public document for this purpose. If the absence of qualification was apparent from the Annual Return, *quaere: ibid.*

[40] *Re Allison* [1904] 2 K.B. 327. But he may be entitled to claim on a *quantum meruit*: *Craven-Ellis* v. *Canons Ltd.* [1936] 2 K.B. 403, C.A.

[41] In *Kerr* v. *Mottram Ltd.* [1940] Ch. 657 the articles made minutes *conclusive* evidence and it was held that it was not open to the plaintiff to adduce evidence to contradict them in the absence of fraud. It is submitted that this decision can only be supported on the assumption that the transaction was between the company and a member as such so that the articles bound the plaintiff as a contract: see Chap. 12, *infra*.

[42] Thompson, in (1956) 11 Univ. of Toronto L.J. 248, expresses this principle by saying that a forgery is not a mere internal irregularity within the meaning of the *Turquand* rule.

[43] See the very helpful discussion by Campbell in (1960) 76 L.Q.R. at pp. 130–136.

[44] [1906] A.C. 439, H.L.

that it was genuine. Even assuming that the secretary might be taken to have impliedly warranted this, he had no colour of authority, actual, usual, or apparent, to do so and therefore the company was not bound.

The case, therefore, decides no more than that the acts of the secretary were outside the scope of his authority, which as we have seen is an extremely restricted one.[45] There is, however, a dictum by Lord Loreburn which suggests that the *Turquand* rule has no application to a forgery. The forged certificate, he said,[46] " is a pure nullity. It is quite true that persons dealing with limited liability companies are not bound to inquire into their indoor management and will not be affected by irregularities of which they have no notice. But this doctrine, which is well established, applies only to irregularities that otherwise might affect a genuine transaction. It cannot apply to a forgery."

In *Lloyd* v. *Grace, Smith & Co.*[47] the House of Lords held that acts might be within the scope of authority of an agent or servant notwithstanding that they were done fraudulently and for his own benefit and not for that of his principal or master. In *Kreditbank Cassel* v. *Schenkers*[48] certain members of the Court of Appeal felt difficulty in reconciling Lord Loreburn's principle with *Lloyd* v. *Grace, Smith & Co.*, but nevertheless adopted it as an alternative ground of their decision. So too did Clauson J. in *S. London Greyhound Racecourses* v. *Wake*,[49] in which he held that a share-certificate, to which the company's seal had been fraudulently affixed in the presence of a director and the secretary, was a forgery since there had been no resolution of the board authorising the sealing.[50]

In these circumstances it was not unreasonable for Wright J. in *Slingsby* v. *District Bank* [51] to draw the conclusion that:

" Though a man may be estopped by conduct from denying that a forgery is his signature,[52] yet as forgery is a crime he cannot authorise it in advance (if indeed it is not a contradiction in terms to authorise a forgery) without being an accessory before the fact. Nor can he agree to be bound by it subsequently, so as to shield a criminal or compound a felony. *Hence an act of forgery*

---

[45] See pp. 142, 143 and 160, *supra*, and *cf. George Whitechurch Ltd.* v. *Cavanagh* [1902] A.C. 117, H.L.; and *Kleinwort, Sons & Co.* v. *Associated Automatic Machine Corporation* (1934) 50 T.L.R. 244, H.L.

[46] [1906] A.C. at p. 443. *Cf.* Stirling L.J. in the C.A. [1904] 2 K.B. at p. 729.

[47] [1912] A.C. 716, H.L.

[48] [1927] 1 K.B. 826, C.A.

[49] [1931] 1 Ch. 496.

[50] This was despite a provision in the articles that in favour of a purchaser or person dealing bona fide with the company such signatures should be conclusive of the fact that the seal had been properly affixed. The learned judge held (rightly on this point it is respectfully submitted) that Wake could not rely on this article, since he did not know of it.

[51] [1931] 2 K.B. 588 (affd. [1932] 1 K.B. 544, C.A.) at p. 605.

[52] This is irrefutable: *Greenwood* v. *Martins Bank* [1933] A.C. 51, H.L.: and see Bills of Exchange Act 1882, ss. 54 (2) and 55 (2).

is a nullity and outside any actual or ostensible authority,[53] and outside the principle of *Lloyd* v. *Grace, Smith & Co.*"

This doctrine has, however, been emphatically rejected by the Court of Appeal in *Uxbridge Building Society* v. *Pickard,*[54] where a solicitor was held liable for the frauds of his managing clerk notwithstanding that they involved forgery. In this case, Greene M.R. felt constrained to explain away the company cases on the ground that the rule in *Turquand's* case does not depend on ordinary agency principles [55] and that it " has always—certainly ever since the days of Lord Hatherley—been held not to apply to cases of fraud." [56] It is respectfully submitted that this view is untenable; the *Turquand* rule has always been expressed as an agency principle, and as for its non-application to fraud, surely Lord Hatherley's famous judgment in *Mahony* v. *East Holyford Mining Co.* was actually made in a case of fraud?

The truth seems to be that there are no reasons why the fact that there is a forgery should exclude the *Turquand* rule. All the decisions can be explained on the ground either that the forged document was not put forward as genuine by an official acting within his usual or apparent authority, or that the outsider was put on inquiry. In *Ruben's* and *Schenkers'* cases this decision was probably justified; in *Wake's* case it probably was not. But, accepting the findings in these cases, all three are reconcilable with principle. Indeed it was on this basis that MacKinnon L.J. explained *Ruben's* and *Schenkers'* cases in *Uxbridge Building Society* v. *Pickard.*[57]

It is therefore submitted that rule 6 rightly expresses the present law.

Summary of common law and statutory protections

In conclusion it may be useful to summarise the various protections which an outsider can invoke when he has dealt with an officer of the company who has exceeded his actual authority:

1. He may be able to rely on the rule in *Royal British Bank* v. *Turquand,* the effect of which is set out above, and which, in reality, is the normal agency principle of usual and apparent authority, modified in its relation to companies, having regard to the publicity given to their constitutional documents.

2. If there is a defect in the officer's appointment, section 180 of the Act may afford protection, but this will rarely help an outsider who could not rely, in any case, on the *Turquand* rule.[58]

---

[53] My italics.
[54] [1939] 2 K.B. 248, C.A.
[55] At p. 257.
[56] In [1939] 2 All E.R. at p. 350. This passage does not appear in the L.R., from which it may be deduced that the learned judge had second thoughts.
[57] [1939] 2 K.B. at p. 258.
[58] *Supra*, pp. 165, 166.

3. The outsider may be able to rely on some special protecting provision in the articles, but only, apparently, if he in fact knows of the provision in question. One such article (Article 105 of Table A) has been dealt with already.[59]   Another, which may be referred to here, is Article 79 of Table A, which limits the directors' powers of borrowing to the nominal amount of the issued share capital, but provides that no one dealing with the company shall be concerned to see whether the limit is observed and that no borrowing shall be invalid " except in the case of express notice to the lender . . . that the limit hereby imposed had been or was thereby exceeded." It would appear that the only circumstances in which this would afford greater protection than the lender already has under *Turquand's* case [60] are where (a) he lends less than the limit,[61] which is exceeded because of existing borrowings of which he has no express [62] notice, and (b) the circumstances are such as to put him on inquiry,[63] and (c) he actually knows of the terms of the article. Clearly this combination of circumstances is unlikely to occur. Nor, for reasons already stated,[64] does it seem that mere knowledge of the existence of an article permitting delegation will entitle an outsider to rely on the fact that the permission has been exercised.

Hence, like paragraph 2, this possibility will rarely be any help.

4. If there is any defect in the sealing of a deed he may be able to rely on section 74 of the Law of Property Act 1925.[65]

5. Finally, if minutes of meetings can be produced which indicate that the transaction was regular, the onus of proof of the contrary will lie on the company.[66]

---

[59] *Ibid.*
[60] Which, as we have seen, established that he was entitled to assume that the borrowing had been approved in general meeting: *supra*, p. 152.
[61] If his own loan is for more than the limit (of which he is presumably deemed to have notice, since the amount of the issued capital will be ascertainable from the returns at the Registry—but see p. 154, *supra*) he must presumably be regarded as having " express notice " that the limit " was thereby exceeded."
[62] *Quaere*, whether registration of a charge would be " express " notice within the meaning of this article.
[63] Thus excluding protection under the *Turquand* rule.
[64] *Supra*, p. 162.
[65] *Supra*, p. 159. But only if the outsider is a " purchaser " and the document is a " deed."
[66] s. 145 (3), *supra*, p. 166.

Chapter 9

COMPANIES AND TAXATION

ONE of the important consequences of incorporation is that it may affect the incidence of taxation. It is beyond the scope of this book to deal with revenue law in any detail.[1] Nevertheless, it is a trite observation that today taxation is one of the main factors for consideration in any legal transaction and this is especially true of company law. Indeed, it is probably fair to say that in the last fifty years more companies have been formed because of the real or imagined taxation advantages than for any other single reason. However, since the fundamental changes introduced by the Finance Act 1965, there has been, in many cases, a movement in the opposite direction: a number of private companies have been liquidated in order that their shareholders can carry on their businesses in partnership with each other. Private investment companies have been particularly harshly treated by the 1965 Act, and are steadily disappearing from the scene. It is therefore essential to glance briefly at the consequences of incorporation in this respect.

For this purpose only direct taxation need be considered; so far as concerns the various forms of indirect taxation (customs and excise duties, purchase tax, and stamp duties [2]) a company is not generally in a different position from a natural person. In these latter cases the tax is imposed on transactions, and those who indulge in them are liable irrespective of their personal status. But a great part of the revenue is raised by taxes on individual incomes and capital gains during life and on capital on death, and here differences between companies and natural persons are almost inevitable—obviously so in the case of death duties, for a company cannot die.

TAXES ON INCOME AND CAPITAL GAINS

General principles

Evolving a system for taxing companies presents more difficulties than evolving a system for taxing individuals. The principal problem

---

[1] On income tax, capital gains tax and corporation tax, see *British Tax Encyclopedia* (ed. G. S. A. Wheatcroft), Vol. I. On corporation tax, see Talbot and Wheatcroft, *Corporation Tax*, and Beattie, *Corporation Tax* (2nd ed.). On death duties, see Green's *Death Duties*, 6th ed., 1967, with supplement; and Dymond's *Death Duties*, 14th ed., 1965, with supplement. Grundy, *Tax and the Family Business* (3rd ed.), seeks in a fairly short compass to indicate, principally to the businessman rather than the lawyer, how the whole tax system affects the small or medium-sized family business, incorporated or otherwise. There is also much of interest in the eminently readable *Tax Planning for the Family Solicitor* (3rd ed.) by J. Philip Lawton.

[2] " Capital duty " (at present 10s. per cent.) is, of course, peculiar to companies (and limited partnerships). In cases of reconstructions or amalgamations special reliefs from stamp duties are available to companies: F.A. 1927, s. 55, as amended, see Chap. 26 at pp. 632, 633.

arises from the relationship between a company and its shareholders, and from the fact that it is neither necessary nor common for the whole of a company's profits to be distributed. In approaching the task of levying taxation by reference to companies, a legislature might adopt any one or more of four different attitudes.

1. It might treat a company in precisely the same way as a natural person. Since the essence of most modern tax systems for individuals is that the tax is charged at progressive rates—the higher the income, the higher the rate of tax—this solution would involve the same element of progression being introduced for companies. Considerable difficulties would follow, particularly in countries like the United Kingdom where the progressive effect is—at the lower levels of income—achieved by means of personal allowances varying in their incidence according to whether the taxpayer is or is not married, does or does not have children, and the like. Accordingly, almost all systems have taxed companies basically at a flat rate, though possibly with some small reductions in the rate where the profits are low.[3]

2. It might have torn aside the veil of incorporation, and, without taxing the company at all, have taxed the shareholders on the company's profits, whether or not distributed to them. This solution would involve the profits being notionally apportioned among the members, and, in cases where the company " ploughs back " its profits instead of distributing them, would be somewhat unfair on the members, except, perhaps, in cases where the members controlled the company and could ensure that distributions were made when they needed money.

3. It could have the same tax for companies as for other taxpayers, but could impose it on the company and not on the shareholders. As a likely corollary, distributions actually made to the shareholders would not be taxed again.

4. It could apply a special tax to the company's profits, and then might or might not impose an entirely different form of tax on distributions made to the members.

In the United Kingdom the legislature has recently, through the introduction of corporation tax by the Finance Act 1965, completely changed its former approach. Previously the tax system involved a combination of the third and fourth possibilities, with some elements of the second also present. Now the fourth possibility has been whole-heartedly adopted, though still supplemented by elements of the second. Another radical change brought about by the Finance Act 1965 was the imposition of tax on capital gains, which formerly had not been taxed in any systematic way. The new tax applies both to companies, which pay corporation tax on their capital gains, and to the shareholders, who pay capital gains tax at rates of up to 30 per cent. on gains on their

---

[3] As was the case with the " abatement " which used to apply for profits tax: see F.A. 1947, s. 33.

shares, unless they are themselves companies, in which case gains on their shares will suffer corporation tax.

Company taxation before the Finance Act 1965

Prior to the 1965 Act a company was liable to two separate taxes: first, to the ordinary income tax as charged on individuals, but payable by companies at the standard rate without any personal allowances; and secondly, to profits tax, a tax peculiar to companies.[4] As with indivi-- duals, capital gains were normally not taxable. In contrast with individuals, companies were not liable to surtax, the progressive tax payable on the higher slices of income of the wealthy.[5] When companies paid dividends these were treated as a distribution of a fund which had already borne income tax (if the dividend was paid out of income profits), or as a distribution of non-taxable capital (if paid out of capital gains). In the normal case of a distribution of income the company notionally deducted income tax at the standard rate from the dividend. The shareholders were accordingly treated as having received income which had already borne income tax at the standard rate, and if their total income was so small that they were not liable to bear the standard rate they could claim a refund from the Revenue. But in determining their total income for tax purposes the dividend was " grossed-up," *i.e.*, treated as the larger amount which, after deduction of tax, left the net amount actually received. If their total income, including that gross amount, brought them within the surtax bracket they had to pay surtax on that basis.

It became apparent at an early date that surtax could be avoided if a company retained its profits instead of distributing them. The members would ultimately realise the benefit of the retained profits either by selling their shares, or on a capital reduction or liquidation, but they would receive it as tax-free capital and not as surtaxable income.[6] To counteract tax avoidance by this use of the corporate entity principle most small and medium-sized companies were made subject to a procedure called a " surtax direction," which was originally introduced by section 21 of the Finance Act 1922.[7] The effect was that, if the company had distributed less than a reasonable amount of its profits,[8] the whole of its income was notionally apportioned among the members, and the

---

4 In 1965–66 the combined rates of income tax and profits tax amounted to 56¼ per cent.
5 At the highest levels of income this is charged at 10s. in £ which, with income tax at 8s. 3d. in the £, means that the total tax on the top slice can be as high as 91¼ per cent.
6 *I.R.C.* v. *Burrell* [1923] 2 K.B. 478; affd. [1924] 2 K.B. 52, C.A. Pending a sale or reduction or liquidation, the members might extract cash by " loans " from the company; see, *e.g.*, *I.R.C.* v. *Sansom* [1921] 2 K.B. 492, C.A.
7 In their final form the surtax direction provisions were contained in I.T.A. 1952, ss. 245 to 262.
8 Except in the case of investment companies, where a surtax direction was automatic whatever the distributions made: *ibid.*, s. 262.

Revenue collected the surtax (usually from the company) which would have been payable if dividends had been declared in accordance with the notional apportionment.

Thus it will be seen that even though the old system of corporate taxation functioned for many years, it nevertheless had several disadvantages. It involved the interaction of two, and sometimes three, different charges, and was of necessity extremely complicated. Moreover, the system whereby the company paid income tax and then distributed its profits with the income tax notionally deducted from them lent itself to avoidance devices—in particular to the " dividend-stripping " technique whereby the recipient of the dividends created an artificial tax loss and claimed relief on it in the form of a repayment of tax from the Revenue.[9] Moreover, as long as income tax applied both to companies and to individuals, it was difficult (though not impossible [10]) to vary the burden of tax falling on companies without affecting individuals, or vice versa. Accordingly, there were powerful arguments in favour of making a complete new departure, and that was done by the Finance Act 1965.

Company taxation after the Finance Act 1965

The general structure

In very broad terms, the Finance Act 1965 [11] changed the previous system of corporate taxation in two fundamental respects. First, it abolished the charge to income tax and profits tax on a company's profits and introduced a charge to a new tax, known as corporation tax. Secondly, it imposed liability to income tax (as well as surtax, which had always applied) on the distributions which a company makes. Corporation tax is levied at a rate lower than the combined rates of income tax and profits tax, and the difference is, in broad terms, made good to the Revenue by the income tax on distributions.

Although the income tax on distributions is, in theory, the shareholders' tax, it is the company which actually has to pay it by deducting it from the distributions and accounting for it to the Revenue. The general effect is to shift part of the tax burden from the company's profits on to its distributions, and to encourage companies [12] to retain and

---

[9] For a (successful) example of dividend stripping in its simplest form, see *Griffiths* v. *J. P. Harrison (Watford) Ltd.* [1963] A.C. 1. For an (unsuccessful) attempt at a more complicated variant (the " forward strip "), see *Bishop* v. *Finsbury Securities Ltd.* [1966] 1 W.L.R. 1402. A battery of legislation, beginning with s. 4 of F. (No. 2) A. 1955 was enacted to try to nullify the tax advantages deriving from dividend stripping. A particularly interesting provision is F.A. 1960, s. 28, by which Parliament, apparently despairing of ever being able to defeat in detail all the elaborations on the basic scheme which could be devised by skilfully advised taxpayers, gave to the Revenue discretionary powers to nullify the effect of " transactions in securities " having certain broadly described characteristics.
[10] The effect coud be produced by adjustments to the rate of profits tax.
[11] ss. 46 to 89, and Scheds. 11 to 21.
[12] Except " close companies," on which see *infra*, p. 177.

plough back their profits instead of distributing them. Taking corporation tax at 45 per cent.[12a] and income tax at 41¼ per cent.,[12b] that part of a company's profits which, after corporation tax, is distributed as dividends costs the company a combined tax bill of just below 68 per cent.[13] Undistributed profits are, initially, subject to corporation tax only, but that is not the end of the story, because the retained profits are reflected in an increased value of the shares in the company. Eventually those shares will be realised by the shareholders—typically by a sale or on liquidation [14]—and the increase in their value emerges as a capital gain liable to capital gains tax. The relationship between retained profits and the value of the shares is more direct in the case of a small company than in the case of a quoted company with numerous shareholders, but exists to some extent for all companies, however large or small.

Corporation tax on profits

A company resident in the United Kingdom [15] is liable to corporation tax on all its profits wherever arising.[16] The " profits " consist of the company's income from various sources,[17] and its capital gains (after deduction of capital losses), less a number of reliefs. The most important relief allows the deduction of " charges on income," [18] which include most types of interest. Dividends and other distributions, on the other hand, cannot be deducted,[19] and the difference in this respect between interest and dividends is having major repercussions on the methods by which companies raise finance. More is said on this later.[20]

Distributions and franked investment income

A major feature of the corporation tax system is the special treatment accorded to distributions, and an extremely wide and complicated definition is given to the term.[21] Its importance is twofold; in the first place, distributions entail the company paying income tax and the shareholders (if individuals with large incomes) paying surtax [22]; and, in the second place, the company cannot, in computing its profits

12a The rate for the year beginning March 1, 1969.

12b *i.e.,* the standard rate of 8s. 3d in the £ for the year 1969–70.

13 *i.e.,* 45 per cent., plus 41¼ per cent. of 55 per cent.

14 There are other occasions, notably gifts (F.A. 1965, s. 22 (4) (*a*)) and death (*ibid.,* s. 24 (1)), on which the shares will be deemed to be disposed of at their market value.

15 A company is resident where its central control and management is situated (normally where the directors meet), see Chap. 10, pp. 207, 208.

16 **F.A.** 1965, ss. 46 (1) (2) (*a*) and 49.

17 An important exception is distributions from other companies, see further, p. 176, *infra.*

18 F.A. 1965, s. 52.

19 *Ibid.,* ss. 52 (2), 53 (5) (*a*).

20 See p. 176 and Chap. 16, p. 353.

21 F.A. 1965, Sched. 11.

22 *Ibid.,* s. 47.

chargeable to corporation tax, deduct anything which ranks as a distribution.[23]

The usual type of distribution is, of course, a dividend, and this now includes a dividend out of capital gains.[24] Simple bonus issues of ordinary shares are not distributions, but exceptional types of bonus issues may be caught. For example, issues of bonus debentures or of bonus redeemable shares are distributions,[25] and this rule is likely to put an end to bonus issues of that type. Also covered by the definition are bonus issues which have been preceded at any time after April 6, 1965, by a repayment of capital [26] (except where the capital repaid consisted of fully paid preference shares [27]). The same applies in reverse: if a company makes a bonus issue and then repays the bonus shares,[28] the repayment is a distribution and attracts an income tax and surtax liability.[29] That apart, however, repayments of capital—whether of redeemable preference shares or pursuant to a reduction of capital confirmed by the court—do not constitute distributions.[30] They are, however, disposals for capital gains tax,[31] and may give rise to some liability to that tax. The same is true of distributions in a liquidation. This is an important practical point, because, where a company has accumulated profits within it, virtually the only methods whereby the shareholders can enjoy those profits subject only to capital gains tax, and not to income tax and surtax, is to liquidate the company [32]—or to sell their shares if they can find a buyer at a price which will reflect the value of the accumulated profits.

Thus bonus issues,[33] repayments of capital, and liquidations do not, as a general rule, amount to distributions. What of payments of interest? Here the question is important, not because it decides whether income tax and surtax is payable—interest is taxable income in any case—but because it decides whether the company can deduct the interest in determining its taxable profits. Interest is, in principle, deductible as a charge on income,[34] but it is disallowed if it is caught by the definition

23 *Ibid.*, ss. 52 (2), 53 (5) (*a*).
24 *Ibid.*, Sched. 11, para. 1 (1) (*a*).
25 *Ibid.*, Sched. 11, para. 1 (1) (*c*).
26 *Ibid.*, Sched. 11, para. 1 (3); the repayment of capital would have occurred on the redemption of redeemable preference shares or on a reduction with the consent of the court.
27 F.A. 1966, Sched. 5, para. 14.
28 Or the shares in respect of which they were issued, or any shares of the same class as either.
29 F.A. 1965, Sched. 11, paras. 1 (2) (*b*), 2 (1).
30 Except to the extent that more than the par value (plus any share premium account) is repaid: *ibid.*, para. 3.   31 F.A. 1965, Sched. 7, para. 3.
32 Even then, if they continue the same business through another company, they could be in danger of attack by the Revenue under F.A. 1960, s. 28, as to which, see p. 173, note 9, *supra*.
33 Nor does a mere bonus issue have any adverse capital gains tax consequences: F.A. 1965, Sched. 7, para. 4. For a general discussion of the tax problems arising from bonus issues, see Carey [1967] *British Tax Review* 127.
34 *Ibid.*, s. 52. After F.A. 1969, this will not be so in the case of interest paid by individuals, but most companies will not be affected.

of distribution.[35]   The general rule is that interest is not a distribution, but, again there are exceptions.   One exception covers interest on bonus debentures.[36]   Others apply to various types of debenture which, though ostensibly such, have many of the characteristics of shares.[37]

Thus it will be seen that, although commercial factors will—particularly in the case of quoted companies—impel most companies to make distributions (usually by way of dividend), the tax consequences to the company making them will be unfavourable.   The converse case is the company which receives a distribution from another.   It would have discouraged companies from investing in other companies, or from dividing their businesses between parent and subsidiary companies, if dividends (which are, of course, paid out of profits which have already borne corporation tax) were to be assessed to corporation tax again. Therefore, distributions received by companies are free of corporation tax.[38]   Usually the distribution will be received after deduction of income tax at the standard rate.[39]   If so, it is called " franked investment income " of the recipient company.[40]   That company is, in principle, not liable to income tax,[41] and, although it is, in general,[42] not allowed to claim from the Revenue in cash the income tax deducted from its franked investment income,[43] it nevertheless has what may be described as a notional credit against the Revenue for that income tax.   It uses that credit to offset its own liability to deduct and account for income tax on the distributions which it, in its turn, makes to its own shareholders.[44] Thus a company which has no franked investment income but wishes to declare dividends to its shareholders can only do so at the cost of an income tax liability; a company which does have some franked investment income can, to the extent of that income, declare dividends without incurring any additional tax burden.

The effect of corporation tax on company financing

The introduction of corporation tax has brought wholly new factors into play in relation to methods of financing companies.   It will be some time yet before the full effects of the changes can be clearly discerned, but it seems that there will be a decided shift towards raising money by borrowing rather than by making issues of shares.[45]

---

[35] *Ibid.*, s. 52 (2).
[36] *Ibid.*, Sched. 11, para. 1 (1) (*d*) (i).
[37] See Chap. 16, p. 353.
[38] F.A. 1965, s. 47 (1).
[39] *Ibid.*, s. 47 (3). There is an exception for dividends paid within a group: *ibid.*, s. 48 (3).
[40] *Ibid.*, s. 48 (1).
[41] *Ibid.*, s. 46 (2).
[42] For exceptions, see *ibid.*, ss. 48 (4) and 62.
[43] *Ibid.*, s. 48 (1).
[44] *Ibid.*, s. 48 (1) (2), Sched. 12, Part I.
[45] See Chap. 16, p. 353.

There is, however, another side to the picture which cannot be ignored. Companies would rather pay interest than dividends, but they would rather receive dividends than interest. Indeed, franked investment income (which, as has been explained, means distributions received from other companies under deduction of tax) is the most attractive type of income which a company can have: it is free from corporation tax, and also enables the company to declare dividends to its own shareholders without having to account for income tax on them. Thus, while most companies seem to prefer to raise money by debenture issues, those which are willing to bear the extra tax burdens which accompany share financing are, other things being equal, assured of a ready reception by other companies which have surplus funds at their disposal available for investment.

Close companies

A striking feature of the corporation tax legislation is the stringent provisions affecting " close " companies.[45a] The philosophy behind them is that the shareholders in small or medium-sized companies might manipulate the company so as to secure fiscal benefits for themselves, but in many cases the provisions can be so severe in their operation as actually to impose fiscal penalties. The definition of " close company " is extremely complicated and far-reaching. Basically it covers any company " controlled " either by five or fewer " participators," participators and their " associates " being counted as one, or by participators who are " directors." [46] However, the meanings attributed to " control," [47] " participator," [48] " associate " [49] and " director " [50] are so extensive, and involve so comprehensive a piercing of the corporate veil, that one writer has said: " The one thing clear about close companies is that practically every family company is going to be one." [51] One might go further and say that practically every private company, except a subsidiary of a public company, is one. Almost the only way out for a family company is to obtain a Stock Exchange quotation, and " go public " to the extent of at least 35 per cent.,[52] and this is undoubtedly a very strong factor in impelling substantial private companies to convert themselves into public companies.

Close companies are subject to a number of handicaps, among which can be mentioned the following.

    (i) There is an even wider definition of " distribution " than there is for other companies.[53] The most important consequence is

45a But the Finance Bill 1969, will relax these.
46 F.A. 1965, Sched. 18, para. 1 (1).   47 *Ibid.*, para. 3
48 *Ibid.*, para. 4. Shareholders and debentureholders are included.
49 *Ibid.*, para. 5.
50 *Ibid.*, para. 6.
51 J. Philip Lawton: *Tax Planning for the Family Solicitor*, 2nd ed., p. 47.
52 F.A. 1965, Sched. 18, para. 1 (3).
53 *Ibid.*, Sched. 11, Part II.

that a close company cannot, except since 1969, within certain
limits, deduct loan interest paid to a member who is a director
(or to his " associates ").[54]   The object is to prevent the shareholders from under-capitalising the company, financing it by
loans, and " creaming-off " the profits as interest payments.

(ii) There were limits on the amounts which the company could
deduct for the salaries and fees of its directors.[55]   But the
Finance Bill 1969 proposes to abolish these limits and this is
a very important change which will greatly ease the tax burden
on close companies.

(iii) If a shareholder incurs a debt to the company it must pay to the
Revenue income tax on the grossed-up amount [56] of the debt.[57]
This, and the prohibition on making loans to directors,[58] which
now applies equally to all companies,[59] have virtually killed
off the practice whereby the individuals who stood behind
a company enjoyed its money by means of so-called " loans." [60]

(iv) To prevent the company avoiding the income tax charged on
distributions by retaining its profits and not making distributions,
every close company has a " required standard of distributions,"
the amount of which varies according to the company's particular
circumstances.   If the company's distributions [61] do not match
up to the required standard, the difference is a " shortfall," and
the company will be assessed to income tax on it.[62]

(v) Where a close company has a shortfall in its distributions, the
amount underdistributed would, but for counteracting legislation, save surtax for the shareholders as well as income tax for
the company.   Accordingly, the shortfall is notionally apportioned among the shareholders, and the Revenue then collect the
surtax which would have been payable if dividends had been
declared in accordance with the apportionment.[63]   The shareholders can pay the surtax if they want to.   If not, the Revenue
can recover it from the company.

The shortfall and surtax apportionment provisions reveal an inherent
inconsistency in the corporation tax provisions.   The imposition of a
separate tax on distributions is intended to encourage companies to
" plough back " profits instead of distributing them as dividends.   On
the other hand, the shortfall provisions put pressure on close companies

---

54 *Ibid.*, Sched. 11, para. 9 (1) (*a*) as proposed to be amended by Finance Bill 1969,
   Sched. 14.   55 *Ibid.*, s. 74.
56 For " grossing-up," see p. 172, *supra*.
57 F.A. 1965, s. 75.   And see Finance Bill 1969, Sched. 14.
58 Companies Act 1948, s. 190.
59 Companies Act 1967, s. 2.
60 *Cf.* p. 172, *supra*, note 6.
61 These include not only dividends, but also directors' loan interest over the limits
   which the company is allowed to deduct.
62 F.A. 1965, s. 77.   63 *Ibid.*, s. 78.

to make distributions. The Act attempts to reconcile the apparent conflict by providing for the company's required standard to be reduced to the extent that it needs to retain its profits in order to maintain and develop its business.[64] The situation is nevertheless somewhat uneasy, and the major tax problem which confronts every close company each year is to resolve its shortfall position to the mutual satisfaction of itself, its shareholders, and its Inspector of Taxes.

Groups of companies

Although taxing statutes frequently pierce the corporate veil and look through a company to its shareholders, the corporation tax legislation nevertheless adheres to the principle of the separate legal entity to the extent that it does not tax a parent company and its subsidiaries as if they were one. Thus, companies in a group make separate tax returns and receive separate assessments on their profits. On the other hand, if commercial reasons rendered it convenient for separate aspects of a business to be split up between several companies, it would be wrong for tax factors to stand in the way. Accordingly, there are a number of favourable provisions for transactions between companies under common control. The main ones permit dividends to be paid from a subsidiary to its parent company without deduction of income tax,[65] assets to be transferred within a group free of corporation tax on capital gains,[66] and losses or charges on income of one company to be used against profits of another within its group.[67] As a result, although a group of companies needs to be rather carefully managed from a tax point of view, its creation need not entail any increase in the total tax liability. These special provisions for groups illustrate the growing recognition of the idea of " enterprise entity " rather than the purist legal theory inherent in the corporate entity principle.

Loss companies

The corporate entity principle can, however, sometimes be used as a means of making profitable use of losses. Business losses can be carried forward and deducted from future profits of the same trade so as to reduce the tax liability in later years. Normally the " benefit " of a loss cannot be sold as an item in itself.[68] However, if the shares in a company with unrelieved trade losses are sold to a purchaser who can cause the company to make profits while it continues to carry on the same trade,

---

[64] *Ibid.*, s. 77 (2).
[65] *Ibid.*, s. 48 (3). Such dividends are " group income." They are, like all distributions, free of corporation tax in the hands of the recipient company (*ibid.*, s. 47 (1)), but, of course, do not constitute franked investment income.
[66] *Ibid.*, Sched. 13, para. 2.
[67] F.A. 1967, s. 20 and Sched. 10. The system is known as " group relief," and replaces an inferior system known as " subvention payments."
[68] Except between companies under common control: F.A. 1965, s. 61 (3).

the losses go with the company and can be used to reduce the taxable profits in future years. This led to quite a thriving market in the share capital of tax-loss companies but this will be curtailed by the Finance Bill 1969 which proposes to deny tax relief where there has been any major change in the nature or conduct of the trade or it became small or negligible. If the trade has genuinely continued but the purchaser does not want to take over the actual company that made the losses it can form a subsidiary, transfer to it the trade and the losses,[69] and then sell the shares to the subsidiary.[70]

However, in this sphere too it must be borne in mind that the separate corporate personality of companies may boomerang. Except within a group of holding and subsidiary companies, losses, even in the same year, of one company cannot be offset against the profits of another or of an individual shareholder. Accordingly the man who carries on two businesses,[71] one of which tends to be profitable and the other unprofitable, will be ill-advised to incorporate one and not the other or to incorporate both without making one the subsidiary of the other or both subsidiaries of a third, holding, company.

Charitable companies

Companies may also be used to obtain the tax advantages extended to charities. Charities are usually thought of as a part of the law of trusts, but it is quite common for a charity to be established in the form of a company (usually limited by guarantee) with objects exclusively charitable. Charities, whether incorporated or not, are exempt from tax on what is commonly called their endowment income [72] (normally income from investments or from deeds of covenant), but the exemption does not usually [73] extend to trading profits. The exemption appears reasonable enough, but it should be remembered that the legal definition of charity [74] is in some respects wider than the lay meaning, and there are many activities which can be carried on either as charities or for private profit. Examples are the running of schools, theatres, opera houses, concert halls and art galleries.

---

[69] The losses go with the trade: *ibid*.

[70] But the details are somewhat tricky and a recent case has shown that if the timing goes wrong the whole operation can fail to achieve its object: *Wood Preservation Ltd.* v. *Prior* [1969] 1 All E.R. 364, C.A.

[71] The farming stock-broker used to be the classic example, but the extent to which farming losses can be deducted from business profits is now severely circumscribed by F.A. 1960, s. 20, and F.A. 1967, s. 22.

[72] I.T.A. 1952, s. 447, F.A. 1965, s. 53 (6).

[73] The exceptions are (a) where the trade is exercised in the course of a primary purpose of the charity (*e.g.*, an educational charity running a school) and (b) where the persons working in the trade are themselves beneficiaries of the charity: I.T.A. 1952, s. 448 (1) (c).

[74] *Cf.* the famous preamble to 43 Eliz. c. 4, and *Commissioners of Income Tax* v. *Pemsel* [1891] A.C. 531 at p. 583 (*per* Lord Macnaghten). Recent cases have stressed the need for public benefit (*e.g.*, *National Anti-Vivisection Society* v. *I.R.C.* [1948] A.C. 31, H.L., and *I.R.C.* v. *Educational Grants Association* [1967] Ch. 993, C.A.), but a wide field is still left. See generally the Report of the Nathan Committee on Charitable Trusts (Cmd. 8710/52).

If the proprietors of such concerns run them in such a way that the profits will ultimately enure for their own benefit the total tax liability will be severe, and probably very little of the profits will be left. If, however, they form a guarantee company with its objects strictly limited to those regarded as charitable (*e.g.*, the promotion of education), and prohibit distribution of profits to the members, the company will be exempt from taxation on its endowment income. Admittedly it may be taxable on its trading profits, but most concerns of this nature trade at a slight loss, which they make good out of their endowment income. In any event, there are devices whereby a trade can be operated in such a way that its profits escape tax and enure for the benefit of a charity.[75]

It is true that, if a proprietor of, say, a school transfers it to a charitable company, he will be precluded from taking a direct share in the returns, but there is nothing to prevent his being employed by the company under a remunerative service agreement. Nor is there anything to prevent his selling an established school (or similar establishment) to the company for a price left outstanding on mortgage. Eventually the price might even be paid out of the tax-free income [75a] which has accumulated within the company, but an operation of that sort, if overdone, is apt to come unstuck.[76]

In America, not only are charities exempt from taxation but, within limits, donations to charities are allowed as deductions from taxable income, and these advantages have led to the popularity of incorporated " charitable " foundations. Thereby substantial taxation advantages can be obtained by a capitalist, without loss of control over his financial empire or, indeed, of all the income for his family, and with the preservation of his name and the advancement of his reputation. This is a development which is still in its infancy in this country, and as yet it seems to have been mainly practised through the medium of the old-fashioned trust rather than the more modern corporation. But the seed has been sown and is likely to germinate. In the meantime the private school and the theatre are more and more resorting to the charitable company in an attempt to avoid extermination or State control.

Conclusions

The changes contained in the Finance Act 1965 have led to a new appraisal of the tax consequences of choosing a company as a business

---

[75] The main method involves the charitable company forming a subsidiary which carries on the trade. The subsidiary then, pursuant to a power in its objects clause, executes a seven-year deed of covenant binding itself to pay the whole or the bulk of its profits to the charity. The covenanted donations to the charity are deducted from the subsidiary's profits (F.A. 1965, s. 52), thereby leaving little to be assessed to corporation tax, and are tax-free endowment income of the charity. The details of the operation, however, are tricky, and it requires careful preparation. For a full discussion, see Potter and Monroe, *Tax Planning* (5th ed.), pp. 238–240.

[75a] Including, since it is an educational charity operating a school, its operating profits and not just its endowment income: see note 73, *supra*.

[76] For an example of an over-ambitious scheme which ultimately failed, see *Campbell* v. *I.R.C.* [1968] 3 W.L.R. 1025, H.L.

medium. This is no bad thing, because it was not uncommon in the past for companies to be formed as a result of a decidedly over-optimistic assessment of their tax advantages. Now there is a danger of the same process in reverse. In some respects there is no doubt that companies—particularly close companies—are adversely treated. That is especially true of private investment companies, whose capital gains are, in effect, taxed twice—once to corporation tax on the company and once to capital gains tax on the shareholders to the extent that the company's gains (even after tax) increase the value of the shares.[77] Such companies, many of which were established in the palmy days when capital gains were tax free, are rapidly being eliminated.

For other companies—typically trading companies—it is not easy to assess the total tax burden involved in corporate status. However, for the family company whose shareholders are also its directors it is necessary to take into account up to four separate taxes—income tax and surtax on the directors' salaries, corporation tax on the company's profits, income tax and surtax on distributions, and capital gains tax on disposals of the shares if their value is increased as a result of retained profits. By way of contrast, the profits of an individual carrying on business alone or in partnership are exposed to income tax and surtax only. Thus there is no doubt that, purely from a taxation point of view, some businesses could be run more advantageously otherwise than through a company. On the other hand, the extent of this factor is sometimes over-estimated,[78] and the impact of surtax on high partnership profits can be very severe. The use of a company—particularly one which can justify a low " required standard " because of the needs of an expanding business—does enable some profits to be accumulated free of surtax. In very broad terms, the effect of the corporation tax system on small to medium-sized companies is to discriminate in favour of the expanding, capital-hungry business, and at the same time to encourage the shareholders of such a company to offer a substantial " slice " of it to the public, thereby removing it from the toils of the close company legislation.

DEATH DUTIES

General principles

Death duties can be dealt with somewhat more briefly. An artificial person cannot die, and although it can be wound up this has never been treated as equivalent to death for revenue purposes. Prima facie, there-

---

[77] Quoted investment trust companies which comply with certain statutory criteria are better placed. Their gains are taxed at 30 per cent. only, and are credited against the shareholders' capital gains tax position: F.A. 1965, ss. 37, 67, 68.

[78] See articles by Peter Bird at [1965] *British Tax Review* 393 and [1968] *ibid.* 346. The calculations in the articles are, however, no longer valid in the light of the proposed abolition (by the Finance Bill 1969) of the limits on directors' remuneration paid by close companies.

fore, a company is completely exempt from death duties, which concern only its human members and their property.[79] Nor ought this to cause any loss of revenue, for the proprietary interests of the members in the company will be property passing on their deaths and liable to duties accordingly.

On the death of a shareholder, estate duty will be payable on the value of his property, including his shares, and the general principle is that property should be valued for duty purposes at the price which it would fetch if sold in the open market at the date of death.[80] In the case of the securities of a public company quoted on a stock exchange, the quoted price at the date of death will therefore govern [81]; this may represent more or less than the break-up value of the holder's share in the company's assets, but this is irrelevant.

If, however, the shares are not quoted, the value will have to be estimated in another way, and the authorities will normally call for the company's accounts and estimate what a willing purchaser would be likely to give, having regard to the prosperity of the company, the values of its underlying assets and liabilities, and the rights conferred by the securities.[82]

Since, therefore, the amount of duty payable depends on the value of the securities as at the time of death, the ingenuity of parties and their advisers has been directed towards evolving methods whereby interests in companies can be retained during life, without holding securities of any value at death.

Arbitrary valuations at date of death

In the case of private companies, restrictions on the right to transfer shares are essential, and these obviously diminish their market value. For a time it was thought that it might be possible virtually to destroy liability to death duties by giving the other members of the company rights of pre-emption at an arbitrary and low price. But the efficacy of this device was reduced when the House of Lords held in 1936 in the *Crossman* case [83] that such shares had to be valued on the assumption

---

[79] But see, now, F.A. 1940, s. 46 *et seq.*, considered below.
[80] F.A. 1894, s. 7 (5).
[81] This may cause hardship where the shares fall in value before the personal representatives obtain a grant to enable them to realise his holdings. If the depreciation can be proved to be due to the death, account must be taken of this, but no allowances can be made because all the shares come on to the market at the same time : F. (1909–1910) Act 1910, s. 60.
[82] For illustrations, see *Re Holt* [1953] 1 W.L.R. 1488 and *Re Lynall* [1969] 1 Ch. 421.
[83] *I. R. C.* v. *Crossman, I. R. C.* v. *Mann* [1937] A.C. 26, H.L. These cases actually concerned the unquoted ordinary shares in a public company. The H.L., by a majority, reversed the majority decision of the C.A. and restored the decision of the judge of first instance. Regarding similar attempts arbitrarily to limit the value of shares in partnerships, see especially *Att.-Gen.* v. *Boden* [1912] 1 K.B. 539 ; *Perpetual Exors. Assn.* v. *Commissioner of Taxes of Australia* [1954] A.C. 114, P.C., and the discussion in Potter & Monroe, *Tax Planning* (5th ed.), pp. 328–335.

that a notional buyer in the open market would be put on the register despite the restrictions, but that he would then hold the shares subject to the same conditions. Hence, addititional devices had to be sought.

A simple method was to transfer assets to a company in consideration of an allotment of shares which would be promptly settled on the founder's children, the founder retaining merely a governing directorship for life at a salary which would absorb the whole income. Or he might retain shares carrying special dividend or voting rights during his life only. Under more complicated arrangements, the founder would take out income disguised as capital, through the medium of redeemable debentures, and several inter-related companies might be formed, thus obscuring the true effect of the transaction.

Finance Act 1940, s. 55

These attempts have been countered by the legislature in two ways, both involving a rift in the veil of incorporation. The statutory provisions only apply where the companies involved are privately controlled, the test for this purpose being that adopted, in connection with the old " surtax directions " under the Income Tax Act 1952, ss. 245–264, but with a slight extension.[84] By section 55 of the Finance Act 1940,[85] where at any time within seven years preceding his death the deceased had control of the company, valuation of his holdings is no longer to be on the basis of their market value, but on a valuation of the company's assets and apportionment amongst the members and debentureholders.[86]

The result of this section, in the case of shares to which it applies, is finally to destroy the efficacy of restraints on transferability as a means of minimising the value of holdings. Let us assume that the deceased held 15,000 out of a total of 30,000 shares of £1 each in a family company of which he was the governing director. And let us suppose that the net assets of the company were worth £90,000 at the date of his death, but that the articles provided that the shares should be offered to the other members at par. As a result of the ruling in

---

[84] F.A. 1940, s. 58 (1). The old definition of companies exposed to surtax directions remains applicable in this context notwithstanding the introduction by the Finance Act 1965 of the new concept of a " close company." The extension brings in foreign companies and those which have *at any time* been controlled by not more than five persons. The provisions of this and later Acts supersede an earlier series commencing with F.A. 1930.

[85] As amended by F.A. 1954, ss. 29–31 and F.A. 1968, s. 35.

[86] This is a much simplified summary of a very complicated section to which reference should be made for details. The section also applies where, although the deceased did not actually have voting control, he was able to exercise powers equivalent to control. But, as a result of F.A. 1954, s. 29, the section only applies in the latter case if the securities pass to a beneficiary who, either alone or with certain relatives, possesses voting control. If the shares are quoted on a stock exchange the section does not apply, provided that there have been dealings in the shares within a year before the death: s. 55 (4). And if there is an arm's-length sale of the securities within three years after the death the price will determine the value: F.A. 1954, s. 30 (1).

Crossman, the personal representatives could not contend that the shares should be valued for death duty purposes only at par. They would have to be valued at the figure which a hypothetical purchaser would pay on the assumption that the shares could be transferred to him but that he would then hold them subject to the like restraint. This figure is obviously more than par, but equally obviously is considerably less than one-half of the value of the company's assets.[87] Now, as a result of section 55, it is the assets value which must be adopted[88]; the deceased's holdings will be deemed to be worth £45,000, or three times the nominal value.

Finance Act 1940, s. 46

This, however, would not have met the situation in which the deceased is left with only a small fraction, if any, of the company's securities but has received disproportionate benefits during his lifetime. If, for example, he had previously transferred his business to a company in consideration of an allotment of shares and debentures and then disposed of all these securities to members of his family, retaining only a life directorship at a salary absorbing the whole of the company's profits,[89] on his death nothing could be apportioned to his estate under section 55, for he had no holdings to which anything could be allocated.[90] Hence, it has been provided[91] that if the company derived any of its property directly or indirectly from the deceased,[92] the latter's estate is charged with estate duty on the proportion of the company's assets which the value of the benefits receivable by him in the seven years preceding his death bears to the total income of the company in those years. And the duties are recoverable from the company itself and not from the estate of the deceased.[93] In practice, the Revenue only invoke these provisions when there has been

---

[87] It might not be much less if the shares were 75 per cent. of the whole, for the purchaser could then put the company into liquidation or alter the articles to remove the restriction.

[88] Assuming, of course, that all the conditions of the section are fulfilled, as they appear to be in the example given. The official view is that the assets should be valued on a " going concern " or " break-up " basis, whichever is the greater.

[89] Or if the consideration for the sale had been redeemable debentures which had been paid off during his life; this was the more likely alternative as it might have enabled him to take out income disguised as capital, thus avoiding surtax. It is possible, however, that the surtax advantages might be nullified under F.A. 1960, s. 28.

[90] Of course, if he died within seven years of the disposition to his family, the securities would be deemed to pass on his death unless the family bought them for full consideration, and the donees would be liable to pay duties thereon: see below.

[91] F.A. 1940, s. 46 *et seq.*, as amended by F.A. 1944, ss. 35–39, F.A. 1950, s. 47, F.A. 1952, s. 72, F.A. 1965, s. 88, and F.A. 1968, s. 35 (1). This again is a much simplified summary of provisions, which Lord Simonds in the leading authority, *St. Aubyn* v. *Att.-Gen.* [1952] A.C. 15, H.L., at p. 30, described as " of unrivalled complexity and difficulty and couched in language so tortuous and obscure that I am tempted to reject them as meaningless."

[92] Even though on a sale for full consideration, or on a cash subscription for shares: F.A. 1952, s. 72 (2), overruling on this point *St. Aubyn* v. *Att.-Gen.*, *supra.*

[93] F.A. 1940, s. 54 (1). The value will be aggregated with the rest of the deceased's estate in order to determine the rate of duty.

some artificial arrangement suggesting an obvious intention to avoid duties. If invoked in the example just given they would mean that virtually the whole [94] of the company's assets would be deemed to pass on his death, he having received the whole of the company's income during the preceding seven years, and duties would be payable accordingly. Obviously, it would have been useless merely to charge the deceased's estate with payment, for his estate would almost certainly not be in a position to pay; hence, as stated, the company itself is made liable.

The joint effect of these two sets of provisions is that duties will normally be payable on the value of the deceased's holdings, assessed under section 55 on the apportioned value of the company's assets, or, exceptionally, on the basis of benefits received, if that is the greater.[95] The only safe course, if the company is not floated off to the public, is to ensure that the proprietor is totally and irrevocably excluded from all benefits for at least seven years prior to his death.

Other examples of the disregard of corporate entity

Of somewhat less practical importance, but of the greatest theoretical interest, are the ancillary provisions contained in section 56 of the Finance Act 1940 and in section 44 of the same Act, as extended by section 46 of the Finance Act 1950. Section 3 (1) of the Finance Act 1894 exempts from estate duty certain transactions which might otherwise be regarded as a " passing of property " within the meaning of the Act. Section 56 provides that where a privately controlled company is concerned, the application of the exemptions shall be tested on the assumption that the company held its property on trust for its members.[96] In other words, revenue law insists on an assumption being made which *Salomon's* case expressly declared to be false. The separate existence of the company is disregarded and it is treated as an alias, agent, trustee or nominee for the members. An exactly similar provision is [97] contained in section 44, dealing with gifts *inter vivos* to relatives. In these cases, therefore, the veil of incorporation has been torn to shreds.

In a few cases the legislature has intervened to counteract the boomerang effect of strict adherence to the corporate entity principle. A reduced rate of estate duty is payable on agricultural property, but if a farmer converts his business into a company, the property passing on

---

[94] In practice it would be slightly less than the whole, for an allowance would be made against the benefits for reasonable remuneration as director: F.A. 1940, s. 51 (4). See also *ibid.*, s. 51 (1), which might also afford some relief.

[95] Provision is made for avoiding recovery of duplicate duties under both heads: F.A. 1940, s. 51, as amended by F.A. 1944, s. 38, and s. 47 of F.A. 1950.

[96] Member includes debentureholder (F.A. 1940, s. 59) and, for the purposes of this section, any other person to whom the company is under any liability incurred otherwise than for the purposes of its business wholly and exclusively (*ibid.* s. 56 (1)). See *St. Aubyn* v. *Att.-Gen., supra*, for the difficulties caused by attempting to apply this " bewildering conception " (*per* Lord Simonds at p. 24) contained in s. 56.

[97] As a result of F.A. 1950. s. 46.

his death is not agricultural property but shares in the company. Hence, prima facie, the abatement is lost, as is the " quick succession " relief on a second death within five years of the first, since this does not apply to shares or debentures in a company.[98]   However, by virtue of the Finance Act 1954,[99] both agricultural abatement and quick succession relief were made available in all cases where the securities fall to be valued on an assets basis under the Finance Act 1940,[1] as was the similar abatement (introduced by that Act [2]), on plant, machinery and industrial hereditaments.

Conclusions

This brief account of the death duty position may be summed up by saying that today companies confer few direct advantages as a means of minimising liability to estate duty.   Just as it is no longer possible, as it was in the good (or bad) old days, easily to use the corporate entity principle as a means of avoiding surtax during life, so it is equally difficult to employ it to minimise the levy on capital on death.   Even if a successful scheme is evolved, the triumph is likely to be short-lived for the Revenue stops the gaps in its defences so soon as the breach becomes apparent—and sometimes with retrospective effect.   And the tax avoider who burns his fingers now gets less sympathy from the courts than he once did.[3]

On the other hand, the formation and flotation of a company is still invaluable as a method of enabling a business to survive, notwithstanding the crippling effect of death duties.   If a business—whether incorporated or not—remains under private control, on the death of the proprietor his personal representatives may be unable to raise sufficient money to pay the duties [4] without resort to the assets of the business.   If the business is unincorporated it will be difficult to find a purchaser at an adequate price, and, in any case, the purchaser will hardly be willing to become a mere sleeping partner.   Hence, even if the business does not have to be liquidated, it will pass into alien control.   If it is incorporated as a private company there is more likelihood of finding a purchaser of the deceased's shares but, once again, the purchaser will normally wish to move in and take an active part in the company's affairs.[5]

---

[98] F.A. 1914, s. 15.

[99] ss. 28 (2) (*b*) and 30 (4).

[1] *i.e.*, under s. 55 (*supra*) as well as under s. 46 (*supra*)—it always applied to valuations under the latter, since then the underlying assets were deemed to pass.

[2] s. 28.

[3] For an interesting survey of fluctuating judicial attitudes in recent years, see M. C. Flesch in [1968] *Current Legal Problems* 215.

[4] The present scales rise to 80 per cent. overall on estates over £1 million.

[5] Estate Duties Investment Trust Ltd. has been formed by the insurance companies specifically for the purpose of providing a possible purchaser who will not seek to disturb the existing control on acquiring interests in private companies.   But naturally EDITH is highly selective.

But if, during the proprietor's lifetime, the company has been converted into a public one, and a public issue made of a controlling block of its shares, the probability is that the dispersed holders of the shares will not disturb the existing management. Of course, the total liability to estate duty will not thereby be reduced. The price received on the issue [6] and any shares retained will, on the proprietor's death, form part of his estate, and the shares, being quoted, will probably be valued more highly than while the company remained a private one. But the liability to estate duty thereon can be avoided if he settles on his family [7] the proceeds and the shares retained, and survives for a further seven years (or one year if he gives them to a charity).[8] Even if he retains a substantial block of shares, these, being quoted, should be readily realisable in order to raise the amount payable in duty.[9] In any case, the business itself will remain intact; the Revenue cannot proceed against its assets as they could in the case of a firm or, in some circumstances, a privately controlled company.

Hence, although corporation tax, particularly in relation to close companies, is not exactly friendly to incorporated business, incorporation is still valuable to safeguard businesses in the private sector against the ravages of death duties and to enable them to survive the fiscal as well as the physical consequences of the demise of their members.

---

[6] Which may, of course, be subject to capital gains tax.
[7] So long, of course, as he parts with all beneficial interest.
[8] F.A. 1968, s. 35 (and earlier legislation amended thereby); F. (1909–10) A. 1910, s. 59 (1), proviso.
[9] One danger is that there may be a substantial fall in the value of the securities between the date of death, when they are valued for duty purposes, and the date when the personal representatives obtain a grant and can sell. If the total estate is valued at over £1 million, this might mean that the whole of it would disappear in duties (in practice the Revenue do not seek to make the personal representatives account for *more* than they have received unless they have been inexcusably dilatory).

CHAPTER 10

LIFTING THE VEIL

HAVING discussed the consequences of incorporation, something must be said on the problem generally described, when it is considered at all,[1] as " lifting the veil "[2]; in other words, on the circumstances in which the law disregards the corporate entity and pays regard instead to the economic realities behind the legal façade. Some of the most extreme examples have already been touched on, particularly in connection with taxation, but it may be convenient if an attempt is now made to collect these and other illustrations. It must be said at once that they illustrate no consistent principle; the only principle is that laid down in *Salomon's* case,[3] and in general the courts have rigidly applied it. Such exceptions as there are represent haphazard refusals by the legislature or the courts to apply logic where it is too flagrantly opposed to justice, convenience or (especially) the interests of the Revenue. In these exceptional cases the law either goes behind the corporate personality to the individual members, or ignores the separate personality of each company in favour of the economic entity constituted by a group of associated concerns; these two types of case cannot be clearly separated and the principle is the same in both.

Before dealing with these exceptions, it must be emphasised that the veil of incorporation never means that the internal affairs of the company are completely concealed from view. On the contrary, the legislature has always made it an essential condition of the recognition of corporate personality that it should be accompanied by the widest publicity. Although third parties dealing with the company will normally have no right of resort against its members, they are nevertheless entitled to see who these members are, what shares they hold and, in the case of a quoted company, the beneficial interests in those shares if substantial. They are also entitled to see who its officers are (so that they know with whom to deal), what its constitution is (so that they know what the company may do and how it may do it), and what its capital is and how it has been obtained (so that they may know whether to trust it). And unless it is an unlimted company they are also

---

[1] It has aroused little attention and less theoretical discussion in this country (see, however, (1968) 31 M.L.R. 481, and (1969) 14 Jur.R.(N.S.) 1), but it is a favourite topic of discussion in America. There is also a considerable Continental literature: see Cohn & Simitis, " Lifting the Veil in the Company Law of the European Continent " (1963) 12 I.C.L.Q. 189.

[2] The " veil " metaphor has been adopted here, but etymologically " mask " might be better since " persona " is derived from the name for a mask worn by a player in the Greek theatre.   [3] [1897] A.C. 22, H.L., *supra*, p. 68.

entitled to see its balance sheet and profit and loss account—again in order to know whether to trust it. Normally, however, third parties are neither bound nor entitled to look behind such information as the law provides shall be made public; in addition to the veil of incorporation, there is something in the nature of a curtain formed by the company's public file, and what goes on behind it is concealed from the public gaze.[4] But sometimes this curtain also may be raised. For example, an inspector may be appointed to investigate the company's affairs,[5] in which case he will have the widest inquisitional powers; indeed, he may even be appointed for the purpose of going behind the company's registers to ascertain who are its true owners.

This, however, is not our present concern, which is to examine the circumstances in which the fundamental principle of corporate personality itself is disregarded. Some of the major examples [6] arising under the express words of a statute will be discussed first.

UNDER EXPRESS STATUTORY PROVISION

Reduction of numbers of members

The Companies Acts themselves have long provided that the members of a company may become personally liable for its debts if their number is allowed to fall below the prescribed minimum. Section 31 of the Companies Act 1948 enacts that if members are reduced below two, in the case of a private company, or below seven in any other case,[7] and the company carries on business for more than six months while the number is so reduced, every person who is a member during the time that it so carries on business after those six months and is cognisant of the fact that it is operating with fewer than the requisite number shall be severally liable for the whole of the debts contracted during that time.

It will be observed that this section does not operate to destroy the separate personality of the company; it still remains an existing entity even though the shareholders are too few [8] or, presumably, although there are none. On the other hand, it goes further than to convert a limited company into an unlimited one, for in an unlimited company debts remain those of the company although the members are liable to contribute towards their payment and are in the position of

---

[4] *Cf.* the rule in *Royal British Bank* v. *Turquand, supra,* Chap. 8, p. 150 *et seq.*
[5] See Chap. 25, *infra.*
[6] There are many other statutory provisions whereby the members or directors may become personally liable to discharge the company's obligations: see, *e.g.,* National Insurance Act 1965, s. 95 (8), and National Insurance (Industrial Injuries) Act 1965, s. 69 (8), regarding directors' liability for unpaid national insurance contributions.
[7] The Jenkins Committee recommended that the number should be reduced to two: Cmnd. 1749, para. 23.
[8] *Jarvis Motors (Harrow) Ltd.* v. *Carabott* [1964] 1 W.L.R. 1101. But the company can be wound up on this ground: s. 222 (*d*).

quasi-sureties. Under section 31 the members may become liable directly to the creditors and, as the section expressly states, " may be severally sued therefor." But the rights of creditors are severely limited; it is only the members who remain after the six months that can be sued (not those whose withdrawal [9] has led to the fall below the minimum), and even they are liable only if they have knowledge of the facts and only in respect of debts contracted after the expiration of the six months. Moreover, the wording suggests that they are liable only in respect of liquidated contractual obligations,[10] but in the absence of authority it cannot be said whether the courts would give this restrictive interpretation to it. It is also noteworthy that the liability only attaches to members, and not, as might have been expected, to the directors as such.

Although the facts giving rise to a possible application of the section are of not infrequent occurrence,[11] it seems rarely, if ever, to be invoked, doubtless because of the limitations considered, and it constitutes an exception to the general rule of theoretical interest rather than practical importance.

Fraudulent trading

Section 332 [12] of the Act contains a further example of far greater practical value. It provides that if, in the course of the winding up of a company, it appears that any business has been carried on with intent to defraud creditors or for any fraudulent purpose, the court, on the application of the Official Receiver, the liquidator, a creditor

---

[9] Thus, if the members of a private company consist of A and B, and B dies and his executors fail to become registered as members, A will be severally liable for debts contracted six months after B's death (unless C is admitted to membership), and there can be no resort against B's estate. It seems that the deceased B cannot be counted as a member, although the shares were registered in his name: *Re Bowling & Welby's Contract* [1895] 1 Ch. 663, C.A.

[10] It talks of "debts contracted" not of "debts contracted or liabilities incurred"; *cf.* s. 332, *infra.*

[11] *e.g.,* in the circumstances suggested in note 9. It may be virtually impossible to keep up membership in such a case, since B's death may have reduced the directors below the quorum, so that there can be no board meeting to pass a transfer of a share from A or to register B's executors. Presumably, the rule that the unanimous consent of the members may be effective without a meeting (see pp. 208–210, *infra*) would not enable A to act on his own and to appoint directors. He could, of course, apply to the court under s. 135 or, in appropriate circumstances, to the Board of Trade under s. 131 (2) to order a "meeting" of himself alone (see Chap. 21, *infra*), and B's executors or any transferee could apply for rectification of the membership register by putting him on it, since, if the articles are in the normal form, the transfer is effective unless the board actively and validly reject it: see Chap. 18, p. 394, *infra.* If both A and B died within six months but a quorum of directors survived, apparently the latter can safely continue to operate the memberless company until it is necessary to hold a general meeting or until someone presents a winding-up petition. The Jenkins Committee recommended that for the purpose of s. 135 the personal representatives of a deceased member should be treated as members, thus enabling the company to appoint directors when all the directors and members had died: Cmnd. 1749, para. 26.

[12] Re-enacting and slightly extending s. 275 of the 1929 Act. The section contains ancillary provisions enabling the court to enforce the liability, *e.g.,* by charging any debts due from the company to the defaulter. Criminal liability is also imposed.

or member, may declare that any persons who were knowingly parties to the fraud shall be personally responsible without any limitation of liability for all or any of the debts or other liabilities of the company. This section is free from the severe limitations of section 31. It expressly covers all liabilities, contractual or otherwise, and imposes liability on the directors or other officers as well as on members. On the other hand, it has limitations of its own, for a creditor seeking to take advantage of it has to discharge the heavy burden of proving fraud.

In *Re William C. Leitch Bros. Ltd.*[13] Maugham J. seemed prepared to give a liberal interpretation to the word " fraud." He said [14]: " If a company continues to carry on business and to incur debts at a time when there is, to the knowledge of the directors, no reasonable prospect of the creditors ever receiving payment of those debts, it is, in general, a proper inference that the company is carrying on business with intent to defraud." He held that the declaration of liability had to be for a definite sum but that this was not necessarily limited to the amounts due to creditors shown to have been defrauded. He accordingly made a declaration that the director was personally liable to the extent of £6,000.[15] In a later case,[16] however, the same judge [17] emphasised that " fraud," for the purposes of the section, connoted " actual dishonesty involving, according to current notions of fair trading among commercial men, real moral blame," and that the onus of proof was on those alleging it. This seems to mark a withdrawal from the attitude revealed in his dictum in the *Leitch* case, and that dictum has been dissented from by the Australian High Court.[18] However, the Jenkins Committee has recommended [19] that the section should be extended so as to apply to reckless, as well as to fraudulent, trading.[20]

On a later application in the *Leitch* case [21] Eve J. held that the moneys recovered formed part of the general assets of the company available for all creditors, not merely for those whose debts were contracted during the time when the business was carried on fraudulently. But in the light of a recent decision of the Court of Appeal in *Re Cyona Distributors Ltd.*[22] it appears that this may not necessarily be so. In that case the claim was made by a creditor (not by the liquidator as in the *Leitch* case) and the payment was made not as the result of any order of the court but prior to any hearing of

---

13 [1932] 2 Ch. 71.
14 At p. 77.
15 Which he charged on a debenture held by the director.
16 *Re Patrick & Lyon Ltd.* [1933] Ch. 786.
17 At pp. 790–791.
18 *Hardie* v. *Hanson* (1960) 105 C.L.R. 451.
19 Cmnd. 1749, para. 503 (*b*).
20 Except as regards the criminal sanction, which, however, should be available where the facts are discovered otherwise than in the course of a winding up (*cf. R.* v. *Rollafson, The Times,* April 3, 1969): *ibid.,* paras. 499 and 503 (*b*) and (*c*).
21 *Re William C. Leitch Ltd.* (*No.* 2) [1933] Ch. 261.
22 [1967] Ch. 889, C.A.

the creditor's application and to help the director to escape more lightly from a criminal charge. It was held, reversing the decision of Plowman J., that the creditor was entitled to retain the money in discharge of the debt to him. Lord Denning M.R. thought that in view of the words of the section there was nothing to require that moneys recovered must be made available for the general body of creditors, although this would usually be the case where proceedings were commenced by the liquidator. Danckwerts L.J. apparently regarded the distinction between applications by a creditor and by the liquidator as decisive. On the other hand, Russell L.J. thought that a recovery under the section " can result only in an accretion to the assets of the company for distribution in due course of winding up." [23] He concurred in the result only because, in his view, the recovery in the instant case had " nothing to do with the section 332 claim." [24]

There is no doubt that in practice this section represents a potent weapon in the hands of creditors which exercises a restraining influence on over-sanguine directors. The mere threat of proceedings under it has been known to result in the directors agreeing to make themselves personally liable for part of the company's debts. Of all the exceptions to the rule in *Salomon's* case it is probably the most serious attempt which has yet been made to protect creditors generally (as opposed to the Revenue) from the abuses inherent in the rigid application of the corporate entity concept. It would be still more effective if widened as the Jenkins Committee recommended.

Misdescription of company

On ordinary agency principles the officers of the company will, of course, make themselves personally liable, notwithstanding that they are in fact acting for the company, if they choose to contract personally, for example, by failing to disclose that they are acting as agents.[25] The Companies Act, however, provides that in certain circumstances they shall incur personal responsibility notwithstanding that they have expressly contracted as agents. This occurs where they have signed or authorised the signature on behalf of the company of any bill of exchange, promissory note, cheque or order for goods or money, and the name of the company is not mentioned thereon in legible characters. Section 108 (4) of the 1948 Act then provides that, in addition to liability to fines, they shall be personally liable to the holder for the amount due unless it is duly paid by the company.

Liability under this section normally arises in connection with bills or cheques, and officers have been held personally liable when the word

---

[23] At p. 908.
[24] At p. 909.
[25] *Cf. Elliott* v. *Bax-Ironside* [1925] 2 K.B. 301, which turned on the effect of s. 26 of the Bills of Exchange Act 1882.

" limited " was omitted,[26] and when the company was described by a
wrong name.[27] The word " holder " is really only appropriate in connection with negotiable instruments, but it has nevertheless been held
that a person to whom an order for goods is given must be deemed to
be the " holder " and can take advantage of the section notwithstanding
that the original order is lost.[28] It seems clear that it makes no
difference that the third party concerned has not been misled by the
misdescription.[29] But the holder's conduct may estop him from
enforcing the liability; for example, where the holder has himself
written the form of acceptance with the misdescription.[30] In any
event the officers concerned merely become liable to pay if the company
does not; they are apparently placed in the position of sureties (with
corresponding rights), in contrast with the primary liability imposed by
the sections previously considered.

The object of this section is plain. As we have seen, the legislature
introduced limited liability on the basis that third parties would realise
that they were dealing with limited companies. Hence great emphasis
has always been placed on the use of the true name of the company
and especially of the word " limited." The provisions just referred to
form part of a wider series of rules designed to ensure that the name
of the company appears wherever it does business, on its seal, and on
all business documents and letters.[31] In general these rules are enforced
by penal sanctions, but these have been supplemented by civil liability
in the cases where it is practicable to do so; and this liability has been
most strictly enforced, particularly in the early days.

Holding and subsidiary companies

The most striking limitation imposed by the Companies Acts on the
recognition of the separate personality of each individual company is,
however, in connection with associated companies within the same
group enterprise. As we have seen, it has become a habit to create
a pyramid of inter-related companies, each of which is theoretically a

---

26 *Penrose* v. *Martyr* (1858) E.B. & E. 499; *Atkins* v. *Wardle* (1889) 5 T.L.R. 734, C.A.
   Cf. Dermatine Co. v. *Ashworth* (1905) 21 T.L.R. 510 and *Stacey* v. *Wallis* (1912)
   106 L.T. 544, where it was held that it suffices if the full and correct name appears
   anywhere on the bill and that the abbreviation " Ltd." can be used.
27 *Nassau Steam Press* v. *Tyler* (1894) 70 L.T. 376; *Scottish & Newcastle Breweries
   Ltd.* v. *Blair*, 1967 S.L.T. 72; *cf. Durham Fancy Goods Ltd.* v. *Michael Jackson
   (Fancy Goods) Ltd.* [1968] 2 Q.B. 839.
28 *Civil Service Co-operative Society* v. *Chapman* (1914) 30 T.L.R. 679.
29 See *Scottish & Newcastle Breweries Ltd.* v. *Blair*, *supra*, where this sentence was
   approved by Lord Hunter at p. 74.
30 *Durham Fancy Goods Ltd.* v. *Michael Jackson (Fancy Goods) Ltd.*, *supra*, where
   the misdescription (" M " instead of " Michael ") was held to be a breach of s. 108
   but not one on which the plaintiffs could rely as they were responsible for it.
   Semble, a similar defence should have prevailed in the *Scottish & Newcastle Brewery*
   case.
31 See s. 108, *passim*. And note that if a company carries on business in a trade name
   it must also register under the Registration of Business Names Act 1916: Companies
   Act 1947, s. 58.

separate entity but in reality part of one concern represented by the group as a whole. The separation of the group into distinct companies is not necessarily in any way improper; it may well be the most economical and convenient arrangement when the concern carries on a number of separate businesses, or when it is desirable to distinguish between the manufacturing and the marketing part of the enterprise or between trade in its various products. It may also enable the advantages of size (*e.g.*, a centralised financial policy) to be obtained without the disadvantages of over-centralisation. And such an arrangement may come about inevitably where one company has gradually expanded its control of an industry by buying up the share capital of existing companies in the same field.

Nevertheless, it is an arrangement which is clearly capable of abuse. As we have seen,[32] it drove a coach and horses through the legislative definition of " private company " and led to a further division of the latter into " exempt " and " non-exempt "—a distinction now, happily, abolished. It is still possible, and indeed usual, for a public company to carry on business through subsidiary operating private companies, but these can no longer escape from the obligation to file copies of their annual balance-sheets and profit and loss accounts with the Registrar of Companies so that they are open for public inspection. This alone, however, would not have prevented the accounts of the public holding company from being presented in such a way as to be totally uninformative or positively misleading as to the true prosperity of the group. This will be clearly seen if we take a simple case of holding company A operating through two wholly owned[33] subsidiary companies B and C.

The principal assets of company A will consist of the shares in companies B and C which, assuming they are private companies with no market quotation, will normally be shown in company A's books at cost. Similarly company A's income will consist of the dividends, if any, paid on the shares in companies B and C. It may be that B will have made a small profit and paid a dividend of, say, £1,000, while company C has traded at a loss of, say, £10,000. In these circumstances company A's profit and loss account will show a profit for the year of £1,000 (less any expenses which it itself has incurred) but in reality the group which it represents will have made a loss of £9,000. Its balance-sheet showing its assets and liabilities may be even more misleading. Company B may have consistently made large profits and ploughed back part of them so that its shares are worth many times their valuation shown in the balance-sheet. Alternatively, company C

---

[32] *Supra*, Chap. 1, p. 13.
[33] To comply with the requirement that there must be at least two members, one or more of the shares will have to be registered in the name of someone other than the holding company; the practice is to vest one share in a director as nominee for the holding company.

may have consistently sustained losses so that its shares are valueless. The position becomes still more complicated where company A has made loans to its subsidiaries or vice versa, or the subsidiaries have made loans to one another.

In circumstances such as those outlined above it is obvious that the accounts of company A alone are valueless to a shareholder or potential investor in that company. No doubt he could obtain some idea of the true position if he spent laborious hours at the Companies' Registry inspecting the published accounts of the subsidiaries, but this would only be possible in a comparatively simple case. The difficulties become insuperable where there are large numbers of English and foreign subsidiaries and sub-subsidiaries making up their accounts to different dates and publishing them in different forms.

The Companies Act 1948 made a determined attempt to tackle this thorny problem. The primary difficulty facing the draftsmen was to define the circumstances in which the relationship of holding-subsidiary companies should be deemed to exist, and for this purpose the element of " control," as recommended by the Cohen Committee,[34] was adopted as the decisive test. But " control " itself is not an easy concept to define satisfactorily; the obvious test—a majority holding of shares—being both too narrow and too wide. It is too narrow because effective control can be exercised in many other ways besides that of a majority holding [35]; for example, through voting rights, which may or may not be commensurate with shareholding, or through a right to appoint and remove the directors. It is too wide in that a majority holding will not confer any effective control if the shares held are non-voting shares, or if the votes are weighted in favour of another class.

Hence section 154 of the 1948 Act [36] adopts a twofold test; a company is said to be the subsidiary of another if that other (the holding company) is a member of it and controls the composition of its board of directors, or if the holding company holds more than half its " equity share capital." Similarly, a subsidiary of a subsidiary (a sub-subsidiary) is in turn regarded as a subsidiary of the head holding company. The reader is referred to the terms of the section itself for the detailed elaboration of this dual test. Here we can only note a few salient points.

In the first place it will be observed that control of the composition of the board (which is defined as the power to appoint *or* remove

---

[34] Cmd. 6659, para. 118.

[35] For an elaborate analysis of the ways in which *de jure* or *de facto* control may be exercised, see Berle & Means, *The Modern Corporation and Private Property*, p. 69 *et seq.* In relation to directors' share dealings (see *infra*, p. 388 *et seq.*) a director is deemed to be interested in shares if he controls the right to more than *one-third* of the votes of a company having an interest in those shares: Companies Act 1967, s. 28 (3) (*b*).

[36] Amplifying and improving an inadequate attempt at definition in Companies Act 1929, s. 127.

a majority of the board [37]) does not suffice of itself; the holding company must also be a member of the subsidiary, although in that case the actual proportion of shares held is irrelevant. Secondly, and rather strangely, shareholdings or powers to appoint and remove directors are to be ignored if held or enjoyed by virtue of a provision in debentures. They are also to be ignored if held or exercisable in a fiduciary capacity—but that is what one would have expected. Thirdly, the section represented the first reception into the legal vocabulary of the business man's expression " equity share capital." This is defined as the issued share capital, disregarding any part which does not carry any right to participate beyond a specified amount in a distribution of capital or income.[38] A majority holding of the equity is deemed automatically to confer control even though it may not confer voting control. Because of the unfortunate growth of non-voting ordinary shares, it is not improbable that in fact it will not confer such control and accordingly the Jenkins Committee recommended the abolition of this limb of the definition.[39] Fourthly, it should be noted that where two companies each hold 50 per cent. of the equity share capital of another, that other will not be the subsidiary of either.[40]

It will be apparent from the foregoing that the statutory definition of control does not cover all the cases in which control can be exercised. Control is a matter of degree, ranging from complete legal control for all purposes over a wholly owned subsidiary to *de facto* control, except in the event of a major scandal, normally exercisable by the existing management even though they may hold few or none of the shares. It may be difficult to detect (particularly when " pyramiding " through numerous subsidiaries and sub-subsidiaries has been resorted to) but it is coming to be recognised as a separate item of property,[41] the value of which will depend upon the degree of its completeness. The statutory definition is undoubtedly right to place the emphasis which it does on the power to control the board, for, as we have seen, the board is the company's head and brains. But *de facto* control over

---

[37] The definition says nothing about control over the exercise of their powers by the directors once appointed, and this section is not one of those which provides that " director " is deemed to include " any person in accordance with whose directions or instructions the directors . . . are accustomed to act."

[36] In other words, ordinary and participating preference shares, but not non-participating preference shares. The business world has long classed the latter with debentures (or mortgages) as " prior charges " in contradistinction to the " equity " subject to those " charges," which economically closely resembles the equity of redemption subject to a mortgage: see Chap. 16, *infra.*

[39] Cmnd. 1749, para. 150. This has not yet been implemented although some related recommendations have been carried out by ss. 3 to 5 of the 1967 Act: see *infra.*

[40] But as regards shares in unlimited companies held by limited companies, see 1967 Act, s. 47 (1) (*a*), *infra,* p. 266, n. 33.

[41] *Cf.* the observations of Lord Uthwatt in *Short* v. *Treasury Commissioners* [1948] A.C. 534 at p. 546, H.L., and *Dean* v. *Prince* [1953] Ch. 590; [1954] Ch. 409, C.A. The question whether it is property which a shareholder should be allowed to deal in for his private profit is discussed *infra,* at pp. 578, 579.

the board can exist without any legal power at all.[42]   Thus, it is well
known that, in a company with a large and dispersed membership, a
comparatively small proportion of the total shares, if held in one
hand, may enable actual control to be exercised, particularly if the hand
is that of the existing management with control over the proxy-voting
machinery.[43]   This and other methods of exercising pressure are
probably incapable of precise legal definition.   But there are other
devices of which this cannot be said.   Thus legal control may be
exercised through agreements divorced from shareholdings, through
weighted voting,[44] through inter-locking directorships, through voting
agreements or through the voting trust so popular in America.[45]   None
of these devices is necessarily caught by either prong of the statutory
definition.

Where the relationship of holding and subsidiary companies exists
the Act makes a number of provisions qualifying the normal rule that
each company constitutes a separate legal entity.   The most important
of these provisions relate to accounts and are designed to meet the
problem outlined above.

By sections 150–153 and the Eighth Schedule, Part II,[46] the holding
company's balance-sheet and profit and loss account are to be presented
in the form of group accounts giving a true and fair view of the state of
affairs of the group as a whole.[47]   Normally consolidated accounts
(*i.e.,* one account for the whole group) must be drawn up in the form
prescribed by paragraphs 17–22 of the Eighth Schedule, but an alternative form may be adopted if the directors consider that this would be
more informative,[48] in which event details must be given of the
subsidiaries' net profits or losses and of shares in or amounts owing
from the subsidiaries.[49]   Similarly the accounts of each subsidiary must

---

[42] Berle & Means, *op. cit.,* p. 69.   "For practical purposes that control lies in the
hands of the individual or group who have the actual power to select the board of
directors (or its majority) either by mobilising the legal right to choose them—
'controlling' a majority of the votes directly or through some legal device—or by
exerting pressure which influences their choice."

[43] See Chap. 21, *infra.*

[44] For an extreme example, see *Investment Trust Corporation* v. *Singapore Traction Co.*
[1935] Ch. 615, C.A., in which one £1 management share could outvote the remaining
399,999 shares.   In this particular case the arrangement would have fallen within the
first prong of the statutory definition, since the share could outvote the others on a
motion to appoint or remove from the board.   But this could have been avoided by
removing such motions from the outvoting power or, *semble,* by expressing it as a
mere negative veto: *cf.* subs. (2) (*a*).

[45] *Semble,* the company whose shares were subject to the voting trust would not
become a subsidiary of the trust corporation since the latter would hold "in a
fiduciary capacity."

[46] A new Sched. 8 was substituted by the Companies Act 1967, Sched. 2.   These provisions represent a very substantial advance on the Companies Act 1929, which
merely provided by s. 126 that the holding company's accounts should state how
profits or losses of subsidiaries had been dealt with.

[47] This requirement may be dispensed with in the circumstances specified in s. 150 (2),
but the consent of the Board of Trade will normally be requisite.

[48] s. 151.

[49] Sched. 8, para. 15.

show details of its indebtedness to and from all other companies within the group.[50] The holding company's directors must also secure that, except where there are good reasons against it, the financial year of each subsidiary coincides with the holding company's own financial year.[51] And, under the Third, Fourth and Fifth Schedules, reports on subsidiary companies' assets, liabilities, profits and losses have to be annexed to prospectuses or statements in lieu of prospectuses.[52]

The Companies Act 1967 carries matters still further. It requires the accounts of the holding company to state in respect of each subsidiary its name, place of incorporation and class and proportion of the issued shares held by the holding company.[53] And the subsidiary has to state the name and place of incorporation of its ultimate holding company.[54] But more important than this is the fact that, although group accounts are required only if the holding-subsidiary relationship is established, it is now recognised that companies may for some purposes be regarded as within the group although they are not legally under the same control. By section 4 of the 1967 Act, if a company holds more than one-tenth of the equity share capital of any other bodies corporate it must, in its accounts, name those bodies corporate, state their places of incorporation and give particulars of the shares held.[55]

It will therefore be seen that the Acts themselves now go some way towards treating all companies within a group as part of the same entity—towards recognising the real business unit of inter-locked companies, rather than the arbitrary legal unit of the single company.[56] But as yet only tentative steps have been made in this direction and it must be emphasised how very limited these provisions are. For example, if one subsidiary company is insolvent there is nothing, beyond the pressure of public and market opinion, to prevent the holding company from putting it into liquidation and leaving its creditors to whistle for their money notwithstanding that the group as a whole is fully solvent. Indeed, it may fairly be said that all that the Companies Acts do is to afford some measure of protection, against the rigid consequence of the rule in *Salomon's* case, to shareholders actual and potential. On the whole, outside creditors are still left to

---

50 *Ibid.* para. 16.
51 s. 153.
52 Additional recognition of the unity of companies within a group is contained in ss. 27, 54, 161 (3), 166 and 196 of the 1948 Act, and ss. 18 (2), 20 (2), 25 (2), 27, 32 (3) and 47 (1) of the 1967 Act. Examples can be found in other legislation ; see, for example, the Landlord and Tenant Act 1954, s. 42 and the Redundancy Payments Act 1965, s. 48.
53 1967 Act, s. 3. Note the limitations in subss. (3)–(5).
54 s. 5. Note the limitation in subs. (2).
55 Note the limitations in subss. (3) and (4).
56 *Cf.* Kahn-Freund in (1946) 9 M.L.R. 235. He points out (at p. 240) the analogy of the German *Konzernrecht*. Developments in this direction have gone further in U.S.A. which has never been fettered by the binding force of the *Salomon* decision.

suffer from the unrestricted application of this rule and shareholders are still allowed the full benefit of it.

Taxation

The only outside creditor in whose favour the *Salomon* rule has been substantially mitigated is the Revenue. A perusal of Chapter 9 will reveal many examples of the lifting of the veil in the Revenue's favour. As regards income tax this applies particularly in the case of close companies, especially in regard to "shortfall" distributions when the company's income may, in effect, be treated for surtax purposes as that of the members. In connection with estate duty there are the very sweeping provisions of the Finance Act 1940.[57] As Devlin J. said[58]: "No doubt the legislature can forge a sledgehammer capable of cracking open the corporate shell; and it can, if it chooses, demand that the courts ignore all the conceptions and principles which are at the root of company law." In the field of taxation, the legislature has done precisely that.

As regards stamp duty the veil has been lifted in the interests of the members. On a reconstruction or amalgamation the capital duty on the newly formed company and the transfer duty on the assignment of the assets to it may be avoided or reduced if the terms of section 55 of the Finance Act 1927[59] are carefully followed. Similarly, transfer duty on transfers of assets within a group may be avoided under section 42 of the Finance Act 1930.

It may therefore be said that not only has the veil been lifted in the interests of the Revenue but further steps have been taken in the interests of members towards recognising "enterprise entity" rather than corporate entity.

Summary

It will therefore be seen that in a number of important respects the legislature has rent the veil woven by the *Salomon* case. Particularly is this so in the sphere of taxation and in the steps which have been taken towards the recognition of enterprise-entity rather than corporate-entity. The courts, however, have only construed statutes as "cracking open the corporate shell" when compelled to do so by the clear words of the statute; indeed they have gone out of their way to avoid this construction whenever possible. Many examples of their reluctance to go further than they are compelled will be found in the discussion that follows. A further illustration of this attitude is the decision of the House of Lords in *Nokes* v. *Doncaster Amalgamated Collieries.*[60]

---

[57] As subsequently amended: see p. 184 *et seq.*
[58] *Bank voor Handel en Scheepvaart N.V.* v. *Slatford* [1953] 1 Q.B. 248 at p. 278: see *infra*, p. 206.
[59] As subsequently amended: see Chap. 26, *infra*, at pp. 632, 633.
[60] [1940] A.C. 1014, H.L. (overruling the unanimous view of the lower courts).

Under what is now section 208 of the Act, the court, when approving a scheme of arrangement or amalgamation, may order the transfer from one company to another of " the property or liabilities of any transferor company," [61] and it is expressly provided that " the expression ' property ' includes property, rights and powers of every description, and the expression ' liabilities ' includes duties." [62] It was nevertheless held that the court's order did not operate to transfer contracts of personal service.[63] With almost passionate rhetoric Lord Atkin declared [64]: " I had fancied that ingrained in the personal status of a citizen under our laws was the right to choose for himself whom he would serve, and that this right of choice constituted the main difference between a servant and a serf." And later [65] he referred to the contrary construction as " tainted with oppression and confiscation." " The principle," he added,[66] " that a man is not to be compelled to serve a master against his will is . . . deep-seated in the common law of this country."

Yet how unreal all this is, when the master is a company, will be apparent when one considers that the transferee company, instead of acquiring the undertaking, might have bought the whole of the shares, changed the management, adopted new articles, amended the objects and other clauses of the memorandum, changed the nature of the business, increased the capital, and, with the consent of the Board of Trade, even have adopted a new name. All this could have been done and the servant would still have been bound to serve the " master " who in theory, but certainly not in fact, remained the same. " The identity of the company is preserved," said Lord Atkin.[67] But how tenuous and unreal this identity is! The actual decision may well have been in accordance with the intentions of the legislature, but to explain it on Lord Atkin's grounds is to mistake the shadow of corporate personality for the substance.

UNDER JUDICIAL INTERPRETATION [68]

Efforts by the judges to lift the veil have, in general, been hamstrung by the *Salomon* case, which finally destroyed the possibility of regarding

---

[61] subs. (1) (*a*).

[62] subs. (4).

[63] *Cf. In the Estate of Skinner, decd.* [1958] 1 W.L.R. 1043, where it was held that a scheme amalgamating two trust corporations could not transfer powers to apply for grants of probate of wills naming them executors.

[64] At p. 1026.

[65] At p. 1030.

[66] At p. 1033.

[67] At p. 1030. Lord Atkin himself was obviously not entirely happy with this explanation, for he added that " in any case, the individual concerned, while he must be prepared to run the one risk, is entitled to say that he is not obliged to run the other." But in practical effect the two risks are identical. In fairness to Lord Atkin it should be said that his words, delivered on August 1, 1940, were probably prompted by contemporary reports of slave labour on the Nazi continent. For a more realistic approach, see the Redundancy Payments Act 1965, s. 48.

[68] This account does not pretend to deal with all the cases in which the courts have lifted the veil. These cases have never been collected and, as the point with which

a " one-man company " as a mere alias of, or agent for, the principal shareholder. Perhaps the most extreme illustration of a refusal to lift the veil is afforded by *Lee* v. *Lee's Air Farming Ltd.*[69] There Lee, for the purpose of carrying on his business of aerial top-dressing, had formed a company of which he beneficially owned all the shares and was sole " governing director." He was also appointed chief pilot. Pursuant to the company's statutory obligations he caused the company to insure against liability to pay compensation under the Workmen's Compensation Act. He was killed in a flying accident. The Court of Appeal of New Zealand held that his widow was not entitled to compensation from the company (*i.e.*, from their insurers) since Lee could not be regarded as a " worker " (*i.e.*, servant) within the meaning of the Act. But the Privy Council reversed that decision, holding that Lee and his company were distinct legal entities which had entered into contractual relationships under which he became, *qua* chief pilot, a servant of the company. In his capacity of governing director he could, on behalf of the company, give himself orders in his other capacity of pilot, and hence the relationship between himself, as pilot, and the company was that of servant and master. In effect the magic of corporate personality enabled him to be master and servant at the same time and to get all the advantages of both—and of limited liability.[70]

Nevertheless, there have been exceptional cases in which the courts have felt themselves able to ignore the corporate entity and to treat the individual shareholders as liable for its acts or entitled to its property, or to regard the various companies of a group as one entity.

Agency

In the first place, there is no reason why, in fact, a company should not act as an agent of its shareholders. Where there is an express agreement to this effect,[71] no difficulty arises. But this will be a rare occurrence. More often the courts will be asked to infer an agency relationship and *Salomon's* case shows how difficult it will be to persuade them to draw this inference. That the difficulty is not insuperable, however, was shown by a line of cases, commencing immediately after the corporate entity principle was first clearly established. These arose

we are now concerned is rarely the major issue, it is impossible to trace them from Digests.

69 [1961] A.C. 12, P.C.

70 Note also *Underwood* v. *Bank of Liverpool* [1924] 1 K.B. 775, C.A., which shows that third parties who are so ill-advised as to regard the members as the same as the company will not only fail to make the members liable to them, but may sometimes incur liability to the company.

71 As in *Southern* v. *Watson* [1940] 3 All E.R. 439, C.A., where, on the conversion of a business into a private company, the sale agreement provided that the company should fulfil existing contracts as agent of the seller, and *Rainham Chemical Works* v. *Belvedere* [1921] 2 A.C. 465, H.L., where the agreement provided that the newly formed company should take possession of land as agents for its vendor promoters.

from the acquisition by English companies of certain American breweries, and the courts refused to disturb the Commissioners' finding that the American companies were in fact merely kept in being as agents of the English companies that had taken them over.[72] But the courts emphasised that merely because an English company had a controlling interest would not have made the business of the foreign company that of the English. Hence, in later tax cases, in which the findings of the Commissioners were more guarded, a contrary decision was reached and the veil of incorporation operated to protect the English shareholder.[73]

In *Smith, Stone & Knight* v. *Birmingham Corporation*,[74] all these authorities were reviewed by Atkinson J. who concluded that it was a question of fact in each case whether the subsidiary company was carrying on the parent company's business or its own. He considered that six points were relevant for determining that question: (1) Were the profits treated as those of the parent company? (2) Were the persons conducting the business appointed by the parent company? (3) Was the parent company the head and brain of the trading venture? (4) Did the parent company govern the adventure and decide what should be done and what capital should be embarked on it? (5) Were the profits made by its skill and direction? (6) Was the parent company in effectual and constant control?[75] The learned judge answered all these questions in the affirmative in the case before him, and accordingly held that the parent company (which, through itself and nominees, held all the shares) was entitled to compensation for removal and disturbance on the compulsory acquisition of the land of its subsidiary.[76]

Re F. G. (Films) Ltd.[77] affords an interesting illustration of the invocation of agency in order to prevent the use of corporate personality for the evasion of statutory regulations. A British company had been

[72] *Apthorpe* v. *Peter Schoenhofen Brewing Co.* (1899) 4 T.C. 41; 80 L.T. 395, C.A. An identical decision was reached by a court of first instance in *U.S. Brewing Co.* v. *Apthorpe* (1898) 4 T.C. 17. *Frank Jones Brewing Co.* v. *Apthorpe, ibid.* 6, is distinguishable as there the land was apparently vested in separate trustees for the English company.

[73] *Kodak* v. *Clark* [1903] 1 K.B. 505, C.A. (in which the English company held 98 per cent. of the shares); *Gramophone & Typewriter Ltd.* v. *Stanley* [1908] 2 K.B. 89, C.A.; and *cf. I. R. C.* v. *Sansom* [1921] 2 K.B. 492, C.A. (in both of which there was a 100 per cent. holding). The last-named decision is a particularly strong case which was followed immediately by s. 21 of the F.A. 1922 (see Chap. 9, *supra*).

[74] [1939] 4 All E.R. 116. See a learned note in (1940) 3 M.L.R. 226.

[75] The weakness of these tests is that all but the first would almost inevitably be answered in the affirmative in every case where the controlling shareholder is also the managing director.

[76] With this decision should be contrasted *Roberts* v. *Coventry Corpn.* [1947] 1 All E.R. 308, in which the court dismissed with something approaching contempt a claim by the controlling director and shareholder for compensation on the compulsory acquisition of land let by her to the company. But in that case there was an independent shareholder. See also, *B. T. H.* v. *Sterling Accessories* [1924] 2 Ch. 33.

[77] [1953] 1 W.L.R. 483. In this case one can perhaps see the first signs of recognition that the under-capitalisation of the subsidiary may be a significant element in deciding whether to treat it as fused with its parent. In the U.S.A. much use is made of this criterion.

formed with £100 capital of which £90 was held by the president of
an American film company. There were three directors, the American
and two British subjects, but no other staff and no place of business
apart from the registered office. By arrangement between the two
companies, a film was then produced in India, nominally by the British
company, but all finance and other facilities were provided by the
American. The Board of Trade refused to recognise that the film was
" made " by the British company and would ¬ot register it as a British
film. On appeal, the court dismissed as a travesty the suggestion that
the powerful American concern had acted as agents of the insignificant
British company. On the contrary, they held that, in so far as the
company had acted at all, it had done so merely as nominee or agent
of the American corporation which was the true maker of the film.

A more recent tax case—*Firestone Tyre and Rubber Co.* v.
Llewellin [78]—also affords an example of an English subsidiary being
treated as the agent of its American parent. The American company
had an arrangement with its distributors on the Continent of Europe
whereby they obtained supplies from the English manufacturers, its
wholly owned subsidiary. The English company credited the American
with the price received after deducting the costs plus 5 per cent. It
was conceded that the subsidiary was a separate legal entity and not a
mere emanation of the American parent,[79] and that it was selling its
own goods. Nevertheless, these sales were a means whereby the
American company carried on its European business, and it was held
that the substance of the arrangement was that the American company
traded in England through the agency of its subsidiary.[80]

With these cases, in which the courts have made use of the agency
concept to pierce the corporate veil, can be contrasted equally striking
illustrations of their refusal to countenance any relaxation of the
Salomon rule. In *Ebbw Vale U.D.C.* v. *S. Wales Traffic Area Licensing
Authority* [81] the Court of Appeal refused to recognise that a service,
provided by a company all of whose shares had vested in the British
Transport Commission under the Transport Act 1947, could be
regarded as provided " by the Commission or by any person acting as
agent for the Commission." In other words, they insisted that the legal
forms should triumph over the realities of nationalisation, holding that:
" Under the ordinary rules of law, a parent company and a subsidiary
company, even a 100 per cent. subsidiary company, are distinct legal

---

[78] [1957] 1 W.L.R. 464, H.L. *Cf. Littlewoods Stores Ltd.* v. *I.R.C., The Times,*
May 6, 1969, C.A.
[79] Contrast the American company in the American brewery cases, *supra.*
[80] *Smith, Stone & Knight* v. *Birmingham Corpn., supra,* was not cited, but it would
appear that the six tests laid down in that case were complied with. See also
Malyon v. *Plummer* [1963] 1 Q.B. 419 where the husband's one-man company and
the wife's appointment as a nominal director were treated as " mere machinery "
whereby part of the husband's earnings was channelled to the wife.
[81] [1951] 2 K.B. 366, C.A.

entities, and in the absence of an agency contract between the two companies one cannot be said to be the agent of the other." [82] In so far as this statement suggests that an express agency contract is needed, it cannot be reconciled with the decisions mentioned above, none of which seems to have been cited.

Similarly, in *Pegler* v. *Craven*,[83] they refused to regard a private company, occupying a shop as licensee of the tenant (its majority shareholder and managing director) as occupying as the tenant's agent, so as to entitle him to a renewal of the tenancy.[84] This case is distinguishable from those previously cited, in that the tenant held considerably less than the whole of the capital, and Evershed M.R. did recognise that the decision might have been different had the holding been more substantial.[85] But this seems very dubious since, in the later case of *Tunstall* v. *Steigmann*,[86] the Court of Appeal held that the landlord could not successfully oppose the grant of a new tenancy on the ground that she required it for the purpose of a business to be carried on by her when, in fact, the business was that of a company in which she owned beneficially all the shares. In that case Ormerod L.J. denied that the veil could ever be lifted except where the company was " a façade concealing the true facts." [87]

Trust

The cases cited above show that in exceptional circumstances creditors have succeeded in persuading the court that the company is acting as an agent for its members. Attempts to rely on *trust* rather than agency have been less successful. It cannot be doubted that a company, if so authorised by its memorandum, may act as a trustee and that the beneficiaries may in fact be the same persons as its members, but the proposition that a company holds its property on trust for its

---

[82] *Per* Cohen L.J. at p. 370, quoting *Salomon's* case and *British Thomson Houston* v. *Sterling Accessories, supra.* Some reliance was placed upon a provision in the Act that for certain purposes " where a body corporate is directly or indirectly controlled by the Commission, anything done by that body shall be deemed to be done by the Commission, and the undertaking of the body shall be deemed to form part of the undertaking of the Commission." This was thought to show that the legislature was well aware of the *Salomon* rule and expressly excluded it when it wanted to do so.

[83] [1952] 2 Q.B. 69, C.A. It is submitted that the court could have held that the director and the company were sharing the accommodation: see *Peebles* v. *Crosthwaite* (1897) 13 T.L.R. 198, C.A., and *Chaplin* v. *Smith* [1926] 1 K.B. 198, C.A. (which do not seem to have been cited) and the later *Willis* v. *Asscn. of Universities of the British Commonwealth* [1965] 1 Q.B. 140, C.A.

[84] Under the Leasehold Property (Temporary Provisions) Act 1951.

[85] At p. 79. For details of the shareholding, see [1952] 1 All E.R. at p. 686.

[86] [1962] 2 Q.B. 593, C.A. This was a case under the Landlord and Tenant Act 1954, Part II. If the landlord had actually held the property on trust for the company the decision would have been different: see s. 41 (2) and *Sevenarts Ltd.* v. *Busvine* [1968] 1 W.L.R. 1929, C.A.

[87] [1962] 2 Q.B. at 602; see also *per* Danckwerts L.J. at 607. But contrast *Willis* v. *Asscn. of Universities of the British Commonwealth* [1965] 1 Q.B. 140, C.A.; *infra*, p. 215.

members *qua* members cannot now be successfully argued.[88] And normally the principle that members have no proprietary interest in the company's assets has been applied with considerable rigidity. Thus, as we have seen, a sole shareholder (and main creditor) of a company has not been regarded as having any insurable interest in its property.[89] And in the case of *Bank voor Handel en Scheepvaart N.V.* v. *Slatford*,[90] Devlin J. described the contrary as " beyond the reach of sustained argument." [91]   In that case the question was whether, for the purposes of a Treaty of Peace Order, property of a Dutch company could be regarded as " belonging " to its shareholders, or as " held or managed " by the company " on behalf of " its shareholders. Devlin J. had no hesitation in holding that it could not.[92]

Nevertheless, a judgment of Danckwerts J.[93] approaches close to such a recognition. In *The Abbey, Malvern Wells Ltd.* v. *Ministry of Local Government and Planning*,[94] the members of an ordinary limited liability company formed to run a school had taken steps to convert it into a non-profit-making charity. This they had done by vesting all the shares in trustees on charitable trusts and by altering the articles to provide that the school was to be run by the trustees. The company applied for a certificate [95] that its land was exempt from the development charge provisions of the Town and Country Planning Act 1947 as being held on charitable trusts. The Minister refused his certificate and the company applied to the court for a declaration that they were entitled to it. This was granted, Danckwerts J. saying that he was entitled, and indeed bound, to look at the constitution of the company to see who in fact was in control, and that this was the trustees. Although the company theoretically had power to make and distribute profits the persons who regulated its operations had no such freedom.

" While the property of the company is held nominally subject to the terms of the memorandum and articles . . . in actual fact [it] is regulated by [them] plus the provisions of the trust deed; and,

---

[88] *Cf.* the dictum of Evershed L.J. in *Short* v. *Treasury Commissioners* [1948] 1 K.B. at p. 122, quoted *supra*, at p. 74, note 36. But *cf.* the strange case of *Re Macartney* [1918] 1 Ch. 300, where a bequest of shares in a company seems to have been treated as if it was the same as a bequest of property owned by the company.

[89] *Macaura* v. *Northern Insurance* [1925] A.C. 619 H.L.(Ir.).   But *cf. Lee* v. *Sheard* [1956] 1 Q.B. 192, C.A., where a director and shareholder of a private company, who had been injured by the negligence of the defendant and prevented from working, was held entitled to recover as damages a sum in respect of the diminution of the distributions received by him from the company.

[90] [1953] 1 Q.B. 248.

[91] At p. 269.

[92] The *American Brewery* and the *Smith, Stone & Knight* cases (*supra*, p. 203) and the *Abbey, Malvern Wells* case (*infra*), which appear to afford most support for the opposite conclusion, were apparently not cited.

[93] See also his judgment in the earlier case of *Re French Protestant Hospital* [1951] Ch. 567.

[94] [1951] Ch. 728.

[95] Town and Country Planning Act 1947, ss. 85 and 92 (1).

therefore, the company is restricted in fact in the application of its property and assets and may only apply [them] for the charitable purposes which are mentioned in the trust deed." [96]

While this decision must be welcomed for its robust determination to cut through red tape, it represents a considerable departure from the normal application of established principle. In effect, it holds that the company may be regarded as holding its property on charitable trusts if all its shares are so held and its governing body are trustees; and this notwithstanding the well-established rule that a company does not hold its property on trust for its members, and the statutory rule that a company is not concerned with the trusts on which shares are held. [97]

Determination of residence

The courts also look behind the façade of the company and its place of registration in order to determine its residence. For this purpose the test laid down has long been the place of its "central management and control," an expression which has now been given statutory authority for certain tax purposes. [98] Normally this place will be where the board of directors function, but it might, no doubt, be the place of business of the managing director (especially if he held a controlling interest), or that of a parent company [99]; once again we are thrown back on the difficult problem of locating "control." The test is purely factual, "to be determined, not according to a scrutiny of this or that regulation or by-law, but upon a scrutiny of the course of business or trading." [1] And it may be satisfied even though the control was "irregular or unauthorised or unlawful." [2]

Residence as thus determined is important mainly in connection with taxation,[3] but it may also govern enemy status [4] or subjection

---

[96] At p. 739.

[97] Companies Act 1948, s. 117. This section is invariably amplified by an article on the lines of Table A, art. 7, which was doubtless incorporated in the present case. With the *Malvern* case, contrast *Butt* v. *Kelson* [1952] Ch. 197, C.A., where it was held that beneficiaries under a trust could not compel the trustees, who were directors of the company, to produce for their inspection company documents not available to the members as such.

[98] I.T.A. 1952, s. 468 (7). Most Double Taxation Conventions use the expression " in which its business is managed and controlled."

[99] *Unit Construction Co. Ltd.* v. *Bullock* [1960] A.C. 351, H.L.

[1] *De Beers Consolidated Mines Ltd.* v. *Howe* [1906] A.C. 455 at 458, H.L.

[2] *Unit Construction Co. Ltd.* v. *Bullock, supra, per* Lord Simonds at p. 363. See also *per* Lord Radcliffe at pp. 363–371.

[3] *Cf. Cesena Sulphur Co.* v. *Nicholson* (1876) 1 Ex.D. 428 ; *De Beers Consolidated Mines* v. *Howe, supra*; *Swedish Central Ry.* v. *Thompson* [1925] A.C. 495, H.L.; *Egyptian Delta Land & Investment Co.* v. *Todd* [1929] A.C. 1, H.L.; *Union Corporation* v. *I. R. C.* [1952] 1 All E.R. 646; affd. [1953] A.C. 482, H.L.; *Unit Construction Co. Ltd.* v. *Bullock, supra.*

[4] *Daimler Co.* v. *Continental Tyre & Rubber Co.* [1916] 2 A.C. 307, H.L.; *Kuenigl* v. *Donnersmarck* [1955] 1 Q.B. 515. *Cf. Part Cargo ex M.V. Glenroy* [1945] A.C. 124, P.C., where a German subsidiary company was treated as " a branch " of its holding company, so as to taint with enemy ownership goods in transit from the holding company to the subsidiary.

to the jurisdiction of English [5] or foreign courts.[6] And, at any rate for taxation purposes, it seems to be well established that a company may have more than one residence,[7] the difficulty of seeing how " central " management can be in more than one place having been met by modifying the " central control " test, so that it becomes a question of finding " where the controlling power and authority, and the exercise of that power and authority, is to some substantial degree to be found." [8]

This, however, is probably not truly to be regarded as an exception to the general principle. As Lord Parker points out in *Daimler* v. *Continental Tyre Co.*,[9] the corporate entity rule does not mean that the law must know nothing about the natural persons who constitute and control the company. " In questions of property [10] and capacity, of acts done and rights acquired or liabilities assumed thereby, this may be always true. Certainly it is for the most part. But the character in which property is held, and the character in which the capacity to act is enjoyed and acts are done, are not *in pari materia*." In other words, it is no more a breach of the *Salomon* principle to look at the corporators to determine the *character* of the corporation as an enemy alien or as a British resident, than it is to look at the members to determine whether the company is a subsidiary.[11]

Ratification of corporate acts

Another series of decisions, which approach more closely to a genuine exception, are those relating to informal ratification by the members of acts done on behalf of the company. As we have seen [12] the law normally insists that only a resolution duly passed at a meeting of the company can be regarded as an act of the company itself. In

---

[5] R.S.C., Ord. 11, r. 1 (*c*). Alternatively, the company may be served in this country under Ord. 65, r. 3, if " present " here, the test of " presence " being the carrying on business from some place in the jurisdiction: see, Chap. 27, *infra*.

[6] *Littauer Glove Corporation* v. *F. W. Millington* (1928) 44 T.L.R. 746; Foreign Judgments (Reciprocal Enforcement) Act 1933, s. 4 (2) (*a*) (iv).

[7] *Swedish Central Ry.* v. *Thompson* [1925] A.C. 495, H.L.; *Union Corpn.* v. *I. R. C.* [1952] 1 All E.R. 646, C.A. (affirmed on other grounds [1953] A.C. 482, H.L.).

[8] *Union Corpn.* v. *I. R. C.*, *supra* (see especially at p. 657), following *Koitaki Para Rubber Estates* v. *Fed. Comm. of Taxation* (1940) 64 C.L.R. 15, 241 (Austr.H.C.). But this test seems inconsistent with previous House of Lords' decisions: see (1952) 68 L.Q.R. 307.

[9] [1916] 2 A.C. at p. 340.

[10] Even as regards deciding whether its property is enemy property: *Bank voor Handel* v. *Slatford*, *supra*; but *cf. Part Cargo ex M.V. Glenroy*, *supra*.

[11] *Elliott* v. *Pierson* [1948] Ch. 452 can also be explained as not really an exception to the general rule. There Elliott had entered into a personal contract to sell a road-house in fact owned by a company of which he was the sole shareholder and director. The purchaser sought to repudiate the contract, but it was held that Elliott was entitled to specific performance because he was in a position to compel the company to convey to the purchaser. The separation of company and shareholder was not denied, but the veil of incorporation did not prevent the court from looking behind it to see whether the seller (the member) could compel the legal owner (the company) to act as he directed.

[12] *Supra*, Chap. 7, p. 127 *et seq*. See further, Chap. 21, *infra*.

a number of cases, however, the question has arisen whether something less formal than a resolution passed at a duly convened meeting will suffice. In other words, can the veil be lifted so as to equate a decision of the members with a decision of the company itself?

In a comparatively early case, *Re George Newman Ltd.*,[13] a strong Court of Appeal held, in a judgment delivered by Lindley L.J., that: " Individual assents given separately may preclude those who have given them from complaining of what they have sanctioned,[14] but for the purpose of binding a company in its corporate capacity individual assents given separately are not equivalent to the assent of a meeting." [15] The court suggested that in any event the acts then assented to (payments to directors) would have been *ultra vires*,[16] but it seems clear that this was not the only, or indeed the main, *ratio decidendi*.

On the other hand, in *Re Express Engineering Works* [17] a later Court of Appeal held that a resolution, passed at a meeting of directors, who were also all the shareholders, could not be impugned notwithstanding that it was beyond the power of the directors as such. Similarly, in *Re Oxted Motor Co.*[18] it was held that all the members might waive the normal length of notice for a meeting; a decision now ratified by the Act which, indeed, permits notice to be waived by 95 per cent. of the members.[19] In both these cases, however, there had in fact been meetings although informally constituted. But in *Parker & Cooper Ltd.* v. *Reading*,[20] there had been no meeting at all; the members had merely informally ratified a debenture granted by the directors acting beyond their powers. Astbury J. nevertheless held that the company was bound. A similar decision was reached in *Re Duomatic Ltd.*[21] where Buckley J. held that the liquidator could not recover directors' salaries paid without the required resolutions but with the consent of all the members *except non-voting preference shareholders*.[22]

In these cases *Re George Newman* [23] was distinguished on the ground that there the act was *ultra vires* the company. Much reliance, too, was placed on the words of Lord Davey in *Salomon's* case [24] itself, that

13 [1895] 1 Ch. 674, C.A.
14 See *Re Pearce Duff & Co. Ltd.* [1960] 1 W.L.R. 1014.
15 At p. 686.
16 *Cf. Pacific Coast Coal Mines* v. *Arbuthnot* [1917] A.C. 607, P.C.
17 [1920] 1 Ch. 466, C.A.
18 [1921] 3 K.B. 32.
19 *i.e.*, by the holders of 95 per cent. in value of the shares carrying a right to vote at the meeting, or, if the company has no share capital, by members representing 95 per cent. of the total voting rights: Companies Act 1948, s. 133 (3). Unanimous consent is still necessary to waive the requirement of 21 days' notice for the annual general meeting: *ibid.* See Chap. 21, p. 477, *infra*.
20 [1926] Ch. 975. And see *Peter Buchanan Ltd.* v. *McVey* [1955] A.C. 516n. at pp. 520–521 (N.Ir.Sup.Ct. 1950).
21 [1969] 2 W.L.R. 114.
22 But payments for compensation for loss of office were recoverable since s. 191 of the 1948 Act (see *infra*, Chap. 25, p. 533) had not been complied with.
23 *Supra.* As already pointed out the *ultra vires* point was clearly not the sole or main *ratio*.
24 [1897] A.C. 22, H.L., at p. 57.

" the company is bound in a matter *intra vires* by the unanimous agreement of its members." It seems, however, that nothing less than 100 per cent. agreement of those entitled to vote will suffice. This was, in fact, decided by the Privy Council in *E. B. M.* v. *Dominion Bank*,[25] in which the facts were very similar to those in *Parker & Cooper* v. *Reading*, except that the holders of two shares in the company had omitted to ratify the debenture. On the other hand, there is an earlier Privy Council case [26] which holds that mere tacit acquiescence over a long period may regularise the absence of a resolution.[27]

It has now become common practice to insert in the articles of a private company an express provision that a written resolution signed by all the members entitled to vote shall be as valid and effective as if it had been passed at a general meeting. Such a provision must clearly be regarded as lawful as it now appears in Part II of Table A.[28] This, however, merely amounts to saying that a company's constitution may expressly provide methods other than a formal meeting for constituting an act of the company. And it would only cover a formal written resolution and not an informal ratification such as that in the *Parker* and *E. B. M.* cases. Whether such a provision is effective in the case of all types of resolution is discussed in a later chapter.[29] In any event, it has nothing to do with our present problem which relates to the binding effect on the corporate person of decisions taken outside the corporation.

Fraud or improper conduct

The above cases represent the nearest approach to any consistent lines of authorities. We now turn to a number of isolated illustrations of circumstances in which the courts have felt themselves free to disregard the corporate entity. The first of these is where there is " fraud or improper conduct." [30] Thus the courts will not allow company promoters to conceal the profits which they are making by operating through dummy companies,[31] and will insist that disclosure of profits must be made not to a board of dummies but to the members, actual and intended.[32] Nor will they allow the holders of 90 per cent.

---

[25] [1937] 3 All E.R. 555, P.C. The Board expressly left open the correctness of *Parker & Cooper* v. *Reading, supra.*

[26] *Ho Tung* v. *Man On Insurance* [1902] A.C. 232, P.C. This decision relied on the early *ultra vires* cases (Chap. 5, pp. 83–87, *supra*) and especially on *Phosphate of Lime Co.* v. *Green* (1871) L.R. 7 C.P. 43, in which it was laid down that acquiescence could be established without proving actual knowledge by each individual member. The whole question of the effect of acquiescence on corporate irregularities is one of immense difficulty: see further, p. 377, notes 33 and 34 and pp. 510, 511.

[27] Even, as there, a special resolution.

[28] Art. 5. It is also accepted inferentially by s. 143 (4) (*c*) of the 1948 Act.

[29] *Infra*, Chap. 21, pp. 496, 497.

[30] The expression used in *Pioneer Laundry* v. *Minister of National Revenue* [1939] 4 All E.R. 254 at 259 E, P.C.

[31] *Re Darby* [1911] 1 K.B. 95; *cf. Patton* v. *Yukon Consolidated Gold Corp.* [1934] 3 D.L.R. 400 (Ont. C.A.) and *Dominion Royalty Corpn.* v. *Goffatt* [1935] 1 D.L.R. 780 (Ont. C.A.); affd. [1935] 4 D.L.R. 736 (Can.S.C.).

[32] *Infra*, Chap. 13, pp. 258–259.

of the shares of a company to expropriate the 10 per cent. minority by the device of forming themselves into another company which then makes an offer for all the shares so that, on their accepting it, section 209 of the 1948 Act [33] can be invoked.[34]

But an even better illustration is afforded by *Gilford Motor Co.* v. *Horne*.[35] There, Horne, a former employee of the plaintiff, had covenanted not to solicit its customers. He formed a company to carry on his business and it undertook the solicitation. An injunction was granted against both him *and the company* to restrain them. The company was described in the judgments as " a device, a stratagem," [36] and as " a mere cloak or sham." [37] The remarkable feature of the case was that an injunction was granted against the company itself notwithstanding that it was not a party to the covenant.[38] In effect, the court treated it as Horne's *alter ego*. This decision was followed in *Jones* v. *Lipman*,[39] where the defendant had attempted to avoid having to complete a sale of his house to the plaintiff by conveying it to a company formed for the purpose. In ordering both the defendant and his company specifically to perform the contract with the plaintiff, Russell J.[40] described the company as: " the creature of the first defendant, a device and a sham, a mask which he holds before his face in an attempt to avoid recognition by the eye of equity."

Public policy

On rather similar principles the court will pay regard to the substance rather than to the form in deciding whether an agreement is void as conflicting with public policy. A good illustration is afforded by the decisions on restraint of trade. The leading case of *Nordenfelt* v. *Maxim Nordenfelt* [41] establishes that covenants in restraint of trade are normally valid when entered into by the seller of goodwill (as opposed to an employee), and that for this purpose covenants by a shareholder and managing director on a sale by the company are treated as covenants by a seller and not subjected to the stricter rules applying to an employee. In *Connors Ltd.* v. *Connors*,[42] the Privy Council extended this rule to the case of a covenant entered into by the

---

[33] See pp. 570 and 644, *infra*.
[34] *Re Bugle Press Ltd.* [1961] Ch. 270, C.A. Harman L.J., at p. 288, described the new company as " nothing but a little hut built round " the majority shareholders and the whole scheme as " a hollow sham."
[35] [1933] Ch. 935, C.A.
[36] At pp. 956 and 961.
[37] At p. 969.
[38] For an example of the reverse situation, see *Benabo* v. *William Jay & Partners* [1941] Ch. 52, where it was held that wilful disobedience by a company of a court order may lead to attachment of its officers or sequestration of their property under (now) R.S.C., Ord. 45, r. 5.
[39] [1962] 1 W.L.R. 832.
[40] At p. 836.
[41] [1894] A.C. 535, H.L.
[42] [1940] 4 All E.R. 179, P.C.

managing director on the sale by him and others of a controlling interest in the share capital of the company.

Quasi-criminal cases

Less easy to follow are the two (virtually irreconcilable) decisions of Divisional Courts in *Wurzel* v. *Houghton Main Home Service Ltd.*[43] and *Trebanog Working Men's Club and Institute Ltd.* v. *Macdonald.*[44] In the first case the question for consideration was whether two mutual benefit societies had infringed the terms of their vehicle licences by " carrying goods for hire or reward " when they delivered coal to their members. One of the two societies was unincorporated and it was held that the terms of the licence had not been broken since the members of the unincorporated society were merely delivering to themselves in vehicles which they owned. The case was held to be on all fours with *Graff* v. *Evans* [45] which decided that a members' club did not require a licence to " sell " liquor to club members. The other society, on the other hand, was incorporated [46] and it was held that it had broken the terms of its licence since it " was and is a legal entity apart from its members." [47] *Newell* v. *Hemingway*,[48] which had applied *Graff* v. *Evans* to the case of an incorporated club, was not followed, Swift J. saying [49] that it had paid insufficient attention to the distinction between a proprietary club, in which purchases are made from the proprietors, and a members' club in which each member draws from the members' common stock.

In the light of this decision *Newell* v. *Hemingway* appeared to be bad law and in conflict with the principles of *Salomon's* case, but its authority was fully re-established by the later *Trebanog Club* case [50] in which the facts were identical. It was there held that the fact that the club property was vested in a corporate body did not (as Swift J. had implied) prevent the club from being a members' club [51] and that, if it was, no justices' licence was required for the sale of liquor. Here therefore, the realities prevailed; the test was held to be the actual nature of the club, not the legal framework. As Lord Hewart said,[52] " We are dealing here with a quasi-criminal case, where the court seeks to deal with the substance of a transaction rather than with the legal form in which it may be clothed." [53] This is admirable. But why was

---

43 [1937] 1 K.B. 380.
44 [1940] 1 K.B. 576.
45 (1882) 8 Q.B.D. 373.
46 Under the Industrial and Provident Societies Acts.
47 *Per* Lord Hewart C.J. at p. 390.
48 (1888) 58 L.J.M.C. 46.
49 At p. 394.
50 Lord Hewart presided over the court in both the *Wurzel* and *Trebanog* cases.
51 So held in *National Sporting Club Ltd.* v. *Cope* (1900) 16 T.L.R. 158.
52 At p. 582.
53 *Cf. R.* v. *McDonnell* [1966] 1 Q.B. 233, holding that a director could not conspire with his one-man company. But he can contract with it even though he acts for

not the same realistic approach adopted in the *Wurzel* case, which was equally quasi-criminal? There the actual, as opposed to the artificial, legal nature of the two societies was identical, but the court seems to have fallen into the temptation of allowing legal formalism to induce it to draw a subtle, but entirely unreal, distinction.

Group enterprises

Consideration of the cases in which the courts have treated a company as the agent of its controlling shareholder [54] suggests that they are more ready to do so where the shares are held by another company. In other words, they are coming to recognise the essential unity of a group enterprise rather than the separate legal entity of each company within the group. Other examples of this can be found. In *The Roberta* [55] a parent company was held liable on a bill of lading signed on behalf of its wholly owned subsidiary, the court saying that the subsidiary was " a separate entity . . . in name alone, and probably for the purposes of taxation." [56] In another case [57] the court found no difficulty in treating a subsidiary as " to all intents and purposes " [58] the same as the parent company which held 90 per cent. of its shares. A licensing authority in exercise of its discretion has been held entitled to have regard to the fact that a parent and subsidiary company, though technically separate legal persons, in fact constituted a single commercial unit.[59] In other cases the courts have been able to arrive at the same result by seizing upon some technicality to evade the effect of the technicality of corporate entity. A good example of this is *Bird & Co.* v. *Thos. Cook & Son* [60] in which an indorsement of a cheque to " Thos. Cook & Son Ltd." was treated as an indorsement to the allied but separate company of Thos. Cook & Son (Bankers) Ltd.. by regarding it as a mere misdescription to be ignored under the principle *falsa demonstratio non nocet.*

Perhaps the most remarkable illustration is afforded by *Holdsworth & Co.* v. *Caddies.*[61] There, Mr. Caddies had been appointed managing director of the parent company upon the terms that he should " perform the duties and exercise the powers in relation to the business of the

the company when making the contract: *Lee* v. *Lee's Air Farming Ltd.* [1961] A.C. 12, P.C., *supra*, p. 202.
[54] *Supra*, pp. 202–205.
[55] (1937) 58 Ll.L.Rep. 159. *Cf. Re Radiation Ltd.'s Appn.* (1930) 47 R.P.C. 37, in which a parent company was allowed to register a trade mark in fact used by various of its subsidiaries.
[56] At p. 169.
[57] *Spittle* v. *Thames Grit & Aggregates Ltd.* [1937] 4 All E.R. 101.
[58] At p. 103.
[59] *Merchandise Transport Ltd.* v. *British Transport Commission* [1962] 2 Q.B. 173, C.A.: see especially, *per* Devlin L.J. at p. 202.
[60] [1937] 2 All E.R. 227. *Cf. Liverpool Corn Trade Assn.* v. *Hurst* [1936] 2 All E.R. 309, in which the word " member " was construed so as to include companies represented by nominee members.
[61] [1955] 1 W.L.R. 352, H.L.(Sc.) (also reported 1955 S.C.(H.L.) 27).

company and the businesses . . . of its existing subsidiary companies . . . which may from time to time be assigned to or vested in him by the board of directors of the company." After disagreements between him and the board he was directed to confine his attentions to one of the subsidiaries only. This was held not to be a breach of contract by the company, notwithstanding that it prevented him from working for the company employing him. The argument " that the subsidiary companies were separate legal entites each under the control of its own board of directors " was described as " too technical," since " an agreement *in re mercatoria* . . . must be construed in the light of the facts and realities of the situation," [62] which were that the parent company had full control of the internal management of its subsidiaries.[63]

But the reactions of the courts to such cases seem quite unpredictable. With *The Roberta* may be contrasted *Wm. Cory & Son* v. *Dorman Long & Co.*,[64] in which, after judgment had been given against the parent company by reason of the negligent navigation by the master of a ship owned by its subsidiary, the parent company was held not to be entitled to limit its liability under the Merchant Shipping Acts, since it was not the owner or charterer by demise. And, as we have seen,[65] the courts have refused to recognise that a parent company has an insurable interest in the property of its subsidiary. Moreover, in the converse case, where there is only one legal entity but it in fact functions in separate branches, the courts seem unwilling even to consider disregarding the legal unity in favour of the actual multiplicity.[66]

Until recently there seemed to be an even greater reluctance to recognise the continuing unity of a business enterprise when, on a reorganisation, a new company takes over from an old, or where a company takes over from an unincorporated firm.[67] Thus in *Pioneer Laundry* v. *Minister of National Revenue*,[68] the Privy Council held that a tax commissioner, in deciding on what was reasonable depreciation, could not take into account any allowance made to the old company on the same assets. Notwithstanding that the commissioner had a discretion,

---

62 *Per* Lord Reid at p. 367. See also Lord Morton at p. 363, but contrast Lord Keith (diss.) at p. 372.

63 See also *Scottish Co-operative Wholesale Society Ltd.* v. *Meyer* [1959] A.C. 324, H.L., especially *per* Lord Keith at p. 361 and *Re Greater London Properties' Lease* [1959] 1 W.L.R. 503 in which Danckwerts J. held a subsidiary company to be a " responsible " assignee because its holding company would not in practice allow it to go to the wall. Its separate legal entity was dismissed as " a point which might be taken by a pedantic chartered accountant ": at p. 507.

64 [1936] 2 All E.R. 386, C.A.

65 *Supra*, p. 71.

66 *Harrods* v. *Lemon* [1931] 2 K.B. 157, C.A.

67 *Davies* v. *Elsby Bros. Ltd.* [1961] 1 W.L.R. 170, C.A.

68 [1940] A.C. 127, P.C., overruling the Supreme Court of Canada. The Canadian courts, as those of the U.S.A., seem more ready to lift the veil but the Privy Council has been alert to correct this heresy. For another example, see *E. B. M.* v. *Dominion Bank* [1937] 3 All E.R. 555, P.C., *supra*.

he was not allowed to " disregard the separate existence of the company " or "inquire as to who its shareholders were and its relation to its predecessors." [69]

However, this step has been taken in some cases. In *Re London Housing Society's Trust Deeds*,[70] an industrial and provident society converted itself into a company under the Companies Act. It had previously established a pension fund for its staff and executed a trust deed vesting the fund in trustees and declaring trusts for the benefit of employees of the society. As a result of the conversion the society as such had ceased to exist, but it was held that the trusts continued nevertheless for the benefit of the same class of persons, now the staff of the company. Farwell J. said [71]:

> " It is no doubt true to say that the registered society and the limited company are, in one sense of the word, separate legal entities, but . . . they are in substance and in truth exactly the same thing with a different structure and a different machinery. . . . In my judgment, the only practical way of dealing with a question of this sort . . . is to treat for this purpose the two things . . . as the same thing in different costume."

In this case, therefore, the court refused to allow a change in legal structure to interfere with third-party rights under a trust. In *Willis* v. *Asscn. of Universities of the British Commonwealth*,[72] the landlords, a registered company, were in process of being wound up on conversion into a chartered corporation. It was held, nevertheless, that they were entitled to oppose the grant of a new tenancy to their tenant [73] on the ground that they required possession for the purposes of a business to be carried on by them. The ground of the decision was that they themselves could occupy for business purposes until they were dissolved, but Pearson L.J. was prepared to say [74] that

> " In form the landlords are a limited company which is being wound up, and a new chartered corporation has been created. In substance, however, there is continuity. The phrase *alter ego* undoubtedly lacks precision for most purposes, but for the present purpose it is a fair description of the landlords in their new guise of the chartered corporation as successors of the landlords in their old guise of the limited company."

---

[69] *Cf. United Steel Companies* v. *Cullington* [1940] A.C. 812, H.L., where, in a similar situation, adherence to the corporate entity principle operated to the taxpayer's disadvantage. And for an example of the same attitude in connection with municipal corporations, see *Magor and St. Mellons R.D.C.* v. *Newport Corpn.* [1950] 2 All E.R. 1226, C.A., especially *per* Denning L.J. (diss.) at p. 1235 *et seq.* and [1952] A.C. 189, H.L.

[70] [1940] Ch. 777.   [71] At pp. 783–784.

[72] [1965] 1 Q.B. 140, C.A.

[73] Under the Landlord and Tenant Act 1954, Part II. *Cf. Tunstall* v. *Steigmann* [1962] 2 Q.B. 593, C.A.; *supra*, p. 205.

[74] At p. 151.

The courts have also shown a reluctance to allow those who have continued to carry on the same business through a new company with the same name to take advantage of the confusion which this is likely to cause to those dealing with them.[74a]

Conclusions

Judicial inroads into the corporate entity principle are few compared with examples of its application. But inroads there have been. It would be idle to pretend that they can be reduced to any consistent principles, but the following tentative conclusions may, perhaps, be drawn—

1. The courts are in general precluded by *Salomon's* case from treating a company as the " alias, agent, trustee or nominee " of its members.[75]

2. They will nevertheless do so if corporate personality is being blatantly used as a cloak for fraud or improper conduct.[76]

3. They will also do so where agency can be established in fact, either in respect of particular transactions, or even as regards the whole of the company's business.

4. They are more ready to hold that agency is established where the controlling shareholder is another company; indeed, there is evidence of a general tendency to ignore the separate legal entities of various companies within a group, and to look instead at the economic entity of the whole group. The courts are here following the lead of the legislature.

5. The courts have found it essential to lift the veil for certain purposes owing to the fact that a company is only an artificial person; this particularly applies to the determination of its residence and to ascertain whether the acts of its agents have been effectively ratified.

6. They have also generally, but not consistently, sought to limit the application of the principle in *Salomon's* case by ignoring it in cases where the facts are sufficiently different. They have, therefore, not felt themselves bound by it, (a) in some criminal or quasi-criminal cases, (b) where trust relationships are involved, (c) where the issue before them is whether an agreement is void as infringing public policy, and (d) where a liberal construction of words enables them to evade it.

7. Since the analogy of *Salomon's* case is remote where the question

---

[74a] *Whittam* v. *W. J. Daniels & Co. Ltd.* [1962] 1 Q.B. 271, C.A.; *Chatsworth Investments Ltd.* v. *Cussins (Contractors) Ltd.* [1969] 1 W.L.R. 1, C.A. *Cf. Davies* v. *Elsby Bros. Ltd.*, *supra.*

[75] See, in addition to the cases quoted in the present chapter, Chap. 4, p. 71, *supra.*

[76] *Cf.* the dictum, which has been so influential in the U.S.A., that " when the notion of legal entity is used to defeat public convenience, justify wrong, protect fraud, or defend crime, the law will regard the corporation as an association of persons ": *U.S.* v. *Milwaukee Refrigerator Transit Co.* (1905) 142 Fed. 247 at p. 255. But we lag far behind the U.S.A. in applying this principle, *e.g.*, we have nothing comparable to the so-called " Deep Rock " doctrine, evolved by the U.S. Supreme Court in a line

is whether the veil can be lifted in the interests of members of the company, the courts have often found it easier to raise it for their benefit than for the benefit of outside creditors.[77] On the other hand, in some cases where they have ignored corporate entity in the interests of third parties, they have refused to allow members to take advantage of this relaxation in similar circumstances.[78] Though unexpressed, there is, perhaps, a very reasonable feeling that those who seek the advantages of corporate personality must accept the corresponding burdens.[79]

8. After a period of rigidity once the effect of *Salomon's* case was fully grasped, there now seem to be some slight signs of greater liberality in the application of its principle. Here again, the courts are merely following the lead of the legislature.

Further than this it is not possible to go in attempting to present in a rational form a development which has been essentially haphazard and irrational. Until very recently, the courts and the legal profession have failed to see the interconnection between the various situations in which the problem arises, with the result that relevant decisions concerning one situation have not been quoted in litigation concerning another.

---

of cases starting with *Taylor* v. *Standard Gas & Electric Co.* (1939) 306 U.S. 307, whereby in a winding up a debt claimed by the controlling shareholder may be postponed even to the claims of the preference shareholders.

[77] Contrast the general failure of the Revenue or other creditors to persuade the court that the business of a subsidiary is that of its parent company with *Smith, Stone & Knight* v. *Birmingham Corporation, supra*; *Trebanog Working Men's Club* v. *Macdonald, supra*; *Re London Housing Society, supra*; and *The Abbey, Malvern Wells* v. *Min. of Local Government, supra*.

[78] Contrast *The Roberta, supra*, and *Wm. Cory & Sons* v. *Dorman Long Ltd., supra*.

[79] This feeling was in fact expressed by Villiers C.J. in the S. African case *Ochberg* v. *C.I.R.* [1931] A.D. 215 at p. 232: "To say that a company sustains a separate persona and yet in the same breath to argue that in substance the person holding the shares is the company is an attempt to have it both ways, which cannot be allowed."

CHAPTER 11

COMPANIES DISTINGUISHED FROM OTHER ASSOCIATIONS

WE have now surveyed the major consequences of incorporation as a company. But, as already pointed out, some of the advantages of incorporation are conferred on other types of association, and formal incorporation may be obtained in other ways besides forming a company. The present Part therefore concludes with a brief account of these other associations in order to explain what alternatives are available and how they are distinguished from companies. These other associations range from clubs and learned societies, the constitution of which is not regulated by any special legislation and which enjoy none of the privileges of incorporation, to industrial and provident societies, building societies, and public corporations which are regulated by special or general statutes and which are incorporated as fully as companies but formed in a different way. Between these two extremes are a number of hybrids which, though not formally incorporated, have had conferred upon them by statute a greater or lesser number of the attributes of incorporation.

Clubs and societies [1]

Unincorporated associations of this type are subject to no statutory regulation. Their constitution depends entirely on the ordinary law of contract, the members expressly or impliedly agreeing to be bound by the rules either in their original form, or, if the rules so provide (as they invariably do), in any form into which they are changed in accordance with their provisions. In the eyes of the law, a club has no existence apart from the members from time to time, but since a distinction has to be drawn between club property and the separate property of the members, the club property is vested in trustees (normally the committee) to be held by them for club purposes in accordance with the rules.[2] By the rules, which are the terms of the

---

[1] See further, Ford, *Unincorporated Non-Profit Associations* (1959); Josling and Alexander, *The Law of Clubs* (1964).

[2] Normally the members will be precluded by implied agreement from dividing up the property among themselves so long as the club functions, but will be entitled to do so once it ceases to operate: *Abbatt* v. *Treasury Solicitor* [1969] 1 W.L.R. 561. Gifts to the committee for club purposes will be valid and not void for uncertainty or perpetuity (*Re Clarke* [1901] 2 Ch. 110; *Re Drummond* [1914] 2 Ch. 90; *Re Jones* [1950] 2 All E.R. 239) unless intended as permanent endowments when they may fail: *Leahy* v. *Att.-Gen. for N.S.W.* [1959] A.C. 457, P.C.

contract between the members, the latter normally delegate executive powers to certain officers and a committee. Whether the members are bound by the acts of the officers or the committee depends on normal agency principles. These principles will also determine whether the members are liable fully or only to the extent of the club funds, whether the officers and members of the committee are liable as such, and, if they are, whether they are entitled to be indemnified either by the members personally or out of club funds. Normally, it seems, contracts by the officers in carrying on the club in the usual way will bind the committee personally [3] (but not the members [4]) and the committee will be entitled to be indemnified out of club funds so far as they will go.[5] In other cases the third party may be held to have agreed that the committee shall not be personally liable beyond the extent of the club funds.[6] A club servant will normally not be liable on club contracts,[7] but acts within the scope of his employment will bind those whose servant he is. In claims in contract he is normally treated as the servant of the committee,[8] but the modern tendency in tort cases seems to be to treat him as the servant of the members as a whole and not of the committee,[9] but in this event the only practical method of enforcing liability is through a representative action,[10] the availability of which is still shrouded in some mystery.[11]

A member who has been wrongfully expelled from the club can obtain redress by way of injunction or declaration and apparently may recover damages if he has suffered any.[12] Normally he will pursue these remedies against the committee, but it seems that he may recover damages directly from the club funds if he can surmount the procedural

---

[3] *Bradley Egg Farm* v. *Clifford* [1943] 2 All E.R. 378, C.A. This case seems difficult to reconcile with (but certainly preferable to) earlier cases which suggest that no one is personally liable unless he has in fact shown a clear intention to pledge his credit: *Jones* v. *Hope* (1880) 3 T.L.R. 247n., C.A.; *Overton* v. *Hewett* (1886) 3 T.L.R. 246; *Steele* v. *Gourley* (1887) 3 T.L.R. 772, C.A.

[4] *Ibid.*

[5] *Wise* v. *Perpetual Trustee Co.* [1903] A.C. 139, P.C. But *cf. Baker* v. *Jones* [1954] 1 W.L.R. 1005 where they were held not to be entitled to indemnification in respect of the costs of libel actions brought against them.

[6] This possibility is recognised by Lindley L.J. in *Steele* v. *Gourley, supra,* 3 T.L.R. at p. 773. There is commonly an express provision to this effect in debentures issued by clubs.

[7] See cases cited note 3, *supra.* But he will be liable if he commits a tort: *Prole* v. *Allen* [1950] 1 All E.R. 476.

[8] *Bradley Egg Farm* v. *Clifford, supra.*

[9] *Prole* v. *Allen* [1950] 1 All E.R. 476; *Campbell* v. *Thompson* [1953] 1 Q.B. 445; *Dodd* v. *Cook* (1956) 4 D.L.R. (2d) 43 (Ont.C.A.); *cf. Shore* v. *Min. of Works* [1950] 2 All E.R. 228, C.A.

[10] Under R.S.C., Ord. 15, r. 12, or C.C.R., Ord. 5, r. 8.

[11] See Lloyd in (1949) 12 M.L.R. 409, and *John* v. *Rees* [1969] 2 All E.R. 274.

[12] On the development of this branch of the law, culminating in *Bonsor* v. *Musicians' Union* [1956] A.C. 104, H.L., see Lloyd in (1950) 13 M.L.R. 281, (1952) 15 M.L.R. 413, (1954) 17 M.L.R. 360, and (1956) 19 M.L.R. 121; and Wedderburn (1957) 20 M.L.R. 105.

difficulties inherent in a representative action.[13]   An expulsion is wrongful if in breach of the club rules or if the rules of natural justice have not been observed in investigating the charges against him.[14]

The above must not be taken to imply that a club can never be carried on through the medium of a company.   On the contrary, such a *modus operandi* is common.   But here again a distinction must be drawn.   In what has been said above it has been assumed that the club is a members' club—that is to say, one in which the club is run by and for the members themselves, they being collectively entitled to the property used by the club.   Alternatively, the club may be a proprietary one,[15] that is to say, it may be owned and operated by one or more persons who, in consideration of the payment of subscriptions, permit the members of the club to enjoy the facilities which they provide.   Although such a club may, and generally will, elect a committee, property will remain vested in the proprietors and it seems that prima facie the proprietors will be liable for any contracts entered into by the committee.   In effect, the proprietors will be carrying on business for profit, will be liable like any other traders for the acts of their servants or partners, and can sue or be sued in the name of the club.[16]   Hence it is common and convenient for the proprietors to be a limited company.

In contrast with this method of operating the club, the members themselves may register a company.   In other words, the so-called club may in fact be a company, normally limited either by shares or guarantee, membership of the company being identical with membership of the club.[17]   When this occurs, the club, of course, ceases to be an unincorporated association.   This arrangement is to be distinguished from a proprietary club run by a company, since, with the latter, there is a body of members mutually bound by the contract contained in the club rules, and in a distinct contractual relationship with the proprietor company.   With an incorporated club, on the other hand, the contractual nexus consists of the memorandum and articles of the company itself, and the members are the proprietors of the company which in turn owns and operates the club.[18]

---

[13] *Bonsor* v. *Musicians' Union, supra.*
[14] See n. 12 and *Davis* v. *Carew-Pole* [1956] 1 W.L.R. 833; *Byrne* v. *Kinematograph Renters Society Ltd.* [1958] 1 W.L.R. 762; *Hiles* v. *Amalgamated Society of Woodworkers* [1968] Ch. 440.
[15] Reference has already been made to this distinction in Chap. 10, p. 212, *supra.*
[16] *Firmin & Sons Ltd.* v. *The International Club* (1889) 5 T.L.R. 694, C.A.
[17] Thus many football clubs are in fact limited companies.
[18] In practice there will probably be club rules supplementing the basic constitution in the company's memorandum and articles.   Hence the distinction between an incorporated members' club and an incorporated proprietary club is a fine one, particularly if, as may well occur, members of an incorporated members' club are admitted to the club without taking up shares in the company.   In addition, working men's clubs may be registered under the Friendly Societies Acts and shop clubs under the Shop Clubs Act 1902.   Both these are referred to under friendly societies, *infra.*   A working men's club might also become incorporated as an industrial and provident society, *infra.*

Hitherto we have spoken of clubs, but what has been said is applicable, *mutatis mutandis,* to learned and similar societies. Most of these will probably be recognised as charitable, thus obtaining certain concessions regarding taxation and local rates. In other respects, however, their constitution is similar to that of clubs in that they may either be unincorporated (with consequences as regards liability similar to that of clubs) or incorporated under the Companies Acts or by Royal Charter. Literary and scientific institutions are, indeed, slightly exceptional in that under the Act of 1854,[19] certain special powers are conferred on them, including that of suing and being sued in the names of their officers. With these exceptions, however, clubs and societies are legally indistinguishable.

However, even as regards these associations the distinction between incorporated bodies, with a separate legal personality, and unincorporated bodies is becoming blurred. Thus, in *Willis* v. *Association of Universities of the British Commonwealth,*[20] Denning M.R. was prepared to recognise that the Universities Central Council on Admissions, though not a body corporate, had a distinct juridical personality as " a body unincorporate." [21]

It will be appreciated that the legality of these unincorporated clubs and societies depends on their not carrying on business for their own gain or for that of their members. Unless this condition is fulfilled they will be illegal if their membership exceeds twenty.[22] The expression " business for gain " has been construed fairly widely; it will include any form of commercial undertaking, even though the distribution of profits is prohibited and indeed even if there is no intention of making a profit. Thus a mutual insurance association[23] or a loan society[24] will be illegal unless registered under the Companies Acts, or some other statute, since the members " gain " by being indemnified from losses or by being permitted to borrow. But the " gain " must result from a " business "; hence a slate club,[25] superannuation fund[26] or a combination to purchase land[27] or investments[28] will be lawful, since these do not involve carrying on a business. " The test appears to me to be

---

[19] Literary and Scientific Institutions Act 1854, s. 21.
[20] [1965] 1 Q.B. 140, C.A. See Wedderburn, " Corporate Personality and Social Policy: The Problem of the Quasi-Corporation " (1965) 28 M.L.R. 62.
[21] At p. 147.
[22] Companies Act 1948, s. 434 (unless formed before 1856 or exempted by Companies Act 1967, ss. 119–121, or regulations made thereunder).
[23] *Re Arthur Average Assn.* (1875) L.R. 10 Ch.App. 542 at p. 545; *Re Padstow Total Loss Association* (1882) 20 Ch.D. 137, C.A. A useful description of the *modus operandi* of these mutual associations will be found in the Final Report of the Royal Commission on Taxation of Profits and Income (Cmd. 9474 of 1955), Chap. 22.
[24] *Greenberg* v. *Cooperstein* [1926] Ch. 657.
[25] *Re One and All Sickness Association* (1909) 25 T.L.R. 674.
[26] *Armour* v. *Liverpool Corpn.* [1939] Ch. 422.
[27] *Re Siddall* (1885) 29 Ch.D. 1, C.A.
[28] *Smith* v. *Anderson* (1880) 15 Ch.D. 247, C.A., *infra,* p. 223.

whether that which is being done is what ordinary persons would describe as the carrying on of a business for gain." [29]

Partnerships

It will have been apparent from the foregoing that clubs and societies, although unincorporated, in effect possess one of the great advantages of corporations, namely, absence of liability of the members for the association's obligations. But they reach this goal by a different route; corporations attain it because they are separate persons from their members; clubs and societies because, in general, the members have not given their committees and other agents power, actual or apparent, to pledge their personal credit. Since associations of this type cannot engage in business for profit, there is no great public danger, but the danger would be great if the same exemption were afforded to the members of the other great type of trading organisation—the partnership. Therefore each partner is deemed to have authorised his fellow-partners to bind him by an act done " in carrying on in the usual way business of the kind carried on by the firm." [30] Whether he be a sleeping or active partner he is personally liable; nor can he place any pecuniary limit on the extent of his liability unless he is a member of a publicly registered limited partnership. [31]

Partnerships differ from clubs in two other respects; they can now sue and be sued in the firm's name, [32] and their membership is normally limited to twenty. [33] Except in these important respects, however, they resemble clubs, and, in England, are not regarded as legal entities separate from their members. [34] The implications need not be further explored here since they have been dealt with sufficiently in the foregoing chapters.

Unit trusts [35]

Technically, unit trusts are not associations at all, but merely an extension of the private trust into the commercial field. Nevertheless

---

[29] *Per* Simonds J. in [1939] Ch. at p. 437. *Quaere* whether the expression has exactly the same meaning as " carrying on business with a view of profit " in Partnership Act 1890, s. 1, and *quaere*, too, whether " ordinary persons " would either make or comprehend the distinctions drawn in the decisions. See further (1962) 26 Conv.(N.S.) 253.

[30] Partnership Act 1890, s. 5.

[31] Under the Limited Partnerships Act 1907, under which one or more of the partners must remain fully liable, and even the limited partner will become so while he takes any part in management: *supra*, p. 73.

[32] R.S.C., Ord. 81; C.C.R., Ord. 5, r. 21 *et seq.*, and Ord. 8, rr. 14 and 15.

[33] Companies Act 1948, s. 434. Ten in the case of banking: *ibid.* s. 429. But for exemptions, see Companies Act 1967, ss. 119–121, and regulations made thereunder.

[34] Partnership Act 1890, s. 4. In Scotland, the firm is recognised as a separate person but, as the agency rules apply equally to Scotland, this makes surprisingly little practical difference between the two countries.

[35] See further *Unit Trusts and How They Work*, by Rosenheim & Merriman (Lond., 1937); Ford (1960) 23 M.L.R. 129; Pennington, *Company Law* (2nd ed., 1967), Chap. 31; Pennington, *The Investor and the Law* (1968), Chap. 8; and Jenkins

they offer to the public an investment practically indistinguishable from shares in a limited company and for this reason alone they require mention. Apart from this, however, they are of absorbing theoretical interest. We have seen how, in the nineteenth century,[36] the marriage of trust and corporation produced the modern limited company; the unit trust is in turn the offspring of a later union between the trust and the limited company.

The basic principle of these trusts is simple; a block of investments is vested in trustees under a trust deed which divides the beneficial ownership into a number of shares, normally described as units, and these the public are invited to purchase. Such an arrangement, then known as a management trust, was not uncommon in the early part of the second half of the nineteenth century and was in fact merely an example of the deed of settlement company, from which it differed only in that the trust held shares in other businesses instead of itself engaging in trade. After the passing of the Companies Acts, forbidding unregistered associations of more than twenty persons carrying on business for profit, Jessel M.R. held [37] that such trusts were illegal, and as a result all but one wound up or registered under the Companies Acts. That one,[38] however, courageously challenged Jessel's ruling and a year later its stand was, rather surprisingly, upheld by the Court of Appeal in the leading case of *Smith* v. *Anderson*.[39] It was there held that there was no " associating " between the holders of the beneficial interests, and that the trustees were not " carrying on business " since holding and varying investments was not a business; hence the trust was not illegal and did not require registration as a company.

For many years no further trusts were established in England; registration under the Companies Acts remained the usual practice, although the parentage of this type of company was recognised by the use of the name " investment *trust* company." Not until 1931 was the trust proper reintroduced into England from America [40] via Switzerland.[41] After the war the industry boomed and there are now well over a hundred trusts with total assets of some £1,400 millions.

Committee Report (Cmnd. 1749), Chap. IX. The best account, however, is still in an unpublished Ph.D. thesis " Unit Trusts," by Chas. H. Walker (1938), available in the British Library of Political Science and the Library of the University of London, to which I must acknowledge my indebtedness. A short but valuable abstract from it was published in (1940) 15 Econ. History 341.

36 *Supra*, Chap. 3.
37 *Sykes* v. *Beadon* (1879) 11 Ch.D. 170. Despite the fact that the great Lord Westbury was one of the trustees and that the trust deed had been settled by Fry, Q.C., the future Lord Justice.
38 The Submarine Cables Trust.
39 (1880) 15 Ch.D. 247, C.A.
40 America had in the meantime evolved an analogous device—the Voting Trust—for effecting a complete separation between " ownership " and " control." Voting rights are vested in trustees, and the former shareholders retain merely their financial interests represented by voting trust certificates.
41 Where an international trust had been formed in 1930.

In England this type of trust is now known as the unit trust, but in essence it is merely a refined version of the type of organisation upheld many years earlier in *Smith* v. *Anderson*. Briefly, what occurs is that the managers of the trust (generally a private company) purchase a block of various investments and vest them in trustees (in practice a trust corporation such as a bank or insurance company), to be held on the terms of an elaborate trust deed. This divides the beneficial interest in the trust fund into a large number of shares or units. In the first instance, the trustees hold the units on trust for the managers who then sell them to the public at a price based on their market value plus a small service charge to cover expenses and a profit for the managers. The managers have power from time to time to increase the number of units by vesting additional securities in the trustees. The managers also provide a market for unit holders by buying back and reselling units. It is the practice for the trust deed to fix a period for the life of the trust (generally about twenty-five years [42]) and, at the end of this period, the underlying investments are realised and the unit holders repaid,[43] unless they elect to continue the trust for a further term or to convert it into an investment trust company.[44]

If the portfolio of underlying investments is fixed and certain or only variable subject to very rigid conditions, the trust is described as a fixed trust.[45] In this event the first panel of investments is generally described as one unit and the aliquot shares that are sold to the public are described as sub-units. The managers then add to the trust by vesting in the trustees from time to time one or more additional units similarly constituted and divided into the same number of sub-units. The first trusts that were introduced into the country were of this type, but the later tendency was in favour of the flexible (or managed) trust in which the managers have power to vary the nature and proportions of the underlying investments either within defined limits or to a virtually unrestricted extent. The trusts at present operating are of this type.

Both fixed and flexible trusts have the advantage, so far as the investor is concerned, of simplicity and of spreading the risk over a wide range of investments. For this reason they appeal particularly

---

[42] It seems that there is no necessity to limit the duration of the trust within the perpetuity period. In *Re A. E. G. Unit Trust (Managers) Ltd.'s Deed* [1957] Ch. 415, it was held that the rule against accumulations had no application to a provision in the trust deed directing that income not distributed should be added to capital. One ground for this decision, that the whole of the unit holders could at any time bring the trusts to an end, would seem equally to prevent the application of the rule against perpetuities.

[43] In fact the trust will probably be unwound gradually, prior to its expiry by effluxion of time, as the managers repurchase units from holders and refrain from reselling.

[44] The trust deeds commonly provide for this and both continuations and conversions to companies have in fact taken place.

[45] For a decision on such a trust, see *Municipal & General Securities Co.* v. *Lloyds Bank* [1950] Ch. 212 (Government Stock issued in substitution of ordinary shares on nationalisation held to remain an authorised investment).

to investors who have only small sums to invest and who accordingly would be unable to secure the advantage of a spread investment by a direct purchase of shares except in an investment trust company. The fixed trust has the further advantage that the investor knows exactly what he is getting, *i.e.*, a share of the beneficial interest in a fixed block of investments. This, however, has the disadvantage that the manager cannot meet changing market conditions by adroit switches of the underlying securities.

The flexible trust avoids the last disadvantage but, as a necessary consequence, causes the investor to be dependent upon the financial integrity and skill of the managers. A completely flexible trust is for practical purposes virtually identical with an ordinary investment trust company. It has, from the viewpoint of the unskilled investor, the advantage that he knows that he is obtaining units at a price which bears a close relationship to the value of the underlying investments. Its disadvantages are that he cannot obtain the benefits of " gearing " [46] as he would if he invested in the equity shares of an investment trust company, has no control over the managers and none of the protections of the Companies Acts. It is true that a relationship of trustee and beneficiary exists between the trustees and the unit holders, but this is less of a protection than might appear, for the real control is vested in the managers, who exercise all initiative and, generally, all voting powers conferred by the shares held. The relationship between the trustees and managers seems most analogous to that between custodian and managing trustees, but it is by no means clear that the managers would in fact be held to owe the duties of trustees to the unit holders. Their position is indeed a somewhat anomalous one, since their role of principals, who stand to gain or lose from operating the trust, is difficult to reconcile with their fiduciary duties to the investors.[47]

These were not the only dangers in this new form of organisation,[48] and accordingly a committee was appointed in 1936 to investigate whether special legislative safeguards were required. The committee's report [47] led to the form of control now embodied in sections 12, 14 and 17 of the Prevention of Fraud (Investments) Act 1958. Under section 14 (3) (*a*) (v) there is an exemption from the general prohibition on the distribution of circulars relating to investments [49] in the case of invitations by or on behalf of the manager of an authorised unit trust scheme [50] in respect of its units. Under section 17, the Board of Trade may declare a trust to be an authorised unit trust scheme if (a) the managers and trustees are incorporated in the United Kingdom and

---

[46] See Chap. 16, p. 356, n. 62, *infra*.
[47] See Report of the Unit Trust Committee (Cmd. 5259/36).
[48] The various dangers are well summarised in the Report of the Unit Trust Committee.
[49] On this, see Chap. 14, *infra*.
[50] " Unit trust scheme " is defined in s. 26 (1) in terms wide enough to cover commodity pools. The Jenkins Committee thought that authorisation should be restricted to trusts of securities and cash : Cmnd. 1749, para. 312.

have a place of business in Great Britain, (b) the managers and trustees are independent of each other, (c) the trust deed provides to the satisfaction of the Board of Trade for the matters specified in Schedule I to the Act [51] and (d) the trustee corporation fulfils certain minimum capital requirements. The authorisation may be revoked.[52] The net result is that it is not feasible to operate a unit trust except under licence from the Board of Trade—a control far more rigorous than that exercised over companies [53] or over issues of their securities. It is not sufficient that the trust deed provides for the matters specified in the Schedule; it must do so to the satisfaction of the Board which, for example, can refuse authorisation if it thinks that the service charge is too high.[54] Indeed, it seems clear that the Board is not restricted to a consideration of matters mentioned in the Schedule, but has a general discretion [54] which it has exercised to insist on additional requirements.[55] The price at which units can be sold is controlled; hence the popular " block offers " are in fact distinctly misleading since no real advantage is obtained by applying within the time stated—units necessarily remain on tap at a price determined by the value of the underlying investments.[56] It will also be observed that the effect of section 17 is to bar all foreign trusts from our shores.[57] Finally, the Board of Trade has power to appoint an inspector of a unit trust,[58] as it has in the case of a company.[59]

In the U.S.A., from which our modern unit trusts sprang, it is now unusual to operate through the device of a trust. The American company can buy its own shares and accordingly it is possible to achieve the same end as that of a unit trust by an open-ended investment trust company or " mutual fund." If a similar arrangement were permitted in the United Kingdom it would lead to a considerable simplification and some saving of expense, and would help to obviate the confusion between the fiduciary duties of the managers and their position as principals. Nevertheless, in evidence to the Jenkins Committee, the majority of the managers opposed the introduction of the mutual fund. Ostensibly their main reason was the alleged protection afforded by the separate trustees. It is very doubtful whether, in fact, that is any great protection. Nevertheless their arguments were accepted by the Committee.[60]

---

51 Under the proviso to s. 17 (1) the Board may dispense with fulfilment of this requirement if this would not prejudice the unit holders.
52 s. 17 (2).
53 With the possible exception of that exercisable over insurance companies since Part II of the Companies Act 1967.
54 *Allied Investors Trusts Ltd.* v. *Board of Trade* [1956] Ch. 232.
55 Cmnd. 1749, para. 308.
56 Cmnd. 1749, para. 324 (vii).
57 The Jenkins Committee did not recommend that this should be changed (Cmnd. 1749, para. 325), but it would presumably have to be if we entered the E.E.C.
58 This power has not been exercised.
59 See Chap. 25, pp. 604–613, *infra.*
60 Cmnd. 1749, paras. 326, 327.

The U.S.A. has also recognised that investment trusts, whether in the form of companies or trusts, and whether open or closed ended, are essentially the same animal which should be distinguished from the ordinary trading company and be specifically regulated.[61] This is a point not yet taken in England, where we have exceptionally rigorous control of unit trusts and no special regulation at all of investment trust companies.

On the other hand, the Jenkins Committee did recommend some rationalisation of the control of unit trusts. Under their proposals the unfettered discretion of the Board of Trade would be removed and, as with public issues of a company's shares or debentures, compliance with prescribed conditions would lead to an entitlement to registration.[62] These conditions would cover qualifications of the managers and trustees,[63] essential provisions of the trust deed,[64] and the banning of undesirable names. No action has yet been taken on these recommendations and it is not clear whether they will be implemented in the next round of company legislation.

Issues of units are, of course, subject to the normal rules of the Borrowing (Control and Guarantees) Act 1946 and the Exchange Control Act 1947.[65] Further, the London Stock Exchange Regulations provide [66] for quotations for units on compliance with conditions similar to those required for a quotation of shares, but very few trusts have taken advantage of this facility. The industry has a professional association, the Association of Unit Trust Managers, which in recent years has become a somewhat more active and effective body than formerly.

Trustee savings banks

This is a convenient place to mention trustee savings banks [67] since they, too, rely on the trust as their legal basis. An ordinary bank, whether or not incorporated, carries on business for profit and the relationship between the banker and the customer is that of debtor and creditor. A trustee savings bank, on the other hand, is a form of association for encouraging small savings,[68] the banker not carrying on business for profit [69] but being a trustee of the savings deposited with him. Statutory recognition and regulation of such banks dates back to 1817 and they are now governed by the Trustee Savings Banks Acts

---

[61] See the (Federal) Investment Company Act 1940; Loss, *Securities Regulation* (2nd ed., 1961 and Supp.), pp. 144–153.
[62] Cmnd. 1749, para. 313.
[63] *Ibid*. para. 316.
[64] *Ibid*. paras. 317–324.
[65] See Chap. 14, pp. 289–291, *infra*.
[66] Appendix 35.
[67] See further, Lawton, *Guide to the Law of Trustee Savings Banks* (3rd ed., 1962).
[68] A limit on the amount to be deposited by one depositor is now fixed by the Treasury.
[69] Though, for certain purposes, undertaking a trade: see *R*. v. *Industrial Disputes Tribunal, ex p. East Anglian Trustee Savings Bank* [1954] 2 All E.R. 730.

1954 to 1968.[70] Like the associations shortly to be considered, the banks are formed by registering approved rules with the Registrar of Friendly Societies, who acts as a domestic tribunal for the settlement of disputes between depositors and the banks. Funds are now vested in custodian trustees [71] and the banks are operated by trustees and managers. The latest Acts seem to imply that the associations have some quasi-corporate status, and that this is so has now been recognised in *Knight & Searle* v. *Dove* [72] where it was held that a trustee savings bank could be sued in tort in its own name. Their independence is limited owing to their close relationships with the National Debt Commissioners (with whom they have facilities for investing funds and who have to approve the creation of new banks) and with the Post Office.[73]

They can be wound up under the Companies Acts [74] and are subject to section 433 of the 1948 Act, which requires them like other banks to publish half-yearly financial statements.[75]

Friendly societies and trade unions

These two types of association may be conveniently treated together since their histories [76] are closely related, their rules are registrable with the same Registrar, and constitutionally they are very similar, being the classic illustrations of associations which, although not corporations, come closest, if registered, to being recognised as *personae juridicae* with most of the advantages and disadvantages of corporations.

The basic object of a friendly society [77] is to raise, by the subscriptions of members, funds out of which advances may be made for the relief and maintenance of members and their families in sickness, infancy, old age or infirmity. The present statutes applying to them are the Friendly Societies Acts 1896 to 1968,[78] which mainly apply only to such societies as choose to register under the Acts by filing approved rules with the Chief Registrar. These Acts apply both to friendly societies in the narrow sense, and also to benevolent societies (which provide benefits for persons other than members and their close relations), cattle insurance societies, shop clubs, working men's clubs, and societies specially authorised by the Treasury. Friendly societies may continue to

---

[70] A new consolidation Act is now before Parliament.

[71] Trustee Savings Bank Act 1954, s. 9.

[72] [1964] 2 Q.B. 631.

[73] Which operates a savings bank under the Post Office Savings Bank Acts 1954 and 1966. Certain Government Departments also have power to establish savings banks, *e.g.*, the Board of Trade for seamen.

[74] Companies Act 1948, s. 398.

[75] In the somewhat attenuated form in Sched. 13 to the 1948 Act.

[76] They can be traced back to a common origin in the medieval guilds.

[77] See further, Halsbury, *Laws of England*, tit. " Friendly Societies."

[78] A long-overdue consolidation is in preparation.

exist without registration [79] (unless their objects involve carrying on business for gain [80]) in which case they will be in virtually the same position as any other unincorporated club or society.

The object of a friendly society is essentially to improve the economic situation of its members through the provision of benefits.[81] A trade union,[82] in contrast, is a combination of workmen or employers for the purpose of regulating a market. Most trade unions are combinations of employees formed with the object of regulating relations between employees and employers.[83] But the legal concept is much wider than this and includes associations between employers and trade associations. Today, unions are governed by the Trade Union Acts 1871 to 1964. These enable trade unions to register their rules with the Registrar of Friendly Societies, but, unlike friendly societies, most of the statutory privileges apply to unions whether registered or not and legalise unions which otherwise may have been unlawful at common law as in undue restraint of trade. They are expressly forbidden to register under the Companies Acts.[84] A peculiar feature of their constitutional organisation is that certain intra-union agreements are not *directly* enforceable by legal proceedings.[85]

The legislature carefully avoided conferring corporate personality on either friendly societies or unions. Instead it was provided that the association's property should be vested in trustees,[86] but something approaching perpetual succession was afforded by enacting that the property should vest in new trustees without formal conveyance or assignment.[87] It was also provided that the trustees could bring or defend actions relating to the association's property.[88]

Judicial interpretation of these provisions has nevertheless produced a situation in which these societies are recognised as corporations for

---

[79] Unless they are thrift funds established for the benefit of workmen, membership of which is a condition of employment: Shop Clubs Act 1902, s. 2. This is of some importance in company law since if a pensions scheme for workmen makes it a condition of their employment that they shall join, the scheme should be registered under the F.S. Acts. In practice this is ignored: see Wedderburn, *The Worker and the Law*, pp. 153–154.

[80] See *supra*, p. 221.

[81] Like trustee savings banks, they, too, will normally have to publish half-yearly financial statements in accordance with the Companies Act 1948, s. 433 and Sched. 13.

[82] On trade unions, see Citrine, *Trade Union Law* (3rd ed., 1967); Grunfeld, *Modern Trade Union Law* (1966); Wedderburn, *The Worker and the Law* (1965) and *Cases and Materials on Labour Law* (1967); and the Report of the (Donovan) Royal Commission on Trade Unions and Employers' Associations 1965–68 (Cmnd 3623) and the White Paper *In Place of Strife* (Cmnd. 3888).

[83] The Donovan Commission recommended that the term should be restricted to this type of association: Cmnd. 3623, paras. 758–767. This recommendation is accepted in the White Paper: Cmnd. 3888, para. 110.

[84] Trade Union Act 1871, s. 5 (3). See Chap. 12, p. 260, *infra*.

[85] *Ibid.* s. 4. But this has been held not to prevent " indirect " enforcement by declaration or injunction.

[86] Friendly Societies Act 1896, s. 49 (1); Trade Union Act 1871, s. 8.

[87] F.S. Act 1896, s. 50; T.U. Act 1871, s. 8 (this does not apply to unregistered unions).

[88] F.S. Act 1896, s. 94; T.U. Act 1871, s. 9.

most purposes except those expressly excluded by the creating statute. This development took place in connection with trade unions, and it is fair to say that political considerations played some part in it. In the famous case of *Taff Vale Ry. Co.* v. *Amalgamated Society of Railway Servants* [89] an action in tort had been brought against a union in its registered name. The House of Lords [90] held that such an action would lie. The decision purported to be based on the clear intention of the legislature, but whatever may be thought of its policy it is difficult to support it on any normal canons of statutory construction. The actual point which it decided was soon overruled by the legislature, and normally unions cannot now be sued in tort.[91] They can sue in tort, however.[92] This judicial attitude towards unions was carried a stage farther in the other milestone in trade union case law, *Amalgamated Society of Railway Servants* v. *Osborne*,[93] in which the House of Lords applied the *ultra vires* doctrine to unions and held that a rule providing for a political levy was void on this ground. This decision was, of course, the beginning of a long-drawn-out and possibly not yet concluded political dispute.[94] In *Cotter* v. *National Union of Seamen*,[95] it was held that a union could sue in its registered name and that, as in the case of companies,[96] only the union, and not an individual member, could sue in respect of some internal irregularity. Finally, in *Bonsor* v. *Musicians' Union*,[97] the House of Lords held that a registered union could be sued by a member who had been wrongfully expelled and an award of damages made against it.

These decisions all relate to registered trade unions. Until recently it seems to have been assumed that they did not extend to friendly societies, and had similar questions arisen in connection with such societies before they arose in relation to trade unions it is probable that they would have been decided differently. However, the

---

[89] [1901] A.C. 426, H.L.
[90] Restoring the judgment of Farwell J. and reversing a unanimous Court of Appeal.
[91] Trade Disputes Act 1906, s. 4. But their officials can be sued (for examples, see *Stratford & Sons Ltd.* v. *Linley* [1965] A.C. 269, H.L. and the *cause célèbre Rookes* v. *Barnard* [1964] A.C. 1129 where, as some think, a novel tort was discovered) unless protected by the Trade Disputes Act 1906 or 1965 (the latter passed as a result of *Rookes* v. *Barnard*). The Donovan Commission recommended that s. 4 should protect trade unions from being sued only in torts arising out of trade disputes (Cmnd. 3623, paras. 902–909) and this recommendation has been accepted by the Government: Cmnd. 3888, para. 113.
[92] *Nat. Union of General & Municipal Workers* v. *Gillian* [1946] K.B. 81, C.A.
[93] [1910] A.C. 87, H.L.
[94] The *ultra vires* doctrine was modified as regards unions by the Trade Union Act 1913, s. 1 (1), and s. 3 conferred power to have rules authorising a political fund, provided that this was approved by a majority poll and that members could " contract out." The Trade Disputes and Trade Unions Act 1927 (passed as a result of the General Strike) provided instead for contracting in (s. 4), but this Act was repealed *in toto* by the Trade Disputes and Trade Unions Act 1946.
[95] [1929] 2 Ch. 58, C.A.
[96] Under the rule in *Foss* v. *Harbottle, infra*, Chap. 25, which was thereby extended to unions on the basis that they, too, were legal entities distinct from their members.
[97] [1956] A.C. 104, H.L., overruling *Kelly* v. *N.S.O.P.A.* (1915) 84 L.J.K.B. 2236. See Lloyd (1956) 19 M.L.R. 121, and Wedderburn (1957) 20 M.L.R. 105.

wording of the friendly societies legislation is, in all material respects, very similar, and in *Longdon-Griffiths* v. *Smith*,[98] the *Taff Vale* and *Osborne* cases were expressly followed in holding that a friendly society could not be sued for defamation in the names of its trustees, but that the society must be sued in its registered name.

In some of these trade union cases certain judges have gone so far as to declare that unions have to be recognised as legal entities separate and distinct from their members.[99] Whether this is correct or not was left somewhat obscure by the House of Lords in *Bonsor* v. *Musicians' Union*,[1] but in the light of later decisions regarding other unincorporated associations [2] there seems little doubt that they are at least separate " bodies unincorporate." [3] In every situation which has yet come before the courts the decision has been the same as if the union had been a true corporation. Whether or not one calls it a legal entity seems to be an argument about terminology rather than substance.[4] The Donovan Commission recommended that trade unions should be granted corporate personality,[5] but this recommendation is rejected in the White Paper.[6] Nevertheless their Report is likely to lead to substantial changes in trade union law and, it is to be hoped, its early consolidation and ultimate codification.[7]

Corporations developed from friendly societies—building societies and industrial and provident societies

There are two types of association analogous to friendly societies which have now graduated into full corporations. The first of these, building societies,[8] are associations whose objects are to raise funds by subscription from members whereby advances may be made on mortgage to members to enable them to acquire small house properties. Instead of forming under the Companies Acts, such bodies may register rules with the Registrar of Friendly Societies under the Building Societies Act 1962, which likewise confers full corporate status with limited liability.

---

98 [1951] 1 K.B. 295.
99 See especially Lord Brampton in the *Taff Vale Case* [1901] A.C. 426 at 442; Romer J. and a unanimous C.A. in *Cotter* v. *National Union of Seamen* [1929] 2 Ch. 58, C.A.; Scott L.J. in *N.U.G.M.W.* v. *Gillian* [1946] K.B. 81 at 86; and Lords Morton and Porter in *Bonsor's* case. See Wedderburn, (1965) 28 M.L.R. 62, who points out the influence of the trade union cases in leading the courts to treat more bodies as "quasi-corporations."
1 [1956] A.C. 104, H.L.
2 *Willis* v. *Association of Universities of the British Commonwealth* [1965] 1 Q.B. 140, C.A., *supra*, p. 221; *Knight & Searle* v. *Dove* [1964] 2 Q.B. 631, *supra*, p. 228.
3 Lord Denning's phrase in [1965] 1 Q.B. at 147.
4 But *cf.* Wedderburn (1957) 20 M.L.R. 105.
5 Cmnd. 3623, para. 782. They also recommended that consideration should be given to enabling all unincorporated associations engaged in business transactions to sue or be sued in the name of the association: *ibid.* para. 784.
6 Cmnd. 3888, para. 111.
7 As recommended by the Commission: Cmnd. 3623, paras. 755, 756.
8 See further, Wurtzburg & Mills, *Law Relating to Building Societies* (12th ed., 1964).

The Registrar, in addition to granting a certificate of incorporation and registering various documents as does the Registrar of Companies, has some of the powers which, in the case of companies, are exercisable by the Board of Trade; for example he may institute inspections [9] and proceedings to wind up a building society under the Companies Act.[10] It should be noted, however, that shares in a building society differ fundamentally from those in a company; shareholders receive interest and do not participate in profits by way of dividend, and may withdraw their capital unless there is an outstanding advance thereon.[11] Despite this, very similar rules now apply regarding meetings.[12]

Of more importance for our purpose is the second type of organisation, industrial and provident societies.[13] Like friendly societies, under whose Acts the early societies registered, they are intended to promote their members' welfare; to be " industrial " in the sense that they make profits by the mutual personal exertion of their members, and " provident " in the sense that they provide for their members' future. Their history is bound up with that of the co-operative movement, for it is co-operative societies that have always been the most important illustration of this type of association. Since 1862 they have been accorded full corporate status, the statutes now governing being the Industrial and Provident Societies Acts 1965–1968. Like building societies, however, they are formed by registering rules with the Registrar of Friendly Societies, and they enjoy certain advantages in comparison with companies. For example, investments in them up to a maximum of £500 can be transferred on death under a written nomination instead of by a formal will and probate—an advantage, indeed, which applies to all friendly societies and most of their offshoots.[14] Similarly, they have certain tax advantages.[15] Moreover, the stringent requirements of the Companies Acts designed for the protection of the public were not included in the Industrial and Provident Societies Acts—doubtless it was thought that they were not needed since trading would be mainly restricted to members of the co-operative enterprise whose shareholdings were limited in size.[16] And, in contrast with companies, shares may be withdrawable; that is, capital may be returned to the members so that the

---

[9] Building Societies Act, s. 53, and may suspend borrowings (ss. 48–50) and prohibit advertising (ss. 51–52).

[10] *Ibid.* ss. 22, 50, 55.

[11] *Ibid.* s. 4 (1) (*c*), (*d*). And see, *Alliance Perpetual Building Society* v. *Clifton* [1962] 1 W.L.R. 1270.

[12] *Ibid.* Sched. 9.

[13] See further, Halsbury, *Laws of England*, tit. " Industrial and Provident Societies."

[14] *i.e.*, to friendly societies, trustee savings banks, and trade unions, but not to building societies (although the latter have statutory power to hand over deposits not exceeding £100 in the event of intestacy without requiring a grant of letters of administration: Building Societies Act 1962, s. 46).

[15] For a description of these, see Final Report of Royal Commission on Taxation (Cmd. 9474 of 1956), Chap. 21.

[16] The limit is now £1,000: 1965 Act, s. 6.

share capital may fluctuate from time to time.[17]   Like companies, they have recently been afforded effective power to borrow on floating charges.[18]

Co-operative societies have captured a considerable part of the retail distributive trade and often deal with all comers (members or not) in effective competition with other traders organised under less favourable codes.   They have entered the fields of banking and insurance and, through the vast Co-operative Wholesale Society, are able to exercise some influence on industry generally.[19]   The distinguishing feature of co-operative enterprise is that profits are distributed, not to shareholders as such, who obtain merely a limited rate of interest on their investments, but in dividends on members' purchases.   They also differ in practice from the normal company organisation in that membership of a local co-operative society is open to all and that members have one vote each, regardless of their capital holdings.

Before the war, the objects for which societies might be formed were ill-defined and it became the practice to register under the Acts in cases where it was far from clear that the purpose of the enterprise was to promote the public welfare.   Particularly was this so in connection with some housing trusts [20]; in the guise of providing cheap houses and flats for the working classes, these sometimes did little more than carry on business as speculative builders financed by debentures which the public could be invited to subscribe for without having to comply with the prospectus provisions of the Companies Acts.

This abuse was taken in hand by the Prevention of Fraud (Investments) Act 1939, now 1958.   By virtue of section 10 of the 1958 Act and later legislation,[21] the Registrar may not register a society's rules unless he is satisfied either that it is a bona fide co-operative society or that, because the society is to be conducted mainly for the purpose of improving the conditions of the working classes or otherwise for the benefit of the community, there are special reasons why it should be registered under the industrial and provident societies legislation rather than under the Companies Act.   The Registrar is also granted powers to deal with societies already registered which offend against the spirit of these provisions.   As a result many housing trusts have either wound

---

[17] A society carrying on the business of banking cannot have withdrawable shares: 1965 Act, s. 7.   Whether banking or not, s. 433 of the Companies Act (requiring publication of half-yearly financial statements) applies.

[18] By the 1967 Act.   The limit on the size of holdings does not apply to loan capital.

[19] Apart from their direct political influence through the Co-operative Party.

[20] Note, once again, the ubiquitous word " trust " used in a sense which has no meaning.   Needless to say, it is not suggested that all housing trusts abused their position; on the contrary, many did a useful job in connection with rehousing and were rightly encouraged by the legislature: see Housing Act 1936, ss. 92–94.

[21] See I. and P. Act 1965, s. 1.

up or converted themselves into companies [22] and the border-line between the two codes has become tolerably clear; registration under the Industrial and Provident Societies Acts has been restricted to its original purpose—for co-operative enterprise or charitable or public activities.

The Prevention of Fraud (Investments) Act 1958 exempts from the general prohibition on the distribution of circulars relating to securities,[23] invitations for shares, loans, or deposits with an industrial and provident society or building society if made by or on behalf of the society.[24] But in the case of a building society the Registrar may, if he thinks it expedient, suspend borrowings and subscriptions or prohibit advertisements.[25]

The result of these developments is that these societies have become assimilated to companies to a far greater extent than the other offshoots of the friendly society and it may well be that the time will come when industrial and provident societies, and perhaps building societies too, will be required to register under the Companies Acts, thus simplifying the somewhat muddled picture of the various legal organisations known to the law. In the meantime, however, each remains organised under its separate code which shows affinities to both the companies' and the friendly societies' legislation.

Public corporations

By the expression " public corporation " is meant the type of body set up to operate nationalised industries or for the organisation of other public enterprises and services. It has already been pointed out,[26] that the practice on nationalisation has not been for the enterprise to be run directly by a Government Department, but for a corporate body to be formed which is a separate entity but subject to a measure of ministerial control. This device of establishing an organisation which is both a public authority and an independent corporation is not new. Nor is it a unique English discovery; on the contrary it has been adopted for similar ends by countries as divergent in their ideas as the U.S.S.R. and the U.S.A., and has also been used extensively in the international sphere. Since the last war, however, it has become especiallly important in this country because of the total or partial nationalisation of the coal,[27]

---

[22] Provisions for the conversion of societies into companies (and vice versa) are contained in the 1965 Act, ss. 52 and 53.

[23] s. 14. See Chap. 14, p. 304 *et seq., infra.*

[24] s. 14 (3) (*a*) (vi). Such societies and friendly societies are similarly exempted from the prohibition on advertising for deposits under s. 2 of the Protection of Depositors Act 1963; see Chap. 14, pp. 306, 307, *infra.* But the anti-fraud s. 1 of that Act applies.

[25] Building Societies Act, ss. 48–52.

[26] *Supra,* Chap. 3, pp. 59–61, where mention is also made of the increasing tendency towards state participation through shareholdings in non-nationalised companies.

[27] Coal Industry Nationalisation Act 1946.

gas,[28] electricity,[29] transport,[30] and iron and steel [31] industries [32] and the forthcoming transformation of the Post Office from a Government Department to a public corporation.[33]

The corporations set up for this purpose have been classified into: (i) " commercial corporations " designed to run an industry or public utility according to commercial principles, although subject to a measure of ministerial control, and (ii) " social service corporations " designed to carry out a particular social service on behalf of the Government.[34] The present discussion concentrates on the former, since it is they that are designed to fulfil the same object as the typical company—the carrying on of a business enterprise. In general, however, what will be said is equally applicable to social service corporations which do not differ fundamentally, but only in detail, although many of the detailed differences are of considerable practical importance.[35]

In some nationalisation schemes, for example, those of Short Bros. Ltd.,[36] the Bank of England,[37] and Cable & Wireless Ltd.,[38] the existing company, chartered or registered, was kept in existence but nationalised by the acquisition of the whole of its share capital.[39] In other cases, however, one or more special *ad hoc* statutory corporations have been formed, and although these differ in detail they all assume basically the same form of " a body corporate . . . with perpetual succession and a common seal." [40] The objects and powers of these corporations are set

---

[28] Gas Acts 1948 and 1965.
[29] Electricity Acts 1947 and 1957.
[30] Transport Act 1962 and 1969 and Air Corporations Act 1967 (replacing earlier legislation).
[31] Iron and Steel Act 1967 (the end, to date, of a chequered career of nationalisation, partial de-nationalisation and re-nationalisation: *cf.* road transport).
[32] These are additional to less sweeping measures such as the Bank of England Act 1946, the Cable and Wireless Act 1946, the Atomic Energy Authority Act 1954, and the Television Act 1964 (consolidating earlier Acts which established the I.T.A.— the B.B.C. is a chartered corporation).
[33] Post Office Bill 1969. It is also proposed to nationalise the major ports under a National Ports Authority (Cmnd. 3903); the Port of London has long been nationalised: see Port of London Authority (Consolidation) Act 1920.
[34] This classification was suggested by Friedmann in (1947) 10 M.L.R. 236–237 and seems to be generally accepted: see, for example, the use of the expression " commercial public corporation " by the C.A. in *Tamlin* v. *Hannaford* [1950] 1 K.B. 18 at 25.
[35] *e.g.*, their relations with the Crown (they may be Crown servants, which commercial corporations are not), and in their subjection to ministerial control. What is of most importance from our point of view is that the commercial corporations are intended to be self-supporting, whereas the social service corporations are mainly financed by the Exchequer and their accounts are audited only by the Comptroller and Auditor-General and not by commercial auditors.
[36] By orders made in 1943 under the Defence (General) Regulations, reg. 78.
[37] Bank of England Act 1946.
[38] Cable and Wireless Act 1946.
[39] The use of registered companies for the purposes of Government Departments is, of course, not new. *E.g.*, R. N. Ltd. was formed under the Companies Acts in 1933 to act as nominees for the Revenue to hold property recovered in respect of tax claims, etc. Extensive use of governmental formed and controlled limited companies was made by the Ministry of Food.
[40] *Cf.* Companies Act 1948, s. 13 (2).

out in much the same way as in the objects clauses of memoranda of association,[41] and in the corporations are vested, normally, the undertakings and assets of the concerns to be nationalised. The iron and steel nationalisation scheme differed in that the operating companies were kept in existence [42] and the whole of their share capital vested in the corporation,[43] which therefore became in effect a vast holding company surmounting a pyramid of wholly owned subsidiaries. The companies or shareholders whose property is thus acquired are compensated by the issue of Government-guaranteed Stock.

In effect, therefore, the corporations are statutory companies differing from others in that neither the Companies Acts [44] nor the Companies Clauses Acts apply to them, the whole statute law applicable being contained in their creating Acts. It seems clear, however, that the general common law of corporations will govern them, except in so far as this is expressly or impliedly modified, and that many of the judge-made principles of company law will be equally applicable to this more recent growth. But in applying common law principles recognition must be given to the consequences flowing from their dual role as commercial enterprises and public authorities. The most obvious and startling difference is that a public corporation has neither shareholders nor share capital. Indeed, it is only nominally that it has any members, for these are appointed and removed by the Minister,[45] and are the same people as the directorate; the dichotomy of management and membership which is characteristic of the public limited company has no meaning in the case of the public corporation. Loan capital it does have; it can issue stock, in compensation for the assets acquired. This stock is its liability,[46] but instead of being charged on its assets, like a company's debentures, it is guaranteed by the Treasury.[47] In effect, it is Government Stock, the servicing of which is made the primary liability of the

---

[41] The provisions in question will be found in the preliminary sections of the various Acts cited above. In general they are less lengthy and detailed than companies' objects clauses but conclude with a wide and elastic formula sometimes expressed subjectively (*e.g.*, " The Board shall have power to do any thing . . . which in their opinion is calculated to facilitate the proper discharge of their duties . . . or is incidental or conducive thereto "—Coal Ind. Nat. Act, s. 1 (3)), and sometimes objectively (*e.g.*, " . . . to do anything which is calculated to facilitate the discharge of their functions . . ."—Air Corporations Act 1967, s. 3 (2)). Often certain activities are expressly excluded or the Minister is empowered to limit the corporations' powers.

[42] On a smaller scale the same occurred under other nationalisation measures, particularly under the transport nationalisation.

[43] But the constitutions of the operating companies were slightly modified.

[44] They are expressly excluded from the application of sections which apply to most registered companies by s. 435 (2) (*a*). On the other hand, it seems that they could in theory be wound up under Part IX of the Act.

[45] " The Minister " is here used to describe whichever of the departmental heads is appropriate.

[46] Except in the case of coal, where Government Stock was issued by way of compensation: Coal Ind. Nat. Act, ss. 21, 32 and 33.

[47] In the case of the Air Corporations and the British Steel Corporation, stock " may " (not " shall ") be guaranteed and in the case of the air corporations *is* charged on the undertaking of the corporations.

corporation for accounting purposes in order to determine whether it is truly self-supporting.

> " The significant difference . . . is that there are no shareholders to subscribe the capital or to have any voice in its affairs. The money which the corporation needs is not raised by the issue of shares but by borrowing; and its borrowing is not secured by debentures but is guaranteed by the Treasury. If it cannot repay, the loss falls on the Consolidated Fund . . . , that is to say on the taxpayer. There are no shareholders to elect the directors or to fix their remuneration. . . . If it should make losses and be unable to pay its debts, its property is liable to execution, but it is not liable to be wound up at the suit of any creditor. The taxpayer would, no doubt, be expected to come to its rescue before the creditors stepped in."

These words of Denning L.J., delivering the judgment of the Court of Appeal in *Tamlin* v. *Hannaford*,[48] admirably summarise the funda-mental difference between the two types of commercial body—and, indeed, the difference between public corporations and the various types of corporate and quasi-corporate organisations mentioned above.

It will be appreciated that the absence of shares and shareholders automatically renders large and important branches of company law totally inapplicable; rules relating to the raising and maintenance of share capital, the control of directors by members, protection of minority shareholders, company meetings and the like can have no relevance. As we have said earlier,[49] the knotty problem of the relationship between the management and the members is solved by the abolition of the latter.

But their abolition leaves a vacuum which has to be filled and which is filled by the Minister. The extent of the Minister's powers over the corporation varies but is always extensive, although commercial corpora-tions have greater independence than those operating the social services. The Minister, in replacing the shareholders, of course does so not for his personal enrichment but as guardian of the public and in particular of the taxpayer and user, and is in turn responsible to Parliament. The judgment of the Court of Appeal, quoted above, after referring to the interests of the taxpayer, continues:

> " But there are other persons who have also a vital interest in its affairs. All those who use the service which it provides—and who does not?—and all those whose supplies depend on it, in short everyone in the land, is concerned in seeing that it is properly run. The protection of the interests of all these—taxpayer, user and beneficiary—is entrusted by Parliament to the Minister. . . . He is given powers . . . which are as great as those possessed by a man

48 [1950] 1 K.B. 18, C.A. at p. 23.
49 *Supra*, Chap. 3, p. 60.

who holds all the shares in a private company, subject, however, as such a man is not, to a duty to account to Parliament for his stewardship. It is the Minister who appoints the directors . . . and fixes their remuneration. They must give him any information he wants; and, lest they should not prove amenable to his suggestions as to the policy they should adopt, he is given power to give them directions of a general nature, in matters which appear to him to affect the national interest, as to which he is the sole judge, and they are then bound to obey." [50]

Commercial public corporations are therefore treated both as public authorities and as commercial concerns. As public authorities they are subject to the normal controls of constitutional and administrative law; to supervision by the Minister, who in turn is answerable to Parliament, and by the courts through the control which they exercise over administrative authorities. This is a peculiarly British attempt to solve the problem of providing adequate, but not stultifying, democratic control over managerial independence. It presents difficulties, particularly as regards parliamentary supervision, which have not yet been wholly eradicated. The Minister can only be questioned on matters within his control, and his control over the corporations is limited.[51] He will, therefore, normally refuse to answer a question relating to day-to-day administration. Lengthy consideration has therefore been given to the problem of making this supervision less ineffective, and in 1956 the House of Commons [52] established a Select Committee on the Nationalised Industries with wide and general terms of reference free from the specific prohibitions which had hamstrung the work of an earlier committee.[53]

Commercial corporations are not Crown agents or servants.[54] " In the eye of the law the corporation is its own master and is answerable as fully as any other person or corporation." [55] Hence it is subject also to the private law control normally exercised over corporate bodies

---

[50] These remarks were specifically directed to the Transport Commission but substantially similar powers of direction and control apply in the other cases. In suggesting that the express power to give directions was intended to supplement an implied power to make suggestions, the judgment probably goes too far. There has been criticism of Ministers' use of informal suggestions, since this enables them to exert pressure without being answerable to Parliament, as they would be for the exercise of their statutory powers of direction.

[51] At times, however, rigorous control has been exercised by the Minister over the nationalised sector of the transport industry even to the extent of vetoing an increase in fares.

[52] 561 H.C.Deb. 5s, 595 (November 29, 1956).

[53] See H.C. 120 of 1955–56. This earlier committee had been set up as the result of the report (H.C. 235 of 1952–53) of a still earlier one appointed in 1951. Reference has already been made to the growing importance of this committee and its periodical reports: Chap. 3, p. 60, *supra*.

[54] *Tamlin* v. *Hannaford, supra.* Hence the Rent Restriction Acts, which do not bind the Crown or its servants (*T. A. A. of London* v. *Nichols* [1949] 1 K.B. 35), apply to commercial public corporations, *ibid.* But social service corporations probably are Crown servants: *Glasgow Corpn.* v. *Central Land Board*, 1956 S.C.(H.L.) 1.

[55] *Tamlin* v. *Hannaford*, at p. 24.

organised for commercial purposes. Despite the necessary modifications, a large field is still left for the application of company law principles. Thus, there is no doubt that the *ultra vires* principle [56] applies to a public corporation precisely as it applies to statutory and registered companies.[57] The only difference in this respect, one of some importance in practice, is that as the corporation has no members other than its directors, those who normally seek to restrain a company from acting *ultra vires* will not be there to do so.[58] And as the company practice of expressing objects widely has been followed in the nationalisation statutes, the opportunities for successfully invoking the *ultra vires* principle will be as rare in the one case as in the other.[59] Its liability to the outside world on contracts and for torts and crimes [60] is the same as that of companies.

The corporations are required to keep normal trading accounts and, although the detailed accounting provisions of the Companies Acts do not directly apply, it is expressly provided that they shall " conform with the best commercial standards " and be audited by professional auditors. Since there is no annual general meeting to which the accounts can be presented, they are to be laid before Parliament and can there be discussed and criticised. Of more importance, perhaps, is the fact that they can be examined by the Committee of Public Accounts of the House of Commons.

It is therefore clear that the corporations are intended to operate in much the same way as public companies. It is true that in *Tamlin* v. *Hannaford* the Court of Appeal said, in effect, that they were not intended to carry on business *for profit*,[61] but this does not seem entirely accurate. Normally they are directed to ensure that their revenue is *at least* equal to their expenditure and they are empowered to establish reserves. The only true difference in this respect is that they cannot distribute profits by way of dividend but must plough the whole of them back into the enterprise.[62] Once adequate reserves are established the consumer or user should benefit either by an improvement in the services or a reduction in costs,[63] and employees by an improvement in their conditions of labour. The result is that if the enterprise makes profits the public benefit in their capacity of consumers, users or employees,

---

[56] See Chap. 5, *supra*.
[57] This is expressly recognised in *Tamlin* v. *Hannaford* [1950] 1 K.B. 18 at 23, and by *Smith* v. *London Transport Executive* [1951] A.C. 555, H.L.
[58] But the point may, it seems, be raised by third parties when their interests are sufficiently affected: see *Smith* v. *London Transport Executive*, *supra*.
[59] *Smith* v. *London Transport Executive*, *supra*. When the subjective formula (see n. 41, *supra*) is adopted, the scope for *ultra vires* is further decreased. But there is still room for its application, particularly in connection with excluded powers and those inherited from the companies nationalised.
[60] In 1951, an electricity authority was heavily fined and its chairman imprisoned.
[61] [1950] 1 K.B. 18 at 23.
[62] Because the corporations are not Government Departments their profits cannot be used in direct relief of taxation as was formerly done in the case of the Post Office.
[63] There is an obvious analogy here to the co-operative principle.

whereas if it consistently makes losses [64] the public suffer; indeed, in the last resort the public in their capacity of taxpayers [65] will have to come to its rescue.   In other words, the public are substituted for the shareholders as profit-sharers and risk-bearers.

It must be confessed, however, that this difference is today becoming more apparent than real.   So far as the profit-sharing aspect is concerned, the incidence of income tax, corporation tax and voluntary or involuntary dividend limitation, is tending to produce a situation in which more of a company's distributable profits is taken for public purposes than is left in the pockets of the members whose position is not very different from that of the holders of stock of public corporations.[66]   Only in the event of winding up will their position differ substantially.   And even as regards losses, it is now accepted that " private " enterprise which is in the public interest may have to be protected from loss by means of Government subsidies, export credit guarantees and the like.

The public corporation therefore recognises openly what the public company is coming to recognise tacitly; that an enterprise should be run for and on behalf of the public as a whole and not merely for the benefit of a small section of it represented by the shareholders.   And there is substituted for the largely nominal control of management by the shareholders a somewhat more effective control by the Minister and Parliament as guardians of the public.   To establish further contact between the corporations and the public most of the nationalisation Acts provide for the establishment of advisory councils to act as a link between supplier and consumer and, in the last resort, to give independent advice to the Minister on behalf of the public generally or such sections as are particularly interested in the enterprise concerned.[67] And to these *de jure* controls is added the *de facto* control of informed (and uninformed) public opinion expressed in the Press and elsewhere; a curb of some potency having regard to the fierce light of publicity in which the corporations are required to function.   That these controls are considerably more effective than those which are exercised over the management of public companies can hardly be doubted.   The power of shareholders over directors is small, the main sanction on irresponsibility being public and market opinion.   Although, in the case of public corporations, market opinion cannot be expressed directly through quoted prices,[68] the greater publicity given to nationalised industries in

---

[64] One of the strongest arguments in favour of the nationalisation of certain enterprises is, of course, that it enables capital to be raised for an essential public purpose even though no adequate economic return on that capital can be expected.

[65] The corporations' " universal guarantors ": [1950] 1 K.B. 18 at 23.

[66] But it should be noted that the higher strata of management obtain a far higher share of the profits of companies than those of public corporations (though thanks to Lord Beeching the latter now do better than they did).

[67] They have not been very effective.

[68] The corporations' stocks are, of course, accorded Stock Exchange quotations but, as the stocks are Government-guaranteed, prices merely represent market opinion on

the financial and general columns of the newspapers more than makes up for this. Whether these controls are truly efficient as well as effective is more doubtful. There is an obvious danger that they will prove so rigorous as to discourage the better type of manager, produce frequent changes of those holding the reins, destroy continuity, initiative and enterprise,[69] and produce what is sometimes (but perhaps unfairly) described as the " civil-service mentality "[70] which it was hoped to avoid by establishing independent bodies. To some extent this danger seems to have been experienced already.

Conclusions

This summary of the legal status of the other associations known to English law will have revealed their great multiplicity and the appallingly complicated state of a great deal of the legislation. Some multiplicity is doubtless necessary since each type of organisation fulfils a different function and therefore requires to be dealt with by its own legal rules. Nevertheless, it seems clear that considerably greater co-ordination and consolidation are possible and desirable. The basic legal frameworks of all the associations under the wing of the Chief Registrar of Friendly Societies are so similar that it should not be difficult to reduce them to a common formula in a Societies (Clauses) Act, leaving only the necessary divergences to be dealt with by separate Acts. As it is, the basic similarities are concealed in differently worded provisions[71] lost in what until recently was (and in some cases still is) a maze of unconsolidated legislation the state of which is a disgrace to the Statute Book. In any clearing up of the legislation, certain legal differences might well be eradicated as no longer fulfilling any useful purpose.

As regards public corporations, there also seems to be scope for co-ordination. Here again there are the closest resemblances between the basic constitutional provisions of the various nationalising statutes, but once more they are hidden by the different arrangement of the various Acts and by needless diversity in terminology. If the common-form provisions were embodied in a Public Corporations Clauses Act (a kind of Table A) it would materially facilitate the task of the administrator and student and assist in the development of a coherent body of legal principles relating to this new form of organisation. Moreover, if we

---

interest rates and the nation's financial situation generally, and in no way reflect on the position of the particular enterprise.

[69] In the words of Roy Campbell, " You use the snaffle and the curb all right, but where's the bloody horse?"

[70] This mentality, it is suggested, is typical, not so much of the civil service but of any enterprise which becomes too large. Hence attempts to meet the danger by increased decentralisation, which, however, has other dangers.

[71] With the result that it was not realised until fifty years later that the interpretation placed, by the H.L. in the *Taff Vale* case, on certain sections of the Trades Unions Acts applied to slightly differently worded sections of the Friendly Societies Acts: see *Longdon-Griffiths* v. *Smith* [1951] 1 K.B. 295, *supra*, p. 231.

are to have any further schemes of nationalisation, it would make it much easier for Parliament to exercise supervision over the necessary legislation, since any divergence from the normal would be immediately apparent.

Moreover, although it may be that each type of association demands some separate legal regulation it is by no means clear that most of them (building societies and industrial and provident societies in particular) could not be assimilated with companies to a considerable extent. Already, under Part IX of the Companies Act 1948, the court may wind up under the Act any " unregistered company," an expression defined [72] as including a trustee savings bank, partnership, association, or company (other than a registered one) provided it consists of not fewer than eight members. Hence, nearly all the associations considered in this chapter [73] can be compulsorily [74] wound up as if they were companies. The only exceptions are unit trusts (which, in law, are not associations at all),[75] trade unions,[76] bodies with fewer than eight members,[77] and associations which are illegal.[78]

The ultimate objective would seem to be to draw a clear-cut distinction between unincorporated associations on the one hand and incorporated associations on the other, and to assimilate all the incorporated bodies under one code. The Companies Act already permits the registration of so many kinds of associations with widely different objects that it should not be impossible to convert it into a corporation code covering most, if not all, of the incorporated associations. Before this occurs, however, all types of *company* will have to be brought within the Companies Acts, for, as we have seen, statutory and chartered companies are still excluded. In this respect, a big step forward was taken by the 1948 Act which extended some of its provisions to most statutory and chartered companies.[79] But the Act is still a long way from being a complete code even of company law, and still further from being a code of corporation law.

All this, moreover, is clearly a very long-term objective,[80] the attainment of which has probably been retarded by the recent influx of public

---

[72] s. 398.
[73] *Semble*, even including public corporations provided they have more than eight members.
[74] They cannot be wound up voluntarily under the Companies Act (s. 399 (4)) except in the case of industrial and provident societies where this is possible as a result of the express wording of the Industrial and Provident Societies Act 1965, s. 55 (a).
[75] Nor, probably, can proprietary clubs (for the same reason) unless, of course, the proprietor is a company.
[76] This appears to be the joint effect of s. 5 of the Trade Unions Act 1871, and s. 459 (9) (b) of the Companies Act 1948.
[77] And not English limited partnerships even if they have more than eight members: s. 398 (d).
[78] e.g., associations infringing s. 429 or 434: *Re Padstow Total Loss Assn.* (1882) 20 Ch.D. 137, C.A.; *Re Ilfracombe Building Society* [1901] 1 Ch. 102.
[79] s. 435 and Sched. 14.
[80] But one which has aroused some support in recent years: see, for example, M. Fogarty, *Company and Corporation—One Law* (1965) Chap. 6; *Companies Beyond*

corporations making confusion worse confounded. Nor is its attainment likely to be made easier by the arguable need to distinguish in the company legislation itself between the small, medium and giant company.[81] The only immediate hope is that the various bodies of legislation will receive a much needed spring-cleaning (rather than mere consolidation) and that some attempt will be made to eradicate pointless divergences between them.

Jenkins (P.E.P. Pamphlet, Vol. XXXI, No. 486, 1965); *A Companies Act 1970?* (P.E.P. Pamphlet, Vol. XXXIII, No. 500, 1967).

[81] *Supra,* Chap. 3, p. 64, n. 58.

PART THREE
FORMATION AND FLOTATION OF COMPANIES

FORMATION AND FLOTATION OF COMPANIES

THIS Part deals with the problems which have to be faced on the company's birth. The first chapter (Formation) considers the steps necessary to secure the company's incorporation and the questions which then arise. The next (Promoters) considers the position of the individuals who are responsible for the formation and their duties towards the new-born company. The third chapter (Flotation) indicates the methods whereby a public company raises its capital from the public. Formerly flotation commonly preceded formation; the promoters would publish a prospectus inviting subscription from the public and the company would be formed only if these invitations were successful. Today, however, this order is invariably reversed; the company is formed first and, after incorporation " floats-off " its capital. Hence the orders of these three chapters. Finally, the fourth chapter (Prospectuses) deals with the responsibility of the company, and its directors, and others who sponsor issues, for the way they represent the company's affairs to the public when raising its share and loan capital.

CHAPTER 12

FORMATION OF COMPANIES

As we have seen today there are three basic types of company—statutory, chartered and registered,[1] and the formalities attending formation vary fundamentally as between each type. Detailed consideration is necessary only in respect of the last, companies registered under the Companies Acts, for these are overwhelmingly the most common and important.

STATUTORY COMPANIES

These are formed by the promotion of a private Act of Parliament which will adopt in whole or in part the provisions of the Companies Clauses Acts 1845–1889 and of any other Clauses Act which may be appropriate to the particular type of undertaking.[2] Details of the procedure therefore appertain to the field of Private Bill legislation rather than to a manual of company law and the reader who is concerned in the formation of such a company is referred to the specialised works on the former topic.[3] In practice the work is monopolised by a few firms of solicitors who specialise as parliamentary agents [4] and by a handful of counsel at the parliamentary bar, and the numbers of both promotions and specialist practitioners are dwindling, having regard to the curtailment of work resulting from nationalisation.

CHARTERED COMPANIES

Here again it is unlikely that there will be any further creations of chartered trading companies [5] except perhaps under Government auspices [6] but the grant of charters to charitable or public bodies is not uncommon. The procedure in such cases is for the members of the body to petition the Crown (through the office of the Lord President of the Council) praying for the grant of a charter, a draft of which is normally annexed to the petition. If the petition is granted the promoters and their successors then become " one body corporate and politic by the

---

[1] Plus, of course, cost book companies, in the unlikely event of any more being formed.
[2] See Chap. 1, p. 6.
[3] *e.g.*, Erskine May, *Parliamentary Practice*, 17th ed., 1964, Book III. For a good short account, primarily directed to local authority Bills, see Jennings, *Parliament*, 2nd ed., 1957, Chap. 13.
[4] For particulars, see the current *Law List*.
[5] It is still theoretically possible for the Crown to grant a charter under the Chartered Companies Act 1837 without formal incorporation, Chap. 1, p. 7, *supra*.
[6] *Cf.* the British South Africa Co. and the British North Borneo Co. (now registered).

name of —— and by that name shall and may sue or be sued plead and be impleaded in all courts whether of law or equity . . . and shall have perpetual succession and a common seal." [7]

Frequently a charter will be granted to the members of an existing guarantee company registered under the Companies Acts in which event the assets of the company will be transferred [8] to the new chartered body, and the company wound up unless the Registrar can be persuaded to exercise his power to strike it off the register under section 353 of the Companies Act 1948, thus avoiding the expense of a formal liquidation.[9]

REGISTERED COMPANIES

In the vast majority of cases the company, whatever its objects, will today be formed under the Companies Acts, and it may be helpful to set out the practice in such cases in some detail.

Types of registered company

The promoters will have to make up their minds which of the many types of registered company they wish to form, for while this will make little difference to the number and types of documents required, it will affect their contents.

First, they must choose between a limited and an unlimited company. The disadvantage of the latter is that its members will be personally liable for its debts and for this reason they are likely to be wary of it if the company intends to trade. If, however, the company is merely to hold land or investments, the absence of limited liability may not matter and may confer certain advantages, for example, as regards returning capital to the members. The absence of limited liability may also render the company more acceptable in certain circles, for example, the turf, stock-broking or jobbing, and finance.[10] Since the 1967 Act the only way in which they can avoid giving publicity to the company's financial affairs is by forming it as an unlimited one and accordingly greater use is now being made of this type. In the case of a small private company the advantages of limited liability tend to be exaggerated, and indeed illusory, since those who afford the company

---

[7] As to the extent to which the company is restricted to the objects specified in the charter, see Chap. 5, *supra*.

[8] It is understood that it is not the practice of the stamp office to claim *ad valorem* stamp duty thereon, although there appears to be no statutory exemption.

[9] See Chap. 27, p. 653, *infra*. The Registrar is reluctant to exercise this power if the company is one which has been granted a licence to dispense with the word " Limited " under s. 19.

[10] An alternative, which in practice is never adopted, is a limited company with unlimited liability on the part of the directors: s. 202. A similar type of association is of considerable importance in some other legal systems, *e.g.*, the German *Kommandit-Gesellschaft auf Aktien* and the French *société en commandite par actions*.

formal credit facilities will in practice insist on personal guarantees from its directors and major shareholders.

If they decide upon a limited company they must then make up their minds whether it is to be limited by shares or guarantee, and as already explained [11] this is really a matter which will be decided for them by the purpose which the company is to fulfil. Only if it is to be a non-profit-making concern are they likely to form a guarantee company which is especially suited to a body of that type.

Overlapping these distinctions, but closely bound up with them, is the further point of whether or not the company should have a share capital. If, as is most probable, the company is to be limited by shares —*cadit quaestio*. But if the company is unlimited or a guarantee company it may or may not have its capital divided into shares; if unlimited it probably will, if a guarantee company it generally will not. Once more, the decision is dependent on the company's purpose; if the company is intended to make and distribute profits a share capital will be appropriate, but otherwise it should be dispensed with as this will reduce the formation expenses.[12]

Advantages and disadvantages of private companies

They will further have to make up their minds whether the company is to be a public or a private one. The differences between the two are now relatively few. But the latter still has the following advantages and disadvantages [13]:

Advantages [14]:

    (a) There need only be two members instead of a minimum of seven[15] and one director instead of a minimum of two.[16]

    (b) It can be formed more simply and therefore more cheaply.[17]

    (c) It can commence business immediately on registration.[18]

---

[11] See Chap. 1, *supra*.

[12] If the company has a share capital the registration fees vary between £20 and £68 according to the amount of the capital, and capital duty of 10s. per cent. is also payable. If the company has no share capital the fees vary between £20 and £38 according to the number of members and no capital duty is payable: Companies Act 1967, Sched. 3, and F.A. 1933, s. 41.

[13] This does not purport to be an exhaustive statement of the differences between the rules applying to public and private companies, but merely of the advantages and disadvantages; *e.g.*, the fact that a proxy can speak as well as vote at a general meeting of a private company (s. 136) is ignored as it is neither beneficial nor the opposite from the point of view of the promoters. It would be an improvement in drafting if the Act stated in one place which of its rules did not apply to private companies.

[14] This does not apply to a deposit-taking private company: Protection of Depositors Act 1963, s. 4, as amended by 1967 Act, Sched. 8, Pt. VII.

[15] 1948 Act, s. 1.

[16] s. 176.

[17] A prospectus or statement in lieu thereof does not have to be filed: s. 48. And directors need not file consents to act, or take up, prior to appointment, such qualification shares as are required by the articles: s. 181.

[18] s. 109.

(d) On formation it will not have to give so much publicity to its affairs.[19]

(e) All its directors can be appointed by a single resolution of a general meeting [20] and normally will not be liable to retire under an age limit.[21]

Disadvantages:

(a) Membership must be limited to fifty, excluding employees and ex-employees who became members while employed.

(b) Restrictions must be imposed on the right to transfer shares, and

(c) It must be prohibited from making any invitation to the public to subscribe for its shares or debentures.[22]

As we have seen,[23] public and private companies are designed to meet different economic needs: the former to raise capital from the public to finance an enterprise, the latter to confer a separate legal personality on the business of a single trader or small partnership. In practice, even if the promoters intend the company to be a public one they will probably form it initially as a private company and then convert it, for this, for reasons explained below,[24] has certain advantages. It is nevertheless advisable to know the ultimate intention of the promoters before framing the articles of association, since in the case of a public company certain clauses will be needed [25] which would probably be inappropriate or inconvenient if the company were to remain private.

It might appear that a company can be private only if it has a share capital since, if it has none, it cannot " restrict the right to transfer its shares " which is one of the essential prerequisites. Nevertheless the Registrar of Companies will be prepared to accept a company as a private one if the prescribed limitations (including a restriction on the transfer of its non-existent shares!) appear in its articles.

The result of the various possible permutations and combinations is that there are five primary types of company to choose from, namely:

(i) Unlimited company not having a share capital.

(ii) Unlimited company having a share capital.

(iii) Company limited by guarantee and not having a share capital.

---

[19] s. 48, *supra*, note 17; and no statutory report or meeting is required: s. 130.

[20] s. 183 (1).

[21] s. 185. This does not apply if the company is the subsidiary of a public company and even a public company can " contract out " by altering its articles.

[22] s. 28. Joint holders are counted as one for the purpose of this section. If, in fact, it breaks these rules it does not cease to be a private company but loses most of the latter's privileges: s. 29.

[23] Chap. 1, p. 11 *et seq.*, *supra*.

[24] p. 304, *infra*.

[25] The articles should be framed so as to comply with the stock exchanges' *Requirements* if it is intended to apply for a quotation for the company's securities. These will, for example, require that the articles shall place a limit on the extent to which the company's borrowing powers can be exercised by the board of directors.

(iv) Company limited by guarantee and having a share capital.

(v) Company limited by shares.

Each of these five can be divided into public and private, so that the final total is no less than ten. But, for reasons already stated the choice is not likely in practice to present any difficulty; a decision will flow almost automatically from the nature of the enterprise and in most cases a public or private company limited by shares will be appropriate.

Name of company

The promoters must next decide on a suitable name. In the case of an artificial person such as a company, the name is of vital importance in identifying it and the 1948 Act provides that it must be stated in the memorandum,[26] on the company's seal, business letters, negotiable instruments and orders for money and goods,[27] and must be affixed outside every office or place in which its business is carried on.[28] It follows, therefore, that it is advisable that the name should be reasonably short. Nor, once the company has been registered, can it change its name as informally as can a natural person; a special resolution coupled with the consent of the Board of Trade is requisite.[29]

The Act provides that " no company shall be registered by a name which in the opinion of the Board of Trade is undesirable," [30] thus giving the Board an unfettered discretion to refuse any name. The Registrar has published *Notes for Guidance* in which he indicates the policy which will be adopted and which in general follows the lines laid down more narrowly in the earlier Acts.[31] The name must not be misleading or suggest a connection with the Crown, a Government Department, or a municipality, and only in exceptional circumstances will names be allowed which include " Imperial," " Commonwealth," " National " or " International." The use of the words " Co-operative " and " Building Society " is also forbidden, for as we have seen, these imply registration under the Industrial and Provident Societies Acts or the Building Societies Acts. Of most importance, however, is the rule that a name will be refused registration if it is too like the name of an existing company.[32] As a result of this rule, registration secures a *de facto* monopoly of corporate trading under that name and, because of this, names which include a proper name which is not the surname of a director will not be allowed except for valid

---

[26] s. 2.
[27] For the consequences of omission, see Chap. 10, pp. 193, 194, *supra*.
[28] s. 108.
[29] s. 18.
[30] s. 17. The initial decision is made by the Registrar but there can be an appeal to the Board against a refusal by him.
[31] See Companies Act 1929, s. 17.
[32] Unless, as earlier Acts expressly stated, that company is in liquidation and signifies its consent.

reasons (*e.g.*, because the company is acquiring a going concern carried on under that name). For the same reason if the proposed name includes a registered trade mark the consent of the owner will be required, and if the Registrar thinks the name is likely to be a registered trade mark he will require to be satisfied to the contrary.

As the Board have a complete discretion it is not possible to be entirely certain that the name will be accepted until the company's documents are lodged for registration, but the practice is to write to the Registrar at any early stage inquiring whether the proposed name is available for registration, and to this he will reply either in the negative or with a guarded affirmative. If the reply is favourable the promoters are reasonably safe in preparing documents incorporating the name and in ordering stationery and the seal; the only risk is that the Registry's officials may not have searched existing registrations with sufficient care, or may have overlooked some other infringement of the accepted principles,[33] or that another company will have registered in the interval with a name unduly similar. To guard against the possibility of a negative reply it is advisable for the promoters to have in mind one or more suitable alternatives. The Jenkins Committee recommended the introduction of a system prevailing in many Commonwealth countries whereby, on payment of a fee, a name can be definitely reserved for a short period.[34] Such reservation is not permitted here.

It has been said that once the company has secured registration in a particular name it secures a virtual monopoly of corporate activity under that name. This, of course, is true only if no other company is in fact already registered with a name identical or too similar; it is just possible that the Registry will allow a name to slip through which should have been rejected on this ground. Should this occur the new company may change its name with the consent of the Board of Trade and must do so if the Board direct within six months of registration.[35] If the Board omit to take action the other company may do so by applying to the courts for an injunction to restrain the new company from carrying on business under its name. More probably, an existing enterprise, not registered under the Companies Acts, such as partnership or private trader,[36] may be carrying on business under a similar name and may bring an action to restrain the company. A passing-off action of this sort is possible only if the two concerns are in the same line of business, so that the new company is in effect cashing in on the reputation of the pre-existing concern and appropriating its goodwill

[33] This happens occasionally, but commendably rarely, and produces disarming apologies from the Registrar.
[34] Cmnd. 1749, para. 450. This recommendation was not implemented in the 1967 Act.
[35] s. 18 (2).
[36] Or, in theory, a statutory or chartered company, although in practice the Registry would probably know of its existence and refuse registration.

and connection [37]; but if this condition is fulfilled and the action succeeds, the new company will not be able to continue trading under that name and will therefore be compelled to change its name or its business.

It must also be stressed that registration only confers protection against subsequent *company* registrations in the same or a closely similar name; it will not prevent a trader or partnership from setting up in business under that name or from registering it under the Registration of Business Names Act 1916. Once again, however, if there is a common field of commercial activity, and consequently an expropriation of the company's trade, a passing-off action by the company may be successful to restrain the new concern from trading under that name even though it be the proper name of one of the associates in the concern.[38] Moreover if at any time the name, in the opinion of the Board of Trade, gives so misleading an indication of the nature of the company's activities as to be likely to cause harm to the public, the Board may now compel it to change its name.[39]

If the company is limited, " Limited " must appear as the last word of the name; this, as we have seen,[40] is intended as a danger signal to those dealing with the company. This applies whether the company is limited by shares or by guarantee, and the only exception is where a licence to dispense with the warning word is obtained from the Board of Trade under section 19 of the 1948 Act. A licence, which is revocable and which may be granted subject to conditions, is obtainable only if the Board are satisfied that the company is formed to promote " commerce, art, science, religion, charity or any other useful object and intends to apply its . . . income in promoting its objects and to prohibit the payment of any dividend to its members." This means that in practice only guarantee companies without share capital make use of this provision. The Board insist that the memorandum and articles shall be settled by counsel on their behalf at the promoter's expense and, as this adds to the cost and delays formation, advantage is not always taken of this possibility even in cases where it would undoubtedly be granted.[41]

Finally, it may be mentioned that if the company proposes to carry on business under another name, for example, when it subsequently

---

[37] For further details relating to passing-off actions the reader is referred to works on the law of torts. For a good illustration in the field of company law, see *Panhard et Levassor* v. *Panhard Levassor Motor Co.* [1901] 2 Ch. 513.

[38] *Tussaud* v. *Tussaud* (1890) 44 Ch.D. 678.

[39] Companies Act 1967, s. 46 (implementing a recommendation of the Jenkins Committee—see Cmnd. 1749, para. 454). There is an appeal to the court: s. 46 (3).

[40] Chap. 3, p. 49, Chap. 10, p. 194, *supra.* Unless duly incorporated with limited liability it is a criminal offence to carry on business under a name of which " limited " is the last word: 1948 Act. s. 439.

[41] A licence will be refused if there is any likelihood of the company competing with another commercial concern. If one is granted the Registrar will expect the company to display extreme punctilio in its observance of the rules; he may, for example, refuse to permit the cheap form of liquidation by striking off the register under s. 353 and insist on a formal liquidation: see p. 249, n. 9, *supra.*

takes over an existing business, it will be required to register under the Registration of Business Names Act 1916.[42] Compliance with that Act will not, of course, obviate the necessity also to affix the company's name outside any premises where the business is carried on.[43]

Memorandum and articles

The next step is to prepare the memorandum and articles of association. Both are necessary unless the company is to be a company limited by shares, in which case Table A, a model set of articles in Schedule I to the Companies Act 1948, automatically applies in the absence of other articles.[44] In the latter case, even if articles are registered, Table A will apply in so far as it is not excluded or modified.[44] But it will be necessary to register articles if the company is to be a private one since such a company must, by its articles, impose the three essential restrictions listed at p. 251, above. Since the 1948 Act, this can be complied with, if desired, by a document of one clause adopting Table A, Part II, which contains the appropriate clauses and a number of other modifications normally found in articles of private companies.

In respect of all other types of company (except an unlimited company not having a share capital for which there is no special statutory form) model forms of memoranda and articles are set out in the various Tables of Schedule I to the 1948 Act. In all cases full memoranda must be registered. As regards the articles it is only Table A that can be adopted by reference, either in whole or in part,[45] so that all companies, other than those limited by shares, must register full articles, except that if they have a share capital they can adopt by reference some of the clauses of Table A.[46] The Act[47] provides that the memoranda and articles shall be " in accordance with the forms set out in [the Tables] or as near thereto as circumstances admit," but this requirement is interpreted with some latitude; provided the basic form of the statutory model is preserved, the widest variations of contents are permitted. Thus, as we have already seen,[48] the objects clauses of the memorandum will in practice be far more detailed than those in the Tables.

[42] As amended by the Companies Act 1947, s. 58—one of the sections of that Act not repealed by the Act of 1948.
[43] Under Companies Act 1948, s. 108, *supra*.
[44] s. 8 (2).
[45] It is only in the case of Table A that adoption by reference is expressly authorised by the Act (compare ss. 8 and 11) and the present practice of the Registrar is to refuse to allow adoption by reference in the case of the other Tables. His conclusion that adoption is not authorised is to some extent supported by the terms of s. 454 (2) which, in authorising alterations to the Tables by Board of Trade regulations, contains a saving for existing Table A companies but not for others. This appears to be a legislative oversight which causes some inconvenience and useless expense.
[46] *Cf.* Table D, art. 2, and Table E, art. 4.
[47] s. 11.
[48] Chap. 5, p. 88, *supra*.

Before preparing the memorandum and articles the draftsman will need to obtain from the promoters information on the following points : —

(a) The nature of the business. This will be required in connection with the objects clauses of the memorandum, and the draftsman will in practice elaborate the purposes expressed by the promoters by surrounding them with a profusion of peripheral objects and subordinate powers which will probably astonish his clients. The motive for this verbosity has already been explained in Chapter 5.

(b) The amount of nominal capital and the denomination of the shares into which it is to be divided (assuming, of course, that it is to have a share capital). These will need to be stated in both the memorandum and articles. For the articles he will also require to know if the shares are to be all of one class and, if not, what special rights are to be attached to each class,[49] as these should be set out in the articles, but preferably not in the memorandum.[49a] In settling the initial capital it should be borne in mind that capital duty will be dependent on its amount and that it can be increased with the greatest of ease. Hence overstatement of probable requirements can only be window-dressing to attract ignorant customers and will be an expensive luxury.

(c) Any other special requirements which deviate from the normal as exemplified by the appropriate Table of the Act. The most likely matters are quorums, and the minimum and maximum numbers of directors.

With the aid of this information the draftsman should have no difficulty in preparing drafts based on precedents from his own experience, reference books, and Tables of the Act. Moreover, most law stationers have their own standard forms set up in print, adaptation of which will reduce printing charges. The main question for consideration in the case of a company limited by shares is the extent to which Table A is to be adopted. If adopted *in toto* this will be the cheapest solution as it will avoid printing charges,[50] but this will not always be possible, for example, where there is no share capital or where there is more than one class of share. Moreover, although the latest Table A is an admirable model, careful consideration should be given to it in each case to ensure that the particular circumstances do not demand some additions or deletions. In the case of a private company it may be desirable to provide that the first directors shall not retire by rotation, and, in order to preserve the existing balance of power, that new issues of shares shall first be offered to the existing shareholders in proportion

---

[49] See further, Chap. 16, *infra*.　　　　　　　　　　　[49a] See Chap. 22, p. 508.

[50] Articles must be printed : s. 9 (*a*). The Act requires the printing of memoranda only if they are subsequently altered : ss. 5 (7) and 23 (3). Although certain cheaper processes (such as type-litho) will be accepted by the Registrar, printing charges may be one of the heaviest items of expenditure on the formation of a small private company.

to their holdings.[51] Another possibility is to adopt Table A with modifications. If this is done, care should be taken to specify exactly which provisions of Table A are excluded and not to leave this to implication by some such formula as " Table A shall apply except in so far as it is varied by or inconsistent with the following provisions "—a formula which inevitably leads to trouble.

Unless economy is a serious consideration, however, it is far better to exclude Table A completely and to have self-contained articles, even if, as will almost certainly be the case, these in most respects merely duplicate the provisions of the Table. By so doing, the company's officials will not be faced with the task of extracting its regulations from two separate documents, one of which, Table A, may become progressively less accessible—for it will be appreciated that it is the Table of the Act extant at the time of incorporation which continues to govern.[52] Hence many existing companies are still governed by Table A of the 1862 or 1908 Act [53] which may not be readily to hand, and which, in any case, is in many respects out of date having regard to the substantive provisions of the later Acts. Adoption of Table A is therefore often a false economy, particularly as some of the larger firms of company solicitors have their own standard forms which are kept up in print by their stationers, thus minimising the costs to their clients.

The distinction between the memorandum and the articles of association has already been dealt with.[54] The effect of the two documents as between the members and the company will be considered later.[55]

Lodgment of documents

The final step is to lodge certain documents at the Companies' Registry.[56] The first of these documents are the *Memorandum* and *Articles* which must have been signed by seven persons [57] (or two if a private company) whose signatures must be attested by a witness.[58]

---

[51] A provision to this effect had appeared in earlier Tables but was omitted from the 1948 Act. Most jurisdictions in the U.S.A. held (on partnership principles) that it was an implied obligation to offer new capital to the existing members, but this view was never taken in England.

[52] This is often overlooked when new articles are adopted; it is the original, not the current, Table A which should be expressly excluded.

[53] Companies formed between 1906 and 1908 are apt to be particularly troublesome, since these are governed by a Table A introduced by S.R. & O. 596/L15 which cannot be found in any Act of Parliament.

[54] Chap. 5, *supra*.

[55] p. 261 *et seq.*, *infra*.

[56] For English companies, at Companies House, 55–71 City Road, London, E.C.1. Documents may be lodged by post but it is more usual to do so by hand.

[57] *Semble*, an infant can be a subscriber (*Re Laxon & Co. (No.* 2) [1892] 3 Ch. 555, C.A.) as can an alien resident abroad (*Reuss* v. *Bos* (1871) L.R. 5 H.L. 176), but if resident outside the sterling area not without Treasury consent (Exchange Control Act 1947, s. 8 (2), and Companies Act 1948, s. 459 (9) (*d*)) at present given generally by Notice E.C. 10 (Third Issue) on which see Chap. 14, *infra*.

[58] ss. 3 and 9.

If the company has a share capital each subscriber to the memorandum must write opposite his name the number of shares he takes and must not take less than one.[59]   In practice he will merely subscribe for one share in the first instance, irrespective of the number which eventually he intends to purchase, and more often than not the requisite number of clerks in the solicitors' office will sign as subscribers rather than the true promoters.   The memorandum and articles must each be stamped as if it was a deed [60] (*i.e.*, 10s.).

The third document, required if the company has a share capital, is a *Statement of Nominal Capital*.   This is not a company form but a Revenue one, its only purpose being to bear the requisite stamp in payment of the capital duty (10s. per cent.).

The fourth is the *Declaration of Compliance*, a statutory declaration, made either by the solicitor engaged in the formation or by a person named in the articles as a director or secretary, that all the requirements of the Act have been complied with.[61]   This declaration can be accepted by the Registrar as sufficient evidence of compliance, but as his staff in fact go through the documents with care, and as those engaged in the formation would hardly lodge the documents unless they thought that they had prepared them properly, it is doubtful whether the declaration fulfils any useful purpose.[62]

The above are the only documents which necessarily have to be lodged in order to secure registration of the company, but in practice two others, which have to be filed within a short time of formation, are lodged at the same time.   The first of these is the *Notice of Situation of Registered Office*.   The memorandum must state whether the registered office is to be in England or Scotland, an unalterable clause which determines whether the company is an English or Scottish company and whether domiciled south or north of the border, but it will not give the actual address, which can be changed within the country as often as the management wish.   Those dealing with the company are obviously vitally interested in this address, if only because it is there that documents may be served on it [63]; hence it is provided [64] that within fourteen days of incorporation notice thereof shall be filed.

Similarly the company must, within fourteen days of the appointment of directors and secretary, send to the Registrar *Particulars of Directors and Secretary*.[65]   The articles generally name the first directors, or provide that they shall be nominated by the subscribers,[66] who, in the

---

[59] s. 2.
[60] ss. 3 and 9.
[61] s. 15 (2).
[62] The Jenkins Committee recommended its abolition: Cmnd. 1749, para. 31 (*h*).
[63] s. 437.
[64] s. 107.   Notice of any change must also be filed within 14 days and, as regards third parties, it seems that the change is ineffective until this has been done: *Ross* v. *Invergordon Distillers Ltd.*, 1961 S.C. 286.
[65] s. 200 (4) and (5).
[66] *Cf.* Table A, art. 75.

latter case, will sign a nomination when they sign the memorandum.[67] Theoretically the secretary can hardly be appointed until the first board meeting after incorporation but, if those interested have decided who he is to be, it is customary to beat the pistol by filing the particulars of both directors and secretary with the documents required to secure registration.

If the company is formed as a public one it may also be necessary to file certain documents whereby the directors consent to act and agree to take up and pay for their qualification shares (if any) [68]; but if the usual practice is adopted of forming as a private company and then converting, this can be avoided.

The separate filing fee of 5s. formerly required on the filing of each document has now been abolished.[69]

Registration and certificate of incorporation

The Registry's officials examine the documents and register them if they are in order. The Registrar then signs and issues the certificate of incorporation,[70] the company's birth certificate. He has no discretion in the matter; if the documents are in order and the objects of the company are lawful, the subscribers have a right to registration enforceable by mandamus.[71]

The Act states [72] that " A certificate of incorporation . . . shall be conclusive evidence that all the requirements . . . in respect of registration *and of matters precedent and incidental thereto* have been complied with, *and that the association is a company authorised to be registered and duly registered* . . ." The courts have, nevertheless, been somewhat reluctant to accept this at its face value. The words italicised did not appear in the 1862 Act, and the courts held that if the company did not fulfil the essential requirements for registration (*e.g.*, because it had less than seven members) the certificate was not conclusive.[73] It appears, however, that the extended wording introduced in 1900 must cover a case of this sort and that once a certificate has been granted no one can question the regularity of the incorporation.[74] To this, however, there is

---

[67] The Jenkins Committee recommended that every company should have two directors and that the first two subscribers to the memorandum should be deemed to be directors until the notice naming at least two directors had been filed: Cmnd. 1749, para. 25.

[68] Under s. 181.

[69] Companies Act 1967, s. 48 and Sched. 3. But note that the fees are alterable by statutory instrument: s. 48 (2)–(4).

[70] 1948 Act, s. 13.

[71] *R.* v. *Registrar of Joint Stock Companies* [1931] 2 K.B. 197, C.A. But if the documents are not in order or if the objects are unlawful it seems clear that he may reject them: see Jenkins Committee Report, Cmnd. 1749, para. 494, where it is recommended that this should be expressly stated in the Act.

[72] s. 15 (1).

[73] *Re National Debenture and Assets Corporation* [1891] 2 Ch. 505, C.A.

[74] *Hammond* v. *Prentice Bros. Ltd.* [1920] 1 Ch. 201. See also *Bell Houses Ltd.* v. *City Wall Properties Ltd.*, *supra*, pp. 88, 89, where the section was invoked to support the legality of subjectively worded objects clauses: [1966] 2 Q.B. 656, C.A., at pp. 685 and 691.

still one exception, namely, that should a trade union succeed in securing
registration as a company, the registration will be ineffective notwithstanding the grant of a certificate [75]; this is because registration of trade
unions is forbidden by section 5 of the Trade Union Act 1871, and the
Companies Act 1948 [76] provides that nothing therein shall affect the
provisions of that Act. Needless to say, the certificate does not conclusively establish that the objects of the company are legal; if they are
not it seems that the Attorney-General could institute proceedings by
way of certiorari to have the registration cancelled.[77] It is also possible
that proceedings in the nature of *scire facias* could be brought to revoke
the registration.[78] These questions, however, are somewhat theoretical,
as the Registrar in practice is careful not to register in such cases.[79]

Nor, in recent years, have the courts been troubled with the converse
problem arising out of defectively formed corporations [80]—a fertile
source of litigation in America. In England this problem could only
arise when a body of persons describe themselves and act as an incorporated company without having secured a certificate of incorporation, or
when an association which is in law a trade union succeeds in registering
as a company. The members of such an association would be liable to
penalties if " Limited " formed part of the name,[81] and, if the association
were formed for gain and the number of members exceeded twenty,[82]
the association would be illegal and no action could be brought by it or
on its behalf.[83] What the position would be if it or its members were
sued is obscure. The old cases on deed of settlement companies [84] imply

---

[75] *British Assn. of Glass Bottle Manufacturers* v. *Nettlefold* (1911) 27 T.L.R. 527;
Performing Right Society v. *London Theatre of Varieties* [1922] 1 K.B. 539; [1922]
2 K.B. 433, C.A., affd. other grounds [1924] A.C. 1, H.L. It seems clear that quite a
number of companies have in fact been registered despite the fact that their objects
bring them within the definition of a trade union: see Hickling, " Trade Unions in
Disguise " (1964) 27 M.L.R. 625.

[76] s. 459 (9) (*d*).

[77] *Bowman* v. *Secular Society* [1917] A.C. 406, H.L., at pp. 439, 440.

[78] *Salomon* v. *Salomon* [1897] A.C. 22, H.L., at p. 30. This, as we have seen, was
the old remedy to lead to the cancellation of a charter and s. 15 (1) is not expressed
to bind the Crown. But it is doubtful if it was appropriate for the cancellation of a
statutory registration. *Scire facias* itself appears to have been abolished by the
Crown Proceedings Act 1947, s. 13 and 1st Sched., but Lord Goddard C.J. stated,
in *Att.-Gen.* v. *Colchester Corporation* [1955] 2 Q.B. at p. 215, that it was still
available for the cancellation of charters.

[79] *Cf. R.* v. *Registrar of Joint Stock Companies* [1931] 2 K.B. 197, C.A., where, on
application for a mandamus, the Registrar's refusal to register a company to deal
in tickets in the Irish sweepstake was upheld, the sweepstake being an illegal lottery
in England. But see note 75, *supra*.

[80] Except as regards pre-incorporation contracts by promoters: see *Kelner* v. *Baxter*
(1866) L.R. 2 C.P. 174 and *Newborne* v. *Sensolid (G.B.) Ltd.* [1954] 1 Q.B. 45,
C.A., discussed in Chap. 13 at p. 281, *infra*.

[81] s. 439.

[82] s. 434 (unless exempted by s. 120 of the 1967 Act or regulations made thereunder)
or ten if the purpose was banking: s. 429 (unless all were authorised by the Board
of Trade and the number did not exceed 20: s. 119 of the 1967 Act).

[83] *Shaw* v. *Benson* (1883) 11 Q.B.D. 563, C.A. *Cf. Re Thomas* (1884) 14 Q.B.D. 379,
where the debtor was held to be estopped by his acquiescence after the association
had registered and thus become legalised. And note that the members *inter se* may
be protected by ordering an account: *Greenberg* v. *Cooperstein* [1926] Ch. 657.

[84] See Chap. 2, *supra*.

that the members would be automatically liable as partners, but later authorities [85] suggest that the question would be answered, on the analogy of unincorporated associations in general,[86] on agency principles and that the members, if numerous, would not necessarily be held personally liable as partners.

Effect of registration : the contract in the memorandum and articles

From the date of incorporation stated in the certificate the company comes into existence as a body corporate " capable forthwith of exercising all the functions of an incorporated company and having perpetual succession and a common seal." [87]   Furthermore, section 20 of the 1948 Act provides that the memorandum and articles " shall, when registered, bind the company and the members thereof to the same extent as if they respectively had been signed and sealed by each member, and contained covenants on the part of each member to observe all " their provisions, and that any sums due from the members to the company under the memorandum or articles shall be specialty debts.

The wording of this section can be traced back with variations to the original Act of 1844 which adopted the existing method of forming an unincorporated joint stock company by deed of settlement (which did of course constitute a contract between the members who sealed it) and merely superimposed incorporation on registration.   The 1856 Act substituted the memorandum and articles for the deed of settlement and introduced a provision on the lines of the present section 20.   Unhappily, full account was not taken of the vital new factor, namely, the fact that the incorporated company was a separate legal entity, and the words " as if . . . signed and sealed by each member " did not have added to them " *and by the company.*"   This oddity has survived into the modern Acts.

Despite the odd wording, however, certain points are clearly established.   First, the memorandum and articles constitute a contract between the company and each member.[88]   This has been called a contract of " the most sacred character " since the shareholder advances his money in reliance upon it.[89]   But it is a contract with various special characteristics.   Section 20 expressly provides that it is subject to the provisions

---

[85] See the inconclusive discussions in *Murray* v. *Scott* (1884) 9 App.Cas. 519, H.L., at pp. 546–548; *Re West London & General Building Society* [1894] 2 Ch. 352; and *Re Ilfracombe Building Society* [1901] 1 Ch. 102.

[86] See Chap. 11, *supra.*

[87] 1948 Act, s. 13 (2).   But in the case of public companies there are further conditions to be fulfilled before they may commence business: see *infra*, pp. 303, 304.   Previous difficulties over a charitable company's holding land without licence in mortmain were swept away by the Charities Act 1960, s. 38 and 7th Sched., Pt. II A.

[88] *Hickman* v. *Kent or Romney Marsh Sheepbreeders' Assoc.* [1915] 1 Ch. 881, where Astbury J. reviewed earlier cases in a judgment which has become the *locus classicus.* An article providing for a reference to arbitration of disputes between members and the company was held to be contractually binding.

[89] *Clark* v. *Workman* [1920] 1 I.R. 107 at p. 112, *per* Ross J.

of the Companies Acts.[90] The latter include the sections which permit
of alterations in the objects clause of the memorandum [91] and in the
articles of association,[92] by means of a special resolution. Thus, the
shareholder is making a contract on terms which are alterable by the
other party by a special majority voting at a general meeting,[93] rather in
the same way that a member of a club agrees to be bound by the club
rules as validly altered from time to time, or a workman agrees to be
employed on the terms of a collective agreement as occasionally varied
by the employers and his trade union. Further, as has been previously
mentioned, normal remedies for breach of contract may not here be
available; for example, rectification is not available where articles are
registered in the wrong form by mistake.[94] The remedies of a member
seem to be restricted to actions for an injunction or declaration or for a
liquidated sum due to him as a member (for example an unpaid dividend
owing to him); damages for breach of the contract are probably not
recoverable from the company.[95] In most of the reported cases a member
has sought to enforce the contract against the company but it is equally
clear that the company can enforce it against the member,[96] and
in principle there is then no reason why all the normal contractual
remedies,[97] including damages, should not be available.

Secondly, the contract under section 20 is enforceable among the
members *inter se*.[98] The history of the section would lead one to expect
that it has this consequence, and recent cases confirm the preponderant
dicta [99] of earlier decisions to that effect. The principal occasions on

[90] Articles cannot therefore contract out of the statutory demand in s. 75 for a written
instrument for the transfer of shares: *Re Greene* [1949] Ch. 333, C.A.

[91] s. 5, *supra*, p. 99 *et seq.*

[92] s. 10.　But note the limits on majority power on alteration of the articles where
it is a " fraud on the minority," *infra*, Chap. 24, pp. 562–578.

[93] *Shuttleworth* v. *Cox* [1927] 2 K.B. 9, C.A., *per* Atkin L.J. at p. 26; *Malleson* v.
National Insurance and Guarantee Corporation [1894] 1 Ch. 200, *per* North J. at
p. 205.

[94] *Scott* v. *Frank Scott (London) Ltd.* [1940] Ch. 794, C.A., *supra*, p. 21. On the
power of the court to rectify the shareholders' *register*, see *infra*, pp. 377, 378.

[95] This is perhaps a facet of the courts' determination to maintain capital: see Chap. 6,
supra.　In that respect it accords with the rationale of *Houldsworth* v. *City of
Glasgow Bank* (1880) 5 App.Cas. 317, H.L., *infra*, p. 319. In *Moffatt* v. *Farquhar*
(1878) 7 Ch.D. 591, Malins V.-C. appears to have allowed recovery of damages;
but the point was not fully argued and the usual view is that stated in the text. As
for actions brought against the company for dividends owing, see *infra*, p. 354.
Where one member is enforcing the contract not against the company but against
another *member*, the objections to an award of damages do not seem to apply; but
even there the plaintiff must probably show loss which is personal to himself, and
not merely damage common to the corporators as a general body: see *Breay* v.
Browne (1896) 41 S.J. 159.

[96] *Lion Mutual Marine Insce. Assoc.* v. *Tucker* (1883) 12 Q.B.D. 176, C.A.; *Hickman*
v. *Kent or Romney Marsh Sheepbreeders' Assoc.*, *supra*.

[97] Except rectification of the memorandum or articles: *Scott* v. *Frank Scott (London)
Ltd.*, *supra*.

[98] *Rayfield* v. *Hands* [1960] Ch. 1.

[99] See, for example, Lord Cairns in *Eley* v. *Positive Govt. Security Life Assoc.* (1876)
1 Ex.D. 88, C.A., at p. 89; Farwell J. in *Borland's Trustee* v. *Steel Bros.* [1901]
1 Ch. 279 at p. 290; Sargant J. in *Re Famatina Devlpt. Corpn.* [1914] 2 Ch. 271
at p. 279; Simonds J. in *Kerr* v. *Mottram* [1940] Ch. 657 at p. 660. Dicta which
appear to oppose this view, such as Lord Herschell's in *Welton* v. *Saffery* [1897]

which this question is likely to be important arise when articles confer on members a right of pre-emption or first refusal where another member wishes to sell his shares,[1] or, more rarely, a duty on remaining members to buy the shares of a retiring member.[2] A direct action between the shareholders concerned is here possible; and for the law to insist on action through the company would merely be to promote multiplicity of actions and involve the company in unnecessary litigation.

Thirdly, it is settled, as an overriding principle, that section 20 gives the memorandum and articles contractual effect only in so far as they confer rights or obligations on the member in his capacity of member.[3] This is as true of the contract between him and his fellow members as it is of his contract with the company.[4] If, therefore, an article provides that someone shall be the company's solicitor, he cannot rely directly on that as a contract to enforce his right to be the solicitor, even if he is in fact also a member; for the article concerns him in his capacity as an outsider, not as member.[5] Nor will a provision that disputes between the company and its members must be referred to arbitration avail a person whose dispute is between the company and himself as a director, even though he happens also to be a member.[6]

" An outsider to whom rights purport to be given by the articles in his capacity as such outsider, whether he is or subsequently becomes a member, cannot sue on those articles treating them as contracts between himself and the company to enforce those rights. . . . [N]o right merely purporting to be given by an article to a person, whether a member or not, in a capacity other than that of a member, as, for instance, as solicitor, promoter, director, can be enforced against the company. . . ."[7]

A.C. 299, H.L., at p. 315, turn out on inspection to be concerned with the difficulties of *enforcement* of a member's rights in the light of the rule in *Foss* v. *Harbottle*, discussed *infra*, Chap. 25.

[1] *Borland's Trustee* v. *Steel* [1901] 1 Ch. 279 (member seeking declaration that rights of pre-emption in articles were valid). *Cf. Lyle & Scott* v. *Scott's Trustees* [1959] A.C. 763, H.L. *infra*, p. 393.

[2] *Rayfield* v. *Hands* (*supra*) where Vaisey J. was prepared to make an order in effect for specific performance.

[3] But not necessarily *qua* shareholder. In *Lion Mutual Marine Insce. Assoc.* v. *Tucker*, *supra*, the members' insurance liabilities were unrelated to their share capital.

[4] *London Sack and Bag Co.* v. *Dixon & Lugton* [1943] 2 All E.R. 763, C.A. In *Rayfield* v. *Hands* (*supra*) the articles placed the obligation to take the shares of retiring members upon the " directors "; but, somewhat surprisingly, Vaisey J. construed this as an obligation falling upon them in their capacity as *members*: see further, Gower (1958) 21 M.L.R. 401 and 657; Wedderburn [1958] Camb.L.J. 148.

[5] *Eley* v. *Positive Govt. Security Life Assoc.* (1876) 1 Ex.D. 88, C.A. So, too, where the articles provide for payment of his expenses as promoter: *Re English & Colonial Produce Co.* [1906] 2 Ch. 435, C.A. If the person concerned is not a shareholder, the ordinary principles of privity of contract of course prevent his relying upon any contract in the articles.

[6] *Beattie* v. *Beattie Ltd. and Beattie* [1938] Ch. 708, C.A. (where the second defendant answered charges made against him as a director and appeared in that capacity in the dispute: see Greene M.R. at pp. 721–722).

[7] *Per* Astbury J. in *Hickman's Case* [1915] 1 Ch. 881 at pp. 897 and 900.

It must, however, be noticed that, although the articles cannot them-selves constitute a contract in respect of what may be termed " outsider-rights " (*i.e.*, rights pertaining to some capacity other than that of member), the terms of the articles may be expressly or tacitly incor-porated into some other contract. Thus, where directors act for the company without express contracts, the court may infer from conduct a contract intended to be on the same terms as the articles, for example, in regard to the directors' tenure or remuneration.[8] Such an inferred contract, however, is deemed to be made on the usual basis that the terms of the articles can by special resolution be altered from time to time; and the director can have no complaint if they (and his contract) are so altered to his detriment.[9] In contrast, where the director has an express contract with his company, no alteration of the articles can excuse a breach of its express terms, even though he cannot by relying upon that contract prevent the company from altering the articles by special resolution in accordance with section 10 of the 1948 Act.[10]

The principles already explained are illustrated in many decisions in which a member has obtained a declaration, injunction or other order to enforce or protect a right which was personal to himself as member and which arose from the contract in the articles, for example, a right to vote attached to his shares,[11] or a right to a dividend duly declared and payable.[12] But it may be that the principle goes further than this, for there is some authority for the view that each member has a general con-tractual right to have his company's affairs conducted in accordance with the provisions of its memorandum and articles.[13] Such a proposition would explain some of the cases where, despite the rule in *Foss* v. *Harbottle*,[14] an individual member has been allowed to challenge the

---

[8] *Re New British Iron Co., ex p. Beckwith* [1898] 1 Ch. 324; *Swabey* v. *Port Darwin Gold Mining Co.* (1889) 1 Meg. 385, C.A.

[9] *Re T. N. Farrer Ltd.* [1937] Ch. 352, *per* Simonds J. at p. 360; *Re City Equitable Fire Ins. Co.* [1925] Ch. 407 at pp. 520–521; *Read* v. *Astoria Garage* [1952] Ch. 637, C.A. (where alteration of the articles as to determination of his office left a director, who had no express contract, at the mercy of the general meeting in respect of removal. As to removal of directors today, see *supra*, pp. 133–136).

[10] *Southern Foundries Ltd.* v. *Shirlaw* [1940] A.C. 701, H.L.; *Shindler* v. *Northern Raincoat Co. Ltd.* [1960] 1 W.L.R. 1038. See for further discussion, *supra*, p. 135.

[11] *Pender* v. *Lushington* (1877) 6 Ch.D. 70. (Chairman refusing member's vote. But see today Table A, art. 66.)

[12] *Wood* v. *Odessa Waterworks Co.* (1889) 42 Ch.D. 636 (injunction to stop payment in bonds when articles required payment in cash); *Burdett* v. *Standard Exploration Co.* (1899) 16 T.L.R. 112 (right to receive share certificate). Class rights (see *infra*, p. 507 *et seq.*) or rights of pre-emption are enforceable on the same basis: see *Grant* v. *John Grant Ltd.* (1950) 82 C.L.R. 1 (H.Ct. Aus.), especially *per* Williams J. at p. 29. The same principle applies to trade union rules: *Edwards* v. *Halliwell* [1950] 2 All E.R. 1064, C.A.

[13] See Wedderburn, " Shareholders' Rights and the Rule in *Foss* v. *Harbottle* " [1957] Camb.L.J. 193 at pp. 210–215; *Re H. R. Harmer Ltd.* [1959] 1 W.L.R. 62, C.A., where the submission that shareholders have a " right as members of the company to have its affairs conducted in accordance with its articles of association " (see p. 84) was accepted impliedly by Jenkins L.J. at p. 85 and expressly by Romer L.J. at p. 87. The case decided that infringement of this right was oppression of *members* within the meaning of s. 210 (see *infra*, Chap. 25).

[14] *Infra*, Chap. 25.

wrongful appointment of directors or the conduct of the company's affairs by an improperly constituted board of directors,[15] or, indeed, the improper conduct of its affairs by a duly constituted board.[16] It would also allow for the indirect enforcement of " outsider rights " by means of a member suing *qua* member to have the articles observed.[17] This seems to be precisely what happened in one case where a member obtained an injunction to prevent his company from completing certain transactions in contravention of an article which specifically required the consent of two managing directors (of whom he happened to be one).[18]

If, however, there is a principle as wide as this it would seem to conflict with some of the other decisions on the rule in *Foss* v. *Harbottle* preventing an individual member from complaining of procedural irregularities.[19] Nor can it easily be reconciled with the apparently well-settled principle that the memorandum and articles confer rights on members only if they relate to them *qua* members.[20] It would, for example, enable a shareholding solicitor indirectly to enforce a provision in the articles that he is to be the company's solicitor [21] by saying, in effect: " As I am a member, I insist that the legal business of the company shall be conducted in manner provided by the articles." [22] And, conversely, it would enable the company to hold him liable for breach of contract if he refused to act.[23]

The fact is that despite the innumerable decisions on section 20 its full implications have still not been worked out.

---

[15] *Catesby* v. *Burnett* [1916] 2 Ch. 325; and see *Theatre Amusement Co.* v. *Stone* (1915) 50 S.L.R. 32 (Can.Sup.Ct.) at pp. 36–37; and *Kraus* v. *J. G. Lloyd Pty. Ltd.* [1965] V.R. 232 (Aust.) at pp. 235–237, where the problem is fully discussed. See generally Chumir in (1965) 4 Alberta L.R. 96.

[16] *Hogg* v. *Cramphorn Ltd.* [1967] Ch. 254; *Bamford* v. *Bamford* [1968] 3 W.L.R. 317; [1969] 2 W.L.R. 1107, C.A.

[17] This may explain *Woodlands Ltd.* v. *Logan* [1948] N.Z.L.R. 230 (N.Z.Sup.Ct.), where the executors (technically " outsiders ") of a deceased managing director (who was a shareholder) enforced his right under the articles to nominate his successor. The court was prepared to prevent any " attempt by irregular means to vary the constitution of the company ": at pp. 235–236. It seems to be generally assumed that a provision in the articles entitling, say, a debentureholder to appoint a director is enforceable.

[18] *Quin & Axtens Ltd.* v. *Salmon* [1909] 1 Ch. 311, C.A., affd. [1909] A.C. 442, H.L. The plaintiff sued on behalf of himself and other *shareholders*.

[19] See, for example, *Mozley* v. *Alston* (1847) 1 Ph. 790, especially at pp. 796 and 799; and *MacDougall* v. *Gardiner* (1875) 1 Ch.D. 13, C.A. Yet he could sue if his personal rights were regarded as being infringed: *Edwards* v. *Halliwell* [1950] 2 All E.R. 1064, C.A. See *infra*, Chap. 25.

[20] *Supra*, p. 263.

[21] As in *Eley* v. *Positive Government Life Assoc., supra.*

[22] Stiebel, *Company Law and Precedents* (3rd ed.), p. 92.

[23] It has been suggested that *Re Richmond Gate Property Co. Ltd.* [1965] 1 W.L.R. 335 supports the proposition that the company can: see Wedderburn (1965) 28 M.L.R. 347, but contrast Marshall Evans (1966) 29 M.L.R. 608 at p. 612. Certainly that case was decided on the basis that the company could rely on a provision in the articles as a contract barring any claim against it for remuneration on a *quantum meruit* basis by its managing director, who was a member.

Re-registration of an existing company

If a private company wishes to convert itself into a public company no re-registration is needed; it merely alters its articles by deleting the provisions which constitute it a private company and files a prospectus or a statement in lieu of prospectus.[24] If, however, it wants to do something more drastic, such as converting from a guarantee company to a company limited by shares it will normally have to form a brand new company and transfer its undertaking to it.[25] But if an unlimited company wishes to convert to a limited one or vice versa this can be done without its being necessary to form a new company. By section 44 of the 1967 Act, replacing section 16 of the 1948 Act, an unlimited company wishing to re-register as limited must pass a special resolution to that effect and apply to the Registrar.[26] The resolution must state the manner in which the members' liability is to be limited and, if it has a share capital, what that capital is to be, and must make such alterations in its memorandum and articles as are requisite to bring it into conformity with the requirements of the 1948 Act as regards that type of company.[27] The application must be accompanied by printed copies of the new memorandum and articles.[28] The Registrar then issues a new certificate of incorporation,[29] which is conclusive evidence that the requirements of the Act have been complied with and that the company has been duly re-registered.[30] But those who were members at the time of conversion remain liable without limitation of liability if the company is wound up within three years.[31]

Until the 1967 Act there was no way in which a limited company could re-register as unlimited. But that Act finally adopted the principle that publicity of a company's financial position should be the price of limited liability in all cases.[32] Hence it was thought necessary to allow the formerly exempt private companies to convert to unlimited if they wished, thus enabling them to escape the need to publicise their balance sheets and profit-and-loss accounts.[33] Application is made to the Registrar[34] setting out the alterations in the memorandum and articles

---

[24] 1948 Act, s. 30. See *infra*, p. 303.
[25] See further, Chap. 26.
[26] 1967 Act, s. 44 (1).
[27] s. 44 (2).
[28] s. 44 (3).
[29] s. 44 (4).
[30] s. 44 (5).
[31] s. 44 (7).
[32] Jenkins Committee Report (Cmnd. 1749), paras. 55–63.
[33] 1967 Act, s. 47. But it is exempt only so long as it is not to its knowledge (a) a subsidiary of a limited company or would have been a subsidiary if shares or powers held by more than one limited company had been held by one only, or (b) a holding company of a limited company, or (c) carrying on business as the promoter of a trading stamp scheme within the meaning of the Trading Stamps Act 1964: s. 47 (1).
[34] 1967 Act, s. 43 (1).

requisite as regards the new type of company.[35]   The application must be accompanied by the prescribed [36] form of assent signed by or on behalf of all the members, and by a statutory declaration by the directors that the signatories constitute all the members and that the directors have taken all reasonable steps to satisfy themselves that where signing was by an agent he was empowered to do so.[37] These requirements are essential safeguards since members are forfeiting the former limitation on their liability.   The application must also be accompanied by printed copies of the new memorandum [38] and of the new [39] or amended [40] articles.   The Registrar then issues a new certificate of incorporation which, once again, is conclusive that the conversion has duly taken place.[41] The members of the company, present and future, then become fully liable for existing and future debts of the company in the same way as if the company had throughout been unlimited.[42]   But one who had ceased to be a member at the time when the application was lodged does not become liable to a greater extent than he would if the company had not been re-registered.[43]

In addition a company not originally formed under the Companies Acts may be able to register under them.   Companies registered under the earlier Companies Acts are, of course, subject to the provisions of the current Act just as if they had been formed under it,[44] except that certain sections [45] are expressed only to apply to companies formed after a specified date.   But certain other associations not at present subject to the Acts may register under them in accordance with Part VIII of the 1948 Act.   Briefly, the associations so authorised to register are pre-1862 companies and any others duly constituted according to law and consisting of seven or more members.[46]   In addition to chartered, statutory and cost-book companies this will apparently include an ordinary partnership of more than seven persons, except that it may

---

[35] s. 43 (2).   The difference in the wording of the subsection according to whether or not the converted company is to have a share capital is because the 1948 Act prescribes a form of memorandum and articles if an unlimited company has a share capital (1948 Act, s. 11 and 1st Sched., Tables B and E) but does not do so if there is no share capital.

[36] The various prescribed forms are set out in the Companies (Forms) Regulations 1967 (S.I. No. 1442).

[37] s. 47 (3) (*a*) and (*b*).   Note subs. (7) as regards personal representatives and trustees in bankruptcy.

[38] s. 43 (3) (*c*).

[39] s. 43 (2) (*b*).

[40] s. 43 (3) (*d*).

[41] s. 43 (4) and (5).

[42] See Companies Act 1948, s. 212.

[43] 1967 Act, s. 43 (6).   *I.e.*, he is not liable until existing members have failed to pay, or for more than the unpaid capital on his shares, and is not liable at all if he ceased to be a member more than a year before the commencement of the winding up or in respect of any debt or liability incurred after he ceased to be a member: 1948 Act, s. 212 (1) (*a*), (*b*), (*c*) and (*d*).

[44] Companies Act 1948, Part VII.

[45] *e.g.*, ss. 176 and 201.

[46] s. 382.   A general meeting of the members must resolve in favour: *ibid.* subs. (1), proviso (v).

not register as a company limited by shares unless previously organised on the joint stock principle [47]—an expression given a highly technical meaning.[48] Copies of the association's constitution and particulars of directors and share capital (if any) must be filed,[49] and if the company is limited it must add " Limited " to its name,[50] which, with the assent of the Board of Trade, may be changed to satisfy the normal requirements of the Registrar.[51] A certificate of incorporation will then be issued in the normal way and with the usual consequences,[52] and all property of the association will vest in the newly registered and incorporated company.[53] It is this last provision that explains the attempts to register under Part VIII instead of forming a company in the normal way and transferring to it the business of the partnership, for by so doing stamp duty on the transfer of property from the members to the new company could be avoided. The efficacy of this ingenious device was partially destroyed, however, when it was held by the Court of Appeal [54] in 1891 that a partnership could not register under what is now Part VIII if it had been expressly formed for this sole purpose. Moreover, as we have seen, a partnership cannot register under Part VIII as a company limited by shares unless already organised on a joint stock basis, and the Registrar will require to be satisfied of this.[55] As it is in the highest degree unlikely that an existing partnership will be organised in this way, Part VIII, as a means of evading stamp duty, appears to be a dead letter.[56]

Registration does not affect any existing liabilities of the company,[57] so that, presumably, unless the company was formerly incorporated with limited liability, its members will remain personally liable for debts existing at the time of registration. After registration it may adopt a memorandum and articles by special resolution,[58] but until it does so its existing constitution will continue to govern. Those provisions of its constitution which, in the case of a normally formed company, would have to be in the memorandum will be treated as if they were in a memorandum and the remainder as if they were in the articles.[59]

It should be noted that in any event the modern tendency is increasingly to subject unregistered companies to the regulatory provisions of

[47] s. 382 (1), proviso (iv).
[48] See s. 383.
[49] ss. 384, 385.
[50] s. 389.
[51] s. 388.
[52] s. 390.
[53] s. 391.
[54] R. v. *Registrar of Joint Stock Companies, ex p. Johnston* [1891] 2 Q.B. 598, C.A.
[55] s. 387.
[56] An existing partnership might presumably reorganise on the joint stock principle and then apply for registration, but it is doubtful whether the Registrar would accept an *ad hoc* conversion of this sort or whether, in the light of the observations in *Ex p. Johnston, supra*, he could be compelled to do so.
[57] s. 392.
[58] s. 395.
[59] s. 394 (2).

the Acts.[60] A large number of sections specified in Schedule 14 to the 1948 Act and section 54 of the 1967 Act apply, with such modifications as may be specified by regulations,[61] to all bodies corporate incorporated in, and having a principal place of business in, Great Britain,[62] unless incorporated under a public general Act,[63] not formed for the purpose of gain by the corporation or its members, or exempted by the Board of Trade.[64] They apply to the like extent to unincorporated bodies of persons entitled to privileges under the Chartered Companies Act 1837.[65] The sections thus made applicable include those relating to publicity and to inspections.

---

[60] 1948 Act, s. 435; 1967 Act, s. 54.
[61] See Companies (Unregistered Companies) Regulations 1967 (S.I. No. 1876).
[62] 1948 Act, s. 435 (1).
[63] Thus excluding the so-called public corporations: see *supra*, Chap. 11, pp. 234–241.
[64] s. 435 (2).
[65] s. 435 (3); on the 1837 Act, see *supra*, p. 7.

CHAPTER 13

PROMOTERS

Meaning of " promoter "

If, in a psycho-analyst's consulting room, we were asked to say what picture formed in our minds at the mention of the expression " company promoter," most of us would probably confess that we envisaged a character of dubious repute and antecedents who infests the commercial *demi-monde* [1] with a menagerie of bulls, bears, stags, and sharks as his familiars, and who, after rising to affluence by preying on the susceptibilities of a gullible public, finally retires from the scene in the blaze of a sensational suicide or Old Bailey trial.[2] In other words, we should envisage someone whose profession it was to form bogus companies and foist them off on the public to the latter's detriment and his own profit. Such figures have existed and it is probably too much to hope that they will ever be entirely eradicated, but even in their Edwardian heyday they formed only the minutest fraction of those whom the law classifies as promoters. A much more typical, if less romantic example, would be the village grocer who converts his business into a limited company. He, of course, is in no sense a professional company promoter, always and increasingly a *rara avis*,[3] but he would be the promoter of his little company, and a moment's thought will make it clear that the difference, however great, between him and a professional promoter is basically one of degree rather than of kind. Both create or help to create the company and seek to sell it something, whether it be their services or a business. Both are obviously so placed that they can easily take advantage of their position by obtaining a recompense grossly in excess of the true value of what they are selling.[4] The only difference is that the grocer is less likely than the professional to abuse his position since he will

---

[1] Somehow associated in our minds with " the curb."

[2] It is perhaps a tribute to the law that we definitely picture him as coming to a sticky end; *cf.* Lord MacNaghten in *Gluckstein* v. *Barnes* [1900] A.C. 240, H.L., at p. 248.

[3] As pointed out in the next chapter, the handling of public issues is now virtually monopolised by a small number of reputable issuing houses. It is the close scrutiny by these and the Stock Exchanges as much as the rigour of the law which has caused the virtual disappearance of the old-time professional promoter whose role the issuing houses have assumed. Too tight a monopoly in the hands of a few issuing houses may, of course, present dangers: *cf.* the (unsuccessful) anti-trust suit brought against certain American houses: *U.S.* v. *Morgan et al.* (1953) 118 F.Supp. 621.

[4] A good (or rather, bad) example of the *modus operandi* is *Re Darby* [1911] 1 K.B. 95, see Chap. 10, p. 210, *supra*.

probably continue to be the majority shareholder in his company, whereas the promoter, if a shareholder at all, will intend to off-load his holdings on to others as soon as possible.

It will have been apparent from the foregoing that the expression " promoter " covers a wide range of persons. Indeed it is still wider. Both the professional promoter and the village grocer are promoters to the fullest extent, in that each " undertakes to form a company with reference to a given project, and to set it going and . . . takes the necessary steps to accomplish that purpose." [5] But a person may be a promoter who has taken a much less active and dominating role; the expression may, for example, cover any individual or company that obtains a director, places shares, or negotiates preliminary agreements. [6] Nor need he necessarily be associated with the initial formation of the company; one who subsequently helps to arrange the " floating off " of its capital (in the manner explained in the next chapter) will equally be regarded as a promoter. [7] On the other hand, those who act in a purely ministerial capacity, such as solicitors and accountants, will not be classified as promoters merely because they undertake their normal professional duties [8]; although they may if, for example, they have agreed to become directors or to find others who will. [9]

Who constitutes a promoter in any particular case is therefore a question of fact. The expression has never been clearly defined either judicially [10] or legislatively, [11] despite the fact that it is frequently used both in decisions and statutes. So far as the promoter himself is concerned this imposes no particular hardship; as we shall see, his duty is merely to act with good faith towards the company and this he should do whether legally compelled or not. But from the point of view of the company the vagueness of the term is apt to be embarrassing. The Companies Acts impose on every public company the duty to disclose

---

[5] *Per* Cockburn C.J. in *Twycross* v. *Grant* (1877) 2 C.P.D. 469 at p. 541, C.A.

[6] *Cf. Bagnall* v. *Carlton* (1877) 6 Ch.D. 371, C.A.; *Emma Silver Mining Co.* v. *Grant* (1879) 11 Ch.D. 918, C.A.; *Whaley Bridge Printing Co.* v. *Green* (1880) 5 Q.B.D. 109; *Lydney & Wigpool Iron Ore Co.* v. *Bird* (1886) 33 Ch.D. 85, C.A.; *Mann* v. *Edinburgh Northern Tramways Co.* [1893] A.C. 69, H.L.; *Jubilee Cotton Mills* v. *Lewis* [1924] A.C. 958, H.L. and cases cited, *infra*.

[7] *Lagunas Nitrate Co.* v. *Lagunas Syndicate* [1899] 2 Ch. 392 at p. 428, C.A.

[8] *Re Great Wheal Polgooth Co.* (1883) 53 L.J.Ch. 42.

[9] *Lydney & Wigpool Iron Ore Co.* v. *Bird* (1886) 33 Ch.D. 85, C.A.; *Bagnall* v. *Carlton* (1877) 6 Ch.D. 371, C.A. Presumably the mere subscription of the memorandum would not make them promoters, *sed quaere*.

[10] In addition to Cockburn C.J.'s description (*supra*), see those of Lindley J. in *Emma Silver Mining Co.* v. *Lewis* (1879) 4 C.P.D. 396 at p. 407, and of Bowen J. in *Whaley Bridge Printing Co.* v. *Green* (1880) 5 Q.B.D. 109 at p. 111.

[11] For the purposes of s. 43 of the Companies Act 1948 (relating to liability for misstatements in a prospectus) it is " defined " as follows: " the expression ' promoter ' means a promoter (!) who was a party to the preparation of the prospectus or of the portion thereof containing the untrue statement, but does not include any person by reason of his acting in a professional capacity for persons engaged in procuring the formation of the company." S. 38 uses instead the expression " any person who is or has been engaged or interested in the formation of the company."

in its prospectus or statement in lieu [12] particulars of any benefit payable to any promoter, and it may be a matter of some delicacy to decide who is to be included, particularly as people are apt to be sensitive about being so described.

Duties of promoters

The early Companies Acts contained no provisions regarding the liabilities of promoters, and even today they are largely silent on the subject, merely imposing liability for untrue statements in prospectuses to which they were parties.[13] The courts, however, were early conscious of the possibilities of abuse inherent in the promoter's position and in a series of cases in the last quarter of the nineteenth century they laid it down that anyone who can properly be regarded as a promoter stands in a fiduciary position towards the company with all the duties of disclosure and accounting which that implies; in particular he must not make any profit out of the promotion without disclosing it to the company. The difficulty, however, is to decide how he is to make this disclosure, the company being an artificial entity. The first leading case on the subject, *Erlanger* v. *New Sombrero Phosphate Co.*,[14] suggested that it was his duty to ensure that the company had an independent board of directors and to make full disclosure to them. In that case Lord Cairns said [15] that the promoters of a company

> " stand . . . undoubtedly in a fiduciary position. They have in their hands the creation and moulding of the company; they have the power of defining how, and when, and in what shape, and under what supervision, it shall start into existence and begin to act as a trading corporation. . . . I do not say that the owner of property may not promote and form a joint stock company and then sell his property to it, but I do say that if he does he is bound to take care that he sells it to the company through the medium of a board of directors who can and do exercise an independent and intelligent judgment on the transaction. . . ."

This rule, however, was obviously too strict; an entirely independent board would be impossible in the case of most private and many public companies, and since *Salomon* v. *Salomon* [16] it has never been doubted that a disclosure to the members would be equally effective. In that famous case it was held that the liquidator of the company could not complain of the sale to it at an obvious over-valuation of Mr. Salomon's business, all the members having acquiesced therein. " After *Salomon's* case I think it impossible to hold that it is the duty of the promoters of

---

[12] Companies Act 1948, Scheds. 3, 4 and 5.
[13] s. 43.
[14] (1878) 3 App.Cas. 1218, H.L.
[15] At p. 1236.
[16] [1897] A.C. 22, H.L.; *supra*, p. 68.

a company to provide it with an independent board of directors if the real truth is disclosed to those who are induced by the promoters to join the company." [17] But the promoter cannot escape liability by disclosing to a few cronies, who constitute the initial members, when it is the intention to float off the company to the public or to induce some other dupes to purchase the shares. This was emphasised by the speeches of the House of Lords in the second great landmark in the development of this branch of the law—*Gluckstein* v. *Barnes*.[18] " It is too absurd," said Lord Halsbury, with his usual bluntness, " to suggest that a disclosure to the parties to this transaction is a disclosure to the company. . . . They were there by the terms of the agreement to do the work of the syndicate, that is to say, to cheat the shareholders; and this forsooth, is to be treated as a disclosure to the company, when they were really there to hoodwink the shareholders."

The position therefore seems to be that disclosure must be made to the company either by making it to an entirely independent board or to the existing and *potential* members as a whole. If the first method is employed the promoter will be under no further liability to the company, although the directors will be liable to the subscribers if the information has not been passed on in the invitation to subscribe; indeed, if the promoter is a party to this invitation,[19] he too will be liable to the subscribers.[20] If the second method is adopted the veil of incorporation is in effect ignored and disclosure must be made in the prospectus, articles, or otherwise, so that those who are or become members, as a result of the transaction in which the promoter was acting as such, have full information regarding it. A partial or incomplete disclosure will not do; the disclosure must be explicit.[21]

It is often stated [22] that the duty of a promoter may be even heavier than that of making full disclosure of any profit made. The suggestion is that if he acquires any property after the commencement of the promotion he is presumed to do so as a trustee of the company so that he must hand it over to the company at the price he gave for it, unless he discloses not merely the profit which he proposes to make but also informs the company of its right to call for the property at its cost price. In theory this is undoubtedly sound. If the promoter broke his duty by attempting to acquire the property beneficially when he should have

---

[17] *Per* Lindley M.R. in *Lagunas Nitrate Co.* v. *Lagunas Syndicate* [1899] 2 Ch. 392, C.A., at p. 426.

[18] [1900] A.C. 240, H.L., at p. 247.

[19] In which event he will find some difficulty in persuading the court that the directors were truly independent of him.

[20] Companies Act 1948, s. 43, replacing the Directors' Liability Act 1890, passed as a result of *Derry* v. *Peek, infra.*

[21] *Gluckstein* v. *Barnes, supra.*

[22] See Palmer, *Company Precedents*, 17th ed., Pt. I, p. 30 *et seq.*

acquired it for the unborn company,[23] then his breach of duty was not merely failure to disclose his profit but was his attempted expropriation of the company's property. Indeed, if this is the situation it appears that nothing short of unanimous consent of all the shareholders of the company when formed should entitle the promoter to retain his ill-gotten gains,[24] for not even a resolution of a general meeting can authorise an expropriation of the company's property.[25] But in fact the English decisions cited in support of this theory [26] do not go anything like so far (although certain dicta in them do [27]). There seems to be no case in which, full disclosure of the profit having been made, the promoter has been held liable to account. The judgments acknowledge the possibility that the promoter may have acquired the property as trustee, but they seem to require something more than the mere acquisition of property after the commencement of the promotion with the intention of re-selling it to the company.[28] In principle it should suffice if the company can show that the promoter acquired the property for himself when it was his duty to acquire it for the company.[29] But in practice all seems to turn on the intentions of the promoter at the time of purchase; on whether he intended to buy for himself for re-sale *to* the company or to buy initially *for* the company.[30] In the former case his only duty is to disclose; in the latter he cannot subsequently change his mind and seek to act as vendor rather than as trustee.

It will be observed that the promoter's duty to the company, even apart from statute, is not merely to refrain from wilfully false statements but actively to disclose the whole truth. His duty to the company is to be contrasted with that which he owes towards people invited to subscribe for the company's shares. At common law his duty to the latter was merely to refrain from falsehoods,[31] and even as a result of statutory intervention, it is doubtful if there is a positive duty to disclose all material facts.[32]

---

23 There seems to be no objection in principle to the establishment of a trust in favour of an unformed company—for there can certainly be a trust in favour of an unborn person—but the decisions display a reluctance to invoke this principle: cf. *Natal Land Co.* v. *Pauline Syndicate* [1904] A.C. 120, P.C.

24 *Cf. Cook* v. *Deeks* [1916] 1 A.C. 554, P.C.; *Canada Safeway Ltd.* v. *Thompson* [1951] 3 D.L.R. 295; [1952] 2 D.L.R. 591 (B.Col.S.C.), *infra*, Chap. 24.

25 See Chap. 24, *infra*.

26 *Tyrrell* v. *Bank of London* (1862) 10 H.L.C. 26; *Re Ambrose Lake Tin Co.* (1880) 14 Ch.D. 390, C.A.; *Re Cape Breton Co.* (1885) 29 Ch.D. 795, C.A., affd. *sub nom. Cavendish Bentinck* v. *Fenn* (1887) 12 App.Cas. 652, H.L.; *Ladywell Mining Co.* v. *Brookes* (1887) 35 Ch.D. 400, C.A.

27 See especially (1887) 35 Ch.D. at p. 413.

28 See especially, *Omnium Electric Palaces* v. *Baines* [1914] 1 Ch. 332, C.A.

29 *Cf. Cook* v. *Deeks* and *Canada Safeway Ltd.* v. *Thompson, supra.*

30 See especially, *per* Sargant J. in [1914] 1 Ch. at p. 347.

31 *Derry* v. *Peek* (1889) 14 App.Cas. 337, H.L. This famous case immediately led to the passing of the Directors' Liability Act, now s. 43 of the Companies Act 1948, which in turn was the forerunner of the Misrepresentation Act 1967.

32 This matter is dealt with more fully below in Chap. 15, where it is pointed out, at pp. 325, 326, that in practice the liability has become almost as extensive.

It seems clear that a promoter cannot effectively contract out of his duties by inserting a clause in the articles whereby the company and the subscribers agree to waive their rights.[33]

Remedies for breach of promoters' duties

Since the promoter owes a duty of disclosure to the company, the primary remedy against him in the event of breach is for the company to bring proceedings for rescission of any contract with him or for the recovery of any secret profits which he has made.

So far as the right to rescind is concerned, this must be exercised on normal contractual principles, that is to say the company must have done nothing to show an intention to ratify the agreement after finding out about the non-disclosure or misrepresentation [34] and *restitutio in integrum* must still be possible.[35] In view of the wide powers now exercised by the court to order financial adjustments when directing rescission, it is doubtful whether the *restitutio in integrum* rule operates as any real restraint, at any rate where the promoter has been fraudulent and where he himself is responsible for the dealings alleged to have resulted in restitution being impossible.[36] The only circumstance where this requirement seems likely to impose a serious limitation is where innocent third parties have acquired rights to the property concerned, and even there a monetary adjustment will often enable the third parties' rights to be discharged.[37] The mere fact that the contract had been performed never seems to have destroyed the right to rescind a contract of this type [38] and since the Misrepresentation Act 1967 any suggestion to that effect seems unarguable.[39]

---

[33] *Gluckstein* v. *Barnes, supra*; *Omnium Electric Palaces* v. *Baines* [1914] 1 Ch. at p. 347, *per* Sargant J. Such "waiver" clauses used to be common and, except as regards actual misrepresentations (on which see Misrepresentation Act 1967, s. 3, *infra*, p. 316), there is still no statutory prohibition of them as there is of similar clauses in prospectuses under Companies Act 1948, s. 38 (2), which, however, might be wide enough to nullify the effect of a clause in the articles so far as subscribers for securities are concerned. S. 205 (invalidating exemption clauses) only covers officers and auditors.

[34] *Lagunas Nitrate Co.* v. *Lagunas Syndicate* [1899] 2 Ch. 392, C.A. Here again "the company" must mean the members or an independent board; clearly ratification by puppet directors cannot be effective.

[35] *Re Leeds & Hanley Theatre of Varieties* [1902] 2 Ch. 809, C.A.; *Steedman* v. *Frigidaire Corpn.* [1933] 1 D.L.R. 161, P.C.; *Dominion Royalty Corpn.* v. *Goffatt* [1935] 1 D.L.R. 780 (Ont.C.A.), affd. [1935] 4 D.L.R. 736 (Can.S.C.).

[36] *Erlanger* v. *New Sombrero Phosphate Co.* (1878) 3 App.Cas. 1218, H.L., and *Spence* v. *Crawford* [1939] 3 All E.R. 271, H.L. These cases suggest that the courts have more restricted powers of financial adjustment when there is no fraud: *sed quaere*, *Armstrong* v. *Jackson* [1917] 2 K.B. 822.

[37] As, perhaps, in *Re Leeds & Hanley Theatre of Varieties, supra*, where the property had been mortgaged to a bank. The mere fact that the company is in liquidation does not prevent it from rescinding; contrast the stricter rule as regards rescission of an allotment of shares in the company, *infra*, p. 327.

[38] As pointed out in the 10th Report of the Law Reform Committee (Cmnd. 1782), paras. 6–9, the extent, if any, of any such rule was doubtful except as regards contracts relating to land. The Misrepresentation Act 1967 is based on this Report.

[39] s. 1 of the Act expressly provides that a contract can be rescinded for misrepresentation notwithstanding that the misrepresentation has become a term of the

If the contract is rescinded the promoter's secret profit will normally disappear as a result, but if he has made a profit on some ancillary transaction there is no doubt that this too may be recovered. Moreover, a secret profit may be recovered although the company elects not to rescind [40]; the classic illustration of this is *Gluckstein* v. *Barnes* [41] itself.

In that case a syndicate had been formed for the purpose of buying and reselling Olympia, then owned by a company in liquidation. The syndicate first bought up at low prices certain charges on the property and then bought the freehold itself for £140,000. They then promoted a company of which they were the directors, and to it they sold the freehold for £180,000 which was raised by a public issue of share and debentures. In the prospectus the profit of £40,000 was disclosed. But in the meantime the promoters had had the charges on the property repaid by the liquidator out of the £140,000 and thereby made a further profit of £20,000. This was not disclosed in the prospectus, though reference was there made to a contract, close scrutiny of which might have revealed that some profit had been made. Four years later the new company went into liquidation and it was held that the promoters must account to the company for this secret profit.

There is, however, authority for saying that if the property on which the profit was made was acquired before the promoter became a promoter, there can be no claim for the recovery of the profit as such.[42] According to this view it may be necessary for this purpose to make the, admittedly difficult, determination of the exact moment of time at which the promotion began. The principle on which this view is based has been most clearly expressed as follows [43]:

> "In any question as to the remedies available against a [promoter] who has sold his own property to the company, regard must be had to the relationship in which the [promoter] stood to the company when he acquired the property. If he was under no obligation at that time to acquire the property for the company

contract or that the contract has been performed. Technically, this has no application to non-disclosure as opposed to a misrepresentation.

40 In this respect the company's rights against a promoter are greater than those of a subscriber against the company, for it has been held, anomalously, that the subscriber cannot recover damages for fraud unless he also rescinds: *Houldsworth* v. *City of Glasgow Bank* (1880) 5 App.Cas. 317, H.L. See p. 319, *infra*.

41 [1900] A.C. 240, H.L. And see *Jubilee Cotton Mills* v. *Lewis* [1924] A.C. 958, H.L.

42 *Re Ambrose Lake Tin Co.* (1880) 14 Ch.D. 390, C.A.; *Re Cape Breton Co.* (1885) 29 Ch.D. 795, C.A., affd. *sub nom. Cavendish Bentinck* v. *Fenn* (1887) 12 App.Cas. 652, H.L.; *Ladywell Mining Co.* v. *Brookes* (1887) 35 Ch.D. 400, C.A.; *Re Lady Forrest (Murchison) Gold Mine* [1901] 1 Ch. 582; *Burland* v. *Earle* [1902] A.C. 83, P.C.; *Jacobus Marler Estates* v. *Marler* (1913) 85 L.J.P.C. 167n.; *Cook* v. *Deeks* [1916] 1 A.C. 554 at pp. 563, 564, P.C.; *Robinson* v. *Randfontein Estates* [1921] A.D. 168 (S.Afr.S.C.App.Div.); *P. & O. Steam Nav. Co.* v. *Johnson* (1938) 60 C.L.R. 189 (Austr.H.C.).

43 The quotation is from the headnote of *Robinson* v. *Randfontein Estates* [1921] A.D. 168 (S.Afr.S.C.App.Div.), summarising the statement of Innes C.J. at p. 179. "Promoter" has been substituted for "director" throughout.

instead of for himself, then his non-disclosure of the fact that the property was his own would entitle the company to repudiate the sale and restore the original position, but would not entitle it to retain the property at a price reduced by a deduction of the [promoter's] profit. When, however, the [promoter's] default extends further than non-disclosure, when a breach of duty attended the original acquisition, the company may, if it chooses, retain the property purchased and also demand a refund of the profits." [44]

Normally this rule works fairly enough. If the company freely elects to affirm the purchase, there would be an element of injustice in making the promoter disgorge the whole of the difference between the price at which he bought—perhaps many years previously—and that at which he sold. No doubt the court could assess the market value at the date of the sale and on that basis force the promoter to account, but this, it has been argued, [45] would be to make a new contract for the parties.

On the other hand, the rule could work grave injustice to the company on the rare occasions when *restitutio in integrum* had become impossible so that the company had lost the right to rescind through circumstances beyond its control. In practice the courts avoided this injustice either by finding that the promoter was fraudulent, and accordingly liable to an action for deceit, or that the promotion had commenced when he acquired the property; indeed, they found both.[46] They even suggested that, in the absence of common law fraud, the promoter would be liable in damages for his failure to disclose,[47] or for negligence in allowing the company to purchase at an excessive price,[48] the damages being the difference between the market value and the contract price.[49] As a result of the Misrepresentation Act 1967 there is a clear legal basis for awarding damages in all cases where the promoter has made an actual misrepresentation and cannot prove that he had reasonable ground to believe and did believe up to the time the contract was made that the facts represented were true.[50] When there is any misrepresentation the Act makes any exclusion clause ineffective to bar

---

[44] As pointed out, *supra*, pp. 273, 274, mere disclosure of the profit should not in principle bar this right, but the cases suggest the contrary.
[45] *Re Cape Breton Co.* (1885) 29 Ch.D. 795, C.A.
[46] *Re Olympia, Ltd.* [1898] 2 Ch. 153, affd. *sub nom. Gluckstein* v. *Barnes, supra*; *Re Leeds and Hanley Theatre of Varieties, supra.* But the mere non-disclosure of the amount of the profit is not misrepresentation: *Re Lady Forrest (Murchison) Gold Mine* [1901] 1 Ch. 582; *Jacobus Marler Estates Ltd.* v. *Marler* (1913) 85 L.J.P.C. 167n.
[47] *Re Leeds and Hanley Theatre of Varieties, supra*; see especially, *per* Vaughan Williams L.J. [1902] 2 Ch. at p. 825.
[48] *Per* Lord Parker in *Jacobus Marler Estates* v. *Marler* (1913) 85 L.J.P.C. at p. 168.
[49] Since *Hedley Byrne & Co. Ltd.* v. *Heller & Partners Ltd.* [1964] A.C. 465, H.L., it is clear that even at common law there may be a remedy in such cases if a misstatement is made negligently.
[50] Misrepresentation Act 1967, s. 2 (1). Moreover, under s. 2 (2) damages may be awarded in lieu of rescission.

any remedy, unless the court allows "reliance on it as being fair and reasonable in the circumstances of the case "[51]—which is most unlikely.

In addition to the remedies of the company, the promoter may be liable to a subscriber in damages for fraud if the promoter has been party to a wilfully false statement inducing subscriptions. Moreover, in the absence of actual fraud, he may be liable to pay compensation to any subscriber if he was a party to a false statement in any prospectus, or to a prospectus lacking the information required by the Companies Act.[52] The liability in this respect is the same as that of a director and is dealt with more fully in Chapter 15, *infra*.

Remuneration of promoters

A promoter is not entitled to recover any remuneration for his services from the company unless there is a valid contract, enabling him to do so, between him and the company. Indeed, without such a contract he is not even entitled to recover his preliminary expenses[53] or the registration fees and capital duties.[54] In this respect the promoter is at the mercy of the directors of the company. Until the company is formed it cannot enter into a valid contract[55] and the promoter therefore has to expend the money without any guarantee that he will be repaid. In practice, however, recovery of preliminary expenses and registration fees does not normally present any difficulty. The articles will contain a provision authorising the directors to pay them,[56] and although this does not constitute any contract between the company and the promoter, it is a sufficient authority to the directors to repay expenses properly incurred.[57] If, as is generally the case, the promoter is one of the directors, he can be reasonably confident that his expenses will be paid.

It may well be, however, that the promoter will not be content merely to recover his expenses; certainly if he is a professional promoter he will expect to be handsomely remunerated. Nor is this unreasonable.

---

[51] *Ibid.* s. 3.
[52] 1948 Act, ss. 43 and 38. The Misrepresentation Act 1967, s. 2 (1), will not afford a remedy in these cases since this subsection applies only where a misrepresentation has been made by a party to the contract, and the promoter will not normally be a party to the contract of subscription with the company. Nor is he likely to be liable under *Hedley Byrne & Co.* v. *Heller & Partners, supra.*
[53] *Re English and Colonial Produce Co.* [1906] 2 Ch. 435, C.A.
[54] *Re National Motor Mail Coach Co.* [1908] 2 Ch. 515, C.A.
[55] *Kelner* v. *Baxter* (1866) L.R. 2 C.P. 174; *Natal Land Co.* v. *Pauline Syndicate* [1904] A.C. 120, P.C. Nor can it ratify a preliminary contract purporting to be made on its behalf: *ibid.* It must enter into a new contract and this ought to be under seal since the consideration rendered by the promoter will be past.
[56] Table A, art. 80.
[57] *Re Rotherham Alum Co.* (1883) 25 Ch.D. 103, C.A.; *Re Englefield Colliery Co.* (1877–1878) 8 Ch.D. 388, C.A. The estimated amount of the expenses and by whom they are payable must be disclosed in any prospectus (Sched. 4, Pt. I, para. 12) or statement in lieu (Sched. 3, Pt. I, and Sched. 5, Pt. I) and, until written off, the actual amount paid or payable must be disclosed in the company's annual balance sheet (Sched. 8, Pt. I, para. 3).

As Lord Hatherly said,[58] " The services of a promoter are very peculiar; great skill, energy and ingenuity may be employed in constructing a plan and in bringing it out to the best advantages." Hence it is perfectly proper for the promoter to be rewarded, provided, as we have seen, that he fully discloses to the company the rewards which he obtains.

The reward may take many forms. The promoter may purchase an undertaking and promote a company to repurchase it from him at a profit, or the undertaking may be sold direct by the former owner to the new company, the promoter receiving a commission from the vendor. A once-popular device was for the company's capital structure to provide for a special class of deferred or founders' shares which would be issued credited as fully paid in consideration of the promoter's services.[59] Such shares would normally provide for the lion's share of the profits available for dividend after the preference and ordinary shares had been paid a dividend of a fixed amount. This had the advantage that the promoter advertised his apparent confidence in the business by retaining a stake in it, but all too often his stake (which probably cost him nothing anyway) was merely window-dressing. And if, in fact, the company proved an outstanding success the promoter might do better than all the other shareholders put together. Today, when the trend is towards simplicity of capital structures, founders' shares are out of favour and, in general, those old companies which originally had them have got rid of them on a reconstruction.[60] Another alternative is for the promoter to be given an option to subscribe for shares at a particular price (*e.g.,* par) within a specified time. If the shares have meanwhile gone to a premium this will obviously be a most valuable right; it is a perfectly legal arrangement,[61] but particulars of the option have to be given in any prospectus [62] or statement in lieu [63] and in a note to the annual balance sheet.[64]

When a public issue is made, most of the functions of the old style professional promoter will be carried out by an issuing house which

---

[58] In *Touche* v. *Metropolitan Ry. Warehousing Co.* (1871) L.R. 6 Ch.App. 671 at p. 676.

[59] The promoter will have to obtain a contract with the company prior to rendering the services, for past services are not valuable consideration: *Re Eddystone Marine Insurance* [1893] 3 Ch. 9, C.A. Hence if the services are rendered before the company was formed the promoter will have to pay for the shares. But provided they are given a very low nominal value this may not be a serious snag.

[60] There have been many interesting battles between holders of founders' shares and the other members. If the holdings of founders' shares are widely dispersed there is obviously a risk of a block being acquired on behalf of the other classes in the hope of outvoting the remaining founders' shareholders at a class meeting to approve a reconstruction. To safeguard their position, in a number of cases the founders' shareholders formed a special company and vested all the founders' shares in it, thus ensuring that they were voted solidly at any meeting.

[61] *Hilder* v. *Dexter* [1902] A.C. 474, H.L.

[62] Sched. 4, Pt. I, para. 7.

[63] Scheds. 3 and 5.

[64] Sched. 8, Pt. I, para. 11. An option to subscribe for shares is not invalidated by the 1967 Act, s. 25.

will, of course, be a promoter in the broad sense previously explained. How the issuing house will be rewarded will be apparent from the discussion in the next chapter.

Whatever the nature of the remuneration it must be fully disclosed not only by the promoter to the company in accordance with the foregoing rules but also by the company in any prospectus so long as the remuneration was paid within two years or remains payable.[65]

Where the promotion is not in the hands of professionals the matter is obviously simpler. If the village grocer is converting his business into a private company his main object will be to secure the advantage of corporate personality, not to make a quick profit. But even in this case he may incidentally make a profit; for example, like Mr. Salomon, he may sell his business to the company at an over-valuation.[66] In principle exactly the same rules apply, but provided that all the members acquiesce all will be in order.[67]

Preliminary contracts by promoters

Until the company has been incorporated it cannot contract or enter into any other act in the law. Nor, once incorporated, can it become liable on or entitled under contracts purporting to be made on its behalf prior to incorporation, for ratification is not possible when the ostensible principal did not exist at the time when the contract was originally entered into.[68] Indeed, as we shall see,[69] if the company is initially formed as a public company it cannot bind itself until after the flotation of its share capital and the granting of a trading certificate.

Hence preliminary arrangements will either have to be left to mere " gentlemen's agreements " or the promoters will have to undertake personal liability. Which of these courses will be adopted depends largely on the demands of the other party. If our village grocer is converting his business into a private company of which he is to be managing director and majority shareholder he will obviously not be concerned to have a binding agreement with anyone. In such a case a draft sale agreement will be drawn up and the main object in the company's memorandum will be to acquire his business as a going concern " and for this purpose to enter into an agreement in the terms of a draft already prepared and for the purpose of identification signed by. . . ." When the incorporation is complete the seller will ensure that the agreement is executed and completed.

---

[65] s. 38 (1) and Sched. 4, Pt. I, para. 13.
[66] Even here there will in reality be no profit to the promoter unless the purchase price is satisfied in cash or debentures as well as shares.
[67] *Salomon* v. *Salomon* [1897] A.C. 22, H.L. Subject, of course, to the possibility of the transaction being set aside by the vendor's trustee in bankruptcy: see *supra*, Chap. 4, p. 69
[68] *Kelner* v. *Baxter* (1866) L.R. 2 C.P. 174; *Natal Land Co.* v. *Pauline Syndicate* [1904] A.C. 120, P.C. See Ziegel (Ed.), *Studies in Canadian Company Law* (1967), Chap. 6.
[69] *Infra*, Chap. 14, pp. 303, 304.

If, however, promoters are arranging for the company to take over someone else's business, the seller will certainly, and the promoter will probably, wish to have a binding agreement immediately. In this event the sale agreement will be made between the vendor and the promoters and it will be provided that the personal liability of the promoters is to cease when the company in process of formation is incorporated and enters into an agreement in similar terms, which, once again, will be referred to in the memorandum.

Agreements of this nature will be a necessary feature of nearly every promotion, and not only must the promoters make full disclosure to the company but, in addition, the company must give particulars of them in any prospectus [70] or statement in lieu.[71] Generally speaking, all material contracts must be disclosed unless entered into more than two years previously and in particular all those relating to property acquired or to be acquired by the company. Further details must, however, be left to the next chapter in which the process of flotation will be explained.

What in practice is a not infrequent source of trouble is that those engaged in the formation of a company cause contracts to be entered into ostensibly by the company but before it has in fact been formed. As we have seen, the company, when formed, cannot ratify or adopt the contract,[72] but the legal position of the promoter and the other party seems to depend on the terminology employed. If the contract is entered into by the promoter and signed by him " for and on behalf of XY Co. Ltd." then, according to the early case of *Kelner* v. *Baxter*,[73] the promoter will be personally liable. If, however, as is much more likely, the promoter signs the proposed name of the company, adding his own name to authenticate it (for example, " Leopold Newborne (London) Ltd. Leopold Newborne ") then, according to *Newborne* v. *Sensolid (Great Britain) Ltd.*[74] there is no contract at all. In that case it was the promoter (now director) of the company who attempted to enforce the agreement and although the defence was entirely unmeritorious (Sensolid wanted to escape from buying because the market had fallen), it may be thought that sympathy need not be wasted on Newborne and his company who were the cause of their misfortunes. But it appears from the judgments that the result would have been the same if the other party had wanted to enforce the contract. That this is indeed so has since been held by the High Court of Australia.[75]

---

[70] Sched. 4, Pt. I, paras. 9 and 14.
[71] Scheds. 3 and 5.
[72] Unless it enters into an entirely new contract. This, of course, does not mean that, in the absence of a new contract, the company or the other party can accept the delivery of the goods or payment without being under any obligation. In such a case there will clearly be a liability in tort for conversion or in quasi-contract for money had and received.
[73] *Supra.*
[74] [1954] 1 Q.B. 45, C.A.
[75] *Black* v. *Smallwood* [1966] A.L.R. 744 (Aust.H.C.). But it is difficult to see why the promoter should not be liable for breach of implied warranty of authority.

The legal position is obviously profoundly unsatisfactory. Many common law countries have now recognised, either by judge-made law or by statute, that the company when formed can validly adopt pre-incorporation contracts by unilateral act. The Jenkins Committee recommended that the British Act should follow suit, and that, unless and until the company did so adopt, the person who purported to act for the company should be entitled to sue and liable to be sued thereon.[76]

---

[76] Cmnd. 1749, para. 44.

CHAPTER 14

FLOTATIONS

SOMETIMES, but rarely, a public company is formed to start a new business or to work a new discovery. Most large commercial concerns, however, have grown from small family businesses which were originally incorporated as private companies, if incorporated at all. At some stage in the company's development the family decided to sell out in whole or in part, perhaps because they could no longer provide from their own resources the capital required for further expansion, or because the need to provide for death duties made it essential for them to invest in more readily realisable assets. At this stage the concern was converted into a public company and its securities offered to the public.

Today, this smooth progression from family concern to publicly owned company is less easily accomplished. For one thing a public issue will be prohibitively expensive unless the issue is a large one, so that there may be a hiatus between the stage when the family are still able and willing to retain full control, and the time when the public can economically be asked to take over. For another, the amount of " new money " available for investment in the hands of the public has increasingly become concentrated in the hands of institutional investors such as banks, insurance companies, unit trusts and trustees of pension funds. Many companies now try to avoid some of the expense of a public issue by placing the securities with these institutions instead of offering them to the public generally.

But institutions of this type naturally tend to be conservative in their investing policy. They cannot take too high a proportion of ordinary shares with fluctuating returns, nor are they prepared to incur undue risks by financing new and untried developments. Moreover, they are likely to insist on the securities being freely marketable, thus involving the company in the expense of obtaining a stock exchange quotation so that the securities become available to the public by purchase even though not by original subscription.

Two major needs have therefore been felt. The first of these is for some organisation able and willing to finance new projects in the early stage of their development and to nurse growing family concerns by privately providing finance until the time has come, by natural growth or amalgamation with other concerns, for a public issue to be made. Under Government encouragement an attempt has been made to meet this need by the formation of two corporations financed mainly by the banks. The first, the Finance Corporation for Industry, is designed to

283

support major projects of re-equipment and development, while the second, the Industrial and Commercial Finance Corporation, provides capital for small and medium-sized companies, where existing facilities are not readily available. More recently, these two semi-official bodies have been supplemented by others, sponsored by various banking and finance houses, which are intended to improve the facilities available for financing concerns until the time is ripe for a public issue. The second need arises directly from the burden of death duties which may force executors prematurely to break up the continuity of control of a private company by a sale to outside interests in order to raise sufficient cash to meet these duties. To meet this need, Estate Duties Investment Trust Ltd. (Edith) was formed in 1953 to provide an organisation of good standing and sound financial position prepared to purchase shares in private companies, to adopt a neutral position in its counsels, and to accept the position of a minority holder. When capital is provided from the sources described in this paragraph it may be possible to dispense with a market quotation and to retain the company for the time being as a private company. But if its business continues to expand it may be assumed that sooner or later its capital will be " floated off " to the general public.

This chapter is concerned primarily with the regulations which have to be complied with, whenever a public issue is made, in order to give the public the fullest possible information about the nature of the concern in which they are being invited to invest. Even if there is no general invitation, the law considers it vital that disclosure shall be made whenever a company is formed as, or converted into, a public company with a share capital, for there is then no legal limit to the number of persons who may acquire its shares. Hence, similar but modified regulations apply to such a case and these too will be discussed here. But with private companies this chapter is not concerned, for, since the public cannot become interested in their securities, the additional safeguards, required in other cases, can be dispensed with. But before the nature of these safeguards can be appreciated it is necessary to understand the various methods which a company may employ when it makes a public issue. Hence, as an introduction to this confusing branch of the law, these methods are briefly explained.

METHODS OF PUBLIC ISSUE [1]

Any company wishing to raise money from the public will almost certainly enlist the aid of one of the financial houses specialising in

---

[1] For a fuller description of the matters here discussed, see F. W. Paish, *Business Finance* (4th ed., 1968), Chap. VII (the whole of this short book may be read with advantage as background literature), and R. R. Pennington, *The Investor and the Law* (1968), Chaps. 6, 7, 15 and 18. Reference may also be made to Chap. IV of R. F. Henderson's *The New Issue Market* (Cambridge, 1951).

public issues.[2] The new issues market is now virtually monopolised by a small number of firms who are experts in this type of transaction and who either devote themselves entirely to it or who combine it with merchant banking and acting as company registrars or the like. Most of these firms are members of the Issuing Houses Association and their high repute, and their determination not to forfeit it, are probably the greatest safeguards which the public have. The nature of the role which they play differs somewhat according to the method of issue employed, but in most cases they will be associated with it either as principals or as agents of the company and, if it is unsuccessful, will incur a risk either to their pockets or their reputations, or both. Hence the close scrutiny which they give to issues which they sponsor is a far more effective restraint on fraudulent or uneconomic issues than any legal regulations.

Direct offers to public

The first method which the company can employ is itself to make a direct offer to the public by publishing a prospectus inviting subscriptions of the securities. If this is done the company will bear the risk of the issue being unsuccessful and will therefore have to arrange for it to be underwritten, *i.e.*, it will have to insure, by negotiating contracts whereby financial houses and syndicates agree to take up such part of the securities as are not applied for by the public.[3] The issuing house assisting the company in the issue will therefore probably appear in the prospectus (if at all) only as an underwriter. In all probability it will underwrite the whole issue and will reinsure by sub-underwriting. Under section 53 of the 1948 Act underwriters may be paid a commission not exceeding 10 per cent. even if this results in shares being issued to them at a discount.

This method, which formerly was the normal procedure, is now comparatively uncommon in the case of issues by companies, although normally adopted still by public authorities. It is generally described as an issue by prospectus and this terminology will be adopted here, with the warning that it is somewhat misleading since a prospectus in the legal sense will be published even if one of the other methods of issue is employed.

Offers for sale

The second method, now sometimes adopted in the case of large original issues, is for the company to sell the whole of the securities

---

[2] The issuing house must not be confused with the new issues department of a bank to which applications and subscription moneys are usually to be sent and which acts in a purely ministerial capacity in sending out allotment letters and checking the payments received. Details regarding issuing houses and their operations are given in *The Times Issuing House Year Book*.

[3] Some part of the issue may be " underwritten firm," *i.e.*, the underwriters may definitely subscribe for it.

to an issuing house which in turn publishes a prospectus inviting the public to purchase the securities from it at a slightly higher price. If the company adopts this course it has no responsibility for the success of the issue; it already has a binding contract whereby the issuing house has subscribed or agreed to subscribe for the securities, thereby, in effect, " underwriting firm " the whole issue. Doubtless the issuing house will insure itself against an unsuccessful issue by arranging underwriting on its own account. Apart from this, the main differences, from the point of view of the issuing house, are that it accepts primary responsibility for the prospectus and that it receives remuneration not by way of commission but by virtue of the profits which it makes on the sale.

It will be appreciated that the issuing house will not normally be registered as holder except in respect of such securities as are not taken up by the public. In practice, renounceable allotment letters will be issued either to the issuing house or directly by the company to the purchasers and underwriters. These enable the allottees to assign their rights to become shareholders [4] by signing forms of renunciation in favour of purchasers from them.

Offers by tender

Whichever method is adopted all the securities of the same class are normally offered to the public at the same fixed price. It is, however, possible to invite tenders and to sell to the highest bidder. Until recently this practice was not adopted by companies, though it sometimes was by statutory authorities, but now, in an attempt to ensure that the best possible price is obtained and to frustrate " stags " who apply for speculative purposes,[5] a new form of offer by tender has become popular. The normal method is to fix a minimum price and to provide that the securities will be allotted at the highest tendered price above this at which all the shares will be taken up. This ensures that all are issued at the same price and that wildly optimistic bidders do not have to pay the full price of their folly.[6]

Placings

Another method commonly adopted is for the company to arrange for the issuing house to purchase the securities and to " place " them with its clients or, alternatively, to " place " them without itself purchasing. If the first alternative is adopted the effect is identical with an offer for sale except that the securities are placed privately

---

4 They are not yet shareholders in the strict sense for they have not yet been entered on the share registers: see Chap. 17.
5 See further on stags, *infra*, p. 302.
6 On the other hand, it encourages those who want to be sure of obtaining shares to put in multiple applications at deliberately inflated prices in the knowledge that the issue price will in fact be determined by the realistic large applications of the institutional investors.

instead of being offered to the public generally. If the issuing house agrees to "place" without purchasing, the effect is similar to a prospectus issue, the issuing house acting as agents for the company in the disposal of the shares which, once again, is effected privately instead of by a general public offer.[7]

This method is, of course, very much cheaper than prospectus issues or offers for sale, but it is only feasible if the issue can be absorbed by a few selected institutions. Moreover, if the securities are to be quoted on a stock exchange, the latter will not permit the issue to be by way of placing, at any rate in the case of equity shares, unless it is so small that the expense of the former methods would be disproportionate. In other cases the view is taken that the public at large should be given an opportunity of subscribing at the issue price and not be forced to purchase on the market when, if all goes well, the shares will be at a premium.[8] Nevertheless, placings of this type are numerically far more common than either offers or direct prospectus issues and rival them in total size.

Normally the obtaining of a stock exchange quotation will be a necessary condition of the placing. In this event, steps to this end will have to be taken by the company; in other words, the placing will be coupled with a stock exchange introduction [9] and the whole transaction is generally described as "a stock exchange placing." In order to obtain a quotation, those handling the placing will have to make an adequate number of securities available for dealings on the stock exchange so that indirectly the public at large will be able to buy, although not necessarily at the placing price.

Rights and conversion issues and open offers

The above are the only methods available on the initial flotation of the company. But thereafter other methods of increasing popularity are available if the company wishes to raise further capital. The company may make an offer, not to the public at large, but to the existing members who are given rights to acquire shares of the new issue in proportion to their existing holdings. By so doing trouble

---

[7] "Issuing house" is here used in a wider sense; placings are often affected by stock-brokers who would not handle on their own a direct public issue: see Rules of London Stock Exchange, r. 164.

[8] Quotation at a premium during the first few weeks is the more likely since the right to the securities can be transferred by renunciation of renounceable allotment letters, thus avoiding the 1 per cent. transfer duty. The London Stock Exchange formerly placed a maximum period of six weeks on renounceability but this is omitted from the present rules, see *Requirements*, Appendix, Sched. III. Difficulties will be experienced with exchange control if renounceable letters of allotment remain in existence for more than six months (see Exchange Control (Deposit of Securities) (Exemption) Order 1968 (S.I. No. 79) and E.C. 10 (Third Issue) Appendix I), but in practice a much shorter period is chosen.

[9] Such an introduction may also take place subsequently to and independently of any issue when the existing holders wish a market to be made for the securities, probably to facilitate a placing or offer for sale by them.

and expense can be minimised and the assistance of an issuing house can sometimes be dispensed with. More new capital is raised by this method than by any other form of issue and in the case of issues of equity shares for cash the stock exchanges insist upon its being adopted by quoted companies unless the shareholders otherwise agree. The normal practice is to offer the shares upon rather more favourable terms than would be adopted on a direct issue to the public, so that the rights are almost certain to be taken up [10] either by the members or by those to whom they sell. But unless the bonus element is substantial it is customary, even in this case, to underwrite the issue through an issuing house. The usual practice will be to issue renounceable letters of right (analogous to renounceable allotment letters) to facilitate sales by members not wishing to retain.

It should perhaps be emphasised that although the costs of either a placing or rights issue will be far less than those of a prospectus issue or offer for sale, the latter may nevertheless be cheaper to the company in the sense that they may enable it to raise more money from an issue of the same nominal amount of securities. On a placing or rights issue the company is less likely to receive the full market price of the securities it issues.

The *modus operandi* described above is known as a " rights issue." A variation of it is the " conversion issue " when holders of one type of redeemable security (*e.g.,* debentures) are offered the right to convert into securities of another type (*e.g.,* ordinary shares) as an alternative to redemption. For all practical purposes the procedure is the same. Another variation is the " open offer "—an offer limited to the security holders of the company but not giving them definite rights proportionate to their existing holdings. In all these cases there will be no general invitation to the public but merely an offer by circular to the security holders concerned.

It should, perhaps, be mentioned that existing share- or debenture-holders, or other special classes (*e.g.,* employees of the company or

---

[10] If shares are offered at the quoted price of the existing shares the rights issue should have no effect on the quotation. If, however, they are issued at below the quoted price this will reduce the subsequent quotation. For example:

Present Share Capital	*Net Value of Assets*		*Quoted Price*
20,000	£40,000	=	£2 (approx.)

Add rights issue on one-for-one basis at 35s.

Increased Share Capital	*Net Value of Assets*		*Quoted Price*
40,000	£75,000 (*i.e.,* £40,000 + £35,000 proceeds of issue)	=	37s. 6d. (approx.)

If, therefore, a shareholder does not take up his rights he stands to lose 2s. 6d. per share. This argument remains basically valid even if, as is probable, the quoted price, being based on yield, is different from what it would be if based on the " net asset " value and, if the quoted price is less than the " net asset " value (as it may well be in circumstances where dividend limitation has been practised), dilution takes place even if the issue is at quoted price.

members of a profession peculiarly associated with its business) are sometimes given preferential rights to subscribe on a prospectus issue or offer for sale; that is to say, their applications may be met in full, before others, in the event of the issue being over-subscribed. Applications from the preferred classes are generally to be made on special forms (coloured pink) to facilitate the work of checking by the bank to which applications are made.

Bonus issues

A rights issue must be distinguished from a bonus or capitalisation issue which is not, in fact, a method of raising new capital but merely of increasing the nominal amount of the issued share capital by using undistributed profits to pay it up. It is mentioned only for the sake of completeness and because of the risk of confusion with a rights issue, particularly as the latter is said to contain a bonus element when issued below the market price of the existing securities. Moreover, many of the following rules apply equally to a bonus issue despite its purely nominal effect.

Issues on take-overs

The question of take-overs is dealt with more fully in Chapter 26. But one of the reasons why a new issue of securities may be made is to enable the company to acquire another company or its business. If the acquisition is to be for cash, the cash needed may well be raised by a normal offering by prospectus, offer for sale, placing or rights issue. But more often the securities of the acquiring company will be offered to the other company or to its shareholders as the price payable to them. In other words, the acquiring company will not so much be selling its shares, but rather be buying shares or assets and paying for them by issuing shares to the sellers. Nevertheless from a practical point of view such an issue raises precisely the same problems as an issue for cash or, *a fortiori*, as a conversion issue, and it is something of an anomaly that, as we shall see, the legal regulations applicable are very different.

REGULATIONS TO BE COMPLIED WITH ON PUBLIC ISSUES

Whichever method of issue is adopted three distinct sets of regulations may have to be complied with.

Treasury consent [11]

During the war years raising of capital was controlled under the Defence Regulations and thereafter this control was put on a semi-

---

[11] This can only be a brief summary of a complicated topic. For further details the reader is referred to Howard, *Exchange and Borrowing Control* (1948) with Supplement (1950).

permanent basis by the Borrowing (Control and Guarantees) Act 1946. Under this Act, Treasury consent is required if more than £10,000 is raised within a period of twelve months.[12] However, since 1958 this control has been virtually in abeyance since a general exemption has been given, the effect of which is that specific authorisation is not required for issues by companies resident in the United Kingdom.[13]

Of rather more immediate practical importance is the control exercised under the Exchange Control Act 1947, though here, too, the restraints have been greatly relaxed.[14] Under the Act, Treasury permission is needed (i) unless the prescribed evidence (a written declaration) is produced that the person to whom the securities are issued is resident in the Scheduled Territories (*i.e.*, the sterling area),[15] (ii) on an issue of bearer securities,[16] or (iii) on an issue which would have the effect of passing control of the company from persons resident in the United Kingdom to persons resident outside the United Kingdom.[17] Specific permission is still required in case (iii), but, subject to certain conditions and exceptions, general permission has been given for issues in the United Kingdom in the other two cases. As regards (i), issues may generally be made without obtaining the prescribed declaration,[18] so long, in most cases, as the documents are lodged by an authorised depositary.[19] There are, however, exceptions: for example, issues to persons outside the sterling area, issues of non-quoted securities or of quoted securities otherwise than for cash, or issues which would result in a non-United Kingdom resident acquiring 10 per cent. or more of the voting rights in the company.[20] As regards (ii), bearer securities may now be issued so long as they are not in exchange for registered securities existing before August 1963.[21] But in general all the documents have to be lodged by an authorised depositary and the securities have to be deposited with him.[22] The

---

[12] Borrowing (Control and Guarantees) Act 1946, s. 1.

[13] Control of Borrowing Order 1958 (S.R. & O. No. 1208 as amended by S.I.s No. 445 of 1959 and No. 69 of 1967). But the Bank of England must approve the timing of issues of £1 million or more: para. 8A (2) (*b*).

[14] The up-to-date position is set out in E.C. Notices issued from time to time by the Bank of England to authorised depositaries and now available on application to one's bank in a loose-leaf binder and described as *United Kingdom Exchange Control Manual*. The most important notice for present purposes is E.C. 10; references here are to the Third Issue (October 31, 1968).

[15] Exchange Control Act 1947, s. 8. For the form of declaration, see S.I. 1968 No. 1232.

[16] *Ibid*. s. 10.

[17] *Ibid*. s. 30 (2).

[18] E.C. 10 (Third Issue), para. 8.

[19] *Ibid*. para. 9. " Authorised depositaries " are banks, stock-brokers, solicitors and the like. The documents do not have to be lodged through them on a bonus issue, or on the issue of provisional documents on a rights issue: *ibid*.

[20] *Ibid*. para. 10.

[21] *Ibid*. paras. 11 and 13.

[22] *Ibid*. para. 12 and Appendix I. This, as we have seen, does not apply to renounceable allotment letters or letters of right which have not been in existence for more than six months: *ibid*. Nor does it apply to bearer shares issued under the Aims of Industry Scheme, but these are subject to strict control: see *ibid*. Appendix II.

relaxation of the former ban on bearer securities has not in fact led to public issues of them by United Kingdom companies.

Stock exchange regulations

In practice it will be necessary to arrange for the securities to be quoted on one or more stock exchanges, since otherwise they will not be freely marketable, and liquidity is one of the main attractions of shares and debentures as investments. Hence the issuing house will insist upon the company taking the necessary steps to obtain a quotation for, and permission to deal in, the securities which will involve compliance with the strict requirements of the exchanges. As a result the stock exchanges' rules, though not " law " in the sense that they lay down norms which will be enforced by the courts, are in practice at least as important as the rules laid down in the Companies Act.

The London Stock Exchange has always been the most important in the United Kingdom and its regulations afforded a model for the others, even though they may have lacked the resources to police them as effectively. After the London and the major provincial exchanges federated in 1965, they unified their requirements for admission of securities for quotation and these are now published, together with various memoranda of guidance, in the 1966 edition of what is sometimes described as the *Yellow Book* (yellow being the colour of its covers) but which is herein referred to as *Requirements*. The regulations themselves are set out in an Appendix [23] to the various memoranda which afford useful guides to the detailed contents of the Appendix and to the practice of the exchanges.[24] The Appendix is divided into two Sections and nine Schedules, the latter detailing the contents of the various documents required. Of the two Sections only the first, Section A, concerns us.[25] Part I of Section A, which is the most stringent, applies where no part of the company's capital is already quoted, Part II where some part is already quoted, and Part III where securities, already quoted on another Federated Exchange, are being introduced without any further issue. In all cases the basic principle is the same as the underlying philosophy of the Companies Act, namely, to ensure that full disclosure is made of all information needed to enable a potential investor to assess the worth of the securities. And the stock exchanges, unlike the Registrar of Companies when a prospectus is

[23] Based on the former (and present) App. 34 of the Rules of the London Stock Exchange.

[24] See especially, Memorandum 1 (*The Admission of Securities to Quotation*) and Memorandum 3 (*Acquisitions and Realisations and Bids and Offers*). These are supplemented from time to time by Notices.

[25] It covers issues by all bodies corporate to which the prospectus provisions of the Companies Act apply; this extends beyond registered companies: see 1948 Act, s. 435 and Sched. 14. Section B concerns issues by governments, local authorities and those statutory bodies to which the prospectus provisions of the Act do not apply.

registered with him, scrutinise the documents before they are finalised and do their best to see that they are clear and accurate. They also impose a rather arbitrary qualitative test by insisting that both the company and the issue concerned are of some size.[26]

Whenever Part I or Part II of the Appendix applies, a prospectus has to be published whatever may have been the method of issue or introduction employed. This must be approved in advance by the exchange and must give the information prescribed in Schedule II, Part A or B.[27] The prescribed information is generally similar to that required by Schedule 4 to the Companies Act, though in a few respects it is less extensive [28] and in others still stricter.[29] But whereas, as we shall see, the Act only requires a full Schedule 4 prospectus where there is a general offer to the public, the requirements of the stock exchanges are not so limited. Where the transaction is to be handled by way of placing or introduction, special permission has to be obtained [30] and the prescribed information normally has to be published in the form of an advertisement circulated in the statistical services of the Exchange Telegraph Company Ltd. and Moodies Services Ltd.,[31] and must bear the following legend [32]:

> "This Advertisement is issued in compliance with the Regulations of the Council of the Stock Exchange [London] for the purpose of giving information to the Public with regard to the Company. The Directors collectively and individually accept full responsibility for the accuracy of the information given and confirm, having made all reasonable enquiries, that to the best of their knowledge and belief there are no other facts the omission of which would make any statement in the Advertisement misleading." [33]

Normally, too, the prospectus or advertisement must be published in two leading newspapers.[34] The main case where this is not required is where the issue of securities of a quoted company is made by circular primarily to existing shareholders or employees.[35] But even in this case

---

[26] The minimum market value of the company must be £250,000 and of the issue £100,000: *Requirements*, App., Section A, Parts I and II, para. I.

[27] *Ibid.* App., Section A, Parts I and II, paras. II (A) and (B).

[28] It omits certain formal information required by Sched. 4 to the Act.

[29] There has been a continuous process of cross-fertilisation between the regulations of the exchanges and of the Act, and many of the present statutory rules first appeared in the regulations of the London Stock Exchange and were adopted by the legislature after they had been subjected to a period of trial by the exchange. One main respect in which the *Requirements* are more stringent is that they require an auditor's report on profits or losses for 10 years past (*Requirements*, App., Sched. II, Part A, paras. 21 and 22, and Part B, para. 14) whereas the Act requires this for only five years (1948 Act, Sched. 4, paras. 19–21).

[30] *Requirements*, App., Section A, Parts I and II, para. I.

[31] *Ibid.* para. II.

[32] *Ibid.* App., Sched. II, Parts A and B, para. 2.

[33] See *infra*, pp. 317, 320, for a discussion on whether this imposes legal liability on the directors.

[34] *Requirements*, App., Section A, Parts I and II, para. II (A) (i).

[35] *Ibid.* Part II, para. II (A) (i), note.

the contents of the circular must contain the information required in Schedule II, Part B, of the Appendix,[36] though some items need not be given on a bonus issue.[37]

Only when Part III of Section A of the Appendix applies, *i.e.*, where there is merely an introduction of securities already quoted on another Federated Exchange, are these requirements relaxed. Renewed publication of a prospectus or advertisement is not then required, that published on the initial introduction being accepted.[38]

The publication of an approved prospectus or advertisement, though the main, is far from being the only, requirement. Copies of various other documents must be submitted [39] and many of these are required to be in a particular form.[40] The articles of association and any debenture trust deed (or debentures) must contain certain prescribed provisions.[41] Moreover, when the company's securities are first quoted it must give a General Undertaking regarding its future behaviour towards its security holders, and towards the exchange, which must be given advance information on various matters and, in some cases, its approval sought.[42] Save in circumstances agreed by the stock exchange to be exceptional, equity share capital must not be issued for cash except to the existing equity shareholders.[43] Moreover, if the authorised capital is being increased prior to the issue the directors must state in the circular accompanying the notice of the meeting whether they have any present intention of issuing any part of the increase and, if the increase is by more than 25 per cent. of the authorised capital, must undertake that it will not be issued so as to change the nature or control of the business without the prior approval of the shareholders.[44]

The application for a quotation must be signed by a broker appointed by the company and, in the case of the London Exchange, supported by two jobbers [45] (except on a rights or bonus issue where securities of the company are already quoted [46]). This affords a further protection, for brokers and jobbers are as reluctant as issuing houses to be

---

[36] Contrast the position under the Companies Act, see *infra*, p. 298.

[37] *Requirements*, App., Section A, Part II, para. II (B).

[38] *Ibid.* Part III, para. II (A).

[39] *Ibid.* Parts I, II and III.

[40] For prescribed forms, see *ibid.* Scheds. I (applications), IV (documents of title), V (particulars of securities), VI (declaration of compliance) and IX (marketing statement on placings).

[41] *Ibid.* Sched. VII, Parts A and B.

[42] *Ibid.* Section A, Part I, para. III (H) (i). For the contents of the Undertaking, see *ibid.* Sched. VIII, Part A, and note that it includes the circulation of interim half-yearly profit statements: *ibid.* para. 5, and see Sched. VII, Part C. The scope of the Undertaking has been progressively widened but companies which have long been quoted may not be subject to the rigours of the latest version.

[43] *Ibid.* Sched. VIII, Part A, para. 15.

[44] *Ibid.* Memorandum 1, para. 6.

[45] *Ibid.* Section A, Parts I, II and III, para. II (A).

[46] *Ibid.* Part II, para. III (A).

associated with a dubious issue. Confirmation regarding the adequacy of working capital may also be required from the issuing house.[47]

The scrutiny of the stock exchanges is the second major safeguard of the interests of investors. It is directed mainly to checking the accuracy and completeness of the information given and not to assessing the financial merits of the offer. Nevertheless it is continuing, whereas that of the issuing house may cease once the securities have been successfully off-loaded on to the public.[48] By virtue of the General Undertaking given by the company the exchanges keep an eye on the company throughout its life and exercise a salutary influence through their power to suspend or cancel quotations [49] or to prohibit dealings.[50] Moreover, it is no longer wholly true to say that the Stock Exchange Requirements are not " law," for since 1948 they have received some recognition by the legislature. Under section 51 of the Act if a prospectus states that application is being made for a quotation,[51] any allotment or sale made in pursuance of the prospectus will be void unless application is made before the third day after the first issue of the prospectus and unless the application is granted. Otherwise the company or vendors must repay all money (which must meanwhile be kept in a separate bank account [52]), and if the company defaults its directors will be personally liable to repay with 5 per cent. interest unless they prove that the default was not due to their misconduct or negligence. Moreover, under section 39, an advertisement complying with the stock exchange regulations may in some circumstances be substituted for a full prospectus complying with Schedule 4 to the Act, and, under section 38, the requirements of the Act are relaxed on an issue of securities uniform with those quoted on a recognised stock exchange. These matters are dealt with more fully in the next part of this chapter.

Statutory provisions protecting investors

Finally, the company and those associated with the issue must comply with the rules of law embodied in the Companies Acts as supplemented by the Prevention of Fraud (Investments) Act 1958 and the Protection of Depositors Act 1963.

---

[47] *Ibid.* Part I, para. III (R) and Part II, para. III (M).
[48] This may, of course, take some time if the bulk of the issue has been left with them as underwriters.
[49] See Rules of London Stock Exchange, r. 159 (7).
[50] *Ibid.* r. 165. This, of course, is more help to potential investors than to the existing members. It is, however, feared by directors who know that it is likely to lead to a revolt against their management, and, probably, to the appointment of a Board of Trade inspector.
[51] This statement must be made if a quotation is in fact being sought: *Requirements,* App., Sched. II, Parts A, B and C, para. 3.
[52] This, it seems, imposes a trust on the moneys so that they can be followed by the subscribers who are not left solely to a personal claim as creditors: *Re Nanwa Gold Mines Ltd.* [1955] 1 W.L.R. 1080 at p. 1085. A trust is definitely imposed if the company can be deemed to have promised the subscribers that the moneys will be earmarked in accordance with the section: *ibid.*

Under the Companies Act

The main regulations are contained in the prospectus and allotment provisions (ss. 37–55 and 417–423) of the Companies Act 1948 and Schedules 3, 4 and 5. These are extremely confusing, largely because they have grown up haphazardly as new safeguards have been added to meet dangers revealed by experience. But the general aim is clear, namely, to ensure that the company gives to the public the essential minimum of information about its position when it is launched into the world, and that whenever it offers its securities to the public it fully and fairly discloses the relevant facts so that the risk of the investment can be assessed. In the explanation which follows, the statutory order will be departed from since it does not appear to be based on any principle of logic or convenience; an attempt at re-arrangement and co-ordination is long overdue. Except where otherwise stated these provisions apply not only to companies registered under the Companies Acts but also to chartered and statutory companies.[53]

(i) **Scope of the provisions.** The prospectus provisions deal primarily with invitations (a) to the public, (b) by or on behalf of a company, (c) to subscribe or purchase (d) the company's shares or debentures.

(a) " Public " is defined extremely widely; by virtue of section 55 (1) it includes " any section of the public, whether selected as members or debentureholders of the company concerned or as clients of the person issuing the prospectus or in any other manner." Hence invitations to participate in rights, conversion or bonus issues are clearly included, as are offers to place securities with the clients of an issuing house or broker. Indeed, the definition is so wide that, unless some limitation were imposed, it would be impossible for any company ever to issue any shares or debentures without making a public issue. And as a result no company could be a private one. Hence subsection (2) limits its ambit by providing that :

> " The foregoing subsection shall not be taken as requiring any offer or invitation to be treated as made to the public if it can properly be regarded in all the circumstances, as not being calculated to result, directly or indirectly, in the shares or debentures becoming available for subscription or purchase by persons other than those receiving [it], or otherwise as being a domestic concern of the persons making and receiving it."

And it adds that, in particular, provisions relating to private companies shall be construed accordingly.

It is therefore clear that an invitation by or on behalf of a private

---

[53] Companies Act 1948, s. 435 and Sched. 14, and Companies (Unregistered Companies) Regulations 1967 (S.I. No. 1876).

company to a few of the promoter's friends and relations will not be deemed to be an offer to the public. Nor, generally, will an offer which can only be accepted by the shareholders of a particular company.[54] On the other hand it is equally clear that an offer of securities in a public company even to a handful of people may be an offer to the public if it is calculated (which presumably means " likely " rather than " intended ") to lead to the securities being subscribed (*i.e.*, applied for on original allotment) or purchased (*i.e.*, bought after original allotment) by persons other than those receiving the initial offer. In particular, if securities are to be issued under renounceable allotment letters or letters of right the invitation to take them up must be deemed to be made to the public, since these securities are obviously liable to be subscribed or purchased by others. Equally, if a purely private placing, without renounceable allotment letters, is nevertheless coupled with a stock exchange advertisement, the latter is obviously calculated to lead to purchases by persons other than those with whom the securities are originally placed. Hence the totality of the documents constituting the invitation will collectively be deemed to be a prospectus, which is defined to include any " notice, circular, advertisement or other invitation." [55]

(b) In general, the provisions of the Companies Act are restricted to cases where the invitation is made by or on behalf of the company, or in relation to an intended company.[56] Prima facie, therefore, they would only affect direct prospectus, rights, bonus and conversion issues, and not offers for sale or placings. In fact, however, they are greatly extended in their ambit by section 45, which provides that where a company allots or agrees to allot any securities with a view to their being offered for sale to the public[57] " any document by which the offer for sale . . . is made shall for all purposes be deemed to be a prospectus issued by the company." This is clearly wide enough to include issues by an offer for sale. It will also include placings, unless of a purely domestic nature without either renounceable allotment letters

---

54 Despite the definition of " public " in s. 55 (1), this will apparently be regarded as of " domestic concern " within the meaning of s. 55 (2), unless the shares are to be issued under renounceable allotment letters: *Governments Stock and Other Securities Invest. Co.* v. *Christopher* [1956] 1 W.L.R. 237 at 242.

55 See definition of " prospectus " in s. 455. Although the Act does not expressly say so, it seems clear that its prospectus provisions only apply where there is a written document of some sort. Purely oral share-hawking is regulated only by the anti-fraud provisions in s. 13 of the Prevention of Fraud (Investments) Act 1958 and s. 19 of the Theft Act 1968, considered *infra*, Chap. 15. The Jenkins Committee drew attention to the dangers of advertising on commercial television but thought that this was adequately controlled by the rules of the I.T.A.: Cmnd. 1749, para. 246.

56 Although, as already pointed out, it is not now the practice to issue a public invitation until after the incorporation, the promoters may seek to prepare the ground, and will have to secure that at least two shares are taken upon formation. The promoters must be careful how far they go, for the sections are still framed to cover invitations made by them if they cast their net too widely.

57 Unless the contrary is proved, an offer for sale within six months after the agreement to allot. or before the whole consideration for the allotment has been received by the company, is evidence (presumably sufficient evidence) that the allotment was with a view to the offer to the public: s. 45 (2).

or a stock exchange introduction; if the placing is not a merely domestic concern the placing letters and stock exchange advertisement will have to be treated as prospectuses issued by or on behalf of the company.

On the other hand, a mere stock exchange introduction of shares already issued,[58] not coupled with any issue, offer for sale or placing, will be outside the ambit of the Act; it is true that the mere fact that there is an advertisement is calculated to lead to purchases of the securities, but no offer of any sort has been made to anyone, certainly not by or on behalf of the company or as a result of an allotment by the company with a view to an offer.[59] Where a public offer is made by shareholders, as opposed to the company, in circumstances not coming within section 45, it appears that certain of the prospectus provisions may apply but not others.[60]

(c) The invitation must be to " subscribe or purchase." [61] " Subscribe " denotes acquiring securities by allotment from the company, " purchase " a subsequent acquisition from the original allottee or a subsequent holder, in either case for a cash payment.[62] Hence when shares are issued as the price of other assets (for example, shares of another company being taken over), the prospectus provisions of the Companies Act do not apply.[63] Such legal control as there is in the latter case is under the Prevention of Fraud (Investments) Act 1958.[64] The Jenkins Committee recommended that this anomaly should be removed by extending the definition of a prospectus so that it would cover documents offering securities for a consideration other than cash, but that in the case of take-over offers compliance with rules which would be made legally binding on all take-overs [65] should be deemed sufficient compliance with the prospectus provisions.[66]

(d) The invitation must relate to " shares or debentures of a company." [67] Despite the fact that " ' debenture ' includes . . . any . . . securities of a company whether constituting a charge on the assets of the company or not," [68] it appears that rights to the repayment of money deposited with a company are not, *per se*, securities, so that advertisements for deposits are not subject to the prospectus provisions of the

---

58 If the original issue was to the public a prospectus will then have been published, and if not a statement in lieu of prospectus will have been filed.
59 The existing holders, who will necessarily have made some arrangement with the jobbers, will have to pay regard to the provisions of the Prevention of Fraud Act (*infra*), but the transaction will normally come under one of its exemptions.
60 See *infra*, p. 301.
61 See definition of " prospectus " in 1948 Act, s. 455.
62 *Arnison* v. *Smith* (1889) 41 Ch.D. 348, C.A.; *Re V. G. M. Holdings Ltd.* [1942] Ch. 235, C.A.; *Governments Stock & Other Securities Invest. Co.* v. *Christopher* [1956] 1 W.L.R. 237.
63 *Governments Stock & Other Securities Invest. Co.* v. *Christopher, supra.*
64 See pp. 304, 305 and Chap. 26, *infra*.
65 As emphasised in Chap. 26, *infra*, the present rules under the 1958 Act apply as a matter of strict law only to a small minority of take-overs.
66 Cmnd. 1749, para. 237.
67 See definition of " prospectus " in 1948 Act, s. 455, and the various prospectus provisions.
68 See definition of " debenture " in 1948 Act, s. 455.

Act.[69] Nor are they " securities " within the ambit of the Prevention of Fraud (Investments) Act 1958.[70] This meant that finance companies, however dubious their antecedents, could freely advertise for deposits, a freedom which led to a number of grave scandals until it was controlled by the Protection of Depositors Act 1963.[71]

(ii) **Authentication of prospectuses.** The Act provides that any prospectus, as above defined, issued by or on behalf of the company or in relation to an intended company, shall be dated,[72] and that before its issue [73] a copy shall be filed with the Registrar of Companies and signed by or on behalf of any person named therein as a director or intended director.[74] If the prospectus includes a statement purporting to be made by an expert [75] he must consent, the prospectus must state that he has done so and not withdrawn his consent,[76] and his consent must be filed with the Registrar.[77] The prospectus must also state that a copy has been delivered to the Registrar.[78]

(iii) **Form of prospectuses issued generally.** The Act then imposes additional requirements in respect of " prospectuses issued generally," *i.e.*, to persons who are not existing members or debentureholders of the company.[79] In such cases the prospectus must comply strictly with Schedule 4,[80] that is to say, it must state the matters specified in Part I thereof and set out the reports specified in Part II. Any condition purporting to bind applicants to waive compliance or binding them with notice of any matter not disclosed is void.[81] There are only two exceptions to the rule requiring a full compliance with the Schedule in the case of a general issue. The first is where the shares or debentures are in all respects uniform with those already issued and quoted on a

---

69 This seems never to have been tested in the courts, perhaps because of the embarrassment that that would have caused the genuine banks. It would have been difficult to sustain the argument that deposits were " securities " in the light of the definition in the 1958 Act: see next note.
70 See definition in s. 26 which includes them only if the deposit is with an industrial and provident society or a building society.
71 See p. 306, *infra*.
72 s. 37. This date is rebuttably presumed to be the true date of publication which is of importance in connection with certain items of information which must be disclosed: see, *e.g.*, Sched. 4, paras. 9 (1) (*c*), 14 and 19 *et seq.*
73 For a somewhat inconclusive discussion of the meaning of " issue," see *Nash* v. *Lynde* [1929] A.C. 158, H.L.
74 s. 41.
75 Defined as including " engineer, valuer, accountant and any other person whose profession gives authority to a statement made by him ": s. 40 (3). By virtue of Sched. 4, and the S. E. *Requirements* a statement by an accountant will be required in most cases.
76 s. 40 (1).
77 s. 41 (1).
78 s. 41 (2).
79 See definition in s. 39 (1) (*a*), and s. 38 (5) (*a*). It makes no difference that the existing members may have a right to renounce; indeed, if they do not the document may not be a prospectus within the meaning of the Act: see note 54, *supra*.
80 s. 38 (1).
81 s. 38 (2).

prescribed stock exchange [82]; the second relates to the grant of a
" certificate of exemption " by a prescribed stock exchange.[83] As regards
the latter, section 39 provides that if an application is to be made for
a quotation, the stock exchange may certify that, having regard to the
size and other circumstances of the issue and to the persons to whom it
is to be made, compliance with the Schedule would be unduly burdensome. If this certificate is granted and an advertisement complying with
the regulations of the stock exchange is duly published, the advertisement will be deemed to be a prospectus complying with the Schedule.
As we have seen, the Stock Exchange *Requirements* are more stringent [84]
but are somewhat shorter, and some expense can be saved if only one
set of regulations has to be complied with instead of two.[85]

The matters which have to be stated to comply with the Schedule
include details of the share capital, directors and their interests, auditors,
underwriting commission, preliminary expenses, payments to promoters,
and material contracts, but certain details can be dispensed with if the
issue is made more than two years after the company is entitled to
commence business.[86] The requirement which causes the most trouble
is that relating to material contracts, for the Act nowhere defines the
meaning of " material "; presumably the test is whether mention of the
contract would be likely to affect in any way (however slight) an intelligent appraisal of the securities offered.[87] Nevertheless, the appropriate
paragraph (14) excludes contracts entered into in the ordinary course
of the company's business *or* more than two years before the date of
issue of the prospectus. This, however, does not mean that contracts
more than two years old can necessarily be ignored. If the contract
relates to property bought by the company, details may have to be given
under another paragraph, (9), unless the purchase was *completed* more
than two years previously. Moreover, as we shall see, there is a general
obligation not to make statements which are misleading in their form
and context, and the failure to mention an important continuing contract,

[82] s. 38 (5) (*b*). Not all the Federated Exchanges are prescribed but only the London
Stock Exchange, the Midlands and Western Stock Exchange Association, the
Northern Stock Exchange Association and the Scottish Stock Exchange Association
(the last three were formed by mergers of a number of provincial exchanges as part
of the federation scheme): Board of Trade, *General Annual Report on Companies*,
1967.
[83] The stock exchanges prescribed for this purpose are now the same as those prescribed
under s. 38: see note 82.
[84] The Jenkins Committee recommended that the provisions of the Schedule should be
extended to accord more closely to the Stock Exchange *Requirements* (Cmnd. 1749,
paras. 243 and 244) and that the Board of Trade should be empowered to amend it
by statutory instrument (*ibid*. para. 245).
[85] The Jenkins Committee recommended that s. 39 should be extended so as to enable
partial, as well as complete, exemption from compliance with Sched. 4 to be given
and so as to empower the Board of Trade to grant exemption when no quotation was
being sought (Cmnd. 1749, para. 249) but that it should be provided that any form of
application must be accompanied by a prospectus complying with the conditions of
the exemption: *ibid*. para. 252 (k).
[86] Sched. 4, para. 22.
[87] If those issuing the prospectus are anxious to omit any reference to a particular
contract this is cogent evidence that it is material.

however long ago it was originally entered into, may well render other statements misleading. Copies of material contracts requiring disclosure must be filed with the Registrar.[88]

Another vital matter which has to be mentioned on an issue of shares to the public is *the minimum subscription*. This is an estimate by the directors of the minimum amount required to be raised to finance any purchase intended to be defrayed out of the proceeds of the issue, plus preliminary expenses and working capital.[89] Section 47 provides that if, on a first issue of the company's shares to the public, this amount is not in fact subscribed and the sum payable on application (which must not be less than 5 per cent. of the nominal value [90]) duly paid, the company shall not proceed to an allotment and all moneys shall be returned.[91] The object of these provisions is to prevent the company getting under way until it has raised the capital needed to carry out the objects in which it has invited the public to participate; it would obviously be iniquitous to force an applicant, who has accepted an invitation to participate in a £1 million issue for the purpose of buying Wembley Stadium, to sink his capital in a company which has only raised enough money to buy a suburban villa. They also afford protection to the creditors by ensuring that a limited company is not able to incur commitments if it is grossly under-capitalised. In this respect they supplement the rules relating to the raising and maintaining of capital as a guarantee fund for creditors—rules which, as has already been pointed out,[92] do not on their own ensure that the capital raised is adequate for the company's needs. Hence the need to state a minimum subscription applies only to an issue of shares—not to an issue of debentures, for debentureholders as creditors are intended to be protected by ensuring that their debtor-company has an adequate paid-up capital to support it. It is, of course, theoretically true that a company might launch itself with a small share capital privately held and seek to raise the whole of its working capital by a public issue of debentures, and in that event there is no legal assurance that the minimum amount required will ever be subscribed. However, those who have in fact subscribed for the debentures will have the legal remedies of a creditor (generally with security) and should therefore be able to get their money back.

In practice, of course, any risk of not reaching the minimum subscription is avoided by underwriting, which normally ensures that the

[88] s. 41 (1) (*b*). If the company is required to hold a statutory meeting (see *infra*) it must not vary any contract referred to in the prospectus except with the consent of the meeting: s. 42.

[89] Sched. 4, para. 4.

[90] s. 47 (3). This 5 per cent. minimum applies to any issue of shares to the public and not merely to the first: s. 47 (6).

[91] There are provisions, similar to those in s. 51 (*supra*, p. 294), relating to the personal liability of directors in the event of default by the company. If an allotment is made in breach of the section it is voidable within one month: s. 49.

[92] Chap. 6, *supra*.

whole issue (and not merely the minimum subscription) will be taken up. These provisions, however, serve the useful purpose of making underwriting virtually compulsory and not merely prudent. And in practice an issue of debentures will also be underwritten.

The reports required by Schedule 4 are those by the company's auditors on the financial position of the company and its subsidiaries (if any) [93] and by accountants named in the prospectus on any business to be acquired.[94] The statutory provisions require these reports to cover the preceding five years but this is in fact extended to ten years by the Stock Exchange *Requirements*.[95] If the auditors or accountants make any adjustments of figures in the accounts they must indicate that they have done so [96] and a written statement of their reasons must be filed with the Registrar.[97]

If section 45 applies to an offer for sale, the prospectus must give additional details showing the price paid to the company for the shares or debentures by the issuing house which offers them to the public and the place and time at which the contract between the issuing house and the company may be inspected.[98]

Section 38 (3) provides that no application forms for shares or debentures shall be issued unless accompanied by a prospectus which complies with Schedule 4 or is deemed to comply by virtue of a certificate of exemption. This subsection is subject to the general limitation in section 38 (5) excluding issues to existing members or debentureholders and issues of securities uniform with those quoted on a prescribed stock exchange. And it does not apply to a bona fide invitation to enter into an underwriting agreement or in relation to securities not offered to the public.[99] But it is apparently not limited to issues made by or on behalf of the company or in relation to an intended company and to issues deemed to be so made by virtue of section 45. If this interpretation is correct, it means that an offer for sale or placing (unless strictly private) made by existing holders always imposes an obligation on them to publish a formal prospectus [1] even though the original issue by the company was not made with this in view. But it seems that in the latter case the prospectus will not have to be registered, since section 41 is definitely limited to company issues.[2]

[93] Sched. 4, paras. 19–21.
[94] *Ibid.* para. 20.
[95] *Supra*, p. 292n.
[96] Sched. 4, para. 29.
[97] s. 41 (1) (*b*) (ii).
[98] s. 45 (3).
[99] s. 38 (3), proviso. For the very wide definition of " public," see *supra*, pp. 295, 296.
[1] See *infra*, Chap. 15, pp. 336–338. This will clearly be so if the existing holders had been " engaged or interested in the formation of the company," for the whole of s. 38 is expressed to apply in such circumstances: s. 38 (1). They might, in any case, be bound to do so under the Prevention of Fraud (Investments) Act 1958, *infra*.
[2] In practice it will be prudent for the company to register it, if application is being made for a quotation. Such application will have to be made by a broker appointed by the company which will necessarily have participated in the preparation of the

(iv) **Acceptance and revocation of applications.** Further, section 50 provides that when a general prospectus has been issued, applications [3] may not be converted into binding contracts until the beginning of the third working day after issue or such later time as may be specified in the prospectus as the time of opening the subscription lists.[4] The object of this is, of course, to give time for consideration, consultation and the study of Press comments before submission of applications.[5] The section further provides that applications shall not be revocable until after the *expiration* of the third working day thereafter.[6] This is designed to curtail the activities of " stags," who apply hoping to sell for a quick profit if the securities rise but who try to revoke their applications if a fall seems likely. Provided the applications are accepted before the expiration of the third day after the opening of the lists, " stags " will now be bound to take up the shares applied for whether they like it or not.[7]

Section 50 specifically applies to all general prospectuses, whether issued by the company or by existing holders on an offer for sale or placing,[8] but not where a certificate of exemption has been given.[9] Apart from this there is no requirement either under the Act or the Stock Exchange *Requirements* to fix a date for the closing of the lists, but in practice this is always done when securities are to be quoted. But there have been issues of unquoted securities which have remained

---

advertisement. It will, therefore, be difficult for the company to disprove that the prospectus was not issued (in part) on its behalf. An interesting illustration occurred in connection with the denationalisation of transport. The British Transport Commission made a public invitation for tenders for the purchase as one unit of all the shares in its parcels delivery company—B.R.S. (Parcels) Ltd.—a private company. The invitation was in the form of a prospectus complying with Sched. 4 and was registered " on the footing that [it] . . . is a prospectus to which s. 41 applies ": see *The Times*, October 25, 1955. This is probably the only case in which shares in a private company have been the subject of a public offering, but the offer did not affect its status as a private company for IT had not made any public invitation.

[3] *i.e.*, applications made pursuant to the prospectus. An underwriting agreement would, of course, be binding. In underwriting and sub-underwriting agreements it is customary irrevocably to appoint someone to apply for the shares left with the (sub)underwriters. This authority, being coupled with an interest, cannot be revoked: *Carmichael's Case* [1896] 2 Ch. 643, C.A.; *Pole's Case* [1920] 2 Ch. 341, C.A. As *Carmichael's* case shows, this is an effective way of protecting the company even if the underwriting contract is entered into before its incorporation.

[4] subss. (1)–(4) and (6).

[5] A waiting period of only two days seems inadequate but the Jenkins Committee rejected a suggestion that it should be extended: Cmnd. 1749, para. 238.

[6] subss. (5) and (6). But applications may be revoked earlier if some person responsible for the prospectus gives notice under s. 43 (*infra*, Chap. 15, p. 331 *et seq.*) disclaiming responsibility.

[7] The Jenkins Committee recommended that the wording should be clarified and the period slightly extended by providing that applications are irrevocable from the date of issue of the prospectus until the expiration of seven working days thereafter: Cmnd. 1749, para. 239.

[8] subs. (4).

[9] subs. (7). It is not easy to understand the reason behind this subsection. The stock exchange can ensure that the company complies with the " waiting period " provisions since this can be made a condition of the certificate of exemption. But it cannot protect the company against withdrawals of applications, for without statutory authority offers cannot be made irrevocable. The Jenkins Committee recommended the repeal of subs. (7): Cmnd. 1749, para. 242.

" on tap " indefinitely. To guard against the risk of the public subscribing on the basis of out-of-date prospectuses, the Jenkins Committee recommended that a time limit of three months should be imposed.[10]

(v) **Foreign companies.** All the above provisions apply only to issues of securities of companies incorporated under the Companies Acts [11] and to unregistered companies, incorporated in Great Britain, having a principal place of business there, and carrying on a business for gain.[12] But they are, in effect, extended by Part X of the Act to companies incorporated outside Great Britain which issue securities here. The relevant sections (417–423) do not require detailed consideration. Briefly they make compulsory the publication of a prospectus complying with Schedule 4, and the registration of any prospectus, in all cases where this would be required of an English company. There is a similar provision for certificates of exemption.

(vi) **Statements in lieu of prospectuses.** The foregoing discussion of the statutory rules has assumed that the securities of a company have in fact been issued to the public. But this need not necessarily ever happen even in the case of a public company, or it may not happen until long after its formation or conversion from a private company. Nevertheless, section 48 provides that a public company having a share capital which does not issue a prospectus on its formation or which publishes a prospectus but does not proceed to allotment [13] must not allot any of its shares or debentures unless, at least three days before, it has filed with the Registrar a statement in lieu of prospectus complying with Schedule 5. Section 30 and Schedule 3 contain similar provisions applying when a private company converts into a public one and does not issue a prospectus within fourteen days. These provisions were inserted in the Act at a time when placings and offers for sale were not covered by the prospectus provisions and they now fulfil no useful purpose in the light of sections 45 and 55. The Jenkins Committee recommended their repeal.[14]

(vii) **Trading certificate, statutory report, statutory meeting and consents of directors.** As a further sanction to secure compliance with the provisions outlined above, it is provided by section 109 that a public company cannot begin to carry on business until one of the directors or the secretary has made a statutory declaration that the various requirements have been fulfilled, and the Registrar has issued a certificate,

---

[10] Cmnd. 1749, para. 240.
[11] See definitions of " company " and " existing company " in s. 455.
[12] s. 435 and Sched. 14.
[13] The abortive prospectus will, of course, already have been filed.
[14] Cmnd. 1749, paras. 247, 248 and 252 (j).

commonly known as the trading certificate, that it is entitled to commence business. Until then any contract is provisional and only becomes binding on the company as from the date of the trading certificate,[15] which is extremely inconvenient. Moreover, under section 130, the company has to make a detailed report (the statutory report) to the members certifying the result of the flotation, and to convene a general meeting (the statutory meeting) for a date not less than one month or more than three from the date when it was entitled to commence business. At this meeting the members present are entitled to discuss any matters relating to the company's formation or arising out of the statutory report. Finally, under section 181, there has to be filed with the Registrar consents to act by the directors and confirmation that they have taken up and agreed to pay for any qualification shares.

But none of these requirements applies to a private company.[16] Moreover, it can easily convert itself from a private to a public company; it merely has to pass a special resolution deleting from its articles one or more of the three essential restrictions entitling it to be a private company. It will thereby avoid many of the requirements needed if it had originally formed as a public company. Hence it has become the common practice to adopt this method, even though the conversion is to take place immediately. As a result sections 109, 130 and 181 have become obsolete and, as this seems to have harmed no one, the Jenkins Committee recommended their repeal.[17]

Under the Prevention of Fraud (Investments) Act 1958

It will be appreciated that the rules of the Companies Act apply primarily to public issues of securities by the company. Although, as already emphasised, they may also regulate public offers for sale or placings by existing holders, in general they do not affect subsequent dealings. Nor, as we have seen, do they regulate issues for a consideration other than cash, such as issues on a take-over. These matters are, however, subject to a measure of legal control under the 1958 Act, which re-enacts the earlier Act of 1939 as amended.

This Act contains provisions for regulating the business of dealing in securities by those who are not members of a recognised stock exchange or otherwise exempted. Dealers and their representatives are required to be licensed,[18] and under section 7 the Board of Trade may make rules for regulating their conduct. The Licensed Dealers (Conduct of Business) Rules 1960,[19] made under this section, contain provisions regarding the contents of all written[20] offers made by a licensed dealer

---

[15] s. 109 (4).   [16] ss. 109 (7), 130 (10) and 181 (5).
[17] Cmnd. 1749, para. 65.
[18] Prevention of Fraud (Investments) Act 1958, s. 1.
[19] S.I. No. 1216 of 1960.
[20] Unwritten offers are subject only to the anti-fraud provisions in s. 13: see p. 313, *infra*.

either to acquire or dispose of securities, and include particularly detailed provisions regarding the contents of take-over offers. Although in practice few take-over offers are made through licensed dealers, the Rules are generally observed in other circumstances also. If, as is commonly the case, the offer is made through an exempted dealer,[21] such as an issuing house, or through a stockbroker on a recognised exchange, he will be expected to observe the rules and will risk losing his exemption or being disciplined by the exchange if he does not. If, another alternative, the offer is made by the offeror company itself [22] the consent of the Board of Trade will be needed to avoid a breach of section 14 of the Act which controls the distribution of circulars relating to investments; and the Board will consent only if the Rules are complied with. If the offeror company is a quoted one, it will be expected to observe the Memorandum of Guidance on Acquisitions and Bids and Offers, the second part of which substantially repeats the Rules and, indeed, amplifies them.[23]   Hence, in an anomalous and indirect fashion,[24] take-over offers are now subject to legal control, a control supplemented by the *Requirements* of the Stock Exchange, and by the *City Code on Take-overs and Mergers* [25] and the Panel which tries, as yet not wholly successfully, to see that it is observed. All these matters are dealt with in some detail in Chapter 26 and need not concern us further at this stage.

The ambit of the Act is, however, much wider than the control of take-overs. Section 14, in effect, forbids the distribution or possession for purposes of distribution of any document offering to acquire or dispose of securities [26] unless the document is a prospectus complying or deemed to comply [27] with Schedule 4 to the Companies Act [28] or unless the person in question is a member of one of the categories of persons authorised to deal in securities.[29]   The main categories are: members of a recognised stock exchange or recognised association of

---

[21] Prevention of Fraud (Investments) Act 1958, s. 16: see *infra*.

[22] Either directly or through the board of directors of the offeree company: the exception from the prohibition in s. 14 (*infra*) of distributions of circulars by a company to its own shareholders is not regarded as covering this.

[23] *Requirements*, Memorandum 3 at p. 17.

[24] The Jenkins Committee recommended that the system of control should be rationalised: see p. 309, *infra*.

[25] Obtainable from the Secretary, The Issuing Houses Association. The present edition is that of April 28, 1969.

[26] Prevention of Fraud (Investments) Act 1958, s. 14, which incorporates the wide classification of transactions specified in s. 13. The wording of s. 14 suggests that it applies only if the circulation is intended to be to more than one person. Newspaper advertisements are included: s. 14 (4). The Jenkins Committee recommended the clarification of this subsection: see Cmnd. 1749, para. 255. They also recommended that the position of circulars giving advice should be clarified by the recognition of a separate category of licensed investment adviser: *ibid*. para. 263.

[27] Because of a certificate of exemption under the Companies Act, s. 39: see *supra*, p. 299.

[28] s. 14 (2).

[29] s. 14 (3).

dealers; those issuing houses, merchant banks and the like who are declared by the Board of Trade under section 16 to be exempted dealers; and licensed dealers. Circulars of a company to its members, employees or creditors or to those of a subsidiary company and relating to securities of the company or the subsidiary are also exempted.[30] In all other cases, however, there can be no distribution without the consent of the Board of Trade.[31]

The effect of section 14 is to close most of the gaps left by the prospectus provisions of the Companies Act as respects disposal of securities and to introduce regulation of offers to acquire as well as offers to dispose. As regards disposals, the section deals primarily with dealings after the securities have been issued,[32] but puts beyond doubt that, whatever may be the position under the Companies Act, a placing by a company will have to be accompanied by a full prospectus unless undertaken through one of the authorised classes of dealers. As regards offers to acquire, it covers a field untouched by the Companies Act. But, in the case of both disposals and acquisitions, the basic approach is different from that of the Companies Act. The latter permits anyone to participate in an issue of securities so long as he complies with the prospectus provisions. The 1958 Act ensures that there is no subsequent disposal or acquisition unless members of the public are approached through a reputable professional dealer. So long as this is so, there is less effort to control in detail the amount of disclosure. Only licensed dealers, a relatively unimportant category, are subject to legal regulation regarding what must be disclosed,[33] although, as we have seen, the other classes of dealers are expected to conform where appropriate, especially as regards take-over offers. To that extent only will members of the public be entitled to something analogous to a prospectus whenever they are invited to buy or sell securities.

Under the Protection of Depositors Act 1963

The main type of invitation not clearly covered either by the prospectus provisions of the Companies Act or by the Prevention of Fraud (Investments) Act is an invitation to deposit money with a company. This loophole was stopped by the Protection of Depositors Act 1963.[34] Subject to various exceptions,[35] advertisements inviting

---

[30] s. 14 (3) (*a*) (iii).
[31] s. 14 (2).
[32] But " securities " within the meaning of the Act has been held to include those of a company in course of formation: *R.* v. *Hamid* [1945] K.B. 540, C.C.A.
[33] Under the Licensed Dealers (Conduct of Business) Rules 1960, *supra.*
[34] Amended by the Companies Act 1967, Sched. 8, Part VII, in the light of that Act's abolition of the exempt private company and general extension of the Board of Trade's powers of investigation.
[35] Protection of Depositors Act 1963, s. 2 (2)–(4). The exceptions include deposits with a banking or discount company (*i.e.,* one " which satisfies the Board of Trade that it ought to be treated for the purposes of this Act as a banking company or a

the public to deposit money are prohibited, unless they comply with regulations made by the Board of Trade [36] and the accounts required by the Act [37] have been duly delivered before the issue of the advertisement, or unless specific permission by the Board of Trade has been given.[38] The regulations so made [39] detail the information to be given in advertisements with the result that, as under the Licensed Dealers (Conduct of Business) Rules, something like a short prospectus will have to be published. If the business of the company is described in the advertisement, as it must be when the prescribed regulations apply,[40] deposits will become repayable on demand if the company carries on another business, and depositors must be informed of the new business and of their right to demand repayment.[41] The Act also imposes obligations regarding the delivery of periodical accounts to the Registrar and the Board of Trade, with copies to depositors,[42] and contains additional grounds on which a deposit-taking company may be compulsorily wound up.[43]

Conclusions

Four main conclusions on investor protection will occur to any reader of this chapter. The first is that England has pinned its faith on a philosophy of disclosure rather than of supervision. Our rules are based upon the assumption, which indeed underlies the whole of our company law, that the best protection of the public lies in publicity. It is assumed that if one gives the investor full information about the company's affairs he will avail himself of it and make an intelligent appraisal of the worth of the security offered. This is a large assumption in the case of the average investor. In the words of Justice Douglas of the U.S. Supreme Court [44]: " those needing investment guidance will receive small comfort from the balance sheets, contracts, or compilation of other data. . . . They either lack the training or intelligence to assimilate them and find them useful, or are so concerned with a speculative profit as to consider them irrelevant." This danger we have attempted to meet by the Prevention of Fraud (Investments) Act,

---

discount company ": Companies Act 1967, s. 127 (3)), and advertisements with respect to a class of deposits exempted by the Board of Trade: see the Protection of Depositors (Exempted Advertisement) Regulations 1963 (S.I. No. 1398).

[36] Under s. 3.

[37] *i.e.*, under s. 5, and by regulations made under s. 13: see the Protection of Depositors (Accounts) Regulations 1963 (S.I. No. 1353) which add to the normal requirements under Sched. 8 to the Companies Act.

[38] s. 2.

[39] The Protection of Depositors (Contents of Advertisements) Regulations 1963 (S.I. No. 1397).

[40] 1963 S.I. No. 1397, reg. 3 (1) (*a*).

[41] s. 12.

[42] ss. 6–11.

[43] s. 16. And see s. 17 as to consequences of failure to comply with the accounting provisions.

[44] (1934) 23 Yale Rev.(N.S.) 521.

designed to ensure that the public are not invited to engage in speculation except through reputable professional advisers who will not " lack the training or intelligence " to assimilate the information supplied. This Act, however, does not preclude a direct public invitation through a prospectus complying with the Companies Act. Moreover, the disclosure philosophy only affords protection if the information supplied is true. As we shall see in the next chapter the penalties of being found out in an untruth are severe, but most rogues would be prepared to risk subsequent exposure if they had a reasonable chance of first collecting the proceeds of their villainy and disappearing with it. Prevention is worth any amount of *ex post facto* penalties.

The second main feature, therefore, of our system is the apparent inadequacy of the arrangements to check the truth of the information disclosed. And if the legal rules stood alone they would indeed be inadequate. The Registrar of Companies cannot, and does not, attempt to check the accuracy of the data in the prospectuses filed with him; he merely ensures that *ex facie* they comply with the statutory regulations. We leave the rest largely to private enterprise; to the stock exchanges, the issuing houses and other City institutions.

This leads to the third point: the extent to which English company law relies on private enterprise and extra-legal techniques in the field of investor protection. Some state intervention there certainly has been: the Companies Act, the Prevention of Fraud (Investments) Act and the Protection of Depositors Act, all confer increasing powers on the Board of Trade. But, in contrast with the Board's powers of investigation into malpractices after they have occurred,[45] control over issues of or dealings in securities is generally exercised by prescribing what must be disclosed and hoping that the prescription will be followed. The Board rarely attempt to play a preventive role by preliminary scrutiny to determine the accuracy of what is disclosed or the fairness of the deal.

The inevitable final conclusion is that our rules are remarkably irrational and confusing, both in their diversity and arrangement. We have three separate Acts, and innumerable different institutions, public and private, dealing with what is essentially a single problem: how should investors, actual or potential, be protected when they acquire or dispose of securities?

In all these respects we lag behind developments elsewhere. In the United States, securities regulation has long been recognised as a subject in itself distinct from company law, and close control over all aspects of it is exercised at the federal level by the Securities and Exchange Commission (S.E.C.),[46] and at the state level by security commissioners operating under the so-called " Blue-Sky " Laws of

---

45 See Chap. 25, at p. 604 *et seq.*
46 See Loss, *Securities Regulation* (2nd ed., 1961 and Supp.).

which there is now a uniform Act.[47] As a result prospectuses and circulars are subjected to a detailed scrutiny before they are released. This method of dealing with the problem has spread from the United States through Canada as far as Israel.

The Jenkins Committee considered whether an independent statutory body like the S.E.C. was needed in Britain, but decided that it was not.[48] Clearly the position in the United States and many other countries is very different in a number of respects, notably perhaps in that there is a large " over-the-counter " market of shares not quoted on a stock exchange. Nevertheless, the Committee recognised that something needed to be done to produce a more co-ordinated, coherent and effective system. Hence, in addition to a number of detailed changes, the more important of which have already been referred to, they suggested that the Consultative Committee, which, as we have seen,[49] had been set up on the recommendation of the Cohen Committee, should be given a bigger role to play. In their view, the Consultative Committee:

" should meet regularly to co-ordinate the experience of the various bodies concerned with the protection of investors; the Committee should advise the Board of Trade of changes which they consider desirable in the administration of the law (including the use of the Board's rule-making powers) or in current practice to protect the investor; the Committee should also be free to advise amendments to the Acts if they thought such action was urgently required." [50]

They also suggested that the provisions relating to issuing and dealing in securities in the Companies Act and the Prevention of Fraud (Investments) Act should be consolidated in one Act,[51] thus producing a co-ordinated Securities Act on the lines of those in North America and elsewhere. The normal prospectus provisions should be made to apply to all issues whether the consideration offered was cash or other assets,[52] except to take-over offers which they propose would be subject to a special code laid down by the Board of Trade in the exercise of its rule-making power and applicable to all offers irrespective of their source.[53] The result, in effect, would be that in all cases issues could be made so long as a proper " prospectus " was published. The present method of control under the 1958 Act, by ensuring that invitations come from an authorised source, would apply only outside the field of public issues and take-overs. To provide some further assurance in cases where

---

[47] See Loss & Cowett, *Blue Sky Law* (1958).
[48] Cmnd. 1749, paras. 219–228.
[49] *Supra*, p. 39n.
[50] Cmnd. 1749, para. 234 (*a*). See also paras. 229 and 230.
[51] *Ibid*. paras. 231, 232 and 234 (*b*). This might with advantage also include the Protection of Depositors Act which is later than the Committee's Report.
[52] *Ibid*. paras. 236–237. They recommended that the Board of Trade should have power to amend Sched. 4 by statutory instrument: *ibid*. para. 245.
[53] *Ibid*. paras. 270–273.

the prospectus would not be scrutinised by a stock exchange, because no quotation was being sought, the Registrar should have power to reject a prospectus when lodged for registration if it did not set out the prescribed information or did so " in a manner likely to create a false impression on the mind of an unwary or inexperienced investor." [54]

At the time when the Jenkins Committee reported (1962), it would probably have been generally accepted that in this field their recommendations went about far enough. Perhaps if their proposals had been implemented promptly that view might still prevail, for it is possible that a revivified Consultative Committee might have taken the bit between its teeth and helped to co-ordinate the activities of the Board of Trade and the City institutions. It is also possible that a legally binding set of take-over rules might have prevented a relapse to the law of the jungle that has prevailed in some take-over battles. Unfortunately their recommendations have still not been implemented. And it is now widely acknowledged that continued reliance on private agencies will not do. It is fair to say that dissatisfaction is in relation to take-overs rather than to normal flotations, but, as the Jenkins Committee recognised, the two cannot be kept wholly distinct. The trouble is that Queensberry rules not subject to legal sanctions are inadequate to preserve a code of conduct, at any rate in the heat of a take-over battle. No rules for disclosure, however all-embracing, no City code, however clearly drafted, and no Panel, however prestigious, can really be an adequate substitute for a single authority with statutory powers over the whole field of securities regulation. The present position, even if modified as recommended by the Jenkins Committee, represents an uneasy compromise whereby public authorities lay down some of the rules and belatedly punish breaches of them, while private agencies lay down some more rules, try to see that all the rules are observed, but have inadequate powers to ensure that they are. And nobody co-ordinates the activities of the public and private agencies. What seems to be needed is a statutory body—a smaller (poor man's) S.E.C.—to which would be transferred the functions in this field of the Board of Trade and the Registrar, and which would be provided with a staff adequate to lay down rules and to police them, and be armed with powers to co-ordinate and supervise the activities of the private agencies.[55]

---

[54] *Ibid.* para. 252. But the Committee acknowledged that " we do not expect the Registrar to do more than reject prospectuses which, on the face of them, appear to be cast in a misleading form. He would not be expected to check the accuracy of the contents ": *ibid.*

[55] The need for this has at last been partially recognised in relation to take-overs. The Board of Trade have agreed to consider exercising their powers to withdraw exemptions and licences of dealers when breaches of the *City Code* are reported to them by the Panel: see statement by Lord Shawcross, the new Chairman of the Panel, in the *Financial Times*, April 29, 1962.

CHAPTER 15

LIABILITIES IN RESPECT OF PROSPECTUSES

THE legal rights of subscribers, and the liabilities of companies and their officers, in respect of omissions from or misstatements in prospectuses (using that expression in the wide sense described in the previous chapter) depend on two sources. First, there are the general rules of common law and equity, which have nowhere been codified in any legislation but which remain of vital importance. Secondly, there are the various statutory rules superimposed upon judge-made law to mitigate its failure to deal with all the opportunities for abuse inherent in joint stock enterprise.

In addition to these legal remedies there are the extra-legal sanctions imposed by the stock exchanges to secure compliance with their regulations and to preserve discipline over their members, and which are in turn supplemented by the issuing houses and the Issuing Houses Association [1] and by the Panel in relation to the *City Code on Take-overs and Mergers*. These need not concern us further; their practical importance has already been stressed, but breach of their rules normally gives rise to no legal liability. The present chapter is concerned only with the legal remedies available when there has been a contravention of the rules outlined in the previous chapter or, more especially, when, irrespective of a breach of these rules, there has been some omission or misstatement in the published prospectus. The criminal sanctions will be dealt with first in order to dispose of them before dealing with the civil liabilities which are our major concern; the possibility of criminal punishment is, of course, a potent protection to the public in that it deters the potential wrongdoer, but it is a poor consolation to the individual investor who has been cheated.

CRIMINAL LIABILITIES

For non-compliance with statutory requirements

As pointed out in the previous chapter, a company and its officers when raising money from the public may have to comply with a number of different statutes: the Borrowing (Control and Guarantees) Act 1946, the Exchange Control Act 1947, the Companies Act 1948,[2]

---

[1] The Issuing Houses Association does not include among its expressed objects the enforcement of a code of conduct, but in practice it seems to be ready to express its views especially when complaints are referred to it by the stock exchanges.

[2] It is again emphasised that the appropriate provisions of the Act apply also to statutory and chartered companies: s. 435 and Sched. 14 and S.I. 1967 No. 1876.

the Prevention of Fraud (Investments) Act 1958 and the Protection of Depositors Act 1963.[3]

Each of these provides its own penalties. It is unnecessary to refer to them in detail, but it may be mentioned that under section 40 of the Companies Act a fine not exceeding £500 may be imposed on the company and on every person who is knowingly a party to the issue of a prospectus containing an expert's statement unless he has given his consent, and not withdrawn it, and the prospectus says so. Breach of the registration provisions in section 41 renders the same persons liable to a fine not exceeding £5 for every day of default, and under section 38 (3) liability to a fine not exceeding £500 is incurred by issuing an application for securities unaccompanied by a full prospectus. Failure to file a statement in lieu of prospectus, when that is requisite, is also punishable by fines,[4] as is a failure to retain subscription money in a separate bank account so long as it is liable to be returned on failure to obtain a stock exchange quotation.[5] In the case of the remaining sections, however, there are no provisions for criminal penalties in the event of default,[6] as opposed to misstatements.

Breaches of section 14 of the Prevention of Fraud Act, relating to the possesssion or distribution of circulars,[7] are punishable more severely, the maximum being two years' imprisonment and a fine of £500, but proceedings may not be brought except with the consent of the Board of Trade or the Director of Public Prosecutions.

For false or misleading statements

People who induce others to subscribe for securities by fraudulent misrepresentations might obviously find themselves liable for one or other of the general offences now reformulated in the Theft Act 1968. In fact, however, there have long been special statutory offences designed to deal with frauds of this nature. At the present day those who put out fraudulent prospectuses are generally prosecuted under one or more of the following:

(a) Section 19 of the Theft Act 1968 (replacing s. 84 of the Larceny Act 1861), under which an officer or person purporting to act as an officer of a body corporate or unincorporated association who, with intent to deceive its members or creditors about its affairs, publishes or concurs in publishing a written statement or account which to his knowledge is or may be misleading, false or deceptive in a material particular, is liable to seven years' imprisonment. It was under the

---

[3] If carrying on a special type of business (*e.g.,* insurance) there may, of course, be further statutory provisions to be observed.
[4] £50 if the statement is required under s. 30 on a conversion from a private company, but £100 under s. 48.
[5] £500. See s. 51 (3).
[6] But see s. 421 as to foreign companies.
[7] For details, see Chap. 14, pp. 304–306, *supra.*

forerunner of this section that Lord Kylsant was convicted in the *Royal Mail* case,[8] notwithstanding that all the statements made in the prospectus were in themselves true, but the omission to state that dividends had been maintained only by drawing on secret reserves resulted in the prospectus as a whole giving a false impression of the company's position.[9]

(b) Section 13 of the Prevention of Fraud (Investments) Act 1958,[10] which provides that any person who, by any promise or forecast which he knows to be misleading, false or deceptive, or by any dishonest concealment of material facts, or by the reckless making (*dishonestly or otherwise*) of any statement, promise or forecast which is misleading, false or deceptive, induces or attempts to induce another person to enter into any agreement for acquiring, disposing, subscribing, or underwriting any securities, or speculating in them or in other property, is guilty of an offence and liable to imprisonment for seven years. Section 1 of the Protection of Depositors Act 1963 contains similar provisions regarding inducements to invest money on deposit.

These sections are worded extremely widely and, unlike section 19 of the Theft Act, extend to promises and forecasts as well as statements, and are not restricted to officers of the company,[11] nor to cases of wilful falsehood. Since the insertion by the 1963 Act of the words italicised, it is clear that *reckless* " must be left to bear its full meaning, and be construed, therefore, as covering also the case where there is a high degree of negligence without dishonesty " [12]; so long as there is " a rash statement or promise . . . made heedless of whether the person making it has any real facts on which to base the statement or promise." [13]

(c) Section 44 of the Companies Act 1948 provides that if a prospectus includes any untrue statement, any person who authorised the issue of the statement shall be liable to imprisonment not exceeding two years and a fine not exceeding £500, unless he proves either that

---

[8] *R.* v. *Kylsant* [1932] 1 K.B. 442, C.C.A., followed in *R.* v. *Bishirgian* [1936] 1 All E.R. 586, C.C.A., where the prospectus omitted to point out that capital was really being raised to finance a colossal gamble attempting to " corner " the world supply of pepper.

[9] If accounts are prepared in accordance with the Companies Acts 1948–1967, concealment of this sort will now be impossible except in the case of banks and shipping companies.

[10] As amended by s. 21 of the Protection of Depositors Act 1963.

[11] In the Specialloid prosecution in 1952 a director of the issuing house was prosecuted under this section, but the magistrates found that he had no case to answer on the particular facts.

[12] *Per* Donovan J. in *R.* v. *Bates* [1952] 2 All E.R. 842 at p. 846 (which arose out of the Specialloid prosecution) prior to the insertion of these words. The suggestion that " reckless " was used as in the definition of deceit in *Derry* v. *Peek* (1889) 14 App.Cas. 337, H.L., was expressly rejected. The C.C.A. (*obiter*) had expressed agreement with Donovan J.'s definition (*ibid.*, *sub nom. R.* v. *Russell* [1953] 1 W.L.R. 77). But Salmon J. in *R.* v. *Mackinnon* [1959] 1 Q.B. 150, had taken the opposite view, and Paull J. in *R.* v. *Grunwald* [1963] 1 Q.B. 935 at p. 939 (1960) had differed from both.

[13] *Per* Paull J. in *R.* v. *Grunwald, supra.*

the statement was immaterial or that he had reasonable ground to believe and did believe that the statement was true.[14] This section is subject to the general provisions of section 46 to the effect that a statement shall be deemed untrue if it is misleading in the form and context in which it is included (thus, in effect, applying the *Kylsant* ruling), and that it shall be deemed to be in a prospectus if it is in any report or memorandum therein, incorporated therein by reference, or issued therewith.

The most notable features of this section, which extend its ambit beyond that of any of the foregoing, are that mere negligence, in the sense of an absence of reasonable grounds for belief, imposes criminal liability, and that the onus of proof is shifted to the accused once the prosecution have proved that a misleading statement has been made in a prospectus issued with his authority. The justification for this latter reversal of the normal rules of our criminal jurisprudence is, of course, that the accused is in a far better position than anyone else to prove the state of his belief and knowledge. As we shall see, there is a similar reversal of the normal onus in civil cases.

In addition to this general provision, the Act also contains other provisions imposing criminal responsibility for misstatements. There is, for example, section 438 whereby any person who, in any document required by or for the purpose of certain sections of the Act specified in Schedule 15, wilfully makes a statement false in any material particular knowing it to be false, is guilty of an offence.[15] The sections referred to in Schedule 15 include 30 and 48, relating to statements in lieu of prospectus. In fact, however, the inclusion fulfils little purpose because, under the sections themselves, he will be liable to similar punishment,[16] and the onus is then shifted to him to prove immateriality or belief on reasonable grounds of the truth of the statements made.[17]

It will be observed that whereas the sections of the Act imposing penalties for non-compliance expressly render liable the company as well as its officers, the sections penalising misstatements refer only to " any person." Under the Interpretation Act 1889, s. 19, the word " person " may include a corporation and hence the company itself should be liable if its managers have made the statements on its behalf.[18] The context, however, seems to make it clear that the company itself is not intended to be included.

Finally, it may be mentioned that, in a number of recent cases, allegations of prospectus offences have led in the first instance to the

---

14 An expert will not be liable merely because he consented to the inclusion of a statement by him: s. 44 (2). But he may, of course, be liable if the falsity is in his statement.
15 Punishment not exceeding two years and a fine (unlimited in amount if on indictment).
16 The only difference is that the maximum fine is £500 under ss. 30 and 48.
17 ss. 30 (4) and 48 (5).
18 See Chap. 8, *supra*.

appointment of Board of Trade Inspectors,[19] criminal proceedings following as a result of their investigations.

CIVIL LIABILITIES

This part of the chapter will deal first with the general rules of common law, equity and statute and then consider the ways in which these have been extended by special statutory rules of company law.

General Remedies

The general law provides two remedies for those who are damnified by misrepresentations: damages, and rescission of any resulting contract. These are equally available to anyone who suffers as a result of misrepresentations in a prospectus, although he may, in addition, have other and better remedies under the provisions of the Companies Act. Generally speaking, in order to recover damages the misrepresentation must be fraudulent, or, in some circumstances, negligent; in order to rescind the contract the misrepresentation need not be either fraudulent or negligent, a completely innocent misrepresentation, so long as it is material, suffices. In the following discussion these basic principles are amplified and illustrated in relation to misrepresentations in prospectuses—using that expression in the broadest sense.

Damages for misrepresentation

(i) **Type of misrepresentation.** To recover damages the misrepresentation must be a misstatement of fact, not a mere promise, forecast or expression of opinion.[20] And there must be a positive misstatement, not a mere omission to state a material fact.[21] However, if the omission causes the prospectus as a whole to give a misleading impression or falsifies one of the statements made in it, this will do.[22] Section 46 of the Companies Act, providing that " a statement shall be deemed to be untrue if it is misleading in the form and context in which it is included," appears to be merely declaratory of the common law.[23] The action of deceit lies only where the misrepresentation is made fraudulently, *i.e.*, with knowledge of its falsity or recklessly, not caring whether it be true or false. This was established by the House of Lords in *Derry*

---

[19] See Chap. 25, *infra.*

[20] Unless, perhaps, the opinion stated is not actually held, so that the maker misrepresents the state of his mind which " is just as much a fact as the state of his digestion ": *per* Bowen L.J. in *Edgington* v. *Fitzmaurice* (1885) 29 Ch.D. 459, C.A., at p. 483.

[21] *Peek* v. *Gurney* (1873) L.R. 6 H.L. 377.

[22] *Ibid.* and *Aaron's Reefs Ltd.* v. *Twiss* [1896] A.C. 273, H.L. In this respect there is no difference between claims for damages and for rescission.

[23] *R.* v. *Kylsant* [1932] 1 K.B. 442, C.C.A., goes at least as far, and civil liability can hardly be less extensive than criminal; indeed, the *Kylsant* ruling was based on dicta in civil cases.

v. *Peek*,[24] a decision which led immediately to its reversal as regards prospectuses by the Directors Liability Act 1890, now section 43 of the Companies Act 1948.[25]

But two developments have occurred recently as a result of which, despite *Derry* v. *Peek*, damages may be recoverable in respect of misstatements which are made negligently and not fraudulently. One of these developments is the Misrepresentation Act 1967.[26] Under section 2 (1) of this, if a person has entered into a contract after a misrepresentation has been made to him by another party thereto and if the maker of the misrepresentation would have been liable to damages if the misrepresentation had been made fraudulently, he is liable despite the absence of fraud unless he proves that he had reasonable ground to believe and did believe, up to the time the contract was made, that the facts represented were true. Both as regards imposing liability for negligence and as regards the reversal of the normal onus of proof, this subsection is based on the analogy of section 43 of the Companies Act.[25] In relation to misrepresentations in prospectuses the latter section will normally afford the better remedy. But the two statutory provisions do not wholly overlap and, as we shall see,[27] it may be that the company itself could be sued under the Misrepresentation Act, which is not possible under section 43. Section 2 (2)[28] of the Misrepresentation Act goes even further, for it entitles the court to award damages in lieu of rescission, thereby making an award of damages possible even though the misrepresentation is neither fraudulent nor negligent. Under section 3, a clause in a contract purporting to exclude or limit liability is ineffective unless the court allows reliance on it as being fair and reasonable in the circumstances.

The other development is the decision of the House of Lords in *Hedley Byrne & Co. Ltd.* v. *Heller & Partners Ltd.*[29] which establishes that even at common law there will be liability for negligent misstatements so long as a duty of care is owed by the maker to the recipient of the statement. Prior to the *Hedley Byrne* case it had been thought, on the authority of *Derry* v. *Peek*, that no duty of care could arise unless there was a pre-existing contractual or fiduciary[30] relationship. It is now clear that it may arise in other circumstances, though it is not yet clear exactly what these circumstances are. In the *Hedley Byrne* case the plaintiffs had sought advice from professional men and it was held that the law will imply a duty of care when the party seeking information from a person possessed of special skill trusts him to

---

[24] (1889) 14 App.Cas. 337.
[25] See *infra*, pp. 331–333.
[26] This Act was designed to implement the 10th Report of the Law Reform Committee: Cmnd. 1782 of 1962.
[27] *Infra*, p. 318 *et seq*.
[28] See further on this subsection, *infra*, at p. 324.
[29] [1964] A.C. 465.
[30] *Nocton* v. *Lord Ashburton* [1914] A.C. 932, H.L.

exercise due care and that person knew or ought to have known that reliance was being placed on his skill and judgment.[31] If the duty cannot arise unless advice or information is sought, it will rarely be possible to establish a duty of care in respect of prospectuses which are often unsolicited by the recipients. But neither the speeches of the Law Lords nor later cases in which *Hedley Byrne* has been considered [32] suggest that it is as narrowly based as that. If the true rule be that a duty of care is owed whenever someone has given advice or information in circumstances in which he knew or ought to have known that reliance was being placed on his care, skill and judgment, the publication of a prospectus would seem to be a perfect illustration. As we have seen, when the prospectus is in the form of a stock exchange advertisement, the rubric which the Stock Exchange *Requirements* insist shall be placed at the head of the advertisement [33] invites the public to place reliance on it and says that the directors accept responsibility.[34] Similarly, an expert, such as a surveyor or accountant, who consents to his report appearing in the prospectus must surely be inviting the public to rely upon his expert opinion. Often the investor will have a better remedy under section 43 of the Companies Act, but, as we shall see,[35] only a subscriber [36] can rely on this. Often, too, he may have a better remedy under the Misrepresentation Act, but this entitles him to sue only the other party to the contract (normally the company and, on an offer for sale, the issuing house) and not, apparently, others responsible for statements in the prospectus.[37] Moreover, unlike all the other remedies, he may be able to succeed in a common law action for negligence without having to establish that there was a misrepresentation of fact; a duty to exercise care may clearly be broken by a careless opinion or forecast.[38]

(ii) **Who can be sued for damages.** The action of deceit lies against all those who made the false statement intending it to be acted upon and having knowledge of its falsity or who were the principals of those

---

[31] In the *Hedley Byrne* case the defendants escaped liability because there had been an express disclaimer of responsibility.

[32] *Clay* v. *A. J. Crump & Sons Ltd.* [1964] 1 Q.B. 533, C.A.; *Clark* v. *Kirby-Smith* [1964] Ch. 506; *Weller & Co.* v. *Foot & Mouth Disease Research Inst.* [1966] 1 Q.B. 569; *Rondel* v. *Worsley* [1969] 1 A.C. 191, H.L.; *Anderson & Sons* v. *Rhodes (Liverpool) Ltd.* [1967] 2 All E.R. 850; *Margarine Union G.m.b.H.* v. *Cambay Prince* [1969] 1 Q.B. 219. See Atiyah (1967) 83 L.Q.R. 248.

[33] See *supra*, p. 292.

[34] Pennington, *Company Law* (2nd ed.), at p. 229, interprets the observations of Lords Morris and Devlin at [1964] A.C. 500–501 and 518–519 as denying that there is any such duty in the case of a prospectus issued generally as opposed to one issued to the existing shareholders. Their speeches do not seem capable of bearing any such interpretation.

[35] See *infra*, pp. 331, 332.

[36] *i.e.*, one who acquires securities from the company for cash: see *supra*, p. 297.

[37] See *infra*, p. 318.

[38] " It cannot matter whether the information consists of fact or of opinion or is a mixture of both . . .": *per* Lord Devlin in *Hedley Byrne & Co. Ltd.* v. *Heller & Partners Ltd.* [1964] A.C. 465 at p. 528.

who fraudulently issued it while acting within the scope of their authority.[39]   In the case of prospectuses this will normally include the company itself if any of its officers have knowledge that the statement is false.   It will certainly do so if the company publishes the prospectus or if it was an offer for sale by an issuing house after an allotment for this purpose by the company.[40]   Even in other cases, the directors, acting on behalf of the company, will normally have to accept responsibility for the prospectus, if not under the Companies Act at any rate under the Stock Exchange *Requirements*.   Hence the company will generally be liable together with participants such as the directors, issuing houses, and any experts as regards reports by them—assuming, of course, that they knew of the falsity of the statements.

As regards liability for negligent misrepresentations under section 2 of the Misrepresentation Act, the range of persons liable is narrower. It appears that only the other party to the contract can be sued and only in respect of statements made by him (or, presumably, by an agent acting within the scope of his authority).   It seems that directors and experts cannot be sued under this Act.[41]   Nor, it seems, can the company itself, unless it is the party from whom the investor has acquired the securities. Even where section 45 of the Companies Act applies to an offer for sale by an issuing house, it is not clear that its wording is sufficiently wide to make the company a party for this purpose to the contract of purchase. On the other hand it could be argued that as, in every case, a new contractual relation between a purchaser and the company will be established when the purchaser is registered as the holder of its shares or debentures, there is a contract with the company entered into after a misrepresentation which will be deemed to be made by the company whenever section 45 applies.

If damages for negligent information are claimed under the common law rule established in *Hedley Byrne & Co. Ltd.* v. *Heller & Partners Ltd.*,[42] the only persons liable will be those who owed and broke a duty of care.   This, it has already been submitted,[43] should include directors, whenever they have accepted responsibility for the prospectus, and experts in respect of reports by them.   It seems doubtful whether the company itself could be sued on this basis; the needed reliance seems to be placed on its directors personally rather than on the company itself, so that it is they, not the company, that owe the duty.

---

[39] *Briess* v. *Woolley* [1954] A.C. 333, H.L., and *cf. Armstrong* v. *Strain* [1952] 1 K.B. 232, C.A.

[40] Companies Act 1948, s. 45, which expressly provides that the prospectus shall then be deemed to be issued by the company (as well as the issuing house) and all " rules of law as to . . . liability in respect of statements in and omissions from prospectuses . . . shall apply and have effect accordingly."

[41] But they will be liable under s. 43 of the Companies Act when that applies.

[42] *Supra.*

[43] *Supra*, p. 317.

On the other hand, when an offer for sale or placing is made by an issuing house or a stockbroker, a strong argument could be raised for saying that trust and reliance is placed on the issuing house or broker.

Prima facie, therefore, damages for misrepresentation in an action of deceit and sometimes under the Misrepresentation Act (though probably not under *Hedley Byrne*) should be recoverable from the company. It is, however, very doubtful whether such a claim has any point. In the case of an issue of debentures, the debentureholders would normally prefer to enforce their security rather than to sue the company for damages. In the case of an issue of shares, it was held by the House of Lords in *Houldsworth* v. *City of Glasgow Bank* [44] that damages for fraud cannot be recovered against the company unless the allotment of shares is also rescinded. Although the reasons for this anomalous rule are not altogether clear,[45] it appears to make a claim against the company for damages altogether pointless. If the shares are obtained from the company, on rescission the subscriber will be entitled to his money back with interest, and usually this is all that he can recover in a claim for damages.[46] If the shares were obtained by a subsequent purchase, the only contract which could be rescinded would presumably be that with the seller; not the original allotment of the shares, which may have taken place years before, or the contract between the purchaser and the company when the latter registered him as a member.

There is no express provision in the Misrepresentation Act which reverses the rule in *Houldsworth* v. *City of Glasgow Bank*. On the other hand section 2 (2) of that Act appears to assume that there is no such rule since it provides, without stating any exception, that the court can award damages in lieu of rescission. If the result is that damages can be awarded where rescission is possible but not granted, whereas they cannot be awarded if it is too late to rescind or rescission is not asked for, the result is highly anomalous and inconsistent with the policy of the Act. Perhaps the Act will encourage the House of Lords to exercise its newly declared freedom to reverse itself and to rule that the *Houldsworth* case was wrongly decided.[47]

For the present, however, it seems safer to assume that damages are not an effective remedy against the company. However, they may still be a valuable remedy against others who are party to the prospectus, including those who have actually offered the securities and, if fraud can be proved, directors, promoters and experts who have assumed responsibility for statements in it, and, even if fraud cannot be proved, against those who can be shown to have broken a duty of care.

---

[44] (1880) 5 App.Cas. 317, H.L.Sc.; followed in *Re Addlestone Linoleum Co. Ltd.* (1887) 37 Ch.D. 191, C.A.

[45] See the exchanges between Professor Hornby and the author in (1956) 19 M.L.R. 54, 61 and 185.

[46] *McConnel* v. *Wright* [1903] 1 Ch. 546, C.A. But see *infra*, p. 330.

[47] This would certainly be a happier solution than a decision that the Misrepresentation Act has impliedly reversed it; especially as that Act does not apply to Scotland.

(iii) **Who can sue.** In order to succeed in an action of deceit the plaintiff must show that the representation was addressed to him; that he was one of a class of persons intended to act upon it. The same clearly applies to actions based on negligence whether under the Misrepresentation Act or under *Hedley Byrne & Co. Ltd.* v. *Heller & Partners Ltd.* In *Peek* v. *Gurney* [48] it was held that an investor who had purchased shares on the market, on the faith of a prospectus published on the issue of the shares, could not recover, since the prospectus was only intended to induce subscriptions of shares from the company and not subsequent purchases on the market. Although the later case of *Andrews* v. *Mockford* [49] shows that this does not apply when it is proved as a fact that the prospectus was intended to induce market dealings, it is usually stated that the rule in *Peek* v. *Gurney* is still that generally applicable. It is submitted, however, that this fails to recognise the result of modern issuing techniques. As was explained in the last chapter, on most types of new issue the prospectus will, to comply with the Stock Exchange *Requirements*, have to be published as an advertisement to lead to the grant of a quotation, and those responsible for the issue will arrange with the company for its publication for this purpose. This being so, it seems impossible to argue that they did not intend it to influence purchasers on the market. They must know that it is likely to be relied on by such purchasers and that the stock exchange insisted on its advertisement expressly for this purpose. As already pointed out, where there is a stock exchange introduction unaccompanied by an issue, the advertisement has to state that the directors accept responsibility for the accuracy of the statements made and this must surely mean that they accept liability to market purchasers who rely on the advertisement. If this is so, it is difficult to see why purchasers should be in a weaker position merely because the advertisement is also an invitation to subscribe. Under modern conditions those who publicly advertise a prospectus know that it will be relied on indiscriminately by investors who apply on allotment and by those who buy on the market.

The point which impressed the House of Lords in *Peek* v. *Gurney*, namely, the difficulty of knowing when the prospectus has spent its force, does not seem to be any objection to the view here contended for. The difficulty is one which the plaintiff will have to surmount, for it is he that will have to satisfy the court that he has in fact relied on the prospectus, and obviously, if a long interval has elapsed since its publication, it may be difficult for him to satisfy the court on this score. But the fact that he has to surmount this difficulty is no reason why directors and promoters should be able to escape liability if in fact he is able to discharge the burden of proof. In any event, this difficulty has not prevented American courts from granting a remedy in such cases. [50]

[48] (1873) L.R. 6 H.L. 377.
[49] [1896] 1 Q.B. 372, C.A.   [50] *Restatement of Torts*, § 531.

If this view is correct, the remedy of an action for damages under the general law may still have considerable practical importance notwithstanding section 43 of the Companies Act (considered below), for that section only affords a remedy to those who are subscribers or who are deemed to be subscribers under section 45. Hence it will not be available to market purchasers who will be thrown back on to their common law remedy if they are to have any relief.

Where there is no public advertisement, but merely a rights, conversion or take-over issue by circular to existing members or debentureholders, there is less ground for contending that market purchasers can rely on misstatements in the circular. Nevertheless, it is submitted that even in such cases if the issue is by renounceable allotment letters or letters of right the remedy of damages [51] is available to those who purchase the letters on the market. By making the issue in this way, those responsible have shown that they envisage the likelihood of the circular being relied on by purchasers.[52] But once the period allowed for renouncing has expired it seems that there can be no liability on the circular to subsequent purchasers.

Not only must the plaintiff have been intended to act on the misstatement, he must actually have done so. In other words, the falsehood must have influenced him; if he never read the prospectus, or did not believe it, or placed no weight on the matter misstated, or was not misled by an ambiguity,[53] he has no remedy. The misstatement need not be the only factor which induced him to subscribe; it is sufficient if it was one (and not even the main one) of several.[54] This appears to be all that is meant, at any rate in this connection,[55] by saying that the misrepresentation must be of a material fact. It expresses the same point objectively instead of subjectively, and in truth the courts adopt both approaches. Their attitude is perhaps best explained by saying that if the misrepresentation is of a fact which would have influenced a reasonable man, the plaintiff will be entitled to succeed unless the defendant proves that the plaintiff was not in fact influenced thereby. Probably the plaintiff will also succeed if he can persuade the court that he is less than reasonable and has been influenced by a misstatement that a rational person would have regarded as irrelevant, for fools are entitled to be protected against rogues—indeed it is they who are most in need of protection. Certain

---

[51] It will also be submitted that they could rely on s. 43 ; see *infra,* p. 331.

[52] The thoroughly unsatisfactory case of *Collins* v. *Associated Greyhound Racecourses* [1930] 1 Ch. 1, C.A., admittedly appears to suggest the contrary.

[53] *Smith* v. *Chadwick* (1884) 9 App.Cas. 187, H.L.

[54] *Edgington* v. *Fitzmaurice* (1885) 29 Ch.D. 459, C.A., where the plaintiff had subscribed for debentures partly because of his own mistake in believing that they were secured by a charge and partly because of a fraudulent misrepresentation of the purpose for which the money was being raised.

[55] It may mean something more in Companies Act 1948, s. 38 (4) (*c*): see *infra,* p. 335.

it is, that he is not bound to verify the facts stated in the prospectus even if invited to do so. In the oft-quoted words of Jessel M.R.[56]:

> " Where men issue a prospectus in which they make statements of the contracts made before the formation of the company, and then say that the contracts themselves may be inspected . . . , it has always been held that those who accepted those false statements as true, were not deprived of their remedy merely because they neglected to go and look at the contracts."

It need hardly be emphasised that it makes no difference whether the matter misrepresented is one which has to be stated in order to comply with the Companies Act or the Stock Exchange *Requirements,* or whether it is one which has been gratuitously inserted. The only question of importance is whether it was material in the sense already explained.[57]

Rescission

The second remedy provided by the general law is rescission of the contract entered into as a result of the misrepresentation. In relation to prospectuses this may arise in two ways. First, the acquirer of the securities may be seeking rescission of the contract with the company whereby he became a shareholder or debentureholder and rectification of the register of members or debentureholders by deleting his name therefrom.[58] Secondly, where he has acquired the securities from a previous holder he may be seeking to rescind the contract whereby he did so.

(i) **Rescission against the company.** Where the company issues securities and publishes a false prospectus, the position is usually straightforward. But difficulties could arise in two situations. The first is where the prospectus is issued by the promoter prior to the formation of the company. The company cannot have any agents prior to its formation and, equally, cannot afterwards ratify acts purporting to be done on its behalf. It is clear, however, that companies cannot be allowed to take advantage of misleading prospectuses previously published, so as to off-load their shares on to a public deceived thereby.

---

[56] *Redgrave* v. *Hurd* (1881) 20 Ch.D. 1, C.A., at p. 14. See also *Aaron's Reefs* v. *Twiss* [1896] A.C. 273, H.L.

[57] If it had to be stated, the plaintiff can argue that the legislature or the stock exchange obviously regarded it as material; if it did not have to be stated, he can argue that the defendants only inserted it because they thought it would be a material inducement.

[58] s. 116 of the Companies Act 1948 provides specifically for rectification by summary procedure of the register of members of a registered company, but it is clear that the court has a general jurisdiction in the case of both members' and debentureholders' registers, and as regards all types of company. If the contract has not been completed by allotment the subscriber need merely defend an action for specific performance, but if he has already paid anything an action for rescission will be necessary unless the company is prepared to release him and refund; and because of the danger of laches he must in any event repudiate the contract in unequivocal terms.

Hence the courts have held that if the officers of the company know that applications are made on the basis of a prospectus, the contract with the company is vitiated by any misrepresentations contained in it, even though the company was not initially responsible for the prospectus.[59]

The second difficulty formerly arose where the prospectus was published by an issuing house on an offer for sale or placing by it, but this has now been solved by the legislature by section 45 of the Act. This, it will be remembered, states that if securities are allotted with a view to a public offer, the prospectus published on that offer shall be deemed for all purposes to be issued by the company and the purchasers shall be deemed to be subscribers.

The position is, therefore, that the company will be liable to an action for rescission:

(a) where the misrepresentations have been made by the directors or other general agents of the company entitled to act and acting on its behalf;

(b) where they have been made by a special agent of the company acting within the scope of his authority;

(c) where the company can be held affected, before the contract is completed, with the knowledge that it is induced by misrepresentations;

(d) where the contract is made to the knowledge of the company on the basis of certain representations which turn out to be material and untrue; and

(e) where the misrepresentations are made in a prospectus deemed, under section 45, to be issued by the company.[60]

The only case in which the subscriber is left without a remedy when the contract has been made with the company is when the misrepresentation is not made by an agent of the company, and the company does not know that the subscription is on the basis of the prospectus, which turns out to be false. But, as already emphasised,[61] *a purchaser*, not deemed to be a subscriber under section 45, will not be able to sue the company for rescission of his contract (it is not with the company) and he will be limited to a claim for damages against the persons responsible, other than the company, or such other remedy as he may have against his seller.[62]

---

[59] *Karberg's Case, Re Metropolitan Coal Consumers Association* [1892] 3 Ch. 1, C.A. *Quaere* whether this should truly be regarded as rescission for misrepresentation or as repudiation for breach of a condition of the contract: see *infra*, p. 328 *et seq.*

[60] (a) to (d) are as stated by Romer J. in *Lynde* v. *Anglo-Italian Hemp Spinning Co.* [1896] 1 Ch. 178, as amended, in the case of (d), by Luxmoore J. in *Collins* v. *Associated Greyhound Racecourses* [1930] 1 Ch. 1. The difference between (c) and (d) is that under (c) the company must know of the falsehood, whereas under (d) it need only know that the contract is based on the representations which it may erroneously believe to be true. But (d) seems wide enough to include (c) which is probably superfluous.

[61] *Supra*, p. 319.

[62] This may include rescission of the contract of sale and purchase.

Where the misrepresentation is contained in an expert's report referred to in the prospectus, this in itself will not be a ground for rescission, at any rate if the company dissociated itself from the expert's statements.[63] But if the company itself makes statements based on the report it will be responsible for them unless it makes it absolutely clear that it does not vouch for the accuracy of the report or the conclusions based on it.[64]

(ii) **Rescission against the transferor of the securities.** Hitherto this has been of little importance, since it was generally believed, on the authority of *Seddon* v. *North Eastern Salt Co.*,[65] that the contract could not be rescinded once it had been executed by the transfer of the securities. If, however, there was any such rule it has now been abolished by section 1 of the Misrepresentation Act 1967. As a result, this remedy has become very much a live one, enabling the acquirer of the securities to rescind *vis-à-vis* his transferor so long as he acts promptly after discovering the truth.[66] As in the case of an action against the company, he will, of course, have to show that the transferor, or his agent, was responsible for the misrepresentation or knew that the contract was entered into on the faith of certain representations, which turn out to be material and untrue.[67]

(iii) **Nature of misrepresentation—need not be fraudulent or negligent.** Whether rescission is sought against the company or against a transferor, the misrepresentation need not be either fraudulent or negligent.[68] It is this that constitutes the important contrast between the remedies of rescission and damages. But the former clear-cut contrast in this respect has been blurred by section 2 (2) of the Misrepresentation Act 1967 which provides that if a contract has been entered into after a misrepresentation has been made, otherwise than fraudulently,[69] which would entitle the person to whom it is made to rescind, and it is claimed, in any proceedings arising out of the contract, that it ought to be or has been rescinded, the court may declare the contract subsisting and award damages in lieu of rescission. This it may do [70] if of opinion " that it would be equitable to do so, having regard to the nature of the misrepre-

---

63 *Re British Burmah Lead Co.* (1887) 56 L.T. 815; *Bentley & Co.* v. *Black* (1893) 9 T.L.R. 580, C.A.
64 *Re Pacaya Rubber Co.* [1914] 1 Ch. 542. This applies particularly if the report is by one of the directors: *Mair* v. *Rio Grande Rubber Estates* [1913] A.C. 853, H.L.
65 [1905] 1 Ch. 326.
66 See *infra*, p. 328.
67 See *supra*, p. 323.
68 Hence the vexed question, of the division of knowledge of the facts between various agents of the company, does not arise. In any event, the questions seem finally (?) to have been set at rest by *Armstrong* v. *Strain* [1952] 1 K.B. 232, C.A., see (1952) 15 M.L.R. 232.
69 The draftsman obviously assumed that damages would be recoverable as of right if the misrepresentation was fraudulent. As we have seen, *supra*, p. 319, this is not necessarily so in the case of company prospectuses because of the curious rule in *Houldsworth* v. *City of Glasgow Bank, supra*.
70 The power is clearly discretionary.

sentation and the loss that would be caused by it if the contract were upheld, as well as to the loss that rescission would cause to the other party." As previously pointed out,[71] this means that damages may be recovered for a misrepresentation that is shown to be neither fraudulent nor negligent. But in that event they cannot be claimed in an action in tort, but may be awarded only in an action under the contract claiming rescission.

Except for the irrelevance of fraud and negligence, the same principles apply as in a claim for damages in deceit or under section 2 (1) of the Misrepresentation Act. Once again the prospectus must have been addressed to the plaintiff unless, even though it was not, it was known that his application for the securities was based upon it.[72] The misrepresentation must be of fact and must be material in the sense that it was one of the factors which induced him to enter into the contract. The date upon which the truth or falsity of the statement is to be determined is that on which the contract was entered into. If the statement was true when the prospectus was issued but changed circumstances rendered it false prior to the finalisation of the contract (which, in the case of an issue by the company, will mean the despatch of allotment letters [73]), the contract can be rescinded.[74] It was formerly doubted whether failure to publish a correction would support an action for damages, but this too now seems to be clear.[75] It never seems to have been questioned in relation to rescission.

It will be appreciated that rescission is not possible merely because there has not been disclosure of all material facts. Contracts to acquire securities, whether from the company itself or from an existing holder, are not within the traditional category of contracts under which there is a positive duty to disclose all material facts.[76] Nevertheless the difference between them and fully fledged contracts *uberrimae fidei* is perhaps more apparent than real. Especially is this so when the content of the prospectus is prescribed by law.[77] And, as we have seen, in every case the prospectus has to be considered as a whole to see whether it gives a misleading impression, and the courts are particularly ready to hold that

---

71 *Supra*, p. 316.
72 *Karberg's Case* [1892] 3 Ch. 1, C.A.
73 *Household Fire Insurance Co.* v. *Grant* (1879) 4 Ex.D. 216, C.A.
74 *Anderson's Case* (1881) 17 Ch.D. 373; *Re Scottish Petroleum Co. Ltd.* (1883) 23 Ch.D. 413, C.A. Perhaps a better way of expressing this is to say that, unless the contrary is clearly stated, a prospectus must be taken to represent what will be the state of facts at the date of allotment: *cf. With* v. *O'Flanagan* [1936] Ch. 575, C.A.
75 In the case of deceit this was left open in *Arkright* v. *Newbold* (1881) 17 Ch.D. 301 at pp. 310, 325 and 329, and by Lord Porter in *Bradford Building Society* v. *Borders* [1941] 2 All E.R. 205, H.L., at p. 228, but seems to have been settled by *Briess* v. *Woolley* [1954] A.C. 333, H.L., see especially at pp. 353–354. In the case of negligent misrepresentations, s. 2 (1) of the Misrepresentation Act specifically requires the defendant to prove that he believed the statement on reasonable grounds up to the time that the contract was entered into.
76 *McKeown* v. *Boudard-Peveril Gear Co.* (1896) 65 L.J.Ch. 735, C.A.
77 *i.e.*, where s. 38 of the Companies Act 1948, or the Licensed Dealers (Conduct of Business) Rules 1960 apply.

suppressio veri results in *suggestio falsi*. In practice, indeed, they appear to be more ready to take this view when the claim is merely for rescission and not for damages, since they are not then called upon to brand anyone as fraudulent or negligent. Hence, a contract to subscribe for shares or debentures has become, as it is sometimes said, one of modified *uberrima fides*.

> " Those who issue a prospectus, holding out to the public the great advantages which will accrue to persons who will take shares in a proposed undertaking, and inviting them to take shares on the faith of the representations therein contained, are bound to state everything with strict and scrupulous accuracy, and not only to abstain from stating as facts that which is not so, but to omit no one fact within their knowledge, the existence of which might in any degree affect the nature, or extent, or quality, of the privileges and advantages which the prospectus holds out as inducements to take shares." [78]

(iv) **Effect of rescission.** If the contract is rescinded the former security holder will be entitled to his money back (normally with interest) and to a refund of any expenses to which he has been put.[79] If his action is against the company he will be entitled to have the company's registers rectified by deleting his name therefrom,[80] and can prove in the company's liquidation for the amount due to him.[81]

(v) **Loss of right to rescind.** The rule which was formerly thought to apply to a contract to buy shares or debentures, that there could be no rescission once the contract was executed, never applied to an allotment of shares or debentures by the company. The mere fact that the shareholder or debentureholder had been entered on the register did not preclude rescission and the rectification of the register. In any case, this rule has, as we have seen,[82] been abolished *in toto* by section 1 of the Misrepresentation Act 1967. That section also expressly provides that the fact that the misrepresentation may have become a term of the contract does not preclude rescission. But the principle that there can be no rescission if the contract has been affirmed after discovering the truth, or if in the meantime third parties have acquired rights, still

---

[78] *Per* Kindersley V.-C. in *New Brunswick & Canada Ry. Co.* v. *Muggeridge* (1860) 1 Dr. & Sm. 363 at p. 381. These words, described by Page Wood V.-C. as a " golden legacy " (*Henderson* v. *Lacon* (1867) L.R. 5 Eq. 249 at p. 262), were adopted by Lord Chelmsford in *Central Ry. of Venezuela* v. *Kisch* (1867) L.R. 2 H.L. 99 at p. 113. See also *Aaron's Reefs* v. *Twiss* [1896] A.C. 273, H.L., and *Greenwood* v. *Leather Shod Wheel Co.* [1900] 1 Ch. 421, C.A.

[79] *Re British Gold Fields of W. Africa Ltd.* [1899] 2 Ch. 7, C.A.

[80] Either by summary procedure under s. 116 of the Companies Act, or by an order obtained in the proceedings (if any) for rescission, or, if need be, by a separate action: see p. 322, n. 58, *supra.*

[81] *Re British Gold Fields of W. Africa Ltd., supra.* Although s. 116 describes the compensation as " damages " they are inherently different from damages in a deceit or negligence claim (*ibid.*) although the amount will normally be the same it seems: see *infra*, p. 329.

[82] See *supra*, p. 324.

applies and does so with particular rigour in the case of contracts to acquire company securities, at any rate in relation to the allotment of shares. This is because the member having subscribed to the share capital has allowed the company to obtain credit on the strength of it. If therefore he wishes to rescind he must take steps promptly, and in any case before the company goes into liquidation, when the rights of creditors are regarded as having crystallised. Unless he has issued a writ or been actually removed from the register by the company, or taken some other unequivocal action before liquidation, he will be too late.[83] In theory, this rule presumably does not apply to a subscriber for debentures (there is no reason for applying it to him [84]) but in practice a debentureholder, normally a secured creditor, will not wish to renounce his debentures after winding up, since this would reduce him to the level of an unsecured creditor in his claim for the return of his money.[85] Whether liquidation will necessarily bar a transferee's right to rescind the contract with his transferor will presumably depend on how far the courts are prepared to take the theory that rights crystallise on winding up. If the shares are fully-paid (so that no contribution can be required from the present holder) and if the transferee is able to restore the former position by retransferring the shares (which may be impossible especially in the case of a compulsory liquidation [86]), there is no obvious reason why liquidation of the company should prevent rescission in this case.

But in any case the allottee or transferee must take action before he has done anything to show an election to affirm the contract. If therefore he accepts dividends,[87] attends and votes at meetings,[88] or sells or attempts to sell his securities,[89] after he has found out the truth he will have lost his right. And, in the case of shares, and because of the sacrosanctity of share capital, even mere delay after ascertaining the truth may be fatal.[90] But, of course, there can be no election until the truth is discovered; until then the only risk is that liquidation may supervene, or that *restitutio in integrum* may have become impossible. In the case of a contract of this sort, however, it is difficult to see how the *restitutio* principle can ever have much application. The sole example of its application when the securities have been obtained from the company

83 *Oakes* v. *Turquand* (1867) L.R. 2 H.L. 325.
84 Unless it can be said that on winding up there is a " crystallisation " from the viewpoint of all interested in the company: see (1955) 71 L.Q.R. 416–417, citing *Burgess's Case* (1880) 15 Ch.D. 507.
85 He could not claim to " follow " his money except in the unlikely event of the subscription moneys still being retained in a separate bank account.
86 See Companies Act 1948, s. 227, under which " any transfer of shares, or alteration in the status of the members of the company, made after the commencement of the winding-up, shall, unless the court otherwise orders, be void."
87 *Scholey* v. *Central Ry. of Venezuela* (1869) L.R. 9 Eq. 266n.
88 *Sharpley* v. *Louth & East Coast Ry.* (1876) 2 Ch.D. 663.
89 *Ex p. Briggs* (1866) L.R. 1 Eq. 483; *Crawley's Case* (1869) L.R. 4 Ch.App. 322 (executing blank transfer).
90 *Re Scottish Petroleum Co.* (1883) 23 Ch.D. 413, C.A.

seems to be when the subscriber has sold the securities even though he did so before discovering the truth. He will then be absolutely barred as regards those he has sold, even (apparently) though he is prepared to acquire and return an equivalent number.[91] Whether he will be barred as regards those he retains is not clear; it seems that he will be barred as regards shares obtained under the same contract [92] but not as regards those obtained under a separate application.[93] Presumably the same principles apply in relation to a contract between a transferor and transferee, but it is questionable whether these strict rules would be followed today in view of the more liberal attitude now adopted towards restitution. One case where the *restitutio* principle might clearly prevent rescission as between transferor and transferee is where the articles of the company contain restrictions on transfer with which the transferee is unable to comply so as to retransfer the shares.

Breach of contract

Hitherto we have assumed that the representation has not been incorporated as a term of a contract. There is, however, no inherent reason why the courts should not hold that a misrepresentation in the prospectus has become a term of the resulting contract to acquire the securities or of a collateral contract. Where securities are brought from an issuing house or from any seller other than the company it seems clear that the purchaser should then have a claim for breach of contract against his seller.

Where, however, the securities are obtained direct from the company it is doubtful whether the prospectus can ever be relied on as a contractual document after allotment and entry in the register. This seems to be regarded as a complete novation [94]; the substitution of a new contract divorced from the prospectus for the old contract based on the prospectus. Certain it is that the rights attaching to the shares or debentures depend on the terms of the memorandum and articles [95] or the debenture,[96] and not on those of any prior prospectus. This, however, does not necessarily mean that the original contract of subscription can-

---

[91] Cf. *Edinburgh United Breweries* v. *Molleson* [1894] A.C. 96, H.L.(Sc.).

[92] *Secus* Kay J. in *Re Mount Morgan Gold Mines Ltd.* (1887) 3 T.L.R. 556.

[93] *Maturin* v. *Tredinnick* (1864) 10 L.T. 331; *Re Metropolitan Coal Consumers Assn. Ltd., Grieb's Case* (1890) 6 T.L.R. 416, C.A.

[94] Cf. Chap. 18, p. 408, *infra.*

[95] These may authorise the terms to be fixed by a company resolution (cf. Table A, art. 2), in which event the resolution will have to be read in conjunction with the articles. But one cannot go further afield, and there seems to be no possibility of rectification: *Scott* v. *Frank Scott (London) Ltd.* [1940] Ch. 794, C.A.

[96] *Re Chicago (etc.) Granaries Ltd.* [1898] 1 Ch. 263; *Re Tewkesbury Gas Co.* [1911] 2 Ch. 279, affd. [1912] 1 Ch. 1, C.A. But cf. *British Equitable Assce.* v. *Baily* [1906] A.C. 35, H.L. (insurance policy); *Jacobs* v. *Batavia & General Plantations Trust* [1924] 2 Ch. 329, C.A. (unsecured loan notes construed in the light of the prospectus, which, it was suggested, might constitute a separate collateral contract) and *R.* v. *International Trustees for Bondholders* [1937] A.C. 500, H.L. (Government bonds). *Semble,* rectification of the debenture may be possible; *per* Parker J. in [1911] 2 Ch. 279 at p. 283.

not still be sued on by the original subscriber, and there are certain decisions which imply that this may be possible.[97]

What, then, might be the advantages of suing for breach of contract rather than for misrepresentation? In the first place, it might enable him to sue for rescission and damages where there has been a breach of a *promise* as opposed to a misrepresentation of existing fact. In practice, however, the opportunities for invoking this possibility are likely to be few, for prospectuses, however much they may " puff " the company's prospects, rarely contain any definite promises. Certainly there is no reported decision in which such a claim has succeeded, although *Re Addlestone Linoleum Co.*[98] appears to recognise its feasibility.

Secondly, it might enable the allottee to recover damages from the company without rescinding. Unfortunately much of the value of this possibility is destroyed by *Re Addlestone Linoleum Co.*[98] It was there held, following *Houldsworth* v. *City of Glasgow Bank,*[99] that damages against the company could be recovered only if the allottee also rescinded and it was assumed that this equally applied to an action in contract.

This leaves only a third possible advantage. As already mentioned, in an action based on fraud the subscriber apparently cannot recover the loss of any expected profit on the shares.[1] This is logical (since the action is in tort the appropriate principle is indemnity against loss) but it is not altogether fair. The allottee has doubtless entered into the transaction because he has been persuaded that he will make a profit, and, as we have seen, new issues are normally quoted at a premium immediately after the closing of the lists. It seems, however, that he will be unable to recover damages in respect of this expected profit. On the other hand, if he can sue for breach of contract he should be able to do so.[2] This seems to be the only real advantage of pleading a claim in breach of contract.

Such a claim will, of course, only be possible against those parties with whom the subscriber has a contract, that is, the company, on an issue made by it,[3] and against the issuing house or other vendors on an

---

[97] *Re Addlestone Linoleum Co.* (1887) 37 Ch.D. 191, C.A.; *Re Railway Time Tables Publishing Co.* (1889) 42 Ch.D. 98, C.A.; *Karberg's Case* [1892] 3 Ch. 1, C.A.

[98] *Supra.*

[99] (1880) 5 App.Cas. 317, H.L., *supra.*

[1] *McConnell* v. *Wright* [1903] 1 Ch. 546, C.A. The same rule applies to claims for compensation under s. 43, *infra; Clark* v. *Urquhart* [1930] A.C. 28, H.L.(N.I.).

[2] *Cf.* Sale of Goods Act 1893, s. 53 (3). Although a claim for rescission is a contractual claim in one sense, the damages which may now be awarded in lieu under s. 2 (2) of the Misrepresentation Act 1967 obviously cannot exceed the indemnity which would have been obtained if rescission had been granted.

[3] Or, possibly, when s. 45 of the Companies Act applies to an offer for sale.

offer for sale or placing by them. It will not be possible to sue the
directors in contract, for they have acted merely as agents. Nor, it
seems, can a stock exchange advertisement published for information
only on a mere introduction (unaccompanied by an offer or placing)
ever be relied on as a contractual document.

On the other hand, although, as now seems to be accepted, loss of
expected profit cannot be recovered in an action in tort,[4] it equally now
seems to be established that, as regards other consequential losses, the
tortious measure of damages may be more generous than the contractual.[5] Hence, whether it will be more advantageous to plead a claim in
contract, where possible, rather than in tort will depend on the nature of
the losses sustained.

Offers to acquire securities

Hitherto we have assumed that the prospectus is of the orthodox type
published on a disposal of securities. But precisely the same common
law and equitable principles apply to an offer, for example, on a take-
over bid, to acquire securities. Here too, if there is a misrepresentation
in the take-over circular, there may be an action for damages (either in
deceit, under the Misrepresentation Act, or, conceivably, under *Hedley
Byrne & Co. Ltd.* v. *Heller & Partners Ltd.*), rescission, or an action for
breach of contract, and the same principles apply. The only difference is
that an offer for shares will necessarily be made by someone other than
the company itself, since a company cannot buy its own shares. Hence
the remedies will have to be pursued against the third-party acquirer
and not against the company.[6]

Company Law Remedies

The principal civil remedy specifically providing for falsehoods in
prospectuses is under section 43 of the Companies Act 1948. In
addition there are various possibilities of claims based on statutory
duties imposed by that Act and the Prevention of Fraud (Investments)
Act 1958 and the Protection of Depositors Act 1963.

---

4 *McConnell* v. *Wright* [1903] 1 Ch. 546, C.A., *per* Collins M.R. at pp. 554–555
(the defendant was the notorious Whitaker Wright, still remembered for his glass-
roofed ballroom beneath a lake and his sensational suicide in court); *Clark* v.
Urquhart [1930] A.C. 28, H.L.(N.I.). But some jurisdictions in the U.S.A. have
allowed such recovery: see Loss, *Securities Regulation* (2nd ed., 1961), pp. 1629, 1630.
5 *Doyle* v. *Olby (Ironmongers) Ltd.* [1969] 2 W.L.R. 673, C.A., where Winn L.J.,
at p. 681, approved the statement in *Mayne & McGregor on Damages* (12th ed.),
para. 955.
6 It is possible that the company itself may be responsible for some of the statements
in the take-over circular and therefore prima facie liable if its officers have been
fraudulent. In that case the rule in *Houldsworth* v. *City of Glasgow Bank* (if it
still survives—see *supra*, p. 319) should not prevent action against the company
since the plaintiff will have ceased to be a member of the company when his shares
were acquired.

Section 43 of the Companies Act 1948

Section 43 [7] re-enacts and extends the provisions of the Directors' Liability Act 1890, which largely superseded common law actions for deceit in cases arising out of misleading prospectuses.

(i) **Scope of remedy.** Anticipating the Misrepresentation Act, this section maintained most of the common law requirements but removed the need to prove fraud and altered the onus of proof in favour of the plaintiff. Once the plaintiff has proved that he has sustained damage by reason of an untrue statement in a prospectus his action will succeed unless the defendant disproves responsibility for the prospectus in one of the ways mentioned below, or unless he proves that he had reasonable ground to believe, and did up to the time of allotment believe, that the statement was true. In other respects most that has been said previously applies to this statutory remedy; there must be a false statement [8] of a fact which is material in the sense that it induced the subscription, and the sanction is damages assessed as in actions for deceit.[9]

There may be one other respect in which the statutory liability is wider than deceit. As already pointed out, damages for fraud or under section 2 (1) of the Misrepresentation Act can be recovered only by those to whom the prospectus was addressed.[10] It is not clear whether a claim for compensation under section 43 is similarly limited. Sub-section (1) says that " where a prospectus invites persons to subscribe," compensation shall be paid " to *all persons who subscribe* . . . on the faith of the prospectus . . ." This does not appear to restrict applications to those originally invited. It is therefore submitted that, whatever the position may be at common law,[10] persons to whom allotment letters or letters of right are renounced, will be entitled to claim compensation if they have in fact relied on the prospectus.[11]

In other respects, however, the scope of the section is narrower than the common law remedy.

Although it is not expressly limited to prospectuses issued by or on behalf of the company, it seems clear that it only applies to them. This construction appears inevitable because the remedy is restricted to persons who " subscribe," [11] as opposed to " purchase," securities on

---

[7] This also applies to prospectuses issued in Great Britain by foreign companies: s. 422.

[8] As defined in s. 46, *supra*.

[9] *Clark* v. *Urquhart*, *supra*, in which it was suggested that the draftsman used the expression " compensation " instead of " damages " to emphasise the fact that there is not necessarily any moral blame.

[10] *Supra*, pp. 320, 321.

[11] " Subscribe " has been held to mean taking or agreeing to take unissued shares for cash: *Arnison* v. *Smith* (1889) 41 Ch.D. 348, C.A.; *Re V. G. M. Holdings Ltd.* [1942] Ch. 235, C.A.; *Governments Stock and Other Securities Invest. Co.* v. *Christopher* [1956] 1 W.L.R. 237. Those to whom newly issued shares are renounced would appear to qualify as subscribers.

the faith of the prospectus and because the primary liability is that of the directors. Hence it will afford no relief on an offer for sale or placing by existing holders unless the company has made the allotment with that in view, so that section 45 applies. Even if, as may well be the case, the company and its directors have published a stock exchange advertisement on the offer or placing, the section will have no application. Nor can it be invoked by market purchasers of securities after the original allotment. And it clearly cannot apply to offers for a non-cash consideration or to offers to acquire securities; hence it has no application to take-over circulars.

(ii) **Who may be sued.** Although the section applies only where the company is responsible for the prospectus, no liability is cast on the company itself. Those liable are the directors, every person who has authorised himself to be named, and is named, as a director in the prospectus, promoters, and every person who has authorised the issue of the prospectus. While the last type of person might, on normal principles of construction, include the company itself, it is quite clear that this is not the intention. Rescission remains the remedy against the company; section 43 gives the investor an additional remedy against the company's directors and other responsible individuals, a remedy of which he can avail himself whether or not he can or does rescind the allotment and whether or not he can prove *mens rea* on anyone's part.

The remedy, then, is available against directors,[12] apparent directors, promoters and others who have authorised the issue of the prospectus. " Promoters " here only includes one who was a party to the preparation of the prospectus.[13] Among those who have authorised the issue will be an expert whose report is included therein and who will therefore be required by section 40 to give his formal consent, but by the proviso to subsection (1) he is not to be liable merely on this account, except as regards any untrue statement purporting to be made by him.

(iii) **Defences.** An expert will escape liability for misstatements in his report if he can prove that he withdrew his consent in writing either (a) before the prospectus was registered, or (b) on becoming aware of the untruth after registration but before allotment, provided, in the latter case, that he gave reasonable public notice of his with-

---

12 Defined in s. 455 as including " any person occupying the position of director by whatever name called."
13 subs. (5). And does not include any person acting in a professional capacity for persons engaged in the formation: *ibid.* This presumably implies that professional advisers are not, as such, included under the other heads unless their formal consent as experts is required under s. 40. *E.g.*, the solicitor who had drafted the prospectus would presumably not be liable as a person who had authorised its issue. On the other hand, a sponsoring issuing house would clearly be liable whether or not it was the actual seller of the securities.

drawal and of his reasons.[14] He will also be absolved if he can prove that he was competent to make the statement and that up to the time of the allotment he believed it on reasonable grounds.[14] Nevertheless, these provisions impose serious risks of liability and, in effect, compel a *soi-disant* expert actually to be competent and careful. They clearly provide a subscriber with a better remedy than an attempt to establish a duty of care under *Hedley Byrne & Co. Ltd.* v. *Heller & Partners Ltd.*[15]

Any of the specified persons, other than the expert, can only escape [16] by proving either that he publicly dissociated himself from the prospectus or that he believed on reasonable grounds that the statement was true. Even if the untrue statement is that of the expert, the other sponsors of the prospectus will have to prove that it fairly represents what the expert said, and that they believed on reasonable grounds that the expert was competent and had consented to its publication.[17] In brief, they are under a duty to be both honest and diligent and have to prove that they have discharged that duty.

The section also contains provisions [18] whereby the directors are required to indemnify anyone made liable because he is named as a director, or because his expert report has been published after he has withdrawn his consent.

Under other sections of the Companies Act 1948 [19]

Certain of the other prospectus provisions of the Act expressly provide for civil liabilities. Thus under section 47, if the minimum subscription has not been received within forty days after the first issue of the prospectus, the company is liable to refund all subscription moneys. If this is not done within a further eight days all the directors are jointly and severally liable to repay with 5 per cent. interest from that day, unless any can prove that default in repayment was not due to misconduct or negligence on his part. Section 51 contains similar provisions when subscription or purchase moneys have become repayable as a result of a failure to obtain a stock exchange quotation when the prospectus states that one is to be applied for. If the quotation is not obtained, any purported allotment or purchase is void. This section specifically applies whether the prospectus is on an issue or sale, and any underwriter of the issue can avail himself of it as if he had applied on the faith of the prospectus.[20]

[14] subs. (3).

[15] [1964] A.C. 465, H.L.; *supra*, p. 316.

[16] subs. (2). The statement in the text is much abbreviated.

[17] In the case of statements culled from official sources it suffices if the extract is an accurate representation of the official publication: subs. (2) (*d*) (iii).

[18] subs. (4).

[19] For details of these sections, see Chap. 14, *supra*.

[20] s. 51 (6).

Section 49 also provides that any allotment made by a company in contravention of section 47 (just mentioned) or section 48 (relating to the filing of a statement in lieu of prospectus by a company which does not issue a prospectus on its formation) shall be voidable within one month, but not later, of the holding of the statutory meeting, or of allotment if a statutory meeting is not required to be held after the allotment. It is expressly stated that winding up will not bar the allottee's rights provided he acts within the month. And if any director knowingly permits the contravention of any of these provisions he is liable to compensate the company and the allottee for any loss, and in this case proceedings may be taken within two years of the allotment.

Section 49, however, gives no remedy because of an inaccuracy or omission from the statement in lieu.[21] Nor do any of the other sections in the Companies Act or any sections in the Prevention of Fraud (Investments) Act 1958 or the Protection of Depositors Act 1963. The question arises, therefore, whether a civil action for damages would lie for breach of the statutory duty imposed by any of these sections.

Breach of statutory duty

The argument that there may be civil liability is difficult to sustain in the case of the Companies Act itself since, as we have seen, it expressly provides civil remedies in some cases and thus seems necessarily to imply that there is to be none in others. Despite this, there is one section (s. 38) where the courts have shown themselves willing to imply that there is a civil remedy.

Section 38 of the Companies Act

Section 38 provides for the matters to be set out in a prospectus issued generally of securities not uniform with those already issued and dealt in on a prescribed stock exchange.[22] This section makes no express provision for either civil or criminal liabilities, except for the criminal sanction imposed by subsection (3) for non-compliance with that subsection. On the other hand, subsection (4) provides that in the event of contravention or non-compliance with any of the requirements of the section " a director or other person responsible for the prospectus shall not incur any liability " if he proves certain specified defences. This can only mean that if he cannot prove one of these defences he will be liable, presumably civilly, and it was so held in *Re South of England Natural Gas Co.*[23] although the House of Lords left the point open in the later case of *Nash* v. *Lynde.*[24]

---

[21] *Re Blair Open Hearth Furnace Co.* [1914] 1 Ch. 390, C.A., "unless the statement is so insufficient as to be illusory and amount to no statement at all."
[22] See *supra*, Chap. 14, p. 298 *et seq.* S. 417 in effect extends s. 38 to offers in Great Britain of securities of foreign companies.
[23] [1911] 1 Ch. 573, following *Re Wimbledon Olympia* [1910] 1 Ch. 630.
[24] [1929] A.C. 158, H.L. In this case the House decided that there had been no omission.

Section 38 therefore becomes a valuable weapon in the investor's armoury. Neither at common law nor under section 43 will a mere omission to state a material fact afford the subscriber any relief. As we have seen, the courts stopped short of imposing a duty of full disclosure, although they gave a liberal application to the maxim *suppressio veri suggestio falsi.* But section 38, by imposing an obligation to state the matters specified in Schedule 4 [25] and, apparently, affording a civil remedy if they are not stated, completes the protective wall around the investor, and any attempt to make subscribers contract-out of their rights under the section is void. [26]

(i) **Who may be sued.** The section raises a number of questions. First, against whom is the remedy available? Swinfen Eady J. in *Re South of England Natural Gas Co.* [23] decided that it gave no right to rescind the allotment or other remedy against the company, and that the subscriber's remedy was an action for damages against the directors and other persons responsible for the prospectus. This interpretation appears to accord with the wording of subsection (4) and to be consistent with the general policy of the legislature and the courts of maintaining capital intact as a fund for outside creditors and limiting claims for damages to proceedings against the responsible individuals.

Less convincing are the reasons advanced by the learned judge, who said [27] : "In my opinion the allottee is not entitled to rescind his contract because of any breach of the statutory requirements which extend to such comparatively unimportant matters as the names and addresses of the company's auditors." But this, with respect, is beside the point. Nobody could suggest that the allottee would necessarily have a remedy because of *any* omission; it must be a material one, [28] otherwise the allottee will have suffered no loss thereby and will be debarred from pursuing a claim for damages. The argument, put at its highest, is that anything which the legislature has required may be presumed to be material, although in some cases (*e.g.*, as regards the auditors) a misstatement may be material when an omission to state anything would not. [29] It may therefore be open to the courts to reconsider whether rescission may not be permissible when the omission is material, but, for the other reasons stated above, it is probably the better view that damages from the responsible individuals is the remedy intended.

Subsection (4) refers to " a director or other person responsible for the prospectus " and this appears to bring within the class of those

---

[25] Or under the Stock Exchange *Requirements* if a certificate of exemption is granted under s. 39.

[26] subs. (2). This finally eradicates the once popular " waiver-clause."

[27] At p. 577.

[28] See subs. (4) (c).

[29] To state falsely that the auditors will be a particular firm (which is in fact the best-known firm in the City) is probably a material inducement ; to fail to state who the auditors will be, can hardly mislead anyone—unless a subscriber can prove that the firm proposed is the one that he distrusts above all others.

potentially liable most of the persons specified in more detail in section 43. In addition to directors, it will clearly include promoters concerned with the issue, sponsoring issuing houses, and the vendors or placers of the securities. But, in contrast with section 43, the onus of proving responsibility for the prospectus appears to be on the plaintiff.

It seems unlikely that an expert as such can incur liability under section 38. Subsection (4) refers to a "person responsible for the prospectus" not, as in section 43, to a "person who has authorised the issue of the prospectus," and the expert is not responsible for the prospectus as a whole. On the other hand, he is responsible for part of it,[30] and it is arguable that, if his report omitted some of the matters specified in Part II of Schedule 4, he would be liable therefor. This, however, involves construing responsibility for "the prospectus" as including responsibility for any part of it, which seems somewhat far-fetched. In any event, it is highly unlikely that an expert's report could contain a material omission without falsifying what was stated, so that the expert would normally be liable under section 43.

(ii) **Defences.** Any director or other person responsible can escape liability by proving,[31] (a) that he was not cognisant of any matter omitted, or (b) that the non-compliance or contravention arose from an honest mistake. The liability, therefore, is less extensive than that under section 43, for ignorance or an honest mistake excuses even though not on reasonable grounds. Indeed, if the omission is of directors' interests in the promotion, the onus of proof is on the plaintiff to show that the defendant had knowledge.[32] He will also be excused if, in the opinion of the court, the error was immaterial or otherwise such as ought reasonably to be excused.[33]

(iii) **To what prospectuses it applies.** The final problem is to determine to what prospectuses the section relates. Because of the statutory definition of "prospectus" it clearly applies only to those offering securities for subscription or purchase and therefore has no application to take-over circulars offering to acquire securities or to issue shares for a non-cash consideration.[34] Subsection (1) suggests that it applies only to prospectuses on issues by or on behalf of a company or by or on behalf of a promoter of it. This, with the extension resulting from section 45, would limit its ambit to offers by

---

[30] Under s. 46 (*b*), if his report is referred to in the prospectus it shall be considered as part of it.

[31] s. 38 (4) (*a*) and (*b*).

[32] subs. (4) proviso.

[33] subs. (4) (*c*). *Cf.* s. 448, which contains a general power similar to that in the Trustee Act, enabling the court to excuse any officer of the company in proceedings for "negligence, default, breach of duty, or breach of trust." This seems sufficiently wide to include proceedings based on breach of the prospectus provisions but it seems never to have been invoked in such cases.

[34] *Governments Stock and Other Securities Investment Co. Ltd.* v. *Christopher* [1956] 1 W.L.R. 237.

promoters, issues by the company itself and offers for sale or placings made after an allotment with that in view. It would not, on this basis, cover other offers for sale or placings by existing holders. But the effect of subsections (3) and (5) seems to be to extend the section to all offers except those specifically excluded in these subsections.[35] In other words, the persons responsible for the invitation are liable unless the form of application for the subscription or purchase of shares or debentures is accompanied by a prospectus disclosing the statutory information, except in four cases:

(a) where the application was issued in connection with a bona fide under-writing agreement;

(b) where there was no offer to the *public* [36];

(c) where the securities are offered to existing members or debenture-holders, whether or not renounceable; and

(d) where the securities are uniform with an existing issue already quoted on a prescribed stock exchange.

In every other case an investor, whether a subscriber or purchaser, seems to be able to rely on the section if there is a material omission of any of the statutory information.

This construction is put forward with some hesitation because, prior to the Misrepresentation Act 1967, it produced the absurd result that in some cases an investor might have a claim for damages for non-disclosure in circumstances in which he would have none if there had been a positive misrepresentation. If the existing holder of shares [37] makes an offer of them to a sufficiently wide class of his acquaintances for it to be regarded as an offer to the public, he will, apparently, have to accompany the offer by a prospectus giving the statutory information. If he does not, or if the prospectus omits any of the required data, he will be liable under section 38. If, however, he accompanies the offer with a prospectus and gives all the information, but gives some of it inaccurately, he will not, apparently, be liable under section 43 (because the prospectus does not offer the securities for *subscription*) or under section 38 which only gives a remedy for " non-compliance with or contravention of " its requirements, and inaccuracy does not appear to be either.[38] However this particular absurdity has been largely removed by the Misrepresentation Act which affords a remedy for negligent misrepresentations against the offeror. Nevertheless, if this interpretation of section 38 is right it means that the section covers much the same ground as section 14 of the Prevention of Fraud Act, which does not, expressly at any rate, impose any civil

---

[35] See *supra*, Chap. 14, p. 301.

[36] For the wide meaning, see Chap. 14, pp. 295, 296, *supra*.

[37] It is assumed that they were not allotted to him with this in view so that s. 45 does not apply, and that they are not quoted on a stock exchange.

[38] *Cf. Re Blair Open Hearth Furnace Co.* [1914] 1 Ch. 390, C.A.

liability for breach of its requirements. It may be, therefore, that contrary to the views expressed in this and the previous chapter the whole of section 38 is intended to be limited to " issue," as opposed to " sale," prospectuses unless the sale is caught under section 45. This interpretation would certainly avoid some absurdity and would prevent the wording of subsection (1) from being " illusory, if not indeed misleading." [39]   But in either event the section is unhappily worded.

The Prevention of Fraud (Investments) Act 1958 and the Protection of Depositors Act 1963

Neither of these Acts makes any express provision for civil remedies for breach of it. But both, as their titles make clear, are intended for the protection of investors and it would be open to the courts to hold that any investor damnified as a result of a breach of their provisions or of regulations made under them has a remedy in damages. If there were such remedy for breach of section 13 or section 14 of the 1958 Act or the equivalent section 1 or section 2 of the 1963 Act or of the Licensed Dealers (Conduct of Business) Rules 1960 it would certainly help to fill some of the gaps in the protective wall. In the light of the reluctance of English courts to make implications of this sort it is perhaps doubtful whether they would be prepared to do so in this case. But, without going so far, they could and, it is submitted, probably would hold that a contract concluded in non-compliance with the statutes or regulations was illegal and unenforceable by the party in breach.[40]

In the absence of authority, it is perhaps unprofitable to speculate on these matters. Three points may, however, be mentioned. First, in the U.S.A. a whole body of valuable law has resulted from the willingness of the courts to allow a civil remedy to individuals who suffer from breach of the comparable statutes and regulations administered by the S.E.C., notwithstanding the absence of any express provision for such a remedy which was clearly not foreseen by the legislators or the draftsmen.[41]   Secondly, the Jenkins Committee [42] recommended in 1962 that the doubt whether there was any civil remedy for breach of section 13 of the 1958 Act should be resolved by an express provision that any person who suffered damage as a result of any untrue statement, promise or forecast in a circular to which that section applies should have a civil remedy unless those responsible could prove that they had reasonable cause to believe and did believe that the

[39] Buckley, *Companies Acts*, 13th ed., p. 94. It would also be more consistent with s. 45 (3).
[40] Since the other party would be one of those intended to be protected there should be no obstacle in the way of his suing on the contract or for restitution.
[41] See Loss, *Securities Regulation* (2nd ed., 1961 and Supp.), pp. 932–946, 1757–1862.
[42] Cmnd. 1749, paras. 254 and 264 (*a*).

statement was true or the promise or forecast justified.[43] Despite the fact that section 13 was amended by the 1963 Act, this recommendation was not implemented in that Act or in the Companies Act 1967. Thirdly, the Law Commission and the Scottish Law Commission have proposed [44] that legislation should clarify the circumstances in which civil liability for breach of a statutory duty is to be implied. If resulting legislation should provide, as the Commissions recommend, for a civil remedy in the absence of an express provision to the contrary, we might expect in the future a considerable extension of civil liability in this and other spheres.

CONCLUSIONS

The foregoing discussion will at least have shown how muddled and unco-ordinated is the present legal position. This emphasises the point made at the beginning of the previous chapter, namely, that the prospectus provisions have grown up haphazardly to meet particular dangers as they have been experienced. This has resulted in a lack of logical consistency between various sections of the Companies Act, and between that Act and the Prevention of Fraud (Investments) Act and the Protection of Depositors Act. Very recently the well-meaning but insufficiently comprehensive reforms in the Misrepresentation Act have accentuated the inconsistency particularly in relation to company prospectuses, to the peculiarities of which no thought seems to have been given.

Many of the difficulties could have been avoided if the courts had been prepared to recognise that a contract to subscribe for a company's securities was a contract *uberrimae fidei* demanding full disclosure. As it is, the courts, aided by the legislature, have produced an untidy approximation to that conclusion. This is an important and valuable step. In other respects, however, the only consistent principles which are discernible are that damages or compensation shall not be obtainable from the company itself, but from its officers and other persons responsible, and that the equitable remedy of rescission shall be restricted within narrow limits when sought in relation to an allotment of shares. This, apparently, is due to the determination to maintain the company's capital as a guarantee fund for outside creditors.

Despite the defects of unnecessary diversity and a considerable measure of uncertainty, the protection now afforded to investors is extensive. But their real protection is initial screening,[45] and thanks

---

[43] *Cf.* Companies Act, s. 43, and Misrepresentation Act 1967, s. 2 (1), and note that neither covers promises or forecasts.

[44] Report on Interpretation of Statutes (Law Com. 21, June 9, 1969), paras. 38 and 78.

[45] It is interesting to note that in the post-war years no investor seems to have had both the courage and the financial resources to bring to court civil proceedings for mis-statements in a prospectus even in those cases where the directors of the company have been convicted of prospectus offences. If this continues, the material in this chapter may be largely of academic interest.

largely to the issuing houses and to the discipline of the stock exchanges, this screening does take place and is generally effective. Hence it is largely to extra-legal techniques that investors owe their present relative immunity from sharp practice. But it must never be forgotten that had it not been for the legal sanctions, civil and criminal, the extra-legal techniques might never have been perfected.

PART FOUR

A COMPANY'S SECURITIES

CHAPTER 16

THE NATURE AND CLASSIFICATION OF COMPANY SECURITIES

FREQUENT references have been made to the securities which a company can issue. It is now necessary to look a little more closely at the exact nature of these securities and to indicate the various forms they may take.

They fall into two primary classes which legal theory tries to keep rigidly separated but which in economic reality merge into each other. The first of these classes is described as shares; the second as debentures. The basic legal distinction between them is that a share constitutes the holder a member of the company,[1] whereas the debentureholder is a creditor of the company but not a member of it.

Legal nature of shares

What, then, is the exact juridical nature of a share? At the present day this is a question more easily asked than answered. In the old deed of settlement company, which was merely an enlarged partnership with the partnership property vested in trustees, it was clear that the members' " shares " entitled them to an equitable interest in the assets. It is true that the exact nature of this equitable interest was not crystal clear, for the members could not, while the firm was a going concern, lay claim to any particular asset or prevent the directors from disposing of it. Even with the modern partnership, no very satisfactory solution to this problem has been found, and the most one can say is that the members have an equitable interest, often described as a lien, which floats over the partnership assets throughout the duration of the firm, although it only crystallises on dissolution. Still, there is admittedly some sort of proprietary nexus (however vague and ill-defined) between the partnership assets and the partners.

At one time it was thought that the same applied to an incorporated company, except that the company itself held its assets as trustee for its members.[2] But, as we have seen,[3] this idea has long since been rejected. Shareholders have ceased to be regarded as having equitable interests in the company's assets and, " shareholders are not, in the eye of the law,

---

[1] A person may, however, become a member without being a shareholder—the company may not have a share capital.

[2] *Child* v. *Hudson's Bay Co.* (1723) 2 P.Wms. 207. As in the case of partnerships it was clear long before the express statutory provisions to this effect (see C.C.A. 1845, s. 7, and Companies Act 1948, s. 73) that shares were personalty and not realty even if the company owned freehold land : see Chap. 2, p. 26n., *supra*.

[3] See *supra*, Chap. 4, p. 74.

part owners of the undertaking." [4] As a result the word " share " has become something of a misnomer, for shareholders no longer share any property in common; at the most they share certain rights in respect of dividends, return of capital on a winding up, voting, and the like.

Today it is generally stated that a share is a chose in action.[5] This, however, is not helpful, for " chose in action " is a notoriously vague term used to describe a mass of interests which have little or nothing in common except that they confer no right to possession of a physical thing, and which range from purely personal rights under a contract to patents, copyrights and trade marks.

It is tempting to equate shares with rights under a contract, for as we have seen [6] the memorandum and articles of association constitute a contract of some sort between the company and its members and it is these documents which directly or indirectly define the rights conferred by the shares. But a share is something far more than a mere contractual right *in personam*. This is sufficiently clear from the rules relating to infant shareholders, who are liable for calls on the shares unless they repudiate the allotment during infancy or on attaining majority,[7] and who cannot recover any money which they have paid unless the shares have been completely valueless.[8] As Parke B. said,[9] " They have been treated, therefore, as persons in a different situation from mere contractors for then they would have been exempt, but in truth they are purchasers who have acquired an interest not in a mere chattel, but in a subject of a permanent nature. . . ." [10]

The definition of a share which is, perhaps, the most widely quoted is that of Farwell J. in *Borland's Trustee* v. *Steel*.[11]

> " A share is the interest of a shareholder in the company measured by a sum of money, for the purpose of liability in the first place, and of interest in the second, but also consisting of a series of mutual covenants entered into by all the shareholders *inter se* in accordance with [section 20 of the Companies Act 1948]. The contract contained in the articles of association is one of the original incidents of the share. A share is not a sum of

---

4 *Per* Evershed L.J. in *Short* v. *Treasury Commissioners* [1948] 1 K.B. at p. 122, C.A.
5 See, for example, *per* Greene M.R. in [1942] Ch. at p. 241, and *Colonial Bank* v. *Whinney* (1886) 11 App.Cas. 426, H.L.
6 *Supra*, Chap. 12, p. 261 *et seq.*
7 *Cork & Brandon Ry.* v. *Cazenove* (1847) 10 Q.B. 935; *N.W. Ry.* v. *M'Michael* and *Birkenhead (etc.) Ry.* v. *Pilcher* (1851) 5 Exch. 114. If they repudiate during infancy it is not clear whether they can be made liable to pay calls due prior thereto: the majority in *Cazenove's* case thought they could, but Parke B. in the later case (at p. 125) stated the contrary.
8 *Steinberg* v. *Scala (Leeds) Ltd.* [1923] 2 Ch. 452, C.A.
9 (1851) 5 Exch. at p. 123.
10 Later he suggested that the shareholder had " a vested interest of a permanent character in all the profits arising from the land and other effects of the company " (at p. 125). This can hardly be supported in view of later cases.
11 [1901] 1 Ch. 279 at p. 288. Approved by C.A. in *Re Paulin* [1935] 1 K.B. 26, and by H.L. *ibid.*, *sub nom.* *I.R.C.* v. *Crossman* [1937] A.C. 26. See also the other definitions canvassed in that case.

money . . . , but is an interest measured by a sum of money and made up of various rights contained in the contract, including the right to a sum of money of a more or less amount."

It will be observed that this definition, though it lays considerable and perhaps disproportionate stress on the contractual nature of the shareholder's rights, also emphasises the fact that he has an interest in the company. The theory seems to be that the contract constituted by the articles of association defines the nature of the rights, which however, are not purely personal rights but instead confer some sort of proprietary interest in the company though not in its property. The company itself is treated not merely as a person, the subject of rights and duties, but also as a *res,* the object of rights and duties.[12] In an attempt to distinguish the *persona* from the *res* the latter is often described as " capital stock " or " share capital," but the use of the vague term " capital " hardly makes for greater precision. It is the fact that the shareholder has rights *in* the company as well as against it, which, in legal theory, distinguishes the member from the debenture-holder whose rights are also defined by contract (this time the debenture itself and not the articles) but are rights *against* the company and if the debenture is secured, in its property, but never *in the company itself.*

Farwell J.'s definition mentions that the interest of a shareholder is measured by a sum of money. Reference has already been made to this [13] and it has been emphasised that the requirement of a nominal monetary value is an arbitrary and illogical one which has been rejected in certain other common law jurisdictions. The nominal value is meaningless and may be misleading, except in so far as it determines the minimum liability. Even as a measure of liability, it is of less importance now that shares are almost invariably issued on terms that they are to be fully paid up on allotment and are frequently issued at a price exceeding their nominal value. But reference to liability is valuable in that it emphasises that shareholders *qua* members may be under obligations to the company as well as having rights against it. In so far as these obligations are financial they are usually strengthened by the express conferment on the company of a lien on the shares or a right to forfeit the shares for non-payment.[14]

This analysis may seem academic and barren, and to some extent it is, for a closer examination of the rights conferred by shares and debentures will show the impossibility of preserving any hard and fast distinction between them which bears any relation to practical reality. Nevertheless the matter is not entirely theoretical, for in a number of

---

[12] " A whole system . . . has been built up on the unconscious assumption that organisations, which from one point of view are considered individuals, from another are storehouses of tangible property ": Arnold, *The Folklore of Capitalism,* p. 353.
[13] *Supra,* Chap. 6.
[14] Problems connected with the company's lien generally arise on the transfer of the shares and hence they will be considered in Chap. 18, *infra.*

cases the courts have been faced with the need to analyse the juridical nature of a shareholder's interest in order to determine the principles on which it should be valued. The most important of these cases are the *Crossman and Paulin* case [15] and *Short* v. *Treasury Commissioners* [16] to which reference has already been made. In the latter, which is particularly interesting, the whole of the shares of Short Bros. were being acquired by the Treasury under a Defence Regulation which provided for payment of their value " as between a willing buyer and a willing seller." [17] They were valued share by share on the basis of the quoted market price, but the shareholders argued that, since all the shares were being acquired, stock exchange prices were not a true criterion and that either the whole undertaking should be valued and the global price thus determined apportioned among the shareholders, or the value should be the price which one buyer would give for the whole block, which price should then be similarly apportioned. The courts upheld the method adopted and rejected both the alternatives suggested, the first because the shareholders were not " part owners of the undertaking " and the second because the regulation implied that each holding was to be separately valued. It was conceded that had any individual shareholder held a sufficient block to give him " control " of the company then he might have been entitled to a higher price than the total stock exchange value of all his shares, [18] since he would then have been selling an item of property—control—additional to his shares. [19] But if no one shareholder has control to sell, a buyer of a number of separate holdings may, as in the *Short* case, be able to acquire control of assets for a fraction of their true value.

While it may be doubtful whether the rights which a share confers on its holder can be classified as " proprietary " in the usual sense, one thing at least is clear: the share itself is an object of dominion, *i.e.*, of rights *in rem*, and not so to regard it would be barren and academic in the extreme. For all practical purposes shares are recognised in law, as well as in fact, as the objects of property which are bought, sold, mortgaged and bequeathed. They are indeed the typical items of property of the modern commercial era and particularly suited to its demands because of their exceptional liquidity. To deny that they are " owned " would be as unreal as to deny, on the basis of feudal theory, that land is owned—far more unreal because the owner's dominion over

---

[15] [1935] 1 K.B. 26, C.A., reversed [1937] A.C. 26   See *supra*, Chap. 9, pp. 183, 184.

[16] [1948] 1 K.B. 116, C.A., affd. [1948] A.C. 534, H.L.

[17] This popular formula is much criticised by economists who argue with some force that the willingness of the buyer and seller depends on the price and not vice versa.

[18] Hence in *Dean* v. *Prince* [1953] Ch. 590 (reversed on the facts [1954] Ch. 409, C.A.) Harman J. held that the " fair value " of a block of shares conferring control must include something above the " break-up " value of the assets, in respect of this control.

[19] This question is further discussed in connection with take-over bids: Chap. 23, pp. 540–546, and Chap. 24, pp. 578, 579.

his shares is likely to be considerably less fettered than that over his land. Nor, today, is the bundle of rights and liabilities making up the share regarded as equitable only. On the contrary, as the next chapter will show, legal ownership is recognised and distinguished from equitable ownership in very much the same way as a legal estate in land is distinguished from equitable interests therein.

Nor must this emphasis on the proprietary and financial aspects of a shareholder's rights obscure the important fact that his shares cause him to become a member of an association with the right to take part in its deliberations by attending and voting at general meetings. These rights as member of an association also distinguish him from the debenture-holder who is not a member of the corporate body and has none of the privileges of an associate in it.

Legal nature of debentures

" I cannot find any precise legal definition of the term [debenture], it is not either in law or commerce a strictly technical term, or what is called a term of art." [20] But despite this discouraging pronouncement it is in fact far easier to fit debentures into the normal legal classifications; it may be difficult to decide what is and what is not a debenture, but the juristic nature of the underlying transaction is never in doubt. The difficulty is the converse of that in the case of shares; there is never any doubt about whether something is a share, but there is considerable doubt about what a share is. There is no doubt about the juristic nature of a debenture, but there may be considerable doubt about whether something ought properly to be described as a debenture.

" Debenture " is a name applied to certain types of document evidencing an indebtedness which is normally, but not necessarily, secured by a charge over property. The rights of the debentureholder, therefore, are simply contractual rights against the company, coupled, if the debenture is not a " naked debenture " without a charge, with rights against some or all of the company's [21] property. Whether or not there is a charge (and only if there is, will there theoretically be any rights *in rem* vested in the holder) the debenture is treated equally with the share as the object of dominion.

Primarily, the expression " debenture " is applied not to the indebtedness itself but to the document evidencing it. But the company, instead of issuing individual debentures, evidencing separate and distinct debts, may create one loan fund known as " debenture stock " divisible among a class of lenders each of whom is given a debenture stock

---

[20] *Per* Chitty J. in *Levy* v. *Abercorris Slate & Slab Co.* (1887) 37 Ch.D. 260 at p. 264.
[21] The word " debenture " is not necessarily restricted to companies' securities. Clubs not infrequently issue debentures and the name may even be applied to securities issued by an individual; for example to the Tichborne Bonds issued by the claimant to finance his attempt to establish his right to the Tichborne inheritance. For an account of this fascinating chapter in legal and social history, see Maugham (Lord): *The Tichborne Case* (1936).

certificate evidencing the aliquot parts of the whole loan to which he is entitled.[22] This debenture stock, which is analogous to the loan stocks of governments and local and public authorities, is then the indebtedness itself, and the certificates evidence the stockholders' interests in it. A consequence of the distinction is that whereas a debenture is a single thing which can be legally transferred only as one entity, debenture stock can be subdivided and transferred in any fractions which the holder wishes. As we shall see, a similar arrangement can be made in the case of shares which, when fully paid, can be converted into " stock " but without, of course, changing the basic rights of the holders or altering them from members to creditors. For the purposes of the Companies Act, " share " includes " stock " and " debenture " includes " debenture stock." [23]

But not every type of indebtedness can properly be described as a debenture. It is here that the imprecision of the term becomes apparent. In practice it is restricted to loans of some permanence.[24] Generally the loan is secured on property of the company, but this is not necessary,[25] although the stock exchanges will not grant permission to deal in an issue of naked debentures if it is to be described as an issue of debentures, but will insist on the term " notes," " unsecured loan stock " or the like.

Because of the technical distinction between securities whose holders are members, and securities whose holders are outside creditors, it follows, as we have seen,[26] that the rules relating to the raising and maintenance of capital apply only to the former. Subject to the exceptions already mentioned, shares impose a liability on the holder to pay in cash or in kind their nominal value, and, while the company remains a going concern, this nominal value must not be reduced by a repayment nor must the holders be paid any return on their outlay except out of profits. But none of these rules applies to debentures. They may be issued at a discount, they may be redeemed, and interest on them may be paid out of the company's capital. In legal theory their holders are not interested *in* the company but are creditors having claims *against* it.

However, when we examine the various classes of securities which a company may issue we find that for practical purposes the various

---

[22] Debenture stock certificate is to debenture stock what debenture is to debt.
[23] Companies Act 1948, s. 455.
[24] A promissory note, bill of exchange or IOU would not be described as a debenture (and the passage of the Protection of Depositors Act 1963, *supra*, pp. 306, 307, implicitly recognises that they are not); nor would a document evidencing a pledge of goods or documents of title to goods. But their exclusion from the legal definition in s. 455 can only be supported if " any other securities " can be construed *ejusdem generis* with " debenture stock " and " bonds."
[25] *Lemon* v. *Austin Friars Investment Trust Ltd.* [1926] Ch. 1, C.A. The dicta in this case that a provision that the moneys should only be payable out of profits constituted a " charge " on the company's property seem untenable.
[26] *Supra*, Chap. 6.

types merge imperceptibly one into another, and that there is in practice far greater similarity between debentures and certain types of shares than there is between all classes of shares.

The presumption of equality between shareholders

The typical company—one limited by shares—must issue some shares, and the initial presumption of the law is that all shares confer equal rights and impose equal liabilities. As in partnership [27] equality is assumed in the absence of evidence to the contrary. Normally the shareholders' rights will fall under three heads: (i) dividends, (ii) return of capital on a winding up (or authorised reduction of capital) and (iii) attendance at meetings and voting, and unless there is some indication to the contrary all the shares will confer the like rights to all three. So far as voting is concerned this is a comparatively recent development, for, on the analogy of the partnership rule, it was long felt that members' rights to control through voting should be divorced from their purely financial interests in respect of dividend and capital, so that the equality should be between members rather than between shares. A stage intermediate between these two ideas is reflected in the Companies Clauses Act 1845 [28] which provides that in the absence of contrary provision in the special statute every shareholder shall have one vote for every share up to ten, one for every additional five up to a hundred and one for every ten thereafter, thus weighting the voting in favour of the smaller holders. However, attempts to reduce the proportion of voting rights as the size of holdings increased were doomed to failure since the requirement could be easily evaded by splitting holdings and vesting them in nominees. It is now recognised that if voting rights are to vary, separate classes of shares must be created so that the different number of votes can be attached to the shares themselves and not to the holder. Even today, however, the older ide' still prevails on a vote by a show of hands, when the common law rule is that each member has one vote irrespective of the number of shares held; a rule which, although it can be altered by the constitution, is normally maintained, if only because the number of an individual's hands cannot be multiplied with his shareholdings.[29]

There is a similar presumption of equality so far as concerns the shareholders' liabilities. As we have seen, in the case of a company limited by shares the only liability *qua* shareholder will normally be to pay the nominal amount of the share, so that if shares are of the same nominal value the holders' liabilities are necessarily the same.[30] And, in

[27] Partnership Act 1890, s. 24 (1).
[28] s. 75.
[29] For the law and practice regarding voting at meetings, see Chap. 21, *infra*.
[30] This does not mean that the shares will necessarily be issued at the same price; different prices, at or above par, may be payable when, for example, issues are made at different times or at the same time by tender.

calling up the unpaid liability, this equality must be preserved; calls must be made *pari passu* unless the articles otherwise provide.[31] If the liability is to differ, different classes of shares must be created.[32]

For many years it was thought that in the absence of express provision in the original constitution the continued equality of all shares was a fundamental condition which could not be abrogated by an alteration of the articles so as to allow the issue of shares preferential to those already issued.[33] This idea was, however, finally destroyed in *Andrews* v. *Gas Meter Co.*[34] which established that in the absence of a prohibition in the memorandum, the articles could be altered so as to authorise such an issue.

In the United States of America the principle of equality, based on the analogy of partnerships, has been carried so far as to confer on the existing shareholders pre-emptive rights on the issue of any new shares so that the existing balance of power is preserved. This rule has now been abrogated or modified in many states.[35] In England it never seems to have been adopted as a common law rule. On the other hand, the Companies Clauses Acts provide [36] that if the existing shares of a statutory company are quoted at a premium any new shares must be offered to the existing holders. As regards registered companies, the optional model in Table A formerly contained similar provisions which applied whether the existing shares were above or below par,[37] but in the latest Table this has been deleted. In the case of a small private company it may be important expressly to incorporate such a provision since otherwise a majority of " partners " who are directors may issue new capital to the detriment of the minority. Similarly it has long been recognised that further issues by public companies of equity shares for cash ought normally to be in the form of rights issues to the existing equity shareholders, and the stock exchanges now require this unless those shareholders otherwise resolve in general meeting.[38]

---

31 *Galloway* v. *Hallé Concerts Society* [1915] 2 Ch. 233. But *cf.* Companies Act 1948, s. 59, and Table A, art. 20. If in fact the directors exercised the power of differentiation conferred by the article the shares would in reality be of different classes. It is also common to provide that shareholders may make payments at interest in advance of calls: *cf.* Table A, art. 21. The resulting position is somewhat anomalous, since the amount so advanced is for some purposes treated as capital and for others as an outside debt. It seems that while it may not be repaid except on an authorised reduction (*London and Northern S.S. Co.* v. *Farmer* [1914] W.N. 200), it ranks for repayment before other capital (*Re Wakefield Co.* [1892] 3 Ch. 165) but after outside debts (*ibid.*, and *Re Exchange Drapery Co.* (1888) 38 Ch.D. 171 at p. 175), and agreed interest may be paid out of capital if there are insufficient profits (*Lock* v. *Queensland Mortgage Co.* [1896] A.C. 461, H.L.).
32 Although they need not necessarily be expressly given different names: *cf. Re United Provident Assurance Co.* [1910] 2 Ch. 477; *Greenhalgh* v. *Arderne Cinemas* [1945] 2 All E.R. 719; affd. [1946] 1 All E.R. 512, C.A.
33 *Hutton* v. *Scarborough Cliff Hotel Co.* (1865) 2 Dr. & Sim. 521.
34 [1897] 1 Ch. 361, C.A.
35 Bearle & Means, *The Modern Corporation and Private Property*, 255 *et seq.*
36 1845 Act, s. 58; 1863 Act, s. 17.
37 *Cf.* Companies Act 1929, Table A, art. 35.
38 *Requirements*, App., Sched. VIII, Part A. (General Undertaking), para. 15. And see Jenkins Report (Cmnd. 1749), paras. 119–121.

The prima facie equality of shares can be modified by special provision, in the memorandum or in the original or amended articles, dividing the shares into different classes with different rights as to dividends, capital and voting or any of them, or with different nominal values and hence with different liability. By ringing the changes on these various incidents the number of possible classes is limited only by the total number of shares.[39]

Tendencies in capital structures

The practice in this respect has gone through three phases. The early companies were still imbued with partnership ideas and hence it was common to have shares of a large nominal value, partly paid and all of one class. This, however, was attractive only to the investor who was prepared to take an active interest in the company. Once it was realised that the great virtue of the limited liability company was that it enabled money to be raised from absentee investors, the tendency was to adopt a capital structure which would provide something to appeal to this type of investor. From about 1880 therefore the prevailing practice was in favour of reducing the amount of unpaid liability (never popular with someone who was merely looking for an investment for a certain sum) and with it the size of the nominal value. This tendency was encouraged when it was found desirable to appeal to the small investor. This development was, however, accompanied by an increase in the various classes of securities. An appeal was made to the investor who was looking for a steady return and a greater measure of security by making use of the practice, popularised by railway and other statutory companies, of issuing preference shares conferring a fixed preferential dividend with or without a corresponding preference as regards capital on a winding up.[40] A leaf was also taken from the statutory companies'[41] book by issuing mortgage debentures, thus appealing to the man in the street who had hitherto invested in the funds but who was seeking a greater return without substantial reduction in security. The popularity of debentures was greatly increased when the legality of the floating charge was finally established in 1870[42]; the advantages to the

---

[39] German jurisprudence for long denied that voting preference could be given unless coupled with some financial preference. No such rule has ever been suggested in England, but certain Dominion Acts now restrain weighted voting: see, for example, S. African Companies Act, No. 46 of 1926 (as amended by Act No. 46 of 1952), s. 62 *quat.*; Indian Companies Act 1956, ss. 87–89.

[40] General permission for statutory companies to issue preference shares was first conferred by the 1863 Act, s. 13, but from 1830 onwards the practice had been widespread under the authority of special Acts.

[41] The practices of statutory companies had already converted the mortgage from a mere short-term loan to a possible long-term investment. A peculiar type of debenture stock is also authorised under the 1863 Act whereby the holder obtains a charge for the interest due to him in the nature of a perpetual annuity with no right to repayment of capital.

[42] *Re Panama, New Zealand and Australian Royal Mail Co.* (1870) L.R. 5 Ch.App. 318.

investor, and the danger to the public,[43] of this form of security have already been stressed.[44]

The number of share classes was increased by three factors. In the first place, the rise of the professional company promoter led to the practice of creating a special class of founders' or deferred shares which the promoters retained, partly by way of remuneration and partly as an advertising gesture to show their ostensible confidence in their flotations. These shares were normally of low nominal value but conferred substantial rights after the other shareholders had received a fixed return. Secondly, the need to raise further capital led, as it had in the case of statutory companies, to the issue of pre-preference shares designed to offer greater attractions than the depreciated existing shares.[45] Thirdly, the proliferation of classes enabled a small minority—normally the original proprietors of a business—to retain voting control despite the fact that their financial interests were far less than those of the public.

In the result the second phase was characterised by companies with highly complicated capital structures comprising shares, and perhaps debentures, of many different classes. The third phase, however, which commenced about 1920 and which still continues, has seen a tendency towards greater simplification. Deferred and founders' shares (after causing their companies great embarrassment) have been almost completely eradicated. So have partly paid shares; even the banks and finance houses are now taking steps to reorganise their capital so as to remove the uncalled liability. Companies with numerous classes of preference and pre-preference shares have proved unpopular with investors and with managements, and have generally reorganised so as to consolidate some or all of the various classes. Today, therefore, it is uncommon to find a public company with more than one, or at the most two, of each of the primary classifications of debentures, preference shares, and ordinary shares. Generally speaking the same applies in even greater measure to private companies which usually have only one class of share.[46]

The other major tendency of the second phase—smaller nominal values—has continued and become ever more noticeable, so that today

---

[43] By 1881 it had become sufficiently common, and its dangers sufficiently appreciated, for the Annual General Meeting of the Associated Chambers of Commerce to urge legislation to ban it: see *III Journal of Inst. of Bankers*, p. 227. These protests continued yearly, but vainly except in so far as they led to publicity by registration of charges and to other measures rendering floating charges vulnerable in some circumstances: see Chap. 19, *infra*.

[44] *Supra*, Chap. 4, p. 78 *et seq.*

[45] The need was especially great since registered, unlike statutory, companies could not issue their shares at a discount: *supra*, Chap. 6, p. 106.

[46] The urge, however, to avoid tax has in some cases led to considerable complication through attempts to divorce voting control from financial reward, but, as we have seen (*supra*, Chap. 9), success in this direction has become an increasingly remote chance.

shares are rarely above £1 in denomination and are often as low as 6d. or 1s.

During this last phase the peculiarities of taxation have also had their effect on capital structures. As we have seen,[47] post-war government policy has been to encourage dividend restraint and accordingly a higher rate of tax has been payable on that part of the profits which is distributed to the shareholders. Companies can scarcely omit to pay their fixed preference dividends if they have made adequate profits, but, if they pay them, the tax liability is increased and the burden of it falls, not on the preference, but on the ordinary, shareholders. The result has been to make preference shares unpopular with those controlling the destinies of companies, who generally think of ordinary shareholders as the true proprietors whose interests must be given primary consideration. Hence the increased popularity of debentures, for here again legal theory becomes important; since the debentureholders are creditors not members, payments to them are normally [48] deductible from profits, and tax liabilities are reduced instead of increased. Rather than issue preference shares in these circumstances several companies have resorted to unsecured loan stock [49] or even subordinated loan stock which on a winding-up ranks after other creditors so that it is in reality a class of preference shares.[50]

Declaration of dividends on shares

Before proceeding further it may be well to say a few preliminary words about the declaration of dividends on shares. Subject to the rule that dividends must not be paid out of capital,[51] the terms on which they are payable, and the method of declaring them, depend entirely on the provisions in the articles. In practice, however, these have become standardised and provide for declaration in general meeting to an amount not exceeding that recommended by the directors.[52] This is coupled with a provision entitling the directors to set aside reserves out of the profits before recommending a dividend.[53] In addition, the directors are empowered to pay interim dividends,[54] that is to say, dividends payable in between two annual general meetings.

---

[47] *Supra*, Chap. 9.
[48] Since F.A. 1965 there are a number of exceptions, *e.g.*, interest on bonus debentures, on non-quoted convertible debentures and, in the case of close companies, on debentures held by certain people concerned in the management.
[49] Formerly there were tax advantages even if the interest on the loan stock was payable only out of profits: see *I.R.C.* v. *Pullman Car Co.* [1954] 1 W.L.R. 1029, but this is no longer so since F.A. 1965. Formerly, too, the stamp duty on an issue of debentures (2s. 6d. per £100) was considerably less than the capital duty on nominal share capital (10s. per £100), but, except for short term borrowings, loan capital duty of 10s. per £100 is now payable on debentures: F.A. 1967, s. 28.
[50] See (1967) 111 Sol.J. 841. But exceptionally high interest rates now make any form of loan capital very expensive.
[51] Chap. 6, *supra*.
[52] Table A, art. 114.
[53] *Ibid*. art. 117.
[54] *Ibid*. art. 115.

The result, once again, is that, although the members in general meeting retain the ultimate theoretical control, the real control is vested in the directors. The members have no say in the matter of interim dividends,[55] and as regards final dividends for the year their control is purely negative; they can reduce the amount recommended by the directors but cannot raise it. Generally this applies equally to all types of dividend (as opposed to interest on debentures); to the fixed dividend on preference shares as well as to the fluctuating return on ordinary shares. But everything depends on the terms of the articles and, as we shall see, these occasionally remove the directors' discretion so far as preference dividends are concerned.

Once the dividend has been lawfully declared the amount due to each shareholder becomes a debt for which he can sue the company.[56] The normal method of payment by public companies is by a dividend warrant which, for most practical and legal purposes, is merely a special form of cheque. Whatever method of payment is adopted the company is bound to attach an explanation of the income tax deductions.[57]

Classes of securities

(i) *Debentures*

Of the three primary types of security, the first in seniority is the debenture which, as already pointed out, embraces any form of long-term borrowing and which is normally secured by a charge on property of the company. In law the debentureholder is a creditor and entitled to all the remedies of a creditor to obtain payment of the sums due to him whether they be principal or interest. The company must repay the principal (but must not repay the shareholders' capital contributions) and the company must pay the prescribed rate of interest whether or not it has made profits (but must not pay dividends to its shareholders unless it has made profits).

On the face of it, therefore, the debentureholder stands entirely aloof from the company and is dependent on its prosperity only to the extent that any creditor is. Such may, indeed, be the position. If the company has landed property on which it borrows, the mortgage may be in the normal form of a mortgage of land and the mortgagee's position will be no different from that of any other mortgagee.

---

[55] *Scott* v. *Scott* [1943] 1 All E.R. 582.

[56] *Re Severn and Wye Ry.* [1896] 1 Ch. 559. This is perhaps the only circumstance in which a member as such has a legal (as opposed to an equitable) remedy against the company. The debt is a specialty and therefore statute-barred after 12 years from the date when it should have been paid : *Re Artizans Land and Mortgage Corpn.* [1904] 1 Ch. 796. The grounds on which this case was decided—that the share certificate was a deed—are unsatisfactory (*cf. Re Northern Ontario Power Co.* [1954] 1 D.L.R. 627, Ont. S.C.), but the decision seems to be correct in view of s. 20 of the Act (see *supra*, pp. 261–265).

[57] I.T.A. 1952, s. 199. The company will be accountable for income tax on the grossed-up amount and is entitled to deduct the tax : F.A. 1965, s. 47, see Chap. 9.

Although in law he will be a debentureholder,[58] he is highly unlikely to think of himself as one, and the interest which he takes in the company will be slight, unless by some mischance the specifically mortgaged property depreciates in value to such an extent that he has to think about the possibility of enforcing the personal covenant against the company.

But the normal debenture is somewhat different; so different that its holder regards himself, whatever the law may say, as one who has an interest in the company different in degree but not in kind from that of a shareholder. For the typical debenture is one of a series each of which confers like rights, thus creating a " class " similar to a class of shareholders. And it is unlikely that the holders individually or collectively will be able, like normal mortgagees, to demand their money back whenever they want it; in all probability the money will be repayable only after a date many years in the future and may not be repayable at all,[59] except on a winding up, or only repayable at the option of the company. Again, they resemble shares in being either registered with the company and transferable by the same simple transfer form, or by being in bearer form, in which case there is a judicially recognised custom that they are negotiable instruments. Moreover, the security may comprise a floating charge which is not practicable in the case of an individual borrower because of the Bills of Sale Acts and the reputed ownership provision of the Bankruptcy Acts.[60] Where there is a floating charge the interests of the debentureholder are tied up with the prosperity of the company almost to the same extent as those of a shareholder—for, if the company trades unprofitably, the debentureholder's security will be placed in jeopardy, whereas, if it flourishes, his security will normally be enhanced. Indeed such a debentureholder is placed very much in the legal position that a shareholder was formerly thought to assume, that of having an equitable interest in the fluctuating property of the company.[61] It is true that he will not be entitled to vote *as a member* at company meetings. He may by the articles be given a right to attend and vote, but his vote cannot be counted on a special or extraordinary resolution since section 141 of the Companies Act expressly refers to " members." However, he may be able to exercise far more effective control, for example, by insisting on a provision in the debenture entitling him to appoint a director.

---

58 *Knightsbridge Estates Trust* v. *Byrne* [1940] A.C. 613, H.L.
59 The normal rule of equity that a mortgage may not be made wholly irredeemable does not apply to registered companies: Companies Act 1948, s. 89. That a debenture may be something more than a mere loan is also recognised by the fact that a contract to take up debentures may be specifically enforced: Companies Act 1948, s. 92.
60 Chap. 4, p. 79, *supra.*
61 So much so that on a scheme of arrangement the debentureholders normally give up some of their rights like the shareholders (obtaining, it is true, some *quid pro quo*), whereas the unsecured creditors (over whom they theoretically have priority) are paid in fuil. See Chap. 26, *infra.*

It is because of these features that in practice debentures are not regarded as necessarily differing fundamentally from shares. A man who has £1,000 to invest on the stock exchange does not say to himself, "Shall I become a member of a company or shall I lend money to a company? " Nor does his stockbroker read him a lecture on the legal distinction between a member and a creditor. On the contrary, the broker seeks to find whether the client is primarily interested in the possibilities of capital appreciation, in the risk of depreciation, or in yield. According to the answers on these points and to the general economic background he will recommend (not either shares or debentures) but either " prior charges " or "equities." The broker, for reasons which will become apparent, lumps together all securities conferring a fixed maximum return, which he describes as " charges " whether there be in law any charge in favour of a creditor or merely a preferential right to dividends in favour of a member. He distinguishes from these " prior charges " the ordinary shares, conferring the residual rights after payment of the " prior charges," which he describes as " equities," thus borrowing and extending, probably without realising it, the lawyer's " equity of redemption." [62]

The stockbroker will draw a distinction between first-class preference shares and debentures only because he realises that in the last resort the lawyer's fine distinctions do have their effect on the risk undertaken. The debentureholder is, after all, a creditor and entitled to sue for his money and to enforce his security if he has any. Even if the debenture is perpetual it will invariably contain provisions for enforcement in circumstances such as non-payment of interest, winding up, or the levying of execution or distress. And the court has a residual power to intervene if the debentureholder's security is " in jeopardy." The shareholder, whether preference or ordinary, is a mere member. Normally his money is returnable only on winding up, he will find it difficult on his own to put the company into liquidation, and even if he succeeds he cannot obtain anything until all the outside creditors have been paid in full. Very different is the position of the debentureholder, who, on a liquidation if not before, ranks at the worst with the other creditors and at the best enforces his security and ignores the claims of unsecured creditors, so far as his security will go, and of shareholders in any event.

Hence, the debenture is potentially the most secure of the company's securities. It appeals to the investor who wants a relatively small but certain return without risk of losing his money. But, having said this,

---

[62] The proportion which the claims of prior charges bear to the total anticipated yield is often referred to as the " gearing " and much thought has been devoted to the question of what is the ideal " gear ratio " in various circumstances. If the total distributable profits each year are expected to be 10 per cent. on the total capital, the higher the proportion of the total capital which can be raised by prior charges at less than 10 per cent., the higher the yield on the equity. But the higher this ratio becomes, the greater becomes the risk of the preference dividend not being paid in full and of the ordinary shareholders receiving nothing.

it must be pointed out that it too is something of an over-simplification. When the true purchasing power of money is depreciating, a debenture, which only entitles the holder to the future return of the nominal value of the money advanced, may be a very inadequate security for the repayment of the true worth of the money invested. An ordinary share in a first-class company may in economic reality be less risky than its debenture, since the nominal value of its assets is likely to appreciate as the value of money falls, so that the nominal amount of the annual yield and capital return will rise proportionately, thus providing, in stock-broker's jargon, " a hedge against inflation." In inflationary conditions all prior charges are highly vulnerable; all one can truly say is that in conditions of stability or, *a fortiori*, of deflation they are less risky, with debentures then the safest of all. The convertible debenture is a useful device for obtaining the best of both worlds; it confers on the holder the initial security appropriate to a debentureholder while conditions seem to make that prudent, but with an option to convert into equity shares if that seems advisable.[63]

In any company there may, of course, be more than one class of debentures each of which may have a charge over different assets or, more probably, successive charges over the same assets. This applies whether the charges are fixed or floating, but it is comparatively unusual to find several classes each with a floating charge, and generally there will be one series of debentures secured by a fixed charge on certain assets and a floating charge over the remainder.

(ii) *Preference shares*

Types of preference share. Next in point of seniority are preference shares of which there are various types, the distinguishing features of all being that they confer on the holders some preference over other classes in respect either of dividend or of repayment of capital or both. As we have seen, this feature causes them to be classed with debentures as " prior charges." They may, however, participate with the other shareholders after their preferential rights have been satisfied. For example, it might be provided that the preference shares shall confer the right to a preferential dividend of 7 per cent.,[64] and to participate with the other shareholders in any dividends after the latter have in turn received 7 per cent. Or, either instead or in addition, it might be provided that the capital paid up on the shares shall be repaid in preference to others, and that they shall in addition participate in surplus

---

[63] Debentures cannot be issued at a discount and made immediately convertible into paid-up shares of the full par value, for this is a colourable device for issuing shares at a discount: *Moseley* v. *Koffyfontein Mines* [1904] 2 Ch. 108, C.A. But there seems to be no objection if they are convertible only when due for repayment, for the company will then owe the holder the full par value.

[64] It is usual to provide for the dividend to be calculated on the paid-up capital, but in the absence of express provision the nominal amount governs: *Oakbank Oil Co.* v. *Crum* (1882) 8 App.Cas. 65, H.L.

assets [65] after the others have also received back their paid-up capital. Such shares are called participating preference (or sometimes preferred ordinary) shares and confer all the advantages of normal prior charges and some or all of the advantages (according to the degree of participation) of equities. [66]

Again, although preference shareholders can be paid dividends only out of profits, it may be provided that arrears shall be made up in subsequent years when profits are available. Or it may be that if the dividend is once passed it is lost for all time. In other words, the shares may be either cumulative or non-cumulative. And, if cumulative, they may or may not be entitled to preferential payment of arrears on a winding up.

Finally, they may be of the anomalous type known as redeemable preference shares [67]; that is to say, they may be repaid, otherwise than on a formal reduction of capital approved by the court, notwithstanding the fundamental principle of the maintenance of share capital. Reference has already been made to this matter in Chapter 6, where it was pointed out that the purity of the latter principle is preserved, in effect if not in name, by the strict provisions contained in section 58 of the Companies Act 1948. These only allow redemption either out of profits or out of the proceeds of a fresh issue and, in the former case, require the establishment of a " capital redemption reserve fund " which is treated as if it were paid-up capital. From the point of view of the holders, however, the similarity to debentures is even more striking than in the case of other preference shares. [68]

Into which of these classes any particular preference shares fall depends solely on the construction of the provisions of the memorandum and articles (or corresponding documents in the case of chartered and statutory companies [69]) and of the resolutions under which they were

---

[65] Once again, in the absence of the normal provision to the contrary, participation will be based on nominal, not paid-up, capital: *Birch* v. *Cropper* (1889) 14 App.Cas. 525, H.L.

[66] Such shares are " equity share capital " within the meaning of the definition in Companies Act 1948, s. 154 (5). If the amount of fixed preference dividend on non-participating shares is very large (*e.g.*, 20 per cent.) it may be less misleading to describe them as " preferred ordinary " despite the fact that, as the right of participation is limited, they will not be " equity share capital " within the meaning of the statutory definition; for an interesting discussion on terminology, see *Re Powell-Cotton's Re-Settlement* [1957] 1 Ch. 159.

[67] And, in the case of statutory companies, redeemable stock issued under the Statutory Companies (Redeemable Stock) Act 1915, which does not require the establishment of a capital redemption reserve fund.

[68] *Quaere*, what is the position when such shares become due for redemption? American authorities suggest that the amount repayable does not become due as a debt (like a properly declared dividend—see *supra*, p. 354), but that shareholders can institute a suit against the company to compel redemption if they can prove that the statutory conditions have been fulfilled.

[69] The C.C.A. 1863 imposes certain limits on the conditions of preference shares in statutory companies, but subject to these limits the rights depend entirely on the construction of the terms under which they are issued: see *Windermere Gas and Water Co.* v. *Whitehead* [1931] 1 Ch. 558.

issued. So do their rights in respect of dividend, capital and voting. If these provisions are clear and comprehensive no difficulty arises; a company is entitled to issue shares conferring any rights it thinks fit,[70] and it only has to express its intention for this to be carried out. But this presupposes that the draftsman of the terms of issue has foreseen and provided without ambiguity for every possible eventuality, and this, unfortunately, has not always proved to be the case.[71] Hence the courts have had to construe provisions of doubtful import, and in the course of doing so have worked out various canons of construction. Unhappily these canons have varied over a period of years, a variation which is particularly unfortunate since it has seriously affected vested proprietary rights.

Participation in income and capital. As we have seen, the initial presumption is that all shares rank equally. Hence if shares are to be preferential at all, there must be some provision to this effect in the documents under which they are issued.[72] Until quite recently it was thought that this presumption of equality should be carried so far that an express provision for preference should not derogate from a right to equal participation after the preference had been obtained; in other words, that preference shares were presumed to be participating in both capital and income. This, indeed, appeared to be the inevitable conclusion to be drawn from the words of Lord Macnaghten in *Birch* v. *Cropper*[73]:

> "Every person who becomes a member of a company limited by shares of equal amount becomes entitled to a proportionate part in the capital of the company, and, unless it be otherwise provided by the regulations of the company, entitled as a necessary consequence to the same proportionate part in all the property of the company. . . ."

And later,[74] he drew a distinction between preference shareholders and debentureholders, saying of the former:

> "But they are not debentureholders at all. For some reason or other the company invited them to come in as shareholders,

---

[70] If the rights of any class are unreasonably curtailed the stock exchange may, of course, refuse to grant a quotation.

[71] The Jenkins Committee rejected a suggestion that a new Companies Act should provide that preference shares should carry certain defined rights in the absence of specific provision to the contrary: Cmnd. 1749, para. 196. *Cf.* Ghana Companies Code 1963 (Act 179), s. 51.

[72] For the sake of simplicity these documents will in future be referred to as the memorandum or articles—the nomenclature appropriate to registered companies. The problem of the extent to which the rights depend on the prospectus if this modifies or supplements the memorandum or articles has already been discussed in Chap. 15, pp. 328, 329. For a brief discussion of the courts' approach to these questions of construction, see pp. 20, 21, *supra.*

[73] (1889) 14 App.Cas. 525, H.L. at p. 543.

[74] At p. 546.

and they must be treated as having all the rights of shareholders, except so far as they renounced those rights on their admission to the company."

However, *Birch* v. *Cropper* left the law in a state of some confusion. The original articles of the company, the Bridgewater Navigation Co., had provided that "the entire net profits of each year shall belong to the holders of the shares of the company " [75] and there was one class of shares only. Later preference shares were created and the amended articles provided that the preference shares should be entitled to a dividend of 5 per cent. taking precedence over the dividends of the original (ordinary) shares.[75] Although not stated expressly, it was pretty clear that the preference shares were to be entitled to a 5 per cent. preferential dividend only, with no further right of participation.[76] The question which arose was how the assets were to be divided between the preference and ordinary shareholders on the winding up of the company. As we have seen, the House of Lords ruled that the preference shareholders were entitled to participate equally with the ordinary shareholders. Subsequently it was necessary to determine whether that ruling applied to three so-called reserve funds [77] which had been set up out of undistributed profits in previous years. The Court of Appeal decided,[78] notwithstanding Lord Macnaghten's dictum, that, as these represented the undistributed profits which the ordinary shareholders might have divided among themselves, they belonged and were payable to the ordinary shareholders alone.

Ten years later it was held at first instance that, in the absence of an express exclusion of participation in surplus assets, preference shareholders were entitled thereto in addition to any preferential right.[79] However, in 1914 the House of Lords in *Will* v. *United Lankat Plantations* [80] decided that where the preference shareholders were given a preferential dividend that, prima facie, was all they were entitled to by way of dividend. For a time it was uncertain whether that applied equally to rights to a return of capital, but after considerable fluctuations of judicial opinion,[81] that question was finally, as it was thought, resolved by the Court of Appeal in *Re William Metcalfe Ltd.*[52] in favour of the preference shareholders. At this stage, therefore, where shares were given a preference as regards both dividends and

---

[75] See the terms quoted in full in the report of the case in the courts below, *sub nom.* *Re Bridgewater Navigation Co.* (1889) 39 Ch.D. 1.
[76] See North J., *ibid.* at pp. 11 and 12.
[77] These did not exist as separate earmarked and invested funds: [1891] 2 Ch. at 326.
[78] *Re Bridgewater Navigation Co.* [1891] 2 Ch. 317, C.A.
[79] *Re Espuela Land and Cattle Co.* [1909] 2 Ch. 187.
[80] [1914] A.C. 11, H.L.
[81] *Cf. Re Fraser & Chalmers Ltd.* [1919] 2 Ch. 114; *Anglo-French Music Co.* v. *Nicoll* [1921] 1 Ch. 386; *Re John Dry Steam Tugs* [1932] 1 Ch. 594 (in favour of the preference shareholders) and *Re National Telephone Co.* [1914] 1 Ch. 755; and *Collaroy Co. Ltd.* v. *Giffard* [1928] Ch. 144 (against the preference shareholders).
[82] [1933] Ch. 142, C.A.

return of capital they were presumed to be non-participating in dividends but participating as regards a return of capital.

In 1949 this anomalous distinction was removed by the House of Lords in the leading case of *Scottish Insurance Corporation* v. *Wilsons and Clyde Coal Co.*[83] which overruled *Re William Metcalfe Ltd.* The present position, therefore, as stated in the subsequent judgments of the Court of Appeal in *Re Isle of Thanet Electric Co.*,[84] can be embodied in the two following propositions [85]:

> "First, that, in construing an article which deals with rights to share in profits, that is, dividend rights, and rights to share in the company's property in a liquidation, the same principle is applicable; and, second, that that principle is that, where the article sets out the rights attached to a class of shares to participate in profits while the company is a going concern, or to share in the property of the company in a liquidation, prima facie, the rights so set out are in each case exhaustive."

In other words, if preference shareholders are given preferential or other express rights to dividends or to a repayment of capital the presumption is that they are non-participating as regards further dividends or capital repayments.

If, however, the articles are silent regarding their rights to either (they can hardly be silent about both, for in that event the shares would not be preference shares) then in that respect they will have the same rights as the other (ordinary) shares. But what of the situation which arose in the *Bridgewater* case, where the surplus assets on winding up represent ploughed back profits of previous years which could have been distributed by way of dividend to the ordinary shareholders but which instead were placed to reserve? Are these to be regarded as belonging to the ordinary shareholders and therefore distributable to them alone, as the Court of Appeal apparently decided in the *Bridgewater* case? [86] This question arose again in *Dimbula Valley (Ceylon) Tea Co. Ltd.* v. *Laurie.*[87] In that case the preference shareholders were entitled to a 6 per cent. cumulative preferential dividend, and on a winding up to a preferential return of capital and arrears of dividend with an express right to participate equally with the ordinary shareholders in surplus assets. Accordingly, as in the *Bridgewater* case, the preference shares were non-participating as regards dividend but participating as regards capital. The first question that Buckley J. had to decide was whether, on a winding up, the preference shareholders would participate in the

[83] [1949] A.C. 462, H.L.
[84] [1950] Ch. 161, C.A.
[85] *Per* Wynn-Parry J. (at p. 171), in whose judgment Evershed M.R. and Asquith L.J. concurred.
[86] A decision followed in N. Ireland in *Re Marshall Bros.* [1956] N.I. 78.
[87] [1961] Ch. 353. See Rice (1961) 24 M.L.R. 525.

distribution of all surplus assets or only in such of them as did not represent ploughed back profits which could have been distributed as dividends to the ordinary shareholders. The Court of Appeal's decision in *Bridgewater* had not been overruled and had indeed been cited with approval by Lord Maugham in the *Wilsons & Clyde Coal Co.* case.[88] However, in that case Lord Simonds had pointed out the absurdity of supposing " that the parties intended a bargain which would involve an investigation of an artificial and elaborate character into the nature and origin of surplus assets." [89] Accordingly, Buckley J. felt able to distinguish *Bridgewater* on the basis that there the articles had expressly provided that undistributed profits should " belong " to the ordinary shareholders,[90] whereas in the instant case they merely said that such profits should be " divisible " among such shareholders.

It is to be hoped that this decision rings the death-knell on the refinement apparently introduced by the Court of Appeal in the *Bridgewater* case.[90a] To attempt to analyse the nature and origin of surplus assets would lead to insuperable difficulties, and, indeed, seems to be quite illogical [91] since under our dividend rules *any* part of the surplus could have been distributed to the shareholders by way of dividend. This, indeed, was illustrated by the *Dimbula Valley* case, for Buckley J. went on to hold [92] that prior to liquidation the company could revalue its assets and distribute any surplus either by way of cash dividend [93] or by way of a bonus issue to the ordinary shareholders, thus depriving the preference shareholders of any participation therein on a winding up. While this can hardly be regarded as wholly satisfactory, it is difficult to see how a better result can be achieved if shares are non-participating as regards dividend but participating as regards capital, for this is an inherently nonsensical arrangement which any company should avoid.[93a]

Ultimately, therefore, reasonable and uniform canons of construction have been adopted, but only after a deplorable history of vacillation in

---

88 [1949] A.C. at p. 482. On the other hand, Lord Morton (at p. 504) appeared to have reservations.
89 At p. 489.
90 In fact, as pointed out above, the articles did not quite say that; they merely said that profits should belong to the shareholders, and, under the original articles, there was only one class of shareholder.
90a This hope has been fulfilled in *Re Saltdean Estate Co. Ltd.* [1968] 1 W.L.R. 1844.
91 It is also inconsistent with the well-established principle that on a winding up all assets are distributed as a fund of capital (see *Staffordshire Coal & Iron Co.* v. *Brogan* [1963] 1 W.L.R. 905, H.L.) and with the line of cases culminating in *Re Wharfedale Brewery Co.* [1952] Ch. 913 considered *infra*, at pp. 366, 367.
92 See Chap. 6 at pp. 118, 119, above.
93 Not following *Westburn Sugar Refineries Ltd.* v. *I.R.C.*, 1960 S.L.T. 297; [1960] T.R. 105. The Jenkins Committee recommended that it should not be permissible to pay a cash dividend out of an unrealised capital surplus but that it should be permissible to capitalise the surplus: Cmnd. 1749, paras. 336–339.
93a Equally nonsensical is an arrangement such as that of the company in *Re Saltdean Estate Co. Ltd.*, *supra*, which had preferred shares participating as regards income but non-participating as regards capital. On a reduction of capital they are paid off on the latter basis, thus losing any share in the accumulated reserves.

a field where certainty and consistency are particularly desirable. The conclusion reached in the *Wilsons & Clyde* case is probably one at which lay investors, if left to themselves, would have arrived. But lay investors have not been left to themselves and the knowledgeable ones among them were entitled, after *Re William Metcalfe Ltd.*, to believe that, in the absence of indication to the contrary, preference shares would confer the valuable right to further participation in capital. Moreover, they would certainly assume that unless their shares were expressly issued as redeemable they would not be repaid while the company remained a going concern. What made the decisions in the *Wilsons & Clyde* case, and in *Prudential Assurance* v. *Chatterley-Whitfield Collieries* [94] which followed it, particularly disturbing is that in these cases it was held that the courts must approve a reduction of capital by the extinguishment of the preference shares provided the statutory requirements are complied with and the preference shareholders receive their rights on a winding up.[94a] The result was that preference shareholders, who in the first case [95] probably thought that they had a right to participate in surplus assets, and who in both cases certainly thought that they had a secure return of a high rate of dividend,[96] found themselves paid off at par for the benefit of the ordinary shareholders who rid themselves of the burden of paying a higher interest rate than that prevailing at the time.[97] Since these decisions the practice has been adopted of expressly providing in the terms of new preference issues by companies whose shares are quoted that in the event of a return of capital the amount repaid shall be tied to the market quotation at the time.[98] In any case, subscribers to new issues know where they stand, but small consolation is afforded to those who bought earlier issues.

The result is, that after lawyers have spent some fifty years trying to teach lay investors that there is a fundamental distinction between

---

[94] [1949] A.C. 512, H.L. See further Chap. 24, p. 636 *et seq.*

[94a] See *Re Saltdean Estate Co. Ltd., supra.*

[95] In the *Chatterley-Whitfield* case the articles expressly stated that there was no right to participate in surplus assets.

[96] That they thought this is shown by the fact that the shares had been quoted considerably above par. The Wilsons & Clyde Coal Co. was to be put into voluntary liquidation but the Chatterley-Whitfield Collieries Co. was to continue in business indefinitely.

[97] The result in these two cases was particularly iniquitous since the repayment was out of compensation received under the Coal Industry Nationalisation Act 1946, which itself contained provisions (s. 25) that regulations might be made adjusting the rights of various classes of shareholders in respect of the compensation. It was, nevertheless, held that this did not oust the jurisdiction of the court under the Companies Act, or prevent the company from taking the law into its own hands.

[98] Under this, the so-called *Spens* formula, the preference shareholders are given effective voting rights on a resolution to reduce capital. Having regard to this, the Jenkins Committee rejected a suggestion that a repayment by way of reduction of capital of irredeemable preference shares should be prohibited by law unless the preference shareholders consented. The Committee recognised that the *Spens* formula was no protection in the case of private companies but did not think there was adequate justification for altering existing contractual rights: See Cmnd. 1749, para. 195.

preference shares and debentures, the lawyers themselves have ended up by being largely converted to the layman's original view that both are really " charges " rather than " equities." Today, preference shares may be expressly created as redeemable and, even if they are not, it seems that they may be redeemed at the option of the company through the medium of a reduction of capital. And, under the canons of construction finally adopted, the probability is that they will confer only a right to a fixed return of both dividend and capital. In both respects they closely resemble debentures. Though their holders are members of the company, it is usual to deny them voting rights except in special circumstances,[99] so that here too they do not greatly differ from debentureholders. That lawyers have effected a *volte-face* was admitted by Evershed M.R. in *Re Isle of Thanet Electric Co.* when he said [1]:

> " I think that during the sixty years which have passed since *Birch* v. *Cropper* was before the House of Lords, the view of the courts may have undergone some change in regard to the relative rights of preference and ordinary shareholders—and to the disadvantage of the preference shareholders whose position has, in that interval of time, become somewhat more approximated to the role which Sir Horace Davey [2] attempted to assign to them, but which Lord Macnaghten rejected in *Birch* v. *Cropper*, namely, that of debentureholders."

But though they share the disadvantages of debentureholders they lack their advantages. They can only receive a return on their money if profits are earned and dividends declared, they rank after creditors on a winding up, and they have less effective remedies for enforcing their rights. Suspended midway between true creditors and true members they get the worst of both worlds.

Cumulative or non-cumulative dividends. Preference dividends are presumed to be cumulative, so that any unpaid arrears accumulate and must be paid in a later year before the payment of any ordinary dividend.[3] In this respect at least the resemblance of preference shares to debentures operates to their advantage. But this presumption can be

---

[99] *e.g.*, when dividends are in arrear or the resolution derogates from their special rights.

[1] [1950] Ch. at p. 175.

[2] One of the counsel in *Birch* v. *Cropper.*

[3] *Webb* v. *Earle* (1875) L.R. 20 Eq. 556. It is unnecessary here to do more than mention the unusual case of two classes of cum. pref. shares ranking *pari passu* as regards dividends payable at different rates. There are conflicting decisions of judges of first instance on what occurs if dividends fall into arrear but in a later year there is sufficient available for dividend to enable part payment of arrears to be made. In *Weymouth Waterworks* v. *Coode & Hasell* [1911] 2 Ch. 520, Parker J. held that payment should be proportionate to the rates of dividend. In *First Garden City* v. *Bonham-Carter* [1928] Ch. 53, Tomlin J. held that payment should be proportionate to the total arrears on each class (the earlier case was not mentioned although Tomlin had been engaged in it as counsel).

rebutted by any words indicating that a preferential dividend for a year is to be payable only out of the profits of that year.[4] If so, a dividend once passed is lost for ever.

Declaration of dividend and arrears on winding up. Difficulties and divergencies of construction have also arisen in connection with two further questions relating to preference dividends. Even if the preferential dividend is cumulative it is, of course, only payable if profits ultimately permit. Moreover, the articles are generally framed so as to restrict the rights of all shareholders to such dividends as are declared by the company. Hence preference shareholders will have no right to payment if the company earns profits sufficient to pay the preferential dividend but instead places these profits to reserve. The articles may be worded so as to entitle the preference shareholders to their dividends once profits are earned,[5] but the presumption seems to be to the contrary,[6] and in this respect preference shares diverge from debentures. In the case of non-cumulative shares there are obvious possibilities for abuse here.[7] With cumulative shares the holders may hope to get their arrears of dividend paid in later years. But suppose the company goes into liquidation with the arrears still unpaid; are the preference shareholders then entitled to payment of arrears? If not, cumulative preference shares are almost as vulnerable as non-cumulative.

Here again the views of the courts have varied from time to time. An early decision of the Court of Appeal [8] laid down the basic principle that, prima facie, cumulative preference shares were not entitled to payment of any arrears once a winding up had commenced. The only exceptions to this were when the articles entitled the shareholders to their dividend once profits had been earned irrespective of a declaration, in which event they would be entitled to payment if the company had accumulated profits in its hands,[9] or when the dividends had actually been declared, though not paid, before the liquidation.

---

[4] *Staples* v. *Eastman Photographic Materials Co.* [1896] 2 Ch. 303, C.A. It is usual and prudent to declare expressly that the dividend is " non-cumulative." It is theoretically possible to provide that the dividend shall be regarded as earned if sufficient profits are made, but that it need not be paid but can be carried forward to a later year, no ordinary dividend being payable until it has been discharged. This produces a cross between cumulative and non-cumulative shares similar to that resulting from the idiosyncratic rules of construction adopted in New Jersey.

[5] *Evling* v. *Israel & Oppenheimer* [1918] 1 Ch. 101.

[6] *Burland* v. *Earle* [1902] A.C. 83, P.C.; *Re Buenos Ayres Great Southern Ry.* [1947] Ch. 384; *Godfrey Phillips Ltd.* v. *Investment Trust Corpn. Ltd.* [1953] Ch. 449. In other words their right is not so much to the payment of a preference dividend as to restrain payments to the ordinary shareholders until they themselves are paid. It seems, therefore, that in the absence of express provision to the contrary non-cumulative shareholders inevitably lose their dividends for the year in which winding up commences, for a dividend (in this sense) cannot be declared after winding up has commenced: *Re Foster & Son* [1942] 1 All E.R. 314; *Re Catalinas Warehouses* [1947] 1 All E.R. 51.

[7] For a discussion of what remedies, if any, the shareholders have, see Chap. 25, *infra.*

[8] *Re Crichton's Oil Co.* [1902] 2 Ch. 86, C.A.

[9] *Re Bridgewater Navigation Co.* [1891] 2 Ch. 317, C.A.

This decision of the Court of Appeal has handicapped attempts to avoid the obvious injustice which may arise and, in the absence of anything at all in the articles indicating the contrary, the courts have been compelled to deny the shareholders their arrears.[10]   But recently the slightest straw has been clutched in order to avoid this conclusion, and provided the court can spell out some reference to payment of dividends in a winding up, the preference shareholders will be protected.[11]   Thus, in *Re F. de Jong & Co. Ltd.*,[12] the Court of Appeal had to construe an article which read " the said Preference shares shall carry the right to a fixed cumulative preferential dividend at the rate of 6 per cent. per annum on the capital for the time being paid up thereon respectively, *and shall have priority as to dividend and capital over the other shares in the capital for the time being*, but shall not carry any further right to participate in the profits or assets."   The court held that the words italicised must all relate to rights in a winding up, the preferential dividend while the company was a going concern having been secured under the earlier part of the clause.   Hence, while paying lip-service to the basic principle, they were able to find for the preference shareholders.[13]   On the other hand they expressed approval of the contrary decision in *Re Wood, Skinner & Co. Ltd.*,[14] in which the only material difference in wording was the omission of the word " preferential " from the earlier part of the clause.   Such fine distinctions reflect no credit on the law, and having regard to the tendency to assimilate preference shares to debentures it may be envisaged that the basic presumption will be reversed when the House of Lords have an opportunity of expressing an opinion on this aspect of the subject.   In the meantime, the prudent draftsman avoids these doubts by expressly providing for prior payment of arrears to the date of winding up or date of repayment " whether earned or declared or not."

One final difficulty has arisen in this connection.   On a winding up are preference shareholders, entitled to arrears under the articles, only able to obtain them to the extent that the assets remaining after payment of debts represent accumulated profits which might have been distributed

---

10   *Re Roberts & Cooper Ltd.* [1929] 2 Ch. 383; *Re Wood, Skinner & Co. Ltd.* [1944] Ch. 323.

11   *Re Walter Symons Ltd.* [1934] Ch. 308; *Re F. de Jong & Co. Ltd.* [1946] Ch. 211, C.A.; *Re E. W. Savory Ltd.* [1951] 2 All E.R. 1036; *Re Wharfedale Brewery Co.* [1952] Ch. 913.

12   *Supra.*

13   In *Re E. W. Savory Ltd., supra,* Wynn-Parry J. came to the same conclusion where the express exclusion of further participation was omitted, for, since the *Scottish Insurance* case, the express exclusion was unnecessary. He also held that arrears were payable up to the date of winding up—not until actual repayment.

14   *Supra,* note 10.   On the other hand *Re Roberts & Cooper Ltd.* (*ibid.*) was not commented on.   It is submitted that the decision in that case cannot be supported. Eve J. there held that the shareholders were not entitled to arrears, notwithstanding that the articles expressly provided " for arrears of dividend due " on the ground that no dividend was due until it had been declared, thus defeating the obvious intention of the provision.

by way of dividend? In *Re W. J. Hall & Co. Ltd.*[15] Swinfen Eady J. held that they were so limited, but his decision has been dissented from in three more recent cases[16] and may safely be taken to be bad law. It is essentially an example of the heresy given its quietus, it is to be hoped, in *Dimbula Valley (Ceylon) Tea Co. Ltd.* v. *Laurie.*[17]

Canons of construction. It is now possible to sum up the various canons of construction which are adopted:

1. Prima facie all shares rank equally.[18] If, therefore, some are to have priority over others there must be provisions to this effect in the regulations under which they are issued.

2. If, however, the shares are expressly divided into separate classes (thus necessarily contradicting the presumed equality) it is a question of construction in each case what the rights of each class are.[19]

3. If nothing is expressly said about the rights of one class in respect of either (a) dividends, (b) return of capital, or (c) attendance at meetings or voting, then, prima facie, that class has the same rights in that respect as the other shareholders. Hence a preference as to dividend will not imply a preference as to capital (or vice versa).[20] Nor will an exclusion of participation in dividends beyond a fixed preferential rate necessarily imply an exclusion of participation in capital (or vice versa) although it will apparently be some indication of it.[21]

4. Where shares are entitled to participate in surplus capital on a winding up, prima facie, they participate in all surplus assets and not merely in that part which does not represent undistributed profits that might have been distributed as dividend to another class.[22]

5. If, however, any rights in respect of any of these matters are expressly stated, that statement is presumed to be exhaustive so far as that matter is concerned. Hence if shares are given a preferential dividend they are presumed to be non-participating as regards further dividends,[23] and if they are given a preferential right to a return of capital they are presumed to be non-participating in surplus assets.[24] The same clearly applies to attendance and voting; if they are given a vote in certain circumstances (*e.g.*, if their dividends are in arrear) it is

---

15 [1909] 1 Ch. 521.
16 *Re New Chinese Antimony Co. Ltd.* [1916] 2 Ch. 115; *Re Springbok Agricultural Estates Ltd.* [1920] 1 Ch. 563; *Re Wharfedale Brewery Co.* [1952] Ch. 913.
17 [1961] Ch. 353, *supra.*
18 *Birch* v. *Cropper* (1889) 14 App.Cas. 525, H.L., 543, 546.
19 *Scottish Insurance Corpn.* v. *Wilsons & Clyde Coal Co.* [1949] A.C. 462, H.L.; *Re Isle of Thanet Electric Co.* [1950] Ch. 161, C.A.
20 *Re London India Rubber Co.* (1868) L.R. 5 Eq. 519; *Re Accrington Corp. Steam Tramways* [1909] 2 Ch. 40.
21 This is implied in the speeches in *The Scottish Insurance* case, *supra*, and in *Dimbula Valley (Ceylon) Tea Co. Ltd.* v. *Laurie* [1961] Ch. 353.
22 *Dimbula Valley (Ceylon) Tea Co. Ltd.* v. *Laurie, supra*; *Re Saltdean Estate Co. Ltd.* [1968] 1 W.L.R. 1844; *cf. Re Bridgewater Navigation Co.* [1891] 2 Ch. 317, C.A.
23 *Will* v. *United Lankat Plantations Co.* [1914] A.C. 11, H.L.
24 *Scottish Insurance Corpn.* v. *Wilsons & Clyde Coal Co., supra*; *Re Isle of Thanet Electric Co., supra.*

implied that they have no vote in other circumstances—*inclusio unius exclusio alterius*.[25] The onus of rebutting this presumption is not lightly discharged and the fact that shares are expressly made participating as regards either dividends or capital is no indication that they are participating as regards the other—indeed it has been taken as evidence to the contrary.[26]

6. If a preferential dividend is provided for, it is presumed to be cumulative.[27] This presumption can be rebutted by any words indicating that the preferential dividend for a year is to be payable only out of the profits of that year.[28]

7. It is presumed that even preferential dividends are payable only if declared.[29]

8. Hence arrears even of cumulative dividend are prima facie not payable in a winding up unless previously declared.[30] But this presumption may be rebutted by the slightest indication to the contrary.[31] When the arrears are payable, the presumption is that they are to be paid provided there are surplus assets available, whether or not these represent accumulated profits which might have been distributed by way of dividend,[32] but that they are payable only to the date of the commencement of the winding up.[33]

(iii) *Ordinary shares*

Ordinary shares (as the name implies) constitute the residuary class in which is vested everything after the special rights of other classes, if any, have been satisfied. They confer a right to the " equity " in the company and, in so far as members can be said to own the company,

---

[25] *Quaere* whether attendance at meetings and voting should not really be treated as two separate rights. *Semble*, however, that express exclusion of a right to vote will take away the right to be summoned to (or presumably to attend) meetings: *Re MacKenzie & Co. Ltd.* [1916] 2 Ch. 450.

[26] *Re National Telephone Co.* [1914] 1 Ch. 755; *Re Isle of Thanet Electric Co., supra.* But this seems illogical. If, as the H.L. suggested in the *Scottish Insurance* case, the fact that shares are non-participating as regards dividends is some indication that they are intended to be non-participating as regards capital (on the ground that the surplus profits have been appropriated to the ordinary shareholders), where the surplus profits belong to both classes while the company is a going concern both should participate in a winding up in order to preserve the *status quo*.

[27] *Webb* v. *Earle* (1875) L.R. 20 Eq. 556.

[28] *Staples* v. *Eastman Photographic Materials Co.* [1896] 2 Ch. 303, C.A.

[29] *Burland* v. *Earle* [1902] A.C. 83, P.C.; *Re Buenos Ayres Gt. Southern Ry.* [1947] Ch. 384; *Godfrey Phillips Ltd.* v. *Investment Trust Ltd.* [1953] 1 W.L.R. 41; *cf. Evling* v. *Israel & Oppenheimer* [1918] 1 Ch. 101. *Semble*, therefore, non-cumulative shares inevitably lose their preferential dividend for the year in which liquidation commences: *Re Foster & Son* [1942] 1 All E.R. 314; *Re Catalinas Warehouses* [1947] 1 All E.R. 51.

[30] *Re Crichton's Oil Co.* [1902] 2 Ch. 86, C.A.; *Re Roberts & Cooper* [1929] 2 Ch. 383; *Re Wood, Skinner & Co. Ltd.* [1944] Ch. 323.

[31] *Re Walter Symons Ltd.* [1934] Ch. 308; *Re F. de Jong & Co. Ltd.* [1946] Ch. 211, C.A.; *Re E. W. Savory Ltd.* [1951] 2 All E.R. 1036; *Re Wharfedale Brewery Co.* [1952] Ch. 913.

[32] *Re New Chinese Antimony Co. Ltd.* [1916] 2 Ch. 115; *Re Springbok Agricultural Estates Ltd.* [1920] 1 Ch. 563; *Re Wharfedale Brewery Co., supra,* not following *Re W. J. Hall & Co. Ltd.* [1909] 1 Ch. 521.

[33] *Re E. W. Savory Ltd., supra.*

the ordinary shareholders are its proprietors. It is they who bear the lion's share of the risk and they who in good years take the lion's share of the profits (after the directors and managers have been remunerated). If, as is often the case, the company's shares are all of one class, then these are necessarily ordinary shares, and if a company has a share capital it must perforce have at least one ordinary share whether or not it also has preference shares or debentures. It is this class alone which is unmistakably distinguished from debentures both in law and fact.

But as we have seen, the ordinary shares may shade off imperceptibly into preference, for, when the latter confer a substantial right of participation in income or capital, or *a fortiori* both, it is largely a matter of taste whether they are designated " preference " or " preferred ordinary " shares. Moreover, distinctions may be drawn between ordinary shares, ranking equally as regards participation, by dividing them nevertheless into separate classes with different voting rights. In this event they will probably be distinguished as " A " " B " " C " (etc.) ordinary shares. In recent years there have been a number of issues of non-voting A ordinary shares. By this device control may be retained by a small proportion of the equity leading to a further rift between ownership and control. This disturbing development (a response to the threat of take-over bids [34]) has given rise to demands that the stock exchanges should refuse to grant quotations for such shares, or, failing that, that the legislature should intervene.[35] The Jenkins Committee was divided on this issue. The majority took the view that the case for banning non-voting ordinary shares had not been made out but that such shares should be clearly labelled [36] and that their holders should be entitled to receive notices of all meetings so as to be kept informed.[37] A minority of three recommended that all equity shareholders should have a right to attend and speak at meetings and that there should be a prohibition on the granting of a quotation for non-voting or restricted-voting equity shares.[38] No legislative action has been taken on either recommendation but the opposition of institutional investors has caused issues of non-voting shares to be less frequent and some companies have enfranchised their non-voting shares.

Again, shares may be of different nominal value, or, in exceptional circumstances, some may be fully paid and others not. Or, again, certain

---

[34] See pp. 540–546, 625–631, *infra.* Thus, after the battle for control of *Savoy Hotel Ltd.* (see *infra,* p. 521) the capital of the company was reorganised so that £21,198 B ordinary stock could outvote £847,912 A ordinary stock. There the A stock *had* voting rights but the votes were so weighted that over 97 per cent. of the equity could be outvoted by the remainder!

[35] Such shares are barred in S. Africa (Companies Act No. 46 of 1926, as amended, s. 62 *quat.*) and in India (Companies Act 1956, s. 87).

[36] The Stock Exchange *Requirements* now provide that non-voting shares must be so designated and that the designation of equity shares with restricted votes must include the words " restricted voting " or " limited voting ": Sched. VII, Part A, para. K.

[37] Cmnd. 1749, paras. 123–140.   [38] *Ibid.* pp. 207–210.

shares may, as already mentioned, be given no right of participation until all others have received a certain return. Such a class is the converse of *preference* shares or *prior* charges; it has a share in the equity, albeit contingent only, but, in view of its extraordinary character, it will probably be distinguished from the normal ordinary, and designated " deferred " or " founders' " shares. Provided that the company's regulations (either in their original form or as validly amended) are complied with, the company has complete freedom as to the creation of classes and as to the names it gives them, and the nature of the rights attaching to each class is a matter of construction of the terms of issue.

(iv) *Special classes*

Although in most cases the shares of a company will fall into one or other of the primary classes of preference or ordinary, it is, of course, possible for the company to create shares for particular purposes and containing terms which cut across the normal classification. An example of this, and perhaps the most important one in practice, is afforded by employees' shares, that is, shares created for issue to employees under a scheme of co-partnership. The main feature of such shares is normally that they are to be issued only to employees and that they are to be transferred to trustees when the holders leave the company's employ.[39] Moreover, they normally have no vote. Apart from this their rights will generally be similar to those of normal preference or ordinary shares, although they may be further limited.

The main weakness of schemes of this sort is that the shares result in co-partnership in the true sense only if the holders' rights approximate to those of the other equity shareholders. In practice companies have been reluctant to concede so much and have restricted the rights in various ways, and especially in respect of voting. This, and the opposition of the trade unions, probably accounts for the failure of such schemes to spread to the extent that had been hoped by those who saw in co-partnership a solution to the problem of harmonising the relations between capital, management, and labour.[40]

(v) *Unclassified shares*

In recent years it has become common, where the whole of the authorised share capital is not issued, to describe the unissued shares as " unclassified shares." This practice, borrowed from the U.S.A., is

---

[39] For precedents, see Palmer's *Company Precedents*, 17th ed., Pt. I, Chap. 22.
[40] I.C.I. Ltd. has a scheme which goes considerably further towards associating employees in ownership than is customary with employees' shares. Whenever an ordinary dividend exceeding 5 per cent. is paid, all employees are to be credited with a cash bonus which will be used to purchase normal ordinary stock with voting rights and this stock will be freely at their disposal whether or not they stay with the company. But in view of the company's colossal share capital it would be idle to pretend that this is likely, in the foreseeable future, to give employees any effective share in the control of the company.

logical in so far as it recognises that until shares are issued they confer no rights at all, and that the rights ultimately attached to them depend on the company's decision at the time of issue. It is to be hoped, however, that it will not lead to any weakening of the practice of setting out the rights of all shares, when issued, in the articles where they are readily ascertainable. If it should become common to rely on an article analogous to Table A, art. 2, and merely to fix the rights by ordinary resolution or, worse still, to give power in the articles to the directors to fix the terms of issue, it would no longer be possible to turn to the public documents in order to ascertain what the rights are. The Australian Act [41] guards against this by providing that the rights of preference shares must be set out in the memorandum or articles.

---

[41] s. 66 of the Uniform Act of 1961.

CHAPTER 17

SHARES

In the previous chapter an attempt was made to define the legal nature of shares, to distinguish them, so far as they are distinguishable, from debentures, and to describe their various classifications. It is now proposed to deal with a number of legal problems and rules relating to shares generally.

Becoming a shareholder

In the case of companies with shares to become a shareholder will normally [1] be the same as to become a member.[2] To become a shareholder, therefore, one must become a member of the company concerned. How does one do this?

The answer is that the first requirement is agreement between the person concerned and the company. In the old deed of settlement company the necessary agreement would have been evidenced, in the case of the original members, by signing the deed of settlement, and, in the case of a transferee from an original member, by taking a transfer and applying for registration in the company's books. The modern registered company has accepted these principles, but modified them so as to secure the maximum publicity which has been regarded as an essential protection to the public.

Subscription of memorandum

The Companies Act 1948, s. 26, provides, first, that the subscribers to the memorandum (corresponding to the signatories of the deed of settlement) shall be deemed to have agreed to become members and, on the registration of the company, shall be entered as members in the register of members which every company is bound to maintain.[3] Section 2 (4) further provides that, in the case of a company with share capital, each subscriber shall state the number of shares, not being

---

[1] A holder of share warrants to bearer is not necessarily a member: see p. 386, *infra.* In the case of a company limited by guarantee but having a share capital there may be guarantor-members who are not shareholders.

[2] Hence the Companies Act 1948 expressly deals only with becoming a member (s. 26) and with the maintenance of a register of members (ss. 110 *et seq.*) and not with becoming a shareholder or with share registers. On the other hand, the C.C.A. 1845 refers only to becoming a shareholder and to the register of shareholders: see ss. 8 and 9.

[3] Under s. 181 (2) an undertaking by a director, to take up and pay for his qualification shares, signed and delivered to the Registrar is equivalent to subscription of the memorandum for that number of shares: *Migotti's case* (1867) L.R. 4 Eq. 238, *per* Romilly M.R. at pp. 240 and 243.

less than one, which he agrees to take. The effect of this provision has been held to be that, on registration of the company, a subscriber automatically becomes a member and holder of the shares for which he has signed, even if the company omits to fulfil its duty to put him on the register or to allot the shares to him.[4]

In other cases entry on the register is necessary; but not here, for publicity is automatically secured by signing the public document itself. The subscriber cannot escape by proving misrepresentation by a promoter[5]; indeed it is submitted that, by signing, the subscriber is estopped from denying that he has agreed and that in the absence of incapacity the agreement is absolutely binding on him.[6]

To this rule, that subscribing the memorandum without more constitutes membership and shareholding, there are only two exceptions. The first is where the company not only fails to allot any shares to the subscriber but allots them all to other persons. Clearly these other persons cannot be deprived of their shares—in any case which of them should be deprived?—and short of forcing the company to increase its share capital, there is little that can be done save to recognise the inevitable. This the courts have done.[7] But presumably the subscriber would be able to sue the company for breach of the contract to allot him the shares. In all the cases on this subject the subscriber has wished to escape liability as a shareholder, and it has been held that he is entitled to do so since the company cannot fulfil its bargain, but if he chooses to hold the company to the bargain, although he cannot get specific performance, he should obtain damages.

The second exception is under a modern statute, the Exchange Control Act 1947. The object of Part III of this Act is to control the registration of securities in the names of residents outside the sterling area or of nominees for them. To this end section 8 (2) provides that a subscription by either class of persons shall be invalid[8] unless Treasury consent is obtained. This section goes further than to restrict the capacity of the foreign resident; the subscription by a lunatic or infant[9] may be voidable,[10] but until it is avoided the subscriber is a member and shareholder. The foreign resident, on the other hand, never becomes either[11] unless a general consent applies or special consent is obtained.

---

[4] *Evans's Case* (1867) L.R. 2 Ch.App. 427.
[5] *Lurgan's Case* [1902] 1 Ch. 707.
[6] *Quaere* could the subscriber set up the defence of *non est factum* if he had been induced to sign in ignorance of the nature of the document?
[7] *Mackley's Case* (1875) 1 Ch.D. 247..
[8] The validity of the incorporation is not affected.
[9] As regards infants, see *supra*, p. 344.
[10] This will depend on the application of normal principles of the law of contract.
[11] *Quaere* whether his subscription produces any contractual effects, as between himself and the company. The section merely says that the subscription shall " be invalid in so far as it would on registration of the memorandum have the effect of making him a member or shareholder."

Agreement and entry on register

Secondly, section 26 provides that every person, other than a subscriber, who agrees to become a member and whose name is entered in its register of members, shall be a member. Here two things are necessary (a) agreement and (b) entry on the register; both must be present before the person concerned becomes a member and shareholder.[12]

Agreement. So far as the agreement is concerned its existence depends on normal principles; whether there is a valid agreement will be decided in precisely the same way as in the case of any other contract and there must be an offer by one party (the company or the potential member) accepted by the other, either personally or through an agent. No particular form is required, the agreement may be either written, oral or implied from conduct.

In practice, however, the procedure follows a recognised course. The acceptance of members and the issue of shares to them is a matter which is invariably delegated to the directors by the company's articles.[13] In the case of an original allotment of shares on a public issue, a prospectus,[14] either in the popular or in the wider legal sense, is first published accompanied by a form of application. This, of course, is not an offer but a mere invitation to submit offers by completing and returning the application form, which, to comply with the Exchange Control Act, may have to be accompanied by the prescribed declaration, that the applicant is not resident outside the " scheduled territories " (the sterling area) or applying on behalf of one so resident.[15] Since the company will not be able to accept every offer in full if the issue is over-subscribed, the form will be worded so that the applicant agrees to accept and pay for the shares applied for or any lesser number. The only difference between it and any other offer is that in the case of " a prospectus issued generally " (*i.e.,* on a public issue in the fullest sense [14]) the offer is not revocable until after the expiration of the third day after the opening of the subscription lists.[16] The board of directors

---

[12] But see *infra,* pp. 386–388, as to share warrants.

[13] In the case of private companies it is sometimes provided that new shares shall be offered to the existing shareholders and it is generally accepted that all new issues of equity shares for cash should be so offered unless otherwise agreed in general meeting: *cf.* S.E. *Requirements,* Sched. VIII, Part A (General Undertaking), para. 15. The Jenkins Committee recommended that all new issues should require prior approval by the company in general meeting: Cmnd. 1749, paras. 119–121 and 122 (h)–(n).

[14] See Chap. 14, *supra.*

[15] Details of Exchange Control requirements and general consents are given from time to time in E.C. Notices (*supra,* p. 290, n. 14) of which the most important is E.C. 10 (Third Issue). As a result of the general consent given by this notice, most issues by U.K. companies of securities quoted on a U.K. stock exchange are permitted without the prescribed declaration provided that applications are lodged by " authorised depositaries "—stockbrokers, solicitors, banks and the like: for list, see E.C. 1 (Eighth Issue).

[16] Companies Act 1948, s. 50. See Chap. 14, p. 302, *supra.*

then consider the various applications and decide whether or not to accept them or some of them, and whether for the full amount or only part—in the case of a public issue the prospectus will normally have stated the policy to be adopted in the event of over-subscription. Their decision to accept is known as allotment, but it has no legal effect until notified to the applicant. This notification will be by dispatch of allotment letters which will often be renounceable for a limited time.[17] Once the allotment letter has been dispatched the agreement is complete.[17a]

But the allottee is still not a shareholder. He has not yet been entered on the register—indeed particular shares identified by number have probably not been appropriated to him. This will not occur until he is duly placed on the register, and if the allotment letter is renounceable he himself may never become a shareholder. At this stage he merely has a contractual right to become a shareholder and this he assigns by renouncing. The company will then have to obtain an agreement to become a shareholder from the person (or persons) in whose favour he renounces. To this end the allotment letter will incorporate a form of renunciation to be signed by the original allottee,[18] and another form to be signed by the acceptor of the renunciation in which he confirms his agreement to take the shares. When these two forms are returned by him to the company there is another completed agreement and it only needs the second step of entry on the register to make the ultimate acceptor of the shares a member and shareholder of the company.

Renounceable allotment letters are in effect the modern form of scrip certificates which it was formerly common for companies to issue prior to the shares themselves. These certificates were generally in bearer form, entitling the holder to the future allotment of a specified number of shares contingently on his registering with the company and paying certain instalments. Issues of scrip are still occasionally made on an offer of government or municipal stocks but never by companies, renounceable allotment letters fulfilling the same function.

---

[17] As pointed out (*supra*, Chap. 14, p. 287, note 8), this avoids the payment of stamp duty on the transfer.

[17a] The above description relates to the ordinary case where shares are issued for cash. Where shares are offered in a take-over circular it may be much more difficult to determine precisely when a binding agreement is entered into.

[18] If he signs the form in blank the letter will in effect be a bearer instrument. In any event it is a " bearer certificate " within the meaning of section 10 of the Exchange Control Act (*infra*) since it is a document recognising the title of securities to be issued and transferable by delivery with or without endorsement (see definition in s. 42 (1)), and therefore renounceable allotment letters cannot be issued without Treasury consent whether or not such consent to the raising of capital would be required under the Borrowing (Control and Guarantees) Act 1946 (see Chap. 14, *supra*). At present there is a general consent subject to exceptions and, in general, renounceable allotment letters do not have to be deposited with authorised depositaries: see Notice E.C. 10 (Third Issue), paras. 11, 12 and App. I.

So far as the underwriters [19] are concerned the company will, of course, have a formal written underwriting agreement whereby the underwriters agree either to take up a specified number of shares (underwritten " firm ") or to take up such shares as the public do not apply for. If the underwriters re-insure themselves against this risk, the sub-underwriting agreement will irrevocably authorise the original underwriters to apply for allotment in the names of the sub-underwriters, and this authority, being coupled with an interest, will be effectively irrevocable.[20]

Needless to say, in the case of a private placing everything will be very much less formal, and on an issue by a private company allotment letters will probably be dispensed with—in any case they cannot be freely renounceable [21]—and the original offer by application may simply be followed by allotment and dispatch of the share-certificates by way of acceptance. In any event all that is needed is an agreement however constituted.[22]

Entry on the register. The second step is entry on the company's register. Under sections 110–123 of the Companies Act 1948, every registered company [23] is required to maintain, normally at its registered office, a register of its members, and this must, if the company has a share capital, give particulars of the shares held by each member.[24] These sections contain detailed rules regarding the place and manner of maintaining the register, which may be closed [25] for a total period of thirty days in any year if newspaper advertisement is given.[26] At other times it is to be open for inspection not only by members but by any member of the public, and the company must supply copies on demand.[27] The register therefore constitutes one of the documents of the company to which the public have access and, although it cannot be seen at the Companies' Registry, notice has to be given to the Registrar stating where the register is kept if this is elsewhere than at the registered office.[28] Moreover the company has to make an annual return to the Registry and

---

19 See further on underwriting: Chap. 14, *supra.*
20 *Carmichael's Case* [1896] 2 Ch. 643, C.A.; *Pole's Case* [1920] 2 Ch. 341, C.A.
21 This is theoretically possible if there are not more than 50 shares; the renunciation is not deemed to be a transfer (*Re Pool Shipping Co.* [1920] 1 Ch. 251) so that there will not be an infringement of the article restricting transfers.
22 If an Exchange Control declaration is required (see *supra*, n. 15) the company's registrar is under a statutory duty to ensure that one is lodged: Exchange Control Act 1947, s. 13.
23 As regards statutory companies see the comparable provisions in C.C.A. 1845, ss. 9 and 10, and 15–20, which provide for a register of shareholders and a separate register of transfers.
24 s. 110 (1).
25 Thus enabling the company to prevent changes of membership during the currency of a notice of a general meeting or while preparing its annual return (referred to, *infra*, Chap. 20, p. 449).
26 The Jenkins Committee recommended certain changes in the relevant sections (Cmnd. 1749, para. 483 (*f*) to (*i*)) but these have not yet been made.
27 s. 113. Members can inspect free, but the company is entitled to charge non-members 1s. Copies may be charged for at 2s. per 100 words: Companies Act 1967, s. 52 (2).
28 s. 110 (3).

this, in the case of a company with a share capital, must give details of membership and shareholdings.[29]

The register is prima facie evidence of the matters entered in it,[30] and hence of the fact of membership and extent of shareholding. But it is not conclusive. If therefore there is no true agreement, and this can be proved. the so-called member will not in fact be a member or shareholder. If the ostensible agreement is merely voidable because of some flaw such as fraud, misrepresentation or incapacity he must, of course, take steps to avoid it, and we have already seen in Chapter 15 [31] that if the flaw is misrepresentation he must act promptly once he finds out the truth and, in any case, before the company goes into liquidation. If the flaw is incapacity he must also act promptly once the incapacity is removed, but it is not clear whether liquidation will preclude him from doing so; in the case of infancy (on which alone there seems to be any authority) it has been held that winding up—far from preventing the infant from renouncing—instead precludes him from confirming (unless the liquidator agrees) on his subsequently attaining full age.[32]

Should there be no semblance of agreement (*e.g.*, his name has been entered on the register to lend a spurious air of respectability to the company) or should the agreement be void (*e.g.*, for mistake) he clearly will never have been a member at all and theoretically there is no need for him to do anything about it.[33] But in practice he will be ill-advised to refrain from taking action, for, as we have seen, the courts place great importance on the need for speedy removal of a name from the register since its presence may act as an inducement to others to subscribe for shares or to allow the company credit. It may well be, therefore, that if he knew his name appeared and took no steps to secure its removal, he would be held estopped from denying that he was a member.[34]

In any event therefore the alleged shareholder should take steps to have his name removed from the register. This he may do by bringing

---

[29] s. 124 and Sched. 6. See *infra*, Chap. 20, p. 449.
[30] s. 118. The Jenkins Committee recommended that its accuracy should not be challenged on the strength of transactions alleged to have taken place 30 years before the challenge: Cmnd. 1749, para. 481.
[31] *Supra*, pp. 326–328.
[32] *Castello's Case* (1869) L.R. 8 Eq. 504; *Symon's Case* (1870) L.R. 5 Ch.App. 298. See further as to infancy, *supra*, p. 344, and for a good general discussion: Burns, " Infants as Shareholders " (1955) 28 Aust.L.J. 407.
[33] *Alabaster's Case* (1868) L.R. 7 Eq. 273; *Gorrissen's Case* (1873) L.R. 8 Ch.App. 507; *Wynne's Case, ibid.*, 1002, C.A.; *Beck's Case* (1874) L.R. 9 Ch.App. 392; *Baillie's Case* [1898] 1 Ch. 110.
[34] In the cases cited in note 33, the allottee had either remained in ignorance until after the winding up or had only found out a short time before. It seems to have been conceded that had there been " acquiescence " the allottee would have been bound: *cf. Re Miller's Dale (etc.) Lime Co.* (1885) 31 Ch.D. 211. It is interesting to note that the implied representation to the public at large causes the ostensible member to become bound to the company—an unusual type of estoppel in which the addressee of the representation is not the same as the beneficiary of it.

an action against the company for rescission or by applying summarily for the rectification of the register under section 116. If the court exercises its jurisdiction under this section [35] it may order the payment of compensation in order to restore the parties to their former position.[36] The Act calls this " damages," but this is a misnomer.[37]

It is normally the alleged shareholder who wishes to disclaim that role; the company will rarely wish to avoid an allotment which it has made or be in a position to do so if it wishes. If the company has been fraudulently induced to issue partly paid shares to someone who is unable to pay the calls it will normally have power under the articles to declare them forfeited for non-payment of calls and this will clearly be a more satisfactory course than attempted rescission. But section 116 specifically recognises that the company itself may apply for rectification and this has in fact occurred where the holder of partly paid shares has fraudulently induced it to pass a transfer to a man of straw [38] and where an official of the company has wrongly completed the register.[39]

Hitherto it has been assumed that the member acquires that position on an original allotment of shares. But he may instead do so by taking a transfer of shares from an existing holder. The procedure in this case will be dealt with when transfers are considered in the next chapter. Once again the two steps of agreement and entry on the register are necessary. The only circumstances in which these requirements are somewhat modified is where share warrants to bearer are issued; this too is dealt with later.

Invalid allotments

An issue or allotment of shares may be invalid either because the company has not complied with the legal requirements for agreement and entry on the register or because it has purported to issue shares in excess of its authorised share capital. In the latter event it seems that shares numbered from one to the maximum authorised number are valid and the rest null.[40] Since the invalidity may not be noticed until some time later, acute embarrassment can be caused to all concerned.

---

[35] It is not bound to do so: see *Re British Sugar Refining Co.* (1857) 3 K. & J. 408. The order may be made retrospective. *Quaere* does this invalidate corporate acts taken as a result of the vote of the quondam " shareholder ": *cf. Re Sussex Brick Co.* [1904] 1 Ch. 598, C.A.

[36] *i.e.,* the return of any moneys paid by the " shareholder " whose name is removed plus interest: *Re Metropolitan Coal Consumers Assn., Wainwright's Case (No. 1)* (1890) 63 L.T. 429, C.A.; *Karberg's Case* [1892] 3 Ch. 1, C.A.

[37] *Re British Gold Fields of West Africa* [1899] 2 Ch. 7, C.A.

[38] See *Re Discoverers Finance Corpn., Lindlar's Case* [1910] 1 Ch. 312, C.A.

[39] *Re Indo-China Steam Navigation Co.* [1917] 2 Ch. 100. The extent to which the company can rectify the register without reference to the court is doubtful: see *Re Derham & Allen* [1946] Ch. 31.

[40] *Moosa* v. *Lalloo,* 1957 (4) S.A. 207 (Nat. P.D.); *cf. Macley's Case* (1875) 1 Ch.D. 247, *supra,* p. 373. If the shares have ceased to be numbered it may be virtually impossible to trace back those which are null.

The Australian Act[41] contains a useful provision, which might well be copied in the next revision of the U.K. Act,[42] whereby the court can make an order validating the issue if it is just and equitable to do so.

Conversion of shares into stock

Once the shares or any class of them are fully paid the company may convert them into stock,[43] that is to say they may be treated as merged into one fund of a nominal value equivalent to that of the total of the shares, and the member, instead of holding particular identified shares (say 100 shares of £1 each numbered 1 to 100) will hold £100 stock.

The only advantage, indeed the only effect, of this from the member's point of view is that stock is theoretically freely divisible into fractions of any amount. While he had shares he could transfer them only in denominations of £1, whereas with stock he can (in theory) transfer any fraction of £1. In practice, however, the company's articles will almost certainly provide that the stock shall not be transferable in units of less than a prescribed amount, since small fractions would give rise to obvious administrative difficulties. In our example, therefore, the probability is that the member will still find that he is unable to transfer his stock in units of less than £1. Hence this advantage is more apparent than real.

But on the company's side, stock formerly greatly simplified the work of maintaining the register and issuing certificates. While the capital was divided into shares the register had to keep track of each share identified by a separate number,[44] and after some years it would be unlikely that the holdings of each member would be in a neat and consecutive run. On conversion into stock this no longer causes difficulty, for the register simply shows the amount of stock held by each member.[45] It is, however, provided by the 1948 Act[46] that if all the issued shares of a class are fully paid, none of those shares need have a distinguishing number so long as it remains fully paid and ranks *pari passu* for all purposes with all the shares of that class.[47] Having regard to this relaxation it is difficult to see what practical purpose is served by converting into stock.

In any event, a conversion of his shares into stock in no way alters the relationship between the holder and the company. He still remains a member and the nature of his interest in the company is

---

[41] Uniform Act, s. 63.
[42] See Jenkins Committee, Cmnd. 1749, para. 474.
[43] Companies Act 1948, s. 61. Notice must be given to the Registrar: s. 62. For statutory companies, see C.C.A. 1845, s. 61; C.C.A. 1863, ss. 12 and 13.
[44] s. 74.   [45] s. 110 (1), proviso.
[46] s. 74, proviso. If quoted, S.E. consent will be needed to dispense with numbers or to convert to stock.
[47] The Jenkins Committee recommended an amendment to the section to avoid the difficulty which arises if a new issue of shares is not to rank for the next dividend but is, in every other respect, *pari passu* with existing unnumbered shares: Cmnd. 1749, para. 473.

unchanged; for the purposes of the Companies Act " share " includes " stock." [48]

It must be emphasised that a registered company cannot make a direct issue of stock—although a statutory company may be authorised so to do by its special Act.[49] The only object of this prohibition is to avoid having partly paid stock, when the divisibility of stock might lead to difficulty and abuse. When shares were normally issued partly paid this prohibition was sensible but, now that they are almost invariably to be fully paid up on allotment, it seems pointless. However, the law still insists that shares must first be issued even if they are immediately afterwards converted into stock. With new companies the point is of little importance since they will probably not bother to convert but will instead rely on the power to dispense with distinguishing numbers. But the rule is a nuisance when, for example, an existing company with stock makes a bonus issue to its stockholders. Notwithstanding that the issue is fully paid it will have to be framed as an issue of shares and unless members are to be left with both shares and stock the issue will have to be followed by a conversion into stock.[50]

The Jenkins Committee recognised that the whole distinction between shares and stock is today merely a source of confusion and recommended that steps should be taken to eradicate the latter term.[51]

Share certificates

The invariable practice is for the company to issue a certificate to the member, certifying that he is the holder of a specified number of shares (giving their distinguishing numbers if they have them and stating the extent to which they are paid up) or of a certain quantity of stock. The purpose of this is to give the shareholder some document which he can use as evidence of his title. It also provides the company with a check on the identity of the registered holder, and the company will not normally register any dealing unless the certificate is produced.

The Companies Act 1948 accordingly provides that " a certificate, under the common seal of the company, specifying any shares held by any member, shall be prima facie evidence of the title of the member to the shares," [52] and that, unless the articles otherwise provide, the company shall issue certificates within two months of original allotment or subsequent transfer.[53] Similar provisions apply to statutory com-

---

[48] See definition in s. 455.

[49] See C.C.A. 1863, ss. 12 and 13.

[50] In practice the whole transaction will be effected by separate resolutions at one meeting and share certificates will never be completed or issued; the stockholders will receive the ultimate stock certificates.

[51] Cmnd. 1749, para. 472.

[52] s. 81.

[53] s. 80. Hence the shareholder is entitled to a certificate unless the articles otherwise provide.

panies.[54] These provisions are generally supplemented by the company's regulations specifying the terms on which any member shall be entitled to more than one certificate in respect of his holding and providing for the issue of a new certificate if the old is lost or destroyed.[55]

Estoppel by share certificate

A share certificate is in no sense a contractual document and, although under the company's seal, it is not a deed.[56] The holder's legal rights depend not on the certificate but upon entry in the register, and the certificate is merely a declaration by the company stating what these rights are and affording prima facie evidence of them.[57] It is totally different from the documents of title of unregistered land, which consist of the deeds disposing of the property itself, but exactly comparable to the land certificate issued by the Land Registrar in respect of registered land—indeed land registration is an attempt to adapt the procedure relating to shares to the more complicated case of land.

Just as mistakes in the land certificate may impose on the Land Registrar liability to compensate those who suffer loss as a result, so may errors in the share certificate, but in this case under common law principles and not, as in the case of the Land Registrar, under specific statutory provisions. Although the certificate is only prima facie evidence of the statements which it contains, these statements are made with the intention that they shall be relied upon in connection with dealings in the shares. Hence if anyone changes his position in reliance on these statements the company may be estopped from denying their truth. In other words, although the statements are at first only prima facie evidence the company may subsequently be prevented from denying them. The situation is exactly comparable to that which arises in connection with bills of lading. If a ship's master signs a bill of lading evidencing receipt on board of goods of a particular description and condition, statute declares[58] that the bill shall be prima facie evidence (no more) of receipt of goods of that description and condition. If, however, the bill is used as a document of title to the goods which are bought on the faith of the statements in it, the master will be estopped from denying receipt of goods in accordance with these statements and will be liable accordingly.[59]

Short though it is, the share certificate contains two statements of vital importance, namely, first, that the member was at the date of

---

[54] C.C.A. 1845, ss. 11, 12 and 13. In this case certificates are to be issued on demand and a charge may be made.
[55] *Cf.* Table A, arts. 8 and 9.
[56] *South London Greyhound Racecourses* v. *Wake* [1931] 1 Ch. 496; *R.* v. *Williams* [1942] A.C. 541, P.C.
[57] Analogous to examination certificates or a solicitor's admission certificate.
[58] Carriage of Goods by Sea Act 1924, Sched., Art. III, para. 4.
[59] This is in fact recognised by another statute—the Bills of Lading Act 1855, s. 3, but the common law principle of estoppel is probably somewhat more extensive.

issue of the certificate the holder of a certain number of shares [60] and, second, the extent to which they are paid up. The company having made these statements with the knowledge and intention that they shall be acted upon will be estopped from denying them to anyone who has changed his position in reliance on them. Hence if B buys shares from A relying on the production of a certificate [61] in favour of A, and it then proves that A never was the registered proprietor so that B never validly acquires title, the company will be liable to compensate B.[62] Similarly if the certificate states that A's shares are fully paid whereas in fact they are not, the company will be estopped from denying that they are fully paid and from making calls on B.[63]

It will be noted that estoppel operates rather differently in the two cases. In the second it provides a defence to a claim for calls made by the company—the classic role of estoppel in acting as a shield and not as a sword. In the first case, however, it enables the person deceived to recover damages from the company. This is the only solution if it is to aid him at all; the company cannot actually recognise him as the holder of the shares, for that would involve depriving the true legal owner and the latter's rights cannot be impeached. Hence damages are awarded to compensate the other who has relied on the false certificate. At first sight this appears to be equivalent to committing the heresy of treating estoppel as a cause of action. This, however, is not so. The certificate itself gives rise to no right of action.[64] The action against the company will be based on something done or omitted by it, such as refusing to register the transferee or subsequently removing him from the register; these acts being wrongful on the basis of the assumed facts which the company is estopped from denying.[65] The measure of damages is the value of the shares at the date of the assumed breach of duty.[66]

An important limitation on the efficacy of the estoppel principle is that a share certificate is not a representation of continuing ownership so long as the certificate remains in existence. " The only representation is that *at the date of the certificate* the person named therein was owner of the shares." [67] If therefore the owner, A, transfers his shares to B,

---

[60] Or, of course, a quantity of stock.

[61] The principle is not limited to share certificates but extends, for example, to allotment letters: *Peterborough Trust Ltd.* v. *Steel Industries of G.B. Ltd.* (1934) 78 S.J. 861. But sending a dividend warrant does not estop the company from denying that the addressee is a shareholder: *Foster* v. *Tyne Pontoon Co.* (1893) 63 L.J.Q.B. 50.

[62] *Re Bahia and San Francisco Ry.* (1868) L.R. 3 Q.B. 584.

[63] *Burkinshaw* v. *Nicholls* (1878) 3 App.Cas. 1004, H.L. This is an anomaly. The company could not issue its shares at a discount but estoppel produces the same result.

[64] It might, of course, support an action of deceit if issued fraudulently.

[65] *Re Ottos Kopje Diamond Mines* [1893] 1 Ch. 618, C.A. This may perhaps be regarded as an award of damages for breach of statutory duty.

[66] *Re Ottos Kopje Diamond Mines, supra.*

[67] Per Romer L.J. in *Rainford* v. *James Keith & Blackman Co. Ltd.* [1905] 2 Ch. 147, C.A., at p. 154. (My italics.)

but retains the certificate and B is registered by the company notwithstanding the absence of the certificate, whereupon A borrows from C
pledging the original certificate, C will have no remedy against the
company.[68]   And this is so even if the certificate has endorsed on it
the customary statement that transfers will not be registered unless the
certificate is produced.[69]   In this respect a share certificate differs
fundamentally from a share warrant.[70]

Availability of the estoppel

The company will be estopped only as against someone who has
changed his position on the strength of the certificate.   Hence it will
never avail anyone who has knowledge of the truth.[71]   If only for this
reason it can rarely help the person to whom the false certificate was
first issued, for he, presumably, will know that he has no title to the
shares or that they are not fully paid.   Indeed, the original recipient has
to surmount two further difficulties.   First, it will be difficult for him
to show that he has changed his position on the faith of the certificate
which, so far as he was concerned, marked the culmination of the transaction and was not a factor inducing it.[72]   Secondly, no one can hold the
company liable if he has put forward a forged transfer; on the contrary
he must then indemnify the company against any liability it may incur.[73]
If, therefore, B forges the signature of A, the registered owner, to a
transfer on a sale to C, and C in all good faith lodges the transfer and
A's certificate (which B had stolen from A) and obtains a new certificate
in his (C's) own name, C cannot make the company liable.   Only a bona
fide purchaser or mortgagee from C can do so.

But, in exceptional circumstances, even the original recipient (as
opposed to a purchaser from him) may succeed.   Thus in *Balkis
Consolidated Co.* v. *Tomkinson*,[74] A, the original proprietor, transferred
to B who was registered.   A then fraudulently transferred to C, who took

---

[68] *Longman* v. *Bath Electric Tramways Ltd.* [1905] 1 Ch. 646, C.A.; *Rainford* v.
James Keith & Blackman Co. Ltd. [1905] 1 Ch. 296; [1905] 2 Ch. 147, C.A.   And
see the Canadian case of *Smith* v. *Walkerville Malleable Iron Co.* (1896) 23 A.R. 95
(Ont. C.A.).   But a dictum of Lord Blackburn in *Colonial Bank* v. *Whinney* (1886)
11 App.Cas. 426, H.L., at p. 438, suggests the contrary, and if the law is in fact as
suggested it is difficult to see the need for the indemnity which companies invariably
demand before they issue a duplicate certificate or register a transfer without its
being produced.

[69] *Rainford* v. *James Keith & Blackman Co. Ltd., supra.*   Articles generally expressly
empower the directors to decline to register unless the certificate is lodged: *cf.*
Table A, art. 25.   In the absence of such an article the directors are clearly entitled
to make reasonable inquiries but probably cannot definitely decline merely because
the certificate is missing.   *Quaere* if they are entitled to demand the usual indemnity?
In the case of statutory companies the answer appears to be no, for s. 12 of the
C.C.A. 1845 expressly provides that "the want of such certificate shall not prevent
the holder of any share from disposing thereof."

[70] See p. 386, *infra.*   [71] *Crickmer's Case* (1875) L.R. 10 Ch.App. 614.

[72] *Re Vulcan Ironworks Co.* [1885] W.N. 120.

[73] *Sheffield Corpn.* v. *Barclay* [1905] A.C. 392, H.L.; *Welch* v. *Bank of England* [1955]
Ch. 508.

[74] [1893] A.C. 396, H.L.

in good faith, and the company issued C with a certificate but never put him on the register. C then contracted to sell to D but was, of course, unable to perform his contract without purchasing other shares. It was held that he was entitled to recover from the company the price paid for these other shares.[75] Similarly in *Dixon* v. *Kennaway & Co.*[76] a broker, who was also a servant of the company, obtained money from a client for the purchase of the shares and procured the issue of a certificate stating that the client was the proprietor of shares in fact owned by another member. When, a year later, his fraud was discovered, he went bankrupt. Again it was held that the company was liable in damages, the client having been put to rest by the certificate until it was too late to recover from the fraudulent broker. But it was emphasised that this reliance and detriment had to be proved by the plaintiff and that even then she would have failed had the company been able to prove that action against the broker would have been fruitless had she been able to pursue it immediately. It will be observed that in both these cases the original recipient of the certificate had in fact changed his position in reliance on the certificate and in neither had he put forward a forged transfer.

Similarly, the original holder of the certificate may occasionally be able to rely on a false statement that shares are fully paid. Thus in *Parbury's* case,[77] P. paid money to his solicitor and instructed him to subscribe on his behalf for shares in a company which the solicitor was engaged in forming. Instead of using the money to pay for the shares the solicitor caused the company to allot to P. some of the shares to which the solicitor was entitled, but which were not fully paid because no contract evidencing the non-cash consideration had been filed as the law then required.[78] The certificate nevertheless described the shares as fully paid. In the subsequent winding up it was held that the company was estopped from alleging that they were not fully paid or from making calls on P.[79] And in *Bloomenthal* v. *Ford*[80] a lender of money to a company who took shares by way of collateral security, the

---

[75] In effect, C was subrogated to D's claim against the company.

[76] [1900] 1 Ch. 833.

[77] [1896] 1 Ch. 100.

[78] Under s. 25 of the Companies Act 1867, shares were fully payable in cash unless the contract was filed before the issue. Now (Companies Act 1948, s. 52) failure to file merely imposes liability to fines on the company's officials.

[79] There are two difficulties about the decision. (1) No consideration seems to have been given to the question whether P. had in fact been prejudiced in pursuing remedies against the solicitor because of relying on the certificate. (2) The solicitor seems to have acted in the application for the shares as P.'s agent. Although P. had no notice that the shares were not effectively paid up, the solicitor presumably had, and one would have supposed that his knowledge would be attributed to the principal P. Neither of these points seems to have been taken.

[80] [1897] A.C. 156, H.L. The decision is difficult to understand for a company cannot lawfully issue its own shares to secure a loan to it and, even if it could, it would afford no security.

certificates stating that they were fully paid, was allowed to hold the company estopped from denying the truth of the allegation on the faith of which the money was advanced. Although he might by inquiry have discovered that nothing had been paid on them, he had no actual notice and acted in all good faith and this was all that mattered.

The cases show that the mere fact that the membership register shows the true position will not be deemed to be notice precluding estoppel; if it were otherwise the importance of the principle would be greatly diminished for often the register will be correct and only the certificate wrong. It is not clear whether this is because the register, although open for public inspection, is not a public document, or because, in any event, the company will not be allowed to set up constructive notice of this sort to contradict a categorical statement made by it.[81] If the former is the true explanation it might be argued that the position would be different if, at the time when the shares were acquired, the true position could be seen from the return of allotments or annual return filed at the Companies' Registry. But this point seems never to have been taken, and, as we have seen, the extent of the public documents of which parties are deemed to have notice is uncertain.[82]

If a holder has shares which have become fully paid by estoppel he can pass an equally good title to others, and the fact that these others have notice has been held to be irrelevant.[83] Some doubts have been expressed on the correctness of this ruling,[84] but, it is submitted, without justification, for if it were otherwise the shares might become unmarketable and the estoppel of little value. But it may be legitimately doubted whether a holder with knowledge can obtain the benefit of the estoppel by transferring the shares to a bona fide purchaser and then buying them back.[85]

Forged certificates

Finally, it must be emphasised that the certificate only estops the company if it is the company's certificate. If therefore the certificate is issued without authority it cannot bind the company in any way.[86] Nevertheless it is submitted that if the genuineness of the certificate has been expressly or impliedly warranted by an official acting within the usual or apparent scope of his authority this warranty will bind the

---

[81] It has already been submitted that directors will be liable for breach of warranty of authority if they categorically state that their actions are within their powers notwithstanding that such acts are *ultra vires* the company and that this is apparent from the memorandum. See Chap. 5, *supra*, p. 95.

[82] *Supra*, Chap. 8, p. 154. It is clearly desirable that its extent should be contained within as narrow limits as possible.

[83] *Barrow's Case* (1880) 14 Ch.D. 432, C.A.

[84] *Re London Celluloid Co.* (1888) 39 Ch.D. 190, C.A., at p. 197; *Re Railway Time Tables Publishing Co.* (1889) 42 Ch.D. 98 at p. 110.

[85] *Simm* v. *Anglo-American Telegraph Co.* (1879) 5 Q.B.D. 188, C.A., implies that he cannot, and Jessel M.R., in *Barrow's Case* (1880) 14 Ch.D. at p. 445, expressly recognised that this would be so if the holder had been fraudulent.

[86] *Ruben* v. *Great Fingall Consolidated* [1906] A.C. 439, H.L.

company even though that official has committed forgery.[87] This point has already been argued fully in an earlier chapter.[88]

Share warrants

Section 83 of the Companies Act 1948 provides that a company limited by shares may, if authorised by its articles, issue a share warrant to bearer in respect of any of its fully paid shares. This means that instead of a share certificate the holder is given a document sealed by the company stating that the bearer is entitled to the shares or stock specified therein. Normally, provision will be made for obtaining dividends by a delivery to the company of coupons detachable from the warrant.

Section 112 provides that on the issue of the warrant the company shall strike out the name of the member from its register of members and shall enter instead merely the fact of the issue of the warrant, a description of the shares, and the date of issue. Subject to any contrary provision in the articles the bearer is entitled to surrender the warrant for cancellation and to have his name restored.[89] But the bearer of the warrant may, if the articles so provide, be deemed to be a member either to the full extent or for any purposes defined in the articles.[90] To this extent, therefore, share warrants lead to exceptions to two general principles stated above. First, to the rule that in companies limited by shares " shareholder " and " member " are synonymous, for the bearer of a warrant is always a shareholder but may not be a member; and secondly, to the rule that, apart from subscribers to the memorandum, a person can be a member or shareholder only if his name is on the register, for the bearer of a warrant will not be on the register but will nevertheless be a shareholder and may be a member.

A share warrant differs from a certificate in two other fundamental aspects. As we have seen a share certificate imposes no liability on the company, except through estoppel, and is in no sense a warranty of the holder's title, but at the most a statement that he once had a title. A warrant, as its name implies, is a warranty that the bearer is the share holder. Provided it is not a forgery,[91] the company will be contractually bound to recognise the bearer's title.

[87] *Lloyd* v. *Grace, Smith & Co.* [1912] A.C. 716, H.L.; *Uxbridge Building Society* v. *Pickard* [1939] 2 K.B. 248, C.A.; *secus, Ruben* v. *Great Fingall Consolidated, supra,* per Lord Loreburn at p. 443; *Kreditbank Cassel* v. *Schenkers* [1927] 1 K.B. 826, C.A.; *S. London Greyhound Racecourses* v. *Wake* [1931] 1 Ch. 496; *Slingsby* v. *District Bank* [1931] 2 K.B. 588.
[88] *Supra*, Chap. 8, pp. 166–168.
[89] s. 112 (2).
[90] s. 112 (5). The articles may, for example, deprive the holders of voting rights but generally they are permitted to vote on lodging their warrants with the company or producing a certificate from a bank that it holds them on their behalf. But a director's qualification cannot be obtained by holding share warrants: s. 182 (2).
[91] If the forgery is by an officer of the company, the same principles apply as in the case of share certificates: *supra*, and Chap. 8, pp. 166–168.

Secondly, it is a negotiable instrument which may pass by delivery free from equities.[92] In point of fact the difference here is mainly in respect of means of transfer rather than of freedom from equities, for, as we shall see, the mechanism of share transfer is such that a transferee, once his transfer is registered, normally takes free from equities affecting the transferor unless he has notice of them. The principal difference in this respect is that the transferee only perfects his title when the transfer is passed and registered; the transfer alone, even if in blank and accompanied by the share certificate, or, as in the American practice, endorsed on the back of the certificate, does not give the holder a clean title and is not regarded as negotiable.[93] In contrast the bona fide purchaser of a share warrant acquires a title free from equities immediately. Hence a private company cannot issue share warrants, without forfeiting its privileges as a private company, because no restriction on transfer is practicable.

Share warrants have never been particularly popular with English companies or investors, for they suffer from a number of obvious disadvantages. In the first place, the company is unable to get into touch with its shareholders except through newspaper advertisement and, if the share warrants confer voting rights, this makes it much more difficult for the management to maintain control through the proxy voting machinery. On the other hand, if the shareholder fails to see the advertisements he may lose his opportunity of voting and will not receive his dividends promptly. Again, there are obviously grave risks of loss or theft, the consequences of which will be far more serious than in the case of share certificates. Finally, the Revenue has taken steps to off-set the loss which it suffers through its failure to collect stamp duty on share transfers. The warrants themselves have to be stamped with three times the amount of the transfer duty,[94] that is with 3 per cent., and this adds considerably to the initial expense.

Despite these disadvantages, bearer securities have always been much in demand by Continental investors,[95] and some English companies have issued share warrants to meet this demand. Although the Exchange Control Act 1947 [96] forbids any issues of bearer securities or coupons without the consent of the Treasury, since 1963 a general consent has been given.[97] But the Act further provides [98] that bearer securities,

---

[92] *Webb, Hale & Co.* v. *Alexandria Water Co.* (1905) 21 T.L.R. 572.
[93] *Colonial Bank* v. *Cady* (1890) 15 App.Cas. 267, H.L. As to the exact effect of an unregistered transfer, see *infra*, Chap. 18, p. 402 *et seq.*
[94] F.A. 1963, s. 59 (1).
[95] This is mainly because of the different organisation and less widespread use of the banking system on the Continent. The quality of transferability greatly facilitated the task of refugees who wished to smuggle their wealth out of countries from which they were forced to flee.
[96] s. 10.
[97] See now Notice E.C. 10 (Third Issue). Specific consent is still required in the case of conversions from registered securities.
[98] ss. 15 and 16.

whether of English or foreign companies, if they are in the United Kingdom or held on behalf of a United Kingdom resident shall be deposited with an authorised depositary [99] to whom all dividends and the like have to be paid. By this means the Treasury is able to maintain its control but, in effect, at the expense of destroying the bearer and negotiable character of the securities.

In present circumstances, therefore, share warrants are of minimal importance so far as English companies are concerned.

Nominee shareholdings

It will be appreciated that the register of members does not enable the company or anyone else to ascertain more than the identity of the registered proprietors of the shares; indeed the Act provides that no notice of any trust shall be entered on the register in the case of companies registered in England.[1] Where share warrants have been issued still less is known. In both cases it may be impossible to find out who are the true beneficial owners of the shares since it is quite common for registered shares to be held by nominee companies as trustees for the true owners. This practice can be highly convenient for the owners but is obviously capable of abuse. For example, it enables directors to traffic in the securities of their companies without this being known, or someone secretly to acquire control or a sizeable holding on which to base a bid for control. The Cohen Committee gave extended consideration to this problem,[2] but all that ultimately resulted in the Companies Act 1948 were provisions for the maintenance of a register of directors' shareholdings and dealings [3] and a power to the Board of Trade to appoint an inspector to investigate the true ownership of a company.[4] The far more sweeping proposal of the Committee, that there should be compulsory disclosure of those entitled beneficially to 1 per cent. or more of the issued capital,[5] was ultimately rejected as impracticable.

However, the matter was again taken up by the Jenkins Committee,[6] which recommended the more practical solution of banning outright one type of transaction by directors, and of improving the provisions for disclosure and extending them from directors to 10 per cent. shareholders. Their suggestions have now been enacted in the Companies Act 1967, ss. 25 and 27–34. For the purposes of these sections " director " includes " any person in accordance with whose directions or instructions the directors of the company are accustomed to act," [7]

---

[99] For exceptions, see E.C. 10 (Third Issue), App. I & II.
[1] s. 117.
[2] Cmd. 6659, paras. 77–87.
[3] s. 195.
[4] s. 172.
[5] Cmd. 6659, paras. 81–82.
[6] Cmnd. 1749, paras. 88 and 91, and 141–147.
[7] ss. 25 (3), 27 (11), 29 (14).

otherwise than " by reason only that [they] act on advice given by him in a professional capacity." [8]

Section 25 makes it a criminal offence to buy a " put " or " call " or " put-and-call " option [9] in any quoted shares or debentures of any company in the group (*i.e.*, the company, any subsidiary company, its holding company, or any other subsidiary of the latter). By section 30 this is extended to the spouse and infant child of a director unless they had no reason to know of the directorship. Thereby the most blatant type of speculation with the advantage of inside information is banned.

The remaining sections provide for disclosure. They are extremely complicated and here can be dealt with in outline only. The complication is partly because shareholdings and dealings by directors and by others have been treated as posing distinct problems. In the U.S.A. directors and 10 per cent. shareholders are dealt with together and dealings by both are treated as raising the single problem of " insider-trading." [10] In contrast, in England, disclosure of holdings and dealings by directors has been regarded as necessary to prevent the abuse of inside information, whereas disclosure by other shareholders has been thought of as required mainly to protect directors (and members and employees) against having their companies taken over without their knowledge. [11]

Sections 27–29 and 31, repealing and replacing section 195 of the 1948 Act, make more effective provision for disclosure in relation to directors. They have to notify the company in writing within fourteen days of acquiring or disposing of any beneficial interest [12] in shares or debentures of companies in the group. [13] The notice must give considerable detail regarding the transaction concerned, including the price. [14] Interests of a spouse or infant child of a director are treated as interests of the director. [15] The company must maintain a register of directors' interests and dealings and must enter thereon the information received within three days. [16] Where the company itself grants a director the right to subscribe for its shares or debentures it must enter details on the register of the rights and of their exercise. [17] This register, and this is the great contrast with the former section 195, is during business hours

[8] s. 56 (3).
[9] *i.e.*, an option to buy or sell at a specified price or, at his option, either to buy or sell: see s. 25 (1). But an option may be granted by the company to its director: s. 25 (4); in the U.S.A. such stock-options are a popular method of remunerating directors and managers but are less prevalent here for tax reasons.
[10] s. 16 of the Securities Exchange Act 1934, on which see Loss: *Securities Regulation* (2nd ed. 1961) pp. 1037–1132.
[11] *Cf.* Jenkins Report, Cmnd. 1749, para. 142.
[12] " Interest " is defined very widely: s. 28.
[13] s. 27 (1).
[14] s. 27 (5), (6) and (7).
[15] s. 31. This blocks a loophole in s. 195 of the 1948 Act.
[16] s. 29 (1) and (4).
[17] s. 29 (2) and (4).

to be open to inspection by members without charge and by others on payment of a fee not exceeding 1s.[18] and copies may be obtained.[19]

Sections 33 and 34 contain corresponding provisions regarding 10 per cent. shareholders. Their coverage is considerably narrower than that applying to directors; because of the concentration on take-over of control,[20] they are restricted to quoted companies,[21] to holdings of shares (not debentures), and moreover to shares which carry unrestricted voting rights.[22] Disclosure is required by anyone who is or becomes beneficially interested in one-tenth or more in nominal value of such shares [23] and, generally speaking, the same rules as those relating to directors apply to the meaning of " interest " (though there are additional exceptions [24]) and to the time within which disclosure is to be made.[25] But the information which has to be given is narrower; in particular the price paid or received on an acquisition or disposal of shares does not have to be disclosed. As already pointed out the object is to enable those interested in the company to see who its actual or potential controllers are, and not, as in the case of directors, to discourage the abuse of inside information. A separate register of these shareholdings and dealings has to be maintained by the company,[26] and this too is open for inspection [27] and copies may be obtained,[28] except in so far as it contains information regarding the holdings of companies incorporated or carrying on business abroad where a dispensation from disclosure in their accounts under section 3 or 4 of the Act has been granted by the Board of Trade.[29] Where a director is entitled to more than 10 per cent.

[18] s. 29 (7). It must also be produced at the annual general meeting (s. 29 (11)) and details of each director's holdings at the beginning and end of each financial year must be given in the directors' report: s. 16 (1) (*e*), *infra*, p. 467. Still more extensive disclosure is required in the case of quoted companies: see *Requirements*, App., Sched. VIII, Part A (General Undertaking), para. 7 (*a*) (*i*): note that this expressly includes interests under a discretionary trust which are excluded under s. 28 (2).

[19] s. 29 (10).

[20] See p. 389, *supra*.

[21] s. 33 (10). This restriction was added during the Bill's passage. In fact the S.E. General Undertaking requires still more extensive annual disclosure: *Requirements*, App., Sched. VIII, Part A, para. 6 (*d*).

[22] See the definition of " relevant share capital " in s. 33 (10).

[23] It is not clear whether this means 10 per cent. of each class of equity shares (as was apparently intended and as the Jenkins Committee recommended: see Cmnd. 1749, para. 143) or merely 10 per cent. of the total equity. If the latter is held to be the correct construction the section is gravely defective since one class may give voting control without being 10 per cent. of the total equity. In any case to make nominal value the test seems inconsistent with the apparent object since there is not necessarily any relation between nominal value and number of votes.

[24] s. 33 (4). Note that both here, and for directors (see s. 27 (1)) the Board of Trade may extend the exceptions and has done so by S.I.s 1594 and 1595 of 1967, and S.I.s 864, 865, and 1533 of 1968.

[25] s. 33 (5).

[26] s. 34.

[27] s. 34 (5).

[28] s. 34 (7).

[29] s. 34 (5) and (7). As regards ss. 3 and 4, see p. 456, *infra*.

of the voting shares his holdings and dealings in them have to appear both in this register and in the register of directors' shareholdings.[30]

Finally it should be mentioned that section 32 confers an additional [31] power on the Board of Trade to appoint an inspector to investigate possible breaches by the directors of their duties under section 27 (or section 25 relating to the buying by directors of put or call options in their companies' shares).[32]

As a result of these new provisions some of the worst abuses flowing from clandestine dealings through nominees should be prevented. But we have still not gone nearly so far as legislation in the U.S.A.[33] In particular there is nothing comparable with section 16 (*b*) of the Securities Exchange Act whereby insiders may have to account to their companies for short-term profits made by dealings in their companies' securities.[34] Nor, as yet,[35] have we anything comparable with rule 10b–5, made under that Act, whereby insiders (and perhaps even their " tippees ") may be liable to those with whom they have had dealings in the company's securities.[36]

---

[30] The recommendation of the Jenkins Committee (Cmnd. 1749, para. 147 (*c*)), that disclosure in the register of directors' shareholdings should suffice, has not been adopted. This duplication would have been avoided had there been but one register for all " insiders."

[31] *i.e.*, additional to ss. 172 and 173 of the 1948 Act. On all these sections see Chap. 25, pp. 606–613, *infra*.

[32] On which see p. 389, *supra*.

[33] See p. 389, *supra*.

[34] As yet we have contented ourselves with disclosures similar to s. 16 (*a*).

[35] But see *infra*, p. 518.

[36] See especially *S.E.C.* v. *Texas Gulf Sulphur Co.*, 401 F. 2d 833 (2d Circ. 1968), cert. denied April 1969.

CHAPTER 18

TRANSFER AND TRANSMISSION OF SHARES

WE now turn to a consideration of some of the problems which arise
in connection with the transfer of shares.[1] The transfer may take place
either voluntarily, or involuntarily on execution or as an element in a
universal assignment of the owner's property on death or bankruptcy—
the last of these being generally described as a transmission. Voluntary
transfers will be considered first.

Restrictions on transferability

Prima facie, companies' shares are freely transferable; as we have
seen,[2] it is this feature which constitutes one of the great advantages
of an incorporated company. Unless the company's regulations provide
otherwise, the shareholder is entitled to transfer to whom he will.[3]

But, as we have also seen, the company's regulations may place
restrictions on the right to transfer and must do so if the company
is a private one.[4] These restrictions may take any form, but in practice
they normally either give the existing members a right of pre-emption or
first refusal, or confer a discretion on the directors to refuse to pass
transfers.[5] The vast body of case law on this subject (of which only
the most important recent decisions are cited in the footnotes) may, it is
thought, be reduced to the following propositions:

(a) The extent of the restriction is solely a matter of construction of
the regulations. But, since shareholders have a prima facie right to
transfer to whomsoever they please, this right is not to be cut down by
uncertain language or doubtful implications.[6] If, therefore, it is not
clear whether a restriction applies to any transfer or only to a transfer
to non-members,[7] or whether a right of pre-emption applies to any

---

1 As pointed out in the next chapter, most of what is here stated is equally applicable
  to transfers and transmissions of debentures and, *a fortiori*, debenture stock.
2 *Supra*, Chap. 4, pp. 77, 78.
3 *Weston's Case* (1868) L.R. 4 Ch.App. 20, C.A. Thus in *De Pass's Case* (1859) 4
  De G. & J. 544 (approved *Lindlar's Case* [1910] 1 Ch. 312, C.A.) it was held that a
  transfer of partly paid shares to a pauper, avowedly for the purpose of escaping
  liability in an impending winding up, was unimpeachable.
4 Restrictions are unusual in the case of a public company except in the case of partly
  paid shares; in other cases a stock exchange quotation will not be granted if there
  are restrictions: *Requirements*, App., Sched. VII, Pt. A, para. A2.
5 The latter restriction is commonly found in conjunction with the former. In the
  U.S.A. it is generally held that the restrictions, being restraints on the alienability of
  personal property, must be reasonable. In England it is clear that there is no such
  rule except, perhaps, when the restrictions are imposed after the shares have been
  issued: *cf.* Chap. 24, p. 567 *et seq.*
6 *Per* Greene M.R. in *Re Smith & Fawcett Ltd.* [1942] Ch. 304, C.A., at p. 306.
7 *Greenhalgh* v. *Mallard* [1943] 2 All E.R. 234, C.A.; *Roberts* v. *Letter " T " Estates
  Ltd.* [1961] A.C. 795, P.C.

392

disposition or only to a sale,[8] the more restrictive construction will be adopted.

(b) On the other hand the courts will not carry a literal construction of the regulations so far as to defeat their obvious purpose. In one case [9] the articles conferred a right of pre-emption on the other shareholders when any shareholder was "desirous of transferring his ordinary shares." Certain shareholders sold their shares to a take-over bidder, received the purchase price and gave him irrevocable proxies to vote on their behalf, but, in the light of the articles, transfers were not to be lodged for registration. The House of Lords held that in the context "transferring" obviously meant assigning the beneficial interest and not the technical process of having a transfer registered.[10] The shareholders had clearly manifested an intention to sell their shares and could not continue with the sale without giving the other shareholders a right to exercise their option under the articles.[11]

(c) Where the regulations confer a discretion on directors with regard to the acceptance of transfers, this discretion, like all the directors' powers, is a fiduciary one [12] to be exercised bona fide in what they consider—not what the court considers—to be in the interest of the company, and not for any collateral purpose.[6] But the court will presume that they have acted bona fide, and the onus of proof of the contrary is on those alleging it and is not easily discharged.[13]

(d) If, on the true construction of the regulations, the directors are only entitled to reject on certain prescribed grounds and it is proved that they have rejected on others, the court will interfere.[14] And interrogatories may be administered to determine on which of certain prescribed grounds the directors have acted, but not as to their reasons for rejecting on these grounds,[15] and not if the articles provide, as they often do, that they shall not be bound to state their reasons.[16] If the directors do state their reasons the court will investigate them to the extent of seeing whether they have acted on the right principles and will overrule their decision if they have acted on considerations which should not have weighed with them, but not merely because the court would

---

[8] *Moodie* v. *Shepherd (Bookbinders) Ltd.* [1949] 2 All E.R. 1044, H.L.Sc.

[9] *Lyle & Scott Ltd.* v. *Scott's Trustees* [1959] A.C. 763, H.L.Sc.

[10] This distinction is all too often overlooked in the drafting of the relative articles.

[11] Cf. *Jarvis Motors (Harrow) Ltd.* v. *Carabott* [1964] 1 W.L.R. 1101, where a right of pre-emption in favour of "other members" was held to operate where there was only one other member.

[12] For a fuller discussion of the directors' fiduciary duties, see Chap. 23, *infra.*

[13] In *Re Smith & Fawcett Ltd.* the directors refused to register the transfer of all the shares but agreed to register the transfer of some if the transferor would sell the balance to one of the directors at a certain price. It was held that this was insufficient evidence of *mala fides.*

[14] *Re Bede Steam Shipping Co.* [1917] 1 Ch. 123, C.A.

[15] *Sutherland* v. *British Dominions Land Settlement Corpn.* [1926] Ch. 746.

[16] *Berry & Stewart* v. *Tottenham Hotspur Football Co.* [1935] Ch. 718. The Jenkins Committee recommended that directors should be required to state reasons, if asked, when they refused to register the personal representatives of a deceased shareholder: Cmnd. 1749, para. 210.

have come to a different conclusion.[17]   If the regulations are so framed as to give the directors an unfettered discretion the court will only interfere with it on proof of bad faith.[18]   Since, in the latter case, the directors will not be bound to disclose either their grounds or their reasons, the difficulty of discharging the onus of proof is especially great, for the objectors have to try to make bricks without straw.

(e) If, as is normal, the regulations merely give the directors power to refuse to register, as opposed to making their passing of transfers a condition precedent to registration,[19] the transferee is entitled to be registered unless the directors resolve as a board to reject.   Hence in *Moodie* v. *Shepherd* (*Bookbinders*) *Ltd.*[20] where the two directors disagreed and neither had a casting vote, the House of Lords held that registration must proceed.   The directors have a reasonable time in which to come to a decision,[21] but in the case of registered companies, section 78 of the Act imposes an obligation on them to give to the transferee notice of rejection within two months of the lodging of the transfer, and, at any rate in the case of such companies, the maximum reasonable period is two months.[22]   The Jenkins Committee recommended that this period should be reduced to five weeks and that the transferee should be entitled, on showing good cause, to apply to the court for an order that the transfer should be registered forthwith.[23]

These rules apply if, but only if, the limitations concerned are validly inserted in the regulations either in their original form or as subsequently altered.   The extent to which such an alteration can be restrained, if made to the detriment of the shareholder subsequently to the issue of the shares to him, is discussed in Chapter 24.

Procedure on transfer

When shares are bought and sold at least three [24] entirely distinct legal transactions are involved.   First, there will be a contract for the sale of the shares, a contract which, if effected through a stockbroker,

---

[17] *Re Bede S.S. Co.*, *supra*; *Re Smith & Fawcett Ltd.*, *supra*.   Similarly if there are rights of pre-emption at a fair value to be certified by the auditors the court can investigate the adequacy of the valuation if (but only if) the auditors give their reasons: *Dean* v. *Prince* [1953] Ch. 590; [1954] Ch. 409, C.A.   The position closely resembles the principles on which the court acts in deciding whether to quash by *certiorari* the decision of a lower court or administrative tribunal.

[18] *Re Smith & Fawcett Ltd.*, *supra*; *Charles Forte Investments Ltd.* v. *Amanda* [1964] Ch. 240, C.A.   *Cf. Re Hafner* [1943] I.R. 264 (Ir.S.C.) where the onus of proof was discharged.

[19] It is common to state that transfers have to be passed by the directors but under the normal articles (*e.g.*, Table A, arts. 24 and 25) this is incorrect.   Unless they decide to *reject* the transferee is entitled to be registered.

[20] [1949] 2 All E.R. 1044, H.L.Sc., approving *Re Hackney Pavilion Ltd.* [1924] 1 Ch. 276.

[21] *Shepherd's Case* (1866) L.R. 2 Ch.App. 16.

[22] *Re Swaledale Cleaners Ltd.* [1968] 1 W.L.R. 1710, C.A.

[23] Cmnd. 1749, para. 476.

[24] If the transactions are effected through a stockbroker there will, of course, additionally be the establishment of agency relationships between the clients and the broker.

will be evidenced by his "bought" and "sold" notes. This alone, however, will not operate to transfer the "property" in the shares, for shares are not like goods and the property in them does not pass as a result of the contract. In this respect they more closely resemble land; just as the contract of sale of land requires to be completed by a convey-ance, so a contract for the sale of shares requires to be completed by transfer.[25]

If the shares are represented by warrants, the transfer of property will simply be effected by delivery of possession of the warrants, the only complication being that today the warrants will have been deposited with a bank or other "authorised depositary" which will either attorn to the buyer or transfer to another authorised depositary, in either event ensuring that the regulations of the Exchange Control Act are complied with. If, however, the shares are registered, a further document will be required and registered companies [26] cannot dispense with the need for one since the Act [27] makes it unlawful for the company to register a transfer unless a proper instrument of transfer has been delivered. The purpose of this peremptory requirement is not to safeguard either com-panies or shareholders but to protect the Revenue by preventing evasion of the 1 per cent. stamp duty required on transfers.[28] The Act specifically states that this requirement shall be "notwithstanding anything in the articles," and it has accordingly been held that an article purporting to introduce an automatic transmission of shares on the death of the holder, otherwise than under the rules of intestacy or by will, is ineffective.[29]

It is therefore an implied obligation of the contract that the seller will deliver to the buyer a validly executed document of transfer. Until the Stock Transfer Act 1963 introduced a simplified form of transfer the form of this depended on the company's regulations, although in practice it had become pretty well standardised. Under that

---

[25] But since specific performance may be ordered of a contract for the sale of shares (*Poole* v. *Middleton* (1861) 29 Beav. 646) the equitable interest passes to the purchaser so soon as the agreement is specifically enforceable. If the agreement is subject to a condition precedent this will not be until the condition is fulfilled unless it is solely for the benefit of the purchaser and he waives it: *Wood Preservation Ltd.* v. *Prior* [1969] 1 All E.R. 364, C.A. (where it is suggested that prior to waiver the beneficial interest may have left the seller but not vested in the buyer!). There are expressions in the judgment of Vaisey J. in *Hawks* v. *McArthur* [1951] 1 All E.R. 22 which suggest that the equitable interest passes whenever there is a binding agreement and payment even though, as in that case, specific performance could hardly be granted because of restrictions on the right of transfer.

[26] As regards statutory companies, C.C.A. 1845, s. 14 *et seq.*, also provides for documents of transfer.

[27] Companies Act 1948, s. 75.

[28] Hence a transfer will not be void under this section though it does not comply with all the provisions of the articles: *Re Paradise Motor Co. Ltd.* [1968] 1 W.L.R. 1125, C.A. The Stamp Act 1891, s. 17, imposes liability to a fine if an improperly stamped transfer is registered, and the directors would not be able to put the transfer in evidence to justify the registration until they had stamped it under penalty. Prior to 1929, however, these safeguards were often evaded by providing in the articles for oral transfers.

[29] *Re Greene* [1949] Ch. 333.

Act the new simplified form suffices in the case of transfers of fully
paid shares of nearly all registered or statutory companies.[30]   Often
the seller will sign the transfer leaving blank the date and the name
of the transferee.   By so doing he impliedly authorises the buyer to
complete the transfer by inserting either his own name or that of a
nominee for him or of a sub-purchaser from him.[31]   This formerly
caused legal difficulties where the transfer was required under the
company's regulations to be by deed, as it was, for example, in the case
of statutory companies,[32] for then the transfer could not lawfully be
completed unless the seller authorised the buyer by a power of attorney
under seal.[33]   But by virtue of the Stock Transfer Act a transfer to
which it applies need not be under seal [34] and it seems that when a deed
is not necessary a transfer bearing a seal will not be treated as a deed.[35]

The seller will also be under an obligation to hand over to the buyer
his document of title, the share certificate, for the company will not
normally register the transfer until it is produced.   The practice where
the seller is unwilling to give the certificate to the buyer, because he is
only selling part of the holding, is explained later.

This normally completes the transaction so far as the seller is
concerned; his only outstanding obligation is not to do anything to
prevent the buyer (or his nominee or sub-purchaser) from becoming
registered and obtaining the full benefit of the shares.[36]   He does not
warrant that registration will be effected and if the directors, having a
discretion, refuse to register, the purchaser cannot get his money back [37]
but the seller will be regarded as holding the shares on trust for him.[38]

But the transaction is still incomplete as between the buyer and
the company.   Before the buyer can become a member and shareholder
there must be an agreement between him and the company and he must
be entered on the register.   To obtain definite evidence of an agreement
the common form of share transfer used to contain a provision whereby
the transferee " agrees to accept the said shares " and most articles
required that it should be executed by the transferee as well as the
transferor.[39]   This need to obtain the signature of the transferee caused
difficulty and delay in stock exchange transactions in which it is

---

[30] It does not apply to guarantee or unlimited companies: Stock Transfer Act 1963,
s. 1 (4).
[31] *Re Tahiti Cotton Co.* (1874) L.R. 17 Eq. 273. *Semble*, the authority being coupled
with an interest will be irrevocable: *Carter* v. *White* (1883) 25 Ch.D. 666, C.A.
[32] C.C.A. 1845, s. 14.
[33] *Powell* v. *London & Provincial Bank* [1893] 2 Ch. 555, C.A.
[34] Stock Transfer Act 1963, s. 1 (1).
[35] *Re Tahiti Cotton Co., supra*; *Ortigosa* v. *Brown* (1878) 47 L.J.Ch. 168.
[36] *Hooper* v. *Herts* [1906] 1 Ch. 549, C.A.
[37] *London Founders' Assocn.* v. *Clarke* (1888) 20 Q.B.D. 576, C.A., and the contract
not being *uberrimae fidei*, the seller is not bound to draw the buyer's attention to
any right to refuse transfers which, being in the public documents, the buyer is
deemed to know.
[38] *Hardoon* v. *Belilios* [1901] A.C. 118, P.C.
[39] *Cf.* Table A, art. 22.

uncommon for there to be a simple transfer from one seller to one buyer. Accordingly the Stock Transfer Act 1963 has done away with the need for execution by the transferee when the shares are fully paid. The new form of transfer need be signed only by the transferor who transfers " the above security out of the name(s) aforesaid to the person(s) named below or to the several persons named in . . . the Brokers' Transfer Forms relating to the above security." If the shares are not transferred in a stock exchange transaction the name of the transferee will be inserted and the transferee or his agent will authenticate the final words of the form whereby he requests " that such entries be made in the register as are necessary to give effect to this transfer." In the case of a stock exchange transaction the seller's broker endorses details of the various sales and the buyers' brokers complete separate brokers' transfer forms with a similar request.[40] The transfer plus the brokers' transfer forms (if any) and the share certificate are then lodged with the company and are treated as adequate evidence of the agreement of the transferee who or whose agent either lodges all the documents or, at least, the brokers' transfer form.[41] However, when the shares are partly paid, the only case where the transferee is likely to dispute his agreement, stronger evidence of his concurrence is thought to be needed and the Stock Transfer Act does not apply. In such circumstances the company's regulations are likely to require that the transfer be executed by the transferee.

It is the normal practice for companies to dispatch a notice to the transferor that a transfer has been lodged for registration. This is some protection against registering a forged transfer, but not necessarily an effective one, because it has been held that failure to reply does not estop the alleged transferor.[42] Companies are highly vulnerable in this respect since they will have to restore the true shareholder to the register and to make good any loss to him,[43] while they may become liable to pay damages to anyone who has relied on the new certificate.[44] They

---

[40] For the forms, see the Schedules to the Act; these can be amended by the Treasury: s. 4.

[41] If it is necessary or profitable to analyse the agreement into offer and acceptance it must be confessed that it is not altogether clear whether the transferee must be regarded as accepting the company's offer or vice versa. If the directors have no power to decline to register, it would appear that the " agreement " is completed when the transferee notifies his acceptance by dispatching the transfer, for the directors can be compelled to register. If, however, they have a discretion presumably the lodging of the transfer is an offer by the transferee which is only accepted when the passing of the transfer is notified.

[42] *Barton* v. *L. & N.W. Ry.* (1889) 24 Q.B.D. 77, C.A.; *Welch* v. *Bank of England* [1955] Ch. 508.

[43] *Ibid.* The company cannot plead the statute of limitations since the forged transfer is a nullity and the true shareholder has remained a member throughout. *Barton's Case* suggests that time would start to run when there was a categorical refusal by the company to restore the shareholder to the register, but Harman J. in *Welch* v. *Bank of England* seemed to think that it would not run even then.

[44] *Supra*, Chap. 17, p. 381 *et seq.*

have, it is true, a claim against the person who lodged the forged transfer,[45] but this remedy may not be worth much and is one which they will be reluctant to pursue if he acted in all innocence.[46]

If the shares are only partly paid, it will be very much in the transferor's interest to ensure that the transfer is registered as soon as possible, for until it is he will remain liable, and the year during which he can be placed on the B list of contributories will only start to run from the date of registration. He will, it is true, have a right to be indemnified by the buyer[47] but this may not be worth much. Hence section 77 of the Companies Act 1948 provides that the company shall register on the application of the transferor " in the same manner and subject to the same conditions as if the application . . . were made by the transferee." This, however, will not be of great assistance to the seller if he has handed over the certificate and transfer to a buyer who refuses to lodge them for registration. Moreover, in the case of partly paid shares, he runs a particular risk that the directors will refuse registration and this he will not know until the transferee tells him, for section 78 merely imposes an obligation to send notice of refusal to the transferee—not to the transferor.[48]

At the present time there is a further precaution which the company must take before registering the transfer. This is to ensure that the rules of the Exchange Control Act 1947[49] have been complied with, for section 13 of that Act makes it an offence to register a transfer unless the regulations appear to have been observed. If both transferor and transferee are resident in the sterling area and are beneficially entitled, no difficulty arises, provided that the transfers are lodged by " authorised depositaries " or the prescribed declarations are made.[50] If, however, either party, or the person for whom he is a nominee, is resident elsewhere, the consent of the Treasury may be required and the company's registration officer and the parties will be guilty of an offence if it is not obtained.[51]

The above account explains briefly the normal procedure on a sale and purchase of shares. When the transfer is by way of gift, on an appointment of new trustees, or the like, there will, of course, be no sale agreement but all that has been said about the other steps is equally applicable.

---

45 *Supra*, p. 383.
46 They will, in that event, have power to compensate him under the Forged Transfer Acts 1891 and 1892, but these Acts are merely permissive.
47 *Hardoon* v. *Belilios* [1901] A.C. 118, P.C.
48 The Jenkins Committee recommended that notice should be sent to both transferor and transferee and that the time should be reduced from two months to five weeks: Cmnd. 1749, para. 476.
49 As regards transfers, see s. 9.
50 Notice, E.C. 10 (Third Issue), para. 17.
51 The innocent registrar and the innocent party will escape liability if the prescribed declarations are made: see ss. 9 and 13.

Certification of transfers

When the transferor is disposing of the totality of his holding included in a share certificate he must hand this over to the transferee for the latter to lodge with the completed transfer. But if he is only disposing of part he will be unwilling to hand over the certificate. To obviate this difficulty a practice has grown up whereby the transferor lodges the certificate and transfer either with the stock exchange or with the company, which then " certifies " the transfer by endorsing a statement to the effect that a share certificate covering those transferred has been lodged. This the transferee accepts in lieu of the certificate itself,[52] which is retained by the company or forwarded to it by the stock exchange concerned. When the transfer is lodged with the company and passed, the company cancels the old certificate and sends a new one, for the shares transferred, to the transferee and a balance certificate, for those retained, to the transferor. A similar practice is adopted when all the shares are disposed of but to two or more transferees. In the case of stock exchange transactions the certification is on the brokers' transfer forms.[53]

The form of the certification makes it clear that it is not a warranty of the transferor's title, nor, it has been held, is it a guarantee that the certificate is genuine [54] or even that the statements in it are true. Hence it does not give the transferee the same protection as he would obtain under the doctrine of estoppel by share certificate [55] if he obtained the certificate itself.[56] But it is a statement that documents showing a prima facie title to the shares transferred have been lodged, and the fraudulent maker of this statement is liable in damages if the transferee acts on it.[57] Unfortunately the efficacy of this rule, when the certifying was done by an official of the company, was largely destroyed when the House of Lords decided in *George Whitechurch Ltd.* v. *Cavanagh* [58] that if the company's secretary fraudulently and for his own purposes certified a transfer when the share certificate had not in fact been lodged, the company was not responsible. This decision appears to have been based on the now obsolete idea that a servant could not be regarded as acting within the scope of his authority so as to bind his master if he was acting for his own benefit and not for that of his master—a notion which was later rejected by the House of Lords in

---

[52] It constitutes good delivery according to the rules of the London Stock Exchange, rule 129.
[53] *Cf.* Stock Transfer Act 1963, s. 2 (2).
[54] It would be unreasonable to expect an official of the stock exchange to check whether the certificate was genuine or not, but there seems no reason why the company should not. However, it was held otherwise: *Longman* v. *Bath Electric Tramways* [1905] 1 Ch. 646, C.A. And see now Companies Act 1948, s. 79.
[55] See pp. 381–386, *supra.*
[56] See the Jenkins Committee's Report (Cmnd. 1749, para. 482) which, however, refrained from making any recommendation.
[57] *Bishop* v. *Balkis Consolidated Co.* (1890) 25 Q.B.D. 512, C.A.
[58] [1902] A.C. 117, H.L.

Lloyd v. *Grace, Smith & Co.*[59]   In view of the latter decision the point
was again fought to the House of Lords in 1934,[60] but the House held
that it was bound by its previous decision in the *Whitechurch* case.   This
anomalous result can only be explained on the somewhat dubious basis
that it is not within the normal scope of a company secretary's duties
to certify transfers—although if this is so, it is difficult to see how anything can be within his normal authority, for certifying transfers is one
of his most common tasks.[61]

However, so far as registered companies are concerned, good sense
has now, somewhat grudgingly, been partially restored by section 79
of the 1948 Act.   This confirms the common law rule as to the limited
nature of the representation, but provides that it shall be deemed to be
made by the company, provided that it is issued by someone having
actual authority to issue certified transfers, and purports to be signed
by any person who has actual authority to certify or by any officer or
servant of the company or of any other company so authorised.[62]   The
apparent result of this section is that if the transfer is sent to and received
back from the secretary's department or that of the registrar *and* the
secretary or registrar has actual authority to certify transfers *and*
the certificate purports to be signed by an official of the company (or of
another company acting as registrars) the company will be responsible
for the representation.   Further, if it is false, whether because of fraud
or negligence, the company will be liable to compensate the transferee.[63]
In particular, the company will not be able to escape liability by alleging
that, although the secretary or registrar has authority to certify, his
authority is limited to cases where a share certificate has in fact been
lodged, or that the signature on the certificate, although that of one of
the company's or registrar's servants, is not that of anyone having
authority to sign.   But it would appear that the company will still escape
if it can prove that it has not in fact authorised its secretary or registrar
to issue certified transfers at all,[64] or that the signature is not that of any
officer of the company or registrar, and not made by anyone else
authorised to use his signature for the purpose of certifying.[65]

---

[59] [1912] A.C. 716, H.L.
[60] *Kleinwort, Sons & Co.* v. *Associated Automatic Machine Corpn.* (1934) 50 T.L.R.
244, H.L.
[61] See *supra*, pp. 143 and 160.
[62] s. 79 (3).   Signature includes initialling.   And note subs. (3) (*c*) (ii) which eases the
burden of proof on the transferee.
[63] s. 79 (2).   Thus creating another statutory example of tortious liability for negligent
statements: *cf.* the prospectus provisions (especially s. 43) discussed in Chap. 15,
supra.   But presumably the negligent officer escapes liability to the transferee, though
he might be bound to indemnify the company.
[64] This seems outrageous, but appears to be the inevitable result of subs. (3) (*b*) (i).
Indeed, it is arguable that the onus of proving this is placed on the transferee!
The Jenkins Committee thought that it should be made clear that the company is
bound by an act of an officer having apparent authority: Cmnd. 1749, para. 482.
[65] Subss. (3) (*b*) (ii) and (3) (*c*).

It will be observed that the section applies only to certification by the company. No difficulty ever seems to have arisen from certification by an official of a stock exchange and, although the rules of the exchanges disclaim liability arising out of certification,[66] it is unlikely that any reputable exchange would in fact take advantage of such a provision in the event of either fraud or negligence of its officials.

The effect of unregistered transfers, as between transferor and transferee [67]

A question that has caused the courts great difficulty is that of deciding what precisely is the legal effect of a transfer executed by the transferor and delivered to the transferee but not yet registered by the company. In considering this question it is essential to keep in mind the dual nature of the transaction; on the one hand it is a straightforward assignment of personal property, on the other it is the release of one person from membership and the admission of another in his place. As between the transferor and the transferee it is the first aspect that is important, while as between the parties and the company it is the second. But while adherence to this distinction may solve problems arising between one set of contracting parties and the company, it does not necessarily do so when other parties are involved, each claiming priority.

So far as the transferor is concerned the transaction is complete as between him and the transferee when he hands over the duly executed transfer and certificate. On a sale and purchase therefore it is clear that the beneficial ownership passes then at the latest; indeed, if the contract of sale is specifically enforceable the purchaser has already become the beneficial owner.[68] But the buyer does not become a member or shareholder until the transfer is registered. Moreover, it is the policy of our company law that the company shall not be concerned with the beneficial ownership but shall only be bound or entitled to recognise the person whose name is on the register. Accordingly, so far as registered companies are concerned, section 117 of the 1948 Act[69] provides that no notice of any trust, expressed, implied or constructive, shall be entered on the register or be receivable by the registrar. And this is invariably supplemented by an article[70] providing that no right shall be recognised by the company except an absolute right to the entirety of the share in the registered holder.

Hence the company will continue to recognise the transferor and to disregard the transferee until the transfer is registered and, if the directors have power to refuse to register, this may never happen. In

---

[66] See rule 129 (2) of London Stock Exchange.
[67] On the subject of this and the following section, see the learned discussion in Wegenast, *Canadian Companies*, Chap. XXIII.
[68] See p. 395, n. 25, *supra*.
[69] Similar provisions apply to statutory companies by virtue of C.C.A. 1845, s. 20.
[70] *Cf.* Table A, art. 7.

the meantime it is clear that, in the case of a sale and purchase, the seller holds as trustee for the purchaser and must account to him for any benefit but is entitled to be indemnified against any obligations and, if unpaid, to exercise voting rights as he thinks will best protect his position.[71] But what is the position if there is no sale or other valid contract and the transfer is merely by way of gift? Until recently it appeared on the authority of the leading case of *Milroy* v. *Lord*[72] that the gift had to be regarded as incomplete and therefore ineffectual since there was " no equity in this court to perfect an imperfect gift." [73]

But two more recent cases (both, by a coincidence, named *Re Rose*[74]) make it clear that the rule in *Milroy* v. *Lord* does not mean that a transfer can never be regarded as a perfect gift until it is registered. It suffices if the transferor has done all that is required of him. This normally involves handing over an executed transfer and the share certificate, but may involve further action, for example, to comply with the Exchange Control regulations.[75] Whether delivery of a transfer without the certificate would suffice is questionable. Presumably, if the articles provided that a transfer would not be registered without it, it would not suffice except in the case of a statutory company governed by the Companies Clauses Act 1845, section 12 of which provides that the absence of the certificate shall not prevent the shareholder from disposing of his shares.

The effect of unregistered transfers—priorities

On the other hand an unregistered transfer is incomplete and unrecognised as between the parties and the company; and this has an important effect so far as third parties are concerned, for the transferee is liable to be defeated if someone else registers a transfer first. Hence various expressions, such as " incomplete " and " inchoate," have been used to describe the title of the transferee prior to its completion by registration, but most commonly he is said, on the analogy of land law, to have the equitable interest, leaving the legal interest outstanding in the transferor.

The analogy to land law is close. Because the company is precluded from receiving notice of the trust, the question of priorities is dealt with much on the same lines as those applying to equitable interests in land

---

71 *Musselwhite* v. *Musselwhite & Son Ltd.* [1962] Ch. 964.
72 (1862) 4 De G.F. & J. 264.
73 *Per* Turner L.J. at p. 274. *Cf.* the intriguing case of *Nanney* v. *Morgan* (1887) 37 Ch.D. 346, C.A., where the trustees who were the registered holders executed an irregular transfer to a beneficiary, A, who purported to settle the shares by assigning them to trustees. It was held that the settlement was effective because A had only an equitable interest which he had effectively assigned. Had the transfer from the original trustees been effective the settlement would have failed because A would then have had the legal interest and failed to transfer it.
74 [1949] Ch. 78; [1952] Ch. 499, C.A.
75 As in *Re Fry* [1946] Ch. 312.

prior to the extension to them of the rule in *Dearle* v. *Hall*.[76] Briefly, the principles governing the priority of rival claimants to shares may be expressed in two rules:

(i) *Where the equities are equal the first to register a valid transfer acquires priority.* This corresponds to the rule of land law that where the equities are equal the law prevails, registration being equivalent to getting in the legal estate.

(ii) *Where the equities are equal and neither is registered the first in time prevails.*

Priority of legal interest

Rule (i) may be illustrated as follows. Shareholder A executes a transfer to B on January 1 and another to C on January 10, C having no notice of the transfer to B. C lodges his transfer and secures registration. C is entitled to the shares free from any rights of B who is relegated to a claim against A.[77] Clearly the risk of B's being defeated in this way is far less if he obtains the share certificate, so much so that Lord Watson in *Colonial Bank* v. *Cady*[78] said that such a transferee had " a title, legal and equitable, which will enable the holder to vest himself with the shares without risk of his right being defeated by any other person deriving title from the registered owner." This, however, seems to go too far, for another transferee may be the innocent recipient of a forged certificate and become registered on the strength of it,[79] or may be put off by some plausible excuse for the absence of the certificate and may succeed in securing registration without it.[80] In such circumstances it appears that he obtains priority, and that people who rely on the original genuine certificate cannot even hold the company estopped thereby.[81]

But this applies only if the equities are equal. Hence a transferee, notwithstanding that he obtains registration, will take subject to the

---

[76] By L.P.A. 1925, s. 137. There are also, of course, resemblances to the modern law of land registration, but, except for the fact that in both cases registration of the transfer is an essential step towards completing the title, the analogies here are less close because the land register can show interests other than those of the owner.

[77] *Shropshire Union Ry.* v. *R.* (1875) L.R. 7 H.L. 496, especially *per* Cairns L.C.; *Guy* v. *Waterlow Bros. & Layton Ltd.* (1909) 25 T.L.R. 515; and see the Canadian case of *Smith* v. *Walkerville Malleable Iron Co.* (1896) 23 A.R. 95 (Ont. C.A.).

[78] (1890) 15 App.Cas. 267, H.L., at p. 278. This case actually concerned a transfer of the American type indorsed on the back of the certificate, a system which, as Lord Watson pointed out, " has the merit of inseparably connecting the certificate with the transfer."

[79] As in *Guy* v. *Waterlow Bros. & Layton Ltd., supra.* Note that the later transferee acquires a good title because he derives it by transfer from the genuine legal owner. As pointed out in the previous chapter, his reliance on the forged certificate gives him no rights against the company unless the latter has warranted its genuineness.

[80] As in *Smith* v. *Walkerville Malleable Iron Co., supra*; although, under an article such as Table A, art. 25, the directors may decline to register a transfer unless the certificate is produced, it is clear that they are not bound to do so and that the validity of the registration is not affected because of the absence of the certificate: *Shropshire Union Ry.* v. *R., supra.*

[81] *Supra*, Chap. 17, pp. 382, 383.

claim of any prior transferee or other holder of an equitable interest of which he has notice.[82] In some of the cases [83] it has been held that the mere fact that someone other than the registered owner hands the transferee a transfer executed in blank by the registered owner is sufficient to give him notice that the equitable title may be elsewhere, but this seems to be incorrect.[84] On the other hand the absence of the share certificate would certainly be sufficient to put the transferee on inquiry, though it is submitted that he would not be affected with notice if his inquiries were met with a plausible explanation. In principle it would seem that notice can be relevant only if the transferee is affected with it at the date of the transfer and that later notice acquired prior to registration is irrelevant.[85] It is, of course, clear that a transferee who secures registration will obtain priority over prior equities only if he is a purchaser for value, for, as in land law, the legal interest only prevails over prior equities in favour of a bona fide purchaser.

A remark of Lord Selborne's in an early case [86] suggests that actual registration may not always be essential in order to obtain the protection of the legal interest, but that " a present absolute unconditional right to have the transfer registered " may suffice. This suggestion is repeated in the later cases, but in none has anything short of complete registration actually been accepted. It has been held [87] insufficient that a transfer has been lodged with the company, the directors of which have no power to refuse to register transfers, and it is highly doubtful whether " anything short of registration would do except under very special circumstances." [88]

Is there, then, no way in which the unregistered transferee or other holder of an equity can protect himself from the possibility of a later transfer being registered and thus defeating his rights? As we have seen, it is no use giving notice to the company, for the notice will merely be returned with a polite letter referring to section 117 and the company's articles.[89] If, however, he is prepared to go to a certain amount of trouble and expense he can secure protection by taking steps under R.S.C., Ord. 50, rr. 11–15, which provide a procedure for obtaining a stop order taking the place of the old writ of distringas. This enables

---

[82] *France* v. *Clark* (1884) 26 Ch.D. 257, C.A.; *Earl of Sheffield* v. *London Joint Stock Bank* (1888) 13 App.Cas. 333, H.L.; *Fox* v. *Martin* (1895) 64 L.J.Ch. 473; *Rainford* v. *James Keith & Blackman Ltd.* [1905] 2 Ch. 147, C.A. But, of course, these equitable claims will not concern the company: *supra*, p. 401.

[83] *France* v. *Clark, supra*; *Fox* v. *Martin, supra*.

[84] See the cases discussed below, pp. 405, 406.

[85] So held in *Dodds* v. *Hills* (1865) 2 Hem. & M. 424. But see *Coleman* v. *London County and Westminster Bank* [1916] 2 Ch. 353. In the latter case, however, the original transaction was merely a pledge of the debentures and it was only when the pledgee found out about the prior equity that he took a transfer and had it registered: *cf. Shropshire Union Ry.* v. *R.* (1875) L.R. 7 H.L. 496 at p. 505.

[86] *Société Génerale de Paris* v. *Walker* (1885) 11 App.Cas. 20, H.L., at p. 28.

[87] *Ireland* v. *Hart* [1902] 1 Ch. 522.

[88] *Ibid., per* Joyce J. at p. 529.

[89] *Supra*, p. 401. But although legally ineffective it may not be altogether useless in practice: see, for example, *Peat* v. *Clayton, infra*, p. 407.

any person having an interest in shares to file an affidavit of his interest and to serve an office copy and notice on the company requiring it not to register a transfer or to pay a dividend on the shares without giving the server notice.[90] If the server is then notified by the company of an application to transfer he has eight days in which to obtain a court order restraining the transfer.

In practice very little use is made of this procedure, but it is valuable if the holder of an equity has reason to suppose that his position is being jeopardised. Obviously it will not be adopted when the holder has an executed transfer, since it will be far simpler to lodge the transfer for registration, but it may be used to protect an equitable mortgagee or beneficiary under a trust, or the like.

In applying rule (i) it must always be borne in mind that registration alone is not conclusive, but only prima facie, evidence of title, and that the register may be rectified. In other words, there must have been a valid transfer of the legal interest before the person who has secured registration has an unimpeachable title, for shares, unless represented by share warrants, are not negotiable instruments and if the transferor has no title he cannot pass one to the transferee. Registration may relieve the transferee from claims available against the transferor and which might have prevailed against the shares in the hands of the transferee prior to registration, but it cannot cure a flaw in the legal title itself. If therefore a thief steals the share certificate and forges the owner's signature on a share transfer, it is clear that the transferee acquires no title at all.[91] And the position would normally be the same if an executed transfer was stolen.

Difficulties in this connection have arisen where the registered owner has been induced by fraud to hand over blank transfers for a particular purpose and they have then been completed and used for another purpose, or where he has handed them over to an agent giving him only a limited authority to complete them and the agent has then exceeded his authority. If a bona fide transferee is to obtain a good title in these circumstances it can only be on the basis that the original owner is estopped from denying the validity of the transfer, and on this point the decisions are difficult to reconcile. Some have applied the so-called rule in *Lickbarrow* v. *Mason*,[92] that wherever one of two innocent persons must suffer from the acts of a third, he who has enabled the third party to cause the loss must bear it. On this basis, the owner by handing over all the indicia of ownership in the form of a blank

---

[90] If the company should fail to do so the server will apparently retain his priority for " the effect of the distringas is notice " (*per* Stuart V.-C. in *Wilkins* v. *Sibley* (1863) 4 Giff. 442 at p. 446)—and notice which the company is not entitled to ignore notwithstanding any provision in its articles.

[91] *Barton* v. *L. & N.W. Ry.* (1889) 24 Q.B.D. 77, C.A.; and see *Powell* v. *London & Provincial Bank* [1893] 2 Ch. 555, C.A., where a blank transfer required to be by deed was held to be ineffective to pass the legal interest.

[92] (1787) 2 T.R. 63 at p. 70.

transfer and share certificate is the one to suffer.[93] In other cases, however, a distinction has been drawn according to whether the blanks have or have not been completed prior to the transfers being handed to the registered transferee. If they are handed over to him still in blank this has been said to affect him with notice of the possibility of equities.[94] But this view appears to ignore the practice regarding the use of blank transfers and to be contrary to the views of the House of Lords in *Colonial Bank* v. *Cady*.[95] Moreover, it was expressly dissented from by the Court of Appeal in *Fry* v. *Smellie*.[96]

It is therefore submitted that if an owner signs and delivers a transfer, whether or not in blank, he will be estopped from denying its validity in favour of a bona fide purchaser who has changed his position on the strength of it. Moreover, if that purchaser secures registration he will then take free from any equities. Hence, as already pointed out, a transfer once registered has much the same effect as a negotiable instrument so far as freedom from equities is concerned.[97] But this result is only reached by a combination of two principles; first, that any interest in the shares other than that of absolute ownership is treated as equitable only, so that it cannot bind a bona fide purchaser of the legal interest, and secondly, estoppel. The former principle makes registration essential to protection, for absolute ownership cannot be obtained without it; hence although blank transfers may pass from hand to hand, like bearer bonds, they are not capable of ousting equitable interests until registered. The second, the estoppel, principle, carries still further the quasi-negotiability of a registered transfer by preventing, in some circumstances, the original registered owner from setting up his legal title. But he can be estopped in this way only as a result of his own conduct—the delivery of an executed transfer. If a transfer is stolen from him, not even a bona fide purchaser who gets on the register can prevail against him, and to this extent the full quality of negotiability is never attained.

[93] *Rimmer* v. *Webster* [1902] 2 Ch. 163 and *Fry* v. *Smellie* [1912] 3 K.B. 282, C.A. (both particularly strong cases as the original owners were postponed to the claims of *later* equities), *Easton* v. *London Joint Stock Bank* (1886) 34 Ch.D. 95, C.A. (reversed *sub nom. Earl of Sheffield* v. *London Joint Stock Bank* (1888) 13 App.Cas. 333, H.L., but only on the ground that there were *other* facts putting the transferee on inquiry).

[94] *France* v. *Clark, supra*; *Fox* v. *Martin, supra* (but in this case the transfer had not in fact been registered so that the dispute was really between two equities).

[95] *Supra.*

[96] *Supra.* The C.A. in this case attempted to distinguish *France* v. *Clark* on the basis of the relationship between the transferor and the original holder of the blank transfer. In *Fry* v. *Smellie* it was an agency relationship; in *France* v. *Clark* that of mortgagor and mortgagee. Yet another view is that estoppel can have no operation since no duty of care is owed as transfers are not negotiable instruments: *per* Greene M.R. in *Wilson & Meeson* v. *Pickering* [1946] K.B. at 427. But it seems clear that estoppel by negligence can be applied to other documents: *cf. Mercantile Credit Co.* v. *Hamblin* [1965] 2 Q.B. 242, C.A.

[97] We are here dealing with " equities " of third parties. For the position where the equity consists of a claim by the company, see *infra*, p. 408 *et seq.*

Priority of time

Rule (ii), that where the equities are equal the first in time prevails, needs little elaboration. It simply means that until a transfer is registered the transferee takes subject to any flaws affecting the shares in the hands of the transferor. If, therefore, the transferor had already made an unregistered transfer to another or held the shares on trust, the transferee will take subject to the rights of the prior transferee or beneficiaries.[98] A good illustration is the queer case of *Peat* v. *Clayton*,[99] in which A, the registered owner, executed a transfer in favour of B but did not hand over the certificates, stating that they were abroad. B gave notice to the company but did not attempt to secure registration. This notice was, of course, of no legal effect. A then transferred to C, handing over the certificates, and C's transfer was lodged with the company and registered. At this stage, therefore, C had an unimpeachable title under Rule (i). But the company then remembered B's notice and took C's name off the register and refused to give her a certificate. C, not wishing to buy a law suit, applied to her brokers for restitution and they bought other shares in the company for her. The brokers then claimed a lien on the original shares to reimburse them for their expenditure. It was held that, although C might have had a legal title which would prevail over B, the brokers had at the most only an equitable lien, and as this had arisen after B's equity it did not prevail against B.[1]

If an earlier equity is to be postponed to a later it can only be as a result of some conduct of the holder of the earlier equity making it inequitable that he should retain priority. Although the principle can be expressed by the same formula as that employed when a later legal interest is postponed to an earlier equity (*i.e.*, that the equities must be equal), the conduct which can make it inequitable to allow a prior holder to retain his priority is necessarily of a different and very much more serious nature. *Ex hypothesi* there is no question of notice, for there can be no notice of something which has not yet taken place; and in practice the conduct must be such as to estop the prior holder from setting up his title. The normal, and in practice probably the only, illustration is where the holder of the prior interest has clothed another with all the indicia of absolute beneficial ownership, and here it will normally be the legal owner, and not merely the holder

[98] *Shropshire Union Ry.* v. *R.* (1875) L.R. 7 H.L. 496, H.L.; *Société Génerale de Paris* v. *Walker* (1885) 11 App.Cas. 20, H.L.; *Roots* v. *Williamson* (1888) 38 Ch.D. 485; *Colonial Bank* v. *Cady* (1890) 15 App.Cas. 267, H.L.; *Moore* v. *North Western Bank* [1891] 2 Ch. 599; *Ireland* v. *Hart* [1902] 1 Ch. 522; *Peat* v. *Clayton* [1906] 1 Ch. 659; *Hawks* v. *McArthur* [1951] 1 All E.R. 22.

[99] [1906] 1 Ch. 659.

[1] See also *Hawks* v. *McArthur* [1951] 1 All E.R. 22, in which purported transfers, which could never have been registered by the company since the parties had failed completely to give effect to the rights of pre-emption conferred on members by the articles, were nevertheless effective to pass an equitable title which prevailed over a later charging order of an execution creditor of the transferor.

of an equity, that will be postponed.[2] The mere failure by a transferee to obtain the share certificate will clearly not result in his being postponed to a later equity.[3]

The company's lien

Rather different considerations apply, however, where the company itself has a claim on the shares. If the shares are represented by share warrants a transferee necessarily takes free of any claim by the company against the transferor, for a share warrant is a negotiable instrument. But in other cases, if a share is treated as a contractual chose in action, the transferee should take subject to all claims by the company against the transferor which arose under the contract prior to the transfer. This rule is generally expressed by saying that an assignee of a chose in action takes subject to " equities," but the word " equities " is a misnomer; the legal assignee takes subject to them because they are not mere equitable interests but legal limitations on the extent of the contractual rights transferred. On general principles an assignee only takes subject to claims which have accrued prior to the date when the other party to the contract receives notice of the assignment; thereafter this other party cannot alter the state of account between himself and the assignor so as to affect the assignee.

When, however, the transfer is registered the effect is more extensive than the completion of a legal assignment. It operates also as a novation; the transferor is discharged from the contract[4] and a new contractual relationship is established between the company and the transferee. Future claims by the company against the transferor can no longer affect the transferee, and the latter will take free from any existing claims unless his liability to these is preserved in the new contract.

General principles produce two limitations on the extent of the company's rights even as regards an unregistered assignee. In the first place, the assignee would only take subject to such of the company's claims as arise under the contract[5] creating the shares, i.e., under the articles, and these claims could normally only be for unpaid calls on the shares. Secondly, even if the company could enforce other claims against the transferee, its only method of doing so would be by set-off—a right exercisable only to the extent of any dividends payable. Accordingly, in the absence of special provisions in the company's regulations, the company's rights are of minimal importance.

---

[2] As in *Rimmer* v. *Webster* [1902] 2 Ch. 163, and *Fry* v. *Smellie* [1912] 3 K.B. 282, C.A. See *supra*, p. 406.

[3] *Cf. Peat* v. *Clayton* [1906] 1 Ch. 659. As already pointed out, share certificates differ fundamentally from the title deeds of land.

[4] Not completely, for if the shares are partly paid he may still be placed on the " B " list of contributories: s. 212. And *cf. Re Consolidated Goldfields of N. Zealand* [1953] Ch. 689.

[5] This apparently would not even include a claim for damages for fraud inducing the entry into the contract: *Stoddart* v. *Union Trust* [1912] 1 K.B. 181, C.A.

Hence these regulations normally seek to improve the company's position in two ways. First, as we have already seen, they provide that the company is entitled to disregard notices, thus prima facie enabling the company to alter the state of account between itself and the registered proprietor without regard to any unregistered assignments. Secondly, they give the company a " first and paramount " lien on the shares, and provide for the enforcement of the lien by sale.[6] Sometimes this lien is limited to unpaid calls in which case it is of little practical importance since the regulations will generally contain more sweeping and effective provisions permitting forfeiture of the shares in the event of non-payment of calls.[7] More commonly, though restricted to partly paid shares, it covers all indebtedness from the shareholder to the company,[8] and in other cases it extends even to fully paid shares.[9]

This so-called lien, in so far as it is anything more than a right of set-off, can only be an equitable charge, for the legal ownership and possession of the shares remain in the shareholder. On the other hand it is a peculiar sort of charge because it arises under the terms on which the shares are held; the potentiality to a charge in favour of the company is initially one of the bundle of rights and obligations which make up the share. Treated as a mere equity the lien should not be effective against any prior equity.[10] Treated, however, as a right under the contract constituting the chose in action it should place the company in an impregnable position when coupled with the other provision in this contract excluding the company from liability to receive notice of equities.

An early case[11] appeared to favour the view that the lien was one of the rights arising under the contract from the moment the shares were issued.[12] But later decisions, including that of the House of Lords in *Bradford Banking Co.* v. *Briggs*,[13] seem to be based on the alternative theory that the lien is an equitable charge which does not arise until the holder of the shares incurs a debt to the company. These cases firmly

[6] As in Table A, arts. 11–14. A provision for forfeiture except for non-payment of calls is invalid as an unauthorised reduction of capital: *Hopkinson* v. *Mortimer, Harley & Co.* [1917] 1 Ch. 646.

[7] As in Table A, arts. 33–39. Lindley, *Company Law*, 6th ed., at p. 635, was of the opinion that the company had such a lien even in the absence of a provision in the articles, by analogy with partners' liens. This, however, seems to be true only in the sense that the unpaid liability is necessarily attached to the shares and that the company may be able to recover by set-off against dividends.

[8] As in Table A, art. 11.

[9] The stock exchanges will not grant a quotation in such cases: see *Requirements,* Sched. VII, Pt. A, A. 2.

[10] *Supra,* pp. 407, 408, *i.e.,* against any equity arising prior to the lien fructifying because of the creation of the debt thereby secured.

[11] *New London & Brazilian Bank* v. *Brocklebank* (1882) 21 Ch.D. 302, C.A.

[12] *Per* Lindley L.J. at p. 307. And see the comments of Farwell J. in *Borland's Trustee* v. *Steel Bros.* [1901] 1 Ch. at p. 289.

[13] (1886) 12 App.Cas. 29, H.L. And see *Rearden* v. *Provincial Bank of Ireland* [1896] 1 I.R. 532 (Ir. C.A.); *Mackereth* v. *Wigan Coal and Iron Co.* [1916] 2 Ch. 293; and *M'Arthur* v. *Gulf Line Ltd.,* 1909 S.C. 732 (Sc.).

establish that if an equitable interest in favour of a third party has arisen and the company has notice of it, the company cannot claim a lien in priority to the third party [14] in respect of ordinary trade debts subsequently incurred by the registered shareholder. For this purpose actual notice binds the company notwithstanding section 117 precluding the company from taking notice of any trust [15] or the common form article which exempts the company from recognising any equitable or partial interest in the shares.[16]

If, however, the company does not have actual notice of the third party's interest when the debt to it is incurred, it is thought that it will be able to claim priority for its lien.[17] Although the lien is later in time, the equities are not equal since the third party is deemed to have notice of the article conferring the right to a lien in respect of debts to the company.[18]

When the lien is for amounts due on the shares themselves as opposed to ordinary commercial debts due from the shareholder,[19] the position may well be different, for then the liability to pay for the shares arises when they are issued [20] even though payments may not be due until calls are made. Hence the lien is presumably to be regarded as prior in time and will prevail over any other equitable interests. This, however, is relatively unimportant since all the lien does is to add a further method of recovering calls to the normal remedy of forfeiture.[21] Indeed it can be strongly argued that the whole concept of the lien is due for abolition; as regards calls it is unnecessary, as regards other debts, undesirable.

Where the company has an existing lien it is obviously advisable that it should not permit the shares to be transferred. It is therefore common practice to give the directors power to decline to register a

---

[14] Or, presumably, anyone claiming under the third party, such as a purchaser of the beneficial interest in the shares when an equitable mortgagee exercises his power of sale.

[15] This, incidentally, prevents the company from establishing a lien for debts due from the beneficial owner of the shares under a trust: *Re Perkins* (1890) 24 Q.B.D. 613, C.A.

[16] See Table A, art. 7.

[17] If the contractual theory were adopted it could be argued that the lien could never be effective as regards ordinary trade debts since, as we have seen (*supra*, p. 263), the articles only constitute a contract as between the company and the member *qua* member and not *qua* trade debtor. The fact that that would invalidate a large part of Table A, art. 11, is an additional reason for rejecting the contractual theory.

[18] The position might be different if, as the Jenkins Committee recommended (Cmnd. 1749, para. 41), the doctrine of constructive notice of the articles were abolished.

[19] As in the Scottish case of *M'Arthur* v. *Gulf Line Ltd.*, *supra*, one may have intermediate cases where the lien is on all shares registered in the name of the member in respect of calls due on *any* shares registered in his name. It was there held that an alteration of the articles to confer such a lien could not bind a transferee of fully paid shares who had lodged his transfer, but not been registered, prior to the alteration.

[20] Query what the position would be if the liability on the shares was subsequently increased under an approved scheme of arrangement or by agreement with the registered shareholder.

[21] See Table A, arts. 33–39.

transfer in such circumstances.[22] What the effect is, if a transfer is in fact registered, is not entirely clear. In one case it was held that the lien must be thrown first on the shares retained by the transferor.[23] In another it was argued that a clean certificate granted by the company might estop the company from setting up a lien in favour of a subsequent bona fide purchaser.[24] But this was doubted by the court which pointed out that since the certificate will expressly state that the shares are held subject to the regulations of the company, it is difficult to see how the company can be estopped from setting up a lien to which it is entitled under the regulations. Estoppel, it is submitted, could only arise if there was a lien for unpaid calls and the certificate described the shares as fully paid.[25] In other circumstances, if the lien is treated primarily as an equitable charge, then it should not prevail against a bona fide purchaser of the legal interest without notice. Hence, once such a purchaser is registered he should take free from a lien irrespective of any estoppel by share certificate—which, in any event, could normally only operate in favour of a subsequent purchaser.[26]

It is sometimes stated that if a company registers a transfer of shares on which it has a lien, it automatically waives this lien. This, however, confuses the case where the company has an express lien (which, though it can be waived if the intention to do so is clear,[27] will certainly not be waived merely by registering transfers), and the case where it has only a right to refuse to register transfers from shareholders indebted to it. This latter right resembles a lien in that it affords the company a weapon which it can use to aid recovery of the debt, but, unlike a lien, it clearly will be lost if the transfer is registered.[28]

Mortgages of shares [29]

Shares, being items of property, can, of course, be disposed of by way of security for a loan as well as sold outright. It follows from what has already been said that the security can be a legal mortgage only if the mortgagee is entered on the register, and that this can only be done if there is an outright transfer to him. Hence a legal mortgage involves a registered transfer which, for the protection of the borrower, should be coupled with a written agreement setting out the terms and containing an undertaking by the lender to retransfer when the borrower redeems by repaying the principal, interest and costs.

---

[22] *Cf.* Table A, art. 24. C.C.A. 1845, s. 16, prohibits transfers by holders who are in arrear with calls, but contains no provision for a lien.
[23] *Gray* v. *Stone* (1893) 69 L.T. 282. Here the transfer had not in fact been registered.
[24] *Re W. Key & Son Ltd.* [1902] 1 Ch. 467.
[25] *Supra*, Chap. 17, pp. 381–385.
[26] *Supra*, Chap. 17, p. 383.
[27] *Bank of Africa* v. *Salisbury Gold Mining Co.* [1892] A.C. 281, P.C.
[28] *Cf. Re Cannock & Rugeley Colliery Co.* (1885) 28 Ch.D. 363, C.A. This would be so, even if the claim was enforceable by set-off, because of the novation: see p. 408, *supra*.
[29] For an excellent account, see Holden, *Securities for Bankers' Advances*, Part III.

In practice, however, a legal mortgage of shares is rarely resorted to, the lender generally resting content with some form of equitable charge. Such a charge can be created quite informally, for anything showing an intention to charge the shares to secure an indebtedness will suffice. But in practice the lender will wish to ensure that his security is as invulnerable as possible and that it is readily realisable in the event of the borrower's default. He will therefore demand the deposit with him of the share certificate, for this will make it difficult, but not, as we have seen,[30] impossible, for someone else to obtain priority over him. And if he wants to be thoroughly safe he should obtain a stop order and serve notice on the company[31]; an ordinary notice is ineffective, except as a protection against the future creation of a lien in favour of the company.[32]

Retention of the share certificate, though some protection against transfer to another, is not in itself sufficient to enable the mortgagee readily to realise his security. If all he has obtained from the borrower is the certificate he will have to go to the court and ask for an order for sale or foreclosure.[33] Unless this is done the shares cannot be registered in his name or that of a purchaser, for, in the absence of a court order, the company must and will insist on a transfer duly signed by the registered owner. This can be obviated by obtaining an irrevocable[34] power of attorney authorising the lender to sign transfers on behalf of the borrower, but a simpler and cheaper method, which in practice is resorted to, is to obtain blank transfers from the borrower. The lender is then entitled to sell after reasonable notice,[35] and has implied authority to complete the blank transfer.[36] This authority, being coupled with an interest, is, it is submitted, one which cannot effectively be revoked either by the borrower or by his death.[37] As we have seen,[38] it is not entirely clear whether the purchaser will obtain a good title if the mortgagee exceeds this authority or acts irregularly, but the better view is that he will.

A judgment creditor can obtain a charging order[39] on the debtor's shares by way of equitable execution. This charge merely vests in the creditor such title as the debtor had at the date of the order,[40] but the court, on independent application,[41] may order a sale.[42]

---

[30] *Supra*, p. 403.   [31] *Supra*, pp. 404, 405.

[32] *Supra*, pp. 401, 410.

[33] It will be appreciated that on a sale the mortgagee will have to account to the borrower for any surplus after he has been repaid; while on foreclosure he becomes the absolute owner. Hence circumspection is displayed before the latter is ordered.

[34] Under L.P.A. 1925, s. 126.   [35] *Stubbs* v. *Slater* [1910] 1 Ch. 632, C.A.

[36] *Re Tahiti Cotton Co.* (1874) L.R. 17 Eq. 273.

[37] *Cf. Carter* v. *White* (1883) 25 Ch.D. 666, C.A.

[38] *Supra*, pp. 405, 406.

[39] Under R.S.C., Ord. 50, r. 2.

[40] *Hawks* v. *McArthur* [1951] 1 All E.R. 22.

[41] *Kolchmann* v. *Meurice* [1903] 1 K.B. 534, C.A.

[42] But not foreclosure: *Daponte* v. *Schubert* [1939] Ch. 958. If notice of the order is given to the company it affects it in the same way as notice of a stop order.

Transmission of shares by operation of law

Someone may, of course, become entitled to shares by operation of law; for example, on bankruptcy or death the shares will vest in the trustee in bankruptcy or personal representative. This is expressly recognised by section 75 of the Companies Act 1948, which provides that the requirement of delivery of a document of transfer shall not prejudice the power of the company to register any person to whom the right to any shares has been transmitted by operation of law.

The transmission to the persons so entitled will take place immediately upon the bankruptcy or death but they cannot become members until their names are placed on the register and when so placed they become, *vis-à-vis* the company, personally liable to the same extent as any other shareholder, for the company is not bound to have regard to their representative capacity. This will obviously not suit trustees in bankruptcy or personal representatives if in fact there is any liability on the shares; for example, where the shares are only partly paid or where the company is an unlimited one.

Hence the law entitles them to realise the shares notwithstanding that they themselves have not been registered. The trustee in bankruptcy may either transfer the shares [43] or, if they are onerous, disclaim them.[44] But a provision in the articles that in the event of bankruptcy the shares shall be sold to a particular person and at a particular price is valid and not obnoxious to the bankruptcy laws, at any rate if the price is a fair one.[45] Similarly on death, the company is bound to accept English [46] probate or letters of administration as sufficient evidence of the personal representative's entitlement [47] and to recognise a transfer from him notwithstanding that he was not registered.[48] But of course the articles may empower the directors to refuse to register transfers even if made by the personal representatives, and there may be effective rights of pre-emption or compulsory purchase.[49] If the trustee or personal representative causes himself to be registered he is entitled to a clean certificate not mentioning his representative capacity or any lien to which the shares are subject,[50] but, as already mentioned, the better view

---

[43] Bankruptcy Act 1914, s. 48 (3).

[44] *Ibid.*, s. 54.

[45] *Borland's Trustee* v. *Steel Bros.* [1901] 1 Ch. 279.

[46] If it recognises the title of anyone without this production, *e.g.*, by accepting a foreign grant, it becomes personally liable for any death duties which may be payable: *New York Breweries Co.* v. *Att.-Gen.* [1899] A.C. 62, H.L. In the case of small estates, companies sometimes agree to dispense with the formality of a grant upon having confirmation from the Estate Duty Office that no duties are payable. But, although irrelevant for revenue purposes, if the deceased, domiciled in England, owned shares in a Scottish company the English grant will have to be resealed in Scotland and a Scottish grant will have to be resealed in England in the converse situation. It is likely that this pointless farce will soon be abolished.

[47] Companies Act 1948, s. 82; C.C.A. 1845, ss. 18, 19.

[48] Companies Act 1948, s. 76.

[49] As we have seen (*supra*, Chap. 9), the arbitrary price payable will not be a decisive test of value for death duty purposes.

[50] *Re W. Key & Son Ltd.* [1902] 1 Ch. 467.

is that this in no way prejudices any lien or right to refuse to register transfers which the company may have.[51]

Until the trustee or personal representative becomes registered or until a transfer from him is registered the legal position is somewhat strange. Although not registered the trustee or representative seems to be regarded as having the legal interest in the shares, for the company must, notwithstanding section 117 of the Act, recognise his title although it cannot make him personally liable as a member. The estate will, however, remain liable, that is to say calls can be proved for in the bankruptcy or recovered from the personal representatives to the extent of the assets, and equally will be entitled to dividends. In the case of bankruptcy, some of the theoretical difficulties can be avoided by regarding the bankrupt as continuing to be a member, and, except when the company is in liquidation,[52] he is entitled to attend meetings and to vote, though he must do so in accordance with the trustee's directions.[53] But when the original holder is dead, membership in respect of the share is perforce in abeyance. The courts have then sometimes construed the articles so that, in effect, the estate is personified, much as in Roman law, and treated as a member.[54] But how far this may go is obscure. The estate is apparently not regarded as a member for the purpose of deciding whether the minimum membership has been maintained,[55] nor is it clear to what extent voting rights can be exercised.[54]

Practical difficulties are generally minimised by express provision in the articles. Thus Table A, art. 32,[56] provides that the trustee or personal representative shall be entitled to the same dividends and other advantages as if he were registered, except that he shall not be entitled to exercise any rights in respect of meetings. It also empowers the directors to serve notice requiring him to elect either to be registered or to transfer the shares, and to withhold all dividends and other payments in respect of the shares until the notice is complied with. The object of the latter provision is, of course, to enable pressure to be exerted to restore the position to normal.

---

51 *Supra*, p. 411. In any event this is certainly so under articles similar to Table A, arts. 30 and 31.
52 When Companies Act 1948, s. 216, provides that the trustee shall represent the bankrupt for all purposes. This, however, does not entitle the trustee to present a winding-up petition: *Re Bolton Engineering Co. Ltd.* [1956] Ch. 577.
53 *Morgan* v. *Gray* [1953] Ch. 83.
54 *Baird's Case* (1870) 5 Ch.App. 725; *New Zealand Gold Extraction Co.* v. *Peacock* [1894] 1 Q.B. 622, C.A.; *James* v. *Buena Ventura Nitrate Syndicate* [1896] 1 Ch. 456, C.A.; *Allen* v. *Gold Reefs of West Africa* [1900] 1 Ch. 656, C.A.; *Howling's Trustee* v. *Smith* (1905) 7 F. 390 (Sc.); *Llewellyn* v. *Kasintoe Rubber Estates* [1914] 2 Ch. 670, C.A.
55 *Re Bowling & Welby's Contract* [1895] 1 Ch. 663, C.A. It has already been pointed out (*supra*, Chap. 10, p. 191) that this may cause grave embarrassment to a small company.
56 *Cf.* C.C.A. 1845, s. 18.

Conclusion

No attempt has here been made to deal exhaustively with the many problems which may arise in connection with shares. For example, virtually nothing at all has been said about " calls," upon which the considerable body of learning is now of little practical importance because of the extreme rarity of partly paid shares. It is believed that enough has been said in the last three chapters to indicate the main principles and to illustrate the true nature of this modern and immensely important form of property. One major problem remains for discussion, namely, that of the protection afforded to shareholders against acts or omissions of those controlling the company. This, clearly, is a matter of vital concern, for upon it depends the true value of the shares. Before discussing it, however, the other primary type of company security—the debenture—must be further examined.

CHAPTER 19

DEBENTURES AND DEBENTURE STOCK

THE general nature of debentures and debenture stock was discussed in Chapter 16 where it was pointed out that the former term covers any acknowledgment of a reasonably long-term borrowing by the company, and the latter the funded loan so raised or an aliquot part of it. As in the Companies Acts, the expression " debenture " will here be used, except where the context otherwise requires, to include debenture stock also and to refer to the obligation acknowledged by the debenture as well as the acknowledgment itself.

Basically, therefore, a debenture, unlike a share, is an entirely orthodox item of property; it is a normal chose in action, a debt, generally secured by a mortgage, and most of the rules relating to it depend on the normal law of personal property, mortgages, and civil procedure. With the details of these rules it would be inappropriate to deal here. The purpose of the present chapter is simply to investigate certain matters which are peculiar to company debentures and which have not already been touched on in Chapter 16.

Applicability of rules already discussed in connection with shares

We have already seen that the debenture may take many forms and that the statutory definition is wide enough to include a single fixed mortgage,[1] but that the typical debenture is one of a series either in bearer form or transferable on a register maintained by the company. In both these latter cases the resemblance to shares is close, particularly as regards transfers and transmission, and much of what has been said in the previous two chapters is equally applicable. Bearer debentures, like share-warrants, are recognised as negotiable instruments [2] and accordingly pass by manual delivery free from equities. They are more often met with than are share-warrants, but the restrictions contained in the Exchange Control Act 1947 (outlined in Chapter 17 [3]) are equally applicable, so that at present bearer debentures normally have to be deposited with an " authorised depositary." Registered debentures, too, are to a considerable extent equated with shares so far as concerns title and transfers. On the initial issue of debentures the register of debentures does not have the same importance as the register of members,

---

[1] *Knightsbridge Estates Trust* v. *Byrne* [1940] A.C. 613, H.L.
[2] *Bechuanaland Exploration Co.* v. *London Trading Bank* [1898] 2 Q.B. 658; *Edelstein* v. *Schuler & Co.* [1902] 2 K.B. 144.
[3] *Supra*, pp. 387, 388. But if expressed in the currency of a country outside the " scheduled territories " (the sterling area) they are exempt from stamp duty: F.A. 1967, s. 30.

since the only essential element in becoming a debentureholder is agreement, and entry on the register is not necessary. But as in the case of shares, this agreement is normally constituted by a prospectus followed by application, allotment, and letter of allotment,[4] superseded in due course by the issue of the debenture itself or a debenture stock certificate.[5] And in practice the debenture will contain provisions for a register of debentures similar to the register of members,[6] and similarly precluding the company from taking notice of " equities," and will be transferable by the same form of transfer as is used for shares.[7]

The result is that on transfer the same procedure is adopted as in the case of shares,[8] the same distinction is drawn between legal ownership of the debenture, obtained by registration, and the equitable ownership of an unregistered transferee, giving rise to the same rules regarding priorities as those explored in the previous chapter.[9] Only in three major respects do the rules differ from those there outlined. In the first place, there will not, in practice, be any question of construing limitations on transferability, debentures invariably being made freely transferable.[10] Secondly, certification of transfers [11] only arises in connection with debenture stock, never with a debenture which cannot be legally transferred except as a whole. Thirdly, the company is never given a lien on its debentures. But this last rule does not mean that questions similar to those discussed in connection with a company's lien [12] cannot occur. Since a debenture is a chose in action, and not, unless in bearer form, a negotiable instrument, it is, prima facie, only transferable subject to the state of account between the company and the transferor.[13] This rule is a much more serious danger in connection with debentures than with shares, for there are far greater opportunities for previous alterations of the state of account between the transferor and the company, and, also, greater opportunities of enforcing a set-off against the transferee; furthermore, registration of the transfer will not, as with shares, operate as a new contract between the company and the transferee so as to wipe

---

[4] See Chap. 17, p. 374 *et seq.* An agreement to subscribe for debentures may be specifically enforced: s. 92. This is an exception to the general principle regarding contracts for loans.

[5] s. 80 of the Act, requiring the issue of certificates within two months of allotment or transfer, applies equally to debentures.

[6] As the Act envisages: see ss. 86 and 87 laying down rules as to where the register shall be kept and who may inspect it. The Jenkins Committee recommended that there should be a statutory obligation to maintain a register: Cmnd. 1749, para. 295.

[7] s. 75 is equally applicable—a transfer may not be registered unless a proper instrument has been lodged: see Chap. 18, p. 395.

[8] See Chap. 18. The Stock Transfer Act 1963 applies to debentures as well as to shares.

[9] *Ibid.,* p. 402 *et seq.* The problem of the priority of rival claimants to the debenture must not be confused with that of the priority of the charge securing the debenture *vis-à-vis* other claimants to the company's property; the latter problem is discussed *infra,* p. 421 *et seq.*

[10] Even in the case of a private company.

[11] *Supra,* p. 399 *et seq.* s. 79 is equally applicable.

[12] *Supra,* p. 408 *et seq.*

[13] *Athenaeum Society* v. *Pooley* (1858) 3 De G. & J. 294.

out any former equities. But whereas in the case of shares, companies have tried to increase their rights by providing for an express lien, in the case of debentures they invariably waive the protection which the general law gives them.[14] This they do by inserting a provision, now common form, that the moneys expressed to be secured by the debenture will be paid, and are to be transferable, free from any equities and claims between the company and the original or any intermediate holder. This is effective to exclude any claim by the company [15] and to place transferees of debentures in the same position as transferees of shares when there is no lien and no right to refuse transfers.

Estoppel by certificate may also occur. It will not arise in connection with debentures in the strict sense, because they themselves constitute the (written) contracts so that estoppel is not needed.[16] But where debenture stock is issued the holder will merely obtain a certificate which is in every way analogous to a share certificate and may impose similar liabilities on the company through estoppel.[17]

However, debentures are to be contrasted with shares in that the company may re-purchase its debentures, thus in effect redeeming them. When it does so it may, in the absence of agreement to the contrary, re-issue them with the original priority.[18]

Advantages of debenture stock

It will have been apparent from the foregoing that the similarity to shares, as regards procedure on transfer and its legal implications, is closest when debenture stock is issued rather than debentures in the narrow sense. Moreover, the practical effect of the distinction between debentures and debenture stock is far greater than that between shares and stock. Little advantage is obtained by the theoretically greater divisibility of stock rather than shares. The conversion of £1 shares into stock is normally on the terms that it shall not be transferable in smaller denominations than £1, and, both before and after conversion, a holder of £100 nominal worth of shares or stock can transfer any multiple of £1 leaving himself and the transferee each with

---

14 This is presumably a reflection of the (real or assumed) greater bargaining power of debentureholders.

15 *Farmer* v. *Goy & Co.* [1900] 2 Ch. 149. But care must be taken in wording; if it merely provides that the money will be *paid* free from equities (and not also that the debentures will be *transferred* free from equities) it will only protect a *registered* transferee: *Christie* v. *Taunton, Delmard & Co.* [1893] 2 Ch. 175; *Re Rhodesia Goldfields Ltd.* [1910] 1 Ch. 239. Note also s. 90, *infra*, note 18.

16 They may, of course, incidentally produce estoppel by deed as regards statements contained in them.

17 Chap. 17, *supra*, p. 381 *et seq.*

18 Companies Act 1948, s. 90. Note subs. (3) which is designed to remove the technical difficulties, revealed in *Re Russian Petroleum & Liquid Fuel Co.* [1907] 2 Ch. 540, C.A., when the company secures its current account by depositing a debenture for a fixed sum. For the advantages of this to the lender, see *Re Regent's Canal Ironworks* (1876) 3 Ch.D. 43, C.A. and *Robinson* v. *Montgomery Brewery* [1896] 2 Ch. 841.

only one certificate. But if he has a debenture for £100 he can only make a legal transfer of the whole of it. If he wants it to be divisible he must insist on obtaining 100 debentures of £1 each—a cumbersome bundle of paper for him and the company to handle. If, however, the issue is of stock—and an initial issue can be made, it does not have to be by way of conversion [19]—the holder merely obtains a certificate for £100 stock, analogous to a share certificate, and can transfer units of £1 or whatever minimum denomination the terms fix. Hence debenture stock is much more convenient and issues of it are much more common; indeed they are almost invariable in the case of public offers.

Debenture stock has a further advantage. If there is a series of debentures, each debenture will prima facie rank for priority according to its date of issue, thus defeating the whole intention, which is that all of the series should rank together. To avoid this it is necessary expressly to provide in each debenture that it is one of a series each of which is to rank *pari passu* in point of charge. If, however, a single fund of debenture stock is raised and interests in it issued to various subscribers the same result is achieved without express provision. In other respects too the document issued to the subscriber—the certificate—is a much simpler and shorter document than a debenture, since the stock will be created by one deed, to the terms of which the certificate will refer, which need not be sent to each holder.[20]

Trustees for debentureholders

The deed required on the creation of debenture stock may be a deed poll executed by the company alone, but it is now invariable practice [21] for the deed to be made with trustees. This, too, is normally done when there is an issue of a series of debentures. In other words, trustees, normally a trust corporation,[22] are interposed between the company and the debentureholders. Any charge can then be in favour of the trustees who hold it on trust for the debentureholders. Such an arrangement has many advantages.

In the first place it will enable the security to be by way of specific legal mortgage or charge on the company's land as well as by way of equitable floating charge on the rest of the assets. Clearly the ideal security is one so constituted, but a legal interest cannot be vested in

---

[19] As we have seen (*supra*, p. 380) this is necessary in the case of shares.

[20] If the deed creates a charge, a copy must be kept available for his inspection at the registered office: s. 103.

[21] Except with unsecured loan stock.

[22] Formerly it was common for banks to undertake this work but they have tended to fight shy of it since *Re Dorman Long & Co.* [1934] Ch. 635 drew attention to the conflict of interest and duty which might arise when the bank was both a creditor in its own right and trustee. Today, therefore, the duties are generally undertaken by other trust corporations, such as insurance companies, though sometimes by the separate trustee companies formed by certain banks. Very occasionally individual trustees are still employed.

thousands of debentureholders,[23] nor can the deeds be split up amongst them. If, however, there are trustees, the legal mortgage can be vested in them, on trust for the beneficiary debentureholders, and they can retain custody of the title deeds. Again, if there is to be a specific charge on shares in subsidiary companies (which may be a necessary precaution) trustees are needed in order that someone independent of the holding company shall be able to exercise the voting rights attached to the shares.

Secondly, it will provide a single corporation or a small body of persons charged with the duty of watching the debentureholders' interests and of intervening if they are in jeopardy. This is obviously far more satisfactory than leaving it to a widely dispersed class each of whom may lack the skill, interest and financial resources required if he is to take action on his own.[24] It will also be possible, by the trust deed, to impose on the company additional obligations, regarding the submission of information and the like, which would not otherwise be practicable. Similarly, the trustees can be empowered to convene meetings of the holders [25] in order to acquaint them with the position and to obtain their instructions. Unhappily complaints have been made in the past that the trustees are all too often content to act as passive recipients of their remuneration rather than as active watch-dogs. The Cohen Committee admitted that these complaints were not altogether unfounded,[26] but all that finally resulted from their deliberations was section 88 of the Act, invalidating provisions in new trust deeds absolving trustees from liability for breach of trust.[27]

Floating charges—English companies

It has already been pointed out in Chapter 16 that a debenture is normally secured either by a fixed or floating charge or, ideally, by both. Fixed charges are normal legal or equitable mortgages, and nothing more need be said about them here. Floating charges, however, being in practice restricted to companies,[28] and possessing certain peculiarities, deserve further mention. They are an invention of English equity and, so far as English law is concerned, their incidents remain

---

23 Since 1925 a legal estate in land cannot be vested in more than four persons.
24 Though there are trustees an individual stockholder can take steps to enforce the security (*infra*, p. 434) but he is not regarded as a creditor with the latter's remedies against the company personally: *Re Dunderland Iron Ore Co.* [1909] 1 Ch. 446.
25 The Jenkins Committee recommended that the statutory provisions relating to company meetings (Companies Act 1948, ss. 132 and 135–138) should be extended to meetings of debentureholders: Cmnd. 1749, para. 297. The Stock Exchange *Requirements* lay down certain conditions in the case of quoted debentures: Sched. VII, Part B.
26 Cmd. 6659, paras. 61–64.
27 The Stock Exchange *Requirements* lay down that unless otherwise agreed with the Council there must be a trustee or trustees one of whom must be a trust corporation having no interest in or relation to the company which might conflict with the position of trustee: Sched. VII, Part B. In U.S.A. under the federal Trust Indenture Act 1939, considerably more stringent obligations are imposed on debenture trustees: see Loss, *Securities Regulation* (2nd ed., 1961), Chap. 4.
28 For reasons stated in Chap. 4, p. 79, *supra*.

the subject of uncodified judge-made law. Their general nature has already been explained [29]; they are equitable charges on some or all of the present and future property of the company, subject to the company's power to deal with it in the ordinary course of business. Such a charge is, therefore, a particularly valuable means whereby a business concern can raise money without removing any of its property from the business. The charge remains floating and the property liquid until some default is made and the debentureholder takes steps to enforce his security, or until winding up commences. When that occurs the charge " crystallises " and is converted into a normal fixed charge on the assets of the company at the time of crystallisation or which come into existence thereafter.[30] Default alone will not suffice to crystallise the charge, the debenture-holders must intervene to determine the licence to the company to deal with the property, normally by appointing a receiver or by applying to the court to do so.[31] But if the company is wound up, no intervention by the debentureholders is necessary; the charge automatically crystallises because the licence is subject to the implied condition that the company carries on business.[32]

No particular form of words is necessary in order to create a floating charge; it suffices that the intention is shown, (a) to impose a charge on property present and future, and (b) to allow the company to continue to deal with that property in the ordinary course of business.[33] But the expression " ordinary course of business " is construed widely: it may even cover a sale of the whole undertaking to another company in exchange for securities in the new company, provided that such a sale is authorised by the objects clause of the company's memorandum.[34] In any event, the company will be allowed to continue to buy and sell in the usual way, to pay its unsecured creditors, and even to grant mortgages on the same property unless it is otherwise provided.

Priority of charges

It follows that peculiar rules apply to the determination of the priority of floating charges. As a floating charge is necessarily equitable, it will clearly be postponed to a later legal mortgage if that mortgagee had no notice of it. But this is of little importance for, as we shall see,

---

[29] Chap. 4, pp. 78–80.
[30] *Robbie & Co.* v. *Witney Warehouse Co.* [1963] 1 W.L.R. 1324, C.A.
[31] *Nelson & Co.* v. *Faber & Co.* [1903] 2 K.B. 367; *Evans* v. *Rival Granite Quarries* [1910] 2 K.B. 979, C.A.
[32] *Wallace* v. *Universal Automatic Machines* [1894] 2 Ch. 547, C.A. Even if the winding up is for purposes of reconstruction: *Re Crompton & Co.* [1914] 1 Ch. 954.
[33] *Illingworth* v. *Houldsworth* [1904] A.C. 355, H.L. In practice it is usual to state specifically that the charge is " by way of floating charge " but it suffices if it is expressed to be on the " undertaking " or the like: *Re Panama Royal Mail Co.* (1870) L.R. 5 Ch.App. 318; *Re Florence Land Co.* (1879) 10 Ch.D. 530, C.A.; *Re Colonial Trusts Corpn.* (1880) 15 Ch.D. 465.
[34] *Re Borax Co.* [1901] 1 Ch. 326, C.A. But this case probably turns on the finding of fact that the sale was in the ordinary course of business and that the company had not ceased to carry on business. *Cf. Hubbuck* v. *Helms* (1887) 56 L.J.Ch. 536.

the floating charge will be invalid unless registered at the Companies' Registry and registration constitutes notice.[35] What makes the floating charge so vulnerable is not so much that it is equitable, as the fact that the debentureholders have impliedly authorised the company to continue to deal with its assets notwithstanding the charge. Because of this authority the floating charge will be postponed to a later fixed charge whether legal or equitable, even if the later chargee has notice of it.[36] Some limit was placed on the ambit of this rule when Sargant J. held [37] that the company could not create another *floating* charge on the same assets ranking in priority to or *pari passu* with the original floating charge. This decision was subsequently approved by the Court of Appeal,[38] but limited to cases where the assets comprised in both charges are the same, and it appears that a general floating charge on the whole undertaking may be postponed to a subsequent floating charge on a particular class of assets.[39]

The debenture itself may, however, restrict the company's power to raise further charges in priority to or *pari passu* with it. Such restrictions, which are quite common but strictly construed,[40] limit the company's actual authority to deal with its assets and accordingly remove the basis on which floating charges are postponed to later equities. Nevertheless, it has been held that they may still be postponed to later mortgages, notwithstanding the limitation of the company's actual authority. If the later mortgage is legal, the mortgagee will obtain priority by virtue of his legal interest unless he has notice not only of the floating charge but of the restriction in it.[41] If it is equitable, he may be preferred on the ground that the company has been allowed to represent that it is free to deal with the assets unincumbered. For example, if the title deeds are left with the company, an equitable mortgagee by deposit will take priority unless he has notice of the restriction in the debenture.[42] Mere registration of the floating charge at the Companies' Registry is not sufficient to give notice of any restric-

---

35 *Wilson* v. *Kelland* [1910] 2 Ch. 306. This appears to be confirmed as a result of the joint effect of Land Charges Act 1925, s. 10 (5), and Law of Property Act 1925, s. 198.
36 *Re Hamilton's Windsor Ironworks* (1879) 12 Ch.D. 707; *Government Stock Co.* v. *Manila Ry.* [1897] A.C. 81, H.L.
37 *Re Benjamin Cope & Co.* [1914] 1 Ch. 800.
38 *Re Automatic Bottle Makers* [1926] Ch. 412, C.A.
39 *Re Automatic Bottle Makers, supra,* implies that this depends on the wording of the charge and of the express provision, if any, relating to the creation of further charges.
40 *Brunton* v. *Electrical Engineering Corpn.* [1892] 1 Ch. 434; *Robson* v. *Smith* [1895] 2 Ch. 118.
41 *English & Scottish Mercantile Investment Co.* v. *Brunton* [1892] 2 Q.B. 700, C.A.
42 *Re Castell & Brown Ltd.* [1898] 1 Ch. 315; *Re Valletort Sanitary Steam Laundry* [1903] 2 Ch. 654. *Quaere* whether this would apply to an equitable charge other than by deposit of title deeds. *Quaere* also whether it would apply to property other than land, *e.g.,* what would have been the position in *Re Automatic Bottle Makers, supra,* if the debentures had forbidden subsequent equitable charges?

tion on the creation of other charges,[43] and it is, therefore, very important that the debentureholders (or their trustees) should ensure that the registered particulars include a note of the restriction. It is submitted that, if this is done, notice is given to all the world, so that neither a legal nor an equitable mortgagee can take priority,[44] but it is a wise precaution to deprive the company of the title deeds of its properties—this is another advantage of having trustees who can take charge of the deeds. A mortgage to secure an advance of the purchase price of after-acquired property will apparently have priority to the floating charge even if the mortgagee has actual notice of the restriction, since the realities of the situation are that the company merely acquired the equity of redemption subject to the mortgage.[45]

Once the charge crystallises it will, of course, give the debentureholders a right to the property charged, free from the claims of the unsecured creditors. But if any such creditor has levied and actually completed execution [46] the debentureholders cannot compel him to restore the money, nor, until the charge has crystallised, can he be restrained from levying execution.[47] Similarly, if the debts due to the company are subject to a floating charge which has crystallised, the debts can only be enforced subject to any rights of set-off which have accrued prior to crystallisation, for a floating charge is not regarded for this purpose as an immediate assignment of the chose in action.[48] And the debentureholders only take over the company's property subject to the rights of anyone claiming by title paramount, so that a landlord can re-enter and can distrain on chattels in the leasehold premises if rent is unpaid, notwithstanding that the chattels are comprised in a charge which has crystallised.[49] But if a receiver has been appointed by the court, the court's leave must be obtained, for it is then in possession through its officer.[50]

Statutory limitations on floating charges

It will therefore be apparent that a floating charge is from its very nature a somewhat vulnerable security. Furthermore, the legislature has seen fit to intervene still further to curtail the protection afforded by the

---

43 *Wilson* v. *Kelland* [1910] 2 Ch. 306. *Cf. Re Mechanisations (Eaglescliffe) Ltd.* [1966] Ch. 20 and *Re Eric Holmes (Property) Ltd.* [1965] Ch. 1052. L.C.A. 1925, s. 10 (5), and L.P.A. 1925, s. 198, do not appear to affect this.
44 This is expressly dealt with in the Companies (Floating Charges) (Scotland) Act 1961: see p. 426, *infra.*
45 *Re Connolly Bros. Ltd. (No. 2)* [1912] 2 Ch. 25, C.A., which still seems to be good law on this question of competing equities notwithstanding *Church of England Building Society* v. *Piskor* [1954] Ch. 553, C.A., and *Capital Finance Co.* v. *Stokes* [1969] 1 Ch. 261, C.A.; see p. 432, *infra.*
46 Seizure alone does not suffice: *Norton* v. *Yates* [1906] 1 K.B. 112.
47 *Evans* v. *Rival Granite Quarries* [1910] 2 K.B. 979, C.A.
48 *Biggerstaff* v. *Rowatt's Wharf* [1896] 2 Ch. 93, C.A.
49 *Re Roundwood Colliery Co.* [1897] 1 Ch. 373, C.A.
50 Leave will normally be granted unless the company is in liquidation, in which case s. 228 applies: *Re Oak Pits Colliery Co.* (1882) 21 Ch.D. 322, C.A.

charge. As already pointed out, debentureholders with a floating charge closely resemble shareholders and form a class of those interested in the company rather than of those who merely have claims against it. Consequently it has been thought unjust that they should obtain priority over employees who have been working for the company and therefore to some extent for the debentureholders. Hence it is provided [51] that on winding up, or if a receiver is appointed, or if the debentureholder takes possession, the debts which have priority over the claims of ordinary creditors [52] shall similarly have priority over any floating charge. Claims in respect of employees, which are thus given preference, include four months' wages, accrued holiday remuneration and National Insurance contributions [53] and anyone who has advanced money to the company to pay wages is subrogated to the rights of the employees so paid.[54] The Act has also ensured that the Revenue is protected by giving preference to twelve months' rates and taxes. It has been held that if a debentureholder, or his receiver, once collects funds out of which preferred debts could have been paid he will be personally liable for breach of his statutory duty if he does not pay them.[55]

It has also been thought unjust to allow an unsecured creditor to obtain priority to the other creditors by obtaining a floating charge when he realises that liquidation is imminent. The temptation and the opportunities to attempt thus to salvage something out of the wreck are particularly great in the case of the directors themselves. So long as assets remain available they will have caused the company to borrow on mortgage, but when the company's credit is exhausted they may have attempted to keep the company afloat by themselves making unsecured loans to it. Finding that their efforts are doomed to failure, what more natural than that they should cause the company to execute a floating charge in their favour so that if anything is left, after the claims of the mortgagees are satisfied, they take it rather than the business creditors.[56] To prevent this, section 322 provides that a floating charge created within twelve months [57] of the commencement of the winding up shall be invalid (except to a limited extent), unless it is proved that the company was solvent [58] immediately after the creation of the charge.

---

51 ss. 94 and 319 (5) (b).
52 Listed in s. 319 and extended by later Acts: see *infra*, p. 658, n. 8.
53 But the preference does not extend to payments due to members of a gang employed under a " labour only " sub-contract—an increasingly common practice in the building and construction industries: *Re C. W. & A. L. Hughes Ltd.* [1966] 1 W.L.R. 1369.
54 s. 319 (4): see *Re Primrose* [1950] Ch. 561; *Re Rutherford (James R.) & Sons Ltd.* [1964] 1 W.L.R. 1211; *Re Rampgill Mill Ltd.* [1967] Ch. 1138.
55 *Westminster City Council* v. *Haste* [1950] Ch. 442.
56 In some cases the company has been deliberately floated with the intention of defrauding creditors by granting floating charges to the promoters and then winding up: see Cohen Report (Cmd. 6659), para. 148.
57 The period was three months in the 1908 Act and six months in the 1929 Act; each was found inadequate in view of the ingenuity displayed in staving off liquidation.
58 *i.e.,* able to pay its debts as they fall due: *Re Patrick & Lyon* [1933] Ch. 786. The onus of proof of solvency is on the chargee.

Otherwise the charge is valid only to the extent of cash paid to the company at the time of or subsequently to the charge [59] and in consideration of it, together with interest at a rate prescribed by the Treasury.[60] Hence those who take a floating charge from a company which cannot be proved to be solvent, and which does not survive for a further year, cannot thereby obtain protection in respect of their existing debts, but only to the extent to which they then advance money which swells the assets of the company, and thus becomes available for creditors generally.[61] The directors, in the example given above, cannot retrospectively convert themselves into secured creditors in respect of moneys which they have previously advanced without demanding security. Nor will it avail them to advance further money on a floating charge on the understanding that this is to be used to repay their existing loans.[62]

It must be emphasised that these two statutory limitations only apply to *floating* charges. To the extent of any fixed charge which they may confer, debentures are not subject to the claims of preferential creditors. Nor is a fixed charge invalid, even though granted by an insolvent company immediately before liquidation—although it may, of course, be attacked on the ground of fraud or as a fraudulent preference. Neither is there any limitation on the rate of interest that may be secured by a fixed charge. But those statutory limitations may affect companies other than those registered under the Act if, but only if, they are being wound up under it.[63]

Floating charges—Scottish companies

Until recently floating charges were unknown to Scottish law. But, following a report by the Law Reform Committee for Scotland,[64] the Companies (Floating Charges) (Scotland) Act 1961 empowered any incorporated company to create such charges. The result is that Scottish law now has a more clearly defined body of legal rules relating to such charges than has English law. The Act describes the nature of such

---

[59] For interesting illustrations of how the rule in *Clayton's Case* ((1816) 1 Mer. 572) may protect a bank when the charge secures a current account, see *Re Thomas Mortimer Ltd.* (1925), now reported in [1965] Ch. 186n.; *Re Yeovil Glove Co.* [1965] Ch. 148, C.A.

[60] At present still only 5 per cent.: S.I. 1865/52.

[61] If some creditors only are paid it may be that the payment could be recovered by the liquidator as a fraudulent preference, but only if liquidation followed within six months of the payments: s. 320.

[62] *Re Destone Fabrics Ltd.* [1941] Ch. 319, C.A., but contrast *Re Matthew Ellis Ltd.* [1933] Ch. 458, C.A. The test seems to be whether there is a genuine cash payment or a mere subterfuge. In the latter event the payment will normally be a fraudulent preference but may not be subject to attack on that ground because the six-month period has elapsed.

[63] *i.e.*, a floating chargee who appoints a receiver of a statutory or chartered company will not be subject to the claims of preferential creditors unless the company goes into compulsory liquidation under Part IX of the Act.

[64] Cmnd. 1017. The working of the 1961 Act has recently been reviewed by a Working Party of the Scottish Law Commission whose report recommends new legislation replacing and amending it: Scottish Law Commission Memorandum No. 10 (1969).

a charge,[65] and prescribes the method whereby it can be created.[66] Most important of all, the rules relating to priority are laid down. A fixed security always has priority over a floating charge unless (a) the floating charge was registered before the fixed security was created and (b) the document creating the floating charge prohibited the creation of any fixed security having priority over, or ranking *pari passu* with, the floating charge.[67] Under the rules relating to registration of charges introduced by the same Act,[68] if there is any such prohibition it has to be registered.[69] When the same property is subject to two floating charges they rank according to date of registration, unless each contains a provision that they are to rank *pari passu*.[70] Accordingly many of the doubts which arise under English law [71] are resolved.

In most respects the Scottish position is the same as the English [72] except that, under the present Act, a floating charge crystallises only on a winding up.[73] This is because receivers also were unknown to Scottish law and it was hoped to be able to introduce floating charges without the additional complication of introducing receiverships. To make this workable an additional ground for compulsory liquidation in Scotland was introduced, namely, if the security of a floating chargee was in jeopardy.[74] However the attempt to dispense with receiverships has not proved wholly satisfactory and the Scottish Law Commission is reconsidering the matter as part of a review of the whole Act.[74a]

Charges on foreign property

The recognition by Scottish law of floating charges has removed the difficulties and conflicts which were liable to arise if a Scottish company purported to grant a floating charge over its English assets.[75] It should be pointed out, however, that similar difficulties and conflicts are liable to arise in the case of other (foreign) companies or if a British company has assets in a foreign country where floating charges are not recognised. True the charge can be enforced in England against the company

---

[65] Companies (Floating Charges) (Scotland) Act 1961, s. 1. Difficulties have arisen because this section only authorises the creation of a floating charge to secure a debt due from the company and not, for example, indebtedness of its holding or subsidiary company.

[66] *Ibid.*, s. 2 and First Schedule.

[67] *Ibid.*, s. 5.

[68] *Ibid.*, s. 6, and Second Schedule which incorporates a new Part IIIA into the Companies Act 1948.

[69] Companies Act 1948, ss. 106A (7) (*e*) and 106D (1) (*b*) (v) (these sections are in the new Part IIIA introduced by the 1961 Act).

[70] Companies (Floating Charges) (Scotland) Act 1961, s. 5 (3).

[71] See pp. 421–423, *supra*.

[72] *e.g.*, floating charges in Scotland are subject to the statutory limitations referred to above.

[73] Companies (Floating Charges) (Scotland) Act 1961, s. 1 (2).

[74] *Ibid.*, s. 4. Subs. (2) of this section defines " jeopardy ": see p. 435, *infra*.

[74a] See Scottish Law Commission Memorandum No. 10: *supra*, note 64.

[75] See *Carse* v. *Coppen*, 1951 S.C. 233, and the discussion in the 2nd ed. of this book at p. 394. But see p. 433, *infra*.

in personam if the company is subject to the jurisdiction of the English courts,[76] but what the debentureholder wants is an effective right *in rem* against the foreign assets and not merely a right of action against the company. Hence it is essential to ensure that local formalities are complied with. This is so whether the charge be fixed or floating, but in the latter case compliance may be impossible if such a charge is unknown to the local law.

Registration of charges

Charges requiring registration

As we have seen, most companies obtain a substantial part of the finance that they need by borrowing it on debentures. If these confer a charge, as they normally do, on the company's assets it is vital that those dealing with the company should be able to find out that its assets are subject to charges. Hence the Companies Act 1948 contains provisions whereby particulars of charges have to be registered on the company's file at the Companies' Registry.[77] The relevant provisions differ slightly according to whether the company is an English or a Scottish one; the following account is primarily directed to the English position but attention is drawn to the major differences in Scotland.

In both countries it is not all mortgages and charges which have to be registered under the Act but only those prescribed.[78] Although this includes most types likely to be met with, and in particular, all floating charges and, in the case of English companies, any " charge for the purpose of securing any issue of debentures," [79] the question whether the charge is one requiring registration has been a fruitful source of litigation.[80] It has been held that it is only charges to secure money that are registrable so that a charge which, if granted by an individual, would require registration under the Bills of Sale Act 1882 will not necessarily be registrable if granted by a company.[81] The Jenkins Committee

---

[76] *British South Africa Co.* v. *De Beers Consolidated Mines* [1910] 2 Ch. 502, C.A.; [1912] A.C. 52, H.L.; *Re Anchor Line Ltd.* [1937] Ch. 483.

[77] For English companies, under Part III; for Scottish companies, under Part IIIA, introduced by the Companies (Floating Charges) (Scotland) Act 1961. In the references which follow sections followed by a capital letter relate to Scotland.

[78] ss. 95 (2) and 106A (2).

[79] s. 95 (2) (*a*). There is no equivalent in s. 106A (2). Presumably " issue of debentures " means " issue of a series of debentures."

[80] A charging order on land to enforce a judgment against the company is not registrable: *Re Overseas Aviation Engineering (G.B.) Ltd.* [1963] Ch. 24, C.A. But charges on hire-purchase agreements with the company are, since these are " book debts " which are specifically mentioned in ss. 95 (2) (*e*) and 106A (2) (*c*): *Independent Automatic Sales* v. *Knowles & Foster* [1962] 1 W.L.R. 974. But a charge on a policy granted by the Export Credit Guarantee Dept. is not registrable; the policy is not a " book debt " as the policy moneys would not be entered in well-kept books until liability thereunder was established: *Paul & Frank Ltd.* v. *Discount Bank (Overseas) Ltd.* [1967] Ch. 348.

[81] *Stoneleigh Finance Ltd.* v. *Phillips* [1965] 2 Q.B. 537, C.A. So held despite the fact that the registration provisions were intended to take the place of registration under the Bills of Sale Act from which incorporated companies were exempt and despite the express reference in s. 95 (2) (*c*) to " a charge . . . which, if executed

rejected a suggestion that all charges should require registration since this would be highly inconvenient if applied to documents of title to goods and negotiable instruments,[82] but they did recommend the inclusion of charges on shares held in a subsidiary company—a serious omission in the present provision.[83]

Registration is required even though the property charged is foreign,[84] and is also required if the company acquires property already subject to a charge of a class requiring registr 'ion.[85]

Method of registration

It is the duty of the company to send the prescribed particulars to the Registrar for registration.[86] The obvious intention is that it shall discharge this duty so that the particulars reach the Registrar within twenty-one days of the creation of the charge or the acquisition of the charged property, or, if the charge was created outside the United Kingdom and comprises property outside the United Kingdom, within twenty-one days of the date within which it or a copy could have been received in due course of post if despatched with due diligence.[87] This is expressly so provided in the case of charges on property acquired by the company.[88] But in the case of charges created by the company all the Act says is that the charge is invalidated if the particulars are not received within that time,[89] and strictly the company does not appear to break its duty if it fails to lodge particulars in time.[90] In the latter case any other person affected (for example the mortgagee) may lodge the particulars instead of the company.[91]

The particulars normally required include the date of creation of the charge or of the acquisition of the property subject to the charge, the amount secured, a short description of the property, and the person entitled to the charge,[92] and, under the Scottish Act, in the case of floating charges a statement of any restriction on the right to create further charges ranking in priority to, or *pari passu* with, the floating

by an individual, would require registration as a bill of sale." Presumably this applies *a fortiori* to Scotland since s. 106A (2) has nothing equivalent to s. 95 (2) (c), Scotland not being plagued with bills of sale legislation.
[82] An alternative solution would be to prescribe those charges which do not have to be registered rather than those that do: see Ghana Companies Code 1963 (Act 179), s. 107 (3).
[83] Cmnd. 1749, para. 301.
[84] This is implied by ss. 95 (3) and (5) and 106A (3) and (4) and a charge on land " wherever situate " is expressly registrable: ss. 95 (2) (d) and 106A (2) (a).
[85] ss. 97 and 106C.
[86] ss. 96, 97, 106B and 106C.
[87] Presumably this applies even though the charge also comprises property in the U.K.
[88] ss. 97 and 106C.
[89] ss. 95 (1) and 106A (1): see below, p. 430.
[90] See Jenkins Report, Cmnd. 1749, para. 306 (i). Hence the company can apparently escape any liability for the fine imposed by ss. 96 (3) and 106B (3).
[91] ss. 96 (1) and 106B (1).
[92] ss. 98 (1) and 106D (1). Note the modification in the case of a charge to secure a series of debentures: ss. 95 (8) and 106A (7). And see also ss. 95 (9) and 106A (8).

charge.[93] Since the particulars have to be accompanied, in the case of English companies by the charge itself and, in the case of Scottish, by a certified copy,[94] it might be supposed that anyone dealing with the company could safely assume that the registered particulars gave him accurate and up-to-date information about the extent of registrable charges affecting the company's property. This, however, is not so, as certain recent cases have graphically revealed. This is because of the weaknesses in the registration requirements. First, the Registrar is required to grant a certificate of registration[95] which is " conclusive evidence that the requirements of this Part of this Act as to registration have been complied with." [96] Hence the charge is effective even though the registered particulars are inaccurate.[97] Secondly there are no provisions for registering changes in the registered particulars except where the whole or part of the secured debt has been paid or part of the property released,[98] and even in that case there is no legal obligation to apply for registration. Accordingly, if the charge is capable of covering further advances it will validly cover such advances whether or not they are mentioned in the registered particulars,[99] and there is no means of registering particulars of those further advances when made.[1] At the best, a searcher will know only that further advances may have been made which will be covered by the security, and will not know even that if the registered particulars omitted to mention them. Similarly if there is a charge to a bank to secure " all sums due or to become due " the searcher will not be able to tell from the register how much is actually secured.

On receipt of the documents from the applicant the Registrar's duty is to enter the prescribed particulars on the register (which is merely a

---

[93] ss. 106A (7) (e) and 106D (1) (b) (v).

[94] ss. 95 (1) and (8) and 106A (1) and (7). The Jenkins Committee recommended that this requirement should be repealed and that instead both chargor and chargee should be required to sign the particulars delivered for registration: Cmnd. 1749, para. 302.

[95] In the case of English companies a copy of this certificate has to be endorsed on every debenture: s. 99. The Jenkins Committee recommended that this burdensome requirement should be abolished: Cmnd. 1749, para. 303. In the case of Scottish companies there is the more sensible requirement that a copy of the certificate is to be sent to each debentureholder: s. 106E.

[96] ss. 98 (2) and 106D (2).

[97] *National Provincial and Union Bank* v. *Charnley* [1924] 1 K.B. 431, C.A. (where property charged incorrectly stated); *Re Mechanisations (Eaglescliffe) Ltd.* [1966] Ch. 20 (amount misstated); *Re Eric Holmes (Property) Ltd.* [1965] Ch. 1052 (date misstated).

[98] ss. 100 and 106F.

[99] *Re Mechanisations (Eaglescliffe) Ltd.*, supra. But the Court of Session in *Archibald Campbell, Hope & King Ltd.*, 1967 S.C. 21 appeared to assume the contrary.

[1] *Archibald Campbell, Hope & King Ltd.*, supra. If, however, further property is charged, even if it is to secure the same debt, there will be a new charge which, if of a registrable class, can and must be registered: *Cornbrook* v. *Law Debenture Corpn.* [1904] 1 Ch. 103, C.A. But *Cunard SS. Co.* v. *Hopwood* [1908] 2 Ch. 564 appears to establish that this does not apply if other property is substituted under provisions in a trust deed particulars of which have been registered under s. 95 (8) or 106A (7): *sed quaere.*

separate part of the file of each company).[2]   The Jenkins Report[3] reveals that the Registrar has been advised that the effect is to impose on him an absolute duty to register accurate particulars and the Committee suggested that if he fails to do so[4] he may be liable to anyone who suffers loss in consequence.[5]   The Committee thought, rightly, that this imposed an unreasonable burden which should be removed.[3]

The charge itself (or in Scotland the copy) is not retained in the Registry but is merely used to check, so far as possible, the accuracy of the particulars delivered and is then returned to the applicant. Hence searchers at the Companies' Registry cannot there inspect the charge itself.   However, the company has to keep at its registered office a copy of every charge requiring registration at the Registry[6] and must there maintain its own register of charges.[7]   These too are open to public inspection.[8]

Effect of non-registration

Failure to comply with the various registration requirements leads, as one would expect, to liability to fines.   But the most potent sanction is that non-registration at the Companies' Registry of charges created by the company (as opposed to existing charges on property acquired by the company) destroys the validity of the charge.[9]   Unless the prescribed particulars and documents are delivered to the Registrar within twenty-one days of the creation of the charge[10] it will, so far as any security on the company's assets is conferred thereby, " be void against the liquidator and any creditor of the company." [11]   The sufferer is, of course, the chargee, not the company; hence the provision authorising the chargee to deliver particulars instead of the company.[12] If, however, neither the company nor the chargee delivers particulars in time[13] the consequences are grave indeed for the chargee; in effect, he

---

[2] ss. 98 and 106D.
[3] Cmnd. 1749, para. 302.
[4] As in the cases cited in note 97, *supra.*
[5] In view of the inherent inadequacy of the registered particulars (see *supra*) it is not easy to see how anyone could establish that a loss flowed from reliance on it.
[6] ss. 103 and 106H.
[7] ss. 104 and 106I.   For some reason the English section (s. 104) is restricted to *limited* companies.
[8] ss. 105 and 106J.
[9] Non-registration in the company's own register has no such dire sanction.
[10] Or, in the case of charges created outside the U.K. comprising property outside the U.K., within 21 days of the date when it could have been received if despatched with due diligence: ss. 95 (3) and 106A (3).
[11] ss. 95 (1) and 106A (1).   For recent examples see *Re Molton Finance Ltd.* [1968] Ch. 325, C.A. and *Capital Finance Co. Ltd.* v. *Stokes* [1969] 1 Ch. 261, C.A., where ingenious, but deservedly vain, attempts were made to persuade the court that although formal charges had become void for non-registration the lenders were entitled to claim (non-registrable) common law liens until repaid.
[12] ss. 96 (1) and 106B (1).   He is entitled to recover the registration fees from the company: ss. 96 (2) and 106B (2).
[13] This happens surprisingly often; for example, because of failure to realise that the charge is of the registrable class, or because both the company and the lender assume

loses his security. To reduce the possible hardship the Act makes two concessions. First, if the security becomes void the money secured thereby becomes immediately payable.[14] Accordingly the lender is not bound to leave his, now unsecured, money on loan until it becomes repayable under the terms of the debentures but can enforce his personal remedies for what they are worth. The second is that the court has power to order that the time for registration be extended or that any error or omission be rectified.[15] So long as the company is not in liquidation [16] such orders are made fairly freely.[17] But the Act empowers the court to impose such conditions as seem just and convenient and it is the invariable practice in England to impose conditions saving the rights of parties acquired prior to the time when registration is in fact completed.[18] It is now established that this protects proprietary rights only and not the inchoate rights of unsecured creditors notwithstanding that they may have granted credit to the company in the belief that its assets were uncharged.[19] But once winding up has commenced it will be too late even to register out of time in pursuance of an order in the usual terms made before the winding up, since on winding up all creditors are regarded as having rights against the company's property.[20] Provided, however, that registration pursuant to an order of the court is effected prior to liquidation, the charge will be fully effective except as against creditors who have previously obtained a charge.

As an alternative to obtaining leave to register out of time the unregistered charge may be scrapped [21] and a new one executed, taking care to register that within the prescribed twenty-one days. The disadvantages of that course are expense, for the stamp duty paid on

that the other will register, or because a charge of registered land is sent first to the Land Registry, instead of the Companies' Registry, and not returned within the 21 days.

[14] ss. 95 (1) and 106A (1). Presumably this means that the money becomes repayable once the 21 days are up and not merely when a liquidation ensues or a secured creditor intervenes. Although, as pointed out below, the unregistered charge does not really become void until then, it would defeat the whole purpose of the provision if the mortgagee had no immediate right to payment.

[15] ss. 101 and 106G. In view of the conclusiveness of the certificate of registration it is difficult to see why one should need to rectify an error or omission: see note 97, *supra*.

[16] Orders are not then made (except perhaps in order to prevent fraud—see *Re Eric Holmes (Property) Ltd., supra*) and if made in the usual terms (see below) would be pointless since the claims of creditors would have become choate.

[17] They may be made notwithstanding that the validity of the charge is being disputed on other grounds: *Re Heathstar Properties Ltd. (No. 2)* [1966] 1 W.L.R. 993.

[18] This practice dates back to *Re Joplin Brewery Co.* [1902] 1 Ch. 79 and is based on that already adopted under the Bills of Sale Act.

[19] *Re Kris Cruisers Ltd.* [1949] Ch. 138. This is not as unfair as it may seem because no sensible person lends without security merely because the borrower has not at the moment granted a charge to anyone else; he may do so next day.

[20] *Re Anglo-Oriental Carpet Co.* [1903] 1 Ch. 914.

[21] If it has been left undated and a false date less than 21 days before is subsequently inserted it seems that the charge if registered will be fully effective: see *Re Eric Holmes (Property) Ltd.* [1965] Ch. 1052, *supra*. But this, of course, would be a grossly improper solution.

the original charge will be wasted, and the possible impact of section 322.[22] This section will invalidate the charge if the company goes into liquidation within a year, unless the company can be proved to be solvent at the date of the charge, since the existing debt will not be cash paid to the company at the time of or subsequently to the charge.

As already pointed out, non-registration does not make the security totally void but void only " against the liquidator and any creditor of the company." [23] Hence the company itself cannot dispute its validity.[24] Nor, it seems, is there any way in which, prior to liquidation, an unsecured creditor can do so or can prevent the mortgagee from realising his security. But once liquidation starts, the charge will be void against the liquidator (*i.e.*, all creditors) and even before liquidation it will be void against secured creditors. This is so even if a later mortgagee has actual notice of the (unregistered) charge.[25] Hence, failure to register may vitally affect the rules relating to priority of charges set out above and there based on the assumption that each of the charges in question was duly registered. If the first charge, whether legal or equitable and whether fixed or floating, becomes void through non-registration any later charge will take priority so long as it is duly registered. This is so even if the first chargee obtains leave in the usual terms to register out of time, for if the second charge is executed before the first is registered the holder's rights are protected by those terms.[26] Moreover, if the charge is a land charge of a type which would require registration under the Land Charges Act 1925 but for section 10 (5) of that Act,[27] it will be void if unregistered against any purchaser of that land.[28]

Where the company acquires property subject to an existing charge, failure to register this does not avoid the charge.[29] This, however, does not protect a charge immediately granted by the company on the acquisition of property to secure part of the purchase price.[30]

Effect of registration

Registration does not cure any formal material flaw in the charge itself which may still be attacked on grounds other than non-registration [31]; the certificate of registration is conclusive evidence only of the

---

22 *Supra*, p. 424.
23 This formula was borrowed from the Bills of Sale Act.
24 *Independent Automatic Sales* v. *Knowles & Foster* [1962] 1 W.L.R. 974.
25 *Re Monolithic Building Co.* [1915] 1 Ch. 643, C.A.
26 *Ibid.* If neither was registered in time, presumably the first to obtain leave and to register would obtain priority. This is clearly so in Scotland in the case of floating charges: Companies (Floating Charges) (Scotland) Act 1961, s. 5 (3).
27 See *infra*, p. 433.
28 L.C.A. 1925, s. 13.
29 Companies Act 1948, ss. 97 and 106C.
30 *Capital Finance Co.* v. *Stokes* [1969] 1 Ch. 261, C.A., following *Church of England Building Society* v. *Piskor* [1954] Ch. 553, C.A., and distinguishing *Re Connolly Bros. Ltd. (No. 2)* [1912] 2 Ch. 25, C.A., *supra*, p. 423.
31 *Cf. Re Heathstar Properties Ltd. (No. 2)*, *supra*.

fact that " the requirements of . . . this Act as to registration have been complied with." [32] But, as already pointed out, it seems that registration at the Companies' Registry is sufficient to give constructive notice of the registered particulars, though not of the contents of charges themselves notwithstanding that these are available for public inspection at the company's registered office. [33]

At present (though this is likely to be altered) registration at the Companies' Registry obviates any need to register the charge at the Land Charges Registry. [34] There is, however, no similar provision in the case of land registered under the Land Registration Act 1925, so that if the charge affects registered land it must first be registered at the Companies' Registry and further protected by the appropriate entry on the Land Register. [35]

Foreign companies

The English registration provisions of Part III of the Act extend to charges on property in England so far as concerns a company incorporated outside England but having an established place of business in England. [36] The corresponding Scottish provisions in Part IIIA are narrower, since they apply only to *floating* charges and then only if the property includes *heritable property* in Scotland and the company has an established place of business in Scotland. [37] Nevertheless the result is that an overseas company which is carrying on business both in England and Scotland may have to register charges in both countries. That perhaps is as it should be. What seems quite unnecessary is that an English or a Scottish company may have to register both in the English and Scottish Registries and that the charge may be avoided in one or other country if it does not. [38] Thus in the recent case of *Amalgamated Securities Ltd.* [39] a Scottish company, with a place of business in England also, granted a charge over its specific landed property in both England and Scotland. It duly registered particulars of the charge on the English property in England [40] and on the Scottish

---

[32] ss. 98 (2) and 106D (2).
[33] *Wilson* v. *Kelland* [1910] 2 Ch. 306.
[34] L.C.A. 1925, s. 10 (5). This is not wholly satisfactory since there are no facilities at the Companies Registry for official searches or priority notices. Hence the Law Commission has recently recommended that s. 10 (5) be repealed except as regards floating charges (Law Com. 18, paras. 67-72) and a provision to this effect is in the Law of Property Bill 1969, cl. 23.
[35] This applies even to a floating charge if there is a restriction on prior charges. An entry should then be placed on the Land Register and the charge should contain a covenant by the company to notify the chargee if any registered land is acquired so that he may register an appropriate entry against the title. But in Scotland a floating charge on heritable property need not be recorded in the Register of Sasines: (Companies (Floating Charges) (Scotland) Act 1961, s. 3.
[36] Companies Act 1948, s. 106.
[37] s. 106K.
[38] This was pointed out by the Jenkins Committee which recommended that this duplication of registration should be avoided: Cmnd. 1749, para. 306 (n).
[39] 1967 S.C. 56 (Sc.).
[40] Under s. 106.

property in Scotland,[41] but did not register in Scotland particulars of the charge on the English property. It was held that the charge on the English property required to be registered in Scotland also [42] and an extension of time was granted to enable this to be done. But for that it seems that the Scottish courts would have regarded the charge on the English property as void [43] and the English courts would have held it valid.

It is to be hoped that these flaws, and the many others in the registration requirements, will be corrected as a result of the review now being carried out by the Scottish Law Commission.[43a]

Enforcement of debentures—receiverships

The methods of enforcing a debenture depend upon the nature of the security which it confers and essentially are in no way peculiar to company law. But, in England,[44] almost invariably the first step is for debentureholders or their trustees to secure the appointment of a receiver.[45] This appointment may either be made out of court, under an express or implied [46] power in the debenture, or by the court. If nothing has occurred to render the security enforceable [47] but the debentureholder's position is nevertheless in jeopardy, an application to the court may be necessary, for the court has a discretionary power to appoint a receiver in such circumstances.[48] The normal procedure is then for one of the debentureholders, on behalf of himself and all other holders, to commence a debentureholders' action, the first step in which will be the appointment of a receiver. " Jeopardy " will be established when, for example, execution is about to be levied against the company,[49] or when it proposes to distribute to its members its one remaining asset.[50] It would be tempting to say that, when there is a floating charge,

---

[41] Under s. 106K.

[42] Under s. 106A (2) (*a*).

[43] *Cf. Archibald Campbell, Hope & King Ltd.*, 1967 S.C. 21, *supra*. But this is erroneous in the view of the English courts, assuming that the charge was effected in one document and that a certificate of registration of particulars of it had been issued: see *National Provincial and Union Bank* v. *Charnley* [1924] 1 K.B. 431, C.A., *supra*.

[43a] See p. 425, note 64, *supra*.

[44] As we have seen, receivers are, as yet, unknown to Scottish law.

[45] If the state of the company is so parlous that it is doubtful whether there will be enough to cover a receiver's remuneration it may be necessary for the trustees to take possession. If the " debenture " is just an ordinary mortgage of particular property the debentureholder may, of course, exercise his power of sale without the preliminary step of appointing a receiver.

[46] *i.e.*, under L.P.A. 1925, s. 101, when applicable.

[47] This will, of course, depend on the terms of the debenture which will specify various events (*e.g.*, if interest is in arrear for six months) on the occurrence of which the security becomes enforceable.

[48] But the court will not normally have any power to appoint a receiver unless the debentures are secured by a charge: *Harris* v. *Beauchamp Bros.* [1894] 1 Q.B. 801, C.A.; *Re Swallow Footwear Ltd., The Times,* October 23, 1956.

[49] *McMahon* v. *North Kent Co.* [1891] 2 Ch. 148; *Edwards* v. *Standard Rolling Stock* [1893] 1 Ch. 574; and see *Re Victoria Steamboats Co.* [1897] 1 Ch. 158.

[50] *Re Tilt Cove Copper Co.* [1913] 2 Ch. 588.

" jeopardy " should be assumed whenever the circumstances make it unreasonable, in the interests of the debentureholder, that the company should retain power to dispose of the property subject to the charge. This is in fact the statutory definition under Scottish law,[51] but the English decisions hardly go so far, for the fact that the assets on realisation would not repay the debentures in full has been held insufficient.[52]

In cases where appointment out of court is possible this is certainly preferable from the viewpoint of the debentureholders as a body. The procedure in a debentureholders' action is lamentably expensive and dilatory, since the receiver, as an officer of the court, will have to work under its closest supervision and constant applications will have to be made in chambers throughout the duration of the receivership, which may last years if a complicated realisation is involved. Since the 1948 Act, which allows a receiver, even though appointed out of court, to obtain the court's directions,[53] it is difficult to envisage circumstances in which an application to the court can be justified if the cheaper alternative is available, and the professional adviser who recommended it would be laying himself open to grave risk of criticism.

The function of a receiver is merely to get in the assets charged, to collect the rents and profits, to exercise the debentureholders' powers of realisation, and to pay the net proceeds to the holders in reduction of their charge. He has no power, as a receiver, to carry on the business of the company and, if the charge is a floating one over all the undertaking, this will obviously be necessary if the security is to be most beneficially realised by its sale as a going concern. For this purpose he will need to be appointed manager as well as receiver, and express power so to appoint is invariably included in the terms of the debenture. Alternatively, the court may appoint under its inherent power. In the discussion which follows, the expression " receiver " includes a receiver and manager.

It is now forbidden for a corporate body[54] or an undischarged bankrupt[55] to act as a receiver, and an attempted appointment is a nullity,[56] but if the company is in liquidation the official receiver may be appointed.[57]

Position of receivers

The appointment of receiver must not be confused with that of

---

[51] Companies (Floating Charges) (Scotland) Act 1961, s. 4 (2). Under that Act " jeopardy " is a ground for winding up by the court: *ibid.*, s. 4 (1).
[52] *Re New York Taxicab Co.* [1913] 1 Ch. 1.
[53] s. 369 (1).
[54] s. 366. There are obvious objections to allowing a small limited liability company to act as a receiver, but it seems unnecessary to forbid a bank or insurance company.
[55] s. 367.
[56] *Portman Building Society* v. *Gallwey* [1955] 1 W.L.R. 96 (an attempted appointment of a company).
[57] s. 368. For the functions of this official, see Chap. 27, *infra.*

liquidator.[58] The company need not go into winding up and, if it does, a different person will normally be appointed liquidator. But, if a receiver and manager is appointed over the whole of the undertaking, the board of directors will, for all practical purposes, become *functus officio* just as on liquidation,[59] and the company will probably be wound up if anyone thinks it worth while to take the necessary steps, that is, if there seems a prospect of something being left over for the unsecured creditors and the members. In that event, the liquidator's task, until the receivership is concluded,[60] is to act as a watchdog over the receivership, and, on its conclusion, to deal with any property that may be left.

A receiver appointed by the court is not an agent of anyone, but an independent officer of the court.[59] A receiver appointed out of court, on the other hand, might be expected to be an agent of the party appointing him, namely, the debentureholder or trustee,[61] but in practice, the debenture will invariably provide, expressly or impliedly,[62] that the receiver shall be deemed to be the agent of the company. Prior to the 1948 Act, this distinction had important consequences, for the former type of receiver would be personally liable on contracts into which he entered, whereas the latter would not, unless he pledged his personal credit. But this difference has now been removed,[63] and for most purposes the position of the two is identical, except that the former must act under the court's supervision, whereas the latter does not,[64] although he can obtain its direction if he wishes.[65] Primarily, his duties are owed to the debentureholders and not to the company, which cannot, for example, complain that on realisation of the assets he has

---

[58] The English receiver for a secured creditor must not be confused with his American namesake who is appointed on the application even of unsecured creditors and who corresponds to our liquidator in a compulsory winding up.

[59] *Moss S.S. Co.* v. *Whinney* [1912] A.C. 254, H.L.

[60] If the company is in liquidation this will not be until all the charged assets have been realised and the proceeds distributed to the debentureholders. But in other cases the debentureholders may discharge the receiver after he has brought their interest payments up to date and, if a manager, pulled the company round. There seems to be no authority on the question whether the crystallised charge then automatically becomes floating again; presumably it does (on the basis that the debentureholders have again restored the company's licence to deal with its assets) unless this is inconsistent with the terms of the debenture.

[61] This is so if no express or implied term to the contrary applies: *Gosling* v. *Gaskell* [1897] A.C. 575, H.L.

[62] *i.e.*, by virtue of L.P.A. 1925, s. 109 (2).

[63] By s. 369 (2).

[64] There is also the difference that interference with a receiver appointed by the court will be contempt of court. But with the leave of the court an action may be brought against him, *e.g.*, by the debentureholder at whose instance he was appointed: *Arthur (Insurance) Ltd.* v. *Sisson* [1966] 1 W.L.R. 1384.

[65] s. 369 (1). And his remunerations may be fixed by the court on application of the liquidator: s. 371. The Jenkins Committee recommended that the court should be empowered to give directions under s. 369 (1) on the application of the debentureholder also: Cmnd. 1749, para. 298.

not held out for the best possible price.[66] Nor can summary misfeasance proceedings [67] be taken against him as an officer of the company.[68]

The present position regarding the receiver's liability on contracts is that he is not bound by those entered into by the company even if he sees that they are performed, as he normally should if abandonment would affect the goodwill.[69] If, however, he enters into new contracts for the purpose of his receivership, he, as well as the company, will be personally liable thereon, unless the contract otherwise provides, but with a right of indemnity out of the assets.[70] The result is that whereas existing unsecured creditors have little chance of recovery once a receiver of the undertaking is appointed, they can enter into new contracts with the receiver with every confidence, for they will have the personal liability of a responsible professional man and, by a process of subrogation, can take advantage of his right of indemnity as a first claim on the assets.[71]

The appointment of a receiver, at any rate if he is appointed out of court, does not automatically terminate contracts of employment with the company,[72] but a sale by him of the business does.[73] If he gives employees notice and offers them re-employment which is accepted, they continue to be regarded as employed by the company whose agent he is.[74]

The receiver appointed out of court will become liable as a trespasser if there is a defect in his appointment [75] or if the charge is for any

---

[66] *Re B. Johnson & Co. Ltd.* [1955] Ch. 634, C.A.

[67] Under s. 333; see *infra*, p. 595.

[68] *Re B. Johnson & Co. Ltd.*, *supra*. This applies even if he is also appointed manager, despite the express reference to " manager " in the section: *ibid.* Contrast the position of the liquidator. But one way in which the company may be able to control him is by resolving that an inspector be appointed under s. 165 (*a*) (i): *R.* v. *Board of Trade (ex p. St. Martins Preserving Co. Ltd.)* [1965] 1 Q.B. 603.

[69] *Re Newdigate Colliery Co.* [1912] 1 Ch. 468, C.A. But the receiver may, if he adopts them, become personally liable by virtue of a novation, and he may perhaps be liable in tort if he induces their breach: *Re Botibol* [1947] 1 All E.R. 26.

[70] s. 369 (2). This is without prejudice to any other right of indemnity which he may have if appointed out of court; *e.g.*, he may expressly stipulate for an indemnity from the debentureholder, and, if the latter's agent, may be entitled to one as such. If a contract is entered into without the authority of the then receiver he will not become personally liable if it is subsequently ratified by a later receiver: *Lawson* v. *Hosemaster Co. Ltd.* [1966] 1 W.L.R. 1300, C.A.

[71] *Re London United Breweries Ltd.* [1907] 2 Ch. 511. But they cannot set-off what becomes due to them from the company against any debts they owe the company since the crystallised floating charge will have attached to those debts: *Robbie & Co. Ltd.* v. *Witney Warehouse Co.* [1963] 1 W.L.R. 1324, C.A.

[72] *Re Mack Trucks (Britain) Ltd.* [1967] 1 W.L.R. 780.

[73] *Re Foster Clark's Indenture* [1966] 1 W.L.R. 125.

[74] *Re Mack Trucks (Britain) Ltd.*, *supra*. This may be important for the purpose of determining the length of notice to which they will be entitled under the Contracts of Employment Act 1963 if they are later dismissed: *ibid.* In these respects the position of a receiver appointed by the court may be different. It may be, though this is obscure, that such an appointment automatically determines all contracts of employment and that a re-engagement will not be deemed to be continued employment with the company.

[75] Hence he should make sure that the necessary formalities are scrupulously observed and that the power to appoint him has become exercisable: *cf. Windsor Refrigerator Co. Ltd.* v. *Branch Nominees* [1961] Ch. 375, C.A.

reason invalid. The Jenkins Committee recommended that the court should be empowered in such circumstances to relieve him of liability and to impose liability on his appointor.[76]

Publicity required of receivers

On the appointment of a receiver notice must be given to the Registrar[77] and all business documents containing the name of the company must contain a statement of his appointment.[78] Further, in recognition of the fact that a receiver in respect of a floating charge over the whole, or substantially the whole, of the undertaking is virtually in the position of a liquidator,[79] accounts and statements similar to those called for on a liquidation are required.[80] In other cases,[81] the duties of disclosure are slightly less stringent, but the receiver has to file at the Registry bi-annual abstracts of his receipts and payments.[82] There are no similar requirements when the debenture-holder enters into possession instead of appointing a receiver. This omission requires correction, for though taking possession is a remedy which mortgagees avoid if possible, there have been cases where the trustees have been forced to do so since no one would act as receiver.[83] There is no obvious reason why this should not impose identical obligations of disclosure on them and the company.[84]

Statutory and chartered companies

The foregoing discussion has been directed primarily to registered companies, but what has been said is generally applicable to other companies except that the provisions of the Companies Act then have no application.[85] But debentures issued by statutory companies subject to the Companies Clauses Acts possess certain peculiarities which can only be referred to here.[86] Having regard to the inconvenience which might be caused if public utilities ran the risk of having their land taken away, the debentureholder cannot either foreclose or sell, so that the appointment of a receiver is normally the only way of enforcing

---

[76] Cmnd. 1749, para. 299.
[77] s. 102 (1). And when the receiver ceases to act he must give notice of this fact: s. 102 (2).
[78] s. 370.
[79] *Cf.* Cohen Report, Cmd. 6659, para. 66.
[80] ss. 372–373 and 375.
[81] *e.g.*, where there is a fixed charge.
[82] ss. 374–375.
[83] See p. 434, note 45, *supra.* This possibility is recognised in s. 94.
[84] The Jenkins Committee recommended that s. 102 should be extended to such a case: Cmnd. 1749, para. 306 (k).
[85] None of the sections cited is included among those which may be extended to unregistered companies. But, as already pointed out, the registration provisions of Parts III and IIIA of the Act apply to charges on property in Britain of foreign companies: ss. 106 and 106K.
[86] See Halsbury, *Laws of England*, 3rd ed., Vol. 6, p. 42 *et seq.*

the security,[87] although judgment in a personal action may be obtained and execution levied,[88] or the company wound up under the Companies Act as an unregistered company. Further, such a company may issue debenture stock, under the Companies Clauses Act 1863, which gives no right to repayment of principal but merely to payment of interest in the form of a perpetual annuity. The remedies of the stockholder are even more circumscribed, for he can only recover judgment in respect of arrears of interest and, if he appoints a receiver, the latter's task will merely be to recover these arrears, not the principal.

[87] *Furness* v. *Caterham Ry.* (1858) 25 Beav. 614. The Act provides for the appointment by J.P.s (C.C.A. 1845, s. 53), but this is without prejudice to the High Court's jurisdiction.

[88] *Bowen* v. *Brecon Ry.* (1867) L.R. 3 Eq. 541; *cf. Furness* v. *Caterham Ry.* (1859) 27 Beav. 358, where an authorised sale by the company enabled the debentureholder to recover against the proceeds.

PART FIVE

INVESTOR AND CREDITOR PROTECTION

INVESTOR AND CREDITOR PROTECTION

THE purpose of this final Part is to consider the protection afforded to investors in, and creditors of, a company. Many of the matters discussed appear in the Companies Act under the heading " Management and Administration," and the orthodox textbook arrangement is to consider them merely as aspects of the company's internal machinery. Such subjects as accounts, audits, meetings and resolutions could well be dealt with in this way, for even in the absence of mandatory legal rules business convenience would demand the voluntary adoption of very similar practices. But in the case of companies these practices have been converted into legal regulations because this has been thought necessary to protect those interested in the company and those having dealings with it. And, from the viewpoint of the lawyer, their primary importance lies in their effectiveness as a means of avoiding disputes and preventing injustices. Hence the discussion which follows is deliberately directed towards this aspect of them.

The danger of this approach is that it may give the erroneous impression that companies are constantly embroiled in internecine strife, and that investors and creditors are habitually maltreated by dishonest or incompetent company controllers. Nothing could be further from the truth; on the contrary, " the great majority of limited companies, both public and private, are honestly and conscientiously managed." [1] The succeeding chapters consider the extent to which the legal rules conduce to this desirable result, and provide adequate redress in the case of the small number of companies less scrupulously operated. If they suggest that the legal sanctions against the abuse of power by company controllers are not wholly adequate, it must be remembered that it is but rarely that power is abused. The British believe they have a genius for constitutional government with a minimum of constitutional laws, and for working majority rule without oppression of minorities. Our company law, with its relative freedom from stringent regulations, reflects this national belief. No system can wholly protect fools from their own folly or from the knavery of others, and the advantages of trying to do so as fully as possible have to be weighed against the disadvantages of imposing fetters on business conducted honestly and efficiently.[1]

The problems of protecting (a) investors, both shareholders and debentureholders, and (b) creditors, cannot be kept entirely distinct.

[1] Cohen Report (Cmd. 6659), para. 5.

And some of the protective devices have already been discussed. Thus, the safeguards provided when securities are first issued have already been dealt with in Part Three and need not be repeated; the present discussion is directed to the position of investors, once they have become holders of shares or debentures, in relation to future acts of the company. The *ultra vires* doctrine and the rules relating to maintenance of capital were discussed in Chapters 5 and 6, but with the conclusion that they were snares rather than true safeguards. We also saw in Chapter 8 how agency principles have been expanded so as to impose on companies an extended range of liability for the acts of their officials, and, in Chapter 10, how creditors can sometimes lift the veil of incorporation so as to strike directly at those in control of the company.

Of the additional safeguards now to be considered the primary one, both to investors and creditors, is the publicity which, to a greater or lesser extent, attends the functioning of the company, and this is the essential basis of all the other safeguards. Hence it forms the subject of the first chapter of this Part. The following six chapters (21–26) are primarily concerned with the protection of investors. The problem here is normally that of protecting the minority against the majority, but to express it thus is an over-simplification. In practice, even a majority interest may be oppressed, for it may be deprived of legal control by a device such as non-voting shares or weighted voting.[2] And even if control exists in law it may be virtually impossible to exercise it in fact because of the difficulty of ousting the existing management with *de facto* control exercised through a small but closely held block of shares.[3] The true nature of the problem, therefore, is to protect investors, be they a majority or a minority, against the acts of those who are *de jure* or *de facto* in control of the company.

Company meetings, dealt with in Chapters 21 and 22, constitute the forum in which the investors are supposed to exercise supervision over the management; they also provide the means whereby the controlling management may vary or abrogate the rights of the investors. However, the controlling management are subject to certain restraints on the exercise of their powers. Accordingly Chapter 23 considers what duties are owed by the directors who are installed by the controllers, and Chapter 24 what duties are owed by the controlling majority when voting directly at general meetings. These duties confer certain rights on investors—but rights are useless without effective remedies;

---

[2] Berle and Means, *The Modern Corporation and Private Property*, is still the best analysis of the various means whereby control may be secured and maintained.

[3] Nevertheless there have in recent years been a number of successful " take-over bids," some of which are referred to in the pages which follow, in which the existing controllers have been ousted. For a racy description of some of the titanic American battles, see Karr, *Fight for Control* (Ballantine Books, 1956) and on the law and practice, see Aranow & Einhorn, *Proxy Contests for Corporate Control* (2nd ed., 1968). Some British battles are described, less excitingly, in G. Bull & A. Vice, *Bid for Power* (Lond. 1958).

accordingly, the all-important question of remedies is discussed in Chapter 25. Finally, Chapter 26 discusses the extraordinary procedures whereby major reconstructions can be effected in the constitution of the company. Here, the position of creditors also is liable to be affected.

Creditors, too, are to some extent affected by the question of remedies discussed in Chapter 25. But their ultimate remedy—and, indeed, the ultimate remedy of investors—is winding up, of which there is a brief description in Chapter 27. And this Part concludes with a short discussion in Chapter 28 of the safeguards provided when foreign companies operate in England.

CHAPTER 20

PUBLICITY, ACCOUNTS AND AUDIT

ON the basis that " forewarned is forearmed " the fundamental principle underlying the Companies Acts has been that of disclosure. If the public and the members were enabled to find out all relevant information about the company, this, thought the founding fathers of our company law, would be a sure shield. The shield may not have proved quite so strong as they had expected, and in more recent times it has been supported by offensive weapons, such as a Board of Trade Inspection, or an application under section 210, and by additional armour in the shape of legal control over certain activities such as the issue of prospectuses. But, basically, disclosure still remains the principal safeguard on which the Companies Acts pin their faith, and every succeeding Act since 1862 has added to the extent of the publicity required, although, not unreasonably, it has varied it according to the type of company concerned.

This publicity is mainly secured in three ways:

(a) By provisions for registration at the Companies' Registry;

(b) By compulsory maintenance of various registers and the like by the company; and

(c) By compulsory disclosure of the financial position in the company's published accounts and by attempting to ensure their accuracy through a professional audit.

In these three ways, and in certain others of less importance which will be referred to briefly, members and the public (which, for practical purposes, means creditors and others who may subsequently have dealings with the company and become its members or creditors) are supposed to be able to obtain the information which they need to make an intelligent appraisal of their risks, and to decide intelligently when and how to exercise the rights and remedies which the law affords them.

Reference has already been made to many of the matters requiring registration whether at the Companies' Registry or by the company itself. Here we can merely collate the more important provisions under each of these heads. Speaking generally, it may be said that every registered company is required to give the public information relating to its constitution, its officials, its home, and its capital structure. It must also make available to its members particulars of its financial position and normally must make these particulars public also. Nor are these rules solely applicable to registered companies; as we shall see in the

446

last section of this chapter and in Chapter 28, they apply to most chartered and statutory companies and to foreign companies operating in Great Britain.

The matters here mentioned are additional to those which the directors of the company have to disclose to the members or creditors in notices or circulars when they invite them to resolve on particular measures. The extent of the disclosure required in those circumstances will be described in later chapters of this Part.

Matters requiring registration at the Companies' Registry

The company's constitution

On formation the company must file its memorandum and articles of association.[1] These documents can only be altered by special resolution or a court order, and copies of these must also be registered.[2] Hence it is possible to ascertain from an inspection of the company's file exactly what its constitution is.

The company's officers

Within fourteen days of their first appointment particulars of the directors and secretary must be filed with the Registrar and notices of changes must be given within fourteen days of their occurring.[3] Similarly if a receiver or manager is appointed by a debentureholder notice of his appointment must be registered,[4] as must the appointment of a liquidator.[5] The company's file will therefore reveal who are the senior officers of the company and this, coupled with an examination of the articles to ensure what their ostensible authority is, should give third parties the information they need under this head.[6]

The company's home

By the expression " home " we mean the office at which its registers have to be kept and where service of process on it may be effected. It is not necessarily its " residence " in the technical sense, for a company registered in England may transfer its residence abroad.[7] But it must retain an office in England—though within England it can change its actual situation as it wishes—and however much its residence may change its English registration fixes its nationality and domicile. The Act provides that notice of the situation of this office must be sent to the Registrar within fourteen days of the company's formation or of any

---

[1] s. 12, see Chap. 12.
[2] s. 143 (see Chap. 21); ss. 69 and 206 (see Chap. 26); s. 210 (see Chap. 25).
[3] s. 200, see Chap. 7.
[4] s. 102, see Chap. 19.
[5] s. 305. It must also be published in the *Gazette*: *ibid.* (see Chap. 27).
[6] See Chap. 8.
[7] See Chap. 10, pp. 207, 208.

change in the situation of the office.[8]   It has been held that *vis-à-vis*
third parties a change is not effective until notice of it is given.[9]   If the
company exercises its right to maintain the register of members or
debentureholders elsewhere than at its registered office it must also file
a notice stating where the register is kept.[10]   The file will therefore show
where it is possible to obtain additional, and, perhaps, more up-to-date [11]
information than is available at the registry, and where writs and notices
can be served on the company.[12]   It will be appreciated, however, that
the file does not show where the company carries on business, for this
will not necessarily be at the registered office which is often simply the
address of the company's solicitor or accountant.

Share capital

If the company has a share capital particulars must be lodged
showing details of its capital—nominal, issued and paid-up.   The initial
nominal capital will, of course, appear in the memorandum.   If it is
increased [13] or reduced,[14] or if the shares are consolidated, sub-divided
or converted into stock,[15] notice must be given to the Registrar.   Details
regarding the issued and paid-up capital must similarly be given in a
return of allotments which must be filed within one month of allotment.[16]
The required details include the names and addresses of the allottees,
but of course, the return will not give details of members to whom the
shares are transferred after allotment.   To ascertain this the inquirer
will have to inspect the company's register of members or rely on the
annual return,[17] if that is sufficiently recent for his purpose.   But as many
of the shares may be held by nominees he may be unable to find out who
the true owners are.[17a]

Financial position

Every company must, within twenty-one days of creating a charge on
any of its property or of acquiring property subject to a charge, lodge
particulars which will be included in the register of charges in its file.[18]

---

[8] s. 107 (see Chap. 12, p. 258).
[9] *Ross* v. *Invergordon Distillers Ltd.*, 1961 S.C. 286 (Sc.).
[10] ss. 110 and 86 (3).
[11] It will be appreciated that a period, normally of 14 or 21 days, is allowed for filing
documents.   Hence a searcher at the registry cannot be certain that no changes
have recently taken place.   *Quaere* whether he is entitled to assume that they have
not: see Chap. 8, p. 164.
[12] s. 437.   Process is validly served if left at the registered office or sent there by either
registered or *ordinary* post: *T. O. Supplies Ltd.* v. *Jerry Creighton Ltd.* [1951] 1
K.B. 42; *Addis* v. *Berkeley Supplies Ltd.* [1964] 1 W.L.R. 943.
[13] s. 63.   [14] s. 69.   And see s. 62 (1) (*e*) and (*f*).
[15] s. 62.   The time allowed under this section is one month.   A simple but much
needed reform of company legislation is the reduction of the various times allowed
for filing documents to a uniform period.
[16] s. 52.   If shares are allotted otherwise than for cash, particulars of the contract must
also be given.
[17] *Infra*, p. 449.   [17a] But see pp. 388–391, *supra*.
[18] Companies Act 1948, Parts III and IIIA: see Chap. 19; as there pointed out, not
all types of charge are registrable.

To anyone proposing to grant credit to the company or to invest in its securities this is perhaps the most valuable safeguard, for he can see to what extent the company's assets are already mortgaged. A public company will also have initially to give a considerable amount of financial information in its filed prospectus,[19] or statement in lieu of prospectus.[20] This information is valuable to anyone contemplating investment in a public issue, or on the initial formation of the company or its conversion into a public company, but it is a " once-for-all " requirement and the information will speedily become too stale to benefit creditors or later purchasers of securities. These will have to rely on the published annual accounts,[21] which, as we shall see, must be filed with the annual returns of all limited companies. Further details will be available once the company has gone into liquidation [22] or had a receiver or manager appointed of substantially the whole of its undertaking,[23] but this information comes somewhat late in the day for most purposes.

Annual returns

In addition to the requirement for registration of the above matters as and when they occur, the 1948 Act contains provisions for an annual return which has to be completed within forty-two days after the annual general meeting for the year.[24] The object of this is to provide an annual consolidation of the periodical information so that a searcher will not generally have to go back beyond the last annual return. At the same time, however, the opportunity is taken of obtaining certain additional information which would otherwise be available only at the company's office if at all.

The form of the return varies according to whether the company has a share capital or not.[25] In the former case not only must the information as to share capital contained in the returns of allotments be consolidated, but the company must also submit a consolidated replica of its register of members.[26] In both cases details of charges and of the company's officers must be given. And normally there must be annexed to the return certified copies of the balance-sheet, profit and

---

[19] ss. 38, 41 and 4th Sched.; see Chap. 14.
[20] ss. 30 and 48 and 3rd and 5th Scheds.; see Chap. 14. The information in these documents extends far beyond mere financial matters and constitutes the most detailed source of information about the company's affairs. Note also the statutory report (s. 130) which, however, is not normally necessary for reasons stated in Chap. 14.
[21] *Infra*, p. 454 *et seq.*
[22] ss. 249, 283, 288–290, 293, 299, 300. See Chap. 27.
[23] ss. 372–374. See Chap. 19.
[24] ss. 124–129.
[25] If it has, s. 124 and the 6th Sched. apply; if not, s. 125.
[26] A full return in this respect is only needed once every three years; in the intervening years it suffices if changes of membership are given: s. 124 (1) (c). The size of a full annual return from a company as big as I.C.I. can be imagined.

loss account, and directors' and auditors' reports.[27] The nature of these documents is considered below; for the present it suffices to say that this requirement compels limited companies to make public the same information relating to their financial positions as they are compelled to prepare and to make available to their members and debentureholders. However, this requirement does not now apply to an unlimited company so long as it is not the holding or subsidiary company of a limited company or carrying on business as the promoter of a trading stamp scheme.[28] Hence companies can avoid making their accounts public only if their members are prepared to accept personal liability for the company's debts.[29]

Enforcement of registration requirements

With the enormous number of companies on the register one serious problem is to secure compliance with the registration requirements, and many companies, especially small private ones, are years in arrear with their annual returns. The penalties provided by the various sections have not proved an effective sanction. The Registrar has, however, two other strings to his bow. If he believes that the company's failure to file returns is due to the fact that it has ceased to operate he may institute the procedure to strike it off the register.[30] Under this procedure a large number of moribund companies are struck off each year. That does not help if the company is in fact in operation but is, deliberately or through inefficiency, failing to afford the public the information which the law requires. In these circumstances, however, the Registrar may proceed under section 428 and obtain a court order requiring the company and its officers to make good the default within a specified time. If the order is not complied with the officers will be in contempt of court and liable to imprisonment until they purge their contempt. In recent years increased resort to this remedy has proved highly effective.

Information to be maintained by the company

Much of the information filed at the Companies' Registry duplicates information which the company itself must maintain at its office. The particulars of directors and secretary are, for example, copies of the registers which companies must maintain.[31] But certain information additional to that at the Registry must be recorded. For example, the company must maintain registers of members and of debentureholders, of which only the former will be belatedly incorporated into the file at the Registry through the annual return. It must also maintain not merely

---

[27] s. 127. s. 129, which formerly made an exception for exempt private companies, was repealed by the Companies Act 1967, s. 2 and Sched. 8, Pt. III.
[28] Companies Act 1967, s. 47.
[29] See Jenkins Committee, Cmnd. 1749, paras. 55–63.
[30] Under s. 353: see pp. 653–654, *infra*.
[31] Companies Act 1948, s. 200.

a register of charges similar to that at the Registry,[32] but must keep copies of all instruments containing any charge requiring registration.[33] Copies, or memoranda of the terms, of directors' service contracts must be kept [34] and a register must be maintained of directors' holdings of shares and debentures in the company or its associated companies.[35] Quoted companies must also maintain registers of holdings of 10 per cent. or more of shares carrying unrestricted voting rights.[36] Banking companies must prepare half-yearly statements of assets and liabilities which must be conspicuously exhibited in every place where they carry on business.[37] Finally, proper books of accounts must be maintained,[38] and minutes of all proceedings of general meetings, and of directors' and managers' meetings must be entered in minute books.[39]

The extent to which these additional requirements benefit members and creditors depends, of course, on the extent to which they provide information which is available for general inspection; this is discussed in the next section.

Inspection and right to copies

In general all information filed at the Companies' Registry is available for public inspection on payment of 1s., and copies of all documents there may be obtained on payment of the prescribed fees.[40] To this there are only two exceptions: First, without the consent of the Board of Trade, certain documents delivered with a prospectus [41] are not available for inspection except within fifteen days after the date of the prospectus.[42] Secondly, only members and existing creditors or their agents are entitled to access to the full statement of affairs filed by a receiver or manager [43]; others have to be content with the summary of it.[44] A copy of any filed document certified by the Registrar is admissible in evidence in all legal proceedings,[45] and this normally obviates the need for production of the original which can only be obtained with leave of the court.[46]

---

[32] s. 104. See Chap. 19. Non-fulfilment of these requirements (as opposed to registration at the Registry) does not affect the validity of the charge.

[33] s. 103. *Ibid.*

[34] Companies Act 1967, s. 26. Chap. 23, p. 533.

[35] Companies Act 1967, ss. 26–31, replacing and extending Companies Act 1948, s. 195. See Chap. 17, pp. 388–391.

[36] Companies Act 1967, ss. 33 and 34. See Chap. 17, pp. 388–391.

[37] s. 433.

[38] s. 147. These books may now be in loose-leaf or mechanically recorded form provided that adequate precautions are taken for guarding against falsification and facilitating discovery: s. 436.

[39] s. 145. s. 436 also applies to minute books.

[40] s. 426.

[41] *i.e.*, material contracts required to be filed under ss. 41 (1) (*b*) (i) and 420 (1) (*b*).

[42] s. 426 (1) (*b*), proviso (i).

[43] Under s. 372.

[44] s. 426 (1) (*b*), proviso (ii).

[45] s. 426 (3).

[46] s. 426 (2).

As regards inspection and copies of documents maintained by the company itself, there are wide divergences. If the information merely duplicates that at the Companies' Registry it is normally available on at least equally favourable terms. Thus the registers of members [47] and directors and secretary [48] are open to inspection by members without fee and by others on payment of 1s. and in the case of the register of charges free search is extended to any creditor.[49] In a number of cases registers which have to be maintained only by the company can be searched on similar terms; this applies to the registers of debenture-holders,[50] of directors' shareholdings,[51] and of 10 per cent. shareholders.[52] But only members are entitled to inspection and copies of minutes of general meetings (but not of directors' or managers' meetings [53]), while the account books are open only to inspection by the directors.[54] Members can also obtain from their company copies of the memorandum and articles of association with all amendments and registrable resolutions,[55] but no one else can demand them from the company notwithstanding that they are obtainable from the registry.[56]

It will therefore be seen that the right of outsiders to pry into the indoor management is severely limited, and the rule in *Royal British Bank* v. *Turquand* [57] is, of course, a corollary of this, since the limitation on their rights is normally coupled with a corresponding freedom from any obligation to investigate. Even the rights of members are restricted, for they do not have access to the books and records as partners have.[58]

Information on business communications

An effective method of ensuring that essential information of a simple character reaches those who need it, is by insisting that it appears in all business communications emanating from the company. Hence, as we have seen, the letter-heading must mention the company's name,[59] and if the company is limited the last word of the name must announce this.[60]

---

[47] s. 113. With a like right to bespeak copies.
[48] s. 200. But with no right to bespeak copies.
[49] s. 105.
[50] s. 87. With a right to bespeak copies.
[51] Companies Act 1967, s. 28. With a right to bespeak copies.
[52] *Ibid.*, s. 34. With a right to bespeak copies.
[53] 1948 Act, s. 146.
[54] s. 147 (3).
[55] ss. 24, 25, 143 (2).
[56] But they can, of course, refuse to have dealings with the company unless copies are supplied. This is the invariable practice of the banks. In such cases the obligation to issue copies with amendments and resolutions (ss. 25 and 143 (2)) will apply.
[57] See Chap. 8, *supra*, p. 150 *et seq.*
[58] *Cf. Butt* v. *Kelson* [1952] Ch. 197, C.A., where it was held that beneficiaries could not compel the trustee, who was a director, to produce the company's books and papers for their inspection. In U.S.A. the partnership analogy was followed so that shareholders are entitled to inspect the books except to the extent to which this right is curtailed, as it now is in many states.
[59] s. 108; see Chap. 10, pp. 193–194, and Chap. 12, p. 252 *et seq.*
[60] s. 2 (1). Unless a charitable or quasi-charitable company obtains a licence to dispense with this: s. 19. See Chap. 12, p. 254.

The names of the directors must also appear,[61] and if the company is in liquidation[62] or in the hands of a receiver[63] this, too, must be mentioned.[64]

Extra-legal requirements

A public company with quoted shares is in practice subjected to a degree of publicity which far transcends these legal obligations. As a condition of obtaining a quotation, it will have had to enter into an undertaking with the stock exchange concerned to make information available. Thus, the general undertaking of the Federation of Stock Exchanges[65] imposes an obligation on such a company to notify the exchange of, *inter alia*, substantial realisations or acquisitions of assets, any changes in the directorate or in the general character of the business of the company or any subsidiary, of all dividends and bonuses which the board decide to recommend, of net profit figures with a comparison with the previous year, and "of any other information necessary to enable the shareholders to appraise the position of the company and to avoid the establishment of a false market in the shares." The stock exchanges take the fulfilment of these obligations very seriously, and try to ensure that managements take investors into their confidence as regards any developments which may affect quotations. If necessary, the sanction of suspension of dealings may be imposed and, indeed, this has been done (sometimes at the company's request), even though there is no definite breach of the undertaking, but dealings have been taking place which suggest that some move is afoot which has not yet been made public.

Over and above this consensual[66] obligation of disclosure is one yet more powerful in fact, although devoid of any basis in law: Press publicity. The financial columnists have their own channels of information and once their interest is aroused they explore these channels with sleuth-like pertinacity. The result may be that what the board had looked upon as a confidential decision or a domestic difference is suddenly brought out into the harsh light of day. This may be embarrassing, and even, in some circumstances, detrimental to the true interests of investors; but if the power of the financial Press is exercised with wisdom and fairness, as, on the whole it undoubtedly is, informed

---

[61] s. 201; see Chap. 7, pp. 127–128, and note that this is not of universal application.
[62] s. 338; see Chap. 27, p. 665.
[63] s. 370; see Chap. 19, p. 438.
[64] And compare the special provisions in s. 433, *supra*, relating to the display of financial statements in bank premises.
[65] *Requirements*, Sched. VIII, Part A. It will be appreciated that the form of the undertaking has varied from time to time so that old-established companies may be subject to no, or to less onerous, obligations.
[66] Probably the undertaking is not intended to be a legally enforceable contract; certainly it is unlikely that anyone will try to enforce it by legal action; as indicated in the text equally powerful sanctions are exercisable by the exchange, making resort to legal action unnecessary.

newspaper comment is perhaps the most potent protection afforded to investors and, to a lesser extent, to creditors.[67] Unfortunately, the Press normally takes an interest only in public companies with quoted shares, so that this safeguard exists only in their case and operates uncertainly even there.

Finally, it should be borne in mind that an unreasonable refusal to supply members with information, even though not of the type which they have any definite legal right to demand, may be regarded by the Board of Trade as a factor for consideration when deciding whether to exercise their power to appoint an inspector.[68]

Accounts

Compulsory disclosure through accounts is a method of providing information about companies which the legislature adopted at a comparatively late stage. It was not until 1908 that companies were compelled to publish their balance-sheets, nor until 1929 that they were made to circulate to their members the perhaps more informative document, the profit and loss account.[69] And it was only by the 1948 Act that a serious attempt was made to lay down in detail how these documents were to be prepared and by the 1967 Act that they were made available to the public in the case of all limited companies. This Act also added substantially to the amount of information which has to be given and substituted a new and amplified Schedule 8 [70] which lays down the details which must appear in the balance-sheet and profit and loss account.

Unfortunately, accounts in general and those of companies in particular are of little immediate help except to the well instructed, who are least in need of protection. To the average investor or creditor—" the man on the Clapham omnibus "—they are cryptograms which he is incapable of solving. He looks to skilled professional assistance to interpret them for him, and one of those to whom he may look is his solicitor. It would, therefore, be agreeable to assume that lawyers are among the select minority by whom accounts can be read like a book. Unhappily, experience suggests that this assumption would not always be true and that, in reality, there is nothing in the lawyer's background or training (except perhaps his battle with " Accounts " in the Law Society's examination [71]) which makes him

---

67 It should be noted that fair and accurate newspaper reports of *general meetings* of companies, other than private companies, are not actionable, in the absence of malice, provided that the paper publishes any reasonable explanation or contradiction: Defamation Act 1952, s. 7, and Sched., Part II. See further, Chap. 21, pp. 498, 499.

68 See Chap. 25, p. 604 *et seq.*

69 The fact that they were not legally compulsory does not, of course, mean that they were not prepared; this is another of the many respects in which law codified, rather than created, good practice.

70 Companies Act 1967, s. 9 and Sched. 2. This implements, with modifications, the accounting recommendations of the Jenkins Committee: Cmnd. 1749, Chap. X.

71 This should at least have given him an inkling of " double-entry " which is one of the confusing elements.

more adept in this respect than any other traveller on the Clapham omnibus. While, therefore, a detailed description of company accounts would be beyond the scope of this book,[72] some attempt must be made to explain how they are framed and what can be gleaned from them. This, it is thought, may be more helpful than a repetition or summary of the statutory rules. The account which follows deals only with the legal requirements relating to companies generally. In the case of certain types of company the Board of Trade can prescribe special accounting rules; this applies, for example, to companies which invite the public to deposit money with them [73] and to insurance companies.[74]

As we have seen, limited companies must annex to their annual returns copies of their balance-sheets and profit and loss accounts [75] with the directors' and auditors' reports, thus making them available to the general public. In addition the directors of *every* company must lay these documents before the company in general meeting,[76] and copies must be sent, not less than twenty-one days before, to every member, debentureholder, and other person entitled to be present at the meeting.[77] In starting with these documents we are, in a sense, putting the cart before the horse, for neither can be prepared unless the company has in fact kept running accounts. But here we are following the example of the statute which contains only the most perfunctory provisions regarding account books. The fact is, of course, that the ends determine the means, which can be left to take care of themselves provided the ends are fixed.[78] All the Act says [79] is that the company shall keep proper books with respect to receipts and expenditure, sales and purchases, and assets and liabilities, but what form of accounting is " proper " is left to the company, so that it may range from the simplest cash book and ledger to the most complicated mechanised type. The only further requirement is that it must give " a true and fair view of the company's affairs " and " explain " its transactions.[80] It may be thought indicative

---

[72] And for reasons appearing in the text (which will seem naïve to the expert) beyond the competence of the author.

[73] See the Protection of Depositors Act 1963.

[74] Insurance Companies Act 1958, as amended by Pt. II of the Companies Act 1967 (ss. 71–78).

[75] Or " Income and Expenditure accounts " in the case of companies not trading for profit.

[76] Companies Act 1948, s. 148. The intervals at which they must do so are linked to the provisions for annual general meetings (*i.e.*, within 18 months of incorporation and thereafter once in every calendar year), but there is as yet no legal requirement that they must be laid at the annual general meeting as the Jenkins Committee recommended: Cmnd. 1749, para. 419. In general the accounts must be made up to a date not earlier than nine months before the meeting.

[77] s. 158. There are a few exceptions of which the only one of any importance is that a member of a company without a share capital need not be sent copies if he is not entitled to attend the meeting. But he can obtain them by asking: s. 158 (2). Normally the only persons other than members entitled to attend the meeting will be the auditors: 1967 Act, s. 14 (7). In interpreting the statutory provisions it is useful to bear in mind that the profit and loss account is one of the documents required to be annexed to the balance sheet: see s. 156.

[78] Just as an examination syllabus too often fixes the lecturing curriculum.

[79] 1948 Act, s. 147 (1).   [80] s. 147 (2).

of the artificial atmosphere in which we are moving that it is apparently recognised that something can be " true " without being " fair " and " fair " without being " true," [81] but what is intended is that the books must show not merely a true story but the full story. Up to this point the Act probably adds little or nothing to the common law and equitable obligation to account, which would in any case bind the directors in their capacity of fiduciary agents, or to the sanction of criminal proceedings against the directors if, on liquidation, inadequate accounts prove to have been maintained.[82]

The 1967 Act has made it necessary for the published accounts and the annexed reports to be much more informative than hitherto regarding the company's relationship to other companies in the same group. If the company has subsidiaries at the end of its financial year, these must be named, and their countries of incorporation and the class and proportion of shares held in each must be stated.[83] The like information has to be given if the company holds in another company, not being a subsidiary, more than one-tenth of the equity share capital of that company or any shares which exceed in stated value more than one-tenth of the stated value of the holding company's assets.[84] And if the company is a subsidiary it must state the name of its ultimate holding company and, if known, its country of incorporation.[85] These provisions enable any member or person dealing with the company to know if it is a part of a larger group and, if so, what the group is. However, since it was thought that the information might be detrimental to companies operating abroad, the Board of Trade can permit it to be dispensed with in particular cases.[86]

Profit and Loss Account

The profit and loss account is an account in the true sense; it presents the figures for a period of activity designed to show the resulting profit or loss. As we saw in Chapter 6,[87] theoretically, " profit " or " loss " is the difference between the net value of the assets at the beginning and end of the accounting period, but in practice it is calculated by comparing the company's earnings during that period with the expenditure incurred in earning them. It therefore

---

[81] A member might argue that while accounts showing a loss of £1m. might be true, they certainly could not be fair; this, however, is hardly what is meant in this context.

[82] s. 331—a section based on the bankruptcy legislation. Subs. (2) gives a general indication of what will be regarded as " proper books of account."

[83] 1967 Act, s. 3.

[84] *Ibid.*, s. 4.

[85] *Ibid.*, s. 5. In each case the information may be given in, or in a note on, or in a statement annexed to, the accounts.

[86] *Ibid.*, ss. 3 (3), 4 (3) and 5 (2). Note also ss. 3 (4) and (5) and 4 (4) and (5) where the subsidiaries are very numerous.

[87] Which should be read in conjunction with the present discussion.

corresponds very much to the income and expenditure account which is its statutory equivalent in the case of companies not trading for profit.[88] It need not be, and normally is not, as complete as the full profit and loss account in the ledger. It will probably omit the important opening section of the full account—the trading account—containing such vital items as sales and purchases. Normally it begins with a net balance of profit or loss on trading. However, since the latest Act [89] these turnover figures have to be shown, in a note or otherwise, if the turnover exceeds £50,000, and even if it does not if the company is a holding or subsidiary company. And the method whereby turnover is arrived at must also be shown. The directors' report [90] must show how turnover is split between various classes of business if the company carries on more than one.[91] There will be added other income, such as interest, dividends on investments and rents receivable, and deducted from it will be other expenditure not debited to the trading account, such as mortgage and debenture interest and income tax. It is, therefore, essentially a revenue account, although a capital profit or loss may exceptionally appear in it.

By itself, the profit and loss account is not necessarily very informative but the study of a series of accounts over a number of years can be most revealing since the trend of profits is the best indication of the prospects of the company, and on the continuation of the business as a going concern the true valuation of its assets depends.[92] The layman undoubtedly finds it easier to study these trends from this account than from the balance-sheet in its traditional and, to him, confusing layout.

As in the case of the account books, the primary principle is that the profit and loss account " shall give a true and fair view of the profit or loss of the company for the financial year." [93] This formula is the golden rule which, as we shall see, applies also to balance-sheets. The details which have to be shown are set out in Schedule 8 as amended by the 1967 Act and set out in its Schedule 2. They include investment income from quoted and unquoted investments respectively, rents receivable (if substantial), interest on loans, the amount charged for depreciation, corporation and other tax, increases of and withdrawals from reserves, hire-rents of plant or machinery, and auditors' remuneration.[94] And either in the account or in a note thereto must be indicated, *inter alia*, the method of providing for renewals if depreciation

[88] s. 149 (7).
[89] Companies Act 1967, Sched. I, para. 14, and para. 13A of substitute Sched. 8 in Sched. 2. There is an exception for banking and discounting companies (businesses in which turnover is hardly a meaningful context) and other businesses that may be prescribed.
[90] See pp. 466, 467, *infra*.
[91] Companies Act 1967, s. 17.
[92] Cohen Report (Cmd. 6659), para. 96.
[93] s. 149 (1).
[94] Sched. 8, Part I, paras. 12–14.

is not charged [95] or the fact that it is not provided for, the basis of computing the charge to tax, and any material respects in which the account is affected by unusual transactions or a change in the basis of accounting.[96] The corresponding amounts for each item in the preceding year must also be shown,[97] thus aiding the study of trends. There are also stringent provisions regarding disclosure of the remuneration of directors and the highest-paid employees. In the accounts or in a statement annexed there must be shown the aggregate of directors' emoluments, pensions and compensation payments for loss of office [98] and, as a result of the 1967 Act, if these exceed £7,500,[99] the actual remuneration of the chairman must be shown, and the number of directors remunerated at the rate of £0–£2,500, £2,500–£5,000 and so on.[1] Similar disclosure has to be made of remuneration which has been waived,[2] and in respect of any employees entitled to more than £10,000.[3] The amount of loans to officers of the company must also be shown.[4]

The profit and loss account strictly so called is normally supplemented by an appropriation account showing the allocation of the profit thus determined and acting as a link between it and the balance-sheet. The statutory provisions treat this account as part of the profit and loss account for they require the latter to show details of these allocations.[5]

In the case of a holding or subsidiary company the requirements of Schedule 8 are modified by the provisions of Part II and, if it is a holding company, group accounts (normally consolidated into one joint account) must be prepared.[6] The object of these provisions and the " control " test of the holding-subsidiary relationship have already been considered in Chapter 10.[7] In Part III there are certain exceptions for banking, discount, shipping and assurance companies and the Board of Trade may authorise others.[8] The exemption of banking and discount companies led to a disagreement among the members of the Jenkins Committee,[9] and the latest Act empowers the Board of Trade to repeal or amend it.[10] The Committee unanimously thought that the case for

---

[95] It is unfortunate that the basis of depreciation does not have to be shown in sufficient detail to enable its adequacy or excessiveness to be assessed.

[96] *Ibid.*, para. 14. The value of the account would be largely destroyed if its basis was secretly changed.

[97] *Ibid.*, para. 14 (5).

[98] s. 196.

[99] And even if they do not, should the company be a holding or subsidiary company: 1967 Act, s. 6 (6).

[1] 1967 Act, s. 6. This does not apply to overseas directors: s. 6 (1) (*b*).

[2] *Ibid.*, s. 7.

[3] *Ibid.*, s. 8; unless they worked wholly or mainly abroad: s. 8 (1) (*b*).

[4] 1948 Act, s. 197.

[5] See Sched. 8, Part I, para. 12 (1) (*f*) and (*h*).

[6] ss. 150–154.

[7] See pp. 194–200, *supra.*

[8] Sched. 8, paras. 12 (2) and 15 (4). This in addition to the Board's general powers to modify under ss. 149 (4), 150 (2), proviso, and 152 (3), proviso.

[9] See Cmnd. 1749, paras. 399–407, and Note of Dissent at p. 211.

[10] Companies Act 1967, s. 12.

exemption by shipping companies had not been made out on commercial grounds,[11] but in fact it has been preserved.[12]

The balance-sheet

The second document—the balance-sheet—is not an account in the strict sense. It is merely a statement of the company's assets and liabilities as at the end of the financial year. Unlike the profit and loss account which deals with a course of events during a period of time, the balance-sheet describes a state of affairs as at a particular point of time. In practice it is its interpretation that the layman finds particularly difficult. He is especially baffled because he is likely to see among the liabilities, items which he would expect to find, if at all, among the assets. This is mainly due to two factors: First to the fact that balance-sheets are traditionally presented in a two-sided form resembling a " trial balance " prepared to test the accuracy of double-entry book-keeping [13]; Secondly, to the complications, peculiar to companies, caused by share capital. The first of these means that a balance-sheet may be presented as a set of debits and credits which balance. In fact the assets and the liabilities (in the sense in which the law and commonsense would use these words) are highly unlikely to balance exactly, and if one or other side of the balance-sheet was concluded by " to (or ' by ') balance " the average reader of it would probably understand it well enough. But mysteriously there is no such item; somehow a perfect equilibrium appears to have been achieved. The second factor causes an item described as " capital " to appear unchanged year after year among the liabilities. Some attempt to explain this latter complication has already been made in Chapter 6, but the explanation of both may become clearer if we take an actual example (much simplified) of a balance-sheet presented in the traditional form (see p. 460).

The vital point to grasp is that, of the items on the liabilities side, those included in I are not true liabilities at all. The figures of the *authorised* capital do not enter into the balance in any way and serve no purpose except to give the rather useless information that the company can issue another 5,000 ordinary shares and 2,000 preference shares without increasing capital. The figures for issued and paid-up [14] capital merely express the sums which the members originally put into the company and show whether there are different classes of members with different rights to return of income and capital. These figures are liabilities only in the artificial sense explained in Chapter 6, namely, that the company, having received these sums from the members, is debited with them.

[11] Cmnd. 1749, paras. 413–416.
[12] Sched. 8, para. 25.
[13] Balance-sheets almost certainly developed from such trial balances and their present form is a relic of their origins.
[14] In the case of A B Co. (like most others) there is no difference between issued and paid-up capital.

A B CO. LTD.

Balance Sheet at 31st December, 1970

LIABILITIES

1969 £			£	£	£
	I. SHARE CAPITAL AND RESERVES				
	CAPITAL				
	Authorised in shares of £1 each				
2,000	5% Preference Shares	2,000			
10,000	Ordinary Shares	10,000			
12,000		12,000			
	Issued in Shares of £1 each all fully paid				
5,000	Ordinary Shares		5,000		
	RESERVES				
1,200	General Reserve	1,500			
300	Unappropriated profit carried forward	500	2,000		
6,500				7,000	
	II. LONG TERM LIABILITIES				
2,000	Debentures secured on Company's Undertaking and Assets			2,000	
	III. CURRENT LIABILITIES AND PROVISIONS				
500	PROVISION FOR DEFERRED REPAIRS		500		
1,500	SUNDRY CREDITORS		1,300		
2,000				1,800	
£10,500				£10,800	

ASSETS

1969 £		£	£	£
	I. FIXED ASSETS			
	PREMISES HELD ON SHORT LEASE			
4,000	AT COST	4,000		
250	*Less* DEPRECIATION	500		
3,750			3,500	
	MOTOR VEHICLES AND OFFICE FURNITURE AT COST	3,000		
3,000	*Less* DEPRECIATION	1,500		
1,000			1,500	
2,000				
5,750				5,000
	II. CURRENT ASSETS			
1,500	STOCK-IN-TRADE	2,500		
1,100	SUNDRY DEBTORS	2,200		
2,150	CASH at Bankers and in Hand	1,100		
4,750				5,800
£10,500				£10,800

Sgd. John Doe } Directors
Richard Roe }

Really, both issued capital and the so-called reserves are mere balancing items. If from the assets (£10,800) we deduct the true liabilities in items II and III (£3,800) we are left with a balance of £7,000, which represents the value of the business to the holders of the 5,000 shares. But for the technicalities of company law the whole of this £7,000 might be described as capital, this being the expression customarily used to describe what remains after liabilities have been deducted from assets,[15] but that solution is not possible because the nominal amount of the issued share capital (£5,000) cannot be altered quite so simply as that. Unless this nominal amount is increased by making a bonus issue of further shares, some other expression has to be used to describe the remainder of the balance (£2,000), and the word normally adopted is " reserves " (and not " surplus " or " balance " which would be clearer). The word " reserves " is undoubtedly unfortunate for it causes the layman to envisage some fund [16] in excess of present requirements which he would expect to find, not among the liabilities, but among the assets. In fact, all it means is that the book figures of the assets exceed the liabilities and share capital by £2,000, indicating that the company has, during its existence, made profits, and for the time being left £2,000 of them in the business. To decide whether there is any fund of liquid assets representing this surplus we have to look at the assets side; in our particular case there is clearly no such earmarked fund—the excess is merged in the general run of current assets [17]—but in another company's balance-sheet we might find, say " Quoted Investments at Market Valuation . . . £500," thus suggesting that it had set aside a fund to balance part of the reserve.[18]

The hypothetical company, whose balance-sheet we have taken by way of example, has clearly proved reasonably profitable, so that its assets are now worth more than its liabilities plus share capital. Had it made losses the liabilities plus share capital would, of course, have exceeded the assets, and the balancing item would then have appeared on the assets side, probably under some such heading as " loss to date." This explains why, to the confusion of the average reasonable man, a loss may appear as an asset.[19]

Having described the general lay-out of the balance-sheet it remains to indicate what sort of information a member or creditor can deduce

---

[15] In accordance with the equation: Assets−Liabilities=Capital. *Cf.* Chap. 6.
[16] *Cf.* gold and dollar reserves.
[17] And, as pointed out below, its most liquid asset, cash, has decreased during the year by £1,050 notwithstanding that its profits and reserves grew by £500.
[18] Quoted and unquoted investments must be distinguished: Sched. 8, para. 8 (1) (*a*).
[19] " Goodwill " may also be used as a balancing item. If a company acquires a business for 10,000 shares of £1 credited as fully paid, and values its physical assets at £7,000, the remaining £3,000 will be entered in the accounts as goodwill, this being the assumed extra value of the business as a going concern. In practice the company will, over the years, try to strengthen its balance-sheet by writing off the goodwill out of profits, for it does not follow that it will ever be able to sell its business as a going concern or that, if it does, anyone else will give £3,000 for it. Hence anyone studying the balance-sheet will wisely ignore this item.

from it. It would be tempting to say that he could ascertain the company's net worth, *i.e.*, what is left after true liabilities have been subtracted from the assets. In our case, this amounts to £7,000, so that the credit of the company seems to be good and the £1 shares each worth about £1 8s. But this is misleading. As already indicated in Chapter 6, the values placed on the assets, particularly the fixed assets,[20] are highly conventional. As our balance-sheet indicates, the fixed assets have been valued at cost less depreciation. We do not know what their true present market value is; it may be very much greater, or very much less,[21] for some fixed assets may be valueless except to the business as a going concern. Nor do we know whether in fact the rate of depreciation is adequate or (a very important consideration today[22]) whether replacement costs would exceed the original cost. " A balance-sheet is thus an historical document and does not as a general rule purport to show the net worth of an undertaking at any particular date or the present realisable value of such items as goodwill, land, buildings, plant and machinery, nor, except in cases where the realisable value is less than cost, does it normally show the realisable value of stock in trade." [23]

What it should show, with much greater accuracy, is the total and types of the company's liabilities, and how its funds are spread between various types of assets. This, in particular, should reveal its all-important liquid position, *i.e.*, to what extent it has assets immediately and readily available to meet claims on it. Our A B Co. Ltd. has current assets of £5,800 to meet current liabilities of £1,800. Even if we assume that the debentures may be called in, the current assets are still more than sufficient. On the face of it, therefore, the liquid position is favourable. The only disturbing feature is that much of it is represented by debtors and little by cash, and that the comparable figures for the previous year[24] indicate that there has been a marked deterioration in this respect. This may account for the fact that the company has used some of its profits for the year to increase its reserves rather than to pay dividends.[25]

---

20 The distinction between "fixed" and "floating" or "current" assets has been described in Chap. 6. A company may, of course, carry out a complete revaluation of assets but even so the information is deceptive " since the value of such assets while the company is a going concern will in most cases have no relation to their value if the undertaking fails ": Cohen Report (Cmd. 6659), para. 98.

21 But see under Directors' Report, *infra*, p. 466.

22 One of the major grouses against the present tax code is that for tax purposes depreciation may not be charged on the basis of replacement costs.

23 Cohen Report, para. 98, quoting the evidence of the Institute of Chartered Accountants.

24 As in the case of the profit and loss accounts, the balance-sheet is far more revealing when used to study trends over a number of years, and corresponding figures for the previous year have to be shown: Sched. 8, Part I, para. 11 (11).

25 The exact source of these increases would have to be shown either in the balance-sheet or profit and loss account: Sched. 8, Part I, para. 7 (1) (*a*). It is assumed that in the appropriation account a profit for the year of £500 was appropriated as

The object of the statutory provisions is to ensure, so far as possible, that the balance-sheet reveals accurately and in some detail sufficient information to enable these deductions to be made. Once again the primary rule is that it must give a " true and fair view," this time of " the state of affairs of the company as at the end of its financial year." [26] And, once again, this is supplemented by the detailed requirements of Schedule 8. Among other rules, it is laid down that fixed assets, current assets and assets that are neither fixed nor current shall be separately identified [27] (as we have seen, this is necessary in order to enable the company's liquidity to be determined). The method used to arrive at the amount of the fixed assets must be stated in some detail.[28] Quoted and unquoted investments must be separately shown, again in some detail,[29] especially as regards unquoted equity shares.[30] If the directors think that any current assets would not realise their stated value they must say so.[31] The aggregate amount of reserves and provisions are to be stated under separate headings.[32] These are defined,[33] and the essential distinction between them is that a provision is an amount set aside to meet a known liability the exact amount of which cannot be determined with accuracy, whereas a reserve is an amount retained to meet unknown eventualities.[34]

It will be observed that these rules are complied with in the specimen balance-sheet on p. 460, and that this contains examples of a provision and two reserves. A provision [35] of £500 is made to meet the cost of repairs which should have been made in the financial year but which have been deferred. Since the exact cost is uncertain, and no contract has been entered into to incur it, it cannot be shown as a debt; nor can it be shown as a reserve, for the liability is certain and definite, and only the amount unknown. Had the repairs not yet been due, a reserve might have been set up to provide for them in the future, but this would

---

to £300 to general reserve and that the balance of £200 was added to the unappropriated profit. If a dividend was declared but unpaid at the end of the accounting year the amount of it would, of course, have to appear in the balance-sheet among current liabilities.

[26] s. 149 (1). But these last words must be read in the light of the consideration that so far as values are concerned the balance-sheet is an historical document only, especially as regards fixed assets.

[27] Sched. 8, Part I, para. 4 (2). The third class is newly introduced by the 1967 Act in recognition that there are some assets that cannot be properly classed as either fixed or current.

[28] *Ibid.*, paras. 4 (3), 5, 8 (1) (*b*), 11(6A),(6B) and (6C). The last of these demands distinguishing between freeholds, long leaseholds and short leaseholds: for definitions of the latter see para. 29.

[29] *Ibid.*, paras. 5A, 8 (1) (*a*) and 11 (8).

[30] *Ibid.*, para. 5A.

[31] *Ibid.*, para. 11 (8).

[32] *Ibid.*, para. 6.

[33] Sched. 8, Part IV, para. 27.

[34] The former confusing distinction between capital and revenue reserves is abolished by the 1967 Act.

[35] The amounts written off fixed assets for depreciation are also provisions and would be so described in the profit and loss account but need not be shown under separate headings in the balance-sheet: Sched. 8, Part I, para. 6.

have been optional, not essential. If, however, the liability would become an obligation of the financial year contingently on the happening of a certain event or on the result, say, of a pending law suit, then, if the balance-sheet was to present a true and fair view of the affairs as at the end of that year, allowance would have to be made somehow; if neither a provision nor a reserve was considered appropriate this might be by way of note.[36]

Then there are reserves totalling £2,000. The directors have chosen to divide this sum into " general reserve—£1,500 " and " undistributed profits—£500." Such a distinction is quite common, though not compulsory. In so far as it means anything, it is simply an indication of the directors' views as to its immediate availability for distribution. The directors obviously think it advisable at the moment to retain £1,500, perhaps for stock replacement in the light of increased prices: the remaining £500 they would be happy to see distributed, but this has not yet been done, perhaps because of the cash position already animadverted on.

A common reason for establishing reserves is to provide a cushion so that dividends can be maintained in bad years out of undistributed profits in past good years. Provided that these reserves are disclosed this is unobjectionable, but if they are concealed the balance-sheet becomes misleading and, as a means of assessing the worth of the shares, even more unreliable than it always is. The profit and loss account is also falsified if the profit available for dividend is depleted by excessive provisions and this, too, artificially deflates the market price of the shares. One of the principal objects of Schedule 8 is therefore to prevent the establishment of secret reserves, which previously was not uncommon,[37] since the view was widely held that the purpose of published accounts was to show that the financial position was at least as good as that stated, and not to guarantee that it was not better.[38] To allow a limited company to appear as more profitable than it really is is obviously objectionable, for it may grievously mislead creditors and investors, actual or potential. But it is a comparatively modern development to regard it as equally objectionable that it should pose as poorer than it really is. Today, however, it is recognised that this is unfair on those whose claims may depend on the extent of the company's profits (*e.g.*, the Revenue and employees) and on shareholders eager for dividends. This the Schedule seeks to prevent by making it compulsory to classify separately provisions and reserve,[39] and to disclose

---

[36] Sched. 8, Part I, para. 11 (5).

[37] It was, of course, this practice, coupled with a misleading statement about it in a prospectus, which got Lord Kylsant into trouble: *R.* v. *Kylsant* [1932] 1 K.B. 442, C.C.A.

[38] There was, indeed, some judicial authority for this view: see dicta in *Newton* v. *B.S.A. Co.* [1906] 2 Ch. 378 at p. 387. But for a summary of the objections to hidden reserves see Cohen Report, para. 101.

[39] Part I, para. 6.

the source of any increase in reserves or provisions and the application of any amounts derived from any decrease,[40] and by providing that any provision in excess of what is reasonably necessary shall be treated instead as a reserve.[41] It was thought that full disclosure in this respect might be detrimental in the case of banking, discount and shipping companies, and it is mainly for this reason that certain exceptions are made in their case by Part III of the Schedule, and that the Board of Trade is authorised to make others in the case of any type of company if satisfied that it is in the public interest to do so.[42]

Only a very few of the many matters specified in the Schedule have been touched on, and reference should be made to the Act for fuller information, which it is hoped that this elementary introduction may have made more intelligible. The only other matters which need be referred to here are that, as in the case of the profit and loss account, the requirements of Schedule 8 are modified by Part II when the company is a holding or a subsidiary company, and that, for reasons stated in Chapter 10,[43] a consolidated balance-sheet is normally required in the case of a holding company in addition to its separate balance-sheet.[44] It may also be mentioned that a balance-sheet must be signed by two directors, or, if there is only one, by that director.[45]

Powers of Board of Trade

In addition to the powers, already referred to, to waive the requirements of various paragraphs of Schedule 8, the Act confers upon the Board of Trade certain general powers to modify the accounting provisions of the Act.[46] The widest of these is section 454 which entitles the Board to alter or add to the requirements by statutory instrument, subject to approval by affirmative resolution of Parliament if the requirements are made more onerous. Section 149 (4) entitles the Board, on the application or with the consent of the directors, to modify in relation to any company any of the statutory requirements as to matters to be stated in the balance-sheet or profit and loss account. But it is expressly stated that this does not extend to any waiver of the golden rule that both documents must present " a true and fair view." The

---

40 *Ibid.*, para. 7.
41 Part IV, para. 27 (2).
42 paras. 6, proviso, and 12 (2). This is in addition to the Board's general powers to modify under ss. 149 (4), 150 (2), proviso, 152 (3), proviso, and 454, as amended by s. 12 of the 1967 Act.
43 *Supra*, pp. 194–200.
44 1948 Act, ss. 150–154.
45 s. 155. Attention may be drawn to the surprising decision in *Jones* v. *Bellgrove Properties Ltd.* [1949] 2 K.B. 700, C.A., to the effect that the item " sundry creditors " may amount to a signed acknowledgment of a debt in fact included therein so as to prevent the period of limitation from running. But in the light of *Re Transplanters (Holding Company) Ltd.* [1958] 1 W.L.R. 822, and, especially, *Consolidated Agencies Ltd.* v. *Bertram Ltd.* [1965] A.C. 470, P.C., it is clear that the decision in *Jones* v. *Bellgrove Ltd.* depended on the special facts.
46 ss. 149 (4), 150 (2), proviso, 152 (3), proviso, and 454.

object is simply to obviate the risk that the new statutory code for companies' accounts might prove unduly inflexible. The code is not intended to act as a strait-jacket preventing reasonable liberty of action, but merely as a foundation garment moulding the form of figures into a presentable shape. When it proves unduly constricting the Board is privileged to unlace it,[47] but only to the extent necessary to reveal, and not to conceal the truth.

Directors' report

To be attached to the balance-sheet, and to be circulated and publicised with it,[48] is a report by the directors " with respect to the state of the company's affairs, the amount, if any, which they recommend should be paid by way of dividend, and the amount, if any, which they propose to carry to reserves. . . ." [49] Until the 1967 Act these reports tended to be formal, colourless and of little value. But now they have been made a source of such information as it is thought should be provided annually but which cannot conveniently be given in the accounts themselves. They must state the names of the directors and the principal activities of the company and its subsidiaries and any significant changes.[50] In particular they must draw attention to changes in fixed assets and, if the balance-sheet value of any land differs substantially from market value, must indicate the difference " with such degree of precision as is practicable." [51] If shares or debentures have been issued, details must be given with reasons for the issues.[52] Disclosure is required of contracts of significance in relation to the company's business in which any director was interested [53] and of any arrangements for enabling directors to acquire benefits by the acquisition of shares or debentures of the company or any other body corporate.[54]

---

[47] Applications to the Board under this section are not infrequent and are granted fairly freely.

[48] Neither the directors' nor the auditor's report is technically " a document annexed . . . to the accounts ": see s. 163. But both have to be annexed to the accounts accompanying the annual return (s. 127) and presented to the general meeting: s. 157. The auditor's report has also to be sent to everyone who has a right to a copy of the balance sheet but, it seems, the directors' report need not (s. 158) unless it contains information which the Act requires either to be in the accounts or in a statement annexed: s. 163. In practice all four documents (balance sheet, profit and loss account, directors' report and auditor's report) are printed and treated as one.

[49] s. 157 (1).

[50] 1967 Act, s. 16 (1).

[51] s. 16 (1) (a). This is an attempt to meet the criticism of the inadequacy of the valuations obtainable from the balance-sheet. It does not include companies exempted under Sched. 8, Part III: s. 16 (2).

[52] s. 16 (1) (b).

[53] s. 16 (1) (c). This does not include service contracts or those with another company in which a director is interested *only* because he is also a director of that other: s. 16 (3). It extends the recommendation of the Jenkins Committee which was limited to management contracts: see Cmnd. 1749, paras. 96 and 122 (a) (vii).

[54] s. 16 (1) (d). This throws the light of publicity on attempts by directors to add to their emoluments by share-acquisition schemes.

The provisions, already considered, relating to disclosure of share-holdings and dealings by directors [55] are supplemented by requiring details of each director's holdings at the beginning and end of the financial year,[56] as are those relating to turnover by requiring details of the proportions of each class of business to total turnover and profitability.[57] Unless the number of employees of the company and its subsidiaries is less than one hundred, the number [58] employed and their aggregate remuneration must be stated.[59] If the company and its subsidiaries have made donations for charitable or political purposes exceeding £50 in all, details must be given of the amounts subscribed for each purpose.[60] And if a company and its subsidiaries have a turnover exceeding £50,000 and their businesses include the supplying of goods, the value of goods exported must be given.[61] These last two requirements, which were not recommended by the Jenkins Committee, have been strongly attacked as political gimmicks but can perhaps be justified on the ground that shareholders have a right to know what charities and political aims are being supported by their money—as perhaps have the public too—and that publication of export figures is an ingenious way of encouraging the export drive. Finally, the report must give particulars of any other matters which are material for the appreciation of the company's affairs by its members, unless disclosure would be harmful to the business of the company or its subsidiaries.[62]

In the case of public companies it has become common to circulate the statement made by the chairman at the annual general meeting and to publish this in the Press. Though these statements are sometimes interlarded with fulminations about nationalisation or aspects of the Government's economic policy, they have in the past tended to be considerably more informative about the company's affairs than the directors' report. The Jenkins Committee recommended that this tendency should be recognised by permitting information to be provided in the chairman's statement rather than in the directors' report.[63] This recommendation, however, has not been adopted. Nevertheless the chairman's statement should never be overlooked as a possible source of additional information.

Auditors' report

Finally there is the auditors' report which must invariably be attached

---

[55] Under ss. 27–31, see *supra*, pp. 388–391.
[56] s. 16 (1) (e). And as regards other substantial shareholders in quoted companies, see *Requirements*, Sched. VIII, Part A (General Undertaking), para. 6 (d).
[57] s. 17.
[58] By weekly average: see s. 18 (1) (a), (2) (a) and (3).
[59] s. 18. But the figures required do not reveal the company's pay-roll structure.
[60] s. 19. Note the definition of "political purposes" in subs. (3) and the exclusion of foreign charities in subs. (4). And contrast the definition of political objects in s. 3 (3) of the Trades Union Act 1913.
[61] s. 20. The Board of Trade can grant exemption if satisfied that disclosure would not be in the national interest (arms?): subs. (4).
[62] s. 16 (1) (f).
[63] Cmnd. 1749, para. 115.

to any circulated or published copies of the accounts.[64]   The auditors
are required to report to the members on the accounts examined by
them and on all balance-sheets, profit and loss accounts, and group
accounts laid before the company.[65]   The form of the report has been
improved and simplified by the 1967 Act which repeals the former
Schedule 9 and replaces it by section 14.   This, in brief, provides that
the report must state whether the accounts have been prepared in
accordance with the Acts of 1948 and 1967 and, except where the
company is entitled to and has availed itself of an exemption in
Part III of Schedule 8, whether they give a true and fair view.[66]   It
further clarifies the auditors' duties by laying down that they must
carry out such investigations as will enable them to form an opinion on
whether proper books have been kept and proper returns adequate for
their audit have been received from branches not visited, and on whether
the balance-sheet and profit and loss account are in agreement with
the books and returns; if not the report must so state.[67]   Every auditor
has a right of access to all books, accounts, and vouchers of the
company and to information and explanation from its officers [68]; if he
fails to get it the auditors' report must say so.[69]   To emphasise the
importance of the report, it is laid down that it shall be read at the
general meeting [70] and be open to inspection by any member.[71]   The
auditors are also entitled to notices and circulars relating to any general
meeting, to attend it, and to be heard on any part of the business which
concerns them.[72]

If, as is usually the case, the auditors give a clean certificate, this
is not so much an independent source of information as some guarantee
of the accuracy of the other sources.[73]   If, however, it is qualified, it
should be treated as a red light.[74]   In either event it fulfils a most
valuable function.   As pointed out in connection with prospectuses,[75]
the disclosure philosophy, adopted in England as the fundamental
principle of investor protection, only works if the information disclosed
can be safely taken as accurate.   Unless checked by some independent
authority this cannot be relied on; so far as the accounts are concerned
the auditors are this independent (and usually reliable) authority

---

[64] 1948 Act, s. 156.
[65] 1967 Act, s. 14 (1).
[66] s. 14 (3).
[67] s. 14 (4).   If the directors do not allow the auditors adequate time to make these
investigations they must either refuse to make a report at all or qualify it: *Re
Thomas Gerrard & Son Ltd*. [1968] Ch. 455 at 477.
[68] s. 14 (5).
[69] s. 14 (6).
[70] If the auditor is present he himself generally reads it.
[71] s. 14 (2).
[72] s. 14 (7).
[73] Or, rather, of the balance-sheet and profit and loss account.   They are not required
to back the directors' report unless, and to the extent that, this contains matters
required to be stated in or with the accounts: s. 163.
[74] It may well lead to a Board of Trade inspection and, perhaps, to criminal proceedings.
[75] *Supra*, Chap. 14, pp. 307–310.

If, however, they are adequately to perform this function their competence, integrity and independence must be assured. To this end the Act provides that they must not be incorporated companies and must be members of one of the recognised professional bodies of accountants. They must not be employees of the company or of any company in the same group, or partners of an employee.[76] This should ensure professional competence and integrity, but would not of itself guarantee independence—for they are professional men whose livelihood is largely dependent on audit work, and they must be protected from the temptation to relax their vigilance rather than risk offending the management and losing their jobs. Hence as we have seen,[77] they are entrenched by the " special notice " procedure which is necessary before they can be removed from their posts, and which gives them ample opportunities to lay their case before the members.[78] Moreover, the appointment and remuneration of auditors rests with the members in general meeting (and if they fail to appoint, with the Board of Trade), and not with the board of directors.[79] Hence, auditors need no longer fear the consequences of offending the management; indeed, it is probable that today no public company would dare to sack its auditors against their will except for manifest incompetence or impropriety.[79a] Even though the management normally have *de facto* control over a general meeting they would be rash to try to wield it in the face of the Press publicity which their action would be likely to arouse.

Although the terms of section 14 have clarified the nature of the auditors' duties, the degree of care and skill which they must display in fulfilling them depends still on various judicial decisions.[80] In the words of a famous judgment of Lopes L.J. [81]:

[76] s. 161 as amended by s. 2 of the 1967 Act which repeals the former exemptions in the case of exempt private companies but subject to the transitional provisions in s. 13.
[77] *Supra*, Chap. 7, pp. 133–134; and see further Chap. 21, pp. 480–482, *infra*.
[78] ss. 142 and 160. These legal provisions are supplemented by a strictly observed rule of etiquette of the accountancy profession whereby an auditorship is not undertaken without prior consultation with the former auditor to ensure that there is no reason why the post should not be accepted.
[79] s. 159. Except for the first year and in the event of a casual vacancy. *Semble* an auditor cannot resign except by giving notice that he does not want to be re-appointed at the next A.G.M., and cannot be dismissed between the dates of A.G.M.s. The Jenkins Committee recommended that the Act should expressly recognise his right to resign (Cmnd. 1749, para. 430) and that if he ceases to be qualified he should automatically relinquish office (*ibid.*, para. 429), but neither recommendation has yet been implemented. Nor have the improvements recommended in paras. 427 and 428 regarding the position where a firm is appointed in the firm's name.
[79a] Or for some plausible business reason; *e.g.*, after a take-over by another company.
[80] Notably those connected with the liquidations of the Kingston Cotton Mill Co. and the Liberator Group of Companies at the end of the last century: *Re Kingston Cotton Mill Co. (No.* 1) [1896] 1 Ch. 6, C.A.; *(No.* 2) [1896] 2 Ch. 279, C.A.; *Re London & General Bank (No.* 1) [1895] 2 Ch. 166, C.A.; *(No.* 2) [1895] 2 Ch. 673, C.A.; and the more recent *Re City Equitable Fire Insurance Co.* [1925] Ch. 407, C.A.; *Fomento (Sterling Area) Ltd.* v. *Selsdon Fountain Pen Co. Ltd.* [1958] 1 W.L.R. 45, H.L., especially *per* Lord Denning at pp. 60–63 (this case was not concerned with a company audit but the terms of the contract were not dissimilar to those of s. 14 (5)); and *Re Thomas Gerrard & Son Ltd.* [1968] Ch. 455.
[81] [1896] 2 Ch. at pp. 288, 289.

"It is the duty of an auditor to bring to bear on the work he has to perform that skill, care and caution which a reasonably competent, careful and cautious auditor would use. What is reasonable skill, care and caution must depend on the particular circumstances of each case. An auditor is not bound to be a detective, or, as was said, to approach his work with suspicion, or with a foregone conclusion that there is something wrong. He is a watchdog, but not a bloodhound. He is justified in believing tried servants of the company in whom confidence is placed by the company. He is entitled to assume that they are honest and to rely upon their representations, provided he takes reasonable care. If there is anything calculated to excite suspicion, he should probe it to the bottom; but in the absence of anything of that kind he is only bound to be reasonably cautious and careful. . . . It is not the duty of an auditor to take stock; he is not a stock expert; there are many matters on which he must rely on the honesty and accuracy of others."

In other words, he must act as the reasonably careful and competent auditor would. The cases illustrate what this duty has been held to demand in particular circumstances; but they are unlikely to give much help when the general principle is applied to future cases. This is especially so because most of the reported cases are old, and professional standards have undoubtedly risen in recent years; for example, notwithstanding the dictum quoted above, it is coming to be accepted that an auditor should not rely wholly on the honesty and accuracy of others even as regards taking stock, and that he should at least satisfy himself that it has been taken on sound principles and, probably, that he should carry out a spot check of at least one sample item.[82] In the words of Lord Denning [83]:

"An auditor is not to be confined to the mechanics of checking vouchers and making arithmetical computations. He is not to be written off as a professional ' adder-upper and subtractor.' His vital task is to take care to see that errors are not made, be they errors of computation, or errors of omission or commission, or downright untruths. To perform this task properly he must come to it with an enquiring mind—not suspicious of dishonesty . . . —but suspecting that someone may have made a mistake somewhere and that a check must be made to ensure that there has been none."

Accordingly in *Re Thomas Gerrard & Sons Ltd.*,[84] where the managing director had falsified the accounts by three methods, one of which

---

[82] As regards checking investments, see *Re City Equitable Fire Insurance Co., supra.*
[83] *Fomento (Sterling Area) Ltd.* v. *Selsdon Fountain Pen Co. Ltd.* [1958] 1 W.L.R. at p. 61.
[84] [1968] Ch. 455.

involved including non-existent stock and another altering invoices, Pennycuick J., while leaving open the question whether the auditors would have been in breach of duty had the falsification of stock stood alone,[85] held that once they had come across the altered invoices they were under a duty to make an exhaustive inquiry. Having failed to do so they were liable to the company for the cost of recovering excess tax paid and for dividends and tax not recovered, since this loss was the natural and probable result of their breach of duty.

To whom does the auditor owe the duty of care? Primarily to the company, with whom alone he is in any contractual relationship. And in all the cases in which he has been held liable, it has been in an action brought by the company—generally through its liquidator.[86] But the auditor's report has to be made to the *members* [87] and not to the company—and this suggests that a duty of care is owed to each individual member [88] who could, accordingly, sue, notwithstanding the rule in *Foss* v. *Harbottle*.[89] If this is correct, we must presumably regard him as standing in a fiduciary relationship not merely to the company but also to its members [90]—in which event his position is in contrast with that of a director.[91] And it is now clear that he owes a duty of care even to a non-member if he knows that his audited accounts are going to be produced in order to induce someone to invest in the company, unless, apparently, there is an express disclaimer of responsibility.[92]

General observations on accounts

As a result of the latest Companies Act it is generally agreed that published accounts are now mines of valuable information, supplying knowledge of the company's financial position in greater detail than is likely to be available from any other source. Clearly, the statutory provisions are not the last word on the subject; but in general they ensure that the vital information is there for those qualified to extract it. Unhappily, as already indicated, the traditional lay-out of a balance-sheet renders its contents inaccessible to the bulk of its readers. The

---

[85] At p. 475.

[86] On a misfeasance summons under s. 333, for which purposes the auditor is regarded as "an officer" of the company: *Re London & General Bank (No.* 1), *supra*; *Re Kingston Cotton Mills Co. (No.* 1), *supra*. The draftsman does not seem to have been able to make up his mind whether the auditor is an officer for all purposes (*cf.* ss. 161 (2), 167 (5), 205 and 455) but it seems that he is unless appointed solely for some limited purpose such as a private audit: *R.* v. *Shacter* [1960] 2 Q.B. 252, C.C.A. He is not normally an *agent* whose acts bind the company: *Re Transplanters (Holding Co.) Ltd.* [1958] 1 W.L.R. 822.

[87] 1967 Act, s. 14 (1). He clearly cannot evade his duty to report by asking not to be re-appointed.

[88] This argument is much strengthened since *Hedley Byrne & Co. Ltd.* v. *Heller & Partners Ltd.* [1964] A.C. 465, H.L. There were dicta in *Candler* v. *Crane, Christmas & Co.* [1951] 2 K.B. 164, C.A., which seem to support this, but others, *e.g.*, by the C.A. in *Re City Equitable Fire Insurance Co.*, *supra*, which suggest the contrary.

[89] *Infra*, Chap. 25.

[90] *Nocton* v. *Ashburton* [1914] A.C. 932, 971.   [91] *Infra*, Chap. 23.

[92] *Hedley Byrne & Co. Ltd.* v. *Heller & Partners Ltd.*, *supra*, overruling *Candler* v. *Crane, Christmas & Co.* [1951] 2 K.B. 164, C.A. (Denning L.J. dissenting).

financial editor, the accountant and (sometimes) the lawyer can extract the gold from the mine, but the average investor lacks the technical skill. And the more detailed accounts become, the greater are his difficulties. In so far as he relies on competent professional advice no great harm is done, but all too often he has his flutter on the stock exchange or fills in his proxy form without taking this precaution. He may subsequently regret it—perhaps almost immediately if comment is excited in the financial Press (if he reads it)—but by then it may be too late. And what is true of the investor is even more true of the creditor. How many traders study published accounts before granting credit? And how many of them would draw the right conclusions if they did?

Published accounts have become the linch-pin of the system of protection through disclosure. Unless, in a Welfare State, this system is to be rejected in favour of some more drastic method, the outstanding need seems to be to ensure that accounts are presented in a form which is more readily intelligible to the layman.[93] This, it seems clear, ought at least to involve rejection of the two-sided layout, and its replacement by a consecutive statement preferably in narrative form and incorporated as an integral part of the director's report. There is, of course, nothing in the statutory code to prevent companies from presenting their accounts in this way and the growing tendency is in this direction. The position cannot be regarded as satisfactory, until the law requires that to be done, for readily understood data are more necessary in the case of the unwilling company, with something to conceal, than with the best companies which are only too eager to put their cards on the table.

Unregistered companies

By virtue of section 435 and Schedule 14 to the 1948 Act, and section 54 of the 1967 Act, and the regulations made thereunder,[94] many of the foregoing provisions apply to British [95] statutory and chartered companies [96] other than those not formed for the purposes of gain [97] or specifically exempted by the Board of Trade. Thus; the prospectus provisions [98] (but not those relating to the statement in lieu of prospectus), those relating to the register of directors and secretaries,[99] and, with slight modifications,[1] those relating to accounts, audit and directors' report all apply. What is more, so do those relating to annual

---

[93] A useful encouragement towards greater clarity and frankness is the annual prize for the best presented set of company accounts awarded by the *Accountant*.

[94] Companies (Unregistered Companies) Regulations 1967 (S.I. No. 1876).

[95] *i.e.*, "incorporated in and having a principal place of business in Great Britain": s. 435 (1).

[96] Including unincorporated companies granted letters patent under the Chartered Companies Act 1837, but not bodies registered under any *general* Act of Parliament: s. 435 (2) and (3).

[97] For the meaning of this expression, see Chap. 11, p. 221.

[98] ss. 37–46, 50, 51 and 55 and Sched. 4.

[99] s. 200.

[1] See Sched. 14 and s. 54 of the 1967 Act.

returns,[2] with the result that nearly all the information required to be filed by a registered company will ultimately become available in the case of an unregistered one, although most of it is only made public in an annual consolidated return and not as changes occur. And, of course, if the company is compulsorily wound up under the Act all its winding-up provisions, including those requiring returns, will apply.

The result is that the " disclosure philosophy," on which incorporation by registration is based, has been applied also to the older methods of incorporation—although still not to the full extent. This is an interesting development which may herald further measures of assimilation.

[2] ss. 124–129 and 432 and Scheds. 6 and 7, and s. 54 of 1967 Act.

CHAPTER 21

MEETINGS AND RESOLUTIONS

THE ultimate control of a company rests with the general meeting. It is therefore essential to a proper understanding of investor protection to appreciate how such meetings are summoned and conducted. Basically this is a matter for the regulations of each individual company, but in practice there is a considerable measure of uniformity; indeed, there now has to be, because recent Companies Acts have laid down an increasing number of rules which must be complied with whatever the company's regulations may say.

The company's regulations will almost invariably distinguish between ordinary meetings held at regular intervals, and extraordinary meetings which can be convened at any time should the need arise.[1] In the case of registered companies, it is now provided [2] that a meeting to be called "the annual general meeting" shall be called in each year, and hence the expression "annual general meeting" has largely superseded "ordinary meeting." In the case of public companies there is a third type of meeting—the statutory meeting—to be held between one and three months of the date at which the company is entitled to commence business.[3] Reference has already been made to this meeting [4] and it need not concern us further; it can only be held once in the life of any company, is not needed in the case of a private company, and in practice is generally dispensed with, even by public companies, by the device of forming as a private company and then converting.[4]

In practice, therefore, there are two types of general meeting, the annual general meeting and the extraordinary general meeting.

The annual general meeting

The Companies Act 1948 provides [5] that a company shall in each year (i.e., each calendar year, not every twelve months [6]) hold an annual general meeting specified as such in the notices convening it, and not more than fifteen months must elapse between one annual general meeting and the next.[7] But it suffices if the first annual

---

[1] Companies Clauses Act 1845, ss. 66–70.
[2] Companies Act 1948, s. 131.
[3] *Ibid.*, s. 130.
[4] *Supra*, Chap. 14, p. 304.
[5] s. 131.
[6] *Gibson* v. *Barton* (1875) L.R. 10 Q.B. 329.
[7] The Jenkins Committee recommended that the Board of Trade should have power to grant a company an extension of the period: Cmnd. 1749, para. 457.

meeting is held within eighteen months of formation even though this is not in the first or second year of incorporation. Penalties are imposed for default,[8] on which the Board of Trade on the application of any member may call a meeting.[9]

Rather surprisingly the Act itself does not say precisely what business must be transacted at the annual general meeting, and the only statutory duty which has to be performed there is the appointment of auditors.[10] However, certain other business must be transacted annually (for example, the presentation of the accounts and directors' and auditors' reports [11]), and the regulations will almost certainly provide for other matters of an annually recurring nature. Indeed, the normal business of an annual general meeting is best indicated by Article 52 of Table A, which implies that it is the declaration of dividends, consideration of the accounts and the directors' and auditors' reports, the appointment of directors in place of those retiring, and the appointment and fixing of the remuneration of auditors. These are the things which have to be done annually and which it is envisaged will be done at the annual general meeting.

The annual general meeting is an important protection to members, for it is the one occasion when they can be sure of having an opportunity of meeting the directors and of questioning them on the accounts, on their report, and on the company's position and prospects. It is at this meeting that, normally, a proportion of the directors will retire and come up for re-election, and at which the members will be able to try to exercise their only real power over the board—that of dismissal. Moreover, it affords members an opportunity of moving resolutions on their own account. Most of these things could, of course, be done at an extraordinary meeting, but the members who want to raise these matters may not be able to insist upon the convening of an extraordinary meeting. The annual general meeting is valuable to them because the directors must hold it whether they want to or not.

It must be emphasised that the business of an annual general meeting need not be restricted to the ordinary matters specified above. The annual general meeting is a general meeting, and anything that can be done at a general meeting can be undertaken at the annual general meeting just as well as at an extraordinary meeting. There is, for example, no reason why a special resolution or an extraordinary resolution should not be considered.[12]

---

[8] s. 131 (5). In practice proceedings for their recovery are unusual. Where the meeting is held after the prescribed time, voting rights are determined as at the actual time of the meeting; not as they would have been if the meeting had been held at the proper time: *Musselwhite* v. *Musselwhite & Son Ltd.* [1962] Ch. 964.

[9] s. 131 (2). [10] s. 159.

[11] ss. 148, 156 and 157.

[12] This point is emphasised for there seems to be a widespread belief that the annual general meeting should be restricted to ordinary business and that if, *e.g.*, a special or extraordinary resolution is to be considered an extraordinary general meeting should be convened even if this is to be held at the same time and place.

Extraordinary general meetings

A company's regulations commonly provide that any meeting other than the annual general meeting (and statutory meeting if applicable) shall be called an extraordinary general meeting, and that it may be convened by the directors whenever they think fit.[13] In the absence of any further statutory requirement the regulations would probably stop there, for the management would like nothing better than to be able to call meetings when it suited them, but to be under no obligation to do so when it did not. But the 1948 Act provides [14] that the directors must convene a meeting on the requisition of holders of not less than one-tenth of the paid-up capital carrying voting rights.[15] If they fail to do so the requisitionists, or any of them representing more than half of their total voting rights, may themselves convene the meeting,[16] and their reasonable expenses shall be paid by the company and recovered from fees of the defaulting directors.[17] The weakness of these provisions is that in a company with a large and dispersed membership it may be a matter of considerable difficulty and expense for one member to enlist the support of sufficient of his fellow-members to be able to make a valid requisition. The requisition must state the objects of the meeting [18] and, unless the articles otherwise provide, it will be impossible to insist on anything else being included in the notice of the meeting.[19]

Finally, the Act provides a residual power whereby the court may convene a meeting if, for any reason, it is otherwise impracticable to do so.[20] So, as we have seen, may the Board of Trade if default is made in holding the annual general meeting.[21] These powers may be particularly valuable in the case of small private companies when the number of available members is reduced to one or when the majority shareholder is being frustrated by the absence of a quorum.[22] The natural meaning of the word " meeting " implies the presence of at least two members [23]; but it is expressly provided that the court or the Board

---

[13] *Cf.* Table A, arts. 48 and 49.

[14] s. 132 (1): " notwithstanding anything in its articles."

[15] Or, if the company has no share capital, members representing not less than one-tenth of the voting rights (*cf.* C. C. Act 1845, s. 70). Note that in the case of a company with a share capital in which some shares have more than one vote no regard is paid to this so far as concerns powers to requisition a meeting.

[16] s. 132 (3). The Jenkins Committee suggested that, to avoid evasion by giving notice for a meeting in the distant future, the requisitionists should be entitled to convene a meeting if the notice given by the directors was for a date more than 28 days ahead: Cmnd. 1749, para. 458. Already, if the articles do not otherwise provide, two or more members holding not less than one-tenth of the issued capital (whether or not with voting rights) may convene a meeting: s. 134 (*b*).

[17] s. 132 (5).   [18] s. 132 (2).

[19] *Ball* v. *Metal Industries Ltd.*, 1957 S.C. 315 (Sc.).

[20] s. 135.

[21] s. 131 (2) and (3).

[22] *Jarvis Motors (Harrow) Ltd.* v. *Carabott* [1964] 1 W.L.R. 1101.

[23] *Sharp* v. *Dawes* (1876) 2 Q.B.D. 26, C.A.; *Re Sanitary Carbon Co.* [1877] W.N. 223, notwithstanding that the one member held proxies from others; *Re London Flats Ltd.* [1969] 1 W.L.R. 711. But *cf. East* v. *Bennett Bros.* [1911] 1 Ch. 163 where one member holding all the shares of a class was held to constitute a class meeting.

of Trade may direct that one member present, whether personally or by proxy, shall be deemed to constitute a meeting.[24]

Notices

The length of notice of meetings, and how and to whom notice shall be given, also depend primarily on the company's regulations. The Companies Clauses Act 1845[25] provides for fourteen days' notice by advertisement, but in the case of registered companies, until the 1948 Act, the only statutory regulation which could not be varied was that twenty-one days' notice was required for a meeting at which a special resolution was to be proposed. In other cases the Act of 1929[26] provided that, unless the articles otherwise directed (which they rarely did) only seven days' notice was needed. The Cohen Committee pointed out[27] that this left far too short a time for opposition to be organised.[28] Hence, it is now provided by section 133 of the Companies Act 1948 that any provision of a company's articles shall be void in so far as it provides for the calling of a meeting by a shorter notice than twenty-one days' notice in writing in the case of an annual general meeting, or a meeting for the passing of a special resolution, or fourteen days' notice in writing in other cases.[29] There is a disagreement between the English and the Scottish courts on whether this means " clear " days, *i.e.*, exclusive both of the day of service and the day of the meeting,[30] and it is wiser to play safe. Meetings (other than annual general meetings) can, however, be convened on shorter notice if it is so agreed by a majority in number of members having a right to attend and vote at the meeting, and holding not less than 95 per cent. in nominal value of the shares giving a right to attend and vote.[31] In the case of a special resolution the members must agree to that specific resolution being passed on short notice.[32] In the case of annual general meetings *all* the members entitled to attend and vote must agree if shorter notice is to be valid.[33]

---

[24] ss. 131 (2) and 135 (1): see *Re El Sombrero Ltd.* [1958] Ch. 900. If there are no members (*e.g.*, because both have been killed in an accident) a meeting will not be possible until a grant has been obtained to the estate of one. Thereafter on compliance with the articles (*e.g.*, Table A, arts. 29–32) the executors should be able to conduct a meeting convened by the court or the B. of T.: see *Re Noel Tedman Holdings Pty. Ltd.* [1967] Qd.R. 561.

[25] s. 71.

[26] s. 115.

[27] Cmd. 6659, para. 126.

[28] Particularly as the period might be reduced still further by provisions requiring proxy forms to be lodged in advance of the meeting.

[29] Seven days in the case of unlimited companies.

[30] *Re Hector Whaling* [1936] Ch. 208 (clear days); *Neil M'Leod & Sons Ltd., Petitioners*, 1967 S.C. 16 (*secus*). See *infra*, p. 478, as to the day of service.

[31] s. 133 (3) (*b*). If the company has no share capital, 95 per cent. of the total voting rights at the meeting must agree.

[32] s. 141 (2), proviso: see *Re Pearce Duff & Co. Ltd.* [1960] 1 W.L.R. 1014.

[33] s. 133 (3) (*a*). The reason for the distinction between annual general meetings and other meetings was given in the Cohen Report (Cmd. 6659, para. 126): " We suggest the longer period of notice for annual general meetings because we attach consider-

These provisions are clearly a great improvement. Even so, fourteen (and even twenty-one) days may be woefully short if opposition has to start from scratch. Moreover, the intention of the provisions is largely defeated because, as we shall see, all too often the result is determined by proxies lodged long before the meeting. Furthermore, although section 133 lays down minimum lengths of notice and states that notice shall be in writing, it does not say to whom the notice is to be given or how it is to be transmitted. Whether any particular class of member has a right to attend meetings depends on the rights attached to the shares as determined by the articles and terms of issue.[34] And, even though the member may have a right to attend, it does not follow that he will ever actually receive the notice, for the method of service is left entirely to the articles which, in theory, might presumably provide that notice should be given by affixing it to a notice-board at the registered office.[35] In practice, however, regulations follow closely those of Table A; indeed, it is expressly provided[36] that Table A shall apply " in so far as the articles of the company do not make other provision in that behalf." This, it will be observed, results in Table A applying even though it has been expressly excluded, unless the regulations which take its place make other provisions for service of notice, and even though the company is not a company limited by shares so that Table A would normally have no relevance. Moreover, and this is a unique provision in the Act, in this context " Table A means that Table as for the time being in force "[36]—not Table A as at the date of incorporation.

The present provisions of Table A (arts. 131–134) provide for service either personally or by post to the member's registered address. Where sent by post, service shall be deemed to be effected twenty-four hours after posting properly addressed and prepaid[36a] letters. Every member (except one with no address in the United Kingdom[37]) and every person to whom a share has devolved on death or bankruptcy is entitled to notice and to attend meetings. These rules will, of course, require revision if some class of members (*e.g.,* preference shareholders) are not to be entitled to attend, or if share warrants to bearer have been issued; in the latter case provision is usually made for newspaper advertisement. It is also wisely provided[38] that the accidental omission

---

able importance to some of the business transacted thereat—and because the company is bound to hold an annual general meeting and little inconvenience should be caused by the necessity to give longer notice of it." Extraordinary meetings, on the other hand, " may need to be summoned in greater haste for urgent business."

[34] See Chap. 16, *supra.* Anyone having a vote at the meeting will clearly have a right to attend, but *quaere* whether a member who has no right to vote is nevertheless entitled to attend unless this right is expressly excluded. *Re MacKenzie & Co. Ltd* [1916] 2 Ch. 450 suggests that he is not.

[35] But if the shares were to be quoted, the stock exchange would obviously object *cf. Requirements,* Sched. VII, Pt. A, H.

[36] s. 134 (*a*).   [36a] *Quaere* whether a 4d. stamp suffices.

[37] A foreign resident is entitled to give an address within the U.K. for the purpose of service of notices: art. 131. *Cf. Re Warden & Hotchkiss Ltd.* [1945] Ch. 270, C.A.

[38] By art. 51.

to give notice to any member or the non-receipt of notice by him shall not invalidate the meeting.[39]

As for the contents of the notice, it is clear that these must indicate not only the time and place, but must state the nature of the business to be transacted at the meeting. But here, again, the articles may make express provision and it is usual to distinguish between special and ordinary business.[40] Thus, Table A provides that notices shall specify the place, day and hour of the meeting and, in the case of special business, the general nature of that business.[41] And it provides [42] that all business transacted at an extraordinary general meeting and all at an annual general meeting other than the ordinary business already described,[43] shall be deemed special. The result is that if an annual general meeting is called solely for the purpose of transacting ordinary business, the notice need do no more than describe it as an annual general meeting and state the place, day and hour. But if anything else is to be done, its general nature must be stated and nothing else can be effectively undertaken.[44]

Formerly, this requirement of notice rendered largely illusory the right of individual shareholders to move their own resolutions at annual general meetings, for there was no way in which they could compel the company to include reference to their resolutions in the notices of the meeting. Hence, they might themselves have to undertake the laborious and expensive task of circulating notices. Only if they were sufficiently numerous to have requisitioned a meeting could they be sure that the notice sent out by the company would cover their resolutions.[45] This is now partially rectified by section 140,[46] which provides that members representing not less than one-twentieth of the total voting rights,[47] or 100 members holding shares on which there has been paid up an average of £100 per member, may require the company to give notice of their resolutions, which can then be dealt with at the next annual general meeting.[48] To take advantage of this facility they must deposit the

---

[39] This covers even a special resolution: *Re West Canadian Collieries Ltd.* [1962] Ch. 370. But not a deliberate omission even though based on a mistaken belief that the member is not entitled to attend: *Musselwhite* v. *Musselwhite & Son Ltd.* [1962] Ch. 964.

[40] Table A, art. 52, C. C. Act 1845, ss. 67 and 71. The draftsman's affection for the word " special " is unfortunate; we now have special business, special notices and special resolutions, none of which is in any way connected with the others.

[41] Art. 50.

[42] Art. 52.

[43] *Supra*, p. 475.

[44] *Re Hampshire Land Co.* [1896] 2 Ch. 743. But third parties may be protected by the rule in *Royal British Bank* v. *Turquand*: *ibid.*

[45] Provided that these were referred to in the requisition: see p. 476, *supra*.

[46] In U.S.A. Federal legislation goes very considerably further in enabling individual stockholders to bring proposals before a general meeting.

[47] *i.e.*, normally half the proportion needed to requisition an extraordinary meeting under s. 132, but in this case regard *is* had to multiple voting rights attached to any shares: *cf.* note 15, p. 476, *supra*.

[48] s. 140 (1) (*a*).

requisition six weeks before the meeting,[49] and (unless the company otherwise resolves[50]) they must pay the expenses, which, however, should be small, since all that is involved is an addition to the company's notice.[51]

There are numerous reported cases considering whether the nature of the business has been stated with sufficient particularity. But in so far as any guiding principle can be deduced from them it seems to amount to nothing clearer than that the notice must convey to ordinary minds sufficient information as to what is proposed to enable the recipients to decide whether they should attend and vote.[52] In the case of special or extraordinary resolutions it appears to be necessary,[53] as it is certainly customary, to set out in the notice the exact terms of the resolutions. This, indeed, is usually done in the case of any resolution not comprised in ordinary business, the accepted formula being " for the purpose of considering and if thought fit passing (with or without modifications[54]) the subjoined resolutions as ―――[55] resolutions of the company." Furthermore it seems that if the effect of the resolution will be to enable the directors to obtain a benefit, the purpose for which the meeting is called will not be properly stated unless the intended benefit is disclosed.[56]

In cases where the law now insists upon the right to attend and vote by proxy, the notice must also state with reasonable prominence the members' rights in this respect.[57]

Special notice

Reference has already been made to the new type of notice, unoriginally and unhelpfully designated " special notice," now required in the case of three types of resolution, *viz.*, to dismiss a director by ordinary resolution,[58] to appoint as auditor someone other than the

---

[49] But the deposit is valid if after its receipt an annual general meeting is convened within the six weeks: s. 140 (4).
[50] Which it is unlikely to do unless the resolution is carried.
[51] The expense only becomes considerable if the members require circulars to be distributed; as we shall see (*infra*, p. 483) this also is possible.
[52] *Alexander* v. *Simpson* (1889) 43 Ch.D. 139 at p. 147, C.A.; *Choppington Collieries Ltd.* v. *Johnson* [1944] 1 All E.R. 762, C.A.; *Robt. Batcheller & Sons* v. *Batcheller* [1945] Ch. 169.
[53] s. 141. *Baillie* v. *Oriental Telephone Co.* [1915] 1 Ch. 503, C.A.; *MacConnell* v. *Prill & Co.* [1916] 2 Ch. 57.
[54] These words are advisable as they draw attention to the possibility of alteration and therefore, perhaps, give greater scope for valid amendments; see *infra*, p. 491.
[55] " Ordinary," " special " or " extraordinary " as the case may be.
[56] *Kaye* v. *Croydon Tramways Co.* [1898] 1 Ch. 358, C.A.; *Tiessen* v. *Henderson* [1899] 1 Ch. 861; *Baillie* v. *Oriental Telephone Co.* [1915] 1 Ch. 503; but *cf. Grant* v. *U.K. Switchback Ry.* (1888) 40 Ch.D. 135, C.A. In the case of notices to approve a scheme of arrangement under s. 206 (see *infra.* p. 619) it is expressly provided that any material interests of the directors and the effect thereon of the scheme must be disclosed: s. 207 (1) (*a*). The Jenkins Committee recommended that a like express statutory provision should apply generally: Cmnd. 1749, paras. 465–467.
[57] s. 136 (2). *Infra*, pp. 485, 486.
[58] s. 184.

retiring auditor or providing that the latter be not reappointed,[59] or to appoint or retain a director liable to retirement under an age limit.[60] " Notice " is here used in a different sense, for it means notice *to* the company of intention to move the resolution at the next meeting,[61] and not notice *by* the company of the meeting. Section 142 provides that such notice must be given not less than twenty-eight days before the meeting. The company must then give its members notice of the resolution with the notice of the meeting or, if that is not practicable,[62] either by newspaper advertisement or in any other mode allowed by the articles, not less than twenty-one days before the meeting. Had the section stopped there, there would have been an obvious loophole, for the managers having received the special notice could then have convened a meeting for less than twenty-eight days after its receipt and thus rendered the notice out of time. Hence, it is expressly provided that in such a case the notice shall still be deemed to have been properly given. Receipt of a special notice will therefore affect the form of the notice of the meeting, which will have to refer to the resolution concerned, presumably setting it out verbatim.[63]

In the case of a resolution to remove a director or auditor the provisions of section 142 are supplemented by further provisions designed to enable the director or auditor whom it is sought to remove to state his case to the members. It is essential that he should be able to do so, not merely because he is being deprived of an office of profit, but because the attempt to remove him probably indicates a disagreement with the board, a disagreement which may well have been caused by his scrupulous determination to safeguard the members' interests. Hence a copy of the notice must be sent to the director [64] or auditor [65] who is entitled to be heard on the resolution at the meeting.[66] Further, the auditor or director is entitled to make representations and to require these to be circulated to the members, and, if this is done in time, the company must, in the notice of the meeting, state that representations have been made, and must send a copy to every member to whom notice of the meeting is sent. If the representations are not sent, because received too late or because the company defaults, the director or auditor may require them to be read out at the meeting.[67] Although the wording

---

[59] s. 160.
[60] s. 185.
[61] The notice must be given no matter whether the resolution is to be moved by the management or the " opposition."
[62] For example, if the notices have already been dispatched although more than 28 days is still to elapse before the meeting.
[63] It is usual to set out the resolution and to state expressly that special notice has been received of the intention to propose it.
[64] s. 184 (2).
[65] s. 160 (2).
[66] ss. 184 (2) and 162 (4).
[67] ss. 184 (3) and 160 (3). The court may order these provisions to be dispensed with if satisfied that they are being abused to secure needless publicity for defamatory matter : *ibid.*

of the sections makes it clear that the mere fact that notices have already been dispatched does not excuse the company from circulating the representations, there is undoubtedly a loophole here. If the board wish to dismiss a director or auditor one of the directors [68] can give special notice to the company twenty-eight days before the meeting. The notices can then be sent out immediately, with proxy forms, without waiting for the victim's representations. When these are received they must admittedly be dispatched if there is time before the meeting and, in any case, the victim can be heard at the meeting. But before then the board will probably have received sufficient proxies to enable them to carry the resolution, and proxies once given are rarely withdrawn.

In practice, however, few public companies would wish to face the Press publicity likely to result from an attempt to take advantage of this loophole, and there is no doubt that these provisions are a reasonable restraint on the new power to remove a director and a valuable protection to the auditor, the watchdog of the shareholders' interests.

Circulars

In practice, the notice will be of a formal nature but, if anything other than ordinary business is to be transacted, it will be accompanied by a circular explaining the reasons for the proposal and giving the opinion of the board thereon. Normally, therefore, the circular will be a reasoned case by the board in favour of their own proposals or in opposition to proposals put forward by others. In deciding whether the nature of special business has been adequately described the notice and circular can, no doubt, be read together. [69] But equally the circular must not misrepresent the facts; there have been many cases in which resolutions have been set aside on the ground that they were passed as a result of a " tricky " circular. [70]

If there is opposition to the board's case, the opposers will doubtless wish to state their case and a battle of circulars will result. It is here, however, that the superiority of the board's position becomes manifest. Even if they do not directly control many votes they are for the moment in control of the company and they can get their say in first and use all the facilities and funds of the company in putting their views across. If it is their proposals that are to be debated they will have set the stage and chosen their moment to ring up the curtain. They will have had all the time in the world in which to prepare a polished and closely reasoned circular and with it they will have been able to dispatch stamped and

---

[68] So long as he is a member of the company entitled to attend the meeting, for otherwise he cannot move a resolution.

[69] *Tiessen* v. *Henderson* [1899] 1 Ch. 861 at p. 867.

[70] *Kaye* v. *Croydon Tramways Co.* [1898] 1 Ch. 358, C.A.; *Tiessen* v. *Henderson* [1899] 1 Ch. 861; and *Baillie* v. *Oriental Telephone Co.* [1915] 1 Ch. 503, C.A. In the case of quoted shares there is a further safeguard in the requirement that proofs of circulars shall be sent to the stock exchange: see *Requirements*, Sched. VIII, Part A (General Undertaking), para. 4.

addressed proxy forms in their own favour. And all this, of course, at the company's expense.[71]

Until the 1948 Act the opposition had none of these advantages and they still lack them in the case of statutory or chartered companies. And even in the case of registered companies, only the most timid steps have been taken towards counteracting the immense advantage enjoyed by those in possession of the company's machinery. Such steps as have been taken are included in section 140. As we have already seen, this entitles members holding one-twentieth of the votes or 100 members holding shares on which there has been paid up an average of £100 each, to use the company's machinery for circulating resolutions to be moved at annual general meetings. In addition it further entitles them to require the company to circulate statements not exceeding 1,000 words in length with respect to any business to be dealt with at any meeting.[72] The opposition, therefore, can now use the company's machinery for the dispatch of circulars whether in support of their own resolutions or in opposition to any proposals of the board. In this case it suffices if the requisition is deposited not less than a week before the meeting.

In practice, however, this provision is of little value. The expense still has to be borne by the opposition—unless the company otherwise resolve[73]—and no substantial saving will result from the use of the company's facilities except in the case of a circular which can go out at the same time as the notices. In other cases, for example, when the circulars are designed to oppose proposals already forwarded by the board, little extra cost will be incurred by acting independently of the company and this will have a number of advantages. It will avoid any difficulty in obtaining sufficient requisitionists and will prevent delay, which may be fatal if notices of the meeting have already been dispatched. It will also obviate the need to cut the circular to 1,000 words and will enable the opposition to accompany it with proxies in their own favour.[74] Moreover, and from a tactical point of view this is vital, the board will not obtain advance information about the opposition's case, nor be able to send out at the same time a circular of their own in reply.

---

[71] *Peel* v. *L.N.W. Ry.* [1907] 1 Ch. 5, C.A. For an excellent description of the relative weakness of the opposition, see *per* Maugham J. in *Re Dorman Long & Co.* [1934] 1 Ch. 635 at pp. 657–658.

[72] s. 140 (1) (*b*). As in the case of the " special notice " procedure, the court can excuse the company from circulating defamatory matter: s. 140 (5).

[73] This implies that where advantage is taken of s. 140 the company may resolve to pay the opposition's costs as well as those of the management. *Quaere*, does this apply generally? In the U.S.A. it has been held that the company may always so resolve, with the result that after successful fights for control the company has been saddled with responsibility for the costs of both sides: see *Steinberg* v. *Adams* (1950) 90 F.Supp. 604; *Rosenfeld* v. *Fairchild Engine and Airplane Corp.* (1955) 309 N.Y. 168; 128 N.E. 2d 291.

[74] There is clearly no reason why a statement circulated under s. 140 should not invite the recipients to cancel any proxies already given and to substitute proxies in favour of the opposition, but it seems that the company could decline to forward the opposition's proxy forms unless, at any rate, the words on them were counted against the total 1,000 allowed.

Hence members determined to do battle with the board are probably well advised to disregard section 140. But whether they do so or not they start with severe handicaps, the least of which is that they will have to draw on their own funds, not on those of the company. Victory normally goes to those who first state their case and first solicit proxies. Unless the board are so foolish as to part with the initiative by failing to comply with a valid requisition for a meeting, it is almost invariably the board that will strike the first blow. In a public company with a large and dispersed membership this is normally sufficient to ensure them victory.[75]

Proxies

It will have been apparent from the foregoing that proxies play a vital part in modern company meetings. At common law attending and voting had to be in person,[76] but it early became the normal practice to allow these duties to be undertaken by an agent or proxy[77] and both the Companies Clauses Acts[78] and the Companies Acts recognise this practice. Until the 1948 Act, however, the right to vote by proxy at a meeting of a registered company was dependent upon express authorisation in the articles. In practice this was almost invariably given; but not infrequently it was limited in some way, generally by providing that the proxy must himself be a member. Where there was such a limitation the scales were further tilted in favour of the board, for a member wishing to appoint a proxy to oppose them might find difficulty in locating a fellow member prepared to attend and vote on his behalf. It has also been customary to provide that proxy forms must be lodged in advance of the meeting. While this is a reasonable provision, inasmuch as it is necessary to check their validity before they are used at the meeting,[79] it too could be used to favour the board if the period allowed for lodging was unreasonably short. Moreover, as already pointed out, it had become the practice for the board to

---

[75] The only effective opposition is likely to come from institutional investors who probably hold large blocks and who tend to act together in accordance with the advice of their associations (*e.g.*, the Association of Investment Trusts and the British Insurance Association's Investment Protection Committee—bodies whose consent managements often secure in advance). Where institutions are interested small shareholders may obtain protection under their umbrella. But *cf. Re Old Silkstone Collieries Ltd.* [1954] Ch. 169, C.A. (at pp. 191–192), for a case where the approbation of these bodies was likely to lull the other shareholders into unwarranted apathy. Attempts to form similar associations to protect the interests of general investors have not proved very successful.

[76] *Harben* v. *Phillips* (1883) 23 Ch.D. 14, C.A.

[77] The word " proxy " is used indiscriminately to describe both the agent and the instrument appointing him. A general proxy to vote at more than one meeting requires to be stamped 10s. but no stamp duty is now payable on a proxy to vote at a single meeting and any adjournment: F.A. 1949, s. 35, and Sched. 8.

[78] C.C.A. 1845, ss. 76–77.

[79] In the U.S.A., where there is no such practice, the meeting may be deliberately prolonged for days in order to enable the management to enlist more proxy votes by high-pressure solicitation.

send out proxy forms in their own favour with the notice of the meeting and for these to be stamped and addressed at the company's expense.

For all these reasons, although proxy voting gave an appearance of democratic freedom, this appearance was often deceptive and in reality the practice helped to enhance the dictatorship of the board. In recognition of this the stock exchanges now require that quoted companies shall send out "two-way" proxies, *i.e.*, forms which enable members to direct the proxy whether to vote for or against any resolution.[80] The Cohen Committee [81] considered whether the two-way proxy should be required by law and whether open recognition should be given to the practical results of the system of circulars and proxies (which had virtually caused a postal referendum to take the place of voting after oral discussion at meetings) by enabling members to cast votes by post. But they rejected both these proposals; though recognising that two-way proxies were a practical move towards giving greater reality to the control by the shareholders over the directors, they felt that it was better to leave such matters to the stock exchanges which could waive or modify their rules in suitable cases, thus providing desirable flexibility.[82] Nevertheless, they made certain recommendations for legislation and these, with minor amendments, now appear in section 136 of the Act.

This section gives members of companies having a share capital [83] a right to attend and vote by a proxy who need not be a member. Except in the case of private companies more than one proxy may be appointed,[84] but proxies may vote only on a poll (not on a show of hands) and may speak at meetings of private companies only [85] or to demand a poll.[86] These rights may be extended by the articles (for example, to companies without a share capital, or so as to enable members of private companies to appoint more than one proxy or so as to

---

[80] *Requirements*, Sched. VIII, Part A (General Undertaking), para. 14. The only exception now is in the case of "resolutions relating to the procedure of the meeting or to the remuneration of the auditors": *ibid.*

[81] Cmd. 6659, para. 132.

[82] But the Jenkins Committee favoured making two-way proxies compulsory: Cmnd. 1749, para. 464.

[83] The Jenkins Committee recommended its extension to companies without a share capital: Cmnd. 1749, para. 462.

[84] This appears to be implied by ss. 136 (1) (*b*) and 136 (2), but presumably he may not appoint more proxies than one per share. The obvious intention is to provide for nominee companies: *cf.* s. 138, *infra*, p. 494. Another interpretation is that "more than one proxy" means more than one in the alternative (*i.e.*, A, whom failing B, etc.), but it is always assumed that this is equally permissible in a private company. The Jenkins Committee recommended that, without prejudice to the right to name alternatives, not more than two proxies should be permissible in the case of both private and public companies: Cmnd. 1749, para. 463. The difficulties that may face one proxy if he represents members, some of whom have instructed him to vote for and others against, are illustrated by *Oliver* v. *Dalgleish* [1963] 1 W.L.R. 1274.

[85] The Cohen Committee had recommended that all proxies should have a right to speak, but it was thought that the meetings might be unduly prolonged if professional advocates could be briefed to represent the various factions at a meeting of a public company. The Jenkins Committee agreed with Cohen: Cmnd. 1749, para. 463.

[86] s. 137 (2).

allow proxies to speak at meetings of public companies) but cannot be
curtailed. And shareholders must be informed of their rights in the
notice of the meeting.[87] Moreover, if proxies are solicited at the company's expense the invitation must be sent to all members entitled to
attend and vote[88]; the board cannot invite only those from whom they
expect a favourable response. Finally, it is no longer permissible to
provide that proxy forms must be lodged more than forty-eight hours
before a meeting or adjourned meeting.[89]

It cannot be said, however, that these provisions have done much
to curtail the tactical advantages possessed by the board. They still
strike the first blow and their solicitation of proxy votes is likely to meet
with a substantial response before the opposition is able to get under
way. Even if the proxies are in the " two-way " form, many members
will complete them after hearing but one side of the case,[90] and only
the most intelligent or obstinate are likely to withstand the impact of
the, as yet, uncontradicted assertions of the directors. It is, of course,
true that once opposition is aroused members may be persuaded to
cancel their proxies, for these are merely appointments of agents and
the agents' authority can be withdrawn[91] either expressly or by personal
attendance and voting.[92] But in practice this rarely happens.

Articles commonly provide that a vote given by a proxy shall be
effective notwithstanding the revocation, by death or otherwise, of
the authority, provided that the company has not received notice of
the revocation,[93] and they sometimes specify that such notice must be
received not later than so many hours before the meeting. Such a
provision is clearly effective as between the company and the member,
and it has even been held that the company must disregard notice of
revocation received out of time.[94] On the other hand it does not prevent
the member from attending and voting in person and the company must
then accept his vote instead of the proxy's.[95] And, on ordinary agency
principles, it is clear that as between the member and his proxy a
revocation is always effective if notified to the proxy before he has

---

[87] s. 136 (2).

[88] s. 136 (4). Overruling as regards registered companies *Wilson* v. *L.M.S. Ry.* [1940]
Ch. 393, C.A.

[89] s. 136 (3). Hence proxies may now validly be lodged between the original date of the
meeting and any adjournment.

[90] Psychologically the fact that the forms are stamped and addressed is of immense
importance. And most two-way proxies provide that if neither *for* nor *against* is
deleted the proxy will be used as the proxy thinks fit (*i.e.*, as the board wish);
Table A, art. 71. The stock exchanges have since April 1967 required this to be
expressly stated.

[91] Unless an authority coupled with an interest (for example, when given to a transferee
prior to registration of his transfer) or when an irrevocable power of attorney under
L.P.A. 1925, s. 126.

[92] *Cousins* v. *International Brick Co.* [1931] 2 Ch. 90, C.A.

[93] Table A, art. 73.

[94] *Spiller* v. *Mayo (Rhodesia) Development Co. Ltd.* [1926] W.N. 78.

[95] *Cousins* v. *International Brick Co., supra.*

voted,[96] and that if he disregards it he usurps an authority and is liable to his principal.

The final question of interest relating to proxies is whether they are compelled to exercise the authority conferred upon them. Unless there is a binding contract or some equitable obligation compelling them to do so, the answer appears to be in the negative. Normally there is only a gratuitous authorisation imposing no positive obligation on the agent, but merely a negative obligation not to vote contrary to the instructions of his principal if he votes at all.[97] But there may be a binding contract, if, for example, the proxy is to be remunerated. Or there may be a fiduciary duty, if, for example, the proxy is the member's professional adviser. Although the directors are not normally in a fiduciary relationship to individual members, it seems that if they are appointed proxies and instructed how to vote they must obey their instructions.[98] It if were otherwise the two-way proxy would be valueless, for the board would only use the favourable proxies and ignore the others. Similarly anyone who solicits proxies stating that he will use them in a certain way or as instructed, will, it is thought, be under a legal obligation to do as he has stated. But failing any such statement or definite instructions from his principal he will have a discretion and if he exercises it in good faith he will not be liable, whichever way he votes or if he refrains from voting.

Corporation's representatives

Since a company or other corporation is an artificial person which must act through agents or servants, it might be supposed that, when a member of another company, it could only attend and vote at meetings of that company by proxy. This, however, is not so. Section 139 provides that the member company may, by a resolution of its directors or other governing body, authorise such person as it thinks fit to act as its representative at meetings and that the representative may exercise the same powers as could his company if it were an individual.[99] It is

---

[96] Unless the agency is irrevocable, see note 91, *supra*.

[97] This was discussed, but not decided, in *Oliver* v. *Dalgleish* [1963] 1 W.L.R. 1274, which also left open the question of how far the company is concerned to see whether the proxy is obeying his instructions.

[98] *Per* Uthwatt J. in *Second Consolidated Trust* v. *Ceylon Amalgamated Estates* [1943] 2 All E.R. 567 at p. 570. So held in the case of proxies solicited under an order of the court in connection with a scheme of arrangement under s. 206: *Re Dorman Long & Co.* [1934] Ch. 635 (this case contains an admirable discussion of the general problem of proxy voting). But in both these cases the proxy holders were present at the meeting; *quaere* whether they can be compelled to attend: see [1934] Ch. at pp. 664–665. The chairman is not entitled to reject properly executed proxy forms because he believes them to have been obtained by misrepresentation: *Holmes* v. *Jackson, The Times*, April 3, 1957. The proper course seems to be to apply to the court for an injunction restraining the proxy-holders from voting the proxies—a not uncommon proceeding in America. Nor can he reject them because of some trifling misstatement in them. *Oliver* v. *Dalgleish, supra*.

[99] This is really a statutory example of an official acting as an organ of the company rather than as a mere agent: *cf.* Chap. 7, *supra*. In the case of meetings of statutory companies subject to the Companies Clauses Acts the representative must

therefore normally preferable for a company to attend and vote by representative rather than by proxy, for the representative is in a stronger position since he may always speak, and vote on a show of hands as well as on a poll.[1]

Conduct of meetings

Although the result of any disputed resolutions is in reality generally determined in advance through the system of proxy votes, the meeting still has to be held. At the meeting the board and the opposition will have an opportunity of repeating the arguments already expressed in their circulars, often succeeding in generating a surprising amount of heat considering that both sides know that it is little more than shadow boxing; little, but nevertheless more, for a mistake at the meeting may still dash the cup of victory from the lips of the triumphant party, since any breach of the regulations governing the conduct of the meeting may cause any resolutions passed to be quashed. Nor are meetings merely a means of passing resolutions, they also give the members an opportunity of asking questions either out of a genuine desire for information for its own sake, or as a tactical move in the next stage of the battle. And, of course, meetings may be, and most often are, held when there is no battle at all, and here they afford an opportunity for the management to report to the members and for the latter to congratulate or commiserate with the former on the results of their labours. Unhappily meetings are rarely attended by more than a handful of members unless there is some dispute, and then the only real excitement arises from the attempts by the party that has lost the battle of circulars to trap the other into some formal irregularity or into revealing information which may enable the validity of the notices to be attacked as misleading or incomplete.

It is therefore necessary to ensure that the rules for the conduct of meetings are scrupulously observed. What these rules are will depend on the regulations of the company construed in the light of the common law as to the conduct of meetings generally. Here attention can only be drawn to the most important matters which will require attention.

Quorums

The first essential is to ensure that a quorum is present, for without a quorum the meeting will be a nullity. It is not clear whether, if the articles are silent on the question, a quorum must remain present throughout [1] or whether it suffices if it is present at the beginning of the

be formally appointed a proxy but need not himself be a shareholder in the statutory company: C.C.A. 1845, s. 76, as amended by C.C.A. 1888 and 1889.

[1] If this is so a disgruntled faction may be able to bring the meeting to a close by withdrawing.

meeting.[2] But under Table A articles it suffices if a quorum is present at the beginning [3] and more than one member remains throughout.[3a] Failing other provision in the articles, in the case of a private company two members personally present, and in the case of any other company three members personally present,[4] constitute a quorum.[5] But the articles may provide that presence by proxy suffices [6]: thus Table A, Part II,[7] article 4, provides that two members present in person or by proxy suffice. For a meeting in the true sense it cannot be validly provided that one member shall constitute a quorum,[8] but the court or the Board of Trade can so declare in the case of a meeting convened by the court [9] or the Board.[10]

Table A further provides [11] that if within half an hour after the time appointed for the meeting a quorum is not present, the meeting, if convened upon the requisition of members, shall be dissolved, and that in every other case it shall stand adjourned for a week when the members [12] actually present shall constitute a quorum.

Chairman

The next step is to provide a chairman to preside over the meeting. Who he shall be again depends on the company's regulations and, if they are silent, the members present may themselves choose.[13] Table A [14] provides that the chairman of the board [15] if present and willing, whom failing one of the directors, whom failing anyone selected by the members present, shall take the chair.

The position is an important and onerous one, for the chairman will be in charge of the meeting and will be responsible for ensuring

---

[2] There seems to be no English authority. In America (where the question is of greater moment because of their practice of requiring large quorums) the decisions are divided but it is generally conceded that the better view is that a quorum need not be present throughout: *Ballantine on Corporations*, 395.

[3] *Re Hartley Baird Ltd.* [1955] Ch. 143.

[3a] *Re London Flats Ltd.* [1969] 1 W.L.R. 711.

[4] The Jenkins Committee recommended that two members personally present should suffice: Cmnd. 1749, para. 458. This was apparently the common law rule: *Sharp* v. *Dawes* (1876) 2 Q.B.D. 26, C.A.

[5] s. 134 (c). It has been held in Scotland that a member present in two capacities (as individual member and as trustee) counts as two members personally present: *Neil M'Leod & Sons Ltd.*, 1967 S.C. 16. *Sed quaere*.

[6] "Present," prima facie, means present in person and presence by proxy will not suffice uness the articles otherwise provide: *M. Harris Ltd.*, 1956 S.C. 207 (Sc.).

[7] *i.e.*, Table A for a private company.

[8] Cohen Report, para. 129. *Re Sanitary Carbon Co.* [1877] W.N. 223, but *cf. East* v. *Bennett Bros.* [1911] 1 Ch. 163, where one member with all the shares of a class was held to constitute a quorum for a " meeting " of that class: *supra*, p. 476.

[9] s. 135.

[10] s. 131 (2).

[11] Art. 54.

[12] *Quaere* if one member will then suffice. It is sometimes argued that one will do, since under the Interpretation Act the plural includes the singular. But *semble* this. is a case where the context otherwise requires.

[13] s. 134 (d), re-enacting the common law rule.

[14] Arts. 55–56.

[15] The board elect a chairman under art. 101.

that its business is properly conducted. This may entail taking snap decisions on points of order, motions, amendments and questions, often deliberately designed to harass him, and upon the correctness of his ruling the validity of the action may depend. He will probably require his legal adviser to be at his elbow, and this is one of the occasions when even the most cautious lawyer will have to give advice without an opportunity of referring to the authorities.[16] Good chairmen are as rare as good statesmen—and almost as valuable, for whether the meeting will be long drawn out and inconclusive, or short and decisive, depends upon them.

Resolutions

The 1948 Act contemplates three types of resolutions—Ordinary, Extraordinary and Special.[17] An ordinary resolution is one passed by a simple majority of those voting, and is used for all matters not requiring an extraordinary or special resolution under the Act or the articles. An extraordinary resolution is one passed by a three-fourths majority but no special period of notice is needed.[18] Under the Act an extraordinary resolution is required only for certain matters connected with winding up,[19] but the articles may require one in other cases, and normally do so when class meetings are asked to agree to a modification of class rights.[20] A special resolution is also one passed by a three-fourths majority, but twenty-one days' notice must be given of the meeting at which it is to be proposed.[21] A special resolution is required before any important constitutional changes can be undertaken[22]; notably to alter the memorandum[23] (where that is permitted), to alter the articles,[24] or to reduce capital with the consent of the court.[25] In the case of both extraordinary and special resolutions the notice of the meeting must specify the intention to propose the resolution as an extraordinary or a special resolution, as the case may be.[26]

It will be observed that in all cases the appropriate majority is of the members entitled to vote, and actually voting either in person or

---

[16] He should appear to be sure of his ground even if he is not and pray that the rule in *Foss* v. *Harbottle* (*infra*, Chap. 25, p. 581 *et seq.*) will make it difficult for any of his rulings to be effectively attacked.

[17] As already emphasised, these distinctions have no relation to the distinction between ordinary and extraordinary meetings.

[18] s. 141 (1).

[19] ss. 278, 303, 306 and 341. The Jenkins Committee recommended its abolition and replacement by a special resolution: Cmnd. 1749, para. 461.

[20] Table A, art. 4.

[21] s. 141 (2).

[22] See (in addition to the sections quoted in the three following footnotes), ss. 60, 65, 165, 203, 204, 222, 278 and 287.

[23] ss. 5, 18 and 23.

[24] s. 10.

[25] s. 66.

[26] s. 141. The formalities for special resolutions were radically changed by the 1929 Act. Until then the resolution had to be passed by a three-fourths majority at one meeting and subsequently confirmed by a simple majority at a second meeting.

by proxy where proxy voting is allowed.[27] This may, and normally will, be much less than a majority of the total membership, and may even be less than a majority of the members present at the meeting, for those who refrain from voting are ignored.[28] To take an extreme case: A meeting of a company with 500,000 preference shares without voting rights, and 500,000 ordinary shares each with one vote, is attended only by five ordinary shareholders, four with one share each and one with a hundred shares. If then a resolution is voted for by three of the holders of one share and against by the fourth shareholder with one share, the holder of the hundred shares abstaining, the resolution will have been duly carried even if it is an extraordinary or special resolution, notwithstanding that only three out of a total of one million shares, three out of five hundred thousand total votes and three out of one hundred and four votes represented at the meeting, have actually been polled in its favour! As we shall see later,[29] the procedure of voting on a show of hands, unless a poll is effectively demanded, may produce even greater anomalies.[29a]

Amendments

After the resolution has been proposed (and normally seconded, although this is not strictly necessary unless required by the regulations) an amendment to it may be moved, and one of the chairman's most difficult tasks may be to decide whether the motion to amend should be allowed or not. The general principle is that amendments are permissible only if they are within the scope of the notice. Clearly, therefore, far greater scope is allowed if the amendment is to a resolution not detailed in the notice but merely included under ordinary business. If, however, the resolution is " special business," the opportunities for valid amendment are far less, particularly if the terms of the resolution have been set out *in extenso* in the notice. Indeed, it is often suggested that no amendment is permissible to an extraordinary or special resolution since the Act [30] specifically requires " notice specifying the intention to propose *the* resolution." [31] This, however, may be too strict an interpretation; until the 1908 Act, amendments to special resolutions were certainly permissible.[32] It is therefore submitted that they are still allowed within the narrow limits indicated below, and that it is advisable to frame the notice so that it indicates the possibility of amendments.[33]

---

[27] s. 141.   [28] *Cf.* s. 141 (4).

[29] *Infra*, pp. 492, 493.

[29a] So may multiple votes attached to the shares of a particular holder: *Bushell* v. *Faith* [1969] 2 W.L.R. 1067, C.A.

[30] s. 141.

[31] See *MacConnell* v. *Prill & Co.* [1916] 2 Ch. 57.

[32] *Torbock* v. *Lord Westbury* [1902] 2 Ch. 871. *Cf. Henderson* v. *Bank of Australasia* (1890) 45 Ch.D. 330, C.A., where a special resolution was held to be ineffective because of the chairman's refusal to allow an amendment to be moved. But at the second confirmatory meeting, required prior to 1929, no amendments were permissible: *Wall* v. *London & Northern Assets Corpn.* [1898] 2 Ch. 469, C.A.

[33] *i.e.,* " To consider and if thought fit pass with or without modifications. . . ."

It has already been suggested [34] that the test of the adequacy of the notice is whether the business is specified in sufficient detail to enable members to decide whether they should attend. And, subject to the doubt as regards extraordinary and special resolutions, the test of validity of an amendment appears to be similar, namely, would the amendment so alter the nature of the business stated as to cause any shareholder who had stayed away reasonably to wish he had not? Thus, if the notice specified consideration of a resolution to increase the directors' remuneration by £10,000, an amendment to reduce this to £5,000 would clearly be valid, since a member who was prepared to swallow a camel could scarcely strain at a gnat. On the other hand, an amendment to increase it to £20,000 would undoubtedly be invalid, since many members might have stayed away because they regarded £10,000 as not unreasonable, but might have dissented violently from a resolution granting the larger sum.[35]

When a proper amendment is moved the correct procedure is to debate and vote on the amendment [36] before considering the substantive resolution. If the amendment is duly carried consideration then proceeds on the resolution as amended, which is finally put to the meeting; if the amendment is lost, the resolution is considered in its original form.

Voting

Unless the company's regulations otherwise provide, voting is in the first instance on a show of hands, *i.e.*, those present indicate their views by raising their hands. Recognising the limitations of human anatomy, regulations generally provide for one vote only per person on a show of hands, irrespective of the number of shares held.[37] Moreover, there is no statutory obligation to allow proxy votes on a show of hands and it is not usual to do so.[38] For both these reasons the result on a show of hands may give a very imperfect picture of the true opinion of the meeting. If the resolution is uncontroversial a vote by show of hands will probably suffice and will save time and trouble, and on such matters the chairman's statement that the resolution is carried will normally be undisputed.[39] But on any disputed question a poll will almost certainly

---

[34] *Supra*, p. 480.

[35] In the *Gordon Hotels* case (not reported on this point, but see (1953) 97 S.J. 465) it was apparently held that if notice had been given of a resolution to elect a number of directors, an amendment could not be moved to resolve on each separately. Hence the resolution was totally ineffective for it could not be passed in its original form (see s. 183) nor could the defect be cured by amendment. *Sed quaere.*

[36] And, strictly, the last amendment of an amendment is put first and so on back to the original motion; but the chairman will be well advised to seek to avoid amendments of amendments (the same result can generally be accomplished in a less confusing way).

[37] In the absence of express provision (*e.g.*, C.C.A. 1845, ss. 75–76) this will apparently be implied: *Ernest* v. *Loma Gold Mines* [1897] 1 Ch. 1, C.A.

[38] Unless the proxy holders are physically segregated from the members personally present it may, in a well-attended meeting, be difficult to enforce this in practice.

[39] s. 141 (3) provides, in the case of special and extraordinary resolutions, that the chairman's declaration shall be conclusive. Table A, art. 58, provides generally that

be demanded [40] by a member, or by the chairman if a resolution proposed by the board has been defeated on a show of hands (as may well
be the case since it is probably only the opposition which will have
attended in person in any strength). It is therefore of considerable
importance to decide whether such a demand is effective.

The regulations of companies invariably direct that a demand by the
chairman shall be effective.[41] This again strengthens the position of
the board, for they run no risk of not being able to use their full voting
power. Further, the Act [42] provides that the articles must not exclude
the right to demand a poll on any question, other than the election of a
chairman or the adjournment of the meeting, nor must it make ineffective
a demand by not less than five members having a right to vote, or by
members representing not less than one-tenth of the total voting rights [43]
or holding shares having a right to vote on which a sum has been paid
up equal to not less than one-tenth of the total sum paid up on all the
shares conferring that right. Further, a proxy may demand or join in
demanding a poll. This provision, therefore, makes it impossible for the
articles to hamstring a sizeable opposition by depriving them of their
opportunity to exercise their full voting strength. Nevertheless, it may
still mean that the members who can outvote all the others will (if less
than five) never have an opportunity of doing so because they cannot
effectively demand a poll. If, in the example given at p. 491, above,
the four holders with one share each had voted in favour and the holder
of 100 shares had voted against, the special resolution would have been
validly passed on a show of hands and the unfortunate dissentient would
have had no right (unless the articles were more liberal than Table A)
to demand a poll so as to reverse this decision. The moral is that a
member should, to be absolutely safe, always split his holdings among
five nominees.[44] It is, however, the duty of the chairman to exercise
his right to demand a poll so that effect is given to the real sense of the

the chairman's decision when recorded in the minutes shall be conclusive: see
Kerr v. *Mottram Ltd.* [1940] Ch. 657, *supra,* Chap. 8, p. 166.

[40] It is a question of construction of the relevant article whether a poll can be
demanded before there has been a vote on a show of hands: *Carruth* v. *I.C.I.*
[1937] A.C. 707, H.L. at pp. 754–755; *Holmes* v. *Keyes* [1959] Ch. 199, C.A.

[41] Table A, art. 58.

[42] s. 137. *Cf.* C.C.A. 1845, s. 80. In the absence of anything in the regulations any
member may demand a poll (*R.* v. *Wimbledon Local Board* (1882) 8 Q.B.D. 459,
C.A.), and, of course, the articles may be more generous than s. 137: see Table A,
art. 58.

[43] This is thought to be the effect of the wording of s. 137 (1) (*b*) (ii) (*cf.* ss. 132 (1)
and 140 (2) (*a*)), but it is susceptible of the interpretation that the demand must be by
one-tenth of the total voting rights of members *present* (for unless present in person
or by proxy a member has no right to vote at that meeting).

[44] It will be no use appointing five different proxies, for these will all represent one
member and only be counted as one for the purpose of demanding a poll. Indeed,
in the particular example quoted, the only result would be that the member would
have disfranchised himself completely since his vote would not be counted at all on
the show of hands!

meeting, and if he realised what the position was it seems that he would be legally bound to direct a poll to be taken.[45]

If a poll is effectively demanded it is for the chairman to decide when and where it shall be taken. The usual course is to direct it to be taken immediately and to postpone the meeting to enable the result to be declared later. Alternatively he may, unless the regulations direct otherwise,[46] direct the poll to be taken on a later date. Whichever course is adopted the resolution will not be deemed to have been passed until the result of the poll is declared and the meeting will be regarded as having continued until then.[47] If the poll is postponed members may vote although not present on the original occasion (for there is no rule that they have to be present throughout), but if the articles provide that proxies shall be lodged forty-eight hours before a meeting or adjourned meeting, it will not be possible to lodge further proxies prior to the poll.[48] The normal method of taking a poll is for the members present in person or by proxy to sign lists or slips indicating whether they vote for or against and the number of votes that they are polling.[49] The number of votes to which each will be entitled depends, of course, on the regulations, but usually it will be one per share.[50] Members are not bound to exercise all their votes; nor need they use them all in the same way.[51] This latter provision is intended for the benefit of the nominee companies and proxy holders, who are thus enabled to give effect to the instructions of their various principals.

Clearly the number of votes cast will require careful checking to ensure that members have not purported to exercise more votes than they in fact have; hence the practice of adjourning to declare the result at a future date.[52] For this purpose it is usual for each side to appoint scrutineers, who agree the result and report to the chairman.

It should be noted that, unless the articles specifically authorise it (which is unusual[53]), voting by postal ballot is not permitted.[54] This may well be thought strange, for clearly such a general referendum is by

---

[45] *Second Consolidated Trust* v. *Ceylon Amalgamated Estates* [1943] 2 All E.R. 567 (in this case the chairman himself held proxies which would have defeated the resolution passed on a show of hands and no quorum was present without counting the proxies).

[46] Table A directs an immediate poll in the case of resolutions for the election of chairmen or an adjournment but leaves it to the chairman in other cases (art. 61).

[47] *Holmes* v. *Keyes* [1959] Ch. 199, C.A.

[48] *Shaw* v. *Tati Concessions Ltd.* [1913] 1 Ch. 292. But the articles may provide that proxies can be lodged up to 24 hours *before the poll*, as Table A, art. 69, now does. If an immediate poll is taken and the meeting is then postponed for a declaration. of the poll, the postponed assembly is not an adjourned meeting but a continuation of the original one so that, unless Table A, art. 69, applies, further proxies cannot be lodged for any business still outstanding: *Jackson* v. *Hamlyn* [1953] Ch. 577 (which arose out of one of the many disputes relating to Gordon Hotels Ltd.).

[49] Table A, art. 59, directs that it shall be taken in such manner as the chairman directs.

[50] s. 134 (*e*).

[51] s. 138.

[52] Hence, also, the impossibility of a secret ballot.

[53] Except in the case of professional associations organised as guarantee companies.

[54] *McMillan* v. *Le Roi Mining Co.* [1906] 1 Ch. 331.

far the best method of obtaining the views of the members as a whole. But the fiction is preserved that the result is determined after oral discussion at a meeting and by those present thereat, although everyone knows that personal attendance is the exception rather than the rule, and that the result is normally determined by proxies lodged before the meeting is even held.[55]

Articles generally give the chairman a second or casting vote in the event of equality.[56] But he has no such right at common law except that, if he has a vote as a member which he has not previously exercised, he may do so to resolve the deadlock.[57]

Adjournments

It may be necessary to adjourn the meeting; for example, because time does not permit its business to be concluded in one day or because a quorum was not present. It is usual for the regulations to provide that in the latter event it shall automatically stand adjourned to the same time and place in the following week, when any members present shall be a quorum.[58] An adjourned meeting is deemed to be a resumption of the original meeting and no further notice is needed unless the regulations otherwise provide,[59] and no business can be transacted except that left over. But the Act now provides that resolutions passed at an adjourned meeting shall be treated as having been passed on the date on which they were in fact passed and not on the date of the original meeting,[60] and the articles cannot forbid the lodging of further proxies up to forty-eight hours before the adjourned meeting.[61]

The regulations normally deal specifically with the question of adjournment. If they are silent it is not clear whether it rests with the meeting or with the chairman to resolve on an adjournment, but the latter cannot capriciously at his own will and pleasure adjourn leaving business uncompleted, and if he purports to do so the meeting may elect another chairman and continue.[62]

Class meetings

In addition to general meetings it may be necessary to convene meetings of separate classes of members or debentureholders (for example,

---

[55] As has been well said in an American case (*Berendt* v. *Bethlehem Steel Corpn.* (1931) 154 Atl. 321 at p. 322) statements made at the meeting to the audience of proxy-holders fall " upon ears not allowed to hear and minds not permitted to judge; upon automatons whose principals are uninformed of their own injury."

[56] Table A, art. 60. *Cf.* C.C.A. 1845, s. 76.

[57] *Nell* v. *Longbottom* [1894] 1 Q.B. 767 at p. 771.

[58] Table A, art. 54. Unless the meeting is requisitioned, when it is dissolved: *ibid.*

[59] *Wills* v. *Murray* (1850) 4 Exch. 843. Table A, art. 57, requires notice if the adjournment is for more than 30 days.

[60] s. 144. This may be important if the resolutions need to be filed within 15 days: see *infra*, p. 498.

[61] s. 136 (3). But note that a postponement to another day may not be regarded as an adjournment: see note 48, *supra*.

[62] *National Dwellings Society* v. *Sykes* [1894] 3 Ch. 159; *John* v. *Rees* [1969] 2 All E.R. 274; *cf. R.* v. *D'Oyly* (1840) 12 Ad. & E. 139.

to consider variations of rights), or of creditors (for example, in connection with a reconstruction or in a winding up). Here again, the rules to be observed will depend on the particular regulations construed in the light of the general law relating to meetings. Statute law is generally silent, but s. 136 (relating to proxies), s. 139 (relating to representation of corporations), and s. 144 (relating to resolutions passed at an adjourned meeting) of the 1948 Act are expressed to cover also meetings of any class of members (but not debentureholders). Moreover, Table A, article 4, provides that to any separate meeting of a class of shareholders all the provisions of the Table relating to general meetings shall apply, subject to an increase in the quorum and a reduction in the number who can demand a poll. In practice, very similar arrangements are incorporated in debentures or debenture trust deeds to regulate the conduct of meetings of debentureholders and the Jenkins Committee recommended that the appropriate sections of the Act should be extended to such meetings.[63]

At class meetings all members other than those of the class ought to be excluded, but if for convenience a joint meeting is held of the company and all separate classes, followed by separate polls, the court will not interfere if no objection has been taken by anyone present.[64]

Written resolutions

Despite the normal rule that resolutions have to be passed at meetings, it has, as we have seen,[65] become common practice to insert in the articles of a private company a provision that a written resolution signed by all the members entitled to vote shall be as valid and effective as if it had been passed at a general meeting, and such a provision is now included in Table A, Part II.[66]

It is by no means clear that this provision can dispense with the need for a meeting in the case of resolutions which the Act provides shall be passed at a general meeting, such as special and extraordinary resolutions. It was generally thought that written resolutions could not be made effective in such circumstances,[67] and the usual practice was expressly to exclude special and extraordinary resolutions from the ambit of the article. But the new Table A leaves the matter uncertain, since it merely provides that the clause is " subject to the provisions of the Act," which is regrettably vague. Section 143 of the Act seems to imply that written resolutions will be effective, since it provides for the registration of " resolutions which have been agreed to by all the members . . . but which, if not so agreed to would not have been

63 Cmnd. 1749, para. 297.
64 *Carruth* v. *I.C.I.* [1937] A.C. 707, H.L.
65 *Supra*, Chap. 10, p. 210.
66 Art. 5. *Cf.* the general regulation relating to directors' resolutions: Table A, Part 1, art. 106.
67 See Buckley, *Companies Act*, 12th ed., p. 337.

effective for their purpose unless . . . they had been passed as special resolutions or as extraordinary resolutions." [68] It is therefore submitted that there are no grounds for drawing a distinction between one type of resolution and another, and that every consideration of convenience and justice is to the contrary. The old rule expressed in *Re George Newman*,[69] that individual consents given separately cannot bind the company, may well have been a logical conclusion from the corporate-entity principle, but that rule has now been departed from with the tacit acquiescence of the legislature and there seem to be no good grounds for the retention of relics of it. Minorities are sufficiently protected by the rule requiring unanimity.

It may well be, however, that the powers conferred by section 61 to alter the share capital cannot be exercised by a written resolution. Subsection (2) of that section provides categorically that "the powers conferred by this section must be exercised by the company in general meeting." This wording seems considerably more peremptory than the references to general meetings in the definitions of special and extra-ordinary resolutions in section 141 and may be what the draftsman of Table A had in mind when he added the qualification "subject to the provisions of this Act." On the other hand, it is difficult to see why these powers should be treated exceptionally.

The Jenkins Committee recommended that the uncertainty should be cured by an express provision that the written resolution should be equivalent to a resolution duly passed at a general meeting, and clearl'' intended that this should cover resolutions under section 61.[70]

Registration of resolutions

Normally, resolutions are a matter of purely domestic concern—part of the company's indoor management. The only statutory requirement is the provision that minutes shall be recorded in a book kept for that purpose.[71] Minutes, if purporting to be signed by the chairman of the meeting or the next succeeding meeting, are evidence (but, of course, not conclusive evidence [72]) of the proceedings,[73] and the meeting is presumed to have been duly held, convened, and regularly conducted.[74] Such minutes are open for inspection by members but not by others.[75]

Certain resolutions, on the other hand, are clearly of concern to third parties, and copies [76] of these have to be filed with the Registrar

---

[68] s. 143 (4) (c).
[69] [1895] 1 Ch. 674. Discussed *supra*, Chap. 10, pp. 208–210.
[70] Cmnd. 1749, para. 460.
[71] s. 145 (1). Loose-leaf books are now permissible providing adequate precautions are taken against falsification: s. 436.
[72] But the articles may so provide; see Table A, art. 58, and *Kerr* v. *Mottram Ltd.* [1940] Ch. 657 (*supra*, Chap. 8, p. 166, n. 41) for an even wider article.
[73] s. 145 (2).
[74] s. 145 (3).
[75] s. 146.
[76] These no longer have to be printed so long as they are in a form approved by the Registrar: Companies Act 1967, s. 51.

within fifteen days of their passing and embodied with all copies of the articles issued after their passing.[77] This requirement applies to extraordinary and special resolutions and to all resolutions agreed to by all the members but which would otherwise have had to be passed as extraordinary or special resolutions, to resolutions of class meetings, and to resolutions for voluntary winding up.[78] All these, it will be appreciated, may well affect third parties, and this is especially so in the case of special resolutions changing the company's constitution by varying the articles. They are, therefore, taken outside the bounds of indoor management and anyone dealing with the company will be deemed to have notice of them when registered, and cannot assume that a needful resolution of one of the prescribed classes has been duly passed if a copy has not been filed.[79]

Privilege and the Press

Since members and their directors clearly have a common interest in matters relating to the company's affairs and a common duty to disclose information, a company meeting is a privileged occasion and statements there made will not be actionable as defamation in the absence of malice.[80] This common law privilege, however, does not extend to statements broadcast to the world at large, and hence newspaper reports relating to a company or its meetings are not generally privileged.[81] At common law the newspaper's only defence against a libel action, if the statements could not be justified, would be a plea of fair comment which could be sustained only if the matter was one of public interest. Nevertheless, as we saw in the previous chapter, Press publicity has become one of the most important factors in investor and creditor protection and it is clearly undesirable that the Press should be discouraged from commenting. Hence it is provided in the Defamation Act 1952[82] that fair and accurate reports of general meetings of companies, other than private companies, are not actionable in the absence of malice, provided that the paper publishes any reasonable explanation or contradiction.

Although the Press still have no legal entitlement to attend company meetings, it has become the practice for public companies with quoted shares to invite reporters to attend, to circulate advance copies of the chairman's speech at the annual general meeting, and even to pay for

[77] s. 143.
[78] s. 143 (4). It also extends to agreements which unless approved unanimously would have required to be adopted in some special manner.
[79] See Chap. 8, p. 156, *supra*.
[80] *Longdon-Griffiths* v. *Smith* [1951] 1 K.B. 295. If a defamatory report is made by the directors, malice on the part of one of them will not destroy the privilege as regards the others: *ibid*. The presence of the Press does not destroy the privilege (*Pittard* v. *Oliver* [1891] 1 Q.B. 474) but may be evidence of malice on the part of those inviting the reporters. The same principles apply to circulars to the members: *Lawless* v. *Anglo-Egyptian Cotton Co.* (1869) L.R. 4 Q.B. 262; *Quartz Hill Consolidated Gold Mining Co.* v. *Beall* (1882) 20 Ch.D. 501, C.A.
[81] *Ponsford* v. *Financial Times* (1900) 16 T.L.R. 248.
[82] s. 7 and Sched., Pt. II.

publication of this and the reports and accounts.[83] Reporters can, however, legally be excluded, though they will probably contrive to secure attendance (perhaps as members' proxies) if they really wish to.[84]

It will be noted that the provisions of the Defamation Act apply only to reports of general meetings and have no application to private companies. Outside the statutory protection the newspaper will have to rely on the defences of justification or fair comment. Clearly it may be difficult to establish that the affairs of a private company are a matter of public interest susceptible of the defence of fair comment. But this defence should be open where comment has been made on the proposals to be submitted to a future meeting of a public company or on the conduct of the board of such a company, and will clearly apply to prospectuses published in the Press. Moreover, it is submitted that this defence would be available in the case of comment on any document filed at the Companies' Registry and there open for public inspection; to this extent it is difficult to see how even a private company can legally suppress fair comment on its business.

Conclusions

General meetings are intended to be the means whereby the members exercise control over the management. But despite the undoubted improvements introduced by the 1948 Act it cannot be said that they are an effective means. In part this is the members' own fault, for most of them are too apathetic to exert themselves to exercise such powers as the law affords them. And even when some disaster jerks them out of their apathy they all too often follow like sheep the course that the management recommend. More often than not they may be right to do so. The complications of a modern commercial enterprise make it virtually essential that matters should be left to experts, and an expert managerial class has grown up to meet this need and has become separated from the so-called proprietors. The latter are merely suppliers of capital which they have entrusted to others, whom they perforce must trust. The danger is that what is best for the managers may not necessarily be best for the individual proprietors, and, in the resulting conflict of interests, which is to prevail? The law has answered this question by saying that it is the company as a whole whose interests shall be paramount, and that, in general, the interest of the majority of the members should be taken to be that of the company. But what the law says, and what in fact occurs, are very different things. In practice the company may be controlled by the majority, but the majority

---

[83] Clearly those responsible for the circulation to the Press could not deny that the matter was of public interest, but others could.

[84] Alternatively they can extract the information from one of the members who attended. It is obviously impossible to keep confidential information revealed to a general meeting of a public company and this may be a legitimate embarrassment to the board.

are in turn controlled by the management which can nearly always persuade the majority to follow their lead unless the majority are well informed, closely knit, and well organised.

The proxy-voting system attempts to restore the balance of power but in fact tilts it still further in favour of the management, thanks to the latter's control of the proxy-voting machinery. Decisions which, in theory, are taken at meetings after discussion, are in practice taken before the meeting is even held, so that it becomes a solemn farce. The real battle, if it takes place at all, occurs in the columns of the financial Press and in rival circulars, of which the oral debate is but a hollow echo. And in this battle of wits all the dice are loaded in favour of the management. It may be that this is desirable; that management which supplies the brains and initiative should prevail, and that in so far as its power needs curtailing it should be in favour of the public as a whole and of the employees, rather than in favour of a small section of the community who happen to have invested in the company—after all, we do not give a man more votes in parliamentary elections because he happens to have invested in government securities.

This, however, is a political rather than a legal question. Accepting that members ought to have *de facto* as well as *de jure* control, the question for the lawyer is how this might be achieved. The answer, it is submitted, is to provide that certain important decisions (perhaps, at any rate as a start, those that require a special or extraordinary resolution and resolutions requiring special notice) should only be taken as a result of a postal ballot held after the meeting. If this were done members would not be able to vote until they had an opportunity of hearing both sides of the argument. And meetings would again become live debates upon the result of which the ballot might depend. It is not suggested that meetings would necessarily be better attended than they are at present, but, in the case of the big public companies, they would be fully reported and commented on by the Press so that the discussion would become known to shareholders sufficiently interested to follow it. The present law, by clinging to the shadow of decision at meetings, has in fact destroyed the substance of meetings. This substance, it is submitted, can only be restored by making meetings a preliminary to voting but not the occasion of voting.[85]

---

[85] For the solution adopted in the U.S.A. under regulations of the Securities and Exchange Commission, see Loss, *Securities Regulation* (2nd ed.), pp. 857–1036, and Aranow & Einhorn, *Proxy Contests for Corporate Control* (2nd ed.), Pt. II. Solicitation of proxies for companies whose shares are listed on a stock exchange may not take place until a proxy statement (giving a great deal of detail about the company and those soliciting the proxies) has been filed with the Commission and sent to all shareholders who are to be circularised. And all campaign material has to be filed with the Commission and cleared by it before it is used.

CHAPTER 22

LIMITATIONS ON THE POWER OF THE GENERAL MEETING

THE primary and residual organ of the company is the general meeting and normally anything resolved upon by a bare majority of those voting at the meeting binds the company and all the members of it. All investors and creditors are subject to the risk of action being taken at a general meeting which will affect their position.

ENTRENCHED RIGHTS

To this general principle there are certain obvious exceptions, for the general law or the company's constitution may entrench certain rights by providing that they shall only be alterable with additional formalities if at all. Thus a statutory company cannot itself alter its statute or a chartered corporation its charter. Similarly a registered company could not originally alter its memorandum and, although it can now do so, except as regards its domicile, additional safeguards are provided.[1] Even as regards alteration of the articles a special, as opposed to an ordinary, resolution is required before the alteration is effective[2]; that is to say, twenty-one days' notice has to be given of the intention to propose the resolution which must then be passed by a three-fourths majority of those voting.[3] Furthermore, it is expressly stated that the power to alter the articles is subject to the conditions of the memorandum.[4] Hence if the alteration of the articles produces a conflict with the memorandum the latter will prevail and the alteration will be ineffective to the extent of the conflict.[5] But the importance of this is minimised because, as we have seen,[6] section 23 now permits provisions in the memorandum to be altered if they could lawfully have been included in the articles rather than the memorandum. Accordingly, all that will normally be necessary is for the company to ensure that it alters the provisions in the memorandum at the same time. It is possible, however, for rights to be effectively entrenched by inserting them in the memorandum and expressly providing that they shall be unalterable; if this is done the power given by section 23 does not

---

[1] See Chap. 5, pp. 99–101, *supra*.
[2] Companies Act 1948, s. 10.
[3] s. 141, *supra*, p. 490. See *Bushell* v. *Faith* [1969] 2 W.L.R. 1067, 1072, C.A.
[4] s. 10 (1).
[5] *Guinness* v. *Land Corpn. of Ireland* (1882) 22 Ch.D. 349, C.A.; *Ashbury* v. *Watson* (1885) 30 Ch.D. 376, C.A.; *Re Duncan Gilmour & Co.* [1952] 2 All E.R. 871.
[6] *Supra*, Chap. 5, p. 101.

apply.[7] Nor does it authorise any " variation or abrogation of the special rights of any class of members "[7]—a limitation to which we shall revert later.[8]

Nor is a member bound by any alteration of the memorandum or articles after the date on which he became a member, if and so far as the alteration requires him to take more shares or increases his liability on those he holds.[9] Again, when an application is made under section 210, considered in detail later,[10] the court may alter the company's memorandum and articles and, unless the order otherwise provides, the company will then have no power to make any further alteration inconsistent with the order except with the court's consent.[11] And, of course, the company cannot effectively resolve upon any action which is inconsistent with the Act itself.[12] Apart from these express statutory limitations on the company's powers it is bound by the ordinary legal restraints. Hence a resolution will be ineffective if illegal or contrary to public policy.[13]

Interference with Contractual Rights [14]

Among the ordinary legal restraints by which the company is bound is that of sanctity of contract. If, therefore, the company has entered into contracts it will be liable if, at the behest of those in control, it breaks the contract,[15] and it cannot justify a breach by alleging that its constitution justified or required it so to act.[16] In considering how far this affords protection to investors it is necessary to deal separately with the position of debentureholders and shareholders.

1. Debentureholders' rights

So far as the debentureholder is concerned, the protection is substantial. Since the debenture constitutes a contract between the holder

---

7 s. 23 (2).

8 *Infra,* p. 507 *et seq.*

9 s. 22. On what is meant by an increase of liability, see a series of cases in New Zealand where it has caused difficulties to agricultural co-operatives: *MacDonald* v. *Normanby Co-op. Dairy Factory Co. Ltd.* [1923] N.Z.L.R. 122; *Shalfoon* v. *Cheddar Valley Co-op. Dairy Co. Ltd.* [1924] N.Z.L.R. 561, C.A.; and *Johnson* v. *Eltham Co-op. Dairy Co. Ltd.* [1931] N.Z.L.R. 216, C.A.

10 *Infra,* Chap. 25, pp. 598–604.

11 s. 210 (3).

12 s. 10, authorising alterations of the articles, is expressly stated to be " subject to the provisions of this Act." See *Re Peveril Gold Mines* [1898] 1 Ch. 122, C.A.; *Re Greene* [1949] Ch. 333.

13 *Pharmaceutical Society of G.B.* v. *Dickson* [1968] 3 W.L.R. 286, H.L.

14 See Rice: (1958) 22 Conv.(N.S.) 126 and 168, and Trebilcock: (1967) 31 Conv.(N.S.) 95.

15 It would be equally liable if it committed a tort but this is of little importance from the aspect of investor and creditor protection.

16 *Southern Foundries Ltd.* v. *Shirlaw* [1940] A.C. 701, H.L. Unless the provisions of the constitution are incorporated into the contract in which event a variation authorised by the constitution is not a breach: see *supra,* Chap. 7, pp. 134–136 and Chap. 12, pp. 261–265.

and the company he is immune from the power of those controlling the company; whatever they do cannot derogate from his contractual rights. Whether his immunity is complete depends, however, on what remedies are available to him in the event of breach. These, normally, will be entirely adequate, for he will be able to enforce his security by appointing a receiver and manager, thus assuming control of the company. If, however, the debenture is unsecured it becomes of some importance to ascertain whether the holder can restrain the breach by injunction or whether he is limited to a claim for payment or damages.

The answer to this question is not entirely clear. To take a concrete example: Suppose the naked debenture contains a clause entitling the holder to appoint a director and that this right is also protected by a provision in the articles. Can the holder restrain by injunction the company from altering its articles by special resolution removing this protection? This question never seems to have arisen in connection with a debenture, but it has in connection with agreements with shareholders and ordinary creditors. In *Punt* v. *Symons & Co.*[17] Byrne J. held that an injunction could not normally be granted because the company had a statutory right to alter its articles[18] and could not contract out of it.[19] On the other hand the Court of Appeal held in *Baily* v. *British Equitable Assurance Co.*[20] that a company could be restrained from adopting articles which infringed the profit-sharing rights of its policy-holders. This decision, was, however, reversed by the House of Lords,[21] but only on the ground that the terms of the articles, and consequently the implied power to alter them by special resolution, were incorporated into the contract in that case. Hence, in *British Murac Syndicate* v. *Alperton Rubber Co.*[22] Sargant J. granted an injunction restraining an alteration in breach of a contract. However, in *Southern Foundries Ltd.* v. *Shirlaw*, Lord Porter[23] said:

> " A company cannot be precluded from altering its articles thereby giving itself power to act upon the provisions of the altered articles—but so to act may nevertheless be a breach of contract if it is contrary to a stipulation in a contract validly made before the alteration. Nor can an injunction be granted to prevent the adoption of the new articles, and in that sense they are binding on all and sundry, but for the company to act upon them will none-

17 [1903] 2 Ch. 506.
18 See now Companies Act 1948, s. 10.
19 In fact, however, he granted an injunction on the ground that the resolution had been passed only as a result of an improper issue of new shares.
20 [1904] 1 Ch. 374, C.A.
21 *Sub nom. British Equitable Assce. Co.* v. *Baily* [1906] A.C. 35.
22 [1915] 2 Ch. 186; followed in Australia in *Fischer* v. *Easthaven Ltd.* [1964] N.S.W.R. 261.
23 [1940] A.C. at pp. 740–741. In this case the new articles entitled the holding company to dismiss directors of the subsidiary, a power which they exercised in breach of an agreement between the subsidiary and its managing director.

theless render it liable in damages if such action is contrary to the previous engagements of the company."

This dictum, for it was no more (an injunction had not been claimed in that case), states categorically that an injunction cannot be granted to restrain the alteration of the articles and clearly implies that the company equally cannot be restrained from acting on the articles as altered. Although it seems to be generally accepted that this is the better view, the second conclusion does not necessarily follow from the first. Since the company has a statutory power to alter its articles it seems logical to hold that it cannot effectively contract out of this power, but it is less easy to see why it should not be restrained from acting on the altered article if by so doing it breaks its contracts. If, as is clear, it cannot justify a breach by pleading the new article, it is submitted that the other party should have the normal remedies of a contracting party, and that, if damages are not an adequate remedy, the court should have a discretion to grant either an injunction or specific performance if these are appropriate remedies. Surely it would not be in any way inconsistent with any statute if a company was restrained from exercising a power in the articles to appoint a managing director in breach of a negative covenant in a debenture that no managing director should be appointed without the consent of the debentureholder? And why should a company be able to avoid an action for specific performance of an agreement for the sale of land by altering its articles to forbid any disposition without, say, the unanimous consent of its members?

Subject, however, to these doubts, which in the case of most debentures are purely academic, it is clear that the investor holding debentures can, by his contract secure adequate protection against those controlling the *company*. But if there is a series of debentures or an issue of debenture stock with the usual provisions for meetings of the holders, he may find himself subjected to a measure of control from those who hold a sufficiently large block to carry a resolution at a meeting, and these may in fact be identical with or allied to those who are in control of the company.

In practice, however, control over a series of debentures can never be as effective as control over the company itself. For one thing, there will almost certainly be trustees whose job it will be to convene the meeting. Since, in practice, the trustees will be a trust corporation of high repute and of complete independence,[24] the circular accompanying the notice of the meeting is likely to be more objective than one emanating from the company's management. For another, if something has occurred to render the security enforceable or in jeopardy, any single

---

[24] There is, of course, a risk that the trustees will not be completely independent: *cf. Re Dorman Long & Co.* [1934] Ch. 635, where the trustees were also the company's bankers and creditors. But, since that case, trust corporations have generally taken care not to allow themselves to be placed in a position where their duties and their interests conflict.

debentureholder, suing on behalf of himself and all other holders and making the company and the trustees defendants, will be permitted to start a debentureholder's action and to secure the appointment of a receiver and manager. In such circumstances the court does not insist on the views of the majority of the debentureholders being ascertained.[25] Hence the principle of majority rule is less important and the opportunities for exercising control are less real, as in consequence are the possibilities of oppression. Where, in practice, the debentureholders are most vulnerable is when a scheme of arrangement is put forward in which they are asked to concur.[26] If the scheme is put forward under section 206 of the Companies Act (which is considered in more detail in Chapter 26), the decision of the majority in number and three-fourths in value may bind the whole. Although the scheme is subject to the approval of the court, both the court and the debentureholders are to some extent in the hands of the company's management, which alone will be fully seised of all the relevant information and which will have put forward the scheme after setting the stage for it.[27] The position is even more serious where advantage is taken of an express clause in the debenture trust deed enabling a specified majority to bind the whole in agreeing to a modification of rights, for then the sanction of the court is not needed.[28] A dissentient seems to have only two remedies open to him; if the security has already become enforceable he can start a debentureholders' action before the meeting is held to approve the scheme. This, however, is unlikely to avail him, for the court will probably stay the action pending the outcome of the meeting.[29] Or he can seek to invoke the " fraud-on-the-minority " principle,[30] but this, as we shall see, is likely to prove a broken reed unless he can show that there was inadequate disclosure. He cannot complain under section 210 on the ground that he is being " oppressed " because this section applies to oppression of members only.

Still, although the individual debentureholder may sometimes be in a weak position, there is no doubt that his contractual rights afford him a

[25] Unless the debentures provide that no action is to be taken without the consent of a majority: see *Pethybridge* v. *Unibifocal Co. Ltd.* [1918] W.N. 278.

[26] It is customary for such schemes to be negotiated between the directors, the trustees and a committee representing the debentureholders. To what extent the existence of a committee is a protection to the individual holder is doubtful: in practice the representatives tend to be those of larger holders who may often be closely allied to the management.

[27] For a good example of debentureholders falling for a scheme which was clearly detrimental to their interests, see *Re Dorman Long & Co.*, *supra*, in which they ultimately succeeded in extricating themselves but only as a result of tireless activity by a small minority. There are innumerable unreported examples where equally detrimental schemes have gone through.

[28] Companies Act 1948, s. 72 (*infra*), does not apply.

[29] Even if a receiver has been appointed in the debentureholders' action, the powers of the meeting will not cease, but the court's approval to the scheme will then be needed: *Re Buenos Aires Tramways* (1920) 89 L.J.Ch. 597.

[30] Chap. 24, *infra*.

considerable measure of protection. The position of a shareholder, to which we now turn, is very different.

2. Shareholders' rights

As we have already seen,[31] shares are regarded as items of property based primarily on a contract between the company and the holder, the terms of the contract normally being in the company's constitution. On the face of it, therefore, the shareholder, equally with the debenture-holder, is protected because he has inviolable contractual rights, and this may be the position in the case of chartered or statutory companies.[32] But, as we have also seen, the contract, in so far as it is dependent on the articles of a registered company, is of a curious type because it is variable at the option of one party which can always alter the original terms of the contract by special resolution. If the company seeks to disregard its contract without having validly varied it, then the individual shareholder can restrain the company from doing so. But if those in control are able to secure the passing of a special resolution, the shareholder is powerless. His only possible remedy would be to obtain an injunction restraining the alteration, but this remedy is not available to him for, as we have seen, the company cannot contract out of its statutory power to alter the articles and this applies *a fortiori* where the only contract is the articles themselves. Thus, in the leading case of *Allen* v. *Gold Reefs of W. Africa*[33] it was held that a company could validly alter its articles so as to impose a lien on fully paid shares even in respect of debts already contracted.[34]

What, then, are the limitations on the powers of those in control to derogate from the shareholder's " contractual " rights in this way?

(a) *Shares all of one class*

Assuming that the shares are all of one class the only limitations are those already adverted to,[35] which restrict the extent to which a company can effectually alter its memorandum or articles. Hence a member cannot be compelled to take up more shares or have his liability increased,[36] and if his rights are embodied in the memorandum they can only be altered subject to compliance with section 23, and not altered at

---

[31] *Supra*, Chap. 16.

[32] Subject to the possibility of a scheme of arrangement under ss. 206 and 306 of the Companies Act 1948, which apply to all companies which can be wound up under the Act (*infra*, Chap. 26), and subject, of course, to any provisions for variation in the special Act or charter.

[33] [1900] 1 Ch. 656, C.A.

[34] It is sometimes said that this case shows that the alteration can be made retrospective. This, however, is misleading. It can, as in the instant case, affect existing rights, but the judgments make it clear that, although the section provides that the alteration shall " be as valid as if originally contained " in the articles, the alteration only takes effect as from the date of the resolution.

[35] *Supra*, pp. 501, 502.

[36] s. 22.

all if expressly declared in the memorandum to be unalterable. Nor can they be altered without the court's consent if an order to that effect has been made under section 210. But these eventualities are all somewhat unlikely to occur. In most cases the rights will not be set out in the memorandum but in the articles, and in that event they are freely alterable unless an order has been made under section 210.

(b) *Shares of various classes*

Suppose, however, that the shares are divided into various classes. Then, as we have seen, section 23 expressly says that the new power, to alter such provisions of the memorandum as could have appeared in the articles, " shall not authorise any variation or abrogation of the special rights of any class of member." [37] This particular provision applies only to alterations of the memorandum and as such is of little importance. But the distinction between normal rights and class rights appears to have a wider application. What then is the exact nature of the distinction?

(i) *Meaning of class rights*

The distinction, it will be observed, is not between the normal incidents of *membership* and the special rights attaching to *shares* in the form of dividends and return of capital; the former idea that these latter rights were always inviolable was rejected in *Andrews* v. *Gas Meter Co.*[38] If, therefore, the memorandum and articles create merely one class of share the company will nevertheless be entitled to take power to issue preference shares, notwithstanding that this necessarily waters down former rights of the existing shares.[39] There cannot be class rights until the shares of the members are somehow divided into separate classes in the sense that some have rights different from those of the others. It would therefore be tempting to assume that the rights which are then specially protected are only those which differ from those enjoyed by every member.[40] But this too appears to be an over-simplification. If, for example, preference shares are given a preference as regards dividends but rank *pari passu* with the ordinary shares as regards voting and return of capital, it is quite clear that their voting and capital rights will be regarded as " special " [41] equally with their

---

[37] s. 23 (2).
[38] [1897] 1 Ch. 361, C.A.
[39] *Andrews* v. *Gas Meter Co., supra.*
[40] There are observations in the judgment of Jenkins L.J. in *Re John Smith's Tadcaster Brewery* [1953] Ch. 308, C.A., which appear to support this view, but it does not seem to be consistent with the approach adopted by the other members of the court or in the other cases. On the other hand, it is difficult to find any definite authority supporting the definition in the text. This, however, appears to follow from the decisions, cited *infra*, dealing with what amounts to a " variation," etc., of class rights, for these decisions imply that the rights concerned were class rights even though they deny that they were varied.
[41] *Re Stewart Precision Carburettor Co.* (1912) 28 T.L.R. 335, which at first sight suggests the contrary, merely held that the right of the ordinary shareholders to

dividend rights. Once a special class of shares has been created then any rights enjoyed by that class will apparently be regarded as special class rights if either, (a) they are expressly described in the memorandum, articles or terms of issue [42] as rights attaching to that class, or (b) they relate to dividends, return of capital or voting rights of that class. And if there is a variation of rights clause in the memorandum or articles providing a procedure for the alteration of class rights, the protection afforded by that clause will also, it seems, be regarded as a class right.[43] What is less clear is whether the residual rights of the ordinary shares will equally be regarded as class rights or as entitled to the protection of the variation of rights clause.[44]

(ii) *Extent of protection*

What, then, is the extent of the additional protection afforded to class rights as so defined?

In the first place it is clear that if the rights are embodied in the memorandum they cannot be varied or abrogated by special resolution under section 23, and that they are inviolable unless the memorandum itself provides a procedure for variation either expressly or by reference to provisions in the accompanying articles.[45] In the absence of any such power they cannot be varied, even with the individual consent of each shareholder,[46] except under a scheme of arrangement approved by the court.[47]

In practice, however, class rights are not set out in the memorandum but are instead embodied in the articles. In the absence, therefore, of any express provisions in the Companies Acts prohibiting the variation of class rights (and the Acts have never contained such provisions) one would suppose that they would be freely alterable by special resolution. But this was not the view which would have prevailed prior to *Andrews*

---

surplus capital was not " a preference or special privilege " within the meaning of s. 45 of the 1908 Act. Eve J. would apparently have agreed that it was a " special right."

[42] Or other appropriate document, *e.g.*, the resolutions in *Re Old Silkstone Collieries* [1954] Ch. 169, C.A.

[43] The Jenkins Committee recommended that this should be made clear: Cmnd. 1749, para. 198 (*b*).

[44] See *Hodge* v. *James Howell & Co.* [1958] C.L.Y. 446, C.A., *The Times*, December 13, 1958, which suggests that they will not.

[45] As in *Re Welsbach Incandescent Gas Light Co.* [1904] 1 Ch. 87, C.A. Two Scottish cases hold that it suffices if a power of variation is included in the articles filed contemporaneously with the memorandum even though not referred to therein: *Oban & Aultmore-Glenlivet Distilleries Ltd.* (1903) 5 F. 1140, and *Marshall Fleming & Co. Ltd.*, 1938 S.C. 873. *Sed quaere.* The furthest the English cases have gone is to concede that the articles may be read in conjunction with the memorandum " so far as may be necessary to explain any ambiguity appearing in the terms of the memorandum or to supplement it upon any matter as to which it is silent ": *per* Sir George Lowndes in *Angostura Bitters Ltd.* v. *Kerr* [1933] A.C. 550 at 554, P.C. The Jenkins Committee recommended that the Scottish rule should apply to both countries: Cmnd. 1749, para. 190.

[46] *Ashbury* v. *Watson* (1885) 30 Ch.D. 376, C.A. But, of course, each shareholder might agree not to enforce his rights.

[47] See Chap. 26, *infra.*

v. *Gas Meter Co.*[48] Before that decision it was thought that the financial interests of shareholders could not be varied unless special provision was made in the articles. Hence the practice had grown up of providing in the articles for variation by the consent of a specified majority of the class or the sanction of a resolution passed by a specified majority at a separate class meeting.[49] And, despite *Andrews* v. *Gas Meter Co.*, and the other decisions, previously cited, holding that a company cannot contract out of its statutory power to alter its articles, it is still widely thought that, in the absence of such express provisions for variation, the class rights of issued shares cannot be varied except with the consent of the individual holders or an authorised scheme of arrangement. In any event, it is generally accepted that, if there is a variation of rights clause in the articles, class rights can be varied only in accordance with that clause.

This view seems to have been accepted by the legislature, for section 72 of the 1948 Act gives a dissenting minority of 15 per cent. or more power to apply to the court where " provision is made by the memorandum or articles for authorising the variation of the rights attached to any class of shares . . . subject to the consent of any specified proportion of the holders . . . or the sanction of a resolution passed at a separate meeting . . ." and the rights have been varied pursuant to such provision. It makes little sense to give this right when the variation has been pursuant to a variation of rights clause but to deny it when there is no provision for variation or, *a fortiori*, when there is such a provision but the company has disregarded it.[50] The legislature must surely have assumed that in either of the latter cases there could be no variation. And, since the power to alter the articles expressed by section 10 is expressly " subject to the provisions of this Act " it is subject to the implied limitations of section 72.

There is no clear English reported case [51] on this subject, though all the recent cases [52] seem to have assumed that if there was a variation of rights clause it must be observed even though such clauses are generally expressed as enabling and not as restrictive. In Australia, however, there are two conflicting decisions in which the question was discussed.[53] In the first,[54] it was held that the company could, under

---

[48] [1897] 1 Ch. 361, C.A., *supra*.

[49] *Cf.* Table A, art. 4.

[50] In the latter case the variation could probably be attacked as a " fraud on the minority ": see *Allen* v. *Gold Reefs of W. Africa Ltd.* [1900] 1 Ch. 656, C.A., at 671, and Chap. 24, *infra*.

[51] But see *Re National Dwellings Society* (1898) 78 L.T. 144 where the articles were altered by inserting a variation of rights clause which was then exercised. The legality of the variation was not disputed on a subsequent application for consent to a reduction of capital.

[52] See in particular, *Greenhalgh* v. *Arderne Cinemas* [1946] 1 All E.R. 512, C.A.; *White* v. *Bristol Aeroplane Co.* [1953] Ch. 65, C.A.; *Re John Smith's Tadcaster Brewery* [1953] Ch. 308, C.A.; *Re Old Silkstone Collieries Ltd.* [1954] Ch. 169, C.A.

[53] See (1967) 31 Conv.(N.S.) 95.

[54] *Fischer* v. *Easthaven Ltd.* [1964] N.S.W.R. 261. But the alteration was restrained on the ground that it was a breach of contract.

its statutory power to alter the articles by special resolution, vary class rights without complying with a variation of rights clause, the contrary arguments summarised above being expressly rejected. In the second,[55] the earlier decision was not followed and the foregoing arguments were adopted.

The Jenkins Committee recommended that these doubts should be resolved as follows:

> (a) Where class rights are attached by the articles and there is no variation of rights clause therein, the articles should be deemed to include a variation of rights clause similar to article 4 of Table A.[56]
>
> (b) Section 10 should be amended to make it clear that the power to alter the articles does not include power to vary or abrogate class rights except in accordance with the provisions (express or implied under (a)) of the articles.[57]

They also recommended that section 72 should be strengthened, principally by increasing the time of application to the court from twenty-one to twenty-eight days, by permitting application to be made by 10, instead of 15 per cent., and by deleting the requirement that the applying minority must not have assented—a requirement that causes difficulty to a nominee-shareholder for several persons, some only of whom dissent.[58]

Hence class rights enjoy a considerable measure of protection (and will be still more secure when the recommendations of the Jenkins Committee are implemented). If set out in the memorandum the rights cannot be varied or abrogated under section 23; if set out in the articles they can probably be varied or abrogated only with the consent of a majority of the class in accordance with a clause to that effect in the articles and, even then, 15 per cent. of the holders can apply to the court under section 72 to disallow the variation. The rule that a company cannot contract out of its statutory power to alter its articles seems to have no application when class rights have been created. The shareholders can then obtain an injunction restraining the alteration.[59] What the position would be if they refrained from applying for an injunction seems never to have been determined. It may be that the

---

55 *Crumpton* v. *Morrine Hall Pty. Ltd.* [1965] N.S.W.R. 240.
56 But with certain amendments: Cmnd. 1749, para. 189. This solution is similar to that reached in *Re National Dwellings Society, supra,* and is fair since the class will thereby have the protection of s. 72.
57 *Ibid.,* para. 192.
58 *Ibid.,* para. 193. They also wished it to be made clear that s. 72 does not derogate from the more general remedy of s. 210.
59 Their position appears to be the exact converse of that of debentureholders or other outside creditors. The latter can sue for damages but apparently cannot obtain an injunction. Shareholders can obtain an injunction or declaration of invalidity but apparently cannot sue for damages.

variation would be completely ineffective, in which event mere lapse of time does not appear to rectify the position, although the shareholders might presumably be bound by subsequent acquiescence, waiver, or estoppel.[60]

(iii) *Meaning of abrogation and variation*

The courts have, however, reduced the extent of this protection by putting a restrictive interpretation on the meaning of the words "abrogated or varied" which are used in both sections 23 and 72.[61] The House of Lords in *Adelaide Electric Co.* v. *Prudential Assurance* [62] held that the alteration in the place of payment of a preferential dividend from England to Australia did not vary the rights of the preference shareholders notwithstanding that the Australian pound was worth less than the English. A subdivision [63] or increase [64] of one class of shares is not deemed to vary the rights of the other notwithstanding that the result is to alter the voting equilibrium of the classes. If preference shares are non-participating as regards dividend but participating as regards capital on a winding up or reduction of capital, a capitalisation of undistributed profits in the form of a bonus issue to the ordinary shareholders is not a variation of the preference shareholders' rights notwithstanding that the effect is to deny them their future participation in those profits on a winding up or reduction.[65] A reduction of capital by repayment of irredeemable preference shares in accordance with their rights on a winding up will not be regarded as a variation or abrogation of their rights.[66] Nor, it seems, will an issue of further shares

---

[60] *Cf. Godfrey Phillips Ltd.* v. *Investment Trust Corpn. Ltd.* [1953] Ch. 449, and p. 210, n. 26, and p. 377, nn. 33 and 34.

[61] s. 72 uses the expression "variation" but defines it in subs. (6) as including abrogation. Table A, art. 4, refers only to rights being varied and it is arguable in the light of *Mercantile Investment Trust* v. *International Co. of Mexico* [1893] 1 Ch. 484n. at 489, that total abrogation is not included. The Jenkins Committee recommended that art. 4 should be amended so as to include abrogation: Cmnd. 1749, para. 189.

[62] [1934] A.C. 122, H.L.

[63] *Greenhalgh* v. *Arderne Cinemas* [1946] 1 All E.R. 512, C.A., where the result of the subdivision was to deprive the holder of one class of his power to block a special resolution: see *infra*, p. 572.

[64] *White* v. *Bristol Aeroplane Co.* [1953] Ch. 65, C.A.; *Re John Smith's Tadcaster Brewery* [1953] Ch. 308, C.A.

[65] *Dimbula Valley (Ceylon) Tea Co.* v. *Laurie* [1961] Ch. 353. And see the startling decision in *Re Mackenzie & Co. Ltd.* [1916] 2 Ch. 450 which implies that a rateable reduction of the nominal preference and ordinary capital (which participated *pari passu* on a winding up) did not modify the rights of the preference shareholders notwithstanding that the effect was to reduce the amount of their fixed dividend while making no difference at all to the ordinary.

[66] *Scottish Insurance Corp.* v. *Wilsons & Clyde Coal Co.* [1949] A.C. 462, H.L.; *Prudential Assurance Co.* v. *Chatterley Whitfield Collieries* [1949] A.C. 512, H.L., *supra*, p. 363, and this is so even if they are participating as regards dividends: *Re Saltdean Estate Co. Ltd.* [1968] 1 W.L.R. 1844. (This, of course, does not apply if they are given special rights on a reduction of capital.) The Jenkins Committee (Cmnd. 1749, para. 195) did not see sufficient justification for altering this since holders of quoted shares are now generally protected by the *Spens* formula: *ibid. Cf. Re Old Silkstone Collieries Ltd.* [1954] Ch. 169, C.A. (*infra*, Chap. 26, p. 636), where the repayment was restrained because it would have destroyed a special right to apply for an adjustment of shares in nationalisation compensation.

ranking *pari passu* with the existing shares of a class.[67]　And, if there are preference and ordinary shares, an issue of preferred ordinary shares ranking ahead of the ordinary but behind the preference will not be a variation of the rights of either existing class.[68]

(iv) *Additional protection in memorandum or articles*

The English cases imply that should the terms of the variation of rights clause cover something more than variation or abrogation the clause will be enforced.　This, it seems, will be so whether the clause is expressed as facultative (" rights may be affected if . . .") or as restrictive (" rights may be affected only if . . .") [69] and certainly this will be so when the recommendations of the Jenkins Committee [70] are implemented.　But very clear wording will have to be used if such a provision is to be construed as affording any greater safeguards than those under the Act and Table A.　In *White* v. *Bristol Aeroplane Co.*[71] and *Re John Smith's Tadcaster Brewery Co.*,[72] the relevant clause referred to class rights being " affected, modified, dealt with or abrogated."　At first instance Danckwerts J.[73] held that a bonus issue to the ordinary shareholders could not be made without the consent of the preference shareholders because, although their rights would not be abrogated or varied, they would be affected since their votes would be worth less in view of the increased voting power of the ordinary shareholders.　But the Court of Appeal reversed his decision. They said that the rights of the preference shareholders would not be affected; the rights themselves—to one vote per share in certain circumstances—remained precisely as before.　All that would occur was that their holders' enjoyment of these rights would be affected.　If that eventuality was to be guarded against more explicit wording would have to be used.

It seems, therefore, that if a clause is effectually to prevent class rights from being " affected as a matter of business " [74]—which one would have supposed is what business men would want—it is necessary

---

[67] This is generally expressly provided in the articles: see Table A, art. 5.　But the position seems to be the same in the absence of express provision: see cases cited in note 64.　*Cf. Re Schweppes Ltd.* [1914] 1 Ch. 322, C.A., which, however, concerned s. 45 of the 1908 Act, which forbade " interference " with the " preference or special privilege " of a class.　On the other hand, the Australian Uniform Act, s. 65 (6), states that an issue of further preference shares ranking *pari passu* with the existing issued shares will be deemed a variation unless the new issue was expressly authorised when the original shares were issued.

[68] *Hodge* v. *James Howell & Co.* [1958] C.L.Y. 446, C.A., *The Times*, December 13, 1958.

[69] But see the Australian case of *Fischer* v. *Easthaven Ltd.* [1964] N.S.W.R. 261, *supra*.

[70] See *supra*, p. 510.

[71] [1953] Ch. 65, C.A.

[72] [1953] Ch. 308, C.A.

[73] Only his judgment in the latter is fully reported: see [1952] 2 All E.R. 751.

[74] The words are those of Greene M.R. in *Greenhalgh* v. *Arderne Cinemas* [1946] 1 All E.R. at 518.

to find a formula which will expressly operate in any event which affects any class of shareholders (as opposed to the rights attached to the shares) or the enjoyment of their rights (as opposed to the rights themselves). This seems less than satisfactory. The distinctions which the courts have drawn are over-subtle and unsuited to matters of practical business as opposed to abstract jurisprudence. In every case where the voting equilibrium is upset it is clear that class rights are " affected as a matter of business," and it is strange to protect a class from having its votes halved while refusing to protect it when the votes of the other class are doubled; the practical effect is the same in both cases.

Conclusions

The position may therefore be summed up as follows—

(1) The fact that debentureholders are creditors of, and contractors with the company normally affords them protection against those who control the company, for their contracts cannot be varied or abrogated without their consent.

(2) But the position of shareholders in registered companies [75] is much less secure. Unless they have control they normally have no protection against subsequent variations of their rights. Although these rights depend on the contract embodied in the memorandum and articles, the contract can be varied by a special resolution. They are safeguarded only to the following extent:

(a) If their rights are embodied in the memorandum and there declared to be unalterable, which is unusual, they cannot be varied.

(b) If there is only one class of shares with rights embodied in the memorandum (but not declared to be unalterable) they can be altered by special resolution, but only subject to the right of a dissenting minority of 15 per cent. to apply to the court which may cancel the alteration.

(c) If the shares are divided into separate classes it seems that the special rights of each class cannot be varied unless there is a variation of rights clause in the memorandum or articles. If there is such a clause the rights can be

---

[75] Shareholders in statutory companies normally enjoy considerably greater protection since there is no general power to alter the statute comparable to that of altering articles. Even if the special Act authorises the creation and issue of further shares and incorporates Part II of the Companies Clauses Act 1863, the issue can only be effected with the sanction of the proportion of the votes of existing members specified in the special Act and, if no proportion is prescribed, of three-fifths: ss. 12 and 13. And if the issue is of preference shares it " shall not affect any guarantee or any preference or priority in the payment of dividend or interest on any [existing] shares or stock ": s. 13, proviso. Further, if the existing ordinary shares are at a premium then, unless the company otherwise resolves, the new shares must be offered to the existing ordinary shareholders at par: s. 17.

varied in accordance therewith subject to the right of a dissenting minority of 15 per cent. to apply to the court which may cancel the alteration. For this purpose it appears to make no difference whether the rights are set out in the memorandum or in the articles.

(d) A shareholder cannot be compelled to take more shares or have his liability increased.

The general rules set out in this chapter are, however, subject to two further qualifications. Although the investor may be protected from the exercise of majority rule by the limitations imposed on the normal power of the general meeting, he may, nevertheless, be vulnerable if those in control are prepared to seek court sanction or to carry out a complete reorganisation. This matter is dealt with in Chapter 26. The investor has, however, an additional protection of greater practical importance than the very narrow restrictions placed on the powers of the general meeting. This consists of the duties owed by the controllers in the exercise of their powers. These duties are primarily owed by them in their capacity of directors and officers, if such they be, and flow from the fact that they then stand in a fiduciary relationship towards the company. But even if the controllers are not directors, but maintain their grip by voting at general meetings, they still remain under certain rather ill-defined duties of good faith. Accordingly, the two following chapters explore the nature of these duties.

CHAPTER 23

DIRECTORS' DUTIES

THE two preceding chapters have dealt with the means whereby investors can exercise such control as they have over the company by attending and voting at meetings, and with the legal limitations on the powers of those meetings. But, as we saw in an earlier chapter,[1] the general meeting is merely one of the company's two primary organs and most of the company's powers are not vested in it but in the board of directors. And, as we also saw, the directors exercise these powers either directly or through managers appointed by them. It is therefore of vital importance to see what duties are owed by directors and managers in the exercise of their powers. It is to this that we now turn.

It is often stated that directors are trustees and that the nature of their duties can be explained on this basis. It is easy to see how this idea arose. Prior to 1844 most joint stock companies were unincorporated and depended for their validity on a deed of settlement vesting the property of the company in trustees.[2] Often the directors were themselves the trustees and even when a distinction was drawn between the passive trustees and the managing board of directors the latter would quite clearly be regarded as trustees in the eyes of a court of equity in so far as they dealt with the trust property.[3]

With directors of incorporated companies the description " trustees " was less apposite but it was not unnatural that the courts should extend it to them by analogy. For one thing, the duties of the directors should obviously be the same whether the company was incorporated or not[4]; for another, courts of equity always tend to apply the label " trustee " to anyone in a fiduciary position.[5] Nevertheless, to describe directors as trustees seems today to be neither strictly correct nor invariably helpful. In the words of Romer J. in *Re City Equitable Fire Insurance Co.*[6]:

[1] Chap. 7.
[2] Chaps. 2 and 3. *Cf.* the various bodies discussed in Chap. 11, whose property is still vested in trustees.
[3] *Cf. Grimes* v. *Harrison* (1859) 26 Beav. 435, where the directors of a building society were held liable for breach of trust, while the actual trustees escaped liability, since they had acted only ministerially under the instructions of the directors.
[4] Moreover, as already pointed out (*supra*, p. 343), it was for long believed that the property of a corporation was held on trust by the corporation for its members, and, since it would be the directors who managed the property, they would be liable as constructive trustees if they misapplied it.
[5] The extent to which the courts were prepared to carry this analogy is well illustrated by *Re German Mining Co., ex p. Chippendale* (1853) 4 De G.M. & G. 19, where directors were afforded a trustee's rights to be indemnified by the members as their beneficiaries. The company in that case had originally been an unincorporated Deed of Settlement company but had become incorporated by registration under the 1844 Act.
[6] [1925] Ch. 407 at p. 426; affd. C.A., *ibid.*

" It has sometimes been said that directors are trustees. If this means no more than that directors in the performance of their duties stand in a fiduciary relationship to the company the statement is true enough. But if the statement is meant to be an indication by way of analogy of what those duties are, it appears to me to be wholly misleading. I can see but little resemblance between the duties of a director and the duties of a trustee of a will or of a marriage settlement."

In truth, directors are agents of the company rather than trustees of it or its property.[7] But as agents they stand, as Romer J. points out, in a fiduciary relationship to their principal, the company. The duties of good faith which this fiduciary relationship imposes are virtually identical with those imposed on trustees, and to this extent the description " trustee " still has validity. It is when we turn to the duties of care and skill that the trustee analogy breaks down. The duty of the trustees of a will or settlement is to be cautious and to avoid all risks to the trust fund. The managers of a business concern must, perforce, take risks; one of their primary duties is to carry on a more or less speculative business in an attempt to earn profits for the company and its members.

Hence the duties of directors can conveniently be discussed under two, more or less distinct, heads: (1) fiduciary duties of loyalty and good faith (analogous to the duties of trustees *stricto sensu*), and (2) duties of care and skill (differing fundamentally from the duties of normal trustees). The nature of the duties is discussed first, leaving, so far as possible, the effect of a breach for consideration at the end of this chapter. Until then it will merely be stated that directors are liable in certain circumstances without indicating in detail what the extent of their liability is. Moreover, until then, no consideration will be given to the obvious head of liability when directors have acted outside the authority conferred upon them, and when they accordingly incur liability like any other agents. In the following discussion it is assumed that the directors are acting *intra vires*—that is, within their powers and, of course, within the powers of the company.

FIDUCIARY DUTIES [8]

General equitable principle

The fiduciary duties of directors are, basically, identical with those applying to any other fiduciary and discussed in works on Trusts and Agency. Such duties have, indeed, already been dealt with briefly in

---

[7] But they will be treated as trustees of the company's property if they misapply it: see *infra*, pp. 554–556.

[8] See Sealy: " Fiduciary Relationships " [1962] C.L.J. 69 and [1963] C.L.J. 119, and " The Director as Trustee " [1967] C.L.J. 83 ; and Gareth Jones, " Unjust Enrichment and the Fiduciary's Duty of Loyalty " (1968) 84 L.Q.R. 472.

connection with another type of fiduciary peculiar to company law, the promoter.[9] But the relevant rules have received particular elaboration in relation to directors and the practical importance of the subject makes it desirable to discuss it here in greater detail.

In the first place it should be noted that whereas the authority of the directors to bind the company as its agents normally depends on their acting collectively as a board,[10] their duties of good faith are owed by each director individually. A single director, as such, will not be an agent of the company with power to saddle it with responsibility for his acts, but he will be a fiduciary of it. To this extent, directors again resemble trustees who must normally act jointly but each of whom severally owes duties of good faith towards the beneficiaries.

Secondly, the fiduciary duties are owed to the company and to the company alone. The difficulties which may be caused by treating a metaphysical entity as the beneficiary, in whose interests the directors must act, are referred to later.[11] Here it suffices to emphasise that, in general, the directors owe no duties to the individual members as such, or, *a fortiori*, to a person who has not yet become a member—such as a potential purchaser of shares in it. This principle is regarded as firmly established by the much-criticised decision in *Percival* v. *Wright*,[12] where directors purchased shares from their members without revealing that negotiations were in progress for a sale of the undertaking at a favourable price. This, however, does not mean that directors can never stand in a fiduciary relationship to the members; they well may if they are authorised by the latter to negotiate on their behalf with, for example, a potential take-over bidder.[13] Nor, as we shall see, does it necessarily follow that if they make a personal profit as a result of the use of inside information in dealings in the company's securities they will not break their fiduciary duty to the company and be liable to account to it. But as yet we lag far behind the American law which, as a result largely of a judicial gloss on rule 10b–5 made under the Securities Exchange Act 1934, has virtually placed directors in a fiduciary relationship to all those with whom they have dealings in their company's securities.[14]

However, the *Percival* v. *Wright* rule may shortly disappear. It was severely criticised by the Cohen Committee,[15] and has been forthrightly

---

9 Chap. 13.

10 Chaps. 7 and 8, *supra*.

11 *Infra*, pp. 521–524.

12 [1902] 2 Ch. 421. This applies even if all the shares are owned by a holding company with whom the directors have service contracts: *Bell* v. *Lever Bros.* [1932] A.C. 161, H.L.

13 *Briess* v. *Woolley* [1954] A.C. 333, H.L.; and see *Allen* v. *Hyatt* (1914) 30 T.L.R. 444, P.C., and *Ferguson* v. *Wallbridge* [1935] 3 D.L.R. 66, P.C.

14 See Loss: *Securities Regulation* (2nd ed.), pp. 1445–1474. This liability to the other party is additional to the statutory liability to account to the company for short-term profits under s. 16 (*b*) of the Securities Exchange Act, on which see *ibid.*, pp. 1040–1070. See p. 391, *supra*.

15 Cmd. 6659, paras. 86 and 87.

rejected by the Jenkins Committee in one of their bolder moods.[16]
They recommended the adoption of a rule which comes close to the
American, namely that:

> " a director . . . who, in any transaction relating to the securities of
> his company or of any other company in the same group, makes
> improper use of a particular piece of confidential information which
> might be expected materially to affect the value of those securities,
> should be liable to compensate a person who suffers from his action
> in so doing unless that information was known to that person." [17]

In the operation of such a provision much will, of course, depend on how
the courts interpret " improper." Furthermore when the transaction
was effected on a stock exchange it may, as the Committee recognise,[18]
be difficult for the other party to establish that he was dealing with a
director. But here the improved arrangements under the 1967 Act for
disclosure by directors of dealings in their company's securities should
help.[19]

It must be emphasised, however, that the suggested rule will merely
lay down one exception or modification—albeit an important one—to
the general principle that it is to the company, and not to its members
or anyone else, that the directors stand in a fiduciary relationship. It
seems that directors of a holding company do not even owe any duties
to its subsidiary, at any rate when that has an independent board of
directors.[20]

Thirdly, these duties, except in so far as they depend on statutory
provisions expressly limited to directors, are not so restricted but apply
equally to any officials of the company who are authorised to act on its
behalf [21] and in particular to those acting in a managerial capacity.
This is a matter of considerable practical importance now that it is
common for the management of public companies to be delegated by the
board to a smaller body. At present the managers to whom the directors
delegate their powers are likely themselves to be managing and other

---

[16] Cmnd. 1749, para. 89.
[17] *Ibid.*, para. 99 (*b*). Note that the 1969 *City Code on Take-Overs and Mergers*
bans any dealings in the shares of offeror or offeree company by any person who is
privy to the discussions until there is an announcement of the bid: rule 30.
[18] *Ibid.* para. 89.
[19] See *supra*, pp. 388–391.
[20] *Lindgren* v. *L. & P. Estates Ltd.* [1968] Ch. 572, C.A. But if the subsidiary's
directors merely act in the interests of the holding company ignoring those of the
minority shareholders, those shareholders may have a remedy under s. 210: see
Scottish Co-operative Wholesale Society v. *Meyer* [1959] A.C. 324, H.L. See,
infra, pp. 548, 601.
[21] *i.e.*, to those who are the company's *agents*, and who therefore stand in a fiduciary
capacity towards it, as opposed to those who are merely its *servants*, who do work
for it but do not act on its behalf. That the latter's duties of good faith are somewhat less extensive seems clearly established: *Bell* v. *Lever Bros.* [1932] A.C. 161,
H.L. But servants, too, owe duties of fidelity which in most respects amount to
much the same: *cf. Reading* v. *Att.-Gen.* [1951] A.C. 507, H.L. These, however,
depend upon the normal law of master and servant and present no peculiarities in
the company law field.

full-time service directors. But the modern tendency seems to be towards a clearer distinction between the management which runs the business and the board of directors which oversees the management and lays down broad lines of policy. This may, in time, lead to the practice of delegating managerial powers to professional managers without seats on the board.[22] In that event certain statutory rules will need amplification but the general principles of equity are already sufficiently all-embracing to deal with most [23] of the resulting possibilities. In the following discussion we shall refer to directors [24] but, except where the context requires otherwise, what is said is equally applicable to all agents of the company; their fiduciary duties are the same but, of course, the lower one goes in the official hierarchy the less opportunity there is for a breach of these duties.

The general principle upon which these duties are based is clear and simple. Directors, once their appointments take effect,[25] are fiduciaries and must therefore display the utmost good faith towards the company in their dealings with it or on its behalf. As the Jenkins Committee pointed out, legislation has to some extent extended and clarified the ambit of those duties, but in the main these are still " determined by extensive and complex case-law which does not find expression in the Act." [26] The Committee thought that a general statement of the basic principles underlying the relationship between a company and its directors, such as appears in a number of Commonwealth and American Acts, " might well be useful to directors and others concerned with company management." [27] The formulation which they recommended is as follows [28]:

> " (i) a director of a company should observe the utmost good faith towards the company in any transaction with it or on its behalf and should act honestly in the exercise of his powers and the duties of his office;
>
> (ii) a director of a company should not make use of any money or other property of the company or of any information acquired by virtue of his position as a director or officer of the company

---

[22] But, no doubt, with comparable prestige by dubbing them " special directors "—see *supra*, p. 130.

[23] Perhaps not all; there is the disquieting possibility of a dominating manager feathering his nest and escaping liability by pleading that he had obtained the consent of the board; *cf.* the position of the solicitor in *Regal (Hastings) Ltd.* v. *Gulliver* [1942] 1 All E.R. 378; [1967] 2 A.C. 134n., H.L., *infra*, p. 535.

[24] It seems better to avoid the technical expression " officer " defined, somewhat inadequately, in Companies Act 1948, s. 455, as including " a director, manager or secretary." While we are primarily concerned with such officials, they are not exhaustive of those who may act on the company's behalf.

[25] *Lindgren* v. *L. & P. Estates Ltd.* [1968] Ch. 572, C.A., which rejected the argument that " directors-elect " are in a fiduciary relationship to the company.

[26] Cmnd. 1749, para. 86.

[27] *Ibid.*, para. 87.

[28] *Ibid.*, para. 99 (*a*).

to gain directly or indirectly an improper advantage for himself at the expense of the company;

(iii) a director who commits a breach of these provisions should be liable to the company for any profit made by him and for any damage suffered by the company as a result of the breach;

(iv) these provisions should be in addition to and not in derogation of any other enactment or rule of law relating to the duties or liabilities of directors of a company." [29]

At present, however, this recommendation has not been implemented and until it is the "extensive and complex case law" still has to be resorted to; indeed this will still be so even if the suggested formulation is enacted in the next Companies Act for, as (iv) stresses, it is not intended to be an exhaustive codification but merely a guide.[30] Even as a statement of general principles it appears, as will be seen, to be in some respects narrower than the existing case-law.

The general principles in their application have four facets which are probably best treated as distinct, though in practice they tend to overlap. First, the directors must act bona fide, that is in what they believe to be the best interests of the company. Secondly, they must exercise their powers for the particular purpose for which they were conferred and not for some extraneous purpose, even though they honestly believe that to be in the best interests of the company. Thirdly, they must not fetter their discretion to exercise their powers from time to time in accordance with the foregoing rules. And finally, despite compliance with the foregoing rules, they must not, without the consent of the company, place themselves in a position in which there is a conflict between their duties and their personal interests.

1. Bona fides

The principle is undoubted that directors must act "bona fide in what they consider—not what a court may consider—is in the interests of the company." [31] In most cases compliance with this rule is tested on common sense principles, the court asking itself whether it is proved that the directors have not done what they honestly believed to be right, and normally accepting that they have unless satisfied that they have not behaved as honest men of business might be expected to act. However, there may be a breach of duty notwithstanding that it is not shown that they have acted with any conscious dishonesty, but have acted as they did, because it was in their own interests or that of some third party,

---

[29] Compare the formulations in the Australian Uniform Act, s. 124, which is generally similar except that it adds a reference to "reasonable diligence," in the Ghana Companies Code (Act 179 of 1963), s. 203 *et seq.* (especially ss. 203–205) which is more exhaustive, and in the new Ontario Business Corporations Bill, s. 131, which, like Ghana, requires skill as well as diligence.

[30] In this respect it follows the Australian pattern but not the Ghanaian which attempts a complete codification.

[31] *Per* Lord Greene M.R. in *Re Smith & Fawcett Ltd.* [1942] Ch. 304 at 306, C.A.

without considering whether it was also in the interests of the company. A good illustration of this is afforded by the recent case of *Re W. & M. Roith Ltd.*[32] There the controlling shareholder and director of two companies wished to make provision for his widow without leaving her his shares. On advice he entered into a service agreement with one of the companies whereby on his death she was to be entitled to a pension for life. On being satisfied that no thought had been given to the question whether the arrangement was for the benefit of that company and that, indeed, the sole object was to make provision for the widow, the court held that the transaction was not binding on the company.[33]

But what exactly is meant by saying that they must act in the interests of the *company*? Despite the separate personality of the company it is clear that directors are not expected to act on the basis of what is for the economic advantage of the corporate entity, disregarding the interests of the members.[34] They are, for example, clearly entitled to recommend the payment of dividends to the members and are not expected to deny them a return on their money by ploughing back all the profits so as to increase the size and wealth of the company. It has been said that " the company " does not mean " the sectional interest of some (it may be a majority) of the present members or even . . . of all the present members, but of present and future members of the company . . . on the footing that it would be continued as a going concern, [balancing] a long-term view against short term interests of present members." [35] If, as will normally be the case, the directors themselves are shareholders they are clearly entitled to have regard to their own interests as such and not to think only of the others. As it was happily put in an Australian case, they are " not required by the law to live in an unreal region of detached altruism and to act in a vague mood of ideal abstraction from obvious facts which must be present to the mind of any honest and intelligent man when he exercises his

---

[32] [1967] 1 W.L.R. 432.

[33] Following *Re Lee, Behrens & Co. Ltd.* [1932] 2 Ch. 46. See also *Alexander* v. *Automatic Telephone Co.* [1900] 2 Ch. 56, C.A.; *Millers (Invercargill) Ltd.* v. *Maddams* [1938] N.Z.L.R. 490 (N.Z.C.A.); and *Ngurli Ltd.* v. *McCann* (1954) 90 C.L.R. 425 (Aust.H.C.); but *cf. Lindgren* v. *L. & P. Estates Ltd.* [1968] Ch. 572, C.A., where it was held that there had been no failure to consider the commercial merits.

[34] In connection with members voting in general meetings, Evershed M.R. in *Greenhalgh* v. *Arderne Cinemas* [1951] Ch. 286, C.A., said at p. 291, " the phrase ' the company as a whole ' does not (at any rate in such a case as the present) mean the company as a commercial entity as distinct from the corporators." This seems equally true in the present context; *cf. Parke* v. *Daily News* [1962] Ch. 927 at 963.

[35] Counsel's advice to the directors in the *Savoy Hotel* case—a *cause célèbre* which never reached the courts but in which a Board of Trade Inspector was appointed to report on the legality of the directors' action in attempting to remove the Berkeley Hotel from the company's control so as to take it beyond the reach of a take-over bidder: see the Inspector's Report (H.M.S.O. 1954) and for a detailed comment thereon (1955) 68 Harv.L.R. 1176.

powers as a director." [36]   But it is apparently only the interests of the members, present and future, to which they are entitled to have regard; the interests of the employees, the consumers of the company's products or the nation as a whole are legally irrelevant.[37]

This, it may be thought, is an increasingly anachronistic view. Directors habitually have regard to these interests; indeed it has become common form for them to declare that industry owes duties to employees, consumers and the nation, as well as to the shareholders.[38] Fortunately, so long as the company remains a going concern the members' interests will normally be served by having regard to the other interests; rebellious staff, hostile trade unions, dissatisfied customers and an aggrieved public or government are not conducive to the future prosperity of the company.[39] Hence it is generally possible to justify generosity to employees, charitable donations[40] and even political contributions,[41] though it seems that the onus will be on the directors to justify any gratuitous payments by showing positively that they were made bona fide for the benefit of the company.[42]

The real difficulty arises when the company's business is about to cease, for then no commercial purpose can be served by keeping other interests happy and the interests of the company can mean only the economic interests of the present members. This was starkly illustrated by *Parke* v. *Daily News Ltd.*[43] which arose out of the sale of the ailing *News Chronicle* and *Star.* The Cadbury family, who controlled the selling company, wished to distribute the whole of the purchase price among the employees who would become redundant. At the suit of one shareholder they were restrained from doing so.[44] To the argument

---

36 *Mills* v. *Mills* (1938) 60 C.L.R. 150 (Aust.H.C.), *per* Latham C.J. at p. 164; *cf.* Dixon J. at pp. 185–186.

37 *Parke* v. *Daily News* [1962] Ch. 927; following *Hutton* v. *W. Cork Ry.* (1883) 23 Ch.D. 654, C.A.

38 No one, except perhaps the late Henry Ford at one time (see *Dodge* v. *Ford Motor Co.* (1919) 204 Mich. 459; 170 N.W. 668), has yet suggested that the shareholders' interests should be totally subordinated to those of the employees, consumers and the public.

39 Conversely, in a once-famous phrase, " What is best for General Motors is best for the U.S.A."

40 Though these and political contributions now have to be disclosed with the accounts (Companies Act 1967, s. 19) there is still no statutory power to make such gifts and " charity has no business to sit at boards of directors *qua* charity ": *per* Bowen L.J. in *Hutton* v. *W. Cork Ry.* (1883) 23 Ch.D. at p. 673. But a gift by a company such as I.C.I. for scientific education can easily be justified (*Evans* v. *Brunner Mond & Co.* [1921] 1 Ch. 359); one for flood relief in Florence would be more difficult to justify in law except on the cynical basis that it is good advertising.

41 The massive contributions disclosed by some highly respectable companies since the 1967 Act show that the directors think they can be justified, presumably on the basis that the policy of the party or pressure group concerned would be good for the company's business.

42 See *Parke* v. *Daily News Ltd.* [1962] Ch. 927 at 954; *Re W. & M. Roith Ltd.* [1967] 1 W.L.R. 432, *supra.*

43 *Supra.* For earlier proceedings see [1961] 1 W.L.R. 493.

44 It was held that the gratuitous payments proposed were illegal and *ultra vires* and could not be made even with the authority of a general meeting; on this see pp. 92, 564, 565. Ultimately the other shareholders participated voluntarily in a scheme whereby their shares of the proceeds were distributed among the employees.

that " the prime duty must be to the shareholders; but boards of directors must take into consideration their duties to employees in these days," Plowman J. answered tersely: " But no authority to support that proposition as a proposition of law was cited to me; I know of none, and in my judgment such is not the law." [45]

A further difficulty arises in the case of a director who, under the articles, is appointed by a special class of shareholders or the debenture-holders. Clearly the intention is that he shall act in what he conceives to be the interest of the security holders who appointed him,[46] and if he does not he is likely to lose his office.[47] But on the law as at present formulated he is in the same position as any other nominee director whose appointment has been engineered by, for example, a large share-holder to watch the latter's interest. " There is nothing wrong in it. It is done every day. Nothing wrong, that is, so long as the director is left free to exercise his best judgment in the interests of the company which he serves." [48] If he does not he will break his duties to the company and, moreover, in determining whether his actions are proper he will have attributed to him any knowledge possessed by the shareholder whose orders he obeys.[49] That he should not be allowed to act as a mere puppet is obviously salutary. But to deny a director, openly appointed under the articles to represent a particular class, the right to think primarily of the interests of that class, instead of exclusively of the members as a whole, may be to defeat the whole object of his appointment. Especially is this so if he represents the debentureholders, for they, apparently, cannot be regarded as part of " the company as a whole." [50]

But can the present formulation be correct? [51] Surely the directors can have regard to the interests of creditors and, indeed, must do so when the company is insolvent, for then the members have little

[45] [1962] Ch. at p. 963.

[46] Any agreement to vote as they instructed him would apparently be unenforceable: *infra*, p. 525. Perhaps the articles might validly authorise him expressly to exercise his discretion in the interests of those appointing him, but it is not the practice so to provide.

[47] He will also be liable to lose office if dismissed by an ordinary resolution: s. 184. Altogether his legal position is an invidious one. For a legislative attempt to deal with these questions see the Ghana Companies Code 1963 (Act 179), s. 203 (3): " In considering whether a particular transaction or course of action is in the best interests of the company as a whole a director may have regard to the interests of the employees, as well as the members, of the company, and when appointed by, or as a representative of, a special class of members, employees or creditors may give special, but not exclusive, consideration to the interests of that class."

[48] *Per* Denning M.R. in *Boulting* v. *A.C.T.A.T.* [1963] 2 Q.B. 606 at 626.

[49] *Selangor United Rubber Estates Ltd.* v. *Cradock (No.* 3) [1968] 1 W.L.R. 1555. For the possible liability of his master, see *infra*, pp. 554, 561.

[50] Similar problems would arise if workers' representatives were appointed to boards of directors: see the Report of the Royal Commission on Trade Unions (Cmnd. 3623 of 1968) Chap. XV, and especially paras. 1002–1005.

[51] Note the statement in the 1969 *City Code on Take-overs and Mergers*: " It is the shareholders' interests taken as a whole which should be considered, *together with those of employees and creditors* ": General Principle 11.

remaining interest to consider. Further developments in the law in this respect seem inevitable—and overdue.

2. Proper purpose

If directors exercise their powers for purposes other than those for which they were conferred, it may be said that they have exceeded their authority and are liable accordingly. But it probably makes for clarity to distinguish between an act *ultra vires* the directors because they have usurped a power which they never had, and an act which prima facie is within the powers delegated to them but which they have abused by exercising it for an improper purpose. Occasionally their purpose may be improper because it is illegal or contrary to public policy.[52] More often the impropriety will merely be because this purpose is not that contemplated by the article conferring it. Thus directors will normally be authorised to issue further capital[53] but they will be liable if they exercise this or any other power for the purpose of maintaining their control of the company, and this notwithstanding that they honestly believe that to be in the best interests of the company.[54] The power is delegated to them in order that they can raise money if the company needs it, not to enable them to keep themselves in the saddle. But if their primary purpose is legitimate, the action will not be invalidated merely because they have an additional subsidiary motive, even though this be to promote their own advantage.[55]

It is for the court to decide on a true interpretation of the articles what the purpose was for which the power was conferred.[56] But, unless it can be shown that the directors have exercised it for some other purpose, their action cannot be impugned notwithstanding that the court may doubt whether the act was best designed to promote that purpose.[57]

---

[52] *Pharmaceutical Society* v. *Dickson* [1968] 3 W.L.R. 286, H.L. (restraint of trade).
[53] But see *supra*, p. 374n., for the recommendations of the Jenkins Committee.
[54] *Punt* v. *Symons & Co.* [1903] 2 Ch. 506; *Piercy* v. *Mills & Co.* [1920] 1 Ch. 77; *Hogg* v. *Cramphorn Ltd.* [1967] Ch. 254 (1963); *Bamford* v. *Bamford* [1969] 2 W.L.R. 1107, C.A. For the application of a similar principle to other powers, see *Stanhope's Case* (1866) L.R. 1 Ch.App. 161 and *Manisty's Case* (1873) 17 S.J. 745 (forfeiture of shares); *Galloway* v. *Halle Concerts Society* [1915] 2 Ch. 233 (calls); *Bennett's Case* (1854) 5 De G.M. & G. 284 (passing transfers); *Legion Oils Ltd.* v. *Barron* [1956] 2 D.L.R. (2d) 337 (Alb.S.C.); and *Hogg* v. *Cramphorn Ltd.*, *supra*, where a loan made as part of the scheme to maintain their control was held invalid as well as the share issue. In the *Savoy Hotel* case, *supra*, note 35, the disposal of an asset was regarded by the Inspector as improper because the object was to deprive the " shareholders of such control as, under the regulations of the company, they may have over the company's assets." Conduct of this sort is contrary to the 1969 *City Code on Take-overs and Mergers*, General Principle 4. But contrast *Re Smith & Fawcett Ltd.* [1942] Ch. 304, C.A., where it was held that the appropriate article was expressed sufficiently widely to enable the directors to exercise the power to refuse transfers for any purpose which they bona fide believed to be in the interests of the company.
[55] *Hirsche* v. *Sims* [1894] A.C. 654; *Hindle* v. *John Cotton Ltd.*, 1919 56 S.L.T. 625 (Sc.); *Mills* v. *Mills* (1938) 60 C.L.R. 150 (Austr.H.C.); *cf. Nash* v. *Lancegaye Safety Glass Ltd.* (1956) 92 Ir.L.T.R. 11 (Ir.H.C.).
[56] See cases cited in note 54.
[57] This seems to follow from the decisions on refusal to register share transfers cited, *supra*, at p. 393.

Provided the directors have correctly interpreted the purpose of their powers and honestly believe that their action will fulfil that purpose and be in the interests of the company they are free from liability under this head. They may, if their error is sufficiently egregious, have broken their duties of care and skill,[58] but not their fiduciary duties.

3. Unfettered discretion

We now turn, under this and the next head, to certain objective standards which must be complied with notwithstanding the presence of good faith and proper motive. Since the directors' powers are held by them in trust for the company they cannot fetter their future discretion. Thus it seems clear as a general principle, despite the paucity of reported cases on the point,[59] that directors cannot validly contract (either with one another or with third parties) as to how they shall vote at future board meetings.[60] This is so even though there is no improper motive or purpose (thus infringing the previous rules) and no personal profit reaped by the directors under the agreement (thus infringing the succeeding rule).

This, however, does not mean that if, in the bona fide exercise of their discretion, the directors have entered into a contract on behalf of the company, they cannot in that contract validly agree to take such further action at board meetings as are necessary to carry out that contract.[61]

" There are many kinds of transaction in which the proper time for the exercise of the directors' discretion is the time of the negotiation of a contract and not the time at which the contract is to be performed. . . . If at the former time they are bona fide of opinion that it is in the best interests of the company that the transaction should be entered into and carried into effect, I can see no reason in law why they should not bind themselves to do whatever under the transaction is to be done by the board." [62]

Indeed, it may be that if there is a voting agreement between all the members and directors which provides that they shall vote together at all meetings, whether general meetings or directors' meetings, the parties to it will be bound *inter se*,[63] and that only if there are other members or directors will they be able to complain.[64] It is submitted, however,

---

58 See on those duties, *infra*, p. 549 *et seq.*
59 But see *Clark* v. *Workman* [1920] 1 Ir.R. 107 and the unreported decision of Morton J. in the *Arderne Cinema* litigation quoted *infra*, Chap. 24, at p. 571.
60 Contrast the position of shareholders who may freely enter into such voting agreements, *infra*, Chap. 24, p. 562.
61 *Thorby* v. *Goldberg* (1964) 112 C.L.R. 597 (Aus.H.C.).
62 *Ibid.*, per Kitto J. at pp. 605–606.   63 *Cf.* Menzies J., *ibid.*, at p. 616.
64 This was discussed, but not clearly settled, by the Canadian Supreme Court in *Ringuet* v. *Bergeron* [1960] S.C.R. 672, where the majority held the voting agreement valid because, in their view, it related only to voting at general meetings. The minority held that it extended also to directors' meetings and was void, but they conceded that the position might have been different had *all* the members originally been parties to the agreement: see at p. 677.

that even if all the then directors and members were parties, the validity of the agreement, and of action taken under it, could be attacked by the company, to whom the fiduciary duties are owed, if at a later stage someone (a new board, a later member or the liquidator) was able to take action on its behalf.

On much the same principle, the board must not, in the absence of express authority, delegate their discretions to others.[65] But in practice wide authority to delegate is invariably conferred by the articles.[66]

4. Conflict of duty and interest

As fiduciaries, directors must not place themselves in a position in which there is a conflict between their duties to the company and their personal interests. Good faith must not only be done but must manifestly be seen to be done, and the law will not allow a fiduciary to place himself in a situation in which his judgment is likely to be biased and then to escape liability by denying that in fact it was biased.

It will be convenient to consider the application of this principle in four connections. And first, in relation to contracts with the company, where it has received its most detailed working out.

(a) Contracts with the company

Effect of equitable principle. By the middle of the last century it had been clearly established that the trustee-like position of directors vitiated any contract which the board entered into on behalf of the company with one of their number. This principle receives its clearest expression in *Aberdeen Ry* v. *Blaikie* [67] in which a contract between the company and a partnership of which one of the directors was a partner was avoided at the instance of the company notwithstanding that its terms were perfectly fair. Lord Cranworth L.C. said on that occasion [68]:

> " A corporate body can only act by agents, and it is, of course, the duty of those agents so to act as best to promote the interests of the corporation whose affairs they are conducting. Such agents have duties to discharge of a fiduciary nature towards their principal. And it is a rule of universal application that no one, having such duties to discharge, shall be allowed to enter into engagements in which he has, or can have, a personal interest conflicting, or which possibly may conflict, with the interests of those whom he is bound to protect.
>
> " So strictly is this principle adhered to that no question is allowed to be raised as to the fairness or unfairness of a contract so entered into. . . .

---

[65] *Cartmells' Case* (1874) L.R. 9 Ch.App. 691.
[66] *Supra*, Chap. 7, pp. 138–142. But a purported delegation may be void as inconsistent with the articles: *Horn* v. *Faulder & Co.* (1908) 99 L.T. 524.
[67] (1854) 1 Macq.H.L. 461 (H.L.Sc.).
[68] At pp. 471–472.

" It may sometimes happen that the terms on which a trustee has dealt or attempted to deal with the estate or interests of those for whom he is a trustee have been as good as could have been obtained from any other person—they may even at the time have been better. But still so inflexible is the rule that no inquiry on that subject is permitted."

Later cases have added little to the general principle thus enunciated. It applies not only to contracts directly with the directors but also to those in which they are in any way interested, whether because they benefit personally however indirectly,[69] or because they are subject to a conflicting duty.[70] The effect of a breach of the principle is discussed in more detail later [71]; here it suffices to say that in general the contract will be voidable at the instance of the company,[72] and any profits made by the directors personally will be recoverable by the company.

The principle is the same as that applying to promoters and already discussed,[73] but the burden of it falls more heavily upon directors. As we have seen, promoters can enter into contracts with the company if they make full disclosure of all material facts either to an independent board or to the members of the company. Any contract which the company then enters into with the promoter will be fully valid and enforceable. The same applies to a contract with any agent of the company other than a director.[74] But the directors themselves cannot escape so easily. Disclosure to themselves is ineffective even if the interested directors refrain from attending and voting leaving an independent quorum to decide, for the company has a right to the unbiased voice and advice of every director.[75] Hence, in the absence of express provision in the company's articles, the only effective step is to make full disclosure to the members of the company and to have the contract entered into or ratified by the company in general meeting.

Disqualification. This need for approval in general meeting was expressly recognised by section 29 of the first Joint Stock Companies Act of 1844. However, this section disappeared from the Act of 1856, to be replaced only by an article in the optional Table B [76] to the effect that

---

[69] For a strong example see *Victors Ltd.* v. *Lingard* [1927] 1 Ch. 323 (issue of a debenture to secure the company's debt which the directors had guaranteed).

[70] *Transvaal Lands Co.* v. *New Belgium (Transvaal) Land and Development Co.* [1914] 2 Ch. 488, C.A.; *Boulting* v. *A.C.T.A.T.* [1963] 2 Q.B. 606, C.A., *per* Upjohn L.J. at pp. 635–636.

[71] *Infra*, p. 552 *et seq.*

[72] The rule is for the protection of the company and cannot be used by the director as a shield to protect himself against a third party: *Boulting* v. *A.C.T.A.T.*, *supra*.

[73] *Supra*, Chap. 13, p. 272 *et seq.*

[74] For example, the solicitor: see *Regal (Hastings) Ltd.* v. *Gulliver* [1942] 1 All E.R. 378; [1967] 2 A.C. 134n., H.L., *infra*, p. 535.

[75] See *Benson* v. *Heathorn* (1842) 1 Y. & C.C.C. 326, *per* Knight-Bruce V.-C. at pp. 341–342, and *Imperial Mercantile Credit Asscn.* v. *Coleman* (1871) L.R. 6 Ch.App. 558, C.A., *per* Hatherley L.C. at pp. 567–568.

[76] Art. 47.

any director directly or indirectly interested in any contract with the company (except an interest merely as shareholder of another company) should be disqualified and vacate office—a provision borrowed from the mandatory provisions in the Companies Clauses Consolidation Act of 1845.[77] Similar provisions for disqualification have caused difficulty in the case of public authorities (from which the provisions were borrowed[78]); they seem even less appropriate in the case of purely commercial ventures. Yet they remained in all Tables A until the 1948 Act. Hence, unless the incorporators remembered to exclude the relevant provision of Table A, there was the risk not only that the contract would be voidable, but also that the directors would vacate office. Not surprisingly, perhaps, the courts tended to construe disqualifying provisions as restrictively as possible. It has been held, for example, that a director of one company who is managing director of another and remunerated only by salary is not disqualified as " interested " in contracts with that other company.[79] This emphasis on conflicting pecuniary advantage, without consideration of the equally important aspect of conflicting duties, is to be contrasted with the more realistic attitude towards the question whether the resulting contract is voidable.[80]

Exclusion clauses in articles. It is not surprising that these strict rules were not acceptable to the business community. Hence it soon became the practice to ensure that the company waived them. So far as the disqualifying rules were concerned this was easy; they had no common law or equitable basis and all that was necessary was to exclude or modify Table A.[81] And in the case of registered companies formed under the 1948 Act not even that is needed, for the new Table A omits the former disqualifying clause, and expressly states that directors are not disqualified by contracting with the company.[82] Hence, disqualification is of little practical importance today, except in the case of statutory companies formed under the Companies Clauses Acts.

The basic equitable principle invalidating contracts was, and is, the more serious snag. Contracts with directors, such as service agreements,

---

[77] ss. 85–87. These provisions were borrowed from the Municipal Corporations Act 1835, s. 28; it was not unnatural to apply to statutory companies running public utilities the same rules as those for local authorities.

[78] See a learned note in (1956) 2 Brit.J. of Adm. Law 90, in which the history of the local government rules is summarised.

[79] *Wilson* v. *L.M.S. Ry.* [1940] Ch. 169, following and applying the similar rule for local authorities laid down in *Lapish* v. *Braithwaite* [1926] A.C. 275, H.L.

[80] *Transvaal Lands Co.* v. *New Belgium (Transvaal) Land Co.*, *supra*.

[81] But note how such provisions have been held to impinge on the basic equitable principle. In *Costa Rica Ry.* v. *Forwood* [1901] 1 Ch. 746, C.A., it was held that a provision that certain types of contract should not disqualify a director impliedly validated the contract, and entitled the director to retain the profits. This followed the judgment of Hatherley L.C. in *Imperial Mercantile Credit Asscn.* v. *Coleman* (1871) L.R. 6 Ch.App. 558, which was reversed on other grounds (1873) L.R. 6 H.L. 189.

[82] Art. 84 (3).

became increasingly common, and contracts in which the directors were interested, for example as directors of another company, more common still. And the directors were unwilling to suffer the delay, embarrassment and possible frustration entailed by having to submit all such contracts to the company in general meeting. But just as the normal obligations of trustees can be waived or modified by express provisions in the trust deed under which they were appointed, so (within limits) can the normal fiduciary duties of directors be modified by express provision in the company's constitution. Such provisions have become common form in the articles of registered companies. The length to which they go varies. At their narrowest they provide that an interested director shall disclose his interest to the board, shall not be counted in determining whether a quorum is present, and shall not vote [83]; at their widest they enable an interested director to attend and vote just as if he were not interested. However wide or narrow the conditions may be, it is invariable to provide that if complied with [84] the contract shall be fully effective, and the director not liable to account for any profit made.[85]

Statutory provisions for disclosure. Alarmed by the growing ambit of exclusion clauses, the legislature by the 1929 Act made mandatory the disclosure of the director's interest. The relative provisions are now embodied in section 199 of the 1948 Act.

Three main questions arise in relation to section 199. First, what is the effect of a failure to disclose in accordance with it? The section itself provides for liability on the part of the defaulting director to a fine not exceeding £100.[86] But over and above this, a breach of its provisions automatically removes any protection afforded by the exclusion clauses in the articles and brings the basic equitable principle into operation; in other words, the contract is voidable by the company and any profits made by the interested director are recoverable.[87] But failure to comply with the section does not make the contract void, it merely becomes voidable under the general equitable principle and if it is too late to rescind it is fully enforceable against the company.[88]

---

[83] This is the basic rule in Table A (considered in more detail *infra*, pp. 533–535), but note the many exceptional cases in which voting is allowed. Stricter rules apply to statutory companies: Companies Clauses Act 1845, ss. 86–87. The stock exchanges will not grant a quotation unless the company's articles prohibit voting by an interested director except as provided by Table A (*Requirements*, Sched. VII, Part A, para. D 2).

[84] The onus of proving this is on the director: *Gray* v. *New Augarita Porcupine Mines* [1952] 3 D.L.R. 1, P.C.

[85] See Table A, art. 84 (3). Such articles do not infringe s. 205 of the 1948 Act (*infra*, p. 532) because they modify the duties of directors and do not exempt from liability for breach of duty.

[86] s. 199 (4).

[87] *Hely Hutchinson* v. *Brayhead Ltd.* [1968] 1 Q.B. 549, C.A. (Lords Denning M.R., Wilberforce and Pearson). See also *Imperial Mercantile Credit Assen.* v. *Coleman* (1873) L.R. 6 H.L. 189, where the failure was to comply with a provision for disclosure in the articles.

[88] *Hely Hutchinson* v. *Brayhead Ltd.*, *supra*.

Secondly, to whom must disclosure be made? In marked contrast with the basic equitable principle,[89] the disclosure required is not to the general meeting but to the board.[90] It hardly seems over-cynical to suggest that disclosure to one's cronies is a less effective restraint on self-seeking than disclosure to those for whom one is a fiduciary. Moreover, the effect of subsection (2) seems to be that disclosure is required only if the contract is brought before the board; many contracts never are.

Thirdly, how extensive must the disclosure be? It is not sufficient to disclose merely that one is interested—the *nature* of the interest (as the section itself says) must also be disclosed. This normally involves disclosing the exact extent of the profit which the director will make as a result of the contract.[91] This, however, is limited to some extent by the section itself, which provides [92] that a general notice that a director is a member of a specified company or firm, and is to be regarded as interested in any contract made with it, shall be deemed to be a sufficient declaration of interest.

Moreover, it is only the nature of the interest—not all material facts—that has to be disclosed. If the exclusion clause in the articles provides, as it invariably will, that, subject to compliance with section 199, contracts with directors shall not be voidable nor the director's profits realised thereunder be recoverable by reason of the director " holding that office or of the fiduciary relation thereby established," [93] the director may freely contract without disclosing any material facts other than his interest.[94] However, if there is an " interest " it has to be disclosed even if it is too small to be material.[95]

Fourthly, what is meant by " interested " for this purpose? As we have seen, it has been held that an interest as trustee is sufficient to bring the basic equitable principle into operation [96]—since the resulting conflict of duties is just as serious as a conflict of pecuniary interests. On the other hand, it has been held that a director of another company remunerated only by salary is not deemed to be " interested " in a

---

[89] And the provisions in the 1844 Act: see p. 527, *supra*.
[90] subs. (1) and (2).
[91] *Imperial Mercantile Credit Asscn.* v. *Coleman, supra*; *Gray* v. *New Augarita Porcupine Mines* [1952] 3 D.L.R. 1, P.C.: " If it is material to their judgment that they should know not merely that he has an interest, but what it is and how far it goes, then he must see to it that they are informed ": *per* Lord Radcliffe at p. 14, citing Lord Cairns in (1873) L.R. 6 H.L. at p. 205.
[92] subs. (3).
[93] Table A, art. 84 (3).
[94] It should be noted that even under the basic equitable principle the obligation to make full disclosure only arises when a contract is to be entered into with the company. Thus a director is not under a general duty to disclose his own breach of other duties: *Healey* v. *S. A. Française Rubastic* [1917] 1 K.B. 946, approved in *Bell* v. *Lever Bros.* [1932] A.C. 161, H.L. On the other hand he may be under a duty to disclose the misdeeds of other directors and officers: see the observations in *Bell* v. *Lever Bros., ibid.* at p. 228. It is, apparently, more blessed to denounce the sins of others than to confess one's own.
[95] subs. (1).
[96] *Transvaal Lands Co.* v. *New Belgium (Transvaal) Land Co., supra*.

contract with that other company for the purposes of a provision requiring an interested director to vacate office.[97] It is, therefore, arguable that a similarly restrictive interpretation should be placed on " interested " in section 199, thus excluding anyone (such as a trustee or salaried director—not being a shareholder) who has no *pecuniary* interest. It would be lamentable if this argument should prevail. It is difficult to distinguish the words used in the respective provisions,[98] but the restrictive interpretation certainly does not seem to have been the intention of the draftsman of the Act.[99] It is, at any rate, clear that the interest does not have to be immediate; the section itself[1] expressly refers to any director " who is in any way, whether directly or indirectly, interested in a contract or proposed contract. . . ."

Finally, it should be emphasised that section 199 has of itself no validating effect on the contract even if it is fully complied with. It is purely negative in its operation, limiting the ambit of any exclusion clause in the articles; the section expressly states[2] that " nothing in this section shall be taken to prejudice the operation of any rule of law restricting directors of a company from having any interest in contracts with the company." If such contracts are to be valid this can only be as a result of ratification in general meeting after full disclosure, or as a result of an exclusion of the general rule under a provision in the articles.

The Jenkins Committee made recommendations[3] which, when implemented, would remove some of the defects of section 199. Disclosure would then be limited to *material* interests but would extend to contracts whether or not they came before the board. A general notice of interests would be permissible and not merely those arising from membership of another company or firm; but in all cases the nature *and extent* of the interest would require to be stated and the general notice would not be sufficient unless, at the time when the contract was first taken into consideration, the extent of the interest was not greater than that stated in the general notice.

Permissible ambit of exclusion clauses. If the exclusion clause covers what has been done, it appears that the mere fact that the contract is

[97] *Wilson* v. *L.M.S. Ry.* and *Lapish* v. *Braithwaite, supra,* note 79.
[98] The only difference is that the Municipal Corporations Act 1882 and the Companies Clauses Consolidation Act 1845 (relevant in *Lapish* v. *Braithwaite* and *Wilson* v. *L.M.S. Ry.* respectively), omit the words " in any way " used in s. 199; but all three statutes expressly refer to " directly or *indirectly* interested."
[99] Art. 84 (2) (*d*) of Table A expressly authorises voting by a director in connection with any contract with another company " in which he is interested only as an officer " or shareholder. This seems to imply that holding an office is a sufficient interest for general purposes and in particular for the purposes of disclosure under s. 199 and art. 84 (1).
[1] subs. (1).
[2] subs. (5).
[3] Cmnd. 1749, paras. 95 and 99 (*c*) and (*m*). They also recommended subsequent public disclosure of certain types of management contracts; paras. 96 and 99 (*n*). ss. 16 (1) (*c*) and 26 of the 1967 Act (see *infra,* p. 533) go considerably further.

disadvantageous to the company will not render it voidable. On the other hand, it is clear on general principles that no clause can protect the directors against the consequences of their own fraud. Furthermore, it is submitted that another statutory provision will prevent the clause from protecting the directors from a considerably lesser degree of fault. Under section 205, any provision in the articles or elsewhere is void in so far as it purports to exempt directors or any employees of the company from liability for " negligence, default, breach of duty or breach of trust." In determining whether there has been a breach of duty or breach of trust regard must be had to the articles. These may allow the director to place himself in a position where his duties and his interests may conflict and may authorise him to be personally interested in contracts with the company so that that alone will not be a breach of duty or trust. But they cannot, it is submitted, relieve the director of his duty to act in good faith, or of his liability if he does not, for that is banned by section 205. For example, although directors will be able, if the articles entitle them to do so, to vote themselves service agreements, these will still be liable to attack if the terms as to remuneration or otherwise are so unfair as not to have been voted in good faith and for a legitimate corporate purpose.

Other statutory restrictions on freedom of contract. Certain other sections of the Act impose further restraints on certain types of contracts or arrangements between a company and its directors. By section 189 a company may not pay a director remuneration (whether as director or otherwise) free of income tax,[4] and any agreement so to do has effect as if it provided for payment, subject to tax, of the sums stated.[5] Loans to directors are normally totally prohibited.[6] Moreover, section 196 requires disclosure to the members, through the annual accounts presented to them, of the aggregate amounts of the directors' emoluments,[7] pensions,[8] and payments by way of compensation for loss of office.[9] And by section 197 similar particulars have to be given of the amount of any loans made by the company [10] to any officer.

These obligations are greatly extended by the 1967 Act which requires disclosure of directors' emoluments, individually in the case of the chairman and within prescribed brackets in the case of others,[11]

---

[4] s. 189 (1). There is an exception in the case of agreements in force on July 18, 1945 (the date of publication of the Cohen Report, which recommended this provision; Cmd. 6659, para. 88).

[5] s. 189 (2).

[6] s. 190 as amended by s. 2 of the 1967 Act. The prohibition includes loans to a director of a holding company.

[7] As defined in s. 196 (2). Note that it includes expense allowances (except in so far as they are not chargeable to income tax), pension fund contributions, and benefits in kind.

[8] As defined in subs. (3).

[9] As defined in subs. (4).

[10] Or by any subsidiary company or by any person under a guarantee or security given by the company or its subsidiary.

[11] 1967 Act, s. 6. And as regards employees paid £10,000 p.a. or more, see s. 8.

and details of waived remuneration.[12] Moreover, and this is a real breakthrough, directors' contracts of service, or memoranda of them if not in writing, have to be made available for inspection by any member of the company without charge.[13] This means that although directors may still be able to vote themselves highly remunerative and long-term service agreements they can no longer conceal details of these from their members. Furthermore, in the directors' report particulars have to be given of any contract of significance in relation to the company's business in which a director has a material interest.[14] This is a valuable supplement to the disclosure to the board required under section 199.[15] Directors and officers are placed under an obligation to give notice to the company of such matters relating to themselves as may be necessary to enable it to comply with these provisions.[16]

But though these sections require *ex post facto* disclosure, they do not demand ratification by the company in general meeting. This, however, is required by section 191 in the case of any payment to a director by way of compensation for loss of office.[17] In this one case,[18] therefore, the statute has reverted to the original principle requiring disclosure to, and ratification by, the company in general meeting.

With these exceptions, provided that the directors act bona fide and remember to disclose their personal interests, there is, today, little effective restraint on their power to enter into contracts with the company. This will be apparent if the present provisions of Table A are examined in more detail. And these provisions, it should be remembered, are an optional model; subject only to sections 189, 190, 191 and 199, there is nothing to prevent the company from going even further in waiving its rights.

Table A articles.[19] Article 84 (2) of Table A contains a general prohibition against voting by a director in respect of any contract or

---

[12] *Ibid.*, s. 7.

[13] *Ibid.*, s. 26. Under the S.E. General Undertaking public disclosure is required annually in the case of quoted companies: *Requirements*, Sched. VIII, Part A, para. 7 (*a*) (2). The words of s. 26, "director whose contract of service," are not too clear. The intention was, presumably, to cover all service contracts with someone who was a director, but it is arguable that only contracts for service as a director are caught.

[14] *Ibid.*, s. 16 (1) (*c*) and (*d*). For further details regarding disclosure in the directors' report, see *supra*, pp. 466, 467.

[15] *Supra*, pp. 529–531.

[16] s. 198.

[17] For similar provisions where the payment is made by another person or company on a take-over bid, see *infra*, p. 540 *et seq.* Note that "any bona fide payment by way of damages for breach of contract or by way of pension in respect of past services" is not included: s. 194 (3). The section is not expressed to cover payments to former directors and it therefore seems possible to evade it by retiring before receiving the compensation. For this and other criticisms see Cmnd. 1749, paras. 92 and 93 and *infra*, p. 543.

[18] There is one other unusual case under s. 190 (2).

[19] These provisions are incorporated into Table D (for a company limited by guarantee and having a share capital) and Table E (for an unlimited company having a share capital) but there is nothing comparable in Table C (for the usual type of guarantee company, that without a share capital).

arrangement in which he is interested. It further provides [20] that he shall not be counted in the quorum present at the meeting.[21] Though Table A (and articles generally) provide that the number needed for a quorum may be fixed by the directors,[22] they cannot validly resolve to reduce the quorum so as to evade this rule.[23] Nor can they get round either rule by splitting what is in reality a single matter, in which they are all interested, into separate parts, in each of which one only appears to be interested.[24]

But to both these prohibitions there are a number of exceptions. Neither applies to granting a security or indemnity to a director in respect of loans to the company or obligations undertaken on its behalf,[25] nor to a contract to subscribe for shares or debentures in the company,[26] nor to any contract with another company in which he is interested only as an officer [27] or share or debentureholder.[28] These exceptions may, perhaps, be regarded as reasonable, but the same can hardly be said of the further exclusion, that of service contracts. A director, notwithstanding his interest, may be counted in the quorum present at any meeting whereat he or any other director is to be appointed to any office or place of profit under the company or whereat the terms are to be arranged, and although he may not vote on his own appointment, he is expressly authorised to do so on any appointment other than his own.[29] This apparently countenances an arrangement whereby at the same meeting all the directors vote themselves service agreements so long as each refrains from voting on his own agreement—a device which would seemingly infringe the general rule against " splitting." [30] This means that there is no need for service agreements to be submitted even to an independent board, let alone to an independent meeting of shareholders. Finally, it is provided that the prohibition may be suspended by ordinary resolution in general meeting either generally or in respect of any particular transaction.[31]

---

[20] This express provision seems to be unnecessary, since it has been held that only directors capable of voting can be counted towards a quorum: *Re Greymouth-Point Elizabeth Ry.* [1904] 1 Ch. 32.

[21] Although for the purposes of a general meeting it generally suffices if a quorum is present at the beginning of the meeting (*Re Hartley Baird* [1955] Ch. 143, *supra*, Chap. 21, p. 489), it seems clear that at a directors' meeting there must be a valid quorum for each separate item of business.

[22] Table A, art. 99.

[23] *Re North Eastern Insurance Co.* [1919] 1 Ch. 198.

[24] Hence a resolution to issue debentures to secure loans by directors cannot validly be taken as separate resolutions to issue part to each director, *ibid.* But under Table A this particular example would now fall within the exceptions to the general rules: art. 84 (2) (*a*).

[25] Art. 84 (2) (*a*) and (*b*).

[26] Art. 84 (2) (*c*).

[27] As already pointed out (*supra*, note 99), this appears to recognise that the holding of an office in another company is a sufficient " interest " in a contract with that company to require disclosure under s. 199, the obligations of which are restated in art. 84 (1).

[28] Art. 84 (2) (*d*).

[29] Art. 84 (4).

[30] *Supra*, notes 23 and 24.   [31] Art. 84 (2), the concluding words

Provided these rules are complied with, any contract or arrangement in which the director is in any way interested cannot be avoided, nor is the director liable to account to the company for any profit made thereout, " by reason of such director holding that office or of the fiduciary relation thereby established." [32] And, *ex abundante cautela,* a clause analogous to the " trustee charging clause " provides that a director may act by himself or his firm in a professional capacity and charge therefor.[33]

(b) Other secret profits

General equitable principle. Waiver claims, such as those of Table A just considered, have removed the sting from the basic equitable principle so far as concerns contracts between the company and its directors, or contracts in which the directors are indirectly interested. In striking contrast is the position where directors profit in some other way as a result of their position. For it has not become the practice to insert waiver clauses excluding liability to account to the company for such profits.[34]

In this respect, therefore, the equitable principle is applied in its full rigour. It applies not only to payments in the nature of bribes, made to directors in the hope of influencing their judgment, but also to any benefit which they would not have reaped but for some use of their special position. An extreme case which illustrates most of the questions which arise is the decision of the House of Lords in *Regal (Hastings) Ltd.* v. *Gulliver.*[35] The facts, briefly, were as follows—

> The company owned one cinema and the directors decided to acquire two others with a view to selling the whole undertaking as a going concern. For this purpose they formed a subsidiary company to take a lease of the other two cinemas. But the owner insisted on a personal guarantee from the directors unless the paid-up capital of the subsidiary was at least £5,000. The company was unable to subscribe in cash for more than 2,000 shares and the directors were not willing to give personal guarantees. Accordingly the original plan was changed; instead of the company subscribing for all the shares in the subsidiary the company took up 2,000 and the remaining 3,000 were taken by the directors and their friends. Later, instead of selling the undertaking, all the shares in both companies were sold, a profit of £2 16s. 1d. being made on each of the shares in the former subsidiary. The new controllers of the company then caused it to bring an action against the former directors to recover the profit they had made.

---

[32] Art. 84 (3).
[33] Art. 84 (5).
[34] The drafting of such a clause would be difficult but if art. 84 (3) can validly entitle directors to retain some profits, it is not clear why they should not be authorised to retain others. [35] [1942] 1 All E.R. 378; [1967] 2 A.C. 134n.

It will be observed that this claim was wholly unmeritorious. Recovery by the company would only benefit the purchasers, who, if the action was successful, would recover an undeserved windfall resulting in a reduction in the price which they had freely agreed to pay.[36] It also appears that the directors had held a majority of the shares in the company so that there would have been no difficulty in obtaining ratification of their action by the company in general meeting [37]; but acting, as it was conceded they had, in perfect good faith and in full belief in the legality and propriety of their action it had not occurred to them to go through this formality. It was also clear that the directors had not deprived the company of any of its property [38] (unless information can be regarded as property [39]), or robbed it of an opportunity which it might have exercised for its own advantage; the 3,000 shares in the subsidiary had never been the company's property and, on the facts as found, the company could not have availed itself of the opportunity to acquire them. Because of this the court of first instance and a unanimous Court of Appeal had dismissed the action. But a unanimous House of Lords reversed this decision. Following the well-known cases on trustees [40] it was held that the directors were liable to account once it was established " (i) that what the directors did was so related to the affairs of the company that it can properly be said to have been done in the course of their management [41] and in utilisation of their opportunities and special knowledge as directors; and (ii) that what they did resulted in a profit to themselves."

This may well be thought to be carrying equitable principles to an inequitable conclusion. Nor does this account exhaust the anomalies inherent in the decision. The chairman (and, apparently the dominant member) of the board, instead of agreeing himself to subscribe for shares in the subsidiary, had merely agreed to find subscribers for £500. Shares to this value had, accordingly, been taken up by two private companies of which he was a member and director, and by a personal friend of his. It was accepted that the companies and friend had subscribed beneficially and not as his nominees and, accordingly, he was held not to be under any liability to account for the profit which they had made.[42] The company's solicitor also escaped; though he had

---

36 Only one of their Lordships seemed to be disturbed by this—Lord Porter at [1967] 2 A.C. p. 157. On this question, see *infra*, pp. 537, 546.

37 See the very cogent editorial note in [1942] 1 All E.R. at 379. It was conceded that had this been done, there could have been no recovery. See on this question Chap. 24, *infra*.

38 Thus bringing the case within what is designated in America the " corporate asset " theory of liability.

39 On this important question, see *infra*, p. 555.

40 Notably the leading case of *Keech* v. *Sandford* (1726) Sel.Cas.Ch. 61.

41 This, of course, does not mean that they must be acting within the scope of their authority: *cf. Reading* v. *Att.-Gen.* [1951] A.C. 507, H.L.

42 The companies and friend had not been sued. Could recovery have been obtained from them had they been joined as parties? See *infra*, p. 554.

subscribed for shares and profited personally he could retain his profit because he had acted with the knowledge and consent of the company exercised through the board of directors. The directors themselves could avoid liability only if a general meeting had ratified, but the solicitor was an outsider [43] who could rely on the consent of the board. And this, despite the fact that the board had acted throughout on his advice. Hence the two men most responsible for what had been done escaped liability, while those who had followed their lead had to pay up.

What seems wrong with the application of the basic principle in this case is that recovery was not from all the right people and, more especially, was in favour of quite the wrong people.[44] Had it not been for the change of ownership it might well have been equitable to order restoration to the company, thus, in effect, causing the directors' profits to be shared among all the members. Certainly it is generally salutary to insist that directors shall not derive secret benefits from their trust. And it is probably well that this should apply whether or not any actual loss is suffered by the company, and whether or not it is deprived of an opportunity of benefiting itself. To allow directors to decide that the company shall not accept the opportunity and then to accept the opportunity themselves might impose too great a strain on their impartiality.

Although *Regal (Hastings) Ltd.* v. *Gulliver* has been followed and applied by a number of courts throughout the Commonwealth [45] it cannot be said that its exact scope is altogether clear. It certainly seems to go further than the Jenkins Committee's suggested formulation of the basic principles,[46] for that would limit accountability to "an improper advantage" obtained "at the expense of the company." In *Regal*, on the facts as found, the advantage was not improper, nor was it at the company's expense. But does it go so far as to establish that "if directors bona fide decide not to invest their company's funds in some proposed investment, a director who thereafter embarks his own money therein is accountable for any profits"? [47]

In 1966 this question was considered by the House of Lords in *Phipps* v. *Boardman* [48] and by the Canadian Supreme Court in *Peso Silver Mines* v. *Cropper.*[49] The former concerned agents acting for

---

[43] This description is used strictly in the technical sense!

[44] Some American courts have, in like circumstances, allowed recovery by the individual shareholders; see note: "Pro-Rata Recovery in Stockholders' Derivative Suits" (1956) 69 Harv.L.R. 1314.

[45] *Zwicker* v. *Stanbury* [1953] 2 S.C.R. 438 (Can.S.C.); *Canada Safeway Ltd.* v. *Thompson* [1951] 3 D.L.R. 295; [1952] 2 D.L.R. 591 (B.Col.S.C.), see (1952) 30 Can.B.R. 179; *Smith Ltd.* v. *Smith* [1952] N.Z.L.R. 470 (N.Z.S.C.); and *Fine Industrial Commodities* v. *Powling* (1954) 71 R.P.C. 253.

[46] See *supra*, pp. 519, 520.

[47] *Per* Lord Russell (quoting Greene M.R.) at [1967] 2 A.C. 152.

[48] [1967] 2 A.C. 46.

[49] (1966) 58 D.L.R. (2d) 1.

trustees in connection with the affairs of a company in which the trust held shares. The agents ultimately acquired the rest of the shares for themselves. *Regal* was followed and the agents were ordered to account for the profit they made—but there was no unanimity on exactly why. Lord Cohen said that the mere use of knowledge or opportunity would not lead to accountability; this depended on the facts of the case. In the instant case, as in *Regal*, the agents were liable because not only did the knowledge come to them while acting as fiduciaries but so did the opportunity to acquire the shares and to make the profit.[50] They were also liable because there was a possibility of a conflict of duty and interest since unprejudiced advice could not be given on whether the trustee-principals should apply to the court for permission to acquire the shares despite the fact that they were not an authorised investment.[51] Lord Hodson stated the relevant proposition in the widest terms:

> " No person standing in a fiduciary position, when a demand is made upon him by the person to whom he stands in the fiduciary relationship to account for profits acquired by him by reason of his fiduciary position and by reason of the opportunity and knowledge, or either, resulting from it, is entitled to defeat the claim upon any ground save that he made the profits with the knowledge and assent of the other person." [52]

But he then qualified this by saying that the knowledge must be " special information " which included confidential information.[53] Lord Guest quoted the speeches of Lords Russell and Wright in *Regal* and held that the principle they had enunciated clearly established that the agents held the shares they had acquired as constructive trustees for the principals and were bound to account. He expressly stated that it was irrelevant that the principals themselves could not have acquired the shares and that the agents were not competing with them.[54] Of the dissentients, one, Lord Dilhorne, in effect, adopted the narrower formula suggested by the Jenkins Committee,[55] holding that the agents were not liable to account since there had been no improper use of information which could have been used for the benefit of the principals.[56] The other, Lord Upjohn, thought the case was distinguishable from *Regal* since it did not concern property which had been " contemplated as the subject-matter of a possible purchase by the trust." [57]

50 [1967] 2 A.C. at pp. 100–103.
51 At pp. 103–104.
52 At p. 105.
53 At p. 109. Note the similarity to the formula suggested by the Jenkins Committee for reversing the rule in *Percival* v. *Wright* and imposing liability on directors who buy or sell their company's securities: see *supra*, p. 518.
54 At p. 117.
55 See *supra*, pp. 519, 520.
56 At pp. 84–94.
57 At p. 125.

In his view there was "no general rule that information learnt by a trustee during the course of his duties is property of the trust and cannot be used by him." [58] He could so use it:

"unless it is confidential information which is given to him (1) in circumstances which, regardless of his position as a trustee, would make it a breach of confidence for him to communicate to anyone . . . or (2) in a fiduciary capacity, and its use would place him in a position where his duty and his interest might possibly conflict." [59]

Disagreeing with the majority more on his assessment of the facts than of the law, he held that neither (1) nor (2) applied to the present case.

One proposition seems to emerge fairly clearly: the *mere* fact that knowledge comes to directors while acting as such does not make them liable to account. But it would appear that, in the view of all but Lord Dilhorne, they will be so liable if the knowledge is presented to them confidentially as a possible investment for the company even though the company does not avail itself of the opportunity.

In the *Peso Silver Mines* case the Canadian Supreme Court gave a definite negative answer to the question posed at page 537. The board of a mining company were approached by a prospector who offered to sell his claims adjoining the ground of the company. The board bona fide rejected this offer, but at the suggestion of the company's geologist some of the directors then agreed to purchase the shares themselves. [60] The company was later taken over and the new controllers claimed that the defendant, one of the directors concerned, was liable to account for his shares in a company which had been formed to operate the claims. The Supreme Court [61] held that he was not liable since there had been no use of confidential information and, in its view, the later approach to the directors was not in their capacity as directors but as individual members of the public. [62]

It appears from these two cases that directors may be entitled to take personal advantage of an opportunity originally offered to the company; but, probably, only if (1) the opportunity was rejected by the company, (2) the directors, if they acted in connection with its rejection, did so bona fide in the interests of the company, (3) the information was not given to them confidentially on behalf of the company, and (4) their subsequent use of the opportunity was not related to their positions as

---

[58] At p. 128.

[59] At p. 129.

[60] One of the reasons given for the purchase was that it was recognised that the claims were important to the company and should be in friendly hands. On the other hand the defendant claimed that the company's interest was "out of his mind" when he agreed to buy.

[61] (1966) 58 D.L.R. (2d) 1, affirming a majority decision of the Br.Col.Ct. of Appeal: (1966) 56 D.L.R. (2d) 117 where the facts are more fully stated.

[62] At p. 8.

directors. It will be a rare case in which the court, as in *Peso*, will be prepared to find that all these conditions are fulfilled.[62a]

Application to take-overs—statutory rules.[63] Just as the equitable principle has received statutory amplification in its relation to directors' contracts, so has it in connection with secret profits. The statutory rules relate to circumstances in which there is a transfer of the company's undertaking or of its capital, that is, to the increasingly prevalent " take-over bid," using that expression in the broadest sense.[64]

Anyone wishing to obtain control of a company may go about it in one of four main ways: (i) he may buy the company's undertaking, (ii) he may make a general offer to the shareholders to purchase their shares or sufficient of them to give control, (iii) he may do a deal with the existing board whereby they sell their shares to him and resign their offices, filling the casual vacancies, thus created, by his nominees [65] or (iv) he may seek to acquire, by purchase on the stock exchange or otherwise, sufficient shares to enable him to wage a successful battle of proxies with the existing management so that they are dismissed and replaced by his nominees. In all except the fourth case it will be necessary, or at least desirable, to have the concurrence of the existing directors. If they receive some special benefits in return for their support, will this be a secret profit for which they must account?

(i) *Sale of undertaking.* This case presents no difficulty. What is involved is a sale by the company for whom the directors are acting.[66] Any payment received by them [67] must therefore be accounted for to the company. This was always the result of applying the general equitable principle [68] and it is now codified by section 192 which says that it is unlawful in connection with the transfer of the whole *or any part* of the undertaking for any payment to be made to a director by way of compensation for loss of office, or in connection with his retirement [69] unless this has been disclosed to the members and approved

---

[62a] For a trenchant criticism of the rigour of these rules, see Gareth Jones, (1968) 84 L.Q.R. 472. He argues persuasively that fiduciaries should not be liable to account unless either they have not acted honestly or they have been unjustly enriched.

[63] For take-overs in general, see Chap. 26; and see further Weinberg, *Take-overs and Amalgamations* (2nd ed., 1967) in which Chap. 25 relates to the problems discussed here.

[64] It is most often used in the sense of case (ii) of the succeeding paragraph.

[65] The *City Code* (on which see Chap. 26, p. 627 *et seq.*) disapproves of this save " in very exceptional circumstances and after consultation with the Panel ": r. 10.

[66] The Jenkins Committee recommended that such a sale should require the specific approval of a general meeting: Cmnd. 1749, paras. 117 and 122 (*e*)–(*g*).

[67] Normally the payment would be made by the bidder; if made by the company itself it would generally also be caught by s. 191. The Jenkins Committee recommended that ratification should require a special, and not, as at present, merely an ordinary, resolution: Cmnd. 1749, para. 93.

[68] *Gaskell* v. *Chambers (No. 3)* (1858) 26 Beav. 360. This equitable principle clearly cannot be evaded, as can ss. 191 and 192 on a literal construction, by retiring from the directorship before receiving the payment.

[69] For the wide construction given to this expression, see s. 194, considered *infra*.

in general meeting. If this is not done the amount received is to be held on trust for the company.[70] The result, unlike that in *Regal (Hastings) Ltd.* v. *Gulliver*,[71] is perfectly equitable for the membership of the company remains unchanged by the transfer of its undertaking, and all the members benefit by the restoration to the company.

(ii) *General offer.* When we turn to a sale of shares, rather than of the undertaking, the problem becomes more difficult. What normally occurs on a take-over bid of this sort is that another company requests the directors to forward an offer to their shareholders to purchase their shares at a specified price,[72] the offer being expressed to be conditional on acceptance by holders of 90 per cent. of the shares.[73] Although there will often have been prior negotiations with the directors to seek to arrive at a price which they will be prepared to accept in respect of their own shares and to recommend to the other shareholders,[74] it is not clear that the directors can really be regarded as acting on behalf of their company. They seem, rather, to be merely a convenient channel of communication between the bidder and the shareholders.[75] On the other hand, the whole basis of this method—and its great virtue as compared with methods (iii) and (iv)—is that all the shareholders should receive the same price.[76] This object will be defeated if the directors can bargain for additional payments to themselves. Section 193 [77] is designed to prevent this.

The section applies where there has been a transfer of shares resulting from: (i) an offer to the general body of shareholders, (ii) an offer by one company with a view to another company becoming its subsidiary,[78] (iii) an offer by an individual with a view to his obtaining the right to exercise or control not less than one-third of the voting power at general meetings, or (iv) any other offer conditional on acceptance to a

---

[70] s. 192 (2).

[71] *Supra.*

[72] To be satisfied either in cash or in shares in the acquiring company or partly in one and partly in the other.

[73] If the offer is made by a company and accepted by not less than 90 per cent., advantage may be taken of the right of pre-emption of the shares of the dissenting minority conferred by s. 209 and of certain stamp duty exemptions: see on these points Chap. 26, pp. 625–633.

[74] Without such a recommendation acceptance by the shareholder is less likely but has occurred in a number of take-overs in recent years: for some statistics see Rose and Newbould, " The 1967 Take-over Boom " in *Moorgate and Wall Street* for Autumn 1967, p. 5 *et seq.*

[75] Hence the Board of Trade take the view that the fact that the offer is so forwarded does not dispense with the need to obtain their consent to the circular to comply with the Prevention of Fraud (Investments) Act, *supra*, Chap. 14, p. 305. But the Board do not object to circulation by an exempted dealer acting on behalf of the bidder. If the circular offers shares to be newly quoted, it must also comply with the S.E. *Requirements, ibid.* In practice, too, the conduct of both sides must comply with the 1969 *City Code* policed by the " watch-dog " Panel: *ibid.* and pp. 626–631, *infra.*

[76] See 1969 *City Code.* General Principle 8. But as regards market purchases, see rr. 29–33.

[77] As amplified by s. 194.

[78] Or a subsidiary of its holding company. For definitions see s. 154, *supra*, p. 196.

given extent.[79]   Hence it invariably covers the method of acquiring
control now under consideration.   It is then the duty of a director to
take all reasonable steps to secure that, in any notice of the offer made
to the shareholders, there shall be included particulars with respect to
payments [80] to be made to him.[81]   Unless this is done and unless, in
addition,[82] the payment is approved by a special meeting of the holders
of the shares to which the offer relates and of other shares of the same
class,[83] any sum received by the director shall be held by him in trust
for any persons who have sold their shares as a result of the offer.[84]

Here, it will be observed, the legislature has faced the problem, met
with in *Regal (Hastings) Ltd.* v. *Gulliver*,[85] of providing for restoration
to those truly damnified, and not to the company thus giving an
undeserved reduction of price to the bidder.   To this extent, therefore,
it has recognised an exception to the general rule that directors are
not trustees for individual shareholders.   They become trustees for
shareholders, but not for all of them, merely for those who have sold.[86]

Section 193 refers, as do sections 191 and 192, to payments " by
way of compensation for loss of office . . . or in connection with his
retirement from office " *i.e.*, to what are known as " golden hand-
shakes "—though the gold is no longer 18 carat.[87]   But this is considerably amplified by section 194.   For the purpose of all these sections a
payment is presumed to be by way of compensation if made in
pursuance of an arrangement which was part of the agreement for the
transfer, or which was made within one year before or two years after
the offer, so long as the company or the bidder was privy to the
arrangement.[88]   This is designed to prevent evasion by pretending to
separate the payment of compensation from the arrangements for the
transfer.   Moreover, and this materially widens the ambit of the

---

[79] s. 193 (1).
[80] See below for a detailed consideration of the nature of the payments covered.
[81] If he does not he is liable to a fine, as is the bidder if he does not comply with
   the request to include it: subs. (2).
[82] The rather tortuous wording of s. 193 (3) and the use of the disjunctive " or "
   obscures the fact that the requirements are cumulative.   This, however, is clear both
   on a careful analysis of the grammatical construction and from a study of the
   legislative history.
[83] Arrangements are made for convening a meeting of this special group if provision
   is not made in the articles: subs. (4).   If a quorum is not present after the original
   meeting and one adjournment, the payment is deemed to be approved; subs. (5).
   The Jenkins Committee recommended that a threequarters majority should be
   required: Cmnd. 1749, para. 93.   Under the Licensed Dealers (Conduct of Business)
   Rules 1960 (S.I. 1216) the offer may not be made conditional on the offerees'
   approving the payment: Sched. 1, Pt. II, para. 1 (3).
[84] s. 193 (3).
[85] *Supra.*
[86] It is arguable that all those to whom the offer was made should share, for those who
   declined the offer might have accepted it had it been increased by the amount payable
   to the director.   On the other hand, they retain their shares which, presumably, are
   worth at least as much as the adjusted price.
[87] Any such payment in excess (normally) of £5,000 is taxable as income for the year:
   F.A. 1960, ss. 37 and 38.
[88] s. 194 (1).

section, if a director is to retire, and the price paid to him for his shares is in excess of the price paid to the other shareholders or any other valuable consideration is given to him, this is deemed to be compensation.[89] In other words, the payment has to be accounted for even though it is expressed to be in respect of his shares,[90] or ostensibly is totally unconnected with the retirement.

On the other hand, it appears that unless the director is to retire from office as director in the particular company concerned [91] an additional payment made to him is not recoverable under the sections. If no change is made in the directorship but, for example, the board are paid £10,000 to persuade them to recommend the offer to the other shareholders, or are paid an increased price for their shares because they hold a large block, it seems there can be no recovery under the sections. Whether reliance can then be placed on the general equitable principle we shall consider after we have seen how far the sections apply to the two remaining methods of acquiring control. Moreover, recoverable payments do not include "any bona fide payment by way of damages for breach of contract or by way of pension in respect of past services." [92] It seems, though this is not entirely clear, that such payments would be excluded notwithstanding that the agreements under which they are paid were made in contemplation of the transfer.[93]

(iii) *Deal with directors.* As already emphasised more than once, *de facto* control of a company can be exercised, especially by the existing board, although they hold considerably less than 50 per cent. of the voting capital. Hence a bidder may be able to acquire effective control by purchasing, say, 20 per cent. of the equity shares from the directors (and others if need be) and arranging with the directors to resign their offices and to fill the casual vacancies thus created by nominees of the

---

[89] s. 194 (2).

[90] *e.g.*, because he has a large block.

[91] It apparently does not at present cover payments by a holding company for loss of a directorship in a subsidiary : see Cmnd. 1749, para. 93.

[92] s. 194 (3). The Jenkins Committee recommended that the total amount receivable should be disclosed if shareholders were asked to ratify any additional payment not legally due: Cmnd. 1749, para. 93. This seems already to be required by the Licensed Dealers (Conduct of Business) Rules 1960, Sched. 1, Pt. II, para. 2 (6) and (7).

[93] Under the recommendations of the Cohen Committee it was clearly otherwise : Cmd. 6659, pp. 49 and 53. But s. 194 (3), seems to exclude bona fide payments of damages or pensions even though they arise under arrangements within subs. (1). If directors suspect that a take-over bid is likely, an obvious step is to vote themselves long-term service agreements. *Semble* this will entitle them to damages even though the agreements are entered into within a year previous to the bid or definitely in contemplation of it. But the payment must be bona fide—so that it might be ill-advised for the old board to settle their own claim for damages, which, as a result of *B.T.C.* v. *Gourley* [1956] A.C. 185, H.L., may not be very large if they are liable to a high rate of surtax. And, of course, it might be possible for the service agreements to be set aside as not made " bona fide in the interests of the company and for a proper purpose." *Quaere* if this would be contrary to the *City Code*, General Principle 4, as action " which could effectively result in any bona fide offer being frustrated."

bidder. Such a transaction would fall completely outside sections 193 and 194 [94] and hence, so far as those sections are concerned, the directors are entitled to demand whatever they can get from the bidder.

(iv) *Deals with outside interests.* Attempts to obtain control by purchase on the stock exchange, or elsewhere, followed by a proxy fight will also normally fall outside the sections. This is of less importance for, *ex hypothesi*, the bidder is fighting the directors and therefore is unlikely to make any payments to them. However, it might happen that a minority on the board were seduced from their allegiance. Or, after frantic buying on both sides, the board might decide to sell out to the bidder at a price in excess of what the outside shareholders had obtained.[95]

Take-over bids—residual application of equitable principle. It will be apparent, therefore, that there are a number of circumstances in which the directors, in connection with a take-over bid, may receive additional payments without being liable to account for them under the statute. The 1969 *City Code* and the supervision of the Panel should, in most cases, prevent this occurring in future in the case of public companies. But it could still occur in the case of private ones where some of the worst abuses have occurred in the past. How far will equitable principles then apply to compel them to disgorge?

There are two possible lines of attack. First it may be argued that they have broken some duty to the individual shareholders. The difficulty here is that, at present,[96] directors normally owe no duty to individual shareholders. Hence, in *Percival* v. *Wright* [97] it was held that they were not liable to members whose shares they bought without disclosing a take-over bid at a higher price. But a later case [98] shows that this must not be taken too far; the board may by their conduct place themselves in a fiduciary position towards shareholders in the course of negotiating terms with the bidder.[99] They may even be expressly appointed by the shareholders to act as their agents,[1] though this would be unusual in the

---

[94] For the four circumstances in which these sections operate, see *supra*, p. 541. For practical purposes none of these will occur if less than one-third of the equity is the subject of an unconditional offer—and the fraction must normally be more than a half if the offer is by a corporation. But since the 1969 *City Code* this is unlikely to occur with a quoted company.

[95] If no general offer were ever made this would seem to fall outside the scope of the *City Code*.

[96] See *supra*, p. 518 for the Jenkins Committee's recommendations.

[97] [1902] 2 Ch. 421.

[98] *Allen* v. *Hyatt* (1914) 30 T.L.R. 444, P.C.

[99] Compare the " special facts " doctrine, widely adopted in the U.S.A., flowing from *Strong* v. *Repide* (1909) 213 U.S. 419. Recently the interpretation placed on S.E.C. rule 10b–5 seems to be universalising the former minority rule that directors are in a fiduciary relationship to individual shareholders: see *Kardon* v. *National Gypsum Co.* (1947) 73 F.Supp. 798 ; *Speed* v. *Transamerica Corpn.* (1951) 99 F.Supp. 808 (and many later proceedings); and Loss: *Securities Regulation* (2nd ed., 1961), pp. 1448–1474.

[1] As in *Briess* v. *Woolley* [1954] A.C. 333, H.L., where, as a result, the shareholders were held liable for the fraud practised by the directors on the bidder.

case of a public company whose shares were widely held. If they have become fiduciaries of the shareholders it is clear that normal equitable principles compel them to restore the profits they have made in respect of the members' shares.[2] It is equally clear that they will then have to account if the bidder pays them something to induce them to persuade the shareholders to accept the offer; this would be nothing less than a bribe and the directors would be liable accordingly.[3] But it is less clear that the shareholders would have any remedy if the bidder paid the directors something as compensation for loss of their offices. This would not seem to be a payment received by them *qua* agents of the shareholders.

In any case, directors will normally have no difficulty in avoiding an implication that they have become anything in the nature of agents for the other shareholders. The mere fact that they negotiate terms and forward them with a recommendation clearly does not suffice. The position will be remedied to some extent if the recommendation of the Jenkins Committee[4] is implemented, for then directors will be liable to anyone whose securities they buy concealing their knowledge of an impending take-over bid.[5]

The second, and legally more hopeful, line is to allege a breach of the directors' fiduciary duties towards the company. Wherever the payments have been made to the directors because, and only because, they were directors there is a strong argument for saying that the principle exemplified in *Regal (Hastings) Ltd.* v. *Gulliver*[6] applies, and that they must account to the company. This should cover the case where the payment is made to secure their resignations even though it is shares that are being sold and not the undertaking. In America the courts have had no difficulty in adopting this view on the narrower ground that their offices are corporate property.[7] A still stronger case can be made out for recovery by the company where there has been trafficking in shares, as in *Percival* v. *Wright*,[8] for then there has been an abuse of confidential information, itself an additional ground for recovery.[9] The position is somewhat more difficult where the payment received is simply to secure their favourable recommendation to the shareholders, for this hardly seems to be a bribe or payment to them *qua* directors,

---

[2] So held in *Allen* v. *Hyatt, supra.*
[3] For the various liabilities incurred in respect of bribes, see *infra,* p. 557.
[4] *Supra,* p. 518.
[5] Having regard to the terms of the *City Code* it seems clear that the court would regard this as " improper " use of confidential information.
[6] *Supra.*
[7] For a leading case see *Gerdes* v. *Reynolds* (1941) 28 N.Y.S. 2d 622, where the directors were held liable not only to account for the sums paid for their resignations but also to restore the loss suffered by the company from the looting of its assets by the new board that they had negligently installed.
[8] *Supra,* p. 517.
[9] See *infra,* pp. 546, 547.

no corporate action being involved.[10] It is more difficult still where they are simply paid something in respect of their (effectively controlling) blocks of shares. But here also the American courts are beginning to come round to the view that directors (or, indeed, other controllers who are not directors) are not entitled to retain the increased price obtained because their shares confer such control.[11] This seems eminently desirable—control is valuable because it enables the company's assets to be dealt with; all members should share rateably in this, not just the lucky few. But this would be a highly novel doctrine in England.

Novelty, however, is no conclusive objection. The difficulty about its reception is twofold. First, it comes close to holding that section 193 is declaratory which, in contrast to section 192, it is not expressed to be.[12] This, however, might be met by drawing attention to section 194 (4) which declares that nothing in section 192 or 193 shall be taken to prejudice the operation of any rule of law requiring disclosure to be made with respect to payments to directors.

The second, and major objection, is the futility of allowing recovery by the company in circumstances where those really damnified are the other shareholders who have sold.[13] The statutory rule meets this difficulty; the judge-made rule does not.[14] While the courts insist that, where a duty to the company has been broken, recovery can be ordered only to the company, an extension of this equitable principle would do little more than punish the directors for their self-dealing—a criminal penalty would serve this purpose better. Here, again, the American courts are ahead of ours by allowing recovery by the individual shareholders who have suffered, notwithstanding that the duty broken was owed to the company.[15]

(c) Abuse of confidence

Directors are not permitted, either during or after their service with

---

[10] But corporate action may be required; for example, if, as in the case of a private company, the directors have a right to refuse transfers of the shares, a payment to secure their acceptance of transfers would clearly be recoverable: *cf. Clark* v. *Workman* [1920] I.R. 107 (Irish). And s. 165 (b) (*infra*, p. 607 *et seq.*) implies that it is the duty of directors to give shareholders "the information which they might reasonably expect." Might not this include notice of a take-over bid?

[11] See especially *Perlman* v. *Feldmann* (1955) 219 F. 2d 173, cert. denied 349 U.S. 952, (1957) 154 F.Supp. 436. For a discussion of this and earlier authorities see Jennings: "Trading in Corporate Control" (1956) 44 Cal.L.R. 1, Leech in (1956) 104 U. of Penn.L.R. 725–841, Berle in (1958) 58 Col.L.R. 1212, and Boyle in (1964) 13 I.C.L.Q. 185; and see *infra*, Chap. 24, pp. 578, 579.

[12] Subs. (3), imposing a trust for *shareholders*, clearly goes further than the common law rule, but this was not in the original section in the 1929 Act which, equally, was not expressed to be declaratory.

[13] It is arguable, see note 86, *supra*, that *all* the other shareholders have suffered—this seems to be the American view. There is certainly a better case for allowing recovery by the company if there are a number of outside shareholders left in the company, for this at least means that others benefit beside the entirely unmeritorious bidder. But unfortunately the larger the proportion of outside shareholders remaining, the less likelihood there is of the new controllers causing the company to take action.

[14] As *Regal (Hastings) Ltd.* v. *Gulliver, supra,* strikingly reveals.

[15] See authorities cited in note 11, *supra*, and (1956) 69 Harv.L.R. 1314.

the company, to use for their own purposes anything entrusted to them for use on behalf of the company. This principle is not restricted to property in the strict sense; it also includes trade secrets [16] and confidential information.[17] This principle, it is submitted, should be wide enough to cover cases, such as *Percival* v. *Wright*,[18] in which directors have used confidential information (for example, knowledge of an impending dividend declaration or take-over bid) to speculate successfully in their company's shares. The fact that the company itself suffers no damage ought, on general principles,[19] to be irrelevant. As yet, however, no company in this country [20] has sought to recover from a director on this ground, and, since *Percival* v. *Wright*,[21] it seems to have been generally assumed that in law directors have *carte blanche* to utilise their inside knowledge in private speculations. This, clearly, is not in accordance with accepted commercial morality as has virtually been recognised by the provisions for disclosure of dealings by directors and insiders in the 1948 and 1967 Acts.[22]

(d) Competition

A fiduciary is normally strictly precluded from entering into competition with his *cestui que trust*.[23] This finds its clearest expression in partnership law, where it is now embodied in section 30 of the Partnership Act 1890. But despite the close analogy between companies and partnerships it is by no means clear that a similar rule applies to the directors of a company.[24] Indeed, it is generally stated that it does not, and there appears to be a clear, if inadequately reported, decision to the effect that a director of one company cannot be restrained from acting as a director of a rival company.[25] This assumes, of course, that it cannot be shown that " he was making to the second company any disclosure of information obtained confidentially by him as a director of the first

---

[16] *British Industrial Plastics* v. *Ferguson* [1938] 4 All E.R. 504, C.A.; *Cranleigh Precision Engineering Ltd.* v. *Bryant* [1965] 1 W.L.R. 1293.

[17] Such as lists of customers or copies of confidential documents for use by a competitor: *Measures Bros.* v. *Measures* [1910] 1 Ch. 336, affd. [1910] 2 Ch. 248, C.A.; *Printers & Finishers Ltd.* v. *Holloway* [1965] 1 W.L.R. 1.

[18] *Supra.* This case merely decides that there can be no recovery by the selling shareholder.

[19] *Cf. Reading* v. *Att.-Gen.* [1951] A.C. 507, H.L., and *Phipps* v. *Boardman* [1967] 2 A.C. 46, H.L.

[20] Contrast America: see *Brophy* v. *Cities Service Co.* (1949) 31 Del.Ch. 241, 70 A. 2d 5, and see also s. 16 (*b*) of the Securities Exchange Act 1934.

[21] *Supra.*

[22] See *supra*, pp. 388–391.

[23] This duty, unlike that considered under head (*c*), only applies during the subsistence of the relationship, not after it has ended. For a discussion of the general question of the survival of fiduciary duties after the cessation of the fiduciary relationship, see *Nordisk Insulinlaboratorium* v. *Gorgate Products* [1953] Ch. 430, C.A.

[24] It clearly does not apply to shareholders, even in a private company, but if they exercise their powers so as to conduct the company's affairs in a manner oppressive to the other members they may fall foul of s. 210: see *infra*, pp. 548, 598–604.

[25] *London & Mashonaland Exploration Co.* v. *New Mashonaland Exploration Co.* [1891] W.N. 165. Approved by Lord Blanesburgh in *Bell* v. *Lever Bros.* [1932] A.C. at 195.

company," [26] thus infringing the rule against abuse of confidence described above. Nor does this seem to be merely a reluctant recognition of the consequences of multiple directorships, for it has been said that: " What he could do for a rival company he could, of course, do for himself." [26]

Admittedly the position may be different as a result of a provision in the articles or in any service contract; for example, a provision that the director shall devote the whole of his time and attention during usual office hours to the business of the company would preclude him from working during those hours for himself or anyone else, and whether or not in a competing business. Furthermore, a later case [27] has established that the duty of fidelity flowing from the relationship of master and servant may preclude the servant from engaging, even in his spare time, in work for a competitor. Having regard to this decision it is submitted that the position of directors requires reconsideration. It is established that the servant's duty of fidelity imposes lesser obligations than the full duty of good faith owed by a director or other fiduciary agent.[28] How then can it be that a director can compete whereas a subordinate servant cannot? It seems clear that, at the very least, a service director is not allowed to do so,[29] and it is suggested that the same should apply to any director.

In any event it is clear that the position has been materially affected by the new remedy against oppression introduced by section 210 of the Companies Act 1948.[30] This is shown by *Scottish Co-operative Wholesale Society Ltd.* v. *Meyer*,[31] where the Society, the controlling shareholder, through their nominee directors, were held by the House of Lords to have conducted the affairs of the company in a manner oppressive to the minority shareholders by running down the business of the company in order to benefit the competing business of the Society. Although the proceedings were against the Society, not the directors, it was essentially the action of the directors, at the Society's instigation, which was regarded as oppressive conduct of the company, and one at least of the Law Lords, Lord Denning, was clearly of opinion that they were guilty of breaches of duty. After pointing out the conflicts of duty which are likely to arise when directors act for two competing concerns,[32] he said:

---

[26] *Per* Lord Blanesburgh in *Bell* v. *Lever Bros.*, *ibid.* On the other hand, it was conceded in *Bell* v. *Lever Bros.* that the directors had broken their fiduciary duties by entering into private transactions under which liability might be incurred by the company.

[27] *Hivac Ltd.* v. *Park Royal Scientific Instruments Ltd.* [1946] Ch. 169, C.A. See Kahn-Freund in (1946) 9 M.L.R. 145 and Arthur Lewis in *ibid.* 280. See also *British Syphon Co.* v. *Homewood* [1956] 1 W.L.R. 1190.

[28] *Bell* v. *Lever Bros., supra.*

[29] His case would be covered, *a fortiori*, by the *Hivac* decision as Lord Denning recognised in *Scottish Co-op. Wholesale Society Ltd.* v. *Meyer* [1959] A.C. 324, H.L. at p. 367.

[30] This section is dealt with in more detail in Chap. 25, *infra.*

[31] [1959] A.C. 324, H.L.(Sc.).   [32] At pp. 366–368.

"Your Lordships were referred to *Bell* v. *Lever Bros. Ltd.* where Lord Blanesburgh said that a director of one company was at liberty to become a director also of a rival company. That may have been so at that time. But it is at the risk now of an application under section 210 if he subordinates the interests of the one company to those of the other." [33]

It seems, however, that the mere acceptance of directorships in competing companies is not a breach of duty or conduct within section 210 [34] so long as he can walk the tightrope by acting fairly to both.

DUTIES OF CARE AND SKILL

This subject can be disposed of briefly, for there is a striking contrast between the directors' heavy duties of loyalty and good faith and their very light obligations of skill and diligence. Directors have to display some degree of both, but the courts have found difficulty in deciding how much. Here, as already pointed out,[35] the trustee analogy breaks down, for the type of skill required of a cautious trustee is quite different from that which an enterprising director needs to display. The courts might, no doubt, have demanded of directors a degree of *diligence* comparable to that of trustees—a high degree particularly where they are paid.[36] But the courts cannot be too far in advance of public opinion, and public opinion has come to recognise that directorships are often little more than sinecures, requiring, at the most, attendance at occasional board meetings.

But if, in this respect, directors are not trustees they are certainly agents. Does the law of agency offer a guide? In agency it is customary to draw a distinction between those exercising a particular trade or profession, who must display a degree of diligence and skill comparable with that of reasonably competent and conscientious members of that trade or profession,[37] and other agents who are merely expected to display such skill as they possess and such diligence as would be displayed by a reasonable man in the circumstances.

Is a directorship a profession within the meaning of this distinction? In favour of this view it may be argued that a directorship is a recognised office of profit. But, once again, the courts have had to face the facts, and the facts are that until recently the possession of a title was often regarded as a greater qualification for office than any amount of business acumen and drive, and that the ordinary part-time director was only

---

[33] At p. 368. *Quaere* whether the *directors of the Society* could have been made liable: cf. *Lindgren* v. *L. & P. Estates Ltd.* [1968] Ch. 572, C.A., *supra.*

[34] *Re Lundie Bros. Ltd.* [1965] 1 W.L.R. 1051.

[35] *Supra,* p. 516.

[36] *National Trustees Co. of Australasia* v. *General Finance Co. of Australasia* [1905] A.C. 373, P.C. ; *Re Windsor Steam Coal Co.* [1929] 1 Ch. 151, C.A.

[37] As in the case of auditors : see *supra,* pp. 469–471.

expected to display such skill (if any) as he happened to possess, and such attention to duty as he thought fit to offer.

The position differs radically with holders of other offices under the company. Full-time employees are obviously bound to devote their whole time and attention (during usual office hours) to the business of the company, and solicitors, accountants, and secretaries are expected to display the normal skill of members of their professions. Full-time managing directors are also expected to display similar *diligence* but it is not yet clear whether there is, so far as they are concerned, any objective standard of *skill* to which they must measure up. The evolution of a class of company managers is one of the distinctive features of the present epoch, but the courts hardly seem prepared to recognise that it has attained professional status and standards.[38]

The judges have faced one further difficulty. Whereas their training and experience make them well equipped to adjudicate on questions of loyalty and good faith, they move with less assurance among complicated problems of economics and business administration. Hence, they display an understandable reluctance to interfere with the directors' business judgment—a reluctance of which many examples will be found throughout the whole area of company law.[39] Perhaps, too, they are conscious of the possible unfairness of attempting to substitute their hindsight for the directors' foresight, and are therefore unwilling to condemn directors even though events have proved them wrong.

In *Re City Equitable Fire Insurance Co.*[40] in 1925 the earlier cases were reviewed by Romer J. in an elaborate judgment in which he reduced the law to three propositions. As in the case of the fiduciary duties previously discussed, the duties of diligence, care and skill described in these propositions are owed only to the company itself [41] and not to the individual members.

The three propositions were:

1. *A director need not exhibit in the performance of his duties a greater degree of skill than may reasonably be expected from a person of his knowledge and experience.*

This proposition lays down the standard of skill to be exhibited in such actions as the director undertakes. It prescribes a test which is

---

[38] Note the speeches of the Law Lords in *Holdsworth & Co.* v. *Caddies* [1955] 1 W.L.R. 352 (also reported 1955 S.C.(H.L.) 27), H.L.Sc., refusing to recognise the " conception of a stratification of a position as managing director," to use the phrase of Lord Kilmuir L.C. at p. 356. But if the managing director can be treated as an employee (see *Trussed Steel Concrete Ltd.* v. *Green* [1946] Ch. 115 at 121) there seems no reason why objective standards of care should not be applied to him.

[39] See especially Chap. 26, p. 635 *et seq., infra.*

[40] [1925] Ch. 407 at p. 428 *et seq.* The arguments and judgments in this case constitute a mine of information on the duties of directors and auditors. The case went to appeal only in respect of the auditor's liability and it is only in that respect that the judgment can technically be said to have been upheld by the C.A. On the duties of auditors see Chap. 20, *supra,* pp. 467–471.

[41] See *supra,* pp. 517–524.

partly objective (the standard of the reasonable man), and partly subjective (the reasonable man is deemed to have the knowledge and experience of the particular individual). Though this may be thought to express a somewhat lowly degree of expertise, it probably puts it higher than is justified by some of the earlier cases. Half a century earlier it had been said [42] that if directors were to be liable they must be " cognisant of such circumstances of such a character, so plain, so manifest, and so simple of appreciation, that no men with any ordinary degree of prudence, acting on their own behalf, would have entered into such a transaction as they entered into." The slightly less contemptuous expressions used by Romer J. doubtless reflect the rise in the standards of business education during the intervening years.

2. *A director is not bound to give continuous attention to the affairs of his company. His duties are of an intermittent nature to be performed at periodical board meetings, and at meetings of any committee of the board upon which he happens to be placed. He is not, however, bound to attend all such meetings, though he ought to attend whenever in the circumstances he is reasonably able to do so.*

Whereas, in the present stage of legal development, proposition 1 probably applies equally to managing directors, this second proposition clearly does not. It is directed solely to holders of ordinary directorships from whom nothing more is expected than attendance at meetings. And though it is said that they ought to attend these meetings whenever they can, the cases suggest that this is little more than a pious hope.[43] As in other walks of life, if anything is going wrong there are great advantages in " not being there." The director who stays away runs the risk of not being reappointed when he next comes up for re-election, but little risk of liability for what is done in his absence. Here, as throughout this branch of the law, questions of causation are of paramount importance; if a director is party to a decision to take a particular course of action it may be possible to show that this led directly to loss by the company,[44] but it will be next to impossible to show that his laziness was the cause of the damage or that the action would have been different had he attended.[45]

---

[42] *Per* Lord Hatherley L.C. in *Overend & Gurney Co.* v. *Gibb* (1872) L.R. 5 H.L. 480 at p. 487.

[43] In *Re Denham & Co.* (1883) 25 Ch.D. 752, the director had not attended any meetings for four years, and in *The Marquis of Bute's Case* [1892] 2 Ch. 100 a trustee of a savings bank had not attended for even longer (but there were 50 trustees); each escaped liability. In the latter case Stirling J. said (at p. 109): " Neglect or omission to attend meetings is not, in my opinion, the same thing as neglect or omission of a duty which ought to be performed at those meetings."

[44] Observe how, in the *City Equitable Case*, specific losses were pleaded as flowing from particular acts or omissions.

[45] This is well brought out in the opinion of Learned Hand J. in the American case of *Barnes* v. *Andrews* (1924) 298 Fed. 614.

3. *In respect of all duties that, having regard to the exigencies of business and the articles of association, may properly be left to some other official, a director is, in the absence of grounds for suspicion, justified in trusting that official to perform such duties honestly.*

Since directors are not required to possess any particular accomplishments and since the successful running of a business requires a measure of skill, ignorant directors must obviously rely on expert officials. These officials are the agents and servants of the company, not of the directors. Hence, the directors are not responsible vicariously for their misdeeds. If the directors are to be made liable it can only be on the basis of their personal negligence, and, as proposition 3 [46] recognises, it is not negligent to trust an official whose previous conduct has given no ground for suspicion. However, duties must not be entrusted to an obviously inappropriate or unqualified official; the handling of the investments of a finance company must not be left to the office boy. One of the grounds on which the *City Equitable* directors were held to have broken their duties was that they had allowed the managing director to usurp functions not delegated to him, and had permitted the company's stockbrokers to retain large sums without security in a manner more appropriate to bankers than to brokers.

Although the *City Equitable* directors were held to have fallen short even of these somewhat lowly standards,[47] they escaped because of a clause absolving them from liability except for wilful default. As we have seen,[48] such a clause would no longer avail them, for section 205 [49] invalidates indemnity clauses of this sort.

EFFECT OF BREACH OF DUTY

This subject also can be dealt with briefly, for nothing peculiar to company law is involved but merely the general principles of common law and equity applicable to agency and trust.

Remedies

A breach by a director of his duties may lead to an order for one or more of the following—

(a) Injunction or declaration;

(b) Damages or compensation;

---

[46] Which is fully supported by the decision of the H.L. in *Dovey* v. *Cory* [1901] A.C. 477, H.L.

[47] Romer J. also thought that the auditor had been negligent but this question was left open by the C.A.

[48] *Supra*, p. 532.

[49] But it does not avoid clauses entitling an officer to be indemnified in respect of the costs of successfully defending proceedings brought against him. On this see pp. 558, 559, *infra*. And on ordinary agency principles he will be entitled to be indemnified in respect of liabilities properly incurred by him in connection with the company's business.

(c) Restoration of the company's property if traceable;

(d) Rescission of a contract;

(e) Account of profits;

(f) Summary dismissal.

In addition, the commission of a criminal offence may incidentally be involved, leading to liability to punishment—but this possibility need not be explored here. For the purpose of this discussion, however, " breach " includes not only a failure to observe the duties of loyalty, care and skill, dealt with above, but also an act exceeding the authority conferred upon the director, or one *ultra vires* the board as a whole, or the company itself.

Which of these orders will be appropriate depends on the nature of the breach.

(a) *Injunction or declaration* is primarily employed where a breach is threatened but has not yet occurred. If action can be taken in time this is obviously the most satisfactory course, and injunctions, permanent or temporary, are extensively employed when, for example, the board is proposing to take some action which is, or is alleged to be, beyond their powers.[50] An injunction may also be appropriate where the breach has already occurred but is likely to continue,[51] or if some of its adverse consequences can thereby be avoided.[52]

(b) *Damages or compensation.* Damages are the appropriate remedy for breach of a common law duty of care: compensation is the equivalent equitable remedy granted against a trustee or other fiduciary to compel restitution for the loss suffered by his breach of fiduciary duty. In practice, the distinction between the two has become blurred,[53] and probably no useful purpose is served by seeking to keep them distinct. The principles governing the award of these remedies will be found fully treated in works on tort and trusts respectively. Here, all that need to be said is that all the directors who participate in the breach [54] are jointly and severally liable with the usual rights of contribution *inter se*.[55]

---

[50] A declaration of invalidity will often fulfil the same purpose and is generally asked for as an alternative to an injunction.

[51] *e.g.*, use of trade secrets, *supra*, p. 547.

[52] *e.g.*, to enjoin the delivery up of confidential documents improperly taken away by a former director: *Measures Bros.* v. *Measures* [1910] 1 Ch. 336; [1910] 2 Ch. 248, C.A.; *Cranleigh Precision Engineering Ltd.* v. *Bryant* [1965] 1 W.L.R. 1293.

[53] Note how, in *Re Leeds & Hanley Theatre of Varieties* [1902] 2 Ch. 809, C.A., the court envisaged the award of " damages " for breach of a fiduciary's duty to disclose: see *supra*, p. 277.

[54] Either actively or by subsequent acquiescence in it: *Re Lands Allotment Co.* [1894] 1 Ch. 616, C.A. Merely protesting will not necessarily disprove acquiescence: *Joint Stock Discount Co.* v. *Brown* (1869) L.R. 8 Eq. 381.

[55] As regards breaches of fiduciary duties the right of contribution always existed in equity; it has now been extended to tortious liability by s. 6 of the Law Reform (Married Women and Tortfeasors) Act 1935.

Third persons who knowingly participate in a breach of directors' fiduciary duties are similarly liable.[56] They need not actually know that what is being done is a breach of duty; it suffices if they assist in a transaction with knowledge of circumstances which would put a reasonable man on inquiry whether a morally reprehensible design is being carried out.[57] Their liability is clearer still if they knowingly induce a breach of such a duty.[58] Where, however, the third party is innocent and does not know of the facts which constitute the breach of duty he cannot normally be made liable under this heading,[59] though recent authority suggests that he may not be safe if he cannot also prove that he gave valuable consideration for a benefit received from a director acting in breach of duty.[60]

(c) *Restoration of property.* Since directors are regarded as trustees of such of the company's property as has or should have come under their control,[61] it may be recovered *in rem* from them and from third parties, who are not purchasers for value, in so far as it is traceable.[62] This includes not only property reduced into the company's possession but also property which it was the directors' duty to acquire for the company [63] or to give the company an opportunity of acquiring.[64] But

---

[56] *Selangor United Rubber Estates Ltd.* v. *Cradock (No. 3)* [1968] 1 W.L.R. 1555; *Gray* v. *Lewis* (1869) L.R. 8 Eq. 526 (later proceedings 8 Ch.App. 1035); *Canada Safeway* v. *Thompson* [1951] 3 D.L.R. 295; [1952] 2 D.L.R. 591 (B.Col.S.C.); *Morrison* v. *Coast Finance Ltd.* (1966) 55 D.L.R. (2d) 710 (B.Col.C.A.), *per* Sheppard J.A. at pp. 724–726.

[57] *Selangor United Rubber Estates Ltd.* v. *Cradock (No. 3), supra.* But clearly if they know that it is a breach of duty it is irrelevant whether they regard it as morally reprehensible.

[58] *Boulting* v. *A.C.T.A.T.* [1963] 2 Q.B. 606, C.A., where the majority found that no breach was proved on the facts. Where the director has a contract this liability will merge into the tort of knowingly inducing breach of contract: *cf. Jasperson* v. *Dominion Tobacco Co.* [1923] A.C. 709, P.C. But only the company can sue for that, not the director: *per* Upjohn L.J. in the *Boulting* case, at p. 640. *Quaere* whether a third party and the director may not be liable for conspiracy to damage the company by unlawful means: *cf. Canada Safeway* v. *Thompson* [1951] 3 D.L.R. at p. 321, *per* Manson J.

[59] *Selangor United Rubber Estates Ltd.* v. *Cradock (No. 3), supra* (where the claim against the Bank of Nova Scotia failed on this ground); *Lindgren* v. *L. & P. Estates Co. Ltd.* [1968] Ch. 572, C.A., *per* Harman L.J. at p. 595. *Cf. McKay* v. *Proprietary Mines Ltd.* [1939] 3 D.L.R. 215 (Ont.C.A.); approved [1941] 1 D.L.R. 240 (Can.S.C.), where the wrongdoing director was made to account for proceeds of shares sold to innocent purchasers.

[60] It is odd if this is the law, since, even where the property concerned is traceable *in rem* in equity, the courts have allowed the innocent volunteer to share *pari passu*, with the claimant owner: *Re Diplock* [1948] Ch. 465 (*infra*, heading (c)). In the situation discussed under this heading the original claim against the director is *in personam* only. Nevertheless, the authorities suggest that the proceeds are impressed with an equity by reason of a director's breach of duty and that the volunteer third party may be accountable: see *G. L. Baker* v. *Medway Building & Supplies Ltd.* [1958] 1 W.L.R. 1216, C.A. (approved [1959] 1 W.L.R. 492, H.L.), discussing *Nelson* v. *Larholt* [1948] 1 K.B. 339 and *Ministry of Health* v. *Simpson* [1951] A.C. 251, H.L.

[61] *Re Forest of Dean Coal Co.* (1879) 10 Ch.D. 450.

[62] *Re Diplock* [1948] Ch. 465, C.A., reveals the ambit of the equitable tracing rules, on which see Goff & Jones: *The Law of Restitution*, pp. 49–52.

[63] As in *Cook* v. *Deeks* [1916] 1 A.C. 554, P.C.

[64] As in *Canada Safeway Ltd.* v. *Thompson* [1951] 3 D.L.R. 295; [1952] 2 D.L.R. 591 (B.Col.S.C.). *Semble* it may even include property which the company has

apparently it does not include all profits made by a director or other agent for which the company has a right to call upon him to account.[65] These profits and the investments made with them will not be regarded as belonging in equity to the company unless they flowed from a use of the company's property.[66] But this poses a major unsolved problem. If information confidential to the company is deemed to be the company's property, in almost every case in which directors are liable to account for profits there will have been a use of the company's property. Information is certainly often treated as property.[67] On that basis the company in *Regal (Hastings) Ltd.* v. *Gulliver*[68] and the beneficiaries in *Phipps* v. *Boardman*[69] could have recovered not merely the profits made but the shares themselves. The Canadian Supreme Court in *Peso Silver Mines Ltd.* v. *Cropper*[70] clearly assumed that this was so. But the speeches in the House of Lords in *Phipps* v. *Boardman* leave this in some doubt. Lord Guest took the view that all information obtained while acting as a fiduciary was " trust property," [71] and that the shares acquired were held on trust.[72] Lord Hodson thought that information was property if it was confidential and capable of being turned to account.[73] Lord Dilhorne considered that it could be regarded as property only if capable of being turned to account by the beneficiary (as opposed to the fiduciary).[74] Lords Cohen [75] and Upjohn [76] held that information was never property in the strict sense. Lord Upjohn said that, though often described as property, " in the end the real truth is that it is not property in any normal sense but equity will restrain its transmission to another if in breach of some confidential relationship." [77] But Lord Upjohn seems to understate its proprietary characteristics. A third party may clearly be restrained from using confidential information,[78] and apparently may be made to disgorge benefits derived from it by means of an action *in rem*, at any rate if he knew that the infor-

---

no present power to acquire, for it may be the directors' duty to cause the objects clause to be amended so that it can do so: *Fine Industrial Commodities* v. *Powling* (1954) 79 R.P.C. 253 at 288.
[65] *Lister & Co.* v. *Stubbs* (1890) 45 Ch.D. 1, C.A., where the court rejected a claim to investments made by an agent out of secret commissions. See also *Powell & Thomas* v. *Evan Jones & Co.* [1905] 1 K.B. 11.
[66] See Goff & Jones, *The Law of Restitution*, pp. 459–460 and *cf.* as regards promoters, *supra*, pp. 273, 274, 276, 277.
[67] See, for example, *Bell Houses* v. *City Wall Properties Ltd.* [1966] 2 Q.B. 656, C.A., where knowledge of sources of finance was held to be an asset of the company.
[68] [1942] 1 All E.R. 378; [1967] 2 A.C. 134n., H.L., *supra*, p. 535.
[69] [1967] 2 A.C. 46, H.L., *supra*, pp. 537–539.
[70] (1966) 58 D.L.R. 1, *supra*, p. 539.
[71] At p. 115.
[72] At p. 114.
[73] At p. 107.
[74] At pp. 89–91.
[75] At p. 102.
[76] At p. 127.
[77] At p. 128.
[78] *Cranleigh Precision Engineering Ltd.* v. *Bryant* [1965] 1 W.L.R. 1293. There the third party was another company controlled by a delinquent director, but the same principle applies to an independent third party: *Saltman Engineering Ltd.* v. *Campbell Engineering Ltd.* [1963] 3 All E.R. 413n., C.A., and *Printers and Finishers Ltd.* v. *Holloway* [1965] 1 W.L.R. 1.

mation was confidential.[79]   Equity certainly seems to come very close
to treating information confidential to the company as the company's
property.

Recovery here is in the form of proceedings *in rem* as opposed
to recovery *in personam* under head (b) or (e).[80]

(d) *Rescission of contracts.*   An agreement with the company which
breaks the rules relating to contracts in which directors are interested [81]
may be avoided, provided that *restitutio in integrum* is possible, and that
the rights of bona fide third parties have not supervened.[82]   This matter
has been sufficiently discussed in connection with promoters' contracts.[83]

(e) *Accounting for profits.*   Reference has already been made to the
strict liability to account for secret profits made by directors.   This
liability may either arise out of a contract made between a director and
the company,[84] or as a result of some contract or arrangement between
the director and a third person.[85]   In the former case, accounting is a
remedy additional to avoidance of the contract and is normally available
whether or not there is rescission.[86]   But as we have seen when discussing promoters' contracts, if a director has sold his own property to
the company, the right to an account of profits will be lost if the company elects not to rescind or is too late to do so.[87]   When the profit arises
out of a contract between the director and a third party there will be no
question of rescinding that contract at the instance of the company,
since the company is not a party to the contract.   Here an account of
profits will be the sole remedy.   In neither case does recovery of the
profit depend on proof of any loss suffered by the company; it is recoverable not as damages or compensation but because the company is
entitled to call upon the director to account to it.[88]

---

[79] *Saltman Engineering Ltd.* v. *Campbell Engineering Ltd., supra*; *Peter Pan Manufacturing Corpn.* v. *Corsets Silhouette Ltd.* [1964] 1 W.L.R. 96.   See Goff & Jones,
The Law of Restitution, p. 455.   On this basis it should be possible to recover from
" tippees " of insiders: *cf.* p. 391, *supra*.

[80] Recovery under one head will, normally, reduce the amount recoverable under
another: contrast the curious situation as regards bribes, *infra*, p. 557.

[81] *Supra*, pp. 526–535.

[82] *Transvaal Lands Co.* v. *New Belgium (Transvaal) Land & Development Co.* [1914]
2 Ch. 488, C.A.

[83] *Supra*, Chap. 13, p. 275 *et seq.*

[84] *Imperial Mercantile Credit Asscn.* v. *Coleman* (1873) L.R. 6 H.L. 189.

[85] *Regal (Hastings) Ltd.* v. *Gulliver* [1942] 1 All E.R. 378; [1967] 2 A.C. 134n., H.L.,
supra, p. 535 *et seq.*

[86] *Gluckstein* v. *Barnes* [1900] A.C. 240, H.L., *supra*, p. 276.

[87] *Re Ambrose Lake Tin Co.* (1880) 11 Ch.D. 390, C.A.; *Re Cape Breton Co.* (1885)
29 Ch.D. 795, C.A. affd. *sub nom. Cavendish Bentinck* v. *Fenn* (1887) 12 App.Cas.
652, H.L.; *Ladywell Mining Co.* v. *Brookes* (1887) 35 Ch.D. 400, C.A.; *Re Lady
Forrest (Murchison) Gold Mine* [1901] 1 Ch. 582; *Burland* v. *Earle* [1902] A.C.
83, P.C.; *Jacobus Marler* v. *Marler* (1913) 85 L.J.P.C. 167n.; *Robinson* v. *Randfontein Estates* [1921] A.C. 168 (S.Afr.S.C.App.Div.); *P. & O. Steam Nav. Co.* v.
Johnson (1938) 60 C.L.R. 189 (Aus.H.C.); *Hely-Hutchinson* v. *Brayhead Ltd.*
[1968] 1 Q.B. 549, C.A. and *cf.* pp. 276, 277, *supra*.

[88] *Boston Deep Sea Fishing & Ice Co.* v. *Ansell* (1888) 39 Ch.D. 339, C.A.; *Regal
(Hastings) Ltd.* v. *Gulliver, supra*.   The question whether third parties can be called
upon to account personally depends on the same principles as in (b), *supra*.

(f) *Summary dismissal.* The right which a master has to dismiss a servant who has been guilty of serious misconduct has no application to a director as such. He can at any time be dismissed from his directorship by ordinary resolution subject to compliance with the provisions of section 184.[89] The provisions of this section are mandatory and clearly cannot be dispensed with because it is alleged that the director has been guilty of misconduct.[90] It is, however, of considerable importance in the case of other officials of the company and of directors who hold some other office such as that of managing director. So far as their offices are concerned it is clear that, notwithstanding that they may hold long-term agreements, they can be dismissed immediately if guilty of misconduct. Any breach of their fiduciary duties clearly suffices[91]; and it may be surmised that negligence, sufficiently gross to infringe the lax standards of skill and care required of a director, would also do so.[92]

Illustration in relation to bribes

The inter-relation of the various orders described above is best illustrated by the position when a director or other official accepts a bribe. " Bribe," for this purpose, does not connote any corrupt motive on the part of either the giver or the receiver,[93] but merely that a third party dealing with a company through one of its officials has given something in cash or in kind to that official without the knowledge and consent of the company.[93] When that has occurred any contract between the company and the third party may be rescinded.[94] Alternatively, it may be affirmed, and the agent and the third party sued for damages, which are conclusively presumed to be equivalent at least to the amount of the bribe.[95] Further, the official may be made to restore to the company the amount of the bribe. This claim for restoration and the claim for damages are entirely independent, and hence the company may recover damages at least to the amount of the bribe from the third party notwithstanding that the official has restored to it the amount of

---

[89] *Supra*, Chap. 7, p 133 *et seq.*

[90] It would be possible to provide in the articles that his office shall be vacated in the event of misconduct but the more usual and effective provision is one to the effect that this shall occur if the board call upon him to resign.

[91] *Boston Deep Sea Fishing & Ice Co.* v. *Ansell, supra. Cf. Bell* v. *Lever Bros.* [1932] A.C. 161, H.L.

[92] Under the general law of master and servant, incompetence or disobedience is a ground for dismissal but whether an isolated act of negligence suffices is a question of fact and degree: *Clouston* v. *Corry* [1906] A.C. 122, P.C.; *Savage* v. *British India Steam Navigation Ltd.* (1930) 46 T.L.R. 294. *Laws* v. *London Chronicle Ltd.* [1959] 1 W.L.R. 698, C.A.; *Sinclair* v. *Neighbour* [1967] 2 Q.B. 279, C.A.

[93] *Industries and General Mortgage Co.* v. *Lewis* [1949] 2 All E.R. 573.

[94] *Shipway* v. *Broadwood* [1899] 1 Q.B. 369, C.A.

[95] *Industries and General Mortgage Co.* v. *Lewis, supra,* and authorities there cited. In order to recover against the third party it appears to be unnecessary to prove that he knew that the officer would not disclose the payment to the company: *Grant* v. *Gold Exploration and Development Co.* [1900] 1 Q.B. 233, C.A.

the bribe.[96] Finally, the official will be liable to instant dismissal [97] and will forfeit any claim he may have to commission on the transaction concerned.[98]

Limitation of actions

Procedural questions arising in relation to actions against directors are, in general, dealt with in Chapter 25. However, it may be convenient to mention here that in claims based upon breaches of their fiduciary duties directors are equated with trustees as regards limitation of actions.[99] Hence, claims against them will be barred after six years,[1] but no period of limitation applies if there is fraud or if the action is to recover the company's property in the director's possession or previously converted to his use.[2]

Relief from liability and indemnification

Section 448 of the Companies Act 1948 empowers the court to relieve, in whole or in part, any director or other officer,[3] or the auditor of the company in respect of his " negligence, default, breach of duty or breach of trust," if it appears that " he has acted honestly and reasonably and that, having regard to all the circumstances of the case, including those connected with his appointment, he ought fairly to be excused. . . ." [4] This extends to company directors a power which the court has under the Trustee Act [5] to relieve trustees. It will be observed, however, that the section extends only to " officers " [3] and applies only to registered companies. It is doubtful whether other officials could invoke the similar provisions of the Trustee Act,[6] or whether directors and officers of statutory and chartered companies could do so.[7]

Where directors successfully defend proceedings brought against them they may be entitled to require the company to indemnify them

---

[96] *Salford Corporation* v. *Lever* [1891] 1 Q.B. 168, C.A.; *Grant* v. *Gold Exploration and Development Co., supra.* If this is correct, it means that the company may do better on the deal because the official has been bribed.

[97] *Supra,* p. 557.

[98] *Andrews* v. *Ramsay & Co.* [1903] 2 K.B. 635, but contrast *Hippesley* v. *Knee Bros.* [1905] 1 K.B. 1 and *Keppel* v. *Wheeler* [1927] 1 K.B. 577, C.A.

[99] *Re Lands Allotment Co.* [1894] 1 Ch. 616, C.A., *Tintin Exploration Syndicate* v. *Sandys* (1947) 177 L.T. 412.

[1] Limitation Act 1939, s. 19 (2).

[2] *Ibid.* s. 19 (1).

[3] For definition (if such it can be called) see s. 455.

[4] In the recent case of *Selangor United Rubber Estates Ltd.* v. *Cradock (No.* 3) [1968] 1 W.L.R. 1555 the court refused to relieve nominee directors who had disposed of virtually the whole of the company's assets without regard to minority shareholders " but blindly at the behest of the majority shareholder who nominated them ": see p. 1660. See also *Re Duomatic Ltd.* [1969] 2 W.L.R. 114.

[5] Trustee Act 1925, s. 61.

[6] Maugham J., in *Re Windsor Steam Coal Co.* [1928] Ch. 609, held that a liquidator was not a trustee within the meaning of the Trustee Act. But the C.A. were prepared to concede (without deciding) that he might be: *ibid.* [1929] 1 Ch. 151.

[7] Having regard to the many dicta that directors are trustees for some purposes there is no obvious reason why they should not be trustees for this purpose. But see Maugham J. in [1928] Ch. at pp. 612–613.

against their costs either under common law principles or by virtue of an express indemnity clause. The common law right will apply only if the proceedings arose out of lawful activities by them as directors, and hence they are not entitled to be reimbursed the expense of successfully defending themselves against allegations that they had done something which they had not done, and which it was not their duty to do.[8] But the indemnity clause in article 136 of Table A appears to give wider protection [9] and not to be limited in this way.[10] A clause which purported to entitle them to an indemnity if their defence was unsuccessful would, of course, be void under section 205.[11] But it may extend to cases where they are relieved under section 448,[12] and article 136 so provides and is not specifically limited to cases where they are *wholly* relieved.[13]

Where, on the other hand, an action is successfully brought by a third party against the company arising out of the wrongful act of the directors or other agents for which the company is made vicariously liable, it appears that they must indemnify the company.[14]

CONCLUSIONS

A description of the legal and equitable rules relating to directors' duties appears to show that their duties of loyalty are exceptionally strict, and their duties of diligence and skill exceptionally lax. This picture is, however, somewhat misleading. In practice their fiduciary duties do not weigh too heavily upon them because, in the most important aspect of contracts between them and their companies, the duties are largely waived in the company's articles. Often all that then remains is an obligation to disclose their interest in the most general terms, and to disclose it in advance merely to their fellow directors, and only after the contract is concluded to the true beneficiaries, the shareholders. Furthermore, a rigid adherence to the corporate entity principle, with its corollary

---

[8] *Tomlinson* v. *Scottish Amalgamated Silks Ltd.*, 1935 S.C.(H.L.) 1. *Cf. Re Famatina Development Corpn.* [1914] 2 Ch. 271, C.A.

[9] And to be wider than the clause in *Tomlinson's* case, *supra*.

[10] Its wording covers any liability incurred by a director or other agent in successfully defending *any* proceedings. Obviously, however, it must be construed as restricted to proceedings against the director or agent in his capacity of director or agent of the company. This, however, would seem to cover circumstances such as those in *Tomlinson's* case. The doubt expressed by Sargant J. in *Re Famatina Development Corpn.*, *supra*, on whether such an indemnity clause could be enforced by the agent, since the articles only constitute a contract between the company and the members as such or between the members *inter se*, would not, it is submitted, prevent the directors enforcing it since they would be deemed to have accepted office on the terms of the articles: see *supra*, Chap. 12, p. 264.

[11] *Supra*, p. 532.

[12] See proviso to s. 205.

[13] Accordingly the court should bear this in mind when granting relief under s. 448 and consider whether terms should not be imposed precluding a claim to indemnity. s. 448 (1) empowers the court to impose terms.

[14] *Cf. Lister* v. *Romford Ice and Cold Storage Ltd.* [1957] A.C. 555, H.L. *Quaere*: would this apply when liability is based on the theory that the act of the directors is the act of the company itself (see Chap. 8, pp. 144–150, *supra*)?

that duties are owed to the company but not to the shareholders, leaves loopholes which the Acts have not yet completely closed. It is true that at times the directors' equitable obligations prove of exemplary severity, but all too often in circumstances where the equity of their application is not obvious. As for the duties of care and skill, these, undoubtedly, are far from strict. But this is because, hitherto, directorships have been part-time, and company management not a recognised profession with objective professional standards. The modern tendency, however, seems to be towards full-time service directorships and towards the evolution of a managerial profession. This tendency may, in time, be reflected in judicial or legislative [15] recognition of considerably stricter standards.

There are, however, two major difficulties in the way of effective enforcement of the directors' duties, be they strict or lax. The first is, that the duties merely apply to what directors undertake *qua* directors without the concurrence of the company in general meeting. It is therefore essential to see how far the directors and others voting at a general meeting are subjected to similar duties. This forms the subject of the following chapter. The second difficulty is procedural. Legal duties are valueless in the absence of effective procedures for invoking them before the court. The nature of these procedures and how far they are effective are discussed in Chapter 25.

---

[15] As we have seen (*supra*, p. 520, note 29) Australia now requires reasonable diligence and Ghana both diligence and skill.

CHAPTER 24

CONTROLLING SHAREHOLDERS' DUTIES

IN the last chapter we saw that, although the directors may be acting within the powers conferred upon them by the company, they nevertheless owe certain duties of good faith and of care and skill in the exercise of these powers. The present chapter discusses whether there are any comparable duties owed by the controllers when acting as members or debentureholders and not as directors. Here it is necessary first to distinguish between cases where the controllers, though not themselves directors, nevertheless instigate or are parties to a breach of duty by the directors whom they have appointed, and cases where shareholders (whether or not they are also directors) act purely in their capacity of members.

PARTICIPATION IN DIRECTORS' MISFEASANCE

As we have seen [1] anyone, and *a fortiori* a dominating shareholder, may be liable if he knowingly participates in a breach of " trust " by the directors. He will equally be liable if without lawful excuse he induces the directors to break any contractual duties which they owe the company.[2] The controllers, therefore, cannot with impunity install men of straw as dummy directors and use them to bleed the company. This, however, falls far short of imposing on the true controllers general liability for the acts and defaults of the directors, and in practice it will be difficult to prove that in any particular transaction the directors have acted merely as puppets for others who have pulled the strings.[3] That this is a serious problem is apparent from a number of recent reports of Board of Trade Inspectors.[4] Those responsible for the drafting of the Acts seem to have toyed with the notion of shifting responsibility onto the shoulders of the true masters of the company's destiny, since, for the purposes of certain sections,[5] " director " is defined as including " any person in accordance with whose directions or instructions the directors of a company are accustomed to act." The sections in question include those relating to the register of directors' shareholdings and to the publi-

---

[1] *Supra*, p. 554.
[2] *Jasperson* v. *Dominion Tobacco Co.* [1923] A.C. 709, P.C.; *Torquay Hotel Co. Ltd.* v. *Cousins* [1969] 2 W.L.R. 289, C.A.; cf. *Boulting* v. *A.C.T.A.T.* [1963] 2 Q.B. 606, C.A.
[3] See *Selangor United Rubber Estates Ltd.* v. *Cradock (No. 3)* [1968] 1 W.L.R. 1555.
[4] See, for example, the Report into Town Centre Properties Ltd. (H.M.S.O. 1967).
[5] 1948 Act, ss. 124, 125, 195, 200 and 201, and 1967 Act, ss. 25, 27 and 29. But it does not include a person " by reason only that the directors act on advice given by him in a professional capacity ": 1948 Act, s. 455 (2), 1967 Act, s. 56 (3).

cation of particulars of the directors—with the queer result that the company may be under a duty to hold out someone to the outside world as a director, although he is not in fact a director at all. We need not consider what the effect of this would be on the person concerned, for it is in the highest degree unlikely that any company will ever admit that its directors are accustomed to act on another's instructions. But the provision is interesting as a tentative recognition by the legislature that it is not always the directors who actually direct.

VOTING AS MEMBERS

Chapter 22 described the limitations on the powers of general meetings. The question now is whether there are any restraints on the members in general meeting when acting within the ambit of their powers. As we have seen,[6] directors must not only act within their powers but must also exercise them " bona fide in what they believe to be in the best interests of the company." Is there any similar restraint on shareholders exercising their powers as members at general meetings?

Scattered throughout the reports are statements that members must exercise their votes " bona fide for the benefit of the company as a whole," [7] a statement which suggests that they are subject to precisely the same rules as directors. But it is clear that this statement is highly misleading, and that the decisions do not support any such rule as a general principle. On the contrary, it has been repeatedly laid down that votes are proprietary rights, to the same extent as any other incidents of the shares, which the holder may exercise in his own selfish interests even if these are opposed to those of the company.[8] He may even bind himself by contract to vote or not to vote in a particular way and his contract may be enforced by injunction.[9]

In all these respects the position of the shareholder is in striking contrast with that of the director. If it were the case that the general meeting could only operate in the few residual matters reserved to it by the company's constitution,[10] this would not be unduly serious. But, as we have seen,[11] the general meeting is regarded as having power to act in place of the board if, for any reason, the board cannot function. If,

---

6 *Supra*, Chap. 23, p. 520 *et seq*
7 The original source of this oft-repeated but misleading expression seems to be Lindley M.R. in *Allen* v. *Gold Reefs of W. Africa* [1900] 1 Ch. at 671. Lord Murray, in the Scottish case of *Harris* v. *A. Harris Ltd.*, 1936 S.C. 183 (Sc.) at p. 205 went so far as to argue that the relationship between members of a company was identical with that between partners.
8 *North-West Transportation* v. *Beatty* (1887) 12 App.Cas. 589, P.C.; *Burland* v. *Earle* [1902] A.C. 83, P.C.; *Goodfellow* v. *Nelson Line* [1912] 2 Ch. 324.
9 *Greenwell* v. *Porter* [1902] 1 Ch. 530; *Puddephatt* v. *Leith* [1916] 1 Ch. 200—in which a mandatory injunction was granted. Voting agreements are not uncommon in this country, although we have nothing comparable to the American voting trust.
10 See Chap. 7, *supra*.
11 Chap. 7 at pp. 136–138.

therefore, a proper quorum cannot be obtained at a directors' meeting or there is a deadlock on the board, the general meeting may act instead.[12] Furthermore, a transaction will not be regarded as a breach of the directors' fiduciary duties if full disclosure is made to the company in general meeting and the company's consent obtained by a resolution passed at that meeting.[13] Hence, although the transaction concerned may relate to ordinary management, and therefore be within the powers of the board, the ratification [14] of it will always be a matter appropriate for the general meeting, which can waive what would otherwise be a breach of duty.[15] As a result, the activities of general meetings may indirectly extend over the whole sphere of the company's operations, and ultimate control revert to shareholders who are free from duties of good faith to which the directors are subject.

What is more startling still is that the directors themselves, even though personally interested, can vote in their capacity of shareholders at that general meeting.[16] As a consequence, when the directors have *de facto* control they can, subject to what follows, disregard their fiduciary duties at their pleasure, provided that they are prepared openly to disclose what they propose to do, and then to force through a confirming resolution by the exercise of their own votes supplemented, if need be, by their control of the proxy voting machinery. It is true that if the transaction to be ratified is one which has increased their voting power the court may order that the increased votes shall not be exercised but it will not, apparently, prevent them from exercising their original votes.[17]

Clearly, therefore, some restraint must be put on the power of those able to command a majority vote. And in fact it is clear that, in some circumstances, the courts will intervene to annul [18] the resulting resolution and to restrain what is generally described as a fraud on the minority.

---

[12] *Barron* v. *Potter* [1914] 1 Ch. 895; *Foster* v. *Foster* [1916] 1 Ch. 532.

[13] See *supra*, Chap. 23.

[14] In Chap. 7 at p. 137 attention was drawn to the elaborate discussion by Plowman J. at first instance in *Bamford* v. *Bamford* [1968] 3 W.L.R. 317, on the assumption that ratification is equivalent to original action. The C.A. [1969] 2 W.L.R. 1107, regarded this assumption as erroneous.

[15] *Irvine* v. *Union Bank of Australia* (1877) 2 App.Cas. 366, P.C.; *Grant* v. *U.K. Switchback Ry.* (1888) 40 Ch.D. 135, C.A.; *Hogg* v. *Cramphorn Ltd.* [1967] Ch. 254 (1963); *Bamford* v. *Bamford, supra.*

[16] *N.W. Transportation Co.* v. *Beatty* (1887) 12 App.Cas. 589, P.C.; *Burland* v. *Earle* [1902] A.C. 83 at 93, P.C.; *Harris* v. *A. Harris Ltd.*, 1936 S.C. 183 (Sc.); *Baird* v. *Baird & Co.*, 1949 S.L.T. 368 (Sc.). James L.J. once lamented, with justification, that there was no procedure for submitting such matters to the vote of independent shareholders only: *Mason* v. *Harris* (1879) 11 Ch.D. 97 at 109, C.A.

[17] *Hogg* v. *Cramphorn Ltd.* [1967] Ch. 254 (1963); *Bamford* v. *Bamford, supra.*

[18] A resolution passed without proper notice, or one exceeding the legal powers of the meeting (described in Chap. 22, *supra*), is probably void *ab initio* (see p. 511, *supra*). But it seems clear that a resolution only impeachable as a fraud on the minority is merely voidable and will be valid until successfully attacked: *cf. Borland's Trustee* v. *Steel Bros.* [1901] 1 Ch. 279 and the observations thereon in *Brown* v. *British Abrasive Wheel Co.* [1919] 1 Ch. 290.

Meaning of fraud on the minority

As we shall see, the exact meaning of the expression " fraud on the minority " is not easy to determine. But at least it is clear that both " fraud " and " minority " are used somewhat loosely. There need not be any actual deceit; if there were, those on whom it was practised would have a common law remedy against those who had wilfully deceived them. " Fraud " here connotes an abuse of power analogous to its meaning in a court of equity to describe a misuse of a fiduciary position. Nor is it necessary that those who are injured should be a minority; indeed, the injured party will normally be the company itself,[19] though sometimes those who have really suffered will be a class or section of members, not necessarily a numerical minority, who are outvoted by the controllers.[20] It covers certain " acts of a fraudulent character "—in the wider sense just described—of which " familiar examples are when the majority are endeavouring directly or indirectly to appropriate to themselves money, property or advantages which belong to the company or in which the other shareholders are entitled to participate." [21] Most of the cases in which the principle has actually been applied appear to fall within one of the following three classes (a)–(c), though there may be a wider class discussed under head (d).

(a) Expropriation of the company's property

The classic illustration of the first type of case is *Menier* v. *Hooper's Telegraph Works.*[22] There the defendants, a rival concern, held a controlling interest in the company which it was alleged that they had exercised so as to compromise a pending action to their own advantage and then put the company into liquidation, leaving them in possession of the company's assets to the exclusion of the minority. It was held that such action could be enjoined at the suit of the minority. This case was later followed in *Cook* v. *Deeks,*[23] in which the directors had diverted to themselves contracts which they should have taken up on behalf of the company, By virtue of their controlling interest they secured the passing of a resolution in general meeting ratifying and approving what they had done. It was held that they must be regarded as holding the benefits of the contracts on trust for the company, for " directors holding a majority of votes would not be permitted to make a present to themselves." [24] The same may apply when the present is not to themselves but to someone else. Thus in *Parke* v. *Daily News* [25] it was held that

---

[19] As in (a) and (b), *infra.* These cases, therefore, should properly be described as frauds on the company.
[20] As in (c) and (d), *infra.*
[21] *Per* Lord Davey in *Burland* v. *Earle* [1902] A.C. 83 at 93, P.C.
[22] (1874) L.R. 9 Ch.App. 350.
[23] [1916] 1 A.C. 554, P.C. See also *Canada Safeway Ltd.* v. *Thompson* [1951] 3 D.L.R. 295; [1952] 2 D.L.R. 591 (B.Col.S.C.)
[24] [1916] 1 A.C. at p. 564.
[25] [1962] Ch. 927, *supra*, pp. 92, 522.

the general meeting could not resolve to give away the company's property to the employees made redundant by the cessation of the company's activities.[26]

Where, then, is the line to be drawn between those cases where shareholder action is improper, and those in which shareholder action has been upheld? How, in particular, can one reconcile *Cook* v. *Deeks* with the many cases in which the liability of directors has been held to disappear as a result of ratification in general meeting, notwithstanding the use of their own votes?[27] Why, in *Regal (Hastings) Ltd.* v. *Gulliver*,[28] did the House of Lords say that the directors would not have been liable to account for their profits had the transaction been ratified, while, in *Cook* v. *Deeks*, the Privy Council made them account notwithstanding such ratification?

The answer, it is submitted, depends first on the distinction between (a) misappropriating the company's property and (b) merely making an incidental profit for which the directors are liable to account to the company. As we have seen,[29] an incidental profit is not treated as the company's property unless it flows from a use of the company's property. *Cook* v. *Deeks* clearly came within (a) for it was the duty of the directors to acquire the contracts on behalf of the company.[30] Hence the company in general meeting could not ratify, at any rate if the directors' own votes caused the resolution to be passed. "Even supposing it be not *ultra vires* of a company to make a present to its directors, it appears quite certain that directors holding a majority of votes would not be permitted to make a present to themselves."[31] In the light of later cases, it seems fairly clear that to make presents to directors or others is not necessarily *ultra vires*,[32] but probably the onus will then be on the directors to show positively that the presents were made and the ratifying resolution passed, bona fide for the benefit of the company as a whole within the meaning of (d) below.[33] Where, as in *Cook* v. *Deeks*, the resolution has been passed only as a result of their votes it will be difficult, if not impossible, to discharge this onus.

On the other hand, in *Regal (Hastings) Ltd.* v. *Gulliver* the directors had not misappropriated any property of the company. Prima facie, therefore, the company could ratify what they had done and enable them to retain the profits. The difficulty, however, is that they had used

---

[26] The payment was said to be *ultra vires* the company: as to this see *supra*, p. 92.

[27] e.g., *N.W. Transportation Co.* v. *Beatty* (1887) 12 App.Cas. 589. P.C.; *Burland* v. *Earle* [1902] A.C. 83, P.C.; *Harris* v. *A. Harris Ltd.*, 1936 S.C. 183 (Sc.); *Baird* v. *Baird & Co.*, 1949 S.L.T. 368 (Sc.).

[28] [1942] 1 All E.R. 378; [1967] 2 A.C. 134n., H.L., *supra*, Chap. 23, p. 535.

[29] *Supra*, p. 555

[30] Or, as in *Canada Safeway Ltd.* v. *Thompson*, *supra*, to give the company an opportunity of deciding whether to acquire them.

[31] [1916] 1 A.C. at 564.

[32] *Supra*, p. 92.

[33] See *Parke* v. *Daily News* [1962] Ch. 927 at p. 954; *Re W. & M. Roith* [1967] 1 W.L.R. 432.

information coming to them as directors, and, as we have seen,[34] it may be that this is to be regarded as the company's property. If so, the shares which they acquired belonged in equity to the company. However, the present to them of the shares would not necessarily have been improper. Since the company was financially unable to acquire the shares there might have been a bona fide decision of its members that it was in the interests of the company to allow the directors to retain the shares and the profits made from them—especially if the directors refrained from voting.[35] In *Cook* v. *Deeks* the directors had profited at the company's expense; in *Regal* they had profited without harming it in any way. To forbid ratification in the former and to allow it in the latter makes some sense. Moreover, in *Cook* v. *Deeks,* unlike *Regal,* the directors had broken their duty to act bona fide in the interests of the company so that that case fell within head (b) as well as head (a). As we shall see, a " fraudulent " breach of this sort cannot be ratified.

(b) Release of directors' duties of good faith

As indicated above, the general meeting can to some extent release the directors from their duties either prospectively or retrospectively.[36] It can permit them to enter into contracts with the company, to profit from their offices, or otherwise to place themselves in a position where their interest may conflict with their duty.[37] Similarly it can ratify an act by the directors in excess of the powers conferred on them,[38] or resolve not to sue in respect of a breach of their duties of care and skill.[39]

But a resolution of a general meeting cannot, either prospectively or retrospectively, authorise the directors to act in fraud of the company.[40] And, here again, " fraud " is used in a wider sense than deceit or dishonesty. If the directors have acted in their own interests or those of a third party rather than in the interests of the company,[40] or have not directed their minds to the question whether what they are doing is in the best interests of the company,[41] a resolution of the general meeting will not protect them.

---

34 *Supra*, p. 555.
35 *Cf. Hogg* v. *Cramphorn Ltd.* [1967] Ch. 254 (1963); *Bamford* v. *Bamford* [1969] 2 W.L.R. 1107, C.A.; and *Rights and Issues Investment Trust Ltd.* v. *Stylo Shoes Ltd.* [1965] Ch. 250, *infra*, p. 575.
36 Provided, of course, that adequate disclosure is given in the notice convening the meeting: *Kaye* v. *Croydon Tramways Co.* [1898] 1 Ch. 358, C.A.; *Tiessen* v. *Henderson* [1899] 1 Ch. 861, *supra*, Chap. 21, p. 482. It never seems to have been argued that an *ad hoc* resolution authorising a particular transaction would be a provision exempting the director from " any liability which by virtue of any rule of law would otherwise attach to him," and therefore avoided by s. 205 of the Act.
37 *Boulting* v. *A.C.T.A.T.* [1963] 2 Q.B. 606, C.A.
38 *Irvine* v. *Union Bank of Australia* (1877) 2 App.Cas. 366, P.C.; *Grant* v. *U.K. Switchback Rys.* (1888) 40 Ch.D. 135, C.A.; *Bamford* v. *Bamford, supra*.
39 *Pavlides* v. *Jensen* [1956] Ch. 565.
40 *Atwool* v. *Merryweather* (1867) L.R. 5 Eq. 464n.; *Mason* v. *Harris* (1879) 11 Ch.D. 97, C.A.
41 *Re W. & M. Roith Ltd.* [1967] 1 W.L.R. 432 (where, though the transaction does not seem to have been formally confirmed in general meeting, the memorandum and articles had been altered to enable the company to enter into it). See also *Alexander*

As we saw, when the directors appropriate the company's property, it seems that their action can be authorised by a resolution of the company if it can be shown positively that this was passed bona fide in the interests of the company. When, however, the directors do not act bona fide in the interests of the company it seems to be impossible to ratify.[42] A resolution authorising the directors not to act bona fide in the interests of the company cannot be in the interests of the company. What, perhaps, might be shown is that a resolution not to sue them for a past breach of duty was bona fide in the interests of the company. But while it might be in the interests of the company not to spend its money on litigation, it is difficult to see how it can be in its interests to release the directors from liability so as to protect them from suit by an individual member suing at his own expense on behalf of the company.[43] In any case such a resolution would appear to be ineffective under section 205.[44] On the other hand that section equally avoids any provision exempting from, or indemnifying against, liability for negligence; yet it has been held that the general meeting can validly resolve not to sue a negligent director.[45] Perhaps, therefore, there is a distinction between " exempting " and " indemnifying " on the one hand, and resolving not to sue on the other.[45] A resolution not to sue even a fraudulent director may, therefore, conceivably be valid if it can positively be shown to have been passed bona fide in the interests of the company. But it will not validate the fraudulent act and the directors will still be liable at the suit of an individual shareholder.[46]

On the other hand, it now seems to be clear that if the directors have acted honestly in what they believe to be the best interests of the company but have exercised a power for a purpose different from that for which they were given it, the general meeting can validly ratify so long as the purpose was a proper one for the company itself and the resolution was passed bona fide in its interests.[47] Since the company might have conferred a power on the directors to act for that purpose it can equally ratify retrospectively.

(c) Expropriation of other members' property

Just as the controllers cannot exercise their voting power so as to

---

v. *Automatic Telephone Co.* [1900] 2 Ch. 56, C.A.; *Millers (Invercargill) Ltd.* v. *Maddams* [1938] N.Z.L.R. 490 (C.A., N.Z.); *Ngurli Ltd.* v. *McCann* (1954) 90 C.L.R. 425 (Aus.H.C.).

[42] In *Bamford* v. *Bamford, supra,* which may appear to suggest the contrary, " not bona fide in the interests of the company " was used in the narrower sense of an act which exceeded the directors' powers because they were not authorised to act for that purpose; the directors' good faith was not questioned.

[43] *i.e.,* in a " derivative action "—see *infra,* p. 587 *et seq.*

[44] See *supra,* p. 532

[45] *Pavlides* v. *Jensen, supra.*

[46] *Cf. Atwool* v. *Merryweather* (1867) L.R. 5 Eq. 464n., *infra,* p. 588.

[47] *Hogg* v. *Cramphorn Ltd.* [1967] Ch. 254 (1963), *supra* (where the directors did not vote in respect of the shares acquired for the improper purpose), and *Bamford* v. *Bamford, supra* (where the company to which the shares had been improperly issued by the directors did not vote them).

deprive the company of its property, so, it is submitted, they are not entitled to use it so as to deprive the other members of their shares in the company. In this case, however, the prohibition is clearly not absolute and will not apply if such expropriation is for fair compensation and required in the interests of the company as a whole.

The authority for this proposition is found in two cases in 1919 and 1920, *Brown* v. *British Abrasive Wheel Co.*[48] and *Dafen Tinplate Co. Ltd.* v. *Llanelly Steel Co.*[49] In the first of these, a public company was in urgent need of further capital which the majority, holding 98 per cent. of the shares, were willing to supply if they could buy out the minority. Having failed to persuade the minority to sell, they proposed to pass a special resolution adding to the articles a clause whereby any shareholder was bound to transfer his shares upon a request in writing of the holders of nine-tenths of the issued capital. Although such a clause could have been validly inserted in the original articles[50] and although the good faith of the majority was not challenged, Astbury J. held that an attempt to add the clause in order to acquire compulsorily the shares of the minority, who had bought when there was no such power, could not be for the benefit of the company as a whole, but was solely for the benefit of the majority. He accordingly granted an injunction restraining the company from passing the resolution.

But doubt was cast on the correctness of this decision by the judgment of the Court of Appeal in *Sidebottom* v. *Kershaw Leese & Co.*[51] There a director-controlled private company had a minority shareholder who was interested in a competing business. It therefore passed a special resolution empowering the directors to require any shareholder who competed with the company to transfer his shares, at their fair value, to nominees of the directors. The Court of Appeal, reversing the trial judge, held that the alteration was valid. The company had statutory power to introduce into its articles anything that could have been validly included in the original articles provided that the alteration was made bona fide for the benefit of the company as a whole. " Bona fides " was not a further test of validity additional to " for the benefit of the company as a whole," [52] and as it was beneficial to the company to be able to rid its membership of a competitor the alteration was valid. *Brown* v. *British Abrasive Wheel Co.*[53] was distinguished as turning on the judge's finding of fact that the alteration was not made " for the benefit of the company as a whole," but the members of the Court of

48 [1919] 1 Ch. 290.
49 [1920] 2 Ch. 124.
50 *Phillips* v. *Manufacturers Securities Ltd.* (1917) 116 L.T. 290. *Cf. Borland's Trustee* v. *Steel Bros.* [1901] 1 Ch. 279 in which an even wider power was incorporated by an amendment of the articles, but there all the existing members had agreed to the amendment.
51 [1920] 1 Ch. 154, C.A.
52 [1920] 1 Ch. 154, especially at p. 172.
53 *Supra.*

Appeal obviously had doubts whether they would have made the same finding.

However, in *Dafen Tinplate Co.* v. *Llanelly Steel Co.*[54] Peterson J. followed *Brown's* case and held that a new article conferring on the majority an unrestricted and unlimited power to buy out any shareholder they might think proper, went much further than was necessary for the protection of the company from conduct detrimental to its interests. The learned judge described his finding as one of fact,[55] and, in deference to the observations of the Court of Appeal in *Sidebottom's* case, he conceded that the alteration would be valid if for the benefit of the company as a whole. But he clearly considered that the onus of proof was on those supporting the resolution, and thought that the test was an objective one and not what the shareholders honestly believed. But this, too, must now be regarded as doubtful, for the Court of Appeal, in a later decision not concerned with expropriation of shares,[56] laid it down that it was for the members, and not the court, to decide what was beneficial to the company and that the court could only interfere if they had not acted in good faith. If the resolution were such that no reasonable man could consider it for the benefit of the company as a whole, this might be a ground for finding lack of good faith.[57]

The suggestion that there is anything approaching a prohibition on expropriating the other members' shares, analogous to the better supported prohibition on expropriation of the company's property, therefore rests primarily on the decisions of two judges at first instance both of which have been somewhat blown upon by decisions of the Court of Appeal. Nevertheless they are believed to be good law and to have been impliedly recognised as such by the legislature. As we shall see in a later chapter,[58] section 209 [59] of the Act confers on a nine-tenths majority rights of compulsory acquisition of the shares of the minority in certain limited circumstances and subject to certain safeguards. Unless the decisions in *Brown's* case and the *Dafen Tinplate* case are right, the statutory power seems to be unnecessary and the statutory safeguards unavailing, for the majority, even if less than nine-tenths, could attain their object by an alteration of the articles provided only that they could not be proved to have acted otherwise than " bona fide for the benefit of the company as a whole." Whatever may have been the position prior to 1929, it is thought that the courts will not today permit compulsory acquisition in disregard of the statutory rules unless, as in

---

[54] [1920] 2 Ch. 124.
[55] At p. 141.
[56] *Shuttleworth* v. *Cox Bros. and Co.* [1927] 2 K.B. 9, C.A., *infra.* See also *Greenhalgh* v. *Arderne Cinemas* [1951] Ch. 286, C.A.
[57] [1927] 2 K.B. at pp. 18, 19, 23, 26 and 27.
[58] Chap. 26, p. 629, *infra.*
[59] Re-enacting and extending s. 155 of the 1929 Act based on the recommendation of the Greene Committee (Cmd. 2657/26, para. 84). The section is intended to prevent the minority from oppressing the majority (*ibid.*) but if the argument in the text is sound it has incidentally achieved the reverse result also.

Sidebottom's case, the power is only exercisable in circumstances which are prima facie beneficial to the company.[60]   Powerful support for this view is afforded by the decision and observations of the Court of Appeal in *Re Bugle Press*.[61]   There the holders of 90 per cent. of the shares, who wished to buy out the holder of the remaining 10 per cent. (but who must have been advised not to attempt to do so by the simple expedient of inserting a power in the articles), formed a company and vested their shares in that company which then made a bid for the remaining shares and purported to acquire them under section 209.   The court refused to permit this, saying that to allow existing shareholders to use the section as a device to get rid of a minority whom they did not happen to like would be contrary to fundamental principles of company law.[62]

(d) A general principle ?

Just as the fiduciary duties of directors impose upon them certain objective restraints to which they are subject irrespective of subjective good faith on their part,[63] so, it seems, do the so-called fiduciary obligations of the controlling shareholders.   As we have seen, they cannot exercise their powers so as to expropriate the company's property,[64] or so as to relieve the directors of their duties of subjective good faith,[65] or, perhaps, so as to expropriate the shares of the minority.[66]   In all these cases the motives of the controllers appear to be irrelevant except to the extent that it may be possible to uphold their action if it can be shown positively that it was taken bona fide in the interests of the company as a whole.   The decisions, however, purport to be examples of an alleged general principle that the majority must always exercise their powers " bona fide for the benefit of the company as a whole."

If there is any such general principle it seems quite clear that in cases falling outside heads (a)–(c) it operates only if it can be shown that the action was not bona fide in the interests of the company as a whole, whereas, in cases falling within heads (a)–(c) it is, at the most, a defence if it can be shown positively that the action was bona fide in the interests of the company.   Certainly there is need for a general principle

---

[60] *Quaere* whether the terms of acquisition must be fair.   In *Brown* v. *British Abrasive Wheel Co.*, *Sidebottom* v. *Kershaw Leese & Co.*, and *Dafen Tinplate Co.* v. *Llanelly Steel Co.*, *supra*, the new articles provided for acquisition at a fair value.   In *Crookston* v. *Lindsey Crookston & Co.*, 1922 S.L.T. 62, an alteration was allowed which compelled any shareholder *who wanted to sell* to offer his shares to the directors at par.   But it was emphasized (see p. 63) that had the shareholders been compelled to sell at par *when called upon to do so* this would have been strong evidence that the alteration was not bona fide for the company's benefit.

[61] [1961] Ch. 270, C.A.   Followed in *Esso Standard (Inter-America) Inc.* v. *J. W. Enterprises Ltd.* [1963] S.C.R. 144 (Can.S.C.).

[62] See Evershed M.R. at p. 287 and Harman L.J. at pp. 287, 288.   But it is not easy to find any such fundamental principle if *Greenhalgh* v. *Arderne Cinemas* [1951] Ch. 286, C.A., *infra* (in which Evershed M.R. presided) is rightly decided.

[63] See Chap. 23, p. 525 *et seq.*, *supra*.

[64] Head (a), *supra*.

[65] Head (b), *supra*.

[66] Head (c), *supra*.

applying outside heads (a)–(c), for it is clear enough that there is nothing in the nature of an objective bar to alterations of members' rights which fall short of an attempted expropriation of their shares. Thus in *Allen* v. *Gold Reefs of West Africa*,[67] the majority were allowed to alter the articles so as to give the company a lien on fully paid shares even in respect of debts incurred prior to the resolution. In *Shuttleworth* v. *Cox Bros. & Co.*,[68] they were permitted to get rid of an unsatisfactory life director by adding to the articles a provision providing that a director should be disqualified if called upon to resign by the other directors. And, finally, in *Greenhalgh* v. *Arderne Cinemas*,[69] they were held entitled to abridge the pre-emptive rights afforded existing shareholders in the original articles.

This last case, however, was merely the culmination of a long battle in the courts which is such an admirable illustration of the vulnerability of a minority shareholder that it is worth while summarising the whole story.

In 1941 Arderne Cinemas Ltd., a private company then controlled by the Mallard family and their associates, was in financial difficulties, and an approach was made to Greenhalgh. The arrangement come to was that Greenhalgh should advance £11,000 on debentures and become a director, and that the unissued shares should be subdivided and allotted to Greenhalgh. Further, there was a collateral voting agreement between Greenhalgh and the Mallards whereby the latter agreed to vote with the former. As a result, of the total 49,820 votes Greenhalgh had 19,213 in his own right and controlled a further 16,062 by virtue of the voting agreement—in all just under three-fourths of the whole and 20,000 more than all the other shareholders.

Unhappily, differences arose almost immediately between Greenhalgh and the Mallards, who denied that the voting agreement bound them since it purported to extend to voting at directors' meetings where any attempt to fetter their fiduciary discretion would be void. Morton J., in an unreported judgment, held that it was nevertheless valid so far as concerned voting at general meetings.

The Mallards then transferred the bulk of their shares to other members not parties to the voting agreement, and Greenhalgh instituted his second action, *Greenhalgh* v. *Mallard*,[70] which went to the Court of Appeal and to which reference has already been made in Chapter 18. It was held that the members' pre-emptive rights conferred by the articles did not extend to transfers to existing

[67] [1900] 1 Ch. 656, C.A.
[68] [1927] 2 K.B. 9, C.A. This and the earlier cases were reviewed in admirable judgments of the High Court of Australia in *Peters American Delicacy Co.* v. *Heath* (1939) 61 C.L.R. 457. See especially *per* Latham C.J. at p. 479 *et seq.*
[69] [1951] Ch. 286, C.A.
[70] [1943] 2 All E.R. 234, C.A.; *supra*, p. 392.

· members, and that the obligation to vote with Greenhalgh was personal to the parties to the agreement and did not run with the shares. Hence, Greenhalgh could not attack the validity of the transfers or enforce the voting agreement against the transferees.

The result of this decision was that Greenhalgh had lost voting control—he now only had about 20,000 votes out of a total of 49,820. But he still had sufficient to block a special resolution. After the disposal of yet a third (unreported) action, caused by disputes as to the exact form of the debentures, the Mallards returned to the attack by securing the passing of an ordinary resolution subdividing the then 10s. shares into 2s. ones. As these shares were held by the Mallard faction the result was that they had acquired sufficient votes to pass any resolution they liked and that Greenhalgh had lost any effective voice in the company's affairs. As we have seen, he instituted a fourth action, *Greenhalgh* v. *Arderne Cinemas*,[71] and carried this to the Court of Appeal, but lost on the ground that there had been no variation of the rights of the class of shares held by him. A further claim for breach of contract also failed because there was no express term in the agreement with the company prohibiting a subdivision.

Greenhalgh then issued a writ against the Mallards alleging malicious conspiracy to defeat the judgment of Morton J. in the first action. Uthwatt J. found that the predominant purpose of the defendants was not to injure Greenhalgh but to protect their own interests, and the Court of Appeal upheld his decision in the Mallards' favour.[72] Nothing daunted, Greenhalgh issued a further writ based on the same alleged conspiracy, but grounded, not on malice, but upon alleged employment of unlawful means to accomplish their object. The defendants asked that the pleadings be struck out on the grounds of *res judicata* and that they were vexatious. This interlocutory point was also taken to the Court of Appeal which upheld the argument of the defendants.[73]

Although the Mallards (after their initial reverse) had proved victorious all along the line, they may well have found litigation on such a scale an expensive hobby and concluded that it was time to get out while the going was good. Be that as it may, one of them, who was chairman of the board, entered into negotiations with a certain Sol Sheckman for the acquisition by him of the Mallard faction's shares. In the result Mr. Sheckman agreed to acquire the Mallards' shares at 6s. per 2s. share [74] and was, apparently, willing

---

[71] [1946] 1 All E.R. 512, C.A. See Chap. 22, at p. 511.
[72] Unreported.
[73] *Greenhalgh* v. *Mallard* [1947] 2 All E.R. 255, C.A.
[74] The fact that, despite ten years' internecine strife, the company's affairs had flourished sufficiently for the shares to appreciate to this extent is one of the most incredible features of this extraordinary story.

to buy any other shares at the same price. The only snag was that the articles still provided that no sale could take place to a non-member but that the shares must be offered to the existing shareholders. It was therefore necessary either to obtain the agreement of all the shareholders to waive this provision (and clearly Greenhalgh would not be amenable) or to alter the articles. A general meeting was accordingly convened to consider a special resolution altering the articles so as to permit any transfer with the sanction of an ordinary resolution. After a somewhat stormy meeting, during which Greenhalgh " asked questions and Mr. Mallard, so far as he could, avoided answering them," [75] the resolution was passed and the transfer to Sheckman authorised by a subsequent ordinary resolution.

Greenhalgh then started his final action [76] (the seventh, and the fifth to go to the Court of Appeal) claiming a declaration that the resolutions were invalid as a fraud on the minority. Though Greenhalgh's shares were not being expropriated he was losing the right to purchase a proportion of any shares which his fellow members wished to sell to outsiders. Moreover, there was no doubt that the chairman had " thought fit to display towards Mr. Greenhalgh (who, like himself, was a shareholder in this company) a singular lack of courage and candour . . ." [77] Despite these considerations it was held that the resolution was not invalid as a fraud on the minority.

However, it was conceded that the resolutions would be invalid if not passed " bona fide for the benefit of the company as a whole " and some attempt was made to define this expression. A definition is important because, as we have seen, in some cases falling under heads (a) and (b) and all cases falling under head (c) the resolution will be valid if it can be positively shown to have been passed bona fide in the interests of the company and, in other cases, it may be invalid if it can be shown that it was not so passed. Evershed M.R. said [78]:

" In the first place it is now plain that ' bona fide for the benefit of the company as a whole ' means not two things but one thing. It means that the shareholder must proceed on what, in his honest opinion, is for the benefit of the company as a whole. [Secondly] the phrase, ' the company as a whole,' does not (at any rate in such a case as the present) mean the company as a commercial entity, distinct from the corporators: it means the corporators as a general body. That is to say, the case may be taken of an individual hypothetical member and it may be asked whether what is proposed

[75] *Per* Evershed M.R. in [1950] 2 All E.R. at p. 1124.
[76] *Greenhalgh* v. *Arderne Cinemas Ltd.* [1951] Ch. 286, C.A., and [1950] 2 All E.R. 1120, where the judgment of Evershed M.R. is reported more fully.
[77] [1950] 2 All E.R. at p. 1122.
[78] [1951] Ch. at p. 291.

is, in the honest opinion of those who voted in its favour, for that person's benefit. I think that the matter can, in practice, be more accurately and precisely stated by looking at the converse and by saying that a special resolution of this kind would be liable to be impeached if the effect of it were to discriminate between the majority shareholders and the minority shareholders, so as to give the former an advantage of which the latter were deprived. When the cases are examined in which the resolution has been successfully attacked, it is on that ground. It is therefore not necessary to require that persons voting for a special resolution should, so to speak, dissociate themselves altogether from their own prospects and consider whether [the proposal is [79]] for the benefit of the company as a going concern."

This restatement restores some virility to a principle which, after *Shuttleworth* v. *Cox Bros. & Co.*,[80] had appeared to be completely impotent. Though shareholders are not expected to divorce themselves wholly from their own personal interests they are bound to ask themselves whether the proposal is beneficial, not only to themselves, but to a hypothetical member who, presumably, has no personal interests apart from those as member.[81] Clearly there must be many cases in which the controllers do not ask themselves this question. Unfortunately it will be virtually impossible to prove it. Moreover the question is somewhat meaningless when the resolution concerns the adjustment of the rights of different interests within the company.[82] Doubtless it was because he was conscious of this that the learned judge suggested an alternative objective test and one which would be more meaningful than that of whether no reasonable person could have regarded the proposal as beneficial. The suggested alternative is that of discrimination, which was said to explain the cases in which the resolutions have been successfully attacked. Unfortunately the only such case specifically mentioned in the judgment is *Dafen Tinplate Co.* v. *Llanelly Steel Co.*[83] Doubtless the *Dafen* case, and *Brown* v. *British Abrasive Wheel Co.*,[84] could be explained on the ground that the resolutions would have resulted in discrimination between majority and minority, since the former could acquire the shares of the latter but not vice versa, but this does not appear to have been the ground on which they were decided. Nor

---

[79] The wording in [1950] 2 All E.R. at p. 1126 is substituted for that given in the *Law Reports* (*viz.*, " what is thought to be ") which does not make sense.
[80] [1927] 2 K.B. 9, C.A., *supra.*
[81] This interpretation of Lord Evershed's statement was expressly adopted by McLelland J. in *Australian Fixed Trusts Pty. Ltd.* v. *Clyde Industries Ltd.* [1959] S.R.(N.S.W.) 33 at p. 56. But he may have meant that the *court* should ask itself the question and could avoid the resolution only if *it* answered in the negative.
[82] *Cf.* Latham C.J. in *Peter's American Delicacy Co.* v. *Heath* (1939) 61 C.L.R. 457 at 481 (Aus.H.C.).
[83] [1920] 2 Ch. 124, *supra.*
[84] [1919] 1 Ch. 290, *supra.*

would it have been a very happy one, for it would seem to follow that the resolutions would have been valid had they empowered the directors to call upon *any* shareholder to transfer his shares—a wording which would have fulfilled the majority's purpose equally well.[85] And if discrimination is the true test, why was the resolution upheld in the *Greenhalgh* case itself? The result of the resolution was that a majority would always be in a position to sell to an outsider whereas the minority would not. Is this not discrimination?

Apart from cases falling under head (a), (b) or (c)—which do not seem to depend solely or primarily on the motives of those voting as members—there appears to have been no English case in the present century in which a resolution has been successfully attacked on this ground. Indeed, there seems to have been only one reported case since *Greenhalgh* v. *Arderne Cinemas Ltd.*[86] in which an attempt to do so has been made. In that case,[87] the previous control of the holders of management shares was preserved, when further shares of the other class were issued, by resolving to increase the votes of the management shares. On that resolution the holders of the management shares refrained from voting. The court refused to intervene, holding that all that had occurred was that the members of the company, other than the holders of the management shares, had decided that it was for the benefit of the company to preserve the existing basis of control and that there had been no " discrimination against or oppression of "[88] some part of the members.

There is, however, one noteworthy Australian decision[89] in which Lord Evershed's discrimination test was applied. The effect of a proposed alteration would have made it difficult if not impossible for shares in the company owned by unit trusts ever to be voted. It was held that the alteration would be invalid since it would deprive those shareholders of an advantage retained by others and there were no grounds upon which reasonable men, if they considered the matters which they ought to have considered, could decide that the resolution was for the benefit of the company as a whole. There is also an earlier decision of the Privy Council on an appeal from Canada.[90] This concerned voting as members of a class of debentureholders on a reconstruction scheme. The requisite majority would not have been obtained but for the vote of one member of the class whose support had been

---

[85] This was in fact the wording used in *Sidebottom* v. *Kershaw Leese & Co.* [1920] 1 Ch. 154, C.A., *supra*. Admittedly the resolution was upheld in that case but not, surely, because it applied to any shareholder but because the exercise of the power was limited to circumstances in which it would be beneficial to the company?

[86] *Supra*.

[87] *Rights & Issues Investment Trust Ltd.* v. *Stylo Shoes Ltd.* [1965] Ch. 250.

[88] The court seemed to think that the formulation of Evershed M.R. involved proof of oppression: see at pp. 255 and 257.

[89] *Australian Fixed Trusts Pty. Ltd.* v. *Clyde Industries Ltd.*, *supra*.

[90] *British America Nickel Corpn.* v. *O'Brien* [1927] A.C. 369, P.C.; *cf. Goodfellow* v. *Nelson Lines* [1912] 2 Ch. 324

obtained by the undisclosed promise to him of a block of ordinary stock. An injunction was granted since that member had not treated the interest of the whole class as the dominant consideration. But some of the remarks made appear to suggest that the duties of the majority at a class meeting are greater than those at a general meeting.[91] This seems wholly unreasonable; if there is any general principle it must surely apply generally, subject only to the qualification that at a class meeting the voting must be " bona fide for the benefit of the class as a whole " rather than " bona fide for the benefit of the company as a whole."

While authority supporting a general principle is meagre apart from dicta, the latter are weighty and numerous and should certainly be supported. What they appear to establish is this:

Unlike directors, members are not fiduciaries and therefore are not required to act bona fide in the interests of others. But, just as directors must not only act bona fide in the interest of the company but must also exercise their powers for a proper purpose, so members, though they need not act bona fide in the interest of the company, must exercise their powers for a proper purpose. As the House of Lords has recently emphasised, a purpose which is contrary to public policy is improper and a resolution designed to achieve that purpose is invalid.[92] But the purpose may be equally improper if, though not contrary to any legal rule, it is obviously contrary or totally unrelated to the welfare of the company and its members. Hence a resolution which purports to expropriate the property of the company or its members or to relieve the directors of their duties of good faith will prima facie be improper and invalid, though exceptionally it may be upheld if it can be shown positively to have been passed for the benefit of the company.[93] In other circumstances the resolution will be valid unless it can be positively shown to have been passed for an improper purpose.[94] And here the test is not whether the court thinks the resolution will accomplish a proper purpose but whether it can be, shown that those who voted for the resolution did not think so.[95] This onus is very difficult to discharge unless the resolution is such that those who voted for it could not reasonably have regarded its purpose as proper.[96]

[91] [1927] A.C. at pp. 371–372.
[92] *Pharmaceutical Society of G.B.* v. *Dickson* [1968] 3 W.L.R. 286, H.L., which concerned a chartered corporation.
[93] As we have seen, expropriation of the company's property may conceivably be proper and expropriation of members' property certainly may, but release of the directors' duties of good faith probably can never be proper.
[94] That the onus of proof of improper purpose is then on those alleging it is clearly established by *Shuttleworth* v. *Cox Bros. & Co.* [1927] 1 K.B. 9, C.A., *supra*; and *Greenhalgh* v. *Arderne Cinemas* [1951] Ch. 286, C.A., *supra*.
[95] See especially *Shuttleworth* v. *Cox Bros. & Co.*, *supra*, where the court over-ruled the judgment of the *jury* and deferred to that of the shareholders.
[96] *Australian Fixed Trusts Pty. Ltd.* v. *Clyde Industries Ltd.* [1959] S.R.(N.S.W.) 33 seems to be the only case in the post-war years in which the onus has been discharged and there the court was satisfied that reasonable men could not have regarded the resolution as beneficial to the company if they had adverted to the matters which they should have taken into consideration: see *supra*, p. 575.

The purpose is proper if it was to benefit [97] the company or the generality of its members or of the class concerned.[98] It is improper if it was primarily to benefit extraneous interests whether of the persons voting for the resolution or of third parties. It is submitted that it will equally be improper if the predominant motive is to injure other members, or even to display power for self-assertion or personal prestige.[99] It is cogent evidence that the purpose was improper if the resolution discriminates between members of the same class.[1]

Accordingly the motives of those voting are relevant and to that extent there is justification for using the expression " bona fide for the benefit of the company " despite the fact that this causes confusion with the wider principle applying to directors. Normally, however, the question will be tested objectively against the standards of the reasonable man (this is almost inevitable when a large number of members have voted, for the individual motives of each will be unascertainable), but with a strong presumption that the members are reasonable men and are the best judges of what is beneficial to them and their company. This presumption is probably reasonable so long as some do not have interests contrary to those of the generality of members. The main interest of the latest English decision on this subject [2] is that the class whose interests might have been thought to conflict with those of the other members refrained from voting.

Another point to notice is that there may be circumstances in which, although the court will not restrain the company from passing a resolution or declare it invalid if passed, it will nevertheless restrain the company from later acting on it in fraud of the minority.[3] Thus an alteration of the articles empowering the company to buy out a shareholder who was interested in a competing business will normally

---

[97] Normally the benefit must be economic but in the case of a non-trading company the test would obviously be whether the resolution was beneficial in the sense that it served to accomplish the company's objects.

[98] Tested by the standards of a hypothetical member having no conflicting interests: see *supra*, p. 574.

[99] In other words, if there is " malice " in a sense similar to that in the law of civil conspiracy: *Crofter Hand Woven Harris Tweed Co.* v. *Veitch* [1942] A.C. 435, H.L. *Cf. Re H. R. Harmer Ltd.* [1959] 1 W.L.R. 62, C.A.

[1] See *Greenhalgh* v. *Arderne Cinemas* and *Australian Fixed Trusts Pty. Ltd.* v. *Clyde Industries Ltd., supra.*

[2] *Rights and Issues Investment Trust Ltd.* v. *Stylo Shoes Ltd.* [1965] Ch. 250, *supra. Cf. Hogg* v. *Cramphorn Ltd.* [1967] Ch. 254 (1963) where the directors were ordered not to vote the shares they had improperly issued to themselves, but were not restrained from voting their original shares, and *Bamford* v. *Bamford* [1969] 2 W.L.R. 1107, C.A., where the holders of the newly issued shares refrained from voting.

[3] This distinction between restraining the alteration and restraining the company from acting on it is not clearly drawn in the cases—rather surprisingly since it would afford a neat way round the argument that under s. 10 the company has a statutory right to make any alteration which would have been valid if in the original articles. From the viewpoint of the minority shareholder the dis-advantage of waiting until the alteration is acted on is that he may then be met by the argument that he has acquiesced in the alteration: *Borland's Trustee* v. *Steel* [1901] 1 Ch. 279.

be valid as beneficial to the company.[4] But if the directors later tried to use it to expropriate a minority shareholder on the pretext that he held a few shares in a public company in the same line of business, it is submitted that this would be restrained as a fraud on the minority even if their action were ratified by the general meeting. This particular exercise of the power would be shown not to be bona fide for the benefit of the company.

Members' Acts Outside General and Class Meetings

The final question which needs brief discussion is whether the fraud on the minority principle can ever operate in respect of acts by the controllers taken outside formal meetings. The principal case when this is likely to arise is in connection with a take-over bid. As we have seen,[5] both at common law and under statute law the directors are placed under fiduciary restraints notwithstanding that it is the shares, and not the undertaking, which are being acquired. Under sections 193 and 194 no additional payment may be made to a director unless this is approved by a meeting of the shareholders. To this meeting, although it is not strictly a general or class meeting of the company, there can be little doubt that the above rules would apply. In other words, although the directors could vote at the meeting in their capacity of shareholders, the court could set aside an approving resolution if it had not been passed " bona fide for the benefit of the class as a whole " as defined above.

But suppose the controlling shareholders are not themselves directors? Can they then sell their controlling block for a larger price than that which the other shareholders can obtain? In England it has always been assumed that they can.[6] In the United States, however, a number of courts have held that they may have to account to the other shareholders on the ground that they are selling control of corporate property.[7] There is, in theory, no reason why the English courts should not adopt the same view; it would be easy to treat this case as an example of expropriation of the company's property [8] as exemplified in *Menier* v. *Hooper's Telegraph Works* [9] and *Cook* v. *Deeks*.[10] And, clearly, there are sound grounds for so doing, for the only reason why they get a larger price is because their shares enable the holders to appoint the board, and thereby to gain control of assets which belong not to themselves but to the company as a whole. However, it would need a substantial change

---

[4] *Sidebottom* v. *Kershaw Leese & Co.* [1920] 1 Ch. 154.
[5] *Supra*, Chap. 23, p. 540 *et seq.*
[6] *Cf. Short* v. *Treasury Commissioners* [1948] A.C. 534, H.L., *supra*, p. 346. But see the 1969 *City Code*, General Principle 8 and Rule 10.
[7] See especially *Perlman* v. *Feldmann* and the learned articles thereon, referred to at p. 546, *supra*, n. 11.
[8] See (a) at pp. 564–566.
[9] (1874) L.R. 9 Ch.App. 350.
[10] [1916] 1 A.C. 554, P.C.

of judicial outlook if such an extension were to be made, and the statutory regulation of this field with its express limitation to payments to directors is likely to make the courts all the more reluctant to engage in judicial legislation. In S. Africa there has been a decision [11] rejecting such an extension. Kuper J., after quoting the earlier part of this paragraph, said:

> " I do not agree with this statement. The action of the majority can only be impeached if they receive a larger price at the expense of other shareholders. If the majority sell their control to a third party the minority is in exactly the same position as it was before the sale except that the control is to be exercised by B instead of A. Of course the position is different if the action of the majority is fraudulent, in the sense in which that word is used in regard to oppression of the minority, but in the absence of that essential the majority must be entitled, without hindrance, to sell their shares as a block at the best price they can obtain for those shares." [12]

This dictum, though it rejects the suggestion that the majority owe fiduciary duties—for in the case of fiduciaries the test of accountability is not whether the beneficiary has been damnified but whether the fiduciary has profited without the permission of the beneficiary—does recognise that the majority may be liable if the result of the sale is to harm the company or the minority. A sale to a competitor might well have that result.

In any event, a course of oppressive conduct on the part of the new controllers may lead to intervention by the courts in the form either of a winding-up order or of the alternative remedy under section 210 of the Act. These remedies, which are dealt with in the next chapter, may fairly be regarded as extensions of the same principle and, indeed, as approaching closer to imposing genuine duties of good faith on those in control, whether they act through the board of directors or the general meeting.[13]

CONCLUSIONS

1. Members or debentureholders voting at company or class meetings are not bound to disregard their own selfish interests, but are generally entitled to vote or refrain from voting in whatever way they think best for themselves.

2. But a resolution will be avoided and the company restrained from acting upon it if it attempts—

    (a) to expropriate the company's property; or

---

[11] *United Trust Pty. Ltd.* v. *S. African Milling Co.*, 1959 (2) S.A. 426 (Wits L.D.).
[12] At pp. 433–434.
[13] See *Scottish Co-op. Wholesale Society Ltd.* v. *Meyer* [1959] A.C. 324, H.L., and especially *per* Lord Keith who, at p. 361, went so far as to say that if the company was in substance, though not in law, a partnership, there must be the utmost good faith between the constituent members.

(b) to waive prospectively or retrospectively, the directors' duties to act bona fide in what they believe to be for the best interests of the company as a whole; or

(c) to enable some members or debentureholders to acquire compulsorily the shares or debentures of others, unless the power of acquisition is exercisable only in circumstances which are, prima facie, beneficial to the company or class as a whole.[14]

3. Further, any resolution will be set aside and the company restrained from acting upon it, if it can be shown that the predominant motive of those voting for it in the form in which it was presented was to benefit interests other than those of the members of the company or class *qua* members of the company or class or to injure the minority or to dominate for the sake of domination.

4. There is as yet no sign of a general extension of these quasi-fiduciary rules to actions by the members or debentureholders other than voting at meetings.

---

[14] It is difficult to see how it could ever be legitimate to enable some *debenture-holders* to acquire the debentures of another; but conceivably this might be so if the holder was using his powers under the debenture to drive the company into liquidation contrary to the wishes of the other holders.

CHAPTER 25

THE ENFORCEMENT OF THE DIRECTORS' AND CONTROLLERS' DUTIES

THE purpose of the present chapter is to discuss the means of enforcing the duties of the directors and controllers.[1] Though incorporation solves many procedural problems it does not wholly remove those which arise when there is a dispute within the company; indeed, it may render them more intractable. If one partner is breaking the duties which he owes to his fellows the latter can call him to account.[2] When, however, the directors or controllers of an incorporated company are breaking their duties, the other members of the company normally have no *locus standi*. The duties are owed not to them but to the company itself; and therefore it is the company itself which should sue. But those against whom the action is to be brought may themselves be the appropriate organ for instigating proceedings in the company's name. Hence some alternative means of enforcement have been made available in certain circumstances as a result of intervention both by the equity courts and the legislature.

In discussing these remedies consideration will not be restricted to court proceedings alone. As we shall see, recent legislative extensions of the Board of Trade's power to appoint an inspector have provided an administrative remedy which may often prove effective either on its own or as a preliminary to legal action. And both this administrative sanction and the right to petition the court under section 210 of the 1948 Act[3] have not only made more effective the legal duties of directors and controllers, but seem indirectly to have extended their ambit by providing a remedy for abuses which formerly were beyond the scope of legal sanctions.

1. ACTION BY COMPANY

If the duty to be enforced is one owed to the company, then the primary remedy for its enforcement is an action by the company against those in default. If, therefore, complaint is made that the directors have

---

[1] *i.e.*, the directors' duties to act within the powers delegated to them and in good faith and with the required degree of care and skill (see Chap. 23), and the controllers' duties to adopt the appropriate procedure at general meetings (Chap. 21), to act within the powers of such meetings (Chap. 22) and to comply with their quasi-fiduciary duties (Chap. 24).

[2] Of course, the position becomes more complicated with an unincorporated association with a large number of members all of whom should be made parties in person or by representation.

[3] *Infra*, p. 598 *et seq.*

broken their duties of loyalty, care, or skill, the company is the proper plaintiff in an action against them.[4] This is the famous rule in *Foss* v. *Harbottle*, so called after the decision in which it was first clearly articulated.[5] Later, however, the rule was extended to cover all cases where what is complained of is some internal irregularity in the operation of the company [6]; for example, to dispute the validity of the appointment of some of the directors,[7] or to attack the refusal to call a poll at a meeting.[8] Though the courts often describe these actions as wrongs done to the company, it is far from clear why they should not instead be regarded as breaches of the rights of each shareholder under the contract established by the memorandum and articles.[9] And, in fact, where the breach is one which could not be remedied by an ordinary resolution of the company, the courts have for some time recognised that it is an infringement of the personal rights of the member in respect of which he can therefore bring proceedings.[10]

The fact is that the courts have ceased to be moved by pure questions of principle but have instead given weight to the practical advantages of the *Foss* v. *Harbottle* rule. And these practical advantages are—

(a) Insistence on action by the company itself prevents multiplicity of suits. If each shareholder were permitted to sue, the company might be harassed by a succession of actions started and discontinued by innumerable plaintiffs.[11]

(b) If the irregularity complained of is one which can be effectively ratified by the general meeting it is futile to have litigation about it except with the consent of the general meeting.[12]

These two reasons, and especially the second, justify the extension

---

4 *Foss* v. *Harbottle* (1843) 2 Hare 461; *Russell* v. *Wakefield Waterworks* (1875) L.R. 20 Eq. 474; *Gray* v. *Lewis* (1873) L.R. 8 Ch.App 1035; *Duckett* v. *Gover* (1877) 6 Ch.D. 82; *Burland* v. *Earle* [1902] A.C. 83, P.C.; *Dominion Cotton Mills* v. *Amyot* [1912] A.C. 546, P.C.; *Foster* v. *Foster* [1916] 1 Ch. 532; *Pavlides* v. *Jensen* [1956] Ch. 565; *Birch* v. *Sullivan* [1957] 1 W.L.R. 1247; *Heyting* v. *Dupont* [1964] 1 W.L.R. 843, C.A.

5 For a full discussion of this rule, see Wedderburn [1957] Cam.L.J. 194 and [1958] Cam.L.J. 93. And for a comparison with America, see Boyle (1965) 28 M.L.R. 317.

6 *Mozley* v. *Alston* (1847) 1 Ph. 790; *MacDougall* v. *Gardiner* (1875) 1 Ch.D. 13; *Campbell* v. *Australian Mutual Provident Society* (1908) 77 L.J.P.C. 117; *Cotter* v. *National Union of Seamen* [1929] 2 Ch. 58, C.A. The extension involved linking the rule with the principle that the courts would not interfere as between partners in respect of internal irregularities which the majority of partners could put right.

7 *Mozley* v. *Alston* (1847) 1 Ph. 790.

8 *MacDougall* v. *Gardiner* (1875) 1 Ch.D. 13, C.A.

9 Companies Act 1948, s. 20; *supra*, Chap. 12, p. 261 *et seq.*

10 *Pender* v. *Lushington* (1877) 6 Ch.D. 70; *Edwards* v. *Halliwell* [1950] 2 All E.R. 1064, C.A.

11 *Gray* v. *Lewis, supra.*

12 *MacDougall* v. *Gardiner, supra.* " If the thing complained of is a thing which in substance the majority of the company are entitled to do, or if something has been done irregularly which the majority of the company are entitled to do regularly or if something has been done illegally which the majority . . . are entitled to do legally, there can be no use in having a litigation about it, the ultimate end of which is only that a meeting has to be called and then ultimately the majority gets its wishes ": *per* Mellish L.J. at p. 25. See also *Harben* v. *Phillips* (1883) 23 Ch.D. 14, C.A., and *Burland* v. *Earle* [1902] A.C. 83, P.C.

of the rule to internal irregularities, as well as wrongs by the directors or controllers to the company itself.

Normally, therefore, the company itself is the proper plaintiff, and the only proper plaintiff, in an action arising out of a dispute within the company. And the appropriate agency to start an action on the company's behalf is the board of directors, to whom this power is delegated as an incident of managing the company.[13] However, it is well established that if the directors cannot or will not start proceedings in the company's name (and if they themselves are the defendants they obviously will not) the power to do so reverts to the general meeting.[14] Hence, the practice has grown up of allowing anyone connected with the company to start proceedings in the company's name subject to the risk that the defendants will challenge his right to do so. In that event, the court will stay proceedings until a general meeting has been called to decide whether or not the company shall sue.[15] If the decision is in favour of continuing, all is well.[15] If, however, the decision is against action the proceedings will be dismissed,[16] and the rash individual and his solicitors on the record will be liable for the costs.[17] In practice, this means that there is little likelihood of prosecuting an action against the directors or other controllers so long as they remain in *de facto* control.[18] Such proceedings are only likely if a new group has assumed control,[19] or if the company has gone into liquidation and thus passed into the control of an independent liquidator,[20] or if the Board of Trade is in a position to take action in the name of the company under its newly extended powers dealt with later in this chapter.[21]

2. ACTION BY SHAREHOLDER

The rule in *Foss* v. *Harbottle* greatly strengthens the position of the majority; indeed, if there were no exceptions to it the minority would

---

[13] *Shaw & Sons (Salford) Ltd.* v. *Shaw* [1935] 2 K.B. 113, C.A.

[14] *Pender* v. *Lushington* (1877) 6 Ch.D. 70; *Imperial Hydropathic Hotel Co.* v. *Hampson* (1882) 23 Ch.D. 1, C.A.; *Danish Mercantile Co. Ltd.* v. *Beaumont* [1951] Ch. 680, C.A. Attention has already been drawn to the difficulty of reconciling this rule with the strict doctrine of the separation of powers as between the board and the general meeting: *supra*, pp. 136, 137.

[15] *Danish Mercantile Co. Ltd.* v. *Beaumont, supra*. If the company is in liquidation the liquidator will be the appropriate person to ratify: *ibid*.

[16] *East Pant Du Mining Co.* v. *Merryweather* (1864) 2 H. & M. 254. In some circumstances where action by minority shareholders is allowed (see below) the name of the company may be struck out as plaintiff and added as defendant: see *Harben* v. *Phillips* (1883) 23 Ch.D. 14, C.A.

[17] *Newbiggin Gas Co.* v. *Armstrong* (1880) 13 Ch.D. 310, C.A.; *La Compagnie de Mayville* v. *Whitley* [1896] 1 Ch. 788, C.A.

[18] Especially as the court probably has no power to prevent the defendants, if shareholders, from voting at the general meeting: *Mason* v. *Harris* (1879) 11 Ch.D. 97, C.A. But *cf. Hogg* v. *Cramphorn Ltd.* [1967] Ch. 254 (1963).

[19] As in *Regal (Hastings) Ltd.* v. *Gulliver* [1942] 1 All E.R. 378, [1967] 2 A.C. 134n., H.L., discussed *supra*, Chap. 23, p. 535 *et seq.*

[20] It is normally only on liquidation that an attempt is made to bring the directors to book. As we shall see, *infra*, p. 595, the Act then provides a summary remedy against officers.

[21] See p. 611, *infra*.

be completely in their hands. Even the limitations imposed by the substantive law on the powers of the majority would be stultified, for so long as the company remained a going concern no action could effectively be brought to enforce them. As for the fiduciary and other duties of the directors these, too, could be disregarded with impunity so long as the directors had voting control. Hence, exceptions have been recognised. In addition to the special statutory procedures outlined below, it is well established that in certain circumstances an individual shareholder or group of shareholders can institute proceedings as plaintiffs, instead of those proceedings having to be instituted in the name of the company. It is, however, one of the most difficult problems in the whole field of company law to determine exactly what are these exceptional circumstances.

When can a shareholder sue ?

It is generally stated that a suit by a shareholder instead of by the company is allowed in four circumstances [22]—

(i) When it is complained that the company is acting or proposing to act *ultra vires*.[23]

(ii) When the act complained of, though not *ultra vires* the company, could be effective only if resolved upon by more than a simple majority vote [24]; *i.e.*, where a special or extraordinary resolution is required and (it is alleged) has not been validly passed.[25]

(iii) Where it is alleged that the personal rights of the plaintiff shareholder have been infringed or are about to be infringed.[26]

---

[22] See, for example, *Edwards* v. *Halliwell* [1950] 2 All E.R. 1064, C.A. The case concerned a registered trade union to which the same principles apply since, whether or not a union should be regarded as a corporation (see *supra*, Chap. 11, pp. 228–231), it can sue or be sued in the union name.

[23] *Bagshaw* v. *The Eastern Union Ry.* (1849) 7 Hare 114, affd. (1850) 2 Mac. & G. 389; *Simpson* v. *Westminster Palace Hotel Co.* (1860) 8 H.L.C. 712; *Hoole* v. *G.W. Ry.* (1867) L.R. 3 Ch.App. 262; *Russell* v. *Wakefield Waterworks Co.* (1875) L.R. 20 Eq. 474; *Hutton* v. *W. Cork Ry.* (1883) 23 Ch.D. 654; *Yorkshire Miners' Asscn.* v. *Howden* [1905] A.C. 256, H.L. As these cases show, *ultra vires* is here used in a broad sense to include any action forbidden to the company either because it is beyond the powers in its memorandum or because of a general legal prohibition.

[24] *Baillie* v. *Oriental Telephone Co.* [1915] 1 Ch. 503, C.A.; *Cotter* v. *National Union of Seamen* [1929] 2 Ch. 58 at 69, 70; *Edwards* v. *Halliwell* [1950] 2 All E.R. 1064, C.A. All the cases on alleged wrongful variation of class rights (*supra*, pp. 507–513) may be regarded as examples of this or the next exception. The fact that anything turned on the nature of the resolution seems to have been ignored in certain of the earlier cases; see, for example, *Campbell* v. *Australian Mutual Provident Society* (1908) 77 L.J.P.C. 117, and *Normandy* v. *Ind Coope & Co. Ltd.* [1908] 1 Ch. 84, in which shareholders were not allowed to sue to attack the validity of special resolutions passed as a result of inadequate notices, there being no allegations of fraud. On this point both cases seem to be impliedly disapproved in *Baillie* v. *Oriental Telephone Co., supra.*

[25] It seems clear that the shareholder may sue notwithstanding proof that those who oppose him are sufficiently numerous to pass the special resolution which is needed.

[26] *Johnson* v. *Lyttle's Iron Agency* (1877) 5 Ch.D. 687, C.A.; *Pender* v. *Lushington* (1877) 6 Ch.D. 70; *Wood* v. *Odessa Waterworks Co.* (1889) 42 Ch.D. 636; *Salmon* v. *Quin & Axtens* [1909] 1 Ch. 311, C.A.; affd. [1909] A.C. 442, H.L.;

(iv) Where those who control the company are perpetrating a fraud on the minority [27] *i.e.*, an act of the type defined in Chapter 24.

As will be seen from the citations in the footnotes there is ample authority for each of these exceptions. There are also certain judicial dicta [28] which would add a further exception—

(v) Any other case where the interests of justice require that the general rule, requiring suit by the company, should be disregarded.

Apart from this fifth exception, if it exists, it is arguable that all these exceptions could be reduced to one by saying that an individual shareholder can always sue, notwithstanding the rule in *Foss* v. *Harbottle*, when what he complains of could not be validly effected or ratified by an ordinary resolution. This formulation covers alleged *ultra vires* acts, which cannot be effected by any resolution or even by unanimous consent of all shareholders. [29] It clearly covers the second exception (indeed, it is the second exception), and likewise the fourth, for, as we have seen, [30] no resolution can justify fraud on the minority.

It is less clear whether it covers the third exception—where it is alleged that the personal rights of the plaintiff shareholder have been infringed. Prima facie, this is wider than our formulation, for a shareholder might have personal rights, notwithstanding that these were liable to be destroyed or modified by an ordinary resolution of the company. For example, since the articles of association constitute a contract between the members and the company, each member would seem to have a personal right to see that they are complied with and to restrain any breach of them. [31] But in general it appears that while this is true if what is done could only be made effective by an alteration of the articles requiring a special resolution, [32] it does not always apply if the act could be effectively ratified by ordinary resolution. [33]

However, the recently reported case of *Hogg* v. *Cramphorn Ltd.* [34] suggested that it is an over-simplification to say that the possibility of ratification by ordinary resolution is always the decisive test. It was

---

British America Nickel Corpn. v. *O'Brien* [1927] A.C. 369, P.C.; *Edwards* v. *Halliwell*, *supra*; *Hayes* v. *Bristol Plant Hire Ltd.* [1957] 1 W.L.R. 499. For a further list of illustrations, see [1957] Cam.L.J. at pp. 210–211.

[27] *Atwool* v. *Merryweather* (1867) L.R. 5 Eq. 464n.; *Menier* v. *Hooper's Telegraph Works* (1874) 9 Ch.App. 350; *Mason* v. *Harris* (1879) 11 Ch.D. 97, C.A.; *Spokes* v. *Grosvenor Hotel* [1897] 2 Q.B. 124, C.A.; *Alexander* v. *Automatic Telephone Co.* [1900] 2 Ch. 56, C.A.; *Burland* v. *Earle* [1902] A.C. 83, P.C. (see especially *per* Lord Davey at p. 93); *Cook* v. *Deeks* [1916] 1 A.C. 554, P.C.

[28] See especially *per* Wigram V.-C. in *Foss* v. *Harbottle* itself (1843) 2 Hare at 492, *per* Jessel M.R. in *Russell* v. *Wakefield Waterworks Co.* (1872) L.R. 20 Eq. 474 at p. 482 and *Heyting* v. *Dupont* [1964] 1 W.L.R. 843, C.A., at pp. 851, 854.

[29] *Ashbury Carriage Co.* v. *Riche* (1875) L.R. 7 H.L. 653; *supra*, Chap. 5.

[30] *Supra*, Chap. 24.

[31] See *supra*, pp. 264, 265.

[32] See cases cited in notes 24 and 26, *supra*.

[33] *Mozley* v. *Alston* (1847) 1 Ph. 790; *MacDougall* v. *Gardiner* (1875) 1 Ch.D. 13; *Foster* v. *Foster* [1916] 1 Ch. 532; *Cotter* v. *National Union of Seamen* [1929] 2 Ch. 58, C.A. For the difficulty of drawing this line, see [1957] Cam.L.J. at 213–215.

[34] [1967] Ch. 254. The case was heard in 1963 but not fully reported until four years later.

there accepted that an individual shareholder could sue when his complaint was that the directors, in issuing further shares, had exercised their powers for an improper purpose.[35]   Yet Buckley J. held that their action could be ratified by a general meeting, and gave the company an opportunity of doing so [36] on the directors' undertaking not to exercise the votes on the new shares.   This decision has been followed and approved by the Court of Appeal in *Bamford* v. *Bamford*.[37]   These sensible decisions avoid the major absurdity of the *Foss* v. *Harbottle* rule—the preventing of a member from complaining of an impropriety merely because it would not have been improper if authorised by the general meeting, notwithstanding that the general meeting has not authorised it or had any opportunity of doing so.   Further development on these lines would mean that the possibility of ratification would cease to be a bar to getting an action on its feet; coupled with the recent recognition by the Court of Appeal of the possibility that, if justice clearly requires, a member might be allowed to sue to restrain misfeasance without alleging fraud,[38] it points the way in which the shackles of the rule might be struck off without awaiting a flank attack on the lines suggested by the Jenkins Committee.[39]   If that development needs a theoretical justification it could, it is thought, be found by saying [40] that every member has, under the contract implied by section 20, a personal right to have the company's affairs properly conducted in accordance with its memorandum and articles.[41]   That would have the effect of greatly widening the scope of the third exception, for every case of improper action by the directors would involve a breach of the member's personal rights.   It would not, however, eradicate the distinction, to which we turn next, between suing on behalf of the company to enforce its rights and suing on the member's own behalf to enforce his rights.   The former will be needed if damages or property are to be recovered on behalf of the company, the latter when all that is wanted is an injunction or a declaration.

---

[35] There was plenty of authority for this: see *Punt* v. *Symons & Co.* [1903] 2 Ch. 506; *Galloway* v. *Halle Concerts Society* [1915] 2 Ch. 233; and *Piercy* v. *Mills* [1920] 1 Ch. 77.

[36] Which it took.   Buckley J. pointed out that in *Punt* v. *Symons & Co.*, *supra*, and *Piercy* v. *Mills*, *supra*, it had been clear that the general meeting would not have ratified unless the new shares were voted.

[37] [1969] 2 W.L.R. 1107.   Here the shares had been issued not to the directors themselves but to another company.   The issue was ratified by the company in general meeting, the other company not voting, and the minority shareholders' action then dismissed.

[38] *Heyting* v. *Dupont* [1964] 1 W.L.R. 843, where, however, it was held that justice did not require since the company had not suffered damage by the alleged misfeasance.

[39] See *infra*, p. 604.

[40] As was suggested by Wedderburn in [1957] Cam.L.J. at 210–215: see also (1967) 30 M.L.R. 77.

[41] See *supra*, pp 264, 265.   It was expressly on this basis that the plaintiffs sued in *Bamford* v. *Bamford* and presumably in *Hogg* v. *Cramphorn Ltd.*

(a) *Enforcing the company's rights—the derivative action*

If confusion has been caused by drawing unnecessary distinctions between the circumstances in which a minority shareholder's action is possible, even greater confusion seems to have arisen from a failure to draw a clear distinction between two different rights in which he may sue. On the one hand there is the type of case, of which *Foss* v. *Harbottle* itself was an example, where a wrong has been done to the company and action is brought to restrain its continuance, or to recover the company's property or damages or compensation due to it. Here the company is the only true plaintiff. The dispute is not an internal one between those interested in the company, but one between the company on the one hand and third parties on the other, and it makes no difference in principle that the third parties happen to be the directors or controlling shareholders of the company. If anyone other than the company is allowed to appear as plaintiff it is an anomaly allowed only as a matter of grace to prevent a serious wrong from going unremedied because the wrongdoers control the company. Where such an action is allowed the member is not really suing on his own behalf nor on behalf of the members generally, but on behalf of the company itself. Although, as we shall see, he will have to frame his action as a representative one on behalf of himself and all the members other than the wrong-doers, this gives a misleading impression of what really occurs. The plaintiff shareholder is not acting as a representative of the other share-holders but as a representative of the company, and the action will necessarily present features quite different from those in the normal representative action. This has been less clearly recognised here than in the United States, where such actions have been infinitely more frequent and the appropriate rules elaborated to an extent unknown here. And there this type of action has been given the distinctive name of a " derivative action," recognising that its true nature is that the individual member sues on behalf of the company to enforce rights derived from it. Here it is proposed to adopt this illuminating nomen-clature, but the reader must be warned that it is, as yet, virtually unknown in this country.

The English courts have recognised that a derivative action may sometimes be brought by an individual member where it is impracticable for the company to do so. The best illustration of this recognition is afforded by the proceedings arising out of the fraudulent promotion of the *East Pant Du Lead Mining Co.* The owners of a derelict mine formed a company, of which they became directors and shareholders, and sold the mine to it for a substantial sum. The outside shareholders sought to relieve the company of the purchase and to recover the money paid to the sellers. An action was commenced in the name of the company but was dismissed when the miscreants secured, through the exercise of their votes, the passing of a resolution directing that the

company should discontinue the proceedings.[42] A shareholder then
started a new action in the name of himself and all other members except
the fraudulent directors. It was held that, notwithstanding *Foss* v.
Harbottle, the court would allow an action framed in this way, since
otherwise it would be impossible to set aside the fraud.[43]

But such an action will only be allowed under stringent conditions
designed to ensure that the advantages of the *Foss* v. *Harbottle* rule are
preserved so far as possible. These conditions are procedural requirements which apply even though the company concerned is a foreign
one.[44] Moreover it has been held that it is the duty of the court to ensure
that they are complied with even though the parties do not object to
the action being brought.[45]

(i) Not every wrong to the company will justify a derivative action
to remedy it. Normally the wrong complained of must be such as to
involve a fraud on the minority, which could not be validly waived by
the company in general meeting. What constitutes such conduct has
been discussed in Chapter 24. Briefly to recapitulate, it appears to cover
conduct of the following types [46]—

    (a) Expropriation of the property of the company or, in some
        circumstances, that of the minority,
    (b) Breach of the directors' duties of subjective good faith, and
    (c) Voting for company resolutions not bona fide in the interests of
        the company as a whole.[47]

It will be observed that all these cases involve either misappropriation
of property or some element of fraud in the sense of an improper
motive. Does this mean that for wrongs of other types done to the
company there is no remedy so long as the wrongdoers control the
company? Some recent cases suggest that this is so. In *Pavlides* v.
Jensen [48] a minority shareholder, who had no voting rights, complained
that the directors had negligently sold an asset of the company at a
gross undervaluation. It was held that a derivative action could not
be brought, since the general meeting could have ratified the directors'
action or resolved not to sue in respect of it. However, in the later case
of *Heyting* v. *Dupont* [49] the Court of Appeal left open the question
whether there might not be cases where, in the interests of justice, an

---

[42] *East Pant Du Lead Mining Co.* v. *Merryweather* (1864) 2 H. & M. 254.
[43] *Atwool* v. *Merryweather* (1867) L.R. 5 Eq. 464n.
[44] *Heyting* v. *Dupont* [1964] 1 W.L.R. 843, C.A.
[45] *Ibid.* There the objection was taken by the judge in the court below: [1963] 1
W.L.R. 1192. Though justified in the particular case, where the litigation was
obviously futile, it will be lamentable if this is generally followed since it might
stifle a friendly action to resolve a disputed question.
[46] *Supra*, pp. 564–578. In some of these cases, however, the member may have a
personal action on the basis that his personal rights are infringed by the "fraud."
[47] For a discussion of the meaning of this expression, see *supra*, Chap. 24, p. 573
et seq.
[48] [1956] Ch. 565. See also *Birch* v. *Sullivan* [1957] 1 W.L.R. 1247.
[49] *Supra.*

action would be allowed in respect of misfeasance without fraud. Unfortunately the court did not suggest that *Pavlides* v. *Jensen* was such a case yet, if the facts there pleaded were true, it is difficult to imagine a stronger example of injustice.

(ii) It must be shown that the alleged wrongdoers control the company.[50] The clearest way of doing this will be to show that both the directors and a general meeting have been invited to institute proceedings in the name of the company and have refused to do so, and that the refusal was because of the votes cast by the wrongdoers.[51] This, in effect, was what had occurred in the case of the *East Pant Du Lead Mining Co.*[52] referred to earlier. However, the English cases recognise that there is no point in formally asking the directors to institute the proceedings if they are to be the defendants, and that it is not necessary to convene a general meeting and to invite it to resolve upon proceedings in the company's name, provided that the court can be satisfied *aliunde* that the wrongdoers are in effective control.[53]

Sometimes this will present no difficulty; for example, if the directors have issued to themselves further shares so as to give themselves voting control,[54] or if the defendants are a majority of the board of directors and it appears from the company's registers that the directors own a clear majority of the voting shares.[55] In other cases it may not be so easy, especially as the courts are not always ready to adopt a wholly realistic view of the extent to which directors can exercise *de facto* control although they have considerably less than a clear majority of shares.[56]

In some circumstances this second requirement might, it is thought, be used as a means of establishing "fraud", proof of which was previously lacking. Let us assume that the shareholder, as in the

---

[50] *Atwool* v. *Merryweather, supra*; *Gray* v. *Lewis* (1873) L.R. 8 Ch.App. 1035; *Menier* v. *Hooper's Telegraph Works* (1874) L.R. 9 Ch.App. 350; *Russell* v. *Wakefield Waterworks* (1875) L.R. 20 Eq. 474; *Mason* v. *Harris* (1879) 11 Ch.D. 97, C.A.; *Alexander* v. *Automatic Telephone Co.* [1900] 2 Ch. 56, C.A.; *Cook* v. *Deeks* [1916] 1 A.C. 554, P.C.; *Ferguson* v. *Wallbridge* [1935] 3 D.L.R. 66, P.C.; *Pavlides* v. *Jensen, supra*; *Birch* v. *Sullivan, supra*.

[51] Thus Wigram V.-C. suggested in *Foss* v. *Harbottle* (1843) 2 Hare 461 at p. 494 that a shareholder could institute proceedings only if all means had been used to put the general meeting in motion and had failed.

[52] *Atwool* v. *Merryweather, supra*.

[53] The American courts are generally stricter in this respect and insist upon proof of an abortive demand made on the directors and, sometimes, a reference to the shareholders in general meeting: *cf.* rule 23.1. of the Federal Rules of Civil Procedure.

[54] *Punt* v. *Symons* [1903] 2 Ch. 506; *Piercy* v. *Mills* [1920] 1 Ch. 77; *Hogg* v. *Cramphorn Ltd.* [1967] Ch. 254.

[55] As in *Mason* v. *Harris, supra*, or, *semble*, exactly 50 per cent.: see *Glass* v. *Atkin* (1967) 65 D.L.R. (2d) 501 (Ont.H.C.). The register of directors' shareholdings should be helpful in this connection since it should show holdings both personally and in the names of nominees.

[56] See *Pavlides* v. *Jensen* [1956] Ch. 565. In order to get the action on its feet it is not necessary to prove control but merely to allege facts which, if proved, would establish control; *ibid.* But the plaintiff will ultimately lose on the merits unless he can prove his allegations at the trial.

Pavlides case,[57] is complaining of alleged negligence on the part of the directors. He first calls on the directors to institute proceedings in the name of the company against themselves.[58] Naturally they refuse. He then asks them to convene a general meeting [59] to consider a resolution that the company shall start proceedings against them. The directors are then in a quandary. If they refuse, it might be open to the shareholder to institute a derivative action alleging that the directors, placing their own interests before those of the company, have refused to allow the company to consider whether to take steps to recover damages due to it. Unless it be the law that the original wrong, as opposed to the failure to sue in respect of it, must be fraudulent (the cases are unclear on this) it seems that this would be a sufficient allegation of bad faith to support the action. To refuse in their own selfish interests to allow the general meeting to decide whether the company shall sue or not, is a breach of the directors' duties of subjective good faith, irrespective of the nature of the original cause of action. If, on the other hand, the directors convene the general meeting which, as a result of their own votes, rejects the resolution, the shareholder again seems to be in a position to institute proceedings alleging this time that the resolution was not passed " bona fide in the interests of the company as a whole " [60]—another example of fraud on the minority. Only if the directors convene the meeting which rejects the resolution by the votes of independent shareholders will the complaining shareholder clearly be denied any remedy [61]—and this is fair enough.

(iii) The company must be made a defendant in the action.[62] As already pointed out, the company is the true plaintiff, and if a money judgment is recovered against the true defendants—the wrongdoing directors or other controllers—this will be in favour of the company and not in favour of the individual shareholder who is nominal plaintiff. The company cannot, in fact, be the plaintiff, because neither of its organs—the board of directors and the general meeting—will authorise suit by it. As the next best thing the court insists upon its being made

---

[57] *Supra.*
[58] Notwithstanding what is said above, he might be well advised to make a formal demand in such circumstances.
[59] It is not thought that he would be compelled himself to seek to enlist sufficient support to demand a general meeting under s. 132.
[60] See *supra*, Chap. 24, p. 570 *et seq.*
[61] *Cf. Hogg* v. *Cramphorn Ltd.* [1967] Ch. 254, *supra*, and *Bamford* v. *Bamford* [1969] 2 W.L.R. 1107, C.A., *supra*, where, however, it was only the improperly issued shares which were not voted.
[62] The need for the company to be a party is clearly recognised in all the cases. The reasons, as stated in the text, are most clearly set out in *Spokes* v. *Grosvenor Hotel* [1897] 2 Q.B. 124, C.A. and by Greene M.R. in *Beattie* v. *Beattie Ltd.* [1938] Ch. 708 at 718. C.A. If the company has ceased to exist and cannot be resuscitated (under s. 352 or 353 (6), *infra*, Chap. 27, pp. 652–654) it seems that no action can be brought: *Clarkson* v. *Davies* [1923] A.C. 100, P.C.; *Ferguson* v. *Wallbridge* [1935] 3 D.L.R. 66, P.C. In the U.S.A. direct recovery by the members has been allowed in such circumstances.

the nominal defendant.[63] So long as the company is a party, judgment can be given in its favour, and any decision in the case becomes *res judicata* so far as the company is concerned, precluding it from bringing a subsequent action on the same cause if there is a later change in control.

(iv) The plaintiff shareholder must sue in a representative capacity on behalf of himself and all the other members other than the real defendants.[64] On the face of it this seems anomalous. As we have already pointed out, the plaintiff is not really suing on behalf of the shareholders, but on behalf of the company. But the requirement fulfils a useful purpose, for it ensures that all the other shareholders are also bound by the result of the action. If, therefore, judgment is given for the defendants a second derivative action cannot be brought by another member, for the matter will be *res judicata* as regards all of them.

This requirement, coupled with the third, therefore preserves so far as possible the advantage of the *Foss* v. *Harbottle* rule that multiplicity of actions is avoided. On the other hand, it is regrettable that the English judges—unlike their American colleagues—have not yet realised that the derivative action differs in kind from the normal representative action where one sues on behalf of a class.[65] Thus, it seems to be assumed that, as in the normal representative action, the plaintiff will be *dominus litis* until judgment,[66] and can discontinue and settle the action at his pleasure.[67] Such a settlement (unless embodied in a formal judgment [68]) or discontinuance will not, it is true, preclude a second action by another plaintiff shareholder.[69] But there are obvious possibilities of abuse which the English courts have not yet considered. Suppose the plaintiff discontinues the action in consideration of a payment made

---

[63] It will then be treated as a party for all purposes including costs and discovery: *Spokes* v. *Grosvenor Hotel, supra.* But the successful plaintiff will only recover from the company and the real defendants costs taxed on a party and party basis—not (as might be more logical) solicitor and client costs on the basis that they are paid out of a common fund: *ibid.* Similarly, if unsuccessful, he will normally have to pay the party and party costs of the real defendants and the company. This potential liability is a serious restraint on actions of this sort and accounts for their rarity in comparison with the position in the U.S.A.

[64] This, too, is recognised in all the cases since *Mozley* v. *Alston* (1847) 1 Ph. 790. Alternatively all the members may actually join as plaintiffs, in which case they will be subject to liability for costs and discovery; members merely represented are not so liable.

[65] Under R.S.C., Ord. 15, r. 12.

[66] Though for adequate reasons (*e.g.*, proof of adverse interest) the plaintiff may be deprived of the conduct of the action in favour of another member of the class who intervenes and applies for it: *Re Services Club Estates Syndicate* [1930] 1 Ch. 78 (a debentureholders' action).

[67] *Re Alpha Co.* [1903] 1 Ch. 203. *Cf. P. & O. Steam Navigation Co.* v. *Johnson* (1938) 60 C.L.R. 189 (Austr.H.C.), where a bona fide settlement by the board with one of their number was held to bar the plaintiff member's action.

[68] And perhaps not even then: see *Re Calgary & Medicine Hat Land Co.* [1908] 2 Ch. 652, C.A., at 662, and *Arsett* v. *Butler Air Transport Ltd.* (*No.* 1) (1957) 75 W.N.(N.S.W.) 299.

[69] *Gray* v. *Lewis* (1873) L.R. 8 Ch.App. 1035, where this is given as a reason for normally insisting on action by the company instead of by a shareholder even in a representative capacity.

to him personally (probably out of the coffers of the company): can he hold on to it? It is submitted that he cannot, and that he must account, for anything that he receives, to the company as whose agent he was really acting.[70] And ought he to be allowed to settle or discontinue at his pleasure? Is there not much to be said for the salutary rule adopted in certain American jurisdictions [71] that this will be allowed only with the court's consent after notice has been given to all the shareholders?

(v) The right to bring a derivative action is afforded the individual member as a matter of grace. Hence the conduct of some shareholder may be regarded by a court of equity as disqualifying him from appearing as plaintiff on the company's behalf. This will be the case, for example, if he participated in the wrong of which he complains.[72] But the mere fact that the plaintiff was not a member at the time of the wrong will not bar him from bringing the action,[73] for he is enforcing the company's rights, not his own, and without his intervention a wrong to the company might go unremedied. But he must be a shareholder of record at the time when he brings his action.[74]

(b) *Enforcing the member's rights—the personal action*

The derivative action, explained in (a) above, lies where a wrong has been done *to* the company. Where, however, a wrong is being done or threatened *by* the company different considerations apply. The company then is not merely a nominal defendant but the real defendant, because judgment is required against it, not for it. And the proper plaintiff is anyone who has a personal right against the company which is being infringed. The reason why the decisions are so confused and confusing on the question whether the action should primarily be by the company or against it, is because the same facts will normally give rise to both possibilities. If the company is proposing to do something *ultra vires* or which infringes its articles, a shareholder may properly sue to restrain it. But, alternatively, the company itself may proceed against its directors to restrain them from taking the proposed action. If the first alternative is adopted the company is properly a defendant, though not necessarily the only one, for the directors may be joined as co-defendants so that they personally are bound by the order of the court. If the second course is adopted, the company is properly the plaintiff, and the directors are the defendants. But the fact that this second alternative is a possible one is no reason for refusing

---

[70] For this purpose it should not matter whether or not the payment is made from the company's funds; a fiduciary cannot make a secret profit from his position.

[71] See, for example, r. 23.1 of the Federal Rules of Civil Procedure.

[72] *Whitwam* v. *Watkin* (1898) 78 L.T. 188; *Towers* v. *African Tug* [1904] 1 Ch. 558, C.A. *Cf. Mosely* v. *Koffyfontein Mines* [1911] 1 Ch. 73, C.A., affd. [1911] A.C. 409, H.L., where he was allowed to sue to restrain *future* illegal acts.

[73] *Seaton* v. *Grant* (1867) L.R. 2 Ch.App. 459; *Bloxam* v. *Metropolitan Ry.* (1868) L.R. 3 Ch.App. 337 (in both of which the plaintiff had bought shares in order to qualify himself).

[74] *Birch* v. *Sullivan* [1957] 1 W.L.R. 1247.

to allow a member to sue the company if he has an independent right to do so.

Thus, it is clear that an action to restrain the company from acting *ultra vires*[75] may be brought by any member[76] as plaintiff in his own right against the company as defendant.[77]

There is then no need to join as defendants the directors or anyone else unless some relief is required against them.[78] The position seems to be precisely the same if action is brought in respect of some internal irregularity. Thus, if the company is attempting to interfere with class rights,[79] to deprive a member of his votes[80] or of some other right conferred upon him by the articles,[81] to act upon an invalid special or extraordinary resolution,[82] or to alter the internal structure of the company in circumstances amounting to a fraud on the minority,[83] a single member may bring an action against the company.[84] In some circumstances he may do so if the directors are exceeding their powers or exercising them for an improper purpose.[85] Here, however, we come up against the rule that he may not be allowed to do so if the transaction concerned is one which could be validly undertaken or ratified by an ordinary resolution of the company.[86] Since *Hogg* v. *Cramphorn Ltd.*[87]

---

[75] Once again, this is used in a broad sense to include acts illegal under the general law as well as acts beyond the powers of the company in its memorandum.

[76] Or, sometimes a debentureholder: *Hutton* v. *West Cork Ry.* (1883) 23 Ch.D. 654; or a holder of scrip not yet registered as a member: *Bagshaw* v. *The Eastern Union Ry.* (1849) 7 Hare 114, affd. (1850) 2 Mac. & G. 389.

[77] *Simpson* v. *Westminster Palace Hotel* (1860) 8 H.L.C. 712; *Hoole* v. *G.W. Ry.* (1867) L.R. 3 Ch.App. 262; *Yorkshire Miners' Assen.* v. *Howden* [1905] A.C. 256, H.L.

[78] It may be desirable to join the other party to an alleged *ultra vires* contract in order to recover restitution in favour of the company.

[79] In none of the cases cited on this topic in Chap. 22, p. 507 *et seq.*, was objection taken to the right of the member to bring proceedings; in most cases it is clear from the reports that the plaintiff sued as representative of the class to which he belonged.

[80] *Pender* v. *Lushington* (1877) 6 Ch.D. 70.

[81] *Johnson* v. *Lyttle's Iron Agency* (1877) 5 Ch.D. 687, C.A.; *Wood* v. *Odessa Waterworks Co.* (1889) 42 Ch.D. 636; *Edwards* v. *Halliwell* [1950] 2 All E.R. 1064, C.A. And see p. 584, n. 26, *supra*.

[82] *Baillie* v. *Oriental Telephone Co.* [1915] 1 Ch. 503, C.A.

[83] *Brown* v. *British Abrasive Wheel Co.* [1919] 1 Ch. 290; *Sidebottom* v. *Kershaw Leese & Co.* [1920] 1 Ch. 154, C.A.; *Dafen Tinplate Co. Ltd.* v. *Llanelly Steel Co. Ltd.* [1920] 2 Ch. 124; *Shuttleworth* v. *Cox Bros. & Co.* [1927] 2 K.B. 9, C.A.; *Greenhalgh* v. *Arderne Cinemas* [1951] Ch. 286, C.A.; *Rights & Issues Investment Trust Ltd.* v. *Stylo Shoes Ltd.* [1965] Ch. 250. See Chap. 24, pp. 567–578, *supra*, where these cases are discussed. In *Brown's* case and the *Dafen* case the plaintiff sued in a representative capacity; in all the others he appears not to have done so.

[84] His right to do so is even clearer if he has a contract independently of the articles: see, for example, *Southern Foundries* v. *Shirlaw* [1940] A.C. 701, H.L.; and *British America Nickel Corpn.* v. *O'Brien* [1927] A.C. 369, P.C. (where suit was by a debentureholder).

[85] *Punt* v. *Symons & Co.* [1903] Ch. 506; *Galloway* v. *Hallé Concerts Society* [1915] 2 Ch. 233; *Piercy* v. *Mills* [1920] 1 Ch. 77; *Hogg* v. *Cramphorn Ltd.* [1967] Ch. 254; *Bamford* v. *Bamford* [1969] 2 W.L.R. 1107, C.A.

[86] See, for example, *Mozley* v. *Alston* (1847) 1 Ph. 790; *MacDougall* v. *Gardiner* (1875) 1 Ch.D. 13; *Foster* v. *Foster* [1916] 1 Ch. 532; *Cotter* v. *National Union of Seamen* [1929] 2 Ch. 58, C.A.

[87] *Supra.*

this does not seem to be an inflexible rule. The member may sue because, as we have seen,[88] the memorandum and articles constitute a contract between him and the company which he has a personal right to enforce.[89] His contractual rights are independent of any which the company may have to sue the directors to restrain them from acting on the irregular scheme.

The mere fact that his rights are identical with those enjoyed by all the other members, or by all members of the same class of shareholders,[90] does not appear to make it necessary that he should sue in a representative capacity on behalf of himself and all the others. It certainly entitles him to proceed in a representative capacity if he wishes to do so, and this is the usual practice. It is also a desirable practice, for it ensures that any judgment is binding on all whom he represents, thus preserving some of the advantages of the *Foss* v. *Harbottle* rule by precluding the possibility of a multiplicity of actions. For this reason it is submitted that the company should be able to insist on the action being a representative one, but this seems to have been lost sight of in the recent cases. Nor does there seem to be any need to join the directors as defendants unless some personal relief is asked for against them. If it is, it seems that they can be added as co-defendants in the member's personal action, notwithstanding that the relief claimed against them is due to the company and not to the individual plaintiff, so long as it arises out of the same series of transactions.[91]

If in any of these cases the action is brought in a representative capacity it is a true representative action. In contrast with the derivative action, in which the plaintiff really represents the company, here the plaintiff truly represents himself and his fellow shareholders and they, not the company, are the actual, and not merely the nominal, plaintiffs.

In contrast with a derivative action to enforce the company's rights,[92] a personal action to enforce the member's own rights obviously cannot be brought in respect of anything which took place prior to the time when the plaintiff became a member, for this could not be a breach of any contract with him. Another contrast is in respect of the remedy

---

[88] *Supra*, Chap. 12, p. 261 *et seq.* and p. 585.

[89] *Bamford* v. *Bamford* [1968] 3 W.L.R. 317 at p. 321H; affd. [1969] 2 W.L.R. 1107, C.A.

[90] *Semble* this must invariably be the case where the complaint is that the articles have been broken, for the articles confer contractual rights only on members *qua* members: *supra*, Chap. 12, p. 263.

[91] See *Hogg* v. *Cramphorn Ltd.*, *supra*. The cases clearly support this in cases of *ultra vires*, per Jessel M.R. in *Russell* v. *Wakefield Waterworks Co.* (1875) L.R. 20 Eq. at 481–482; and see, for example, *Bagshaw* v. *The Eastern Union Ry.* (1849) 7 Hare 114, affd. 2 Mac. & G. 389 where *Foss* v. *Harbottle* was held not to bar a claim for an injunction to restrain *ultra vires* actions and for restitution by the directors in respect of breaches of trust by them. But it may be different where the *ultra vires* transaction is completed and the sole remedy claimed is repayment to the company: *Eales* v. *Turner*, 1928 W.L.D. 173 (S.Afr.). Where the claims against the directors arise out of different facts it may be necessary to plead each claim separately and to fulfil the conditions necessary for a derivative action as regards the claim against the directors: see *Foster* v. *Foster* [1916] 1 Ch. 532.

[92] *Supra*, p. 592.

claimed. A derivative action may often lead to a monetary judgment in favour of the company; a shareholder's personal action based on the contract in the memorandum and articles can rarely, if ever,[93] lead to a money judgment against the company.[94] The appropriate remedy will be an injunction or a declaration.

Finally, it should perhaps be pointed out that one may occasionally have circumstances in which a member or debentureholder can complain that the directors have broken a duty owed personally to him and his fellows. An example of this would be where the directors have placed themselves in a fiduciary relationship towards the members as such.[95] On the rare occasions when this occurs he could sue the directors, either personally or as representative of his class, and the company would not appear to be a necessary party either as plaintiff or defendant.[96]

3. WINDING UP

The foregoing remedies are available only when some wrongful act has been committed or is threatened—something which is a breach of the duties of the directors, controllers or the company, or something which is beyond their powers. We now turn to a series of statutory remedies which may be available not only when some wrongful act has occurred but also when there has been a course of oppressive conduct, whether or not this has involved any particular wrongful act. The provision of such remedies has resulted in a considerable extension of the protection afforded to members of the company, and thereby has imposed greater duties on the controllers and made all their duties more readily enforceable. The first of these remedies is the winding up of the company. This subject is afforded fuller treatment in Chapter 27, but at the present stage attention must be drawn to two matters which are of direct relevance to the subject under discussion.

(a) Misfeasance summonses

Once a liquidation has begun, then, whatever the type of winding up, section 333 of the Act provides a summary and effective remedy for certain past breaches of duty owed to the company. The section applies where any promoter, director, manager or officer of the company or the liquidator himself [97] " has misapplied or retained or become liable or

---

[93] Probably the only case where it might, is where a dividend has been properly declared but not paid.

[94] This seems to be a consequence of the refusal to allow capital to be returned to the members. A debentureholder's action or any other claim based on a contract independent of the articles, might, of course, lead to a money judgment: see, *e.g., British America Nickel Corpn.* v. *O'Brien* [1927] A.C. 369; P.C.; *Southern Foundries* v. *Shirlaw* [1940] A.C. 701, H.L.

[95] For example, as a result of s. 193 (3) or in circumstances such as those in *Allen* v. *Hyatt* (1914) 30 T.L.R. 444, P.C.

[96] *Allen* v. *Hyatt, supra.*

[97] But not a receiver and manager appointed by debentureholders: *Re B. Johnson & Co. (Builders) Ltd.* [1955] Ch. 634, C.A.

accountable for any money or property of the company, or been guilty of any misfeasance or breach of trust in relation to the company." [98] This has been held to cover breaches of fiduciary duties but not common law negligence.[99]   Application may be made to the court by the official receiver or the liquidator (the normal applicant) or by any creditor or member [1]—who is, therefore, no longer handicapped by the rule in *Foss* v. *Harbottle*—and the court may compel the miscreants to repay or restore any money misapplied or to pay compensation.[1a]

Because of the practical difficulties of proceeding against the directors so long as they remain in control, a summons under this section is the most commonly used method of enforcing the directors' duties. Occasionally it may be possible in the liquidation to invoke a still more extensive remedy—that under section 332, whereby those responsible for knowingly carrying on the business of the company with intent to defraud may be made personally liable for its debts without limitation of liability.[2]

(b) Winding up to end oppression

The misfeasance summons is designed to deal with actual breaches of trust which come to light in the course of winding up.   But putting the company into liquidation may itself be a means of ending a course of oppression by those formerly in control, and among the grounds upon which winding up may be ordered is one peculiarly appropriate for use in such circumstances.   Under the 1948 Act, s. 222 (*f*), the court may order the company to be wound up if it is of the opinion that that is " just and equitable." [3]   The courts have so ordered when satisfied that this is essential if the members or any of them are to be protected from oppression.[4]   In particular, they have done so when the

---

[98] s. 333 (1).
[99] *Re B. Johnson & Co. (Builders) Ltd., supra.* The Jenkins Committee recommended that for " breach of trust " should be substituted a reference to any breach of duty, thus affording a remedy for negligence: Cmnd. 1749, para. 503 (d).
[1] The section uses the expression " contributory " the definition of which in s. 213 appears to restrict it to holders of partly paid shares.   But it has been held that here and elsewhere it has a wider meaning and is synonymous with " past or present member ": see Chap. 27, p. 648, note 10, *infra.*   Unless registered as a member, the trustee in bankruptcy of a shareholder is not included: *Re Bolton Engineering Co.* [1956] Ch. 577 (but this can be got round by requiring the bankrupt to petition: *Re K/9 Meat Suppliers (Guildford) Ltd.* [1966] 1 W.L.R. 1112).   Nor, probably, is the personal representative of a deceased shareholder: *Re C. Cooper & Sons Ltd.* [1937] Ch. 392 (where the point was discussed but not decided).   The Jenkins Committee recommended that it should be expressly provided that the trustee or personal representative could petition to wind up and obviously intended that he should be treated as a " contributory " for this purpose: see Cmnd. 1749, paras. 502 and 503 (g).   *Re Bolton Engineering Co.* has been dissented from in Australia: see *Re Meyer Douglas Pty. Ltd.* [1965] V.R. 638.
[1a] The respondents may claim indemnity or contribution *inter se*: *Re Morecambe Bowling Ltd.* [1969] 1 W.L.R. 133.
[2] For a discussion of this section see Chap. 10 at pp. 191–193, *supra.*
[3] This is another relic of partnership law; *cf.* Partnership Act 1890, s. 35 (*f*).
[4] See especially, *Re Brinsmead* [1897] 1 Ch. 406, C.A.; *Re Consolidated South Rand Mines Deep Ltd.* [1909] 1 Ch. 491; *Re Bleriot Manufacturing Aircraft*

conduct of those in control suggests that they are trying to make intolerable the position of the other members so as to be able to acquire their shares on favourable terms.[5] Once again, the *Foss* v. *Harbottle* rule has no application; any member [6] (or creditor) has an individual right to petition.[7] But a *member* has no *locus standi* to petition if the company is insolvent [8]; while if it is solvent, to wind it up contrary to the wishes of the majority shareholders is a serious step which the courts will only take if a strong case is made out.[9] Indeed, until the 1948 Act, it was not their practice to do so if any other remedy was available.[10] Hence, proof of some wrongful act in relation to the operation of the company was a reason against, rather than a reason for, a winding-up order since the complaining member ought instead to bring a minority shareholders' action against the company.

Following the recommendations of the Cohen Committee,[11] the mere fact that an alternative remedy is available is not a ground for refusing a winding-up order. Section 225 (2) now provides that the order shall not be refused unless the court is of the opinion both that some other

Co. (1916) 32 T.L.R. 253; *Loch* v. *John Blackwood Ltd.* [1924] A.C. 783, P.C.; *Re Davis & Collett* [1935] Ch. 693; *Re Newman & Howard Ltd.* [1962] Ch. 257 (which shows how the mere filing of the petition may lead to removal of the oppression by, *e.g.*, causing accounts to be rendered); *Re Lundie Bros. Ltd.* [1965] 1 W.L.R. 1051. And see the Scottish cases *Baird* v. *Lees*, 1924 S.C. 83 and *Thomson* v. *Drysdale*, 1925 S.C. 311, and the Canadian case of *Re National Drive-in Theatres* [1954] 2 D.L.R. 55 (B.Col.S.C.). The section is not, of course, limited in its application to such cases but is commonly invoked in cases of deadlock: see *Re Yenidje Tobacco Co.* [1916] 2 Ch. 426, C.A. But though the company may be a quasi-partnership it is on the terms of the articles and the court will not intervene if what is being done is in accordance therewith or if the deadlock can be resolved thereunder: *Charles Forte Investments Ltd.* v. *Amanda* [1964] Ch. 240, C.A.; *Re Expanded Plugs Ltd.* [1966] 1 W.L.R. 514; *Re K/9 Meat Supplies (Guildford) Ltd.*, *supra*. See (1964) 27 M.L.R. 282.

[5] *Loch* v. *John Blackwood Ltd.*, *supra*; *Re Davis & Collett Ltd.*, *supra*. This latter case, *Re National Drive-in Theatres*, *supra*, and *Re Lundie Bros. Ltd.*, *supra*, are excellent illustrations of the fact that it is not necessarily a minority in the strict sense that alone needs protection; in each case the oppressed members held 50 per cent. of the shares but had been ousted from any effective voice in the company's affairs.

[6] Provided he is an original allottee or has held his shares for six months: s. 224 (1) (*a*). This requirement is strictly construed: *Re Gattopardo Ltd.* [1969] 1 W.L.R. 619, C.A. For the extended meaning of " contributory " (the word used in the section), see n. 1, *supra*.

[7] s. 224. The company itself may also petition, *e.g.*, if a majority want to wind up but cannot secure the passing of a special resolution for voluntary liquidation; *cf. Re Anglo-Continental Produce Co.* [1939] 1 All E.R. 99, where a majority favoured a winding up but were opposed by a minority large enough to block the special resolution required for a voluntary liquidation. And so may the Board of Trade in some circumstances: see *infra*, p. 611.

[8] *Re Othery Construction Co. Ltd.* [1966] 1 W.L.R. 69; *Re Expanded Plugs Ltd.*, *supra*. The Jenkins Committee recommended the reversal of this rule: Cmnd. 1749, para. 503 (*h*).

[9] They refused, for example, in *Re Cuthbert Cooper & Sons Ltd.* [1937] Ch. 392, where the main complaint was a refusal to register as members the personal representatives of a deceased shareholder in a private company (but in *Re Swaledale Cleaners Ltd.* [1968] 1 W.L.R. 1710, C.A., Danckwerts L.J. disapproved this decision), and in *Re Anglo-Continental Produce Co.*, *supra*. And see *Re Davis Investments (East Ham) Ltd.* [1961] 1 W.L.R. 1396, C.A.

[10] See Cohen Report (Cmd. 6659), para. 59.

[11] *Ibid.*, paras. 60 and 152 and p. 95.

remedy is available, and that the petitioners are acting unreasonably in seeking to have the company wound up instead of pursuing that other remedy.[12] This makes a winding up more easily attainable but it does not make it any more inviting. Killing the company is a singularly clumsy method of ending oppression in its operation and it may be suicidal for the petitioners.[13] Hence the Cohen Committee recommended[14] an alternative and less drastic expedient which is now embodied in section 210 of the Act.

4. ORDER UNDER SECTION 210

(a) Nature of the remedy

Under section 210 any member who complains that the affairs of the company are being conducted in a manner oppressive to some part of the members (including himself) may petition the court which, if satisfied that the facts would justify a winding-up order but that this would unduly prejudice that part of the members, may make such order as it thinks fit. The order may regulate the conduct of the company's affairs in future, may order the purchase of some members' shares by others,[15] or by the company itself with a consequent reduction of capital, or may otherwise bring the matters complained of to an end. Where an alteration of the memorandum or articles is ordered, the company may not make any further alteration inconsistent therewith without the leave of the court.[16]

The Cohen Report[17] makes it clear that it was the intention that the court should have " power to impose upon the parties whatever settlement the court considers just and equitable." While recognising that the court could not " be expected in every case to find and impose a solution," it was thought that its discretion " must be unfettered, for it is impossible to lay down a general guide to the solution of what are essentially individual cases." Unfortunately our High Court procedure is ill-adapted for the exercise of the inquisitorial and salvationist role thus imposed upon the judges and, doubtless in recognition of this, it has been held[18] that the petitioner cannot just ask the court to exercise its

---

12 For an illustration, see *Charles Forte Investments Ltd.* v. *Amanda, supra.* The Jenkins Committee recommended that these limitations should be removed: Cmnd. 1749, para. 503 (*i*).
13 Cmd. 6659, para. 60. As the Report pointed out, " the break-up value of the assets may be small or the only available purchaser may be the very majority whose oppression has driven the minority to seek redress." It is significant that the indefatigable Mr. Greenhalgh (*supra*, Chap. 24, p. 571 *et seq.*) never sought this form of redress.
14 *Ibid.* p. 95.
15 It seems clear that either faction may be ordered to purchase the shares of the other.
16 s. 210 (3).
17 Cmd. 6659, para. 60.
18 *Re Antigen Laboratories Ltd.* [1951] 1 All E.R. 110. " [W]e have not been constituted an earthly Providence in matters of this kind, and it is for the petitioners

discretion but must indicate the nature of the relief wanted. This, though perhaps inevitable, seems regrettable and inconsistent with the intention that the court should have power " to find and impose a solution." Furthermore the wording of the section is unfortunate in a number of respects, and the courts, despite two bold decisions,[19] have, on the whole, construed it narrowly.

Nevertheless, the remedy is of undoubted value and has already been extensively and effectively invoked as a threat to induce those in control to behave reasonably towards all interests; as a weapon in the shareholder's armoury it will probably always prove more potent when brandished *in terrorem* than when actually used to strike. But it is particularly useful in the case of small companies, when it will normally be superior to any of the preceding remedies, and available in circumstances where they might be impracticable or disadvantageous.

(b) To whom available ?

The petition may be by any member; in other words, the rule in *Foss* v. *Harbottle* has no application, and an individual member has a personal right to institute proceedings in a non-representative capacity. The section appears in the Act under the heading *Minorities*, but the section itself scrupulously avoids the use of the word and refers to " oppression to some part of the members." It seems clear, therefore, that the draftsman has rightly recognised that oppression may be exercised by those in control even though they lack a majority holding, and that the section affords protection in such a case.[20] On the other hand, it may not be possible to use the section if the only oppression is that of the majority of one class on the other members of that class, for here it might be argued that it could not be said that " the affairs of *the company are being conducted* in a manner oppressive to some part of the members." But if, as is likely to be the case, the class exercising oppression is that which controls the company this difficulty should not arise. An oppressed director,[21] or debentureholder or other

---

to state what they primarily want. . . .": *per* Lord Cooper in *Meyer* v. *Scottish Textile & Manufacturing Co.*, 1954 S.C. 381 at 388 (Sc.).
[19] *Scottish Co-operative Wholesale Society* v. *Meyer* [1959] A.C. 324, H.L.; *Re H. R. Harmer Ltd.* [1959] 1 W.L.R. 62, C.A.
[20] The above passage was expressly adopted and applied in Australia by Joske J. in *Re Associated Tool Industries Ltd.* [1964] A.L.R. 73 at 82 (S.C.A.C.T.) and there is a S. African decision to the like effect: *Benjamin* v. *Elysium Investments (Pty.) Ltd.* 1960 (3) S.A. 467 (E.C.D.), see (1961) 24 M.L.R. 368. In *Re H. R. Harmer* [1959] 1 W.L.R. 62 the oppressor had only a minority of the equity but, with his wife, had voting control.
[21] *Elder* v. *Elder & Watson*, 1952 S.C. 49; *Re Bellador Silk Ltd.* [1965] 1 All E.R. 667; *Re Lundie Bros. Ltd.* [1965] 1 W.L.R. 1051; *Re Five Minute Car Wash Service Ltd.* [1966] 1 W.L.R. 745. And see to the like effect *Taylor* v. *Welkon Theatres Ltd.*, 1954 (3) S.A. 339 (O.F.S., P.D.); *Ex p. Bates*, 1955 (4) S.A. 81 (S. Rhodesia); and *Re B.C. Aircraft Propellor & Engine Co. Ltd.* (1968) 66 D.L.R. (2d) 628 (B.C.). But *cf. Re H. R. Harmer Ltd.* [1959] 1 W.L.R. 62, C.A., where, although the oppression was in relation to the management of the company, the controller had disregarded the provisions of the articles of association and thereby oppressively

creditor [22] cannot obtain an order under section 210 for this is expressly limited to oppression of *members*, and this is so even if the director or creditor is a member but is being oppressed only in his capacity of director or creditor.[21] Nor, it would seem, can a trustee in bankruptcy or personal representative unless he is registered as a member.[23] In the case of bankruptcy this difficulty could doubtless be avoided by petitioning in the name of the bankrupt member,[24] but this expedient is not available to the personal representatives of a deceased shareholder.[25]

In addition to members, the Board of Trade may petition after an investigation of the company's affairs or an inspection of its accounts.[26]

(c) In what circumstances will relief be given ?

The Cohen Report [27] itself instances two situations envisaged for the employment of the section; the first where controlling directors unreasonably refuse to register transfers of the minority's holdings so as to force a sale to themselves at a low price,[28] and the second where they take excessive remuneration so as to leave nothing for distribution by way of dividend. But these were expressly stated to be but illustrations of a general problem.[29] The Jenkins Committee added two further illustrations [30]; the issue of shares to directors and others on advantageous terms [31] and the passing of non-cumulative preference dividends on shares held by the minority.

In fact, however, in the only two reported cases in the United Kingdom where the section has been successfully invoked the facts were very different from those envisaged by the Cohen and Jenkins Committees, and it has failed to bite in a number of others where the

infringed the minority's membership rights; *Marshall* v. *Marshall (Pty.) Ltd.,* 1954 (3) S.A. 571 (N.P.D.) and *Benjamin* v. *Elysium Investments (Pty.) Ltd.,* 1960 (3) S.A. 467 (E.C.D.).
[22] *Re Bellador Silk Ltd., supra; Irvin & Johnson Ltd.* v. *Oelofse Fisheries Ltd.,* 1954 (1) S.A. 231 (E.D.L.D.).
[23] It is arguable that, notwithstanding *Re Bolton Engineering Co. Ltd.* [1956] Ch. 577, the common form article equivalent to Table A, art. 32, might entitle him to petition, but see *Re Meyer Douglas Pty. Ltd.* [1965] V.R. 638, when it was held that a personal representative could not petition under the equivalent Australian section.
[24] *Cf. Re K/9 Meat Supplies (Guildford) Ltd.* [1966] 1 W.L.R. 1112, *supra,* p. 596, n. 1.
[25] Yet, as the Jenkins Committee stressed, a common example of oppression in private companies is a refusal to register personal representatives so as to force a sale at an inadequate price: Cmnd. 1749, para. 205. The Committee recommended that the section should be amended so as to put beyond doubt the right to petition of those to whom shares are transmitted by operation of law: *ibid.,* para. 209.
[26] s. 210 (1), as extended by 1967 Act, s. 35 (2).
[27] Cmd. 6659, paras. 58 and 59.
[28] This was also used as an illustration by Lord Cooper in *Elder* v. *Elder & Watson,* 1952 S.C. 49, *infra.*
[29] para. 60.
[30] Cmnd. 1749, para. 205.
[31] But it seems very doubtful whether this would in fact be caught by the section as at present worded unless it was done habitually.

facts were much closer.[32] The first successful application, and the only one to reach the House of Lords, was *Scottish Co-operative Wholesale Society* v. *Meyer*.[33] There the two petitioners were managing directors and minority shareholders of a subsidiary company formed by the co-operative society to enable it to enter the rayon industry. Later the need to operate through a separate company ceased and the society, through its nominee directors and otherwise, pursued a deliberate policy of running down the subsidiary's business with the result that its shares became valueless. The House of Lords, affirming decisions of the Court of Session,[34] held that the petitioners' case had been established and the society was ordered to buy out the two minority shareholders at £3 15s. per share, the fair value had there not been oppression.[35] This decision was followed by the Court of Appeal in *Re H. R. Harmer Ltd.*[36] which concerned the well-known firm of stamp dealers. The founder of the firm had incorporated it in 1947 and he and his sons were life directors. As a result of gifts of shares by the father the sons had become the majority shareholders, but the father and his wife, who did what he told her, had voting control. The father continued to run the business as if it was his own and to disregard the wishes of his fellow shareholders and of his co-directors and resolutions of the board. This, he asserted, he was entitled to do. As a result of his autocratic and unbusinesslike behaviour it became impossible for the company to be carried on successfully. Roxburgh J. held that a case of oppression had been made out.[37] He ordered that the father should be employed as a consultant only, should not interfere in the affairs of the company otherwise than in accordance with valid decisions of the board, but should, as a face-saving device, be appointed life " president " [38] of the company without any duties, rights or powers as such. The Court of Appeal unanimously affirmed his decision.

These two decisions proclaimed a determination to apply the section liberally. The judgments also contain authoritative statements on its interpretation which have been influential in later cases. " Oppression "

---

[32] See note 21, *supra*. Closer still is the S. African case of *Marsh* v. *Odendaalstus Cold Storages Ltd.*, 1963 (2) S.A. 263 (Wits L.D.) where the petition, based on alleged excessive remuneration, failed because there had been no departure from proper standards of fair dealing.

[33] [1959] A.C. 324.

[34] 1954 S.C. 381; 1957 S.C. 110.

[35] This was their estimated value at the date of the petition, which suggests that it is unwise to delay if the value of the shares is falling. For similar decisions on equivalent sections in other jurisdictions, see *Livanos* v. *Swartzberg*, 1962 (4) S.A. 395 (Wits L.D.); the remarkable case of *Re British Columbia Electric Co. Ltd.* (1964) 47 D.L.R. (2d) 724 (B.C.) where the oppression was by government-appointed directors under a statute later declared unconstitutional; and *Re Associated Tool Industries Ltd.* [1964] A.L.R. 73 (Aust.).

[36] [1959] 1 W.L.R. 62, C.A.

[37] It was irrelevant that the misconduct was not for financial gain but simply due to the father's " overwhelming desire for power and control."

[38] An unhappy choice as it would suggest to the firm's many American clients that he was the top executive.

is said to mean " burdensome, harsh and wrongful." [39]   The conduct must relate to the complainant (or complainants) in his capacity as a member and to the conduct of the affairs of the company.[40]   As the wording of the section implies, there must be a continuing course of conduct, not merely an isolated act of impropriety, and, as it specifically states, the conduct must be such as to make it just and equitable to wind up the company.[41]   In the later English cases a somewhat rigid application of these various conditions has frustrated attempts to use the section. In *Re Bellador Silk Ltd.*,[42] the petitioner failed on three grounds, (1) the petition was brought for the collateral purpose of forcing the repayment of loans to other companies in which the petitioner was interested and was therefore an abuse of process; (2) in so far as the conduct related to the petitioner himself it concerned him as director rather than member; and (3) the circumstances were not such as to justify a winding up at the suit of the petitioner because the company was insolvent and the shareholders had no tangible interest.   In *Re Lundie Bros. Ltd.*[43] it was just and equitable to wind up the company and this was done,[44] but an order under section 210 was denied because there was no proof of oppression to the petitioner in his capacity of member.   In *Re Five Minute Car Wash Service Ltd.*[45] although the managing director had been " unwise, inefficient and careless," [46] and although the controlling shareholders had failed to exercise their control to curtail his damaging activities, it was held that oppression had not been established since the managing director had not " acted unscrupulously, unfairly, or with any lack of probity," [46] and mere acts of omission of the controlling shareholders were not " designed to achieve some unfair advantage." [47]

If these decisions are correct the section fails to achieve all that was intended of it.   The interpretation placed on the requirement that it

---

[39] *Per* Lord Simonds in [1959] A.C. at p. 342, a definition cited approvingly in all the later cases.   Lord Simonds described this as " the dictionary meaning of the word " but difficulty has been experienced in tracing the dictionary from which he took it: see *Re Bright Pine Mills Pty. Ltd.* (Victoria Full Court—unreported)   It appears to be an adaptation of the S.O.E.D.'s " unjustly burdensome, harsh or merciless." Other much-quoted definitions are : " a visible departure from the standards of fair dealing, and a violation of the conditions of fair play on which every shareholder who entrusts his money to a company is entitled to rely " : *per* Lord Cooper in *Elder* v. *Elder & Watson*, 1952 S.C. 49 at 55 ; and " lack of probity or fair dealing " : *per* Lord Keith, *ibid.*, p. 60.   Oppression is not " necessarily confined to cases of discrimination " : *per* Jenkins L.J. in *Re H. R. Harmer* [1959] 1 W.L.R. at 836.   In both *Harmer* and *Meyer* all the shareholders, *qua* shareholders, were equally oppressed.
[40] But may relate to anyone in fact taking part in the conduct of its affairs : normally this will be a director and controlling shareholder but it clearly might be a receiver and manager (*cf. R.* v. *Board of Trade, ex p. St. Martins Preserving Co.* [1965] 1 Q.B. 603, *infra*, p. 606, note 77).
[41] *i.e.*, under s. 222 (*f*), *supra*.   [42] [1965] 1 All E.R. 667.
[43] [1965] 1 W.L.R. 1051.
[44] On the ground that there was a complete deadlock.
[45] [1966] 1 W.L.R. 745.
[46] *Per* Buckley J. at p. 752.
[47] *Ibid.* at p. 753.   *Cf. Re Broadcasting Stn. 2 G.B.* [1964–5] N.S.W.R. 1648 where failing proof of mala fides, a course of conduct showing a determination to maintain control was held not to establish oppression.

must be just as equitable to wind up the company is particularly unfortunate. It seems clear that this was intended to relate merely to proof of grounds and not, as held in *Re Bellador Silk Ltd.*, to require the petitioner to show that he was entitled to a winding-up order.[48] That amounts to saying that if the oppression of the minority has been so successful that the minority's interest has been destroyed there is no remedy—a proposition denied by Lords Keith [49] and Denning [50] in *Scottish Co-operative Wholesale Society Ltd.* v. *Meyer.*[51] Nor is it satisfactory that, as in *Re Lundie Bros. Ltd.*, the minority should be relegated to a disadvantageous winding up, or as in *Re Five Minute Car Wash Service Ltd.*, be denied any remedy at all, merely because it cannot be shown that the petitioners were oppressed *qua* members rather than *qua* creditors or directors, or that the availability of the remedy should turn on whether, as in *Re H. R. Harmer Ltd.*, there has been a breach of the membership rights under the articles or, as in *Re Bellador Silk Ltd.*, *Re Lundie Bros. Ltd.* and *Re Five Minute Car Wash Service Ltd.*, an equally damaging course of conduct that has avoided such a breach.

Some of the weaknesses in the section will be cured if the recommendations of the Jenkins Committee [52] are implemented. They recommended, first, that the link with the winding-up provision should be broken so that the remedy would be available whether or not it was just and equitable to wind up.[53] They suggested, secondly, that the wording of the basic conditions should be amended to make it clear that the section covers isolated acts as well as a course of conduct,[54] and thirdly, that provision should be made to enable the court to restrain the commission or continuance of any act which would suffice to support a petition under the section.[55] Fourthly, " in a manner oppressive " should be widened by adding words such as " or unfairly prejudicial." [56] Fifthly, the section should expressly enable personal representatives, trustees in bankruptcy and others to whom shares are transmitted by

---

[48] This goes even further than the S. African case of *Irvin & Johnson Ltd.* v. *Oelofse Fisheries Ltd.*, 1954 (1) S.A. 231 (E.D.L.D.) where an order was refused since the controlling majority were creditors, entitled to a winding up as such, so that the company could not survive.

[49] [1959] A.C. at p. 364.   [50] *Ibid.* at pp. 368–369.

[51] In this respect *Re Bellador Silk Ltd.* seems inconsistent with the decision in *Meyer* where, at the time of judgment, though not perhaps when the proceedings were instituted, the interests of the minority were admittedly worthless.

[52] Cmnd. 1749, paras. 200–212.

[53] paras. 201 and 212 (*a*): *i.e.*, s. 210 (2) (*b*) would be totally repealed thus making it clear that it is not necessary to establish either grounds or a right to petition for a winding up.

[54] paras. 202 and 212 (*b*).

[55] paras. 208 and 212 (*d*). A continuance could already be restrained as a result of a petition under the section but the suggested amendment would for the first time enable the court to restrain an anticipated act or course of oppression.

[56] paras. 202–204 and 212 (*c*). The intention was to make it clear that the section does not necessarily " postulate actual illegality or invasion of legal rights " but " is satisfied by conduct which, without being actually illegal could, nevertheless, be described as reprehensible ": para. 203. As the Committee recognised, this seemed to be clear since *Meyer's* case; but later cases show the need for the amendment: (1966) 29 M.L.R. 321.

process of law to present a petition or seek an injunction.[57] Implementa-
tion of these proposals will remove most of the difficulties apart from
that of showing that the oppression or prejudicial acts affect members *qua*
members.   Had the recent cases reviewed above been decided before
the Committee reported it seems inconceivable that they would not have
also recommended that the section should be made available in respect
of oppression of members in whatever capacity and to oppression of
directors and creditors [58] whether or not they were members.

Of even greater interest is the recommendation of the Committee
designed to make use of section 210 to circumvent the excessive
restrictions of the *Foss* v. *Harbottle* rule.[59]   They thought it unjust that
a member cannot sue to remedy a wrong done to the company unless the
wrong is of a fraudulent character and control is being used to prevent the
company from suing, in such a way as to constitute a fraud on the
minority.   Hence they suggested that section 210 should be extended to
give the court an express power, upon the hearing of a petition under it,
to authorise proceedings to be brought against a third party in the name
of the company by such person or persons and on such terms as the
court may direct.[60]   They added: " It is not our intention to encourage
litigation in cases in which, for instance, an independent majority has
reached a bona fide decision to the effect that in the interests of the
company as a whole no action should be taken." [61]   Seemingly, therefore,
the result would be to extend to wrongs to the company and to the
company alone, a practice which the courts have now reached in the
case of " ratifiable " wrongs done to members,[62] *i.e.*, to allow proceedings unless and until there has been a bona fide ratification.[63]   Imple-
mentation of this recommendation, when coupled with those enabling
a petition to be based on a single act and empowering the court to grant
an injunction, would certainly strengthen the position of a minority.

5. Board of Trade Investigations

The Board of Trade now have extensive powers to investigate companies,
and the existence of these powers is of outstanding importance both as a
remedy against oppression and as a preliminary to civil or criminal

---

[57] paras. 209 and 212 (*f*). This was coupled with a recommendation, to which reference
has already been made (*supra*, p. 393, n. 16), entitling personal representatives to a
statement in writing of the directors' reasons if they declined to register the personal
representatives: paras. 210 and 212 (*g*).
[58] Debentureholders are subject to oppression equally with shareholders—though
admittedly they may have remedies *qua* creditors which are denied to members.
[59] *Supra*, pp. 583–595.
[60] paras. 206 and 212 (*e*). They thought that the court's discretion and the probable
liability for costs if unsuccessful would be adequate safeguards against abuse:
para. 207.
[61] para. 207.
[62] It is not clear whether the Committee contemplated that their recommendation would
apply to wrongs to members or only to wrongs to the company itself.
[63] *Hogg* v. *Cramphorn Ltd.* [1967] Ch. 254 (1963); *Bamford* v. *Bamford* [1969] 2
W.L.R. 1107, C.A.; *supra*, pp. 585, 586.

proceedings against the miscreants. Until recently these powers were exercisable only by the formal appointment of an inspector to investigate the company's affairs. Such an appointment was likely to excite considerable publicity and itself to cause further damage to the company. Hence the Board were understandably reluctant to make an appointment [63a]; they required a strong prima facie case to be established [64] and normally made inquiries of the directors before appointing. Though these inquiries might cause the oppression to end, they might equally well lead to excessive delay during which evidence could be suppressed or fabricated. Hence the Jenkins Committee recommended that the Board should have a further power to require the production of books and papers, a power which could be exercised with less publicity and which might suffice in itself or lead to a formal appointment of an inspector if the facts elicited showed that that was needed.[65] This suggestion was implemented as regards companies inviting deposits by the Protection of Depositors Act 1963, ss. 18 and 19, and has now been extended to all companies by Part III of the Companies Act 1967. Hence the Board now have two distinct, but inter-related, sets of powers.

(a) Production of books and papers

The Board of Trade may, at any time, if they think there is good reason to do so, give directions to any company requiring it to produce to the Board or any authorised officer of theirs any specified books or papers.[66] A like direction may be made to any person who appears to be in possession of those books or papers.[67] Copies or extracts of them may be taken and any person in possession or past or present officer or employee of the company may be required to provide an explanation of them.[68] If the documents are not produced the person required to produce them must state where he believes them to be,[69] and

---

[63a] Figures relating to applications and appointments in the years 1950–1966 are conveniently set out in Hadden, *The Control of Company Fraud* (PEP Broadsheet No. 503) Table IV (with a highly critical account of the utility of inspections).

[64] But, as the Jenkins Committee pointed out, it was dangerous to have too clear a case: " [I]f the applicants for an inspection have few facts to support their suspicions the Board of Trade are likely to send them away empty-handed with the explanation that inspections cannot be set on foot on the basis of vague suspicions. If, on the other hand, the applicants present a substantial prima facie case they are likely to be told that they already have sufficient information to institute proceedings against the directors and that the appointment of an inspector is therefore not appropriate ": Cmnd. 1749, para. 214.

[65] Cmnd. 1749, paras. 213–215. There were precedents for a power of this nature in s. 173 of the 1948 Act (see *infra*, p. 608), in the Insurance Companies Act 1958, s. 14, and in the Acts of certain Commonwealth countries.

[66] 1967 Act, s. 109 (1).

[67] s. 109 (2). Failure to produce is a criminal offence unless it is proved that the documents were not in his possession or under his control and that it is not reasonably practicable to comply with the direction: s. 109 (4). Statements made by a person in compliance with the section may be used in evidence against him: s. 109 (5).

[68] s. 109 (3) (*a*).

[69] s. 109 (3) (*b*).

a search warrant may be obtained to find them.[70] Provisions are made to prevent publication or excessive disclosure.[71] A solicitor is not compelled to produce a document containing privileged communications made to him in that capacity [72] and there is a, less extensive, protection for banks.[73] It is made a criminal offence for any officer of a company to be party to the destruction, mutilation or falsification of any document affecting or relating to its property or affairs unless he proves that he had no intention to conceal the state of affairs of the company or to defeat the law, or fraudulently to part with, alter or make an omission from any such document.[74] It is also an offence knowingly or recklessly to make a false explanation or statement in response to directions of the Board.[75]

As we shall see, inquiries under Part III of the 1967 Act may, if necessary, be followed up under the provisions of the 1948 Act (as amended and supplemented by the 1967 Act) by the appointment of an inspector or by the institution of civil or criminal proceedings without more ado.

(b) Appointment of inspectors

The Board of Trade have a number of overlapping [76] powers to appoint an inspector to investigate and report on " the affairs of a company." " Affairs " has been held to mean its business affairs—its goodwill, profits or losses, contracts and assets, including its control over subsidiaries—and it makes no difference who is conducting those affairs.[77] Under section 165 (a) of the 1948 Act the Board *shall* appoint one or more competent inspectors if the company by special resolution or the court by order declares that its affairs ought to be investigated by an inspector appointed by the Board. Provided the resolution has been passed or order made, the Board have no discretion and the duty to appoint can be enforced by mandamus.[77] It is very uncommon for an application to be made to the court for an order [78] since it is cheaper,

---

[70] s. 110.

[71] s. 111.

[72] s. 116 (1). Apparently this is so even if the client, whose privilege it is, waives it: see, on the corresponding Australian provision, *Re Stanhill Consolidated Ltd.* [1967] V.R. 749.

[73] s. 116 (2).

[74] s. 113. In contrast with s. 114 this is expressed quite generally and clearly applies whether or not a direction has been made under s. 109.

[75] s. 114.

[76] The Jenkins Committee recommended that the overlap between the various sections, which have been added to from time to time, should be eradicated: Cmnd. 1749, paras. 216 and 218 (a) and (b). This has not yet been done.

[77] *R.* v. *Board of Trade, ex p. St. Martins Preserving Co. Ltd.* [1965] 1 Q.B. 603, where the debentureholders had appointed a receiver and manager and the object of the application under s. 165 (a) was to enable the directors and members to keep a check on the way the receiver conducted the company's affairs and to investigate his disposal of the shareholding in a sub-subsidiary.

[78] For a discussion of the considerations to which the court should have regard if an application is made, see *Irvin & Johnson Ltd.* v. *Gelcer & Co. (Pty.) Ltd.*, 1958 (2) S.A. 59 (Cape P.D.).

quicker and normally easier to apply direct to the Board to exercise their power under section 165 (*b*). Nor is much use made of the right to obtain an appointment by passing a special resolution. Occasionally, however, this affords a means of securing an independent inquiry when in the company there is general agreement that this would be useful. It has also been used as a means whereby the company can keep check on the activities of a receiver.[77]

In addition the Board have a number of powers to appoint in their discretion. First, under section 164 they may do so on the application of 200 members or members holding not less than one-tenth of the issued capital.[79] The applicants must satisfy the Board that they have good reason for the application and may be required to give security for an amount not exceeding £100 for the costs of the investigation. This section is virtually obsolete since on successful application the Board almost invariably proceed under their other discretionary power in section 165 (*b*). Accordingly the Jenkins Committee recommended [80] that it should be repealed and replaced by a mandatory duty to appoint, if requested by over 200 members or holders of one-quarter or more of the holders of the issued shares,[81] unless the Board considered the application vexatious or unnecessary because the applicants already knew sufficient facts to assert their rights. This recommendation has not been implemented.

Secondly, under section 165 (*b*), the Board may appoint if it appears to them :

    (i) that there are circumstances suggesting that its business is being or has been [82] conducted with intent to defraud creditors or for a fraudulent or unlawful purpose or in a manner oppressive of any part of its members, or that it was formed for any fraudulent or unlawful purpose; or

    (ii) that persons concerned with its formation or management have been guilty of fraud, misfeasance or other misconduct toward it or its members; or

    (iii) that its members have not been given all the information with regard to its affairs which they might reasonably expect.

An appointment may be made notwithstanding that the company is in course of being voluntarily wound up.[83] This statutory provision is invoked far more frequently than all the others and is of the greatest importance in relation to the enforcement of the controllers' duties and

---

[79] If the company has no share capital, one-fifth of the members can apply.
[80] Cmnd. 1749, paras. 216 and 218 (*a*) and (*b*).
[81] Or, if the company has no share capital, one-quarter of the members.
[82] " Or has been " was inserted by s. 38 of the 1967 Act, thus putting beyond doubt the legality of an appointment such as that made in the *Savoy Hotel* case (*supra*, p. 521) where at the date of the appointment the improper scheme had been dropped and the status quo restored.
[83] 1967 Act, s. 38.

to minority protection. Anyone may draw the attention of the Board to the alleged scandal and seek to persuade them to make an appointment. In most cases the allegation will be one which, if proved, would lead to a civil or criminal remedy—the wording of the paragraph contains the familiar expressions " fraud," " misfeasance," [84] " other misconduct " [85] and " oppression " [86] and it will be observed that in relation to the last of these, the oppression, as under section 210, must be towards its members (not creditors or directors). But the Board is entitled, under sub-paragraph (iii), to appoint in circumstances where there has not been any legal wrong, for information which the members " might reasonably require " is clearly wider than information to which they " are legally entitled." Whether the Board could appoint when there is no suspicion of anything worse than negligence is still in doubt. It is to be hoped so, for it is precisely in such a case that the need may be greatest because of the rule in *Foss* v. *Harbottle* and the absence of any other remedy [87] while the directors remain in power.[88]

Under sections 172–174, the Board have power to investigate the true ownership or control of companies. Under section 172 an inspector may be appointed to investigate and report on the membership of a company for the purpose of determining who are financially interested in it or able to control or influence its policy.[89] Alternatively, under section 173, the Board may take the less drastic step of themselves demanding information on this point. Whether they proceed under section 172 or 173 they are, by section 174, given the powerful sanction of ordering that the shares shall be subject to restrictions which prevent rights in respect of them being exercised or enjoyed until the holders have given full information.[90] These sections are relics of the abortive attempt by the Cohen Committee to ban secrecy through nominee shareholdings.[91] It was thought that they might be useful in relation to foreign control or the control of newspapers, but in fact in most of the

---

[84] This would presumably be given the same interpretation as in s. 333 and will therefore exclude mere negligence : *supra*, p. 596.

[85] *Quaere*, will this, being interpreted *ejusdem generis*, also exclude negligence : see *Selangor United Rubber Estates Ltd.* v. *Cradock* [1967] 1 W.L.R. 1168 at 1173, 1174.

[86] Which will clearly be interpreted as under s. 210; *supra*, p. 602.

[87] Until s. 210 is extended as reccomended by the Jenkins Committee : *supra*, p. 604.

[88] *Cf. Pavlides* v. *Jensen* [1956] Ch. 565, *supra*, p. 588. In that case the plaintiff subsequently applied to the Board for the appointment of an inspector which was refused, but on the merits rather than on the grounds of absence of power.

[89] This is a summarised account of the section to which reference should be made for its exact terms. The Board must appoint if application is made by sufficient members to have required an appointment under s. 164 unless the Board are satisfied that the application is vexatious : s. 172 (3). It is the practice of the Board to ask the applicants to state their reasons in order that they may consider whether the application is vexatious, but *quaere* whether this is justified by the wording of the subsection.

[90] But in Australia the inadequacy of the powers under these sections was revealed by an investigation into *Ducon Industries Ltd.* (Govt. Printer N.S.W. No. 198 of 1962–3) and in 1964 a stronger section than s. 173 was inserted as s. 178 into the Australian Uniform Act.

[91] Cmd. 6659, para. 77 *et seq.*

very few cases where section 172 has been invoked [92] it has been to enable the existing controllers to ascertain the identity of a potential take-over bidder.[93]

Finally, by virtue of section 32 of the 1967 Act the Board now have power to appoint an inspector to investigate whether or not contraventions have occurred of section 25 or 27 of that Act, *i.e.*, those relating to share dealings by directors and dealt with in Chapter 17.[94]

(c) Conduct of investigation

When the Board of Trade exercise their new powers under Part III of the 1967 Act to require the production of a company's books and papers they act through their own officers, and attempts are being made to increase the staff of their inspectorate for this purpose. As we have seen, the Board's officers have extensive inquisitorial powers and may obtain a search warrant enabling the police to enter premises, by force if necessary, to obtain the documents required.[95] No formal report of the investigation is published; indeed the Act provides for the security of the information elicited which may not be disclosed except so far as is necessary for the follow-up procedure referred to under (d) below.[96]

When the Board appoint an inspector, whether after an examination of the books and papers or independently of that, once again an officer of the Board may be appointed, but usually the inspector will be a Queen's Counsel or chartered accountant or, more commonly, both. The investigation is conducted in private but the inspectors are entitled to the assistance of any persons (for example shorthand writers) whose presence is reasonably necessary.[97] Where the appointment is under section 164, 165 or 172, the inspectors may carry the investigation into the affairs of related companies [98] and report thereon so far as relevant to the investigation of the company itself.[99] All officers and agents, past and present,[1] of any company being investigated must produce all documents in their custody or control, attend when summoned before the inspectors, and give all assistance which they are reasonably able to give.[2] If they refuse they may be brought before the court which may punish them as if they had been guilty of contempt of court.[3] The

---

[92] No use has yet been made of s. 173 or 174.
[93] As in the *Savoy Hotel* case (see the Report of Mr. J. B. Lindon, Q.C., H.M.S.O. 1953).
[94] *Supra*, pp. 388–391.
[95] 1967 Act, s. 110.
[96] *Ibid.*, s. 111.
[97] *Re Gaumont-British Picture Corpn.* [1940] 1 Ch. 506.
[98] As defined in 1948 Act, s. 166.
[99] 1948 Act, ss. 166 and 172. Alternatively they can invite the Board to extend their appointment to other companies.
[1] s. 167 (5), which also contains a wide definition of " agents." In an investigation under s. 172 or 1967 Act, s. 32, these obligations are extended still further: see s. 172 (5) and 1967 Act, s. 32 (3), which brings in stockbrokers and dealers.
[2] s. 167 (1) as amended by 1967 Act, s. 39.
[3] s. 167 (3) as amended by 1967 Act, s. 39.

inspectors may examine them on oath.[4] If it is necessary to examine other persons on oath they may be brought before the court for this purpose.[5] In either case answers to questions are admissible in evidence against the maker.[6] But solicitors are not obliged to disclose privileged communications made to them [7] and there is a more limited protection for banks.[8]

The inspectors report to the Board of Trade,[9] and their report may be (and generally is) published.[10] Moreover, except in the case of an investigation of share dealings under section 32 of the 1967 Act, a copy of the report has to be sent to the company and in some circumstances to others.[11] And in the case of an investigation under section 164 or 165 the report is " admissible in any legal proceedings as evidence of the opinion of the inspectors in relation to any matter contained in the report." [12] These provisions have given rise to some disquiet as the report may make highly damaging allegations based on evidence not all of which would otherwise necessarily be admissible in a court of law. Where criminal proceedings are contemplated it is the practice of the Board of Trade not to publish the report until after the conclusion of those proceedings, but a copy has to be sent to the company [13] and this itself may be embarrassing.[14]

The costs of an investigation under section 172 or section 32 of the 1967 Act are borne by the Board of Trade.[15] So, in the first instance, are the expenses of investigations under section 164 or 165. But in the case of applications under section 164 the Board may require the applicants to give security for costs not exceeding £100,[16] and the applicants are liable for costs to such extent as the Board directs unless a prosecution is instituted as a result of the investigation.[17] Where,

[4] ss. 167 (2) and 172 (5) and 1967 Act, s. 32 (3).
[5] ss. 167 (4) and 172 (5) and 1967 Act, s. 32 (3).
[6] s. 167 (4) and 1967 Act, s. 50: see *Selangor United Rubber Estates Ltd.* v. *Cradock* (*No.* 2) [1968] 1 W.L.R. 319. But it seems that a mere refusal to answer a question on the ground that it might incriminate will not be punished as contempt: *ibid.* and *McClelland, Pope and Langley Ltd.* v. *Howard* [1968] 1 All E.R. 569n., H.L. But *semble* this cannot be so if the question is put or allowed by the court: *cf. Re Atherton* [1912] 2 K.B. 251.
[7] It appears that this is so even if the client waives the privilege: see note 72, *supra.*
[8] s. 175 and 1967 Act, s. 32 (6).
[9] ss. 168 (1), 172 (5) and 1967 Act, s. 32 (4). They may also make interim reports (*ibid.*) and, in an investigation under s. 164 or 165 inform the Board from time to time of any matters tending to show that an offence has been committed: 1967 Act, s. 41.
[10] ss. 168 (2), 172 (5) and 1967 Act, s. 32 (5).
[11] ss. 168 (2) and 172 (5).
[12] s. 171. The exact meaning of this is somewhat obscure: see *Re A.B.C. Coupler & Engineering Co. Ltd.* [1962] 1 W.L.R. 1236; *Re Travel & Holiday Clubs Ltd.* [1967] 1 W.L.R. 711; *Re S.B.A. Properties Ltd., ibid.* 799; *Re Allied Produce Co. Ltd., ibid.* 1469.
[13] s. 168 (2).
[14] See the Jenkins Report, Cmnd. 1749, para. 217. The Committee recommended that the Board should have a discretion whether to send a copy to the company (para. 218 (*g*)), but this recommendation was not implemented in the 1967 Act.
[15] s. 172 (6): s. 32 (7).
[16] s. 164 (2).
[17] s. 170 (1) (*d*), as amended by 1967 Act, s. 40.

however, the inspector is appointed under section 165 (*b*) those who drew the matter to the Board's attention cannot in any circumstances be liable for the costs. After an investigation under section 164 or 165 costs may be recoverable from any people successfully prosecuted or against whom successful civil proceedings are brought,[18] from a company in whose names proceedings are brought to the extent of property recovered,[19] and from the company investigated unless the inspector was appointed of the Board's own motion.[20]

(d) Action following production of documents or investigation

The follow-up powers have also been considerably widened by the 1967 Act. The special provisions in section 169 (1) and (2) of the 1948 Act regarding reference to the Director of Public Prosecutions and institution of proceedings by him have been repealed as unnecessary,[21] but, of course, a criminal prosecution may ensue either by the Director, the police [22] or, indeed, a private prosecutor. Of greater importance for our purposes are the powers of the Board themselves, following either an investigation of books under Part III of the 1967 Act [23] or an inspector's report, to institute civil proceedings. First the Board may, if they think this is in the public interest, petition the court to wind up the company on the just and equitable ground.[24] This they may do unless the company is already being wound up *by the court.*[25] On such a petition the evidence of the inspector's report may be accepted as sufficient evidence,[26] unless, perhaps, the petition is opposed by the company.[27] Secondly, they may petition for the alternative remedy under section 210.[28] Again any inspector's report is clearly admissible in evidence, but since the petition is likely to be opposed it alone may not suffice.[27] Thirdly, if it appears to the Board that any civil proceedings ought, in the public interest, to be brought by a company they may themselves bring such proceedings in the name and on behalf of the

[18] s. 170 (1) (*a*), as amended by 1967 Act, s. 36 (*b*).
[19] s. 170 (1) (*b*).
[20] s. 170 (1) (*c*), as amended by 1967 Act, s. 40. For rights of indemnity and contribution *inter se* of those liable, see s. 170 (5).
[21] By 1967 Act, s. 36.
[22] Frequently there will have been investigations by the Fraud Squad at the same time as an investigation by the Board of Trade.
[23] Or under the Protection of Depositors Act 1963, s. 18 or 19.
[24] *i.e.*, s. 222 (*f*), see *supra*, pp. 596–598: see 1967 Act, s. 35 (1), and 1948 Act, s. 224 (1), proviso (*d*).
[25] 1967 Act, s. 35 (1).
[26] *Re Travel & Holiday Clubs Ltd.* [1967] 1 W.L.R. 711; *Re S.B.A. Properties Ltd., ibid.* 799; *Re Allied Produce Co. Ltd., ibid.* 1469.
[27] *Re A.B.C. Coupler & Engineering Co. Ltd.* [1962] 1 W.L.R. 1236; *Re Allied Produce Co. Ltd., supra.* But in any event if a winding up is ordered the liquidator may obtain a transcript of the evidence before the inspectors: *Re Rolls Razor Ltd.* [1968] 3 All E.R. 698.
[28] 1967 Act, s. 36 (2), replacing 1948 Act, s. 169 (3), and 1948 Act, s. 210, on which see *supra*, pp. 598–604. The Board will have to establish that the conditions of s. 210 are fulfilled, including proof that there are grounds for winding up.

company.[29]   The Board must indemnify the company against the costs [30] which are recoverable to the same extent and from the same persons as costs of an inspection.[31]

(e) Advantages of Board of Trade investigations

The Board of Trade's powers may help a member in three ways.

(i) They may enable him to obtain further information.   To this extent they supplement the basic disclosure philosophy on which the Companies Acts have always been based.   Not only may they help the member to get information to which he was already legally entitled; they add somewhat to his legal entitlement.   As we have seen, a ground for appointing under section 165 (b) is that the members of the company " have not been given the information with respect to its affairs which they might reasonably expect." [32]   This comes close to imposing on directors an obligation to make reasonably full disclosure not merely to the company but to the members.   The obtaining of information may (as under sections 172 and 173) be an end in itself.   Alternatively it may be needed to establish that the member's rights have been infringed; one of the great weaknesses of a shareholder who wishes to do battle with the directors is that they have access to the company's books and records and he has not.   Hence the second purpose of inspections :

(ii) They may provide a further remedy, or supplement the other remedies, against oppression.   And not only may they provide the member with the ammunition which he needs to do battle; he himself may not need to use it, for, as we have seen, the Board of Trade may do it for him without any expense to himself.   Hence a complaint to the Board with a view to their exercising their powers has a number of advantages.   Like a petition by a member under section 210 it can be made by a single member without regard to the rule in *Foss* v. *Harbottle*, but, unlike the invocation of section 210, it may lead to a successful conclusion entirely without expense or trouble to the complainant. Moreover, the Board in exercising their follow-up powers may be in a stronger position than the member, for on a petition to wind up or under section 210 they, unlike him, will not have to show that there will be something left in the company for the members.[33]

---

[29] 1967 Act, s. 37.   The new power is wider than that in 1948 Act, s. 169 (3), which it replaces, and free from the limitations revealed in *S.B.A. Properties Ltd.* v. *Cradock* [1967] 1 W.L.R. 716.   For ultimately successful proceedings under the old subsection, see *Selangor United Rubber Estates Ltd.* v. *Cradock (No.* 1) [1967] 1 W.L.R. 1168, *(No.* 2) [1968] 1 W.L.R. 319, *(No.* 3) [1968] 1 W.L.R. 1555.

[30] s. 37 (2).   This includes costs payable to other parties, and moneys paid by the Board in respect thereof do not form part of the company's assets available for creditors generally : *Selangor United Rubber Estates Ltd.* v. *Cradock (No.* 1), *supra.*

[31] 1948 Act, s. 170 (3), as amended by 1967 Act, s. 37 (3).

[32] s. 165 (b) (iii).

[33] See *supra*, pp. 597, 602, 603.

(iii) The Board's inquisitorial powers, especially the new ones under Part III of the 1967 Act, may be a preventive rather than a mere cure after the disease has taken its toll. If exercised speedily enough, they may prevent oppression from occurring; litigation, all too often, merely locks the door long after everything of value has been spirited away.

6. AVAILABILITY OF REMEDIES TO UNREGISTERED COMPANIES

It is clear that most of these remedies are available irrespective of the nature of the company; that is to say, they apply to statutory and chartered companies as well as to those registered under the Companies Acts. This is certainly so in the case of actions by the company or by minority shareholders, for these depend on general equitable principles and not on the Companies Acts themselves.[34] Similarly, the remedy of winding up is available in the case of any company liable to be wound up by the court under the Act and this, as we have seen, includes all types of companies and certain other bodies.[35] Again, a Board of Trade inspector may be appointed in the case of most unregistered companies, since the appropriate sections of the Acts are among those which have been extended to them.[36] Indeed, sections 165 to 171 and 175 now apply, subject to any modifications made by regulations, to all foreign bodies corporate which are carrying on, or have carried on, business in Great Britain.[37] Part III of the 1967 Act does not apply quite so widely but it too extends to foreign companies which carry on or have carried on business here.[38] It is only the alternative remedy under section 210 which appears not to be available except in the case of a registered company. The section is not among those which have been extended to unregistered companies,[39] and, although it is intended as an alternative remedy to winding up, it does not appear to be regarded as a provision " with respect to winding up "[40] applicable to an unregistered company. If this interpretation is correct the situation is certainly anomalous. Nor does it seem consistent with section 35 of the 1967 Act, which provides that, after a Board of Trade investigation, the Board may " in the case of any body corporate liable to be wound up under

---

[34] One possible difference is that a member of a statutory or chartered company seeking to sue on the basis that his personal rights were infringed would not be able to point to s. 20 of the Companies Act 1948 as establishing a contract between him and the company.

[35] s. 399. See Chap. 11, p. 242, *supra*.

[36] 1948 Act, s. 435 and 14th Sched., as amended by 1967 Act, s. 54.

[37] 1967 Act, s. 42.

[38] 1967 Act, s. 109 (1).

[39] *i.e.*, it is not included in 14th Sched.

[40] s. 399 (1). s. 210 is in Part IV of the Act, not in Part V containing the winding-up sections (where the Cohen Committee would certainly have put it: see Cmd. 6659, p. 95), and the fact that it was thought necessary to provide in s. 210 (5) that it should, for the purposes of Part V of the Economy (Miscellaneous Provisions) Act 1926 (relating to fees), " be deemed to be proceedings . . . in relation to the winding up of companies " seems to imply that it cannot be regarded as winding-up proceedings for other purposes.

the principal Act" present a petition under section 210. Perhaps we must conclude that a member of an unregistered company cannot petition under section 210, but that the Board of Trade can do so.

CONCLUSIONS

A member now has an impressive array of remedies at his disposal, especially where fraud or oppression is alleged. But an effective sanction against breach of the controlling directors' duties of care and skill is still lacking, for the rule in *Foss* v. *Harbottle* will normally bar an action at the suit of the minority, and it is not clear that any of the other remedies will be available to a minority. The relative laxity of these duties, in comparison with the duties of loyalty, is reflected, whether or not as a matter of deliberate policy, in the procedural sphere also.

The two major developments in recent years have been the provision of an alternative remedy under section 210, which is especially useful in the case of private companies, and the increase in the inquisitorial powers of the Board of Trade. This latter use of administrative techniques to supplement the judicial remedies is an interesting attempt to solve one of the major problems—that of expense—which has proved an excessive deterrent to adequate legal enforcement of managerial duties.[41] It may be surmised that the enforcement of these duties in relation to public companies will be left increasingly to the Board of Trade—a further illustration of the protective mantle of the welfare state. A future historian of that department may conclude that it has ceased to be merely a vigilant onlooker,[42] and become a watch-dog with sharp teeth.

---

[41] Almost the only type of shareholder financially able to support company litigation on a large scale is the institutional investor whose policy generally seems to be to sell out rather than to litigate. If we ever develop a shareholding democracy the Legal Aid Scheme may conceivably make itself felt here.

[42] See p. 39, *supra*.

CHAPTER 26

RECONSTRUCTIONS AND TAKE-OVERS

IT will have been apparent from the previous chapters that investors, and especially shareholders, are highly vulnerable to the machinations of those controlling the company. But certain of their rights are entrenched; for example, class rights are subject to some measure of protection, and debentureholders are normally secure. Even these entrenched rights are, however, liable to be modified or abrogated if exceptional procedure is adopted. Such exceptional changes are variously described as reconstructions, reorganisations, schemes of arrangement, amalgamations, mergers or take-overs, but none of these expressions is a term of art with a clearly defined and distinguishable legal meaning. In general, the expression " reconstruction," " reorganisation " or " scheme of arrangement " is employed when only one company is involved and the rights of its investors and, sometimes, of its general creditors are varied—the last expression being more commonly employed when creditors' rights are affected. Under an amalgamation, merger or take-over two (or more) companies are merged, either *de jure* by a consolidation of their undertakings, or *de facto* by the acquisition of a controlling interest in the share capital of one by the other or of the capital of both by a new company. Where this occurs in the case of large companies the provisions of the Monopolies and Mergers Act 1965, to which brief reference is made below,[1] may be relevant.

The scope of the present chapter is therefore wider than that of the previous discussion. For, under some types of reconstruction, creditors generally, as well as investors, may be affected, so that creditor protection is involved as well as investor protection. In practice, however, reconstructions mainly affect share- and debentureholders; indeed ordinary trade creditors are far less likely to suffer under a reconstruction than are debentureholders despite the fact that the latter are secured creditors.

Before considering the major points of principle that arise under reconstructions, it is well to indicate briefly the various legal methods which companies may employ to effect the desired changes.[2]

---

[1] *Infra*, p. 633.

[2] In addition to the changes dealt with in this chapter it should be remembered that a limited company may now be re-registered as unlimited (Companies Act 1967, s. 43), but only with the consent of all the members (s. 43 (3)), and that an unlimited company may re-register as limited (*ibid.*, s. 44, replacing 1948 Act, s. 16) but with a preservation of the former members' liability (s. 44 (7)). See Chap. 12, pp. 266, 267, *supra*.

Types of Reconstruction

(1) Reduction of capital

Assuming that all that is required is the reduction of share capital, either with or without a repayment to the members, advantage may be taken of sections 66–71 of the 1948 Act, already referred to in Chapter 6. These apply only to a limited company registered under the Companies Acts and having a share capital.[3] Such a company may reduce its capital in any way by passing a special resolution and subsequently obtaining the confirmation of the court. It must, however, be authorised so to do by its articles (authority in the memorandum will not do[4]) but the articles may be altered in the ordinary way so as to add such authority if it is not originally included.[5] Section 66 specifies three methods of reducing, but states that these are without prejudice to the generality of the power to reduce in any way.[6] The three methods are:

(a) the extinguishment or reduction of uncalled capital,

(b) the cancellation of capital " which is lost or unrepresented by available assets," [7] and,

(c) the repayment of capital in excess of the company's wants.[8]

After the passing of the special resolution application must be made to the court for confirmation. The procedure varies according to whether creditors are affected or not. If the reduction is of type (a) or (c) they clearly are affected and hence, in those two cases (unless the court otherwise directs) and in any other case if the court so directs, an inquiry is made as to creditors and they are entitled to object.[9] Only if all creditors entitled to object have consented or been paid or had their debts secured may the court make an order confirming the reduction on such terms and conditions as it thinks fit.[10] It may insist on the company adding the words " and reduced " to its name, or publishing an explanation of the reduction,[11] but it is not now usual for this to be done. The order, and a minute approved by the court showing the new particulars

---

[3] As we have seen (Chap. 6, *supra*) unlimited companies may reduce capital in any way if so authorised by their articles. Statutory companies may issue shares at a discount but presumably neither they nor chartered companies may reduce paid-up capital unless expressly authorised by their statute or charter.

[4] *Re Dexine Packing Co.* (1903) 88 L.T. 791.

[5] *Re Patent Invert Sugar Co.* (1885) 31 Ch.D. 166, C.A.

[6] Hence capital may be cancelled even though not lost: *Poole* v. *National Bank of China* [1907] A.C. 229, H.L.

[7] Chap. 6, *supra*, should have made it clear that " capital " (a notional liability) cannot truly be " lost," it can only be " unrepresented by available assets ": but see *Re Hoare & Co.* [1904] 2 Ch. 208, C.A.

[8] Repayment may be made in assets other than cash even though the value of the assets exceeds the nominal value of the reduction: *Ex p. Westburn Sugar Refineries Ltd.* [1951] A.C. 625, H.L.(Sc.).

[9] s. 67.

[10] s. 68 (1).

[11] s. 68 (2). The Jenkins Committee recommended the repeal of this provision: Cmnd. 1749, para. 159.

of the share capital,[12] must then be lodged with the Registrar who will issue a certificate, which is conclusive evidence that all the requirements of the Act have been complied with, and the registered minute is then deemed to be substituted for the corresponding part of the memorandum of association.[13] If uncalled liability is thus reduced any creditor erroneously omitted from the list may be able to insist on members at the time of the reduction continuing to be liable to the former extent.[14]

Although it would seem that a reduction may be validly effected without separate class meetings notwithstanding that shareholders are not treated in strict accordance with their rights,[15] it is clear that the court will not normally confirm such a reduction unless class rights are validly varied in accordance with a variation of rights clause in the memorandum or articles (*i.e.*, under method (2) below) or by a scheme of arrangement under method (3).[16] But as we have seen,[17] the courts have put a very narrow construction on the meaning of class rights so that a reduction may operate most adversely on one class without its separate consent.[18]

(2) Variations of rights under the memorandum or articles

The extent to which shareholders' rights can be validly varied by a special resolution of the company has already been discussed in Chapter 22. As we saw, the position depends on whether the rights are set out in the memorandum, or only in the articles of association, and on whether there is a variation of rights clause.

In practice, it is customary for the rights attaching to shares to be set out in the articles only, and for the articles to provide that, where shares are divided into separate classes, rights can be varied or abrogated with the consent of a prescribed majority of the class. Hence, if the reconstruction is merely designed to alter the rights of *shareholders* this can normally be effected simply by class meetings and a special resolution, subject to the possibility that a dissenting minority of a class will apply to the court under section 72. Under this section, holders

---

[12] But not any reduction of share premium a/c (or presumably capital redemption reserve fund) as this does not appear in the memorandum of association: *Re Paringa Mining & Exploration Co. Ltd.* [1957] 1 W.L.R. 1143.

[13] s. 69. The reduction becomes effective only on registration of the minute: *Re Castiglione Erskine & Co. Ltd.* [1958] 1 W.L.R. 688. It has been held in Scotland that if the capital is repaid prior to the court's confirmation the repayment is *ultra vires* and the court cannot confirm the reduction: *Alexander Henderson Ltd.*, 1967 S.L.T. (Notes) 17.

[14] s. 70.

[15] *British & American Trustee Corpn.* v. *Couper* [1894] A.C. 399, H.L.; *Carruth* v. *I.C.I.* [1937] A.C. 707, H.L., at pp. 744, 749; *Fife Coal Co.*, 1948 S.C. 505 (Sc.); *William Dixon Ltd.*, ibid. 511 (Sc.); *Re Robert Stephen Holdings Ltd.* [1968] 1 W.L.R. 522; and *Re William Jones & Sons Ltd.* [1969] 1 W.L.R. 146.

[16] *Cf. Re MacKenzie & Co. Ltd.* [1916] 2 Ch. 450; *Scottish Insurance Corpn.* v. *Wilsons & Clyde Coal Co.* [1949] A.C. 462, H.L.(Sc.); *Prudential Assurance* v. *Chatterley-Whitfield Collieries*, ibid. 512, H.L.; *Re Old Silkstone Collieries* [1954] Ch. 169, C.A.; *Re Robert Stephen Holdings Ltd.*, supra.

[17] *Supra*, Chap. 22, p. 507 *et seq.*

[18] See, for example, *Re Saltdean Estate Co. Ltd.* [1968] 1 W.L.R. 1844.

of not less than 15 per cent. of the issued shares of the class, if they have not assented to the alteration, may apply to the court within twenty-one days of the date when their fellow-members agreed to the variation of rights.[19] The court will then hear the applicants " and any other persons who apply to be heard and appear to the court to be interested in the application," and may, if satisfied that the variation would unfairly prejudice the shareholders of the class represented by the applicants, disallow the variation, but shall, if not so satisfied, confirm it.[20] It is expressly declared that the decision of the court is final,[21] which probably means that the result cannot be subsequently attacked in separate proceedings based, for example, on the " fraud-on-the-minority " principle, and that there cannot be an appeal.[22]

If there is only one class of share this section is not available to the dissentients, and normally their only right will be to embark on a perilous action based on fraud-on-the-minority or oppression[23] or, perhaps, a petition under section 210.[24] If, however, their rights are specified in the memorandum then, although these are now variable unless expressly declared not to be, they may have a right to apply to the court under section 23.[25] This entitles application to be made within twenty-one days by a like proportion (15 per cent.)[26] to that specified under section 72, but gives the court wider powers, for it may confirm either in whole or in part, and on such terms and conditions as it thinks fit,[27] whereas under section 72 it must either confirm or reject.

These sections apply only to registered companies. Moreover, they do not enable any variation to be made of the rights of creditors, including debentureholders, for a variation of the company's constitution cannot derogate from the terms of any contract entered into with third parties.[28] In practice, however, a similar variation clause will often be found in the trust deed of debenture stock or a series of debentures, in which event the terms may be varied in accordance with the clause without any right of dissentients to apply to the court under section 72; " fraud-on-the-minority " will be the dissentients' only remedy.[29]

---

19 The Jenkins Committee recommended that the proportion should be reduced to 10 per cent., the time extended to 28 days, and the non-assenting requirement repealed because it caused difficulty when shares were held by nominees: Cmnd. 1749, para. 193.

20 s. 72 (3).

21 s. 72 (4).

22 The recommendation of the Greene Committee on which the section is based (Cmd. 2657/26, para. 23) makes it clear that the intention is certainly to bar an appeal.

23 *Supra*, Chap. 24. Such an action is, of course, possible even if there are different classes so that s. 72 could be invoked: see *Rights and Issues Investment Trust Ltd.* v. *Stylo Shoes Ltd.* [1965] Ch. 250.

24 *Supra*, Chap. 24.

25 Incorporating the procedure of s. 5; see *supra*, Chap. 5, pp. 99–101.

26 The Jenkins Committee made recommendations similar to those referred to in note 19 above, but suggested reducing the proportion to 5 per cent: Cmnd. 1749, para. 49.

27 s. 5 (4).

28 *Supra*, Chap. 22, p. 502 *et seq.*

29 s. 210 will not apply: see *supra*, pp. 599, 600.

(3) Schemes of arrangement under sections 206–208

The methods described so far are available only in an extremely limited range of cases. They apply only to registered companies and do not enable the rights of debentureholders or other creditors to be affected. Further, they do not provide a means for effecting an amalgamation between two or more companies, nor enable the liability of shareholders to be increased without their individual consents. We now turn to the first of a number of sections which can be resorted to when the reconstruction is far more radical.

Section 206 applies to any company liable to be wound up under the Act,[30] and to any compromise or arrangement [31] between a company and its creditors or members or any class of them. The procedure is for application [32] to be made to the court either by the company (the normal course) or by its liquidator, a creditor, or member, The court then directs meetings to be convened of the classes concerned and, under section 207, the notice convening the meetings must be accompanied by a circular explaining the scheme, and disclosing any material interests of the directors [33] and of the trustees for debentureholders.[34] If at a meeting of each class a majority in number representing three-fourths in value of those present and voting in person or by proxy [35] approve the scheme, then, if subsequently sanctioned by the court,[36] it becomes binding on all once an office copy of the court order has been delivered to the Registrar.[37] It has now been established that the " compromises and arrangements " covered by this section are of the widest character, ranging from a simple composition or moratorium to an amalgamation of various companies, with a complete reorganisation of their share and loan capital. The rights of debentureholders and other creditors may be modified, as may those of shareholders even though embodied in the

---

[30] s. 206 (6). As we have seen (Chap. 11, p. 242) this includes statutory, chartered and other unregistered companies. It is clear that the section is intended to apply to all associations liable to be wound up under the Act, *i.e.*, to refer to s. 398, although the actual wording seems defective, for unregistered companies are not " companies " as defined in s. 455.

[31] See definition in subs. (6).

[32] *Ex parte* by originating summons.

[33] This has been held to include directors' shareholdings: *Coltness Iron Co. Ltd.*, 1951 S.L.T. 344 (Sc.).

[34] Although the section provides for penalties it has been held in Scotland that the provisions are mandatory and that non-compliance precludes the grant of approval: *Rankin and Blackmore Ltd.*, 1950 S.C. 218; *Peter Scott & Co. Ltd., ibid.* 507; *Coltness Iron Co., supra*; *City Property Investment Trust*, 1951 S.L.T. 371. But *cf. Second Scottish Investment Trust Ltd.*, 1962 S.L.T. 392.

[35] Forms of " two-way " proxy are settled in chambers, and these must be dispatched with the notice, but the members and creditors are not bound to use the form so settled: *Re Dorman Long & Co.* [1934] Ch. 635.

[36] Application is made by petition after the necessary majorities have been obtained at the meetings.

[37] s. 206 (3). The Canadian Supreme Court has held that this means that thereafter there cannot be a successful appeal: *Norcan Oils Ltd.* v. *Fogler* [1965] S.C.R. 36. A copy must be annexed to all copies of the memorandum or equivalent document: s. 206 (3).

memorandum and therein declared to be unalterable [38] and their liability may be increased. The scheme may involve in essence the acquisition by one company of the whole of the share capital of another notwithstanding that less than 90 per cent. of the shareholders agree, so that, if the operation had been effected under method (5) below, section 209 could not have been invoked.[39] The only limitations are that the scheme cannot authorise something contrary to the general law [40] or wholly *ultra vires* the company,[41] and that if capital is to be reduced the formalities of sections 66–71 must also be complied with.

To take advantage of the sections it is not now necessary that the company should go into liquidation. If it is in liquidation it can either proceed under these sections or rely on certain additional powers of compromising claims.[42] Further, a company which is about to be or is being wound up may enter into arrangements with its creditors which will be similarly binding on the company, if sanctioned by an extraordinary resolution, and on the creditors if acceded to by three-fourths in number and value.[43] But this latter provision is far less effective, since it is necessary to obtain the consent of three-fourths in value of *all* the creditors, and not merely of those present and voting *at* a meeting, and procedure under sections 206–208 is almost invariably employed instead.

If, as is often the case, the scheme under section 206 involves the transfer of the company's undertaking to another company, the court may make orders under section 208 for transfer of all the company's assets and liabilities and for its dissolution.[44] Hence the procedure may be adopted, not only for the reconstruction of companies in financial difficulties, but also as a convenient means of merging fully solvent concerns. The scheme may provide for the formation of a new company [45] to take over the undertaking of the old or, on an amalgamation,

---

[38] An argument that s. 23 had destroyed this former power under s. 206 was rejected in *City Property Investment Trust*, 1951 S.L.T. 371.

[39] *Re National Bank Ltd.* [1966] 1 W.L.R. 819. For the advantages of proceeding by a s. 206 scheme, see Weinberg: *Take-Overs and Amalgamations* (2nd ed. 1967), paras. 613–623.

[40] Which has been held to include the conversion of issued shares into redeemable preference shares since s. 58 merely authorises new issues of such shares: *Re St. James' Court Estates Ltd.* [1944] Ch. 6. But this could be got round by cancelling the old shares and issuing redeemable ones in their place.

[41] *Re Oceanic Steam Navigation Co.* [1939] Ch. 41. If the members of the company agree to the scheme this difficulty can be avoided by amending the objects clause of the memorandum under s. 5. But this solution is not available where, as in the instant case, the members get nothing under the scheme, and therefore have no inducement to change the objects. The result is to enable the members to hold the creditors up to ransom. If, however, it is clear that there is no equity left for the members, their consent can be disposed with to a scheme *intra vires* the company: *ibid.*

[42] ss. 245, 303, 315.

[43] s. 306. The court's sanction is not essential, but a creditor or contributory may appeal to the court which can confirm, reject or modify.

[44] See *infra,* p. 623 *et seq.* for a discussion of the relationship between ss. 206 and 287.

[45] Or, of course, the acquiring company may be an existing company which may have to increase its own capital.

to acquire the undertakings of a number of companies, the members and creditors of which accept shares or debentures in the new company in substitution for their former rights. All consequential orders for completing the transaction can then be made by the court. But this is subject to two limitations. In the first place, section 208 applies only when all the companies concerned are registered companies,[46] and secondly, notwithstanding its wide provisions, it does not enable contracts of a personal nature to be transferred.[47] Hence arrangements will have to be made to secure a voluntary novation of contracts of service and the like. If the reorganisation merely affects members, meetings of creditors will not be needed, but the court will not make orders under section 208 without ensuring that creditors are protected.[48]

Another practical difficulty is to secure the accession of trade and other unsecured creditors who lack a common interest such as prevails between shareholders and debentureholders. This difficulty is aggravated by the need to hold separate meetings of the various classes of creditors, and it may not be easy to determine whether all unsecured creditors can be treated as one class, or whether their rights are so different as to make it essential to divide them into separate classes.[49] For these reasons it is quite customary for the scheme to provide for the payment off in full of unsecured creditors, thus dispensing with the need for their consent, notwithstanding that there is a variation of the rights of debentureholders. This, of course, is an extreme illustration of the extent to which debentureholders are equated with shareholders in economic reality notwithstanding their legal position as secured creditors.

(4) Reconstructions under section 287

In straightforward cases the company may proceed instead under section 287. The procedure then is for the company to resolve upon a voluntary winding up and, by special resolution, to authorise the liquidator to sell to another company (normally, but not necessarily one newly formed for the purpose) receiving in payment shares or other securities of that company for distribution *in specie* among the members of the company in liquidation. Such an arrangement is binding on the members of the transferor company,[50] but any of them who did not vote in favour of the special resolution may within seven days express his dissent in writing to the liquidator and require him either to abstain from carrying the resolution into effect or to purchase his interest at a price to be determined by agreement or arbitration.[51]

---

[46] s. 208 (5).
[47] *Nokes* v. *Doncaster Amalgamated Collieries* [1940] A.C. 1014, H.L. See Chap. 10, pp. 200, 201, *supra*.
[48] *Clydesdale Bank*, 1950 S.C. 30.
[49] See *Sovereign Life Assurance Co.* v. *Dodd* [1892] 2 Q.B. 573, C.A. The responsibility of deciding on this is the applicant's: Practice Note [1934] W.N. 142.
[50] s. 287 (2).
[51] s. 287 (3).

Procedure under this section differs from that under sections 206–208 in the following respects:

(a) The transferor company must be put into liquidation, and the normal liquidation procedure has to be carried out except that assenting members will receive shares in the acquiring company instead of cash. There is no procedure similar to section 208 for dispensing with formal assignments of property or of winding up.

(b) There can be no variation of creditors' rights. Creditors are still entitled to prove in the liquidation of the old company and the liquidator must ensure that claims are met to the extent of the company's assets and cannot rely upon any indemnity given by the acquiring company.[52] The sale of the undertaking will, however, be binding on the creditors [53] who will have to look to the securities obtained in payment instead of to the former assets. Since this may affect them most adversely, particularly if the securities consist of unquoted shares, it is provided that if an order is made within a year for the winding up of the old company, compulsorily or under supervision, the special resolution shall not be valid unless sanctioned by the court.[54] If, therefore, the creditors are doubtful about repayment they should petition for a winding-up order within the year. In exceptional circumstances this procedure may even be invoked by dissenting shareholders.[55]

(c) The extent to which there can be a variation of the rights of members is also limited. The shares in the new company may, of course, be very different from those in the old; they may, for example, be partly paid, thus affording an opportunity for raising further capital. But they must be distributed among the members of the old company in strict accordance with their class rights on a winding up.[56] This makes it difficult to apply the section unless all the shares in the old company have equal rights on a winding up or unless all those with special rights expressly agree, or dissent and elect to be paid out.

(d) Shareholders cannot be forced against their will to accept new shares. If they dissent the liquidator will either have to drop the whole scheme or to pay them out in accordance with their previous rights.

(e) On the other hand, the scheme can be implemented without the need to apply to the court for confirmation. It is, therefore, the only method of reconstruction which can be employed without involving

---

[52] *Pulsford* v. *Devenish* [1903] 2 Ch. 625.
[53] *Re City & County Investment Co.* (1879) 13 Ch.D. 475, C.A.
[54] s. 287 (5).
[55] As in *Re Consolidated South Rand Mines Deep Ltd.* [1909] 1 Ch. 491.
[56] *Griffith* v. *Paget* (*No. 1*) (1877) 5 Ch.D. 894. But the narrow meaning given to " variation of class rights " makes this a less serious difficulty than might appear and since preference shareholders may have no vote at the company meeting they may find that their economic interests suffer severely. See *Griffith* v. *Paget* (*No. 2*) (1877) 6 Ch.D. 511, where the result was that for the future the preferred shareholders lost their former preferred dividend.

an application to the court for confirmation or affording dissentients a special statutory right to apply to the court.[57]

(f) Only registered companies can take advantage of section 287 itself, since it is expressly limited to voluntary liquidation,[58] and an unregistered company can only be wound up compulsorily.[59] On the other hand, it is expressly provided that the company to whom the undertaking is to be transferred need not be a company within the meaning of the Act.[60]

The section is therefore narrower in its application than sections 206–208. On the other hand, the fact that application to the court is dispensed with may make it cheaper and more convenient, and it is especially useful in straightforward amalgamations when a new company can be formed to take over the undertakings of the various companies to be merged. But it is subject to the serious snag that dissenting shareholders can insist upon being paid out. Attempts to evade this requirement have proceeded on two lines. In the first place it is common to provide in the objects clause of the memorandum that the company may sell its business to another company in consideration of shares therein, and this is commonly coupled with a provision in the articles authorising a liquidator to distribute the company's assets *in specie* among the members. It was for long believed that a sale for shares under the memorandum would enable the transaction to be carried out so as to avoid compliance with the rights of dissentients under section 287. This belief was, however, exploded by the Court of Appeal in the leading case of *Bisgood* v. *Henderson's Transvaal Estates*,[61] in which those in control had attempted by this means to force members to accept shares with increased liability. The court made it clear that a sale for shares might be *intra vires* and valid, but if the transaction was intended as a sale and distribution it could only be effected under what is now section 287.[62]

This loophole having been stopped up, companies sought to rely on sections 206–208 as a means of evading shareholders' rights to dissent under section 287. It will be appreciated that, although many schemes can only be carried out under the former sections,[63] there are others which could, on the face of it, be carried out under either. It is, however, by no means clear whether the courts will permit the rights of dissenting

---

[57] Despite action under s. 287 there may, of course, be an application to the court by dissentients who contend that their rights are being infringed, as in *Griffith* v. *Paget, supra*, and *Re Consolidated South Rand Mines Deep Ltd.*, *supra*.

[58] s. 287 (1). Whether members' or creditors': see s. 298. But *semble* that in a compulsory liquidation the court could approve a similar arrangement under s. 245 and in this way unregistered companies might adopt a like procedure.

[59] s. 399 (4).

[60] s. 287 (1). But the sale must be to a company, not an individual.

[61] [1908] 1 Ch. 743, C.A.

[62] See especially *per* Buckley L.J. at p. 762.

[63] *e.g.*, those in which creditors are to be affected or in which members are not to be treated in strict accordance with their class rights in a winding up.

members under section 287 to be evaded by a resort to sections 206–208. Astbury J.,[64] reviewing the conflicting decisions, has concluded that the position is as follows:

(a) If the scheme is really a sale, *simpliciter*, under section 287, it must be implemented under that section and the rights of dissentients cannot be evaded by resorting to a scheme under section 206.[65]

(b) If the scheme cannot be carried out under section 287, though it involves a sale for shares to be distributed, the court can sanction it under section 206, and may, if it thinks fit, insist as a term of its approval that dissentients shall be protected in similar manner to that provided for in section 287,[66] but need not do so.[67]

In view, however, of the wide meaning placed on the word " arrangement " in section 206, it is difficult to understand why a scheme should cease to be an arrangement merely because it is one which could be carried out under section 287, and it is therefore submitted that the court always has a discretion as in proposition (b), and that the case [65] which holds that section 206 affords no jurisdiction is wrongly decided.

In any event, it is problematical whether the protection afforded to dissentients under section 287 is of much value to them. The section provides that their interests shall be purchased at a price to be determined by arbitration in default of agreement.[68] The intention clearly is that the shareholder shall obtain what he would have received had liquidation proceeded by realisation of the company's assets in the usual way,[69] and the actual transfer should be ignored since, *ex hypothesi*, he has effectively dissented from it. But in practice it will be extraordinarily difficult for him to prove what he is entitled to on this, a purely hypothetical, basis. His difficulty is aggravated by the fact that it has been held that he is not entitled to examine the books [70] or the directors [71] to obtain evidence for this purpose. He is therefore very much in the position of having to make bricks without straw, his only straw being his nuisance value, which will depend upon the total number of dissentients. If they are numerous, they may be a grave embarrassment to the liquidator, particularly if the new shares are not readily marketable.

---

[64] In *Re Anglo-Continental Supply Co.* [1922] 2 Ch. 723.

[65] *Re General Motor Cab Co.* [1913] 1 Ch. 377, C.A. But it is difficult to see how the scheme in that case could have been carried out under s. 287 as the shares were not to be distributed in strict accordance with class rights.

[66] As in *Re Sandwell Park Colliery Co.* [1914] 1 Ch. 589, and *Re Anglo-Continental Supply Co., supra.*

[67] *Sorsbie* v. *Tea Corporation* [1904] 1 Ch. 12, C.A.; *Re Guardian Assurance Co.* [1917] 1 Ch. 431, C.A. The court would be unlikely to sanction a scheme which forced shareholders to take shares with an increased liability.

[68] s. 287 (3) and (6). For the method of arbitration, see C.C.A. 1845, ss. 128–134, which provide for two arbitrators and an umpire, and Arbitration Act 1950, s. 31. s. 287 (6) expressly applies this procedure to registered companies.

[69] *Re Mysore West Gold Mining Co.* (1889) 42 Ch.D. 535.

[70] *Morgan's Case* (1884) 28 Ch.D. 620.

[71] *Re British Building Stone Co.* [1908] 2 Ch. 450.

Sometimes quite as great a nuisance are those members who, without formally dissenting, fail positively to agree to take up their shares in the new company, for they cannot be compelled to do so,[72] and the new company will not be entitled to register them as members without their agreement. If, therefore, the new shares are partly paid, inert shareholders may defeat the scheme quite as effectively as active dissentients unless effective arrangements are made for underwriting.[73]

The liquidator will therefore have to deal with three classes of shareholder: (a) Those who agree to accept the new shares. These cause no difficulty and the shares will normally be allotted direct to them. (b) Those who actively dissent. These will have to be bought out for cash, unless the scheme is dropped, and the liquidator will have to retain sufficient assets to enable them to be paid. (c) Those who neither agree nor actively dissent. It is normally provided that shares to which they are entitled shall be sold by the liquidator and that they shall be entitled to the proceeds.[74] But apparently the scheme may provide that they shall forfeit all rights unless they accept the new shares within a fixed time.[75] The real difficulty in all these cases is that stamp duty concessions may be lost.[76]

Although section 287 contains no provisions similar to section 207 as regards explanatory circulars, the major factor—disclosure of directors' interests—is partially secured by section 192 which makes illegal any payment to a director by way of compensation for loss of office unless it is both disclosed and approved in general meeting.[77] And this is expressly declared to be without prejudice to any general rule of law requiring disclosure[78]; as we have seen, the courts have been ready to declare resolutions invalid if information on this point is suppressed.[79]

(5) Take-overs by acquisition of shares[80]

This final method is the "take-over bid," as popularly understood, which has already been referred to in relation to the duties of directors.[81]

---

[72] *Re Bank of Hindustan, China & Japan* (1865) 2 Hem. & M. 657.
[73] There were formerly difficulties in valid underwriting in cases of this sort but the wording of s. 53 is now wide enough to avoid them: *Barrow* v. *Paringa Mines* [1909] 2 Ch. 658.
[74] *Cf. Fuller* v. *White Feather Reward* [1906] 1 Ch. 823.
[75] *Re Bank of Hindustan, China & Japan* (1865) 2 Hem. & M. 657; *Burdett-Coutts* v. *True Blue Gold Mine* [1899] 2 Ch. 616, C.A.; and *per* Buckley L.J. in *Bisgood* v. *Henderson's Transvaal Estates* [1908] 1 Ch. 743 at p. 760. The argument is that this does not amount to an unlawful expropriation without compensation, since the shareholder has received the same as all the others who have not formally dissented, namely, an option to take up the new shares. All in all, the lot of an opposing shareholder, whether he formally dissents or remains aloof, is not a happy one. Hence a threat of resort to s. 287 has sometimes been found effective to induce a class to agree to a variation under some other method.
[76] See pp. 632, 633, *infra.*
[77] See Chap. 23, pp. 541–543, *supra.*
[78] s. 194 (4).
[79] Chap. 21, p. 480, n. 56, *supra.*
[80] On these see Weinberg: *Take-overs and Amalgamations* (2nd ed., 1967) and the Jenkins Report, Cmnd. 1749, paras. 265–293.
[81] *Supra*, pp. 540–546.

It differs from the methods previously described in that in strict law the company that is being taken over does not itself participate in the operation. All that occurs is that one company (or for that matter an individual bidder [82]) makes an offer to the shareholders of another to buy their shares either for cash, or for its own shares or debentures, or for a mixture of both. Normally the offer will be expressed to be conditional on acceptance by a stated proportion of shareholders [83] in such a way that those accepting become bound to sell but the offeror does not become bound to buy until the condition is fulfilled.[84] If, as a result, the acquiring company obtains a controlling interest in the taken-over company, the latter will become a subsidiary of the former and a merger will have been achieved. If the consideration was shares in the acquiring company the shareholders in the taken-over company will become shareholders in the acquiring company in much the same way as they might under a scheme under section 206 or 287. Hence an arrangement by this method may, in reality, achieve precisely the same result as one under the methods considered earlier.

Of course the take-over bid is not always employed as a means of merging two or more companies which are going concerns. The bidding company may merely wish to acquire the control of another which is ripe for take-over because its shares, for one reason or another, are quoted at a price much below the actual or potential value of its business.[85] Less legitimately the object may be to acquire a " shell " company with no active business but with large liquid assets which it is hoped, despite section 54, to use to pay for the shares and later to extract permanently from the company.[86]

The Companies Acts are, at present, completely silent on the matter except for section 209 of the 1948 Act which, as we shall see, enables the acquiring company compulsorily to acquire a minority of shareholders who do not accept the offer. The only legal control over the circulars relating to the bid is under rules [87] made by the Board of Trade under the Prevention of Fraud (Investments) Act 1958. More anomalously still, these rules very rarely have any legal application since they apply only to licensed dealers through whom few bids are made. Mostly they are made through members of a recognised stock

---

[82] In practice, for a variety of reasons, the bid will be made by a company.

[83] Normally 90 per cent., because of s. 209 (*infra*). But the acquiring company may be content with less, though partial bids are frowned on by the City.

[84] Despite the doctrinal objections to contracts in which one side is bound and the other not, this is, apparently, legally effective: see *Ridge Nominees Ltd.* v. *I.R.C.* [1962] Ch. 376, *per* Buckley J. at 382–383. But under rule 21 of the *City Code* an acceptor must be allowed to withdraw after 21 days from the original closing date.

[85] This may be because the management is inefficient, or has pursued a policy of dividend limitation, or has not revalued the fixed assets.

[86] For an illustration of the *modus operandi*, see *Selangor United Rubber Estates* v. *Cradock (No. 3)* [1968] 1 W.L.R. 1555, where the main sufferers in the end were the banks who, oblivious of s. 54, had provided the bridging finance.

[87] The Licensed Dealers (Conduct of Business) Rules 1960 (S.I. No. 1216).

exchange, or issuing houses which are exempted dealers,[88] and thus permitted to distribute circulars. The expectation, which is generally fulfilled, is that they will voluntarily act in accordance with the rules. But the main control that applies to them is the *City Code on Take-Overs and Mergers*,[89] laying down rules of commercial morality in this sphere. This has no legal force but is now policed, not as yet very effectively, by the Take-over Panel representative of various City institutions.[90] One might have expected that the first rule in the Code would be an insistence on obedience to the Board of Trade's rules. Not so. It is indicative of the lamentable absence of co-ordination in this field [91] that the Code does not contain a single mention of those rules.[92]

The Jenkins Committee [93] recommended that the system should be rationalised by regulating take-over offers broadly speaking in the same way as prospectuses. In other words the Companies Act would lay down what information had to be given in the circulars containing the bid and in any circulars from the directors of the company recommending acceptance.[94] The stock exchanges and the City would, of course, be expected to supplement those minimum legal requirements. This would indeed be a desirable rationalisation, but doubts are being widely expressed on whether it goes far enough. It would still mean that take-overs would be dealt with very differently from other types of merger and with legal protection of the security holders left exclusively to disclosure as opposed to supervision. It is coming to be accepted that unless the Take-over Panel can show that it is able to produce and enforce observance of a strict code of conduct, supervision through a state organ—a miniature SEC—will be inevitable.

At present, however, the legal control consists only of the Board of Trade rules. These apply to any written offer to acquire or dispose of

---

[88] If not made through any dealers but by the bidder, directly or through the directors of the company being taken over, the consent of the Board of Trade will be required under s. 14 of the Prevention of Fraud (Investments) Act 1958, and the Board will insist on compliance with the rules.

[89] A revised edition was published in April 1969. The Code applies, in principle, to mergers however effected but a merger by take-over bid is the method envisaged and it would be unlikely to have much relevance to one effected under s. 287 or s. 206.

[90] Including the Bank of England, the issuing houses, the British Insurance Association, the pension funds, the clearing banks, the C.B.I. and the London Stock Exchange. Attempts have recently been made to strengthen the Panel and its sanctions. If the securities concerned are, or are to be, quoted, or either of the companies involved has quoted shares, a further measure of extra-legal control is provided by the stock exchange regulations: there is a special Memorandum of Guidance on this subject: see *Requirements*, pp. 17–27, and Weinberg, *op. cit.*, Appendix E.

[91] But see p. 310, n. 55, *supra*. The Jenkins Committee had hoped, as yet in vain, that co-ordination would be achieved through a strengthened Companies Act Consultative Committee: see Cmnd. 1749, paras. 229–230. *Supra*, p. 309.

[92] Apart from a possible, but very oblique, reference in the Introduction.

[93] Cmnd. 1749, paras. 270–282. See also Chapter 14, pp. 304–306.

[94] The Committee thought it would be impracticable to control the contents of circulars recommending rejection: *ibid.*, para. 273.

securities but contain additional provisions applying to a take-over offer, defined as one " calculated to result in any person acquiring or becoming entitled to acquire, control . . ." [95] and " control " means control over " the exercise of a majority of the voting power." [96] What has to be included in the circular containing the bid is set out in Schedules to the rules. Part I of the First Schedule (details relating to the shares) is common to all offers to acquire and Part II sets out additional requirements in respect of take-over offers. The Second Schedule lists the requirements in respect of offers to dispose of securities and will be relevant where the take-over is to be paid for by securities in the acquiring company. The Third Schedule details the requirements in respect of recommendations by the board of directors of the offeree company that the offer be accepted—circulars recommending rejection are free from control. [97] The basic philosophy is one of full disclosure, [98] but in a number of respects the rules go beyond this by prescribing, for example, the minimum period for which the offer must remain open, [99] that it must not be conditional on acceptors agreeing to compensation for directors losing office, [1] and that on a partial bid all shareholders must be treated alike. [2] These mandatory requirements are carried still further by the extra-legal rules in the *City Code*. There are twelve General Principles and thirty-five Rules which elaborate those Principles. [3] Particular emphasis is placed on treating all shareholders alike [4]; in particular they provide that if more than the bid price is paid to any shareholder the increased price must be paid to all. [5] There are also exhortations regarding the duties of the board of directors to give impartial consideration to all offers [6] and the need for care and accuracy in all circulars including those recommending rejection. [7]

It should be mentioned that the Board of Trade rules and, of course, the *City Code* apply not only to registered companies but to all corporate bodies. But, as the Introduction to the Code states, it was drafted with public companies, especially quoted ones, particularly in view,

[95] r. 18 (1).

[96] *Ibid.* Hence a bid which will result in acquisition of less than 50 per cent. of the voting shares is not a take-over offer for this purpose.

[97] This is often thought to place the board opposing a take-over bid at an unfair advantage compared with the bidder.

[98] Note that it includes compulsory disclosure of the name of the principal on whose behalf the bid is made: r. 1 (*a*).

[99] 21 days: First Sched., Part II, 1 (1).

[1] *Ibid.* 1 (3).

[2] *Ibid.* 1 (4).

[3] The exact relationship of the Principles and the Rules is not crystal clear. The apparent intention is that the Principles shall be observed in the spirit and the letter even if not specifically covered by a Rule.

[4] General Principle 8.

[5] Rule 31. In this respect and generally the Code, so far as it can, carries out the recommendations of the Jenkins Committee in Cmnd. 1749, paras. 276–282.

[6] Rules 9–12.

[7] Rules 13–19.

though it adds that " the Rules and their spirit may also be relevant to transactions in shares of private companies." [8]

Where the object of the bid is to take over the company as a wholly-owned subsidiary, the failure by a few shareholders to accept the offer could frustrate the scheme, for an outstanding minority may be a grave embarrassment to the parent company wishing to operate the subsidiary for the benefit of the group as a whole and not just of its own members. Equally, non-acceptors may wish to change their minds when they find, contrary to their expectations, that the offer has been accepted by sufficient of their fellow-shareholders to cause it to be made unconditional. Section 209 of the 1948 Act is designed to meet these two situations.

The effect of the first subsection is that if, under a scheme or contract,[9] an offer by a company [10] to acquire the shares or any class of shares of a registered company has been accepted within four months of the offer [11] by the holders of 90 per cent. in value of the shares involved (other than shares already held), the acquiring company can, within a further two months,[12] give notice to any non-accepting shareholder that it wishes to acquire his shares. The acquiring company is then entitled and bound to acquire his shares on the same terms unless the court, on application by the shareholder within one month,[13] orders otherwise. Provisions are made for executing transfers on behalf of recalcitrant shareholders.[14] The procedure is available even though the acquiring company already owns more than one-tenth of the shares, but in that event the same terms must be offered to all the holders whose shares are involved,[15] and the offer must be accepted by three-fourths in number as well as nine-tenths in value.[16]

---

[8] It is to be hoped that this means that the Panel will be prepared to invoke such disciplinary powers as it can call upon to punish breaches of the Code in relation to take-overs of private companies; there have been some deplorable examples.

[9] *Quaere* whether these words have any limiting effect on the type of take-over within the section: see *Re Bugle Press Ltd.* [1961] Ch. 270, C.A.

[10] Whether a registered company or not. But the section has no application to a bid by an individual or partnership or, according to a recent decision of the Privy Council, to one by a consortium of several companies: *Blue Metal Industries Ltd.* v. *Dilley,* May 5, 1969 (not yet reported).

[11] This does not mean that the offer must remain open for four months (normally a much shorter time-limit (21 days) is set) but merely that it must have been accepted within four months: *Re Western Manufacturing (Reading) Ltd.* [1956] Ch. 436.

[12] *i.e.,* the right must be exercised within six months of the original offer: *Musson* v. *Howard Glasgow Associates Ltd.,* 1960 S.C. 371.

[13] Application is made to the court having jurisdiction to wind up the company being taken over: *Re Samuel Heap & Son Ltd.* [1965] 1 W.L.R. 1458 (where Courtaulds (the offeror company) found themselves dragged to the County Palatine of Lancaster).

[14] s. 209 (3) and (4). Unless an exemption applies (see p. 632, *infra*), the transfers will bear stamp duty as a transfer on sale: *Ridge Nominees Ltd.* v. *I.R.C.* [1962] Ch. 376, C.A. But various devices can be employed to minimise this: see Weinberg: *op. cit.,* paras. 1520–1525.

[15] s. 209 (1), proviso (*a*). This unhappily suggests that different terms can be offered in other circumstances which can hardly have been intended: see Jenkins Report, Cmnd. 1749, paras. 283 and 288.

[16] s. 209 (1), proviso (*b*). The Jenkins Committee recommended that this should be repealed: Cmnd. 1749, para. 288.

Section 209 (2) is designed to give the non-accepting minority a further opportunity to extricate themselves. When the nine-tenths of the shares have been transferred notice must be given to the remaining shareholders within one month and they or any of them can within three months serve a counter-notice requiring the transferee company to acquire their shares. These shares must then be bought on the same terms, or on such other terms as may be agreed or as the court, on the application of either the transferee company or the shareholder, shall order.[17] It will be observed that shareholders have no right to an extension of time for acceptance unless nine-tenths have been acquired. If, however, an offer is made unconditional on acquisition of a lesser fraction, or if for any other reason the subsection does not apply,[18] the *City Code*[19] requires that the offer shall be extended for at least fourteen days unless a prior notice to the contrary has been given.

The whole of section 209 is notoriously badly drafted and the Jenkins Committee made various recommendations,[20] which have not yet been implemented, designed to clarify and improve it.

It will be appreciated that when the terms of the bid are agreed by the boards of the two companies, and no other company makes a counter-bid, the whole operation can be carried out relatively simply and inexpensively. When, however, the bid is opposed or there are competing bids, a long, bitter and expensive battle may result. One problem which is then of some importance in theory, though it does not seem to cause much concern in practice, is who is to bear the expense. It is arguable that if the directors of the company decide to oppose a bid they are not entitled to do so at the company's expense since the identity of holders of fully paid shares is not a matter which concerns the company.[21] However, the only English case directly in point[22] suggests that they are entitled to do so if they consider that that is in the interests of the company, *i.e.*, the long-term interests of the shareholders present and future. In practice they always do treat this as a corporate expense and this practice is accepted by City opinion and acquiesced in by bidders, successful or unsuccessful. It would be unfair if they were not entitled to be reimbursed since the board of the bidding company are clearly entitled to treat expenses they incur as those of that company.[23]

---

[17] It will be observed that under subs. (2) the court can vary the terms; under subs. (1) it can only confirm or deny a right to acquire on the terms of the bid.
[18] As the Jenkins Committee pointed out, it appears to be possible to evade s. 190 (2) by making the offer through a subsidiary: Cmnd. 1749, para. 291.
[19] Rule 22.
[20] Cmnd. 1749, paras. 283–293.
[21] *Morgan* v. *Tate & Lyle Ltd.* [1955] A.C. 21, H.L.
[22] *Peel* v. *L.N.W. Ry.* [1907] 1 Ch. 5.
[23] In the U.S.A. there is authority for the view that if the bidders are successful they can recover from the coffers of the company taken over if this is authorised in general meeting. But the author's views that this might be followed in England (see Vol. 2, *Law in Action* at p. 229) have been exposed by Weinberg, *op. cit.*, para. 2455, as heretical in the light of common law principles and s. 54.

The Jenkins Committee recommended that the matter should be put beyond doubt by providing that they should have a right to be reimbursed in respect of " expenses properly incurred . . . on behalf of, and in the interests of, the members of the offeree company in connection with a take-over offer." [24]

CHOICE OF METHOD—TAXATION CONSIDERATIONS

The choice of method to be employed will sometimes be dictated by circumstances. If, for example, it is desired to reduce capital or to have an arrangement with the company's creditors, there will be no option but to proceed under sections 66–71 or sections 207–208 respectively. In other circumstances, however, particularly in relation to mergers, a variety of methods may be available.[25] Once again, the choice may depend on circumstances. Clearly one cannot proceed under section 287 or sections 206–208 without the concurrence of the directors of the company being taken over. Without this, a bid for the shares will be the only method available. Even if the merger is an agreed one a bid for the shares is in practice the method most commonly employed although another method may be substituted for it or used in addition because, for example, 100 per cent. control is essential and this cannot be obtained, even with the aid of section 209.

Among the most potent factors that are likely to decide what method is adopted when a choice is available are tax and stamp duty considerations. The general nature of the tax considerations should be apparent from a perusal of Chapter 9. Occasionally, indeed, tax considerations may provide the motive for the take-over; for example, where there is a " tax loss " company whose past losses can be set off for tax purposes against the profits of the company taking it over.[25a] Normally, however, tax considerations are relevant only in deciding on the choice of method. The main question will probably be whether it would be more advantageous to transfer the undertaking, *i.e.*, to sell it under a power in the memorandum, or to transfer it under a reconstruction under section 287 or sections 206–208, or to transfer the share capital. If the company being taken over is a " close company " it may be safer to take over its undertaking rather than its shares in view of the potential liability to income tax on any shortfall in past distributions or to a surtax apportionment.[26] Since the introduction of capital gains tax it is virtually impossible for there to be an acquisition of shares for cash which will not render the shareholders liable for short- or long-term capital gains tax on any profit they make, or to acquire the undertaking

---

[24] Cmnd. 1749, para. 279.
[25] For a list of the various choices, see Weinberg, *op. cit.*, Chap. 4.
[25a] But see p. 180, *supra*.
[26] But it may be possible to guard against these, or liability under F.A. 1960, s. 28, by obtaining a clearance from the Revenue.

for cash in a way which will enable the shareholders to escape such a liability on the subsequent liquidation of the company whose undertaking has been acquired. Hence, in order to obtain adequate acceptances it is now almost essential either to acquire for shares alone or to offer the option of shares or cash. It would be inappropriate to go more deeply into these questions here,[27] but it would be unrealistic not to draw attention to them.

Whichever method is adopted it will be very important to set up the scheme in such a way that advantage can be taken of concessions relating to stamp duty on the transfers of the shares or undertaking and to capital duty on the increased share capital raised in order to implement the scheme. These concessions turn primarily on section 55 of the Finance Act 1927.[28] This applies only where a new company is formed or an existing company increases its capital to acquire the whole or part of the undertaking, or not less than 90 per cent. of the share capital of an existing company,[29] and the consideration consists as to at least 90 per cent. of shares in the acquiring company. The nominal capital of the acquiring company is then deemed for the purposes of capital duty to be reduced by the amount of the capital of the company taken over, or a proportion of it equivalent to the proportion of the undertaking [30] being acquired, and any conveyances and transfers are exempt from stamp duty. It will be observed that the concession operates only if the consideration is shares, not cash, so that once again cash offers are discouraged. Moreover, the shares must be actually issued to the taken-over company or its shareholders,[31] so that the concession is likely to be lost if renounceable allotment letters are issued.[32] However, once the shares are registered in the names of the shareholders they are free to sell them even though this is in pursuance of a previous arrangement whereby the offer is underwritten for cash.[33] If, however, the shares are issued to the company, as opposed to its shareholders, the company must retain all [34] of them for two years, unless it goes into liquidation; and similarly the acquiring company must retain any shares in the taken-over company which it acquired.[35]

---

[27] They are discussed in Weinberg, *op. cit.*, Chaps. 16 and, especially, 17.
[28] As amended by F.A. 1928, s. 31, and F.A. 1930, s. 41. For a detailed account, see Weinberg, *op. cit.*, Chap. 15.
[29] Both companies must be English or Scottish (not N. Irish) companies: *Nestlé & Co.* v. *I.R.C.* [1953] Ch. 395, C.A.
[30] *i.e.*, the gross assets without deducting liabilities: *Gomme Ltd.* v. *I.R.C.* [1964] 1 W.L.R. 1348.
[31] *Oswald Tillotson* v. *I.R.C.* [1933] 1 K.B. 134, C.A.; *Brotex Cellulose Fibres* v. *I.R.C.*, *ibid.* 158; *Murex Ltd.* v. *I.R.C.*, *ibid.* 173.
[32] But for the devices that may be adopted to minimise the duty, see Weinberg, *op. cit.*, paras. 1521–1523.
[33] But more sophisticated underwriting arrangements may cause the concession to be lost: *Central & District Properties Ltd.* v. *I.R.C.* [1966] 1 W.L.R. 1015, H.L.
[34] *Att.-Gen.* v. *London Stadiums* [1950] 1 K.B. 387, C.A.
[35] F.A. 1927, s. 55 (6) (*b*) and (*c*).

The conditions of the section are construed very strictly.[36] As stamp and capital duties may be a heavy item on a reconstruction or take-over the greatest care should be taken to ensure that the scheme complies with the conditions if that is practicable. Apart from section 55, exemption from transfer duty, though not capital duty, may sometimes be obtained under section 42 of the Finance Act 1930,[37] which exempts from stamp duty inter-group transfers where the parent company holds at least 90 per cent. of the issued capital of the subsidiaries. The main advantage of this is that the most advantageous method of initial take-over can be employed in reliance on the fact that there can later be a re-shuffling within the group without further stamp duty liability.[38]

MERGERS AND THE PUBLIC INTEREST

Before returning to the question of investor and creditor protection attention should be drawn to certain legislative provisions designed to protect the national interest. First there is the Exchange Control Act 1947 under which the consent of the Treasury, acting through the Bank of England, is required for a transfer of shares to a resident outside the sterling area. The object of the legislation is to protect the strength of our currency, but it may have the additional effect of protecting our industry from passing into foreign ownership.

Of more importance in the case of mergers of large companies is the Monopolies and Mergers Act 1965.[39] This is a somewhat belated recognition of the fact that if monopolies are contrary to the public interest it is more sensible to prevent the mergers which cause them rather than merely to subject the resulting situation to a leisurely investigation by the Monopolies Commission under the Monopolies and Restrictive Practices (Inquiry and Control) Act 1948. Accordingly, under section 6, if it appears to the Board of Trade that a merger is proposed or has occurred within the preceding six months which will result either in the concentration in one enterprise of at least one-third of the supply of particular goods or services [40] or in the taking over of assets exceeding £5 million,[41] the Board may refer the matter to the Monopolies Commission for a report by them within a prescribed time not exceeding six months.[42] The Commission must investigate and report whether the conditions are in fact fulfilled and, if so, whether the merger may be expected to operate against the public interest and, if so,

---

[36] See the cases cited in notes 29–34, *supra*, and *Lever Bros.* v. *I.R.C.* [1938] 2 K.B. 518, C.A. (the concession cannot be obtained if the acquiring company already has more than 10 per cent. of the shares).

[37] As amended by F.A. 1938, s. 50.

[38] But this section also is construed strictly and has been held not to apply to a transfer from a wholly-owned subsidiary to a wholly-owned sub-subsidiary of another wholly-owned subsidiary: *Rodwell Securities Ltd.* v. *I.R.C.* [1968] 1 All E.R. 257.

[39] See Weinberg, *op. cit.*, paras. 1348–1369.

[40] This is a summary, not wholly accurate, of s. 6 (1) (*b*) (i) of the 1965 Act.

[41] This amount may be varied by statutory instrument: s. 6 (3).

[42] There may, for special reasons, be an extension not exceeding three months: s. 6 (6).

what action they recommend. The Board are then given wide powers, not limited to action recommended by the Commission, to prohibit or unscramble the merger. During the course of the reference the Board may ensure the maintenance of the status quo.

The Board of Trade have already made references in the case of a number of proposed take-overs and, as a result, a few have been stopped. In no case has it yet been necessary to undertake the difficult process of unscrambling a merger after it has occurred and, to obviate this risk, the practice is to refer a proposed merger to the Board in any case where it seems possible that the prescribed conditions may apply. If this is done, the Board may give a clearance which will enable the take-over to proceed without risk.[43]

Reference may also be made in this connection to the activities of the Industrial Reorganisation Corporation,[44] established by statute in 1966.[45] In its task of facilitating the rationalisation of industry the Corporation has, in a few cases, intervened decisively in the course of a take-over battle.

One section of the community whose interests as such are not afforded any protection, either under this head or by virtue of the provisions for investor or creditor protection, are the workers and employees of the taken-over company.[46] This is a particularly unfortunate facet of the principle that the interest of the company means only the interest of the members, and not of those whose livelihood is in practice much more closely involved. The Jenkins Committee [47] recognised this, but felt that it could not appropriately be dealt with by amendments of company law. They considered whether a take-over bidder should be required by statute to disclose his intentions regarding the future of the company and its employees, but felt that, though a statement of intentions was desirable if possible, it could not be made mandatory.[48] The position of employees who lose their jobs as a result of the take-over has, however, been somewhat improved financially, as they may now be entitled to compensation under the Redundancy Payments Act 1965.[49]

---

[43] This, of course, does not obviate the risk that the activities of the merged enterprises may later be referred under the 1948 Act if a monopoly situation arises.

[44] " I.R.C.," but not to be confused, as it inevitably will be, with the Inland Revenue Commissioners or the new Commission on Industrial Relations suggested by the Royal Commission on Trade Unions (Cmnd. 3623).

[45] Industrial Reorganisation Corporation Act 1966. Attention has already been drawn to the different, and somewhat conflicting, philosophies of this Act and the Monopolies and Mergers Act: see Chap. 3 at pp. 58, 59.

[46] The effect on morale and on future personnel relations may be deplorable if the employees first hear of the take-over by reading about it in the Press and never have it properly explained to them: see *The Human Effects of Mergers* (Acton Society Trust, 1966).

[47] Cmnd. 1749, para. 267.

[48] A recommendation that such a statement should be made was dropped from the 1968 and 1969 versions of the *City Code*.

[49] Speaking generally, the compensation is one or one-and-a-half weeks' wages for each year of employment.

INVESTOR AND CREDITOR PROTECTION
AND THE ATTITUDE OF THE COURTS

The first protection of investors and creditors under any reconstruction is that it normally involves at least the passing of a resolution by a substantial majority. For a reduction of capital and for a scheme under section 287 a special resolution must be passed; for a variation of rights under the memorandum or articles there must also be a special resolution, plus the consent of the various classes by the majority (normally three-fourths) prescribed in the variation of rights clause; and for a scheme of arrangement under sections 206–208 there must be resolutions at meetings of the classes concerned passed by a majority in number representing three-fourths in value. A take-over by the acquisition of shares involves the consent of those whose shares are acquired, though powers of compulsory acquisition under section 209 may be exercised, but only if 90 per cent. acceptances have been obtained. In general, therefore, one may say that no radical alteration in the company's constitution can take place without at least a company resolution passed by a three-fourths majority, and if there is to be a variation of the rights of a class of investors or creditors [50] without a similar majority at a class meeting. To these meetings all that was said in Chapters 21 and 22 will apply; as there pointed out, it is not in practice so difficult as might be thought for those in control of the company and its proxy-voting machinery to secure the passing of the necessary resolutions, particularly as these merely require a three-fourths majority of those voting, and not of the whole membership or class.

A second safeguard is that in some cases there are more stringent requirements of full disclosure in the notices of the meeting. Thus for a scheme under sections 206–208 there are the provisions in section 207 relating to circulars, and for sales under sections 287 and 209 the provisions in sections 192–194 relating to disclosure and approval of payments to directors.[51]

Thirdly, in every case except under section 287 the court's sanction is either necessary or its veto can in some circumstances be invoked on application by those dissenting. This is not needed under section 287 because dissentients then have a right to be bought out and because liquidation is essential and the court has general power of control over liquidators. In other cases the court's discretion is clearly intended to be the vital safeguard of the interests of those affected and the protection of the minority against the possibility of being sacrificed to the interests of the majority. The question which we now consider is the extent to

---

[50] *i.e.*, of their *legal* rights. Their interests may well be affected commercially without their having any say in the matter; *e.g.*, where a new management acquire control by action under s. 209, debentureholders and other creditors will have no say. And *cf.* the cases on the meaning of "variation" discussed in Chap. 22, p. 511 *et seq.*, *supra*.

[51] See Chap. 23, pp. 540–544, *supra*.

which this safeguard has proved effective. We shall consider first those cases in which the court's sanction has to be sought (that is, on reductions of capital under sections 66–71 and under schemes of arrangement under sections 206–208), and secondly those cases in which there is an appeal to the court (that is, under sections 72 and 209).

Reductions of capital

The position here is summed up with admirable clarity and devastating candour by Lord Cooper in his dissenting judgment in the Court of Session in *Scottish Insurance Corpn.* v. *Wilsons & Clyde Coal Co.*[52]—a case to which reference has already been made. Lord Cooper said [53]:

> "Every major Companies Act, beginning with the Act of 1867, has required that reduction of share capital (except by certain methods which are not in point) should be confirmed by the court. . . .
>
> "Emphasis was again and again laid by the House of Lords upon the proposition that the courts had a ' discretion ' to confirm or not to confirm which it was their duty to apply in ' every proper case,' and that this discretion fell to be exercised by reference to . . . whether the scheme would be ' fair and equitable,' ' just and equitable,' ' fair and reasonable ' or ' not unjust or inequitable,' expressions sometimes qualified and explained by the addition of the words ' in the ordinary sense of the term,' or ' as a matter of business.' . . . Nothing could be clearer and more reassuring than those formulations of the duties of the court. Nothing could be more disappointing than the reported instances of their subsequent exercise. Examples abound of the refusal of the courts to entertain the plea that a scheme was not fair or equitable, but it is very hard to find in recent times any clear and instructive instance of the acceptance of such an objection."

And he concludes:

> "The circumstances of the present case impress me as so exceptional that, if the power to refuse confirmation is not to be exercised here, I have difficulty in figuring circumstances in which it will ever be worth invoking it again."

Having regard to the facts of the case before Lord Cooper (discussed in Chapter 16, *supra*), one may agree that it is indeed difficult to envisage circumstances in which the courts will ever reject a reduction on the ground of unfairness. And, indeed, there is only one reported case [54]

[52] 1948 S.C. 360, affd. [1949] A.C. 462, H.L., *supra*, pp. 361–363.
[53] 1948 S.C. at p. 375 *et seq.*
[54] And diligent search has failed to reveal an unreported one either. *Re Barrow Haematite Steel Co.* [1900] 2 Ch. 846; [1901] 2 Ch. 746, C.A., is often cited as an

in the present century in which they have expressed their willingness to do so. This case, *Re Old Silkstone Collieries Ltd.*,[55] gives some slight grounds for hoping that the courts may be willing to take a firmer line. But the circumstances were exceptional, and the ground of unfairness was merely a makeweight (almost certainly *obiter*) thrown in after the court had already rejected the scheme because of its failure to treat the various classes of shareholders in accordance with their rights.

There is, therefore, little concrete evidence of more than lip service to the principle that the courts have a discretion to refuse confirmation if the scheme seems inequitable. Though some cases suggest that the onus of proving fairness is on the petitioning company,[56] this does not appear to be so unless, on the reduction, classes of shareholders are not being treated in strict accordance with their class rights. In the latter event, as the *Silkstone* case shows, the court will probably decline to confirm, unless the rights are first varied in accordance with a variation of right clause (if any) or by a scheme under sections 206–208, although it has power to do so if it is positively established that the scheme is fair.[57] But if the reduction treats shareholders in accordance with their class rights,[58] or if these rights are first varied[59] it now seems to be admitted in theory as well as in practice that the court must confirm unless there is some formal flaw or unless it is positively established that the reduction is unfair.[60]

This formulation seems to recognise that a reduction may be unfair to a class, although it treats that class in strict accordance with its rights, but unhappily this recognition is not translated into practice. The lack of examples of the exercise of the discretion cannot be explained on the ground that in the last century all reductions have been scrupulously fair; on the contrary, they have sometimes treated preference shareholders abominably. Possibly the *Scottish Insurance* and the *Chatterley-*

example, but the grounds of the decision were that the loss of capital was not established which was then thought to be a decisive bar. It is true that Cozens-Hardy J. indicated that he would not have confirmed the reduction anyway as it had not been proved to his satisfaction to be equitable as between the shareholders, but the Court of Appeal refused to express any opinion on this.

[55] [1954] Ch. 169, C.A.

[56] See, for example, *Re Barrow Haematite Steel Co.*, *supra*.

[57] See p. 617, note 15, *supra*. In *Re Old Silkstone Collieries Ltd.* [1954] Ch. 169, the Court of Appeal seemed to think that it had no power to sanction the scheme once it had been shown that classes had not been treated in accordance with their rights; but see now the definite decision to the contrary by Buckley J. in *Re William Jones & Sons Ltd.* [1969] 1 W.L.R. 146, where, however, the petition was unopposed.

[58] *Scottish Insurance* v. *Wilsons & Clyde Coal Co.* [1949] A.C. 462, H.L.; *Prudential Assurance* v. *Chatterley-Whitfield Collieries* [1949] A.C. 512, H.L. This means their rights on a winding up (*ibid.*, and *Re Saltdean Estate Co. Ltd.* [1968] 1 W.L.R. 1844) unless there is some protection under the *Spens* formula: see Chap. 16 at p. 363.

[59] *Carruth* v. *I.C.I* [1937] A.C. 707, H.L., see especially *per* Lord Maugham at p. 764 *et seq.*

[60] *Re Old Silkstone Collieries* [1954] Ch. 169, C.A.

Whitfield cases [61] are illustrations, but an even clearer example of unfairness is afforded by *Re MacKenzie & Co. Ltd.*[62] There the issued share capital of the company was divided into preference and ordinary shares, all of £20 each and ranking *pari passu* on a repayment of capital on a winding up. The preference shares were entitled to a 4 per cent. preferential dividend on the capital paid up thereon, but had no vote except when their dividends were in arrear. In recent years the company had made losses but had never passed its preference dividend. A scheme of reduction of capital was put forward whereby the nominal and paid-up value of all the shares was to be reduced by £8, £3 of which was actually repaid. Astbury J. held that this was not a variation of the special rights of the preference shareholders so as to require their separate consent as a class, and, the resolution having been duly passed as a special resolution by the ordinary shareholders, he confirmed the reduction without more ado. Yet under this reduction the ordinary shareholders gave up nothing, whereas the preference shareholders sacrificed a large fraction of their annual dividend for the benefit of the ordinary shareholders.

At one time the Scottish courts were prepared to refuse to confirm a reduction because, for example, its purpose was tax avoidance [63] or to protect the company against the possibility of being nationalised.[64] But this has been denounced as a heresy by the House of Lords [65] which has made it clear that in so far as the public interest is relevant it means simply the interest of " persons who may in the future have dealings with the company or be minded to invest in its securities." [66] In other words, the courts will not sanction a reduction by repayment of capital if this will defeat the whole object of the principle of maintenance of capital (considered in Chapter 6) by enabling the capital fund to be returned to the members to the detriment of those having dealings with the company.

It therefore appears that action by the courts has not lived up to their words. There seems to be no case in the present century where the English courts have refused to confirm on the merits alone, and although

---

[61] *Supra.* These cases are considered in more detail in Chap. 16, p. 361 *et seq.* They show that irredeemable preference shares can be paid off at the whim of those able to secure the passing of a special resolution and that no class consents are necessary, provided that the preference shareholders receive the capital to which they would be entitled on a winding up. In those cases their rights to capital were held to be much less than they had been assumed to be under an earlier Court of Appeal decision. It is now the practice for terms of issue of quoted companies to afford some protection by use of the *Spens* formula which ties the redemption price to the current quotation. But for a recent example of an unquoted company, see *Re Saltdean Estate Co. Ltd., supra.*

[62] [1916] 2 Ch. 450. This decision was cited with apparent approval by the Court of Appeal in *White* v. *Bristol Aeroplane Co.* [1953] Ch. 65, C.A. and *Re John Smith's Tadcaster Breweries* [1953] Ch. 308, C.A.

[63] *A. & D. Fraser Ltd.,* 1951 S.C. 394, but see now *David Bell Ltd.,* 1954 S.C. 33.

[64] See *Ex p. Westburn Sugar Refineries Ltd.* [1951] A.C. 625, H.L.

[65] *Ex p. Westburn Sugar Refineries Ltd., supra.*

[66] *Ibid.* at p. 635.

the Scottish courts have proved somewhat bolder [67] their efforts have been effectually frustrated by the House of Lords.

In practice the action of the courts has been reduced to ensuring that the necessary formalities have been complied with. This, of course, is useful so far as it goes, especially as the formalities are designed to secure that the rights of creditors are fully protected.[68] As we have seen, the court is authorised to sanction a reduction of uncalled liability or a repayment of capital only if satisfied that creditors have agreed, or been paid, or had their debts secured.[69] And the court may take similar action in other types of reduction also,[70] and may, as the *Westburn* case recognises, consider the interests of future creditors as well as of existing ones—although here again there is more evidence of lip service than practical application. But, in straightforward reduction schemes, there has been a considerable relaxation in every respect and it is rare today to find a reduction rejected even on technical grounds.[71] Indeed, the freedom with which the courts rubber-stamp reductions of capital adds further to the doubts whether the elaborate rules for the raising and maintenance of share capital (dealt with in Chapter 6) really fulfil any purpose.

Schemes of arrangements

Although the court's discretion has not always proved an effective protection in reductions of capital, at least reductions alone have not often permitted an alteration of admitted class rights or derogation from the rights of creditors. Unless such rights can be altered under a variation of rights clause they normally remain sacrosanct apart from the possibility of modification under a scheme of arrangement under sections 206–208. These sections also require the sanction of the court, and we should hope to find that its discretion is then exercised more effectively. This, unfortunately, is only true in part.

In considering the functions of the court under these sections, Maugham J. *in Re Dorman Long & Co.*[72] said:

> " It is plain that the duties of the court are twofold. The first is to see that the resolutions are passed by the statutory majority in value and number . . . at a meeting or meetings duly convened and held. The other duty is in the nature of a discretionary power [73] . . . In my opinion, then, so far as this second duty is

---

[67] See, for example, *Ex p. Westburn Sugar Refineries, supra,* and *A. & D. Fraser, supra.*

[68] ss. 67 (2), 68 (1), 70 and 71.

[69] s. 68 (1).

[70] s. 67 (2).

[71] Thus the court will not necessarily refuse confirmation, as it did in *Re Barrow Haematite Steel Co.* [1901] 2 Ch. 746, C.A., because loss of capital is not proved: *Poole* v. *National Bank of China* [1907] A.C. 229, H.L.; *Caldwell* v. *Caldwell & Co.,* 1916 S.C.(H.L.) 120. But see *Re Lucania Temperance Billiard Halls* [1966] Ch. 98.

[72] [1934] Ch. 635.   [73] At p. 655.

concerned what I have to see is whether the proposal is such that an intelligent and honest man, a member of the class concerned and acting in respect of his interest, might reasonably approve." [74]

And, as the same learned judge [75] pointed out in the House of Lords in a later case,[76] too much weight should not be placed on the size of the majorities when it is shown that " the majority of the class has voted, or may have voted, in the way it did, because of its interests as shareholders of another class." [77]

Examples can easily be found of the rejection of schemes on the first ground. The *Dorman Long* case itself is one, for there sanction was refused on the grounds that the circulars were insufficient and that the resolutions were not in fact passed by the requisite majority. And, as we have seen,[78] the Scottish courts have in a number of recent cases thrown out schemes on the ground that the provisions as to circulars in section 207 have not been adequately complied with. On the other hand, in the recent case of *Re National Bank Ltd.*,[79] the court approved a scheme notwithstanding that the value of the assets was not disclosed in reliance on the bank's exemption under Schedule 8. Notwithstanding the absence of this vital information, the requisite majorities had been obtained on the strength of assurances by the directors and three eminent firms of accountants (to whom there had been full disclosure) that the scheme was fair. These assurances also satisfied the court, and the scheme was confirmed.

As regards the second ground, the court's discretionary power, the observations of Lord Cooper [80] are equally applicable:

> " Nothing could be clearer and more reassuring than those formulations of the duties of the court. Nothing could be more disappointing than the reported instances of their subsequent exercise. Examples abound of the refusal of the courts to entertain the plea that a scheme was not fair or equitable, but it is very hard to find in recent times any clear and instructive instance of the acceptance of such an objection."

To suggest that the courts adopt quite the same *laissez-faire* attitude as they apply to reductions would be unfair. In practice they investigate the scheme as closely as they are able and regard the initial onus as being on the company [81] to establish its prima facie fairness. The trouble is that English High Court procedure is ill-adapted to the inquisitorial role thus thrust upon the judges. The company will have set the stage for

[74] At p. 657.
[75] Then Lord Maugham.
[76] *Carruth* v. *I.C.I.* [1937] A.C. 707, H.L.
[77] At p. 769.
[78] *Supra*, p. 619, note 34.
[79] [1966] 1 W.L.R. 819.
[80] Already quoted, *supra*, p. 636.
[81] Or other applicant for confirmation.

the scheme and will have little difficulty in establishing its prima facie fairness—indeed, the mere fact that it has been passed with the requisite majority is sufficient to raise a strong inference of fairness, an inference which the objectors are rarely able to rebut. The court cannot readily investigate the indoor management of the company and therefore it tends to take refuge in the facile but fatal rule first enunciated by Lindley L.J. in *Re English, Scottish and Australian Chartered Bank* [82]:

> " If the creditors are acting on sufficient information [83] and with time to consider what they are about, and are acting honestly, they are, I apprehend, much better judges of what is to their commercial advantage than the court can be."

This dictum, that creditors or shareholders know best, is repeated in almost every case relating to every type of reconstruction and it affords, of course, a perfect answer to any suggestion that the court should do more than ensure that the formal requirements have been complied with. Unhappily it is based on the fundamentally false assumption that a vote of a meeting necessarily represents the informed opinion of the majority of members of the class concerned unprejudiced by any conflicting interests. The courts realise this and occasionally their realisation finds expression,[84] but all too often they have to renounce any attempt to form an independent judgment in the face of the harsh fact that they are in scarcely a better position than the investor to pass an informed judgment.

Certainly when one takes a sample of schemes which have been duly ratified and confirmed and considers them in the light of the company's subsequent history, little confidence can be felt in the court's discretion.[85] Still, if one seeks in vain for any case of out-and-out rejection on the merits, there are at least numerous cases [86] in which the courts have made it a condition of confirmation that certain modifications shall be made to the scheme as originally put before them.[87] Moreover, the courts will always listen to the objections of any creditor or member who is affected and will almost invariably decree that his costs be paid by the company.[88] It may. be, therefore, that the need for the court's sanction in the face of the likelihood of hostile argument exercises some

---

[82] [1893] 3 Ch. 385, C.A., at p. 409.

[83] Or, sometimes, even if they are not: see *Re National Bank Ltd., supra.*

[84] As in the dictum of Lord Maugham in *Carruth* v. *I.C.I., supra,* note 76.

[85] For a revealing analysis on these lines, see (1944) 5 U. Toronto L.J. 282.

[86] They are rarely reported. But see *Re Mortgage Insurance Corpn.* [1896] W.N. 4, *Re Land Mortgage Bank of Florida, ibid.* 48, and *Re Anglo-Continental Supply Co.* [1922] 2 Ch. 723.

[87] To cover this eventuality and to avoid further meetings it is usual to frame the resolutions so that they cover the scheme with any modifications required by the court. In practice the modifications tend to be relatively unimportant and often they are suggested by the company.

[88] In this respect their position is much more favourable than in the case of a reduction where unsuccessful objectors have less assurance of being allowed costs.

restraining influence on company managers who might otherwise attempt to force through schemes of greater unfairness.

But, in the main, the court's sanction is valuable for the same reason as in the case of reductions—that it secures strict compliance with the formalities, including, generally,[89] adequate disclosure. Under schemes of arrangement varying creditors' and class rights this is even more necessary than under a straightforward reduction scheme, and the legislature[90] and the courts[91] have done their best to ensure that it is forthcoming.

Modifications of rights

If the court's discretion has proved ineffective to protect minorities in cases where its consent is necessary, we should expect to find it even less effective in cases where it is not needed but where dissentients have a right of appeal. And we should be right.

Where there has been a modification of rights, the remedy (apart from statute) of any dissentients is to appeal to the court either attacking the formal validity of the alteration or alleging a fraud on the minority. If they can show some flaw in the procedure the alteration is invalid, but if they cannot and have to rely on " fraud-on-the-minority " their state is parlous, for as we have seen, the onus of proof is heavy and rarely discharged when alterations to the articles are in issue. These matters have already been discussed in earlier chapters.

If, however, class rights of shareholders are varied under a clause in the memorandum or articles, dissentients amounting to 15 per cent. of the class have a special statutory right to appeal to the court under section 72. This section makes it clear that the onus of proof is on the applicants, who have to satisfy the court that the variation would " unfairly prejudice the shareholders of the class represented." This wording suggests that the onus is little different from that in an action based on " fraud-on-the-minority," and this seems to have been the view of Lord Maugham.[92] But apart from his dictim there is a complete dearth of authority, largely due to the fact that prior to the commencement of the action the applicant must have obtained the written consents of the 15 per cent. minority,[93] and that until 1948 the action had to be commenced within seven days. The time has now been extended to twenty-one days, thus rendering procedure under the section somewhat more practicable. Whether the courts will hold the onus of proof to be

---

[89] But see, *Re National Bank Ltd., supra.*
[90] s. 207.
[91] *Cf. Re Dorman Long & Co., supra,* and the Scottish decisions *Rankin & Blackmore Ltd.,* 1950 S.C. 218; *Peter Scott & Co. Ltd., ibid.* 507; *Coltness Iron Co.,* 1951 S.L.T. 344; *City Property Investment Trust, ibid.* 371.
[92] In *Carruth* v. *I.C.I.* [1937] A.C. 707 at p. 765.
[93] The petition will be struck out unless these consents are obtained (*Re Suburban Stores Ltd.* [1943] Ch. 156, C.A.) and communicated to the applicant prior to the commencement of the action (*Re Sound City Films Ltd.* [1947] Ch. 169).

lighter than in an action based on " fraud " remains to be seen; after the failure of the only two reported cases [93] on the section, the plaintiffs in *Rights & Issues Investment Trust Ltd.* v. *Stylo Shoes Ltd.*[94] apparently thought they might do better to start an action alleging oppression.[95]

As already pointed out,[96] section 23 may be invoked in connection with a modification of rights. If there is only one class of share the rights of which are stated in the memorandum and not declared to be unalterable, these rights may be altered by special resolution but, once again, a dissenting minority of 15 per cent. may apply to the court. The wording of this section (read in conjunction with section 5) suggests that the court has a freer discretion [97] but how it will be exercised remains to be seen. At the best it can hardly confer greater protection than that under sections 206–208.

Acquisitions of shares

Finally, there is the right to appeal to the court conferred on a dissenting minority whose shares are being acquired under section 209. This appeal may be exercised in two sets of circumstances : first, to object to the terms where the acquiring company gives notice to acquire the minority's shares,[98] and, secondly, to settle the terms when the dissentient has served notice electing to be bought out after all.[99] There are a considerable number of reported cases,[1] all relating to the first ground of objection, but, with one exception, where the section was being palpably abused rather than used,[2] all unsuccessful. They make it clear that the onus is normally on the applicants affirmatively to establish the unfairness of the terms and that it is a very heavy one to discharge. As Maugham J. pointed out in the first of these cases, the offer has, *ex hypothesi*, been accepted by over 90 per cent. of the shareholders concerned so that :

" Prima facie the court ought to regard the scheme as a fair one inasmuch as it seems . . . impossible to suppose that the court, in

---

[94] [1965] Ch. 250, *supra*, p. 575.
[95] But failed, too.
[96] *Supra*, p. 618.
[97] See s. 5 (4).
[98] s. 209 (1).
[99] s. 209 (2). The transferee company also may apply to the court.
[1] *Re Hoare & Co. Ltd.* (1933) 150 L.T. 374; *Re Evertite Locknuts Ltd.* [1945] Ch. 220; *Re Press Caps Ltd.* [1949] Ch. 434, C.A.; *Re Western Manufacturing (Reading) Ltd.* [1956] Ch. 436; *Re Trinidad Oil Co. Ltd., The Times*, April 13, 1957; *Re Sussex Brick Co. Ltd.* [1961] Ch. 289n. (1959); *Re Bugle Press Ltd.* [1961] Ch. 270, C.A.; *Nidditch* v. *Calico Printers' Association*, 1961 S.L.T. 282; *Re Hinde & Sons Ltd., The Times*, April 23, 1966; *Re Grierson, Oldham & Adams Ltd.* [1968] Ch. 17. The cases make it clear that unless the applicants have acted unreasonably they will probably not be ordered to pay the offeror company's costs though they probably will not recover their costs.
[2] *Re Bugle Press Ltd., supra*. And see *Musson* v. *Howard Glasgow Associates Ltd.*, 1960 S.C. 371, where the applicant succeeded on the ground that the offeror company's notice was out of time.

the absence of very strong grounds, is to be entitled to set up its own view of the fairness of the scheme in opposition to so very large a majority of the shareholders who are concerned." [3]

Indeed, in a later case [4] Vaisey J. refused to intervene notwithstanding that he was apparently satisfied that " a better scheme might have been evolved " and he went so far as to say that the court would do so only if the offer was " obviously unfair, patently unfair, unfair to the meanest intelligence." [5] It seems that the absence of full disclosure will not suffice [6] and that the applicants must set forth the grounds on which they rely [7] and will not be entitled to discovery to assist them.[8] Nor, apparently, will a palpable breach of the accepted rules of good behaviour be sufficient to induce the court to intervene.[9] Unfairness has to be tested in relation to the general body of shareholders and not the particular circumstances of the individual applicant,[10] and to the value of each share, ignoring the value attributable to the control that will pass to the acquiring company.[11]

However, the Court of Appeal has held that the position is different when the 90 per cent. acceptors are themselves interested in the acquiring company. In *Re Bugle Press Ltd.*[12] a 90 per cent. majority attempted to use section 209 (1) to get rid of the minority. This they did by forming another company which made an offer; this they accepted and then caused the new company to invoke the section. The court held that if the section had any application in such circumstances, the onus was on the acquiring company to persuade the court not to exercise its discretion to " order otherwise." [13] Mere proof that the price was a fair one would not suffice.[14] What is not clear is how far this would be

---

[3] *Re Hoare & Co. Ltd.* (1933) 150 L.T. at p. 375.

[4] *Re Sussex Brick Co. Ltd., supra.*

[5] [1961] Ch. at p. 292. If this is right it is difficult to see how a case of unfairness can ever be established unless it is possible to prove that the 90 per cent. acceptors are complete morons.

[6] *Re Evertite Locknuts Ltd., supra.*

[7] *Nidditch* v. *Calico Printers' Association, supra.*

[8] *Re Press Caps Ltd.* [1948] 2 All E.R. 638, *per* Vaisey J. (but the C.A., [1949] Ch. 434, expressed no opinion on this point).

[9] *Re Hinde & Sons Ltd., supra,* where the issuing house, to placate one shareholder, had bought him out at about 40 per cent. above the bid price (but this was without reference to their clients on behalf of whom the bid was made).

[10] *Re Grierson, Oldham & Adams Ltd., supra,* where the applicant made a loss because he had bought his shares at a higher price.

[11] *Re Grierson, Oldham & Adams Ltd., supra;* see also the views of the C.A. in *Re Press Caps Ltd., supra,* and *cf. Short* v. *Treasury Commissioners* [1948] A.C. 534, H.L., *supra,* p. 346, in relation to nationalisation.

[12] [1961] Ch. 270. This decision was followed on similar facts by the Canadian Supreme Court in *Esso Standard (Inter-American) Inc.* v. *J.W. Enterprises Ltd.* [1963] S.C.R. 144. See also *supra,* p. 570.

[13] Which perhaps it might do if " the minority shareholder was in some way acting in a manner destructive or highly damaging to the interests of the company from some motives entirely of his own ": at p. 287. If this could be shown a power of expropriation could apparently be inserted in the articles and then exercised: see Chap. 24, *supra.*

[14] The shares had been valued by an independent and distinguished firm of chartered accountants.

taken; presumably the burden of proof of unfairness is not reversed merely because some shareholders in the bidding company own shares in the company for which the bid is made.

It seems clear, therefore, that the court's discretion under this section is exercised on much the same lines as in a " fraud " action and that, once again, save in very exceptional circumstances, the only effective function of the court is to ensure that the necessary formalities have been complied with.[15]

Conclusions

The conclusion seems inevitable that the present safeguards are not always enough. The need for special majorities is inadequate protection since, for reasons explored in earlier chapters, those in control can in practice force their will on a minority. The proxy voting system places a weapon in the hands of the controllers which is so potent that its force is hardly blunted by the special provisions for disclosure. Even the right to contract out, conferred on dissenting members in reconstructions under section 287, is of dubious value because of the practical difficulties in proving the true value of their shares. Finally, the protection on which the greatest store has been set—the discretion of the court—has not always proved effective. For this the judges cannot fairly be blamed, for the truth is that our court procedure is ill-fitted for enabling them properly to pass judgment on the economic merits of schemes and to make the valuations and accounting investigations necessary before they can do so. Hence they are naturally reluctant to substitute their opinions for those reached by large majorities of the members. The most they can do is to ensure that the prescribed formalities have been strictly observed and that decisions have been reached after full and fair disclosure. They are also astute to pick on some flaw in the procedure if, notwithstanding the vote, they have serious doubts about the fairness of any scheme.[16] This, and the scrutiny to which reconstructions are subjected by the professional advisers, who will have to support them in court, are very real safeguards.

The difficulty, however, is that the courts and counsel are primarily concerned with the legal rights of the parties. Provided these rights are not infringed it is difficult for them to intervene effectively, however inequitable the results may be. It is this which has resulted in the undoubted hardship in some cases. If unfairness is always to be

---

[15] *e.g.*, strict compliance with the time limits: *Musson* v. *Howard Glasgow Associates Ltd.*, 1960 S.C. 371.

[16] See, for example, *Re Dorman Long & Co.* [1934] Ch. 635; the admirable decision of Uthwatt J. in *Second Consolidated Trust* v. *Ceylon Amalgamated Estates* [1943] 2 All E.R. 567; and the Scottish decisions cited *supra* at p. 619, note 34. Note also *Re Consolidated South Rand Mines Deep Ltd.* [1909] 1 Ch. 491, where the court ordered a compulsory liquidation on the application of dissenting shareholders so as to prevent their being damnified under a s. 287 scheme which " was eminently an unfair one."

prevented the role of the courts needs to be replaced or, better still, supplemented by an administrative agency similar to a Board of Trade inspector. In recognition of this the Scottish courts make a practice of referring schemes to a reporter (generally he will be a charterered accountant or solicitor) whose report they consider before confirming. This practice may account for the fact that the intervention of the Scottish courts seems to have been somewhat more effective than that of the English. In the case of mergers and take-overs the City has established the Panel to police the *City Code*, but the Panel lacks teeth and, in any case, its role is to see that the rules are observed, not that the terms of the scheme are fair. In U.S.A., under Chapter X of their Federal Bankruptcy Act, an administrative agency—the Securities and Exchange Commission—acts in reconstructions as impartial representative of investors and expert adviser of the courts. It is arguable that some such solution should be attempted in England. If, as is the case under the Trade Unions (Amalgamations, etc.) Act 1964, the Registrar of Friendly Societies can exercise supervisory powers over trade union amalgamations, it is difficult to see why the Companies Department of the Board of Trade should not do likewise with company mergers.

But it may be that this would be like taking a steam-hammer to crack a nut. Most companies are not controlled by crooks and most schemes are carefully considered and are meant to be fair. The real protection of investors and creditors is the force of public opinion represented by informed criticism in the financial Press, and the improved standards of commercial morality which it has produced. Though the courts may be relaxing their control, there is no doubt that in the last thirty years the general standards of fairness displayed in reconstruction schemes have improved.

CHAPTER 27

LIQUIDATIONS

THE liquidation or winding up (the two terms are used indiscriminately) of a company is the process whereby its life is ended and its property administered for the benefit of its creditors and members. The closest analogy to what occurs is afforded by the administration of a deceased's estate; an administrator, called a liquidator, is appointed and he takes control of the company, collects its assets, pays its debts and finally distributes any surplus among the members in accordance with their rights. But the process differs from the administration of a deceased's estate in that the estate being administered is that of a person still living. Only at the end of the winding up will the company be dissolved; administration precedes death, not vice versa.

The process also resembles bankruptcy and follows its rules closely if the company is insolvent. A company cannot be made bankrupt; instead it must be wound up under a separate but not dissimilar procedure. But here the differences are more marked. If a company is put into liquidation it cannot, like a bankrupt individual, obtain its discharge and continue freed from the burden of its debts. The liquidation winds up its affairs and then kills it—although, under a reconstruction [1] it may rise like a phoenix from the ashes of its funeral pyre.

Further, the company's property does not vest in the liquidator,[2] as a bankrupt's vests in the trustee in bankruptcy; all that occurs is that the liquidator assumes all the functions of the directors. And, finally, even in the administration of the assets of an insolvent company, the rules applicable are not identical with those in bankruptcy. For example, the " reputed ownership " clause has no application.[3] It must be emphasised, however, that the assumption of the directors' powers by the liquidator occurs even if the company is fully solvent; in this respect it differs fundamentally from the dissolution of a partnership where the partners themselves wind up their affairs unless they are made bankrupt or a receiver is appointed.

It will have been apparent from the foregoing that winding up is a large and complicated topic. Like administration of estates or bankruptcy it is a subject in itself on which a separate book could be written. Here it is not proposed to deal with it in any detail, but merely to

---

[1] See Chap. 26, *supra.*
[2] Unless the court so orders under s. 244.
[3] *Supra*, Chap. 4, p. 79. Nor has the provision (Bankruptcy Act 1914, s. 16) protecting an author on the bankruptcy of the publisher: *Re Health Promotion Ltd.* [1932] 1 Ch. 65.

consider it as an aspect of investor and creditor protection in which it has pre-eminent importance as constituting the ultimate remedy of both these classes. It is, moreover, a remedy available not only in the case of registered companies, but, as already emphasised, for all types of company (including foreign ones [4]) and certain other associations [5] which can be wound up compulsorily [6] under the Companies Act 1948, Part IX. But before dealing with the principal respects in which it operates as a protection it is necessary, if what follows is to be intelligible, to explain briefly the various types of winding up and the position of the liquidator.

TYPES OF WINDING UP

There are two main types of liquidation, compulsory under an order of the court and voluntary under a resolution of the company.[7] Speaking generally one may say that the former occurs when the directors or those in control do not want the company to be liquidated,[8] whereas the second occurs when they do.

(a) Compulsory liquidation [9]

The company, or any creditor, or any member [10] may petition the court [11] to wind up the company on any of the grounds specified in section 222. Of these grounds the only two which need particular mention are (e) that the company is unable to pay its debts (the most common ground), and (f) that it is just and equitable (which, as we have

---

[4] *Infra*, Chap. 28.

[5] *Supra*, Chap. 11, p. 242.

[6] But not in any other way: s. 399 (4).

[7] s. 211. As there stated, there is also the hybrid " winding up subject to supervision," but this is hardly ever used and the Jenkins Committee recommended that it should be abolished: Cmnd. 1749, para. 503 (v).

[8] But a company may resolve by special resolution on a compulsory liquidation: s. 222 (a). Though unlikely, this might occur where, for example, those in control had lost faith in the directors.

[9] In 1967, 1,280 compulsory liquidations were begun in Great Britain: Board of Trade General Annual Report on Companies 1967.

[10] The Act (s. 224) refers to " a contributory," which is defined (in s. 213) as " every person liable to contribute to the assets of the company in the event of its being wound up," *i.e.*, apparently a holder of partly paid shares or the guarantor of a company limited by guarantee. But this definition has been construed so as to include every past or present member: *Re Anglesea Colliery Co.* (1866) L.R. 1 Ch.App. 555, C.A.; *Re Aidall Ltd.* [1933] Ch. 323, C.A.; *Re Consolidated Goldfields of New Zealand* [1953] Ch. 689. Apparently, therefore, even a past member could petition, but it is assumed that the court would not view his action favourably unless he was liable to be placed on the B list of contributories, on which see *infra*, p. 663. As to personal representatives and trustees in bankruptcy, see *supra*, p. 596, n. 1. The Board of Trade may also petition following an investigation by them: s. 224 (1) (d) and 1967 Act, s. 35 (1); see *supra*, p. 611. And so may the Official Receiver if the company is already in voluntary liquidation which cannot be continued " with due regard to the interests of creditors or contributories ": s. 224 (2) on which see *Re J. Russell Electronics Ltd.* [1968] 2 All E.R. 559. The Board of Trade may also petition under s. 16 of the Protection of Depositors Act 1963, and as regards insurance companies under 1967 Act, s. 81.

[11] The county court has jurisdiction if the paid-up capital does not exceed £10,000: s. 218.

seen, may be useful in the event of oppression or deadlock [12] or if the substratum of the company has been destroyed [13]). The petition is normally brought by a creditor, very rarely by the company (which would obviously prefer voluntary liquidation), but sometimes by a member. A member, however, can petition only if he is an original allottee or the holder of shares registered in his name for six months during the preceding eighteen months or which devolved on him on the death of a former holder.[14] Moreover, the member will generally have to show that there will be a surplus available for the members after the creditors have been paid.[15] This, however, will not apply if it is alleged that it is just and equitable to wind up because of a failure to supply the accounts and information to which the members are entitled so that the petitioner does not know whether the company is solvent or not.[16] The Act facilitates proof of the company's inability to pay its debts by providing that it shall be deemed unable to do so if it defaults in complying with a written demand for payment served by a creditor to whom more than £50 is due, or if unsatisfied execution has been levied.[17] The court may, however, accept other evidence,[18] but will not allow the petition to proceed if the debt is seriously disputed.[19]

In a compulsory winding up, the liquidator is appointed by the court [20] and must act under its supervision,[21] and under that of the committee of inspection [22] appointed by the creditors and members,[23] and of the Board of Trade.[24] An official receiver (an official of the

---

[12] *Supra*, Chap. 25, pp. 596–598. Proceedings under s. 210 are normally preferable: *ibid.*, p. 598 *et seq.*

[13] *Supra*, Chap. 5, p. 90.

[14] s. 224 (1) (*a*) (ii). See *Re Gattopardo Ltd.* [1969] 1 W.L.R. 619, C.A., where the provision was applied notwithstanding that a court order had been obtained more than six months previously that the petitioner was entitled to be registered. But the position would probably have been different if the company had been a party to the action in which the order had been made: *ibid.* and *Re Patent Steam Engine Co.* (1878) 8 Ch.D. 464. The provision does not apply if the number of members is reduced below the minimum (s. 224 (1) (*a*) (i)) when, *semble*, even a past member, however long ago he had parted with his shares, could petition: *cf. Re Anglesea Colliery, supra; Re Consolidated Goldfields of New Zealand, supra.*

[15] *Re Rica Gold Washing Co.* (1879) 11 Ch.D. 36, C.A.; *Re Othery Construction Ltd.* [1966] 1 W.L.R. 69; *Re Expanded Plugs Ltd., ibid.* 514.

[16] *Re Newman & Howard Ltd.* [1962] Ch. 257. But it does not suffice merely to show that matters in relation to the company require investigation: *Re Othery Construction Ltd., supra; Re Expanded Plugs Ltd., supra.* The Jenkins Committee recommended that a petition should not fail merely because there would be no assets for contributors: Cmnd. 1749, para. 503 (*h*).

[17] s. 223 (*a*) (*b*) and (*c*). As regards insurance companies, see 1967 Act, s. 79 (1).

[18] s. 223 (*d*). But the court has a discretion and will not make an order if this is opposed for reasons that are shown to be reasonable by the majority of the creditors: *Re A.B.C. Coupler and Engineering Co. Ltd.* [1961] 1 W.L.R. 243, *cf. Re P. & J. Macrae Ltd., ibid.* p. 229, C.A. (leave to appeal refused, *ibid.* 328, H.L.).

[19] *Re Welsh Brick Industries Ltd.* [1946] 2 All E.R. 197, C.A.; *Mann* v. *Goldstein* [1968] 1 W.L.R. 1091 (even if the company is insolvent). *Cf. Re Tweeds Garages Ltd.* [1962] Ch. 406 where the dispute was merely as to exact amount of the debt.

[20] ss. 237–238.

[21] ss. 245 (3), 256 *et seq.*

[22] ss. 245–246. And of any general meeting of creditors or members: ss. 246, 346.

[23] ss. 252–253.

[24] ss. 248–251, 254.

Board of Trade attached to the court) becomes provisional liquidator until another is appointed or it is decided that the liquidation shall be left permanently in his hands.[25] The company's officers must submit to him a statement of the company's affairs,[26] and he must report thereon to the court.[27] All this involves considerable expense, and the Jenkins Committee recommended that the court should be empowered to direct that the liquidation should be conducted as if it were a creditors' voluntary winding up.[28]

(b) Voluntary liquidation [29]

Under section 278, voluntary liquidation of a registered company occurs if it passes a special resolution to that effect, or an extraordinary resolution that it cannot by reason of its liabilities continue its business and that it is advisable to wind up.[30] The purpose of allowing an extraordinary, as opposed to a special, resolution in the latter case is to dispense with twenty-one days' notice when the company is insolvent so that winding up is urgent.[31]

Where it is proposed to wind up voluntarily, the majority of the directors may at a board meeting make a statutory declaration that having made full inquiry into the affairs of the company, they have formed the opinion that the company will be able to pay its debts in full within a specified period not exceeding twelve months.[32] If this declaration of solvency is made the liquidation proceeds as a Members' Voluntary Winding Up [33] and the members appoint the liquidator [34] who is not subject to the supervision of the creditors. Otherwise the winding up is a Creditors' Voluntary Liquidation [35] and the directors must make a financial report to the creditors. The creditors then have the final choice on who shall be liquidator [36] (if they choose to exercise it [37]) and

---

[25] s. 239. Another person may be appointed either provisionally or finally: s. 238.
[26] s. 235.
[27] s. 236.
[28] See Cmnd. 1749, para. 503 (*l*).
[29] In 1967, 7,589 voluntary liquidations were begun in Great Britain, 5,224 members' liquidations and 2,365 creditors' liquidations: Board of Trade General Annual Report on Companies, 1967.
[30] An ordinary resolution suffices if the articles specify the company's duration and it has ended: s. 278 (*a*). But it is most uncommon for articles so to specify.
[31] The Jenkins Committee recommended an alternative procedure consequential on their proposal that extraordinary resolutions should be abolished: Cmnd. 1749, para. 503 (*r*) and (*s*).
[32] s. 283 (1).
[33] s. 283 (4).
[34] s. 285.
[35] s. 293.
[36] s. 294. Provided that a majority in both number and value can agree on whom to appoint; if not, the members' nominee will prevail: *Re Caston Cushioning Ltd.* [1955] 1 W.L.R. 163. This anomalous result illustrates the unhappy consequences of the common, but ill-conceived, requirement in bankruptcy and liquidation practice of a majority in both number and value which will often be unobtainable. If from any cause there is no liquidator acting the court may appoint (s. 304 (1)), and may remove a liquidator and appoint another (s. 304 (2)) though this is done only in the event of impropriety or evidence of bias.
[37] *Re Centrebind Ltd.* [1967] 1 W.L.R. 337.

can appoint a committee of inspection to assist and supervise him.[38] In neither case does the official receiver assume office as in a compulsory liquidation.

Clearly the directors would much prefer a members' winding up, for this means that, through their *de facto* control, their nominee is likely to be appointed (commonly the company's secretary or accountant) and he will probably not investigate their past conduct too closely. Hence it has been said that declarations have sometimes been made " recklessly or even fraudulently . . . in order to retain control of liquidations which have resulted in heavy losses to creditors." [39] But as a result of the recommendations of the Cohen Committee [40] the penalties for this abuse are severe and much greater particularity is required in making the declaration. It must now be made within five weeks preceding the date of the resolution,[41] so that far-seeing directors cannot make it when the company is solvent and keep it in reserve for use in the less prosperous future, and it must embody an up-to-date statement of assets and liabilities.[42] Further, if the declaration is made without reasonable grounds, the makers of it are liable to imprisonment or a fine or both,[43] *and the fact that the debts are not paid in full within the stipulated time raises a presumption that they did not have reasonable grounds.*[44]

The fact that a voluntary winding up has commenced does not prevent the court from making an order for a compulsory liquidation.[45]

DISSOLUTION OF THE COMPANY

For the details relating to the conduct of liquidation, the reader is referred to the Act, to the Companies (Winding-Up) Rules 1949 [46] and to the specialised books on this topic. The salient points, for our purposes, will appear in the following sections of this chapter.

On the conclusion of the administration, the company is dissolved with surprisingly little ceremony. In a compulsory winding up the normal practice now is for the Registrar to strike the company off the

---

[38] s. 295. The members of the company can also appoint representatives to the committee: *ibid.*

[39] Cohen Report (Cmd. 6659), para. 143. The Committee thought that the extent of this abuse had been exaggerated.

[40] *Ibid.*, paras. 144–145.

[41] s. 283 (2) (a). It must be filed with the Registrar *before* the date of the resolution: *ibid.* The Jenkins Committee recommended that filing at the same time should suffice: Cmnd. 1749, para. 503 (n).

[42] s. 283 (2) (b).

[43] Maximum—6 months and £500.

[44] s. 283 (3). And note the duty of the liquidator under s. 288 to call a meeting of creditors if the debts are not likely to be paid within the stated time. The Jenkins Committee recommended that this should be strengthened by empowering the creditors to substitute another liquidator and to convert the liquidation into a creditors' one: Cmnd. 1749, para. 503 (q).

[45] ss. 224 (2) and 310. For a recent example, see *Re Ryder Installations Ltd.* [1966] 1 W.L.R. 524. Such an order will not normally be made if opposed by a majority of the creditors: *Re B. Karsberg Ltd.* [1956] 1 W.L.R. 57, C.A.

[46] S.I. 330 of 1949, as amended.

register when the administration is complete.[47] In a members' voluntary winding up, the liquidator presents his final accounts to a meeting of the members, sends to the Registrar a copy of the accounts and a return of the holding of the meeting, and three months later the company is deemed to be dissolved unless the court otherwise orders.[48] In a creditors' winding up the procedure is the same except that the accounts have to be presented to separate meetings of creditors and members.[49] And if, in a members' liquidation, the liquidator decides that it will not be possible to pay the debts in full within the time stated in the declaration of solvency, he must lay annual [50] and final accounts before the creditors as in a creditors' winding up.[51] Arrangements should be made for the disposal of the books and papers of the company,[52] and for payment of any unclaimed distributions into the Companies Liquidation Account at the Bank of England.[53] Any undisposed-of property of the company vests in the Crown as *bona vacantia*,[54] subject to its right to disclaim.[55]

A dissolved company may, however, be resuscitated if the court so orders within two years of its dissolution.[56] The order, which can be on such terms as the court thinks fit, may be made on the application of the liquidator or any other person who appears to the court to be interested, and has the effect of divesting any property from the Crown and of enabling the company to sue or be sued.[57] so that it is useful if any property, claims, or debts due, are subsequently discovered. But it does not validate acts purporting to have been done by or on behalf of the company prior to its revival.[58]

[47] s. 353 (4). The effect of this practice is to avoid the necessity of an application for a court order under s. 274, but to give rise to the possibility of reviving the company within 20 years of its dissolution instead of the normal limit of two years: *infra.* The Jenkins Committee recommended a simple procedure on the lines of that in voluntary liquidations: Cmnd. 1749, para. 503.

[48] s. 290. Even if there are debts of which the liquidator is not aware: *Re Cornish Manures Ltd.* [1967] 1 W.L.R. 807.

[49] s. 300.

[50] ss. 288 and 299.

[51] ss. 291 and 300.

[52] s. 341.

[53] s. 343.

[54] s. 354.

[55] s. 355. What happens to the property if the Crown disclaims? See (1954) 70 L.Q.R. 25.

[56] s. 352. Or within 20 years if struck off under s. 353. Note the absurd anomaly that had the liquidation in *Re Cornish Manures Ltd., supra*, been a compulsory one which would have been followed by striking-off under s. 353, the Revenue could have succeeded in reviving the company; but, as the liquidation was voluntary and s. 352 applied, they failed.

[57] *Re C. W. Dixon Ltd.* [1947] Ch. 251; *Re M. Belmont & Co.* [1951] 2 All E.R. 898. The Attorney-General must be a party or consent to the order (*ibid.*) but an order can be made notwithstanding his opposition: *Re Azoff-Don Commercial Bank* [1954] Ch. 315.

[58] *Morris* v. *Harris* [1927] A.C. 252, H.L.; *Re Lewis & Smart Ltd.* [1954] 1 W.L.R. 755. And it will not be ordered if the company is subsequently left a legacy, for this would mean divesting the residuary legatees: *Re Servers of the Blind League* [1960] 1 W.L.R. 564.

Striking off the register

Attention may here be drawn to a method of dissolving a moribund company without the need for a winding up. Under section 353 if the Registrar has reasonable cause to believe that the company has ceased to operate, he may inquire of the company and if he receives no reply to two letters or a reply to the effect that the company is not in fact carrying on business, he may publish in the *Gazette*, and send to the company, a notice that unless cause is shown the company will, at the expiration of three months, be struck off the register and dissolved.[59] Unless such cause is shown the company will be struck off and dissolved by like notice. The same procedure may be adopted where a company is being formally wound up if the Registrar has reason to believe that no liquidator is acting or that the winding up is complete apart from the formal steps to lead to a dissolution. The wording of the section shows that it is envisaged that the Registrar will set this process in motion as a result, for example, of the company's failure to file its annual returns. Often, however, the company itself invites the Registrar to exercise his powers, since the procedure is a cheap and simple method of dissolving a private company which has fulfilled its purpose.[60] Numerically this method of dissolution is now the most common of all.[61]

It is, however, a method which robs the members and creditors of all the protection afforded to them by a winding up. Hence it is specifically provided that the liability of every officer and member of the company shall continue as if the company had not been dissolved, and that the court can wind up the company notwithstanding that it has been struck off.[62] Further, the court, on the application of the company or any member or creditor, may within twenty years order the company to be restored to the register, whereupon it shall be deemed to have continued in existence.[63] Restoration under this provision has a more extensive effect than an avoidance of dissolution under the earlier section 352, for everything done by the company in the intervening period is effective.[64] On the other hand, application can be made only by the company

---

[59] This procedure has in practice rendered obsolete compulsory liquidation under s. 222 (c).

[60] But see p. 254, note 41.

[61] In the year 1967, 16 companies were dissolved by court order, 6,444 after voluntary liquidations, and 11,289 were struck off after under s. 353: Board of Trade General Annual Report on Companies 1967. The 11,289 must have included about 800 struck off after compulsory liquidations under the practice referred to above.

[62] s. 353 (5). The correct procedure is first to restore it to the register under subs. (6) so as to revest in it any property which has passed to the Crown as *bona vacantia*: *Re Cambridge Coffee Room Ltd.* [1951] 2 T.L.R. 1155.

[63] s. 353 (6).

[64] *Tymans Ltd.* v. *Craven* [1952] 2 Q.B. 100, C.A. Contrast *Morris* v. *Harris, supra.* The court can insert a provision in the order that time shall not continue to run against creditors during the period between dissolution and restoration. If it does not, the cases leave it in some doubt whether time runs or not: *Re Donald Kenyon Ltd.* [1956] 1 W.L.R. 1397; *Re Vickers & Bott Ltd.* [1968] 2 All E.R. 264n.; *Re Huntingdon Poultry Ltd.* [1969] 1 W.L.R. 204.

or any member or creditor [65] and hence, notwithstanding that the company was struck off under section 353, it may be necessary to apply within two years for restoration under section 352 as a "person interested," for example, where the debt to the applicant is disputed.[66]

THE STATUS OF THE LIQUIDATOR

The exact legal status of the liquidator is difficult to define. The closest analogy seems to be that of directors, whose functions he assumes on appointment, and like them he is probably best described as a fiduciary agent of the company.[67] Again, like directors, he is often described as a trustee, but this appears to be equally inaccurate in his case.[68] As already mentioned the property of the company does not vest in him [69]; the company continues in existence and when he makes a contract he does so on behalf of the company.[70] Unlike the receiver for debenture-holders,[71] the liquidator is therefore not normally personally liable on his contracts.[72]

On the other hand, the liquidator has special statutory duties [73] imposed on him and is in a fiduciary relationship not only to the company but also to the creditors as a body, though not to individual creditors.[74] And if he breaks these duties he is liable either to an action at the suit of the person damnified by breach of a statutory duty owed to him [75] or to a misfeasance summons under section 333.[76] If appointed in a compulsory liquidation he is an officer of the court [77] but not if appointed by the members or creditors in a voluntary

---

[65] This has been held to mean a member or creditor at the time of the striking-off and not a subsequent transferee or assignee: *Re New Timbiqui Gold Mines Ltd.* [1961] Ch. 319 (and *cf. Re M. Belmont & Co., supra*). On the other hand, Megarry J. in *Re Harvest Lane Motor Bodies Ltd.* [1968] 3 W.L.R. 220 (in which *Timbiqui* and *Belmont* were not cited) has held that "creditor" should be given a wide meaning to include a contingent or prospective creditor (there a claimant for unliquidated damages under the Fatal Accidents Act).

[66] As in *Re M. Belmont & Co., supra*.

[67] *Knowles* v. *Scott* [1891] 1 Ch. 717.

[68] *Ibid. Re Windsor Steam Coal Co.* [1928] 1 Ch. 609; [1929] 1 Ch. 151, C.A.

[69] Unless the court otherwise orders: s. 244.

[70] *Re Anglo-Moravian Co.* (1875) 1 Ch.D. 130, C.A. If he carries on the business as he may for the purpose of beneficial realisation (ss. 245 (1) (*b*), 281) the post-liquidation creditors have priority over the pre-liquidation debts: *Re Great Eastern Electric Co.* [1941] Ch. 241.

[71] See Chap. 19, p. 437, *supra*.

[72] *Stead Hazel & Co.* v. *Cooper* [1933] 1 K.B. 840.

[73] And is under express obligations as regards profiting from his position: see Winding-Up Rules 1949, rr. 159–162.

[74] *Knowles* v. *Scott* [1891] 1 Ch. 717; *Leon* v. *York-O-Matic Ltd.* [1966] 1 W.L.R. 1450. But individual members have rights under certain sections of the Act to apply to the court to control his activities.

[75] *Pulsford* v. *Devenish* [1903] 2 Ch. 625. *Cf. Austin Securities* v. *Northgate* [1969] 1 W.L.R. 529, C.A.

[76] *Re Windsor Steam Coal Co.* [1929] 1 Ch. 151, C.A. See Chap. 25, pp. 595, 596.

[77] *Cf. Re Regent Finance & Guarantee Corpn. Ltd.* [1930] W.N. 84.

liquidation [78]; in this respect his position is similar to that of a receiver.[79] A body corporate may not be appointed as liquidator.[80]

SPECIAL PROVISIONS PROTECTING INVESTORS AND CREDITORS

We now turn to the main purpose of this chapter, a consideration of the special provisions applying during the liquidation for the protection of those who have invested in or had dealings with the company.

(a) Ouster of directors and management

Perhaps the most important rule of all is the basic principle of company liquidation, namely, that on winding up the board of directors becomes *functus officio* and its powers are assumed by the liquidator. As we have seen, it is those in control who have the power to cause harm, *i.e.*, generally the directors, or someone for whom they are nominees. Their removal is therefore almost invariably an essential preliminary to any remedial action, and this removal automatically occurs on liquidation.[80a]

It is, however, only a complete removal on a compulsory winding up when, not only do the directors cease to have any powers, but all the service agreements with the company are deemed to be repudiated.[81] In a voluntary winding up, on the contrary, the powers of the directors may in certain circumstances [82] be allowed to continue and, it seems, the winding-up resolution does not necessarily and automatically operate to determine the employment of all the company's officials.[83] This is of no great importance in the case of a creditors' voluntary winding up, for the powers of the directors can continue only if the committee of inspection or the creditors agree,[84] and the liquidator, being the nominee of the creditors, will presumably be independent and can always dismiss employees if he wants to.[85] But in the case of a members' winding up the position is very different. Here it is the company in general meeting that appoints the liquidator, and the general meeting is likely to remain under the *de facto* domination of the directors. Moreover, the directors' own powers may be allowed to continue if this is sanctioned by a general

---

[78] *Re Hill's Waterfall Co.* [1896] 1 Ch. 947, 954.
[79] *Supra*, Chap. 19, p. 436.
[80] s. 335. Note also s. 336 forbidding the offering of bribes to secure appointment as liquidator, and see Winding-Up Rules 1949, r. 151, forbidding solicitation of proxies.
[80a] But even in a compulsory liquidation the directors may exceptionally be allowed to continue the business as " special managers " appointed by the court under s. 263: see *Re Mawcon Ltd.* [1969] 1 W.L.R. 78.
[81] See Graham, " The Effect of Liquidation on Contracts of Service " (1952) 15 M.L.R. 48. The liquidator can, of course, re-engage them, otherwise they will be entitled to claim in the liquidation for damages for breach of contract.
[82] ss. 285 (2) and 296 (2).
[83] See Graham, *loc. cit. Cf.* as regards the appointment of a receiver, *Re Foster Clark's Indenture* [1966] 1 W.L.R. 125; *Re Mack Trucks (Britain) Ltd.* [1967] 1 W.L.R. 780.
[84] s. 296 (2).
[85] If Graham's formulation (*loc. cit.*) is correct, they will probably have been automatically dismissed since the fact that the winding up is a creditors' one will make it clear that the company cannot fulfil its obligations.

meeting or the liquidator.[86] Hence, what usually occurs is that the directors secure the appointment of an associate who will normally allow the *de facto* control of the directors and management to continue uninterrupted. Unless the liquidator is unusually strong-minded there is not likely to be any close investigation of the past or even any clear break in a course of oppressive conduct.

(b) Investigation of officers' conduct

The Act contains a number of provisions enabling the conduct of the directors and managers to be investigated and any of their ill-gotten gains to be recovered. For reasons already explained, the efficacy of these provisions is dependent on the independence of the liquidator and is therefore likely to be greatest in a compulsory liquidation, especially because of the supervision then exercised by the official receiver and the Board of Trade.[87] Moreover, there is widespread criticism that even in compulsory liquidations those concerned in the management of the company are likely to escape very much more lightly than does an individual trader on bankruptcy. The Jenkins Committee recognised the force of this criticism and made a number of not very far-reaching recommendations which were designed to meet it.[88]

Reference has already been made to the fact that on a compulsory winding up, the official receiver must make a report to the court, and in this he must, *inter alia*, state whether, in his opinion, further inquiry is desirable into the conduct of the company's business. He may then make a further report on the manner in which the company was formed, stating whether he thinks any fraud has been committed by any officer or promoter.[89] If he states that in his opinion a fraud has been committed the court may, after consideration of his report, order any person accused of fraud to attend before the court for public examination.[90] The power to conduct a public examination is only exercisable if the further report alleging fraud has been considered,[91] but in any case the court may summon for private examination any person suspected of having in his possession property of the company, or supposed to be

---

[86] s. 285 (2).

[87] Especially if the company is wound up on the petition of the Board of Trade.

[88] Cmnd. 1749, paras. 497–500 and 503 (*a*)–(*d*). For a forthright criticism of the present inadequacy of the legal and organisational arrangements for dealing with company frauds, see Hadden, *The Control of Company Fraud* (P.E.P. Broadsheet No. 503, 1968).

[89] s. 236.

[90] s. 270: see *Tejani* v. *Official Receiver* [1963] 1 W.L.R. 59, P.C. The Jenkins Committee recommended that this section should be extended to recklessness and incompetence (Cmnd. 1749, para. 503 (*a*)) with a similar extension of s. 188 enabling orders to be made disqualifying culprits from acting in corporate management: *ibid.* and para. 85 (*b*). Depositions taken at a public examination are admissible in the subsequent trial of the officer: Winding-Up Rules 1949, r. 71. Contrast r. 74 as to private examination under s. 268.

[91] *Re Great Kruger Gold Mining Co.* [1892] 3 Ch. 307, C.A.

indebted to the company, or thought to be capable of giving relevant information.[92]

These powers may be exercised in a voluntary liquidation also, on the application of the liquidator, member, or creditor,[93] notwithstanding that reports by the official receiver cannot then have been submitted.[94] Furthermore, in a voluntary winding up there is a duty on the liquidator to refer any case of an apparent criminal offence to the Director of Public Prosecutions, who may either prosecute or refer the matter to the Board of Trade for further investigation.[95] And the Companies Act itself supplements the normal criminal law by imposing penalties on various types of improper conduct which may come to light during the liquidation.[96]

(c) Civil remedies against officers

Of more importance, for our purposes, than criminal sanctions are the additional civil liabilities imposed on officers of companies in liquidation. These, however, have already been dealt with sufficiently fully. Here it is only necessary to draw attention once more to the two principal sections, 332 and 333. Section 332 enables the court to impose personal responsibility on those who were knowingly parties to the continuation of the company's business with intent to defraud creditors or for other fraudulent purposes.[97] Section 333 provides the remedy by way of misfeasance summons[98] under which the court may investigate any alleged misappropriation or breach of trust by any promoter or officer,[99] and compel him to restore or pay compensation. It will be appreciated that in practice the likelihood of action under either of these sections is dependent on investigations having been made, and that this is more likely to have occurred on a compulsory liquidation, under the provisions mentioned above, or when a fully independent liquidator is in the saddle under a creditors' winding up.[100]

---

[92] s. 268.

[93] s. 307 (1).

[94] See *Re Campbell Coverings Ltd.* (*No.* 1) [1953] Ch. 488, C.A.; (*No.* 2) [1954] Ch. 225.

[95] s. 334 (2). Under subs. (3) the Board may apply to the court for an order conferring on them all such powers as are exercisable by the court on a compulsory liquidation. This enables them to obtain information in the same way as the official receiver can under s. 235, but not to conduct a public or private examination under s. 270 or 268: *Re Campbell Coverings Ltd.* (*No.* 1), *supra.*

[96] ss. 328–331 and see s. 441.

[97] Chap 10, pp. 191–193, *supra.* The Jenkins Committee would extend this to reckless trading: Cmnd. 1749, para. 503 (*b*).

[98] See Chap. 25, pp. 595, 596, *supra.* The Jenkins Committee would extend this to any breach of duty: Cmnd. 1749, para. 503 (*d*).

[99] This expressly includes the liquidator himself.

[100] Especially if the liquidation has been preceded by a Board of Trade investigation, in which event the liquidator may obtain a transcript of the evidence: *Re Rolls Razor Ltd.* [1968] 3 All E.R. 698.

(d) Proof of debts

In a winding up creditors may normally prove for all debts whether
due immediately or payable contingently, and for all claims present,
future, vested, or contingent, ascertained or sounding only in damages,
a valuation being placed on them where necessary.[1] Prima facie, therefore, every sort of claim, whether in contract, tort or otherwise, can be
proved. This is, however, subject to an important limitation in the
case of insolvent companies, for there " the same rules shall prevail . . .
with regard to the respective rights of secured and unsecured creditors,[2]
and to debts provable,[3] and to valuation of . . . future and contingent
liabilities " as are in force under the law of bankruptcy.[4] This does
not have the effect of incorporating all the rules of bankruptcy law, but
only those applying to the three matters specifically mentioned. But
it does mean that a debt not provable in bankruptcy cannot be proved,
and this excludes claims for unliquidated damages arising otherwise than
by reason of contract or breach of trust,[5] for example, unliquidated
damages in tort.

It is therefore vital that a creditor whose sole claim is in tort, should
not delay in enforcing his rights against a company if its financial
stability is in doubt. Should it go into liquidation before his claim has
become liquidated by a judgment or agreement he will be barred unless
it proves to be solvent.[6] His position is even worse than in the case of
bankruptcy, where his claim, not being provable, will not be ended by
the bankrupt's discharge so that he could sue him thereafter. This,
however, will not be open to him in the case of a company's winding up,
for the company will cease to exist.[7]

As in bankruptcy, certain debts are expressly given preference and
must be paid, *pari passu* between themselves, before others.[8] In the

---

[1] s. 316. See, for example, *Re Armstrong Whitworth Securities Co.* [1947] Ch. 673.
But the liquidator must not pay debts barred by the Limitation Acts (*Re Art
Reproductions Co.* [1952] Ch. 89) or foreign taxation even if owed to another
Commonwealth country (*Government of India* v. *Taylor* [1955] A.C. 491, H.L.).
For an even more extreme example (and a not unamusing one) of the court's refusal
to permit the recovery of a foreign tax claim, see *Peter Buchanan* v. *McVey, ibid.,*
516n. (N.Ir.Sup.Ct., 1950). For a review of the position where the company is
tenant of leasehold premises, see *Re House Property and Investment Co. Ltd.* [1954]
Ch. 576.

[2] Hence a secured creditor must either value or realise his security and prove for any
balance, or rely on his security and not prove at all, or surrender his security and
prove for the whole: Bankruptcy Act 1914, Sched. II, rr. 10–18.

[3] This has the effect of incorporating the wider rules relating to set-off which apply in
bankruptcy: *Mersey Steel and Iron Co.* v. *Naylor Benzon & Co.* (1884) 9 App.Cas.
434, H.L.

[4] s. 317. This applies whether the liquidation is voluntary or compulsory. The
adaptation of bankruptcy rules to make them applicable to companies may present
difficulties. For the technique, see *Re Eros Films Ltd.* [1963] Ch. 565.

[5] Bankruptcy Act 1914, s. 30.

[6] *Re Newman, ex p. Brooke* (1876) 3 Ch.D. 494.

[7] Fortunately he will have a claim, for what it is worth, against the human agent of the
company who committed the tort.

[8] s. 319, as amended by F. A. 1952, s. 30; National Insurance Act 1965, s. 61 (1);
and Land Commission Act 1967, s. 77. See Chap. 19, p. 424, *supra.* As there
pointed out they have priority over a floating charge. Moreover, money received

main these relate to payments due to the Revenue or to employees,[9] but also include, and this is very important in practice, money advanced, normally by the bank, for the purpose of paying current wages.[10] Thereafter the remaining debts provable in bankruptcy are paid *pari passu*,[11] and if there is then anything left, the non-provable debts.[12] Finally, if anything remains it is divided among the members according to their rights.[13] For the purpose of adjusting the rights of the members it may be necessary for the liquidator to make calls although these are not needed for payment of debts, but this will depend on the rights attaching to the shares and, in view of the rarity of partly paid shares, the rules of interpretation need not be explored here. It should, however, again be emphasised that the return which members receive is, for tax purposes, treated as capital even if it exceeds the capital originally subscribed. Recent tax changes,[14] have made this less advantageous than of yore.

(e) Effects on property

The winding up of a company does not have quite the same effects on the company's property as does a bankruptcy and, as we have seen,[15] the property is not automatically divested from the company and vested in the liquidator. On the other hand, the Act contains provisions designed to preserve for creditors the assets existing at the commencement of the winding up, so much so that the courts seem to support the theory that from then on the creditors and members have crystallised rights to these assets.[16] Furthermore, although a winding up does not

under a distress levied within three months before the liquidation is subject to a charge in favour of the preferred creditors but the distraining landlord is subrogated to the claim of the creditors whom he pays: s. 319 (7).

[9] Not including those working on " labour only " contracts: *Re C. W. & A. L. Hughes Ltd.* [1966] 1 W.L.R. 1369.

[10] s. 319 (4). This has given rise to much litigation and many nice legal problems: see, for example, *Re E. J. Morel (1934) Ltd.* [1962] Ch. 21; *Re James R. Rutherford & Sons Ltd.* [1964] 1 W.L.R. 1211; *Re Yeovil Glove Co. Ltd.* [1965] Ch. 148, C.A.; *Re William Hall (Contractors) Ltd.* [1967] 1 W.L.R. 948; and *Re Rampgill Mill Ltd.* [1967] Ch. 1138.

[11] In bankruptcy certain debts are *deferred*, *e.g.*, those due to a lender in consideration of a share of profits of a business: Partnership Act 1890, s. 3. Whether these rules are incorporated into a company's winding up is not wholly clear. The C.A. in *Re Leng* [1895] 1 Ch. 652 thought that the provision " must include all rules as to priorities expressly enacted by any statute and made applicable in the event of bankruptcy ": *per* Lindley L.J. at p. 657. Despite this it was generally believed that the deferment of claims to interest in excess of 5 per cent. (B. A. 1914, s. 66) was not incorporated: but the contrary must now be taken to have been established: see *Re Theo. Garvin Ltd.* [1968] 2 W.L.R. 683.

[12] This is clearly so if there is sufficient to pay them in full, for the company is then solvent and s. 316 applies: *cf. Re Fine Industrial Commodities Ltd.* [1956] Ch. 256. If insufficient is left for full payment and there is a *casus omissus*, but it is submitted that common sense should prevail and that they should be paid abating rateably.

[13] ss. 265 and 302, and see Chap. 16, *supra*, p. 359 *et seq.*

[14] See Chap. 9, *supra*.

[15] *Supra*, p. 654.

[16] See, for example, the cases on registration of charges out of time, *supra*, Chap. 19, p. 431.

" relate back " to the same extent as bankruptcy, it has, as we shall see, a certain retroactive operation.

Dispositions, actions and executions

In a compulsory winding up any disposition of property made after the commencement of the winding up is void unless the court otherwise orders [17] and any execution after that date is totally invalid.[18] Further, once a winding-up order has been made, no action may be commenced or proceeded with against the company except by leave of the court,[19] and the court may stay actions at any time after the presentation of the petition and before a winding-up order has been made.[20] The same rules apply in a winding up subject to the court's supervision.[21] Winding up is deemed to commence not when the order is made, but when the petition is presented,[22] or, if a resolution has previously been passed for voluntary liquidation, when that resolution was passed.[23]

The effect of a voluntary liquidation is less extensive. There is no express prohibition of dispositions,[24] but, of course, once a liquidator is appointed the authority of the directors to part with the company's property without his consent will cease, unless the liquidator or the creditors (in a creditors' winding up), or the shareholders' meeting (in a members' winding up) otherwise resolve.[25] Nor are actions and executions automatically stayed, but the liquidator or a creditor or member may apply to the court to stay proceedings,[26] and it may, and normally will, do so if these are instituted after the winding-up resolution,[27] when the liquidation is deemed to commence.[28]

But as regard executions commenced but not completed [29] before the beginning of the winding up, sections 325 and 326, which apply to every type of liquidation, make special provisions avoiding the execution unless the court otherwise orders. Although a purchaser of goods from

---

[17] s. 227, which also invalidates any transfer of shares. The court has a wide discretion to allow the disposition to stand and will do so whenever it seems just and fair having regard to the good faith of the applicant: *Re Steane's (Bournemouth) Ltd.* [1950] 1 All E.R. 21; *Re T. W. Construction Ltd.* [1954] 1 W.L.R. 540. For the Jenkins Committee's recommended amendments to this section, see Cmnd. 1749, para. 503 (*k*).

[18] s. 228.

[19] s. 231. Including a counterclaim in excess of the company's claim: *Langley Constructions* v. *Wells* [1969] 1 W.L.R. 503, C.A.

[20] s. 226.

[21] ss. 312, 313.

[22] Compare the relation back in bankruptcy to the first available act of bankruptcy (Bankruptcy Act 1914, s. 37) and note that there are no provisions comparable to the Bankruptcy Act 1914, s. 45, protecting bona fide transactions without notice (except s. 325 (1) (*b*), *infra*).

[23] s. 229.

[24] But a transfer of shares requires the liquidator's sanction: s. 282.

[25] ss. 285 (2), 296.

[26] Under s. 307.

[27] See, *e.g., Re Margot Bywaters* [1942] Ch. 121.

[28] s. 280.

[29] For meaning, see s. 325 (2) as amended by the Administration of Justice Act 1956, s. 36 (4), and *Re Overseas Aviation Engineering (G.B.) Ltd.* [1962] Ch. 738, C.A.

the sheriff obtains a good title,[30] the creditor is not allowed to retain the benefit of the execution unless the court so orders.[31] And even if the execution is completed before the beginning of the liquidation a creditor who already had notice that a meeting had been called to consider a resolution for a voluntary winding up will not be protected.[32] Moreover, the sheriff must account to the liquidator, though he is protected as regards his costs of the abortive execution.[33]

Fraudulent preferences

Although the bankruptcy rules, which swell the assets by giving the trustee in bankruptcy a better title to property than the bankrupt, do not, as such, apply to company liquidations,[34] similar provisions relating to fraudulent preferences are expressly incorporated.[35] The effect of these is to avoid any payment or disposition made within six months [36] of the winding up with the intention of giving a creditor or his surety a preference over the other creditors.[37] It is, however, difficult to invoke this rule, for the onus is on the liquidator to prove that the disposition was made with the dominant motive of preferring [38] and not, for example, in order to quieten a particularly pressing creditor or to keep on good terms with him in the hope of future financial assistance.[39]

Moreover, the effect of successfully invoking it may be to injure not the person preferred but an entirely innocent third party. If, for example, the company's overdraft is guaranteed by a director, a payment may be made to the bank in order to relieve the director and the payment may then be avoided so that the bank has to refund the amount paid.[40] The bank is then left with such rights as it may have against the guarantor, and, although it will normally have a claim against the latter where he has accepted personal liability, cases occur where he

---

30 s. 325 (1) (*b*).

31 s. 325 (1) (*c*). The court has an unfettered discretion but will not normally interfere with the general rule whereby all unsecured creditors should rank *pari passu*: *Re Caribbean Products (Yam Importers) Ltd.* [1966] Ch. 331, C.A.

32 s. 325 (1) (*a*).

33 s. 326; see *Bluston & Bramley Ltd.* v. *Leigh* [1950] 2 K.B. 548; *Engineering Industry Training Board* v. *S. Talbot (Engineers) Ltd.* [1969] 2 W.L.R. 464; and cf. *Re T. D. Walton Ltd.* [1966] 1 W.L.R. 869.

34 *Gorringe* v. *Irwell Rubber Co.* (1886) 34 Ch.D. 128, C.A.

35 s. 320.

36 Extended from three months as a result of the Cohen Report: Cmd. 6659, para. 146.

37 " Fraudulent " is therefore used in an artificial sense, not necessarily involving anything immoral.

38 *Peat* v. *Gresham Trust* [1934] A.C. 252, H.L.; *Re M. Kushler Ltd.* [1943] Ch. 248, C.A.; *Re Eric Holmes (Property) Ltd.* [1965] Ch. 1052.

39 *Re F.L.E. Holdings Ltd.* [1967] 1 W.L.R. 1409. But an intention to prefer will be readily inferred if a charge has been granted pursuant to a promise to execute one on request: *Re Eric Holmes (Property) Ltd., supra.* Secus if a legal charge is granted pursuant to an obligation to do so in an existing equitable charge: *Re William Hall (Contractors) Ltd.* [1967] 1 W.L.R. 948.

40 As in *Re M. Kushler Ltd., supra. Semble,* the liquidator has no direct claim against the surety: *Re Conley* [1937] 4 All E.R. 438 and [1938] 2 All E.R. 127 at p. 139, C.A.

has merely charged his securities but not undertaken personal responsibility.[41]   But if the bank released the securities when the overdraft was discharged it was far from clear, before the 1948 Act, whether the bank would have any remedy except, of course, proof in the liquidation.   This point is now dealt with by section 321, which provides that the person preferred who has charged property shall be subject to the same liabilities and shall have the same rights as a surety, to the extent of his interest in the property charged.[42]   He will, therefore, be liable to the bank and entitled to prove against the principal debtor, the company.

A fraudulent preference can be set aside only for the benefit of the general body of creditors and money recovered by the liquidator is impressed with a trust in their favour and cannot be recovered by the receiver for debentureholders as part of the property charged.[43]

Floating charges

Closely allied to the setting aside of fraudulent preferences is the invalidation of floating charges created by insolvent companies within a year of liquidation, except to the extent of money then or thereafter advanced under the charge and 5 per cent. interest.[44]   This subject has, however, been discussed sufficiently in Chapter 19,[45] and here it is only necessary to emphasise that, although the debenture conferring the floating charge may often be a fraudulent preference, if it is to be set aside as such liquidation must follow within six months, whereas its liability to be invalidated under the present rule continues for a year. Because of this and, more especially, because of the great difference in the burden of proof, this ground of invalidation has in practice superseded attempted reliance on fraudulent preference so far as floating, as opposed to fixed, charges are concerned.

Uncalled capital

In the case of registered companies it is in practice impossible for creditors directly to benefit from uncalled capital, a valuable asset in the rare cases where it exists.   While the company is a going concern it rests with the directors to make calls, and without putting the company into liquidation there is no way in which the creditors can compel them to do so, nor can they directly levy execution on the uncalled capital.[46] Moreover, the uncalled capital may be expressly converted into reserve

---

[41] *Re Conley* [1938] 2 All E.R. 127, C.A.

[42] The guarantor may be joined as a third party in the proceedings: s. 321 (3), overruling *Re Singer & Co.* [1943] Ch. 121.

[43] *Re Yagerphone Co.* [1935] 1 Ch. 392.

[44] s. 322.

[45] *Supra*, pp. 424, 425.

[46] Unless it is charged to debentureholders whose receiver can then ensure that a call is made.   If a call has been made but not paid creditors can levy execution on this.

capital,[47] so that it can only be called up in a liquidation. In the case of statutory companies, the Companies Clauses Act 1845 [48] provides for the possibility of direct execution against holders of partly paid shares, and the old cases on chartered corporations suggest that, by a process of subrogation, creditors may have a similar remedy there.[49] But, in connection with overwhelmingly the most important type of company, a liquidation is an essential step before unsecured creditors can avail themselves of the uncalled capital.

It is then the task of the liquidator to prepare A and B lists of contributories.[50] On the A list will be placed those who are the present members. They are primarily liable but, in the case of a limited company, only to the extent of the unpaid capital on their shares.[51] On the B list are placed those who have been members within one year [52] of the commencement of the winding up. The A list contributories are liable to contribute within the amount of their uncalled liability to the extent needed to pay all debts and costs of the liquidation, and to adjust the rights of the members *inter se*. Those on the B list are only liable to the extent that, (a) the amount recovered from the A contributories is insufficient, (b) contribution is needed to meet debts contracted prior to the time when they ceased to be members, and (c) if the company is limited by shares, the present holders of their shares have not been successfully made to pay them up.

In view of the rarity of uncalled capital in the case of limited companies it is unnecessary to explore these rules further.[53] They will, however, become of greater importance in view of the growing number of unlimited companies since the 1967 Act. To such companies the same rules apply except, of course, that past and present members will be liable to calls beyond the extent of the uncalled capital on their shares. But the liability of a past member at the time when application was made to re-register under the 1967 Act is not increased as a result of the re-registration.[54]

Disclaimer

The Companies Act also expressly incorporates rules similar to those in bankruptcy as regards the disclaimer of onerous property.[55] These

---

[47] Under s. 60. See Chap. 6, *supra*, p. 105.

[48] s. 36.

[49] See Chap. 2, *supra*, p. 26.

[50] See s. 212, as amended by 1967 Act, s. 44 (7), regarding unlimited companies re-registered as limited.

[51] Or the amount of their guarantee in the case of a company limited by guarantee.

[52] Three years in the case of unlimited companies which have re-registered as limited under the 1967 Act: 1967 Act, s. 44 (7) (*a*). And see s. 44 (7) (*b*) and (*c*).

[53] But very occasionally they give rise to knotty problems: see *Re Apex Film Distributors Ltd.* [1960] Ch. 378, C.A.

[54] 1967 Act, s. 43 (6).

[55] s. 323.

enable the liquidator, with the leave of the court,[56] to terminate the rights and liabilities of the company in any onerous property or unprofitable contract. Disclaimer is, therefore, a method whereby the members and the creditors as a whole benefit by ridding the company of something which, on balance, is a liability rather than an asset, thereby greatly facilitating the conclusion of the winding up. But if the general body of creditors gains, one particular creditor inevitably loses, and his only remedy is to prove in the liquidation for the amount of the injury which he suffers.[57] The liquidator has a year [58] in which to decide whether to disclaim or not, but so that the other interested party shall not be kept on tenterhooks the latter may serve a notice on the liquidator requiring him to make up his mind within twenty-eight days.[59] The court has power to make any vesting orders required, and the interests of underlessees and the like are protected.[60]

(f) Publicity

The importance to creditors and investors of full publicity, particularly in connection with accounts, was stressed in Chapter 20. Once liquidation begins the duties of disclosure are greatly enhanced and, although this may smack of locking the stable door after the horse has escaped, it at least enables creditors and investors to ensure that the liquidator does not treat them unfairly however much the directors may previously have done so.

In a compulsory liquidation, the Winding-up Rules make provisions for Press advertisement [61] of the various decisive steps in the proceedings; for example, the petition,[62] the winding-up order,[63] and the appointment of the liquidator.[64] They entitle every member and creditor to inspect the court's file of proceedings [65] and, indeed, to attend hearings if they wish to do so.[66] Further, creditors and members are entitled to inspect the statement of affairs submitted to the official receiver by the

---

[56] Leave is always required irrespective of the type of liquidation. A trustee in bankruptcy may sometimes disclaim without leave—not so a liquidator.
[57] s. 323 (7). And see subs. (5).
[58] The year dates from the commencement of the winding up or from the time when the property comes to the knowledge of the liquidator if that is not within the first month. The court may extend the period: s. 323 (1).
[59] s. 323 (4). The 28 days may be extended by the court.
[60] s. 323 (6). *Re Katherine et cie* [1932] 1 Ch. 70 appears to imply that if a lease is disclaimed the future liability of any guarantor of the rent and covenants is ended notwithstanding the concluding words of s. 323 (2); *sed quaere.*
[61] In addition to Gazetting, which is required even more frequently.
[62] Companies (Winding-Up) Rules 1949, r. 28.
[63] r. 42. A copy of the order must also be sent to the Companies' Registry and minuted there: s. 230.
[64] r. 58.
[65] r. 19.
[66] r. 157. Unless they are actually petitioners or respondents they will, of course, have to do so at their own expense. Should it be advisable to have any particular class represented on the consideration of some question the court may appoint one or more members or creditors as representatives and then they will be entitled to their costs: r. 157 (2).

company,[67] and the minute books which have to be maintained by the liquidator.[68] Indeed, the court may allow them inspection of any of the books and papers of the company,[69] thus giving them far greater powers to investigate the company's indoor management than they had while the company was a going concern. As regards financial information during the liquidation, it is provided that the liquidator shall send half-yearly accounts to the Board of Trade which the Board shall have audited. These audited accounts are available for public inspection and a summary is sent to every member and creditor.[70]

In a voluntary liquidation, the winding-up resolution will, of course, require to be filed at the Companies' Registry, and notice of it must also be advertised in the *Gazette*.[71] If there is a declaration of solvency this too must be filed.[72] The liquidator must within fourteen days of his appointment advertise it in the *Gazette* and file notice of it at the Companies' Registry.[73] At the end of each year and at the conclusion of the winding up he must summon meetings of the members, and also of the creditors if it is a creditors' liquidation, and lay before them an account of the conduct of the liquidation.[74]

Further, in every type of liquidation all business communications from the company must contain a statement that the company is being wound up,[75] and where the liquidation is not concluded within a year the liquidator must file with the Registrar financial statements at prescribed intervals.[76] So far as compulsory liquidations are concerned, this last requirement is satisfied by filing a copy of the audited half-yearly accounts.[77] In a voluntary liquidation the rules provide for financial statements at similar intervals [78] but there is no compulsory audit.[79] On the final dissolution of the company the court order,[80] or final accounts and liquidator's return [81] are filed with the Registrar.

(g) Supervision of liquidator

As already emphasised, the extent to which the foregoing provisions are in practice an effective protection depends largely on the degree of skill and determination displayed by the liquidator. It is therefore

---

[67] s. 235 (6). The official receiver must send them a summary and his observations thereon: r. 126.
[68] s. 247.
[69] s. 266.
[70] s. 249 and rr. 174–179.
[71] s. 279.
[72] s. 283.
[73] s. 305.
[74] ss. 289–291, 299–300.
[75] s. 338.
[76] s. 342.
[77] r. 177.
[78] Rule 197. This applies equally to winding up under supervision.
[79] But the Board of Trade may require an audit: r. 201; and see recommendations of the Jenkins Committee: Cmnd. 1749, para. 503 (*m*).
[80] s. 274.
[81] ss. 290, 300.

relevant to consider to what extent he is subject to supervision in the exercise of his duties. One of the dangers of our company law is that directors are not under any really effective control. Does the same apply to liquidators?

In compulsory liquidations it certainly does not. The liquidator is then subject to control by the court, whose consent he must obtain before taking some of the major steps in the liquidation. He is also subject to close day-to-day supervision by the Board of Trade [82] and by the committee of inspection (if any), and he is bound to have regard to any directions given by a general meeting of members or creditors.[83] If there is any complaint on this score it is not that he is too free from control but rather that his independence of action is too fettered so that winding up becomes excessively dilatory and expensive.

In a voluntary liquidation the situation is very different. Although application must be made to the court before the liquidator can exercise certain powers (for example, disclaimer) and although there is a general power to apply to the court for directions,[84] the liquidator has a relatively free hand subject only to the supervision of the committee of inspection (if any) and of the creditors and members (in a creditors' liquidation) or of the members (in a members' liquidation). Here it may be argued that the sacrifice of outside control, in the interests of economy and self-determination, has gone too far, particularly in a members' winding up.

It is also significant that the courts place considerable weight on the principle of self-determination in every type of liquidation. The theory that the members and creditors are the best judges of what is in their own interests is still invoked,[85] and although the rules [86] provide for the conduct of meetings they do little to meet the danger that the interests of the many may be sacrificed to those of the controlling few. And the powers of a majority [87] remain considerable, even to the extent of agreeing upon a compromise with creditors.[88]

To this, however, there are two highly important limitations. The first is that on every winding up, other than a members' voluntary

---

[82] Indeed in the great majority of small cases the official receiver (an officer of the Board of Trade) is appointed liquidator: see General Annual Report on Companies for 1967, Table VII.

[83] ss. 246, 346.

[84] Under s. 307.

[85] See, for example, *Re Agricultural Industries Ltd.* [1952] 1 All E.R. 1188, C.A.; *Re B. Karsberg Ltd.* [1956] 1 W.L.R. 57, C.A.; *Re A.B.C. Coupler & Engineering Co. Ltd.* [1961] 1 W.L.R. 243. *Cf.* the similar attitude adopted towards reconstructions: Chap. 26 at p. 641.

[86] Winding-Up Rules 1949, rr. 127–156.

[87] Note that resolutions require a majority both in number and value of those voting: r. 134.

[88] s. 306. This requires a three-fourths majority in total number and value and any member or creditor may appeal against it to the court. But resort can be had to ss. 206–208, under which the majorities are merely of those voting: see Chap. 26, p. 619 *et seq., supra*

liquidation, the control shifts to the creditors.[89] The majority of the members can no longer oppress the minority, though the majority of creditors may oppress the members and the minority of the creditors. The second is that the procedural rule in *Foss* v. *Harbottle* [90] ceases to exercise a stranglehold on the individual member, for the court can always be applied to, even in a members' voluntary liquidation,[91] by an individual member. On the other hand, although the procedural fetter is lifted, the substantive principle which it embodies remains in the background, for the court is invited in the Act to " have regard to the wishes of the creditors or contributories," and, for the purpose of ascertaining those wishes " to direct meetings of the creditors or contributories to be called." [92] The power of the majority therefore remains but is less powerful, though still too potent in a members' winding up.

CONCLUSIONS

Winding up is the ultimate remedy of the investor or creditor. If the winding up is by the court all interests can be sure of even-handed justice but at a price which may be heavy. Moreover, it is justice according to law, and shareholders should only invoke this remedy if satisfied that the legal rights attaching to their shares will give them a good slice off the goose which might have laid a golden egg had they not killed it. A creditors' voluntary liquidation is almost equally effective, and can be more economical,[93] as a method of protecting the creditors as a whole from the machinations of those formerly in control of the company. It is, however, less satisfactory from the viewpoint of the members, who merely pass from subjection to one master—the board of directors—to domination by another—the creditors and their nominee, the liquidator. In a members' winding up the creditors are unlikely to suffer now that the regulations for declarations of solvency have been tightened up, and theoretically this is the most beneficial method for the members, though in practice their former subjection to the directors is unlikely to be greatly weakened. Still, they have better opportunities of gaining information and easier methods of exercising their rights.

At the worst, liquidation is like the extraction of a tooth—it puts an end to the victim's agony and may even enable him to bite back. But it cannot guarantee him a square meal, and may be painful at the time, particularly if the operation is delayed too long.

---

[89] But note how this control may be stultified if a majority in number and value cannot agree: *supra*, p. 650, note 36.

[90] Chap. 25, *supra*.

[91] See s. 307.

[92] s. 346.

[93] In the liquidation of a large public company it is questionable whether, in practice, a voluntary liquidation will prove to be cheaper than a compulsory one in which the Board of Trade are able to watch and challenge the liquidator's remuneration: r. 159 (2).

CHAPTER 28

FOREIGN COMPANIES

THIS chapter is not intended to deal exhaustively with what is an important and difficult subject, but merely to draw attention to some of its implications. It is an addendum to this part of the book rather than an integral chapter of it.

Meaning of foreign company

First, it is necessary to explain that by the term " foreign company " is here meant a company incorporated otherwise than in England. A company formed in England may, as we have seen,[1] change its residence to a foreign country,[2] but it nevertheless remains an English company, subject to the jurisdiction of the English courts, domiciled in England, and, if a registered company, bound to comply with the provisions of the Companies Acts. Nor are we much concerned here with companies registered in Scotland, for although these are undoubtedly foreign companies in the eyes of an English court, difficulties and conflicts are normally avoided because most provisions of the Companies Acts are equally applicable to them. Only where the relevant Scottish common law principles differ from the English are serious difficulties likely to arise, and the main example of this, concerning charges on property, has already been sufficiently explored.[3]

Our concern is with companies which form themselves under the law of another state but nevertheless carry on business in England or, at least, have dealings with people in England. And, just as the treatment of English companies has been limited to associations that are incorporated, so here we are primarily concerned with foreign associations that are corporate entities. If the " company " has no corporate personality (and, as we shall see, whether it has or not depends upon the law of the place of its formation) it cannot carry on business in England or anywhere else, because " it " does not exist. The business, and the consequent liabilities, are those of the human associates and hence some of the problems, discussed below, cannot arise. On the other hand, this does not necessarily solve the practical difficulty of recovering from those associates, and in recognition of this the 1948 Act[4] treats any

---

[1] Chap. 10, pp. 207, 208, *supra.*
[2] For a learned discussion, see Farnsworth, *The Residence and Domicile of Corporations* (1939).
[3] Chap. 19, pp. 433, 434, *supra.*
[4] Part IX, see p. 674 *et seq., infra.*

foreign association, whether incorporated or not, as an unregistered company which may be wound up under the Act.

The company's personal law

The problems caused by foreign companies operating in the domestic jurisdiction have exercised the minds of the jurists of all countries. The obvious guiding principle, to which, on the whole, the Anglo-American countries have subscribed, is to say that, as a corporation is an artificial entity, its existence and powers should be determined by the law of the country to which it claims to owe its existence, the country of its alleged incorporation.[5] If, however, this principle is carried to logical extremes there are patent opportunities for abuse; promoters will incorporate their companies in the country having the laxest corporation laws and then operate in the harsher climate of other lands, shielded by the cloak of their personal laws—a protection denied to domestic concerns with which they compete.[6] Clearly, therefore, those other countries must, in the interest of their own citizens, impose some limitation on the extent to which foreign companies can operate within their boundaries and invoke foreign personal laws. In some countries this limitation has taken the form of prohibiting or restricting trade by foreign companies; in others the personal law of incorporation has been rejected in favour of that of its central administration or principal place of business.

Various attempts have been made to resolve these difficulties by international action. In 1951 the Hague Conference began an examination of companies in private international law and drafted a Convention on mutual recognition. Between 1952 and 1960 the International Law Association associated themselves with this work and produced a Draft covering other conflicts questions.[7] More recently the Institute of International Law have adopted a set of rules[8] and the Council of Europe have published a European Convention,[9] covering much the same ground in still greater detail. In the meantime, the Common Market countries, in accordance with their obligations under the Treaty of Rome, have made some slight progress with co-ordination of their company laws[10] and rules for mutual recognition.[11] But their most ambitious and interesting project has been the production by Professor

---

[5] " What you have to do is to find out what this statutory creature is and what it is meant to do; and to find out . . . you must look at the statute only, because there and there only is found the definition of this new creature ": *per* Bowen L.J. in *Baroness Wenlock* v. *River Dee Co.* (1883) 36 Ch.D. at p. 685n.

[6] Thus a great many American companies are formed in Delaware, irrespective of their intended place of operation, that state having had the most accommodating corporation law; its exchequer and its lawyers have found this highly profitable. Similarly the Principality of Liechtenstein (with a favourable tax code) is said to have more corporate than natural citizens!

[7] For text, see Report of the 49th (1960) Conference of the I.L.A. at pp. 93–95.

[8] For an account of these, see Thomas C. Drucker in (1968) 17 I.C.L.Q. 28.

[9] European Treaty Series No. 57.

[10] The Council issued its " First Directive on Co-ordination " in March 1968.

[11] The first of a proposed series of Conventions was signed in February 1968.

Pieter Sanders and a team of experts of a draft statute for a new type of " European company " which would be entitled as such to operate in all the member-states of the E.E.C. and freely to change its *siège social* from one to another.[12]

Hitherto the United Kingdom has remained somewhat aloof from these activities; but they will obviously be of vital concern if we ever succeed in entering the Common Market. In the meantime we have, perhaps, been less plagued by difficulties because of the relatively restricted role which our rules of conflict of laws accord to the " personal law "; in England the law of the domicile. In the main this law is important only in connection with matrimonial relations and succession on death, and, happily, neither of these can arise in the case of an artificial person. On the other hand, the law of the domicile does, to some extent, govern questions of capacity and these may arise with companies rather more readily than with human beings. The latter will normally be of full capacity throughout the greater part of their lives, whereas corporations may have their capacity permanently restricted— and will if incorporated in countries which adopt the *ultra vires* doctrine.

One thing at least is clear: the question whether a company exists or not as a corporate body depends, according to English law, on the law of the place of its alleged incorporation.[13] English law will always recognise it as a corporate body if it is duly incorporated according to the laws of a foreign state, whether or not it complies with the rules referred to below [14] regarding foreign companies with a place of business here. And if the foreign company has ceased to have any corporate existence according to its personal law, English law will accept that it no longer exists.[15] We have even given effect to foreign legislation substituting a new company as universal successor of another.[16]

It is also generally stated that English law will treat the question whether a company's transactions are *ultra vires* as governed by the law of the place of incorporation.[17] This, no doubt, is generally true. But strictly it appears that its capacity is limited both by its constitution, construed in the light of the law of the country of its incorporation, and

---

12 The text was published in December 1966. For a convenient brief account, see Drucker in (1968) 118 New L.J. 691.

13 The *Russian Bank* cases are clear on this: " The will of the sovereign authority which created it can also destroy it ": *per* Lord Wright in *Lazard Bros.* v. *Midland Bank* [1933] A.C. 289 at 297, H.L. And, of course, purported liquidation in some other country will be disregarded: *National Trust Co.* v. *Ebro Irrigation and Power Co.* [1954] 3 D.L.R. 326 (Ont.H.C.).

14 pp. 673, 674.

15 Subject to the possibility of statutory resurrection, *infra*, p. 675.

16 *National Bank of Greece & Athens* v. *Metliss* [1958] A.C. 509, H.L. But whether the new company is discharged from the liabilities which vested in it depends on the proper law of those liabilities: *Adams* v. *National Bank of Greece* [1961] A.C. 255, H L.

17 Cheshire, *Private International Law*, 7th ed., p. 180, citing *Risdon Iron Works* v. *Furness* [1906] 1 K.B. 49 at pp. 56–57, C.A. (which, however, is not really concerned with *ultra vires* at all).

by the law governing the transaction in question.[18] Moreover, it does not follow that an English court would allow a foreign company to escape liability on an English contract by proving that its personal law recognised an even stricter *ultra vires* doctrine than that of England.[19] Formerly a foreign corporation could not hold land in England, unless it complied with the provisions of Part X of the Companies Act 1948,[20] even if it had capacity to do so according to the law of its incorporation.[21] This restriction has now been removed,[22] but it may be that the former complications would still arise if there was a purported vesting of English land in a foreign company which, under the law of its incorporation, had no power to hold land.

A number of other matters peculiar to companies also raise problems analogous to questions of incapacity. There are, for example, the questions whether the human members are personally liable for the company's debts,[23] and what constitute its agents or organs with power to act for it.[24] The authorities establish clearly that in these two instances the law of the place of incorporation governs,[23 24] and for practical purposes it hardly matters whether it governs as the law of the domicile, or, as seems more consistent with principle, as the proper law of the contract establishing the company.[25] In either event, it seems clear that the country whose law governs cannot change, though the legal rules of that country may.[26] If it is the proper law that governs, it is presumably determined once and for all at the time when the contract is entered into[27]; if it is the *lex domicilii*, a company, unlike a natural person, cannot change its domicile.[28]

---

[18] Dicey & Morris, *Conflict of Laws*, 8th ed., pp. 484, 485.

[19] The better view is that questions of capacity in mercantile contracts are governed by the law of the country with which the contract has the closest connection: Dicey, & Morris, p. 744, Cheshire, p. 201. If this country were England the incapacity under the foreign law might be ignored. Alternatively, the principle might be invoked that the English courts will not enforce a foreign law conflicting with English public policy.

[20] s. 408.

[21] See *Morelle Ltd.* v. *Wakeling* [1955] 2 Q.B. 379, C.A.; *Att.-Gen.* v. *Parsons* [1956] A.C. 421, H.L.

[22] By s. 38 (1) and Sched. VII, Pt. II, of the Charities Act 1960.

[23] *General Steam Navigation* v. *Guillou* (1843) 11 M. & W. 877; *Risdon Iron Works* v. *Furness, supra*.

[24] *Banco de Bilbao* v. *Sancha* [1938] 2 K.B. 176, C.A.; *Carl Zeiss Stiftung* v. *Rayner & Keeler Ltd. (No.* 2) [1967] A.C. 853, H.L.

[25] This seems to be favoured by the C.A. in *Banco de Bilbao* v. *Sancha*: " The question what body of directors have the legal right of representing the Banco de Bilbao, a commercial entity organised under the laws prevailing in Bilbao, and having its corporate home in Bilbao, must depend in the first place on the articles under which it is constituted. The interpretation of those articles and the operation of them, having regard to the general law, must be governed by the *lex loci contractus* . . ., i.e., by the law from time to time prevailing at the place where the corporate home (*domicilio social*) was set up ": per Clauson L.J. at pp. 194–195.

[26] As in *Banco de Bilbao* v. *Sancha, supra*.

[27] But the dictum cited in note 25 suggests that a change of " corporate home " might change the proper law, *sed quaere*.

[28] *Kuenigl* v. *Donnersmarck* [1955] 1 Q.B. 515. " The domicile of origin, or the domicile of birth, using with respect to a company a familiar metaphor, clings to it throughout its existence ": per Macnaghten J. in *Gasque* v. *I.R.C.* [1940] 2 K.B. 80 at p. 84.

Further, it seems generally true to say that all internal questions arising between the company and its members will be governed by the law of the place of incorporation.[29]   But here it definitely is the accepted view of the English courts that this law governs as the proper law of the contract rather than as the company's personal law,[30] and, since English law is wedded to the theory that parties to a contract can select their own proper law,[31] it is theoretically possible that the rights of members might be submitted to some other law.[32]   This emphasis on the proper law is doubtless the result of the historical development of English companies from partnerships; instead of regarding the formation of a company as a unilateral transaction creating a *persona juridica* and giving rise to questions of status, the English lawyer treats it as an agreement of the parties to be dealt with in accordance with principles appropriate to contract.   Nevertheless, by a different route the same result is normally reached.

But although the law of incorporation is relevant as respects the company's internal relations, it is only to the very limited extent, already indicated, where questions of capacity arise, that this law has any direct relevance as regards relations with outsiders.   If the company operates in England, most of its contracts are likely to be English contracts by reason of the real or assumed intention of the parties,[33] and, as we have seen,[34] it will be liable to be sued in the English courts if it can be regarded as " present " here.

Hence, it is only in a minority of cases that the foreign company's personal law causes difficulty and, except incidentally as a result of

---

[29] *Pickering* v. *Stephenson* (1872) L.R. 14 Eq. 322; *Spiller* v. *Turner* [1897] 1 Ch. 911; *Brailey* v. *Rhodesia Consolidated Ltd.* [1910] 2 Ch. 95; *Indian and General Investment Trust* v. *Borax Consolidated Ltd.* [1920] 1 K.B. 539; *London and S. American Investment Trust* v. *British Tobacco Co.* [1927] 1 Ch. 107; *Adelaide Electric Supply Co.* v. *Prudential Assurance* [1934] A.C. 122, H.L.

[30] This interpretation was adopted by the Ont.H.C. in *Brown, Gow, Wilson* v. *Beleggings-Societeit N.V.* (1961) 29 D.L.R. (2d) 673 at pp. 694–695.

[31] *R.* v. *International Trustee for Bondholders* [1937] A.C. 500, H.L., see especially p. 529; *Vita Food Products* v. *Unus Shipping Co.* [1939] A.C. 277, P.C.

[32] See cases cited in note 29, which, however, indicate how strong is the presumption in favour of the law of incorporation.   But it seems that if shares were issued in another country and transferable upon a register kept there the law of that other country might be the proper law: *cf. Indian and General Investment Trust* v. *Borax Consolidated Ltd.*—which concerned debentures, not shares.   It is submitted that it is necessary to draw a distinction between (a) the contract of incorporation (the memorandum and articles of association) and (b) the subsidiary contract issuing the shares.   The proper law of (a) must almost invariably be the law of incorporation; the proper law of (b) need not be, but the rights of the shareholders necessarily depend on (a) as well as on (b)—*e.g.*, in cases of conflict between holders of two issues with different proper laws.   " The contracts of the shareholders were, no doubt, actually executed in various places; but the bond between them was intended to be Turkish. . . .   The rights of the members of the association as between themselves are therefore to be determined by the Turkish law ": (1872) L.R. 14 Eq. at p. 393, *per* Wickens V.-C., who proceeded to apply English rules (which might have surprised a Turk) under the rule that in default of proof to the contrary a foreign law is to be taken as the same as English!

[33] And torts committed here will be governed solely by English law, *i.e.*, normal rules of English private international law will be applied.

[34] *Supra,* Chap. 10, pp. 207, 208.

Exchange Control regulations, no serious obstacle has been placed in the way of a foreign company wishing to operate here. But clearly it ought not to be allowed to do so without making disclosure comparable to that required of a domestic company, for recognition of its corporate capacity under a foreign law should not exempt it from regulations to which English companies are subject and which are designed to safeguard those having dealings with it in England.

Disclosure by foreign companies

Accordingly, Part X of the Companies Act extends the obligation of disclosure to companies operating here, but incorporated abroad, " abroad " here meaning anywhere except in England *or Scotland*.[35] If such a company establishes a place of business here it must, under section 407, file with the Registrar (a) a copy of its instrument of incorporation,[36] (b) a list of directors and secretary, and (c) the names and addresses of one or more persons authorised to accept service; and must notify any alterations within twenty-one days after notice of the change could with reasonable diligence have been received in Great Britain.[37] Of these requirements, (c) transcends mere disclosure of information about the company, for it also compels it to submit to the jurisdiction of the English courts and to nominate someone to accept service on its behalf[38]; this, in itself, is a valuable protection to creditors. Furthermore, the registration of the constitution and of particulars of directors may well imply a practical limitation on the general principle that it is the law of incorporation which determines who are the company's organs and what their authority is. An English court would, it is submitted, apply the rule in *Royal British Bank* v. *Turquand*[39] and hold that an English transaction with the named

---

[35] Scottish companies are subject to the same obligations as English ones except that the registration office is in Edinburgh. If they carry on business in England they may be served with process at the principal place of business in England: s. 437 (2). Companies incorporated in the Channel Islands or the Isle of Man must file all documents required from an English company if they establish a place of business here: s. 416. N. Ireland companies are treated in the same way as other overseas companies. Throughout most of the Commonwealth, company law closely follows the British model as regards basic common law principles and, to a diminishing extent, as regards statute law.

[36] A certified copy with a certified translation if the original is not in English: s. 407 (1) (a).

[37] s. 409 and Companies (Forms) Order 1949 (S.I. 382).

[38] If default is made in filing and maintaining up-to-date information, service may be effected at the place of business (s. 412), but only if there still is a place of business in England: *Deverall* v. *Grant Advertising Inc.* [1955] Ch. 111, C.A.; see (1955) 18 M.L.R. 180 and 4 I.C.L.Q. 228. Prior to this section it was clear that service on the person nominated was effective even if he refused to accept it (*Employers' Liability Assurance Corpn.* v. *Sedgwick Collins & Co.* [1927] A.C. 95, H.L.), but having regard to the wording of the section this must now be regarded as doubtful. If, however, the person named accepts service *semble* that the company cannot dispute the jurisdiction even though it has ceased to carry on business in England: *Sabatier* v. *The Trading Co.* [1927] 1 Ch. 495. Anomalously, there seems to be no procedure for removing the name from the file except by substituting another. See the Report of the Jenkins Committee, Cmnd. 1749, para. 516.

[39] *Supra*, Chap. 8, p. 150 *et seq.*

directors in a matter which appeared to be within their usual authority was binding on the company whatever the law of incorporation might say.[40]

Furthermore, the company must prepare and file a balance-sheet, profit and loss account and accompanying documents complying with the English provisions subject to any prescribed exceptions.[41] It must exhibit its name in the same way as an English company and, if the liability of its members is limited, state this,[42] and it must comply with the registration provisions in Part III of the Act as regards charges on its English property.[43]

These requirements apply only if the company has established a place of business here. Other requirements, however, are wider. Thus the prospectus provisions of the Act are extended to any issues in this country [44] and the provisions of the Prevention of Fraud (Investments) Act 1958 and the Borrowing (Control and Guarantees) Act 1946 are equally applicable to dealings and issues in securities of foreign companies.[45] Moreover, most of the provisions relating to the Board of Trade's powers of investigation [46] have now been extended to all bodies corporate incorporated outside Great Britain which are carrying on business in Great Britain or have at any time done so.[47]

Winding up [48]

Finally, a foreign company may be compulsorily wound up as an unregistered company under Part IX of the Act, and on winding up English rules will be applied in connection with the administration of its assets.[49] The fact that the foreign company has already ceased to exist under its personal law is no bar to an English winding-up order [50]; indeed, the fact that it has been dissolved is one of the grounds on which an order may be made, the others being inability to pay its

---

[40] Cf. *Employers' Liability Assurance Corpn.* v. *Sedgwick Collins & Co.* [1927] A.C. 95, H.L.

[41] s. 410. For the exceptions see the Overseas Companies (Accounts) (Exceptions) Order 1968, S.I. No. 69. This excepts the directors' report and details of turnover.

[42] s. 411.

[43] s. 106. See further on charges by foreign companies, Chap. 19, pp. 433, 434.

[44] ss. 417–423.

[45] *Supra*, Chap. 14. The rules of the English stock exchanges as regards advertisements will also have to be complied with if shares are introduced here. The general problem of the conflict of laws rules applying to the transfer of securities is too vast a subject to be considered here.

[46] See Chap. 25, pp. 604–613.

[47] Companies Act 1967, ss. 42 (1) and 109 (1) (*e*). But ss. 172 and 173 have not been extended to foreign companies and in the case of ss. 165 to 171 and 175 the extension is subject to any modifications made by regulations: see 1967 Act, s. 42 (no such regulations have been made).

[48] See, generally, Lipstein, " Jurisdiction to Wind Up Foreign Companies " (1952) 11 Cam.L.J. 198; M. Mann, " The Dissolved Foreign Corporation " (1955) 18 M.L.R. 8; and F. A. Mann, " The Confiscation of Corporations " (1962) 11 I.C.L.Q. 471.

[49] *Re Suidair International Airways Ltd.* [1951] Ch. 165. But the court may give directions regarding collection or non-collection of assets outside England: *Re Hibernian Merchants Ltd.* [1958] Ch. 76.

[50] s. 400.

debts, and that winding up is just and equitable.[51] When the winding-up order is made the dissolved company is revived and its English assets, which will have vested in the Crown as *bona vacantia*, will revest in it.[52] The exact effect of this is still not wholly clear.[53] A particularly Gilbertian result was achieved in relation to the winding up of the *Banque des Marchands de Moscou* where it was held that the claims of *creditors* were barred because they had been discharged by the proper law (Russian),[54] but that the *members* were entitled to the property rather than the Crown.[55] Moreover, it is obscure whether the revival validates transactions into which the officers of the company have purported to enter on its behalf since its dissolution in the country of its incorporation.[56] A winding-up order may be made even though the company never had a place of business in this country [57] provided that there are " assets here to administer and persons subject, or at least submitting, to the jurisdiction who are concerned or interested in the proper distribution of the assets." [58]

This winding-up jurisdiction therefore fills the most conspicuous gap in the wall erected for the protection of outsiders having dealings with foreign companies. The registration provisions of Part X may prove inadequate, either because they are not complied with when they should be, or because they do not apply since no place of business is established here. In these circumstances, those having dealings with the company will not only lack full information about the company but may find difficulty in serving process on the company if forced to sue it. Irrespective of the provisions in Part X, a company can be served with process if present here and the courts have tested " presence " by seeing whether the company has done business from some place here.[59] But this will not avail a creditor if the company has merely conducted business *with* England (as opposed to *in* England [60]). Sometimes it may be possible to obtain leave to serve process out of the jurisdiction under R.S.C., Ord. 11, but the conditions of that Order may not be fulfilled, or leave may be refused, and then the only remedy of the creditor will be to pursue the company to its foreign home, which may be an expensive

---

[51] s. 399 (5).
[52] *Re Azoff-Don Commercial Bank* [1954] Ch. 315.
[53] See further M. Mann in (1952) 15 M.L.R. 479, (1955) 18 M.L.R. 8, 25–27, and (1955) 4 I.C.L.Q. 226; and F. A. Mann in (1955) 71 L.Q.R. 186, and (1962) 11 I.C.L.Q. 471. Compare the position under ss. 352 and 353 discussed in Chap. 27 at pp. 652–654.
[54] *Re Banque des Marchands de Moscou* [1952] 1 All E.R. 1269; *ibid.* [1954] 1 W.L.R. 1108.
[55] *Ibid.* [1958] Ch. 182.
[56] Vaisey J. in [1952] 1 All E.R. 1269 held that it did not, as did Roxburgh J. in *Re Russian Commercial and Industrial Bank* (1963) 107 S.J. 415, but Wynn-Parry J. had held the contrary in *ibid.* [1955] Ch. 148.
[57] *Banque des Marchands de Moscou* v. *Kindersley* [1951] Ch. 112, C.A. But the court has a discretion: *Re Hibernian Merchants Ltd., supra.*
[58] *Per* Evershed M.R. [1951] Ch. 112 at p. 126.
[59] *Okura & Co. Ltd.* v. *Forsbacka* [1914] 1 K.B. 715, C.A.
[60] Even if through an agent here, provided he merely transmits offers to his foreign principal or has no place of business, however temporary: *ibid.*

and risky business. In any event, no suit can be brought, either in England [61] or, *a fortiori*, in its foreign home, if it has already ceased to exist under its personal law. But if an English winding-up order is obtained these difficulties disappear; the English liquidator can collect the assets and the creditor, on proving his debt, will receive payment so far as the assets permit.[62]

Furthermore, for the purpose of invoking the winding-up jurisdiction it is irrevelant whether the foreign company is incorporated or not. As we have seen,[63] it is recognised, even in the case of English associations, that winding up under the Act may be the most convenient method of liquidation whenever any considerable body of persons is involved, irrespective of whether their association was registered under the Act. In the case of foreign concerns, the jurisdiction is even wider, for it embraces any association even though a partnership of fewer than eight persons.[64]

CONCLUSIONS

Although English law recognises that the place of incorporation determines a company's personal law, those having dealings with a foreign company are afforded considerable protection against the dangers inherent in this recognition. This protection takes three forms. First, English private international law allows the foreign personal law as such little say in regulating the company's relations with outsiders. Secondly, companies which establish a place of business in England are forced to comply with many of the English rules as to disclosure of material information. Thirdly, foreign companies may be wound up in England according to English rules even though they have no place of business here and have ceased to exist in their native country.

The protection of a shareholder, as opposed to an outside creditor, is less extensive for, as we have seen, his rights will normally depend on the place of incorporation as the proper law of the contract with him. Nor will he necessarily be protected by disclosure, for the provisions regarding registration of documents apply only if the company has a place of business here; the mere fact that it has English shareholders is irrelevant. If there is a public issue in England full information will initially have to be disclosed through compliance with the prospectus provisions but, subject to that, the view is taken that one who chooses to invest in a foreign company must expect that the foreign law will govern. But he, too, may as a last resort invoke the winding-up

---

[61] *Lazard Bros.* v. *Midland Bank* [1933] A.C. 289, H.L. Nor can it sue: *ibid.*

[62] *Russian and English Bank* v. *Baring Bros.* [1936] A.C. 405, H.L. (Subject to the doubts expressed above regarding debts discharged under their proper law and those contracted since the original dissolution.)

[63] Chap. 11, p. 242, *supra.*

[64] s. 398. English partnerships of fewer than eight members and any limited partnership registered in England or N. Ireland are excluded by paras. (*c*) and (*d*) of that section.

jurisdiction, for a petition can be brought by a member as well as by a creditor.[65]

Winding up is therefore the ultimate remedy of both creditor and member. This, as we have seen,[66] is true also of English companies, but with foreign companies its role is even more important, for it may often be the only available remedy.

---

[65] s. 224. This is clearly so if the company has not already been dissolved in its home country. Presumably if a " creditor " of a non-existent company can petition as a creditor, so can a " member " as a contributory. And he may be able to persuade the Board of Trade to exercise their investigating powers.

[66] Chap. 27.

INDEX

Members—*cont.*
general meeting,
  acts outside, 578–579
  control of management by, 499–
    500
  proxies, 484–487
informal consent, 163
interests of,
  employees, preferred to, 522–523
  interests of company equated with,
    521–522
liability of,
  debts of company, 71
  fixed value of shares, 106
  fraudulent trading, 191–193
  minimum, 106
  misdescription of company, 193–
    194
majority,
  fraud on the minority, 564
majority decisions,
  acts of company, 127
majority holding,
  appointment of directors, 128
meetings,
  right to attend, 478
memorandum of association,
  alteration of, 502, 506–507
  rights embodied in, 506–507
  subscription of, 372–373
minimum number, 190
minority,
  expropriation of shares, 567–570
notice of meetings,
  service of, 478–479
oppression,
  order under s. 210...598–604
order under s. 210,
  petition for, 599–600
outsider, as, 263–264
personal rights of, 263, 264–265
purchaser of shares,
  registration of, 396–397
ratification of corporate acts,
  informal, 208–210
reduction of numbers, 190–191
register of, 376–378, 450
relationship *inter se*, 127
remedies,
  extent of, 614
  order under s. 210...598–604
  winding up, 596–598
repayment to, 112
resolutions,
  notice of, 479–480
rights of,
  enforcement of, 592–595
  infringement, ratification of, 593–
    594
  ultra vires action, 592–593
shareholder, 343
  rights of, 347
shares,
  first refusal, right of, 392
  pre-emption, right of, 392

Members—*cont.*
transfer of shares, by, 378
trustee for,
  company as, 205
unanimous agreement of,
  intra vires matter, 209–210
variation of rights,
  meaning of, 511–512
  section 287, reconstruction under,
    622
voluntary winding up, 650
voting,
  bona fides, 562
  freedom as to, 579–580
winding up,
  right to petition for, 597
written resolution of, 210, 496–497
See also SHAREHOLDERS.
Memorandum of Association,
alteration of, 85–86, 501–502
  order under s. 210...598
amendment of, 16–17
articles of association,
  distinction blurred, 100
class rights, 508
  protection of, 512–513
Companies' Registry,
  deposit of, 447
contents, 16
contract, as,
  company and member, between,
    261–265
dividend, payment of, 121
entrenched rights, 501–502
entrenchment of provisions, 101
form of, 255
function of, 15–16
lodgment of, 257
member,
  rights of, 506–507
name of company, 252
nominal capital, 256
objects clause,
  expansion of, 88–89
  nature of business, 256
  subjective form of, 88–89
preparation of, 255–257
registration at the Companies' Registry, 254, 257, 447
rights clause,
  variation of, 508
share capital,
  statement of, 105
stamp duty, 258
statutory requirements, 101
subscriber to,
  allotment of shares to persons
    other than, 373
  appointment of directors, 128
  subscription of, 372–373
  variation of rights under, 617–618
Mens Rea, 146
Merchant Adventurers, 24–25

Shareholder—*cont.*
allotment letter,
contractual right to become, 375
allottee of shares, 375
becoming, 372–379
capital, return of,
right to, 349
class rights. *See* CLASS RIGHTS.
Companies' Registry,
annual returns, 376–377
company,
distinct from, 132
obligations to, 345
taxation problems, 171
company's assets,
interest in, 343–344
contract, rights under, 513–514
contractual rights of,
interference with, 506–513
controlling,
duties of, 561 *et seq. See also*
CONTROLLING SHAREHOLDERS.
death of, 183
derivative action,
company joined as defendant, 590–591
disqualification, 592
fraud on the minority, 588–589
personal action contrasted, 594–595
proof of control by wrongdoers, 589–590
representative action distinguished, 591–592
representative capacity, 591–592
directors, 388–389
voting as, 563
distribution to,
taxation, 171
dividends,
right to, 349, 354
division of assets between,
preference shares, 360
equality of, 53
presumption of, 349–351
exercise of control by, 56
function of, 9–10
infant, 344
interest of,
sum of money, measured by, 345
liability,
equality of, 349–350
loan to,
close company, 178
management by, 56
members, as, 343
rights of, 347
memorandum of association,
subscription of, 372–373
minority,
appeal by dissenting, 643–645
expropriation of shares, 567–570
Greenhalgh v. *Arderne Cinemas*, 571–574
opposition to take-over, 629
take-overs, 626
voting control, 352

Shareholder—*cont.*
modification of rights,
court, appeal to, 642–643
ordinary,
proprietors, as, 368–369
owners of undertaking, not, 343–344
personal action,
derivative action, contrasted, 594–595
personal rights of,
infringement, 584, 585
plaintiffs, as,
multiplicity of actions, 582
preference,
debenture holders, distinguished from, 359–360
protection of,
foreign companies, 676–677
purchaser of shares,
registration of, 396–397
quasi-partner, as, 10
reconstruction,
dissent, 622, 623–624
section 287, under, 625
register of members,
entry on, 376–378
registration of,
directors, refusal by, 394
repayment to, 356
representative of company, as,
legal action by, 587
rights of, 349
variation, of, 617–618
supplier of capital, as, 10
surtax,
avoidance of, 172–173
take-over,
non-acceptance of, 629–630
ten per cent., 390
director, 390–391
variation of rights,
court, appeal to, 642–643
voting rights, 349
See also MEMBERS.

Shares, 343 *et seq.*
acquisition of,
court, appeal to, 643–645
dissenting minority, 643–645
allotment letter, 375
renounceable, 375
allotment of,
invalid, 378–379
voidable, 334
application for,
acceptance, 302–303
revocation, 302–303
application form for, 374–375
prospectus accompanying, 301
bankruptcy,
transmission on, 413–414
blank transfer,
delivery of, 405–406
mortgagee, held by, 412
bonus issue, 110, 289